BANKING
THEORY AND PRACTICE

DR. PREM KUMAR SRIVASTAVA
Faculty of Commerce and Management Studies,
Sukhadia University,
Udaipur.

Himalaya Publishing House
ISO 9001:2015 CERTIFIED

Third Edition	:	1981
Fourth Edition	:	1983
Fifth Edition	:	1986
Sixth Edition	:	1994
Seventh Edition	:	1997
Eighth Edition	:	2000
Ninth Edition	:	2003
Tenth Revised Edition	:	2007
Eleventh Revised Edition	:	2008
Reprint	:	2009, 2010
Twelfth Revised Edition	:	2013
Edition	:	2016, 2018
Edition	**:**	**2020**

Published by : Mrs. Meena Pandey for **Himalaya Publishing House Pvt. Ltd.,**
Ramdoot, Dr. Bhalerao Marg, Girgaon, Mumbai - 400 004
Phone: 022-23860170/23863863; **Fax:** 022-23877178
E-mail: himpub@bharatmail.co.in; **Website:** www.himpub.com

Branch Offices :

New Delhi : Pooja Apartments, 4-B, Murari Lal Street, Ansari Road, Darya Ganj, New Delhi - 110 002. Phone: 011-23270392, 23278631; Fax: 011-23256286

Nagpur : Kundanlal Chandak Industrial Estate, Ghat Road, Nagpur - 440 018. Phone: 0712-2738731, 3296733; Telefax: 0712-2721216

Bengaluru : Plot No. 91-33, 2nd Main Road, Seshadripuram, Behind Nataraja Theatre, Bengaluru - 560 020. Phone: 080-41138821; Mobile: 09379847017, 09379847005

Hyderabad : No. 3-4-184, Lingampally, Besides Raghavendra Swamy Matham, Kachiguda, Hyderabad - 500 027. Phone: 040-27560041, 27550139

Chennai : New No. 48/2, Old No. 28/2, Ground Floor, Sarangapani Street, T. Nagar, Chennai-600 017. Mobile: 09380460419

Pune : First Floor, Laksha Apartment, No. 527, Mehunpura, Shaniwarpeth (Near Prabhat Theatre), Pune - 411 030. Phone: 020-24496323, 24496333; Mobile: 09370579333

Lucknow : House No. 731, Shekhupura Colony, Near B.D. Convent School, Aliganj, Lucknow - 226 022. Phone: 0522-4012353; Mobile: 09307501549

Ahmedabad : 114, SHAIL, 1st Floor, Opp. Madhu Sudan House, C.G. Road, Navrang Pura, Ahmedabad - 380 009. Phone: 079-26560126; Mobile: 09377088847

Ernakulam : 39/176 (New No. 60/251), 1st Floor, Karikkamuri Road, Ernakulam, Kochi - 682011. Phone: 0484-2378012, 2378016; Mobile: 09387122121

Cuttack : New LIC Colony, Behind Kamala Mandap, Badambadi, Cuttack - 753 012, Odisha. Mobile: 9338746007

Kolkata : 108/4, Beliaghata Main Road, Near ID Hospital, Opp. SBI Bank, Kolkata - 700 010, Phone: 033-32449649; Mobile: 07439040301

Printed at : Geetanjali Press Pvt. Ltd., Nagpur, on behalf of HPH.

Preface to the Twelfth Edition

Rapid changes are taking place in almost all the sectors of Indian economy. The country is on a threshold of economic growth. In such a scenario, the Banking sector is witnessing a sea change. The eleventh edition of the book was thoroughly revised and updated to cover all these aspects. The last edition of the book got an overwhelming response from diverse sections, *viz.*, academicians, students, banking practitioners and professionals.

We have tried to incorporate the latest data and information about the increasing role of Reserve Bank of India. Some new important terms have been added, *e.g.*, Gift cheques and Traveller's cheques, Travellers' cheques and credit cards, etc. Short notes have been added on new topics, *viz.* — CRISIL, Electronic clearing service, Stock invest, Phishing, Reverse Mortgage Schemes, Nigerian 419 scams, Ancillary services provided by banks, Consumer Protection Act and Banking Sector, etc.

I am grateful to Dr. S.K.P. Agrawal and Dr. (Mrs.) Kaneez Fatima Sadriwala for the help and suggestions.

I hope, this edition will be beneficial to researchers, bankers and students. Further I welcome constructive comments and suggestions for improvement of the book.

P.K. Srivastava,

Kumar Kutir,

47, Arvind Nagar,

Udaipur 313003 (Raj.)

Phone: 0294 – 2490443

E-mail: rajivkumar_2504@yahoo.com.

CONTENTS

Part I

INDIAN BANKING SYSTEM

Part II

BANKER AND CUSTOMER

PART - I

INDIAN BANKING SYSTEM

CHAPTER

1 Commercial Banking in India — A Retrospect

☞ Indian Banking

The Indian banking can be broadly categorized into nationalized (government owned), private banks and specialized banking institutions. The Reserve Bank of India acts as a centralized body monitoring any discrepancies and shortcomings in the system. Since the nationalization of banks in 1969, the public sector banks or the nationalized banks have acquired a place of prominence and has since then seen tremendous progress. The need to become highly customer focused has forced the slow-moving public sector banks to adopt a fast track approach. The unleashing of products and services through the net has galvanized players at all levels of the banking and financial institutions market grid to look anew at their existing portfolio offering. Conservative banking practices allowed Indian banks to be insulated partially from the Asian currency crisis, Indian banks are now quoting at higher valuation when compared to banks in other Asian countries (*viz.*, Hong Kong, Singapore, Philippines, etc.), that have major problems linked to huge Non-performing Assets (NPAs) and payment defaults. Cooperative banks are nimble footed in approach and armed with efficient branch networks focus primarily on the 'high revenue' niche retail segments.

The Indian banking has finally worked up to the competitive dynamics of the 'new' Indian market and is addressing the relevant issues to take on the multifarious challenges of globalization. Banks that employ IT solutions are perceived to be 'futuristic' and proactive players capable of meeting the multifarious requirements of the large customers' base. Private banks have been fast on the uptake and are reorienting their strategies using the internet as a medium. The internet has emerged as the new and challenging frontier of marketing with the conventional physical world, tenets being just as applicable like in any other marketing medium.

The Indian banking has come a long way from being a sleepy business institution to a highly proactive and dynamic entity. This transformation has been largely brought about by the large dose of liberalization and economic reforms that allowed banks to explore new business opportunities rather than generating revenues from conventional streams (*i.e.*, borrowing and lending). The banking in India is highly fragmented with 30 banking units contributing to almost 50% of deposits and 60% of advances. Indian nationalized banks (banks owned by the government) continue to be the major lenders in the economy due to their sheer size and penetrative networks which assures them high deposit mobilization. The Indian banking can be broadly categorized into nationalized, private banks and specialized banking institutions.

The Reserve Bank of India act as a centralized body monitoring any discrepancies and shortcomings in the system. It is the foremost monitoring body in the Indian financial sector. The nationalized banks (*i.e.,* government-owned banks) continue to dominate the Indian banking arena. Industry estimates indicate that out of 274 commercial banks operating in India, 223 banks are in the public sector and 51 are in the private sector. The private sector bank grid also includes 24 foreign banks that have started their operations here. Under the ambit of the nationalized banks come the specialized banking institutions. These co-operatives, rural banks focus on areas of agriculture, rural development etc.

☞ Progress of Banking in India

India had a system of indigenous banking from very early times, though it was not similar to banking of modern times. There is evidence to show that money lending existed even during the *Vedic* period. With the advent of the English traders in the seventeenth century and the establishment of trading centres by the East India Company, indigenous bankers for their position precarious. Unable to use indigenous bankers for their trading and banking purposes, the East India Company encouraged the establishment of what were known as the *agency houses* — trading firms which undertook banking operations for the benefit of their constituents. Some of the important agency houses established during the period were Alexander & Co. and Fergusson & Co. These firms combined banking with other kinds of business, and both were the predecessors of the early joint stock banks in India. The Bank of Hindustan, a mere appendage of the former, was the earliest bank under European direction in India.

☞ Presidency Banks

The Government of India did not awaken to the need for banks till 1809, the year in which the Bank of Bengal was established. The Bank of Bombay was first constituted in 1840, with a capital of ₹ 52,25,000. The Bank of Madras was formed in 1843 with a capital of ₹ 30 lakh. To each banks, the Government had subscribed ₹ 3 lakh. A new era in the history of public banks in India came in 1860, when the principle of limited liability was first applied to joint stock banks. Till then, little or no banking legislation existed in India. Many banks had sprung up like mushrooms and failed mostly because of speculation, mis-management and fraud on the part of those responsible for their floatation, organisation and management.

Joint Stock Banks

Following the *Swadeshi* movement, many Indian *entrepreneurs* started banking institutions. The number of Indian joint stock banks increased remarkably during the boom of 1906-13. On the one hand, first half of the twentieth century witnessed a mushroom growth of banks; on the other, there was a failure of many banks because of mismanagement and irrational credit policies; as a result, 1917, 1932 and 1939 were the years of banking crisis in India. *Some of the important causes of bank failures during the period were:*

(i) Many of the managers as well as directors of the banks were incompetent and had little knowledge either of the principles or of the practice of banking.

(ii) There was keen competition and rivalry among them to attract deposits. This led them to offer much higher rates of interest than they could really afford.

(iii) In order to be able to pay the high rates of interest, they employed the funds at their disposal in hazardous enterprises.

(iv) There was also a great paucity of funds with these banks, which mostly depended on deposits which could be used only for giving short-term loans and advances.

(v) Most of these banks had locked up too large a proportion of their deposits in industrial investments. As a result, when their depositors got frightened and wanted to withdraw money, the bank's resources proved to be inadequate, and they failed.

(vi) Many banks had blocked large sums in speculative dealings in silver, pearls and other commodities. During the period of depression, therefore, they had to suffer huge losses as a result of which they had to close their doors.

(vii) These banks used to keep very low cash reserves. Even the liquid assets of many were small and precarious. Till 1913, there was no Act for regulating banking companies. Again, till the beginning of 1937, joint-stock banks in India were registered under the Indian Companies Act, 1913, and were governed by its general regulations, with the exception that in a few matters, the Act made a distinction between banks and other companies. But the provisions of this Act were very inadequate for the regulation of banking and had left many banking institutions altogether free from regulation.

(viii) There was no central bank in India till 1934 to control, supervise and help the joint stock banks in times of crisis.

☞ Exchange Banks

In addition to the Indian joint stock banks, a number of foreign banks, with head offices in parent countries, carried on business in India through their branches. They financed the foreign trade of the country by purchasing and discounting foreign bills of exchange, by making advances against shipping documents and by issuing foreign letters of credit. Because they were financed and offered by non-Indians, the Central Banking Inquiry Committee suggested that they should be required to take out a licence and should undertake to appoint Indians to executive posts.

☞ Imperial Bank and State Bank of India

The Presidency Banks referred to above were amalgamated into the Imperial Bank of India, which was brought into existence on 27th January, 1921 by the Imperial Bank of India Act, 1920. This Act, however, gave the Bank no power to issue notes and thus left it without control over the currency of the country. But it was allowed to hold Government balances and to manage public debt and clearing houses till the establishment of the Reserve Bank of India in 1935 which apart from taking overall these functions from the Imperial Bank of India, was given the privilege of acting as an agent of the latter in places where it had no branches. After independence there was a strong demand for the nationalisation of the Imperial Bank of India. Government, however, was not in favour of it because of two reasons. First, the bank had branches outside India which created political problems of great magniturde; secondly, it was thought that nationalisation was likely to divest the bank of its useful commercial functions. The Rural Banking Enquiry Committee (1950), too, recommended against its nationalisation. But the Rural Credit Survey Committee recommended the nationalisation of the Imperial Bank of India.

In pursuance of this recommendation, the Government of India set up the State Bank of India on July 1, 1955, which tookover the business of the Imperial Bank of India.

☞ Social Control on Banks

A demand for the nationalisation of commercial banks was made time and again and even a strong section of the ruling Congress Party supported nationalisation. It was felt that nationalisation was the only way to solve the problems of banking in the private sector. At the Bhubaneshwar session of the Congress Party in 1964, a twelve-point programme of achievements, as a result of nationalisation of banks was placed which covered measures to mitigate the entire range of economic and social evils and to achieve all aspirations.

The Government was not opposed to the move for bank nationalisation. But the decision to nationalise the banks was not taken because of administrative difficulties and also the consequential effects on the economy of the country. As an alternative, the Government tried to reform the commercial banking system through legislative and other measures from time to time. One such important measure was social control on banks. A comprehensive scheme of social control on banks was enforced through legislative measures on 1st Feb., 1969 to serve the cause of economic growth and fulfil our social objectives more effectively. The aim of social control was to bring about changes in the management and credit policy of the commercial banks. The close link between big business houses and big banks was intended to be snapped or at least made ineffective by the reconstitution of the boards of directors with the effect that at least 51% of the directors were to have special knowledge or practical experience in accountancy, agriculture and rural economy, banking, cooperation, finance, economics, law, small-scale industry and any other matters as may be useful to the banking company. To professionalise the top management, provision was made for the appointment of a whole-time chairman with special knowledge and practical experience of the working of commercial bank or financial, economic or business administration. Another step to avoid undesirable flow of credit to units in which directors were interested was to impose restrictions on loans granted to the directors' concerns. Provision was also made for the takeover of banks under certain circumstances.

A National Credit Council was set up to perform the following functions in the direction of credit planning:

(i) to assess the demand for bank credit from various sectors of the economy;

(ii) to determine priorities for grant of loans and advances and for investment having regard to the availability of resources and requirements of priority sectors; and

(iii) to coordinate lending and investment policies as between commercial banks and cooperative banks and other specialised agencies to ensure the optimum and efficient use of the overall resources.

The actual implementation of the scheme of Social Control on Banks started much earlier than the formal enforcement of the Banking Laws (Amendment) Act, 1969. In many cases, the General Managers of the banks were appointed as chairmen and the boards were reconstituted in accordance with the above-mentioned provisions. The banks also embarked upon various schemes to provide finance to priority sectors of agriculture and small-scale industries in compliance with the targets fixed by the National Credit Council.

Nationalisation of Banks: There are two important disadvantages of capitalism, *i.e.,* clash of interests and occasional crisis. The nationalisation of banks has restored harmony of interest and softened the intensity of booms and depressions. In a country which has embarked on economic planning based on a socialist pattern of society, it is not only desirable but also necessary to nationalise some important banking institutions to serve the larger interests of the nation. Nationalisation of banks began with the passing of the Reserve Bank (Transfer of Public Ownership) Act, 1948, which became law on the 3rd September, 1948. It was thought desirable to nationalise the bank to ensure greater co-ordination of monetary, economic and fiscal policies. The nationalisation of the Reserve Bank was, indeed, necessary in the interests of large-scale planning upon which the Union Government had embarked. The Five-Year Plans envisaged an important role for the bank. The second major attempt at nationalisation of banking in India was made in 1955 which came to be known as the State Bank of India. An important statutory function assigned to the State Bank is the promotion of banking through the establishment of an effective machinery of branches spread over the whole country.

The third major attempt was made when 14 leading commercial banks, with deposits exceeding ₹ 50 crore each, were nationalised on 19th July, 1969 by Mrs. Indira Gandhi, the then Prime Minister. Their takeover was intended "to serve better the needs of development of the economy in conformity with national priorities and objectives". The banks which were nationalised are:

(i) Central Bank of India;

(ii) Bank of India;

(iii) Punjab National Bank;

(iv) Bank of Baroda;

(v) United Commercial Bank;

(vi) Canara Bank;

(vii) United Bank of India;

(viii) Dena Bank;

(ix) Syndicate Bank;

(x) Union Bank of India;

(xi) Allahabad Bank;

(xii) Indian Bank;

(xiii) Bank of Maharashtra; and

(xiv) Indian Overseas Bank.

Over 85 per cent of the total deposits with the banking system passed into public control with the nationalisation of these 14 banks. The total deposits with banks at the end of June 1969 were of the order of ₹ 4,600 crore; of this, deposits amounting to ₹ 2,700 crore were accounted for by the 14 nationalised banks. The State Bank and its subsidiaries had deposits amounting to ₹ 1,300 crore. Thus, the nationalised sector of banking possessed ₹ 4,000 crore out of the total deposits of ₹ 4,600 crore.

On 15th April, 1980, six more banks in the private sector were nationalised. The six banks were:

1. The Andhra Bank Ltd.,
2. Corporation Bank Ltd.,
3. The New Bank of India Ltd.,
4. The Oriental Bank of Commerce Ltd.,
5. The Punjab and Sind Bank Ltd.,
6. Vijaya Bank Ltd.,

The demand and time liabilities of these banks on 14 March, 1980 were about ₹ 200 crore. The objective of this nationalisation was to enhance the ability of the banking system to meet more effectively the needs of the development of the economy and to promote the welfare of the people more adequately. The amount to be paid in respect of the transfer of undertakings of the above six banks was ₹ 18.50 crore. With the nationalisation of the above six banks, the number of public sector banks increased to 28 (comprising the State Bank of India and its 7 subsidiaries and 20 nationalised banks) exclusive of Regional Rural Banks. These banks accounted for 91 per cent of the total deposits and credit of commercial banks in April, 1980.

Before the steps of nationalisation of Indian banks, only State Bank of India (SBI) was nationalised. It took place in July 1955 under the SBI Act of 1955. Nationalisation of seven State Banks of India (formed subsidiary) took place on 19th July, 1960.

The State Bank of India is India's largest commercial bank and is ranked one of the top five banks worldwide. It serves 90 million customers through a network of 9,000 branches and it offers — either directly or through subsidiaries — a wide range of banking services.

Till 1980, approximately 80% of the banking segment in India were under Government ownership.

After the nationalisation of banks in India, the branches of the public sector banks rose to approximately 800% in deposits and advances took a huge jump by 11,000%.

- 1955 : Nationalisation of State Bank of India.
- 1959 : Nationalisation of SBI subsidiaries.
- 1969 : Nationalisation of 14 major banks.
- 1980 : Nationalisation of six banks with deposits over ₹ 200 crore.

The Indian banking industry is still very traditional in practice and outlook and is not particularly well-endowed with managerial competence, particularly of the innovative kind required to break new ground and make credit a more purposeful instrument of social policy. This requires an altogether different kind of expertise and experience at various levels, which is in short supply at present. That is the reason why the National Institute of Bank Management, Bombay, and many Bankers' Training Colleges have been opened to conduct research and train bank officials.

The nationalised banks play a new and pioneering role in helping the public sector get on its feet. Current notions of public accountability have made severe inroads into the autonomy of public undertakings, while close association with the Secretariat in terms of officials, protocol, procedures and personnel has resulted in a certain bureaucratisation in their outlook. It should be possible to cut the umbilical cord that binds the public sector to the Government and to forge a new commercial and techno-economic nexus between the public sector and the nationalised banks. In such a situation, public undertakings would turn to the banks for financial assistance which would only be advanced on the basis of the techno-economic feasibility and commercial viability of any given proposal or project. Banks would probably be in a better position to evaluate the working of a project than the Secretariat and would not have to answer questions on the manner of management in Parliament every other day.

In order that it may become an effective instrument for the mobilisation of savings and the distribution of credit along socially desirable lines, bank nationalisation must be related to a larger policy framework from which a series of mutually compatible programmes derive. It may not be correct to assume that nationalisation would necessarily make the economy more socialist. Everything will depend on how the nationalised banks are managed, the type of supporting policies adopted, and how vigorously they are implemented. In their actual working, it is even possible for the nationalised banks to build-up and support interests in agriculture and industry which are "very different from those that the advocates of nationalisation had in mind". If effectively implemented and followed up, nationalisation could prove an extremely important step in the management of credit. On the other hand, if banks do not function effectively, nationalisation may promote serious dislocations and distortions in the economy, and a transfer of deposits may take place from the nationalised banks to the smaller banks which are still in the private sector.

☞ Reasons for Nationalisation

The broad objectives of the Governments decision to nationalise the 14 major banks in 1969 were summed up by Prime Minister Indira Gandhi in the Parliament on July 21, 1969, as follows:

"While the nation is committed to establish a socialist pattern of society, the Government felt that the public ownership and control of the commanding heights of the national economy and its strategic sectors were essential and important aspects of the new social order which we are trying to build. As the financial institutions are amongst the most important levers for the achievement of its social objectives, the nationalisation of major banks was felt a significant step in the process of public ownership over the principal institutions for the mobilisation of people's savings and canalising them towards productive purposes. The Government felt that the public ownership of the major banks will help in the most effective mobilisation and development of national resources so that our objectives can be realised with a great degree of assurance".

The important reasons for the nationalisation of major banks in India can be enumerated as follows:

(a) Equitable distribution of economic power: Before nationalisation, most of the major banks in the country were owned and managed by industrialists and businessmen and, therefore, they used to get the major portion of credit granted by the banks. That is why, the most important reason for the nationalisation of banks was to equitably distribute the economic power, so far concentrated in the hands of a small minority. Even the Monopolies Enquiry Commission, 1965, observed that big business had an advantage over small businesses in obtaining assistance from banks.

(b) To provide finance to neglected sectors of agriculture, small-scale industries, etc.: Some important sectors of Indian economy like agriculture and small-scale industries were not provided with sufficient amount of credit by banks because of risk involved in financing these sectors. Public ownership and control of large banks was felt essential to bring about such changes in the banking policies and practices which may provide finance to neglected sectors.

(c) Removal of malpractices: One of the reasons of nationalisation was to remove the malpractices adopted by banks to favour industrialists and big businessmen. It was not possible to completely stop such malpractices till the top management of the banks remained in the hands of industrialists and big businessmen.

(d) Expansion of banking facilities: Banks in India mostly confined their activities to urban areas with the result that rural areas remained outside their purview. Most of the commercial banks did not expand their business to small towns and rural areas because it was not a profitable proposition in the initial years. This was one of the reasons for the nationalisation of banks so that a massive programme of branch expansion be launched to mobilise deposits and provide credit facilities in rural areas.

In addition to the economic reasons stated above, there was also a need for a change in attitude, outlook and objectives of the banks. Banking institutions are not ordinary commercial enterprises but they provide essential public utility services and also help in the achievement of the social objectives and, therefore, they ought to be under public ownership.

The primary objective of nationalisation of banks was to shift vast financial resources from the hands of a few large business houses (controlling these banks) to the true and rightful claimants, *i.e.*, all sections of society especially the sections so far neglected by the banks. The nationalisation process thus heralded the beginning of social banking, mass banking and innovative banking.

Questions

1. Discuss the rationale of nationalisation of banks in India.
2. When and why were the first fourteen banks nationalised? What do you think has been achieved by the nationalisation of these banks so far? Why was it found necessary to nationalise six more banks recently?
   (I.I.B. Part I, Nov. 1980)
3. What are the social objectives for which the big commercial banks in India were nationalised?
4. What are the broad objectives of the Government in nationalising 14 major commercial banks? In what respect does it differ from social control which had prevailed earlier?
5. Discuss the compelling economic reasons for nationalisation of banks in India.

CHAPTER

2 Present Banking System in India

☞ History of Banking In India

Without a sound and effective banking system in India, it cannot have a healthy economy. The banking system of India should not only be hassle free but it should be able to meet new challenges posed by the technology and any other external and internal factors.

For the past three decades, India's banking system has several outstanding achievements to its credit. The most striking is its extensive reach. It is no longer confined to only metropolitans or cosmopolitans in India. In fact, Indian banking system has reached even to the remote corners of the country. This is one of the main reason of India's growth process.

The governments regular policy for Indian Bank since 1969 has been rich dividends with the nationalisation of 14 major private banks of India.

Not long ago, an accountholder had to wait for hours at the bank counters for getting a draft or for withdrawing his own money. Today, he has a choice. Gone are the days when the most efficient bank transferred money from one branch to other in two days. Now, it is simple as instant messaging or dial a pizza. Money have become the order of the day.

The first bank in India, though conservative, was established in 1786. From 1786 till today, the journey of Indian Banking System can be segregated into three distinct phases. They are as mentioned below:

- Early phase from 1786 to 1969 of Indian Banks.
- Nationalisation of Indian Banks and up to 1991 prior to Indian Banking Sector Reforms.
- New phase of Indian Banking System with the advent of Indian Financial and Banking Sector Reforms after 1991.

(To make this write-up more explanatory, the whole scenario has been prefixed as Phase I, Phase II and Phase III.)

☞ Phase I

The General Bank of India was set up in the year 1786. Next came Bank of Hindustan and Bengal Bank. The East India Company established Bank of Bengal (1809), Bank of Bombay (1840) and Bank of Madras (1843) as independent units and called it Presidency Banks. These three banks were amalgamated in 1920 and Imperial Bank of India was established which started as private shareholders banks, mostly European shareholders.

In 1865, Allahabad Bank was established and first time exclusively by Indians. Punjab National Bank Ltd., was set up in 1894 with headquarters at Lahore. Between 1906 and 1913, Bank of India, Central Bank of India, Bank of Baroda, Canara Bank, Indian Bank, and Bank of Mysore were set up. Reserve Bank of India came in 1935.

During the first phase, the growth was very slow and banks also experienced periodic failures between 1913 and 1948. There were approximately 1,100 banks, mostly small. To streamline the functioning and activities of commercial banks, the Government of India came up with the Banking Companies Act, 1949 which was later changed to Banking Regulation Act, 1949 as per amending Act of 1965 (Act No. 23 of 1965) Reserve Bank of India was vested with extensive powers for the supervision of banking in India as the Central Banking Authority.

During those days, public had lesser confidence in the banks. As an aftermath, deposit mobilisation was slow. Abreast of it, the savings bank facility provided by the Postal department was comparatively safer. Moreover, funds were largely given to traders.

☞ Phase II

Government took major steps in this Indian Banking Sector Reform after independence. In 1955, it nationalised Imperial Bank of India with extensive banking facilities on a large-scale, specially in rural and semi-urban areas. It formed State Bank of India to act as the principal agent of RBI and to handle banking transactions of the Union and State Governments all over the country.

Seven banks forming subsidiary of State Bank of India was nationalised in 1960 on 19th July, 1969, major process of nationalisation was carried out. It was the effort of the then Prime Minister of India, Mrs. Indira Gandhi, 14 major commercial banks in the country were nationalised.

Second phase of nationalisation in Indian Banking Sector Reform was carried out in 1980 with seven more banks. This step brought 80% of the banking segment in India under Government ownership.

The following are the steps taken by the Government of India to Regulate Banking Institutions in the country:

- 1949: Enactment of Banking Regulation Act.
- 1955: Nationalisation of State Bank of India.
- 1959: Nationalisation of SBI subsidiaries.
- 1961: Insurance cover extended to deposits.
- 1969: Nationalisation of 14 major banks.
- 1971: Creation of credit guarantee corporation.
- 1975: Creation of regional rural banks.
- 1980: Nationalisation of six banks with deposits over ₹ 200 crore.

After the nationalisation of banks, the branches of the public sector bank, India rose to approximately 800% in deposits and advances took a huge jump by 11,000%.

Banking in the sunshine of Government ownership gave the public implicit faith and immense confidence about the sustainability of these institutions.

☞ Phase III

This phase has introduced many more products and facilities in the banking sector in its reforms measure. In 1991, under the chairmanship of M. Narasimham, a committee was set up by his name which worked for the liberalisation of banking practices.

The country is flooded with foreign banks and their ATM stations. Efforts are being put to give a satisfactory service to customers. Phone banking and net banking is introduced. The entire system became more convenient and swift. Time is given more importance than money.

The financial system of India has shown a great deal of resilience. It is sheltered from any crisis triggered by any external macroeconomics shock as other East Asian countries suffered. This is all due to a flexible exchange rate regime, the foreign reserves are high, the capital account is not yet fully convertible, and banks and their customers have limited foreign exchange exposure.

In the economic development of a nation, banks occupy an important place. Banking institutions form an important part of the money market and are indispensable in a modern developing society. Indian money market comprises both organised as well as unorganised sectors. The unorganised sector includes moneylenders and indigenous bankers and largely caters to the needs of persons living in villages and small towns. It is estimated that about one-third of the total credit requirements of the country are met by the unorganised sector. Financial institutions in the organised sector have grown significantly in the last three decades. Amongst the institutions in the organised sector of the Indian money market, commercial banks and cooperative banks have been in existence for a pretty long time. An important development in the organised sector was the formation of Regional Rural Banks (RRBs) in the seventies, to cater to the financial needs of rural areas. Commercial banks have also expanded their activities in multifarious ways, *i.e.,* geographical expansion, amount of credit, types of credit facilities and to different new types of customers. Thus, quantitatively as well as qualitatively these banking institutions have increased their services tremendously in recent years.

Besides the cooperative banks, commercial banks and Regional Rural Banks, a variety of specialised financial institutions have been set up in the country to cater to the specific needs of trade, commerce, agriculture, industry and other activities.

In the field of agricultural finance and allied activities, cooperative credit societies and central co-operative banks have been in operation since long. After nationalisation in 1969, commercial banks also have expanded their activities to rural areas and provide finance for agriculture and allied activities. Another important specialised institution which provides long and medium-term credit to farmers is Land Development Bank. Land Development Banks have a two-tier structure — primary Land Development Bank at the district level and State Land Development Banks at the State level. National Bank for Agriculture and Rural Development (NABARD) is the apex institution in the field of agriculture and rural development. The chart given here states the different types of banking institutions which comprise the organised sector of the Indian banking system/Indian money market.

In the field of industrial finance, the Industrial Development Bank of India (IDBI) was established in the year 1964 as the apex bank whose responsibilities are to provide direct finance to big industrial project and provide refinancing facilities for the term loans granted by other financial institutions including commercial banks. Three important national level institutions in this field are Industrial Finance Corporation of India (IFCI), the Industrial Credit and Investment Corporation of India (ICICI) and the Industrial Reconstruction Corporation of India (IRCI). At the state level there are State Finance Corporations (SFCs) and State Industrial Development Corporations (SIDCs) which have been set up to meet the requirements of small and medium-scale industries in the respective states. All these banking institutions differ from the traditional commercial banks, in a sense that they provide finance mostly for developmental purposes and are, therefore, called "development banks". These development banks have filled up the much needed gap in the Indian banking system, *i.e.,* that of industrial finance. In the last few years the contribution of development banks in the industrial growth of the country has been significant. Export-Import Bank of India was set up on January 1, 1982 mainly to cater to the need of foreign trade of the country.

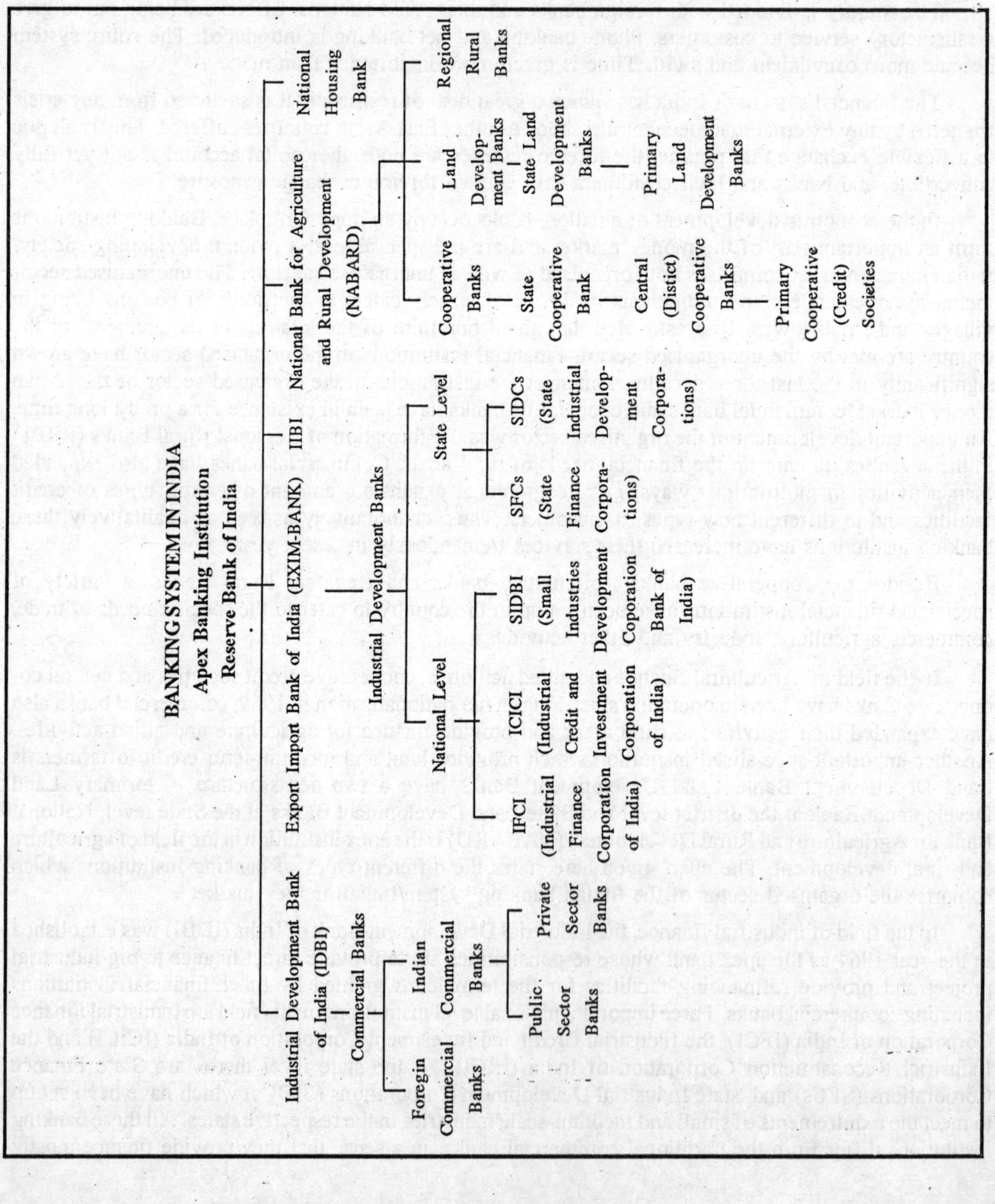

During 1988 two important financial institutions were established. National Housing Bank was set up in July 1988 as the apex banking institution in the field of housing finance. Discount and Finance of India Ltd., was stabilised to deal in money market instruments in order to provide liquidity in the money market.

The above-mentioned banking institutions provide financial assistance to the various segments of the society. In addition to these institutions, there are certain other institutions which provide investment finance to Government, Semi-government and Corporate securities. Such institutions include two insurance institutions — Life Insurance Corporation of India (LIC), the General Insurance Corporation of India (GIC) and the Unit Trust of India (UTI). These institutional investors mobilise the savings of the people and channelise them into desirable securities and, therefore, are called investing institutions.

Two other institutions have been set up in recent years to foster the growth of banking services and to facilitate the banking habit. The Deposit Insurance and Credit Guarantee Corporation of India performs two important functions of extending the insurance cover to the depositors in banks and protecting the interests of banks by providing guarantees in respect of advances granted by them to small-scale industries and the priority and neglected sectors of the economy. The Export Credit Guarantee Corporation (ECGC) provides protection to the banks in respect of risks inherent in financing the export trade. Now with the establishment of all these institutions, the banking system of India has become a highly organised and efficient banking system and is in no way less than the banking systems of developed countries. An institution-wise discussion of the various units of the Indian Banking System has been given in the following paragraphs:

☞ Scheduled Commercial Banks in India

The commercial banking structure in India consists of:

- Scheduled Commercial Banks in India
- Unscheduled Banks in India.

Scheduled Banks in India constitute those banks which have been included in the Second Schedule of Reserve Bank of India (RBI) Act, 1934. RBI in turn includes only those banks in this schedule which satisfy the criteria laid down vide Section 42 (6) (a) of the Act.

As on 30th June, 1999, there were 300 scheduled banks in India having a total network of 64,918 branches. The scheduled commercial banks in India comprise of State Bank of India and its associates (8), nationalised banks (19), foreign banks (45), private sector banks (32), cooperative banks and regional rural banks.

"Scheduled banks in India" means the State Bank of India constituted under the State Bank of India Act, 1955 (23 of 1955), a subsidiary bank as defined in the State Bank of India (Subsidiary Banks) Act, 1959 (38 of 1959), a corresponding new bank constituted under Section 3 of the Banking Companies (Acquisition and Transfer of Undertakings) Act, 1970 (5 of 1970), or under Section 3 of the Banking Companies (Acquisition and Transfer of Undertakings) Act, 1980 (40 of 1980), or any other bank being a bank included in the Second Schedule to the Reserve Bank of India Act, 1934 (2 of 1934), but does not include a cooperative bank.

"Non-scheduled bank in India" means a banking company as defined in Clause (c) of Section 5 of the Banking Regulation Act, 1949 (10 of 1949), which is not a scheduled bank.

The following are the Scheduled Banks in India (Public Sector):

- State Bank of India
- State Bank of Bikaner and Jaipur

- State Bank of Hyderabad
- State Bank of Indore
- State Bank of Mysore
- State Bank of Patiala
- State Bank of Saurashtra
- State Bank of Travancore
- Andhra Bank
- Allahabad Bank
- Bank of Baroda
- Bank of India
- Bank of Maharashtra
- Canara Bank
- Central Bank of India
- Corporation Bank
- Dena Bank
- Indian Overseas Bank
- Indian Bank
- Oriental Bank of Commerce
- Punjab National Bank
- Punjab and Sind Bank
- Syndicate Bank
- Union Bank of India
- United Bank of India
- UCO Bank
- Vijaya Bank

The following are the Scheduled Banks in India (Private Sector):

- Vysya Bank Ltd.
- UTI Bank Ltd.
- IndusInd Bank Ltd.
- ICICI Banking Corporation Bank Ltd.
- Global Trust Bank Ltd.
- HDFC Bank Ltd.
- Centurion Bank Ltd.
- Bank of Punjab Ltd.
- IDBI Bank Ltd.

The following are the Scheduled Foreign Banks in India:

- American Express Bank Ltd.
- ANZ Grindlays Bank Plc.
- Bank of America N.T. and S.A.
- Bank of Tokyo Ltd.
- Banquc Nationale de Paris
- Barclays Bank Plc.
- Citi Bank N.C.
- Deutsche Bank A.G.
- Hong Kong and Shanghai Banking Corporation
- Standard Chartered Bank
- The Chase Manhattan Bank Ltd.
- Dresdner Bank A.G.

In India the banks are being segregated in different groups. Each group has their own benefits and limitations in operating in India. Each has their own dedicated target market. Few of them only work in rural sector, while others in both rural as well as urban. Many even are only catering in cities. Some are of Indian origin and some are foreign players.

All these details and many more is discussed over here. The banks and its relation with the customers, their mode of operation, the names of banks under different groups and other such useful informations are talked about.

One more section has been taken note of is the upcoming foreign banks in India. The RBI has shown certain interest to involve more of foreign banks than the existing ones recently. This step has paved a way for few more foreign banks to start business in India.

☛ Major Banks in India

- ABN-AMRO Bank
- Abu Dhabi Commercial Bank
- American Express Bank
- Andhra Bank
- Allahabad Bank
- AXIS Bank (Earlier UTI Bank)
- Bank of Baroda
- Bank of India
- Bank of Maharashtra
- Bank of Punjab
- Bank of Rajasthan
- Bank of Ceylon
- BNP Paribas Bank
- Canara Bank
- Catholic Syrian Bank
- Central Bank of India
- Centurion Bank
- China Trust Commercial Bank
- Citi Bank
- City Union Bank
- Corporation Bank
- Dena Bank
- Deutsche Bank
- Development Credit Bank
- Dhanalakshmi Bank
- Federal Bank

- HDFC Bank
- HSBC ICICI Bank
- IDBI Bank
- Indian Bank
- Indian overseas Bank
- Indus Ind Bank
- ING Vysya Bank
- Jammu and Kashmir Bank
- JP Morgan Chase Bank
- Karnataka Bank
- Karur Vysya Bank
- Laxmi Vilas Bank
- Oriental Bank of Commerce
- Punjab National Bank
- Punjab and Sind Bank
- Scotia Bank
- South Indian Bank
- Standard Chartered Bank
- State Bank of India (SBI)
- State Bank of Bikaner and Jaipur
- State Bank of Hyderabad
- State Bank of Indore
- State Bank of Mysore
- State Bank of Saurashtra
- State Bank of Travancore
- Syndicate Bank
- Taib Sank
- UCO Bank
- Union Bank of India
- United Bank of India
- United Western Bank
- Vijaya Bank

Among the Public Sector Banks in India, United Bank of India is one of the 14 major banks which was nationalised on July 19, 1969. Its predecessor, in the Public Sector Banks, the United Bank of India Ltd., was formed in 1950 with the amalgamation of four banks, *viz.,* Comilla Banking Corporation Ltd., (1914), Bengal Central Bank Ltd., (1918), Comilla Union Bank Ltd., (1922) and Hooghly Bank Ltd., (1932).

Oriental Bank of Commerce (OBC), a Government of India Undertaking offers Domestic, NRI and Commercial banking services. OBC is implementing a GRAMEEN PROJECT in Dehradun District (UP) and Hanumangarh District (Rajasthan) disbursing small loans. This Public Sector Bank of India has implemented 14 point action plans for strengthening of credit delivery to women and has designated 5 branches as specialized branches for women entrepreneurs.

The following are the list of Public Sector Banks in India:

- Allahabad Bank
- Andhra Bank
- Bank of Baroda
- Bank of India
- Bank of Maharashtra
- Canara Bank
- Central Bank of India
- Corporation Bank
- Dena Bank
- Indian Bank
- Indian Overseas Bank

- Oriental Bank of Commerce
- Punjab and Sind Bank
- Punjab National Bank
- Syndicate Bank
- UCO Bank
- Union Bank of India
- United Bank of India
- Vijaya Bank

☞ List of State Bank of India and its Subsidiary, a Public Sector Banks

- **State Bank of India**
    - State Bank of Bikaner and Jaipur
    - State Bank of Hyderabad
    - State Bank of Indore
    - State Bank of Mysore
    - State Bank of Saurashtra
    - State Bank of Travancore

Private banking in India was practiced since the beginning of banking system in India. The first private bank in India to be set up in Private Sector Banks was IndusInd Bank. It is one of the fastest growing Private Sector Banks in India. IDBI ranks the tenth largest development bank in the world as Private Banks in India and has promoted a world-class institutions in India.

The first private bank in India to receive an in principle approval from the Reserve Bank of India was Housing Development Finance Corporation Limited, to set up a bank in the private sector banks in India as part of the RBI's liberalisation of the Indian Banking Industry. It was incorporated in August 1994 as HDFC Bank Limited with registered office in Mumbai and commenced operations as Scheduled Commercial Bank in January 1995.

ING Vysya, yet another Private Bank of India was incorporated in the year 1930. Bangalore has a pride of place for having the first branch inception in the year 1934. With successive years of patronage and constantly setting new standards in banking, ING Vysya Bank has many credits to its account.

List of Private Banks in India

- Bank of Punjab
- Bank of Rajasthan
- Catholic Syrian Bank
- Centurion Bank
- City Union Bank
- Dhanalakshmi Bank

- Development Credit Bank
- Federal Bank
- HDFC Bank
- ICICI Bank
- Indus Ind Bank
- ING Vysya Bank
- Jammu and Kashmir Bank
- Karnataka Bank
- Karur Vysya Bank
- Laxmi Vilas Bank
- South Indian Bank
- United Western Bank
- UTI Bank

☞ Nationalised Banks vs. The State Bank of India

The points of differences between the nationalised banks and the State Bank of India are given on the following:

1. Separate Statutes

All the 27 commercial banks were joint stock companies registered under the Indian Companies Act and were later nationalised under the Banking Companies (Acquisition and Transfer of Undertakings) Act, 1970. The State Bank of India was established under the State Bank of India Act, 1955, and the subsidiary banks under the State Bank of India (Subsidiary Banks) Act, 1959. Thus, these banks are governed by their respective statutes.

2. Ownership

All the 20 nationalised banks are fully owned by the Government of India, whereas, the State Bank of India is owned, to a large extent, by the Reserve Bank of India. There is still some private ownership in the share capital of the State Bank. The subsidiary banks are owned by the State Bank of India. Some of the nationalised banks like Oriental Bank of Commerce, Dena Bank, Bank of India, etc., have enlarged their capital by issuing share to the public.

3. Functions

One of the important functions of the State Bank of India is to act as an agent of the Reserve Bank of India. Under Section 45 of the Reserve Bank of India Act, 1934, "The Reserve Bank shall appoint the State Bank as its sole agent at all places in India where it does not have an office or branch of its banking department and there is a branch of the State Bank or branch of a subsidiary bank". The 20 nationalised banks have not been entrusted with this function of acting as an agent of Reserve Bank. But with the enforcement of the Banking Laws (Amendment) Act, 1983, the Reserve Bank has been empowered to appoint any nationalised bank to act as its agent at all the places in India where it has a branch for the following purposes:

(a) Paying, receiving, collecting and remitting money, bullion and securities on behalf of Government; and

(b) Undertaking and transacting any other business entrusted by the Reserve Bank from time-to-time.

☞ Cooperative Banks

Farmers in India are scattered all over the country and need short-term small borrowings for agricultural purposes. This need is not fulfilled by commercial banks which are unsuited for financing agriculture. Land which these farmers can offer to cover bank advances is not generally accepted as security by commercial banks. Therefore, special types of banks are necessary for the financing of agriculture. Cooperative banks are best suited for this purpose. The object of cooperative banks is to offer banking facilities to persons of limited means requiring credit for productive purposes in the use of the land and labour at their disposal. In 1914, the Government of India appointed a committee under Sir Edward Maclagan to survey the progress of cooperation in the country. The Committee submitted its report in 1915, in which it made several recommendations, the principal one being the institution of Provincial Cooperative Banks to serve as apex banks in the hierarchy of the cooperative pyramid. The present organisation in India is based upon the findings of this report. In 1919, the Montague-Chelmsford Act made cooperation a provincial subject. Since then, all the State Governments have passed their own separate Cooperative Societies Acts.

The cooperative banking structure in India may be divided into three component parts, *viz.*, *(i)* Primary Credit Societies at the base, *(ii)* Central Cooperative Banks at the district level in the middle, and *(iii)* Provincial or State Cooperative Banks (also called apex banks) at the top.

☞ Primary Cooperative Credit Societies

The primary cooperative credit society is an association of borrowers and non-borrowers residing in a particular locality. The funds of the society are derived from the share capital and deposits of members and loans from Central Cooperative Banks. The borrowing power of the members as well as of the society is fixed. The loans are given to members for the purchase of cattle, fodder, fertilisers, pesticides, implements, etc.

☞ Central Cooperative Banks

These are the federations of primary credit societies in a district, and are of two types — those having a membership of primary societies only and those having a membership of societies as well as individuals. The funds of the bank consist of share capital, deposits, loans and overdrafts from State Co-operative Banks and joint stocks. These banks finance member societies within the limits of the borrowing capacity of societies. They also conduct all the business of a joint-stock bank.

☞ State Cooperative Banks

The State Cooperative Bank is a federation of central cooperative banks and acts as a watchdog of the cooperative banking structure in the State. Its funds are obtained from share capital, deposits, loans and overdrafts from the Reserve Bank of India. The State Cooperative Banks lend money to central cooperative banks and primary societies and not directly to farmers.

☞ The Regional Rural Banks

Another set of new banking institutions which have been added to the Indian Banking system since Oct. 1975 are the Regional Rural Banks. The main objectives of RRBs are to develop the rural economy by providing for the purpose of development of agriculture and allied activities, village industries and other productive activities in rural areas, credit and other facilities, particularly to the small and marginal farmers, agricultural labourers, artisans and small entrepreneurs.

Regional Rural Banks have been established by the Government of India in terms of the provisions of the Regional Rural Banks Act, 1976. The necessity of such banks was felt because the existing credit institutions — the cooperative banks and the commercial banks — were unable to fully meet the needs of rural areas.

There are 196 Regional Rural Banks in all states of the country except Sikkim covering 392 of the total of 478 districts having a network of 14,539 branches. Up to March, 1992 these banks mobilised deposits of ₹ 5,867.83 crore in 345.26 lakh deposit accounts. Rural banks extended loans worth ₹ 4,090.86 crore to 123.99 lakh borrowers up to March, 1992.

Although Regional Rural Banks have achieved the basic objectives for which they were set up, they have not so far been able to achieve the economic viability. The accumulated losses of 194 banks amounted to ₹ 101.04 crore as on 31st March, 1989. The reasons for the Regional Rural Banks incurring losses mainly are:

(i) impact of narrow spread,

(ii) restriction on the choice of clientele,

(iii) area of operation as well as other restrictions on the profitability.

Other features of these banks are that out of the 115 districts identified under the Tribal Sub-plan Area in whole of the country, as many as 94 districts have been covered by the Regional Rural Banks.

Regional Rural Banks can be made viable through a process of amalgamation. Merging them with the sponsoring banks is certainly not the solution as the latter have enough problems in their hands. Merger of RRBs at the state level into separate banks would be a more feasible proposition. The other alternative can be the takeover of these banks by NABARD. It would enable NABARD to have grass-root level presence as against its present city based structure. Instead of being only an apex refinancing agency, it can assert itself as the real rural bank with over 14,000 outlets.

☞ Performance of RRBs in the Spatial Dimension

☞ Some Stylised Facts

The RRBs, over the years have made impressive strides on various business indicators. For instance, deposits of RRBs have grown by 18 times and advances by 13 times between 1980 and 1990. Between 1990 and 2004, deposits and advances grew by 14 times and 7 times, respectively (Table 1). Between the year 2000 and 2004, loans disbursed by RRBs more than doubled reflecting the efforts taken by the banks to improve credit flow to the rural sector. The average per branch advances also increased from ₹ 25 lakh in March 1990 to ₹ 154 lakh in March 2003. When one considers the deployment of credit relative to the mobilisation of resources, the credit-deposit (C-D) ratio of RRBs were more than 100 per cent during the first decade of their operations up to 1987. Though the C-D ratio subsequently became lower, of late, it has shown an improvement and went up from around 39 per cent in March 2000 to 44.5 per cent in March 2004.

Table 2.1

EVOLUTION OF RRBs: SELECT INDICATORS

(₹ *in Crore*)

Parameter	*1980*	*1985*	*1990*	*1995*	*1996*	*1997*	*1998*	*1999*	*2000*	*2001*	*2002*	*2003*	*2004*
No. of RRBs	85	188	196	196	196	196	196	196	196	196	196	196	196
Capital	21	46	91	166	358	705	1,118	1,380	1,959	2,049	2,143	2,141	2,221
Deposits	222	1,315	4,023	11,141	14,171	17,976	22,191	27,059	32,226	38,294	44,539	49,582	56,295
Investments	20	164	60	1,348	2,879	3,891	5,280	6,680	7,760	8,800	9,471	17,138	21,286
Advances	262	1,405	3,384	5,987	7,057	7,908	9,021	10,559	12,427	15,050	17,710	20,934	25,038
Total Assets	426	2,320	6,081	14,886	18,969	24,376	29,468	35,820	42,236	49,596	56,802	62,500	70,195
Interest Earned	NA	NA	480	1,158	1,421	2,033	2,624	3,281	3,938	4,619	5,191	5,391	5,535
Other income	NA	NA	113	72	89	103	136	151	207	240	370	430	697
Total Income	NA	NA	593	1,230	1,511	2,136	2,760	3,432	4,145	4,859	5,561	5,821	6,231
Interest expended	NA	NA	326	851	1,065	1,462	1,773	2,131	2,565	2,966	3,329	3,440	3,363
Operating expenses	NA	NA	254	657	726	804	845	982	1,056	1,165	1,459	1,667	1,825
Provisions and contingencies	NA	NA	NA	120	171	673	72	99	96	128	163	132	289
Total expenses	NA	NA	581	1,509	1,791	2,265	2,617	3,113	3,621	4,130	4,787	5,107	5,187
Operating Profit	NA	NA	12	–279	–280	–129	143	319	524	729	774	714	1,044

Note: Total expenses are excluding provisions and contingencies.

Source: Reserve Bank of India.

☞ HIGHLIGHTS 2004-2005

☞ Credit Operations

➢ Short-term credit limits sanctioned during 2004-05:

- For SCBs, RRBs — seasonal agricultural operations — ₹ 10,185.06 crore.
- For RRBs — other than seasonal agricultural operations — ₹ 216.83 crore.
- For SCBs — financing Weavers' Cooperative Societies — ₹ 349.89 crore.

➢ Long-term loans sanctioned to 7 State Governments for contribution to the share capital of cooperative credit institutions aggregated ₹ 32.98 crore.

➢ Liquidity support to SCBs — ₹ 1,914.24 crore.

➢ Liquidity support to RRBs — ₹ 158.78 crore.

➢ Investment Credit to CBs, SCARDBs, SCBs, RRBs and other eligible institutions — ₹ 7,605.29 crore.

☞ Kisan Credit Card Scheme

➢ During the year (up to February 2005), 70.43 lakh cards issue by co-operative banks, RRBs and commercial banks.

➢ Since inception in 1998-99, 4.84 crore cards issued.

☞ Rural Infrastructure Development Fund

➢ GoI announced ₹ 8,000 crore for RIDF XI (2005-06).

➢ As at the end of March 2005, RIDF sanctions under all the branches of RIDF amounted to ₹ **42,948.51** crore against which the disbursements were ₹ **25,384.02** crore.

☞ Financial Highlights

NABARD was set up under an Act of Parliament, NABARD Act, 1981 and has a capital base of ₹ 2,000 crore contributed by RBI and Government of India, as on 31 March 2004, the highlights are asunder:

- Total Assets of ₹ 55,889 crore of which owned funds are ₹ 22,660 crore.
- Net profit before tax stood at ₹ 1,460 crore.
- A high Capital Adequacy Ratio of 39.41% as against a minimum of 9% stipulated by RBI.
- NPA as low as 0.0014% of advances as on 31 March 2004.

☞ Land Developments Banks

The Land Development Banks meet the long-term credit requirements of the farmers for developmental purposes, *viz.,* purchase of equipments like pump sets, tractors and other machineries, reclamation of land, fencing, digging up new wells, and repairs of old wells etc. Land Development Banks are cooperative institutions and they grant loans on the security of mortgage of immovable property of the farmers. These banks have a two-tier organisational structure — at the State level, there are Central Land Development Banks and at the district or taluka level, there are Primary Land Development Banks. In some States like Gujarat, Jammu and Kashmir and UP, the structure is unitary, *i.e.,* there are Apex Land Development Banks which operate directly through their own branches at the district level.

The financial resources of the Central Land Development Banks are raised by floating debentures in the market. Such debentures carry the guarantee of the State Government and are subscribed by the Central and State Governments, Commercial Banks, Life Insurance Corporation and other Land Development Banks as a measure of mutual support. Land Development Banks also avail of the refinancing facilities provided by the National Bank for Agriculture and Rural Development in respect of the term loans granted by them for the schemes of agricultural development. They also secure short-term accommodation from the State Governments, Commercial Banks and the State Cooperative Banks.

☞ Development Banks

Another important feature of the structure and organisation of Indian banking system is the establishment of many financial corporations, which provide finance to those sectors of the economy to which commercial banks do not provide finance.

It becomes difficult for commercial banks to participate in the financing of long-term requirements of the industry. Mixed banking also has certain disadvantages. Although mixed banking was successful in Germany and some other countries, it cannot be relied upon in a developing country like India where banking habits are still in a nascent stage. At best, our bigger banks can resort to term lending in a limited way. Therefore, certain special institutions are necessary to handle the problem of long-term financing of industries. Broadly speaking, such institutions are known as, "Development Banks".

In a general sense, the term "Development Bank" is used to include both development banks proper and finance corporations. The difference between these two lies in the fact that the former are primarily concerned with long-term loan, capital, while the latter deal with equity capital and assume responsibility for fostering and managing individual companies. However, the objective of both the development banks and of finance corporations is to provide long-term industrial finance. Both may, therefore, be broadly grouped as development banks.

The need for such special institutions was felt long ago, but they have been established only after 1948. Except the Industrial Finance Corporation of India which was set up in 1948, all the other financial institutions were established in the third quarter of the twentieth century (1950-1975). Some of these development banks are: State Finance Corporations, the Industrial Credit and Investment Corporation, the National Industrial Development Corporation, the Industrial Development Bank of India, the Unit Trust of India, etc. The share of commercial banks in the share capital of these institutions is about one quarter and their contribution to the total value of bonds issued by them is 80 per cent. A brief description of these Corporations is given below:

☞ Industrial Finance Corporation

The Industrial Finance Corporation of India was set up in 1948 "for the purpose of making medium and long-term credits more readily available to industrial concerns in India, particularly in circumstances where normal banking accommodation is inappropriate or recourse to capital issue methods is impracticable". The Corporation was meant to solve the problem of finance for new floatations or for expansion.

It has a paid-up capital of ₹ 7 crore (originally, when the Corporation was established, the paid-up capital was ₹ 5 crore, which was increased in 1962 by the issue of additional shares of ₹ 2 crore), a part of which is subscribed by scheduled banks. The activities of the Corporation were enlarged by the Amendment Act of 1960. The Amendment Act, among other things, extends the powers given to the Corporation regarding of loans to —

(i) Loans raised by industrial concerns from banks or State Cooperative Banks;

(ii) Deferred payments due from any industrial concern in connection with the purchase of capital goods within India; and

(iii) With the prior approval of the Central Government, loans raised in foreign currency by industrial concerns from institutions outside India.

It also empowers the Corporation to subscribe directly to the stocks or shares of any industrial concern which it was previously prohibited from doing, and also to convert, at its option, the loans granted or debentures subscribed to by it into stocks or shares of the concern. With effect from August 1964, the Industrial Development Bank of India has acquired a 50 per cent interest in the Industrial Finance Corporation. The Corporation acts in close collaboration with commercial banks and other sister institutions such as the Life Insurance Corporation, the Industrial Credit and Investment Corporation and the State Bank of India, and has financed some of the bigger projects in partnership with them. While the Corporation's financial assistance in the initial years was in the form of rupee loans, it has gradually extended its operations to cover deferred payment guarantees and guarantees for foreign loans and has ventured forth into promotional activities. IFCI's role now extends to the entire industrial spectrum in the country. The facilities and services being provided by it can be deemed to fall broadly under: *(a)* Project finance, *(b)* Financial services, and *(c)* Promotional services. Under its project finance and financial services, upto the end of 31st Dec., 1992, the IFCI had sanctioned assistance of the order of ₹ 14,608.65 crore to 4,211 industrial projects.

IFCI's paid-up capital as at the end of June, 2002 was ₹ 6,386.76 crore and its reserves on that date were of the order of ₹ 327.42 crore. Up to 31st March, 1990, IFCI had utilised a sum of ₹ 39.28 crore on its Variegated Promotional Schemes.

☞ State Finance Corporations

The State Finance Corporations Act, 1951, authorised the State Governments to establish similar Corporations for assistance on a small-scale, by guaranteeing a minimum dividend and repayment of capital. These Corporations can do the following kinds of business:

(i) The guaranteeing of loans raised by industrial concerns repayable within a period not exceeding 20 years and floated in the public market.

(ii) The underwriting of the issues of stocks, shares, bonds or debentures by industrial concerns.

(iii) The granting of loans or advances to, or the subscribing to debentures of industrial concerns and repayable within a period not exceeding 20 years.

In order to facilitate the expansion of the activities of these Corporations, the State Financial Corporation Act, 1951, was amended in March 1962, authorising them —

(i) To render financial assistance to hotels and transport industries and also to concerns engaged in the development of any contiguous area of land as an industrial estate;

(ii) To borrow funds from the Reserve Bank for periods not exceeding 18 months up to 60 per cent of the paid-up capital as well as from State Governments and any notified financial institutions;

(iii) To undertake the business of guaranteeing —

(a) deferred payments due from any industrial concern in connection with the purchase of capital goods within India, and

(b) loans raised by industrial concerns from scheduled banks and State Cooperative Banks.

(iv) To act as an agent of any financial institution notified by the Central Government in respect of loans and advances granted or debentures subscribed by such an institution.

At present eighteen State Finance Corporations including the Tamil Nadu Industrial and Investment Corporation supply industrial finance to medium and small-scale sectors. The total loans sanctioned by them during 1991-92 amounted to ₹ 2,178.1 crore.

☞ State Industrial Development Corporations

State Industrial Development Corporations have been established by the State Governments to finance as well as promote industrialisation in their states. They provide financial assistance to industrial concerns by way of loans, subscription, underwriting and guarantees shares and debentures; SIDCs undertake promotional activities like conducting techno-economic surveys, project identification, preparation of feasibility studies and selection and training of entrepreneurs. They also collaborate in joint sector projects. Another function performed by SIDCs is the development of industrial areas, construction of sheds, provision of infrastructural facilities and development of new growth centres. Incentive schemes of the State Government are also administered by them.

State Industrial Development Corporations are established as joint stock companies fully owned by the State Governments. At present 22 SIDCs are functioning in India. Industrial Development Bank of India provides refinance facilities to SIDCs for the term loans granted by them. SIDCs accept deposits, borrow from the banks and also issue bonds to augment their resources.

☞ Industrial Credit and Investment Corporation of India Limited (ICICI Bank)

ICICI Bank is India's second-largest bank with total assets of about ₹ 2,513.89 bn (US $ 56.3 bn) at March 31, 2006 and profit after tax of ₹ 25.40 bn (US $ 569 mn) for the year ended March 31, 2006 (₹ 20.05 bn US $ 449 mn) for the year ended March 31, 2005. ICICI Bank has a network of about 614 branches and extension counters and over 2,200 ATMs. ICICI Bank offers a wide range of banking products and financial services to corporate and retail customers through a variety of delivery channels and through its sepcialised subsidiaries and affiliates in the areas of investment banking, life and non-life insurance, venture capital and asset management. ICICI Bank set up its international banking group in fiscal 2002 to cater to the cross-border needs of clients and leverage on its domestic banking strengths to offer products internationally. ICICI Bank currently has subsidiaries in the United Kingdom, Russia and Canada, branches in Singapore, Bahrain, Hong Kong, Sri Lanka and Dubai International Finance Centre and representative offices in the United States, United Arab Emirates, China, South Africa and Bangladesh. Our UK subsidiary has established a branch in Belgium. ICICI Bank is the most valuable bank in India in terms of market capitalisation.

ICICI Bank's equity shares are listed in India on the Bombay Stock Exchange and the National Stock Exchange of India Limited and its American Depository Receipts (ADRs) are listed on the New York Stock Exchange (NYSE).

At June 5, 2006, ICICI Bank, with free float market capitalisations* of about ₹ 480.00 billion (US $ 10.8 billion) ranked third amongst all the companies listed on the Indian stock exchanges.

ICICI bank was originally promoted in 1994 by ICICI Limited, an Indian financial institution, and was its wholly-owned subsidiary. ICICI's shareholding in ICICI Bank was reduced to 46% through a public offering of shares in India in fiscal 1998, an equity offering in the form of ADRs listed on the NYSE in fiscal 2000, ICICI Bank's acquisition of Bank of Madura Limited in an all-stock amalgamation in fiscal 2001, and secondary market sales by ICICI to institutional investors in fiscal 2001 and fiscal 2002. ICICI was formed in 1955 at the initiative of the World Bank, the Government of India and representatives of Indian industry. The principal objective was to create a development financial institution for providing medium-term and long-term project financing to Indian businesses. In the 1990s ICICI transformed its business from a development financial institution offering only project finance to a diversified financial services group offering a wide variety of products and services, both directly and through a number of subsidiaries and affiliates like ICICI Bank. In 1999, ICICI became the first Indian company and the first bank or financial institution from non-Japan Asia to be listed on the NYSE.

☞ Industrial Development Bank of India (IDBI)

Industrial Development Bank of India (IDBI) is the tenth largest bank in the world in terms of development. The National Stock Exchange (NSE), The National Securities Depository Services Ltd. (NSDL), Stock Holding Corporation of India, (SHCIL) are some of the institutions which has been built by IDBI. IDBI is a strategic investor in a plethora of institutions which have revolutionised the Indian Financial Markets.

IDBI Bank, promoted by IDBI Group started in November 1995 with a branch at Indore with an equity capital base of ₹ 1,000 million.

☞ Main Functions of IDBI

IDBI is vested with the responsibility of coordinating the working of institutions engaged in financing, promoting and developing industries. It has evolved an appropriate mechanism for this purpose. IDBI also undertakes/supports wide-ranging promotional activities including entrepreneurship development programmes for new entrepreneurs, provision of consultancy services for small and medium enterprises, upgradation of technology and programmes for economic upliftment of the underprivileged.

☞ IDBI's Role as a Catalyst

IDBI's role as a catalyst to industrial development encompasses a wide spectrum of activities. IDBI can finance all types of industrial concerns covered under the provisions of the

IDBI Act. With over three decades of service to the industry, IDBI has grown substantially in terms of size of operations and portfolio.

☞ Developmental Activities of IDBI

Promotional Activities: In fulfilment of its developmental role, the Bank continues to perform a wide range of promotional activities relating to developmental programmes for new entrepreneurs, consultancy services for small and medium enterprises and programmes designed for accredited voluntary agencies for the economic upliftment of the underprivileged. These include entrepreneurship development, self-employment and wage employment in the industrial sector for the weaker sections of society through voluntary agencies, support to Science and Technology Entrepreneurs' Parks, Energy Conservation, Common Quality Testing Centres for small industries.

Technical Consultancy Organisations: With a view to making available at a reasonable cost, consultancy and advisory services to entrepreneurs, particularly to new and small entrepreneurs, IDBI, in collaboration with other All-India Financial Institutions, has set up a network of Technical Consultancy Organisations (TCOs) covering the entire country. TCOs offer diversified services to small and medium enterprises in the selection, formulation and appraisal of projects, their implementation and review.

Entrepreneurship Development Institute: Realising that entrepreneurship development is the key to industrial development, IDBI played a prime role in setting up of the Entrepreneurship Development Institute of India for fostering entrepreneurship in the country. It has also established similar institutes in Bihar, Odisha, Madhya Pradesh and Uttar Pradesh. IDBI also extends financial support to various organisations in conduct studies or surveys of relevance to industrial development.

In January 1992, IDBI accessed domestic retail debt market for the first time with innovative Deep Discount Bonds and registered path-breaking success. In December 1993, IDBI set up IDBI Capital Market Services Ltd., as a wholly-owned subsidiary to offer a broad range of financial services, including Bond Trading, Equity Broking, Client Asset Management and Depository Services.

In September 1984, in response to RBI's policy of opening up domestic banking sector to private participation, IDBI in association with SIDBI set up IDBI Bank Ltd. Today, IDBI bank has a network of 161 branches, 369 ATMs, and 8 Extension Counters spread over 95 cities.

Website of IDBI *www.idibibank.com*

☞ UTI Bank

UTI Bank was the first of the new private banks to have begun operations in 1994, after the Government of India allowed new private banks to be established. The Bank was promoted jointly by the Administrator of the specified undertaking of the Unit Trust of India (UTI-I). Life

Insurance Corporation of India (LIC) and General Insurance Corporation Ltd., and its associates *viz.,* National Insurance Company Ltd. The New India Assurance Company, the Oriental Insurance Corporation and United Insurance Company Ltd.

The Bank today is capitalised to the extent of ₹ 278.89 crore with the public holding (other than promoters) at 72.28%.

The Bank's Registered Office is at Ahmedabad and its Central Office is located at Mumbai. Presetly, the Bank has a very wide network of more than 450 branch offices and extension counters. The Bank has a network of over 1,891 ATMs providing 24 hrs a day banking convenience to its customers. This is one of the largest ATM networks in the country.

The Bank has strengths in both retail and corporate banking and is committed to adopting the best industry practices internationally in order to achieve excellence.

☞ Promoters

UTI Bank Ltd., has been promoted by the largest and the best Financial Institution of the country, UTI. The Bank was set up with a capital of ₹ 115 crore, with UTI contributing ₹ 100 crore. LIC ₹ 7.5 crore and GIC and its four subsidiaries contributing ₹ 1.5 crore each.

☞ UTI — Shareholding 27.72%

UTI is the largest mutual fund in India. UTI presently occupies a special position in Indian capital market. With a servicing and distribution network of more than 53 branch offices, 320 Chief Representatives and about 90,000 agents, UTI provides the complete range of services to its investors.

☞ SIDBI

SIDBI was established on April 2, 1990. The Charter establishing it, The Small Industries Development Bank of India Act, 1989 envisaged SIDBI to be "the principal financial institution for the promotion, financing and development of industry in the small-scale sector and to co-ordinate the functions of the institutions engaged in the promotion and financing or developing industry in the small-scale sector and for matters connected therewith or incidental thereto.

SMALL INDUSTRIES DEVELOPMENT BANK OF INDIA

(Established under the Small Industries Development Bank of India Act, 1989)
Head Office : SIDBI Tower, 15, Ashok Marg, Lucknow-226 001.

UNAUDITED FINANCIAL RESULTS FOR THE QUARTER ENDED JUNE 30, 2007

(₹ in Crore)

Sr. No.	Particulars	Quarter ended 30.06.2007 (Reviewed)	Quarter ended 30.06.2006 (Reviewed)	Yearended 31.03.2007 (Audited)
1	Income from Operations	324	251	1,167
2	Other Income	—	9	20
Total Income [1 + 2]		**324**	**260**	**1,187**
3	Interest Expenses	207	142	585
4	(a) Establishment Expenses [Staff Cost]	17	11	89
	(b) Other Expenses	13	6	54
Total Expenditure [3 + 4]		**237**	**159**	**728**
5	Depreciation	2	2	10
6	**Profit before Tax (1 + 2 – 3 – 4 – 5)**	**85**	**99**	**449**
7	Provision for Taxation (incl. FBT and Deferred Tax Adjustment)	24	30	151
8	**Net Profit**	**61**	**69**	**298**
9	Paid-up Share Capital [comprising equity shares having face value of ₹ 10/- each]	450	450	450
10	Reserves (excluding Revaluation Reserves)			4,259
11	Earning Per Share (₹)	1.35	1.53	6.63
12	**Shareholding**	**No. of shares**	**% of shareholding**	
Financial Institutions		28,900,000	6.42	
Insurance Companies		96,450,000	21.43	
PSU Banks		324,650,000	72.15	
Total		**450,000,000**	**100.00**	

The business domain of SIDBI consists of small-scale industrial units, which contribute significantly to the national economy in terms of production, employment and exports. Small-scale industries are the industrial units in which the investment in plant and machinery does not exceed ₹ 10 million.

About 3.1 million such units, employing 17.2 million persons account for a share of 36 per cent of India's exports and 40 per cent of industrial manufacture. In addition, SIDBI's assistance flows to the transport, health care and tourism sectors and also to the professional and self-employed persons setting up small-sized professional ventures.

☞ LIC India

The Life Insurance Corporation Act on the 19th of June, 1956, and the Life Insurance Corporation of India was created on 1st September, 1956, with the objective of spreading life insurance much more widely and in particular to the rural areas with a view to reach all insurable persons in the country, providing them adequate financial cover at a reasonable cost.

LIC had 5 zonal offices, 33 divisional offices and 212 branch offices, apart from its corporate office in the year 1956. Since life insurance contracts are long-term contracts and during the currency of the policy it requires a variety of services need was felt, in the later years to expand the operations and place a branch office at each district headquarter. Reorganisation of LIC took place and large number of new branch offices were opened. As a result of reorganisation servicing functions were transferred to the branches, and branches were made accounting units. It worked wonders with the performance of the corporation. It may be seen that from about 200.00 of New Business in 1957 the corporation crossed 1000.00 crore only in the year 1969-70, and it took another 10 years for LIC to cross 2000.00 crore mark of new business. But with reorganisation happening in the early eighties, by 1985-86 LIC had already crossed 7000.00 crore sum Assured on new policies.

Today, LIC functions with 2,048 fully computerised branch offices, 100 divisional offices, 7 zonal offices and the Corporate office. LIC's Wide Area Network covers 100 divisional offices and connects all the branches through a Metro Area Network. LIC has tied up with some Banks and Service providers to offer on line premium collection facility in selected cities. LIC ECS and ATM premium payment facility is an addition to customer convenience. Apart from on line Kisoks and IVRS, Info Centres have been commissioned at Mumbai, Ahmedabad, Bangalore, Chennai, Hyderabad, Kolkata, New Delhi, Pune and many other cities. With a vision of providing easy access to its policyholders, LIC has launched its SATELLITE SAMPARK offices. The satellite offices are smaller, leaner and closer to the customer. The digitalised records of the satellite offices will facilitate anywhere servicing and many other convenience in the future.

LIC continues to be the dominant life insurer even in the liberalised scenario of Indian insurance and is moving fast on a new growth trajectory surpassing its own past records. LIC has issued over one crore policies during the current year. It has crossed the milestone of issuing 1,01,32,955 new policies by 15th Oct., 2005, posting a healthy growth rate of 16.67% over the corresponding period of the previous year.

☞ Deposit Insurance

Deposit Insurance Act, 1961 came into force on January 1, 1962.

The Deposit Insurance Scheme was initially extended to functioning commercial banks only. This included the State Bank of India and its subsidiaries, other commercial banks and the branches of the foreign banks operating in India.

The Reserve Bank of India also promoted a public limited company on January 14, 1971, named the Credit Guarantee Corporation of India Ltd., (CGCI). The main thrust of the Credit Guarantee Schemes, introduced by the Credit Guarantee Corporation of India Ltd., was aimed at encouraging the commercial banks to cater to the credit needs of the hitherto neglected sectors, particularly the weaker sections of the society engaged in non-industrial activities, by providing guarantee cover to the loans and advances granted by the credit institutions to small and needy borrowers covered under the priority sector.

With a view to integrating the functions of deposit insurance and credit guarantee, the above two organisations (DIC and CGCI) were merged and the present Deposit Insurance and Credit Guarantee

Corporation (DICGC) came into existence on July 15, 1978. Consequently, the title of Deposit Insurance Act, 1961 was changed to 'The Deposit Insurance and Credit Guarantee Corporation Act, 1961'.

Effective from April 1, 1981, the Corporation extended its guarantee support to credit granted to small-scale industries also, after the cancellation of the Government of India's credit guarantee scheme. With effect from April 1, 1989, guarantee cover was extended to the entire priority sector advances, as per the definition of the Reserve Bank of India. However, effective from April 1, 1995, all housing loans have been excluded from the purview of guarantee cover by the Corporation.

The authorised capital of the Corporation is ₹ 50 crore, which is fully issued and subscribed by the Reserve Bank of India (RBI).

☞ New Private Sector Banks

ICICI: It is the commercial banking arm of ICICI Group. It received its banking licence from RBI on 17th May 1994 and the first branch was established in Chennai in June 1994. It has 540 branches, 1,000 ATM 15 and 16 extension counters. This network is complemented by technology driven delivering channels which include call centres, mobile phone banking and internet banking.

IDBI: IDBI promoted by IDBI and SIDBI. It was established in 1994 to offer full range of commercial banking products to corporates and other business segments. IDBI and SIDBI hold 57.14% and 14.27% respectively of the equity of IDBI Bank. The bank has 39 computerised branches spread across 27 cities in India.

Indus Industrial Bank: It is the number one among the new private sector banks since inspections and has highest productivity in the Indian Banking Industry. It commenced operation in April 1994 with a capital base of 1000 million. It has a network of 23 branches covering 19 centres. All the branches are computerised and networked through VSATs offering anywhere banking.

HDFC: HDFC Bank was incorporated in August 1994 with registered office in Mumbai. The Housing Development Finance Corporation is the promoter of the bank. It has authorised capital of ₹ 300 crore and paid-up capital of ₹ 200 crore. The bank has network of 111 branches and ATM 13 spread over the country.

☞ Unit Trust of India

The Unit Trust of India was established in 1964. It is a financial intermediary which pools the investible resources of numerous subscribers, particularly the small investors and invest these on their behalf, in a wide range of securities. The income from these investments and the realised capital appreciation are distributed to the unitholders after the expenses of running the Trust have been met. The Unit Trust is always to buyback units from investors at market value. This gives a high degree of liquidity to the unitholders. Besides, the Unit Trust minimises the risk involved in investment through diversification and offers the benefits of expert management. It was established with the objective of mobilising the savings of the community and channelling them into productive investments, and more importantly, for encouraging widespread and diffused ownership of industry by affording investors, particularly the small investors, a means of acquiring equity stock assured of a reasonable return with minimum risk.

The Trust was established with a initial capital of ₹ 5 crore, which was contributed by different institutions as follows:

(i)	Scheduled banks and other financial institutions	₹ 1 crore
(ii)	The Reserve Bank of India	₹ 2.5 crore

(iii) The Life Insurance Corporation ₹ 75 lakh

(iv) State Bank and its subsidiaries ₹ 75 lakh

Provision has also been made in the Act for refunding the whole or any part of the subscribed capital by the contributing institutions if the Trust finds that the capital is in excess of its requirements.

Unit Trust of India has formulated three schemes for selling 'units', namely, unit scheme 1964, unit scheme 1971, and unit scheme 1976. In order to cater to specific investment needs of different types of investors, UTI framed specific savings plans linked to the unit schemes, *viz.,* Reinvestment Plan 1966, Children's Gift Plan 1970 and Unit Linked Insurance Plan 1971. For the year ended 30 June, 1981, the Trust had declared a dividend of 11.5 per cent on the unit scheme of 1964.

The Unit Trust of India has so far introduced 72 different schemes to suit the preferences of various class of investors. The main scheme of the UTI is the Unit Scheme, 1964. The UTI is at present managing "Two Country Funds of India". The first called "The India Fund" was launched abroad by the UTI and Merrill Lynch Capital Markets in July, 1986, for enabling Non-resident Indians and other persons outside India to invest in the securities markets of India. The shares of the fund are listed on the London Stock Exchange. The second fund called "The India Growth Fund Inc." was launched abroad by the UTI and Merril Lynch in August, 1988. This fund is registered with the Securities and Exchange Commission (SEC) of the United States. The shares of the fund are listed on the New York Stock Exchange. The investible funds of the UTI up to 1990 were ₹ 17,496 crore.

Apart from UTI there are six Mutual Funds operating at present in India. These funds have been set up by the Life Insurance Corporation of India, the State Bank of India, Canara Bank, Indian Bank, Punjab National Bank and Bank of India.

UTI manages funds of ₹ 49,655.37 crore being market value of investments as on 28th June 2002 from 28.96 million investors. The bank has 79 branches, all computerised and networking through VSAT.

Position as on 31.03.2000	*Amt. ₹ in crore*
Deposits	5,720
Advances	3,506.62
Net profit	51.06
Dividend	12%

☞ THE UTI BANK is now AXIS BANK

AXIS Bank was the first of the new private banks to have begun operations in 1994, after the Government of India allowed new private banks to be established. The Bank was promoted jointly by the Administrator of the specified undertaking of the Unit Trust of India (UTI-1), Life Insurance Corporation of India (LIC) and General Insurance Corporation Ltd., and other four PSU companies, *i.e.,* National Insurance Company Ltd., The New India Assurance Company, The Oriental Insurance Corporation and United Insurance Company Ltd.

The Bank today is capitalized to the extent of ₹ 356.22 crore with the public holding (other than promoters) at 57.32%.

The Bank's Registered Office is at Ahmedabad and its Central Office is located at Mumbai. Presently, the Bank has a very wide network of more than 576 branch offices and extension counters. The Bank has a network of over 2,475 ATMs providing 24 hours a day banking convenience to its customers. This is one of the largest ATM networks in the country.

The Bank has strengths in both retail and corporate banking and is committed to adopting the best industry practices internationally in order to achieve excellence.

☞ Deposit Insurance and Credit Guarantee Corporation

Deposit insurance, as we know it today, was introduced in India in 1962. India was the second country in the world to introduce such a scheme — the first being the United States in 1933. Banking crises and bank failures in the 19th as well as the early 20th century (1913-14) had, from time-to-time, underscored the need for depositor protection in India. After the setting up of the Reserve Bank of India, the issue came to the fore in 1938 when the Travancore National and Quilon Bank, the largest bank in the Travancore region, failed. As a result, interim measures relating to banking legislation and reform were instituted in the early 1940s. The banking crisis in Bengal between 1946 and 1948, once again revived the issue of deposit insurance. It was, however, felt that the measures be held in abeyance till the Banking Companies Act, 1949 came into force and comprehensive arrangements were made for the supervision and inspection of banks by the Reserve Bank.

It was in 1960, that the failure of Laxmi Bank and the subsequent failure of the Palai Central Bank catalyzed the introduction of deposit insurance in India. The Deposit Insurance Corporation (DIC) Bill was introduced in the Parliament on August 21, 1961 and received the assent of the President on December 7, 1961. The Deposit Insurance Corporation commenced functioning on January 1, 1962.

The Deposit Insurance Scheme was initially extended to functioning commercial banks. Deposit insurance was seen as a measure of protection to depositors, particularly small depositors, from the risk of loss of their savings arising from bank failures. The purpose was to avoid panic and to promote greater stability and growth of the banking system — what in today's argot are termed financial stability concerns. In the 1960s, it was also felt that an additional purpose of the scheme was to increase the confidence of the depositors in the banking system and facilitate the mobilisation of deposits to catalyst growth and development.

When the DIC commenced operations in the early 1960s, 287 banks registered with it as insured banks. By the end of 1967, this number was reduced to 100, largely as a result of the Reserve Bank of India's policy of the reconstruction and amalgamation of small and financially weak banks, so as to make the banking sector more viable. In 1968, the Deposit Insurance Corporation Act was amended to extend deposit insurance to 'eligible cooperative banks'. The process of extention to cooperative banks, however took a while, it was necessary for State Governments to amend their cooperative laws. The amended laws would enable the Reserve Bank to order the Registrar of Cooperative Societies of a State to wind up a co-operative bank or to supersede its Committee of Management and to require the Registrar not to take any action for winding up, amalgamation or reconstruction of a cooperative bank without prior sanction in writing from the Reserve Bank of India. Enfolding the cooperative banks had implications for the DIC — in 1968 there were over 1,000 cooperative banks as against the 83 commercial banks that were in its fold. As a result, the DIC had to expand its operations very considerably.

The 1960s and 1970s were a period of institution building. 1971 witnessed the establishment of another institution, the Credit Guarantee Corporation of India Ltd., (CGCI). While Deposit Insurance had been introduced in India out of concerns to protect depositors, ensure financial stability, instill confidence in the banking system and help mobilise deposits, the establishment of the Credit Guarantee Corporation was essentially in the realm of affirmative action to ensure that the credit needs of the hitherto neglected sectors and weaker sections were met. The essential concern was to persuade banks to make available credit to not so creditworthy clients.

In 1978, the DIC and the CGCI were merged to form the Deposit Insurance and Credit Guarantee Corporation (DICGC). Consequently, the title of Deposit Insurance Act, 1961 was changed to the

Deposit Insurance and Credit Guarantee Corporation Act, 1961. The merger was with a view to integrating the functions of deposit insurance and credit guarantee prompted in no small measure by the financial needs of the erstwhile CGCI.

After the merger, the focus of the DICGC had shifted onto credit guarantees. This owed in part to the fact that most large banks were nationalised. With the financial sector reforms undertaken in the 1990s, credit guarantees have been gradually phased out and the focus of the Corporation is veering back to its core function of Deposit Insurance with the objective of averting panics reducing systemic risk, and ensuring financial stability.

The Credit Guarantee Corporation of India Ltd. was established to give protection to banks and other financial institutions against risks, if any, in meeting the credit needs of the smaller borrowers in the priority and hitherto neglected sectors — farming, small-scale industries, small business ventures, road transport and self-employed professionals or technicians engaged in productive enterprises. The Corporation was registered as a joint stock company under the Indian Companies Act, 1956, on 14th January 1971. Its authorised capital is ₹ 10 crore and issued, subscribed and paid-up capital ₹ 2 crore. The Reserve Bank of India and scheduled commercial banks have contributed to this capital.

The Corporation introduced three separate guarantee schemes providing guarantee to credit institutions for all their loans, advances and other credit facilities. The guarantee fee was fixed at one-half of one per cent per annum, to be calculated on the credit facilities actually outstanding. In the event of a loss arising on account of a guaranteed credit facility, the Corporation is to bear 75 per cent of the loss, subject to ceilings wherever prescribed. The main features of the three schemes are given below:

(i) Credit Guarantee Corporation of India (Small Loans) Guarantee Scheme 1971: This scheme, introduced in April 1971, covers credit facilities provided by scheduled commercial banks to transport operators, dealers in fertilisers, traders, professional and self-employed persons, owners of business enterprises and farmers and agriculturists.

(ii) Credit Guarantee Corporation of India Small Loans (Financial Corporation) Guarantee Scheme, 1971: This scheme, introduced in July 1971, is an extension of the first scheme to State Financial Corporations. It covers credit facilities extended by these financial corporations to transport operators, small hoteliers, business enterprises engaged in the generation or distribution of electricity or any other form of power, or in the development or management of any contiguous area of land as an industrial estate, *i.e.,* to borrowers to whom financial corporations are in a position to grant financial assistance and who are not already covered under the credit guarantee scheme for small-scale industries administered by the Reserve Bank of India on behalf of the Central Government.

(iii) Credit Guarantee Corporation of India (Service Cooperative Societies) Guarantee Scheme, 1971: This scheme, introduced from 1st October, 1971, guarantees credit facilities to service co-operative societies which assist artisans and workers engaged in any kind of industrial activity. Besides all the scheduled commercial banks in the country, other credit institutions, eligible to participate in this scheme are the State and Central cooperative banks.

In May 1978, the Credit Guarantee Corporation of India Ltd. was merged with the Deposit Insurance Corporation by an Act of Parliament, in order to serve better and provide credit guarantee of commercial banks. The undertaking has been renamed as the Deposit Insurance and Credit Guarantee Corporation. Up to June 1983, out of 18,15,00,000 accounts, the number of fully protected accounts was 17,85,00,000. Likewise out of 50,797 crore of total assessable deposits the amount of insured deposit was ₹ 37,746 crore.

☞ Life Insurance Corporation of India

Life Insurance Corporation was established on 1st Sept., 1956. It is the biggest institutional investor in India. The investments of LIC are regulated by Section 27A of the Insurance Act, 1938. A major part of the investments of LIC are in Government and other approved securities and in loans to socially oriented sectors. The Corporate sector of the country gets financial assistance from LIC in the following ways:

- *(a)* LIC subscribes and underwrites the shares, loans and debentures of corporate sector.
- *(b)* LIC subscribes to the shares and bonds issued by Development Banks like IDBI, IFCI, ICICI, SFCs.
- *(c)* LIC also provides loans to companies.

☞ General Insurance Corporation of India

The management of General Insurance business in India was taken over by the Government in 1971 and nationalised with the passing of General Insurance Business (Nationalisation) Act, 1973.

As per the guidelines issued by the Government, 70% of the accretions to the GIC Fund have to be invested in socially-oriented sectors, which include Central and State Government securities and loans to various public institutions engaged in housing. GIC also subscribes and underwrites the new issues of shares and debentures of companies. It also grants term loans to companies.

☞ National Bank for Agriculture and Rural Development (NABARD)

The National Bank for Agriculture and Rural Development (NABARD) came into existence on 12th July, 1982. It tookover functions of the erstwhile Agriculture Credit Department, Rural Planning and Credit Cell of the Reserve Bank of India and Agricultural Refinance and Development Corporation. Its subscribed and paid-up capital is ₹ 100 crore, contributed by the Central Govt. and the Reserve Bank of India in equal proportion. NABARD was established for providing credit for promotion of agriculture, small-scale industries, cottage and village industries, handicrafts and other allied economic activities in rural areas with a view to promoting integrated rural development and securing prosperity of rural areas and for matters connected therewith or incidental thereto.

NABARD is an apex institution accredited with all matters concerning policy, planning and operations in the field of credit for agriculture and other economic activities in the rural areas.

The main functions of NABARD are to —

- *(i)* serve as an apex refinancing agency for institutions providing investment and production credit for promoting various developmental activities in the rural areas.
- *(ii)* take measures towards institution building for improving absorption capacity of credit delivery system including monitoring, formulation of rehabilitation schemes, restructuring of credit institutions, training of personnel, etc.
- *(iii)* coordinate rural financing activities of all institutions engaged in the developmental work at field level and maintain liaison with Central Government/State Governments, Reserve Bank of India and other national institutions concerned with policy formulation.
- *(iv)* undertake monitoring and evaluation of projects refinanced by it

NABARD's refinance is available to the State Land Development Banks, State Cooperative Banks, Scheduled Commercial Banks, and Regional Rural Banks. While the ultimate beneficiaries of investment credit can be individuals, partnership concerns, companies and state-owned corporations or co-operative societies; production credit is generally given to individuals. Term credit disbursement of NABARD by way of refinance under schematic lendings was ₹ 1,702 crore during 1989-90. Refinance commitments under the new schemes approved during the same period were ₹ 2,039 crore. Refinance provided for implementation of Integrated Rural Development Programme was ₹ 549 crore during 1989-90.

Thus, NABARD is set up as an apex Development Bank with a mandate for facilitating credit flow for promotion and development of agriculture, small-scale industries, cottage and village industries, handicrafts and other rural crafts. It also has the mandate to support all other allied economic activities in rural areas, promote integrated and sustainable rural development and secure prosperity of rural areas. In discharging its role as a facilitator for rural prosperity, NABARD is entrusted with:

1. Providing refinance to lending institutions in rural areas
2. Bringing about or promoting institutional development, and
3. Evaluating, monitoring and inspecting the client banks.

Besides this pivotal role, NABARD also:

- Acts as a coordinator in the operations of rural credit institutions.
- Extends assistance to the government, the **Reserve Bank of India** and other organisations in matters relating to rural development.
- Offers training and research facilities for banks, cooperatives and organisations working in the field of rural development.
- Helps the State Governments in reaching their targets of providing assistance to eligible institutions in agriculture and rural development.
- Acts as regulator for cooperative banks and RRBs.

☞ Some of the Milestones in NABARD's Activities are:

- With its effective overseeing and monitoring of the implementation of the Government of India's programme to double the flow of credit to agriculture over a three-year period from 2004-2005, the total disbursement of credit reached ₹ 1,25,309 during 2004-2005. Ground level credit flow to agriculture and allied activities reached ₹ 1,57,480 crore in 2005-2006.
- Refinance disbursement to commercial banks, state cooperative banks, state cooperative agriculture and rural development banks, RRBs and other eligible financial institutions aggregated ₹ 8,622.37 crore.
- As on 31st January 2007, through the **Rural Infrastructure Development Fund (RIDF)**, ₹ 59,795.35 crore have been sanctioned for 2,31,702 projects covering irrigation, rural roads and bridges, health and education, soil conservation, drinking water schemes, etc. Developing among hosts of other infrastructures, RIDF will create 20,971 schools, 6,239 primary health centres and provide drinking water supply in 7,267 villages.
- **Watershed Development Fund,** with cumulative sanctions of ₹ 578.95 crore for 427 projects in 124 districts of 14 states, has created a People's Movement in rural India.
- Farmers now enjoy financial access and security through 582.50 lakh **Kisan Credit Cards** that have been issued through a vast rural banking network. The Kisan Credit Card (KCC) scheme introduced in August 1998, has facilitated in augmenting the GLC flow for crop loans. During the year, cooperative banks, RRBs and commercial banks issued 22.97 lakh, 14.06

lakh and 37.67 lakh cards, respectively. Of the total 665.63 lakh cards issued as on 31st March 2007, cooperative banks accounted for 49 per cent of the share, followed by commercial banks (38%) and RRBs (13%).

➢ District Rural Industries Project (DRIP) has generated employment for 23.34 lakh persons with 10.95 lakh units in 105 districts.

☞ Land Development Banks

The long-term credit needs of the agricultural sector are met by another type of cooperative institutions known as Land Development Banks. The structure of these banks is a two-tier one — at the State level, there are Central Land Development Banks and at the district or taluka level, there are Primary Land Development Banks. In a few States, e.g.,Gujarat, Jammu and Kashmir and UP, the structure is unitary, i.e., there are Apex Land Development Banks which operate direct through their own branches at the district level.

The Land Development Banks meet the requirements of the farmer for developmental purposes, i.e., provision of equipment like pump-sets, tractors and machinery and land improvement in the form of levelling, bunding, reclamation of land, fencing, sinking of new wells and repairs to old wells. Loans are granted on the security of mortgage of immovable property of the farmers.

The Central Land Development Banks raise their resources by floating debentures in the market. These debentures carry the guarantee of the State Government and are subscribed by the Central and State Governments, Commercial Banks, Life Insurance Corporation and other Land Development Banks as a measure of mutual support. The Land Development Banks have availed of the refinancing facilities provided by the National Bank for Agriculture and Rural Development in respect of the term loans granted by them for the schemes of agricultural development. They also secure short-term accommodation from the State Governments, Commercial Banks and the State Cooperative Banks.

☞ The Export Import Bank of India (EXIM BANK)

The Export Import Bank of India was established on January 1, 1982, as a statutory corporation, wholly-owned by the Union Government.

☞ Objectives

The main objectives of the Exim Bank are:

(i) to ensure an integrated and coordinated approach to solve the problems of exporters, providing special attention to capital goods and project exports, joint ventures and export of technical services and international merchant banking;

(ii) to extend buyer's credit and lines of credit; and

(iii) to tap domestic and overseas markets for resources for undertaking developmental and financing activities in the area of exports.

☞ Promotional Activities

The promotional activities of the bank are the following:

(i) Planning, promoting and developing exports and imports;

(ii) Providing technical, administrative and managerial assistance for promotion, management and expansion of exports; and

(iii) Undertaking market and investment surveys and techno-economic studies related to development of exports of goods and services.

☞ Export Promotion Schemes

The bank mainly gives term credit for export of goods and services on deferred terms. The bank commenced its lending operations on March 1, 1982. It has introduced a variety of schemes for the promotion of exports of engineering/capital goods and technology consultancy services. It offers financial assistance of flexible and responsive credit terms to enable Indian exporters to compete in international markets. It also operates schemes for financial assistance to overseas buyers for the purchase of engineering goods and to Indian promoters towards their equity contribution in joint ventures obroad.

☞ Resources

The authorised capital of the bank is ₹ 500 crore and paid-up capital is ₹ 233.80 crore as on 31st March, 1990. The Government of India has given a long-term loan of ₹ 20 crore. The bank is authorised to borrow from the Government of India and Reserve Bank and can also raise resources in domestic and international markets.

☞ Management

The Bank is managed by a 17 member Board of Directors, with Chairman and Managing Director as the Chief Executive and full-time director. The Board of Directors comprises representatives from Government of India, the Reserve Bank of India, IDBI, ECGC, Commercial bank and the exporting community.

☞ Operations

Since commencing operations from March 1, 1982, till June 30, 1982, the Bank has extended assistance to the tune of ₹ 133 crore consisting of ₹ 24 crore of medium and long-term loans; guarantees amounting to ₹ 32 crore and rediscounting of export bills aggregating ₹ 77 crore. During the same period, the Bank cleared 99 bids valued at more than ₹ 3,700 crore in respect of construction contracts, turnkey projects and supplies which would involve the total commitment of ₹ 852 crore for bank.

EXIM BANK YEAR 2000

Export contracts supported by EXIM amounted to ₹ 41.62 billion. This was an increase of 127%.

Loan sanctions	₹ 42.41 billions - 95%
Reimbursement	₹ 34.53 billions - 82%
Loan outstanding	₹ 66.10 billions - 17%.

☞ Small Industries Developmental Bank of India (SIDBI)

Small Industries Development Bank of India (SIDBI) was established as wholly-owned subsidiary of the Industrial Development Bank of India (IDBI) under the Small Industries Development Bank of India Act, 1989, as the principal financial institution for promotion, financing and development of industries in the small-scale sector as also for coordinating the functions of institutions engaged in promotion, financing and development of industries in the small-scale sector. SIDBI started its operations from 2nd April, 1990, and small-scale industrial sector in the country through other institutions like State Financial Corporations, Commercial Banks, State Industrial Development Corporations etc.

The paid-up capital of SIDBI which is wholly subscribed by IDBI is at present ₹ 12.5 crore. The outstanding portfolio of IDBI totalling about ₹ 4,000 crore relating to the small-scale sector as on 31st

March, 1990, was transferred to SIDBI from 2nd April, 1990. During the year 1992-93 SIDBI introduced three more schemes: *(a)* Scheme of assistance under Venture Capital Fund, *(b)* Equipment finance scheme for assiting profit-making companies with good track record, and *(c)* Refinance scheme for rehabilitation of NTC workers.

☛ National Housing Bank

National Housing Bank was established in 1988 with a paid-up capital of ₹ 150 crore (provided by the Reserve Bank of India) for the development of Housing Finance in the country. The paid-up capital has now been increased to ₹ 200 crore. Reserve Bank of India has also sanctioned a long-term loan of ₹ 125 crore out of National Housing Credit (Long-term operations) Fund established by the Reserve Bank of India.

— NHB has also issued 20-year Bonds with 11.5 per cent interest worth of ₹ 160 crore.

— In July, 1990 NHB has launched a three year Non-transferable/Non-negotiable Capital Gain Bonds Scheme carrying nine per cent interest rate per annum and providing 100 per cent tax exemption on capital gains arising out of sale/transfer of long-term capital assets like land, building, shares and securities, jewellery, etc.

— NHB has secured a loan from Overseas Economic Cooperation Fund (OECF), Japan for 2,979 billion yen, *i.e.,* ₹ 40 crore (approx.) at the current exchange rate.

— National Housing Bank launched the Home Loan Account (HLA) scheme on July 1, 1989, with a view to mobilising resources fiom the households, specifically for construction of houses/flats. About three lakh people have become HLA scheme members till the end of August, 1990 and the amount of deposits collected through the Public Sector Banks totalled ₹ 35 crore.

— By Jan. 1991, refinance assistance provided by NHB to all categories of eligible primary lenders, *i.e.,* scheduled commercial banks, State Cooperative Banks, Housing finance companies, State level Apex cooperative banks amounted to ₹ 300 crore.

— In its land development and shelter projects, it has till December, 1990, approved 26 detailed project reports costing ₹ 18.04 crore in seven states and involving development of 14,000 plots and construction of over 15,000 dwelling units of various categories.

— NHB has also approved a project for manufacturing of sand-lime brick with a project cost of ₹ 9 crore for equity participation of ₹ 25 lakh under its policy to support building material industry as a part of real sector intervention.

☛ Tourism Finance Corporation of India Ltd., (TFCI)

Tourism Finance Corporation of India Ltd., (TFCI), is an All India financial institution sponsored by the Industrial Finance Corporation of India at the instance of the Government of India and set up as a public limited company in early 1989 for funding tourism and related projects. The authorised capital of TFCI is ₹ 100 crore and paid-up capital is ₹ 50 crore contributed by the All India Financial/ Investment institutions and Public sector banks. TFCI provides all forms of financial assistance for new projects, expansion and modernisation of projects with capital cost of ₹ one crore and above for setting up and for development of tourism, related activities, facilities and services which *inter alia* include hotels, resorts, amusement parks, safari parks, ropeways, convention halls, transport-travel and tour-operating agencies etc. Under the Extant Interest Subsidy Scheme of the Department of Tourism in the Government of India, four to five star category hotels get one per cent interest subsidy on loan upto ₹ 75 lakh and one, two and three star category hotels get interest subsidy of three per cent on the entire rupee term loan. Cumulative sanctions and disbursements by the Tourism Finance Corporation of India Ltd. amounted to ₹ 96.27 crore (66 Projects) and ₹ 28.31 crore respectively upto November, 1990.

☞ Composition of Present Banking System in India

Commercial Banking System in India consisted 274 scheduled commercial banks and four non-scheduled commercial banks at the end of June 1989. Of the scheduled commercial banks, 224 are in the public sector and these account for 90 per cent of the commercial banking system. In the public sector banking system there are 196 Regional rural banks, specially set up to increase the flow of credit to small borrowers in the rural areas. These banks have specified areas of operations usually limited to two to three districts. Their lending operations are also directed toward specified weaker sections. They undertake some other commercial banking business. The remaining 28 banks in public sector are regular commercial banks and transact all types of commercial banking business.

Amongst the public sector banks (as at the end of December 1989), State Bank of India was the biggest unit with 8,113 branches and deposits of ` 38,693 crore and advances of ` 25,477 crore. Apart from the State Bank of India, there are seven other banks called Associate Banks of the State Bank of India. In these banks, SBI owns either the entire or the majority of share capital. The State Bank and its associate banks as a group account roughly for one-third of aggregate banking business conducted by the Public Sector Banks (aggregate of deposits and advances) and around 33 per cent of the aggregate business of the centre banking system. Other 20 banks in the public sector are nationalised banks, 14 of them came in the public sector on 19th July, 1969 and six others on 15th April, 1980.

Term Lending Institutions

(Development Finance Institution)

Aggregate assistance sanctioned and disbursed by the term lending financial institutions (Development Finance Institutions) in 1990-91 shows continuance of an increasing trend. In the three-year period (1988-89 to 1990-91) aggregate assistance sanctioned by them recorded an average annual growth rate of 31 per cent while aggregate disbursements of assistance rose at an annual average rate of 22.5 per cent. Among the All India financial institutions, *viz.,* Industrial Development Bank of India (IDBI), Industrial Finance Corporation of India (IFCI), Industrial Credit and Investment Corporation of India (ICICI), Small Industries Development Bank of India (SIDBI), Life Insurance Corporation of India (LIC), General Insurance Corporation of India (GIC) and Unit Trust of India (UTI), together accounted for the major share of the total assistance sanctioned (` 20,033 crore) and disbursed (` 12,471 crore) by all financial institutions in 1990-91.

☞ Questions

1. Give a brief account of the different types of institutions, all of which together constitute the Indian banking system.
2. Discuss the recent trends in Indian banking.
3. Point out the main defects in the present banking organisation of India. Indicate the future lines of its improvement.
4. Write an essay on "Amalgamation and Nationalisation of Banks in India".
5. Enumerate the main defects in the present banking system of India and suggest measures for reform.
6. Discuss fully the objects, constitution and functions of the Industrial Finance Corporation of India.
7. What are the sources from which industries get their finance in India? Discuss the recent measures adopted to remove the defects of industrial finance in India.
8. Bring out the main points of difference between:
   (i) Cooperative bank and a commercial bank.
   (ii) State Bank of India and Nationalised banks. *[I.I.B., Part I]*
9. What is the broad difference in the functioning of:
   (a) The Reserve Bank of India
   (b) The State Bank of India

(c) The Nationalised Commercial Banks

(d) The Cooperative Banks *[I.I.B., Part I]*

10. Describe briefly the functions of the following financial institutions explaining how they help in the economic development of the country:

(a) Industrial Development Bank of India

(b) Agricultural Finance Corporation

(c) Industrial Finance Corporation

(d) Rural Banks *[I.I.B., Part I]*

11. What is the latest addition to financial institutions in India? When did it come into existence? What are going to be its functions? *[I.I.B., Part I]*
12. Write what you know about the National Bank for Agriculture and Rural Development (NABARD). What are its functions? *[I.I.B., Part I]*
13. What are the main agencies that provide industrial finance in our country? Write a short note on each of the agencies.

[I.I.B., Part I]

↙↙↙

CHAPTER

3 The Changing Profile of Indian Banking

☞ Trends: Achievements and Drawbacks

A study of banking system of different countries of the world shows that along with the process of economic development, the banking system adapts to the structure and needs of the particular economy. The philosophy behind the economic policy of India has been visualised from the goals inherent and enshrined in the Directive Principles of Constitution and was bequeathed to the nation as an instrument of socio-economic revolution by Pandit Jawaharlal Nehru. At the time of nationalisation of banks in 1969, Prime Minister Smt. Indira Gandhi had assigned specific tasks to the banks through her broadcast to the nation on 19th July, 1969, announcing the objectives of nationalisation in pursuance of the Government's policy of achieving maximum economic growth with social justice and self-reliance. To quote the words of Prime Minister in her broadcast ". . . . . An institution, such as the banking system which touches — and should touch — the lives of millions, has necessarily to be inspired by a larger social purpose and has to subserve national priorities and objectives... to the millions of small farmers, artisans and other self-employed persons, a bank can be a source of credit which is the very basis of any effort to improve their meagre economic lot".

We have to examine the changing role of Indian banking in recent years in the light of this background. The Indian system is at present undergoing a significant change from the traditional banking to a modern multifaced banking system in line with the need to achieve rapid socio-economic progress. Some of the noticeable features and achievements of Indian banking system in recent years are discussed below:

☞ Important Features and Achievements of Indian Banking System

1. Organisational Changes

The activities of banks have increased tremendously in the last decade and have brought about a realisation about the dynamic concept of banking. To meet effectively and efficiently this increasing burden of work, many banks have started launching organisational changes. The range of such changes include the redesigning — the organisational structure, introduction of new administrative procedures, decentralisation of authority and introduction of sophisticated performance budgeting systems. There is more emphasis on training of employees and providing them with better equipments.

2. Change from Wholesale Character to Retail Character of Banking

There is a clear change in the philosophy and techniques specially in the field of lending from the wholesale nature to retail character of banking activities. The Governor of the Reserve Bank of India in his address to the Indian Banks Association observed about this change as follows: "Commensurate with the growth of branch banking in the rural areas and the larger involvement of banks with agriculture and small industrial clients, we have had an attitudinal change on the part of bankers, a change symbolised by banking going retail instead of its erstwhile wholesale character and the system itself shedding its elitist image to become more truly an operation for the masses rather than for the classes. Social control sought to break the link between those who owned the banks and the satisfaction of their credit needs. It was realised that a system, where the grant of credit was a matter of privilege, had to be replaced by one where the requirements of credit were assessed on the basis of genuine production need and on impersonal norms related to the repayment capacity.

3. Purpose Orientation in Lending

Traditionally, banks have been lending money on the basis of tangible security or the creditworthiness of a borrower. But under the changing social concept, it is not enough for the banks to provide finance to men of means only. On the contrary, banks should provide finance to make people creditworthy, through productive efforts on their part, and to turn them into men of means. Following this new concept of banking there is a marked shift in the approach of Indian banks in their lendings from security orientation to purpose orientation. Technical competence of the borrower, operational feasibility and economic viability of the project rather than security which the borrower can offer are becoming more popular criteria in evaluating a loan proposal. Important examples of this changing orientation in bank lending are financing of small-scale and cottage industries, self-employed persons, priority and weaker sections of the society, etc.

4. Credit Planning

Another significant development in recent years has been the introduction of credit planning by Indian banks to allocate their available funds among various sectors according to the priorities in terms of overall national policies. This is a welcome development, because a fruitful orientation of banking policy requires a credit plan in conformity with the targets of investment and production laid down in the Five Year Plans. Successful implementation of economic planning presupposes an effective coordination between the credit mechanism and the planning mechanism. The District Credit Plans (DCP) prepared by the Lead banks contain development schemes in the various sectors of the economy, which are financed by the commercial and cooperative banks and other financial agencies operating at the district level according to the targets and quota's fixed for different institutions. The credit plan is prepared according to the agro-climate and physiographic conditions of the area, the availability of natural resources and the needs of the people of that area. Planners ensure that all the schemes included in the credit plan are technically feasible and economically viable. Government, local agencies and financial institutions are associated in the planning process.

5. Reduction of Regional Imbalances

To achieve the socio-economic objectives, all the big commercial banks have opened a network of branches in the unbanked or underbanked areas of the country. As against 8,262 branches at the end of June, 1969, the total number of commercial bank branches at the end of December 1989, was 58,417. The net increase in the number of functioning offices between June 1969, and December 1989, was 50,155. Consequently, the banking coverage in the country as a whole has improved from one office for 65,000 persons in June 1969, to one office for 12,000 persons by the end of December 1989.

To reduce the regional imbalances in banking facilities, the main thrust of branch expansion in the post-nationalisation period has been on improving of banking facilities in rural areas. Of the addition to the branch network during June 1969, and December 1983, nearly 63 per cent were at rural centres having population of less than 10,000 persons. The number of branches located in rural areas which was 1,832 as at the end of June 1969, rose to 33,640 in December 1989, accounting for 55.3 per cent of the total branch network. Greater attention is paid by banks on special distribution of branches — opening of branches at unbanked centres in under-banked areas in community development blocks to improve intra-district imbalances.

6. Development of Banking Habit and Deposit Mobilisation

As a natural corollary to the development of banking facilities throughout the country, a marked development is noticeable in the banking habit of the people. In the last decade, banks have made sustained efforts to induce people to keep a part of their savings as bank deposits and to expand and diversify their lending portfolio to cover a considerably larger number of borrowers than before. The extent to which the banking system has been able to spread banking habits to the rural areas is evident from the fact that growth of deposits in rural areas has been much faster than that of the total deposits. The rapid development of banking habit is also evident by the considerable increase in the use of cheques in recent years. Another important factor which indicates a trend of growing banking habit is the growth of credit.

There has been a significant increase in the deposits of scheduled commercial banks — from ₹ 4,646 crore in June, 1969 (about 15.5 per cent of the national income at current prices) to ₹ 1,84,824 crore by the end of Dec. 1990. It may be noted that although the Indian banking system has been instrumental in developing the banking habits in the country much more needs to be done before the system can catch up with its counterparts in other advanced countries.

7. Increase in the Volume of Credit

Advances — in whatever form — constitute the end objective of bank's operation. There has been a marked increase in the volume of credit provided by the Indian banks to different sectors of the economy in recent years. During the last sixteen years, the advances of scheduled commercial banks increased from a low level of ₹ 3,599 crore in 1969 to ₹ 1,08,935 crore in 1990.

8. Increase in Advances to Priority Sector and Weaker Sectors

More significant than the increase in the volume of bank credit in India are the changes in the sectoral deployment. Before nationalisation of banks in 1969, large and medium industry and wholesale trade accounted for over 78 per cent of the bank credit. By November 1983, the share of these sectors (excluding credit for public food procurement) had declined to about 43 per cent. Correspondingly, the share of priority sectors, food procurement agencies, etc., has shown significant increase. One of the major tasks undertaken by banks is the extension of credit to small borrowers in the hitherto neglected sectors of the economy. Various schemes have been drawn up and implemented by banks in India to extend credit to small borrowers in sectors like agriculture, small-scale industry, road and water transport, retail trade and small business which traditionally had very little share in the credit extended in the past. Taking into account the need to provide resources, requirements of the weaker sections for specific needs, consumption credit (with certain limits for specific needs) has been incorporated in the priority sectors. Small housing loans (not exceeding ₹ 5,000) to scheduled castes/and scheduled tribes and other weaker sections are also considered priority sector advances.

In recent years, the banks have not only been enlarging the total volume of credit, but have also increased — the proportion of it going to small and poor borrowers of the weaker sections of the society. Banks are making special efforts to assist weaker sections to enable them to undertake self-employment ventures or acquire income-generating capital assets to improve their standard of living. Another measure of the thrust of the bank's lending efforts towards weaker sections is their involvement in and support to the integrated Rural Development Programme which is directed towards those below the poverty line. The programme envisages capital subsidy and credit assistance to identified poor families for acquiring income generating assets to come up above the poverty line.

Extension of credit to small borrowers in the hitherto neglected sectors of the economy has been one of the major tasks assigned to the public sector banks in the post-nationalisation period. To achieve this objective banks have drawn up schemes to extend credit to small borrowers in sectors like agriculture, small-scale industry, road and water transport, retail trade and small business, which traditionally had very little share in the credit extended by banks. Taking into account the need to provide resource requirements to weaker sections, for specific needs, consumption credit (with certain limits) has been included in priority sectors. Similarly, small housing loans (not exceeding ₹ 5,000) to scheduled castes, scheduled tribes and other weaker sections are also classified as priority sector advances. Number of borrowal accounts with the public sector banks for these categories of borrowers increased from 2.60 lakh to 355 lakh between June 1969 and September 1990. Amount outstanding during the same period increased from ₹ 441 crore to ₹ 39,833 crore. Public sector banks accounted for 42.7 per cent of the total bank credit by September, 1990.

9. Credit to Weaker Sections

To increase credit flow to small and poor borrowers, weaker sections comprising of small and marginal farmers, landless labourers, tenant farmers, and share-croppers, artisans, village and cottage industries, Beneficiaries of Integrated Rural Development Programme, scheduled castes and scheduled tribes, a Different Rate of Interest (DRI) Scheme has been evolved. This scheme was stated to receive not less than 10 per cent of net bank credit by March 1985. By September 1990, weaker sections had received ₹ 9,961 crore and accounted for 10.7 per cent of aggregate advances of Public sector banks.

10. Advances to Scheduled Caste/Scheduled Tribe Borrowers

People belonging to the SC/ST have been recognised as the most vulnerable sections. Banks have been asked to make special efforts to assist them with adequate credit to enable them to undertake self-employment ventures to acquire income generating capital assets so as to improve their standard of living. Up to September 1989, public sector banks provided credit worth ₹ 3,142 crore to 90.23 lakh SC/ST borrowers.

11. Integrated Rural Development Programme

The Integrated Rural Development Programme envisages capital subsidy and credit assistance to the identified poor families for acquiring income generating assets to come up above poverty line. The programme envisaged a capital subsidy flow of ₹ 1,500 crore during the Sixth Plan period with a matching credit mobilisation of ₹ 3,000 crore to benefit 1.50 crore families. As against this Banking system had mobilised term credit of ₹ 3,102 crore assisting 1.66 crore beneficiary families. Provisional target for the Seventh Plan had been set to assist 2 crore beneficiary families. During the Seventh Plan, *i.e.*, 1985-90, the banking system had assisted 1.82 crore beneficiary families involving term credit of ₹ 5,380.53 crore. Banking system assisted 33.51 lakh beneficiary families during 1989-90 with ₹ 1,228.53 crore.

12. Self-employment Scheme for the Educated Unemployed Youth

The self-employment scheme for the educated unemployed youth was introduced in 1983-84 to create self-employment opportunities and to motivate educated young men and women to take up self-employment ventures. The scheme was extended to all areas of the country except cities with more than ten lakh population as per 1981 census. Under the scheme, composite loans not exceeding ₹ 35,000 for Industrial ventures, ₹ 25,000 for Service Ventures and ₹ 15,000 for Business Ventures are granted. Banks are not to ask for any margin money or seek collateral security or third party guarantee for the loan.

The annual target of banks was to assist 2.5 lakh beneficiaries from 1983-84 to 1986-87 and 1988-89. For the years 1987-88 and 1989-90, the target was 1.25 lakh beneficiaries to be covered by the banks. Against this, banks had assisted 2.42 lakh, 2.29 lakhs, 2.21 lakh and 2.19 lakh during the years 1983-84, 1984-85, 1985-86 and 1986-87 respectively. During 1988-89, 1.91 beneficiaries were assisted. The amounts of loan sanctioned were 401.54 crore, 429.53 crore, 429.99 crore and 455.12 crore for 1983-84, 1984-85, 1985-86 and 1986-87 respectively. Loans sanctioned during 1988-89 were ₹ 404.32 crore.

13. Self-employment Programme for the Urban Poor

Self-employment programme for the urban poor (SEPUP) was launched from Sept. 1, 1986. It covers all cities/towns with a population exceeding 10,000 as per 1981 census and areas which are not covered under Integrated Rural Development Programme (IRDP). One beneficiary for every 300 population (1981 census) is to be assisted at each urban centre. Persons whose total family income does not exceed ₹ 600 per month are eligible for assistance to undertake any economically viable activity. A borrower is eligible for a maximum loan of ₹ 5,000 at an interest rate of 10 per cent per annum. A capital subsidy at the rate of 25 per cent of the amount of assistance is provided by the Central Government. No collateral security or third party guarantee or margin money is needed. Repayment of loan is in 33 equal monthly instalments after a grace period of three months. In 1989-90 the number of beneficiaries were 3.02 lakh and amount sanctioned ₹ 117.20 crore.

14. Differential Rate of Interest Scheme

Public sector banks are operating a scheme of Differential Rate of Interest (DRI) since 1972. The scheme covers poor borrowers having an annual family income of not more than ₹ 6,400 in rural areas and ₹ 7,200 in other areas and not owing more than 2.5 acre of unirrigated or one acre of irrigated land. They are given credit support of four per cent per annum rate of interest for sums up to ₹ 6,500 as term loan and working capital loan for productive ventures. The public sector banks had an outstanding of DRI credit of ₹ 708.03 crore in 42.87 lakh borrowal accounts as at the end of June 1990.

15. Housing Finance

The Reserve Bank of India has liberalised the terms and conditions for housing loans from time-to-time, the last in March 1990. Under the current guidelines for housing finance of the RBI, each bank should compute its share of the housing finance allocation for 1990-91 at 1.5 per cent of the incremental deposits as on the last reporting Friday of March 1990, over the corresponding figures of the last reporting Friday of March 1989. However, the banks can exceed this level up to a reasonable limit having regard to its resources position and compliance with the statutory reserve requirements. Thirty per cent of the total allocation should be reserved for direct lending of this at least half, *i.e.,* 15 per cent of the total allocation should be given as direct housing loan in the rural and semi-urban areas. Further 30 per cent of the allocation be channelled by way of term loans to Housing Finance Companies, Housing Boards and other public housing agencies primarily for augmenting the supply of serviced land and constructed units. The balance of 40 per cent of the allocation will be available for subscription to the Guaranteed Bonds and Debentures of the National Housing Bank and Housing and Urban Development Corporation. Commercial banks had provided housing finance amounting to ₹ 237.00 crore in 1988 and about ₹ 322 crore up to March, 1990.

16. Leasing

Commercial banks in India have realised the significance of leasing finance and are fast entering into the arena. The entry of banks into leasing business confirms the importance of this business and lends legitimacy to it. What with the presence of about 500 leasing companies, the leasing business in the country is estimated to run to nearly ₹ 2,000 crore and its scope for expansion seems to be almost unlimited.

Types of Leasing

A lease may be defined as a special type of transaction in which a party owning the asset (called the lesser) provides the asset for use over a certain period of time to another (called the lessee) for consideration in the form of periodic payment (rent)' with or without a further down payment at the end of lease period.

A lease can be distinguished from a sale and hire purchase. Unlike in a sale where once the transaction is completed, the relationship between the seller and buyer comes to an end; in a lease the relationship between the parties continue and each of them bears some of the incidence of ownership, during the lease period. A lease is different from a hire purchase transaction, in that the ultimate purpose of a hire purchase is to obtain ownership, whereas a lessee aims at having only the use of the equipment.

The term lease denotes time bound contract between a lessor, the owner of the asset and the lessee, the user of the asset within a particular timeframe for a consideration called lease rental.

Lease rentals are of two types. One is upfronted lease, where rentals are higher in the initial years and lower in the later years. The other is the Back Ended Lease which is an inverse transaction to the first. At the end of the lease contract the asset reverts to the lesser who becomes the legal owner. Leasing facilitates the use of an asset and not ownership.

There are basically three types of leasing.

(1) Operating Lease

Here the lease period is significantly less than the useful life of the equipment and the lease rentals payable during this period are insufficient to cover fully the equipment cost. Computers, vehicles and copies are generally leased under this method. Though fairly popular abroad, operating lease is yet to get recognition in India.

(2) Financial Lease Capital Lease

Under this form a firm sells an asset owned by it to another party and this party leases it back to the firm. As a result the lessee received the purchase consideration for the asset and he is able to augment his liquidity position as well as retain the use of the asset in return for periodic lease payment.

(3) Leaveraged Leasing

Here the transaction is among three parties who enter into a contract to make periodic payments over the basic lease period during which they are entitled to use the asset over that period. An equity investment by the lesser finances a part of the asset and the remaining is financed by a long-term lender. The loan is usually secured by a mortgage on the assets and sometimes the lease guarantees the debt.

Banks and Lease Finance

Consequent on the issue of notification under Section 6(i)(o) of Banking Regulation Act, 1949 by the Govt. of India on Aug. 14,1984, commercial banks are now permitted to undertake the business of equipment leasing as one of the activities apart from those specifically set out in Clauses (a) to (n) of Sub-section (i) of that section. Similarly, with the amendment of Section 19 (i) of Banking Regulation Act, 1949, a bank can set up a subsidiary unit for undertaking every type of activity which banks themselves can be engaged in, under Section 6 of that Act.

The banks are now allowed to set up a subsidiary with not less than 51 per cent of shareholding for transacting equipment leasing business, or to invest in shares of a leasing company within the limits specified in Section 19 (2) of the above Act.

The subsidiary, however, is prohibited from transacting hire purchase business and financing of other companies or concerns engaged in equipment leasing business. The Reserve Bank has also stipulated that banks themselves should not:

(a) undertake departmentally the business of equipment leasing, and

(b) act as promoters of companies in which they make portfolio investment.

The aggregate investment of a bank in a subsidiary and/or in shares of other leasing companies should not exceed 10 per cent of the paid-up capital and reserves of the bank. As at the end of June, 1989 with the approval of Reserve Bank, six equipment leasing-cum-merchant banking subsidiaries had been set up by Indian banks.

17. Innovations

Industrial Credit and Investment Corporation of India (ICICI) visualises its role as a catalyst in the growth of a healthy capital and money market. ICICI's development banking activities have not been only limited to providing finance to industry but have also extended to other areas as project promotion, rural development, human resource development and publications. It has identified, over the years, many of the requirements of the financing infrastructure of the country and promoted organisations to fulfil these needs. Among the innovative institutions set up by ICICI are:

1. Housing Development Finance Corporation Ltd., (HDFC).
2. The Shipping Credit and Investment Company of India Ltd., (SCICI).
3. The Credit Rating Information Services of India Ltd., (CRISIL).
4. Technology Development and Information Company of India Ltd., (TDICI).
5. The OTC Exchange of India (OTCEI).

Over the years, ICICI has grown into a commercially successful development finance institution with strong financial base.

The globalization of international markets, the liberalization measures introduced for the Indian industry and the financial system have set the stage for an era of growth opportunities. At the same time, these deregulation trends are expected to induce greater level of competition. ICICI would be required to mobilize resources directly from the market at competitive rates. ICICI with its development ethos, decades of rich experience and close links with the industry is well geared to deal with the emerging market conditions and maintain steady growth in its operations and profits.

18. Risk and Venture Capital Financing

It is relevant here to note the contributions made by the financial institutions to the growth of risk and venture capital assistance in our country.

Risk Capital and Technology Finance Corporation Limited (RCTC): Risk Capital and Technology Finance Corporation Ltd., (RCTC) was established in 1988 after reconstitution of Risk Capital Foundation (RCF) set up earlier in 1975 by IFCI. This corporation provides risk capital assistance to first generation entrepreneurs on soft terms under risk capital scheme and also supplies conventional loans and interest free conditional loans under Technology Finance Scheme to projects that envisage adaptation and commercialisation of new technologies, up to March 1991, RCTC has provided financial assistance of ₹ 29.8 crore.

Technology Development and Information Company of India (TDICI): Technology Development and Information Company of India (TDICI) was set up by Industrial Credit and Investment Corporation of India (ICICI) and Unit Trust of India (UTI) in July 1988 as India's first venture finance company. It primarily assists small and medium scale projects conceived by technocrat-entrepreneurs by providing project finance in the form of equity or conditional loans, apart from offering technology information service. Up to March 1991 TDICI has provided financial assistance of ₹ 24.7 crore.

19. Institutional Developments in the Financial Sector

Discount and Finance House of India (DFHI): Discount and Finance House of India which was set up on April 25, 1988 seeks to develop an active secondary market for the money market instruments and integrate various segments of the market in order to facilitate the smoothening of short-term liquidity imbalances. In its operations, the emphasis is placed on a high turnover in the money market instruments rather than on being their repository.

Apart from making 182 days Treasury Bills, a highly liquid instrument, DFHI operates in:

(a) inter-bank call money and short notice money market,

(b) inter-bank term deposit (15-90 days) market, both as lender and borrower and as a borrower,

(c) commercial papers (CP) and certificates of deposits (CD).

The spread/margin on its money market instruments is not very large but sufficient profits for the DFHI are generated because of large turnover. In 1991-92, DFHI enhanced its paid up capital from ₹ 150 crore to ₹ 200 crore to augment its resources. Besides DFHI enjoys refinance facilities from RBI against the holdings of commercial Bills/derivative usance promissory notes (at 13-18 per cent interest rate). It also continues to avail of a line of credit of ₹ 100 crore (at a minimum of 20 per cent interest) from the consortium of public sector banks for rediscounting of commercial bills.

At present DFHI's activities are restricted to:

(i) Dealing in 91 days and 364 days Treasury Bills.

(ii) Rediscounting short-term commercial bills.

(iii) Participating in the inter-bank call money, notice money and term deposits, and

(iv) Dealing in Commercial Paper and Certificates of Deposits.

(v) Government dated Securities.

(i) Treasury Bills: Treasury Bills are issued by Reserve Bank of India on behalf of the Government of India. Such bills are sold at fortnightly auctions. The Discount House regularly participates in such auctions. Moreover, it provides a ready market to either institutions/individuals to buy or sell the Treasury Bills. It purchases the same either as outright purchase or on repos basis. Repos means with the right to repurchase the same bills again. For this purpose, the DFHI quotes two-way prices with fine spread. Such operation in Treasury Bills imparts greater flexibility to banks in their funds management. Moreover, with the creation of secondary market for Treasury Bills, corporate bodies and other institutions could also invest their short-term surplus funds in such bills.

(ii) Rediscounting of Commercial Bills: The Discount House aims at imparting liquidity to commercial bills which have already been discounted by banks and financial institutions. It further rediscounts them and also enables banks and other institutions to rediscount from it such bills. For this purpose DFHI announces its bid and offers rediscount rates on a fortnightly basis.

(iii) Call Money Market and Term Deposit: DFHI has been permitted by the Reserve Bank of India to operate in the inter-bank call money market, both as lender and borrower of overnight call and notice money up to 14 days. DFHI also renders services to banks in the call money market by arranging or placing funds for banks.

The DFHI is authorised to augment its resources with lines of credit from public sector banks and refinance lines from the Reserve Bank. The amount and the rate of interest charged by Reserve Bank on refinance would be flexible, so that Reserve Bank can have its impact on the money market by varying the quantum of refinance and the rate of interest thereon.

20. New Private Sector Banks: RBI Guidelines

After giving free field to nationalised banks which account for 91 per cent of total bank branches and handle 86 per cent of the banking business in the country for over two decades now, the Reserve Bank has decided to permit setting up of new private sector banks.

It laid down conditions for setting up of new private banks. Such banks must subserve the underlying goals of financial sector reforms which are to provide competitive, efficient and low cost financial intermediation services for the society at large. They should be financially viable. Their presence should result in upgradation of technology in the banking sector. They should be equipped to avoid the shortcomings such as unfair pre-emption and concentration of credit, monopolisation of economic power, cross holdings with industrial groups, etc., which beset the private sector banks prior to nationalisation. Freedom of entry in the banking sector may have to be managed carefully and judiciously.

RBI has laid down detailed guidelines of establishment of new banks in the private sector. Such a bank should be registered as a public limited company under the Companies Act, 1956. The RBI may, on merits, grant a licence under the Banking Regulation Act, 1949 for such a bank. The bank may also be included in the second schedule of the Reserve Bank of India Act, 1934 at the appropriate time. The decision of the RBI in these matters shall be final.

The bank will be governed by the provisions of the Banking Regulation Act, 1949 in regard to its authorised, subscribed and paid-up capital. The minimum paid-up capital for such a bank shall be ₹ 100 crore. The promoters' contribution for such a bank shall be determined by the RBI and will also be subject to other applicable regulations. The shares of the bank should be listed on stock exchanges.

To avoid concentration of the headquarters of new banks in metropolitan cities and other overbanked areas, while granting a licence preference would be given to those the headquarters of which are proposed to be located in a centre which does not have the headquarters of any other bank. Voting rights of an individual shareholder shall be governed by the ceiling of one per cent of the total voting rights as stipulated by Section 12(2) of the Banking Regulation Act. However, exemption from this ceiling may be granted under Section 53 of the said Act, to public financial institutions.

The new bank shall not be allowed to have as a director any person who is a director of any other banking company, or of companies which among themselves are entitled to exercise voting rights in excess of 20 per cent of the total voting rights of all the shareholders of the banking company, as laid down in the Banking Regulation Act, 1949. The bank will be governed by the provisions of the Reserve Bank of India Act, 1934, the Banking Regulation Act, 1949 and other relevant statutes, in regard to its management set up, liquidity requirements and the scope of its activity. The directives, instructions, guidelines and advices given by the RBI shall be applicable to such a bank as in the case of other banks. It would be ensured that a new bank would concentrate on core banking activities initially.

Such a bank shall be subject to prudential norms in respect of banking operations, accounting policies and other policies as are laid down by RBI.

The Reserve Bank of India issued specific guidelines on 22nd Jan., 1993 for the entry of new private sector banks:

1. The bank shall be registered as a public limited company under the Companies Act, 1956.
2. The RBI may, on merits, grant a licence under the Banking Regulation Act, 1949 for a bank. The bank may also be included in the Second Schedule of the Reserve Bank of India Act, 1934 at the appropriate time. The decision of the RBI in these matters shall be final.
3. The bank will be governed by the provisions of the Banking Regulation Act, 1949, in regard to its authorised, subscribed and paid-up capital. The minimum paid-up capital shall be ₹ 100 crore. The promoters' contribution shall be determined by the RBI and will also be subject to other applicable regulations.
4. The shares of the bank should be listed on Stock Exchanges.
5. To avoid concentration of the headquarters of new banks in metropolitan cities and other overbanked areas, while granting a licence, preference may be given to those, the headquarters of which are proposed to be located in a centre which does not have the headquarters of any other bank.
6. Voting rights of an individual shareholder shall be governed by the ceiling of 1% of the total voting rights as stipulated by Section 12(2) of the Banking Regulation Act. However, exemption from this ceiling may be granted under Section 53 of the said Act, to public financial institutions.
7. The bank shall not be allowed to have as a director, any person who is a director of any other banking company, or of companies which among themselves are entitled to exercise voting rights in excess of 20% of the total voting rights of all the shareholders of the banking company, as laid down in the Banking Regulation Act, 1949.
8. The bank will be governed by the Provisions of the Reserve Bank of India Act, 1934, the Banking Regulation Act, 1949 and other relevant statutes, in regard to its management setup, liquidity requirements and scope of its activities. The directives, instructions, guidelines and advices given by the RBI, shall be applicable to such a bank as in the case of other banks. It would be ensured that a new bank would concentrate on core banking activities initially.
9. The bank shall be subject to prudential norms in respect of banking operations, accounting policies and other policies as laid down by RBI. The bank will have to achieve capital adequacy of 8% of the risk weighted assets from the very beginning. Similarly, norms for income recognition, asset classification and provisioning will also be applicable to it from the beginning. So will be the single borrower and group borrower exposure limits that will be in force from time-to-time.
10. The bank shall have to observe priority sector lending targets as applicable to other domestic banks. However, in recognition of the fact that new entrants may require sometime to lend to all categories of the priority sector, some modification in the composition of the priority sector lending may be considered by the RBI for an initial period of three years.
11. The bank will also have to comply with such directions of the RBI as are applicable to existing banks in the matter of export credit. As a facilitation of this, it may be issued an authorised dealer's licence to deal in foreign exchange, when applied for.

12. A new bank shall not be allowed to set up a subsidiary or mutual fund for at least three years after its establishment. The holding of such a bank in the equity of other companies shall be governed by the existing provisions applicable to other banks, *viz.*,

    (i) 30% of the bank's or the investee company's capital funds, whichever is less, as set out under the Banking Regulation Act, 1949, and

    (ii) 1.5% of the bank's incremental deposits during a year as per RBI guidelines.

    The aggregate of such investments in the subsidiaries and mutual fund (if and when set up) and portfolio investments in other companies shall not exceed 20% of the bank's own paid-up capital and reserves.

13. In regard to branch opening, it shall be governed by the existing policy that banks are free to open branches at various centres including urban/metropolitan centres without the prior approval of the RBI once they satisfy the capital adequacy and prudential accounting norms. However, to avoid over-concentration of their branches in metropolitan areas and cities, a new bank will be required to open rural and semi-urban branches also, as may be laid down by RBI.

14. The bank shall have to lay down its loan policy within the overall policy guidelines of RBI. While doing so, it shall specifically provide prudential norms covering related party transactions.

15. The bank shall make full use of modern infrastructural facilities in office equipment, computer, telecommunications, etc., in order to provide good customer service. The Bank should have a high-powered customer grievances cell to handle customer complaints.

16. The bank shall have to satisfy such other conditions as RBI may prescribe from time-to-time.

21. Money Market Mutual Funds

Scheduled commercial banks and their subsidiaries have been allowed to set up Money Market Mutual Funds (MMMFs) to provide an additional short-term avenue to investors and to bring money market instruments within the reach of individuals and small bodies. The MMMFs are a special genre of mutual funds which invest only in high quality money market instruments of a short-term nature. The recent introduction of several new money market instruments like the Certificates of Deposit (CD), the Commercial Paper (CP) and the 182 days Treasury Bills, was essentially meant to tap bulk funds and as such a relatively high minimum transaction amount had been stipulated. By bringing a wide range of short-term money market instruments within the reach of individual investors, the MMMFs would undertake a size intermediation. It was in this context that MMMFs assumed significance. The broad framework of the scheme for MMMFs is as follows:

1. Only banks and their subsidiaries would be permitted to set up MMMFs.
2. Individuals and other bodies would be permitted to invest their resources in MMMFs in the form of negotiable/transferable instruments and MMMFs deposit accounts. Suitable ceilings may be fixed on mobilisation of such funds by banks and their subsidiaries (this could in the first instance be equivalent to one per cent of aggregate deposits).
3. The minimum of size of investment would be ₹ one lakh and repurchases could be subject to a minimum lock-in period of 3 months.
4. MMMFs could be allowed to invest only in specified short-term money market instruments (CDs, CPs, 182 days Treasury Bills, rediscounting of commercial bills and call and short

notice money) as lenders. A minimum of 20 per cent of the MMMFs Funds could be required to be held in 182 days Treasury Bills and a maximum of 20 per cent in call and short notice money.

5. The funds mobilised by MMMFs would not be subject to reserve requirements as these funds are in turn invested in money market instruments.
6. The question of stamp duty would need to be examined.

To fully develop this broad framework and to study the implication of such a scheme a Task Force consisting of representatives of banks and the Reserve Bank of India is to be set up by the Reserve Bank to work out the detailed operative guidelines and documentation of MMMFs.

22. Credit Cards

Several banks, both Indian and foreign, have moved into the credit card business. Also known as "Plastic money", it offers the individual an opportunity to buy rail/air tickets, make purchases from shops, have meals and stay at hotels when they need it. And pay at leisure.

The diagram given below is a graphic description of a credit card business cycle (Fig. 3.1).

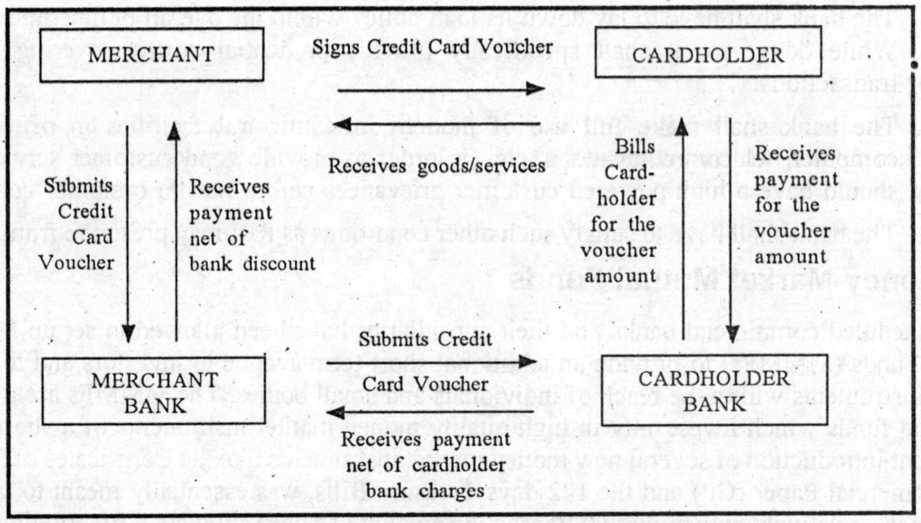

Fig. 3.1 Credit Card Business Cycle

Plastic Money

Credit Card/Debit Card

Credit Card

Credit cards in India is gaining ground. A number of banks in India are encouraging people to use credit card. The concept of credit card was used in 1950 with the launch of charge cards in USA by Diners Club and American Express Credit Card, however, became more popular with use of magnetic strip in 1970.

Credit card in India became popular with the introduction of foreign banks in the country.

Credit cards are financial instruments, which can be used more than once to borrow money or buy products and services on credit. Basically banks, retail stores and other business issue these.

Major Banks issuing Credit Card in India

- State Bank of India credit card (SBI credit card)
- Bank of Baroda credit card or BoB credit card
- ICICI credit card
- HDFC credit card
- IDBI credit card
- ABN-AMRO credit card
- Standard Chartered credit card
- HSBC credit card
- Citibank credit card

Precautions taken after receiving credit card

To Avoid:

- Bending the Card.
- Exposure to electronic devices and gadgets.
- Direct exposure to sunlight.
- Be cautious about disclosing your account number over the phone unless you know you're dealing with a reputable company.
- Never put your account number on the outside of an envelope or on a postcard.
- Draw a line through blank spaces on charge or debt slips above the total so the amount cannot be changed.
- Don't sign a blank charge or debit slip.
- Tear up carbons and save your receipts to check against your monthly statements.
- Cut up old cards — cutting through the account number — before disposing them.
- Open monthly statements promptly and compare them with your receipts. Report mistakes or discrepancies as soon as possible to the special address listed on your statement for inquiries. Under the FCBA (credit cards) and the EFTA (ATM or debit cards), the card issuer must investigate errors reported to them within 60 days of the date your statement was mailed to you.
- Keep a record — in a safe place separate from your cards — of your account numbers, expiration dates, and the telephone numbers of each card issuer so you can report a loss quickly.
- Carry only those cards that you anticipate you'll need.

To Do:

- Please sign on the signature panel on the reverse of the Card immediately with a non-eraseable ball-point pen (preferably in black ink). This will ensure that the benefits of membership are yours and yours alone.
- Keep the card in a prominent place in your wallet. You will notice if it is missing.

Reasons credit card being rejected at retail outlet:

- One may have exceeded the borrowing limit or defaulted (constantly) on minimum payment due.
- The card is hotlisted.
- The card has crossed its expiration date.
- Non-receipt of dues of one-card blocks future transactions on any other card(s) held of the same card-issuing bank.
- The magnetic stripe on the reverse of the card is damaged, i.e., has been scratched or exposed to continuous heat/direct sunlight or magnetic field-like card kept near a TV set/other electronic appliances.
- Systems or technology failures have in rare instances also led to non-acceptance of cards when swiped through an Electronic Terminal.

Global player in credit card market

Master Card

Master Card is a product of Master Card International and along with VISA are distributed by financial institutions around the world. Cardholders borrow money against a line of credit and pay it back with interest if the balance is carried over from month-to-month. Its products are issued by 23,000 financial institutions in 220 countries and territories. In 1998, it had almost 700 million cards in circulation, whose users spent $ 650 billion in more than 16.2 million locations.

VISA Card

VISA Cards is a product of VISA USA and along with Master Cards is distributed by financial institutions around the world. A VISA cardholder borrows money against a credit line and repays the money with interest if the balance is carried over from month-to-month in a revolving line of credit. Nearly 600 million cards carry one of the VISA brands and more than 14 million locations accept VISA cards.

American Express

The world's favourite card is American Express Credit Card. More than 57 million cards are in circulation and growing and it is still growing further. Around US $ 123 billion was spent last year through American Express Cards and it is poised to be the world's No. 1 card in the year's future. In a regressive US economy last year, the total amount spent on American Express Cards rose by 4 per cent. American Express Cards are very popular in the US, Canada, Europe and Asia and are used widely in the retail and everybody expenses segment.

Diners Club International

Diners Club is the world's No. 1 Charge Card. Diners Club cardholders reside all over the world and the Diners Card is an alltime favourite for corporates. There are more than 8 billion Diners Club cardholders. They are affluent and are frequent travellers in premier businesses and institutions, including *Fortune 500* companies and leading global corporations.

JCB Cards

The JCB Card has a merchant network of 10.93 million in approximately 189 countries. It is supported by over 320 financial institutions worldwide and serves more than 48 million cardholders in eighteen countries worldwide. The JCB philosophy of "identify the customer's needs and please the customer with Service from the Heart" is paying rich dividends as their customers spend US $ 43 billion annually on their JCB cards.

Grace/Interest Free Period

The number of days you have on a card before a card issuer starts charging you interest is called grace period. Usually this period is the number of days between the statement date and the due date of payment. Grace periods on credit cards are usually 2-3 weeks. However, there is likely to be no grace for balances carried forward from previous month and fresh purchases thereafter if any.

The following are some of the varieties of credit cards in India:

- ANZ — Gold
- ANZ — Silver
- Bank of India — Indiacard
- BoI — Taj Premium
- BoI — Gold
- BoB — Exclusive
- Bob — Premium
- Canara Bank — Cancard
- Citibank — Gold
- Citibank — Silver
- Citibank WWF Card
- Citibank Visa Card for Women
- Citibank Cry Card
- Citibank Silver International Credit Card
- Citibank Women's International Credit Card
- Citibank Gold International Credit Card
- Citibank Electronic Credit Card
- Citibank Maruti International Credit Card
- Citibank Times Gold
- Citibank Indian Oil International Credit Card
- Citibank Citi Diners Club Card
- HSBC — Gold
- HSBC — Classic
- ICICI Sterling Silver Credit Card
- ICICI Solid Gold Credit Card
- ICICI True Blue Credit Card
- SBI Card
- Stanchart — Gold
- Stanchart — Executive
- Stanchart — Classic
- Thomas Cook Standard Chartered Global Credit Card

Standard Suggestion of Credit Cards

- Standard Chart — It is the most basic card (sans all frills) offered by issuers.
- Classic Card — Brand name for the standard card issued by VISA.
- Gold Card/Executive Card — A credit card that offers a higher line of credit than a standard card. Income eligibility is also higher. In addition, issuers provides extra perks or incentives to cardholders.
- Platinum Card — A credit card with a higher limit and additional perks than a gold card.
- Titanium Card — A card with an even higher limit than a platinum card.

The following are some of the plus features of credit card in India:

- Hotel discounts
- Travel fare discounts
- Free global calling card
- Lost baggage insurance
- Accident insurance
- Insurance on goods purchased
- Waiver of payment in case of accidental death
- Household insurance

Some Facts of Credit Cards

- The first card was issued in India by Visa in 1981.
- The country's first Gold Card was also issued from Visa in 1986.
- The first international credit card was issued to a restricted number of customers by Andhra Bank in 1987 through the Visa programme after getting special permission from the Reserve Bank of India.
- The credit cards shape and size, are as specified by the ISD 7810 standard. It is generally of plastic quality. It is also sometimes known as Plastic Money.

Debit Card

Debit cards, also known as check cards, looks like credit cards or ATM cards (automated teller machine card). It operates like cash or a personal cheque. Debit cards are different from credit cards. Credit card is a way to "pay later", whereas debit card is a way to "pay now", When we use a debit card, out money is quickly deducted from the bank account.

Debit cards are accepted at many locations, including grocery stores, retail stores, gasoline stations, and restaurants. Its an alternative to carrying a checque book or cash.

With debit card, we use our own money and not the issuer's money.

In India almost all the banks issue debit card to its accountholders.

Features of Debit Card

- Obtaining a debit card is often easier than obtaining a credit card.
- Using a debit card instead of writing cheques saves you from showing identification or giving out personal information at the time of the transaction.

- Using a debit card frees you from carrying cash or a cheque book.
- Using a debit card means you no longer have to stock up on travellers' cheques or cash when you travel.
- Debit cards may be more readily accepted by merchants than cheques, especially in other states or countries wherever your card brand is accepted.
- The debit card is a quick, "pay now" product, giving you no grace period.
- Using a debit card may mean you have less protection than with a credit card purchase for items which are never delivered, are defective, or were misrepresented. But, as with credit cards, you may dispute unauthorised charges or other mistakes within 60 days. You should contact the card issuer if a problem cannot be resolved with the merchant.
- Returning goods or cancelling services purchased with a debit card is treated as if the purchase were made with cash or a cheque.

Tips for responsible use of Debit Card

- If your card is lost or stolen, report the loss immediately to your financial institution.
- If you suspect your card is being fraudulently used, report it immediately to your financial institution.
- Hold on to your receipts from your debit card transactions. A thief may get your name and debit card number from a receipt and order goods by mail or over the telephone. Your card does not have to be missing in order for it to be misused.
- If you have a PIN number, memorise it. Do not keep your PIN number with your card. Also, don't choose a PIN number that a smart thief could figure out, such as your phone number or birthday.
- Never give your PIN number to anyone. Keep your PIN private.
- Always know how much money you have available in your account. Don't forget that your debit card may allow you to access money that you have set aside to cover a cheque which has not cleared your bank yet.
- Keep your receipts in one place — for easy retrieval and better oversight of your bank account.

23. Technology Power for Financial Products

The growth of banking concept has been dramatic in recent times. While banks have been instrumental for various technological innovations, they have also been adapting the breakthrough to further their services by adding newer dimensions.

Apart from the extensive use of computers for accounting purpose and communications network of the general order, banks have introduced innovative concepts like Magnetic Ink Character Recognition (MICR) cheques, Bankers Automated Clearing Services (BACS), Clearing House Automated Payment Systems (CHAPS), Cash Dispensers (CDs), Automated Teller Machines (ATMs) are towards instant operational convenience, including cash withdrawals, Point-of-sale (POS) terminals facilitate instant retail banking transactions. Laser Cards have enhanced the utility of credit cards. The formation of Society for Worldwide Inter Financial Telecommunications (SWIFT) coordinates international banking transactions through Satellite communications.

☞ Drawbacks of Indian Banking System

Indian banking system has achieved a remarkable all-round growth during the last fifteen years, as discussed in the preceding paragraphs, but some inherent weaknesses and shortcomings remain there or have cropped up, and efforts should be made to overcome them as early as possible. Some of the weaker points of Indian banking system are discussed below:

1. Poor Capital Base

The survival success and growth of a bank depends on capital resources and their efficient use. In line with the enlargement and elaboration of financial markets, the demand for capital in the banks has risen to unprecedented levels. The business of most of Indian banks has continued to expand and they are experiencing an unprecedented expansion and diversification of their business. Against this background, it may be pointed out that the capital base of almost all Indian banks are very low in comparison with international standards. It forms about 1 to 2.0 per cent of the banks' deposits and other liabilities. Therefore, it is necessary that capital base of all the banks is strengthened. A welcome step in this direction is the announcement in the Lok Sabha on December 13, 1985, by Shri Janardhan Poojari, Minister of State for Finance, Government of India, of Government's decision to augment the capital base of 29 public sector banks. The authorised capital of the State Bank of India has been raised to ₹ 200 crore.

2. Inefficient Organisational Structure

An unprecedented and multifarous growth in the activities of banks in India in the last decade have put up to so much of stresses and strains that the organisational structure has become inefficient and ineffective. The organisational structure of the banks requires changes according to the changing and developmental needs, for example, greater delegation of power, decentralisation of control and constant monitoring of performance. Financing of rural development, priority and weaker sectors by banks require modified organisational structure, pragmatic operational policies, sophisticated control mechanism and skilled personnel to strengthen the system to meet the objective of such financing. Effective coordination between branches and an effective Management Information System are other important requirements.

3. Institutional Overlapping

Some of the problems like unhealthy competition, double financing, uncertainty of operational areas have cropped up because of institutional overlapping of different financial agencies in rural areas. Even in small and big cities there is keen competition between banks and many branches are incurring huge losses. There is an urgent need to demarcate and define the areas and activities of commercial banks, cooperative banks, and regional rural banks.

4. Poor and Declining Customer Service

An important side effect of the growth of banking in India has been a sharp decline in the customer service. The service to the customer is becoming more and more impersonal, indifferent and inefficient. The extent of corruption among bank employees is also on the increase.

5. Declining Profitability

It is correct that objective of banking in the present context is not merely to earn profit but also to achieve larger socio-economic goals. But social banking and profit making need not necessarily be contradictory. As a matter of fact, the ability of the banking system to fulfil social objectives depends, to a great extent, on their commercial viability. Banks should always have a positive approach to profitability planning both at the macro and micro-levels. An unfortunate trend of declining profitability in Indian banks is noticeable in recent years.

According to the "Reserve Bank of India's Report on Trend and Progress of Banking in India — 1984-85", the rate of growth of aggregate profits of the 78 scheduled commercial banks (after providing for taxation, bonus and ex-gratia payment to staff) fell to 8.3 per cent in 1983, from 23.4 per cent in 1982 and 24.5 per cent in 1981. The rate of growth of 20 nationalised banks was a measly 2.6 per cent against 26.3 per cent and 11.4 per cent in 1982 and 1981 respectively. The eight units of the State Bank group too fared badly, but their rate of growth of profits did not fall below 15.1 per cent against 24.5 and 24 per cent in 1982 and 1981 respectively.

6. Recovery of Advances

One of the most important problems faced by banks in India in recent years is the problem of recovery of loans. The rate of recovery in some areas of the country and some types of loans have ranged between 40 and 50 per cent, which is not a good sign of banking development. Naturally, this curtails the recycling of funds and affects the profitability of banks. It does not mean that banks should become indifferent to the needs of priority sectors or weaker sections of society, but any laxity in recovery would be self-defeating. It is necessary to take a fresh look at the existing legal provisions and introduce penal action against wilful defaulters. Some suggestions, like recovery of term loans under the Public Demands Recovery Act, appointment of special officers exclusively to look after the recovery and the extension of the period of limitation from 3 to 6 years, were made by the Indian Banks Association to the Reserve Bank to reduce increase percentage of recovery.

Increasing industrial sickness of bank financed units and disturbing trends in recovery of term sector loans threaten to further set up the already eroded profitability of banks in the country. According to the Annual Report of the Reserve Bank of India, 1985, while agricultural loans have gone up, the recovery rate has decreased from 53.2 per cent to 51.3 per cent despite two successive good agricultural years. An amount of ₹ 3,217.50 crore of bank funds is locked-in sick industrial units. Expert studies show that 4,85,733 of the bank financed small-scale industrial units have little chance of escape from doom. The Reserve Bank of India has advised banks, who provide "loan tonic" to the economy, to adopt a three-pronged strategy to regain financial health:

(i) Efficient recycling of resources;

(ii) Improvement of productivity; and

(iii) Streamlining of overseas branch operations.

☞ RBI Parameters to Banks Regarding Aid to Sick Units

The Reserve Bank of India has suggested to all scheduled commercial banks the following parameters within which they must operate while providing assistance for rehabilitation of sick units that are considered viable.

(i) Interest on term loans may be reduced where necessary, but not more than 2 per cent below the prevailing rate charged by banks and term lending institutions.

(ii) Funded interest should not be free of interest. Interest may be charged on funded interest at the rate of 10 per cent subject to annual review. Wherever a lower rate of interest is felt necessary in exceptional cases, it should be referred to Reserve Bank of India for prior approval.

(iii) Past cash losses should be funded separately into a working capital term loan and should be borne by the banks themselves. The cash inputs required for meeting a part of overdue

statutory liabilities, workers' due and pressing creditors forming part of the rehabilitation package may be shared by participating banks and institutions on 50:50 basis.

Further cash losses, i.e., losses from the time of implementation of the package till the point of break even, should be borne by financial institutions, which will also provide the margin money for working capital. In cases where no term lending institutions are involved, cash inputs as also cash loans should be borne by the Industrial Reconstruction Bank of India.

(iv) Working capital requirement must be worked out as per inventory norms and receivables and should not exceed the permissible bank finance. Interest on working capital be charged at the commercial rate, i.e., between 16.5 per cent and 17.5 per cent at present. Banks ought to consider charging a lower rate wherever concessions are available from the State Government.

(v) The cost of rationalisation of labour should be shared between banks and term lending financial institutions.

(vi) The rehabilitation programme should have an outer limit of seven years. In certain cases, where a limit is considered viable, the period of repayment of restructured debts may extend up to a maximum period of 10 years.

(vii) The promoter's contribution should comprise fresh injection of funds. In cases involving the change of management and professional management, the promoters should be required to bring in 15 per cent of the additional long-term requirements envisaged. In other cases, it should be 20 per cent. At least 10 per cent should be brought immediately and the balance 10 or 5 per cent, as the case may be, within six months. Such funds should be on non-interest bearing basis.

(viii) When a sick unit turns corner and the rehabilitation is successfully completed, the sacrifices made by financial institutions and banks could be recouped from the units out of their further profits and cash accruals. Alternately, there may be provisions for equity participations.

To overcome the present drawbacks in the Indian banking system, like — strained organisational structure, bad customer service, slow and inefficient recovery programmes, overlapping of financial institutions and absence of long-term planning — there is a need of structural reorganisation at the micro-level of an individual bank and at macro-level of the entire banking system, including all the financial institutions.

ECONOMIC LIBERALISATION POLICY AND ITS IMPACT

The Union budget of 1991-92 which was presented on 24th July, 1991 is an important landmark in the economic history of India because it signalled important changes in the economic policies of the Government which are now popularly known as "Policy of Economic Liberalisation". The main features of the policy reforms made in 1991 are given below:

☞ Trade Policy Reforms

New initiatives were taken in trade policy to create an environment which would provide a stimulus to export while at the same time reducing the degree of regulation and licensing control on foreign trade. The exchange rate adjustment of 18 per cent in the value of the rupee was designed to provide a substantial stimulus to exports. This change was accompanied by several other changes in trade policy. Important trade policy reforms introduced in 1991-92 were as follows:

(i) A large part of administered licensing of imports was replaced by import entitlements linked to export earnings. These import entitlements, renamed EXIMSCRIPS are freely tradeable

and attract a premium in the market. For most exports a uniform rate of 30 per cent of Eximscrips was made applicable, though some exports were entitled to higher rates.

(ii) Eximscrips could be used to import any item in the limited permissible limit, the non-sensitive canalized list, all OGL (Open General Licence) items for actual users and Non-OGL capital goods which were not in the restricted list.

(iii) The Advance Licensing System for export, was simplified so as to improve exporters' access to imported inputs at duty free rates.

(iv) Permission to import capital goods was given without clearance from the indigenous availability angle provided this import was fully covered by foreign equity or was up to 25 per cent of the value of plant and machinery subject to a maximum of ₹ 2 crore.

(v) Export and Trading House and State Trading Houses were permitted a larger range of imports. 51 per cent foreign equity is also now allowed in Trading Houses.

(vi) The scope of canalization for both exports and imports was narrowed.

(vii) Actual user requirements for the import of capital goods, raw materials and components under OGL was removed, and

(viii) Established exporters were permitted to maintain foreign currency accounts and to raise external credits to finance their trade transactions.

The object of these reforms was to:

— Reduce the degree of licensing in import trade.

— Broaden, enhance and harmonize export incentives.

— Introduce a self-balancing mechanism where imports would be automatically regulated by the availability of Eximscrips through export earnings.

☞ Industrial Policy Reforms

In order to consolidate the gains already achieved during the 1980s and to provide greater competitive stimulus to the domestic industry, a series of reforms were introduced in Industrial Policy. *The New Industrial Policy* of 24th July, 1991 sought substantially to deregulate industry so as to promote the growth of a more efficient and competitive industrial economy. Industrial Policy reforms announced in July 1991, should be seen as being complementary to those undertaken in trade and fiscal policies and in the management of the exchange rate and the financial sector. The central elements of these reforms were as follows:

(i) Industrial licensing was abolished for all projects except in 18 industries where strategic or environmental concerns are paramount or where industries produce goods with exceptionally high import content. With this 80 per cent of industry has been taken out of the licensing framework.

(ii) The MRTP Act was amended to eliminate the need for prior approval by large companies for capacity expansion or diversification. This will enable Indian firms to become large enough to compete effectively in global markets.

(iii) The requirement of phased manufacturing programmes was discontinued for all new projects.

(iv) Areas reserved for public sector were narrowed down, and greater participation by private sector was permitted in core and basic industries. In the place of 17 areas earlier reserved

for investment by the public sector, only 8 such areas are now reserved. These eight are mainly those involving strategic and security concerns.

(v) Government clearance for the location of projects was dispensed with except in the case of 23 cities with a population of more than one million.

(vi) Small-scale enterprises were given the option to offer up to 24 per cent of their shareholding to large-scale and other industrial undertakings. This will provide them with greater access to capital and technology.

(vii) Loan agreements of the financial institutions with privately managed firms were earlier required to provide for the right of the financial institutions to convert the loans into equity. In August 1991, the institutions were permitted not to insist on this provision in future loans unless they felt it necessary for commercial reasons. In December, 1991, the institutions were permitted to delete the provision from past loans also subject to a revision of the interest rate where appropriate.

(viii) A National Renewal Fund has been set up with a corpus of ₹ 200 crore to ensure that the costs of technological change and modernization of industry would not be borne by workers. It will be used to provide a safety net to workers in sick and non-viable enterprises, and to finance their retraining and redeployment.

☞ Foreign Technology and Investment

A long with a reform of industrial policies, steps were also taken to facilitate the inflow of direct foreign investment. These non-debt creating inflows will reduce reliance on fixed-interest debt and also bring in new technology, marketing expertise and modern managerial practices. The following measures were taken in this context:

(i) The limit of foreign equity holdings was raised from 40 to 51 per cent in a wide range of priority industries. However, foreign exchange outflow on account of dividends on additional equity will be balanced on export earnings. Such foreign equity participation now has automatic approval and is cleared by Reserve Bank of India.

(ii) The procedures for investment in non-priority industries have been streamlined. The Foreign Investment Promotion Board has been established to negotiate with large international firms and to expedite the clearances required. The FIPB also considers individual cases involving foreign equity participation over 51 per cent.

(iii) Technology imports for priority industries are automatically approved for royalty payments up to 5 per cent of domestic sales and 8 per cent of export sales or for lump sum payments of ₹ 1 crore.

Deregulation will reduce the role of Govt. regulatory agencies. They will be reorganised and their staff redeployed. For the economy as a whole, delays in project implementation will be greatly reduced. Increased competition will lead to enhanced pressure on enterprises to reduce their costs and to improve quality.

☞ Public Sector Reforms

The public sector was originally conceived as holding the commanding heights of the economy and leading technological advance. It was also intended to generate investible surpluses and become an engine for self-reliant growth. The public sector has contributed significantly to the diversification of India's industrial structure. But its contribution in terms of generating internal resources for further expansion has fallen short of expectations, and its inability to do so has now become a major constraint on economic growth.

It is imperative that the public sector attains the objective originally set for it. This will require a sustained improvement in productivity and profitability. The budgetary support to public sector enterprises will need to be scaled down and they will be expected to maintain financial discipline in their operation. The sector should be exposed to competitive pressures wherever possible. Some of the enterprises can be restructured so as to improve their capital base and access to the market.

To enable the public sector to work efficiently, the public sector units have to be given the greatest autonomy in their operations. A system of full responsibility and complete accountability will have to be enforced on public sector managements. In 1991-92 the Government undertook a limited disinvestment of a part of public sector equity to the public through public financial institutions and mutual funds in order to raise non-inflationary finance for development. The disinvestment will also bring in greater public accountability and help to create a new culture in their working which would improve efficiency. The objective of public sector policy is to improve the operational efficiency of these units and return them to their original goods. Recognizing that sickness is a serious problem in many public sector units, the Government amended the 'Sick Industrial Companies Act' to bring public sector undertakings also within their purview. This makes sick public sector units subject to the same discipline as private sector units including reference to the BIFR for identification of a viable restructuring package or closure as the case may be.

☞ Balance of Payments Financing

The measures of fiscal correction and structural reform described above were expected to bring about an improvement in the balance of payments in the medium-term. However, for the immediate future substantial financing of balance of payments was unavoidable if import compression was to be relaxed. Accordingly, the Govt. attempted to mobilise support for the balance of payments from multilateral financial institutions, the International Monetary Fund, the World Bank and the Asian Development Bank — as well as from bilateral donors.

As pressure on the reserves mounted, the Government availed itself of the facilities available from International Monetary Fund.

- In July-Sept. 1990, it withdrew the Reserve Tranche (RT) of SDR 490 million.
- In Dec. 1990, it applied for the First Credit Tranche (FCT) of SDR 552 million.
- Govt. negotiated drawals under the Contingency Compensatory Finance Facility (CCFF) which totalled SDR 1.352 billion between Jan.-Sept. 91.
- Drawals of SDR 270 million and SDR 461 million upper credit trenche standby arrangement.
- In 1992 a Structural Adjustment Loan of $ 500 million was negotiated with the World Bank of which $ 300 million has been drawn.
- Additional fast disbursing assistance was tied up with the Asian Development Bank and with some of the bilateral donors.

Another important initiative taken by the Government to meet the urgent need for balance of payments financing was the announcement of two schemes designed to encourage the inflow of capital funds from abroad.

1. India Development Bond Scheme, and
2. Immunity Scheme.

The schemes were introduced in October 1991, for repatriation of funds held abroad. The schemes have proved to be highly successful. India Development Bonds mobilised $ 1.605 billion, and Immunity Scheme $ 793 million.

The New Economic Policy comprises various policy measures and changes introduced since July 1991. The objective is simple and that is to improve the efficiency of the system. The regulatory mechanism involving multitudes of control has fragmented capacity and reduced competition even in the private sectors. The thrust of New Economical Policy is towards creating a more competitive environment in the economy as a means to improving the productivity and efficiency of the system. This is to be achieved by removing the barriers to entry and the restrictions on the growth of firms. While the Industrial Policy seeks to bring about a greater competitive environment domestically, the trade policy seeks to improve international competitiveness subject to the protection offered by tariffs. Private sector is being given a larger space to operate in as some of the areas reserved exclusively for the public sector are also now allowed to private sector. In these areas the public sector will have to compete with private sector even though the public sector may continue to play the dominant role. What is sought to be achieved is an improvement in the functioning of the various entities whether they be in the private or public sector by injecting an element of competition.

The policy changes fall broadly into two categories:

(1) Stabilisation Policy

Stabilisation policies are intended to correct the lapses and put the house in order in the short-term.

(2) Structural Reform Policies

Structural reform policies are intended to accelerate economic growth over the medium-term. Structural reforms are broadly in the area of industrial licensing and regulations, foreign trade and investment and financial sector.

FINANCIAL LIBERALISATION

Narasimham Committee Report, 1991, on the financial system has recommended many important changes in our banking system. Some of the committees' recommendations have already been implemented and other recommendations, more crucial and important, will also be implemented sooner or later. Financial liberalisation is concerned with two important tasks which are necessary and interconnected.

1. Rehabilitation of Weak Banks

The first task is the rehabilitation of weak banks, essentially the nationalised banks and the regional rural banks. Nationalised banks have a creditable record in branch expansion, encouragement of saving and service to the weak and the neglected sectors, also suffer from a lot of internal and external problems like politicisation, direct investment on concessional terms, administered rates of interest and constant Government or political interference in management. There is overstaffing and undermechanisation. The quality of staff and service at all levels has deteriorated. The payments, settlements and clearance system is in shambles. Professional and institutional pride which did exist before nationalisation and which is so essential to competition and efficiency is not there. The different nationalised banks are different today only in name; and if they differ in the degree of their weaknesses, they all are still on the same downward incline.

The task of rehabilitation of banks is difficult and complex and has both short-term and long-term aspects. It is easy to suggest how to clean up a sick bank; but it is very difficult even to actually do the first cleansing especially when the owner is a public sector unit.

2. Effective and Free Competition

The second aspect of financial liberalisation relates to creating conditions of effective and free competition. Such competition is conducive to the financial institutions performing the essential function of promoting savings and directing them to the most productive investments and thus accelerating economic growth. This contribution presupposes that conditions of free and effective competition prevail simultaneously in real markets, *i.e.,* in the markets for goods and labour; and this contribution will be more if in addition, financial and real markets internally are linked freely with international markets.

Financial institutions promote savings and productive investment in many ways: by creating confidence among savers and investors by their own soundness — which is the main justification for rehabilitation of weak institutions; by keeping the cost of intermediation, *i.e.,* the difference between what the saver receives and the investor pays to a minimum; by providing different types of instruments that combine various degrees of yield, liquidity and risk to suit different needs, by providing marketability so that savers and investors can shift from one investment to another according to their need or perception of yield, liquidity and risk changes; by providing quick and transparent settlement of claims and in the case of banks, by serving as a provider of money or means of payment or settlement; by the intimate knowledge of investment opportunities and the financial and managerial capacity of individual firms and hence by managing risk as rationally as possible; and also by discovering and nurturing true entrepreneurial talent. Like products and other services, credit also has to be effectively marketed and, indeed, a good market created for it if financial institutions are to serve and grow.

Financial liberalisation can contribute to growth only to the extent that it enables financial institutions to perform each of the above-mentioned tasks better. There should be free competition for both buyers and sellers. The supply side of financial services should include not only freedom of entry and exit or expansion and contraction but of diversification of products and services as well. This means breaking down the traditional functional barriers between banks, merchant banks, mutual funds, investment houses, security firms and even insurance and mortgage business and the freedom to innovate. The question of freedom of buyers of financial services is equally important. There are questions of removal of exchange control over capital transaction; removal of administered interest rates and directed credit and other aspects of macroeconomic management such as fiscal deficits which have a bearing on financial liberalisation and *vice versa*. Whether in reforms or in day-to-day execution, fiscal, monetary and exchange rate policies and also policies of rehabilitation, regulation and deregulation are a part of the total programme of liberalisation, reform and development.

☞ Top Banks in India

With the advancement of technology and the birth of competition, banks are in the race of becoming the best in the country. With an eye upon customer satisfaction policy, they are providing best of the best services with the minimum hazards.

Banks like ABN-AMRO introduced banking with a coffee. It made a tie-up with one of the best coffee bar in the country. Barista and remained open till late evening for customers with a set up of a coffee bar in the premises.

Few banks have introduced world ATM card to make travellers across the globe more safe and secure. What else, Internet and Phone Banking is the call of the day for banks.

This is a race towards the best.

☞ Indian Banks Association

The Indian Banks Association (IBA) was formed on the 26th September, 1946 with 22 members. Today, IBA has more than 156 members comprising of Public Sector Banks. Private Sector Banks, Foreign banks having offices in India. Urban Cooperative Banks Developmental Financial Institutions. Federations, merchant banks, mutual funds, housing finance corporations, etc.

☞ The Functioning of IBA

- ➢ To promote sound and progressive banking principles and practices.
- ➢ To render assistance and to provide common services to members.
- ➢ To organise coordination and cooperation on procedural, legal, technical, administrative and professional matters,
- ➢ To collect, classify and circulate statistical and other information.
- ➢ To pool together expertise towards common purposes such as reduction in costs, increase in efficiency, productivity and improve systems, procedures and banking practices.
- ➢ To project good public image of banking through publicity and public relations.
- ➢ To encourage sports and cultural activities among bank employees.

The Offices of IBA

Stadium House,

Block II and III, 6th Floor, Veer Nariman Road, Mumbai-400 020

Tel: 91-22--22894500, Fax: 91-22-22835638

World Trade Centre Complex, Centre I, Units 1, 2 and 4

6th Floor, Cuffe Parade, Mumbai-400 005.

Tel: 91-22-22174040, Telex: 011 85146, Fax: 91-22-22184222.

☞ The Organisational Structure of IBA

The Managing Committee manages the affairs, business and funds of IBA. The managing committee is elected by the Ordinary members of the Association, and is the highest management and policy-making body of the Association.

The Chairman of the Association heads upon the working of the Association. He provides guidelines to the Association. The administrative head of IBA is the Chief Executive of IBA. He is also the Secretary to the Managing Committee. He leads a team of executives, officers and other staff members.

☞ The Contract Details of IBA

At World Trade Centre Complex	Direct Nos.
Legal	91-22-22187946 91-22-22174006
Banking Policy	91-22-22182217 91-22-22174014
Payment Systems	91-22-22182196 91-22-22174013
Banking Operations	91-22-22182247 91-22-22174012
Publicity	91-22-22180821 91-22-22174015
Technology	91-22-22182196 91-22-22174011
Library	91-22-22182288 91-22-22174009
At Stadium House:	
Personnel (HR and IR)	91-22-22028525 91-22-22894502 91-22-22831636 91-22-22894501
Administration and Accounts:	91-22-22824846 91-22-22894518

IBA constitutes standing committees/task forces/small groups/committee of experts from member banks for the examining of various aspects relating to industry level issues to get solutions.

Recommendations of these groups/committees, are communicated to members with the approval of the managing committee or taken up with the concerned authorities for action.

☞ Proxy Banking in India

Indian villages were miles away from mutual funds, insurance and even equity trading. Thanks to Internet Kiosk and the ATM duo which has made it possible for rural India. This Kiosk has been set up by ICICI Bank in partnership with network n-Logue Communications in remote villages of Southern part of the country. This is known as Proxy Banking. With the help of fibre optic cables, this Kiosk works on wireless in local loop technology.

☞ Reasons for Settingup of Proxy Banking

- 58% of rural households still do not have bank accounts.
- Only 21% of rural households have access to credit from a formal source.
- 70% of marginal farmers do not have deposit account.
- 87% households have no formal credit.

- Only 1% rural households rely on a loan from a financial intermediary. The loans take between 24 to 33 weeks to get sanctioned.
- Consumers bribe officials to get loans approved which varies between 10 and 20 per cent of the loan amount.
- Branch banking in rurals is a loss-making.

☞ Benefits to Rurals

- Small loans given for buying buffaloes.
- Loans for setting up a tea shop.
- Life and non-life insurance provided.
- Whether insurance given to farmers.
- Insurance policies sold to farmers like groundnut, castor, soya, paddy crop. etc.

The Proxy Banking is an innovative approach to rural lending and will add to the government's expanding base of kisan credit cards and the good old guidelines for agricultural lending.

☞ Fact Files of Banks in India

The first, the oldest, the largest, the biggest, get all such types of informations about Banking in India in this section.

The first bank in India to be given an ISO Certification	Canara Bank
The first bank in Northern India to get ISO 9002 certification for their selected branches	Punjab and Sind Bank
The first Indian bank to have been started solely with Indian capital	Punjab National Bank
The first among the private sector banks in Kerala to become a scheduled bank in 1946 under the RBI Act	South Indian Bank
India's oldest, largest and most successful commercial bank, offering the widest possible range of domestic, international and NRI products and services, through its vast network in India and overseas	State Bank of India
India's second largest private sector bank and is now the largest scheduled commercial bank of India	The Federal Bank Limited
Bank which stated as private shareholders banks mostly European shareholders	Imperial Bank of India
The first Indian bank to open a branch outside India in London in 1946 and the first to open a branch in continental Europe at Paris in 1974	Bank of India, founded in 1906 in Mumbai
The oldest public sector bank in India having branches all over India and serving the customers for the last 132 years	Allahabad Bank
The first Indian commercial bank which was wholly-owned and managed by Indians	

Bank of India was founded in 1906 in Mumbai. It became the first Indian bank to open a branch outside India in London in 1946 and the first to open a branch in continental Europe at Paris in 1974.

☞ The Changing Scenario of Indian Banking: Vision for the Next Decade

The banking scenario in India is rapidly changing and in order to succeed amidst the rapid changes and arrive, one would need a vision. A *"Vision is a mental articulation about the future state of things.* It provides direction to an organization or a country. India is gradually integrating with the world economy and the world is becoming more and more interdependent. Gradually, globalisation of financial markets is taking place. The increasing international flows, mainly initiated by large mutual funds, pension funds and in recent times, hedge funds, have been matched by the growing penetration of domestic markets by foreign financial institutions. The host of financial instruments now available allow both borrowers and lenders to obtain precisely the combination of return, risk and liquidity they desire with single firms operating worldwide and in different time zones, highly independent markets in financial instruments operate 24 hours a day.

As currency traders move their immense resources electronically, instantenously from country-to-country, governments and central banks watch helplessly. In the cybertech globalised world, money has become free of its place and it has become a product which is bought and sold. The net effect is that world financial system has become vulnerable to technological break down and risks of speculation.

The trends envisaged during the next decade may be summarised as follows:

— Technology will be the prime driver of change. These include telematrics (Computers, communications and electronics).

— Global interdependence to increase.

— Spectacular growth of online banking.

— Digital signatures will be accepted in most countries.

— Huge growth of wireless banking and payment services using next generation mobile phones.

— Emergence of a world currency (already Visa and Master Card allow people to buy around the world without conversion of local currency).

— Internationally recognised "Smart Cards" to bring the world closer to global currency.

The above trends are likely to result through more use of technology. If we look at the trends in the Indian banking sector, the nationalisation era from 1969 to 1989 could be seen as a period of rapid expansion with little emphasis on operational efficiency. But the 1990s saw consolidation of gains and efforts at rationalisation of branches as well as human resources. Banks went slow on fresh recruitments and eventually in November 2000, the banks implemented the voluntary retirement scheme. At present banks are giving more importance to technology development to provide better services to customers and also to bring down the cost of transactions.

➢ ABN-AMRO Bank	➢ Dena Bank	➢ South Indian Bank
➢ Abu Dhabi Commercial Bank	➢ Deutsche Bank	➢ Standard Chartered Bank
➢ American Express Bank	➢ Development Credit Bank	➢ State Bank of India (SBI)
➢ Andhra Bank	➢ Dhanalakshmi Bank	➢ State Bank of Bikaner and Jaipur
➢ Allahabad Bank	➢ Federal Bank	➢ State Bank of Hyderabad
➢ Bank of Baroda	➢ HDFC Bank	➢ State Bank of Indore
➢ Bank of India	➢ HSBC ICICI Bank	➢ State Bank of Mysore
➢ Bank of Maharashtra	➢ IDBI Bank	➢ State Bank of Saurashtra
➢ Bank of Punjab	➢ Indian Bank	➢ State Bank of Travancore
➢ Bank of Rajasthan	➢ Indian Overseas Bank	➢ Syndicate Bank
➢ Bank of Ceylon	➢ IndusInd Bank	➢ Taib Bank
➢ BNP Paribas Bank	➢ ING Vysya Bank	➢ UCO Bank
➢ Canara Bank	➢ Jammu and Kashmir Bank	➢ Union Bank of India
➢ Catholic Syrian Bank	➢ J.P. Morgan Chase Bank	➢ United Bank of India
➢ Central Bank of India	➢ Karnataka Bank	➢ United Western Bank
➢ Centurion Bank	➢ Karur Vysya Bank	➢ UTI Bank
➢ China Trust Commercial Bank	➢ Laxmi Vilas Bank	➢ Vijaya Bank
➢ Citi Bank	➢ Oriental Bank of Commerce	
➢ City Union Bank	➢ Punjab National Bank	
➢ Corporation Bank	➢ Punjab and Sind Bank	
	➢ Scotia Bank	

☞ The Upcoming Foreign Banks in India

The RBI has shown certain interest to involve more of foreign banks than the existing one recently. This step has paved a way for few more foreign banks to start business in India.

MAJOR BANKS IN INDIA

☞ Banking Services in India

With years, banks are also adding services to their customers. The Indian banking industry is passing through a phase of customers market. The customers have move choices in choosing their banks. A competition has been established within the banks operating in India.

With stiff competition and advancement of technology, the services provided by banks has become more easy and convenient. The past days are witness to an hour wait before withdrawing cash from accounts or a cheque from north of the country being cleared in one month in the south.

This section of banking deals with the latest discovery in the banking instruments along with the polished version of their old systems.

☞ Financial and Banking Sector Reforms

This last decade witnessed the maturity of India's financial markets. Since 1991, Governments of India took major steps in reforming the financial sector of the country. The important achievements in the following fields is discussed under separate heads:

- Financial markets
- Regulators
- The banking system
- Non-banking finance companies
- The capital market
- Mutual funds
- Overall approach to reforms
- Deregulation of banking system
- Capital market developments
- Consolidation imperative

Now let us discuss each segment separately.

☞ Financial Markets

In the last decade, Private Sector Institutions played an important role. They grew rapidly in commercial banking and asset management business. With the openings in the insurance sector for these institutions, they started making debt in the market.

Competition among financial intermediaries gradually helped the interest rates to decline. Deregulation added to it. The real interest rate was maintained. The borrowers did not pay high price while depositors had incentives to save. It was something between the nominal rate of interest and the expected rate of inflation.

☞ Regulators

The Finance Ministry continuously formulated major policies in the field of financial sector of the country. The Government accepted the important role of regulators. The Reserve Bank of India (RBI) has become more independent. Securities and Exchange Board of India (SEBI) and the Insurance Regulatory and Development Authority (IRDA) became important institutions. Opinions are also there that there should be a super-regulator for the financial services sector instead of multiplicity of regulators.

☞ The Banking System

Almost 80% of the business are still controlled by Public Sector Banks (PSBs). PSBs are still dominating the commercial banking system. Shares of the leading PSBs are already listed on the stock exchanges.

The RBI has given licences to new private sector banks as part of the liberalisation process. The RBI has also been granting licences to industrial houses. Many banks are successfully running in the retail and consumer segments but are yet to deliver services to industrial finance, retail trade, small business and agricultural finance.

The PSBs will play an important role in the industry due to its number of branches and foreign banks facing the constraint of limited number of branches. Hence, in order to achieve an efficient banking system, the onus is on the Government to encourage the PSBs to be run on professional lines.

☞ Development Finance Institutions

FIs' access to SLR funds reduced. Now they have to approach the capital market for debt and equity funds.

Convertibility clause no longer obligatory for assistance to corporates sanctioned by term-lending institutions.

Capital adequacy norms extended in financial institutions. DFIs such as IDBI and ICICI have entered other segments of financial services such as commercial banking, asset management and insurance through separate ventures. The move to universal banking has started.

☞ Non-banking Finance Companies

In the case of new NBFCs seeking registration with the RBI, the requirement of minimum net owned funds, has been raised to ₹ 2 crore.

Until recently, the money market in India was narrow and circumscribed by tight regulations over interest rates and participants. The secondary market was underdeveloped and lacked liquidity. Several measures have been initiated and include new money market instruments, strengthening of existing instruments and setting up of the Discount and Finance House of India (DFHI).

The RBI conducts its sales of dated securities and Treasury Bills through its open market operations (OMO) window. Primary dealers bid for these securities and also trade in them. The DFHI is the principal agency for developing a secondary market for money market instruments and Government of India Treasury Bills. The RBI has introduced a liquidity adjustment facility (LAF) in which liquidity is injected through reverse repo auctions and liquidity is sucked out through repo auctions.

On account of the substantial issue of government debt, the gilt-edged market occupies an important position in the financial set-up. The Securities Trading Corporation of India (STCI), which started operations in June 1994, has a mandate to develop the secondary market in Government securities.

Long-term debt market. The development of a long-term debt market is crucial to the financing of infrastructure. After bringing some order to the equity market, the SEBI has now decided to concentrate on the development of the debt market. Stamp duty is being withdrawn at the time of dematerialisation of debt instruments in order to encourage paperless trading.

☞ The Capital Market

The number of shareholders in India is estimated at 25 million. However, only an estimated two lakh persons actively trade in stocks. There has been a dramatic improvement in the country's stock market trading infrastructure during the last few years. Expectations are that India will be an attractive emerging market with tremendous potential. Unfortunately, during recent times the stock markets have been constrained by some unsavoury developments which has led to retail investors deserting the stock markets.

☞ Mutual Funds

The mutual funds industry is now regulated under SEBI (Mutual Funds) Regulations, 1996 and amendments thereto. With the issuance of SEBI guidelines, the industry had a framework for the establishment of many more players, both Indian and foreign players.

The Unit Trust of India remains easily the biggest mutual funds controlling a corpus of nearly ₹ 70,000 crore but its share is going down. The biggest shock to the mutual fund industry during recent times was the insecurity generated in the minds of investors regarding the US 64 Scheme. With the growth in the securities markets and tax advantages granted for investment in mutual fund units, mutual funds started becoming popular.

The foreign owned AMCs are the ones which are now setting the pace for the industry. They are introducing new products, setting new standards of customer service, improving disclosure standards and experimenting with new types of distribution.

The insurance industry is the latest to be thrown open to competition from the private sector including foreign players. Foreign companies can only enter joint ventures with Indian companies, with participation restricted to 26 per cent of equity. It is too early to conclude whether the erstwhile public sector monopolies will successfully be able to face up to the competition posed by the new players, but it can be expected that the customer will gain from improved service.

The new players will need to bring in innovative products as well as fresh ideas on marketing and distribution, in order to improve the low per capita insurance coverage. Good regulation will, of course, be essential.

☞ Overall Approach to Reforms

The last ten years have seen major improvements in the working of various financial market participants. The government and the regulatory authorities have followed a step-by-step approach, not a big bang one. The entry of foreign players has assisted in the introduction of international practices and systems. Technology developments have improved customer service. Some gaps, however, remain (for example: lack of an inter-bank interest rate benchmark, an active corporate debt market and a development derivatives market). On which, the cumulative effect on the developments since 1991 has been quite encouraging. An indication of the strength of the reformed Indian financial system can be seen from the way India was not affected by the Southeast Asian crisis.

However, financial liberalisation alone will not ensure stable economic growth. Some tough decisions still need to be taken. Without fiscal control, financial stability cannot be ensured. The fate of the Fiscal Responsibility Bill remains unknown and high fiscal deficits continue. In the case of financial institutions, the political and legal structures have to ensure that borrower repay on time the loans they have taken. The phenomenon of rich industrialists and bankrupt companies continue. Further, frauds cannot be totally prevented even with the best of regulation. However, punishment has to follow crime, which is often not the case in India.

☞ Deregulation of Banking System

Prudential norms were introduced for income recognition, asset classification, provisioning for delinquent loans and for capital adequacy. In order to reach the stipulated capital adequacy norms, substantial capital were provided by the Government of PSBs.

Government pre-emption of banks' resources through statutory liquidity ratio (SLR) and cash reserve ratio (CRR) brought down in steps. Interest rates on the deposits and lending sides almost entirely were deregulated.

New private sector banks allowed to promote and encourage competition. PSBs were encouraged to approach the public for raising resources. Recovery of debts due to banks and the Financial Institutions Act, 1993 was passed and special recovery tribunals set up to facilitate quicker recovery of loan arrears.

Bank lending norms liberalised and a loan system to ensure better control over credit introduced. Banks asked to set up asset liability management (ALM) systems. RBI guidelines issued by risk management systems in banks encompassing credit, market and operational risks.

A credit information bureau being established to identify bad risks. Derivative products such as forward rate agreements (FRAs) and interest rate swaps (IRSs) introduced.

☞ Capital Market Developments

A Capital Issue (Control) Act, 1947, repealed, office of the Controller of Capital Issues were abolished and the initial share pricing were decontrolled. SEBI, the capital market regulator was established in 1992.

Foreign institutional investors (FIIs) were allowed to invest in Indian capital markets after registration with the SEBI. Indian companies were permitted to access international capital markets through euro issues.

The National Stock Exchange (NSE), with nationwide stock trading and electronic display, clearing and settlement facilities was established. Several local stock exchanges changed over from floor-based trading to screen-based trading.

☞ Private Mutual Funds Permitted

The Depositories Act had given a legal framework for the establishment of depositories to record ownership deals in book entry form. Dematerialisation of stocks encouraged paperless trading. Companies were required to disclose all material facts and specific risk factors associated with their projects while making public issues.

To reduce the cost of issue, underwriting by the issuer were made optional subject to conditions. The practice of making preferential allotment of shares at prices unrelated to the prevailing market prices stopped and fresh guidelines were issued by SEBI.

SEBI reconstituted governing boards of the stock exchanges, introduced capital adequacy norms for brokers, and made rules for making client or broker relationship more transparent which included separation of client and broker accounts.

☞ Buyback of Shares Allowed

The SEBI started insisting on greater corporate disclosures. Steps were taken to improve corporate governance based on the report of a committee. SEBI issued detailed employee stock option scheme and employee stock purchases scheme for listed companies.

Standard denomination for equity shares of ₹ 10 and ₹ 100 were abolished. Companies given the freedom to issue dematerialised shares in any denomination.

Derivatives trading starts with index options and futures. A system of rolling settlements introduced. SEBI empowered to register and regulate venture capital funds.

The SEBI (Credit Rating Agencies) Regulations, 1999 issued for regulating new credit rating agencies as well as introducing a code of conduct for all credit rating agencies operating in India.

☞ Consolidation Imperative

Another aspect of the financial sector reforms in India is the consolidation of existing institutions which is especially applicable to the commercial banks. In India the banks are in huge quantity. First, there is no need for 27 PSBs with branches all over India. A number of them can be managed. The merger of Punjab National Bank and New Bank of India was a difficult one, but the situation is different now. No one expected so many employees to take voluntary retirement from PSBs, which at one time were much sought after jobs. Private sector banks will be self-consolidated, while cooperative and rural banks will be encouraged for consolidation, and anyway play only a niche role.

In the case of insurance, the Life Insurance Corporation of India is a behemoth, while the four public sector general insurance companies will probably move towards consolidation with a bit of nudging. The UTI is yet again a big institution, even though facing difficult times, and most other public sector players are already existing the mutual fund business. There are a number of small mutual fund players in the private sector, but the business being comparatively new for the private players, it will take sometime.

We finally come to convergence in the financial sector, the new buzzword internationally. Hi-tech and the need to meet increasing consumer needs is encouraging convergence, even though it has not always been a success till date. In India organisations such as IDBI, ICICI, HDFC and SEBI are already trying to offer various services to the customers under one umbrella. This phenomenon is expected to grow rapidly in the coming years. Where mergers may not be possible, alliances between organisations may be effective. Various forms of bancassurance are being introduced, with the RBI having already to come out with detailed guidelines for entry of banks into insurance. The LIC has bought into Corporation Bank in order to spread its insurance distribution network. Both banks and insurance companies have started entering the asset management business, as there is a great deal of synergy among these businesses. The pensions market is expected to open up fresh opportunities for insurance companies and mutual funds.

It is not possible to play the role of the Oracle of Delphi when a vast nation like India is involved. However, a few trends are evident, and the coming decade should be as interesting as the last one.

☞ Easy Banking

This section is fully dedicated to the Tech Banking. A decade before, it was tough to believe that banking sector will be at a finger tip. Now its possible. A mobile handset with a connection is the only instrument needed to make a gateway to your banking transaction, the latest innovation of technology.

Apart from the Mobile Banking, including of SMS Banking, Net Banking and ATMs are the major steps taken by the banks in India towards modernisation. With all these devises and systems, there is a complete freedom to experience.

Check your account, transfer your fund, make payments and what more, do anything of everything what has been followed in physical banking since ages. But this time no standing for hours in front of cash counter and no time boundation in withdrawing your own money.

☞ Banking Services for NRIs in India

Almost all the Indian Banks provide services to the NRIs. There are different types of accounts for them. They are:

- Non-resident (Ordinary) Account — NRO A/c
- Non-resident (External) Rupee Account — NRE A/c
- Non-resident (Foreign Currency) Account — FCNR A/c

An Indian resident who is earning foreign exchange can also maintain Foreign Currency account in the country with an authorised dealer bank but only to the maximum limit of 50% of such foreign exchange earnings, under the Exchange Earners Foreign Currency Account (EEFC) Scheme.

The last decade witnessed sea changes in the Indian banking sector. Norms were gradually relaxed, regulations were brought in line with globally acceptable standards and interest rates were deregulated. As new players who entered the banking sector in the 1990s aggressively expanded network and business, new instruments came into existence and newer methods of banking were encouraged.

☞ Banking Facilities

Gone are the days when you had to trek to a bank branch and stand in long queues for conducting transactions. Almost all commercial banks offer Internet Banking, Mobile Banking and ATM Banking facilities that make it possible for you to do banking from anywhere, at anytime. Internet Banking has made it possible to check balances, transfer funds, open new accounts and make investments from any location. Mobile Banking too offers similar facilities through the handset, in a secure way. ATM, irrespective of which bank you have account with.

Banks have also linked up with other organizations to extend enormous transaction convenience. For example, you could pay taxes online from your account, make travel booking, do online shopping directly using net banking, buy insurance covers and much more. Instruments such as debit cards and credit cards have enhanced payment convenience.

Asset-based lending products such as home loans and car loans have grown in variety. Plain vanilla products have been replaced with a range of customized and sophisticated products tailored to the specific needs of the customer.

Insurance-linked products such as bank assurance have also been offered to consumers on the liability side, services such as 'no frills accounts' have been introduced to enhance the choice of the customers. Banks have also morphed into one stop shops for a range of financial planning solutions.

In short, a trusted bank can completely handle all your financial needs, either by itself or through its associates and partners.

Technology

The considerable widening and deepening of the Indian financial system coupled with the increasing globalization of financial services, has inevitably led to massive advances in technology involved in banking.

Technology has been used in two different avenues in Banking – in Communication and Connectivity and in Business Process Re-engineering. Technology has enabled sophisticated:

1. Product Development
2. Better Market Infrastructure
3. Implementation of reliable techniques for control of risks. Besides, it has also helped banks to reach
4. Geographically distant and diversified markets.

Technology has changed the contours of three major functions performed by banks:

1. Access to liquidity
2. Transformation of assets, and
3. Monitoring of risks

Communication networking systems have had a crucial bearing on the efficiency of money and foreign exchange markets, managed by banks.

For the consumer, this has meant easier access, better deals on funds kept with banks and trend-spotting by the banks to assess emerging needs of the customer, etc. Technology-enabled funds transfer mechanisms such as National Electronic funds Transfer (NEFT) and Electronic Clearing Service (ECS) have made remitting funds from one bank to another far quicker, enabling savings in time.

It is not just the cities and metros that have gained from the strides of technology in banking. Even the rural customer has gained. For instance, standalone ATMs in rural areas have made it possible for small vendors and artisans to deposit and withdraw money after a day's, work. This has substantially enhanced the safety of their monies. ATM machines in rural areas have been customized for the environment for example, the customized ATMs are enabled to dispense slightly wrinkled notes, since new currency notes are looked upon with suspicion in rural areas.

☞ Questions

1. What are the chief defects in the organisation of joint stock banking in India? What suggestions would you offer to improve it?
2. Discuss the recent trends in the organisation, capital structure and investment of Indian joint stock banks.
3. Describe the role of commercial banks in extending credit to priority sectors.
4. Describe the major achievements of banks in India in recent years.
5. Discuss the salient features of the Indian banking system.
6. What are the important drawbacks in the banking system in India?
7. Write short note on DFHI.
8. Critically evaluate the performance of the Regional rural banks during the past 15 years. Explain the problems being faced by them in their functioning and suggest measures for improvement.

[I.I.B. Pt-I]

9. Write short notes on:
   (a) Discount and Finance House of India Ltd.
   (b) CRISIL
   (c) National Housing Bank

[I.IB. Pt-I]

CHAPTER 4

The Reserve Bank of India

The need for a central bank to control and coordinate currency and credit was felt for a very long time. The Reserve Bank of India Act was passed in 1934. In the beginning, it was a shareholders' bank with a capital of ₹ 5 crore divided into shares of ₹ 100 each. In 1948, in accordance with the Reserve Bank (Transfer to Public Ownership) Act, 1948, the Reserve Bank of India was nationalised, and all its shares were purchased by the Government of India.

☞ Management

The general superintendence and direction of the affairs and business of the bank are entrusted to a Central Board of Directors consisting of 20 directors, including:

(a) A Governor and four Deputy Governors, appointed as whole-time officers of the bank by the Central Government for a term not exceeding five years;

(b) Four directors nominated by the Central Government, one from each of the four Local Boards constituted as given below;

(c) Ten directors nominated by the Central Government for a term of four years; these directors are experts in business, industry, finance and cooperation; and

(d) One official nominated by the Government of India (Secretary, Finance Ministry, Government of India).

All the powers of the Bank are exercised by the Central Board which must meet at least six times each year and at least once in each quarter.

The whole country has been divided into four areas: the Western Area, the Eastern Area, the Northern Area, and the Southern Area, having headquarters at Mumbai, Kolkata, New Delhi and Chennai respectively. For each of these four areas, there is a Local Board consisting of five members appointed by the Central Government for a term of four years, to represent, as far as possible, territorial and economic interests and the interests of cooperative and indigenous banks. The function of the local board is to advise the Central Bank on such matters as may be generally or specially referred to it and to perform such duties as the Central Board may delegate to it.

☞ Departments

RBI functions with the help of several departments. These departments are managed mainly by their respective General Managers or Advisers. These departments are as under:

1. Department of Administration and Personal Management.
2. Department of Banking Operations and Development
3. Financial Markets Department
4. Department of Payment and Settlement Systems
5. Department of Banking Supervision
6. Department of Currency Management
7. Secretary's Department
8. Human Resource Development Department
9. Internal Debt Management Department
10. Department of Expenditure and Budgetary Control
11. Monetary Policy Department
12. Department of Government and Bank Accounts
13. Urban Banks Development
14. Department of Non-banking Supervision
15. Rural Planning and Credit Department
16. Department of Statistics and Information Management
17. Department of Economic Analysis and Policy
18. Inspection Department
19. Department of Information Technology
20. Foreign Exchange Department
21. Premises Department
22. Customer Service Department
23. Legal Department
24. Financial stability Unit
25. Deposit Insurance and Credit Guarantee Corporation
26. Rajbhasha Department
27. Department of Communication

Historical Journey of Reserve Bank of India 1935-2010 (Celebrating Platinum Jubilee)

1935 Operations begin on April 1.

1949 Nationalisation of Reserve Bank, Banking Regulation Act enacted.

1950 India embarks on planned economic development.

The Reserve Bank becomes active agent and participant.

1966	Co-operative banks came under RBI Regulation.
1969	Nationalisation of 14 commercial banks (six 06 more were nationalised in 1980).
1973	RBI strengthens exchange control by amending Foreign Exchange Regulation Act CFERA).
1974	Introduction of Priority sector lending targets.
1975	Regional Rural Banks set up.
1985	Financial Market Reforms begin with Sukhamoy Chakravarty and Vaghul Committee Reports.
1991	India faces balance of Payments crisis, pledges gold to shore up reserves. Rupee devalred.
1993	Exchange rate becomes market determined.
1994	Board for Financial Supervision set up.
1997	*(i)* Ad from Treasury bills phased out ending automatic mometisation.
	(ii) Regulation of Non-banking Finance Companies strengthened.
1998	Multiple indicator approach for monetary policy adopted.
2000	Foreign Exchange Management Act replaces FERA.
2002	Clearing Corporation of India Limited (CCIL).
	Commences clearing and settlement in Government securities.
2003	Fiscal Responsibility and Budget Management Act enacted.
2004	*(i)* Transition to a full-fledged daily liquidity adjustment facility (LAF) completed. Market Stabilisation Scheme (MSS) introduced to sterilise capital flows.
	(ii) Real Time Gross Settlement System Commences.
2005	Focus on Financial inclusion and increasing the outreach of the banking sector.
2006	RBI empowered to regulate money, fore, G-Sec. and gold related securities market.
2007	RBI empowered to regulate payment system.
2008-09	Pro-active efforts to minimise impact of global financial crisis.
2010	Celebrating Platinum Jubilee.

Functions of the Reserve Bank of India

The functions of the Reserve Bank of India may be divided under two categories —

(A) Central Banking Functions; and

(B) Other Functions.

(A) Central Banking Functions

(i) Issue of Bank Notes: Under Section 22*(i)* of the Reserve Bank of India Act, 1934, the Bank was given the sole monopoly of the issue of bank notes in India from 1st April, 1935. For this purpose, the Bank maintains a separate department known as the Issue Department. Notes are issued on a basis of a minimum currency reserve system. By the Reserve Bank Amendment Act, 1956, a provision was made for a minimum of reserve of ₹ 400 crore in foreign securities and a minimum reserve of gold

of the value of ₹ 115 crore — a total of ₹ 515 crore. This minimum currency reserve has since been fixed at ₹ 200 crore by the Reserve Bank Amendment Act of 1957. Out of ₹ 200 crore, there must be a reserve of gold of the value of ₹ 115 crore and securities of the value of ₹ 85 crore.

As per the requirements of the Reserve Bank of India Act, the issue of notes and the general banking business of the Bank are undertaken by two separate departments of the Bank. The issue department is responsible for the issue of new notes. The currency of our country consists of coins and one rupee notes issued by the Government of India and bank notes (two rupee, five rupee, ten rupee, twenty rupee, fifty rupee and hundred rupee notes) issued by the Reserve Bank. One rupee notes and coins issued by the Government of India are put into circulation through Reserve Bank only. The notes issued by the Reserve Bank are unlimited legal tender.

Currency Chest

For proper distribution of currency notes and coins, adequate arrangements have been made by the Reserve Bank. There are offices of the Issue Department in ten big cities. To facilitate expansion and contraction of currency in the country, currency chests are maintained all over the country. Currency chests are boxes or containers in which stocks of new or reissuable notes are stored along with rupee coins. The total number of currency chests and repositories run by the Reserve Bank, State Bank and its subsidiaries, public sector banks and Government Treasuries and Sub-treasuries, as at the end of June 1981 was 3,841. Thus, a stock of new currency notes is held in currency chests scattered over the entire country and maintained by the Reserve Bank or other public sector banks on behalf of Reserve Bank. Some of the important advantages of maintaining currency chests or treasuries to the bank are as follows:

(a) If payments, on a particular day, exceed the balance with the bank, it can withdraw funds from the chest. Similarly, if there is surplus, due to less payments, the surplus funds may be deposited into the chest. This avoids the physical transfer of cash at frequent intervals from one place to another. It facilitates the treasuries and bank branches to work with relatively small balances.

(b) The currency chests facilitate the exchange of rupee coins for notes and supply of notes of lower denomination for those of higher denominations and *vice versa* and also the issue of new notes for old and soiled notes.

(c) The currency chests also serve as the basis for providing remittances facilities to banks and the public.

(ii) Bankers' Bank: Another important function of the Bank is the regulation of banking. All the scheduled banks are required to keep with the Reserve Bank a consolidated 3 per cent of their total deposits, and the Reserve Bank has power to increase this percentage up to 15. These banks must have capital and reserves of not less than ₹ 5 lakh. The accumulation of these balances with the Reserve Bank places it in a position to use them freely in emergencies to support the scheduled banks themselves in times of need as the lender of last resort. To a certain extent, it is also possible for the Reserve Bank to influence the credit policy, of scheduled banks by means of an open market operations policy, that is, by the purchase and sale of securities or bills in the market. The Reserve Bank has another instrument of control in the form of the bank rate, which it publishes from time-to-time.

Further, the Bank has been given the following special powers to control banking companies under the Banking Companies Act, 1949:

(a) The power to issue licences to banks operating in India.

(b) The power to have supervision and inspection of banks.

(c) The power to control the opening of new branches.

(*d*) The power to examine and sanction schemes of arrangement and amalgamation.

(*e*) The power to recommend the liquidation of weak banking companies.

(*f*) The power to receive and scrutinise prescribed returns, and to call for any other information relating to the banking business.

(*g*) The power to caution or prohibit banking companies generally or any banking company in particular from entering into any particular transaction or transactions.

(*h*) The power to control the lending policy of, and advances by, banking companies or any particular bank in the public interest and to give directions as to the purpose for which advances may or may not be made, the margins to be maintained in respect of secured advances and the interest to be charged on advances.

(iii) Government Banker: The Reserve Bank of India also acts as a banker to Central and State Governments. As a banker, it is obliged to keep money on account for the Central and State Governments; to make payments up to the amounts standing to the credit of their accounts respectively; to carry out their exchange remittance and other banking operations; and manage the public debt. It has to transact the business of the Central Government without any remuneration. The Bank also floats loans and Treasury Bills on behalf of the Central and State Governments and advises Government on all financial matters.

(iv) Foreign Exchange: As the central bank of the country, the Reserve Bank is entrusted with the responsibility of maintaining the external stability of the rupee. It has been given the monopoly to control and regulate foreign exchange. For example, any person who wants to buy or sell foreign exchange has to take permission from the Reserve Bank.

(v) Miscellaneous Central Banking Functions: Apart from the fundamental central banking functions mentioned above, the Reserve Bank performs a number of subsidiary or ancillary functions incidental to its position as the apex bank of the country. These include:

(*a*) Supply of different forms of currency;

(*b*) The extension of remittance facilities;

(*c*) The management of the clearing house; and

(*d*) Tendering advice on financial matters, collection and dissemination of banking statistics, etc.

(B) Other Functions

The Reserve Bank is authorised to transact the following ordinary banking business:

(*a*) Acceptance of money on deposits without interest from the Central and State Governments, banks, local bodies and any other person.

(*b*) The purchase, sale and rediscount of bills of exchange and promissory notes drawn and payable in India and arising out of bonafide transactions, bearing two or more signatures, one of which must be that of a scheduled bank, and maturing within 90 days from the date of purchase or rediscount.

(*c*) The purchase, sale and rediscount of bills, drawn and payable in India for financing agricultural operations or marketing of crops, and maturing within 15 months from the date of purchase or rediscount.

(*d*) The purchase, sale and rediscount of bills issued or drawn for holding or trading in securities of the Central or State Governments and maturing within 90 days.

(e) The making of loans and advances to States, local bodies, scheduled banks and State co-operative banks.

(f) The making of ways and means advances to Central and State Governments.

(g) The purchase and sale of securities of the Central and State Governments.

(h) The issue of demand drafts made payable at its own offices or agencies and making, issuing and circulating bank post bills.

(i) The borrowing of money from a scheduled bank in India or from central banks in other countries.

(j) The opening of an account, or making of an agency agreement, with central banks in other countries and acting as their agent and investing funds in their shares.

(k) The purchase and sale of gold and bullion.

(l) RBI also plays an important role in the maintenance of exchange value of the rupee and acts as an Agent of the Government in respect of India's membership of International Monetary Fund.

(m) All such functions as may be incidental to or consequential upon the exercise of its powers or the discharge of its duties under the Act.

☞ Achievements of the Reserve Bank

As a Government banker, the Reserve Bank has achieved a remarkable measure of success in the management of the public debt. In addition, it has floated loans for the Central and State Governments at low rates. From time-to-time, it has also provided ways and means to State Governments through the sale of Treasury Bills. As a lender of last resort, the Bank has advanced large amounts to scheduled banks during periods of crisis.

In the field of industrial finance, the Reserve Bank has played a very important role in organising the Industrial Finance Corporation, the State Financial Corporations and the Industrial Development Bank of India as agencies for providing long-term finance to industry.

In the field of agricultural finance, the Reserve Bank has done a very valuable work by developing rural credit in India and maintaining a special department to render expert advice to Government on co-operative credit.

In the field of research, the Bank's Department of Research and Statistics, which is staffed by competent economists and statisticians, has been doing a useful service to the country.

As regards the control and supervision of banking institutions the Reserve Bank, in exercise of the powers vested in it under the Banking Companies Act of 1949, has taken steps to promote sound banking practices in the country. Constant vigilance by the Reserve Bank and sustained efforts on its part to remove defects have tended to strengthen individual banks, and to inspire public confidence in the banking system as a whole.

☞ Failures of the Reserve Bank

In certain fields, the Reserve Bank of India has not been able to perform its functions successfully.

It has failed to stabilise the internal value of the currency, which is admittedly an important function of a central bank. It has also failed to maintain the external value of the Rupee.

It has failed to control and coordinate the services of the various credit agencies and cooperative societies, smaller bankers and indigenous bankers, who are still outside its purview and supervision.

It has failed to develop an organised bill market to provide rediscounting facilities to scheduled banks and to enable them to invest their surplus funds profitably.

The Reserve Bank has not succeeded in reducing the differences between the bank rate and other money market rates. Despite these failures, however, the Reserve Bank of India has ushered in a new era of financial stability and banking reform.

☞ Control of Credit by the Reserve Bank

It has been provided in the Preamble to the Reserve Bank of India Act that one of the functions of the Bank is to control currency and credit. The control that a Central Bank is able to exercise on the monetary system largely depends upon the control that it is able to exercise on the constituents of the purchasing power. In all countries, including India, token coins and currency notes form the bulk of the purchasing power, the latter being more important than the former. In countries where banking has developed, the deposit currency also plays an important role in the creation of credit and purchasing power.

The methods of credit control are usually categorised into: *(i)* General (or) quantitative methods, and *(ii)* Selective (or qualitative) methods. The Bank Rate Policy, variable reserve requirements, statutory liquidity requirements, and open market operations policy fall in the category of general credit control method. The various directives issued by the Reserve Bank restricting the quantum and other terms of granting credit against certain specified commodities constitute the selective control method.

The main difference between the general and selective credit control methods is that the former influence the cost and overall volume of credit granted by banks. They affect credit granted to the whole economy, whereas the selective controls affect the flow of credit to only a specified sector of the economy, wherein speculative tendency and rising trend of prices, due to excessive bank credit, is noticed.

The general credit control measures affect the: *(i)* cost, and *(ii)* availability (or quantum) of bank credit. The cost of credit is influenced by the Bank Rate at which the central bank provides refinance to the banks. During recent years the Reserve Bank has relied upon its powers to regulate the interest rates on the bank advances and is directly regulating the interest rates of banks rather than through the instrument of Bank Rate.

The overall quantum of credit created by banks depends on their cash reserves, comprising cash in hand and balance with the Reserve Bank. The cash reserve increase through: *(i)* a rise in deposit resources of banks, *(ii)* borrowing from the Reserve Bank, or *(iii)* by sale of their investments. Regulation of credit by the Reserve Bank means regulations of quantum of cash reserves of commercial banks. These control measures exert their influence on the assets pattern of commercial banks. When the Reserve Bank desires to control, it adopts various methods, whereby the quantum of refinance is restricted and the flow of bank resources to investments and statutory reserves with the Reserve Bank is enhanced, thereby curtailing the availability of loanable resources with the bank.

☞ Control of Currency

The Reserve Bank of India has been given the monopoly of note issue to enable it to exercise control over the volume of bank notes. Ordinarily, the expansion or contraction of currency is effected under Section 33 (i) by increasing or decreasing the assets of the Issue Department, which are kept in the form of rupee coins, including rupee notes, gold coin and bullion, rupee securities, including Treasury Bills and foreign securities. An expansion in currency can be effected by increasing any of these forms of assets and issuing notes of equal value from the Issue Department. A contraction in currency can be similarly effected withdrawing notes from circulation and reducing any of the assets held by the Reserve Bank. Ordinarily, when it wants to expand currency, the Bank increases the assets of the Issue Department by transferring rupee or foreign securities or both from the Banking Department to the Issue Department or by cancelling *ad hoc* Treasury Bills held in the Issue Department. Sometimes, currency is expanded or contracted as a result of a revaluation of securities held in the Issue Department.

☞ Control of Credit

The Reserve Bank of India, like other central banks, controls, credit by the following methods:

REFINANCING POLICY OF RESERVE BANK

The central bank of the country, the Reserve Bank is the lender of last resort to the banking system. Its refinancing policy, therefore has great significance of the commercial banks. Changes in this policy are carried to the commercial banks. Changes in this policy are carried out in two ways:

(i) by varying the cost of borrowings through a variation in its Bank Rate, and

(ii) by varying the availability (i.e., quantum) of credit to the banks.

(1) The Bank Rate Policy

Section 49 of the Reserve Bank of India Act, 1934, defines Bank Rate as, "the standard rate at which it (the Reserve Bank) is prepared to buy or rediscount bills of exchange or other commercial paper eligible for purchase under this Act". As the provision regarding rediscounting of bills by the Reserve Bank had remained inoperative for a long time in the past, the rate charged by the Reserve Bank on its advances to banks has been treated as the Bank Rate.

A change in the Bank Rate — upward or downward — usually has an immediate effect on the cost of credit available to the commercial banks from the central bank. A high Bank Rate is intended to raise the cost of Reserve Bank accommodation to banks, which in turn raises their own lending rates to the borrowers. Discouraged by high rate of interest, the borrowing will consequently reduce the level of their borrowing from the banks, which in turn brings down the level of refinance secured by them from the central bank. Thus, a high Bank Rate is intended to result in contraction of bank credit.

Theoretically, the Bank Rate happens to be the prime rate — it is a pace setter to all other rates of interest in the money market, *i.e.,* all other rates of interest generally move in the same direction in which the Bank Rate moves. When the central bank intends to follow the policy of high cost of money, it raises the Bank rate first, which is followed by rise in all other rates of interest. Such a policy is called the policy of dear money. The objective of such a policy happens to make money scarce and costly so as to restrict its use to the deserving purpose only.

The Reserve Bank of India resorted to the policy of varying its Bank Rate several times since 1951 when it was changed from 3 per cent to 3.5 per cent for the first time. After several revisions, the Bank Rate was raised from 5 to 6 per cent on January 8, 1971 in view of the need for credit restraint and for minimising the resort to refinance from the Reserve Bank. The Bank Rate was raised to 7 per cent on May 30, 1973, because of highly disquieting increase in the wholesale prices and the excessive use of bank credit by borrowers, particularly for building up inventories. The subsequent months witnessed unprecedented rise in prices and serious inflationary situation developed in the country. To meet such a situation, along with a number of fiscal measures introduced by the Government, the Reserve Bank resorted to the policy of dear money on July 22, 1974 and announced a two percentage point rise in bank rate to 9%, followed by upward revision in deposit and lending rates. There were two objectives of such dear money policy:

(a) *High cost of bank credit was intended to reduce its demand from businessmen and traders and to act as disincentive to be improved.*

(b) *High rate of interest on bank deposits was intended to induce the people to save more and to reduce their consumption expenditure.*

The Bank Rate was further raised to 10% on July 11, 1981, together with certain other measures to contain the inflationary pressure in the economy. Though the Bank rate remained at this level during the next decade, different rate of interest were charged by the Reserve Bank on the refinance provided by it against different types of credit granted by banks. The interest rates on deposits and advances of commercial banks were also prescribed by the Reserve Bank of India without varying the Bank Rate itself. The Bank Rate in India thus ceased to be an effective rate influencing other rates in the banking system and was of limited significance.

Limitations of Bank Rate Policy: A higher Bank Rate is intended to act as an anti-inflationary device, because it is expected to influence the inventory holding through a rise in the cost of such holding. But the efficacy of Bank rate is not without its limitations. If the demand for bank credit is interest-elastic, a high interest rate policy (*i.e.,* high cost of bank credit) will not deter the inventory accumulation. On the other hand, high lending rates push up the cost of production/cost of maintaining the stocks of the genuine borrowers, who in turn raise the selling prices of their products. Thus, the cost-push effect of dear money adversely affects the whole range of industries and trades. Intended to be an anti-inflationary step, the high Bank Rate policy, in reality, proves to be inflationary in character. This seems to be the reason why the Reserve Bank has, during recent years, tightened the availability of its accommodation to the banks as discussed below:

After retaining the Bank Rate at 10% for a decade (1981-91), the Reserve Bank hiked it to 11% with effect from July 4, 1991. The Reserve Bank also hiked the lending and deposit interest rates of the banks. These steps were preceded by the devaluation of Indian rupee in two instalments on 1st and 3rd July, 1991. The overall objective was to curb the imports and to reduce aggregate demand in the economy.

Bank rate was further raised to 12% on October 10, 1991. The two percentage points increase in the Bank Rate within a period of 3 months indicated the commencement of dear money policy by the Reserve Bank of India. At the same time, the Reserve Bank of India withdrew all refinancing facilities to the banks (except refinance facilities on export finance) and increased bank deposits and lending rates also.

In April 1997, Reserve Bank of India felt the necessity of making the Bank Rate an effective signal rate as well as a reference rate. Accordingly, the Bank Rate was reduced by one percentage point to 11% per annum. The objective was that changes in the Bank Rate reflect the stance of monetary policy. Reserve Bank also revised penal rate on shortfalls in reserve requirements that are linked with the Bank Rate. Interest rates on other categories of accommodation from Reserve Bank, which were not linked with the Bank rate, are now linked with it. Ceiling on Deposit rates up to 1 year was also linked with the Bank Rate. The role of Bank Rate as an effective signal rate was restored.

The Reserve Bank of India further reduced the Bank Rate to 10% with effect from June 26, 1997. All rates linked with the Bank Rate were consequently reduced by one percentage point.

With effect from October 22, 1997, Bank Rate was further reduced by one percentage point to 9%. But on 16th January, 1998, Bank Rate was hiked by 2 percentage points to 11% because of the significant pressure on the external value of the rupee. On 18th March, 1998, Bank Rate was reduced to 10% and further to 10% on 2nd April, 1998. It was followed by another reduction of one percentage point to 9% on 29th April, 1998. With the variation in Bank Rate, all other rates linked with the Bank Rate also vary in the same direction.

During the last two years (1999-2001), Bank Rate has moved in both the directions. It was reduced from 9% to 8% on March 2, 1999 and further to 7% with effect from April 1, 2000. Consistently low prevailing inflation rate led the Reserve Bank to curtail the Bank Rate. Another objective has been to cut the cost of bank credit. But shortly thereafter the Bank Rate was raised to 8% on July 21, 2000 mainly to stabilise the value of the rupee *vis-a-vis* US dollar.

During the first quarter of 2001, Reserve Bank of India reduced the Bank Rate twice — from 8% to 7½% on Feb. 16 and further to 7% effective March 1, 2001. It has been reduced by 0.25 percentage point from 6.5% with effect from Oct. 29, 2002.

(2) Refinance Policy

Section 17 of the Reserve Bank of India Act, 1934, permits the Reserve Bank to provide accommodation to commercial banks by way of rediscounting of eligible bills or as advances against approved securities. But such lending as subject to the policy formulated by the Bank in this regard; banks cannot claim such facility as a matter of right. The Reserve Bank of India has restricted the availability of its refinance to banks through the various methods followed by it from time-to-time since 1960. During recent years, the Reserve Bank of India provided refinance to banks on a restricted scale as follows:

(a) Food Credit Refinance: Reserve Bank provided to the banks against food credit provided by them. But such refinance was restricted to an amount equal to the excess of total food credit by all the banks over a minimum level of such credit. Such minimum level of credit was called the threshold level, which was fixed by the Reserve Bank from time-to-time. Banks used to get 100% refinance in respect of their food credit in excess of the threshold level. Food credit refinance was provided at the Bank Rate. This rate was 11.5% till 5th July, 1991 when it was hiked to 14%. Subsequently, in October 1991 this refinance facility was withdrawn.

(b) Export Credit Refinance: Export refinance is also provided by Reserve Bank, but its quantum is determined on the basis of the increase in export credit of a bank over the level of such credit reached in the base year. In the past such base year has been brought forward from time-to-time, for calculating the export refinance limits of banks. Till November 4, 1989, export credit refinance was made available to the banks equal to 100 per cent of the increase in export credit over the monthly average for 1987. With effect from 4th November, 1989, export credit refinance was curtailed to 75% of the increase in export credit over the monthly average for 1987. The base for determining export refinance was brought forward to the financial year 1988-89 (Instead of the calendar year 1987) effective 25th August, 1990. The quantum of refinance remained unchanged at 75%. Reserve Bank of India has introduced a two-tier system of refinancing export credit with effect from July 27, 1991. Banks were provided refinance facility in respect of the increase in export finance provided by them as follows:

(i) at the rate of 50% of the increase in monthly average in 1989-90 over the monthly average during 1988-89, and

(ii) at the rate of 100% of the monthly average in 1990-91 over 1989-90.

With effect from April 26, 1997, Scheduled commercial banks are provided export credit refinance to the extent of 100 per cent of the increase in outstanding export credit eligible for refinance over the level of such credit as on February 16, 1996. The rate of interest on export credit refinance will be at the Bank Rate (i.e., 10% per annum).

(c) Discretionary Refinance: Such credit is essentially temporary accommodation. To provide easier access to the discretionary refinance facility, Reserve Bank permitted all licensed scheduled commercial banks (excluding the Regional Rural Banks) to draw discretionary refinance without prior sanction by the Reserve Bank up to an amount equal to 0.5% of the bank's average deposits in 1985-

86 (April-March) at a rate of interest of 14% p.a. for a period not exceeding 14 days. For banks requiring such refinance for a period of more than 14 days or an amount in excess of the stipulated limit, prior sanction of the Reserve Bank was necessary.

In December 1987, the limit of such discretionary refinance was raised to 1% of the Bank's average aggregate deposits in 1986-87. The revised limit were provided under 3 tranches and for 3 blocks of 4 weeks each. The interest rates on such refinance varied between 14 per cent and 16 per cent depending upon the period and the amount of refinance. This facility was also withdrawn in Oct. 1991.

(d) Standby Refinance: It was provided by the Reserve Bank at 11% interest rate for not more than 3 days at a time and was mainly intended to assist banks to meet clearing imbalances. This facility was available against the collateral of Government and Trustee securities only. This facility has also been withdrawn.

(e) 182 Days Treasury Bills Refinance Facility: Reserve Bank of India introduced this facility in April 1987. Under this facility refinance is provided to the extent of 50% of the holding of the bank's 182 Days Treasury Bills. The rate of interest charged by the Reserve Bank was enhanced from 10.75% p.a. to 11.25% in view of the rise in cut-off yields on these bills.

(f) Government Securities Refinance Facility: This refinance facility was introduced with effect from October 31, 1992. Under this facility refinance was limited to half a percentage point of bank's fortnightly average outstanding aggregate deposits in 1991-92. This facility was granted against the collateral over the statutory liquidity requirement. Interest was charged @ 14% per annum. This refinance facility aimed at the development of government securities market. In September, 1995, the base rate for determining the refinance limits to banks was brought forward from the end of 1991-92 to the end of 1994-95 and the limit of refinance for each bank was also raised from 0.5% to 1% of aggregate deposits. The refinance limit was equally divided under two separate limits against Treasury Bills and Government dated securities respectively.

This refinance facility was withdrawn on July 6, 1996 following the appointment of primary dealers in Government securities and reduction in Cash Reserve Ratio.

(g) General Refinance Facility: A new refinance facility has been introduced by Reserve Bank of India effective April 26, 1997. This facility enables banks to tide over their temporary liquidity shortage. Under this facility all scheduled commercial banks are provided outstanding aggregate deposits in 1996-97 under Section 17 (3B) of the Reserve Bank of India Act, 1934.

Under this facility, general refinance is provided for two blocks of four weeks each. For the first 4 weeks interest would be charged at Bank Rate and for the next 4 weeks at Bank Rate plus 1% point. Banks will be able to avail of general refinance facility afresh after a gap of two weeks during which there has been no borrowing from Reserve Bank under this scheme. Banks which avail of this facility beyond eight weeks would face an automatic debiting of their current accounts with the Reserve Bank.

In addition to the above, the Reserve Bank of India provided special refinance against shipping loans and duty drawbacks. The latter refinance is provided free of cost.

☞ Interim Liquidity Adjustment Facility (ILAF)

Reserve Bank of India had introduced Interim Liquidity Adjustment Facility (ILAF) in April 1999. The features of this facility were as follows:

(1) The general refinance facility (discussed above) was withdrawn and replaced by a collateralised lending facility (CLF) up to 0.25 per cent of the fortnightly average outstanding aggregate deposits in 1997-98 which was made available for two weeks at the Bank Rate. An

additional collateralised lending facility (ACLF) for an amount equivalent of CLF was also made available at the bank rate plus 2 per cent. CLF and ACLF which were for periods beyond two weeks was subject to a penal rate of 2% for an additional two week period. There was a cooling period of two weeks thereafter, *i.e.,* no drawals were permitted during this period.

(2) The existing facility for export refinance at the Bank rate continued.

(3) For the Primary Dealers in Government securities, liquidity support against collateral of Government securities was made available at the Bank Rate and the amount was constant throughout the year. Each drawal was subject to restriction of repayment within 90 days.

(4) Additional liquidity support against collateral of Government securities was also provided to Primary Dealers for a period not exceeding two weeks at a time and the interest rate was 2 per cent over the Bank Rate.

(5) Absorption of liquidity in the market continued to be through fixed rate repos.

(6) The above facilities were supplemented by Open Market Operations in Government securities and Treasury Bills by Reserve Bank of India.

Thus, ILAF was intended to provide a mechanism by which liquidity was injected at various interest rates and absorbed when necessary at fixed rate repo. It was thus expected that volatility on the money market would be minimised. In October 1999, the requirement of cooling period was removed to impart flexibility to the scheme.

As the ILAF served its purpose as a transitional measure for providing reasonable access to liquid funds at set rates of interest, Reserve Bank of India decided in April 2000 to implement a full-fledged LAF in convenient stages in order to ensure smooth transition.

☞ Liquidity Adjustment Facility (LAF) Introduced

Accepting the recommendation of the Narasimham Committee on Banking Reforms, Reserve Bank of India introduced Liquidity Adjustment Facility with effect from June 5, 2000. It is a mechanism by which the Reserve Bank of India draws funds from the money market at a time of surplus and infuses liquidity whenever there is a temporary shortage. For this purpose Reserve Bank of India asks banks and primary dealers to bid for funds if there is a shortage and borrows from them if there is a surplus.

In the first stage, effective June 5, 2000, the additional CLF and level II support to Primary Dealers (as discussed above) have been replaced by variable rate reverse repo auctions with same day settlement. Repos are a mode of borrowing where the borrower sells securities with an agreement to buy them back the next day at a predetermined price. The difference between the sale and repurchase price indicates the interest cost on the funds.

Under LAF system, Reserve Bank of India assesses the liquidity position daily on the basis of various factors, *e.g.,* the conversion of the foreign currencies into rupee, the turnover in the call market the previous day, the CRR requirements of the banking system and the quantum of funds existing in the system such as advance payment of taxes.

Under LAF facility, funds are made available through reverse repo auctions. It is just opposite of repo. The lender buys securities with an agreement to sell them back at a predetermined rate. In the auction, borrowers bid for funds indicating the amount they want to borrow and the rate they are willing to pay. The Reserve Bank of India has the right to reject the bids of any borrower.

Initially repos/reverse repo auctions were conducted on a daily basis from Monday to Friday and with one day maturity (except on Friday and before holidays). In August 2000, multiple repo/reverse repo auctions with 3 to 7 days maturity were introduced. Interest rates in case of both are the cut-off yields emerging from auctions conducted on a uniform price basis.

Under LAF, the quantum of adjustment and also the rates would be flexible, responding immediately to the needs of the system. Funds made available by Reserve Bank of India would meet primarily the day-to-day liquidity mismatches in the system and not the normal financing requirements of banks. Short-term interest rates will move within a corridor and will have greater stability.

☞ The Second Stage of LAF

The LAF, worked satisfactorily as a flexible instrument for injecting/absorbing liquidity and also as an interest rate signal for the short-term money market. Reserve Bank of India felt that it can be made fully effective only when it becomes the primary instrument of liquidity adjustment and other forms of liquidity support are gradually replaced with LAF over a reasonable period of time. In order to move in this direction Reserve Bank of India made the following modifications while announcing its credit policy on April 19, 2001.

(A) Liquidity Support Facilities

(1) The standing liquidity support facilities available to banks from Reserve Bank of India will be split into two parts. *viz., (i)* normal facility and *(ii)* back-stop facility. Accordingly the total quantum of support available to banks in CLF and export credit refinance and quantum of support available to PDS will be split into these two components. Normal facility would initially constitute about 2/3rd and back-stop facility about 1/3rd. PD-wise and bank-wise limits will be fixed separately.

(2) The normal facility will be provided at the Bank Rate.

(3) The back-stop facility will be provided at a variable daily rate, which woul:l be linked to cut-off rates emerging in regular LAF auctions and in the absence of such rates, to NSE-Mumbai Inter Bank Offer Rate (NSE-MIBOR) are as follows:

(a) The variable rate for the back-stop facility to be fixed on a daily basis would be 1% point over the reverse repo cut-off rate at which funds were injected earlier during the day under LAF repo auctions.

(b) If no reverse repo bid was accepted as part of LAF auction, the rate will be 2 to 3 per cent points over the repo cut-off rate of the day emerged in LAF auction, as may be decided by Reserve Bank of India.

(c) In the absence of both *(a)* and *(b)* above, the rate will be 2 to 3 per cent points over NSE-MIBOR as decided by Reserve Bank of India.

(B) Export Credit Refinance

Export Credit Refinance facility has been rationalised. With effect from May 5, 2001, scheduled commercial banks will be provided export credit refinance to the extent of 15% of the outstanding export credit eligible for refinance as at the end of second preceding fortnight. Further, the existing refinance limits as on May 4, 2001, as per the current formula will constitute the minimum limit available for banks up to March 31, 2002.

(C) Changes in LAF Operating Procedure

(i) The minimum bid size for LAF has been reduced from the existing ₹ 10 crore to ₹ 5 crore to enable small operators to participate.

(ii) The LAF timing has been advanced by 30 minutes — 10.30 A.M. for receipt of bids and 12 noon for announcement of result.

(iii) The market would be provided with information on the scheduled commercial banks' aggregate cash balances maintained with Reserve Bank on a cumulative basis during the fortnight with a lag of 2 days.

(iv) Reserve Bank of India will have an additional option to switch over to fixed rate repos on overnight basis. The rate of interest intended to be offered would be announced on the previous evening or before 10 A.M. on the day of auction, if necessary.

(v) In addition to overnight repos, Reserve Bank will also have the discretion to introduce longer term repos up to 14 days as and when required.

(vi) It was decided to introduce multiple price auction (in place of existing uniform price auction) on an experimental basis for one month during May 2001. Under the multiple price auction, bidders get differential rates in accordance with their need and assessment of cost. Thus, greater commitment to bidding is likely to be ensured. Intensity of demand in the market is clearly reflected in the bidding pattern.

Medium term objective is to move over gradually to liquidity adjustment through LAF combined with back-stop facility at variable rates and to do away with the various specific liquidity facilities available at Bank Rate.

☞ Cost of Credit

As regards the cost of credit made available by the Reserve Bank, in the early years, all accommodation was provided uniformly at the Bank Rate, barring ways and means, advances to Central and State Governments, which were made at one per cent below the Bank Rate. Subsequently, concessional rates were offered for agriculture and later on for certain other priority sectors, for example, exports. Further, under the present system of lending to commercial banks, the rate varies from bank-to-bank in accordance with their liquidity ratios. In effect, therefore, there is at present a multiplicity of rates in India.

☞ Open Market Operation

The Reserve Bank has the power to resort to open market operations if it thinks that conditions warrant their application. The weapon operates by enlarging or contracting the cash basis of the commercial banks as a result of the purchase or sale of Government securities by the Bank. The success of these operations depends upon two factors, *viz.*, the resources the central bank has at its disposal and, secondly, the capacity and the responsiveness of the market in which they are sought to be carried out. The Reserve Bank of India resorted to open market operations in 1948-49, 1950-51, 1956, 1957 and 1960.

In most of the subsequent years, the Reserve Bank's sales of securities to the public have exceeded its purchases. Sales were particularly heavy from 1964-65 to 1968-69, the net sales being of the order of ₹ 320 crore. Apart from outright purchase or sales, the Bank engages extensively in *switch* operations, that is, in the purchase of one loan against the sale of another and *vice versa.* This is done to maintain an orderly pattern of yields and to cater to the varying requirements of investors with respect to the maturity distribution policy.

☞ Variable Reserve Ratios

In order to control the credit and currency system effectively and to correlate the two in the interest of national economy, the Reserve Bank is empowered to use the cash balances of all the scheduled banks. According to Section 42(i) of the Reserve Bank of India Act, each bank has to maintain an interest-free balance of not less than 5 per cent of its demand liabilities and 2 per cent of its time liabilities. By an Amendment Act in 1956, the Reserve Bank was empowered to vary the required reserves between 5 per cent and 20 per cent in respect of demand liabilities and between 2 per cent and 8 per cent in respect of time liabilities.

The Reserve Bank of India used this method of credit control for the first time on 11th March, 1960, when it was made compulsory for all the scheduled banks to deposit with the bank 25 per cent of the additions to their "time and demand liabilities". On 6th May, 1960, this was increased to 50 per cent. From 11th January, 1961, this method of additional deposits was altogether abandoned.

Under an Amendment Act of September 1962, a consolidated 3 per cent of the total deposits of all the scheduled banks has to be deposited with the Reserve Bank, which has the power to increase this percentage up to 15. The Cash Reserve Ratio (CRR) was raised from 6.5% to 7% of the net demand and time liabilities from August 21, 1981. The CRR was raised to 7.5% with effect from May 27, 1983 and further to 8% from July 29, 1983. It was further raised to 9% with effect from Feb. 4, 1984. The rate of interest paid by Reserve Bank to Scheduled Banks on additional average balance has been raised to 9% per annum with effect from May 1, 1983.

CRR was raised to 9.5 per cent on 1987, 10.5 per cent from July 2, 1988; 11% from July 30, 1988. Foreign currency (Non-resident) accounts have been subjected to CRR at a lower rate. In July 1988, the rate applicable to them was also raised from 9.5% to 10%. Banks are required to maintain CRR @ 3% on Non-resident (External) Rupee accounts. In January, 1977, the Reserve Bank made effective use of the power to impose additional reserve requirement. Scheduled banks were required to make an additional statutory reserve equal to 10% of the incremental deposits after Jan. 14, 1977. To enable the banks to use the incremental reserves for credit purposes, RBI exempted the banks from maintaining additional reserves with effect from 31st Oct. 1980, but the deposits already unmobilised with the Reserve Bank were not permitted to be withdrawn by the banks, only 20% of the impounded deposits were released to banks in 1984. The RBI again asked the Scheduled Commercial banks to maintain incremental Cash Reserve Ratio (CRR) of 10% of the increase in net demand and time liabilities over the level as on Nov. 11, 1983. This system of multiple prescriptions in respect of CRR was replaced by a single prescription from July 1, 1989. Banks are now required to maintain CRR @ 15% on their entire net demand and time liabilities. After the amendment of RBI Act, the ceiling of 15% has been enhanced to 20%. Subsequently, RBI has directed the banks to maintain with effect from May 4, 1991, an incremental cash reserve ratio of 10% of the increase in net demand and time liabilities over the level as on 3rd May, 1991. This will be in addition to the existing cash reserve ratio of 15% of net demand and time liabilities.

CASH RESERVE REQUIREMENT (CRR)

A scheduled bank is under an obligation to keep cash reserve called the Statutory Cash Reserve with the Reserve Bank under Section 42 of the Reserve Bank of India Act, 1934. Every scheduled bank is required to maintain with the Reserve Bank an average daily balance equal to at least 3% of its demand and time liabilities. Average daily balance means the average of balance held at the close of business on each day of the fortnight. The Reserve Bank is empowered to increase the rate of statutory cash reserve from 3% up to 20% of the net liabilities.

Liabilities of a scheduled bank exclude: *(i)* its paid-up capital and reserve, and *(ii)* loans taken from the Reserve Bank or Industrial Development Bank or National Bank for Agriculture and Rural Development, or the Export-Import Bank of India. *(iii)* the aggregate of the liabilities of a scheduled commercial bank to the State Bank or its subsidiary bank, any nationalised bank or a banking company or a cooperative bank or any other financial institutions notified by the Central Government in this behalf shall be reduced by the aggregate of the liabilities of all such banks and institutions to the concerned scheduled bank. Thus, the entire amount of inter-bank liabilities for the purpose of Section 42 are excluded and the net liability of a scheduled bank to the entire banking system (*i.e.,* after deducting the balance maintained by it with all other banks from its gross liabilities to them) will be deemed to be its liabilities to the system.

Additional Cash Reserve: The Reserve Bank is authorised to direct every scheduled bank to maintain with it, in addition to the above an additional average daily balance at a rate specified by it. This additional cash reserve is not to be maintained on the entire amount of demand and time liabilities but on the excess of such liabilities over the level of the total liabilities at the close of business on the date specified in the notification. For example, the Reserve Bank may direct the banks to keep an additional reserve equal to 25 per cent of the net increase in the total deposit liabilities after a stipulated date, say 1st July1992. In such a case, a bank whose deposit liabilities increase by, say, ₹ 8 lakh between 1st July and 1st August, will be required to keep an additional cash reserve of ₹ 2 lakh (25% of ₹ 8 lakh). This requirement is subject to two limitations:

(i) The additional cash balance to be deposited with Reserve Bank shall in no case be more than the excess of the total deposit liabilities over the level of specified date. In the above example, the Reserve Bank may ask the bank concerned to make additional cash reserve up to the maximum amount of ₹ 8 lakh in the given period and not in excess of that amount.

(ii) The amount of both — the cash reserve and the additional cash reserve — shall not together exceed the limit of 20% of the total demand and liabilities.

The Reserve Bank may pay interest to the scheduled banks on —

(i) the cash reserve maintained by the latter in excess of the statutory minimum of 3% of their total liabilities (if such excess is required by the Reserve Banks), and

(ii) the additional cash reserves: But they shall be entitled to such interest if they maintain the above cash reserves to the full extent as required by the Reserve Bank. If a bank maintains a balance in excess of the enhanced reserve requirement or additional reserve requirement, no interest shall be payable on that excess amount.

Under Section 42 (2) every scheduled bank is required to send to the Reserve Bank a return showing the following:

(i) the amount of its demand and time liabilities and the amount of its borrowing from banks in India;

(ii) the total amount of legal tender notes and coins held by it in India;

(iii) the balance held by it at the Reserve Bank in India;

(iv) the balance held by it at other banks in current accounts and money at call and short notice in India;

(v) the investment (at book value) in Central and State Government securities including Tsreasury Bills and Treasury deposit receipts;

(vi) the amount of advances in India;

(vii) the inland and foreign bills purchased and discounted in India.

The data in the return should relate to the business at the close of each Friday and the return must be sent within the next five days.

Section 42 (3) prescribes penalties for not complying with the above-mentioned requirements. If the balance maintained by a bank during any fortnight is below the minimum prescribed under both the cash reserve requirements, such bank shall be liable to pay the Reserve Bank penal interest at a rate 3% above the Bank Rate on the amount of the short fall in the same fortnight. The penal interest rate goes up to 5% over the Bank Rate in the succeeding fortnights if the shortfall in the cash balance continues. In addition to the above, when penal interest at the increased rate of five per cent above the Bank Rate becomes payable by a scheduled bank, if the average daily balance during the next succeeding fortnight is still below the prescribed minimum, every director, manager or secretary of the bank who is, knowingly and wilfully, a party to the default, shall also be punishable with fine up to ₹ 500 and with a further fine up to ₹ 500 for each subsequent fortnight during which the default continues. The Bank may prohibit the scheduled bank from receiving any fresh deposits after that fortnight. The Reserve Bank may not demand the payment of penal interest or the penalty if it is satisfied that the defaulting bank had sufficient causes for its failure to maintain the cash balance required.

☞ Interest Rate on CRR

Reserve Bank of India pay interest to the scheduled bank on their cash reserves maintained with it (in excess of the statutory minimum of 3 per cent). The rate of interest was gradually raised till it reached the level of 10.5% per cent per annum. With effect from April 12, 1990 interest on banks cash balances with the Reserve Bank is paid on a two-tier formula as follows:

(i) @ 10.5% p.a. on the eligible cash balances based on the net demand and time liabilities as on March 23, 1990, and

(ii) on the eligible cash balances on the basis of increase in net demand and time liabilities after March 23, 1993, no interest is payable since Oct. 9, 1992. The rate of interest on this category of cash reserve was fixed at 8% in April 1990 but it was gradually reduced to nil in October 1992. The banks have been advised to pay interest on eligible CRR balances on a monthly basis with effect from April 2003. To facilitate this, banks have been urged to put in place proper technology including adoption of the software package enabling transmission of Form A data banks directly to RBI.

☞ Scheme of Graduated Penalties

We have already noted that banks suffered dual loss whenever there happened to be a shortfall in the maintenance of CRR. First, no interest was payable to them by the Reserve Bank on the entire amount of cash maintained by them with the Reserve Bank, and second, they were liable to pay penal interest on the amount of shortfall in CRR. To alleviate the impact of such losses in cash of small and involuntary defaults, the Reserve Bank introduced a scheme of graduated penalties with effect from January 1, 1982. This scheme has been revised with effect from April 1, 1990 to give further relief to the banks. Under the scheme no penal interest rate on the shortfall is to be levied if the shortfall does not exceed 10 per cent of the absolute amount of cash balance required to be maintained. For example, if a bank is required to maintain CRR at ₹ 100 crore, but it actually maintains it at ₹ 90 crore (*i.e.,* within 10% limit) no penal interest is to be charged on shortfall of ₹ 10 crore. On the other hand, banks are paid interest on the eligible amount of CRR actually held by them on a graduated scale as follows:

Shortfall during a fortnight as % of the absolute amount of CRR required to be maintained (up to and inclusive of)	*Rate of Interest payable on amount of above statutory minimum of 3% actually maintained (% p.a.)*
0	10.50
2.0	10.00
4.0	9.25
6.0	8.50
8.0	7.00
10.0	6.00
over 10.0	0.00

☞ Recent Changes in Statutory Cash Reserve with Reserve Bank

The Reserve Bank of India accepted the recommendation of the Narasimham Committee on the financial sector that Reserve Bank of India should consider progressively reducing the CRR from the high level. In its opinion the Reserve Bank should have the flexibility to operate the instrument of CRR to serve the monetary policy objectives.

In its credit policy for the first half of 1993-94 the Reserve Bank of India reduced CRR maintained by scheduled commercial banks from 15% to 14% in two phases. Certificates of Deposits issued by banks over the pre-May 1992 level were made subject to CRR.

The main objective of this reduction was to enlarge the availability of credit to trade and industry which was felt necessary for strong industrial revival. Such reduction was expected to augment lendable resources of banks by about ₹ 2,800 crore, for meeting the credit requirements of the productive sectors of the economy.

In its Credit Policy for the first half of 1994-95, the Reserve Bank of India stepped up CRR by 1 per cent point. It has been raised in phases of 14.5% on June 11, to 14.75% on July 9 and finally to 15% on August 6, 1994. Reserve Bank has explained that this increase in CRR intended to be a short-term measure to curb inflation and to neutralise the excess liquidity in the economy and is not a deviation from the policy of reducing CRR over a period of time.

With effect from January 7, 1995 banks are required to maintain at least 85 per cent of the CRR balance required to be maintained on each of the first 13 days of the reporting fortnight. Otherwise they will not be paid interest for that/those day/days, even though there is no shortfall in the maintenance of CRR. Banks are allowed to maintain less than 85% of the required cash balances to the required level.

This step was taken to avoid wider fluctuation in the demand for funds in the call money market by banks during the closing days of the fortnight. Banks used to maintain lower cash balances with the Reserve Bank during the earlier part of a fortnight and used to borrow heavily during the closing days of the fortnight to meet the CRR requirement.

The Reserve Bank of India reduced Cash Reserve Ratio substantially in stages from 15% in 1995 to 10% in January 1997. These changes took place in view of the changing requirements of the banking system and in compliance with the recommendation of the Narasimham Committee. The CRR was reduced as following during this period:

November 11, 1955	15.0% to 14.5%
December 9, 1995	14.5% to 14.0%
April 27, 1996	14.0% to 13.5%
May 11, 1996	13.5% to 13.0%
July 6, 1996	13.0% to 12.0%
October 26, 1996	12.0% to 11.5%
November 9, 1996	11.5% to 11.0%
January 4, 1997	11.0% to 10.5%
January 18, 1997	10.5% to 10.0%

In April 1997, Reserve Bank of India made the following modifications in the requirements of CRR:

(a) Net inter-bank liabilities of a bank (i.e., liabilities of a bank towards all other banks as reduced by the liabilities of all other banks to the banks concerned) were exempted from CRR. This step was taken to develop term money market.

(b) CRR @ 10% imposed on the increase in liabilities under FCNR(B) Scheme, NRE (Accounts) Scheme, and NRNR Accounts Scheme over the level outstanding as on April 11, 1997.

On October 21, 1997, Reserve Bank of India announced reduction in CRR by 2 percentage points to 8% in eight phases of 0.25% each. Consequently it declined to 9.5% on November 22, 1997 after the second phase of reduction. But on December 6, 1997, CRR was hiked to 10% in the face of the falling external value of the Rupee. Reserve Bank has also done away with CRR requirement on NRE and NRNR rupee deposits to attract more dollar funds through these deposits. CRR was raised to push up the cost to short-term money to break the arbitrage between the money and foreign exchange markets.

CRR was further raised to 10.5% on January 17, 1998. On 23rd March, 1998, Reserve Bank announced a cut in CRR by half a percentage point to 10% in two phases of 0.25% each. Thus, with effect from 11th April, 1998, CRR was reduced to 10% of net domestic liabilities.

During the last two years, Reserve Bank has further reduced the cash reserve requirement of the scheduled banks. On 6th November, 1999, CRR was reduced to 9.5% and further to 9% with effect from 20th November, 1999. With effect from April 1, 2000, cash reserve requirement was further reduced to 8%, which augmented the resources of the banks by ₹ 7,200 crore. This also facilitated the government borrowing scheduled for the current year.

On July 21, 2000, Reserve Bank of India announced an increase in CRR by 0.5 percentage point to 8.5% in two stages by 0.25% point each effective from July 29 and August 12, 2000. The obvious objective of this rise was to absorb resources of scheduled commercial banks to the extent of ₹ 1,900 crore at each stage. This step was taken keeping in view the developments in international and domestic financial markets (including foreign exchange market), CRR was reduced by 0.5% point to 8% in two stages, *i.e.,* by 0.25% point w.e.f. February 24 and March 10, 2001. This measure released approximately ₹ 2,050 crore at each stage.

For the computation of CRR to be maintained by banks during a fortnight a significant change was introduced by Reserve Bank of India effective from November 6, 1999. Till then, banks were required to maintain CRR on an average daily basis during a fortnight, on the basis of their net demand and time liabilities as on Friday of the previous fortnight. Reserve Bank introduced a lagged reserve system, whereby banks have to maintain CRR on the net demand and time liabilities of the second preceding fortnight. For example, during the fortnight (17th June to 30th June, 2000) banks were required to base their CRR on the Net Demand and Time Liabilities as on 2nd June, 2000 (instead of

16th June earlier). With this change banks now get sufficient time to assess their exact liabilities and the corresponding reserve requirements.

In the credit policy announced in April, 2000, Reserve Bank of India provided further flexibility to the banks in maintaining CRR. Hitherto banks were required to maintain at least 85% of the CRR balance required to be maintained on each of the first 13 days of the reporting fortnight. This percentage has been reduced from 85 to 65 with effect from May 6, 2000.

In its credit policy announced on April 19, 2001, Reserve Bank of India announced the following two modifications as regards Cash Reserve Ratio, which will come into force with effect from August 11, 2001:

(i) The percentage of daily minimum requirement has been reduced from 65% to 50% for the first seven days of the reporting fortnight. In the second week of the fortnight it will continue to be 65% for all the seven days including the reporting Friday. It is expected to reduce volatility in the call money market. Banks will have flexibility in holding reserves depending upon their intra-period cash flows.

(ii) Inter-bank term liabilities with maturity of 15 days and above have been exempted from the prescription of minimum CRR of 3 per cent. It is expected to help in developing inter-bank term money market.

The Reserve Bank of India further reduced the CRR by 0.5% point to 7.5 per cent effective May 19, 2001, thus releasing ₹ 4,500 crore extra cash into the system.

CRR has been reduced from 5% to 4.75% effective from Nov. 16, 2002. With this reduction CRR has been reduced by as much as 3.75% over the past two years.

☞ Statutory Liquidity Requirements

The Reserve Bank has taken certain measures to prevent banks from offsetting the impact of variable reserve requirements by liquidating Government security holdings. According to Section 24 of the Banking Regulation Act, banks have to maintain liquid assets in cash, gold or unencumbered approved securities amounting to not less than 20 per cent of their total demand and time liabilities. This enables them to liquidate their Government security holdings when their cash reserve requirements are raised and thus to minimise the impact of this instrument. The Banking Regulation Act was amended in 1962, requiring all banks to maintain a minimum amount of liquid assets equal to not less than 25 per cent of their demand and time liabilities in India, exclusive of the balances maintained by them under Section 42 of the Reserve Bank of India Act in the case of scheduled banks, and exclusive of the cash balances maintained under Section 18 of the Banking Regulation Act in the case of non-scheduled banks. By this Amendment, it was ensured that, with every increase in the cash reserve requirements, the overall liquidity obligations were also correspondingly raised. The Statutory Liquidity Ratio (SLR) which was 34% since Dec. 1978, was raised to 35% in two phases — 34% from Sept. 25, 1981, and 35% from Oct. 30, 1981.

With the Banking Laws (Amendment) Act, 1983, the Reserve Bank has been empowered to step up this ratio up to 40 per cent. The Statutory Liquidity Ratio was increased to 36% per cent from Sept. 1, 1984. During 1985 the SLR was again raised to 37 per cent from July 6 and 37.5 per cent from 25 April, 1987 and 38 per cent from Jan. 2, 1988. It was further raised to 38.5 per cent with effect from Sept. 22, 1990.

(a) Basis for Maintenance of SLR

SLR is to be maintained as at the close of business everyday. It means that SLR is to be maintained on a daily basis. It should not be less than 25 per cent of the net demand and time liabilities as obtaining on the last Friday of the second preceding fortnight. For instance, during the period from Saturday, the 24th March, 1990 to Friday the 6th April, 1990 SLR will have to be maintained each day, at the prescribed rate, of the net Demand and Time Liabilities (DTL) as on Friday, the 9th March 1990 (*i.e.*, the last Friday of the second preceding fortnight). The Reserve Bank is empowered to raise the percentage of SLR to a higher level but not exceeding 40%.

(b) Valuation of Securities

(*i*) The 1983 amendment not only conferred on the Reserve Bank the power to increase S.L.R. but has also given it the power to decide the mode of valuation of the securities held by the banks. Up to 1983 the Act required that gold and approved securities were to be valued at a price not exceeding the current market price. According to the amended section the approved securities are to be valued at a price determined in accordance with such one or more of or combination of the following methods of valuation, namely, valuation with reference to cost price, market price, book value, or face value as may be specified by the Reserve Bank from time-to-time. Thus, the Reserve Bank possesses the power to specify the mode of valuation of approved securities. As regards the market price, the date of such price is also to be notified by the Reserve Bank in respect of any class or classes of securities. It may be the price as on the date of issue of notification or as on any earlier or later date.

(*ii*) Approved securities means the securities in which the trustees may invest trust moneys under Clauses (a) to (d) of Section 20 of the India Trusts Act, 1882 and such securities which are authorised by the Central Government under Clauses (f) Section 20 of the said Act.

(*iii*) For the purpose of this Section unencumbered approved securities of a banking company include its approved securities lodged with other institutions for securing an advance or any other credit arrangement to the extent to which such securities have not been drawn against or availed of. For example, if a banking company has taken a loan of ₹ 20,000 only and pledged Government securities of the market value of ₹ 50,000, the balance of the value of the securities (₹ 50,000 – ₹ 20,000 = ₹ 30,000) would be counted as the value of unencumbered securities for the purpose of Section 24.

(c) Liabilities in India

For the purpose of this section the term liabilities in India shall not include the following:

(*i*) the paid-up capital or the reserve or any credit balance in the profit and loss account of the banking company; and

(*ii*) any advance taken from the Reserve Bank, State Bank of India, Industrial Development Bank of India, NABARD or any other bank notified by the Central Government (Explanation to Section 18).

(d) SLR shall exclude CRR

The banking companies are required to maintain liquid assets including cash, under this section, in addition to:

(*i*) the statutory reserves (*i.e.*, the average daily balance) which a scheduled bank is required to maintain under Section 42 of the Reserve Bank of India Act, 1934; and

(*ii*) the cash reserves which a non-scheduled bank is required to maintain under Section 18 of the Banking Regulation Act, 1949.

(e) Definition of Cash Maintained in India

The following shall be included in the term cash maintained in India under this section:

(i) Any balances maintained by a scheduled bank with the Reserve Bank in excess of the balances required to be maintained by it under Section 42. For example, if a banking company maintains an average balance of ₹ 1.5 lakh with the Reserve Bank under Section 42 while it is required to maintain ₹ 1 lakh only, average excess amount of ₹ 50,000 shall be deemed as cash for the purpose of Section 24.

(ii) The 'net balance' in current accounts maintained in India by a Scheduled Bank: The concept of net balance in current accounts was introduced in 1983 so as to reduce the balances of a bank in current accounts with other banks to the extent the bank itself has borrowed from other banks.

(iii) The cash or balances maintained by a non-scheduled bank with itself or with Reserve Bank of India, or by way of net balance in current account excess of the requirement of Section 18.

(iv) The deposit made by a banking company incorporated outside India with the Reserve Bank under Section 11.

(v) Any balances maintained by a Regional Rural Bank in call or fixed deposit with its Sponsor Bank.

(f) Submission of Monthly Return on Form VIII

Every banking company shall submit to the Reserve Bank a monthly return showing particulars of its assets maintained in accordance with this Section and its demand and time liabilities in India at the close of business on each alternate Friday during the month. This return shall be submitted within 20 days after the end of the month. Besides, the Reserve Bank may also require a banking company to submit a return showing these figures on each day or one month.

(g) Penalties for Default in Maintenance of Liquid Assets

The clause relating to imposition of penalties was inserted in 1993. Now, for calculating the amount of liquid assets, the base shall be the figures of demand and time liabilities in India as on the last Friday of the second preceding fortnight. If on any alternate Friday (or preceding working day if Friday is a holiday), the amount maintained by a banking company at the close of business on that day falls below the minimum prescribed under this section, such banking company shall be liable to pay to the Reserve Bank, in respect of that day's default, penal interest for that day at the rate of 3% per annum above the Bank Rate on the amount of shortfall.

If default occurs again on the next succeeding alternate Friday and continues on succeeding alternate Fridays, the rate of penal interest shall be increased to 5% per annum above the Bank Rate on each shortfall in respect of that alternate Friday and each succeeding alternate Friday on which the default continues.

Even after penal interest at 5% above Bank rate becomes payable, if the default still occurs, every director, manager or secretary of the banking company, who is knowingly and wilfully a party to the default, shall be punishable with fine up to ₹ 500 and with a further fine which may extend to ₹ 500 for each subsequent alternate Friday on which the default continues. Reserve Bank is also empowered not to charge penal interest if it is satisfied with the reason for default.

The Reserve Bank of India has notified the method of valuation of securities as follows:

(1) Before the enforcement of the Amendment Act of 1983, those securities which were held by the banks to maintain the minimum SLR of 25% (inclusive of cash and gold) were valued at the market price on that date or at market price prevailing on the date on which compliance as to SLR was reckoned.

The balance of the securities held on March 29, 1995 were valued at book value, less provision, if any, made to the extent of depreciation in the market price as on March 29, 1985 or at current market price.

(2) Securities acquired after March 29, 1985 shall be valued at face value or cost price, whichever is lower, and will continue to be valued so, irrespective of change in their market value.

Though before the enforcement of amendment of Section 24 in March 1985, the Banking Regulation Act did not empower the Reserve Bank to enhance the Statutory Liquidity Requirement from the statutory minimum level of 25% ; in fact, exercising its power of moral suasion, it had in the past raised SLR successively to higher levels. It stood at 36% when the Amendment Act of 1993 was enforced in March 1985.

After the enforcement of the Banking Laws (Amendment) Act, 1983, the Statutory Liquidity Ratio has been raised to higher levels as follows:

From 36% to 36.5% of the net DTL, with effect from June 8, 1985.

From 36.5% to 37% with effect from July 6, 1985.

From 37.0% to 37.5% with effect from April 25, 1987.

From 37.5% to 38% with effect from January 2, 1988.

The Reserve Bank of India further raised SLR by half a percentage point from 38 per cent of net demand and time liabilities to 38.5 per cent with effect from September 22, 1990. This step was taken as usual to curb monetary expansion and to moderate the pace of reserve money creation.

The deposit liabilities of the banks from Non-resident Indians under the Non-resident External Rupee Accounts and Foreign Currency (non-resident) Accounts have been subject to SLR at a lower rate of 25%. It has also been raised to 30% with effect from July 28, 1990.

☞ Effect of Higher SLR

The Reserve Bank has used the instrument of SLR as a credit control method, because with every increase in SLR, the banks are required to maintain a larger portion of their funds in liquid assets, mainly the Government and other approved securities. Consequently, the loanable resources of the banks contract and their capacity to grant credit is reduced correspondingly. Thus, by raising the SLR, bank funds are diverted from loans and advances to investment in Government and other approved securities. The instrument of SLR thus boosts up the flow of funds in the gilt-edged securities and ensures the success of the floatation of loans by the Government.

As the yield on gilt-edged securities was much lower than the interest charged on loans and advances, banks' profitability was adversely affected as a consequence of a rise in SLR.

☞ Reduction in SLR in 1992

Accepting the recommendation of the Narasimham Committee, the Reserve Bank of India reduced SLR to 30% on the incremental deposits over the level as on April 1, 1992. Deposits as on that date continued to be subject to SLR at the existing rate of 38.5%. SLR was reduced by 0.75% on this category of deposits in 3 stages of 0.25 per cent each beginning with fortnight dated January 9, February 6 and March 6, 1993.

During 1993, Reserve Bank of India further stepped down SLR two times. First, it was reduced from 37.75% to 36.75% in four phases; from October 16, 1993 it was further reduced to 34.75% on the level of outstanding liabilities as on September 17, 1993. In respect of any increase in liabilities above September 17, 1993 level SLR was reduced to 25%, SLR was reduced to 34.25% on August 20, 1994 and further to 33.75% on September 17, 1994. The base date for SLR on domestic NDTL was brought forward from September 17, 1993 to September 30, 1994 and SLR was fixed at 31.5%.

With effect from April 26, 1997, all scheduled commercial banks are exempted from maintenance of SLR on their net liabilities to the banking system (just as in case of CRR).

With effect from October 25, 1997, all scheduled commercial banks are required to maintain a uniform statutory liquidity ratio of 25 per cent of their net demand and time liabilities. This is the minimum stipulated rate under Section 24 of the Banking Regulation Act, 1949. The reduction in SLR over these years has resulted in the improvement in profitability of banks as they have utilised their funds more profitably in loans and advances.

☞ Differential Rates and the Quota System

The Reserve Bank has also experienced with the system of differential rates for the borrowing of scheduled banks with a view to avoiding an increase in the general Bank Rate and overcoming the effect of variable reserve ratios. The banks used to resort to large borrowings from the Reserve Bank, which penalised such excess borrowing by raising its cost. A straight increase in the Bank Rate, it was felt, might have adverse repercussions on the gilt-edged market. Therefore, before 1960-64, a system of lending rates on a slab basis was operated by the Bank. Under this system, banks were given a basic quota equal to specific percentage of statutory reserve requirements. Up to this quota, the banks could borrow at the Reserve Bank Rate. Additional quotas attracted higher rates. This system was not considered to be sufficiently effective in restraining bank borrowings from the Reserve Bank. In the first place, the assets distribution of banks was not considered under the system. Secondly, the rise in the cost of borrowing was small and banks could easily pass on this higher cost to their customers.

☞ Net Liquidity Ratio System

Under these circumstances, a new system of sliding scale of interest rates based on the net liquidity ratios of the borrowing banks was introduced in September 1964.

☞ Net Liquidity

This is defined as the total of a banker's cash and balances with the Reserve Bank and other notified banks, balances in current account with other banks and investments in Government and other approved securities, less borrowings from the Reserve Bank, the State Bank of India and the Industrial Development Bank. In other words, *net liquidity means:*

(A) Statutory Liquidity Ratio:

(*i*) Total of the bank's cash ......

(*ii*) Balances with the Reserve bank ......

(*iii*) Balances with other notified banks ......

(*iv*) Balances in Current A/c with other banks ......

(v) Investments in Government and other approved securities ......

Total ....

(B) Less Borrowings From:

(i) The Reserve Bank ......

(ii) The State Bank ......

(iii) The Industrial Development Bank

Net Liquidity ......

The minimum net liquidity ratio was put at 28 per cent and for every percentage point drop in the ratio, the cost of borrowing from the Reserve Bank on the entire amount went up by half per cent. Along with this, a ceiling of 9 per cent was prescribed for the lending rate of foreign banks and larger Indian scheduled banks with demand and time liabilities of ₹ 50 crore or above to discourage banks from borrowing from the Bank at higher rates.

In May 1970, the minimum net liquidity ratio was fixed at 33 per cent and the rate charged on borrowings from the Reserve Bank rose by one per cent above the Bank Rate for every drop of one point or a fraction thereof in the net liquidity ratio. The penal rates are charged only on borrowings in excess of the amount which a bank is entitled to raise from the Reserve Bank at the Bank Rate or at the concessional rate, except for temporary periods. If the excess borrowings continue beyond a week, a higher rate applies, the actual rate being determined by the level of the net liquidity ratio. At present the Net Liquidity Ratio is 39%.

☞ Selective Credit Controls

The primary objective of *selective credit controls* has been to prevent speculative hoarding of commodities like foodgrains and essential raw materials so as to prevent or control inflationary pressures in these areas. Under Sections 21, 35 and 36 of the Banking Companies Act of 1949, the Reserve Bank has powers to control the advances given by banks. On May 17, 1956, it issued a directive to banks to refrain from excessive lending against commodities in general; not to grant fresh advances or credit limits to individual parties in excess of ₹ 50,000 against paddy and rice, and to raise the existing margins in respect of loans against paddy and rice by 10 per cent. Similar restrictions were imposed in 1957, 1958, 1959, 1962, 1964, 1965, 1966 and 1967 on the advances of banks against the security of commodities. The overall effect of these various directives has been more preventive than curative. Selective credit controls have played only a negative part, in the sense that they are applied with the sole objective of curbing excessive advances to particular sectors of the economy. Recent experiments in advanced countries suggest that they can be used to make credit more purpose-oriented.

The advances made by banks against the following commodities are covered by selective credit controls:

1. Foodgrains
2. Vanaspati
3. Oilseeds and Oil
4. Sugar, Khandsari and Gur
5. Cotton
6. Cotton Textiles.

The following three methods are used in selective credit control:

1. Fixation of Party-wise Ceiling on Credit

After taking into consideration the crop prospects, supply position and price trends credit limits are fixed on party-wise basis. The banks are required to seek prior permission of the Reserve Bank for:

(a) granting loans to new borrowers, and

(b) increasing the credit limits of existing borrowers.

(c) imposition of minimum margin. In case of advances against commodities subject to selective control, higher margins are prescribed in order to restrict to borrowing capacity of the borrowers. With higher margin, a borrower can get less credit from banks against a certain quantity of stock and thus can finance only a smaller part of it through bank finance. Moreover, different margins may be prescribed for different types of borrowers against the security of the same commodity. A higher margin is generally fixed for those borrowers whose need for credit is not so urgent or larger flow of credit to whom it is likely to aggravate the price situation. For example, minimum margins were prescribed for advances against foodgrains, pulses and oilseeds (w.e.f. 19th October, 87) at 45% for processing units/mills and against warehouse receipt and at 60% for others.

2. Fixation of Minimum Lending Rate

Minimum lending rate has been prescribed in case of most of the commodities. But the following types of loans and advances are exempt from the minimum lending rates:

1. Loans granted under DIR (Differential Interest Rate) scheme.
2. Loans for financing exports.
3. Loans for financing food procurement operations of FCI or other agencies.
4. Loans covered under the schemes of Credit Guarantee Corporation of India.
5. Loans against approved securities as defined in Section 5(a) of Banking Regulation Act, 1949.
6. Loans to bank employees, cooperative banks or other banking institutions, etc.

Credit Monitoring Arrangement

RBI exercise a great deal of control over the functioning of commercial banks in the country. These guidelines relate to the key areas of deposits, cash management and credit. Earlier to the introduction of Credit Monitoring Aggrangement (CMA), banks were required to obtain the Reserve Banks's prior permission for providing credit beyond stipulated levels under its Credit Authorisation Scheme (CAS).

☞ Credit Authorisation Scheme

The CAS was introduced by the RBI in November 1965. Originally banks were required to obtain RBI prior authorisation for sanctioning any fresh WC limit of ₹ 1 crore or more to any single party or any limit that would take the total limits enjoyed by such a party from the entire banking system to ₹ 1 crore or more on secured and or unsecured basis. This scheme was modified from time-to-time in the light of developments in the economy. In July 1987, the banks, under the 'Fast Track' procedure, were permitted to release the entire additional amount of WC finance sanctioned by their Boards to CAS borrowers provided they complied with the basic disciplines of *(i)* maintainning the current ratio of 1.33, *(ii)* submission of statements under the QIS, and *(iii)* adherence to inventory/receivable's norms.

☞ Credit Monitoring Arrangement

With the improvement in the financial discipline followed by banks, the system of prior authorisation under the CAS for sanction of WC limits above the cut-off points was withdrawn and in its place a scheme of CMA was introduced on 10th October, 1988. CMA involves post sanction scrutiny of proposals relating to sanction of term loans as well as WC limits beyond stipulated levels. The cut-off points for reporting to the RBI has been increased in December 1992 from ₹ 5 crore to ₹ 10 crore for fund based WC facilities and from ₹ 2 crore to ₹ 5 crore for term loans.

CMA is practically administered by Central Office of RBI at Mumbai through its Industrial and Export Credit Department. The reporting under CMA is to be done by the Head Office of a bank or by Regional/Zonal Office of the bank at Mumbai. From 1st April, 1991 new forms have been prescribed for assessment of WC requirement. Briefy the forms are asunder:

Form I : Particulars of the existing proposed limits from the banking system

Form II : Operating Statement (Profit and Loss A/c)

Form III : Analysis of Balance Sheet

Form IV : Comparative statement of current assets and current liabilities

Form V : Computation of MPBF for WC

Form VI : Funds Flow statement

The above statements contain data for:

(a) Two years preceding the current year.

(b) Current year estimates.

(c) Projections for following years.

FINANCIAL STATEMENT

The classification of assets and liabilities as per the balance sheet drawn under the provisions of the Company Act, 1956 differs from the bankers, which is based on the guidelines prescribed by the RBI. As per the balance sheet, the classification is done under the following main heads:

Liabilities	**Assets**
Share Capital	Fixed Assets
Reserves and Surplus	Investments
Secured Loans	Current Assets, Loans and Advances
Unsecured Loans	Miscellaneous Expenditure and Losses
Current Liabilities and Provisions	

The classification adopted by the bankers is done under the following broad heads:

Liabilities	**Assets**
Current Liabilities	Current Assets
Term Liabilities	Fixed Assets
Owned Funds	Other Non-current Assets
	Intangible Assets

The balance sheet classification is sometimes given in the columnar form under sources of funds and uses of funds. Items like capital, reserves, secured and unsecured loans are shown under sources of funds, while the fixed assets, investments and current assets are shown under applications of funds. At times instead of showing current assets and current liabilities separately, a figure 'Net Current Assets' is shown which is equal to total current assets minus total current liabilities.

The classification adopted by the bankers differ from that as per the Company Act in the following respects:

(1) Share Capital: All accounts of share capital are included under one head as per the format of balance sheet under the Company Act. Preference shares redeemable within 1 year are treated by bankers as current liabilities while those redeemable between 1 year and 12 years are treated as term liabilities and beyond 12 years. They form a part of the net worth Preference shares redeemable within 12 years and are not treated as equity but are classified as debt as they have to be redeemed or repaid.

(2) Secured and Unsecured: The balance sheet classification is done on the basis of security and both term loan and WC advances are clubbed together. Also debentures are included as secured loans in the balance sheet. The classification of loans adopted by the bankers is generally based on the period if the loan is repayable in one year, irrespective of the security, it is classified under current liabilities and that repayable after one year is classified under term liabilities. It would be correct to say that bankers classify under current liabilities all WC advances (including WC term loans) and instalments of term loan/deferred payment credits/debentures which are repayable within one year.

(3) Bills Purchases and Discounted: These are normally shown as contingent liabilities or indicated in the footnote in the balance sheet. As per the classification followed by the bankers, the amount involved is treated as short-term borrowings from bank under current liabilities and as receivables under current assets.

(4) Current Liabilities and Provisions: The classification in the Company Act format does not meet fully with the banker's requirements. For example, details of statutory liabilities like exise duty, sales tax, obligations towards workers considered as statutory may not be separately shown in the Company Act format, while these have to be specifically indicated in the classification followed by the bankers.

(5) Fixed Assets: Under fixed assets goodwill, patent rights, etc., are also included as per the Company Act format. However, as per the banker's classification, these items are classified as intangible items. As such while working out tangible net worth, they are reduced from the figures of net worth.

(6) Investments: Under this item only govt. and trustee securities and fixed deposits with banks are normally included as per the bank's classification. The investment in govt. and trustee securities and fixed deposits are made for long-term purpose like sinking fund, gratuity fund, etc., Such investments are excluded from investment under current assets. As per Company Act format, shares held by the borrowing companies in their subsidiaries or others are classified as non-current assets.

(7) Current Liabilities: The main items included by the bank under this head are:

- *(a)* Short-term borrowings from banks (including bills purchased and discounted and excess borrowings spliced on repayment basis, i.e., WCTL).
- *(b)* Short-term borrowings from others.
- *(c)* Deposits (maturing within I year).

  Deposits maturing after I year are to be classified under term liabilities. It is agreed that deposits due within I year need not be classified as current liabilities as these deposits would be renewed but this argument is not correct. Manufacturers of automobiles, two-wheelers, etc., who accept deposits while booking orders for new vehicles are required under the govt. rules to earmark a part of such VW in certain approved securities, etc.

(d) Sundry Creditors (trade).

(e) Unsecured loans.

Unsecured loans taken from the Directors of the borrowing company, where no period is mentioned, are to be treated as current liabilities.

(f) Advance payment from customers.

In the case of construction company, the advance payments received against work-in-progress may be set off and only the net position should be shown either as a current liability or a current asset.

(g) Interest and other charges accrued but not due for payment.

(h) Provision for taxation.

(8) Dividend Payable: If dividend is only recommended and not appropriated from profit, pending approval of shareholders in the AGM, the amount may be shown hereafter deducting it from general reserve and/or surplus in the profit and loss account.

(9) Other Statutory Liabilities (due within 1 year): When provision for excise duty is made it should be classified as current liability. The disputed excise liability shown as contingent liability will not be treated as current liability unless it has been collected or provided for in the accounts of the borrowers. Provision for disputed excise duty may be classified under current liabilities unless the amount is payable in instalment. Where the provision made for disputed excise duty is invested separately, in fixed deposits with banks, such provision may be set-off against the relative investment. Instalment of term loans/redeemable preference shares (due within one year).

(10) Other current liabilities and provisions: In case specific provisions have not been made for known liabilities like dividend payable, tax payable, etc., estimates thereof should be made for eventual payment during the year and the amounts, though not provided should be shown as current liabilities.

(11) Term Liabilities:

(a) Debentures (not maturing within one year)

(b) Redeemable preference share (not maturing within one year but of maturity)

(c) Term loans (exclusive of installment payable within one year)

(d) Deferred payment credits (exclusive of installments payable within one year)

(e) Term deposits (repayable after one year)

(f) Other term liabilities.

(12) Net Worth:

(a) Ordinary share capital

(b) Preference share capital (maturing after 12 years)

(c) General reserve (excluding provision)

(d) Development rebate reserve

(e) Other reserve (excluding provision)

(f) Surplus (+) or deficit in profit and loss account

(13) Current Assets:

(*a*) Cash and bank balances

(*b*) Investment (other than long-term investment, *e.g.*, sinking fund, gratuity funds, etc.)

(*i*) Govt. and other trustee securities

(*ii*) Fixed deposits with bank.

Investment in shares in subsidiaries and other companies should not be included under this head. Shares in which the borrowing company has made investments may be highly marketable but such investments are to be treated as non-current assets of bank finance.

(14) Receivables:

(*a*) Receivables other than deferred and export receivables (including bills purchased and discounted by banks).

(*b*) Export receivables (including bills purchases and discounted by banks). Bills purchased or discounted though not shown as liabilities or assets in the balance sheet should be classified as such as indicated earlier. Under CAS forms receivables realisable within 12 months may be classified under current assets. However, some banks taking conservative view, do not treat receivables outstanding for more than six months as current assets.

Receivables from subsidiary/sister/associate concern will be included, provided these receivables arise in the normal course of business and represent dues for sales made to them in the ordinary course of business on usual credit term.

As per the extent instructions, export receivables are to be included in the receivables but for the purpose of the calculations the maximun permissible level of banking finance, export receivables are to be deducted from the total current assets for arriving at the minimum stipulated net working capital (25% of total current assets under the second method of lending).

In case, the excise duty component is very large, the level of receivables may become distorted in relation to the past trend. In order to make a meaningful study of the position, data related to the excise duty component may be furnished separately. Similarly, if the sales tax element included is large, separate figure thereof may also be furnished.

(15) Inventory:

(*a*) Raw materials (Including stores and other items used in the process of manufaturing).

(*b*) Stock-in-process: Except in industry where the process cycle is long and involve various stages, the classsification is fairly uncomplicated.

(*c*) Finished Goods: In certain cases, where the excise duty component is very large (*e.g.*, tobacco industry), including of duty paid of stock in finished goods and relating its cost of sales which does not include excise duty creates distortion in the level of holding. In such a case, data related excise duty may be shown separately.

(*d*) Other consumable spares: Normally loose tools or spares for machinery are not included but unused dies in a printing press or in extrusion plant causes a problem. If utilised within the maximun period of one year, such items may be classified under this head. Spares should not be linked to the inventory level but we should go by the consumption pattern in the industry. Spares should not excced 12 months consumption for imported items and 9 months consumption for indigeneous items. Beyond this level they should be considered as non-current assets and shown under non-current assets.

"Dead Inventory", *i.e.,* slow moving or obsolete items should not be classiffed as current assets. In certain industries where the operating cycle is beyond 12 months, inventories held during such longer operating cycle will be treated as current assets.

(16) Fixed Assets:

(a) Gross Block (land, buildings, machinery, construction in progress, etc.)

(b) Depreciation to date.

(c) Net Block.

Depreciation will normally be included in actual balances of depreciation. If, however, it is not provided and the arrears of depreciation are indicated in the notes to the balance sheet, extreme conservatism will dictate that such arrears should be included and to that extent, accumulated profits or general reserves would be reduced. But in actual practice, this is not done. However, this fact should be amplified in a footnote.

(17) Other Non-current Assets:

(a) Investments/book debts/advances, deposits, which are not current assets.

(b) Advances to the other firms or companies.

(c) Non-consumables' stores.

(18) Intangible Assets: (Patents, Goodwill, Preliminary and formation expenses, Bad/debts not provided for, etc.)

The basic objectives of CMA is to scientifically arrive at:

- MPBF
- Fund position of the borrower.
- Evaluate the proposal in light of two years' performance.
- Margin of 25% to be brought in from long-term sources.

While calculation MPBF current asset and current liability levels are automatically assessed. The operating statement (Form II) gives a good idea of the cost component and accruals from the operations.

The important ratios in a CMA statement are:

1. Net profit percentage
2. Current Ratio
3. Leverage Ratio
4. Returned profit as a percentage of net profit
5. Net sales to total tangible assets
6. Individual stock level in terms of months.

Thus, the CMA lays a special emphasis on short-term solvency. It is very easy to assume that by showing higher current asset levels more bank borrowing could be requested, but by doing so the following implications arise:

1. The holdings levels have to be justified in relations with the industry.
2. Margin money requirement will go up. Bank always have data of companies in the same line of business and any abnormal deviation is easily noticeable.

☞ Direct Action

In accordance with Section 36 of the Banking Companies Act, 1949, the Reserve Bank may caution or prohibit banking companies generally or any individual banking company in particular from entering into any particular transaction or class of transactions. It has now the power to inspect any banking company and its books and accounts. On a report by the Reserve Bank, the Central Government may prohibit any banking company from receiving fresh deposits or direct the Reserve Bank to apply for the winding-up of the banking company.

☞ Publicity and Moral Persuasion

Publicity has been used as a fruitful weapon in some of the advanced countries, specially America. Its scope in India for controlling the credit of member banks must obviously be very limited. The reason is that these banks do not yet use central banking credit to an appreciable extent. But normal persuasion, in the sense of effecting an improvement in banking standards and practices as a result of representation or instructions offered by the Reserve Bank, can be, and has indeed been of considerable practical effect.

With the advent of planned economic development in the country in 1951, the range of the Reserve Bank's functions has steadily widened. It now performs a variety of developmental and promotional functions, which were previously considered to be outside the purview of a central bank. The Reserve Bank is now responsible not only for the regulation of the banking system, but also for the institutionalisation of savings through the promotion of the banking habit, extension of the banking system and the establishment or promotion of new specialised financing agencies.

The Reserve Bank of India has taken the initiative to set up —

(a) The Deposit Insurance Corporation in 1962, and

(b) The Unit Trust of India in 1964.

Since its inception, the Bank has also been responsible for the provision and expansion of agricultural credit facilities. It has not only encouraged and helped cooperatives to provide short-term agricultural credit, but has also established a separate institution, the Agricultural Refinance Corporation, for the provision of long-term finance.

With a view to increasing the facilities for the provision of industrial finance, the Reserve Bank took the initiative to assist in the establishment of special financing institutions such as the Industrial Finance Corporation of India and State Financial Corporations, and also setting up the Industrial Development Bank of India as its wholly-owned subsidiary.

During the last two decades, wide powers have been given to the Reserve Bank to control and supervise the banking system by keeping in view the country's needs for economic development. The original Act, which gave regulatory powers to the Reserve Bank, was the Banking Companies Act, 1949. This Act has been amended several times in 1960, 1963 and 1965. The title of the Act also changed to "Banking Regulation Act" and "Banking Loans (Application to Cooperative Societies) Act, 1965". These amendments empowered the Reserve Bank to:

(i) Amalgamate banks;

(ii) Restrict the control exercised by particular groups of persons over the affairs of banks and to restrict loans and advances as well as guarantees given by banks to or on behalf of any one company, firm, association of persons or individuals;

(iii) Control the appointment and removal of a bank's executive personnel.

In the last few years, our banking system has made commendable progress, both functionally and geographically. Nevertheless, there are many rural and semi-urban areas which are without banking facilities.

Moreover, a major part of bank advances are still directed towards: *(a)* large and medium-scale industries, and *(b)* big and established business houses, while such priority sectors as agriculture, small-scale industries, and exports have not been getting their due share. To bring about the required change in bank lending, a scheme of *social control* was initiated in December 1967. The Boards of Directors of commercial banks were reconstituted, providing for a majority of members having specialised knowledge or practical experience in the fields of economics, law, cooperation, agriculture and rural economy, banking, small-scale industry, etc. In addition, the chairmen of banks who were to be appointed as whole-time executives had to be professional bankers and not industrialists or businessmen. The banks were also prohibited from advancing loans to their directors or concerns in which their directors were interested. The Reserve Bank was given further power over the management of banks.

A National Credit Council was set up in February 1968 with the Finance Minister as Chairman and the Governor of the Reserve Bank as Vice-chairman, and consisting of representatives of industry, trade, agriculture, banking, the cooperative sector and professionals, including economists, to assess periodically the demand for bank credit and to provide guidelines for a purposeful and equitable distribution of Bank credit.

☞ Incentives for Priority Sectors

The Reserve Bank has provided certain incentives in the form of concessional finance to banks to increase their lending to such priority sectors as agriculture, small-scale industries and exports.

In 1958, the Reserve Bank extended the Bill Market Scheme to export bills to enable banks to extend credit facilities to exporters on a more liberal basis. The Bank introduced the Export Bills Credit Scheme in March 1963. Under this scheme, advances could be made by the Reserve Bank to scheduled banks against their promissory notes repayable on demand and upon their declarations of holdings of eligible usance export bills drawn in foreign currencies or Indian rupees and purchased or negotiated by them.

Refinance is made available to agriculture and small-scale industries at 4½ per cent, irrespective of the net liquidity ratio, up to an amount equivalent to the total of a bank's short-term outstanding advances to agriculture (sale and distribution operations in respect of chemical fertilisers and pesticides, short-term loans to farmers and loans for financing fisheries, dairies, poultries, cold storage, etc.), and small-scale industries covered by the guarantee of the Credit Guarantee Corporation. From February 1970, refinance has been provided to the three priority sectors up to an amount equivalent to the increase in such credit over the prescribed base period. Refinance is offered at 4½ per cent, irrespective of the net liquidity ratio, against:

(i) Credit to exporters at the pre-shipment and post-shipment stages, i.e., in respect of packing credit advances and all post-shipment credits; and

(ii) Lending to primary cooperative credit societies in selective districts in certain states.

Increases in short-term lending to small-scale industries covered by the guarantee of the Credit Guarantee Corporation and in short-term direct lending to agriculturists are refinanced at the Bank Rate, irrespective of the net liquidity ratio.

REGULATION OF BANK'S LENDING RATES

Under Sections 21 and 35 A of the Banking Regulation Act, 1949 the Reserve Bank of India possesses statutory authority to regulate the interest rate charged by banks. During recent past the Bank has relied upon its power of direct control on interest rates, rather than influencing them only through variations in the Bank rate. The Bank had enforced both minimum lending rates and maximum lending rates in the past.

The Reserve Bank of India made significant changes in the interest rate structure from time-to-time in the past.

☞ Interest Rates for Advances of Scheduled Commercial Banks

The interest rates on advances granted by scheduled commercial banks were prescribed by Reserve Bank of India and revised by it from time to time. With effect from 18th October, 1994 Reserve Bank of India has abolished the minimum lending rate for advances of over ₹ 2 lakh. Banks are now free to fix their own Prime Lending Rate which will be their Minimum Lending Rate. Concessional rate of interest for advances up to ₹ 2 lakh were revised by the Reserve Bank of India as shown below:

LENDING RATES OF SCHEDULED COMMERCIAL BANKS

Size of Limit	*Effective 2.9.93*	*Effective 18.10.94*	*1997*
		(p.c., p.a.)	
(a) Up to ₹ 25,000	12.0	12.0	12.0
(b) Over ₹ 25,000 and up to ₹ 2 lakh	15.0	13.5	Not exceeding 13.5
(c) Over ₹ 2 lakh	15.0 (minimum)	Free	Free
Lending rate for commodities Subject to selective credit controls	15.0 (minimum)		

In October, 1996, Reserve Bank asked the banks to announce the maximum spread over the Prime Lending Rate for all advances other than consumer credit. While announcing their Prime Lending Rate, banks have been permitted to prescribe their spreads over prime lending rate separately for the loan component and cash credit component. This was intended to encourage borrowers to prefer loan component over cash credit component because of a higher spread in case of the latter. In pursuance of this directive, State Bank of India has recently prescribed maximum interest spread of 3.5% on loans and 3.75% on cash credits.

In April 1999, Reserve Bank of India permitted the banks to offer tenor-linked prime lending rates, *i.e.,* They can offer different Prime Lending Rates on loans for different maturities.

In October, 1999, Reserve Bank of India permitted the banks to charge interest rates without reference to their Prime Lending Rate in respect of the following categories of loans:

(i) Loans covered by refinancing schemes of term lending institutions

(ii) Lending to intermediary agencies

(iii) Discounting of bills

(iv) Advances/overdrafts against domestic/NRE/FCNR deposits.

The permission granted to banks to grant fixed rate loans for project finance was extended by Reserve Bank to all loans in April, 2000. Now banks are free to offer all loans on fixed or floating rate basis. But they have to ensure that PLR stipulations as applicable are complied with.

To provide further flexibility to commercial banks to decide their lending rates in April 2001. Reserve Bank of India permitted them to offer loans at below Prime Lending Rates to exporters or other creditworthy borrowers including public enterprises on the lines of a transparent and objective policy approved by their Boards.

Small loans up to ₹ 2 lakh still continue to be granted at rates not exceeding the Prime Lending Rate of relevant maturity.

Open Market Operations

Under the open market operations the Reserve Bank sells or purchases Government securities and thus reduces or increases the cash resources of the commercial banks. Open market operations have been used to provide seasonal finance to banks. The banks invest their surplus funds in Government securities during the slack season to increase their credit to industry and commerce.

Selective Credit Controls

The Banking Regulation Act confers wide powers on the Reserve Bank of India to control the level and pattern of bank's advances in general or on a selective basis. Under Section 21 of the Banking Regulation Act, 1949, the Reserve Bank is empowered to issue directions to the banking companies to determine the policy in relation to advances to be followed by them either generally or by any of them in particular. The Reserve Bank's directive may relate to any/or all of the following:

(a) the purposes for which advances may or may not be made.

(b) the margins to be maintained in respect of secured advances.

(c) the maximum amount of advances to any company, firm, individual, etc.

(d) the rate of interest and other terms and conditions on which advances and other financial accommodation may be given.

The Reserve Bank of India has been operating selective controls since 1956 in respect of certain commodities which have been sensitive or in short supply. These controls are being enforced with the objective to discourage the use of bank finance for the hoarding of such commodities so as to check an undue rise in their prices.

The Reserve Bank of India has been operating selective controls since 1956 in respect of certain commodities which have been sensitive or in short supply. These controls are being enforced with the objective to discourage the use of bank finance for the hoarding of such commodities so as to check an undue rise in their prices.

Advances against: *(i)* Foodgrains, *(ii)* Pulses, *(iii)* Oilseeds, *(iv)* Vegetable Oils, *(v)* Cotton and Kapas, and *(vi)* Sugar, Gur and Khandsari have been covered by selective credit controls.

The framework of selective credit controls consists of the following three instruments:

(a) Fixation of party-wise ceiling on credit: The ceilings are fixed keeping in view the crop prospects, supply position and price trends.

After the fixation of ceiling of credit on a party-wise basis since November, 1972, banks are required to seek the prior permission of the Reserve Bank for: *(i)* granting loans to new borrowers, and *(ii)* or increasing the credit limits in case of existing borrowers. Thus, one bank cannot takeover a commodity account which is subject to credit control from another bank without seeking prior approval of the Reserve Bank.

(b) Imposition of minimum margin: In case of advances against commodities subject to selective control, higher margins are prescribed in order to restrict the borrowing capacity of the borrowers. With higher margin, a borrower can get less credit from banks against a certain quantity of stock and thus can finance only a smaller part of it through bank finance. Moreover, different margins may be prescribed for different types of borrowers against the security of the same commodity. A higher margin is generally fixed for those borrowers whose need for credit is not so urgent or larger flow of credit to whom is likely to aggravate the price situation. For example, minimum margins were prescribed for advances against foodgrains, pulses and oilseeds (w.e.f. 19th October, 1987) at 45% for processing units/mills and against warehouse receipts and at 60% for others.

(c) Fixation of minimum lending rate: Though the Reserve Bank had prescribed the interest rates on various categories of commercial bank advances (which include the maximum rates of interest to be charged in certain cases), the minimum lending rate was prescribed for advances for commodities subject to selective controls.

In order to make selective credit controls more effective, clean credit facilities are not allowed to any borrower affected by selective credit controls. Appropriate exemptions from the requirements of the selective credit controls are, however, granted so as to avoid unnecessary hardship to the deserving borrowers. *e.g.,* State agencies like the Food Corporation of India and State Trading Corporation, are exempted from the application of the directives. Exports are exempted from the purview of selective controls. These restrictions are generally less severe in respect of credit granted to the manufacturing and processing units and are tighter in case of traders. Similarly advance against the security of or by way of purchase of demand documentary.

LOAN SYSTEM FOR DELIVERY OF BANK CREDIT

In April 1995, Reserve Bank of India introduced a loan system for the delivery of bank credit. Its objective was to bring about discipline in the utilisation of bank credit and to gain better control over the flow of credit. The salient features of the directive issued by the Reserve Bank (as revised in April 1997) are as follows:

(1) It is mandatory for banks/consortium/syndicate to restrict the cash credit component and to increase the loan component in case of borrowers with minimum permissible bank finance from the banking system of ₹ 10 crore and above. The proportion of the cash credit component has been gradually reduced and that of the loan component correspondingly increased during the past two years.

The present prescription is as follows:

Limit for Maximum Permissible Bank Finance	*Cash Credit Component*	*Loan Component*
(a) ₹ 10 crore and above but less than ₹ 20 crore	25%	75%
(b) ₹ 20 crore and above	20%	80%

As regards borrowers with a limit of less than ₹ 10 crore, the Reserve Bank has permitted that the level of loan and cash credit component may be ideally settled between the bank and the customer. The Reserve Bank has also permitted the banks to identify the business activities which may be exempted from the loan system of delivery on the ground that the business activities are cyclical and seasonal in nature or have inherent volatility.

(2) The maximum permissible bank finance is to be bifurcated into cash credit and loan components as stated above. Reserve Bank has however, permitted that a borrower can avail

of the loan component for working capital purposes at more than the above specified level. In such cases the cash credit component will stand reduced. A borrower can also draw the loan component first.

(3) In case of existing borrowers, if the cash credit limit has been utilised in excess of the permissible level, the cash credit component should be converted and sanctioned as loan component.

(4) *Ad hoc* credit limit may be sanctioned only after the borrower has fully utilised the cash credit and the loan component.

(5) In case of a consortium/syndicate, member banks should share the cash credit component and the loan component on a *prorata* basis depending on their individual shares of MPBF.

(6) Banks shall have the freedom to charge interest rate on loan and cash credit components subject to the observance of the prime lending rate fixed by individual banks.

(7) Till April 1997 the minimum period of the short-term loan for working capital purposes was not to be less than one year (six months in case of seasonal industries). The Reserve Bank has now permitted the banks to fix the minimum period of loans. The loan may be spread over various maturities, subject to roll over.

(8) Bill limit for inland bills should be carved out of the loan component.

(9) Banks may stipulate repayment of the short-term loan either in instalment or by way of a buffer payment. If a loan is repaid before the due date, such repayment may be credited to the cash credit account.

(10) For borrowers with MPBF of ₹ crore or above but less than ₹ 20 crore, the amount of commercial paper that can be issued is restricted to 75% of the cash credit component. For borrowers with limits above ₹ 20 crore, this limit is fixed equal to 100% of cash credit component. The cash credit limit will be reduced *pro tanto* an issuance of commercial paper.

(11) In April 1997 the Reserve Bank has allowed the banks to permit the borrowers to invest their short-term/temporary surplus in short-term money market instrument like commercial paper, certificates of deposits, and in term deposit with bank etc.

(12) Export credit limits (pre-shipment and post-shipment) are to be excluded from MPBF for the purpose of bifurcation of the credit limits into loan and cash credit components.

☞ Monetary and Credit Policy 1999-2000

The Reserve Bank announced in April 1999 its monetary and fixed policy for 1999-2000. The measures include:

(1) Cash Reserve Ratio (CRR) cut by 0.5 per cent with effect from May 8, 1999.

(2) Prime Lending Rate (PLR) for different maturities: In cases where deposit rate bring in excess of PLR, advances to depositors against fixed deposits can be made by banks without reference to the ceiling of PLR and banks can charge suitable interest rates.

(3) Fixed rate loans for project finance term loan.

(4) Bank's boards to delegate necessary powers to Asset Liability Management Committee (ALMC) for fixing interest rates on deposits and advances.

(5) Waiting period of two years in case of rescheduled loan agreements to be reduced to one year.

(6) General refinance facility withdrawn with immediate effect and replaced by a collateral lending facility.

(7) Banks permitted to issue inter-institutional guarantees.

Reserve Bank of India
Central Office, Shaheed Bhagat Singh Road,
Mumbai-4001 001.

Website of Reserve Bank of India
www.rbi,org.in

☞ Publications of the Reserve Bank of India

Annual

- Annual Report
- Report on currency and Finance
- Report on Trend and Progress of Banking in India
- Handbook of statistics on the Indian Economy
- State Finances: A study of Budgets
- Statistical Tables Relating to Banks in India
- Basic Statistical Returns of Scheduled Commercial Banks in India

Quarterly

- Microeconomics and Monetary Development
- Occasional Papers
- Quarterly Statistics on Deposits and Credit of Scheduled Commercial Banks

Monthly

- RBI Bulletin
- Monetary and Credit Information Review

Weekly

- Weekly Statistical Supplement.

☞ Reserve Bank guidelines to follow-up bank credit

The availability of bank credit to industry is a present subject matter of regulation and control. This is required to ensure equitable distribution to various sectors of the Indian economy. The reports submitted by the following four committees are very pertinent in this respect.

(1) Dehejia Committee Report, 1969
(2) Tandon Committee Report, 1975
(3) Chore Committee Report, 1980
(4) Marathe Committee Report, 1984

Dehejia Committee

A committee under the chairmanship of Shri V.T. Dehejia was constituted in 1968 by the National Credit Council to determine the extent to which credit needs of the industry and trade are likely to be inflated and how such trends could be checked. However, the committee made the following recommedations to bring about improvement in the lending system.

(i) Credit applications received by the bankers should be evaluated with reference to the present and projected total financial position submitted by borrowers, (ii) The total cash credit requirement of the borrowers should be segregated into hardcore component and 'short-term' component. While the hard-core component represents the minimum level of raw materials, finished goods and stores which the industry is required to maintain a given level of production, the short-term, component represents the requirements of funds for temporary purposes such as short-term increase in inventories, tax, dividends and bonus payments and (iii) The dealings of a customer should be confined to one bank only for avoiding the possibility of double or multiple financing. However, the adoption of consortium arrangement has been recommended in the case of large borrowers.

Tandon Committees

As a result of the failure of implementing Dehejia Committee recommendations, another committee was appointed by the Reserve Bank of India (RBI) in July 1974, under the chairmanship of Shri P.L Tandon for the urgent necessity of reviewing the existing credit system. The Committee submitted its report on 9th August, 1975. It is a landmark in the history of financing of working capital by commercial banks in India and is based on the following three principles:

(i) The borrowed should observe a proper financial discipline. This is required to be insured by the banker through a realistic appraisal of operational plans submitted by the borrower well in advance, *(ii)* The banker should supplement the borrower's resources to carry on acceptable level of current assetss and *(iii)* The loan is used only for the purpose for which it is made. How, the bank should know the end-use of bank credit.

The unique features of the Tandon Committee's recommendation relate to the fixation of norms and style of credit for bank lending to industry.

Chore Committee

During the slow implementation of the recommendation of the Tandon Committee, another Committee was appointed by the RBI in March 1979 under the chairmanship of Shri K.B. Chore, Chief Officer, Department Banking of Operations and Development, RBI.

The following are the important recommendations of the Committee:

(1) The existing system of three types of lending, namely, cash credits, loans and bills should continue.

(2) There is no bifurcation of cash credit accounts. This is because for seasonal industries, the difference is too high and for non-seasonal industries the difference is too low.

(3) The banks have been asked to fix separate credit limits for peak level and non-peak level credit requirements.

(4) All borrowers (except sick units) with working capital requirements of ₹ 10 lakh and above should be placed under second method of lending recommended by Tandon Committee.

(5) The flow of information from borrower to banks should be simplified, and

(6) A portion of of raw material financing should be taken up by banks through drawee bills.

The majors suggested above should be made compulsory for all borrowers having aggregate working capital limit of ₹ 50 lakh and above from the banking system. However, steps should be taken by banks to enforce the same discipline in stage on borrowers who are enjoying credit limits of less than ₹ 50 lakh from banking system.

Marathe Committee:

Reserve Bank of India in 1982 appointed a committee under the chairmanship of Marathe to suggest measures for providing meaningful direction to the credit management functions of the RBI. The following are the two major recommendations which have been accepted to the RBI with some modification.

(i) The third method of lending as suggested by the Tandon Committee has been declared to be impractical. Thus, in future, the banks should continu to provide credit for working capital to trade and industries as per the second method of lending.

(ii) The introduction of the concept of 'Fast Track' has been suggested. The concept of 'Fast Track' implies that subject to fulfilment of some conditions, banks can release, without priont approval of RBI, 50 per cent (75 per cent in the case of predominantly export-oriented manufacturing units) of the additional credit required by the borrowers falling within the amount of the credit authorisation scheme. Thus, the credit disbursement is on a faster rate and hence, it has been termed as the "Fast Track Scheme".

In order to place on the 'Fast Track' the concerned borrower should comply with the following five requirements:

(1) Reasonableness of estimates in regard to sales, chargeable current assets, current liabilities and networking capital.

(2) Classification of current assets, current liabilities in conformity with the guidelines issued by RBI.

(3) Maintenance of minimum current ratio of 1.33:1 except under exempted categories.

(4) Prompt submission of operating statements, and

(5) Submission of annual accounts and review of accounts.

☞ Questions

1. Point out the chief defects in the working of the Reserve Bank of India and suggest methods of overcoming them.
2. What are the central banking functions of the Reserve Bank of India? How does it exercise control on other banks in the country?
3. What is the scope for, and significance of, the control of credit in Indian conditions?
4. Give a brief account of the various methods by which the Reserve Bank of India seeks to contract and expand the total volume of bank credit in the country from time-to-time.
5. What part does the Reserve Bank of India play in the banking system of the country? How does it control currency and credit in the country?
6. Explain briefly the constitution and functions of the Reserve Bank of India. How does it exercise control over currency and credit in the country?
7. Write a critical note on the working of the Reserve Bank of India.
8. Trace the main developments in the short-term, medium-term and long-term credit facilities for agriculture in India brought about by the Reserve Bank of India in recent years.
9. "The objective of the Reserve Bank's credit policy has continued to be one of adequate financing of economic growth and at the same time ensuring reasonable price stability." Explain the above with reference to conditions in India since 1956.
10. Discuss the functions of Reserve Bank of India. *[I.I.B., Part I]*
11. "Reserve Bank of India is not only a controller of credit but also a promoter of credit." Explain. *[I.I.B., Part I]*
12. Explain the role of Reserve Bank of India in development, control and functioning of commercial banks in India. *[I.I.B., Part I, May 1988, June 1996]*

13. Explain the organisational set-up of Reserve Bank of India and its promotional role in the overall economic growth of the country. *[I.I.B., Part I]*
14. Bring out clearly the main difference between Statutory Liquidity Ratio and Cash Reserve Ratio. *[I.I.B., Part I]*
15. Explain how the Reserve Bank of India controls the activities of commercial banks. *[I.I.B., Part I]*
16. What are the scheduled banks? State the advantages a bank enjoys being a scheduled bank. *[I.I.B. Part. I]*
17. What are the important features of Chore Committee Report? How are they different from Tandon Committee recommendations? *[I.I.B. P-II]*
18. Chore Committee recommendations are extension of Tandon Committee recommendations with certain improvements. Please explain. *[I.I.B. P-II]*
19. Write short notes on Tandon Committee norms. *[I.I.B. P-II]*
20. Describe the salient features of Chore Committee recommendations. *[I.I.B. P-II]*

CHAPTER

5 The Banking Regulation Act, 1949

The Banking Companies Act, 1949, was passed to amend and consolidate the law relating to banking companies. The need for such an Act was felt to check the abuse of power by managers of banks and also to safeguard the interests of depositors and the interests of the country in general. The provisions of this Act are "in addition to, and not, save as expressly provided, in derogation of the Companies Act, 1956, and any other law for the time-being in force" (Section 2).

Since its enactment in 1949, this Act was suitably amended a number of times (1950, 1953, 1956, 1959, 1960, 1961, 1962, 1963 and 1964): new provisions were inserted and existing ones amended to suit the needs of changing circumstances. The Amending Act No. 23, which came into force on March 1, 1956, changed the name of the Act from the Banking Companies Act to the Banking Regulation Act, and made it applicable to certain cooperative societies as well, the principal business of which was banking. The latest amendment of 1968, which came into force on February 1, 1969, introduced *social control* on banks.

☞ Main Provisions of the Act

The Banking Regulation Act, 1949, as amended up to date is divided into the following five parts:

- Part I — Preliminary (Sections 1 to 5A);
- Part II — Business of Banking Companies (Sections 6 to 36A);
- Part IIA — Control over the Management (Sections 36AA to 36C);
- Part IIB — Prohibition of Certain Activities in Relation to Banking Companies (Section 36 AD);
- Part IIC — Acquisition of the Undertakings of Banking Companies in Certain Cases (Sections 36 AC to AJ);
- Part III — Suspension of Business and Winding up of Banking Companies (Sections 36 to 45);
- Part IIIA — Special Provisions for Speedy Disposal of Winding up Proceedings (Sections 45A to 45X);
- Part IV — Miscellaneous (Sections 46 to 55A); and
- Part V — Application of the Act to Cooperative Banks.

☞ Definition of Banking

"Under Section 5(c) a *"Banking Company"* is defined as, *any Company which transacts the business of banking in India."*

The word *Banking* is defined as, *"accepting, for the purpose of lending or investment, deposits of money from the public, repayable on demand or otherwise and withdrawable by cheque, draft, order or otherwise"* (Section 5b).

☞ Important Features of the Definition

The definition of banking in Section 5(1)(b) makes it clear that: *(i)* acceptance of deposits, and *(ii)* lending or investing them are the essential functions of a banking company. A business will not be called a banking business if the purpose of accepting deposits is not to lend or invest. The explanation to Section 5(c) makes it clear that any company, which is engaged in the manufacture of goods or carries on any trade and which accepts deposits of money from the public merely for the purpose of financing its business as such shall not be deemed to transact the business of banking.

The phrase *'deposits of money from the public'* implies that a banker accepts deposits from anyone who offers his/her money for such purpose.

The basic principle of the banking business is thus acceptance of deposits which are to be utilised for lending and/or investment purposes. The banker, therefore, acts as an intermediary who deals in the money belonging to the public. A number of other institutions — the Industrial Finance Corporation of India and State Finance Corporations — are not banks because they do not accept deposits in the prescribed manner and for the presented purpose as a regular business.

☞ Kinds of Business Banking Company Cannot Engage in

Prohibition about Trading: Section 8 prohibits a banking company from engaging in some kinds of business. According to Section 8, a banking company cannot directly or indirectly deal in the buying or selling or bartering of goods, except in connection with the realisation of security given to or held by it, or engage in any trade, or buy, sell or barter goods for others otherwise than in connection with the bills of exchange received for collection or negotiation or with the undertaking of the administration of estates as executor, trustee or otherwise.

Prohibition about Non-banking Assets: Section 9 prohibits a banking company from holding any immovable property, howsoever acquired, except for its own use, for period exceeding seven years from its acquisition. The Reserve Bank may extend this period by another five years. The banking company shall be required to dispose of such property within the above-mentioned period.

Prohibition on Certain Types of Employment: A banking company cannot employ any person —

(a) who is, or at anytime has been, adjudicated insolvent or has suspended payment or has compounded with his creditors, or who is or has been convicted by a criminal court of an offence involving moral turpitude, or

(b) whose remuneration or part of whose remuneration takes the form of commission or of a share in the profits of the company (this does not, however, apply to the payment of any bonus by a banking company in pursuance of a settlement or award under any law relating to industrial disputes or of a scheme framed by a banking company or in accordance with the usual practice prevailing in banking business. It also does not apply to any payment of commission to any broker (including a guarantee broker), cashier, contractor, clearing and forwarding agent, auctioneer, or any other person employed by the banking company under a contract otherwise than as a regular member of its staff, or

(c) whose remuneration is, in the opinion of the Reserve Bank, excessive, or

(*d*) to manage Company if he —

(*i*) is a director of any other company, not being a subsidiary company of the banking company or a company registered under Section 25 of the Companies Act, 1956 (this provision is not applicable to a director for a temporary period of three months or such further period not exceeding nine months as may be allowed by the Reserve Bank), or

(*ii*) is engaged in any other business or vocation, or

(*iii*) whose term of office as a person managing the company is for a period exceeding five years at any one time (Section 10).

Prohibition of Charge on Paid-up Capital: According to Section 14A (added by the Amendment Act of 1959), a banking company is now prohibited from charging its paid-up capital. It provides that no banking company can create a floating charge on the undertaking or any property of the company or any part thereof without a certificate in writing from the Reserve Bank, that such floating charge is not detrimental to the interests of the depositors of such company. Unless such a certificate is obtained, the charge will be invalid.

☞ Minimum Paid-up Capital and Reserves

The Act makes certain important provisions for minimum paid-up capital and reserves. The following statement shows the requirements of the aggregate value of paid-up capital and reserves.

BANKING COMPANY INCORPORATED IN INDIA — AGGREGATE VALUE OF PAID-UP CAPITAL AND RESERVES

		₹
I. (*a*)	For a banking company in India having places of business in more than one State	5,00,000
(*b*)	If any such place or places of business is or are situated in the City of Mumbai or Kolkata or both	10,00,000
II.	If all the places of business are in one State but none of which is in Mumbai City or Kolkata	
(*a*)	For the principal place of business in one State (except in the City of Mumbai or Kolkata)	1,00,000
	Plus	
(*b*)	For every other places of business in the same district	10,000
	Plus	
(*c*)	For each entry place of business situated outside that district	25,000
	Subject to a total of	5,00,000
	Plus	
(*d*)	For having only one place of business	50,000
III.	If all places of business are in one State	
(*a*)	One or more of which is/are in the City of Mumbai or Kolkata	5,00,000
	Plus	
(*b*)	In respect of each place of business situated outside the City of Mumbai or Kolkata	25,000
	Subject to a total of	1,00,0000
Banking Companies Incorporated outside India		
(*a*)	If it has no place of business in Mumbai City or Kolkata	15,00,000
(*b*)	If it has a place of business in Mumbai City or Kolkata or both	20,00,000

☞ Capital and Voting Rights

All the banking companies must satisfy the following conditions:

(i) The subscribed capital of the company should be at least one-half of the authorised capital and the paid-up capital at least one-half of the subscribed capital.

(ii) The capital of the company should consist of ordinary shares only.

(iii) The voting rights of any one shareholder should not exceed one per cent of the total voting rights of the shareholders.

☞ Commission on the Sale of Shares

According to Section 13A, a banking company cannot pay — directly or indirectly by way of commission, brokerage, discount or remuneration in any form in respect of any shares issued by — any amount exceeding in the aggregate 2½ per cent of the paid-up value of the said shares.

☞ Payment of Dividend

A banking company cannot pay dividend on its shares until all its capitalised expenses (which include preliminary expenses, share-selling commission, brokerage, amounts of losses incurred and any other item of expenditure not represented by tangible assets) have been completely written-off.

According to Section 15 of the Amendment Act of 1959, a banking company is allowed to pay dividend on its shares without writing off the following:

(a) Depreciation, if any, in the value of its investments in approved securities where such depreciation has not actually been capitalised or otherwise been accounted for as a loss;

(b) Depreciation, if any, in the value of its investments in shares, debentures or bonds (other than in approved securities), where adequate provision for such depreciation has been made to the satisfaction of the auditor of the banking company; and

(c) Bad debts, if any, where adequate provision for such debts has been made to the satisfaction of the auditor of the banking company.

☞ Common Directors

A person cannot become a director of a bank if he/she is already a director (*i*) of another bank or (*ii*) of companies which among themselves are entitled to exercise voting rights in excess of twenty per cent of the total voting rights of all the shareholders of the bank. However, this provision does not apply to directors appointed by the Reserve Bank (Section 16).

☞ Reserve Fund

Section 17 of the Act as amended in 1962 requires every banking company incorporated in India to transfer to its reserve fund a sum equivalent to not less than 20 per cent of its profits irrespective of whether or not its reserves have equalled the paid-up capital. This provision was made to check the policy of banks to declare large dividends to satisfy their shareholders.

☞ Cash Reserves

According to Section 18 of the Act, "Every banking company, not being a scheduled bank, shall maintain in India by way of cash reserves with itself or in current account opened with the Reserve Bank or the State Bank of India — partly in cash with itself and partly in such accounts, a sum equivalent to at least three per cent of the total of its time and demand liabilities in India."

For the purposes of Section 18 and Section 24, liabilities in India shall not include —

(i) the paid-up capital or the reserves or any credit balance in the profit and loss account of the banking company;

(ii) any advance taken from the Reserve Bank, the State Bank of India, the Industrial Development Bank of India, the Agricultural Refinance Corporation or from any bank notified by the Central Government under Clause (c) of the Explanation to Section 42 (i) of the Reserve Bank of India Act.

☞ Scheduled Banks

Under Section 42(i) of the Reserve Bank of India Act, every scheduled bank is required to hold in India, by way of credit balance in an account with the Reserve Bank or the State Bank of India or other notified banks, the aforesaid percentage of its liabilities. The cash held with itself is not taken into account for compliance with the provision. However, the Reserve Bank may by notification in the *Gazette of India* increase the said rate which shall not exceed 20 per cent in the case of demand liabilities and 8 per cent in the case of time liabilities.

☞ Definition of Scheduled Bank

Under Section 2(e) of the Reserve Bank of India Act, a scheduled bank means a bank included in the second schedule of that Act. That schedule lists a number of banks. The Reserve Bank of India is empowered to include other banks as scheduled banks in that list. Normally, a bank with a paid-up capital and reserve of an aggregate value of not less than ₹ 5,00,000 is included in the scheduled banks.

☞ Control over Advances

Section 21 of the Act empowers the Reserve Bank to control advances by banks in the public interest or in the interest of depositors. By an Amending Act of 1968, another consideration has been added for control over advances, *i.e.,* banking policy. The term *banking policy* is defined as "any policy which is specified from time-to-time by the Reserve Bank in the interest of the banking system or in the interest of monetary stability of sound economic growth, having due regard to the interests of the depositors, the volume of deposits and other resources of the bank and the need for equitable allocation and efficient use of these deposits and resources". Sub-section (2) of Section 21 specifies the purpose, margins, maximum amount of advance, maximum amount of guarantee and the rate of interest, etc.

☞ Liquid Assets

Section 24 of the Act, as amended in 1962, requires every banking company to maintain — in gold, cash or unencumbered securities, valued at a price not exceeding the current market price an amount of not less than 25 per cent of its total time and demand liabilities. This provision is intended to ensure the liquidity of bank assets.

☞ Licensing of Banks

According to Section 22, every bank is required to obtain a license from the Reserve Bank for carrying on or for commencing business in India. The Reserve Bank will issue a license only if it is satisfied that the bank fulfils all or any of the following conditions:

(i) The bank is or will be in a position to pay its present or future depositors in full as their claims accrue;

(ii) The affairs of the bank are not being, or are likely not to be, conducted in a manner detrimental to the interests of its present or future depositors; and

(iii) In case of foreign banks, the carrying on of banking business by such banks in India will be in the public interest and that the Government or the law of the country in which it is incorporated does not discriminate in any way against the banks registered in India and that the company complies with all the provisions of the Act applicable to foreign banks.

☞ Opening of New Branches

According to Section 27, every bank (Indian as well as foreign) is required to take the prior permission of the Reserve Bank for opening a new place of business in India or to change the location of an existing place of business in India. In granting such permission, the Reserve Bank considers the following factors:

(i) the past history and financial position of the bank;

(ii) the general character of its management;

(iii) the adequacy of its capital structure and earning prospects; and

(iv) the public interest.

☞ Returns to Reserve Bank

All the banking companies are required to submit the following returns to the Reserve Bank of India in the prescribed form and manner as at the close of business on the last Friday of every month, or if that Friday is a public holiday under the Negotiable Instruments Act, 1881, at the close of business on the preceding working day.

(i) Return of Liquid Assets and Liabilities (Monthly): According to Section 24(3), every banking company is required to furnish to the Reserve Bank a monthly return showing particulars of its assets and its time and demand liabilities in India.

(ii) Return of Assets and Liabilities (Quarterly): According to Section 25, every banking company is required to submit a return to the Reserve Bank within one month from the end of every quarter, showing that the assets in India are not less than 75 per cent of its demand and time liabilities in India.

(iii) Return of Assets and Liabilities (Monthly): Under Section 27(i), every banking company is required to submit a monthly return showing its assets and liabilities in India.

(iv) Return to Unclaimed Deposits: Under Section 26, every banking company is required to submit a return to the Reserve Bank of all accounts which have not been operated for ten years. In the case of current and savings bank accounts, ten years will be counted from the date of the last transaction, while in the case of fixed deposits the period of ten years will be counted from the date of expiry of the fixed deposit receipt. The return must be submitted within thirty days from the end of each calendar year.

(v) Other Statements: Under Section 27(2), the Reserve Bank has powers to direct a banking company to furnish such information as it considers necessary. The bank has powers to call for information every half-year about the investments of a banking company and the classification of its advances to industry, commerce and agriculture.

☞ Final Accounts and Balance Sheet

All banking companies are required to prepare their final accounts and balance sheets in the prescribed forms given in the Third Schedule of the Act. Such final accounts and balance sheets must be prepared at the end of each calendar year as on 31st December, and must be signed by the principal officer and at least three directors of the company. The annual accounts and the balance sheet, together with auditor's report, should be published in the prescribed manner. Three copies of such accounts, balance sheets and auditor's report should be submitted to the Reserve Bank within three months.

☞ Audit

Section 30 of the Banking Companies Act requires that the balance sheet and the profit and loss account of a banking company must be audited by a duly qualified auditor. Under the Companies Act, 1956, and the Chartered Accountants Act, 1949, a person who is a chartered accountant is qualified to be the auditor of a banking company. The appointment, re-appointment or removal of any auditor of a banking company can only be done with the prior approval of the Reserve Bank. [Section 30(1A)].

☞ Documents of Confidential Nature

The Amending Act of 1960 introduced Section 34A to prevent any authority under the Industrial Disputes Act, 1947, from compelling a banking company to disclose information of a confidential nature. Under this provision, a banking company cannot be compelled to produce, or allow inspection of any of its books of account or other documents or furnish or disclose any statement of information if the banking company claims that such documents, statements or information are of a confidential nature and that their production or inspection or disclosure would involve disclosure of information relating to unpublished reserves or any particulars not shown in the balance sheet or in respect of provisions made for bad and doubtful debts and other usual or necessary provisions.

☞ Inspection by Reserve Bank

Under Section 35, the Reserve Bank either at its own initiative or at the instance of the Central Government, is empowered to cause an inspection to be made, by one or more of its officers, of any banking company and its books and accounts. Every director, officer or employee of a banking company under inspection must produce all books, accounts and other documents, etc., required by the inspecting officer. The Reserve Bank has also powers to examine on oath any director, officer or employee of a banking company.

☞ Powers to Issue Directions by Reserve Bank

Under Section 35A, the Reserve Bank has powers to issue directions to banking companies generally or to any banking company in particular when it deems it necessary, to do so —

(i) in the public interest; or

(ii) to prevent the affairs of any banking company from being conducted in a manner detrimental to interests of its depositors or prejudicial to the interests of banking company; or

(iii) to secure a proper management of banking company generally; or

(iv) in the interest of banking policy.

Under Section 36, more powers have been given to the Reserve Bank to caution or prohibit banking companies generally or any banking company in particular against entering into any particular transactions or class of transactions, and may even give general advice to any banking company. During or after inspection, the Reserve Bank may also pass orders:

(i) requiring the banking company to call a meeting of its directors to consider any matter regarding its affairs;

(ii) requiring any officer of such company to discuss any matter with an officer of the Reserve Bank;

(iii) deputing its officer to watch the proceedings of any meeting of directors or committee of the banking company and be heard at such meetings;

(iv) requiring notices to be sent to such officer;

(v) appointing its officer to observe the manner in which the affairs of the banking company or its officers or branches are being conducted and make a report thereon; and

(vi) requiring such changes in the management as it may consider necessary in consequence of the state of affairs disclosed during an inspection.

Under Section 36, the Reserve Bank is required to make an annual report to the Central Government on the trends in, and progress of banking in the country, including its suggestions, if any, for the strengthening of the banking business.

☞ Control Over Management of Bank

Removal of Officers of Banks: Under Section 36AA, the Reserve Bank has powers to remove from office the chairman or a director, or any officer or employee of a banking company. The Bank may appoint a suitable substitute to hold office for a period not exceeding three years at a time. It may also appoint additional directors (not exceeding five at anytime) of a banking company.

Suspension of Business and Winding up of Bank: Under Section 37, a High Court has discretion to grant a moratorium up to six months to a banking company which is temporarily unable to meet its obligations. By the Amendment Act of 1959, it has been provided that if the Reserve Bank is satisfied that the affairs of a banking company, in respect of which a moratorium has been granted, are being conducted in a manner detrimental to the interests of the depositors, it may apply to a High Court for the winding up of the company.

An order for the winding up of a banking company can be given by a High Court in the following cases:

(i) Where a banking company is unable to pay its debts;

(ii) Where an application for its winding up has been made by the Reserve Bank under Section 37 or Section 38.

Under Section 38, the Reserve Bank may make an application for the winding up of a banking company:

(a) if a banking company:

  (i) has failed to comply with the requirements of Section 11; or

  (ii) has, by reason of Section 22, become entitled to carry on banking business in India; or

  (iii) has been prohibited from receiving fresh deposits by an order under Section 35(4)(a) or under Section 42(3A)(b) of the Reserve Bank of India Act; or

  (iv) having failed to comply with the requirements or contravened the provisions of this Act, has continued such failure or contravention beyond the period specified in that behalf by the

(b) if, in the opinion of the Reserve Bank —

  (i) a compromise or arrangement sanctioned by a court in respect of a banking company cannot be worked satisfactorily with or without modification; or

  (ii) the returns, statements or information furnished to it under or in pursuance of the provisions of this Act disclose that a banking company is unable to pay its debts; or

  (iii) the continuance of the banking company is prejudicial to the interests of its depositors.

☞ Acquisition of Bank

The Reserve Bank of India and the Government of India have powers to acquire any banking company under the Banking Laws (Amendment) Act, 1968. On a report from the Reserve Bank, the Central Government may take over any bank if it has, on more than one occasion, failed to comply with the directions given to it under Section 21 or Section 35A, in so far as such directions relate to banking policy or if it is being managed in a manner detrimental to the interest of its depositors. In addition to this, Central Government must also be satisfied, before taking over a bank, that such a step will be in the interest of the depositors of the bank or in the interest of the banking policy or for the better provision of credit generally or of credit to any particular section of the community or in any particular area. The procedure of takeover and payment of compensation to the shareholders of the acquired bank are given in Section 36AE to Section AJ.

☞ Questions

1. State the provisions of the Banking Regulation Act, 1949, regarding licensing of banking companies and minimum paid-up capital and reserve.
2. Critically analyse the Banking Regulation Act, 1949, with regard to (*a*) Branch expansion. (*b*) Licensing of Banks in India.
3. Discuss the provisions of the Banking Regulation Act, 1949, under the following heads:
   (i) Licensing of banks.
   (ii) Restrictions of loans and advances.
   (iii) Regulation of paid-up, subscribed and authorised capital and voting rights of shareholders.
   (iv) Requirements as to minimum paid-up capital and reserve.
4. Discuss the main powers of the Reserve Bank of India under the Banking Regulation Act, 1949.
5. Attempt a brief review of the working of the Banking Regulation Act, 1949. How far in your view has banking regulation in India contributed to the growth and development of banking of the country?

↙ ↙ ↙

CHAPTER

6 Banking Companies (Acquisition and Transfer of Undertakings) Act, 1970

The Banking Companies (Acquisition and Transfer of Undertakings) Act, 1970, provides for the transfer of the control of fourteen banks, which were nationalised on 19th July 1969, to the Board of Directors appointed or nominated by the Government. The Act provides for the payment of compensation to the shareholders of the banks which were taken over and contains provisions regarding the structure, working and management of the nationalised banks.

As the nationalised banks are no longer companies as defined in the Companies Act, 1956, all the sections of the Banking Regulation Act of 1949 are now not applicable to them. The following sections of the Banking Regulation Act of 1949, however, have been made applicable to the nationalised banks:

Sections 10, 13 to 15, 17, 19 to 21, 23, 29 [excluding Sub-section (3)], 31, 34, 35-A, 36 [excluding Clause (d) of Sub-section (1)], 46 to 48, 50, 52, and 53. In other words, apart from aforesaid sections of the Banking Regulation Act, the nationalised banks are governed by the provisions of the Banking Companies (Acquisition and Transfer of Undertakings) Act, 1970.

☞ New Banks

According to Section 4 of the Banking Companies (Acquisition and Transfer of Undertakings) Act,1970, the control and management of existing banks were transferred to and vested in the corresponding new banks. The names of the new banks remained the same as those of the existing banks except that the words "The" and "Limited" were dropped. Although the new banks have retained their separate identity, Section (2) (c) of the Act empowers the Central Government to prepare schemes for their reconstitution into two or more corporations, for the amalgamation of any of them with another nationlised bank or any other bank, and for the transfer of the whole or a part of a new bank to any other bank or *vice versa*.

☞ Compensation

Section 11 of the Act provides for the payment of compensation to the shareholders of every nationalised banks in one of the following ways:

(i) Three equal instalments in cash with interest @ 4 per cent per annum; or

(ii) In saleable or transferable promissory notes or stock certificates of the Central Government issued at par and maturing at the end of 10 and 30 years, and carrying interest @ 4½% and 5½% respectively; or

(iii) Partly in the form of cash and partly in saleable or transferable promissory notes or stock certificates.

Ten out of 14 banks opted for compensation in 30-year securities; two opted for cash compensation amounting to ₹ 5.60 crore; and the remaining two banks opted for an interim payment in cash and balance in securities of both kinds.

☞ Capital

The total capital of all the 14 nationalised banks stands vested in and allotted to the Central Government. Section 9 of the Act authorises Central Government to prepare schemes which may provide for the capital structure of the nationalised banks. But the paid-up capital of any such bank shall not exceed ₹ 15 crore [Section 9(2).]

☞ Management

Board of Directors: The general superintendence, direction and management of the affairs and business of each nationalised bank vests in the Board of Directors. This Board shall include respresentatives of the employees and of depositors of the banks, and persons representing the interests of farmers, workers, and artisans. The Board is authorised to exercise all such powers and do all such acts and things as the nationlised banks are authorised to exercise and do. It is competent to make regulations to provide for all matters concerning the working of the bank. But it shall do so after consultation with the Reserve Bank and with the previous sanction of the Central Government. Each Board of Directors shall have:

(i) Not more than two whole-time directors, of whom one shall be the Managing Director;

(ii) One director from the workmen employees of the nationalised bank, who will be appointed by the Central Government from panel of three employees recommended by the workers' representative union;

(iii) One director from the non-workmen employees;

(iv) One director to represent the interests of the depositors;

(v) Three directors to represent the interests of farmers, workers and artisans;

(vi) Not more than five directors from persons having special knowledge or practical experience of one or more matters which are likely to be useful for the working of the nationalised bank; and

(vii) Two directors — one an official of the Reserve Bank and one an official of the Central Government.

One of the directors shall be appointed Chairman of the Board, who will preside over the meetings of the Board. The Managing Director shall be the Chief Executive Officer of the bank. Both the offices, however, may be held by one and the same person.

☞ Managing Committee

The Managing Committee of a nationalised bank shall consist of the Chairman, the Managing Director, the directors appointed as representatives of the Reserve Bank and the Central Government, and not more than 4 other directors nominated by the Central Government. The Committee shall exercise such powers as may be delegated to it by the Board.

☞ Advisory Committees

The Board may constitute *advisory committees* to advise it on such matters as are referred to them and to perform such duties as the Board may entrust to them. Persons other than the directors of the bank may also be members of such committees.

☞ Regional Consultative Committees

Regional consultative committees shall be appointed for each of the five regions to review banking developments within the region and to make suitable recommendations for the consideration of the Government and the Reserve Bank. These committees shall consist of the representatives of the States concerned and the nationalised banks, in addition to the persons nominated by the Central Government.

☞ Profit

According to Section 19 (7) of the Act, after making provisions for bad and doubtful debts, contributions to the staff and superannuation funds and other necessary and useful provisions and reserves, the nationalised banks shall transfer the balance of profit to the Central Government.

☞ Accounts and Audit

The account books of the banks shall be closed and balanced on 31st December every year. Auditors qualified to act as auditors of a company shall be appointed by all the banks with the previous approval of the Reserve Bank. Their remuneration shall be fixed by the Reserve Bank in consultation with the Central Government. The auditors shall have access to books, accounts and other documents of the banks at all reasonable times. They may employ accountants or other persons to assist them in investigating accounts at the expense of the banks. The auditors shall also have the authority to examine any officer or employee of the banks about such accounts. They shall report, besides the usual matters, whether or not the transactions of the banks, which have come to their notice, have been within the powers of each nationalised bank. The auditors' report shall be submitted to the Central Government and a copy forwarded to the Reserve Bank and the management of the bank whose accounts have been audited in conformity with the procedure outlined above.

☞ Bank's Obligations to Fidelity and Secrecy

Under Section 13 of the Act, all the nationalised banks are required to observe, except as otherwise required by law, the practice and usages customary among bankers. They shall not divulge any information about the affairs of their constituents except in circumstances in which it is necessary or appropriate for them to do so in accordance with law or practice and usage customary among bankers. Every director, auditor, officer or employee of the nationalised bank shall make a declaration of fidelity and secrecy in the prescribed form before taking charge of his office.

☞ Administration of Banking Legislation

All the banking institutions in the country are controlled and regulated by the following Acts:

(i) The Reserve Bank of India Act, 1934;

(ii) The Banking Regulation Act, 1949;

(iii) The State Bank of India Act, 1955;

(iv) The State Bank of India (Subsidiary Banks) Act, 1956;

(v) The Banking Companies (Acquisition and Transfer of Undertakings) Act, 1970; and

(vi) The Banking Companies (Acquisition and Transfer of Undertakings) Ordinance, 1980.

(a) Reserve Bank of India: The Department of Banking Operations and Development, Reserve Bank of India, is responsible for the supervision, control and development of all the commercial banks, including the nationalised banks, under the Reserve Bank of India Act and the above-mentioned Acts. The functions of this department have been discussed in the Chapter on Reserve Bank of India.

(b) Department of Banking, Ministry of Finance, Government of India: The Central Government has created a Department of Banking in the Ministry of Finance to look after the banking industry as a whole. The functions of this department are to look after:

(i) All the Indian banks and foreign banks so far as their operations in India are concerned;

(ii) All matters relating to the Reserve Bank of India;

(iii) All matters relating to cooperative banks;

(iv) All matters relating to financial institutions, including the Life Insurance Corporation and the Unit Trust of India; and

(v) All matters relating to banking in India, and the administration of all statutes, regulations and other laws concerned with the above.

☞ The Banking Companies (Acquisition and Transfer of Undertakings) Ordinance, 1980

By an ordinance dated April 15, 1980, the Central Government acquired another six scheduled commercial banks whose demand and time liabilities exceeded ₹ 200 crore as on 14th March, 1980. These banks are:

(i) Andhra Bank Ltd.

(ii) Corporation Bank Ltd.

(iii) New Bank of India Ltd.

(iv) Oriental Bank of Commerce Ltd.

(v) Punjab and Sind Bank Ltd.

(vi) Vijaya Bank Ltd.

The total demand and time liabilities of these banks, as on 14th March, 1980, amounted to over ₹ 2,356 crore. The scheme of acquisition of these banks ensures the necessary degree of continuity in their normal operations to avoid any disruption in the relations of depositors and borrowers.

According to the ordinance, "the undertaking of each of the existing banks shall be transferred to, and shall vest, in a corresponding new bank which will be a new body corporate with separate identity".

The chairman or, where there is no chairman, the Chief Executive Officer of the existing bank, holding office as such immediately before the promulgation of the ordinance, shall be the custodian of the corresponding new bank.

The Central Government shall soon constitute Board of Directors for each of the corresponding new banks in consultation with the Reserve Bank of India.

At the time of the takeover of the 14 commercial banks in 1969, it had been stipulated that such Indian commercial banks as had not been nationalised would be taken over as and when the assets of each crossed the limit of ₹ 200 crore. The ordinance was promulgated to implement this provision of the bank takeover Act of 1969.

The Banking Companies (Acquisition and Transfer of Undertakings) Amendment Bill, 1993, seeks to allow the Public sector banks to enter the capital market to mobilise resources as a part of the Group's liberalisation of the financial sector. The main thrust of the bill is to open up the public sector banks not only to the Indian private sector, but also to the private sector of foreign countries.

PART - II

BANKER AND CUSTOMER

CHAPTER 7

Nature of Banking and Functions of a Banker

Banking has played a very important role in the economic development of all the nations of the world. In fact, banking is the life blood of modern commerce. It may truly be said that modern commerce is so dependent upon banking that any cessation of banking activity, even for a day or two, would completely paralyse the economic life of a nation. From its original narrow scope and modest purpose of taking care of other people's money and lending a part of it, banking has developed to such an extent that, in countries like England, France and the USA, there is hardly a business deal in which the assistance of a bank is sought in one form or another.

☞ Definition of Bank

The word *bank* has been derived from the Latin word *bancus* or from *banque,* which means a bench in English. The early bankers transacted their business at benches in a marketplace. When a banker failed, his bench was broken up by the people. According to some authorities, the word *bank* was originally derived from the German word *bank* meaning a joint stock fund, which was Italianised into *banco* when the Germans were masters of a great part of Italy. In India, the Hilton Young Commission recommended that the word *bank* or *banker* should be interpreted as meaning every person, firm or company accepting deposits of money subject to withdrawal by cheque, draft or order. The Indian Banking Companies Act, 1949, defines a "banking company as a company which transacts the business of banking in any State of India", and the word *banking* has been defined as "the acceptance, for the purpose of lending or investment, of deposits of money from the public repayable on demand or otherwise, and withdrawal by cheque, draft, order or otherwise". Under the provisions of Section 6 of the Act, in addition to the business of banking, a banking company may engage in other forms of business mentioned in this Section.

☞ Functions of Banker

Commercial banking grew out of the need of the people for a safe place of deposit. It did not take much time for those who held other people's surplus money to realise that their business could be made profitable if they lent out again what was received by them, provided that it was returned when it was required. Gradually, they learnt from experience that daily payments were more than counter-balanced by daily receipts, and hence there was no need for relending the amounts held by them. Of course, they had to depend on their own judgement in granting credit, and took proper security for such loans. From all these facts, it is evident that borrowing and lending constitute the banking business, and that these are the two basic functions of a bank. There are many other functions which a modern banker performs. All these functions and services may be grouped under the following heads:

(1) Raising Funds

(2) Lending Money

(3) Discounting Bills

(4) Agency Services

(5) Miscellaneous Services

1. Raising Funds

A banker is a dealer in credit. He collects the surplus balances of individuals and firms by issuing his own shares and by offering facilities for opening different types of deposit accounts. The lending power of a banker depends largely on the amounts he can borrow by way of deposits. Bank deposits are of three types: Fixed Deposits, Savings Bank Deposits, and Current Deposits.

☞ Fixed Deposits

The term *fixed deposits* means deposits repayable after the expiry of a certain period, which ordinarily varies from three months to five years. They are also known as *time deposits,* a term which is more commonly used in the United States of America. Customers usually offer their money as fixed deposits to a banker with a view to earning a higher rate of interest. They can withdraw the entire amount on the expiry of the stipulated period in case they happen to require it either to meet certain expenses or to employ it in a more remunerative manner. The majority of small investors in India prefer this form of investment to industrial securities, about which they know nothing, and also because they do not want to run the risk of any depreciation of their capital.

The rate of interest on fixed deposits varies with the period for which money is deposited. The current prevailing rates of interest effective from June 10, 1998 offered by Indian banks on fixed deposits are:

PERIOD	RATE OF INTEREST
1 year but less than 2 years	10 per cent
2 years but less than 3 years	11 per cent
3 years and above	11.5 per cent

Bankers occasionally allow their customers to take advances against the security of their fixed deposits. Banks charge 2% more than FDR rate on advances against fixed deposits. When depositing his money, a customer receives a receipt which is usually marked *not negotiable.* It can, of course, be transferred by way of assignment to a third party, but a deposit receipt, not being a negotiable instrument, cannot pass to a transferee a better title than that of the transferer, and therefore, such receipts cannot be treated like negotiable instruments.

The law of limitation does not apply to a fixed deposit as long as interest is paid on it, or as long as the deposit receipt is renewed from time-to-time. If the deposit receipt has not been renewed, however, the period of limitation runs from the date on which the depositor was entitled to be repaid. Bankers also accept deposits jointly in the names of two or more persons; and the conditions subject to which such deposits are accepted, regulate the manner of their withdrawal.

☞ Savings Bank Deposits

This type of account is suited to those who want to deposit their small savings in a bank, which they need to withdraw only occasionally, and not everyday or many times a day. The interest allowed on savings bank deposits is certainly lower than that allowed on *fixed deposit accounts,* and is calculated on the lowest balance kept during the month. The prevailing interest rates allowed by banks in India on savings bank deposits are 5 per cent on the balance maintained from 10th to the last day of the month, subject to not more than 60 withdrawals in six months.

Deposits received on these accounts have become a very large part of the total deposits of banks. The main aim of this deposit is to promote thrift among lower-income, middle-income and salaried people. The balance of a savings bank account is not allowed to go beyond a certain maximum. It can be opened by anybody on his own behalf, on behalf of any minor relative or on behalf of any minor of whom he is the guardian, etc. Almost all the banks allow the facility of cheques to their savings bank depositors. But a certain minimum balance must be maintained in the account before a depositor can avail himself of this facility.

When a person wants to open a savings bank account, he is supplied with a copy of rules and a printed form. He has to fill in the form and make a declaration therein that he has read the rules of the savings bank account. The depositor has also to give his specimen signature to the bank. The amount deposited is then entered into a pass book, which is handed over to the depositor. When the depositor wants to withdraw money, he or his agent must present the pass book together with a duly filled withdrawal form or cheque. When a cheque is drawn, the pass book need not be presented to the bank at the same time.

☞ Home Safe Account

A home safe account is akin to a savings bank deposit account. The main objective of this account is to promote the habit of savings among children and low-income persons. When this account is opened, the customer is supplied with a toy safe by the bank, which he takes home, and in which he places money from time-to-time. The safe is periodically taken to the bank to be opened, and the contents are then credited to the customer's account. Interest is allowed on the minimum balance of this account, as on a savings bank account.

☞ Current Deposits

Although current deposits did not formerly contribute to the capital of banks in India as fixed deposits did, the position has undergone a considerable change in recent years, for the amount of demand liabilities of scheduled banks has increased enormously in recent years.

In the case of a current account, a customer is allowed to deposit or withdraw moneys as and when he likes; he may do so several times a day, if he so chooses. No interest is allowed by first class banks on current account deposits, but some banks do allow interest if the balance does not fall below a certain minimum limit. Some banks charge one or two rupees per half year with a view to meeting the expense of maintaining such an account. This charge is known as bank charge or incidental charge. There are banks which insist that the balance in a current account must not be allowed to go below a certain limit. A minimum balance of ₹ 500 in urban areas and ₹ 300 in rural areas must be kept. In case it does, they charge interest on the balance or, in the alternative, impose a bank charge.

When a person wants to open a current account with a bank he has to fill in a form. The details in this form are such as to enable the bank to establish the respectability of the applicant. For example, the form contains a declaration that the rules of the bank have been read and understood by the applicant, and he has to sign this declaration. The customer is also required to furnish his specimen signatures, which are preserved in an autograph book of the bank for future reference. When a cheque is received by the bank, it carefully compares the signature of the customer on the cheque with that in the bank's autograph book, and it is only when it is satisfied that the signature is genuine that the payment is made. A new depositor must be introduced to the bank by one of its existing customers. For savings bank and current account deposits, the bank gives three books to the customer: a pay-in-slip book for depositing money, a pass book for keeping a record of transactions and a cheque book for withdrawing money.

☞ Other Accounts

Banks also receive deposits from their customers in certain other accounts. In one such account, the *recurring deposit account,* the customer is required to deposit a fixed sum of money every month for a specific period of time. After the completion of the specified period, he gets back all his deposits along with the cumulative interest which has accrued on them. The recurring deposits may vary from ₹ 5.00 to ₹ 500.00 or more per month, and the total period of account may vary from twelve months to five years or more. The purpose of this account is to encourage customers to save some money compulsorily every month and get a large accumulated sum after a specified period. Without this binding of compulsory deposits every month, he may not save otherwise. After opening this account, the customer willingly forces himself to save. Cumulative interest is allowed on these accounts, and the rate of interest is higher than on savings bank deposits and, in some cases, higher even than on fixed deposit accounts. The rates range between 7½ per cent to 10 per cent.

Banks also allow the facility of certain other types of deposits. Private deposit accounts may be opened, the sole purpose of which may be to defray expenses of a purely personal or private nature. Special accounts for special purposes can also be opened with banks, such as a marriage account in which money is regularly deposited, and withdrawn only at the time of marriage.

☞ Nature of Deposits

There are various ways in which bank deposits arise. Customers may deposit actual cash or they may deposit rights to receive cash; these rights to receive cash may be in the form of a cheque, a bill, a promissory note owing to them, etc. But all the banks insist that while opening a new account, the first deposit must be in the form of cash. When a banker receives a cheque, bill or promissory note from a customer, he collects on it and credits the customer's account with the proceeds. Deposits may also arise out of loans granted by the bank or through the process of discounting a customer's bills. In this case, they are known as *created deposits.* In actual practice, the amount of such deposits is much larger than that of the deposits received in hard cash or in the form of rights to receive cash. It is, therefore, wrong to think that the amount of deposits which appears in the bank's balance sheets is so much amount of cash. These deposits are the credit the banker has created in exchange for the cash and bills which figures on the other side of the balance sheet as assets. Whenever a customer (generally a business man) requires funds, he approaches the banker for a loan, overdraft, cash credit or the discounting of a bill. The banker knows that the money in such cases is required for making payments and not for the purpose of hoarding. He grants accommodation on the understanding that the actual cash will not be immediately withdrawn, but that the borrower shall draw cheques upon him whenever he wants to make payments. This right to draw cheques is also common to cash deposits. Hence, we may say that this right may be created either by the customer, or by the banker. It is created by the customer when he deposits the actual cash, and by the banker when he grants a loan. But the banker's power to create deposits is limited by the cash reserves he holds. Prof. J.M. Keynes has, therefore, rightly said, "Loans are the children of deposits and deposits are the children of loans".

2. Lending of Money

The second important function of a banker is to lend money. The business of lending is usually done in the form of loans and advances, overdrafts, cash credit, and discounting of bills of exchange. It is this function of a banker's activities which is the largest contributor to the bank's profit.

Advances by a banker may be either clean advances against personal credit with a second signature on the pronote, or against tangible or marketable securities, lodged or pledged with him. Advances generally take three forms — cash credits, overdrafts, and loans.

☞ Cash Credit

A cash credit is an arrangement by which a banker allows his customer to borrow money up to a certain limit against either a bond of credit by one or more sureties or against securities. This is the most common mode of borrowing by large commercial and industrial houses in India because of the advantage that a customer need not borrow the whole amount at one time but may draw such amounts as he requires at different times. He may deposit in the bank such surplus amount as may be with him for the time-being. The banker, while granting cash credit and overdraft facilities, has to estimate the amount of the customer's requirement. If the actual drawings fall much below his estimate, he may lose interest on the funds that remain unused. In order to minimise such losses, a banker's cash credit agreements generally provide a half or quarter interest clause, according to which the customer has to pay interest on at least half or quarter of the amount of cash credit allowed to him, even when he does not use that amount. Interest rates on cash credit range from 12.5% to 16.25%.

☞ Overdraft

When a customer requires temporary accommodation, he may be allowed to overdraw on his current account, usually against collateral securities, and pay interest on the amount actually used by him. The essential difference between a cash credit and an overdraft is that the latter is a form of bank credit to be made use of occasionally, while the former is used for long terms by commercial and industrial concerns doing regular business. Banks charge 18% interest on overdrafts.

☞ Loans

When a banker makes an advance in a lump sum which cannot be paid wholly or partly and which the customer has permission to withdraw subsequently, it is called a loan. If the customer repays it, either wholly or partly, and wishes to have subsequent accommodation, the latter will be treated as a separate transaction to be entered into if the bank agrees to do so, and subject to such terms as it may want to impose. Thus, the bank does not suffer any loss of interest as a result of carrying excessive cash, as it may be in the case of credits and overdrafts.

TABLE 7.1
RATE OF INTEREST CHARGED BY BANKS ON DIFFERENT TYPES OF LOANS

	Rate of Interest (%)	*Inclusive of Interest Levy (%)*
Small Business Finance		
(i) Accounts covered under LGC	14	15.10
(ii) Other Accounts	15	16.15
Small-scale Industries		
(i) Limit up to ₹ 25,000	11	11.85
(ii) Limit between ₹ 25,000 and ₹ 1,00,000	12½	13.50
(iii) Limit between ₹ 1,00,000 and ₹ 2,00,000	13½	14.55
(iv) Limit between ₹ 2,00,000 and ₹ 10 lakh	14	15.10
(v) Over ₹ 10 lakh	15	16.15
Term Loans		
(i) Covered under CGO	11	11.85
(ii) Term loan to sick units	11	11.85
(iii) Entrepreneur Scheme up to ₹ 25,000	11	11.85
(iv) Entrepreneur Scheme from ₹ 25,000 to ₹ 2 lakh	12½	13.50
(v) Differential Interest Rates (DIR) Scheme	4	4

Cash credit and term loan rate of interest w.e.f. 4.5.98 (SIB segment)

up to 2 lakh	
(i) up to 25,000/-	12.5%
(ii) above 25,000/- and up to 2 lakh	13.5%
above 2 lakh	
(i) above 2 lakh and up to 25 lakh	15%
(ii) over 25 lakh	16.25%

☞ Loans

Banks in India with the way of development have become easy to apply in loan market. The following loans are given by almost all the banks in the country:

➢ Personal Loan
➢ Car Loan or Auto Loan
➢ Loan against Shares
➢ Home Loan
➢ Educational Loan or Student Loan

In personal loan, one can get a sanctioned loan amount between ₹ 25,000 to 10,00,000 depending upon the profile of the person applying for the loan. SBI, ICICI, HDFC, HSBC are some of the leading banks which deals in personal loan.

Almost all the banks have jumped into the market of car loan which is also sometimes termed as auto loan. It is one of the fast moving financial product of banks. Car loan/auto loan are sanctioned to the extent of 85% upon the ex-showroom price of the car with some simple paper works and a small amount of processing fee.

Loan against shares is very easy to get because liquid guarantee is involved in it.

- Home loan is the latest craze in the banking sector with the development of the infrastructure. Now people are moving to township outside the city. More number of townships are coming up to meet the demand of 'house for all'. The RBI has also liberalised the interest rates of home loan in order to match the repayment capability of even middle-class people. Almost all banks are dealing in home loan. Again SBI, ICICI, HDFC, HSBC are leading.

The educational loan, rather to be termed as student loan, is a good banking product for the mass. Students with certain academic brilliance studying at recognised colleges/universities in India and abroad are generally given educational loan/student loan so as to meet the expenses on tuition fee/ maintenance cost/books and other equipment.

☞ Money Transfer

Besides lending and depositing money, banks also carry money from one corner of the globe to another. This act of banks is known as transfer of money. This activity is termed as remittance business. Banks generally issue Demand Drafts, Banker's Cheque, Money Orders or other such instruments for transferring the money. This is a type of Telegraphic Transfer or Tele Cash Orders.

It has been only a couple of years that banks have jumped into the money transfer businesses in India. The international money transfer market grew 9.3% from 2003 to 2004, i.e., from US $ 213 bn. in 2004. Economists say that the market of money transfer will further grow at a cumulative 10.15% average growth rate through 2008.

With the use of high technology and varieties of products, it seems that "Free" money transfers will become commonplace. We will see more bundling of tailored money services by banks and non-traditional entrants that will include "free" money transfers. Many banks will even use money transfer services as loss-leaders in order to generate account openings and cross-sell opportunities. The price evolution of money transfer products for banks will be similar to that of consumer bill pay–the product is worth giving away as an account acquisition tool to win overall market share and establish banking relationships.

ATM money transfer card products have had terrible bank adoption rates since being introduced in the last three to four years. Remittees who are highly educated and have been exposed to ATM technology in receiving countries tend to have an interest in this product. Money transfer to India is one of the most important part played by the banks. This service provide peace of mind to either the NRIs or to the visitors to India. Many Indian banks have ATMs (automatic teller machines), enable to draw foreign currency in India.

By 2007, we will see a good per cent of all foreign-born, households doing some level of online banking. First-mover banks will start having a window of opportunity to include online transfer functionally within the next couple of years, which currently frequents traditional money transmitters such as Western Union. There is a terrific opportunity for banks and non-banks to offer more robust global inter-institutional funds transfer services online. More than half of Western Union's customers today are already banked, and most do not have an alternative product marketed by their bank that is painless, quick, and cost-effective. That will change as banks offer transfer services through their online channel.

The following are the details of few banks to check for transferring money to India.

Name	*Address*	*Telephone*	*E-mail*	*Website*
Punjab National Bank	7, Bhikaji Cama Place, New Delhi-110 066	9111-2617-6297	pnbibd@ndf.vsnl.net.in	www.pnbindia.com
Reserve Bank of India	Main Building, P.O. Box 901, Shahid Bhagat Singh Road, Mumbai-400 001	9122-2266-0500	rdmumbai@rbi.org.in	www.rbi.org.in
State Bank of India				www.sbi.co.in
UCO Bank	D. N. Road, Mumbai		ro.mumbai@ucobank.co.in	www.ucobank.com

☞ Money Transfer to India

Apart from banks few financial institutions and online portals gives services of money transfer to India. Some of them are asunder:

- Western Union Money Transfer
- Union Money Transfer
- IKobo Money Transfer
- Cash2india.com
- Remit2india
- Samachar Money Transfer
- Timesoftmoney.com
- Wells Fergo International Money Transfer
- Travellers Express
- Money Gram International

☞ Visa Money Transfer

Visa has recently introduced the 'Visa Money Transfer' option for its savings and current accountholder of any bank with a visa debit card. This facility helps its customer to transfer funds from his bank account to any visa card, either debit or credit within India.

A Visa Money Transfer is of similar kind, in many respects, to the third-party fund transfer option given by some banks to its accountholders through e-cheque, but this is restricted to only visa cardholders.

☞ How to Transfer Money?

- Long on to your bank account through your respective bank websites.
- Fill the beneficiary details like visa card numbers, name, address and then specify the amount that needs to be transferred. For bank account specify the visa card number and credit card number for paying credit card bill.

- Click on to VISA Transfer Payments button.
- Transfer immediately or on schedule date. Your account will be debited according to the date mentioned.

☞ Notable Points of Visa Money Transfer

- The time taken for money transfers could be the same or even more than that of a demand draft, *i.e.,* two or three days or even more.
- Currently there are no charges but limits has been set by certain banks on the current transfers.
- It is available in 150 cities across the country now.
- The transferred amount can neither be changed nor stopped once it is initiated.

3. Discounting of Bills

This is the most important form in which a banker advances money. The bills of exchange discounted with a bank may be clear or documentary. The personal security of the drawer and acceptor is the only security in the case of clean bill. If the bill happens to be a documentary one, it is followed either by a railway receipt, bill of lading, or a wharfinger's certificate, etc., which means that the security of the drawer and the acceptor is further strengthened by the goods which are lying with the railway, shop or wharfinger. This type of advance by bankers is becoming more and more popular. The reasons for this popularity are:

(i) A fixed and unalterable amount, irrespective of any fall in the value of securities;

(ii) Certainty of payment on the due date;

(iii) Continuous supply of funds through planned arrangement;

(iv) Rediscount of facilities by the central bank at bank rate;

(v) Deduction of discount from the advance.

4. Agency Services

The fourth important function of a banker is the services performed by him as an agent. The services which he generally renders as an agent are:

(i) Collection and Payment of cheques, bills and promissory notes.

(ii) Execution of Standing Orders: A customer may leave standing instructions with his banker for the payment of sums to various persons or institutions against his account. Such orders are usually given in respect of payments of insurance premiums, subscriptions to clubs and societies and similar payments of a regularly recurring nature. The banker may charge a small fee for rendering such services.

(iii) Collection of Dividend and Interest: The customer may instruct the issuer of securities that he should pay the interest or dividend that may be declared on them to his own bank. He will thus avoid the trouble of endorsing and paying in such dividend warrants. The banker usually levies a very small charge for the collection of dividend and interest on behalf of his customer.

(iv) Purchase and Sale of Securities: Although it is not usual practice for the banker to advise his customer regarding investments, he does furnish him with such information as he has obtained from stock exchanges. He also undertakes to purchase or sell stocks or shares on behalf of his customers.

(*v*) *Remittance of Funds:* All the big commercial banks have a network of branches throughout the country. With this facility banks can conveniently provide the service of transfer of funds from one place to another. Remittances of funds by banks are simple, convenient, safe and inexpensive. Important methods of transfer of funds are:

(*a*) Mail Transfers;

(*b*) Telegrahic Transfers; and

(*c*) Bank Drafts.

(a) Mail Transfers

Banks provide the facility of sending money through mail transfer to any person at any place where the bank has a branch and the person has an account in any other branch of the same bank. For this purpose the sender shall have to furnish details like the name of the beneficiary, his/her account number, the amount to be transferred and the name of the branch where the account is maintained.

(b) Telegraphic Transfers

If the money is to be sent urgently, the bank may be requested for telegraphic transfers on payment of a nominal charge and telegram charges. But the facility of telegraphic transfer are available at selected branches only. In case of both telegraphic transfer and mail transfer, money can also be made payable to a beneficiary on identification. For this purpose, beneficiary's address is also given.

(c) Bank Drafts

Banks issue bank drafts or demand drafts on their branch at the place of destination for remitting money from one place to another. A bank draft is an order from one bank to another branch of the same bank to pay a specified sum of money to a person named therein or to his order. A draft is always payable on demand. According to Section 85-A of the Negotiable Instruments Act, a bank draft is "an order to pay money, drawn by one office of the bank upon another office of the same bank for a sum of money payable to order on demand".

Specimen of a Bank Draft

No. 815618

BANK OF BARODA
Bapu Bazar, Udaipur

₹ .... Date ....

On demand pay to ....

.... Rupees ....

.... for value received.

To

Bank of Baroda ....

.... Accountant

....Manager

Any person who wants to remit money has to purchase a draft from the bank by paying the amount in advance to the bank. The bank then issues the draft. The purchaser of the draft then sends the draft to the payee's place of residence/office by post for the purpose of encashment at the drawee branch of the bank. The bank issuing the draft charges a commission for rendering this service; the amount of the commission is according to the amount of the draft.

There are three parties to a bank draft:

(i) The drawer branch

(ii) The drawee branch

(iii) The payee.

The purchaser of the draft acquires the instrument after paying consideration thereof, but does not remain a party to the instrument. The purchaser of a draft may not be a customer or accountholder of the bank. The service is provided by the bank to the public in general.

☞ Legal Status of a Bank Draft

Section 13 of the Negotiable Instrument Act does not specifically mention bank draft as a negotiable instrument. But as per Section 5 of the same Act, the draft has a semblance of a bill of exchange. In *S.N. Shukla Vs. The Punjab National Bank Ltd.,* the Allahabad High Court held* that a bank draft is a bill of exchange because it fulfils all the essential requisites of a bill, *e.g.,* it is an instrument in writing containing an unconditional order and is signed by its maker. Section 5 requires that the drawer of the bill directs a *'certain person'* to pay a certain sum of money. The words 'certain person' does not mean *'another person'* different from the drawer. Hence a bank draft, which is an order by one branch of a bank to its another branch, fulfils this condition and has all the attributes of a bill of exchange.

The Calcutta High Court upheld this view in another case. The court observed: "ordinarily different branches of a bank and their Head Office constitute one legal entity, a branch being only an agency of the Head Office, but for certain purposes, the branches are treated as distinct entities. When a customer draws a cheque, he does not draw it upon the bank generally but upon the particular branch at which he keeps his account and one branch is, therefore, not compelled to pay the cheques drawn upon another branch. Therefore, in a demand draft by a branch of a bank on its Head Office, the drawer and the drawee are two different entities and thus it is a bill of exchange."[1]

Two important provisions in the Negotiable Instruments Act give the same status to a bank draft as given to a bill of exchange or a cheque. Section 85A grants statutory protection to banks against forged or unauthorised endorsements on drafts also.

Section 131A of the Negotiable Instruments Act treats the draft as a cheque for providing statutory protection to the collecting banker. According to Section 131A "the provisions of this chapter (Chapter XIV on Crossed Cheques) shall apply to any draft, as defined in Section 85A, as if the draft were a cheque".

☞ Loss of a Draft

In case a draft is lost by a purchaser, and the purchaser reports to the issuing banker the loss of the draft without any endorsement, the banker may safely refuse payment of the same. Any endorsement thereon, on behalf of the payee, would be deemed to be a forged endorsement and the title of the holder would not be considered good. The issuing bank should immediately inform the drawee branch about the loss of the draft. When presented for payment, the drawee should return it with the remarks: "Draft reported to be lost. Payee's endorsement requires verification."

In all cases of loss of drafts, banker should take all precautions and the payment should be made only when the banker feels fully satisfied about the valid title of the holder.

**Malik Barkat Ali Vs. Imperial Bank of India,* A.I.R. 1945, Lahore 213.

1.*State Bank of India and Another Vs. Jyoti Ranjan Mazumdar,* A.I.R. 1970, Calcutta, 503.

☞ Issue of Duplicate Draft

In case of loss of draft and a request by the purchaser for the issue of a duplicate draft, the banker should be very careful, and may issue a duplicate draft only after completing the following precautionary measures:

(a) The banker should satisfy himself that the request for a duplicate draft is genuine and has been made in good faith.

(b) The banker should obtain confirmation from the drawee branch that the draft has not been paid.

(c) The banker should get an indemnity bond filled in by the purchaser and/or payee.

☞ Cancellation of Draft

Many times the purchaser of a draft does not send it to the payee and brings back the draft to the issuing banker with a request to cancel it and refund the amount. The banker is fully justified in complying with such request of the purchaser, if he is satisfied that the draft has not been delivered to the payee. The contract between the bank and the payee of a draft is incomplete and revocable unless and until the draft is delivered to the payee. According to Section 46 of the Negotiable Instruments Act "the making note, bill of exchange or cheque is completed by delivery, actual or constructive". In case of an order instrument mere endorsement without delivery does not pass on the title to the endorsee. Delivery of the instrument, actual or constructive, from one person to another is essential.

A banker may cancel a draft so long as it is not delivered to the payee; but after a draft has been delivered to the payee, the banker becomes liable to pay the draft to the payee or to his order and he cannot cancel the draft without the confirmation of the payee. The moment a draft is sent to the payee the purchaser loses the right to get the draft cancelled. In *S.N. Shukla Vs. The Punjab National Bank Ltd.,* the court held: "It is only after the draft has been delivered the payee and his rights have come in that the purchaser's right to claim the money and to stop the payment becomes disputable. At that stage, the bank can reasonably say that in order to have an effective discharge from liability, it is necessary to have the consent of the payee before the amount can be paid to the purchaser."

☞ Purchaser's Request for Stop Payment of Draft

Under what circumstances the purchaser of a draft can ask the issuing bank or drawee bank to stop payment to the payee? This was considered by the Bombay High Court in *Tukaram Bapuji Nigam Vs. The Belgaum Bank Ltd.,* (A.I.R. 1976 Bombay — 185). The Court after consideration of Sections 85-A and 10 observed that: "The relationship of the purchaser of a draft with the bank from which that draft has been purchased is merely that of the debtor and the creditor. The purchaser can, therefore, call upon the bank to cancel the draft and payback the money to him at anytime before the draft has been delivered to the payee. Ordinarily, a bank issuing a draft cannot refuse to pay the amount thereof, unless there was some doubt about the identity of the person presenting it as being or properly representing the person in whose favour it was drawn. In other words, unless there is reasonable ground for disputing the title of the person presenting the draft, the banker must pay the amount of the draft. Once the draft has been delivered to the payee or his agent, the purchaser is not entitled to ask the issuing bank to stop payment of the draft to the payee on the grounds such as matters relating to consideration. The issuing bank can thereafter payback the amount of the draft to the purchaser of the draft only with the consent of the payee."

In the above case, the purchaser of the draft, asked the drawee bank to stop payment of the draft on the ground of dispute regarding consideration. It was held that the purchaser was not entitled to ask the drawee bank to stop payment. On the question of delivery of the draft by post, the High Court relied upon the decision of the *Supreme Court in Shri Jagdish Mills Ltd., Vs. I.T. Commissioner* (A.I.R. 1959, S.C. 8160) that — "where parties were at two different towns separated by some distance, there was imported by necessary implication on implied request to send the cheque by post — thus constituting the Post Office its (Payee's) agent for the purpose of receiving those payments". The High Court held that the post office in the present case was the agent of the payee and when the draft was posted, the act of posting itself amounted to delivery of the draft to the payee. Thus, it must be held that the draft had reached the payee before payment was purported to be stopped by the purchaser of the draft. Hence, the purchaser was not entitled to stop payment.

As mentioned earlier, the Negotiable Instruments Act treats bank draft equal to a cheque for certain purposes only. But so far as issuing bank's position is concerned, there are important differences between draft and a cheque. A cheque is drawn by the drawer on his banker and the drawer possesses the right to stop its payment, before it is actually made. But the purchaser of a draft does not possess this right at par with the drawer of a cheque. As a matter of fact, the purchaser of a draft is not deemed to be a party to the instrument. By issuing a bank draft, the banker takes upon himself a commitment in favour of a third party (the payee) to pay a certain sum of money. Although, the undertaking to pay the amount is given by the bank at the request of the purchaser of the draft after payment of due consideration; but in actual practice a bank draft is a promissory note issued by a banker and it is accepted and honoured on the basis of the goodwill and reputation of the issuing banker.

When a bank draft is delivered to the payee, he acquires a right in the instrument, which cannot be set aside by the "stop payment" order issued by the purchaser. If the payee has endorsed the draft in good faith and for value to a third party, the latter acquires rights enforceable against the banker. This right of the payee or his endorsee will not be affected, if the draft is delivered to him and subsequently a dispute arises between the payee and the purchaser of the draft as regards the payment of money remitted through the draft. In *Malik Barkat Ali Vs. Imperial Bank of India,** it was held that the purchaser of a draft had no authority to *countermand* payment of the draft if it had been delivered to the payee and the banker was under no obligation to comply with "stop payment" orders of the purchaser. Any dispute between the two parties must be settled between themselves.

☛ Payment of Draft

The bank issuing a draft sends an advice to the drawee branch, intimating about the issue of the draft. The drawee branch after verifying the signatures of the authorised officials (signatures of officers authorised to sign bank drafts are circulated to all the branches) makes the payment. The drawee branch should not make the payment if the signature on the draft appears to be forged.

The Reserve Bank of India has accepted the recommendations of the "Working Group on Customer Service" and on the basis of the recommendations, the banks have been advised to follow the following rules:

(i) Payment of drafts should not be refused because of non-receipt of drawing advice.

(ii) Just one authorised signature on the draft should be sufficient.

(iii) The validity period of demand drafts may be clearly indicated on the draft forms.

(iv) Acting as Trustee or Executor: The administration of a will or of a settlement requires specialised knowledge; and a banker undertakes, for a small fee, these complicated duties on behalf of such customers as may desire to nominate him in such capacities.

---

* *Malik Barkat Ali Vs. Imperial Bank of India,* A.I.R. 1945, Lahore 213.

(v) Acting as Agent, Correspondent or Representative of his customers and of other banks and financial houses at home or abroad.

5. Miscellaneous Services

A banker performs many general, utility, personal or miscellaneous services for his customers. Of these, the important ones are:

(i) Letters of Credit: A banker issues personal as well as commercial letters of credit. These enable the customer to profit by the superior credit of the bank. Thus, money can be promptly paid out to a customer or to his agent, and bills drawn by his creditor can be accepted by the bank or any of its branches, agencies or correspondents.

(ii) Foreign Exchange: The banks also deal in foreign exchange transactions. The commercial community receives facilities for its dealings with foreign nationals — a fact which is also a profitable business for a banker. In assisting foreign trade by discounting foreign bills of exchange, a bank has sometimes to arrange for the transport, insurance and warehousing of goods. A freight and insurance department, therefore, is a common feature of many commercial banks. In most foreign countries, the business in foreign exchange is handled by ordinary commercial banks. In India, however, there is a group of specialised institutions known as exchange banks, which handle the business in foreign exchange.

(iii) Safe Custody of Valuables and Securities: A bank undertakes the safe custody of a client's valuables and important documents against theft and fire. These are kept in specially constructed strong rooms, and the bank acts as a bailee of the goods entrusted to its keeping.

Normally, there are two methods of ensuring safety of customers' valuables.

(a) Bank accepts the valuables, *e.g.,* documents of title, jewellery, *etc.,* for safe custody, and

(b) Bank provides safe deposit vaults (lockers) on hire to the customers.

Safe Custody

One of the services provided by a banker is to keep the valuables of customers in safe custody. When a customer avails of this service by keeping valuables with the banker for the specific purpose of safe custody, such valuables are not subject to the general lien of the banker, and the banker is placed in the position of a bailee. The customer may handover the articles for safe custody either openly or in a sealed cover or box. If the customer gives the particulars about the articles they are recorded in the Safe Custody Register. If particulars about the articles are not declared by the customer, the description of sealed cover or box is recorded in a register. A receipt is issued by the bank and customer's signature is taken on the counterfoil or the duplicate copy. When the customer wants to withdraw the valuables, he has to duly discharge the receipt and surrender it to the bank. In case the receipt is lost by the customer, he has to give due discharge on a duplicate receipt and also to fill a letter of indemnity.

☞ Banker's Liability

For articles received by banker for safe custody, the position of banker is that of a bailee. The banker must take due care of the articles placed under his bailment. Sections 151 and 152 of the Indian Contract Act deal with the liability of a bailee. Section 151 says, "In all cases of bailment the bailee is bound to take as much care of the goods bailed to him as a man of ordinary prudence would under similar circumstances take of his own goods of the same bulk, quality and value as the goods bailed".

According to Section 152, the bailee is not liable for any loss, destruction or deterioration of the goods bailed to him provided:

(i) He has taken care of the same as prescribed under Section 151, and

(ii) There is no special contract between them which makes the bailee's liabilities absolute.

The above section of the Indian Contract Act clearly implies that the banker is bound to take a reasonable degree of care of the articles placed in his safe custody. If the banker does so and thereafter there is loss or destruction of the valuable, he shall not be held liable, provided there is no special contract to the contrary. Such special contract may increase the bailee's liability, but cannot reduce the same. Thus, the liability of a banker, as regards the valuables accepted by him for safe custody, shall arise in the following cases:

(a) *Negligence:* If the banker is negligent in ensuring proper safety of valuables, e.g., safe deposit vaults are not strong and thefts are possible or safe deposit vaults are left unlocked by negligence and valuables removed by someone or unrestricted entry to the room where safe deposit vaults are kept.

(b) *Conversion:* If the articles kept for safe custody are delivered by bank to a person other than the depositor, he shall be held liable for conversion.

(c) *Fraud:* The bank shall be held liable for any fraud committed by any of its employees dealing with the articles kept for safe custody.

Safe Deposit Vaults

At many branches banks provide the facility of safe deposit vaults kept in strong rooms. Lockers of different sizes are given to the public on hire. A person who hires a locker is required to execute a 'Lease Agreement' which contains all the terms and conditions on which the locker is hired. In hiring a safe deposit vault, the relationship between a banker and customer is that of a lessor and a lessee. The customer (lessee) promises to pay the annual rental charges and lessor in return provides the facilities of locker. A locker may be hired by two or more persons, the banker takes clear instructions from all the hirers. Any changes in the instructions must be made with the consent of all the hirers.

A locker can be opened by two keys. One of the key is given to the hirer and the other the master key is retained by the banker. The hirer is required to sign the safe deposit vault register every time he opens the locker. The banker simply keeps a record of the visits of the hirer but does not know about the contents of the lockers. In case the customer (lessee) dies, the banker should deliver the contents of the locker to the successor of the deceased after securing a legal representation from the court.

☞ Nomination

By the Banking Laws (Amendment) Act, 1983, some new provisions have been added in the Banking Regulation Act, 1949, which enable the hirers of lockers to avail of the facility of nomination in the following manner. According to Section 45-ZE, an individual hirer of a locker may nominate one person to whom, in the case of the death of the hirer, the banking company may give access to the locker and liberty to remove the contents of the locker. In case the locker is hired jointly by two or more individuals and operated under the joint signatures of two or more of such hirers, they may nominate one or more persons, to whom in the event of the death of such joint hirer or hirers, the bank may give jointly with the surviving joint hirer or joint hirers, access to the locker and liberty to remove the contents of such locker.

Acting as a Referee: A banker sometimes acts as a referee as to the respectability and financial standing of his customers. This is a very valuable service to businessmen, for it enables them to obtain reliable and speedy information about the general standing of people with whom they have business transaction with a view to avoiding any loss through giving credit to persons of little or no financial worth. The information is collected by a banker with great care and is supplied under conditions of the utmost secrecy.

Information and Statistics: Many big banks have opened a separate information and statistical department, which collects information relating to trade and business, and places it at the disposal of its customers. Sometimes a bank publishes a monthly review, which contains economic and financial information and statistics of great value to the commercial community.

Underwriting: Banks often act as bankers to local and municipal authorities or other public bodies, companies and corporations and also underwrite issues of Government loans and loans raised by local and municipal authorities, besides industrial securities. There appears to be a good scope for the expansion of this kind of business in India.

The foregoing discussion is only a brief resume of the innumerable services rendered by a modern bank, which places at the disposal of its customers all its resources and facilities, so that they may be most useful to the community in general. A modern banker performs all the services relating to money for its customers. That is the reason why it is said that a country having a sound banking system possesses one of the most essential foundations of prosperity.

Merchant Banking: Indian banks have started new line of activity in recent years and this is known as Merchant banking. Merchant banking comprises many non-banking type of services rendered by banks to the industrial and business houses. Some of the services provided by the Merchant banking departments of banks include counselling about new projects relating to location, foreign collaboration, tax benefits, etc. Preparation of feasibility reports, help in the procurement of letter of intent and other statutory permissions, appraisal of working capital requirements, arrangement of foreign currency loans, help in negotiating joint ventures abroad and advice about Government regulations, etc. State Bank of India was the first bank in the country to start Merchant banking services. Now some other banks also provide this service.

Bid Bonds and Performance Guarantees: Another new activity which the banks started in recent years is that they provide guarantees on behalf of their customers to third parties specially the Government departments and foreign importers. Such guarantees given by bank are called the bid-bond guarantees and performance guarantees. When a Government department or Public sector undertaking or a foreign party invites tenders for the supply of certain materials or for executing a certain type of work, the interested parties send their tenders quoting their terms, etc. Such firms are required to give a cash deposit equal to 2 to 5 per cent of the total value of the contract. The Government department, or public sector undertaking and foreign parties also accept, instead of cash deposit, a bond issued by a bank on behalf of the firm, undertaking a guarantee that if the contract is entered into with its customer named therein, he will be able to execute the same. This bond is called bid-bond.

After the tender of the successful bidder is accepted and a contract is entered into between the two parties for the supply or execution of a contract, a performance guarantee is required from a bank equal to 5 to 10 per cent of the total value of the contract. The bank providing the performance guarantee gives an undertaking about the completion of the performance of the contract by the customer. Banks, in turn, take a security from the customer by way of deposit of cash, Government securities or a guarantee by a third party. This safeguards the interest of the banker in the event the performance guarantee given by the banker is invoked.

The service of the bank in the form of bid-bonds and performance guarantee is now being increasingly utilised in case of export of goods and overseas construction contracts. The Export Credit Guarantee Corporation (ECGC) extends 90 per cent cover for bid bonds only on the condition that banks give an undertaking not to insist on cash margin. According to Reserve Bank of India, the practice of taking cash margin immobilises to that extent exporter's funds which that party could have otherwise utilised for executing the contract. This practice also does not improve in any substantial manner the bank's security position as the ECGC settle any claims that may arise at the agreed percentage only. The Reserve Bank, therefore, asked the bank not to ask for any cash margin in respect of bid-bonds and performance guarantees, counter-guarantees by ECGC. In other cases where such counter-guarantees of ECGC are not available, the banks may stipulate a reasonable cash margin, where it is considered absolutely necessary. Banks, before issuing bid-bonds and performance guarantees, satisfy themselves about the capacity and financial position of the exporter or the undertaker of a construction contract.

☞ Liability of the Bank Issuing Bid-bond or Performance Guarantee

The liability of the bank providing the issue of bid-bond or performance guarantee services depend upon the terms of the guarantee contract between the bank and the customer.

In *Texmaco Ltd., Vs. State Bank of India and Others** the State Bank of India issued a guarantee whereby it irrevocably and unconditionally guaranteed due performance in an orderly manner of the contractual obligations of its customer Texmaco Ltd. In the contract of guarantee the bank undertook, in the event of default, to pay on first demand the guaranteed amount without any contestation, demure or protest and/or without any reference to customer and/or without questioning the legal relationship subsisting between the customer and the beneficiary of the guarantee, *i.e.*, State Trading Corporation. The State Trading Corporation invoked the bank guarantee and the customer filed a suit for injunction restraining the bank from making any payment pursuant to the bank guarantee.

The Calcutta High Court rejected the contention of the customer and held that in terms of the contract of guarantee the bank was under an obligation to pay irrespective of any dispute as to whether there has been performance in an orderly manner of the contractual obligation by the party. It is, therefore, clear that an injunction restraining the bank from making payment under a bank guarantee cannot be issued, if under the terms of the bank guarantee, the bank has undertaken to make payment on default and without proof or conditions, unless there is a clear fraud of which the bank has notice.

☞ General Structure and Methods of Commercial Banking

Banks are institutions which deal in money. They accept money from the public in the form of deposits which are used for lending and investment operations to earn profits, but a part of these funds are kept in cash or in the form of other liquid assets to enable the bank to fulfil the legal requirements as well as to meet the obligations towards the depositors. In the allocation of funds for various purposes, *i.e.*, income earning and other purposes, the bank is guided by statutory requirements, Reserve Bank's directives and many other considerations.

☞ Sources of Funds

Just like any other business enterprise, the bank mobilises funds from the following two categories of sources:

1. **Funds from Own Sources:** This source consists of funds owned by the banking institution, *viz.*, share capital, reserve fund and other reserves, etc.
2. **Borrowed Funds:** This source consists of deposits in various types of accounts and borrowings from other banks, the Reserve Bank and other sources.

* *Texmaco Ltd., Vs. State Bank of India and Others* (A.I.R. 1979, Calcutta 44).

In case of banks, the borrowed funds, mainly the deposits in various types of accounts, constitute the major part of bank's funds in comparison with the owned funds in the form of capital and reserves. Therefore, borrowed funds are the main basis of banking operations.

☞ Obligation Towards Depositors

One of the basic functions of a banker is acceptance of deposits from the public. By accepting deposits the banker undertakes upon himself two important obligations towards the depositors.

1. An obligation to return the deposits on demand by the customers according to the terms of deposits.
2. An obligation to pay interest on deposits at prescribed rates (except on current accounts).

These two obligations are important and have a direct impact on the way the funds are employed. For example, in case of fixed deposits, the rate of interest is high but the amount cannot be withdrawn by the customer before the date of maturity. In case of current accounts, no interest is paid but the deposits can be withdrawn by the customer anytime. This clearly shows that the funds with the bank can be employed only according to the pattern of deposits.

☞ Importance of Liquidity in Banking Business

The term liquidity means the capacity to pay cash on demand. It is the ability of a banker to satisfy the demands of customers for cash in exchange for deposits. Bankers have to keep a certain percentage of deposits in the form of liquid cash as reserve in its own offices and with the Central Bank. Liquid cash does not earn any interest. Successful banking depends upon the capacity of such liquid reserve to meet the immediate needs and on their not being unnecessarily large. After making provision for immediate liquidity, banker should invest some money in assets which are liquid in nature and at the same time which earn some income. Liquid assets are those assets which can be quickly and easily turned into cash without loss to meet the obligation of customers. In employment of funds, banker should pay regard both to profitability and liquidity.

☞ Employment of Funds by Commercial Banks

Generally, the banks employ their funds in the following assets. These are given in order of liquidity.

1. Cash in hand (Cash balance)
2. Money at call and short notice
3. Bill discounted
4. Investments
5. Advances to customers.

I. Cash in Hand (Cash Balances)

The first item appearing on the asset side of a bank's balance sheet is cash in hand, including statutory cash reserve with the Reserve Bank and deposits with other banks. This is the most liquid asset of a bank. Cash reserves kept with the bank are called the first line of defence, because of their role in defending the solvency, reputation and goodwill of the Bank. Demands of the customers are immediately met by the bank from the cash balances.

In determining the actual amount of cash balance to be kept, the banker has to be very cautious and farsighted. From the point of view of profitability, he is tempted to minimise his cash holdings, whereas, from the point of view of liquidity, he is tempted to maximise his cash holdings. Therefore, an important task of the banker is to determine the adequate size of cash balance. In this task, on the one hand, he is guided by the conventions followed by the banking community, in this regard, on the other hand, he has to abide by the legal requirements. The English bankers usually maintain a cash ratio of 8 per cent, while in India a higher ratio is desirable owing to the undeveloped and unpredictable nature of the money market.

☞ Factor Influencing the Determination of Cash Balances

Some of the important factors which influence the determination of the amount of cash balances maintained by a banker are as follows:

1. **Banking Habit:** The need to maintain large amount of liquid cash will not be there if the customers are highly banking minded, because in that case depositors will seldom demand the payment of legal tender currency and will content themselves by the transfer of rights which the bank can do by mere book entries.
2. **Local Business and Economic Conditions:** The habits of the customers, and the business conditions of the area have an important bearing on the cash reserves. Some types of businesses carried on by the depositors may make heavy occasional demands which the banker will have to meet with adequate provision of liquid cash.
3. **Banker's Clearing House:** Existence of banker's clearing house greatly reduces the need of liquid cash to be kept by a bank because he has only to provide for the difference between the cheques drawn on him by other banks and the cheques drawn by him on other banks.
4. **Nature of Accounts:** The types of customer deposits in current accounts, Savings Bank accounts and fixed deposit accounts and the average size of deposits also determine the amount of cash balance. For fixed deposits, the time of withdrawal is known therefore, banker need not keep large cash balance. If the accounts are of a fluctuating nature, a higher cash reserve may be required. A banker having only a few large deposits, will also have to keep large cash reserve, because there may be heavy demands frequently. If there are a large number of small-sized deposits, the danger of large withdrawals by an individual customer will be less and hence it need not keep a large amount of liquid cash.
5. **Nature of Advances:** The nature of different types of advances made by the banker and the refinancing facilities provided by the Reserve Bank also affect the cash reserve. The Reserve Bank provides advances and rediscounting facilities to banks. A banker may employ more funds in discounting of bills and rediscount the same bills from the Reserve Bank and thereby keep less cash reserve.

☞ Statutory Cash Reserve with Reserve Bank

The Scheduled Banks are required under Section 42(1) of the Reserve Bank of India Act, 1934, to maintain with the Reserve Bank a minimum cash reserve equal to 3% of the aggregate demand and time liabilities. Reserve Bank is also empowered to vary the cash reserve ratio between 3% and 15% of the total demand and time liabilities. Although, the statutory cash reserve, kept with the Reserve Bank, is considered as liquid asset of a bank, in reality it is not a liquid asset, because it is a statutory obligation and the minimum cash reserve cannot be withdrawn.

☞ Balances with Other Banks

Scheduled Commercial Banks keep balances in current accounts with other Banks in India and abroad. According to Section 18 of the Banking Regulation Act, 1949, Non-scheduled Banks are required to maintain a minimum balance of cash with themselves or in current accounts with the Reserve Bank, the State Bank or its subsidiaries or partly with themselves and partly with these banks, equivalent to 3 per cent of the total of their demand and time liabilities in India. The balances held with other banks in current accounts are as liquid as the balances held by the non-scheduled banks themselves and may be withdrawn as soon as needed.

II. Money at Call and Short Notice

The item represents overnight or very short period lending by a bank to other banks, discount market or to the stock exchange. Such amounts are recoverable either on demand or on serving a short notice. The inter-bank call money market provides a means of making the surpluses of some banks available to other banks which are in deficit. This asset has an advantage over cash reserves, in so far as it satisfies, to a certain extent, both the attributes of a sound banking asset, *viz.,* profitability as well as liquidity. It is liquid in the sense that it is recoverable at call or short notice; it is profitable in the sense that it earns interest. This asset constitutes the banker's second line of defence.

III. Bills Discounted

The use of bank's funds in discounting bills, is considered as a highly earning liquid asset and is included among the money market assets. Bills discounted can be rediscounted with the Reserve Bank without much loss because of the very short length of life of such a bill. It is one of the most earning liquid assets, satisfying both the conditions of an ideal banking asset.

IV. Investments

Banks also invest a part of their funds in stock exchange securities like Government securities, Semi-government securities and shares and debentures of joint stock companies. In addition, a small part is also invested in fixed deposits, units and capital of the Unit Trust of India. Investments enable the bank to obtain more earnings than that afforded by 'Money at call and short notice' or 'Bills discounted', although they are less liquid. There is a statutory obligation on banks, under Section 24 of Banking Regulation Act, 1949 to employ no less than 25% of their demand and time liabilities in liquid assets including the approved securities. Securities also provide a convenient medium of employment of bank's funds during the traditional slack season when demand for funds from commercial and industrial concerns is at a low level.

When investing in securities, the banker gives importance not only to the safety of the investment but also to the possibility of each conversion into cash without loss. The important principles which guide the banker in the selection of securities for investment are — safety of capital, easy marketability or liquidity; profitability or yield and stability of price. In buying these securities the banker's primary aim is not to gain by a possible rise in prices of these securities. Generally, bankers prefer Government securities to the shares and stock of Joint stock companies, because firstly, the repayment is assured, secondly, the yield is steady and reasonable and thirdly, they can be easily sold without causing a glut in their market prices.

V. Advances to Customers

The use of bank's funds in giving loans and advances to customers is the most profitable of a banker's assets. Major part of banker's earnings are mainly derived from these assets. But there is a lack of liquidity in these assets. A loan may be covered by a mortgaged property, but the banker may find it difficult to convert the mortgaged property into liquid cash when needed. Herein lies the meaning of the quoted statement, "The art of banking lies in knowing the difference between a mortgage and a bill of exchange." In the case of a bill of exchange, it is of a self-liquidating character and offers an ideal security for a banker's investment.

In making loans and advances the banker should be guided by the following principles:

(i) Margin of safety offered by the security.

(ii) Possibility of fluctuations in the value of security.

(iii) Character, capacity and capital of the customer.

(iv) Loans should be spread as widely as possible over many industries and territories.

(v) Smaller sums should be advanced to a large number of customers than large sums to a small number of customers.

In addition to the items discussed above, the Balance Sheet of a bank contains certain other items also on the assets side, *viz.*, "acceptance and endorsements as per contra", and "Furniture", "premises", etc. Acceptance and endorsements as per contra refers to the amount due from the customers on whose behalf the bank has accepted the bill of exchange. These amounts are due from the customers and hence they are considered as assets. In a way this item represents a liability of the bank also, because the liability to honour these obligations will fall upon the banker if the customers fail to meet them. The other items "Furnitures and fixtures" and "Buildings" are not important from the point of view of the investment portfolio of a bank, as they are the least liquid of all the assets. Moreover, they are not intended for conversion into cash to meet an emergency.

☞ Creation of Credit by Banks

It is always the objective of bankers to minimise their cash holdings to the lowest extent possible. To achieve this objective they inadvertently increase the total amount of money in circulation in the society. It does not mean that they increase legal tender currency, which they cannot do. They create 'Credit money' which is called the creation of credit by bank, *viz.*, "Banks create credit" or "Loans create deposits". We have explained in the following paragraphs how it is done.

When a banker lends money it is given in the form of deposit in the account of borrower who gets a right to draw cheques against it. Thus, the borrower acquires a claim against the bank, just as a sum of money deposited by him with the banker creates a claim against the bank. When the borrower draws cheques in favour of other parties, they pay these cheques to their banks for collection and deposit in their own accounts and with this their deposits go up. This proves the correctness of Martley Withers saying "every loan creates a deposit". Thus, the commercial banks as a system can and increase the total amount of money in circulation, by increasing the purchasing power of the people through the deposit money created by them.

It will be better to explain the mechanism of the creation of credit by banks with the help of an analytical illustration. Let us take the case of a small community, where there is only one bank and people are highly bank minded so that all the transactions are settled by means of cheques. Further, let us assume that the total amount of money in circulation is ₹ 1,00,000 and the banker knows by experience that 10% of its deposits as reserves is sufficient to meet the demands from customers.

Since there is only one bank for the whole community, all the members of the community will deposit their money in that particular bank. The balance sheet of the bank would be as follows:

BALANCE SHEET OF X BANK LTD.

Liabilities	₹	*Assets*	₹
Deposits	1,00,000	Cash in hand	₹ 1,00,000

As we have assumed, the banker is required to maintain a cash reserve of only 10% of its total deposits to meet the demands of customers and can safely lend the balance of ₹ 90,000 to the persons who wants to borrow from the bank. So, in this case the banker will lend ₹ 90,000 to the borrowers and will place this sum to the credit of borrowers' accounts, thereby giving them the right to operate their accounts with cheques. The total deposits of the bank would consequently go up by this amount. The Balance Sheet of the bank after these advances would be as follows:

BALANCE SHEET OF X BANK LTD.

Liabilities	₹	*Assets*	₹
Deposits (Original)	1,00,000	Cash in hand	1,00,000
Deposits(Credit Balance in borrowers' accounts)	90,000	Loans	90,000
Total	1,90,000	Total	1,90,000

These deposits are now credit balances in the accounts of borrowers, and can be demanded by the borrowers from the bank whenever they want, and hence they command a purchasing power and, therefore, they may be considered as good as money. Now suppose the borrowers draw cheques in favour of their creditors. Their creditors will deposit these cheques with the bank for collection. So, actually what happens is merely a transfer of the credit balance of the borrowers to the credit of the accounts of the payees of their cheques. Although, the total amount of legal tender currency in circulation is only ₹ 1,00,000, the banker, by the process of creating additional deposit money, has brought into effective circulation an additional amount of ₹ 90,000, thereby raising the total supply of money from ₹ 1,00,000 to ₹ 1,90,000.

The power of the bank to increase credit does not end here. As we have assumed that the banker should maintain a cash deposit ratio of only 10%. To maintain this the banker has to provide an additional amount of ₹ 9,000 over and above the amount of ₹ 10,000 previously maintained. Even after this a balance of ₹ 81,000 can be advanced by the bank without any risk. Now the balance sheet of the bank would be as follows:

BALANCE SHEET OF X BANK LTD.

Liabilities	₹	*Assets*		₹
Deposits (Original)	1,00,000	Cash in Hand		1,00,000
Deposits (deposited by the payees of the first borrowers' cheques)	90,000	Loans	90,000 81,000	
Deposits (Credit balance of borrowers)	81,000			1,71,000
Total	2,71,000	Total		2,71,000

Now, if the banker is interested in the creation of further credit, he has to keep an additional cash reserve of ₹ 8,100. The total cash reserve will increase to ₹ 27,100 (10,000 + 9,000 + 8,100). The banker will have still loanable funds amounting to ₹ 72,900. In this way, the banker can go on increasing credit. But there is a limit up to which banks can create credit.

☞ Limit of Credit Creation by Banks

The power of banks to create credit is limited by the cash reserves which they are required to keep against their total demand and time liabilities and the total amount of legal tender currency issued by the Central Bank. Every bank has to keep a reserve of liquid cash to meet the demands of customers to pay cash as and when demanded. In societies where the banking habits of people are not well developed, a higher cash reserve is needed and in societies where the banking habits of the people are well developed, a lower amount of cash reserve may be sufficient. But a working reserve of liquid cash according to the needs of the society is always necessary, and this acts as a limit on the power of banks to create credit. In the illustration cited above the banker can go on creating credit money, till he has no more liquid cash to maintain the 10% cash ratio. In most of the countries the law prescribes a minimum cash reserve ratio to be maintained by every bank. Thus, a banker's power to create credit is limited by two factors, *viz.*, the minimum cash reserve ratio and the total amount of currency in the country.

Banking Systems

There has been a rapid development in the banking institutions in the last few decades throughout the world. According to differences in organisational structures, different types of banking systems have developed and are in operation in different parts of the world. Some of the important banking systems and practices currently in operation are discussed in the following paragraphs.

☞ Unit Banking and Branch Banking

Unit banking is a method of carrying on banking business through a single office, or in some cases a few offices in a limited area. It is another name for localised banking. The United States of America still retains some of the original features of unit banking, *i.e.*, banking restricted to a single office, though supplemented by the 'correspondent banking system'.

Branch banking is a method of carrying on banking business by big banking companies having several branches throughout a country or territory. For example, in United Kingdom, most part of the banking business is in the hands of five big banks.

A comparison between unit banking and branch banking is essentially a comparison between small-scale and large-scale operations.

☞ Advantages of Branch Banking or Disadvantages of Unit Banking

(1) Branch banking possesses the advantages and economies of large-scale operations.

(2) Advantages of managing with lower cash reserve in each office.

(3) Remittances of funds from one place to another at a lesser cost than unit banking.

(4) Risks can be spread geographically more effectively than by unit banking.

☞ Disadvantages of Branch Banking or Advantages of Unit Banking

(1) In branch banking there is always difficulty in efficient management, supervision and control. In unit banking management and control is efficient.

(2) Branch banking is expensive.

(3) Branch managers have to refer loan application to Head Office which causes delay and red-tapism. In unit banking quick decisions can be given.

In brief, branch banking has more advantages and in most part of the world this system is prevalent.

☞ Group Banking and Chain Banking

If the affairs of a group of banking companies are controlled by a holding company it is known as Group banking. In case a number of banks are controlled by one or few individuals and interlocking directorate through purchase of shares of such banks, it is known as chain banking. The group banking and chain banking systems are commonly found in the USA. The main objectives of such arrangements are to achieve the advantages of large-scale operations or to grab more powers.

☞ Investing Banking and Mixed Banking

Investment banks invest or help investment of funds in the shares or bonds of joint stock companies. These banks act as intermediaries between business corporations and investors. Generally, they purchase entire issue of new securities of Companies or Government Institutions and reissue them for public subscription at a higher price. Sometimes, they may act as agents on commission basis, but as a rule, they underwrite the issue of securities. Investment banks are classified as originators, underwriters and retailers. As originators they bring out new issues of the securities, as underwriters, they underwrite the issues, and as retailers, they retail the securities to individual and institutional investors. An investment banker, thus, performs a highly useful service to the business world by providing the necessary capital for long-term capital needs of industry.

Mixed banking is the extension of the operations of investment banking to the commercial banking area. The combination of investment banking with Commercial banking is known as 'mixed banking'. Mixed banking has certain important shortcomings. Commercial banks have to be very careful about liquidity of assets. Investment banks have to use their assets for longer investments and risky ventures. Many Governments have recognised the incomparability of mixing investment banking with commercial banking and have enacted legislations, accepting the principle of bifurcation of these two systems of banking.

NON-BANKING FINANCE COMPANIES

A non-banking finance company may be defined as an institution which mobilises the savings of the community and diverts them for financing different activities. A bank also performs similar type of activities. Then what is the difference between bank and non-banking finance company? The difference can be seen from two point of views.

Firstly, from the legal point of view, bank may be defined as an institution which is governed by the Banking Regulation Act, 1949.

Secondly, a more practical definition of a bank may be that it is an institution which accepts, short and long-term (including demand deposits) deposits up to an unlimited extent, and money can be withdrawn by drawing a cheque on any accounts maintained with it.

A non-banking financial intermediary does not fulfil any of these two criteria. The activities of non-banking companies are similar to those of banks and they are often referred to as para-banking institutions. Such intermediaries cover a wide range of institutions differing in their main activities and the services they offer, the one essential feature being the same, *viz.*, mobilisation of the savings of the public and their utilisation for financing various types of economic activities.

Depending on the nature of their major activity, the non-banking financial intermediaries may be classified into the following four categories:

1. Hire-purchase finance companies.
2. Investment companies.

3. Chit fund companies.
4. Nidhis or Mutual benefit finance companies.

1. Hire-purchase Finance Companies

Hire-purchase or instalment credit is needed by transport operators, farmers and professionals needing equipment who find it difficult to offer security to the lending institutions. In this form of credit, the goods themselves serve a security because they remain the property of the lender until the loan has been repaid. A Hire Purchase Act, 1972, was enacted to control and regulate this type of finances. This Act puts limitation on hire-purchase charges and also imposes restrictions on owners' right to recover possession of goods otherwise than through court. The Hire-purchase companies charge a flat rate which is calculated on the entire amount of advance and not on the diminishing balance basis. The true rate of interest is, therefore, far in excess of the flat rate indicated. According to Section 7 of the Hire Purchase Act, 1972, the statutory charges (Hire-purchase finance charges) shall be calculated at the rate of 30% per annum (true rate of interest) or on such lower rate as may be fixed by the Central Government in consultation with the Reserve Bank, but not less than 10% per annum.

Hire-purchase credit in India is given by institutions in the organised sector like commercial banks, hire-purchase companies and State Finance Corporations as well as in the non-organised sector consisting of a large number of firms and individuals.

2. Investment Companies and Unit Trusts

Investment Companies in India owe their origin to the prevalence of the Managing Agency System in the country. There are two types of investment companies in India:

(i) Holding Companies connected with large industrial groups, and

(ii) Other investment companies, which collect deposits from the public and invest in shares and debentures.

Holding companies control a group of companies by providing funds, giving guarantees and facilitating transfer of funds from between companies under their control. Such companies are incorporated as Private Limited Company.

Other investment companies collect deposits from the public and invest in shares and debentures. Such companies are very few and have got a limited role to play.

3. Chit Fund Companies

One of the oldest form of indigenous financial institutions in India are chit fund also known as kuries. Such institutions have their origin and are more popular in South India. The word chit means a written note on a small piece of paper. Chit funds may be broadly classified into the following three categories:

(i) Simple chit: Total subscription of all members goes in turn to one member who is determined by lot. There are no deductions from the total subscription funds and each member gets his/her chance.

(ii) Prize chit: Prize chit is just like a lottery. The amount collected through subscription of members is distributed to members whose number is selected by taking out a lottery after specified period of time.

(iii) Business chit: All the members subscribe a fixed amount every month to the common pool. The number of members of a group and the number of draws are equal. The draws are held after regular intervals. At the time of draw the total monthly subscription is either:

(a) allotted by drawing lots, or

(b) auctioned to the lowest bidder.

In case the amount is distributed by allotment of lots, a fixed amount of discount is deducted for meeting the expenses of conducting the chit. In case of auction to the lowest bidder, the difference between the total subscription and the amount of the bid is distributed to all the members after deducting the necessary expenses. A member who gets the chit once is not entitled to getting it again but has to go on paying his periodical subscriptions. Thus, each member in turn gets a chance to claim the chit. The Central Bureau of Investigation in its report on the working of chit funds had observed that a substantial portion of the contributions made by subscribers to chit funds were diverted or misused. In this report submitted by CBI to the Govt. in 1967, the CBI suggested enactment of uniform legislation throughout the country. The same type of view were expressed by the Banking Commission.

4. Nidhis or Mutual Benefit Finance Companies

Nidhis or Mutual Benefit Finance Companies are one of the oldest forms of non-financial companies. Some of the important objectives of Nidhis are to enable the members to save money, to invest their savings and to secure loans at favourable rates of interest. Nidhis help in encouraging people to save more. They work on the principles of complete mutuality of interest and are generally well-managed. Because, the Nidhis inculcate the idea of thrift and savings among the middle and lower class people, the Government have granted certain concessions under Section 620A of the Companies Act.

☞ Control of Non-banking Financial Intermediaries

Although operations of non-banking finance companies are very small in comparison with commercial banks, but still from the point of view of mobilisation of savings and meeting the credit needs of a large section of people they have their own importance. An important question is whether these companies are efficient savings and credit institutions. Because of the risks involved in their operations their lending and savings rates are more than the commercial banks but less than indigenous bankers or unorganised sector of Indian money market. For the healthy growth of Indian money market, it is necessary that these companies should be brought under control of the Reserve Bank of India. This will help not only in protecting the interests of the depositors, but also in mobilising savings and investing them according to the socio-economic needs and goals of our country.

The Banking Commission in its report submitted on Feb. 9, 1972, gave some useful suggestions regarding the operations of non-banking financial intermediaries. According to the Banking Commission, the non-banking financial intermediaries may be classified into two groups approved and non-approved. The institutions which satisfy the prescribed conditions may be given favourable treatment. About chit fund companies, the commission felt that their removal without offering alternative schemes will create a gap. The commission suggested the following measures to regulate the chit fund companies:

(i) There should be uniform chit fund legislation applicable to the whole country.

(ii) Only public limited companies should be allowed to run chit funds.

(iii) Commercial banks also can run chit funds, subject to appropriate safeguards formulated by the Reserve Bank.

(iv) The administration of banking regulation over financing institutions may be left to an independent agency which should be closely associated with Reserve Bank.

☞ Questions

1. In addition to its usual functions of acceptance of deposits and granting of loans, a commercial bank offers many other agency and general utility services to its customers. Enumerate, and give a brief account of such subsidiary services.
2. Give a brief description of the functions of a commercial bank.
3. What are the different classes of accounts in which deposits are received by a bank? Mention the important characteristics of each.
4. What are the different ways in which bank deposits arise? State how far they provide a source of strength to a banker.
5. According to Keynes, "Loans are the children of deposits and deposits are the children of loans". How far do you agree with this view?
6. Give a short description of the various forms which a bank loan may take. Why is the discounting business so popular with bankers?
7. Among the services rendered by a bank are:
   (i) Accepting valuables for safe custody,
   (ii) Issuing credit cards,
   (iii) Providing Safe Deposit Lockers,
   (iv) Collecting interest and dividends under a mandate.
   State, giving examples, what do you understand in respect of each of these services.
8. Explain why it is necessary for a banker to ask for an introductory reference before opening a current account for a person or a firm.
9. Mention the major functions of a bank and state why a banker asks for a suitable introduction before opening a current account of an applicant.
10. Discuss the various functions performed by a modern commercial bank and bring out their importance in the economic development of a country.
11. How the funds of a bank are employed? Describe the importance of liquidity in banking business.
12. Explain the method of creation of credit by banks. Illustrate it with the help of an example. Is there any limit of such credit creation?
13. Distinguish between:
    (a) Group Banking and Chain Banking.
    (b) Investment Banking and Mixed Banking.
    (c) Unit Banking and Branch Banking.
14. Write short notes on:
    (i) Hire-purchase Finance Companies
    (ii) Investment Companies
    (iii) Chit Fund Companies
    (iv) Nidhis or Mutual Benefit Finance Companies.
15. Besides accepting deposits and making advances, banks render certain subsidiary services to their customers. Describe four of the most important services. *[I.I.B., Part I]*
16. Write an explanatory note on: *(i)* Merchant banking and *(ii)* Bid and Performance bonds. *[I.I.B., Part I]*
17. What action would you take in the following circumstances:
    (i) A purchases a Demand Draft from your branch on another branch in favour of B and sends it to him by post. A few days later, he turns up at your office, complains that the goods supplied to him by B in payment for which he had sent the draft have been found to be defective and requests you to stop payment of the draft and refund the amount to him.
    (ii) C purchases a Demand Draft from your branch on another branch in favour of D. The next day he comes back to your office, says that he has since changed his mind about remitting the amount, surrender the Draft and requests refund of amount.

(iii) X purchases a Demand Draft from your branch on another branch in favour of Y and sends it to him by post. A month later he comes to your office, says that Y has written to him that he has not received the Draft which is presumed to have been lost in transit and, therefore, requests you to issue a Duplicate Draft.

[I.I.B., Part I]

18. Describe the steps which will be taken by you on receiving information that a draft purchased by your client from you is reported missing and you are requested by the client to issue a duplicate draft. *[I.I.B., Part I]*

19. A Demand Draft for ₹ 51,000 in favour of Rupchand Gupta was issued on 5th August, 1981, by Delhi Branch of a bank on its Mumbai Office. The draft is presented on 6 Aug., 1981, for cash payment at the counter by the payee. For identification he presented his signature on the letterhead of the Delhi branch duly verified by the officers who signed the draft along with the rubber stamp of the branch. Although the signatures on the letterhead and the draft are identical, they differ considerably from the specimens on record of the Mumbai branch. The advice for the issue of the draft is not received by the branch. The payee insists on immediate payment. How will you deal with this situation? *[I.I.B., Part I]*

20. A person tells at a branch office and presents a Demand Draft for ₹ 5,000 issued by an upcountry branch of the same bank and requests for payment across the counter in cash. The D.D. is uncrossed. The person who claims to be payee of the D.D. offers to provide introduction/identification from an accountholder of the same branch. How will you, as a branch manager, examine and decide? *[I.I.B., Part I]*

21. (*a*) At the time of review and renewal of the cash credit account it is necessary among other things to study the "run of the A/c" by arriving at the Minimum, Average and Maximum balance and the turnover of the account, total debts and total credits and sales and purchases in relation to the limits sanctioned. Please explain how this information is useful to determine whether the limit is properly utilised and the Advance is safe or otherwise.

(*b*) In the following cases, please explain whether you consider the points in favour or against the borrower and why.

(i) Maximum balance and Minimum balance very close to each other with limit fully drawn and poor turnover.

(ii) Large variation in Minimum balance very close to each other with limit fully drawn and poor turnover. *[I.I.B., Part I]*

8 The Banker-customer Relationship

It is necessary to explain the legal meaning of the terms *banker* and *customer* before examining the relationship between the two.

☞ Banker

The functions of a banker are so varied that it is difficult to give a satisfactory definition of the word. According to Macleod, "the essential business of a banker is to buy money and debts, by creating other debts. A banker is, therefore, essentially a dealer in debts or credit."

The Hilton Young Commission asserts that "the term *bank* or *banker* should be interpreted as meaning every person, firm or company, using in its description or its title *bank* or *banker or* banking and every company accepting deposits of money subject to withdrawal by cheque, draft or order".

Section 3 of the Indian Negotiable Instruments Act, 1881, says that the word "banker includes any person acting as banker and any post office savings bank".According to Section 2 of the Bill of Exchange Act, 1882, the word "banker includes a body of persons, whether incorporated or not, who carry on the business of banking".

Before 1949, there was no statutory definition of banking. The Banking Companies Act, passed in 1949, defines the term banking in Section 5 as follows:

"A banking company means any company which transacts the business of banking." "Banking means the accepting, for the purpose of lending or investment, of deposits of money from the public, payable on demand or otherwise, and withdrawable by cheque, draft or otherwise."

According to Sir John Paget, "No person or body, corporate or otherwise, can be a banker who does not: *(i)* take deposit accounts, *(ii)* take current accounts, *(iii)* issue and pay cheques, and *(iv)* collect cheques, crossed and uncrossed, for his customers". This definition points out the four essential functions of the banking business. Sir John Paget also lays emphasis on the performance of the above functions in a regular and recognised manner. According to him, "one claiming to be a banker must profess himself to be one and the public must accept him as such; his main business must be that of banking from which, generally, he should be able to earn his living".

Under the provisions of Section 6 of the Act, in addition to the business of banking, a banking company may engage in any one or more of the following forms of business, namely:

(i) Borrowing, raising or taking up of money; lending or advancing of money either upon or without security; drawing, making, accepting, discounting, buying, selling, collecting and dealing in bills of exchange, hundis, promissory notes, coupons, drafts, bills of lading, railway receipts, warrants, debentures, certificates, scrips and other instruments, and securities, whether transferable or negotiable or not; grant or issue of letters of credit, travellers' cheques and circular notes; buying and selling and dealing in bullion and species; buying and selling foreign exchange, including foreign bank notes; acquiring, holding, issuing on commission, underwriting and dealing in stocks, funds, debentures, bonds, obligations, securities and investments of all kinds; purchasing and selling bonds, scrips, or valuables on deposits or for safe custody or otherwise; providing safe deposit vaults; collecting and transmitting of money and securities.

(ii) Acting as agents for any Government or local authority or any other person or persons; carrying on agency business of any description, including clearing and forwarding of goods, giving receipts and discharges and otherwise acting as an attorney on behalf of customers, but excluding the business of a managing agent or secretary or treasurer of a company.

(iii) Contracting for public and private loans and negotiating and issuing them.

(iv) Effecting, insuring, guaranteeing, underwriting, participating in managing and carrying out of any issue, public or private, of State, municipal or other loans or shares, stocks, debentures, or debenture stock of any company, corporation or association, and lending money for the purpose of any such issue.

(v) Carrying on and transacting every kind of guarantee and indemnity business.

(vi) Managing, selling and realising the value of any property which may come into its possession in satisfaction of any of its claims.

(vii) Acquiring and holding and generally dealing with any property or any right, title or interest in any such property which may form a security or part of a security for any loans or which may be connected with any such security.

(viii) Undertaking and executing trusts.

(ix) Undertaking the administration of estates as executor, trustee or otherwise.

(x) Establishing and supporting, or aiding in the establishment and support of associations, institutions, funds, trusts, and conveniences created to benefit the employees or ex-employees of a company or the dependants or connections of such persons; granting pensions and allowances and making payments towards insurance; subscribing to or guaranteeing money for charitable or benevolent purposes or for any exhibition or for any public, general or useful object.

(xi) The acquisition, construction, maintenance and alteration of any building or works necessary or convenient for the purpose of a company.

(xii) Selling, improving, managing, developing, exchanging, leasing, mortgaging, disposing of or turning into account or otherwise dealing with all or any part or parts of the property and rights of a company.

(xiii) Acquiring or undertaking the whole or any part of the business of any person or company, when such business is of a nature enumerated or described in this sub-section.

(xiv) Doing all such other things as are incidental or conducive to the promotion or advancement of the business of a company.

(xv) Any other form of business which the Central Government may, by notification in the *Official Gazette,* specify as a form of business in which it is lawful for a banking company to engage.

No banking company shall engage in any form of business other than the forms referred to above.

Some of the above provisions were first inserted in the Indian Companies Amendment Act, 1936. The forms of business under the above provisions are, however, sufficiently comprehensive for a banking company and are in consonance with the accepted principles and practices of banking followed in industrially advanced countries.

☞ Business Prohibited for a Banking Company

Some provisions of the Banking Regulations Act, 1949, prohibit banking companies from doing some type of business activities. According to Section 8 of Banking Regulation Act, 1949, a banking company cannot engage directly or indirectly in trading activities or undertake trading risks. No banking company can directly or indirectly deal in buying or selling or bartering of goods or engage in any trade or buy, sell or barter goods for others. A banking company, however is permitted to do so for the following purposes:

(a) to realise the securities given to it or held by it for a loan, if need arises for the realisation of the amount lent,

(b) to buy or sell or barter for others in connection with: *(i)* bills of exchange received for collection or negotiation, and *(ii)* undertaking the administration of estates as executor, trustee etc. For the purpose of this section 'goods' means every kind of movable property, other than auctionable claims, stocks, shares, money, bullion and specie and all instruments referred to in clause *(a)* of Sub-section *(i)* of Section 6.

Section 9 of the Banking Regulation Act, 1949, prohibits a banking company from holding any immovable property, howsoever acquired, except as is required for its own use, for a period exceeding seven years from the acquisition of the Property. The Reserve Bank may extend this period by another five years, if it is satisfied that such extensions would be in the interest of the depositors of the banking company. The banking company shall be required to dispose of such property within the above-mentioned period. Section 6(f) and (g) of the same Act permit a banking company to manage, sell and realise any property which may come into its possession in satisfaction of any of its claims and to acquire, hold and deal with any property which may form part of the security for any loans or advances or which may be connected with any such security.

☞ Restrictions about Subsidiary Cos. of Banking Cos.

According to Section 19(i) of the Banking Regulations Act, 1949, a banking company could form a subsidiary company only for the following purposes:

(i) for undertaking and executing of trusts;

(ii) for undertaking of the administration of estates as executor, trustee or otherwise;

(iii) for providing the safe deposit vaults; or

(iv) for carrying on the business of banking exclusively outside India with the prior permission of the Reserve Bank.

Section 19 was amended in the Banking Laws (Amendment) Act, 1983, and according to the Amended Act, a banking company may form a subsidiary company for one or more of the following purposes:

(a) for undertaking of any business permitted for a banking company under Clauses (a) to (o) of Sub-section (i) of Section 6;

(b) for carrying on the business of banking exclusively outside India (with the previous permission of the Reserve Bank of India);

(c) for undertaking of such other business which in the opinion of the Reserve Bank would be conducive to the spread of banking in India, or to be otherwise useful or necessary in the public interest.

The business carried on by such subsidiary company shall not be deemed to be the business of the banking company for the purpose of Section 8.

Reserve Bank of India has stipulated that banks can set up subsidiaries to transact equipment leasing business and/or invest in shares of equipment leasing companies within specified limits after obtaining the prior approval of the Reserve Bank of India. Banks are precluded from undertaking directly, *i.e.,* departmentally, the business of equipment leasing.

While a number of banks have been permitted by the Reserve Bank to make portfolio investment in equipment leasing companies, the State Bank of India has entered into this business in a significant way by establishing a subsidiary company, named SBI Capital Markets Ltd., on 1st August, 1986. SBICAP, as it is called, has taken over the business of Merchant Banking Division of the State Bank of India. It provides a range of new services including project advisory services and equipment leasing.

☞ Customer

There is no statutory definition of the term *customer*. There are two schools of thought (old and new) regarding the meaning of this term. According to the old view, as expressed by Sir John Paget, "To constitute a customer there must be some recognisable course or habit of dealing in the nature of regular banking business.... It is difficult to reconcile the idea of a single transaction with that of a customer. The word surely predicates, even grammatically, some minimum of custom antithetic to an isolated act. It is believed that tradesmen differentiate between a customer and a casual purchaser." (*Mathews vs. William Brown & Co.*, 1894.)

According to the new school of thought, the relation of banker and customer begins as soon as the cheque is paid in and accepted for collection and not merely when it is paid. (*Ladbroke vs. Todd,* 1914.) The word *customer* signifies a relationship in which duration is not of the essence. The contract is not between a habitual and a new customer, but between a person who has an account of his own at the bank. (*Commissioner of Taxation vs. English, Scottish and Austrian Bank,* 1920).

Thus, a person who has an account in a bank in his own name and for whom a banker undertakes to provide facilities as a banker, is considered to be a *customer*. It is not essential that the account should have been operated for sometime, but it is presumed that the customer will deal regularly with his banker in future.

Another condition which determines the status of a person as a customer is the nature of his dealings with the banker. The dealings between a banker and a customer must be related to the business of banking.

A customer of a banker need not necessarily be a person. A firm, joint stock company, a society or any separate legal entity may be a customer. Explanation to Section 45-Z of the Banking Regulation Act,1949, classifies that in that section "Customer" includes a Government department and a corporation incorporated by or under any law.

☞ Services Rendered to Depositors and Borrowers

Banks open various types of deposit accounts and render the following services to the depositors and borrowers:

(1) Collection of cheques, demand drafts, bills of exchange, promissory notes, hundis and foreign documentary and clean bills.

(2) Purchase of local and foreign currency documentary/clean bills, negotiation of bills under inland and foreign letters of credit, advising of inland and foreign letters of credit established by branches and correspondents.

(3) Carrying out the standing instructions for the payment of insurance premia, subscriptions, certain taxes and gift remittances.

☞ Ancillary Services

(1) Performance Guarantee and Financial Guarantees.

(2) Safe Custody of Deeds and Securities.

(3) Safe Deposit Vault.

(4) Purchase and Sale of Securities.

(5) Collection of Interest on Securities/Debentures and Dividend on Shares, Collection of Pension Bills.

(6) Remittance of Funds — Bank Drafts, Mail Transfers, Telegraphic Transfers.

(7) Executor and Trustees.

(8) Personal Tax Assistance, preparing Income Tax, Sales Tax, Wealth Tax Returns.

(9) Investment Facilities — Underwriting, Banker to new issues, Guidance to investment, Stock Exchange assistance.

(10) Credit Transfer.

(11) Credit Cards.

(12) Travellers' Cheques and Gift Cheques.

(13) Emergency Vouchers.

(14) Sale of Units of Unit Trust of India.

☞ General Relationship

(1) Debtor and Creditor: The opening of an account with a bank and a banker's acceptance thereof involve a contractual relationship by implication. The depositor is only a creditor, and there is no entrustment to the bank for any particular purpose. The bank is liable to refund the money when demanded; but the money deposited belongs to the bank and the bank is entitled to deal with it as it likes. Thus, a banker when he deals with his customer is primarily in the position of a debtor to his creditor, or *vice versa*, when the customer had an overdraft.

The basis of the general relationship between a banker and a customer is clearly that of a debtor and a creditor. This was described in the *Folley vs. Hill*, 1848, as follows:

"Money, when paid into a bank, ceases altogether to be the money of the principal; it is the money of the banker, who is bound to return an equivalent by paying a similar sum to that deposited with him when he is asked for it. The money paid into the banker's is money known by the principal to be placed there for the purpose of being under the control of the banker; it is then the banker's money; he is known to deal with it as his own; he makes what profit he can, which profit he retains to himself, paying back only the principal, according to the custom of bankers in some places, or the principal and a small rate of interest, according to the custom of bankers in other places...That being established to be the relative situation of banker and customer, the banker is not an agent or factor but is a debtor."

☞ A Debt by a Bank vs. an Ordinary Commercial Debt

There is a difference between the bank-customer relationship and the ordinary commercial debtor-creditor relationship. The debt due from a banker to his customer differs from ordinary commercial debts in one important respect, *viz.,* that the general rule by which a request by the creditor for payments is unnecessary does not apply. In *Joachimson vs. Swiss Banking Corporation, 1921*, it was held that in case of a debt due from a bank, an express demand for repayment by the customer is necessary. In this case, the learned judge described the creation of an indivisible contract as follows:

"The bank undertakes to receive money and to collect bills for its customer's account. The proceeds so received are not to be held in trust for the customer, but the bank borrows the proceeds and undertakes to repay them. The promise to repay is to repay at the branch of the bank where the account is kept, and during banking hours. It includes a promise to repay any part of the amount due against the written order of the customer addressed to the bank at the branch, and as such written orders may be outstanding in the ordinary course of business from two or three days, it is a term of the contract that the bank will not cease to do business with the customer except upon reasonable notice. The customer on his part undertakes to exercise reasonable care in executing his written orders so as to mislead the bank or to facilitate forgery. I think it is a necessary term of such a contract that the bank is not liable to pay the customer the full amount of his balance until he demands payment from the bank at the branch at which the current account is kept.

Although the relationship between a banker and a customer is mainly that of debtor and creditor, it differs from similar relationship of debtor and creditor of ordinary commercial debts in the following respects:

(a) The creditor (customer) must demand payment from debtor (banker): In a banker-customer relationship, the customer (creditor) must demand payment from the bank (debtor), whereas in the case of an ordinary commercial debt, the debtor must pay the amount on the specified date as per the terms of the contract.

(b) The creditor (customer) must demand payment at the proper place and time: A proper place means the office or branch of a bank in which the customer has an account. A bank may have many offices or branches, but the customer can demand payment only from the office or branch where he has an account. In *Indo Allied Industries Ltd., vs. National Bank Ltd.,* (A.I.R., 1970, Allahabad 108), the Allahabad High Court observed that in the absence of an express contract to the contrary, there was an implied contract with a customer who opened an account with the branch of a banking concern, which carried with it the duty of the bank to pay the customer only at the branch where the account was kept, subject to instructions to transfer the amount elsewhere.

(c) The creditor (customer) must demand from the debtor (banker) in a proper manner: The customer can demand payment from the bank only in the manner prescribed by the rules of a bank or in accordance with usage. The statutory definition of a bank itself shows that deposits are withdrawable by cheques, drafts, orders or otherwise.

The Law of Limitation (conflict of views between different High Courts removed): Articles 59 and 60 of the Indian Limitation Act, 1908, define the law of limitation. Article 59 originally provided a period of three years for the recovery of money lent under an agreement and payable on demand from the time when the loan was made. Article 60 originally provided the same period for "money deposited under an agreement".

Under the Limitation Act, 1963, Articles 59 and 60 of the Indian Limitation Act, 1908, have become Articles 21 and 22 respectively. There was a difference of opinion in the views of the Bombay and Allahabad High Courts. According to the High Courts of Bombay and Allahabad (*Ichha vs. Natha,*

13 B. 388, at p. 342; *Dharamdas vs. Gangadevi*, 29A, 773 at p.778), the legal relationship between an indigenous banker and his customer was that of borrower and lender within the meaning of Section 59, and, therefore, no express demand was necessary for the debt recoverable from an indigenous banker. On the other hand, the High Courts of Calcutta and Madras held that the legal relationship in such cases was that of the depositee and depositor within the meaning of Article 60, and consequently a demand was necessary before the cause of action for a suit to recover a debt from a banker could arise [*Isher vs. Jiban*, 16 C.25(28); *Perundeviataya vs. Nam,* 18 M. 390].

This conflict of views between different High Courts was removed by an amendment of Article 60, in which the words "including money of a customer in the hands of his bankers so payable" have been added after the words "payable on demand". The effect of the amendment is to make an express demand a necessary condition for a cause of action to recover a debt due from a banker *(Juggi vs. Kishan, 37A, 292; Bhīma vs. Veni,* 28 Bombay, L.R. 73).

☞ Banker's Right of Set-off

The right of set-off is a statutory right which enables a banker to combine two accounts in the name of the same customer and to adjust the debit balance on one account with the credit balance in the other. The following points must be noted in connection with the use of this right by a bank.

A bank may exercise the right of set-off not only in the case of two accounts of a customer in the same branch of the bank but also in the case of two or more accounts of the same customer in different branches of the same bank. The right of set-off may be exercised subject to the fulfilment of the following conditions:

(a) Both the accounts of the customer must be in the same name and in the same right. The same right means that the capacity of the accountholder in both or all the accounts must be the same. The underlying principle in the rule of "the same right" is that funds belonging to someone else but standing in the name of the accountholders should not be made available to satisfy his personal debts.

(b) For example, the funds in a Trust Account are deemed to be in different rights, and, therefore, a debit balance in a personal account cannot be set-off against the credit balance in the Trust Account which may be in the name of the customer.

(c) The right of set-off may be exercised by a bank only in respect of debts due to and not in respect of future debts or contingent debts.

(d) The right of set-off may be exercised by a bank only if there is no agreement to the contrary.

☞ A Customer has no Right of Set-off or an Appropriation

Although a banker has the right of set-off between two or more accounts of a customer before making any payment to him, a customer has no such facility of getting his two or more accounts considered before the banker pays his cheque. In *Mohammed Hussain vs. Chartered Bank,* 1965, the appellant had an account in a Madras branch of the Chartered Bank and another in its Karachi branch. The banker agreed to provide ₹ 3.50 lakh overdrafts to the appellant, which was later reduced to ₹ 2.50 lakh. The appellant wrote one cheque on the Madras branch which was returned with the remark: "Cheque is far more than overdraft amount". The customer claimed that he had enough funds in the account of the Karachi branch and if that was taken into account, the cheque would never have been dishonoured. The Court held that the banker had the right to set-off between different accounts of a customer, but that the customer had no such right.

☞ Banker's Right of Appropriation

In normal course of business, a banker receives payments from customers. In case a customer has taken more than one loan or has more than one loans or has more than one account with the bank, the question of appropriating the amount deposited by the customer arises. The customer has, naturally, the right to direct the bank to appropriate the amount to any of the accounts of the customer. In the absence of any such direction from the customer, the banker shall have the right to appropriate the payment to any debt or account according to his discretion. But the banker should inform the customer accordingly.

☞ Banker's Right to Charge Interest and Other Charges, etc.

A banker has the implied right to charge interest on loans given to the customers, because when a banker grants a loan to a customer, he becomes a creditor and the customer a debtor. The normal practice followed by the bankers is to debit the customer's account periodically with the amount of interest due from the customer. In some cases, the agreement between the banker and the customer may, on the other hand, stipulate that interest may be charged at compound rate also. In *Konakalla Venkata Satyanarayana and Others vs. State Bank of India* (AIR 1975, A.P., 113) the agreement provided that "interest . . . shall be calculated on the daily balance of such account and shall be charged to such account on the last working day of each month". The customer availed the overdraft facilities for many years and periodical statements of accounts were being sent to the customer showing that interest was being charged and debited at compound rate and no objection was raised at any time. It was held by the High Court in this case that there was no doubt that the customer had agreed to the compound rate of interest being charged and debited to his account. The customer need not pay the amount of interest in cash. The interest amount is debited in the account of the customer and it is deemed as the debt due from the customer to the banker and interest accrued on this amount also along with the debt. Similar practice is followed in allowing interest on savings bank accounts.

(1) Trustee: In the case of securities and valuables deposited in a bank for safe custody, the position of the banker is that of a trustee, and he is liable to return them to the customer when demanded. For example, when a customer pays into his bank a cheque drawn upon another bank, such a chequeis received by the bank as a bill for collection (BC); the customer, therefore, is entitled to claim the cheque, if the collecting bank fails before the bank has collected it and the proceeds of the cheque, if it has credited the amount to his account. If, on the other hand, the deposit has been made for a specific purpose, the banker stops the payment before applying it to such purpose, and the depositor cannot claim the money paid and must content himself with his right of proof as a general creditor. [*In re: Barned's Banking Co.* (1871) 40 L.J. Ch. 730].

Normally, a banker requires articles for safe custody to be delivered in a sealed packet or box, and he has to return it with all the seals intact to the deposit or to one who has his order for the purpose. It has been held in several cases that wrong delivery of articles, kept with the banker for safe custody, to an unauthorised person is nothing less than a conversion, i.e., putting the goods bailed to one's own use, and is, as such, punishable under the law.

☞ Case where the Banker is a Trustee

There are cases where a banker places himself in the position of a trustee. In the case, the *Official Assignee of Madras vs. J.W. Iron,* 8 M.L.T. 99, a remittance was sent to a banker with instructions to purchase shares in a certain company. The bank brought some shares, but before completing the rest of the purchase, it failed. It was held that the bank stood in the position of a trustee to the remitter and therefore, he was entitled a refund of the unspent balance of the amount.

In another case, a banker received money from one party on behalf of another (the latter not being a customer) and wrote to the latter inquiring what was to be done with it, intimating at the same time that the amount was held in suspense. It was held that the relationship of debtor and creditor not being established, the latter can recover the amount in full out of the bank's assets in the event of its failure. (*Official Assignee of Madras vs. D. Rajaram Aiyar,* 33 Mad., 299).

In a case where a person had a deposit account with a banker and asked the banker to buy certain securities out of the money which the banker agreed to do, but the bank failed before he did so, it was held that this agreement did not make the bank a trustee for the amount in deposit *(Official Assignee of Madras vs. The Society for Providing Christian Knowledge,* 8 M.L.T. 52).

Where a banker, pursuant to instructions, express or implied, has credited the proceeds of a bill or other document entrusted to him for collection, the relationship of debtor and creditor arises from the time of his doing so. Where, however, the banker has suspended his business before receipt of such amount, he holds the money as a trustee for the customer, irrespective of whether or not the latter had an account with him on the date of the receipt of the money and whether or not the money had been credited in that account. (*Jinj Sports Ltd., vs. New Bank of India Ltd.,* 1948 Comp. Cas. 253).

(2) Agent: In the course of business incidental to banking, a banker undertakes to perform many services for the customer such as —

(i) buying and selling securities on his behalf;

(ii) collection of cheques, dividends, bills or promissory notes on his behalf;

(iii) acting as a trustee, attorney, executor, correspondent or a representative of a customer.

In the performance of all these functions, the banker acts as an agent of the customer.

(3) Adviser: Bankers also advise customers on their investments in the shares and debentures of joint stock companies and other securities. In performing this function, they act as advisers to customers. When some advice is given by a bank officially, it must be given with the ordinary care and skill that a bank official is expected to exercise and possess, even when such advice is given to a person who is not a customer at that time. In one case, a bank had advertised that expert advice was one of the advantages it offered to customers. The advice was honestly given, but there was no reasonable ground for advising the plaintiff in his own interest to make certain investments. The bank was held liable (as also the manager himself) for the loss occasioned by the advice. [*Woods vs. Martins Bank Ltd., and Anr.* (958) 3 All. E. R. 166].

☞ Special Relationship

(1) Banker's Obligation to Honour Cheques: A banker is under statutory obligation to honour the cheque drawn by a customer so long as his balance is sufficient, provided that the cheques are presented within a reasonable time after the ostensible dates of their issue, and provided that no prohibitory order of a Court is standing against the account of the customer. This duty is imposed upon the banker by Section 31 of the Negotiable Instruments Act, 1881, which reads as follows:

"The drawee of a cheque, having sufficient funds of the drawer in his hands, properly applicable to the payment of such cheques, must pay the cheque when duly required so to do and in default of such payment must compensate the drawer for any loss or damage caused by such default."

The obligation to honour a customer's cheques may be extended by an agreement, expressed or implied, to the amount of overdraft agreed upon; otherwise the banker is not liable for dishonouring his customer's cheques for the meeting of which the latter has not sufficient funds with the former.

☞ Reasonable Time

It is the duty of a customer to ensure that a cheque is complete in all respects, and is presented within a reasonable time. According to custom and practice in India, a reasonable time for the presentation of a cheque is six months after the date of issue.

☞ Collection of Cheques

When a customer gives a cheque to a banker for collection, what should be the reasonable time for crediting funds before they can be drawn upon? A banker is not bound to credit his customer's account with the amount of cheques or drafts upon other banks, sent in for collection, before they are realised. The amount must, however, be credited to the customer's account within a reasonable time after realisation. The question what constitutes a reasonable time depends upon the circumstances in each case.

☞ Garnishee Order

The banker's obligation to honour a customer's cheques is extinguished on receipt of a Court order known as the *Garnishee Order,* which is issued under Order 21, Rule 46 of the Code of Civil Procedure, 1908. A Garnishee Order is an order of a Court to a bank prohibiting it from making any payment from the customer's account. It is issued in two parts. In the first part, the Court directs the banker to stop payment from the account of the customer (judgement-debtor). This order, which is called *Order Nisi,* also seeks an explanation from the banker as to why the funds in the said account should not be utilised to meet the judgement-creditor's claim. On receiving the *Order Nisi,* the banker should immediately inform the customer so that the latter may not issue any cheques which may be dishonoured. The second part of the order, which is called *Order Absolute,* is the final order by which the entire balance in the account or a specific amount is attached and is to be handed over to the judgement-creditor. After receiving such an order, the banker is bound to pay the ordered amount to the judgement-creditor, and his liability towards the customer is discharged to that extent.

☞ Application of Garnishee Order on Joint Account

An account which is opened in the name of two or more persons is called a joint account. This account cannot be attached under the Garnishee Order if only one of the accountholders is a judgement-debtor. But if both or all the accountholders are judgement-debtors in any legal proceedings, the joint account can be attached.

☞ Partnership Account

For the debts incurred by a partnership firm, the personal accounts of all the partners can also be attached in addition to the account of the firm, because the liability of the partners is both joint and several. When a partner is a judgement-debtor in his individual capacity, only his individual account may be attached and not that of the firm or of another partner.

☞ Trust Account

A trust account, though standing in the name of a person in his capacity as a trustee, cannot be utilised for the payment of his personal liabilities.

☞ Attachment of Bank Account Under Income Tax Act

Section 226(3) of the Income Tax Act, 1961, authorises an Income-tax Officer to attach the credit balance in the account of a customer if he makes a default in the payment of the tax due from him.

This section authorises an Income-tax Officer "to require by notice in writing any person from whom money is due or may become due to the assessee, or any person who holds or may subsequently hold money for or on account of the assessee, to pay to the Income-tax Officer an amount equal to the amount of the arrears of tax or the whole amount, if it is equal to or less than the amount of such arrears".

☞ Wrongful Dishonour

If a banker, without justification, dishonours his customer's cheque, he makes himself liable to compensate the customer for injury to his credit (*Marzetti vs. Williams,* 1830). According to Section 31 of the Negotiable Instruments Act, 1881, the words "loss or damage" do not mean only pecuniary loss, but also loss of credit or injury to reputation. The loss can be of two types:

(i) Nominal loss;

(ii) Special or substantial loss.

If a customer is a trader or a businessman, the damages may be substantial; but a non-trader is not entitled to recover substantial damages for the wrongful dishonour of his cheque unless the damage he has suffered is alleged and proved as special damage.

The amount of damages will not necessarily be large only because the amount of the cheque dishonoured is large, for a customer is supposed to suffer more in credit if his cheque for a small amount is dishonoured than if it is one for a large amount. (*Davidson vs. Barclay's Bank Ltd.,* 1940).

Traders and businessmen are entitled to claim from the bank not only general damages, but substantial damages for such loss of credit or reputation even without proving the special loss or damage suffered by them because, in their case, loss or damage is presumed. But if a special loss or damage can be proved, this fact, too, would be taken into consideration for arriving at the exact amount of damages. In *New Central Hall vs. United Commercial Bank Ltd.,* (A.I.R. 1959) Madras 159, the Madras High Court held: "In case where a cheque issued by a trader-customer is wrongly dishonoured, even a special damage could be awarded without proof of special loss or damage. The fact that such dishonour took place due to a mistake of the bank is no excuse, nor can the offer of the bank to write and apologise to the payees of such dishonoured cheques affect the liability of the bank to pay damages for their wrongful act."

The liability of a bank for a wrongful dishonour of a cheque is towards the drawer and not the payee. The payee or the holder of the cheque cannot make the banker liable for such dishonour. (*Meghiya Malsa Ltd., vs. P.S. Commen,* A.I.R. 1963, Kerala 306).

In the case of a wrongful dishonour of a non-trader customer's cheque, the loss of credit or reputation is not to be taken into account. Hence he is entitled to nominal damages.

(1) Banker's Lien: Another important feature of the relationship between a banker and a customer is that a banker may, in the absence of an agreement to the contrary, retain as a security for a general balance of the account any goods and securities bailed to him (Indian Contract Act, 1872, Sec. 171).

A lien is the right of a person in possession of goods to retain them until the debts due to him have been paid.

☞ General Lien

This is a right to retain goods not only for the debt incurred in connection with them but also for the general balance owing by the owner of the goods to the person exercising the right of lien.

☞ Particular Lien

This is a right to retain the goods in respect of which the debt arises.

A banker has a general lien on all securities deposited with him by a customer unless there is an express contract, or unless there are circumstances showing an implied contract inconsistent with the lien. (*Brando vs. Barnett,* 1864). This general lien of the banker is an implied pledge, and may be exercised by him on bills, notes, cheques, bonds, coupons and dividend warrants. The right of sale extends to all the properties and securities belonging to a customer in the hands of the banker, except the title deeds of immovable property which cannot be sold. But a banker has a right to retain even the title deeds.

A banker cannot exercise the right of lien on safe custody deposits, on deposits for a special purpose, on valuables left with the bank by mistake, on valuables left to cover an advance which was not granted, on securities handed over to the bank for sale; nor on trust money with the customer.

☞ No Agreement Necessary

According to Section 171 of the Indian Contract Act, 1872, an agreement for the creation of a lien is implied, and, therefore, no agreement is necessary to create the right of lien. In order that the lien should arise: *(a)* the property must come into the hands of the banker in his capacity as a banker; *(b)* there should be no entrustment for a special purpose inconsistent with the lien; *(c)* the possession of the property must be lawfully obtained in his capacity as a banker; and *(d)* there should be no agreement inconsistent with the lien.

The law of limitation does not bar a banker's right of lien. The effect of the limitation of law is only to bar the remedy and not to discharge the debt. Therefore, it does not affect property over which the banker has a lien. The banker has no right of lien on a trust account which is separately maintained by a customer. *(Exparte Kingston L.R. 6 Ch. 632: ORM* vs. *Nagappa Chettiar,* 43 Boni L.R. 440, P.C.) A lien can be exercised if a banker has no knowledge, and during the currency of the account has received no notice of the trust character of the funds. (*Union Bank of Australia Ltd., vs. Murra Ayusley* 1898 A.C. 693).

☞ General vs. Particular Lien

There is a principle that a particular lien defeats a general lien, and, therefore, where a banker has a particular lien, he cannot also claim a general lien. For example, supposing that securities worth ₹ 2,00,000 were deposited with a banker to secure a debt of ₹ 1,50,000. Here, the banker gets a particular lien to the extent of ₹ 1,50,000 plus interest. In case the customer fails to pay this amount, the banker can recover it out of these securities of ₹ 2,00,000; but he cannot claim a general lien on the balance of ₹ 50,000 for some other debt which the customer owes him. The customer is entitled to have the securities, deposited by him for specific advances, returned to him on payment of those advances. (*Wilkinson and Others vs. London & County Banking Co.* 1984, I.T.L.R. 637). If, however, the securities are allowed to remain with the banker after the specific loan is paid up, the banker will acquire a general lien. (*In re: London & Globe Finance Corporation,* 1902, 2 Ch. 416 at p.424). But if a specific pledge cannot be proved under Section 171 of the Indian Contract Act, 1872, a general lien will apply. (*Kunhan Mayan vs. Bank of Madras,* 19 Mad. 234).

(2) Secrecy of Accounts: A banker should take care not to disclose the condition of his customer's account except on reasonable and proper occasions. This obligation to observe secrecy of account does not end even with the closing of a customer's account. (*Tousier Case 1924*). It is an implied contract between a banker and his customer that the former will not divulge to a third person the state of the latter's account without his express or implied consent.

Reasonable and proper occasions for disclosure may be:

(i) Under compulsion of law: For example, under orders of the Government, a Court or of Income Tax authorities, etc.

(ii) Under the Income Tax Act, 1961: Vide Sections 131 and 133, Income Tax authorities have powers to call for the attendance of any person or for necessary information from a banker for the purpose of assessment of the bank's customers.

(iii) Under the Companies Act, 1956: When the Central Government appoints an inspector to investigate the affairs of any joint-stock company under Section 135 or Section 137, the banker must produce all books and papers relating to the company.

(iv) Court's Order under the Banker's Books Evidence Act, 1891: A Court may also order a banker to disclose information relating to a customer's accounts. The Banker's Books Evidence Act, 1891, provides that certified copies of entries in the banker's books are to be treated as sufficient evidence, and the production of the books in the Court cannot be forced upon him. This protects a banker against the inconvenience of attending in a Court and producing his account books as evidence. According to Section 9 of the Act, "a certified copy of any entry in a banker's book shall in all legal proceedings be received as *prima facie* evidence of the existence of such entry and shall be admitted as evidence of the matter, transaction and accounts therein recorded in every case where, and to the same extent as, the original entry itself is now by law assembled, but not further or otherwise".

(v) Under the Reserve Bank of India Act, 1934: The Reserve Bank of India collects credit information from banking companies and also furnishes consolidated credit information to any banking company. Every banking company is under a statutory obligation under Section 45B of the Reserve Bank of India Act, 1934, to furnish such credit information to the Reserve Bank.

(vi) Under the Banking Regulation Act, 1949: According to Section 26 of the Banking Regulation Act, 1949, every banking company is required to submit an annual return of all such accounts in India which have not been operated upon for 10 years. Banks are required to give particulars of the deposits to the credit of each account.

(vii) Under the Gift Tax Act, 1958: Section 36 of the Gift Tax Act, 1958, confers on the Gift tax authorities powers similar to those conferred on Income Tax authorities under Section 131 of the Income Tax Act.

(viii) Disclosure to Police: Under Section (3) of the Criminal Procedure Code, a banker is not exempted from producing his account books before the police. The police officers conducting an investigation may also inspect a banker's books for the purpose of such investigations. (Section 5, Banker's Books Evidence Act, 1891).

(ix) Under the Foreign Exchange Regulation Act, 1933: Banking companies dealing in foreign exchange business are designated as authorised dealers in foreign exchange. Section 43 of the above Act empowers the officers of the Directorate of Enforcement and the Reserve Bank to inspect the books and accounts and other documents of any authorised dealer and also to examine on oath such dealer or director of a bank or an official in relation to its business.

Reasonable and proper occasions for disclosure may be:

(i) Under compulsion of law, *e.g.,* under orders of the Government, Court or Income Tax authorities, etc.

(ii) *Information to the Proposed Guarantor:* A guarantor has a right to be informed of the extent of his liability and the banker is justified in disclosing to him information about a customer's account so far as it is necessary for the purpose.

(iii) A banker is under a public duty to disclose information in case of danger of treason to the State.

(iv) Where a customer gives the name of his banker for reference, the latter will be justified in answering trade references.

(v) When a banker's own interests are in jeopardy, he can disclose the state of a customer's account.

Risks of Unwarranted and Unjustifiable Disclosure: The obligation of the banker to keep secrecy of his customer's accounts – except in circumstances noted above – continue even after the account is closed. If a banker discloses information unjustifiably, he shall be liable to his customer and the third party as follows:

(a) *Liability to the customer:* The customer may sue the banker for the damages suffered by him as a result of such disclosure. Substantial amount may be claimed if the customer has suffered material damages. Such damages may be suffered as a result of unjustifiable disclosure of any information or extremely unfavourable opinion about the customer being expressed by the banker.

(b) *Liability to third parties:* The banker is responsible to the third parties also to whom such information is given, if —

(i) The banker furnishes such information with the knowledge that it is false, and

(ii) Such party relies on the information and suffers losses.

Such third party may require the banker to compensate him for the losses suffered by him for relying on such information. But the banker shall be liable only if it is proved that he furnished the wrong or exaggerated information deliberately and intentionally. Thus, he will be liable to the third party on the charge of fraud but not for innocent misrepresentation. Mere negligence on his part will not make him liable to a third party.

This point was very clearly decided by the House of Lords in *Hedley Byrne and Co. vs. Heller and Partners Ltd.,* (1964). In this case the banker of a company, in reply to an enquiry from a firm of advertising agents, gave his opinion as follows: "The company was a respectably constituted company, considered good for its ordinary business engagements". The banker also added that the figure of 100,000 (mentioned by the enquirer) was larger than they were accustomed to see. The banker also stated that the opinion was given without responsibility on the part of the answering bank or its officials. The company subsequently went into liquidation and the advertising firm suffered a loss of 17,000 and sued the company's banker for the recovery of this amount on the ground that the replies were given negligently and in breach of duty to exercise care in giving them.

The Trial Court held that though the banker was negligent in his assessment of the position of the company but dismissed the claim on the ground that the banker owed no duty of care to the advertising firm. The House of Lords upheld this decision. Lord Reid stated that in general an innocent and negligent misrepresentation given by itself was no cause of action and that there must be something more than mere mis-statement in order to fasten liability on the person making it. Lord Morris observed that the banker, of whom the reference was made, was not expected to make a detailed inquiry and produce a well-balanced report. All that was expected was that he should answer honestly the question put to him from what he knew from the books and accounts before him.

The general conclusions of the Court can be summarised as follows:

(i) A banker answering a reference from another banker on behalf of the latter's constitution owes a duty of honesty to the said constituent.

(ii) If a banker gives a reference in the form of a brief expression of opinion in regard to creditworthiness, he does not accept and there is not expected of him any higher duty than that of giving an honest answer.

(iii) If the banker stipulates in his reply that it is without responsibility, he cannot be held liable for negligence in respect of the reference.

(3) Banker's Right to Claim Incidental Charges: As long as the banker-customer relationship exists, a banker has an implied right to charge a commission, interest and other charges for the various services rendered by him to a customer. Subject to an agreement to the contrary, a banker has the right to charge six-monthly compound interest on overdrawn amounts.

(4) Law of Limitation on Bank Deposits: Under the Law of Limitation, a creditor forgoes the right to recover the amount due from a debtor after the expiry of the period of limitation. In the case of bank deposits, however, the period of limitation does not begin till a demand for payment is made by the customer, and not from the time of receipt of deposits. *(Joachimson vs. The Swiss Bank Corporation,* 1921).

Under the provisions of Section 26 of the Banking Regulation Act, 1949, banking companies have to submit an annual return of all accounts which have not been operated for ten years, giving particulars of the deposits standing to the credit of each such account; but in the case of money deposited for a fixed period, the period of ten years will be counted from the date of expiry of such fixed period.

(5) Entries in the Pass Book: Another important feature of banker-customer relationship is whether entries in the pass book are finally binding on the customer. According to Sir John Paget: "The proper function which the pass book ought to fulfil is to constitute a conclusive and unquestionable record of transactions between the banker and the customer, and it should be recognised as such. After full opportunity of examination on the part of the customer, all entries, at least to his debit, ought to be final, and not liable to be subsequently reopened, at any rate to the detriment of the banker."

The legal position in connection with entries in the pass book is not satisfactory because of some conflict in Court decisions. But it is generally accepted that entries in the pass book are not finally binding on the customer. It was laid down in *Bank of England vs. Valiano 1891* as follows:

"The mere fact that a customer of a bank takes his pass book out from the bank and returns it without objection to any of the entries contained therein, being a pencil entry of the balance, does not amount to a settlement of account in between him and the banker in respect of these entries."

☞ Wrong Entries

Wrong entries in the pass book are of two types:

(i) Entries in favour of the customer; and

(ii) Entries in favour of the bank.

(i) Wrong Entries in Favour of Customer: In the case of that class of customers who spend all their income and do not keep a balance in the account, if a banker, by an error, credits such a customer with an amount and the customer, relying on the accuracy of the pass book draws cheques, and thus alters the position, the banker cannot subsequently debit him and recover this amount. (*Skyring vs. Greenwood, 1925, Holf vs. Markham, 1923*).

(ii) Wrong Entries in Favour of Bank: Where a banker, on the other hand, makes an erroneous entry in favour of himself which will have to be rectified unless he proves that the account was settled

as between himself and his customer, in what circumstances will the account be considered as settled? The only course open to the banker is to get in writing from the customer that an erroneous entry was made in the pass book. This is generally done by bankers periodically sending letters to customers stating the balance at the close of a particular period, to which are attached blank forms of acknowledgement as to the correctness of the amount which they are requested to fill in, sign and return. But the customer cannot be compelled to sign such a statement.

☞ Questions

1. What are the different forms of relationship that arise between a banker and his customer? Discuss the characteristic features of principal relationship between them.
2. What do you understand by a banker's lien? Point out the difference between a general and a special lien in this connection.
3. Can a banker exercise his lien in the following cases:
   (a) Sealed box kept by a customer for safe custody;
   (b) Dividend warrants handed over to him for collection on X's behalf, when X's account with him is overdrawn;
   (c) Where A, who is indebted to him, has a current account jointly with B;
   (d) A partnership firm ABC and Co. are indebted to him and A, a partner of the firm, carries a large balance in his current account.
4. "The pass book by itself cannot be relied upon as a settled account." Discuss the statement with reference to the general liability of a banker in respect of entries made by him in his customer's pass book.
5. Differentiate between a stale cheque and a post-dated cheque. Discuss the position of a banker who encashes a post-dated cheque.
6. Describe the relationship between a banker and a customer in regard to the following:
   (a) a current account;
   (b) a loan account;
   (c) a fixed deposit account;
   (d) a safe custody account; and
   (e) sale and purchase of securities on behalf of a customer.
7. What is a banker? When does the relationship of banker and customer commence? Is it a fiduciary relationship?
8. When and how may a banker disclose information regarding his customer's account?
9. What is the object of a banker when he supplies a pass book or a statement of account to his customer? Discuss the consequences of any erroneous entries made therein so far as they affect the banker and the customer. *[C.A.I.I.B., Part I]*
10. A cheque for ₹ 1,000, drawn by your customer, is presented for clearing on 27th January, 1970, for payment when the balance in the account is only ₹ 501. The customer happens to have a fixed deposit with the bank of a sum of ₹ 500. It is, however, observed that the cheque is dated Sunday, 25th January, 1970. How will you act in the circumstances?
11. "The relationship between a banker and a customer is that of a debtor and creditor." Explain the implications of this statement.
12. "The proper function of a pass book is to constitute a conclusive and unquestionable record of the transactions between a banker and his customer and it should be recognised as such." Discuss.
13. Examine the effect of entries made in the pass book on the banker and on the customer.
14. "The pass book belongs to the customer and the entries made therein by the banker are statements on which the customer is entitled to act." Discuss.
15. Are the entries in a pass book made by a banker binding on a customer? Discuss briefly why banks periodically send to their customers letters intimating the balance in their accounts at the close of a period and request the customer to confirm in writing the correctness of the balance.
16. To what extent does an entry in the pass book bind —
    (a) the banker; and
    (b) the customer?

17. A, a solicitor, has two current accounts at your branch; the first in his name, and the second also in his name with the addition of the words 'Clients account' as required under the Court's rules. He has drawn a cheque on the Clients' account in favour of a third party. Before the cheque is presented for payment, the Bank is served with a garnishee order in respect of a decree against A. How will you act? *[I.I.B., Part II]*
18. B, who has a current account at your branch, remits cash, expressly to meet, on re-presentation, a cheque which had been returned by your branch on the previous day with the remark "Refer to drawer, Please re-present". Before the said cheque is actually re-presented, garnishee order is served on the bank in respect of B's account. Will you pay the cheque when re-presented? *[I.I.B., Part II]*
19. On the day on which a garnishee order is served on your branch in respect of the account of C, the proceeds of certain shares and securities belonging to him which, on his instructions, had been sold by the Bank for settlement on that day, have not yet come to hand. When the sale proceeds are received subsequently, are they attached by the garnishee order? *[I.I.B., Part II]*
20. The account of a firm is overdrawn but each of the partners has a private account with a credit balance. Under what circumstances could the bank set-off those balances against the firm's debts? *[I.I.B., Part II]*
21. State three principles giving a practical example of each in which a banker would be justified by law in disclosing information concerning his customer's account. *[I.I.B., Part II]*
22. An advocate has 3 separate current accounts in your bank: *(i)* Personal account, *(ii)* Office account, and *(iii)* Clients' account. In expectation of good balances in clients' account, your bank had allowed him a clean advance of ₹ 25,000 in his personal account. For some reasons, the bank grew unhappy with this arrangement and, therefore, recalled the advance. When the advocate failed to respond to the bank's notice to repay, it decided to recourse against the other accounts for recovery of the outstanding balance of ₹ 25,000 in the personal account. The bank found that there was a credit balance of ₹ 15,000 in the client's account and also a credit balance of ₹ 2,000 in the office account. The advocate has also safe deposit locker in your bank, in the joint names of himself and his wife, with operations by Either or Survivor. He had a Fixed Deposit of ₹ 5,000 maturing after 4 months. He had also left some shares with the bank of the approximate value of ₹ 3,000 with instructions to sell them at or above a fixed price. The shares were still lying unsold.
    Consider the recourse which the bank can have on the balances and securities, etc., as detailed above for settlement of its dues in his personal account. *[I.I.B., Part II]*
23. On 19th May, 1977, your branch receives a garnishee order attaching all sums owing by the Bank to your customer X. At the time of the receipt of the order, X has got the following accounts:
    (i) A current account in the name of X with a balance of ₹ 3,000. Included in the balance, however, is a sum of 500 representing a cheque on another local bank which has been sent earlier in the day for collection through clearing, but which has not been realised.
    (ii) A fixed deposit for ₹ 5,000 deposited on 25th May, 1976, for one year in the name of X and maturing for payment on 25th May, 1977.
    (iii) A joint current account in the names of X and Y with a balance of ₹ 7,500.
    (iv) A current account in the name of 'X', executor to the estate of late Mr. 'Z' with a balance of ₹ 10,000.
    (v) An overdue unsecured loan account in the name of X wherein he owes the Bank ₹ 1,000. In view of the garnishe order, explain with reasons, how you would deal with each of the above accounts. *[I.I.B., Part I]*
24. A banker is under strict obligation not to disclose the state of his customer's account to any third party. There are, however, exceptions to this rule. Enumerate all such exceptions. *[I.I.B., Part I]*
25. Discuss a banker's right of set-off in the following cases:
    (i) There is a credit balance in the account of A. The banker wishes to set this off against an overdraft in the joint name of A and B.
    (ii) D is a guarantor for a loan granted by the Bank to S. The loan has become sticky. There is a credit balance in D's account. The banker wishes to set it off against D's liability as a guarantor.
    (iii) There is a surplus of insurance policy amount available with the Bank after adjustment of the balance in the deceased borrower R's loan account secured by the policy. The banker wishes to set off this surplus against a debit balance in R's clean overdraft account.

(iv) X has an account with the bank which has remained overdrawn for long despite many reminders. Meanwhile, X obtains legal representation to the estate of his deceased uncle Y, who too had a current account with the same bank. By virtue of such legal representation, X goes to the bank to withdraw the credit balance in Y's account, but the bank manager wants to set it off against the overdraft in X's account. *[I.I.B., Part II]*

26. An open bearer cheque for ₹ 7,000 drawn by your customer is presented for payment. The balance in his account is ₹ 6,600. The presenter while talking to the ledger keeper comes to know that the balance is short by ₹ 500. He pays into the account ₹ 500 by a pay-in-slip and informs the ledger keeper about the credit and gets his cheque for ₹ 7,000 passed. The drawer, when he comes to know of this, complains to the Manager and asks for a refund of the sum of ₹ 7,000.

    How will you as a banker deal with the situation? *[I.I.B., Part II]*

27. What is a banker's lien? Explain with examples the distinction between General Lien and Particular Lien. *[I.I.B., Part I]*

28. What is relationship between a banker and his customer? Discuss the special features of this relationship. *[I.I.B., Part I]*

29. Bring out clearly the main difference between:
    (a) Right of set-off and Banker's Lien.
    (b) Garnishee order and Attachment order. *[I.I.B., Part I]*

30. *(a)* The Banker's duty of secrecy is not absolute but qualified. Explain this statement with examples.
    (b) How would you deal with the following situation as a banker?
    (i) You have a joint savings bank account in the names of Mr. and Mrs. M.N. Desai 'payable jointly.' Mrs. Desai approaches the bank for knowing the balance in the account.
    (ii) An Income Tax Officer approaches you and requests to let him know the balances in the accounts of three valuable customers of your branch. He informs that he requires this information as the Income Tax Department has to recover arrears of tax payable by them.
    (iii) An overdraft limit of ₹ 20,000/- is granted to Mr. J.K. Mehta with the guarantee of Mr. C.C. Patel. This account shows a debit balance of ₹ 10,000 on 1st Feb., 1991. The guarantor Mr. Patel approaches you for letting him know the balance in the overdraft account of Mr. Mehta.
    (iv) You have a current account in the name of M/s. A.B. Patel & Co. The account is operated by either of the two partners. Later on, a minor son of Mr. A.B. Patel is admitted as a partner on 30th April, 1990. On 1st May, 1990, the minor son who is admitted as a partner approaches you with a request to let him know the balance in the account. *[I.I.B., Part I]*

31. How would you deal with the following cases:
    (i) An attachment order is received from the Income Tax Office impounding an amount of ₹ 10,000 in the account of A. A does not have an account in his own name but also a joint account with B (styled either or survior) which shows a balance of ₹ 20,000. *[I.I.B., Part. I]*
    (ii) A has an overdraft of ₹ 10,000 with your Mumbai Office. The overdraft has become stickly. Subsequently, A opened a Saving Bank Account with your Kolkata branch. The balance in the account was ₹ 15,000. An amount of ₹ 10,000 was transferred by your Kolkata office from A's account to liquidate his overdraft account with your Mumbai office. Meanwhile, a cheque for ₹ 12,000 received at Kolkata office was dishonoured for want of balance. *[I.I.B., Part I]*
    (iii) A maintains an account in his sole name and enjoys an overdraft which he does not repay despite demands. The bank adjusts the overdraft from the credit balance held in the account in the joint names of A& B. B challenges such adjustment and demands restoration of the amount. *[I.I.B., Part I]*
    (iv) A Court prohibitory/attachment order prohibiting the Bank from paying away any money on a constituent's Cash Credit Account in debit balance where sufficient drawing power is available, is received. *[I.I.B., Part I]*
    (v) An attachment order is received from the Income Tax Office for ₹ 5,000 in the name of Mr. A. A has only one joint account with B and C, payable to former and survivor which shows a balance of ₹ 9,000. *[I.I.B., Part I]*

CHAPTER 9

Operation of Bank Accounts

The two main functions of a banker are borrowing and lending. It is difficult nowadays to find any large-scale business which is carried on only with a proprietor's investments. But in the case of banking business, borrowing is much more important and relevant because a banker deals in money. The major part of the profits of a bank are earned by the use of funds borrowed from the general public or, in other words, deposited by the general public with the bank. This is the reason why we find that, in the case of the capital structure of banks, the percentage of deposits is much higher than that of the paid-up capital. The major part of the resource of a bank are, therefore, in the form of deposits accepted from the general public. To attract such deposits, banks offer different types of facilities and privileges to members of the public in different walks of life, engaged in numerous economic activities and having a different financial status.

In India, banks generally accept deposits in four types of accounts, namely:

(1) Fixed Deposit Accounts;

(2) Savings Deposit Accounts;

(3) Recurring Deposit Accounts or Cumulative Deposit Accounts; and

(4) Current Deposit Accounts.

In recent years a few types of accounts, have also been introduced. A few to be mentioned are Students Deposit Accounts, Multipurpose Deposit Scheme, Super Savings Scheme, Janta Deposit Scheme, Re-investment Plan and Pigmy Deposit Scheme.

Opening Bank Account

The most common and first service of the banking sector.

- Bank Savings Account — Bank Savings Account can be opened for eligible person/persons and certain organisations/agencies (as advised by Reserve Bank of India (RBI) from time-to-time)
- Bank Current Account — Bank Current Account can be opened by individuals/partnership firms/Private and Public limited Companies/HUFs/Specified Associates/Societies/Trusts, etc.
- Bank Term Deposits Account — Bank Term Deposits Account can be opened by individuals/ partnership firms/Private Limited Companies/HUFs/Specified Associates/Societies/Trusts, etc.

- Bank Account Online — With the advancement of technology, the major banks in the public and private sector has facilitated their customer to open bank account online. Bank account online is registered through a PC with an internet connection. The advent of bank account online has saved both the cost of operation for banks as well as the time taken in opening an account.

Note: A minors' account can be opened but jointly with a guardian and only the guardian would be allowed to operate the account.

☞ General Procedure to Open an Account

- The Bank will provide you with details of various types of accounts that you may open with the Bank.
- You can have your choice on what type of account would best suit you, based on your needs and requirements.
- The Bank will, prior to opening an account, require documentation and information as prescribed by the "Know Your Customer" (KYC) guidelines issued by RBI and or such other norms or procedures adopted by the Bank prior to opening the account.
- The due diligence process that the Bank would follow, will involve providing documentation verifying your identity, verifying your address, and information on your occupation or business and source of funds. As part of the due diligence process the Bank may also require an introduction from a person acceptable to the Bank if they so deem necessary and will need your recent photographs.
- The Bank is required by law to obtain Permanent Account Number (PAN) or General Index Register (GIR) Number or, where you do not possess such registrations, declaration in form No. 60 or 61 as specified under the Income Tax Rules.
- In the event that the account opening process is likely to take longer than normal, the Bank will inform you of the revised timeline.
- You can also call your branch or the executive for any queries that you may have and the branch/executive will revert on the query at the earliest.
- The Bank will provide you with the account opening forms and other relevant material to enable you queries that you may have and the branch/executive will revert on the open the account. Bank personnel will advise you on the complete details of information that would be required by the Bank for the verification process.
- The Bank reserves the right, at its sole discretion, to open any account and at such terms as the Bank may prescribe from time-to-time.

☞ Regulation of Competition in Banking

Competition in the business of accepting deposits takes two forms:

(i) Improvement in the customer services, and *(ii)* Offer of higher rates of interest to the depositors. Such competition, though essential for the growth of industry, is undesirable if it becomes unhealthy. Bankers realised the urgency of regulating competition amongst themselves in the field deposit mobilisation as early as 1958 when the leading banks in the country entered into a voluntary agreement.

The Inter-bank Agreement on Deposit Rates prescribed the maximum rates of interest payable by member-banks. Modifications in such rates were made as and when felt necessary. After the nationalisation of 14 major commercial banks in July 1969, the Reserve bank of India exercised its right to issue directives to the banks in regard to the deposit rates. The Inter-Bank withdrawal Agreement, was, therefore with effect from 1st April, 1970. The rates of interest on various types of deposit account and other terms, etc., were thereafter prescribed by the Reserve Bank through its directives was that the freedom to compete in the banking business was controlled and regulated rather than completely abolished. The smaller banks with comparatively less deposits were unable to compete with the bigger banks by offering the same rates of interest. In the directives of the Reserve Bank, therefore, smaller banks were permitted to compete with the bigger ones by offering reasonably higher rates of interest. Thus, both the maximum and minimum rates of interest payable on deposits were prescribed for smaller banks. These banks were at liberty to determine their own rates within the limits prescribed by the Reserve Bank according to their own judgement and discretion.

(1) FIXED DEPOSITS

In the case of fixed deposits or time deposits, the depositor agrees not to withdraw the amount deposited for a specified period, which ordinarily varies from three months to five years. The fixing of the period enables the banker to invest the money, without having to keep a reserve, and this is one of the reasons why "fixed deposits" or "term deposits" are so popular. The fixed deposits are also termed "time liabilities", which means that the withdrawable deposits are subject to a notice and not on demand. In the Banking Companies Act, 1949, the term "fixed deposits" is not mentioned anywhere.

☞ Legal Position

In the case of fixed deposits, the legal position of a banker is that of a debtor who is not bound to repay the amount before its due date. The banker continues to be a debtor even though the period fixed for the deposit has expired and the depositor has not withdrawn it. [*(i) Official Assignee of Madras vs. Smith,* 1908; *(ii) Subramanian vs. Kadirisan*].

☞ Transferability

When money is deposited in this account, the banker issues a receipt known as a "Fixed Deposit Receipt", which is usually marked "not negotiable". This receipt is not recognised as a negotiable instrument, or as giving the transferee the right to use the bank in his own name. It may be transferred by way of assignment to a third party, but since it is not a negotiable instrument, the transferee cannot have a better title than the transferor. Hence, such receipts cannot be treated like cheques.

☞ Loss of Deposit Receipt

If a fixed deposit receipt is lost, the amount can safely be paid by the bank on obtaining an ordinary indemnity bond signed by the depositor.

☞ Deposit in Joint Names

Bankers frequently receive fixed deposits in joint names of two or more persons. In such cases, both or all the parties should jointly withdraw except where one has died, in which case the property in the usual course passes to the survivor or survivors, to whom a banker can safely pay, provided he has no knowledge of any trust.

SPECIMEN OF THE BACKSIDE OF FIXED DEPOSIT RECEIPT

<table>
<tr><th rowspan="2">Memorandum</th><th colspan="4">Payment of Interest</th></tr>
<tr><th>Date</th><th>Half year ended</th><th>Amount</th><th>Signature of Authorised Official</th></tr>
<tr><td>1. The Fixed Deposit receipt duly discharged should be surrendered at the time of payment or renewal of deposit. To prevent loss of interest, the receipt intended for renewal should be sent on the due date.

2. The Fixed Deposit Receipt is not transferable by endorsement. In the absence of special instructions, the amount of the Deposit Receipt can be paid only to the depositor in person. Payment to any third party must be authorised by the depositor through a letter which should accompany the fixed deposit receipt duly discharged.

Rate of interest overleaf is subject to Reserve Bank's directives issued from time-to-time.

Received payment/Please renew for . . . months/years

Signature of Depositor</td><td></td><td></td><td></td><td></td></tr>
</table>

Request for Duplicate Receipt: In case one of the joint depositors informs the bank about the loss of the FDR and requests it to issue a duplicate one, the banker should insist that such request should be signed by all the depositors. It is possible that there might be a dispute between the depositors and the FDR might be in the possession of the other depositor.

☞ *Donatio Mortis Causa* (Donation of Receipt)

A deposit receipt is held to be a good subject of a *donatio mortis causa*; and on the death of the donor, the gift will pass to the donee, although it is expressly said to be not transferable. (*Amis vs. Witt, 1863*). When a fixed deposit is placed with a banker, the banker gives a receipt. A specimen of such a receipt is given below:

FDR/UA/313716

Notice of withdrawal given 4.9.1992 Due 4.9.1993
Central Bank of India
Head Office
Mahatma Gandhi Road, Bombay
Fixed Deposit Receipt
(Issued subject to conditions printed on reverse)
UDAIPUR.

No. 11/220 4.9.1990

Received from Shri. Rajiv Kumar

Rupees One thousand only as a deposit at the rate of twelve per cent per annum, to remain till notice of twelve months on either side expires.

Sd/-Agent
Sd/- Accountant

₹ 1,000

It is necessary to produce the receipt at the time of asking for payment on the due date. But it does not mean that the banker can decline to pay in case the deposit receipt is lost or destroyed. He would, in such a case, be entitled to ask for an indemnity bond with a proper security, or guarantee, from the customer. The fixed deposit receipts are not required to be stamped in India and England. An FDR may be offered as a security for an advance. While accepting an FDR as a security, a banker should see to it that it is discharged by the depositor and a memorandum of deposit is taken, setting forth the conditions under which it is lodged with the banker.

☞ Interest on Fixed Deposits

The terms and conditions and the rate of interest on fixed deposits are governed by Sections 21 and 35A of the Banking Regulation Act, 1949. Till April 21, 1992 fixed deposits were classified into four categories with varying periods of maturity starting from 46 days. The creation of various categories of fixed deposit with higher rates of interest for each successive category was intended to induce the depositors to take advantage of higher rates of interest by parting with liquidity for longer periods. The Reserve Bank of India revised the rates of interest on fixed deposits several times. During 1991 Reserve Bank made upward revision in the interest rates on deposits twice, along with rise in the Bank Rate. The main object of the step was to make bank deposits more attractive as compared to other savings instruments. These steps were undertaken as anti-inflationary measures when the inflationary pressure was mounting up.

With effect from April 22, 1992 Reserve Bank of India permitted the banks to prescribe their own rates of interest on fixed deposit of different maturities but the maximum rate of interest was not to exceed 13 per cent per annum. This rate was reduced on 12% w.e.f. 9th October, 1992 and further to 11% on March 1993. This step was taken to encourage competition amongst the banks by offering varying rates.

The maximum rate of interest on fixed deposits was further reduced to 10% effective Sept., 2, 1993. But thereafter it was raised to 11% effective Feb., 10, 1995. and further to 12% effective April 18, 1995.

In October 1995 Reserve Bank permitted the Scheduled Commercial Banks to fix their own interest rates on domestic term deposits with a maturity of over 2 years. Interest rate on domestic term deposits of 46 days and up to 2 years continued to be subject to the maximum rate "not exceeding 12% per annum".

On July 2, 1996 interest rates on deposits over one year were deregulated and banks were permitted to fix their own rates on term deposits with a maturity of over one year.

In July 1996 the minimum period of term deposit was reduced from 46 days to 30 days and the interest rate on term deposits of 30 days and up to one year was prescribed at not exceeding 11% which was subsequently reduced to 10% with effect from October 2, 1996. With effect from April 1997 the above ceiling rate has been linked to Bank Rate and has been fixed at two percentage point below the Bank Rate, which itself was reduced from 12% to 11% and again to 10% on July 1997.

In October 1997, the above ceiling was also withdrawn and thus the deposit interest rates were totally freed from Reserve Bank's regulations. Banks are now free to fix their own interest rates on fixed deposits of different maturities. Further, on April 29, 1998, the minimum period of maturity of term deposits has been reduced from 30 days to 15 days. Hitherto a restriction was imposed on the banks that they must offer the same rate on deposits of the same maturity irrespective of the size of such deposits. This restriction has also been removed since April 29, 1998. Banks are now free to allow different rates of interest varying with the size of the amount of the deposits for the same maturity. According to Reserve Bank's instructions permission to offer varying rates of interest for deposits of the same maturity will apply to domestic deposits of ₹ 15 lakh and above. Banks are required to disclose in advance the schedule of interest rates payable on deposits. Interest should be paid as per the schedule and should not be negotiated between the banker and depositor.

Consequently, banks have prescribed their own rates of interest and have also permitted higher rates on deposits above the specified amount, *viz.*, ₹ 15 lakh. In its credit policy announced on April 19, 2001, Reserve Bank of India permitted the banks to reduce the minimum maturity period for term deposits to 7 days (instead of 15 days) at the discretion of individual banks. This would be applicable to wholesale deposits of ₹ 15 lakh and above, on which banks may offer higher rates of interest. This will enable the non-bank investors to invest their short-term surplus funds in a more flexible manner when they will be phased out of the call money market.

☞ Fixed Deposit Schemes for Senior Citizens

Reserve Bank of India has also permitted the banks to formulate fixed deposit schemes specially meant for senior citizens on which they may offer higher and fixed rates of interest as compared with normal deposits.

These schemes will also incorporate simple procedure for automatic transfer of deposits to nominees of such depositors in the event of death.

Renewal Before Maturity: The Reserve Bank has permitted the banks to renew an existing term deposit before maturity without invoking the penalty provided:

(i) it is renewed before the date of maturity, and

(ii) the period of renewal is longer than the remaining period of the original deposits.

In such cases interest will be payable as follows:

(i) on the original deposit at the rate applicable to the period of which the deposit has actually run (*i.e.,* from the date of deposit to the date of renewal), prevailing at the time of original deposit (without levying any penalty);

(ii) interest for the period from the date of renewal will be allowed at the rate of prevailing on the date of renewal.

RATES OF INTEREST ON FIXED DEPOSITS W.E.F. 1.12.2002

		For Senior Citizens
15 days to 45 days	4.50%	
46 days to 90 days	5.50%	
91 days to 179 days	5.50%	
180 days to less than one year	5.79%	
1 year to less than two years	6.39%	6.92%
2 years to less than three years	6.60%	7.16%
Three years and above	7.11%	7.72%

Banks are now free to fix their own interest rates on deposits of various maturities, subject to the ceiling prescribed for short-term deposits of one year.

☞ Special Interest Rate Concessions

The Reserve Bank of India has permitted Regional Rural Banks to give an additional half per cent over the above rates. Similarly, cooperative banks are allowed to pay at their discretion an additional rate on fixed deposits as follows:

1. State Cooperative Banks in all Union territories and in the States of Manipur, Meghalaya, Nagaland, Arunachal Pradesh and Tripura 0.5%
2. State Cooperative Banks in other areas 0.25%
3. Central Cooperative Banks 0.5%
4. Primary Cooperative Banks 1.0%

In respect of the fixed deposits maintained by the following, the banks have been permitted to pay interest at half per cent above the rates which they are required or permitted to pay:

(i) Charitable or religious institutions;

(ii) Hospitals and medical institutions, educational institutions and those providing relief to the poor sections of society and not working for profit and whose income is exempt from income tax; and

(iii) Ex-servicemen disabled during 1971 Indo-Pak Conflict and/or widows/dependents of the defence personnel killed in action.

Scheduled commercial banks incorporated in India and having aggregate demand and times liabilities of less than ₹ 25 crore to pay, at their discretion have been permitted to pay a rate higher by 0.25 per cent per annum over the prescribed rates on all term deposits of less than three years.

☞ Payment of Interest

Normally, the interest accrued on fixed deposits is payable at maturity, but banks pay interest quarterly or half-yearly at the request of the depositor. The interest earned during a quarter is paid to the depositor in cash or is credited to his savings bank account.

☞ Interest after Maturity of Fixed Deposits

On the maturity of a fixed deposit, interest ceases to accrue, but the bank may, at its discretion, allow interest, if the deposit is renewed. According to the directive of the Reserve Bank, a banker may at his discretion, allow interest on matured fixed deposits for the overdue period provided that:

(a) the deposit is renewed with effect from the date on which it matured for payment, and

(b) the rate of interest allowed does not exceed the appropriate rate applicable to the period for which the deposit is proposed to be renewed as ruling on the date of maturity of the deposit.

In case, where only a part of the deposit is to be renewed, the bank may allow interest, for the overdue period, only on such part of the deposit, which is proposed to be renewed.

☞ Liability of the Bank (Legal Position)

Whether the bank is liable to pay interest on the amount of fixed deposit after the expiry of the period of deposit, this point was considered in '*The Hindustan Commercial Bank Ltd., vs. Jagtar Singh (AIR 1974, Punjab and Haryana 208)*'. In this case X deposited with the bank a sum of money in fixed deposit for 12 months in the name of Y, minor son of M. Y died before the maturity of the deposit. Y's father M obtained a succession certificate from the court empowering him to receive the amount of deposit with interest. X filed a suit against M and the bank, in which he claimed that he is the true owner of the amount of deposit. A temporary injunction was issued by the court restraining the bank from making payment to M.

On an application made by M, the court ordered the bank, during the pendency of suit, to either agree to pay interest on deposit or deposit the amount in court for being invested in securities. But the amount was not deposited by bank in court. In the judgement, the court declared M entitled to recover the amount. The bank paid the amount of deposit with 12 months' interest to M. Later M filed a suit for the recovery of interest for the subsequent period during which the amount remained with the bank.

In this case, it was contested on behalf of the bank that after the expiry of the period of deposit, the fixed deposit became a demand deposit and ceased to carry any interest, and that the claim of M for interest for the period after the maturity of deposit was not correct as there was no implied agreement between the parties to pay the overdue interest. It was held by the High Court that the question of whether a fixed deposit remains a deposit or becomes a loan after the expiry of the period of deposit, depends upon the intention of the parties and the implied agreement. The court held that deposits in banks are normally treated by the banks as payable on demand after the expiry of the period of the deposit. Thus, it remains a deposit and not a loan. The court further held that M suffered a loss of interest because the bank did not deposit the money in court for investment in securities. The bank having retained the amount was liable to pay interest.

☞ Renewal Before Maturity

The Reserve Bank has permitted the banks to renew an existing term deposit before maturity without invoking the penalty provided.

(i) it is renewed before the date of maturity, and

(ii) the period of renewal is longer than the remaining period of the original deposit.

In such cases interest will be payable as follows:

(i) On the original deposit the rate applicable to the period for which the deposit has actually run (i.e., from the date of deposit to the date of renewal); prevailing at the time of original deposit (without levying any penalty);

(ii) interest for the period from the date of renewal will be allowed at the rate prevailing on the date of renewal.

☞ Advance Against Fixed Deposit

The banker may also grant a loan to the depositor on the security of the Fixed Deposit receipt.

As regards interest rate on advances against fixed deposit receipts, Reserve Bank of India stipulated on April 29, 1998 that banks charge interest rate equal to Prime Lending Rate or less. In view of the decline in the Prime Lending Rate subsequently, the Reserve Bank decided in April 1999 that in case of deposit rate being in excess of the Prime Lending Rate, advances to depositors against Fixed Deposit Receipts can be made by banks without reference to the ceiling of PLR. Banks are permitted to charge suitable interest rates in such cases.

The Reserve Bank has advised the banks that they can give loans to depositors against FDR. maintained with them, up to 75 per cent of the total of: *(i)* actual deposits and *(ii)* the interest accrued thereon up to the time the loans are advanced.

The Fixed Deposit Receipts are marked 'Not Transferable' and cannot be transferred by endorsement. But the amount can be paid to a third party authorised by the depositor through a letter which should accompany the Receipt duly discharged. Thus, the ownership of the Receipt cannot be transferred to a third party but the latter may be deputed by the owner to collect the money on its due date. The debt represented by the Receipt may be assigned like any other debt, but a notice of assignment is to be served on the banker for this purpose.

☞ Liability of the Banker on Fixed Deposit Receipt

The liability of the banker in respect of fixed deposit receipt was decided by the Punjab High Court and the Supreme Court in the *United Commercial Bank Ltd., (Appellant) vs. Okara Grain Buyers Syndicate Ltd. (Respondent)* AIR, 1968 Supreme Court 1115). The Syndicate deposited a sum of ₹ 40,000 with the Bank in fixed deposit and the Receipt stated that the amount was received from the Syndicate A/c District Magistrate, Montogomery as the Syndicate was required to make such deposit for performing the procurement of foodgrains. On the due date, the Syndicate served a notice of withdrawal on the Bank and after making an endorsement on that behalf handed over the Receipt to the District Magistrate. Thereafter, the respondent migrated to India leaving all the property and set up a new place of business at Amritsar. On refusal to pay the amount, the Syndicate appealed to the Punjab High Court which held that the *deposit was subject to the conditions expressly mentioned in the receipt and no others* and the District Magistrate was not given any dominion over the amount of deposit. The High Court ordered for the payment of the deposit money to the Syndicate, which was also required to give an indemnity for restitution of the amount in case the Bank was required to pay the amount to the District Magistrate.

On appeal, the Supreme Court upheld the above decision and observed that the deposit receipt was in the name of the Syndicate merely because it was made out A/c District Magistrate was not by itself sufficient to create any interest in favour of the District Magistrate. *In law the District Magistrate was not constituted the owner of the money deposited by virtue of mere delivery of the receipt.* In the books of the Bank, the Syndicate was the owner thereof and was alone entitled to demand payment. In terms of the deposit receipt, the receipt was non-transferable and payment of the amount had to be made to the Syndicate. In the absence of any obligation-contractual or fiduciary-undertaken by the Bank in favour of the District Magistrate, the Bank could not withhold payment of money after the expiry of the period of notice. The Supreme Court also upheld the decision of the High Court directing the Syndicate to give an indemnity to the Bank against any possible loss.

☞ Payment of Fixed Deposit Before Maturity

Although, normally fixed deposit is payable on or after the date of maturity, banks allow the depositor premature encashment if he so desires. In premature encashments of fixed deposit the rate of interest is calculated asunder: First, the rate of interest applicable for the deposit on the basis of the period for which it retained with the bank is determined. Then the said rate is reduced by one per cent point. This penalty for premature withdrawal of term deposits was reduced from two per cent to one per cent with effect from May 1, 1983.

The Reserve Bank has permitted with effect from 19th September, 1981, that if a term deposit is repaid prematurely on the death of a depositor to the heirs or legal representatives, this penalty is not to be imposed by banks.

☞ Premature Repayment in Joint Named Fixed Deposits

If a fixed deposit is in the name of two or more depositors, and one of the depositors requests the banker for repayment before the date of maturity, the banker should make such payment only after obtaining the consent of all other joint depositors. One depositor has no right to ask for the withdrawal of money before the date of maturity. The mandate "payable to either or survivor" is intended to be applicable only at the time of maturity of the deposit. Till then it remains a joint debt, which may be withdrawn with the consent of the depositors.

☞ Request for Change in Names in FDR

A fixed deposit receipt is issued in the name/names of depositors who deposit money with the bank for a fixed period. Many times depositors request the banker for additions or deletion of names in the FDR. In making any changes in names in an FDR the banker should take due precaution and examine the legal implications in each case. If an FDR is issued in the name of one person and he wants to add the name of another person, the banker should have no objection to the compliance of the mandate of the customer. In case an FDR is issued in the name of an unmarried woman and after marriage she requests the banker to change her surname in the receipt, the request of the lady should be complied by the bankers.

In case an FDR is issued in the names of two or more persons, and one of the depositors wants to add a new name, the banker should not add the name without the consent of all other depositors. In case a depositor dies, the banks permit the addition of name/names of legal heir or legal representatives jointly or individually. Such deposits can be split up equally in the names of each legal heirs or can be held jointly in the names of all the legal heirs. In such cases, if the original term of the deposit is not reduced, it is not considered as renewal of deposit or its premature payment.

☞ Repayment of Fixed Deposits

To bring about an effective control over 'benami deposits' with banks and companies and also to check tax evasion, an amendment has been made in the Income Tax Act from 1981. Vide this amendment all the banks, companies, cooperative societies and partnership firms are required to repay deposits made with them by Account Payee cheques or Account Payee drafts if the amounts of such deposits repayable together with interest is ₹ 10,000 or more. This rule does not apply to savings bank and current deposits. If the depositor has an account with the same bank, the amount of fixed deposit can be credited to his account and in such a case there is no need to pay the amount of FDR by an Account Payee cheque unless the depositor wants payment of the amount. Failure to comply with this rule provides for imprisonment up to a term of two years and a fine up to the amount of deposit.

The Direct Tax Laws (Amendment) Act, 1987 provides that a banking company or a cooperative shall pay any deposit by an account payee cheque or draft if the deposit together with interest, if any, payable or the aggregate of the deposits held by a person together with interest, if any payable on such deposits is ₹ 20,000 or more.

The bank can also repay such deposits by crediting the amount to the Savings or Current account of the same depositor. If this requirement is not complied a penalty amounting to the sum equal to the amount of deposit shall be imposed. There is also provision for imprisonment up to a term of two years and a fine up to the amount of deposits, in case of failure to comply with this requirement.

☞ Deduction of Tax at Source

Section 194A of the Income Tax Act provides for deduction of tax at source from interest of time deposits, payable by a bank or cooperative society where it exceeds ₹ 10,000 in a financial year. For this purpose, time deposit means a deposit repayable after the expiry of a fixed period and excludes recurring deposits. Moreover, interest on time deposits with a primary agricultural credit society, primary credit society, a cooperative land development bank will not be subject to tax deduction at source. Deduction of tax will not be made in case of depositors who furnish an affidavit or statement that their income is below taxable limit or that the tax on their estimated income would be nil.

Tax is to be deducted at source at the prescribed rates. At present these rates are: 10% for a resident other than a company and 20% for a domestic company.

☞ New Schemes of Liquidity for Term Deposits

Some leading banks, specially foreign banks, new private sector banks and State Bank of India have recently started new schemes to attract the depositors by providing additional liquidity to their Term Deposits. State Bank of India has launched a Multi Purpose Deposit Scheme wherein the Term Deposits/Special Term Deposit Accountholder is permitted to withdraw from Term Deposit through savings Bank A/c in units of ₹ 1,000 without attracting any penal rate of interest. For this facility the Term Deposit should be for a minimum amount of ₹ 10,000 and thereafter in multiples of ₹ 1,000.

(2) SAVINGS DEPOSIT ACCOUNT

This type of account is suited to those who want to deposit their small savings in bank, which they need to withdraw only occasionally. The interest rates on savings deposits is lower than that allowed on fixed deposits, but higher than that allowed on current deposits. It is calculated on the lowest balance kept during a month.

To open a savings bank account, a person has to fill in a prescribed form and make a declaration therein that he has read the rules governing the savings bank account. He has also to give his specimen signatures. The customer is given a pass book, a cheque book for withdrawals and pay-in-slip book for deposits.

Banks have introduced the practice of imposing a service charge of ₹ 10 per annum on those savings accounts whose minimum balance is not maintained, number of withdrawals exceeds the specified limit. Banks waive this charge in case of respectable customers.

☞ Restrictions on Savings Bank Deposits

Any amount, subject to a minimum of ₹ 50 may be deposited in the savings bank account. Minimum opening amount for semi-urban area is ₹ 200, whereas for urban area it is ₹ 500. Minimum balance for cheque book account. in semi-urban area is ₹ 250 whereas in urban area it is ₹ 500.

☞ Restrictions on Withdrawals

Banks impose restrictions on the right of the depositor to withdraw money within a specified period of time. In one year, the number of withdrawals is limited to 150. But bank may allow more withdrawals in special cases according to their discretion. Depositors are not allowed to withdraw a sum which is less than ₹ 50 or a sum which is not multiple of rupee one unless the account of depositor is being closed.

☞ Interest on Savings Bank Account

The rate of interest to be paid by banks to depositors on saving bank deposits is prescribed by the Reserve Bank of India. At present the rate of interest on savings bank account is 4.5%. Scheduled Banks with less than ₹ 25 crore deposits are permitted to give quarter per cent more interest than the prescribed rate on savings bank deposits. Similarly, Cooperative Banks and Regional Rural Banks have been allowed to give half per cent more interest than the normal interest rate prescribed by the Reserve Bank. Interest is calculated at quarterly or half-yearly rates, on the minimum balance to the credit of the account during the period from the tenth day to the last day of each calendar month on every complete sum of ₹ 10 and is credited to the account.

Savings accounts should not be opened by the banks in the name of Government Departments, Municipal Corporations, Panchayat Samitis, State Cooperative Societies, State Housing Boards, State Textbook Publishing Corporations and Metropolitan Development Authority.

☞ Payment of Interest

The rate of interest payable by the banks on deposits maintained in savings accounts is prescribed by the Reserve Bank. At present the rate of interest on savings deposits is 4.5%. Scheduled commercial banks with deposits less than ₹ 25 crore may, at their discretion, give an additional interest of quarter per cent. Regional Rural Banks may give an additional half per cent. The above rate of interest is payable irrespective of whether cheque facility is extended or not.

Interest is calculated at quarterly or longer rests on the minimum balance to the credit of the account during the period from the tenth day to the last day of each calender month on every complete sum of ₹ 10 and is credited to the account. The State Bank of India credits interest once in a year.

The Reserve Bank of India has prohibited the banks to open a savings bank account in the name of any trading or business concern whether such concern is a proprietary one or a partnership firm, a company or an association. The banks should also not open a savings account in the name of:

(i) government departments,

(ii) bodies depending upon budgetary allocations for performance of their functions[1] (*i.e.,* which receive grants, loans, subsidies or subscription to its share capital from Government).

---

1. This prohibition does not apply in case of the following organisations:

(i) A primary cooperative credit society which is being financed by that bank. *(ii)* Societies registered under the Societies Registration Act, 1980 or any State Law; *(iii)* Companies licensed by the Central Government under Section 25 of the Companies Act, 1956, and permitted not to add to their names the words 'limited' or 'private limited'; *(iv)* Institutions which render social or economic assistance to weaker and underprivileged sections of society; *(v)* Institutions which are not liable to pay income-tax under the Income Tax Act, 1961. Banks are required to get approval of the Reserve Bank for opening such accounts.

Banks have been prohibited to pay interest, on savings bank accounts opened in the name of any trading or business concern, by the Reserve Bank of India. It is immaterial, for the purpose of this restriction, whether the concern is sole trader, partnership firm, a company or an association. But with the prior approval of the Reserve Bank, a scheduled commercial bank may pay interest on the savings bank deposit accounts opened by primary cooperative credit society, society registered under Societies Registration Act, companies licensed under Section 25 of the Companies Act, 1956, institutions which render social and economic assistance to weaker and privileged sections of society and institutions which are not liable to pay income tax.

(3) RECURRING DEPOSIT ACCOUNT OR CUMULATIVE DEPOSIT ACCOUNT

In recent years, a new type of account has been introduced by most of the banks in India which is known as the Recurring Deposit Account. The purpose of this account is to encourage people to save regularly and get a higher rate of interest from banks on such savings. A customer who opens a recurring deposit account in a bank is required to deposit a fixed sum, generally a multiple of ₹ 5, 10, 20 etc., in the bank every month for a specified period which may be one or two to five years or ten to twenty to sixty months.

The rate of interest offered by banks on a recurring deposit account is higher than the rate of interest on a saving bank account, because the former is like a fixed deposit and the money from this account cannot be withdrawn before the date of maturity. The rate of interest on this account is almost equal to that of fixed deposit account, *i.e.,* 6 per cent to 10 per cent compound interest payable on 12 months to 60 months series.

In the case of premature payments, interest at simple rates is allowed at the rates mentioned below:

If the account has remained with the bank

	Rates effective 1-12-2002
(i) For 15 days to 45 days	4.50%
(ii) For 46 days to 90 days	5.5%
(iii) For 91 days to 179 days	5.50%
(iv) For 180 days to less than one year	5.79%
(v) For 1 year to less than two years	6.39%
(vi) For 2 years to less than three years	6.60%
(vii) For 3 years and above	7.4%

A recurring deposit account can be transferred from one branch to another without any charge. It may be opened in the name of one person, jointly in the names of two or more persons, or by minor or by a guardian in the name of a minor. The depositor is given a pass book by the bank in which entries of deposits are made. The accumulated amount, together with interest, is payable one month after the payment of the last instalment.

(4) CURRENT DEPOSIT ACCOUNT

In the case of deposits in current accounts, also called *Demand Deposits,* the banker incurs the obligation of paying all cheques drawn against him as long as there is enough money to the credit of his customer. The customer, on the other hand, pays money in the form of cash, cheques, postal orders, etc., into his current account. The banker supplies to the customer a pass book, a pay-in-slip book for deposit and a cheque book for withdrawals.

The customer is allowed to deposit or withdraw money as and when he likes. No interest is allowed by most banks on current account deposits; but banks do allow interest if the balance does not fall below a certain minimum limit. Some banks charge one or two rupees every half year with a view to meeting the expense of maintaining such an account. This charge is known as a *bank charge* or an *incidental charge*. Some banks insist that the balance in a current account must not be allowed to go below a certain level.

Banks may pay interest on current account of Regional Rural Banks and half per cent below the borrowing rate fixed for the RRB by the sponsor bank.

Since May 1983, banks have been permitted to pay interest on balances lying in current accounts in the name of a deceased depositor from the date of death of the depositor till payment to the legal heirs. Interest on such amount shall be payable at savings banks deposit rate.

The State Bank makes no charge for keeping an account provided the balance maintained is sufficient to compensate the bank for the work involved. In case of unremunerative accounts involving lot of work but without the maintenance of sufficient balances, the banker charges incidental expenses from the customer. The public sector banks now impose a uniform 'ledger folio charge' of ₹ 20 per folio (*i.e.,* one side of the ledger page) on accounts having average balance below ₹ 25,000.

A current account carries certain privileges which are not given to a Saving bank account holder, *e.g.*:

(i) Third Party cheques and cheques with endorsement may be deposited in the current account for collection and credit.

(ii) Overdraft facilities are given in case of current accounts only.

(iii) The loans and advances granted by the banks to their customers are not given in the form of cash but through the current accounts. Current accounts thus earn interest on all types of advances granted by the banker.

Bankers frequently allow customers to overdraw on their current accounts if they also have a fixed deposit account; in these circumstances, they rely for security on their right to set-off between the current and deposit accounts. This right of set-off may be exercised even though the customer, after drawing the said overdraft cheques, becomes insolvent.

☞ Rules in Clayton's Case

The general rule with regard to the approprition of payments is that the party paying the money, *i.e.*, the debtor, has the right to appropriate the payment to whatever debt he likes. Therefore, if the customer instructs his banker to appropriate the money he is paying for a specific debt, the banker is bound to appropriate it accordingly. If the debtor, at the time of payment, makes no specific or implied appropriation, the creditor may appropriate the payment even to a debt barred by the period of limitation. In this case, as soon as the creditor's appropriation is notified to the debtor, it becomes irrevocable. These rules of appropriation apply to current accounts as well. If no specific appropriation is made, whether by the debtor or the creditor, the law appropriates the payment by discharging or reducing the first item on the debit side of the current account by the first item on its credit side. Thus, under this rule, the sum first paid is the sum that is first paid out. [*Sir W. Grant M.R., in Clayton's Case* (1816) 1 Meivale 572]. This rule is popularly known as the *Rule in Clayton's Case* and vitally affects current accounts, especially when overdrawn.

The rule in Clayton's Case applies only when the account is still running and not broken. Therefore, the banker who wants to avoid the application of this rule must break the account and open a new account distinct from the ruled off account and, if possible, get the written consent of the customer for opening such a new account. (*Deely vs. Lloyds Bank Ltd., 1912*). When this is done and payments in and out are credited and debited to such a new account, the rule in Clayton's Case will not apply so far as the old account is concerned.

New Deposit/Savings Schemes Introduced by Banks

In recent years banks have introduced many new attractive savings schemes. Some of the important schemes are discussed below:

1. Super Savings Package

This is a scheme of long-term savings in which the depositor has to deposit every month a specified sum for a long period say 10 to 40 years, and after the expiry of that period the total amount along with accumulated interest is paid back to him.

2. Cash Certificates

Cash certificates of different face values are issued by banks. These certificates are payable after a specified period of maturity. The issue price and the period of maturity is specified in advance, for example, a cash certificate with face value of ₹ 500 for 12 months can be purchased at ₹ 456.

3. Annuity Deposit

In this scheme the depositor makes an initial deposit of a specified amount and therefore receives monthly annuity amount for a specific time period. The depositor has to opt for a monthly annuity for 24, 36, 48, 84 or 120 months and the amount of initial deposit depends upon the period of annuity. For example, by making an initial deposit of ₹ 1,551.50, one gets a monthly annuity of ₹ 50 for 36 months, which includes the amount of deposit as well as interest.

4. Reinvestment Plan

This savings scheme is similar to fixed deposits, the only difference is that interest on deposit is calculated periodically and is reinvested/added to the deposit. The depositor gets the interest only at the time of maturity along with the principal amount. The period of deposit may range from one year to ten years. According to the directive of the Reserve Bank, in case of withdrawal of deposit before maturity, compound interest with quarterly rests at prescribed rate is to be allowed. In case a depositor takes an advance against deposit, accrued interest is also to be taken into account for determining the margin.

5. Perennial Pension Plan

In the Perennial Pension Plan, the depositor deposits a specified sum every month for 84 months. From the 86th month the bank pays a monthly pension. The banker agrees to pay a specified sum to the depositor when pension is discontinued.

6. Education Plan

This is a plan to motivate the depositors to save for the education of their children. The depositor is required to deposit ₹ 100 per month during the period his child studies from nursery to seventh class. After this period, the bank pays a specified sum annually up to the time the child completes university education. In the same plan, there are provisions for higher education or even education abroad.

☞ Deposit Schemes for Indians Living Abroad

In the last few decades a large number of Indians have gone abroad either temporarily on a job or have permanently settled there. Most of them earn and save and even repatriate large sums of money to their dependents or relations in India. To mobilise such savings and attract the savings as deposits in Indian banks, the Government have offered many concessions and incentives, to Indian citizens and persons of Indian origin living abroad, on their remittances to India.

☞ Definition of Non-resident Indians

To open an account under any of the schemes meant for non-resident Indians, one must qualify as a non-resident Indian, by fulfilling any one of the conditions as given in the Foreign Exchange Regulation Act:

1. He is an Indian citizen, who stays abroad for employment or for carrying on a business or vocation, or for any other purpose in circumstances indicating an indefinite period of stay outside India.
2. He is an Indian citizen working abroad with international organisation like the UNO, IMF, etc.
3. He is an official of Central/State Government and public sector undertaking deputed abroad for temporary assignments.
4. He is a person of Indian origin. A person is deemed to be of Indian origin if he at any time held an Indian passport or he or either of his parents or any of his grand parents was an Indian and a permanent resident in undivided India at any time. Wife of a citizen of India or of a person of Indian origin is all deemed to be of Indian origin even though her parents are non-Indians.

At present, banks in India operate the following two types of deposit accounts for Indians living in foreign countries:

1. Non-resident (External) Accounts, and
2. Foreign Currency (Non-resident) accounts.

☞ Non-resident (External) Accounts Scheme

Non-resident Indians or aliens of Indian origin can open current or savings bank account in rupee units in India under this scheme. The capital and interest earned on these accounts are freely irrepatriable at the prevailing rate of exchange. The amount deposited in such accounts can be invested in Government securities, National Savings Certificates, units of an Unit Trust of India, etc. The principal amount invested along with the income earned on such investments are also freely repatriable. Interest earned on these accounts is tax free.

☞ Foreign Currency (Non-resident) Accounts Scheme

Under this scheme, Indians living abroad are permitted to open accounts in foreign currencies in India. At present deposits in US dollars, Pound-sterling, Yen, Franc and DM are accepted. The amount to be deposited may be remitted by the depositor by a bank draft, cheque, mail transfer or telegraphic transfer. Interest on deposits is free of income tax. Amount of deposit and interest are repatriable in the currency in which the account is maintained. This protects the depositor from any loss arising from fluctuations in exchange rates. Interest is payable every six months (except in case of deposits for less than 12 months) or on maturity whichever is earlier. Interest rates on deposits are the same as prescribed for deposits from Indian nationals. On deposits for one year and above, in both types of accounts of Indian living abroad, the banks pay an additional interest of two per cent more than the rates paid on domestic local currency deposits of the same period. Any loan or advance against such deposits can be given only after prior approval of Reserve Bank of India. Interest on such advance shall be 2 per cent higher than the interest paid on deposit, and a margin of not less than 25% of the amount of deposit shall be maintained.

☞ Classification of Deposits

Deposits of the commercial bank have been classified by the Reserve Bank into two broad categories, namely, *(i)* Demand deposits, and *(ii)* Time deposits. It is in these two heads, the data about deposits with banks are published by the Reserve Bank of India. The details of the types of deposits included under each category are given below:

☞ Demand Deposits

(i) Current deposits
(ii) Demand liabilities portion of savings bank deposits
(iii) Margins held against letter of credit/guarantees (if payable on demand)
(iv) Balances in overdue fixed deposits
(v) Cash certificates
(vi) Recurring deposits
(vii) Outstanding telegraphic and mail transfers, demand drafts
(viii) Unclaimed deposits
(ix) Credit balances in cash credit accounts
(x) Deposits held as security for advances which are repayable on demand.

☞ Time Deposits

(i) Fixed deposits
(ii) Cash certificates
(iii) Recurring deposits
(iv) Time liabilities portion of savings bank deposits
(v) Staff security deposits
(vi) Margins held against letter of credit if not payable on demand, and
(vii) Fixed deposits held as security for advances.

☞ Nomination by Depositor

Some of the recommendations of the Banking Commission, accepted by the Government, were incorporated in the Banking Laws (Amendment) Act, 1983, by which a new insertion, Part IIB, has been made in the Banking Regulation Act, 1949, which provides for the facility of nomination by depositors in banks as follows: According to this provision, a single depositor, or all the joint depositors together, may nominate, in the prescribed manner, a person to whom, in the event of death of the depositor or all the joint depositors, the amount to his/their credit may be paid by the banking company. A nomination made by a depositor in the prescribed manner will confer upon the nominee right to receive the amount of deposit from the bank. The nominee shall become entitled to all the rights of the depositor/depositors, to the exclusion of all other persons on the death of depositor/depositors. If the nominee is a minor, the depositor may appoint any person to receive the amount of deposit in the event of his death during the minority of the nominee. The depositor may amend or cancel nomination in a prescribed manner. If a banker makes a payment to a nominee, according to the provisions of this section, he shall be fully discharged from its liability, and claim of any other person against the nominee shall not be accepted by such payment.

☞ Status of a Nominee

The question regarding the legal status of a nominee is an important one. Whether the nominee becomes the absolute owner of the amount received by him or other legal heirs of the deceased can put forward their claims. This problem relates to nomination in general — whether it is bank deposit or insurance policy or any other property. The decision in a recent Supreme Court case makes the point clear. In *Sarbati Devi vs. Usha Devi* AIR, 1984, SC. 346, the deceased had nominated his wife in case of his insurance policy. His mother and minor son claimed their shares from the insurance money received by the wife from the Life Insurance Corporation of India. The Supreme Court held that:

"A mere nomination made under Section 39 of the Insurance Act, does not have the effect of conferring on the nominee any beneficial interest in the amount payable under the life insurance policy on the death of the assured." "The nomination only indicates the hand which is authorised to receive the amount, on the payment of which the insurer gets a valid discharge of its liability under the policy. The amount, however, can be claimed by the heirs of the assured in accordance with the Law of Succession governing them."

According to this judgement of the Supreme Court, even after nomination, the law of succession will still prevail, and the nominee does not become the absolute owner of the amount received by him.

☞ Opening of New Account

Opening an account with the banker, a customer enters into relationship with a banker. As already noted in the previous chapter, the special features of this relationship impose several obligations on the banker. He should, therefore be very careful in opening an account in the name of a customer. Though any person may apply for opening an account in his name but the banker reserves the right to do so in being satisfied about the identity of the customer. The following precautions should be taken in this regard :

1. Application on the Prescribed Form: The request for opening a savings or current account is made on the prescribed form of the bank concerned. Bank provides separate application forms for opening savings and current accounts for individuals, partnership firms and companies. The applicant is required to mention his name, occupation, full address, specimen signature and the name and signature of a referee. He also undertakes to comply with the bank's rules in force from time-to-time for the conduct of the account. It may be changed or modified by the bankers and such modified rules shall be acceptable to the customer. The applicant is also required to submit three copies of his Passport Size Photographs.

2. Introduction of the Applicant: Before opening a savings or current account in the name of an intending customer, the banker must get true identity of the former in order to ensure that he is a respectable person. The banker, thus, reserves the right not to open an account in the name of a person whose true identity has not been established or who is considered to be an undesirable person, *e.g.*, a thief, robber, etc. The applicant may be introduced to the banker in any of the three ways:

(*i*) A respectable person — either a customer of the same branch of the bank or who is known to the staff of the branch — introduces him by signing on the application form itself along with his full address.

(ii) The applicant may give the name of any respectable person or that of another bank as referee. The banker enquires from the said referee about the integrity, honesty, respectability and financial standing of the applicant and his past experience in dealing with the applicant. If the referee sends no reply, the banker should not open the account unless satisfactory introduction is given otherwise.

(iii) The Reserve Bank had advised the banks that pay books or postal identification cards or identity cards of armed forces/police/government departments or passports may be considered sufficient for establishing the identity of persons desiring to open deposit accounts without cheques facility.

☞ Operating the Bank Account

The word 'operate' in relation to a bank account means that the customer deposits further sums of money and cheques, etc., into the bank and withdraws money according to his need or convenience. A special feature of banking business is that each and every transaction of money with the customer is supported by a separate slip or document. A customer is, therefore, required to make use of *(i)* pay-in-slips for depositing money, and *(ii)* cheques for withdrawing money from the bank.

(i) The Pay-in-slip-book contains slips with perforated counterfoils to be filled in by the depositor himself or by his agent at the time of depositing cash, cheques, drafts, bills, etc., to the credit of his accounts. Usually every bank supplies free of cost to the customers separate pay-in-slips for depositing *(i)* cash, and *(ii)* cheques, etc. Through the size and design of such slips vary from bank-to-bank but the contents include information relating to the date of deposit, name and account number of the customer, amount to be deposited, the denomination of currency notes, etc., (in case of cash only), the cheque number and the name of the drawee (in case of cheques, etc.)

After filling in all such details on the foil and the counterfoil, the customer hands over the same together with cash to the cashier (in case of cash) or cheques, etc., to any other responsible officer (in case of cheque) who acknowledges receipt of the same by signing the counterfoil along with the stamp of the bank and returns it to the customer. The slip retained by the bank is passed on to the clerk concerned for making necessary credit entries in the account of the customer.

(ii) The Cheque Book contains blank forms of cheques which are used as an instrument to withdraw money from the bank. In case of savings bank account a cheque book is provided to only those customers who undertake to maintain minimum balance to their credit. Other customers may withdraw from their savings bank account through a withdrawal form available from the bank. But in the latter case it is essential that the pass book must accompany the withdrawal form every time. The blank form of cheques and their counterfoils are serially numbered. The cheque book also contains a requisition slip which, duly filled in, is presented by the customer for obtaining another cheque book from the bank.

(iii) The Pass Book is a small handy book issued by a banker to his customer to record all dealings between them. In fact, it is an authenticated copy of the customer's account in the account books of the banker. The purpose of issuing a pass book to a customer is to acquaint him periodically with the state of affairs of his account with the bank. The pass book also contains rules and regulations governing the savings account. The customer deposits the pass book periodically with the bank for the purpose of recording entries therein. As it passes from the hands of the customer to the banker and *vice versa*, it is called a 'Pass Book'.

A pass book is very important to a customer because it enables him to know some of the entries made by the banker in his ledger account, *e.g.*, the amount of interest allowed or charged, the incidental or other charges made by the banker. In business where such entries are many, businessmen prepare

Bank Reconciliation Statements with the help of the pass book to tally the balance shown in the cash book with that given in the pass book. A specimen of pass book is given.

The following points are important in this connection:

1. Entries in the pass book are to be recorded by the clerk of the bank and must bear the initials of the accountant. The customer should not write any entry himself, even for the purpose of reconciling the bank balance.
2. Whenever the banker sends a pass book to the customer, it must show up to date entries.
3. If the pass book is lost by the customer, a duplicate pass book may be issued by the banker and marked as 'Duplicate.'
4. In case of a savings bank account, the pass book must accompany the withdrawal form everytime when money is withdrawn through a withdrawal form.

Some banks, send to the customers a Statement of Account periodically, *i.e.,* fortnightly or monthly, in place of providing the customer with a pass book. Such statement shows the relevant entries in the customer's account during the given period and are filed by the customer.

SPECIMEN OF BANK PASS BOOK

NAME
ADDRESS

A/c. No...........

IN SAVINGS FUND ACCOUNT WITH

PUNJAB NATIONAL BANK........

DATE	PARTICULARS	Dr. ₹ P.	Cr. ₹ P.	Balance ₹ P.	Acctt's Initials
	Carried over				

In fact this viewpoint rests on the presumption that the customer is under an obligation to verify the entries made in the pass book periodically and if he detects any mistake, he ought to bring it to the notice of the banker within a reasonable period. If he does not do so and remains silent after the receipt of the pass book, customer's concurrence with correctness of the entries is taken for granted. In some of the legal judgments, specially in the United States, this viewpoint was upheld by the Courts. According to this viewpoint negligence or omission on the part of the customer to examine the correctness of the entries in the pass book is a fault on his part and thus renders pass book record as an evidence of an accepted account.

Divergent Viewpoint: The implied obligation on the customer to examine the pass book has not been supported in many other judicial decisions in England and India. In the absence of such obligation on the customer, the entries in the pass book cannot be treated as a conclusive proof of their accuracy and as settled account. The customer is competent to point out the mistakes or omissions in the pass book at any time he happens to know about them. Thus, the entries in the Pass Book do not form the conclusive evidence of their correctness or accuracy. The entries erroneously made or wrongly omitted may be either advantageous to the customer or the banker. Both the parties, may, therefore, indicate the mistakes or omissions therein and get them rectified. The legal position in this regard is as follows:

LEGAL ASPECTS OF ENTRIES IN THE PASS BOOK

Though the pass book contains true and authenticated record of the customer's account with the banker, no unanimous view prevails regarding the validity of the entries in the pass book. The banker may err in recording the entries in the pass book. The question, therefore, arises whether the pass book constitutes a conclusive proof of the accuracy of the entries made therein.

Sir John Paget's View: According to Sir John Paget, "The proper function which the pass book ought to fulfil is to constitute a conclusive and unquestionable record of transactions between the banker and the customer and it should be recognised as such. After full opportunity of examination on the part of the customer of all entries".

Effect of Entries to the Advantage of the Customer: The account of a customer may sometimes wrongly show a credit balance, which is larger than the correct balance because of duplication of credit entries or incorrectly entering higher amounts for such entries or due to omission of any debit entry. The legal position of the banker and his customer shall be as follows:

(i) The pass book is written by the banker and hence the entries therein may form an evidence against the banker. The customer is rightly entitled to believe them as correct and to act on the basis of such entries. If the pass book shows a higher balance and the customer withdraws such balance treating it as his own and subsequently spends it away, the banker shall not be entitled to recover such amount wrongly paid to the customer. But the customer shall have to prove that: *(a)* he acted in such manner relying on the correctness of the balance shown in the pass book and had no knowledge of the mistakes therein, and *(b)* he altered his position by spending the same. This benefit has been given to the customer in various judgments because of the presumption that normally a person spends what he presumes to belong to him and if the banker permits him to withdraw excess money on the above presumption, it would be a great prejudice to him, if he is called to pay them back.

(ii) There are some exceptions to the above-mentioned principle of estoppel. If the customer regularly maintains his account books and the bank regularly sends him the pass book (or statement in lieu of the pass book) the customer cannot act on the basis of the above presumption. Though it is not obligatory for him to check the Pass Book (or the statements), but in such circumstances, it is difficult to establish that he was ignorant about the mistake in the Pass Book, because he regularly maintained the account books. In such circumstances, a constructive notice of the mistake is supposed to have been given to him.

The decision of the Madras High Court in *Oakley Bowden and Co. vs. The Indian Bank Ltd.,* (A.I.R. 1964, Madras 202) may be cited in this connection. The brief facts of the case were as follows:

Oakley Bowden and Co. had a current account with the Indian Bank Ltd., at its head office at Madras. The company had dealings with two customers at Guntur, who used to pay into the Guntur branch of the Bank amounts payable by them to the Company and the said branch used to send advice of the amounts so paid to the head office which used to credit the said amounts to the current accounts of the Company with it.

The Guntur branch of the bank received two deposits for the credit of the Company in 1952. Each of these credits was advised by a telegram by the Guntur branch to the head office, which credited the account of the Company accordingly. The very same two credits were advised by the Guntur branch to the head office by ordinary post also. The head office did not apparently realise that the two credits advised by post related to the identical credits covered by the telegrams. The head office advised the Company by mistake of four credits instead of two. The mistake was detected by the Bank in 1954 and filed a suit against the company for the recovery of the amounts covered by the duplicate credit entries.

The Company in the meanwhile settled its accounts with the customers at Guntur on the basis of these entries communicated to it by the Bank. The Company, therefore, raised the point that the Bank was estopped from claiming that the two entries were duplicate entries.

The trial Court and the first Appellate Court held that the Company had the means of knowledge and therefore, every opportunity to know the real position and, therefore, it could not plead estopped against the Bank. The Courts were of the view that it was possible for the Company to have detected the duplicate credit from perusal of the accounts.

On appeal, the Madras High Court held that: "Generally speaking a bank owes a duty to its customer to maintain proper and accurate accounts of credits and debits. If a bank makes wrong credit entries without knowing the fact at time the entries were made and intimate to its customer the credit entries and the customer acting upon the intimation of credit entries, alters his position to his prejudice, the bank, therefore, will be stopped from contending that the credit entries were wrongly made and that the amounts covered by them should be refunded to it by the customer. Such an intimation by the bank is obviously a representation made to the customer which the customer is at liberty, in fact entitled, to act upon. Once it is acted upon by the customer *bonafide*, of course, it will then be too late for the bank to resile from the credit entries they made mistakenly and seek to have recompense by means of adjustment in the accounts or recovery of the amounts from the customer."

The Court observed that if the Company has even cursorily scrutinised the periodic statements received by it from two customers, it would have detected that two of the credit entries were in fact only duplicate entries. The Court held that the Company was negligent in scrutinising the accounts and that it had constructive notice of the duplicate entries and, therefore, it could not raise the plea of estoppel against the Bank. It was held that the Bank could recover the amounts in question.

In *S. Kotrabasappa vs. Indian Bank (1990) 69 Company Case 683*, the Karnataka High Court held that the customer who has taken unfair advantage of a mistaken credit made by the bank is bound to return or repay the amount according to Section 72 of the Indian Contract Act which states that "A person to whom money has been paid or anything delivered by mistake or under coercion, must repay or return it".

☞ Effect of the Customer Signing Confirmation Slips

The pass book itself is not a conclusive proof of a settled account. Banks nowadays periodically issue to the customers confirmation slip, which give the balance in the account as on a given date. By putting his signature on the confirmation slip, the customer accepts and confirms such balance. The legal effect of a customer's signing the confirmation slip was considered by the Kerala High Court in *Essa Ismail vs. Indian Bank Ltd., (1963)*. The Court observed that "unless there is evidence to show that the practice or the custom indicated a stated or settled account, the customer is not precluded from questioning the debit entries in a pass book but, when confirmation slips are sent and signed by the customer, he will be bound by the debits made". In this case, the confirmation slip was signed by the customer or his authorised agent. Hence, the same were binding on him and his heirs and could not be challenged by them.

Effect of Wrong Entries in Favour of the Banker: When a credit entry has been totally omitted or its figure has been wrongly stated or any debit entry has been erroneously made in the account of the customer, such entries are favourable to the banker and against the customer. The customer is entitled to get the mistake rectified as soon as he happens to detect it. This right of the customer does not lapse even if he returns the pass book without raising objection regarding any entry or he remains silent after the receipt of the pass book periodically and regularly. He is entitled to recover the amount wrongly debited to, or omitted to be credited to his account. The right of the customer to get the mistake rectified is however, subject to one limitation. If the customer comes to know about the forgery in the cheque and he does not inform the bank, it will constitute a negligence on his part. The customer will, therefore, not be entitled to recover the amount paid by the banker on the forged cheque.

The most important point to note is that the negligence on the part of the customer should have been actually proved. In *Canara Bank vs. Canara Sales Corporation and Others (1974) Company Cases, p.6*, the Mysore High Court held that there was no duty on the part of the customer to examine his pass book and to report to the bank that payment has been made on forged cheque and that neglect in that regard would not deprive him of the right to recover subsequently the sums paid on forged cheques. *The High Court further observed that while considering the fact of silence or omission to speak it has to be seen whether there was any occasion for words and any reasonable explanation for the silence.* Citing the facts of the case, the High Court held that as the Corporation was not aware of the fraud (*i.e.,* forgery by the Chief Accounts Officer of the signature of the Managing Director on 42 cheques favouring himself during 1957-61), until 1961, it could not be shared that it was negligent in bringing the forgery to the notice of the bank. The High Court also held that an implied contract as to settlement of accounts does not arise between a customer and his banker merely by reason of the banker sending the pass book to the customer with the accounts written up and the customer failing to point out any irregularities therein.

The Bank filed an appeal before the Supreme Court and contested that after reasonable opportunity was given to the customer to examine the Bank's statements, its debit entries should be deemed to be final and should not be open for reconstruction to the detriment of the Bank. The Supreme Court rejected the appeal and held (AIR 1987 SC 1603) that the Bank can escape liability only if it can establish knowledge to the customer of the forgery in the cheques. Inaction for continuously long period cannot by itself afford a satisfactory ground for the bank to escape the liability. The court further held that there was no duty for a customer to inform to the Bank of fraud committed on him of which he was unaware. Nor can inaction for a reasonably long time in not discovering fraud or irregularity be made a defence to defeat a customer in an action for loss.

It is pertinent to note in this connection that the current account rules of the banks usually lay such obligation on the customer. For example, "On a pass book or statement of account being received by a customer, the entries should be carefully examined and any error or omission should immediately be brought to the notice of the Bank: otherwise, the return of the pass book or rendering of the statement of account to the customer will be treated settlement of the account and acknowledgement of its correctness to date. The Bank will not be responsible for any loss arising from the neglect of these precautions." (Bank of Baroda Current Account Rule No. 15).

Similarly, the State Bank of India requires that —

"The entries should be carefully examined by the constituent and if any errors or omissions are discovered, the attention of the Bank must be drawn to them immediately. The Bank will not be responsible for any loss arising from neglect of this precaution."

It is thus apparent that the current account rules, which form the basis of agreement between the banker and customer, impose a duty on the customer to carefully examine the entries. If he is negligent in performing this duty and thereby some loss is caused, the banker shall not be liable for the same.

☞ Effect of False Entry in the Pass Book

The liability of a banker to his customer in case his employee commits an act of embezzlement and makes false entries in the pass book was considered by the Supreme Court in *State Bank of India vs. Shyama Devi* (A.I.R. 1978 S.C. 12). The brief facts of the case were as follows:

A lady opened a savings bank account in State Bank of India with the introduction by an employee of the bank, who was a close neighbour and fast friend of her husband. The customer entrusted to the said employee moneys and cheques, duly endorsed, for being credited to her account. The employee misappropriated the same and to cover up his fraud made false entries in the pass book. It was argued on behalf of the customer that the entries in the pass book showing the deposit of these amounts in the savings bank account had admittedly been made by the employee of the Bank. It was further pointed out that this employee had manipulated the accounts of three other depositors also that the Bank had reimbursed those customers for the loss. It was urged that the entries in the Pass Book were *prima facie* sufficient to establish the customer's claim.

The Bank argues that the customer had entrusted the employee moneys from time-to-time for depositing in her saving account. In such a situation the employee could not be said to have been acting in due course of his employment or as an agent of the Bank. He was only an agent of the customer. If he did not deposit those amounts as directed by the customer and misappropriated the same and to cover up his fraud made false entries in the pass book, the Bank could not be held liable for the loss.

The Supreme Court, therefore, considered the question whether the amounts were handed over by the customer to the said employee in the course of the bank's business, *i.e.,* whether the employee acted as an agent of the customer or of the Bank in the course of employment.

It was established that the said employment was not, at the relevant time, in charge of the savings bank counter at which the saving accounts of the customer was dealt with. In such a situation he acted as an agent of the customer. His act of misappropriation could not be said to have been committed in the course of his employment with the Bank. Similarly, it cannot be said that false and fictitious entries made by the employee to cover up his fraud made the embezzlement an act committed by the employee in the course of his employment with the Bank. The Bank was, therefore, not held liable to make good the loss caused to the customer. The Supreme Court laid down the legal principle which governs liability of an employer for the loss caused to a customer through the misdemeanour or negligence of an employee as follows: The empolyer is not liable for the act of the servant if the cause of the loss or damage arose without his actual fault or privity or without the fault or neglect of his agent or servant in the course of his employment.

☞ Precautions to be Taken by the Banker and the Customer

1. The pass book must be sent by the customer to the Bank periodically and regularly for recording the necessary entries, so that mistakes, if any, may be detected by the customer soon thereafter. Reserve Bank has advised the Banks to issue a simple receipt to the tenderer of savings bank pass book if it is retained by the bank for updating.
2. The pass book must be initialled by the accountant or other responsible officer of the Bank, who must ascertain the accuracy of the balance on the date of recording the entries, otherwise the customer will be entitled to act upon the same, if it is wrongly stated.
3. The customer must tally the entries with his own record either the account books or the counterfoils of pay-in-slips and cheques, etc. If any inaccuracy is found, the customer must inform the Bank immediately to get the mistake rectified.
4. While sending the pass book to the customer, the banker should take steps to ensure the secrecy of its contents. The pass book must be sent in a closed cover.

CLOSING OF A BANK ACCOUNT

The relationship between a banker and his customer is a contractual one and continues as long as both of them so desire. The relationship may be terminated by either of them by giving notice of his intention to the other party. Moreover, the banker is bound to suspend payment out of the customer's account under the compulsions of law. The right and obligations of a banker in this regard are as follows:

1. If a customer directs the banker in writing to close his account, the banker is bound to comply with such direction. The latter need not ask the reasons for the former's direction. The account must be closed with immediate effect and the customer be required to return the unused cheques.
2. If an account remains unoperated for a very long period, the banker may request the customer to withdraw the money. Such step is taken on the presumption that the customer no longer needs the account. If the customer could not be traced after reasonable effort, the banker usually transfers the balance to an "Unclaimed Deposit Account" and the account is closed. The balance is paid to the customer as and when he is traced.
3. The banker is also competent to terminate his relationship with the customer, if he finds that the latter is no more a desirable customer. The banker takes this extreme step in circumstances when the customer is guilty of conducting his account in an unsatisfactory manner, *i.e.*, if the customer is convicted for forging cheques or bills or if he issues cheques without sufficient funds or does not fulfil his commitment to pay back the loans or overdrafts, etc. The banker should take the following steps for closing such an account:

   (a) The banker should give to the customer due notice of his intention to close the account and request him to withdraw the balance standing to his credit. The notice should give sufficient time to the customer to make alternative arrangements. The banker should not, on his own, close the account without such notice or transfer the same to any other branch.

   (b) If the customer does not close the account on receipt of the aforesaid notice, the banks should give another notice intimating the exact date by which the account be closed otherwise the banker himself will close the account. During this notice period the banker can safely refuse to accept further credit from the customer and can also refuse to issue fresh cheque book to him. Such steps will not make him liable to the customer and will be in consonance with the intention of the notice to close the account by a specified date.

   The banker should, however, not refuse to honour the cheques issued by the customer, so long as his account has a credit balance which will suffice to pay the cheque. If the banker dishonours any cheque without sufficient reasons, he will be held liable to pay damages to his customer under Section 31 of the Negotiable Instruments Act, 1881.

   (c) In case of default by the customer to close the account the banker should close the account and send the money by draft to the customer. He will not be liable for dishonouring cheques presented for payment subsequently.
4. On receipt of the notice of death of a customer the banker must stop the operation of his account because the authority of the customer terminates as he dies.
5. If a banker receives a notice regarding the insanity of his customer, he is bound to stop payment from his account.

6. The relationship between the banker and his customer is also affected if the customer becomes insolvent or the corporate customer goes into liquidation. The credit balance of the customer is transferred to the official Receiver of the insolvent customer.
7. On receipt of a Garnishee Order from the Court, the banker is bound to suspend payment from the account of the customer. If the order prohibits the payment of a specified sum from the account, the banker may honour the cheques out of the remainder amount.
8. When the banker has received a notice of assignment of the credit balance in the account of a customer to a third party, the banker is bound to pay the same amount to the said third party.

There have been cases where frauds have been committed by persons in possession of a cheque book. In one such case, a person approached a bank manager with a request that he be allowed to open an account. He told the manager that he had forgotten to bring the money and requested him to issue a cheque book to him, promising to send the money the next day. After obtaining possession of the cheque book, he succeeded in persuading certain merchants to part with their goods in exchange for his cheques, which were subsequently found to be worthless, for their drawer had no account with the bank upon which they were drawn.

If a banker fails to make the usual enquiries about a new customer, he may be deprived of the statutory protection given to him under Section 131 of the Negotiable Instruments Act, 1881. (*Ladbroke vs. Todd,* 1914). In this case, the learned Judge observed: "The bank acted negligently, for they did not make ordinary enquiries which ordinary reasonable people should make in opening an account".

☞ Insurance of Bank Deposits

After the failure of Palai Central Bank in 1960, a strong need was felt to insure the deposits in the banks. A scheme of deposit insurance was introduced in 1962, with the formation of Deposit Insurance Corporation of India. With effect from July 15, 1978, the Corporation has been renamed as Deposit Insurance and Credit Guarantee Corporation, and Credit Guarantee functions have also been added to the activities of this corporation.

An important feature of Indian banking is that deposits of the public with the banks are insured up to the limit of ₹ 1 lakh in each accounts.

☞ Salient Features of Deposit Insurance

(i) The scheme of deposit insurance applies since its inception to all commercial banks in India, scheduled and non-scheduled. The deposit insurance cover has been extended to co-operative banks also in 21 States and 3 Union Territories. The Regional Rural Banks have also been included in this scheme. All these banks are called insured banks.

(ii) The Insurance cover is extended to all deposits with the insured banks except the deposits of the Central and State Governments, foreign Governments and the commercial banks.

(iii) The deposits with the insured banks are insured up to a special limit only. The insurance cover is available in respect of all unpaid balances due to depositors held in a bank in the same capacity and in the same right up to ₹ 1 lakh. This means that every account of a depositor in every insured bank is insured to the extent of ₹ 1 lakh. The accounts with credit balance up to ₹ 1 lakh each are called fully protected accounts.

(iv) The Corporation reimburses the depositors in case the insured bank fails or is amalgamated with another bank and defaults in paying fully the balances due to the depositors in cash or by crediting the same to the full extent in the books of the transferee bank. The difference

between the amount so paid or credited and the limit of insurance cover per account is paid by the Corporation. For example, if bank X, on its merger with bank Y, gives a credit equal to 75% of the deposits, a depositor having a credit balance of ₹ 10,000 will get credit of ₹ 7,500. The balance of ₹ 2,500 will be reimbursed to him by the Corporation.

(v) The rate of insurance premium is 5 paise per annum for every hundred rupees of assessable deposits. It is payable by the issuer banks and not by the depositors at half-yearly intervals. Assessable deposits are those deposits to which the cover of insurance is extended under *(ii)* above. Premium is thus payable on total assessable deposits, whereas the insured deposits are those which are below the limit of insurance cover, *i.e.,* ₹ 1 lakh in each account.

(vi) The Corporation maintains two funds: *(a)* Deposit Insurance Fund, and *(b)* General Fund. The income from insurance premia is credited to the Deposit Insurance Fund and is invested in the Central Government securities. Income from such investments is credited to and the insurance losses are debited to the Revenue Account of the Fund. The General Fund meets all other expenses of the Corporation.

CERTIFICATES OF DEPOSIT

As suggested the Working Group on the Money Market (Chairman N. Vaghul), Reserve Bank of India has permitted the banks to issue Certificates of Deposit. Reserve Bank has issued guidelines also in this regard, which have been relaxed from time-to-time.

Certificates of Deposit can be issued by scheduled commercial banks only and not by the Regional Rural Banks. Through CDs banks accept short-term deposits of substantial amounts from the investors who have liquid funds for temporary period. Such CDs can be issued to individuals, corporations, companies, trusts, funds, associations, etc. Non-resident Indians (NRIs) may subscribe such Certificates but on a non-repatriable basis and such CDs cannot be endorsed to another NRI in the secondary market.

According to RBI guidelines the maturity period of CDs should not be less than three months and not more than one year. CDs are to be issued at a discount on the face value — the discount rate can be freely determined by the issuing bank. But banks are required to maintain CRR and SLR on the total issue over the pre May 2, 1992 limit (*i.e.,* equal to 5% of the fortnightly average outstanding aggregate deposit in 1989-90) from CRR. The CDs are freely transferable by endorsement and delivery only after 45 days of the date of issue Banks are prohibited from granting loans against CDs or from buying back their own CDs before maturity.

The Reserve Bank has prescribed that the minimum amount of a CD issued to a single investor should not be less than ₹ 10 lakh and thereafter in multiple of ₹ 5 lakh. The Reserve Bank has also restricted the overall amount of such CDs outstanding at any point of time. Earlier the amount of such CDs was not to exceed two per cent of the fortnightly average of aggregate deposits of a bank during the financial year 1988-89. Later on, this limit was raised to 5% of the fortnightly average outstanding aggregate deposits. The limit for issue of such certificates was enhanced to 7 per cent of the fortnightly average outstanding aggregate deposits in 1989-90 with effect from May 2, 1992 and further to 10% in Oct. 1992. Thus, the Bank are now permitted to issue CDs to a large extent. The upward revision of the ceiling limits is an indication of the favourable attitude of the Reserve Bank to popularise this new instrument in the money market in India.

☞ Repayment of Deposits

With the enactment of Income Tax (Second Amendment) Act, 1981, which came into force from September 19, 1981, it is obligatory on all banks to repay deposits by account payee cheque or drafts or by credit to saving bank account or current account of the depositor, if the aggregate of all deposits together with interest held by a person either in his own name or jointly with any other person with a branch of a bank is ₹ 10,000 or more on the date of payment.

Though the purpose of this amendment was to stop the use of banking system as a conduit for unaccounted money, it is doubtful, whether it has served the purpose. The objective of this legislation though laudable, the lacuna that still exists in the Negotiable Instrument Act, 1881, may defeat the purpose.

Though there is no mention of account payee crossing either in the Bills of Exchange Act or in the Negotiable Instruments Act, both governing the commercial world represented by promissory notes, bills of exchange and cheques, this crossing has been in practice since 1852 and has come to be accepted as a direction to the collecting banker to collect and deposit the proceeds of cheque in the account of the named payee only, irrespective of the fact whether the cheque is order or bearer. Despite the fact that there have been judicial pronouncements recognising this crossing, statutorily it has not been made non-negotiable, leading to different interpretations and thus defeating the purpose of the Income Tax (Second Amendment) Act, 1981.

Deposit Schemes For Non-resident Indians

To attract foreign exchange in the form of bank deposits in India, certain concessions and incentives are offered to non-resident Indians to remit money to India for investment. These accounts can be maintained with banks which are authorised dealers in foreign exchange or which are specifically authorised in this behalf by the Reserve Bank. Permission of Reserve Bank is not required to open these accounts which fall in two categories:

(A) Rupee Accounts

Three types of rupee accounts are permitted to be opened in the names of Non-resident Indians:

(1) Non-resident Ordinary Rupee Accounts (NRO Accounts)

This is just like an account opened by a resident Indian to which the local funds (funds from sources in India) are credited. These funds do not qualify for remittance outside India. These accounts can be maintained in any form, *i.e.,* current, savings or fixed accounts. Banks are free to determine the interest rates on these deposits, as in the case of domestic deposits.

(2) Non-resident (External) Accounts Scheme

The non-resident (external) accounts facility was introduced by leading commercial banks several years ago. Indian nationals abroad are permitted to open current, savings or fixed deposit accounts in India. Under this scheme the unit of accounts are freely repatriable at the prevailing rate of exchange. Money in these accounts can also be invested in the Units of the UTI, NSC, Govt. securities, etc. The income earned from these investments as well as the principal realised on maturity are also repatriable. Interest on these accounts is tax free. These accounts can be opened by: *(i)* non-resident Indians or *(ii)* aliens of Indian origin. Other foreigners are not permitted to open such an account. The greatest drawback of this scheme is that the amount of principal and interest is repatriated at the current rate of exchange and hence the exchange risk is borne by the depositors, *i.e.,* Indian national abroad. Effective April 16, 1997 banks are free to determine their own rates of interest on fixed deposits of over one year under this scheme. But for the term deposits of 6 months and up to one year, the rate of interest not to exceed bank rate minus two percentage points (*i.e.,* 10% – 2% = 8%).

(3) Non-resident (Non-repatriable) Rupee Deposit Scheme (NRNR)

Under this scheme, which came into force on 15th June, 1992, accounts are to be opened in Indian rupees with the authorised dealers by remitting funds in freely convertible foreign exchange from abroad or by transfer of funds from the existing Non-resident (external)/FONR accounts. Other features of this scheme are as follows:

(a) Authorised dealers are free to fix the maturity period of the deposit between 6 months and 3 years and also the rate of interest payable on such deposits. Banks have prescribed interest rates on these deposits which are higher than those on domestic deposits.

(b) On maturity, the principal amount of deposit will not qualify for repatriation outside India at any time. Interest accruing on such deposits w.e.f. Oct. 1, 1994 is eligible for repatriation.

(c) The deposits may be renewed and may also be shifted from one bank to another, but if the amount is withdrawn or invested in other schemes, it will not qualify for renewal under the scheme.

(d) These deposits will not be considered as part of net demand and time liabilities for the purpose of CRR and SLR. Hence, these deposits will be free from any reserve requirements.

(e) Lending against these deposits will not be considered as part of net bank credit for the purpose of determining priority sector lending.

(f) Authorised dealers may allow premature withdrawal of the deposits and levy penalty for premature withdrawal as per their descretion.

(B) Foreign Currency Accounts

Foreign Currency Non-residents (Banks) Scheme, 1993

This scheme was introduced with effect from May 15, 1993. Under this scheme banks provide the exchange rate guarantee to the depositors. Deposits of six months and above and up to 3 years are permitted to be accepted under this scheme. The banks are not required to surrender the deposits mobilised under this scheme to the Reserve Bank. The amount collected under the scheme can be swapped either in the domestic market or with the Reserve Bank of India. Authorised dealers are also permitted to lend the foreign currency mobilised under the scheme for certain approved purposes.

The loans under the scheme are not subject to the lending rate stipulations of the Reserve Bank of India and will not be considered as a part of net bank credit for the purpose of determining priority sector lending.

Under the scheme fixed deposits in four currencies — US dollars, pound sterling, Deutsche mark and Japanese yen — are accepted by banks for maturities ranging from six months to 3 years.

The interest rates under the scheme were prescribed by Reserve Bank of India for specified maturities. With a view to give more flexibility to the banks, Reserve Bank of India decided that with effect from April 16, 1997 banks may determine interest rates on such deposits subject to a ceiling prescribed by Reserve Bank of India from time-to-time.

☞ Questions

1. Why is it necessary for a banker to insist on a suitable introduction before opening a current account? What should the banker do when a customer —

   (a) dies,

   (b) becomes insolvent, or

   (c) becomes insane?

2. Under what circumstances should a banker close the account of his customer and to whom should he pay the balance?
3. What precautions should a banker take in opening a current account in the name of a trading partnership firm? If, at a later date, one of the partners retires or becomes insolvent or dies, how should he deal with the firm's account —
   (*i*) if it is in credit, and
   (*ii*) if it is overdrawn?
4. (*a*) The Principal of AB College is authorised to operate the account of the college in M Bank. He has also his personal account in the same bank. He sends to the bank for collection and credit to his personal account a cheque drawn by a donor on S Bank in favour of "The Principal, AB College". What action should the manager of M Bank take, and why?
   (*b*) The same Principal draws a cheque on the said account of AB College in favour of a firm of automobile dealers for the purchase of a motor car for his personal use. Can the cheque be paid or not? Give reasons.
5. (*a*) Two individuals, who are not trading partners, want to open a joint current account in your bank and seek your guidance regarding the manner of operation of the account. What advice would you give them? And why? What forms would you take from them to facilitate its smooth operation and to protect the bank's interests?
   (*b*) What steps would you take to obtain repayment of an overdraft in a joint current account if one of the joint accountholder dies, becomes insane or is adjudged bankrupt?
6. Explain, why it is necessary for a banker to ask for an introductory reference before opening a current account for a party.
7. (*a*) A minor wants to open a current account in his own name in your branch. Would your permit it? If the minor wants an overdraft arrangement and offers to secure the guarantee of a substantial third party, would you grant this facility?
   (*b*) What are the precautions which a banker should take in the opening and conduct of current accounts in the names of executors and administrators?
8. Mrs. K, a widow, maintains a fixed deposit of ₹ 25,000 with your branch. The fixed deposit is due to mature in May, 1974. She has taken a loan of ₹ 20,000 against this fixed deposit. She approaches you with a request to add the name of her minor daughter Miss M in the fixed deposit receipt. How will you deal with this situation? *[I.I.B., Part I]*
9. Miss Saroja Sunderrajan has a fixed deposit account with you and requests to change the name in the fixed deposit receipt to Mrs. Saroj Vaidyanathan. Will you accept this request? *[I.I.B., Part I]*
10. Your branch has issued a Fixed Deposit Receipt for ₹ 10,000 in the joint names of Mr. and Mrs. M.B. Dalvi, payable to either or survivor for a period of 12 months maturing on 30th September, 1979. Mrs. Dalvi approaches you on 11th December, 1978 with a request to issue a duplicate receipt since the original receipt is lost by her. How would you deal? *[I.I.B., Part I]*
11. Why is introduction considered necessary for opening a new current account?
    (*a*) Where only cash operations are permitted.
    (*b*) Where withdrawals by cheque are allowed.
    (*c*) Where deposit of cheques and other instruments is allowed, including those in favour of third parties. Give reasons in each case.
12. Why does a Banker insist on introduction to open a current account but not to open a fixed deposit or a savings bank account? *[I.I.B., Part I]*
13. What do you understand by Non-resident (external) accounts? *[I.I.B., Part II]*
14. What are the rules and regulations governing the opening and conduct of Non-resident (external) accounts? *[I.I.B., Part II]*
15. Please state —
    (1) The categories of deposits under the broad heads 'Demand Deposits' and 'Time Deposits'.
    (2) Schemes formulated and measures taken by Urban Banks to attract (mobilise) urban and rural deposits. *[I.I.B., Part I]*
16. (*a*) Write a short note on Non-resident account.
    (*b*) Answer the following:
        (*i*) Present rate of interest in Savings Bank Account;

(ii) Margin for advances against Bank's own Fixed Deposit Receipts;

(iii) Number of nationalised banks;

(iv) Rate of interest on Bank's fixed deposit for 5 years. *[I.I.B., Part I, Nov.]*

17. A good customer of your Bank's branch in Bombay has lost a fixed deposit receipt for ₹ 3,000 issued by the branch in his favour and falling due for payment on 10th December, 1976. He approaches you for necessary action in the matter. How would you proceed?

18. A bank has issued a fixed deposit receipt for ₹ 7,000 for 2 years with interest @ 8% to X and Y payable to either or survivor.

    On completion of one year, X approaches the bank for repayment of the fixed deposit or in the alternative to grant him a loan for the maximum amount, as he is in urgently need of money. As Manager of the Bank, how would you proceed in the matter? What documents would you take for the loan and how much interest would you charge? *[I.I.B., Part I]*

19. A fixed deposit receipt in the names of A and B payable to either or survivor is presented for prepayment, discharged by A alone. How will you deal with the situation and why? *[I.I.B., Part I]*

20. Mrs. A approaches you with a request to pay to her the amount of a fixed deposit of ₹ 5,000 standing in the name of her husband Mr. A. The fixed deposit is matured. Mrs. A claims that Mr. A is reported missing for 5 years. How will you deal with this situation? *[I.I.B., Part I]*

21. What do you understand by Non-resident (external) accounts? *[I.I.B., Part II]*

22. What are the rules and regulations governing the opening and conduct of Non-Resident (External) Accounts? *[I.I.B., Part II]*

23. Please classify categories of deposits under two headings:

    (i) Time deposits, and *(ii)* Demand deposits. *[I.I.B., Part I]*

24. Under what circumstances would a bank like to close a current account of his customer? What procedure could a banker follow in case he decides to close the current account of his customer? *[I.I.B., Part I]*

25. Shri. A holds one year Fixed Deposit Receipt dated 5th July, 1984 issued in his favour by your branch. He calls at the branch on 1st Sept. 1986 and explains circumstances under which he could not attend to renewal of FDR.

    He seeks to know as to what should be done, under the rules of the bank, to protect his interests. What will be your advice? *[I.I.B., Part I]*

26. A grandfather wants to open a Savings Bank Account in the names of his grandchild (aged 6 years) and himself. How would you deal in this case? *[I.I.B., Part I]*

27. The representation of: *(i)* M/s Bhogilal Nathalal & Co, and *(ii)* B.N. Desai & Co. Ltd. approach you for opening two separate current accounts. What fonnalities are required to be completed and what documents would you obtain? *[I.I.B., Part I]*

28. Mr. Sunil and Mr. Sudhir are the partners of the firm M/s. Sunil Sudhir & Co., who maintain a good Current Account with your Branch. The A/c is operated individually by any one of the partners for and on behalf of the firm as provided for in the partnership deed.

    (i) On 12th December 1992, Mr. Sunil drew a cheque for ₹ 2 lakh and transferred this amount to a fixed deposit for 2 years in the name of the firm. He collected the deposit receipt from you signing on behalf of the firm.

    (ii) On 13th February 1993, a cheque for ₹ 1,50,000 drawn on the Current Account by Mr. Sudhir on behalf of the firm in favour of their supplier was presented for payment when there was a balance of only ₹ 25,000. When contacted, Mr. Sudhir came to the Bank and requested for a Temporary Overdraft of ₹ 1,25,000. He made the request in writing on the firm's letterhead and signed in the capacity of the partner of the firm. The cheque was honoured by granting a debit balance of ₹ 1,25,000 in the Books of the Bank.

    (iii) On 23rd March, 1993, Mr. Sudhir suddenly died. The Bank issued a notice to the surviving partner, Mr. Sunil, to repay the outstanding debit balance which he promptly declined on the ground that, the Bank should have obtained his consent before granting the temporary overdraft.

    The Assistant Manager in the Credit Department of your Branch feels that the Bank has no case, since —

    (a) The partnership stands dissolved on the death of one of the partners and so no claim could be lodged with the firm.

    (b) The partnership deed though provided for availing of the Bank finance makes no mention specifically of the temporary overdraft facility.

    (c) The Bank had not obtained proper documents while granting the TOD.

    (d) Though there is a fixed deposit for ₹ 2,00,000 in the name of the firm, the Bank cannot exercise general lien as

the deposit is retained by the party and one of the ingredients of the banker's lien is the right to retain the good whereas in this case, the Bank is not in possession of the deposit receipt.

(i) Now, you as the Branch Manager, please examine these issues one by one carefully and state whether or not you agree with the Assistant Manager's views. (Each sub-question carries 3 marks).

(ii) Also please state how you would proceed further in the matter. *[I.I.B., Part I]*

29.

FASHION DRESSES

BALANCE SHEET AS AT 31st MARCH, 1993

(Rupees in Lakhs)

Capital			Fixed Assets		
Partner A	10		Machinery	2	
Partner B	20	30	Shed	3	5
Reserves		10	Current Assets		
Loan Secured			Inventory	12	
(i) From Finance Company			Debtors	53	
(Against the Mortgage of			Duty Draw Back		
A's residential flat valued			Receivable	5	
₹ 75 lakhs)		15	Cash and Bank	5	75
(ii) Others		10			
Sundry Creditors		15			
Total		80	Total		80

The firm is a well established garment exporter.

They have approached you as the Branch Manager for a Packing Credit Limit of ₹ 40 lakh and have supplied the following information:

(i) Turnover for the past three years:

1990-1991	*1991-1992*	*1992-1993*
₹ 130 lakh	₹ 135 lakh	₹ 145 lakh

(ii) They do not enjoy any credit facility in any bank and are running the show themselves with a strong capital base of ₹ 30 lakh + Reserves of ₹ 10 lakh.

(iii) One of the partners had mortgaged his residential flat valued at ₹ 75 lakh as a security to the finance company, when export bills referred to below (item vi) were unpaid, he had to borrow this amount.

(iv) The other partner owned 2 sheds in an industrial estate in Bombay valued at ₹ 25 lakh.

(v) The firm has an Export LC for US $ 65,000 and the limit sought is to finance the current shipment.

(vi) In December 1992, a shipment was delayed due to the disturbances in Bombay. The buyer refused to pay for the shipment of ₹ 70 lakh as it was delayed. However, he agreed to sell the goods and remit sale proceeds. By the end of March 1993, he had remitted ₹ 5 lakh and out of the balance amount he remitted ₹ 30 lakh at the end of August 1993. For the final balance of ₹ 35 lakh he has not given any definite date of repayment. The firm has approached you as the Branch Manager for the Packing Credit Limit projecting the sales of ₹ 200 lakh against the confirmed Export L.Cs.

You are requested to examine the information furnished and decide whether to grant PC facility. In case you agree to consider the proposal, please state the Limit you will consider and the reasons therefore. In case you decide to decline the proposal, give reasons for rejection. *[I.I.B., Part I]*

30. What are the effects of entries in the pass book made by mistake? *[I.I.B., Part I]*

31. Is it essential to obtain proper introduction before opening a Bank account? If so why? Explain ways and means of obtaining proper introduction. *[I.I.B., Sept.]*

32. *(a)* What are the circumstances leading to closure of customer's accounts at the instance of the bank and procedure thereof ?

(b) What are the factors responsible for perpetration of fraud through the medium of newly opened, savings A c and Current account. *[I.I.B., Part I]*

33. Who is a non-resident Indian according to FERA? What is the procedure to be followed for opening:

(i) NRO (non-resident ordinary) Account.

(ii) NRE Account.

(iii) FCNR Account. *[I.I.B., Part I]*

(a) What are dormant accounts? What precautions would you take in dealing with them?

(b) There is a dormant savings bank account at your branch in the names of Mr. J.B. Mahajan and Mrs. Ansuya J. Mahajan payable to either or survivor, with a balance of ₹ 7,500 since 1995. The account was opened in 1952.

In January 1979, one Mr. Vasudev (aged 21 years) claiming to be the only son of Mr. J.B. Mahajan approaches you and informs asunder:

(a) He holds the pass book of this account.

(b) His mother Ansuya died in 1970.

(c) His father has left the house since 1960 and his whereabouts are not known.

(d) He has information that a safe deposit locker was also in their names.

The key of the locker is not traceable.

He requests you, as Branch Manager, to make payment of the balance in the account to him and also to deliver the articles lying in the locker to him. How will you deal with the matter?

34. What would you do with the following cases:

(i) Mr. X held a FDR for ₹ 25,000 jointly with his son A styled Either or Survivor. Mr. X died while he was staying with his son B. Mr. B meets the Branch Manager of the branch issuing FDR, produces the relative FDR and claims the proceeds of FDR on the ground that money invested in FDR belonged to his deceased father. *[I.I.B., Part I]*

(ii) A letter is received by you from A requesting you to add the name of C in the fixed Deposit Receipt for ₹ 5,000 only in the joint names of A and B. C is the major son of A and B. *[I.I.B., Part I]*

(iii) A reputed client of your branch informs you in writing that Shri Prakash who has opened and deposited ₹ 2,000 in S.B. account which represents stolen money and as such Banks should not part with the money. He further requests the Bank to provide account particulars of Prakash to enable him to lodge an FIR with the police. *[I.I.B., Part I]*

(iv) A Fixed Deposit Receipt was issued for 180 days @ 11% p.a. The rate of interest was subsequently reduced to 9% for 180 days and 10% for one year. On 160th day the depositor requests you to extend the tenure of the existing deposit to one year from the date of issue to get the advantage of the higher rate which was prevailing on that date. *[I.I.B., Part I]*

(v) A pensioner having a Savings Bank A/c payment of pension requests you to add the name of his wife and convert the same into a joint A/c. He also wishes to give a mandate in favour of his son. *[I.I.B., Part I]*

(vi) A TDR was issued in the name of Mrs. Sujata Roy for ₹ 10,000 for one year. She died three months after the deposit was made in the Bank. Nomination was registered in the books of the Bank in favour of her husband Mr. Kunal Roy. Mr. Roy approaches the Bank for premature encashment of FDR. *[I.I.B., Part I]*

↙ ↙ ↙

CHAPTER

10 Special Types of Customers

A banking institution solicits deposits of money from the members of the public. An account in a bank for this purpose may be opened by any person who *(i)* is legally capable of entering into a valid contract; *(ii)* applies to the banks in the proper manners, *i.e.,* he follows the procedure laid down by the banks, and *(iii)* accepts the terms and conditions stipulated by the latter. The banker, however, possesses the right to reject an application for opening an account, if he is not satisfied with the identity of the applicants, *i.e.,* if the latter is deemed to be an undesirable person. Some persons like the minor, lunatics and drunkards are not competent to enter into valid contracts, some persons who act on behalf of others have limited powers to contract, *e.g.,* the agents, trustees, executors, etc., institutions like schools, colleges, clubs, societies and corporate bodies are the impersonal customers of a banker. The authority power and functions of the persons managing these institutions are embodied in their respective constitutions. The banker should, therefore, take special care and precautions to ensure that the accounts of these institutions are being conducted in accordance with the provisions of their respective charters.

TYPE OF CUSTOMERS

MINOR | AGENT | LUNATIC | DRUNKARD | MARRIED WOMAN

☛ MINOR

A person who has not completed 18 years of age is a minor. If a guardian of his person or property is appointed by the Court before he completes 18th year, he remains minor till he completes his 21st year. According to the Indian Contract Act, 1872, a minor is not capable of entering into a valid contract and a contract entered into by a minor is void. A contract for the supply of necessaries of life to a minor is, however, a valid contract. In case of all other contracts, a minor may repudiate his promise or consent.

1. A banker should, therefore, be very careful in dealing with a minor and take the following precautions. The banker may open a savings bank account (and not a current account) in the name of a minor, in any of the following ways:

(i) In the name of the minor, to be operated upon by the natural guardian of the minor or the guardian appointed by the Court. Such account can also be opened in the joint names of two or more minors, to be operated upon by the guardian.

(ii) In the name of the minor, to be operated upon by himself, if he has attained the age of 12 years. Two such minors can jointly open such an account, to be operated upon by them jointly.

2. The bank records the date of birth of the minor as given by the minor or his/her guardian. On the attainment of majority, the account of the minor in the name of the guardian should be closed and the balance paid to the minor (then major) or be transferred to a new account in his/her own name. In case of a joint account the minor is also permitted to operate the account and his signature is taken on the account opening form.
3. If the father of a Hindu minor dies, his mother becomes his natural guardian. After the death of the mother, during the minority of the boy there is either the testamentary guardian or the guardian appointed by the Court. The banker may return the money to such guardian.
4. In case the minor dies, the balance in the account is permitted to be withdrawn by the guardian and in case of joint account the balance will be held at the absolute disposal of the guardian.
5. No risk is involved if an account is opened in the name of a minor so long as the account is not overdrawn by mistake or unintentionally, the banker has no legal remedy to recover the amount from the minor. The assets of a minor pledged with the banker as security for the advance taken by the minor are not legally available to the banker because such pledge itself is invalid. The banker shall have to return these securities to the minor and he cannot exercise his right of sale in case of default by the minor.
6. If an advance is granted to a minor on the guarantee of a third party, such advance cannot be recovered from the guarantor also because the contract of guarantee is invalid on the ground that the contract between the creditor and the principal debtor (minor) itself is a void contract. According to Section 128 of the Indian Contract Act, 1872, the liability of the surety is co-extensive with that of the principal debtor, unless it is otherwise provided by the contract. The surety, therefore, cannot be held liable on a guarantee given for default by a minor. According to the law a minor cannot enter into valid contract and he cannot undertake a liability upon himself. Thus he cannot default. Surety's liability is a secondary one and does not arise, if the liability of the primary debtor does not arise. In *Edavan Nambiar vs. Moolakai Raman* (A.I.R. 1957 Madras 164), the Madras High Court also upheld the above viewpoint. The liability of a surety is ancillary. It materialises if there is a valid obligation on the part of the debtor whose debt or obligation is guaranteed. However, if the contract of guarantee specially provides contrary to the above, the guarantor may be held liable for the debts of a minor.

   But if minor enters into an agreement by repesenting himself as major and later on claims such a contract as void on account of his minority at the time of entering into contract, the minor must restore the benefit derived by him under the agreement. In *M/s. Thiru Arooram Sugars Ltd., vs. State Bank of India*, the High Court observed as above on the basis of Section 65 of the Indian Contract Act which states that "when an agreement is discovered to be void or when a contract becomes void, any person who has received any advantage under such agreement or contract is bound to restore it or to make compensation for it to the person from whom he recovered it".
7. A minor may draw, endorse or negotiate a cheque or a bill but be cannot be held liable on such cheque or bill. He cannot be used in respect of a bill accepted by him during the minority.

Such bill or cheque, nevertheless, will be a valid instrument and all other parties will be liable in their respective capacities (Section 26 of the Negotiable Instruments Act, 1881). The banker should, therefore, be very cautious in dealing with a negotiable instrument, to which a minor is a party.

8. A minor can be admitted to the benefit of partnership with the consent of all the partners but he will not be liable for the losses or debts of the firm. Within six months after he attains majority he should repudiate his liability as partner otherwise the will be held liable as a partner of the firm from the date he was admitted to the benefit of the partnership (Section 30(7) (a) of the Indian Partnership Act, 1932).
9. A minor may be appointed as an agent to act on behalf of his principal. According to Section 184 of the Indian Contract Act, 1872: "as between the principal and third person, any person may become an agent; but no person who is not of the age of majority and of sound mind can be appointed as an agent, so as to be responsible to his principal". Thus, a minor agent cannot be held responsible to his principal. The principal may be held responsible to the third parties in respect of the acts of his minor agent. Therefore, all of his dealings with the banker will be valid and binding on his principal. The banker should obtain written authority of the principal specifying the power and the extent of authority entrusted to the agent in this regard and should see that the minor agent does not deal beyond such delegated power.

☞ Legal Provisions Regarding Guardianship of a Minor

The guardian of a minor may be either —

(i) a natural guardian, or

(ii) a testamentary guardian, or

(iii) a guardian appointed by the Court.

The first two types of guardians are governed by the provisions of the Hindu Minority and Guardianship Act, 1956, whereas a guardian is appointed by a Court under the Guardians and Wards Act, 1890.

(i) Natural Guardian: According to Section 6 of the Hindu Minority and Guardianship Act, 1956, in case of a minor boy or an unmarried girl, his/her father and after him the mother shall be the natural guardian. In case of a married girl (minor), her husband shall be the natural guardian. The term father or mother does not include step-father or step-mother. If the father becomes a *sanyasi* or does not remain Hindu, he shall not be entitled to remain as guardian. If the father is alive and is not removed from guardianship, the mother does not become the natural guardian of her minor child.

(ii) Testamentary Guardian: A Hindu father, who is entitled to act as the natural guardian of his minor legitimate children may, by will, appoint a guardian for any of them in respect of the minor's person or property. Such guardian acts after the death of the father or the mother.

(iii) Guardian Appointed by Court: A guardian may be appointed by the Court under the Guardians and Wards Act, 1890, but the Court shall not be authorised to appoint or declare a guardian of the person of a minor, if his father is alive and is not, in the opinion of the Court, unfit to be guardian of the person of a minor. Similar is the case with the minor girl, whose husband is not, in the opinion of the Court, unfit to be guardian of her person. Thus, the father (or the husband in case of a married girl) is exclusively entitled to be the guardian. The welfare of the minor shall be a paramount consideration of the court while appointing a guardian.

☞ Reserve Bank's Directive

Reserve Bank has advised the banks to allow opening of minor's accounts (fixed, saving and recurring deposit accounts) with mother as guardian. Thus, banks are now permitted to open account of minors in the guardianship of the mother, even if the father of the minor is alive. A minor may open a bank account in his name. As long as this account is in credit, the banker runs no risk in dealing with him. A minor can draw or endorse a cheque or a bill and the instrument so drawn or endorsed by him is nevertheless valid against all parties except himself [Section 26*(b)* of Negotiable Instruments Act]. Since he has no contractual capacity, if money is advanced to him by a bank, not only is the amount unrecoverable, but any securities pledged by him will also have to be returned. Even if a third party deposits a security with a bank for a loan to a minor, the depositor can reclaim the securities without paying off the debt.

A minor can become a partner in a firm with the consent of all the other partners. But he can be admitted only to the benefits of partnership and cannot be held liable for any debts of the partnership incurred before he attains his majority. On the other hand, unless he expressly repudiates the contract of partnership within six months of his attaining majority, he will be regarded as having ratified the agreement and will become liable as a general partner for all the debts incurred by the partnership since he was admitted to the benefits of partnership.

☞ As Agent

A minor can act as an agent for another person who is competent to contract, provided his principal has duly authorised him to do so. For example, a minor son may make contracts, besides endorsing cheques and bills, on behalf of his father, if his father has duly authorised him to act as his agent.

☞ Lunatic

According to Section 12 of the Indian Contract Act, 1872, "a person is said to be of sound mind for the purpose of making a contract, if at the time when he makes it, he is capable of understanding the nature and effect of the same and of forming a rational judgement as to its effects upon his interests". This definition should act as a guide in deciding whether a person is a lunatic or not. As soon as a banker comes to know of the insanity of his customer, it is absolutely necessary that he should not honour his cheques (*Drew vs. Nunn*). If the customer is confined to a lunatic asylum or is judicially declared a lunatic by a competent Court under the Lunacy Act, the banker is safe in stopping the account. Otherwise, he should take care to see that he does not stop the account in a hurry and thereby place himself in a difficult position. The banker should, as far as possible, avoid opening an account of a person of unsound mind.

☞ Drunkard

Generally, drunkenness is not considered to affect a person's power to contract; yet, with a view to preventing people from taking any undue advantage of a drunken person, he is allowed to evade liability to the person who improperly induces him to sign an instrument, provided that the Court is satisfied that the person was so drunk as to be unable to know what he was doing. The position of a drunkard is similar to that of a lunatic in some respects. It is no doubt difficult to judge whether a person is so inebriated as to be incapable of understanding the nature and effect of his act. In the circumstances, if such a customer comes in to cash a cheque, the banker should take care to see to it that the payment is witnessed by some responsible person who is not in the service of the bank.

☞ Married Woman

A Hindu married woman can enter into contracts and bind her estate (*stridhan*) (*Govindji vs. Kalidas, 1880*). A Mohammedan married woman is not disqualified from entering into contracts by reason of her marriage (Section 20 of the Indian Succession Act, 1925). Married women of other communities in India are given the same power of holding separate properties by Section 4 of the Indian Succession Act, 1925, and Section 4 of the Married Women's Property Act, 1874. A contract by a married woman would bind her husband only if it is for the purchase of her necessities.

A married woman can open a current account with a banker in her own name, which would form part of her separate estate. She can thus draw bills, etc., in connection with her separate estate and arrange for all obligations, including overdrafts with her banker. These obligations, however, will bind her separate estate and not her husband's so long as the husband has no interest in the transaction. A married woman in India, possessing separate property, may be adjudicated insolvent in connection with debts contracted by her, irrespective of whether she belongs to a Hindu, Mohammedan or to any religious community.

☞ Pardanashin Woman

A pardanashin woman observes complete seclusion in accordance with the custom of her own community. She does not deal with the people other than the members of her own family. As she remains completely secluded, a presumption in law exists that:

(i) any contract entered into by her might have been subject to undue influence; and

(ii) the same might not have been made with her free will and with full understanding of what the contract actually means.

Thus, a contract entered into by a pardanashin woman is not a contract free from all defects. The other party to the contract shall have to prove that the contract with her was free from the above-mentioned defects in order to enforce the same. The banker should, therefore, take due precaution in opening an account in the name of a pardanashin woman. As the identity of such a woman cannot be ascertained, the banker generally refuses to open an account in her name.

Illiterate Persons

Illiterate persons cannot sign their names and hence the bankers take their thumb impressions as a substitute for signature, and also a copy of their recent photograph. The application form and the photograph should be attested by an approved witness. For withdrawing money, he must attend personally and affix his thumb impression in the presence of an official of the bank, for the purpose of identification.

JOINT ACCOUNT

☞ Power to Draw Cheques and Death of a Joint Accountholder

When a joint account is opened with a banker, he should take precise instructions in writing as to which members are entitled to draw cheques, and whether the balance in the account has to be paid to the survivor in the event of the death of any of the parties to the joint account, or whether it is to be dealt with in any other manner. This written document should be signed by all the parties in whose name the joint account is opened.

☞ Insolvency

In the event of the insolvency of a joint accountholder, the operations on the account will cease. Payments from such an account should be made only at the joint direction of the insolvent accountholder and the solvent party.

☞ Insanity

In case of mental disorder of any one of the joint accountholders, it would not be safe for the bank to part with the money to the other party.

☞ Survivors

Where no special instructions are given to a banker, the survivor or the survivors of a joint account are entitled to the whole balance in the account on that date.

☞ Overdraft

The instructions by joint accountholders should also indicate clearly whether the person or persons authorised to operate the account have the power to overdraw on the account. Authority is given to incur debts on a joint account. It is important that the "several" liability should also be established. In the event of a joint liability, the creditor can bring only one action, whereas in the case of a "several" liabilities, he has as many rights of action as the number of joint accountholders. Moreover, the banker can prefer a claim against the estate of the deceased joint debtor as well, to the extent of the debt outstanding at the time of his death.

☞ Joint Account of Husband and Wife

In the case of a joint account of husband and wife, when the husband dies, the question whether his wife should take money by survivorship is a question of intention. If the intention was that the husband opened such an account with the deliberate purpose of leaving his money to his wife, she would no doubt come in by survivorship; but if it was shown that this was only a method of keeping and working the account for convenience, the position would be different. In order to avoid any such difficulty, the banker should take in writing from the parties concerned this intention about the disposal of the balance in the account. In *Marshall vs. Crutwell* (1857), it was decided that, in the event of the death of the husband, the balance belonged to the husband's estate. In the case of the death of his wife, the husband would take the balance by survivorship.

A joint account in the name of a Hindu husband and wife, on the terms that the same is payable to either or survivor, does not on the death of the husband constitute a gift to his wife. (*Guran Dutta vs. Ram Ditta,* 55 Cal. 994.) In a case, a husband deposited one lakh of rupees with a bank which formed a part of his self-acquired property. The deposit was made in the joint names of himself and his wife. The husband died, leaving his wife and three sons survivors. The wife withdrew the money with interest through her son, whereupon the other brothers filed a suit objecting to this withdrawal. It was held that though this money was a deposit by a Hindu in the joint names of himself and his wife, on the terms that the same was to be payable to either or survivor, that fact did not constitute a gift by the Hindu husband to his wife.

In *Shantimoyee vs. Bengal Central Bank* 53 C. W. N. 680, a joint account was opened in the bank in the names of husband and wife and payable to either or survivor. It was held that, on the death of the husband, the account could be operated by the wife and there was no resulting trust in favour of the husband's estate as there was no evidence that the amounts deposited in the bank were the property of the husband. Unlike in English law, a presumption of advancement of gift in favour of a wife or child cannot be extended to Hindus or Muslims in India due to the widespread practice of *benami* in this country. It is well established that where it is proved or admitted that the money deposited in a bank was husband's property, there can be no presumption of advancement in favour of the wife simply because the instructions to the bank are that the money is payable to either or survivor. However, it must be established that the amounts deposited were the moneys of the husband alone. When the instructions to the bank are to pay either or survivor, the bank must carry-out the mandate unless a competent court issues an injunction before the presentation of the cheque to the bank by the survivor.

☞ Death of a Joint Accountholder

In respect of a joint account opened in the bank, the law seems to be well settled that on the death of one, there is a resulting thrust in favour of his heirs and legal representatives unless there are special facts and circumstances to show contrary intention (*Krishandas Nagindas Bhate vs. Bhagwandas and Others* AIR 1976, Bombay 153).

In *Padmanabhan Bhawani and Others vs. Govindas Bhawani and Another* — (AIR 1975 Kerala 1983) the high court held that on the death of the depositor, the amounts deposited in the joint names, payable to either or survivor, could not be treated as a gift to the survivor, because the depositor continues to be the owner of the amounts in question till his death. In such cases without any declaration of trust, there is resulting trust in favour of the depositor in the absence of any contrary intention or unless it can be proved that an actual gift of the amount was intended. The burden of proving a contrary intention of gift is on the person who seeks to rebut the resulting trust in favour of the person who makes the deposit.

About the rule of the banks that on the death of one, the account would be converted into a single account to be operated by the survivor, the High Court observed that such provisions were designed only to regulate easy operation of accounts and payment of money to the survivor. The provisions did not touch the rights *inter-se* among the depositors or the rights of inheritance.

Nomination: A new Section 45(2A) has been inserted in The Banking Law's (Amendment) Act, 1983, which provides for the facility of nomination by depositors. Such facility shall also be available in case of joint accounts. In the case of joint accounts, all the joint depositors together may nominate, in the prescribed manner, one person to whom in the event of death of all the depositors, the amount of deposit may be returned by the banking company. Such nominee shall become entitled to all the rights of the depositors in relation to such deposit. The banking company shall be discharged of its liability in respect of the deposit by making payment to the nominee.

JOINT HINDU FAMILY

A joint Hindu family possesses ancestral properties and carries on ancestral business. The ownership of such property passes on to the member of the family according to the Hindu law. In case of a joint Hindu family governed by the Mitakshara School of Hindu law, every male member of a family acquires an interest in the joint property by birth. After the enforcement of the Hindu Succession Act, 1956, the share of a deceased coparcener, who was member of the joint Hindu family, is also divisible amongst his wife, daughters and other female relatives as given in the Act. While dealing with the account of a joint Hindu family and granting it a loan, the banker is naturally faced with a difficult task of ascertaining the right of the coparceners in the joint family. The following legal precautions should be taken by the banker in this regard:

1. The family business and its assets are managed by the eldest male member as the Karta. According to the law, the Karta has an implied authority to take a loan, execute necessary documents and pledge the securities on behalf of the family for the purpose of the business

of the family. However, to be on the safe side, the loan documents should be executed by all the adult male members of the family or with their consent by the head of the family in his capacity as its Karta or manager.

2. The power of the Karta to borrow money on the security of the family property is subject to one limitation, *i.e.,* the loan is taken for the purpose necessary for or beneficial to the family. He can take a loan and pledge the property of the family for the purpose of meeting the needs of the usual business of the family and not for any speculative business or for starting a new business. Other coparceners will not be liable for a loan contracted for a purpose other than that in the interest of the family business. The principles of a law which govern borrowings by the Karta of a joint Hindu family were clearly enunciated by the Rajasthan High Court as follows (in *Ram Dayal and Others vs. Bhanwarlal and Others* (AIR 1973, Raj. 173).

   (i) The manager of a joint Hindu family has power to alienate (*i.e.,* transfer for value) joint family property, so as to bind the interests of both adult and minor coparceners in the property, provided that the alternation is made for legal necessity or for the benefit of the estate. The payments of debts incurred for family business or other necessary purpose constitute a legal necessity.

   (ii) The burden of proving legal necessity to support alienation is upon the alience (transferee).

   (iii) The alience can succeed in *(ii)* above, not only on proof of legal necessity but also on the proof that the alience made reasonable enquiries and was satisfied as to the existence of legal necessity. In case of a dispute on this point, the burden of proof that the bank was satisfied before granting a loan, that the loan was sought for the benefit of the family business lies on the banker himself. He should therefore, be very careful in ascertaining the purpose of the loan sanctioned on the security of joint family assets.

3. The coparceners' liability in case of loans granted to a joint Hindu family is limited to the extent of their interest in the joint property. But if the adult coparceners themselves contract along with the Karta or ratify the contract entered into by the Karta become personally liable for the loan.

   If a suit is brought in a representative capacity as a manager of the joint family, and a decree is granted in pursuance thereof, other members of the family are held to be substantial parties to the suit through the manager of the joint family. The fact that they are not *co-nominee* parties to the suit will not render the decree in the suit any the less binding on them. A decree against the manager in such a suit will be binding on the undivided coparceners and the entire joint family properties can be taken in execution of such a decree even if the junior coparcener is not a party to the suit [*T.A. Sankarlingam vs. T.N. Mani* (AIR 1975, Madras 206)].

4. If there is a minor coparcener in a joint family, his guardian must sign the documents on his behalf. When the minor coparcener attains majority, he should also sign the documents to give his assent to the undertaking given by major coparceners.

☛ Partnership

The mere existence of a business partnership is no warranty that a partner has authority to bind the firm by opening a bank account on its behalf in his own name. (*Alliance Bank vs. Kearsley,* 1871). It is important, therefore, that a banker should always open a firm's account in the firm's name and it is in his interest to endeavour to get a letter signed by all the partners stating the nature of the firm's business, the names and addresses of all the partners and the names of those authorised to operate the account in the name of the firm. The authority should include powers to draw, endorse and accept bills, and mortgage and sell property belonging to the firm. If this is done, a dormant partner cannot evade his liability and the banker is not put to the trouble of proving the interest of all the partners in the firm.

☞ Operation of Account

A firm's account can be operated by one or more partners authorised to do so, and the bank is justified in honouring cheques signed by such partners. A notice to the banker by one or more partners cancelling the authority of a partner to operate the account is sufficient for the banker to act upon. Similarly, any partner has an implied authority to stop the payment of a cheque drawn on the partnership account by another, and the banker is bound to comply with the instructions issued by that partner.

☞ Immovable Property

Section 19 of the Indian Partnership Act, 1932, expressly states that the implied authority of a partner does not extend to the transfer of the immovable property belonging to the firm.

☞ Mortgage

A banker should see to it that the partner executing the mortgage is vested with the power to do so on behalf of his co-partners. In a case where a partner gave a legal mortgage without authority, it was held that while he had no power to bind the firm by a deed, it could be regarded as an equitable assignment under hand. (*Merchant vs. Morton Dawn & Co.* 1901).

☞ Transactions on Private Account

A banker should be careful while accepting cheques payable to a firm in the interest of the credit of the private account of a partner. If a banker fails to take the necessary precaution, he may lose the statutory protection that he enjoys under Section 131 of the Negotiable Instruments Act, 1881.

☞ Retirement of a Partner

In the event of the retirement of a partner, the liability of the retiring partner to the bank ceases in respect of transactions after the date of retirement. If notice of retirement is not given to the bank, the liability of the partner will continue, even for advances after retirement.

☞ Death or Insolvency of a Partner

In the event of the death or insolvency of a partner, the firm is dissolved unless there is an express provision against it in the partnership agreement. The remaining partners are bound to close the books of account and will be accountable to the representative of the deceased or the official assignee of the insolvent for his share in the assets of the firm.

If, however, in the event of the death, insolvency or retirement of a partner, the banker wants to retain his lien for any money due to him, he should stop the account, and the continuing partners should be asked to open a new account, because if the banker fails to do that, the rule in Clayton's Case will come into operation — according to which a payment shall discharge the earliest debt, whether of the customer or of the banker, that remains unpaid *(Clayton's Case, 1816)*.

In the event of the insolvency of a partner, the insolvent partner has no right to use partnership funds. Therefore, cheques drawn by him on the partnership account must be refused by the banker. The other partners may, however, use the credit balance of the firm's account. The banker is not concerned whether or not the remaining partners render account to the trustee in bankruptcy or official assignee for the share of the insolvent partner in the assets of the firm. Cheques drawn by the insolvent partner before his adjudication may be paid by the bank, but it is better to obtain the confirmation of the other partners first. The solvent partners should be permitted to operate the account only to the extent to which it is necessary for the winding up of the old firm. Where the remaining partners desire to continue the partnership business, a new account should be opened for transactions not connected with such a winding up.

☞ Lunacy or Other Disability of a Partner

In case of lunacy or other disability of a partner, partnership is not dissolved *ipso facto,* for an order of a competent Court is required for that purpose.

☞ Limited Liability Company

A limited company is established by means of a statute and enjoys a good many of the attributes of a person; its entity is separate from that of its shareholders. A current account may be opened in the name of the company, whether trading or non-trading; but before opening an account in the name of a company, a banker should examine, under the Companies Act:

(i) The Certificate of Incorporation, and Certificate of Commencement, together with the Memorandum of Association and Articles of Association;

(ii) He should also ask for a copy of the resolution passed by the directors of the company, appointing him as banker to the company and naming the person or persons authorised to operate the account;

(iii) He should obtain the specimen signatures of the persons authorised to operate the account of the company.

☞ Borrowing Powers

The powers of joint-stock companies regarding borrowing, lending, carrying on of business, drawing, accepting and endorsing bills of exchange, promissory notes, cheques, etc., largely depend on their constitution, which is outlined in the Memorandum and Articles of Association of each company and the nature of the business conducted by it. A trading company, for example, has an implied power to borrow even if its constitution does not give such express powers.

It is important for the banker to know and to be sure as to what are the powers of the company, particularly those of its directors and managers who can act on its behalf. He should see to it that the directors do not exceed their powers in any transaction, *i.e.*, act in *ultra vires* fashion because if they do so, that act will not bind the company.

☞ Non-trading Concerns

Accounts are also opened in banks in the names of associations, societies or institutions. Before opening an account in the name of such associations, the banker should follow the same procedure as in the case of joint-stock companies, *viz.,* the banker should examine —

(i) The statute under which such an Association has been established;

(ii) Certification of Incorporation and Commencement and Memorandum and Articles of Association;

(iii) A copy of the resolution passed by the directors or members of the executive of the concern, appointing him as banker to the concern and naming the person or persons authorised to operate the account; and

(iv) Obtain specimen signatures of the person authorised to operate the account of the concern.

The borrowing powers of unregistered associations, clubs and societies depend entirely upon the nature of the rules or constitution of such Associations.

☞ Executors and Administrators

An executor is a person to whom the execution of a will is entrusted by the testator. A banker should avoid opening accounts of executors and administrators; but if the accounts are in their personal capacities, there should be no objection to his doing so. The banker should thoroughly acquaint himself with the documents appointing them and should have no dealings with the estate until the official probate or letters of administration have been inspected by him. In case a banker comes to know that trust funds are being misappropriated, he cannot escape liability on the ground that the bank account was in the name of the trustee. Therefore, the banker should take proper and adequate steps for the protection of the interests of the beneficiaries; otherwise he may be held liable for any fraud committed by the trustees.

The executor's or administrator's account is to be regarded by the banker as that of the deceased's estate. He should take a mandate signed by all the executors as to how cheques and bills are to be signed and endorsed, and hold all the executors jointly and severally liable for any overdraft. The mandate should be strictly followed; where it provides for the signature of only one of them. Where no instructions are given, but one of the executors informs the bankers that cheques must be signed by all the executors, the banker must follow these instructions. One executor can effectively countermand payment even when all the executors are required to sign cheques together.

The operation of an account by executors is for many purposes like that of a partnership. For instance, each executor can deal with the assets and can open and operate a banking account; but the other executors can countermand his actions.

On notice of the death of a customer, the banker should stop payment of his cheques until a probate or letters of administration, or a succession certificate is produced. Before stopping payment, however, he should be absolutely certain of the customer's death. Cheques cashed prior to the notice of death may be debited to the account of the deceased customer as well as those which the banker had "marked" at the customer's request. As soon as the executor or administrator obtains probate or letters of administration, the bank opens an account in the executor's or administrator's own name, to which account the balance of the deceased's account is transferred. The probate is made up of a copy of the will with the sealed certificate of the Court, testifying to its genuineness. On its production, the banker should, for future reference and guidance, note in a special register the directions which the deceased in his will has given in regard to the disposal of his property. In the case of letters of administration also, full particulars should be recorded in the register, together with details. It should also be noted that if the executors or administrators carry on the business of the deceased, they would be personally liable, unless the will directs and authorises them to do so. In the latter case, the executors and administrators can reimburse themselves from the estate; but if the estate is not sufficient to meet the debts, they would be personally responsible.

The law regards the executors and administrators as one person. Therefore, any one executor or administrator can act on behalf of himself or his co-executor or co-administrator, so that one of them can give a valid discharge for a debt or a receipt for money paid into or handed over to the account of the estate.

The insolvency of an executor will not terminate his appointment, and, therefore, the banker need not stop the account if that happens. He should, however, stop the account if it has been overdrawn on the insolvent's personal security. This is to prevent the operation of the Rule in Clayton's Case and to retain the liability of the insolvent executor.

The lunacy of an executor will, however, terminate his authority, and the banker must not pay cheques drawn by such an executor without first obtaining the consent of the other representatives.

When an executor or administrator wants an advance from a banker for the purpose paying the estate, the banker can only advance the amount by taking a proper security. This is because an advance made prior to the obtaining of probate may place the banker in an awkward position if as a result of some technical flaw, the will or appointment is nullified. Of course, after the grant of probate or letters of administration, the executors or administrators are able to exercise their usual powers in connection with the estate. They can pledge the estate of deceased for the purpose of raising a loan to meet the expenses or debts of the deceased.

CUSTOMER'S ATTORNEY

A customer may appoint an attorney to deal with his bank account. The power of attorney is a general notice and an authority for this purpose. It is different from an ordinary mandate authorising a person to operate his bank account.

The power of attorney may be either special or general. In the former case the person so authorised gets powers in regard to certain matters only, *e.g.,* sale or purchase of property, etc. In case of the general power of attorney, the grantor of such power authorises the other person generally, to act on his behalf in all matters concerning his business.

While opening an account in the name of an attorney for a person the banker should take the following precautions:

(1) The power of attorney should be duly stamped and registered with the Registrar of Documents or attested by a Notary Public. The banker must retain with him its attested copy for his own record.

(2) The power of attorney must be in force at the time of opening the account. The power of attorney may be granted for a specific period or for a particular purpose. The banker should ensure that such specific period has not expired or the specific purpose not fulfilled at the time of opening the account. The period for which authority has been granted must be noted at the top of the account so that the account does not continue beyond such period.

(3) The banker should note all the terms of the Power of Attorney which are likely to be of concern to him at any time in future.

(4) The banker should find out what specific powers have been entrusted by the principal to the attorney, *i.e.,* to open accounts, to draw and endorse cheques and to overdraw the account. If the power to overdraw is not entrusted the fact should be specifically recorded.

(5) The person presenting the power of attorney for opening the account must be properly identified and his address noted.

(6) The account opening form should be signed as far as possible by the principal. He should attest the signature of the attorney. If the power of attorney authorises the attorney to open a bank account the bank may open an account at his request. Confirmation from the principal must be obtained before actual operation of the account is allowed.

(7) The account should be opened in the name of the principal with the following heading: "XYZ (principal) by his agent ABC."

Inclusion of the words "constituted attorney" are not necessary. If the agent signs "Per Pro XYZ", it indicates that the agent has limited authority only to sign such cheques. The bankers should ensure that the act of the agent is not beyond the powers conferred upon him.

(8) The banker should also see that the Power of Attorney does not contain any condition or event on the occurrence of which it will be enforceable. A condition like "During my absence from India" implies that the power of attorney is automatically cancelled as soon as the principal returns to india. The banker should not accept such condition.

(9) According to Section 201 of the Indian Contract Act, an agency is terminated in the following cases:

(i) If the principal revokes his authority:

(ii) If the agent renounces the business of agency;

(iii) If the business of agency is completed; and

(iv) If the principal or the agent dies, becomes insolvent or of unsound mind.

It is to be noted that the death, insolvency or insanity of the principal revokes the authority vested in the agent and the latter ceases to act as agent of the principal.

TRUST ACCOUNTS

☞ Definition

According to Section 3 of the Indian Trusts Act of 1882, a trust is an obligation annexed to the ownership of property and arising out of the confidence reposed in and accepted by a person or persons for the benefit of another or others and the owner of the property. "The person who reposes the trust is called the author of the trust." A trustee is the person in whom the confidence is reposed. "The person for whose benefit the trust is formed is called the beneficiary." A trust, therefore, implies the possession of certain assets for the benefit of others.

☞ Creation of Trust

A trust may be created by a person when he is alive. The person who creates a trust is called the settler and may also be the sole or one of the trustees. A trust is created by a Trust Deed.

A trust may also be created under a will. In that case, the settler is also known as the donor or settler. The executor of the estate of the deceased have to prepare a scheme of arrangements which has to be approved by a court. The scheme and the court's order of sanction then take the place of the trust deed; they are as good as a trust deed.

☞ Trustees and Their Appointments

Trustees may be appointed by the author of the trust, or where the trust specifically provides for a fresh appointment, by the retiring/continuing trustees. Such appointment should be in writing and duly accepted by the fresh trustees.

☞ Death of Trustees

If one or more of the trustees die or retire, the authority vested in the remaining trustees is derived from the provisions of the trust deed. If the number of surviving trustees does not fall below the stipulated minimum, or if the minimum number of trustees has not been fixed, the operations in the account are allowed as usual. Cheques signed by the deceased trustee are not paid by the bank. When all the trustees are dead, new trustees may be appointed by the Court.

☞ Types of Trust Accounts

(a) *Private Trusts:* These are trusts which are created for the benefit of specified individuals (like wife, children, etc.)

(b) *Public Trusts:* These are created for the benefit of the general public or a particular community; for example, charitable trusts. They come under the authority of the Charity Commissioner or a similar officer.

A transfer of trust funds should not be allowed for the personal benefit of the trustees. Cheques drawn in favour of the trust must not be credited to the personal accounts of the trustees or executors, specially when the private account is overdrawn. *The banker shall be liable for the misuse of the trust money if the same is within his knowledge.*

The insolvency of a trustee is no cause for him to vacate the office. The creditors of the trustee cannot recover their claims from the trust property. In case the trustee continues to operate upon the account, such operations should be carefully watched.

The trustees may borrow from the bank and pledge or mortgage the trust property, *provided that such borrowing powers are given to them in the trust deed.* It would be safer if the advance is also personally guaranteed by the trustees (if they are respectable persons).

The delegation of powers in regard to the signing of cheques must be mentioned in the trust deed. If it is not, all the trustees should jointly operate the account.

When a trustee is found to be a lunatic, he should not be allowed to operate the account.

JOINT STOCK COMPANIES

Modern businesses are generally organised as joint stock companies incorporated under the Companies Act, 1956. A joint stock company is an artificial person with perpetual succession brought into existence under the provisions of the Companies Act. Legally, a company is considered as an entity separate from its members and hence it possesses all power to enter into valid contract. It can own property in its own name, carry on lawful business and incur liabilities in its name. While opening an account in the name of a company, the banker must satisfy himself about the following:

1. Examination of Documents: As a company is an artificial person, its constitution, powers and objectives, rules and regulations etc., are contained in the following important documents. The banker should thoroughly and carefully examine these documents:

(i) *Certificate of Incorporation and Certificate of Commencement of Business:* These certificates, issued by the Registrar of Companies, provide conclusive proof that the company is a duly incorporated body and all the necessary formalities regarding its formation have been fulfilled by the promoters. A private limited company is not required to obtain the Certificate of Commencement of Business. On its registration under the Companies Act, a company is given recognition as an entity separate from its members and acquires all powers to enter into contracts and to commence its business. The banker should ensure from these certificates that the company applying for opening an account is a duly registered and incorporated body.

(ii) *Memorandum of Association:* The Memorandum of Association is the main document of a company, which embodies its constitution and is called the charter of the company. It contains the name of the company, its authorised capital, the name of the State in which the registered office of the company is to be situated, the object of the company and the liability of its members, which is generally limited to the extent of their shareholdings. The banker should examine the Memorandum specially to note objective for which the company is incorporated because any contract entered into by a company which serves an object other than the objects mentioned in the Memorandum is unenforceable at law and *ultra vires.* Such a contract cannot be ratified by the members of the company at their meeting even by a unanimous vote.

(iii) Articles of Association: The Articles of Association contain the rules and regulations of a company regarding its internal management. It contains in detail all matters which are concerned with the conduct of day-to-day business of the company. For example, the Articles contain the right and powers of the directors, rules regarding the conduct of company meetings, the business that can be transacted by the company and the form in which it is to be done. Every person, including a banker, who is dealing with a company or intends to deal with a company is presumed to have the knowledge of the contents of these two documents and he should take care that his dealings with the company are not inconsistent with the provisions of these documents. This is known as constructive notice. The banker should, therefore, scrutinise these documents very carefully in regard to the following:

(a) The powers of the directors in conducting the affairs of the company.

(b) The procedure for borrowing and the limit on borrowings, if any.

(c) The power vested in the directors to borrow money for the company and to mortgage the company's assets.

(d) The procedure and authority to draw and endorse cheques, bills, etc., on behalf of the company.

The banker should also obtain printed and certified copies of the Memorandum and Articles of Association for the purpose of its own record.

2. Copy of the Board's Resolution: Along with the application to open an account in the company's name, the banker should obtain a certified copy of the resolution passed by the Board of Directors of the company containing the following in regards to the opening of a bank account:

(a) appointing the bank concerned as the banker of the company;

(b) naming the person or persons who are authorised to operate the bank account on behalf of the company;

(c) Stating the name of the persons who are authorised to execute the documents on behalf of the company, or in whose presence the seal of the company will be affixed on the documents;

(d) authorising the advance and stating all details of such advance, *e.g.,* limit, security, rate of interest, etc.; and

(e) stating the names of the persons who are authorised to deposit the title deeds in case of equitable mortgage.

3. The Borrowing Power of the Company: All joint stock companies engaged in trade or industry have the implied power to borrow money for the purpose of carrying on their businesses. The borrowing power of the company may be restricted by its Memorandum of Association. Section 293 (1) (d) of the Companies Act, 1956, provides that the Board of Directors of a public company or of a private company which is a subsidiary of a public company shall not, except with the consent of such public company or subsidiary in general meeting, borrow money in excess of the aggregate of the paid-up capital of the company and its free reserve, *i.e.,* reserves not set apart for any specific purpose. The temporary loans obtained from the company's bankers in the ordinary course of business are excluded in computing total borrowing of the company for this purpose. The term 'temporary loan' means loans repayable on demand or within six months from the date of the loan; such as, short-term cash credit arrangement, the discounting of bills and other short-term loans of seasonal character, but does not include loans raised for the purpose of financing expenditure of capital nature. Thus, the limit imposed by Section 293(1) (d) does not apply to the short-term and seasonal loans. For borrowing in excess of this limit, a resolution shall specify the total amount up to which money may be borrowed by the Board of Directors.

Banker should be very careful in ensuring that the total borrowing of the company do not exceed the above limit because under Section 293(5) of the Companies Act, "No debt incurred by the company is effectual, unless the lender proves that he advanced the loan in good faith and without knowledge that the limit imposed had been exceeded".

According to Section 292, the Board of Directors of a Company shall exercise the power to borrow money otherwise than on debentures only by means of resolutions passed at the meeting of the Board. The Board may, by a resolution, delegate the power of the Board. The Board may, by a resolution, delegate the power to borrow to any committee of directors, the managing director, secretaries and treasurer, etc., and shall specify the total amount outstanding at any one time up to which money may be borrowed by the delegate. The resolution of the Board of Directors, exercising the power to borrow, should mention the *arrangement to be made by the Company with its bankers* for the borrowing of money by way of overdraft or cash credit or otherwise and not the actual day-to-day operation of these accounts by means of which the arrangement so made is actually to be availed of.

Borrowing by Directors without Authorisation: The question whether the amount borrowed by the directors without authority and used for the benefit of the company can be recovered from the company or not, was considered by the Patna High Court in *Kumar Krishan Rohatgi and Others vs. State Bank of India and Others* (1980)50 Comp. Cases 722 (Patna). In this case the company contested the suit filed by the State Bank of India on the ground that the Managing Director of the Company had no authority to execute the pronote in the absence of a resolution duly adopted by the Board of Directors and hence it was not binding on the Company.

"The Division Bench of the High Court concurred with the proposition of law that when an agent borrows money for a principal without the authority of the principal and if the principal takes benefit of the money so borrowed or when the money so borrowed has gone into the coffers of the principal, the law implies a promise to repay". This principle applies to joint stock companies as well, it was, therefore held that the company cannot repudiate its liability to repay.

It is to be noted that any borrowing by the company may be *ultra vires* the directors but not *ultra vires* the company. In such cases money can be recovered from the company.

☞ Precautions to be taken by the Banker

(i) The banker should ascertain that the company borrows only for the purpose mentioned in its Memorandum of Association and within the limits, if any, specified therein.

(ii) A certified copy of the resolution of the Board of Directors passed under Section 292 should be obtained by the banker for his own record.

(iii) The Board of Directors should also pass a resolution certifying that the Company's borrowings, including the proposed borrowing, are within the limit specified by the Companies Act, or the limit sanctioned by the shareholders at the general meeting.

4. Registration of charges under the Companies Act: Section 125 of the Companies Act, 1956, requires that every charge created by joint stock company, falling within the following categories, must be registered with the Registrar of Joint Stock Companies within 30 days of its creation, otherwise it shall be void against the liquidator or any creditor of the company.

(a) a charge for the purpose of securing any issue of debentures;

(b) a charge on any immovable property or any interest therein;

(c) a charge on any book debts of the company;

(d) a charge, not being a pledge, on any movable property of the company;

(e) a floating charge on the undertaking or any property of the company including stock in trade;

(f) a charge on calls made but not paid;

(g) a charge on a ship or any share in a ship; and

(h) a charge on goodwill, a patent or a licence under a patent, a trade mark, or a copyright, or a licence under a copyright.

It is to be noted that a charge on any book debts of the company is required to be registered while it is not necessary in case of a charge created by the pledge of any movable property of the company. The question whether the charge created over the fixed deposits is required to be registered under Section 125 was considered in *Shree Meenakshi Mills vs. Registrar of Companies* (1965) l. Comp. L.J. 266. The Registrar of Companies contended that the amount of Fixed Deposits was a book debt of the company and so a charge created thereon was required to be registered. On the other hand, the company argued that the transaction was a pledge of movable property, namely, the fixed deposit receipt, and so the charge was not required to be registered. The High Court held that the fixed deposits would also be movable property. If the company could, treating the transaction as a pledge, avoid registration of the charge, it was not necessary for it to register the charge merely because it could also be registered as a charge on book debts.

The company must file the prescribed particulars of the charge together with the instruments, if any, by which the charge is created or a vertified copy thereof within the prescribed time. Failure to get the charge registered will render the charge void against the liquidator and any creditor of the company, so far as any security on the company's property is conferred by the charge. This implies that if a charge which is required to be registered under Section 125 is not registered it does not mean that the transaction itself becomes void or the debt is not recoverable. The non-registration of the charge shall have the effect that the security created by it becomes void as against the liquidator and/or other creditors. In other words, such debt becomes an unsecured one when a liquidator is appointed and such security is made available to meet the claims of all unsecured creditors.

In State Bank of India vs. Viswaniryas (1987(2) *Kerala Law Times*-317), the Kerala High Court held that want of registration under Section 125 of the Companies Act would affect the holder of an unregistered charge in case of winding up proceedings and that too against the official liquidator. Such a holder of an unregistered charge would not be entitled to claim a preferential right and would not be entitled to stand outside the winding up proceedings. The Court further held that so long as the company was a going concern, the unregistered charge would not become void against an unsecured creditor of the company.

The consequence of non-registration of charge under Section 125 continues even if the mortagagee has obtained a decree prior to the issue of order winding up the company. In the case of *Official Receiver of Kamani Brothers (P) Ltd., vs. Suryakani Natvarlal Surati and Others,* a decree was passed and the mortgaged property was to be sold by public auction in the event of the company committing default in payment of the sum by the due date. In the meanwhile, the company was ordered to be wound up. In the circumstances of the case, the Bombay High Court held that the unregistered charge in favour of the mortgagee was kept alive hence the mortagee was not allowed to sell the property. The charge of mortgagee would have been extinguished if the sale had taken place before the winding up order was issued.

The banker should ensure that the charge over the assets of the company created in his favour is duly registered with the Registrar of Joint Stock Companies within the prescribed period. Though the company is not under any legal obligation to register such charge, the registration of the charge safeguards the interests of the creditors, including the bankers. According to Section 126, where any charge on any property of a company has been registered under Section 125, any person acquiring such property or any part thereof or any share or interest therein shall be deemed to have notice of the charge as from *the date of its registration and not from the date of its creation.* For example, a company borrows from X on 1st January and from Y on 15th January and mortagages the same property to both. But if the charge in favour of Y is registered on 16th January while that in favour of X is registered on 20th January (*i.e.,* within the permissible period of 30 days after the creation), the charge in favour of Y will have precedence over the charge created in favour of X because the former was registered earlier than the latter.

Precautions regarding prior charge over the assets : Generally, banker grants secured loans on the basis of a fixed charge on the fixed asset of the company and a floating charge over its stock-in-trade, book debts and other movable assets. Sometimes, in addtion to the above, personal guarantee is also secured from the directors of the company as a collateral security.

While granting a loan on the basis of a fixed or floating charge over the assets of a company, the banker should be careful about any prior charge —fixed or floating over the same assets. In some cases debentures are secured by floating charge over the assets of the company with a stipulation that the company cannot create any other charge over the assets ranking above or at par with the charge in favour of the debentureholders. A charge by the company subsequently will, therefore, not have priority over the earlier charge. The banker should, therefore, be very careful in finding out the existence of any prior charge over the assets of the Company by inspecting the Register of Charges, which every company is required to maintain at its registered office.

The banker should also inspect the Register of Mortgage and Charges maintained at the office of the Registrar of Joint Stock Companies, which contains all the details of the charge registered under Section 125 of the Companies Act.

5. Director's personal account: The banker of a company having personal accounts of the directors of the company must handle the latter with care. If a director, who is authorised to operate the company's account and to endorse cheques on its behalf, deposits cheques drawn in favour of the Company to be credited to his personal account the banker should first enquire the purpose for which such cheques are intended to be credited to his personal account and on being satisfied about the genuine reason, credit them to his account. If the banker does not make an enquiry in such a case or credits the amount in the personal account of the director despite unsatisfactory reasons given by him, he shall be liable to refund the money credited to the director's account.

☞ Additional Precautions in case of Private Limited Companies

The banker should be very careful in advancing loans to a private limited company which has recently been incorporated by conversion of the business of a sole-trader. In such cases the creditors of the sole-trader cannot recover their dues from the company which is deemed to be an entity separate from its shareholders. Sometimes, sole-traders convert their business into private limited companies primarily to "defeat or defraud" their creditors, to whom they owe large sums. According to the Insolvency Act, such transfer of assets is considered to be an act of insolvency and the insolvency proceedings may be instituted against such person. When a trader is declared insolvent, all transfers made by him within a period of two years become void against the Official Receiver or Assisgnee except in the following circumstanes:

(a) Transfer made before and in consideration of marriage, or

(b) Transfer to a purchaser in good faith and for valuable consideration.

The Official Receiver gets title to the property of the insolvent with effect from the date on which an act of insolvency takes place. This is called the "Doctrine of Relation Back". According to this doctrine the dealing of the insolvent from the date of the act of insolvency will not be valid and all such property sold or transferred shall vest in the Official Receiver. The banker should, therefore, make enquiries to avoid a situation.

CLUBS, SOCIETIES AND CHARITABLE INSTITUTIONS

Clubs, societies, charitable and religious institutions, libraries, schools, colleges, etc., not engaged in trading activities, maintain their account with the banks. The banks should observe the following precautions in dealing with them:

(i) *The Society must be Incorporated:* The Society Registration Act, 1860, provides for the registration of societies for the promotion of literature, science, fine arts or for charitable purposes. Such institutions may also be incorporated under the Companies Act 1956, or the Cooperative Societies Acts. A society gets the legal recognition as an entity separate from the members only after its incorporation under any of these Acts. Thereafter, it is empowered to enter into valid contracts and to sue or be sued. The banker should therefore ensure that the applicant society is a properly incorporated body. The unregistered society cannot be sued in law.

(ii) *Rules and by-laws of the Society:* A registered society is governed by the provisions of the Act under which it has been registered. It may have its own Constitution. Charter or Memorandum of Association and rules and by-laws etc., to carry on its activities. A copy of the same should be furnished by the society to the banker to acquaint the latter with the power and functions of the persons managing its affairs. The banks should ensure that these rules are observed by the persons responsible for managing the society.

(iii) *Resolution of the Managing Committee:* For opening bank account, the Managing Committee of the society must pass a resolution —

(a) appointing the bank concerned as a banker of the society;

(b) mentioning the name/names of the person or persons, who are authorised to operate the account; and

(c) giving any other directions for the operation of the said account;

A copy of the solution must be obtained by the bank for its own record.

(iv) *Borrowing Power of the Society:* In case a registered society intends to borrow, the bankers must ascertain the borrowing power of the society from its Charter or Memorandum. The purpose for which such borrowing is permissible must also be noted and the powers of the managing committee or its office-bearers to create a charge over the assets of the society for the purpose of borrowing should be enquired into. A resolution must be passed by the Managing Committee for this purpose and a copy thereof must be sent to the banker.

(v) *Death or Resignation:* In case the person authorised to operate the account on behalf of a society dies or resigns, the banker should stop the operation of the society accounts till the society nominates another person to operate its accounts.

(vi) *Care to be Exercised in case of Personal Accounts:* If the person authorised to operate the society's account is also having his personal account with the same branch of the bank, the banker is under an obligation to ensure that the funds of the society are not being credited to the personal account of the said person or office bearer. For example, the principal of a College is authorised to operate the account of the college with bank X. He also has his personal account with the same bank. He sends to the bank for collection and credit to his personal account a cheque drawn by a donor in favour of the College. The banker is under an obligation to ensure that he receives payment on behalf of the true owner of the said cheque, *i.e.,* on behalf of the college. If he fails to do so he will be held guilty of negligence and shall not be able to avail of the statutory protection under Section 131 of the Negotiable Instruments Act. In these circumstances, the banker should not collect such cheques for crediting the same to the account of the principal.

☞ Questions

1. What precautions should a banker take in opening accounts with a —
   (a) Minor,
   (b) Married woman,
   (c) A joint stock company,
   (d) An illiterate person,
   (e) A club, and
   (f) A charitable trust?
2. What precautions should a banker take in opening a current account in the name of a trading partnership firm? If, at a later date, one of the partner's retires or becomes insolvent or dies, how should he deal with the firm's account —
   (i) if it is credit, and
   (ii) if it is overdrawn?
3. *(a)* The Principal of AB College is authorised to operate the account of the college in M Bank. He has also his personal account in the same bank. He sends to the bank for collection and credit to his personal account a cheque drawn by a donor on S Bank in favour of "The Principal, AB College" What action should the manager of M Bank take, and why?
   (b) The same Principal draws a cheque on the said account of AB College in favour of a firm of automobile dealers for the purchase of a motor car for his personal use. Can the cheque be paid or not? Give reasons.
4. *(a)* Two individuals, who are not trading partners, want to open a joint current account in your bank and seek your guidance regarding the manner of operation of the account. What advice would you give them? And why? What forms would you take from them to facilitate its smooth operation and to protect the bank's interests.
   (b) What steps would you take to obtain repayment of an overdraft in a joint current account if one of the joint accountholder dies, becomes insane or is adjudged bankrupt?
5. Explain why it is necessary for a banker to ask for an introductory reference before opening a current account for a party.
6. *(a)* A minor wants to open a current account in his own name in your branch. Would you permit it? If the minor wants an overdraft arrangement and offers to secure the guarantee of a substantial third party, would you grant this facility?
   (b) What are the precautions which a banker should take in the opening and conduct of current accounts in the names of executors and administrators?
7. What are the precautions to be taken by a banker in regard to the opening and conduct of a current account in the name of a Trust? If one of the Trustee dies or becomes insolvent or insane, how should the account be dealt with? *[C.A.I.I.B., Part I]*
8. B comes to your bank with a power of attorney granted to him by A and requests you to open a current account in the name of A to be operated by B as his constituted attorney. How will you deal with this request and what are the points in the power of attorney to which you request and what are the points in the power of attorney to which you would pay special attention? *[C.A.I.I.B., Part I]*
9. On the death of a partner, should the operations on his firm's account be stopped if it is *(i)* in credit, *(ii)* overdrawn? Give reasons. *[C.A.I.I.B., Part I]*

10. As a branch manager, what procedure would you follow in the following cases:
    (i) Examination Company Ltd., requests to open a current account in its name.
    (ii) Exporters Brothers, a firm consisting of four partners, wants a current account to be opened and also an overdraft arrangement for one lakh of rupees against shares of the Terrywool Co. Ltd., standing in the name of one of the partner's and his wife. *[C.A.I.I.B., Part I]*
11. *(a)* What are the points which a banker has to bear in mind in the opening and operation of a current account in the name of a Club, Society or an Association?
    (b) A customer, who has an account at your branch, has issued a Power of Attorney in favour of his representative. What are the main features of the Power of Attorney in favour of his representative. What are the main features of the Power of Attorney to which you, as a banker, should pay special attention? *[C.A.I.I.B., Part I]*
12. What are the formalities to be observed while opening the Current Account of a Public Limited Company? *[C.A.I.I.B., Part I]*
13. What formalities would you observe and what precautions would you take in the opening and subsequent conduct of an account in the name of an illiterate person? *[C.A.I.I.B., Part I]*
14. *(a)* State briefly the procedure for opening an account of an illiterate person.
    (b) State the important documents required to be furnished to the bank by Public Ltd. Co. for opening a current account. *[I.I.B., Part I]*
15. Please state the procedure and formalities for opening account of a club or an association as also the precautions and care a bank may take relating to operation of such accounts. *[I.I.B., Part I]*
16. Please state difference between partnership firm and Joint Hindu family accounts in terms of constitution and operation of bank account. *[I.I.B., Part I]*
17. What precautions should a banker take while opening current accounts in the names of:
    (a) A Joint Stock Company
    (b) Secretary, Jaipur University Students Union,
    (c) Ram aged 12 years *[Rajasthan]*
18. What precautions should a banker take in opening current account in the names of the following:
    (a) A Pardanashin lady
    (b) Registrar, Jodhpur University *[Newly established]*
    (c) A. B. Co. Ltd., *[Rajasthan]*
19. *(a)* What precautions should a banker take in opening account of: *(i)* a partnership firm, *(ii)* a Pardanashin lady?
    (b) What should a banker do on hearing of the death of a customer? *[Rajasthan)*
20. What procedure and precaution should a banker observe in opening and handling the following types of accounts:
    (i) Trusts,
    (ii) Minor,
    (iii) Limited Companies,
    (iv) Attorneys,
    (v) Unregistered Associations. *[Delhi]*
21. How will a banker examine the power to borrow of the following classes of borrowers:
    (i) Joint Stock Companies,
    (ii) Partnership,
    (iii) Agent and attorneys. *[Madras, B.Com., I.I.B]*
22. What precautions should a banker take in dealing with the following classes of customers :
    (i) Minors
    (ii) Married Women
    (iii) Clubs? *[Bombay]*
23. Explain the procedure and practice followed and precautions exercised while opening a Savings Bank A/c in the name of a Trust. *[I.I.B., Part I]*

24. What precautions would you take while opening accounts in the names of the following:
    (a) Married Woman
    (b) Illiterate person
    (c) Joint account
    (d) Trusts
    (e) Clubs
    (f) Society and Associations. *[I.I.B., Part. I]*
25. State and explain the special precautions to be taken while granting advances to a company? Discuss the provision relating to registration of charges created by the company. What are the restrictions on the grant of advance by a banking company to its directors or firm/company in which its directors are interested? *[I.I.B., Part I]*
26. Discuss the procedure to be followed when an attachment order is received at the branch. What will you do if such an order is received in the names of:
    (i) Trust
    (ii) Joint A/c
    (iii) Partnership Firm *[I.I.B., Part I]*
27. State and explain the formalities to be completed and precautions to be taken while opening accounts in the names of:
    (i) Minor
    (ii) Trust
    (iii) Public Limited Companies, and
    (iv) Club, School, College and Charitable Organisations. *(C.A.I.I.B.)*
28. What precautions would you take while opening accounts of the following customers?
    (i) Minor
    (ii) Hindu undivided family
    (iii) Trust
    (iv) Public Limited Company. *[I.I.B., Part I]*
29. What are the precautions to be taken at the time of opening a current account in the name of the following? Answer any three:
    (i) Married Women
    (ii) Drunkards
    (iii) Minor
    (iv) Liquidator
    (v) Mercantile Agents. *[I.I.B., Part I]*
30. *(a)* The partners of M/s. Hiralal and Co. approach you with a request to open a current account in the name of the firm. Explain the procedure that you would follow for opening the account of the firm, what documents, if any, would you obtain for opening the account?
    (b) You have a current account in the name of M/s Hiralalw and Co. with instructions to pay to either or survivor. The account shows a credit balance of ₹ 50,000 on 1st March, 1987. On 3rd March, 1987 you receive a letter from Mr. Hiralal B. Shah, a partner of the firm, requesting you not to allow the other two partners in the firm to operate upon the account in view of certain differences among them. You receive on 4th March, 1987 a cheque for ₹ 30,000/- signed by Smt. Hiralal Shah favouring the Commissioner of Income-tax. What action would you take as a banker. Give reasons for your answer. *[I.I.B., Part I]*
31. How would you deal with the following case:

    M/s. Ravindra Batra and Co., a firm consisting of four partners, maintains current account with your branch for the last two years to be operated by any one partner. A partner of the firm gives a Power of Attorney in favour of Mr. Mehrotra authorising him to operate his personal account as well as the said firm's account. The power of attorney is produced to the bank along with specimen signature of Mr. Mehrotra duly verified by the partner concerned. Attorney requests to allow him to operate the account. *[I.I.B., Part I]*
32. How will you, as a Banker, deal with the following situations?
    (i) You have opened a Saving Bank Account jointly in the names of Mrs. Bharti M. Desai and her minor son Ajay

Desai aged 12 years. The account shows a credit balance of ₹ 5,000 on 1st January, 1981. You are informed of the death of Mrs. Desai on 3rd January, 1981. Her minor son who is the only child of the family approaches you on 10th January, 1981 asking you to pay him the balance of ₹ 5,000 lying in the joint account as he wants to go out of India with his uncle.

(ii) You have opened a current account jointly in the names of Mr. and Mrs. Patil with instruction to pay to either or survivor. The account shows a credit balance of ₹ 3,500 on 1st March, 1981. On 2nd March, 1981, you receive a letter from Mr. Patil to say that you should not allow Mrs. Patil to operate on the account as the court has passed a decree of divorce. He further instructs you to pay every month ₹ 50 to the court for payment to be made to Mrs. Patil for her maintenance.

(iii) A partner of M/s. H. J. Patil and Co., approaches you with a request to open current account in the name of the firm. In course of your conversation with him you find that one of the partners is a minor aged 15 years, anotherpartner has gone abroad and would be returning after six months. In all there are five partners. Would you open an account in the name of the firm and what precautions would you take in case you decide to open the account ? *[I.I.B., Part I]*

(iv) A man approaches you for opening a joint Savings Bank Account in the name of his two minor sons aged 8 years and 5 years to be operated by him as father and guardian. *[I.I.B., Part I]*

(v) What action would you take as a Banker. Give reasons for your answer. *[I.I.B., Part I]*

33. *(a)* The father of a student, who has been admitted to a school with hostel intends to open through Bombay branch, a Saving Bank A/c in the name of his minor son with School Branch of the Bank. Explain the procedure and other points as you may like to make in the form of a letter.

(b) A paying cashier observes that the person who is to receive cash as bearer of a cheque for ₹ 2,000 passed for cash payment is a major. The bearer confirms that his age is 14 years. What would be the decision of the Branch Manager in this matter? *[I.I.B., Part I]*

34. How would you deal with the following cases:

(i) M/s. ABC is a partnership firm with the partners A, B and C sharing profit and loss in the ratio 5:3:2. The firm has been granted a cash credit limit of ₹ 1 lakh, which has been duty utilised. As the firm is not doing well the advance has been recalled. Partner C approaches the Bank with the request to discharge him of his liability by paying ₹ 20,000 as his share in the profit and loss of 20%. *[I.I.B., Part I]*

(ii) The borrower X was granted an overdraft facility which was *inter alia*, backed by a promissory note executed not only by the borrower X, but also by his minor daughter. In course of time the advance becomes bad and the bank served a legal notice on the borrower. The latter contended that the note was not valid as the same was signed by his minor daughter too and therefore no rights could arise against him. *[I.I.B., Part I]*

(iii) A man approaches you for opening a joint Saving Bank A/c in the name of his two minor sons aged 7 years and 5 years to be operated by him as father and guardian. *[I.I.B., Part I]*

(iv) Your Branch received a remittance from third party for the credit of A. Having no account in the sole name of A, you had credited the amount to an account held in the joint name of A and B opened on either or survivor terms. B withdraws the money. A challenges the payment. *[I.I.B., Part I]*

(v) A, B, and C are partners of ABC and Co. who have a current account with you. At the request of B a cheque for ₹ 5,000 favouring ABC and Co., is purchased by you. The said cheque is returned unpaid. You find that C is the only partner having sufficient worth from whom the cheque amount can be recovered. But C pleads that he had retired from partnership before the cheque was purchased by the bank. As such he is not liable to the Bank. *[I.I.B., Part I]*

(vi) A young boy of 14 years of age approaches you with a request to open a Saving Bank A/c. in his personal name and he gets you a cheque issued in his favour by his father as a deposit for opening the account. The cheque is issued by the father on his account with your Branch. *[I.I.B., Part I]*

(vii) A and B are having a joint account at your Branch. They have given a Power of Attorney in favour of C for operating the account. C has been operating that account for sometime. On 18-9-95 you have been informed that B has died. On 19.9.95, a cheque for ₹ 10,000 signed by C is presented for payment. Sufficient balance is available in the account. *[I.I.B., Part I]*

CHAPTER 11

Termination of Banker — Customer Relationship

A banker-customer relationship is established by a mutual agreement between both the parties, which can be discontinued by mutual agreement. The relationship between a banker and his customer is terminated by the following methods:

(i) By mutual agreement;

(ii) By giving notice to the other party;

(iii) On the death of the customer;

(iv) On the insolvency of the customer;

(v) On the insanity of the customer;

(vi) In the case of closure of a business by a banker or his customer;

(vii) By the assignment of balance in the customer's account; and

(viii) By a Garnishee Order on the customer's account.

(i) Mutual Agreement: Differences may arise between a banker and a customer in their dealings with each other. A customer may want some special services which the banker may not be willing to give, or may not be in a position to give such as: a customer drawing cheques on the banker without any funds in his account; giving cheques or bills for collection to the banker on which he has no legal right; or deals with his banker in a manner which may put the banker in a difficult or risky situation.

In the above circumstances, it is better to terminate the relationship. If a customer wants to terminate the relationship with a banker, he gives a written notice to the banker about it. If he has a current account or a savings bank account with the banker, it can be closed immediately; but if he has a fixed deposit account, it can be closed only on the expiry of the period of the fixed deposit.

In case a banker wants to close a customer's account he sends a written notice to him about it. If the customer does not close his account after receipt of the notice, the banker will send him a cheque for the full amount in his account. In case the customer does not encash that cheque, the banker will continue to honour cheques drawn on the account till the funds last, but will not accept any deposits in the account.

(ii) Notice: The banker should give a reasonable period of notice to his customer to close his account, so that the latter may be able to make some other arrangements regarding his business dealings. In the case of foreign customers, more time should be given. What is a reasonable period of time depends on the nature of the business of the customer and other circumstances. Prosperity Ltd., had started an insurance scheme in which many participants had to deposit premium money in the Lloyds Bank. After sometime, the bank gave one month's notice to Prosperity Ltd., to close their account. It was held that considering the vast business of Prosperity Ltd., one month's notice was not a reasonable notice.

(iii) Death of Customer: As soon as the banker receives information about the death of a customer, his account should be closed, and no payment should be made from such account. Even cheques written before his death but presented after it should not be honoured. After the death of the customer, his legal heir inherits the rights on his account and the banker has to act in accordance with his instructions after the legal heir has obtained a succession certificate from a competent court.

(iv) Insanity of Customer: The banker has to close a customer's account as soon as he hears about his insanity. But this account can be reopened when he is declared to be normal by a competent authority. The banker, however, has to be very cautious because it is very difficult to ascertain whether a person is really insane.

(v) Insolvency of Customer: The account of a customer should be closed as soon as his banker gets information about his insolvency. Such an account can be operated only under instructions of the Receiver or Administrator appointed to handle the affairs of the insolvent customer.

(vi) Winding up of Business: In case a partnership is dissolved or a company is liquidated, the banker, on receiving information about such dissolution or liquidation, has to close the account of such partnership firm or company. These accounts can be operated only under instructions of the official liquidator appointed for the liquidation process.

(vii) Assignment of Balance in Customer's Account: In some cases, a customer may assign the credit balance in his account to some other person and may give notice of such assignment to the banker. After the receipt of such notice, the banker will not honour the cheques received on the credit balance assigned or up to the extent of the balance assigned. In case where a part of the credit balance is assigned, the relationship between the banker and customer is not terminated, and the banker may honour the cheques on the remaining part of the credit balance in the customer's account.

(viii) Garnishee Order on Customer's Account: If a bank receives an order from a court to stop payment from a customer's account (Garnishee Order), the banker must not honour cheques drawn by the customer on such account. If the order is to attach the whole balance in the account, the banker can honour no cheques of the customer. If, on the other hand, the order attaches a part of the balance, cheques may be honoured only up to the amount that would remain after the Garnishee Order has been enforced. The relationship between the banker and his customer is re-established after the Garnishee Order is lifted by the court.

☞ Questions

1. When can a banker close the account of a customer? What precautions should be taken before closing the account of an undesirable customer?
2. Discuss the circumstances in which a banker should close the account of a customer. To whom should he pay the balance?

CHAPTER

12 Banker's Clearing House

Clearing is a process by which a banker exchanges cheque drawn against another banker and received by him for collection or clearance from his customer. A banker's clearing house is an institution where their reciprocal liabilities are balanced against one another. The old practice was to send clerks with bundles of cheques to different banks for the collection of cash. This method was found to be very wasteful as well as laborious, with the result that informal meetings of these clerks used to be held, at which they exchanged these cheques. Ultimately, this led to the establishment of a Clearing House. The London Clearing House was established in 1775.

This practice of clearing balances between banks has been adopted by all the central banks as a part of their duty which has been laid down by law. In some countries where clearing arrangement had been made by the commercial banks themselves long before the establishment of a central bank, or where the central banks did not take initiative in the matter in the beginning, there are independent clearing houses. But in these countries also, the central banks, apart from being their members, have to perform the functions of settling the difference between the banks at the end of each clearing.

☞ Process of Working

The process of the working of a clearing house is simple. Supposing there are five clearing banks, namely, I, II, III, IV and V. Each of these banks keeps specially ruled sheets known as *summary sheets of out-clearing*, wherein a record of all the cheques or bills which it has to realise from other banks is kept. Thus, if Bank I, on sorting out the cheques and drafts in its possession, finds that it has claims against Bank II, it will enter these on the sheet; claims against Banks III, IV and V will be similarly entered. A separate sheet is used for each bank. The cheques and drafts are then carefully checked and sorted out into separate bundles, which are then taken to the clearing house and placed on the clearing desks of the five respective banks. There the clerks of these respective banks maintain their own record in the *summary sheet of in-clearing* in the same way as it had been done in the summary sheets of out-clearing. If the total of out-clearing of Bank I against Bank II is greater than the total of its in-clearing, it has to receive a balance, and *vice versa.* These balances are then entered on a list which is known as the *general balance sheet* of the particular bank. This list contains the printed names of the above banks, with debit and credit columns on the left and right side respectively. If an account is to be received from a bank, it is entered on the debit side against the particular bank's name, and *vice versa.* A balance is then struck between the debit and credit totals, and instructions for transfers are given to the Central Bank. For instance, if Bank III has to receive a balance, it directs the Central Bank to transfer the same from the clearing house account to its own account, and *vice versa.* Thus, the entries in the accounts of the clearing banks with the Central Bank are made, as also the entries in the account in the name of the clearing house.

☞ Advantages

A clearing house organisation is advantageous both to the banker and the society at large.

☞ Banker

(i) He is not required to send his men to each bank separately.

(ii) He is not required to receive or pay in cash unnecessarily.

(iii) Because of the above two advantages, banks do not have to keep large sums in hand.

☞ Society

The clearing house system is advantageous to society also, for it helps in the extension of credit following an increasing use of cheques.

☞ British Clearing House System

In Britain, there are independent clearing houses. All the banks settle their clearing differences by drawing cheques on their accounts with the Bank of England.

☞ The London Clearing House

The work at the London Clearing House is divided into three sections:

(i) Town Clearing;

(ii) County Clearing; and

(iii) Metropolitan Clearing.

(i) Town Clearing: A town clearing covers all the instruments drawn upon and paid into a town office or branch of one of the clearing banks. There are two clearings daily, one in the morning and the other in the afternoon, and the settlement of a day's work is done at the close of the afternoon session. Each bank sends to the clearing house a settlement known as the *summary sheet* or *balance sheet* which has one column for the name of each clearing bank, subdivided into debit and credit columns. These summary sheets or balance sheets are exchanged and the totals verified. A balance is then struck between the in-clearing and out-clearings from and to each bank. This balance is then entered in the *general balance sheet* on the debit and credit side as the case may be, against the name of each bank printed therein. The two columns are then added up, the difference between the two representing the total sum owing to or by the bank in question. Each bank keeps an account at the Bank of England. There is also an account called the clearing banker's account; and the differences are settled by transfers between these accounts. When some of the cheques thus cleared are returned unpaid for one reason or the other, they must be returned by the end of the day of presentation in the case of town clearing. All the cheques, which are presented for payment by one clearing bank to another, are to be presented through the clearing house. In the case of cheques that are received later for presentation on the day they are received, they may be sent to be *marked* or *certified* by the banker on whom they are drawn and are then presented for payment at the clearing house the next morning. These *marked* or *certified* cheques will then have priority over other cheques which are presented on that morning. The

difference between the London clearing and the New York clearing is that, in the former, bundles of cheques are allowed to be gradually brought in throughout the working hours of the day, while in New York, a time is fixed when they are to be delivered at the House in one batch. New York has also a system of fines which are inflicted for various reasons, a peculiarity which is unknown in London.

(ii) County Clearing: All the clearing business of every bank in England outside the metropolitan district comes under county clearing. Even county bank appoints a clearing bank in the city of London as its agent for this business. They, therefore, receive cheques drawn on other county banks from their branches and agents. The process of county clearing is the same as that of town clearing. There is only one county clearing on each day. The general balance ascertained from the general balance sheet is not settled directly but through the two clearing on the next day.

(iii) Metropolitan Clearing: This type of clearing work was started later than town and county clearing work. Metropolitan clearing includes cheques and drafts received from the branches or agents of the clearing banks outside the town and county clearing areas and drawn upon the banks situated therein. These are sorted out and presented to the head offices of the branches and agents of the other banks. The balance in the general balance sheet of metropolitan clearing is transferred to the general balance sheet of the town clearing on the next day. As in county clearing, there is only one metropolitan clearing each day. Each clearing bank, on receiving the cheques, sorts them out and sends them to the drawee banks for having them honoured. Information about this is received the next day. In case any cheque or draft is returned or dishonoured, it is regarded as an instrument for out-clearing of that particular clearing.

☞ Clearing in India

The work of clearing in India was done by the Imperial Bank of India (now the State Bank of India) up to the time when the Reserve Bank of India, which is statutorily responsible for this work started functioning. Clearing in India is effected more or less in the same way as in England, the clearing house associations working mostly under the control of the Reserve Bank of India or its representative, the State Bank of India. The rules and regulations of clearing applicable to all those clearing houses are more or less the same. The Reserve Bank or its agent, the State Bank, conducts clearing operations on its premises and arranges for the settlement of balances due to or by the different banks, as is done by the Bank of England, by debiting or crediting the account of the members concerned. Every member is generally required to keep with the supervising bank a statutory deposit of about ₹ 1 lakh.

The Reserve Bank entrusted with the responsibility of clearing for the simple reason that it has now been recognised all over the world, particularly in Europe and the United States, that central banks are specially suited for acting as clearing houses because they are the currency authorities and have to arrange for the provision of such currency and credit as the conditions of trading and commerce of a country require.

☞ Clearing Houses in Europe and America

The functions of clearing houses in the United States are much wider than those of their counterparts in Europe and Asia. They fix the minimum rates of interest to be paid to depositors and issue certificates of banks on the basis of which they can borrow. All the clearing houses work in co-operation and ultimately arrive at established correlated clearing centres all over the United States. In European countries, too, clearing is done through the Central Bank of each country, as is done in India and other Asian countries.

☞ Questions

1. What is a clearing house? State and explain the organisation and working of a clearing house in India.
2. What is meant by the clearing of cheques? Discuss the importance of clearing facilities.
3. Write short notes on —
   (a) Inward and outward clearing;
   (b) Clearing banks.

PART - III

NEGOTIABLE INSTRUMENTS

CHAPTER 13 Negotiable Instruments

Different authors have defined what a "negotiable instrument" is, but no satisfactory definition is available. Section 13 of the Negotiable Instruments Act specifies certain instruments which, when drawn up in a particular manner, would be regarded as negotiable. The best available definition, probably, is the one given by Thomas in his book *Principles of Banking.* He says: *"A negotiable instrument is one which is, by a legally recognised custom of trade or law, transferable by delivery, or by endorsement and delivery, in such circumstances that: (a) the holder of it for the time-being may sue on it in his own name, and (b) the property in it passes, free from equities, to a bonafide transferee for value, notwithstanding any defect in the title of the transferor".*

The Negotiable Instrument Act does not define a negotiable instrument and merely states that, "A negotiable instrument means a promissory note, bill of exchange or cheque payable either to order or bearer".

Justice K.C. Wills defines a negotiable instrument as "One of the property in which is acquired by anyone who takes it *bonafide* and for value not with standing any defect of title in the person from whom he took it".

☞ Negotiation

"Negotiation" means the transfer of the right, title and interest of the holder of a negotiable instrument, so as to give the transferee a good title, if he (transferee) be a holder in due course, even though the transferor has a bad or defective title, except in the case of forgery of the holder's signature if the instrument is payable to order, or in the case of an instrument void *ab initio,* or except in the case of an instrument completed and transferred after it is stolen and which was not at all delivered by the maker or drawer to anybody.

In the case of a negotiable instrument payable to order, negotiation of the instrument takes place by endorsement of the holder's signature on the instrument and by delivery of the same to the endorsee or the person to whom it is handed over. In the case of a negotiable instrument payable to bearer, negotiation takes place by mere delivery without any endorsement.

☞ Characteristics of Negotiable Instruments

The following are the characteristics of negotiable instruments which distinguish them from other forms of written contracts:

1. No formalities are necessary in transferring the right in a negotiable instrument. In other words, the rights in a negotiable instrument can be transferred by mere delivery (in the case of a bearer instrument) or by endorsement and delivery (in the case of an order instrument).
2. The transferee of the instrument can sue on the instrument in his own name and without making the transferor a part to the suit.
3. It is not necessary to give to the party, liable on the instrument, notice of its transfer to ensure that he makes payment only to the transferee.
4. A *bonafide* transferee of a negotiable instrument, who is the "holder in due course", gets even a better title than the transferor. This is one of the fundamental characteristics of negotiability and is an exception to the general rule that no one can give a better title than he has.

☞ Negotiable Instruments

The Negotiable Instruments Act, 1881, mentions only three instruments — promissory notes, bills and cheques; but in actual practice, because of business customs, many other instruments come under the category of negotiable instruments, and are accepted in dealings as well as by the Courts in cases of disputes. Section 137 of the Transfer of Property Act speaks of *"instruments which are for the time-being, by law or custom, negotiable"*, implying thereby that the Courts keep on extending the character of negotiability to instruments other than those enumerated in the Negotiable Instruments Act. The following are the examples of instruments of credit that are deemed to possess the characteristics of negotiability:

1. Promissory Notes;
2. Bills of Exchange;
3. Cheques;
4. Government Securities;
5. Dividend Warrants;
6. Hundis;
7. Bank Drafts;
8. Share Warrants;
9. Circular Notes.

☞ Negotiability

Negotiability is an essential feature of a negotiable instrument. Section 14 defines it as follows:

"When a promissory note, bill of exchange or cheque is transferred to any person, so as to constitute that person, the holder thereof, the instrument is said to be negotiated." The property of a negotiable instrument is that it is acquired by every person who takes it *bonafide* and for value, not withstanding any defect in the title of the person from whom he takes it. Such transfer of property is done by delivery or by an endorsement and delivery, as the case may be. The holder in due course of a negotiable instrument is not affected by the defect in the title of his transferor or any previous party. He may sue in his own name and need not give notice to the debtor that he has become the holder. He is not affected by certain defects — for example, fraud — to which he is not a party.

☞ Presumptions Regarding Negotiable Instruments

Certain facts appearing on a negotiable instrument are considered to be true unless they have been proved to the contrary. The burden of proving the contrary rests on the person who challenges it. These are called presumptions and are provided in the Act (vide Sections 118 to 120). These presumptions are:

1. That every negotiable instrument was made or drawn for consideration, and that every such instrument, when it has been accepted, endorsed, negotiated or transferred for consideration;
2. That every negotiable instrument bearing a date was made or drawn on that date;
3. That every accepted bill of exchange was accepted within a reasonable time after its date and before its maturity;
4. That every transfer of a negotiable instrument was made before its maturity;
5. That the endorsements appearing upon a negotiable instrument were made in the order in which they appear thereon;
6. That a lost promissory note, bill of exchange or cheque was duly stamped (the Stamp duty on cheques has since been abolished);
7. That the holder of a negotiable instrument is a holder in due course; provided that where the instrument has been obtained from its lawful owner, or from any person in lawful custody thereof, by means of an offence or fraud, or has been obtained from the maker or acceptor thereof by means of an offence or fraud, or for lawful consideration, the burden of proving that the holder is a holder in due course lies on him;
8. In a suit upon an instrument which has been dishonoured, the court shall, on proof of the protest, presume the fact of dishonour, unless and until such fact is disproved;
9. No marks of a promissory note, and no drawer of a bill of exchange or cheque, and no acceptor of a bill of exchange by a holder in due course be permitted to deny the validity of the instrument as originally made or drawn;
10. No marks of a promissory note and no acceptor of a bill of exchange payable to order shall, in a suit thereon by a holder in due course, be permitted to deny the payee's capacity at the date of the note or bills, to endorse the same; and
11. No endorser of a negotiable instrument, in a suit thereon be a subsequent holder, shall be permitted to deny the signature or capacity to contract of any prior party to the instrument.

☞ Different Types of Negotiable Instruments

Cheques, bills of exchange and promissory notes are different kinds of negotiable instruments in accordance with the provisions of the Negotiable Instruments Act. However, certain other instruments, through usage and custom of trade, have been recognized as negotiable instruments; for example, hundis.

A comparison of cheques, bills of exchange and promissory notes is given in Table 13.1 below:

TABLE 13.1
COMPARISON OF CHEQUE, BILL OF EXCHANGE AND PROMISSORY NOTE

Points of Comparison	*Cheque*	*Bill of Exchange*	*Promissory Note*
(1)	(2)	(3)	(4)
1. Parties to the instrument	Three — Drawer, Drawee and Payee	Three — Drawer, Drawee and Payee	Two — Maker and Payee
2. By whom drawn	Customers of bank only	Any person	Any person
3. On whom drawn	The bank	Any person	Any person
4. Nature of the instrument	Unconditional order to pay	Unconditional order to pay	Unconditional undertaking to pay
5. Time when payable	On demand	On demand or after a period of time	On demand or after a period of time
6. Acceptance	Not necessary	Necessary	Not necessary
7. Crossing	Can be crossed	Cannot be crossed	Cannot be crossed
8. Grace days	Not available Always payable on demand	3 days for usance bills	3 days for usance promissory notes
9. Provisions relating to acceptance of honour, drawee in case of need, etc.	Not applicable	Applicable	Not applicable
10. Countermanding payment	Can be countermanded at anytime before payment	Once accepted cannot be countermanded	Not applicable
11. Drawing in sets	Cannot be drawn in sets	Can be drawn in sets	Cannot be drawn in sets
12. Non-presentment to make parties liable	Delay in presentment does not discharge the drawer unless the delay has caused a loss to him.	Non-presentment where required discharges the drawer and endorsers.	Non-presentment discharges endorsers; Presentment is not necessary to make drawer liable except where it is payable at a particular place.

☞ Difference between Negotiability and Assignability

In the case of negotiation, the transferee gets even a better title than the transferor has; in the case of assignment, the assignee does not get a better title than the assignor has.

In the case of negotiation, notice of transfer is not required. But in the case of assignment, notice of assignment is required by law.

In the case of negotiation, consideration is presumed unless the contrary is proved, but in the case of assignment, consideration is not presumed and has to be proved by the plaintiff.

Negotiating and discounting bills

☞ Negotiating

A bill is said to have been negotiated when all the rights and titles therein are transferred by endorsement or endorsement and delivery.

☞ Discounting

A bill, on the other hand, is said to have been discounted when there is a liability to meet the bill should the same be dishonoured, and only the amount of the bill is received in advance after the deduction of discounting charges.

☞ Transfer of Negotiable Instrument

A negotiable instrument may be transferred in two ways, *viz.,*

(a) By negotiation under the Negotiable Instruments Act;

(b) By assignment of the instrument under Section 130 of the Transfer of Property Act.

It is always wiser and safer to take a negotiable instrument under an endorsement than under an assignment. In the case of assignment, the assignee does not acquire the rights of a holder in due course, but gets only the right, title and interest of his assignor. On the other hand, in the case of a transfer by negotiation, the transferee acquires all the rights of a holder in due course, *i.e.,* he gets a better title than his transferor had therein (*Muhammed Khumarali vs. Ranga Rao,* 24 M, 654).

☞ Inchoate Instrument

According to Section 20 of the Negotiable Instruments Act, an inchoate instrument is one which is signed and stamped as required by law, but which has not been completely filled up by the maker. A person signing and delivering such an instrument is deemed, *prima facie*, to have authorised the person to whom it is delivered to complete the instrument up to the amount covered by the stamp. However, the delivery of the instrument is essential to make the drawer thereof liable in respect thereof. Delivery may be actual or constructive; but a signed and stamped instrument, which has been stolen, cannot create any liability upon it because it was not delivered. If the maker of an inchoate instrument, asks the person to whom it is delivered to fill up a certain amount, such a limitation will be binding upon him. In such a case, if the party fills up a larger amount, the drawer will not be liable even though the bill is for an amount warranted by the amount for which it is stamped. He, however, would not be able to deny his liability to the holder in due course, since he would not be bound by any private instructions given by the maker. If an inchoate instrument is filled up for an amount exceeding the value of the stamp, it would not be valid. It should be noted here that an inchoate instrument is not a negotiable instrument until it is completed.

☞ Loss of Negotiable Instrument

According to Section 58 of the Negotiable Instruments Act, the owner of a negotiable instrument which is lost can claim it from the finder thereof if that is practicable. The finder, or a person delivering title through him, cannot acquire any title to the instrument from the drawer, provided the owner is prepared to give such indemnity or security as the drawer may require. In the case of loss of instrument, the owner should give a public notice of the loss in important newspapers, and also individual notices to the parties liable upon the instrument, more particularly to the acceptor, to ensure that the acceptor does not make payment to a fraudulent person. If such notice has not been given and payment of the instrument is made in due course, the payer will be discharged from liability.

☞ Alternation of Negotiable Instruments

Normally, a written contract cannot be unilaterally altered. If a contract in writing has been executed, it can only be altered by a voluntary act by both parties as evidenced by their signatures to the alterations. This rule applies equally to negotiable instruments. In the case of negotiable instruments, alterations may be divided into the following three categories:

(a) Material alterations;

(b) Immaterial alterations; and

(c) Alterations which can be made unilaterally.

☞ Material Alteration

As regards a material alteration (an alteration which makes significant variations in the rights and liabilities of the parties), the parties who have not agreed to such an alteration are absolved from liability on the instrument. Therefore, material alterations cannot be made by one party without the consent of the other party. These material alterations include:

(i) Date;

(ii) Name;

(iii) Time or place of payment;

(iv) Rate of interest; and

(v) Addition of new parties to the instrument, etc.

☞ Immaterial Alteration

An immaterial alteration or an alteration which is not significant may be made by any party without the consent of the other party, if it does not have the effect of varying the rights and liabilities of any other party, *e.g.*, crossing a "t" or dotting an "i" in the original instrument or correcting a spelling mistake or some other obvious error in the body of the instrument.

☞ Unilaterally Allowed Alterations

There are certain alterations to an instrument which are allowed to be made by one party without the consent of the other party. A few examples of such alterations are, crossing an instrument which is uncrossed, altering words which make it payable to order, covering blank endorsement into full endorsements, filling in blanks in inchoate stamped instruments, altering a general crossing to a special crossing.

☞ Meaning of Holder

The holder of a negotiable instrument is any person who is for the time-being entitled in his own name and right to the possession of the instrument and to receive and recover the amount due on the instrument. (*Bojiainra vs. Venkatramayya,* Mad. 30).

According to Section 8 of the Negotiable Instruments Act, the holder of a promissory note, bill of exchange or cheque is, "a person entitled in his name to the possession thereof and to receive or recover the amount due thereon from the parties thereto".

A person can become the holder of a negotiable instrument only if the following conditions are satisfied:

(i) He must be entitled to the possession of the instrument in his own name and under a legal title.

(ii) He must be entitled to receive or recover the amount from the parties concerned in his own name. In the case of an order instrument, the name of the holder appears on the document as payee or endorsee. In the case of a bearer instrument, the bearer may claim the money without having his name mentioned on the cheque.

According to Section 8, the holder is competent to receive payment or recover the amount by filing a suit in own name against other parties, to negotiate the instrument and to give a valid discharge. If a bill, promissory note or cheque is lost or destroyed, its holder is the person so entitled at the time of such loss or destruction.

☞ Kinds of Holders

There are two kinds of holders:

(i) A *de jure* holder who is a holder of a negotiable instrument as a matter of legal right;

(ii) A *de facto* holder who is a holder of a negotiable instrument merely by virtue of possession but not entitled in his own right or name.

A clerk or a servant possessing an instrument for collection or custody is a holder *de facto* but not a holder de jure.

(iii) A holder in due course is a person who holds a negotiable instrument in his own right for value and who acquired it before the instrument became mature for payment, and without any notice of defect in the title of the transferor from whom he took the instrument. In order that the person may be a holder in due course, the following three conditions must be satisfied:

(a) There must be some consideration for the instrument and the holder must not have taken it as a gift;

(b) The holder must have taken the instrument in good faith and without negligence or suspicion regarding any defect in the title of the transferor; and

(c) The instrument must not have become mature for payment at the time the holder took it or acquired it.

☞ Rights and Privileges of Holder in Due Course

The holder in due course possesses a good title on the negotiable instrument, free from all defects. His title is better than that of his transferor or any of the previous parties. He can pass on the good title that he possesses to other parties. According to Section 53, "a holder of a negotiable instrument, who derives title from a holder in due course, has the rights thereon of that holder in due course". According to Section 36, "every prior party to a negotiable instrument, *i.e.,* its maker or drawer, acceptor or endorser, is liable thereon to a holder in due course until the instrument is duly satisfied".

In the case of an inchoate instrument, if a subsequent transferor, while completing the instrument, writes down a sum which is greater than the maker intended, the right of a holder in due course to recover the money of the instrument is not at all affected (Section 20).

In the case of a bill drawn on behalf of a fictitious person and payable to his order, the acceptor is not relieved of his liability to a holder in due course because of such fictitious name. But it is essential that the holder in due course proves that the document bears the endorsement with signature purporting to be made by the drawer (Section 42).

According to Section 58, a person liable on a negotiable instrument cannot defend himself on the ground that the instrument was lost or obtained from him by means of an offence or fraud or for an unlawful consideration against a holder in due course.

☞ Right of Estoppel

Section 120 lays down that, "no maker of a promissory note and no drawer of a bill of exchange or cheque and no acceptor of a bill of exchange for the honour of the drawer shall, in a suit thereon by a holder in due course, be permitted to deny the validity of the instrument as originally made or drawn".

Section 121 provides that, "no maker of a promissory note and no acceptor of a bill of exchange payable to order shall, in a suit thereon by a holder in due course, be permitted to deny the payee's capacity, at the date of note or bill, to endorse the same". According to Section 122, no endorser of a negotiable instrument shall, in a suit thereon by a subsequent holder, be permitted to deny the signature or capacity of any prior party to the instrument.

Cheques, Bills of Exchange and Promissory Notes

☞ Cheques

A cheque is a bill of exchange drawn on a specified bank and not expressed to be payable otherwise than on demand (Section 6, Negotiable Instruments Act). That is to say, it is a bill drawn on a banker which is payable on demand.

☞ Bills of Exchange

A bill of exchange is an instrument in writing containing an unconditional order, signed by the maker, directing a certain person to pay a certain sum of money only to, or to the order of, certain person or to the bearer of the instrument (Section 5, Negotiable Instruments Act).

☞ Promissory Notes

A promissory note is an instrument in writing (not being a bank note or a currency note) containing an unconditional undertaking, signed by the maker, to pay a certain sum of money only to, or to the order of, a certain person, or to the bearer of the instrument (Section 4, *ibid.*).

The main features of a Promissory Note are:

1. There must be an undertaking to pay and not merely an acknowledgement of indebtedness. Therefore, an IOU is not a promissory note.
2. The promise to pay must be unconditional.
3. The promise must be to pay a definite sum of money.
4. The payee must be a definite person (a person other than the Reserve Bank or the Central Government cannot issue promissory notes payable to bearer).
5. The promise to pay must be in writing, not verbal.
6. The instrument must be signed by the maker.

SPECIMEN OF A PROMISSORY NOTE

Udaipur,
June 25, 1993

Stamp ₹ 1,000

One month after date, I promise to pay Shri Jag Mohan Dave the sum of ₹ 1,000 only, value received.

Rakesh Sharma

SPECIMEN OF PROMISSORY NOTE (JOINT)

> Jaipur,
> May 30, 1993
>
> Stamp ₹ 1,500
>
> On demand we promise to pay to Shri. Sudhir Chandra the sum of ₹ 1,500 only, value received.
>
> Sant Prasad Gupta
> Mahendra Dayal Mathur

SPECIMEN OF A PROMISSORY NOTE
(Joint and Several)

> Ajmer,
> May 25, 1993
>
> Stamp ₹ 500
>
> Three months after date, we jointly and severally promise to pay Shri. Gur Saran Das Tyagi or order the sum of ₹ 500 only, value received.
>
> Shiv Pujan Sahai
> Devki Nandan Kapoor

The essentials of a Promissory Note were considered by the Punjab and Haryana High Court in *Bal Mukand vs. Munna Lal Ramji Lal and Others (*AIR 1970). The High Court observed as follows:

"Before a document can be treated as a Promissory Note it should be promissory note both in form and in intent. If the indebtedness is acknowledged in a document in a defined sum of money payable on demand that is enough to make the document a promissory note and the document need not necessarily say that the debtor promises to repay the amount. Merely because the document says that payment is to be made when demanded, the undertaking to repay the amount does not become conditional. The absence of the words "I promise to pay" makes no difference in the tenor of the instrument provided it fulfils other conditions of a promissory note.

In another case, the promisee of P/N acknowledged the receipt of a sum and stated that it will be repaid on demand. Below the signature of the promisee, there was an endorsement by a surety guaranteeing the repayment of the sum. It was contested, in this case, that because of the acknowledgement of the receipt of the amount and of the guarantor's endorsement, the document was not a promissory note. The language used in the document under dispute was as follows:

"We have received the sum of ₹ 9,240 from Shri. Ram Ratan Sharma. The above amount will be repaid on demand. We have received ₹ 9,240 in cash today."

In this case *Surjit Singh and Others vs. Ram Batan Sharma* (AIR, 1975, Gauhati) it was held by the High Court that an acknowledgement of a receipt of the amount does not take away document from the category of a promissory note. The guarantor's endorsement was entirely a different agreement and the promise to pay on demand was independent of the guarantee, and the document was a promissory note.

☞ Presentation of Promissory Notes

In the case of promissory notes, presentation for acceptance is not needed. A promissory note is payable on demand and not at any specified place; presentation is not necessary for fixing the liability on the maker because it is the duty of the debtor to seek out his creditor. However, in the following cases, presentation of a promissory note is necessary:

(*a*) where the promissory note is payable after a certain period "after sight", it must be presented within a reasonable time and during business hours on a business day (Section 64);

(*b*) a promissory note must be presented for payment, if it is a demand note, within a reasonable time, after it has been received by the holder, and in other cases within a reasonable time after maturity (Section 74). Delay in presentation owing to avoidable cause can be condoned (Section 75);

(*c*) a promissory note, which is payable in instalments, must be presented on the due dates of instalments (Section 67);

(*d*) a promissory note, which is payable at a specified place, must be presented for payment at that place (Section 68).

☞ Bill of Exchange

From the foregoing definition of a bill of exchange, it will be noticed that, it is necessary that, no condition shall be attached to a bill of exchange. But a promise or order to pay is not regarded as being conditional, simply because the time for payment is expressed by reference to the occurrence of a specified event which is certain to occur, but which at the time could not be determined in advance, *e.g.,* by reference to death. The reference to an event which is not certain to occur (marriage of a certain person) would, however, involve a condition which would vitiate a bill of exchange.

The sum of money expressed in a bill of exchange must be certain, but that does not prevent the amount from being stated as inclusive of the amount of interest to be subsequently determined. The amount also is regarded as being *certain* even though it is expressed to be payable at a rate of exchange which will be determined subsequently.

A bill of exchange contains an order to pay; that is to say, a mere request to pay or the use of other polite words will not suffice. If a document, which purports to be a bill of exchange or a promissory note, fails to satisfy the necessary conditions, it can still be made use of as an evidence of an ordinary contract, although it cannot be acted upon as a negotiable instrument. A bill of exchange or a promissory note payable to bearer on demand cannot be drawn.

SPECIMEN OF A BILL TO EXCHANGE

Specimen of an Inland Bill

Indore,
September 5, 1993

Stamp ₹ 900

Three months after date, pay to Shri. Narain Singh Dubey or order the sum of ₹ 900 only, value received.

To

Shri. Prem Lal
25/41, Mahatma Gandhi Road,
Bhopal.

Jamuna Prasad

Specimen of a Foreign Bill

First of Exchange

Bombay

October 5, 1992

Stamp £ 100

Ninety days after sight of this First Exchange (second and third of the same tenor and date unpaid), pay to the State Bank of India the sum of £ 100 only, value received.

To

Mr. Jack Lunch

31, Woodrow Street,

London S.W.

Jagat Narain Lal

☞ Different Classes of Bills of Exchange

***(i)* Inland and Foreign Bill:** A bill which is drawn in India and which is either payable in India or is drawn on a person resident in India is known as an inland bill and all bills other than inland bills are foreign bills (Sections 11 and 13). An inland bill does not cease to be such because it is endorsed in a foreign country or is in circulation therein. Thus, a bill drawn in Jaipur payable in Ajmer on a person in London is an inland bill. Likewise, a bill drawn in Jaipur on a person in Ajmer but payable in London is also an inland bill. On the other hand, a bill drawn in London on a person in Jaipur payable at Ajmer is a foreign bill.

***(ii)* Documentary Bills:** These are bills (usually, but not necessarily, foreign bills) to which shipping documents (such as bill of lading or railway receipt, invoice, certificate of origin, consular invoice, insurance policy), etc., are attached. Such bills are usually drawn in triplicate, or at least in duplicate, and are, usually, negotiated through a bank which is instructed to deliver the documents to the consignee, either against payment of the bill (Documents against Payment D/P) or against acceptance of the bill (Documents against Acceptance D/A). A letter of hypothecation is sometimes attached to the documentary bill in order to give the bank the right to deal with the goods if the consignee dishonours the bill and if the bank has advanced money against the bill to the consignor (drawer of the bill).

***(iii)* Usance or Time Bills:** "Usance" denotes the time fixed by custom within which bills drawn in one country and made payable in another country are to be paid. This period varies in different countries. In a majority of the Continental countries, the period is generally three months.

***(iv)* Accommodation Bills:** A bill of exchange, which does not originate in pursuance of a commercial transaction like sale of goods or lending of money, and is drawn, accepted or endorsed without consideration merely to help a business associate, is referred to an accommodation bill. In this case, the acceptor just lends out his name to the other so that the latter may obtain credit. The party accommodating is described as the "accommodating party", and the party accommodated as the "accommodated party."

The accommodating party is liable to a holder of the instrument for value even though the holder may have known that the party was only an accommodating party. If the accommodating party is called upon to pay the bill, he can claim to be reimbursed by the accommodated party (Section 43).

☞ Parties to a Bill of Exchange

The drawer is the person who draws the bill. He must sign it. Though there is no objection to its being accepted before the drawer places his signature on it, it remains incomplete and cannot be issued. (*M. Cole vs. Tayler 1865*).

☞ Drawee

A *drawee* is a person on whom the bill is drawn. He becomes the "acceptor" after he has signified his assent to the order of the drawer by writing the word "accepted" right across the face of the bill with his signature and date.

☞ Payee

The *payee* is the person to whom or to whose order the money is directed by the instrument to be paid. The drawer may make the bill payable to himself or may name another person in the bill to whom it has to be paid.

☞ Holder

The *holder* means any person entitled in his own name to the possession of the instrument and to receive or recover the amount thereon from the parties thereto (Section 8).

The holder of the bill may be the original payee named in the bill, or one to whom the bill is endorsed over by the original payee. In the case of a bill or a promissory note payable to bearer, the bearer is the holder.

☞ Acceptance of a Bill

An acceptance is the signature of the drawee of a bill who has signed his assent upon the bill and delivered it or given notice of such signing to the holder or to some person on his behalf. The acceptor is the drawee who has signed his assent upon the bill and delivered it to the holder or has given notice of his so doing to the holder.

Only the drawee can be the acceptor, or a person named as drawee in case of need, or an acceptor for honour (Section 33). The acceptance may be general or qualified.

☞ General Acceptance

A general acceptance is effected when the drawee signs his name on the bill with or without the word "accepted", thereby signifying his assent to the bill.

As a general rule, the bill must always be accepted generally, and if the acceptor adds any qualification to it, it becomes a conditional acceptance or treat the bill as dishonoured by non-acceptance. A banker, who is given a bill by his customer to procure acceptance and ultimately collect, should not take a qualified acceptance without the consent of his customer.

☞ Qualified Acceptance

An acceptance may be qualified in various ways, *i.e.*, qualified as to the amount, time, place, etc. Section 86 mentions the following cases of qualified acceptance:

(a) Where it is conditional, declaring the payment to be dependent upon the happening of an event therein stated;

(b) Where it undertakes the payment of a part only of the sum ordered to be paid;

(c) Where no place of payment being specified on the order, it undertakes the payment at a specified place, and not otherwise or elsewhere; or where a place of payment being specified in the order, it undertakes the payment at some other place and otherwise or elsewhere; and

(d) Where it undertakes the payment at a time other than that at which under the order it would be legally due.

The drawer or holder of a bill is not bound to agree to an acceptance which is qualified. He can treat the bill as dishonoured. If, however, the holder of a bill of exchange acquieses in a qualified acceptance, all previous parties whose consent is not obtained to such acceptance are discharged as against the holder and those claiming under him unless on notice given by the holder they assent to such acceptance (Section 86).

☞ Acceptance by Agent

A bill may be accepted by the drawee's agent on behalf of the drawee, but the agent so accepting must make that point clear; otherwise he will be personally liable.

☞ Acceptance of Honour

When a bill has been noted or protested for non-acceptance, and any person accepts it super protest for the honour of the drawer or of any one of the endorsers, such acceptance is called, "acceptance for honour".

After the acceptor for honour has accepted the bill, the holder at the due date has to present the bill first to the drawee for payment and if it is dishonoured by the drawee and noted or protested as the case may be, it should then be presented to the acceptor for honour for payment.

A person desiring to accept for honour must, by writing on the bill under his hand, declare that he accepts under protest the protested bill for the honour of the drawer or of a particular endorser whom he names, or generally for honour. When the acceptor does not express for whose honour it is made, it shall be deemed to be made for the honour of the drawer.

☞ Drawee in Case of Need

Generally, in the case of foreign bills, the drawer includes another party to a bill of exchange, who is known as, "drawee in case of need". The name of the drawee in case of need is stated by the drawer or any of the endorsers on the bill. The drawee in case of need is to be referred to by the holder, in case the drawee refuses to accept the bill or dishonours it by non-payment after acceptance. The drawee in case of need is generally the agent of the drawer in the foreign country where the bill is made payable.

☞ Difference Between Bill of Exchange and Promissory Note

(i) A bill of exchange contains an order to pay, whereas a promissory note contains a promise to pay.

(ii) In the case of a bill of exchange, the primary liability is that of the drawee after he has accepted the bill; the drawer's liability is secondary. In the case of a promissory note, the primary liability is that of the maker who signs the note.

(iii) A bill can be drawn payable to bearer, provided it is not payable on demand. A promissory note cannot be made payable to bearer.

(iv) In the case of promissory note, the necessity for acceptance does not arise since the maker of the note is already liable upon it.

(v) Bills of exchange are sometimes drawn in sets; the position is not the same in the case of promissory notes.

(vi) A bill of exchange cannot be drawn conditionally, but it can be accepted conditionally with the consent of the holder. A promissory note can never be conditional.

(vii) In the case of a bill of exchange, notice of dishonour, noting and protesting are required to prove dishonour, but these are unnecessary in respect of a promissory note.

☞ Difference between Bill of Exchange and Cheque

(i) In the case of a bill of exchange, the drawee may be any person, whereas in the case of a cheque, the drawee, *i.e.,* the person on whom the bill is drawn, must always be a banker (see Table 2).

(ii) A cheque, as a rule, is payable on demand and no days of grace are allowed.

(iii) In the case of a bill, a notice of dishonour is usually required, whereas a notice of dishonour is not necessary when a cheque is dishonoured.

(iv) A bill cannot be drawn to bearer if it is made payable on demand, but a cheque can be drawn to bearer and made payable on demand.

(v) In the case of bills, presentation is sometimes required for acceptance, and it is always advisable to present it for acceptance even when it is not essential to do so. In the case of a cheque, it is not necessary to present it for acceptance.

(vi) Bills must be stamped according to the law. Cheques do not require to be stamped in India. In several countries, however, cheques are required to be stamped.

☞ Essentials of a Cheque

(1) **Instrument in Writing:** A cheque must be an instrument in writing.

(2) **Unconditional Order:** A cheque must obtain an unconditional order. It is not necessary that the word "order" or its equivalent must be used in the cheque. Generally, the order to a bank is expressed by the word "Pay".

(3) **On a Specified Banker Only:** A cheque must be drawn on a specified bank. In other words, it should be drawn on a bank and not on any other person, and the name of the bank should be specified with a view to avoiding any mistake regarding the institution from which the payment of the cheque is to be demanded.

(4) **Specified Sum of Money:** A cheque must be an order to pay a "specified sum of money only". In other words, the sum of money to be paid must be certain.

(5) **Payable on Demand:** A cheque must be an order to pay a certain sum of money on demand. It is not necessary that the words "on demand" or their equivalent should be used, as and when the drawer of an instrument asks the drawee to pay and does not specify the time for its payment. The instrument, according to Section 19 of the Negotiable Instrument Act, is payable on demand.

☞ Ante-dated and Post-dated Cheques

A cheque can be dated with a date earlier or later than the one on which it is actually drawn. A cheque which bears a date before the date of issue is ante-dated and a cheque which bears a date later than the date of issue is post-dated. A post-dated cheque is not an instrument payable on demand, but when it is presented on or after the date given on it, the paying banker cannot refuse to honour it merely on the ground of its being originally post-dated. A post-dated cheque is as much a negotiable instrument as a cheque for which payment is due immediately on presentation, and there is no authority for holding that a person in whose favour such a cheque is endorsed before the date of payment is not a holder in due course *(Haji Mohd. Haneef Saheb & Co., vs. Abu Bucher and Others 1956).*

☞ Printed Cheque Forms

Printed cheque forms are supplied by banks to their customers because this practice has several advantages:

(i) Forgery becomes difficult as the forger will have to obtain the printed forms first before he can forge the signature of a customer.

(ii) Alterations can more easily be detected on a printed cheque form than on an ordinary piece of paper.

(iii) By referring to the cheque book records, a banker can easily know the name of the drawer if the signature is not legible.

(iv) It saves the customer the trouble of drafting cheques in accordance with the requirements of the law.

(v) It becomes easier to instruct the banker to stop the payment of a certain cheque by giving him its number.

(vi) The counterfoils in the cheque book can be used as a record of the various payments made by the customer by means of such cheques.

☞ Bank Draft

A bank draft is an order drawn by an office of a bank upon another office of the same bank. It is, in a sense, an order drawn by one person upon himself, whereas, in the case of bills, they are drawn by one person upon another person. A draft is drawn either against cash deposited at the time of its purchase or against debit to the buyer's current or savings account with the bank. The buyer of the draft generally furnishes the particulars of the person to whom the amount thereof should be paid. The draft can be made payable to the drawer on demand, as in the case of a cheque. When a draft purports to have been endorsed by or on behalf of the payee, the paying bank is discharged from liability by its payment in due course, even when the endorsement of the payee has been forged. This affords great protection to the paying banker, for it is not always possible for him to identify the signature of the payee.

☞ MICR Cheque/Drafts

With a view to speeding up the cheque clearing process, both local as well as inter-city, the Reserve Bank of India has introduced mechanised cheque processing system using MICR (Magnetic Ink Character Recognition) technology initially in the four metropolitan cities of Mumbai, Kolkata, Chennai and New Delhi. Under this system, the cheques are processed at high speed on machines. Banks issue cheque, draft and other payment instrument in MICR format using the special quality paper and printing specifications. On MICR instruments, there is code line at the bottom containing information printed in magnetic ink, which is required for mechanical processing. The code line contains the following information:

(i) First six number indicate the Cheque Number

(ii) Next three number indicate city code

(iii) Next three number indicate bank code

(iv) Next three numbers indicate branch code.

After some space there is the number for transaction code (*i.e.,* whether the transaction is for a saving or current account).

This magnetised portion, when placed under MICR equipment, allows for instant readability and identification.

MICR cheque should not be folded. Pins, staples, etc., should only be used on top left hand corner of the cheque. Signature of the drawer, rubber stamp, etc., should be affixed above the code line. Nothing should be written on the code line. In place of the counterfoils, MICR cheque books provide for Record slips at the end which are used for recording the details of every cheque issued.

☞ Dividend Warrants

Big joint-stock companies generally distribute dividends to shareholders by issuing dividend warrants. The amount mentioned in the dividend warrant can be drawn from the company's bankers. A dividend warrant is a cheque drawn by a company upon its banker in payment of dividends to its shareholders. They are quasi-negotiable instruments and have acquired negotiability by custom. So far, no Court judgement is available regarding the negotiability of dividend warrants, but the Courts recognise this fact on the basis of the evidence of such custom.

SPECIMEN OF A CHEQUE WITH COUNTERFOIL

Counterfoil

No $\frac{AM}{29}$ 756087

Date...

In favour of ....

....

....

Previous Balance		
Deposits, if any		
Total		
Less this Cheque		
Balance		

Cheque

CODE No.

State Bank of India

DARYAGANJ, NEW DELHI.

No. $\frac{AM}{29}$ 756083

Pay to.. or Bearer

Rupees.................................... ₹

Savings Bank Account No................

☞ Interest Warrants

Interest warrants are drafts for the payment of the interest due on Government securities, debentures, etc. They are also quasi-negotiable instruments and have acquired negotiability by custom.

☞ Postal Orders

Postal orders are not cheques for the simple reason that they are drawn by one post office on another post office. They are generally marked, "Not Negotiable". If a postal order is crossed, according to post office regulations, it becomes payable to a bank only, as if it were a crossed cheque. Thus, a postal order does not come under the category of a negotiable instrument.

Endorsement

Section 15 of the Negotiable Instruments Act defines endorsement thus: *"When the maker or holder of a negotiable instrument signs the same, otherwise than as a maker, for the purpose of negotiation, on the back or face thereof, or on a slip of paper annexed thereto, or signs for the same purpose a stamped paper intended to be completed as a negotiable instrument, he is said to endorse the same and is called the endorser".*

The person in whose favour the instrument is endorsed is described as the endorsee. It is not necessary to use a particular form of words for endorsement *(Sivaram Krishna Pattar vs. Moideen Mudaliar* 33 Mad. 34). But it must be in conformity with the name mentioned in the bill. A bill in favour of P.K. Mathur or order cannot be said to have been properly endorsed if the endorsement is signed as only Mathur or P. Mathur. If the name of the endorsee is incorrectly stated, the endorsee can endorse the bill by signing in the same way and thereafter signing it with his correct name *(Wills vs. Barret,* 1816, 2 Stark 26, *Leonard vs. Wilson* 1834, 2 Cr and M. 489). The endorsement must be made with the object of negotiating the instrument. When a person hands over a bill to another for a special purpose together with a proper endorsement thereon, such a handling over will not amount to negotiation. The endorsement of a promissory note, bill of exchange or cheque is completed only by delivery, actual or constructive, made by the endorser or by his duly constituted agent with the intention of passing the property therein (Section 46 of the Negotiable Instruments Act; *Denton vs. Peters 1870 LR 5 Q B. 475).* Until such delivery, the contract being incomplete, may be revoked at any time *(Brind vs. Hampshire,* 1836, I.M. and W. 365, 373).

An endorsement made on the face of an instrument is not wrong (vide Section 15 quoted above), but it is expedient in view of the time-honoured practice that all instruments should be endorsed on their back. According to Section 6 of the Indian Securities Act, 1886, an endorsement inscribed elsewhere and not on the back of the security itself, is not valid.

☞ Allonge

If the back of the instrument is filled up by endorsements, the holder, in order to provide space for any' endorsements, may tag or paste on it a piece of paper called *allonge*, and subsequent endorsements may be made thereon.

☞ Kinds of Endorsements

(i) **Blank Endorsement:** In the case of a blank endorsement, the endorser puts his signature on the back of the instrument without mentioning the name of any specified person in whose favour the endorsement is made. In this type of instrument, the instrument is payable to bearer, and consequently, it can be negotiated by mere delivery.

(ii) **Special Endorsement or Full Endorsement:** In the case of special or full endorsement, the endorser mentions the name of a specified person or to the order of that person, *e.g.,*

Pay to Rajiv Kumar or order

Sd/- Rajesh Kumar

(iii) **Partial Endorsement:** In the case of a partial endorsement, only a part of the amount of the instrument is transferred. This does not operate as a negotiation of the instrument, but may authorise

the endorsee to receive payment of the amount specified. In the case of a bill of exchange, if part payment has already been received by the holder, it can be endorsed for the remaining unpaid amount. However, the law lays down that an endorsement must relate to the whole instrument.

***(iv)* Restrictive Endorsement:** In the case of a restrictive endorsement, the endorser restricts the further negotiation of the instrument, *e.g.,*

To pay Arjun Prasad only

Sd/- Ram Saran Sinha.

or the endorser restricts the endorsee to deal with the bill as directed by the former, *e.g.,*

Pay to Sheo Saran Sinha or order for collection

Sd/- Gur Dayal Sinha.

In the case of restrictive endorsement, an endorsement must in express words restrict or exclude the right of the endorsee.

***(v)* Sans Recourse Endorsement:** In the case of a sans recourse endorsement, the endorser removes himself from his liability to the endorsee by making it clear that the endorsee, or any subsequent holder, should not look to him for payment in case the bill is dishonoured, *e.g.,*

Pay to H.P. Verma without recourse to me

Sd/- S. Prasad.

In the above case, if S. Prasad endorses the bill "without recourse" to H.P. Verma and H.P. Verma agrees to take it with such an endorsement, he takes it with the understanding that in case he fails to recover the money from the acceptor or any of the previous endorsers to S. Prasad (H.P. Verma) cannot sue S. Prasad on the instrument.

***(vi)* Conditional Endorsement:** In the case of a conditional endorsement, the transfer of property in the instrument is made to depend on the fulfilment of a specified condition, *e.g.,*

Pay to Prema Nandlal on arrival of ship "Godavari"

Sd/- Nirmal Kumar.

According to English law, the condition may be disregarded by the payer and the payment to the endorsee is valid, whether the condition has been fulfilled or not. In India, however, if the drawee accepts a bill after it was conditionally endorsed, he should respect the condition.

***(vii)* Facultative Endorsement:** In the case of a facultative endorsement, the endorser waives some of his rights, *e.g.,*

Pay to Kamta Prasad, Notice of dishonour waived

Sd/- Ram Saran Sinha.

In such an endorsement, the endorsee need not give him notice of dishonour.

***(viii)* Sans Frais Endorsement:** In the case of sans frais endorsement, the endorser does not want any expense to be incurred on his account on the bill.

☞ Liability of the Endorser

Section 35 of the Negotiable Instruments Act defines the liability of the endorser as follows: "In the absence of a contract to the contrary, whoever endorses and delivers a negotiable instrument before maturity, without, in such endorsement, expressly excluding or making conditional his own liability, is bound thereby to every subsequent holder, in case of dishonour by the drawee, acceptor or maker to compensate such holder for any loss or damage caused to him by such dishonour, provided due notice of dishonour has been given to or received by such endorser as hereinafter provided".

Crossing of Cheques

A crossed cheque is a cheque across the face of which two parallel transverse lines are drawn with or without the words "and Co." or any abbreviation thereof, or some other words, the effect of which is that the banker on whom it is drawn shall not pay the same otherwise than to a banker.

A cheque may be crossed generally or specially.

☞ General Crossing

A cheque is crossed generally if it bears two parallel lines without any words or with the words "and Co." or its abbreviation thereof, and with or without the words "Not Negotiable" (Section 123).

By crossing a cheque generally, the banker is directed not to make payment except through another banker and thus a person, who is not entitled to receive its payment, is prevented from getting the cheque cashed at the counter of the paying banker.

☞ Special Crossing

A cheque is crossed specially, if it bears across its face two parallel lines and an addition of the name of a banker, either with or without the words "Not Negotiable" (Section 124).

A special crossing makes the cheque safer, as a person having no claim will find it difficult to obtain payment except through the banker named in the crossing, who is likely to know the payee, and, therefore, will not collect it for any other person.

It may be noted that a crossing is operative only on a cheque and a postal order. If a bill of exchange other than a cheque is crossed, the crossing is inoperative and the acceptor or party liable can pay the same to any person even though that person is not a banker.

When a cheque, as originally issued, is uncrossed, it is permissible for the holder to cross it generally or specially. Where a cheque is crossed specially, the banker to whom it is so crossed may again cross it specially to another banker or his agent for collection.

☞ Not Negotiable Crossing

In the case of a cheque crossed generally or specially and bearing, in either case, the words, "Not Negotiable", the position would be that such instrument shall not have, and shall not be capable of giving, a better title to the holder than that which the person from whom it was taken had (Section 130).

The effect of a "Not Negotiable" crossing is to deprive the instrument of the special advantage which a negotiable instrument as such enjoys. The special advantage of a negotiable instrument is that the holder in due course, who receives it for value in good faith, complete and regular on the face of it, and without any notice as to defect in the title of a previous holder, receives it free from all defects in the title of a previous holder.

An instrument crossed "Not Negotiable" may, of course, be endorsed any number of times as far as its transferability is concerned. The effect of adding the words "Not Negotiable" to a cheque is not to impede transfer, but to perpetuate in the hands of any transferee whatever defect or infirmity of title the endorser had who first transferred the cheque with those words on it.

Payee	*Regular*	*Irregular*	*Ramarks*
INDIVIDUAL			
1. Shri. Ram Prasad Jain	Ram Prasad Jain	R. P. Jain Ram Prasad Shri. Ram Prasad Jain	Full signatures should be given. Shri is a courtesy title.
2. Shri. R. P. Jain	R. P. Jain Ram Prasad Jain	R. P. J.	Full signature should be given and not only initials.
3. Mr. Jain	R. P. Jain	Mr. Jain	Full signature should be given.
4. Shri. Ram Prasad Jain	Ram Prasad Jain Rama Prasad Jain	Ram Prasad Jain Rama Prasad Jain	Correct name should be given only after writing incorrect name.
5. Miss Mathur	Shantha Mathur	Miss Mathur	Miss is simply a description and it should be dropped.
6. Mrs. Mathur	Shanta Mathur wife of Shri P. N. Mathur or Mrs. Shanta Mathur	Mrs. Mathur or Mrs. P. N. Mathur	Name of the husband should also be given.
7. Miss S. Mathur (now married)	S. Sinha (nee Mathur)	Mrs. S. Sinha	Endorsement after marriage should bear the surname of the husband as well as that of the father.
ILLITERATE PERSONS			
8. Ghasi Ram	Ghasi Ram's thumb impression	Ghasi Ram's thumb impression	The witness should be an independent party known both to the endorser and the paying Witness Prem Shanker, banker. He should also sign his name and Bapu Bazar, Udaipur address clearly.

Payee	*Regular*	*Irregular*	*Ramarks*
JOINT PAYEES			
9. M/s. Ram Kumar Prem Kumar Rajiv Kumar	Ram Kumar Prem Kumar and Rajiv Kumar	Ram Kumar Rajiv Kumar	All payees should sign.
10. Messrs. Agrawal	Prem Nath Agrawal Ram Nath Agrawal	Prem Nath Agrawal	Messrs. denotes more than one payee, as such a single signature is apparently an incomplete endorsement.
11. Mr. & Mrs. Jain	Suraj Mal Jain Shantha Jain, wife of Suraj Mal Jain	Suraj Mal Jain Mrs. Suraj Mal Jain	Mrs. Jain should give her name in the signature and also mention her relationship with Suraj Mal Jain.
FIRMS			
12. Lodha & Sons	For Lodha & Sons M. Lodha, Partner	Lodha Partner or For Lodha & Sons Lodha	The endorser should clearly state that he is signing as a partner for a particular firm.
AGENT			
13. R.P. Chowdhry	For R.P. Chowdhry P. Ram Agent	For R.P. Chowdhry P. Ram or on behalf of R.P. Chowdhry P. Ram	For or Pro is no indication of authority. The word 'Agent' must be mentioned.
CLUBS, COLLEGES, etc.			
14. M.B. College, Udaipur	For and on behalf of M.B. College, Udaipur Bhim Sen Principal	Bhim Sen Principal M.B. College Udaipur	The designation is simply a description and does not indicate that the cheque has been endorsed on behalf of the college.
15. Principal M.B. College, Udaipur	Bhim Sen, Principal M.B. College Udaipur	Principal M.B. College, Udaipur	Designation without signature is irregular.

Payee	*Regular*	*Irregular*	*Ramarks*
16. Fields Club, Udaipur	For and on behalf of Fields Club, Udaipur Rajesh Kumar Secretary	Rajesh Kumar, Secretary, Fields Club, Udaipur	The designation is only a description and does not specify that the endorsement is on behalf of the Club.
JOINT STOCK COMPANIES			
17. Prakash Industries Ltd.,	Per Pro Prakash Industries Ltd., Rajiv Kumar Secretary	Prakash Industries Ltd.,	Endorsement should be made by an authorised person on behalf of the company.
	or		
	For Prakash Industries Ltd., Rajiv Kumar Secretary	For Praksah Industries Ltd., Rajiv Kumar	The authorised person should also mention his designation.
TRUSTEES			
18. The Trustees of Late Shri M. Prasad	M. Gopal R. Gopal Trustee of Late Shri. M. Prasad	For Self and Co. Trustees of Late Shri M. Prasad R. Gopal	All the trustees should sign.
19. R. Gopal, Trustee of Late Shri M. Prasad	R. Gopal, Sole Trustee of Late Shri. M. Prasad	R. Gopal, Trustee of Late Shri M. Prasad	In the case of a single trust, it should be specified.
OFFICIALS			
20. The I.T.O. Udaipur	T. Nath I.T.O. Udaipur	Per Pro I.T.O. Udaipur, D. Saran	It is necessary to give the official designation.

DIFFERENT FORMS OF CROSSING

☞ General Crossing

1

& Co.

2

& Co.

3

Not Negotiable

4

Payee's Accounts

☞ Special Crossing

5

Punjab National Bank

6

Central Bank of India
Account Payee

7

Not Negotiable
Cental Bank of India

☞ Account Payee

This direction of crossing a cheque "Account Payee Only" to a banker may be ignored by a banker, though in actual practice, the banker who collects such a cheque does see to it that the instruction is carried out. In other words, the amount mentioned in such a cheque is deposited only in the account of the payee. Even if such a cheque is endorsed, the amount can be deposited only in the account of the payee and of no other person.

☞ Double Crossing

When the names of two bankers are written in crossing, it is known as double crossing. A double crossing by an individual is not permitted. According to Sections 125 and 127 of the Negotiable Instruments Act, a double crossing even in the case of bankers is permissible only when it is shown that the second crossing was placed by the collecting banker for the purpose of the clearing house.

Permissible

Central Bank of India
To
The Bank of Rajasthan Ltd., Udaipur
as agent for Collection

Not Permissible

Central Bank of India
To
The Bank of Rajasthan Ltd., Udaipur

WHO CAN CROSS A CHEQUE?

☞ Drawer

In the first instance, the drawer of a cheque, if he likes, can cross it.

☞ Holder

When a drawer issues an open cheque, any holder of it can cross it generally, convert a general crossing into a special one, or add the words, "Not Negotiable".

☞ Banker

When a cheque is crossed specially, the banker in whose favour it is crossed may again cross it specially to another banker, the latter acting as agent for collection for the former.

☞ Cancelling of Crossing

If a cheque is crossed by the drawer, he has the right to cancel the crossing by writing the words "Pay Cash" across the cheque and by putting down his full signature on the cheque.

☞ Loss of Cheque in Transit

If a bearer, uncrossed or generally crossed cheque is sent by ordinary post at the request of the payee, and the payment of such a cheque is received by a thief, the loss will have to be borne by the payee, on the ground that he employed the post office as his agent. However, according to Section 46 of the Negotiable Instruments Act, the mere sending of a cheque by post does not amount to delivery.

☞ Payment of Lost Cheque to be Stopped Through its Drawer

The drawer of a cheque can ask his banker to stop payment of his cheque. If a cheque is lost by a holder, he has to ask the drawer to instruct the banker to stop payment; otherwise the paying banker may refuse to act according to the instructions of the holder of the cheque. The paying banker is bound by statute to honour his customer's cheque, or in case of wrongful dishonour, he makes himself liable to pay damages to his customer. In the absence of instructions from his customer, he has no means of knowing how far the statement of a person who represents himself to be the holder of a cheque is correct. However, as a rule, bankers take precautions before honouring cheques reported to have been lost.

☞ Marking or Certification of Cheques

If a banker certifies a cheque by writing on it words like "Approved" or "Good" or by initialling the cheque, such cheques are called "marked cheques" or "certified cheques." Occasionally cheques are marked or certified by the banker on whom they are drawn. This marking of a cheque, however, does not convert the banker into an acceptor or make him liable on the instrument; but it does constitute a representation by him on which he may be held liable that the cheque will be paid as drawn if presented within a reasonable time. The effect on the cheque is to give it additional currency by showing on its face that it was drawn in good faith on funds sufficient to meet its payment and by adding to the credit of the drawer, the credit of the banker on whom it is drawn.

The object and effect of a banker's marking of cheques is to facilitate a ready acceptance of the instrument by providing evidence on the face of it that it is drawn in good faith and that there are funds sufficient and available to meet and by adding the credit of the drawee bank to that of the drawer.

☞ Marking for a Drawer

In the case of a cheque marked or certified by a banker at the request of the drawer, the banker can retain money to meet such a cheque and dishonour any cheques presented subsequently if the balance remaining, after providing for the marked cheque, is insufficient to cover these subsequent cheques.

☞ Marking for Another Banker

The marking between bankers is considered as a promise or understanding to pay. It is, however, doubtful whether a customer can countermand payment after a banker has marked the cheque for another banker. The authorities seem to have conflicting views on this point though, of course, the right of the customer to countermand payment previous to such a marking is clearly acknowledged.

☞ Marking for a Holder

Another type of marking can be by a holder or payee presenting a cheque to the banker and getting it marked. Such a marking constitutes nothing more than an intimation that at the time of marking, the banker had a sufficient balance to the credit of the drawer and that there was no appropriation by the banker.

☞ Liability of the Paying Banker on Crossed Cheques

The paying banker on whom a crossed cheque is drawn must make payment thereof in accordance with the crossing. Section 126 lays down this duty of the paying banker as follows:

"Where a cheque is crossed generally, the banker on whom it is down shall not pay it otherwise than to a banker and where a cheque is crossed specially, the banker on whom it is drawn shall not pay it otherwise than to the banker to whom it is crossed or his agent for collection."

Thus, the payment of a crossed cheque is to be made to a banker only. It is presented for payment at the counter of the paying bank, the latter will be justified in refusing its payments. If the payee or the holder of a crossed cheque has an account with the paying banker and presents a crossed cheque for payment at the counter, the banker should not comply with such request and the cheque should be paid through his account.

If the paying banker defaults in making payment of a crossed cheque as stated in Section 126, he shall bear the liability specified in Section 129 as follows:

"Any banker paying a cheque crossed generally, otherwise than to a banker, or a cheque crossed specially, otherwise than to the banker to whom the same is crossed, or his agent for collection being a banker, shall be liable to the true owner of the cheque for any loss he may sustain owing to the cheque having been so paid."

The paying banker shall be liable to the true owner of the cheque and to the drawer as follows:

☞ Liability to the True Owner of the Cheque

Generally, the paying banker is not responsible to the payee or the holder of a cheque, as there is no contract between the two, but if the paying banker makes payment of a crossed cheque in contravention of the direction of the drawer conveyed through the crossing, the banker shall be liable to the true owner of the cheque for any loss sustained by him as a result of such payment. If a crossed cheque is lost by the true owner and its finder gets its payment at the counter of the paying banker, the true owner will be entitled to recover the amount of the cheque from the person who received its payment from the bank. Whatever is the loss suffered by the true owner or are the expenses incurred by him will be reimbursed by the banker.

☞ Liability to the Drawer

If the banker fails to make payment of a crossed cheque in accordance with Section 126, the payment is not deemed to be made as per the mandate of the customer. The banker will, therefore, not be entitled to debit his customer's account with the amount of such cheque, if the payment happens to be made to a wrong person.

Moreoever, the paying banker shall lose the statutory protection granted to him under Section 128, as such payment is not deemed to be payment in due course.

☞ Questions

1. Discuss fully the difference between "Negotiability" and "Transferability". Are the following negotiable?
   (i) Government of India Treasury Bills;
   (ii) Bill of Lading;
   (iii) Fixed Deposit Receipts;
   (iv) Letters of Credit.
2. What is acceptance? Is it necessary that every instrument should be presented for acceptance before it is presented for payment? What are the advantages of presenting an instrument for acceptance when it is not obligatory to do so?
3. Define a cheque and discuss its essential characteristics. Explain the various points which a banker should carefully examine before paying the customer's cheque.
4. Define "Acceptance for Honour". Explain the acceptor's rights and liabilities.
5. Examine the undermentioned statements and state which of them are promoters. Give reasons.
   (a) A promises to pay ₹ 500 seven days after his marriage with C.
   (b) I have taken ₹ 1,000 from you. Whenever you ask for it, I have to pay it together with interest.
   (c) I acknowledge to be indebted to B for ₹ 1,000.
   (d) I promise to pay B or order ₹ 1,000.
6. Explain the various kinds of endorsements on cheques and illustrate them with examples. Is an endorsement valid\ when made with an impressed stamp purporting to be a facsimile of the payee's signature?
7. What are the rules prescribed in the Negotiable Instruments Act for calculating the maturity of a promissory note or a Bill of Exchange expressly payable —
   (i) so many months after date or sight?
   (ii) so many days after date or sight?
   Illustrate your answer with examples.
8. *(a)* What are the correct endorsements for cheques drawn payable to the following:
   (i) Miss Sharda Basu or order (she has since been married to Mr. Ghosh);
   (ii) Lala Jagmohan Mehta or order;
   (iii) Bearer my wife or order (Drawn by C. Jones);
   (iv) Messrs. Hiralal Sharma and Jairam Chopra or order (Joint Payees);
   (v) D.C.B. School or order;

(vi) M.V. "Victoria" or order;

(vii) Income-Tax Officer or order?

(b) What do you understand by a "Per Pro endorsement"? As a paying banker, how would you deal with a cheque bearing such an endorsement if it is received:

(i) through clearing?

(ii) across the counter?

9. What is meant by the "crossing" of a cheque and what is its significance? What are the different types of crossings and their special features? Illustrate with examples.

10. *(a)* Define "Endorsement". What are the requirements of a valid endorsement?

(b) Explain the following endorsements on "order" cheques and explain whether they are regular or irregular. Where they are irregular, explain why and give the correct endorsements.

Payee	*Endorsement*
(i) Apex Commercial Co. Ltd.,	Arthur Jones, Manager
(ii) Ram Pratap & Sons	Ram Pratap Sons
(iii) Trustee of late Arvind Mukherjee	For self and Co-trustees of late Arvind Mukherjee Sudhir Bose
(iv) James Robertson	James Robertson per pro R. Smith
(v) Miss Hirachand	Sar

11. *(a)* What is "Payment in Due Course"? Give three examples of payments not made in due course.

(b) Discuss the effects of crossing a cheque with the words "Not Negotiable" written across its face. *[C.A.I.I.B., Part I]*

12. *(a)* What will be the due dates for the following instruments?

(i) A Bill of Exchange dated 20th Nov. 1982 payable 4 months after date.

(ii) A Promissory Note dated 27th Nov. 1982 payable 60 days after date, without date.

(iii) A Bill of Exchange dated 28th Aug. 1982 payable 180 days after the date.

(iv) A Bill of Exchange dated 1st Feb. 1982, payable after 45 days after sight.

The Bill was accepted on 6th Feb. 1982.

(b) Answer with one word only whether the following statements are True or False.

(i) A Fixed Deposit Receipt due on a Sunday or Bank holiday may be paid on the previous working day.

(ii) A cheque marked "Not Negotiable" is transferable.

(iii) A minor can act as an agent for another person competent to contract provided the former is duly authorised by the latter.

(iv) A cheque can be termed as a bill of exchange *[C.A.I.I.B., Part I]*

13. *(a)* If you consider a customer to be undesirable, what steps would you take as a banker to close his account?

(b) When replying to an enquiry about the creditworthiness of a customer what precautions should a banker take? Under what circumstances would a banker be released from his obligation to maintain secrecy about a customer's account?

14. The Manager of a bank purchases from a person well-known to him certain crossed and uncrossed cheques drawn on other banks. The person has no account with the bank. Is the bank protected if the cheques turn out to have been fraudulently acquired by the person? Give reasons for your answer.

15. Distinguish between the crossing "Not Transferable", "Not Negotiable" and "Payee's Account."

16. A crossed and order cheque marked "Not Negotiable", bearing several endorsements, is presented to your bank through a clearing house. In view of the "Not Negotiable" crossing, would you or would you not pay the cheque?

17. Define the crossing of a cheque and explain its significance. What are the different types of crossings and their special features? How are they to be dealt with by the collecting banker and the paying banker?

18. What are negotiable instruments and their characteristics? Would you consider the following as Negotiable Instruments? Give reasons.

(i) Bill of Lading,

(ii) Railway Receipt,

(iii) Life Insurance Policy,

(iv) Share Certificate,

(v) Promissory Note. [I.I.B., Part I]

19. Who is a 'holder' in due course? What precautions should the transferee of a negotiable instrument take to qualify as a "holder in due course"? [I.I.B., Part I]

20. (a) Define "Endorsement". What are the different types of endorsements? Give examples.

(b) Should a cheque endorsed in pencil be paid? [I.I.B., Part I]

21. Explain the meaning of the following terms:

(a) Allonge,

(b) Sans Recourse. [I.I.B., Part I]

22. Discuss the effects of crossing a cheque with the words "Not Negotiable" written across its face.

23. Bring out the main differencs between "Account Payee" and "Not Negotiable" Cheques. [I.I.B., Part I]

24. Bring out clearly the main difference between

(a) "Payees Account" cheques and "Not Negotiable" cheques.

(b) "Order" cheque and "Crossed Cheque." [I.I.B., Part I]

25. What are negotiable instruments and their characteristices? Would you consider the following a negotiable instrument? Give reasons.

(a) Bill of lading

(b) Postal Order

(c) A Promissory note

(d) A Debenture. [Osmania: I.I.B., Part I]

26. Negotiable instrument take to qualify as a holder in due course? [I.I.B., Part I]

(a) Explain the main characteristics of negotiable instruments.

(b) Indicate, with reasons, whether the following documents are negotiable Instruments:

(i) A ten rupee note issued by the Reserve Bank of India.

(ii) A fixed deposit receipt for ₹ 50,000 issued by a nationalised bank in favour of its customer.

(iii) 100 Equity shares of the face value of ₹ 10 each issued by a public limited company.

(iv) A bill of lading issued by a shipping Co. covering the export of cashewnuts from India to London. [I.I.B., Part I]

27. Write short notes on:

(i) Payment in due course [I.I.B., Part I]

(ii) MICR Cheques/drafts [I.I.B., Part I]

28. Explain different kinds of endorsements. When and how should cheques be endorsed?

29. (a) What are the implications of an endorsement on a cheque?

(b) Spell out the appropriate endorsements for cheques drawn payable to the following:

(i) Lock, Stock and Barrel Ltd. (In Liquidation)

(ii) The Gymkhana Club

(iii) Commissioner of Income Tax

(iv) Messrs. Lila Ram Natwar Lal

(v) N.P. Chakravarty

(vi) Cash

(vii) John Paget and Co. Ltd.

(viii) Miss Kamla Arora.

30. Give the correct forms of endorsement for cheques made payable to the order of:

(a) Dr. Ram Chander MBBS

(b) Miss Asha Rastogi (now married to Mr. Gupta)

(c) XYZ Co. Ltd.,

(d) Krishna (illiterate)

(e) Secretary, Jaipur Club (Rajasthan)

31. Please state whether the following endorsements are correct. If not, please give correct endorsements.

Name	*Endorsement*
(i) Padmashri Krishna Rao	Padmashri Krishna Rao
(ii) Fire and General Insurance Co. Ltd.	Per Pro Fire and General Insurance Co. Ltd Rustamjee Dalal Constituted Attorney
(iii) Kum Aruna Maitra	Aruna wife of Subhash Malhotra (Formerly, Miss Aruna Maitra)
(iv) Manav Mandir Trust	For Manav Mandir Trust Ramadevi Managing Trustee
(v) Dr. Keshavlal Bhatt	Without recourse to me Keshavlal Jamna Das Bhatt.

[I.I.B., Part I]

32. Give the correct endorsements on the cheques payable to the order of
   (i) Bombay Shroff's Association
   (ii) Shah Nathalal and Bros.
   (iii) Raman Lal & Co. by the proprietor 'C' Mehta & Co. Ltd., a Ltd. Company
   (iv) Bangalore Banker's Club
   (v) Bombay Cochin Transport Co. Ltd.

33. Please state whether the following endorsements are correct. If not give correct endorsements and give reasons.

Name	*Endorsement*
(i) Messrs. Jamnadas Ratanchand	Jamnadas Ratanchand
(ii) Messrs. Shroff and Co.	Shroff & Co.
(iii) Principal B. D. Commerce College	For B. D. Commerce College Vice-principal
(iv) Trustees of late Dalichand Gadumal	C. K. Zaveri
(v) Dr. Keshavlal Bhatt MBBS	Keshavlal D. Bhatt MBBS

[I.I.B., Part I]

34. *(a)* Define Endorsements. What are the different types of endorsements? Give examples.
   (b) Give correct endorsement on cheques payable to the order of
      (i) Smt. R. Bakshi
      (ii) M/s. S. Bhattacharya & Co.
      (iii) K.L.K. & Co. Ltd., (In Liquidation)
      (iv) Padmashri Rustomjee Sorabjee
      (v) Trustees of late Gujarmal Mehta *[I.I.B., Part I]*

35. A cheque for ₹ 2,000 which had been crossed originally carries below the crossing the words "Crossing Cancelled". and signed by the drawer and is presented for cash payment on the counter. How would you deal with this situation? *[I.I.B., Part I]*

36. Bring out the main difference between Account Payee and Not Negotiable cheques. *[I.I.B., Part I, May, 1989]*

37. A cheque for ₹ 2,000 which has been crossed originally carries below the crossing the words "Crossing Cancelled" and signed by the drawer is presented for cash payment by a bearer on the counter. What would you do? *[I.I.B., Part I]*

CHAPTER 14 Collection and Payment of Cheques and Bills

One of the most important functions of a modern banker is the collection of cheques presented by customers drawn upon other bankers. In performing this function, he acts as an agent of his customer, and is bound to use reasonable skill, care and diligence.

In the case of collection of cheques, a banker is:

(1) A Holder for Value: In the case of uncrossed or open cheques, he occupies exactly the same position as any other person who so acquires them. The following are some of the situations in which the banker becomes a holder for value:

(a) When he gives cash in exchange for a cheque drawn on another banker;

(b) When he credits his customer with the amount of cheque as soon as it is paid in and allows him to draw at once against the amount; and

(c) When the cheque is expressly paid in to reduce the amount of an overdraft.

(2) An Agent: A banker, while collecting a cheque for a customer, cannot assert any right of a holder for value, for he is acting only as an agent. In doing so, he gets the same title on the cheque as that of his customer. Thus, a banker who is collecting for his customer a cheque belonging to another person may be held liable for conversion, unless he can prove that he acted in good faith and without negligence, and that the cheque was crossed before it came into his hands.

From the foregoing discussion, it is clear that a banker performs the function of collection of cheques as an agent of the customer as a holder for value. As long as the title of the customer is good, the banker incurs no risk. But if the title of the customer is defective and, after collection, he withdraws the amount of the cheque from the bank, the banker may be held liable to pay the money to the true owner of the cheque. The words of Justice Lindley J. may be quoted here:

"Take the position of a collecting bank. A collecting bank receives from its customers crossed cheques: they must collect them, or leave them alone; practically, of course, they do collect them. Then it comes to this — what is the consequence if they do collect and the customer who sends the cheque to them happens to have a bad title? It is, to my mind, a little hard in any case that a banker who merely collects the money for his customer should be liable for the money. I do not mean to say that, as the law stood before, the banker is not liable; but it is a little hard, and it appeared to be only reasonable, at all events, that the legislature should relieve bankers from some of the consequences against which no amount of foresight could possibly guard."*

It will be seen that it is not possible for a paying banker to know whether or not the endorsement on a cheque drawn upon him is genuine. Nor is it possible for a collecting banker to know about the genuineness of the endorsements on the cheques given to him for collection.

☞ Statutory Protection

According to Section 131 of the Negotiable Instruments Act, 1881, *"a banker, who has in good faith and without negligence received payment for a customer on a cheque crossed generally or specially to himself, shall not, in case the title to the cheque proves defective, incur any liability to the true owner of the cheque by reason only of having received such payment".*

This section no doubt gives ample protection, in normal circumstances, to the banker who collects cheques on behalf of his customers so long as cheque happens to be crossed generally or specially to himself when he receives it. He will, however, not get any protection if the cheque is received uncrossed and the banker puts the crossing himself. In other words, this statutory protection is available to a banker only in the case of a "crossed" cheque. In the case of an "uncrossed" or "open" cheque, the collecting banker's position is that of any other holder for value or holder in due course. Again, a banker will be protected only if the collection of the cheque is made on behalf of a customer; in the case of collection for a person who is not a customer of the bank, he will not be protected.

The onus of proving *good faith* and *absence of negligence* is on the banker claiming protection under Section 131. The explanation to Section 131 lays down that the position of the banker is the same, notwithstanding that "he credits his customer's account with the amount of the cheque before receiving payment thereof". The net result is that if a banker receives a crossed cheque for collection, he will be protected under Section 131 of the Negotiable Instruments Act, 1881, as an agent for collection, whether he first credits and then collects or first collects and then credits the cheque as long as he acts: *(i)* in good faith, *(ii)* without negligence, and *(iii)* on behalf of a customer.

☞ Conversion

Conversion may be defined as the lawful taking, using, depositing or destroying of goods, which is inconsistent with the owner's right of possession. In other words, conversion is wrongful interference with goods, as by taking, using or destroying them is inconsistent with the owner's right of possession. According to Dr. Hart, "conversion is the wrongful intermedling with the goods of another for the purpose of taking them away from the party entitled to them."**

It may be noted that, if there were no statutory protection, a banker would be liable for conversion if he paid a cheque on a forged endorsement, or collected a bill, note or cheque bearing a forged endorsement. As banking business is vital to the economic life of a community, and as the doctrine of conversion exposes bankers to the risks and hazards of indeterminable claims, the purpose of the law has been to grant them a conditional immunity or concession which is not enjoyed by the world at large. A banker, however, who takes as a holder for value a bill or a cheque marked "not negotiable" will be liable in conversion, because there is no protection, statutory or otherwise, in such a case.

---

* Bhashyam and Adiga's *Negotiable Instruments Act*, 8th Ed., p. 509.

** Hart's Law of Banking, 4th Ed., p. 609.

☞ Collecting Banker's Duties and Responsibilities

1. It is the duty of the collecting banker to exercise the same care and precaution in the interests of the true owner of a cheque as a reasonable businessman would exercise in his own interests. Failure to obtain references or letters of introduction at the time of the opening of a current account in the name of a person whose title to the cheques collected turned out to be defective was held to amount to negligence sufficient enough to deprive the collecting banker of statutory protection. *(Ladbroke and Co. vs. Todd 1914.)*
2. Another duty of the collecting banker is to verify endorsements on an order cheque. In the case of an irregular endorsement, he may be held to be guilty of negligence.
3. A banker should make proper investigation of "Per Pro" endorsements because collection of such cheques without investigation may amount to negligence on his part. *(Brisel & Co. vs. Fox Brothers & Co.)*
4. A banker will be liable for negligence if he disregards the warning conveyed by the form of instrument itself, apart from any knowledge possessed by him of the customer's position that the customer is either committing a breach of trust or is misappropriating money belonging to somebody else.

   The following examples illustrate the cases where a banker was held liable for negligence:

   (a) Solicitor Terrington drew cheques on Reckitt's account pursuant to the power of attorney and paid them into his private account with the Midland Bank who collected them for him. The bank was held guilty of negligence because there was notice on the face of the cheques that Terrington was applying the plaintiff's money to his private purposes. *(Midland Bank Ltd. vs., Reckitt, 1933).*

   (b) The Chief Accountant of Lloyds Bank in Bombay was authorised to draw cheques on the account kept by the Lloyds Bank with the then Imperial Bank of India. Pursuant to this authority, the Chief Accountant drew certain cheques for large sums on the then Imperial Bank and made them payable to the Chartered Bank where he had a private account. These cheques were handed over to the Chartered Bank with the express direction of the Chief Accountant that the proceeds after collection should be credited to his private account. The Chartered Bank was held guilty of negligence. *(Lloyds Bank vs. Chartered Bank of India Ltd., 1929.)*

   (c) The sole director of one-man company endorsed, in the name of the company, cheques drawn by third parties in favour of the company and paid them into his personal account with the defendant bank which collected them on his behalf and credited his account with their proceeds. The bank was held liable in this case as the name of the payee and the Per Pro endorsements clearly showed that the director, in all probability, was misappropriating the company's money. *(Underwood Ltd. vs. Bank Liverpool, 1924.)*

   (d) A cheque, which was made payable to a partnership firm, was endorsed by one partner on behalf of the firm and was paid into his private account for collection with the defendant bank. The bank was held liable. *(Beven vs. National Bank Ltd., 1906.)*
5. In collecting third party cheques (cheques of which the customer is not the payee but the endorsee), a banker should take extra precautions to safeguard the interests of the true owner.

The legal position of a banker, in the performance of his duties as a collecting banker, was mentioned by the *Supreme Court in Kesharichand Jaisukhlal vs. Shillong Banking Corporation Ltd.,* (AIR 1965 SC. 514). "A banker entrusted by his customer with the collection of a cheque is bound to act according to the directions given by the customer, and in the absence of such directions, according to usages prevailing at the place, where the banker conducts his business and applicable to the matter in hand. The banker is also bound to use reasonable skill and diligence in presenting and securing payment of the cheque and placing the proceeds to his customer's account and in taking such other steps as may be proper, to secure the customer's account and in taking such other steps as may be proper, to secure the customer's interest."

In this case, the collecting banker accepted cheque from the drawee banker instead of cash, without information and consent of the customer. Since the cheque was dishonoured the collecting banker demanded payment from the drawee banker, and with the consent of customer, accepted a demand draft drawn by drawee banker in its head office. The drawee bank in the meantime closed its business and the draft remained uncashed. The collecting banker preferred a claim, in respect of the draft, in the liquidation of the drawee bank and was admitted as a preferential creditor. The plea of the customer was that the collecting banker accepted the draft on its own responsibility and was bound to give credit for the full amount. It was held by the Supreme Court that in accepting a cheque from the drawee bank instead of cash the collecting banker acted in good faith in the interest of the customer. The draft was accepted by the collecting banker on the instructions of the customer. It was, therefore, not open to the customer to take the stand that the collecting banker had accepted the cheque or draft on its own and not as an agent for the customer.

☞ Collection of Bills

Although there is no legal binding on a banker to collect bills for customer, no banker can afford to refuse to render this service. And he does so not only for the convenience of his customer but also because it adds to his own profits, for he generally levies a charge for the collection of bills. By offering this facility, a banker attracts customer who deal in bills and finds it easy to pay their acceptances through a bank.

In the case of collection of bills, a banker does not get the statutory protection afforded to collecting bankers by Section 131 of the Negotiable Instruments Act, 1881. Thus, if the title of the customer to a bill collected by him turns out to be defective, the owner can claim the amount of the bill from the banker, who in turn can look to his customer for making good the loss he has incurred on his account.

☞ Presentment for Acceptance

When a banker receives an unaccepted bill for presentation on behalf of a customer, he should present it for acceptance as early as possible. If a customer suffers a loss owing to the banker's failure to present a bill for acceptance or for payment, he may be held responsible. As far as possible, the banker should present the bill for acceptance on the day of its receipt. If this is not possible, it must be presented within a reasonable time. Section 75A lays down the rules regarding excuse for delay in the presentment for acceptance or payment: the delay is excused if it is caused by circumstances beyond the control of the holder, and is not imputable to his default, misconduct or negligence. When the cause of delay ceases to operate, presentment must be made within a reasonable time.

Section 61 of the Negotiable Instruments Act lays down the provisions regarding presentment for acceptance. According to this Section:

"A bill of exchange payable after sight must, if no time or place is specified therein for presentment, be presented to the drawer thereof for acceptance, if he can, after reasonable search, be found by a person entitled to demand acceptance within a reasonable time after it is drawn in business hours on a business day. In default of such presentment, no party thereto is liable thereon to the person making such default."

If the drawee cannot be found, after a reasonable search, the bill is dishonoured. If the bill is directed to the drawee at a particular place, it must be presented at that place; and if at the due date for presentment he cannot be found after a reasonable search, the bill is dishonoured. Where authorised by agreement or usage, a presentment through the Post Office by means of a registered letter is sufficient.

Presentment for acceptance is excused when the drawee cannot be found after a reasonable search, or when the drawer is a fictitious person, or when the drawer is incapable of contracting or when, although the presentment is irregular, acceptance has been refused on some other ground.

Presentment for acceptance is necessary in case of:

(a) a bill payable after sight, and

(b) a bill in which there is an express stipulation that it shall be presented for acceptance before it is presented for payment.

Presentment for acceptance is not necessary in the case of a bill payable on demand or on a fixed date. However, it is always desirable to get a bill accepted as early as possible even when it is not necessary because of:

(i) Assurance of payment on due date;

(ii) Evidence in case of dispute;

(iii) Facility in negotiation;

(iv) Drawee (or Acceptor) knowing his liability;

(v) Easy discounting of such bills from a bank.

The banker should present a bill for acceptance to the following:

(i) Drawee;

(ii) Authorised agent of the drawee;

(iii) Legal representative, if the drawee is dead;

(iv) Official Receiver, when the drawee has been declared an insolvent;

(v) All the drawees, if there are several drawees, unless any one of them has the proper authority to accept it on behalf of all.

☞ Rules Regarding Presentment for Payment

Sections 62 to 75 of the Negotiable Instruments Act lay down the rules for the presentment of a negotiable instrument for payment.

A promissory note, payable at a certain period after sight, must be presented to the maker thereof for sight (if, after reasonable search, he can be found) by a person entitled to demand payment, within a reasonable time. In default of such presentment, no party thereto is liable thereon to the person making such default (Sec. 62).

Promissory notes, bills of exchange and cheques must be presented for payment to the maker, acceptor or drawee thereof respectively, by or on behalf of the presentment, the other parties thereto are not liable thereon to such holder.

Where authorised by agreement or usage, a presentment through the post by means of a registered letter is sufficient (Sec. 64).

A presentment for payment must be made during the usual hours of business, or during banking hours (Sec. 65).

A promissory note or bill of exchange made payable at a specified period after date of sight thereof must be presented for payment at maturity (Sec. 66).

A promissory note payable by instalments must be presented for payment on the third day after the date fixed for the payment of each instalment. The non-payment on such presentment has the same effect as the non-payment of a note at maturity (Sec. 67).

A promissory note, bill of exchange or cheque made, drawn or accepted, payable at a specified place and not elsewhere, must, in order to charge any party thereto, be presented for payment at that place (Sec. 68).

A promissory note or bill of exchange made, drawn or accepted, and payable at a specified place, must, in order to charge the maker or drawer thereof, be presented for payment at that place (Sec. 69).

A promissory note or bill of exchange not made payable as mentioned in Sections 68 and 69 must be presented for payment at the place of business (if any), or at the usual residence, of the maker, drawee or acceptor thereof, as the case may be (Sec. 70).

If the maker, drawee or acceptor of a negotiable instrument has no known place of business or fixed residence, and no place is specified in the instrument for presentment for acceptance or payment, such presentment may be made to him in person wherever he can be found (Sec. 71).

Subject to the provisions of Section 84, a cheque must, in order to charge the drawer, be presented at the bank upon which it is drawn before the relation between the drawer and his banker has been altered to the prejudice of the drawer (Sec. 72).

A cheque must, in order to charge any person except the drawer, be presented within a reasonable time after delivery thereof by such person (Sec. 73).

Subject to the provisions of Section 31, a negotiable instrument, payable on demand, must be presented for payment within a reasonable time after it is received by the holder (Sec. 74).

A presentment for acceptance or payment may be made to the duly authorised agent of the drawee, maker or acceptor, and if he has died, to his legal representative, or if he has been declared insolvent, to his assignee (Sec. 75).

A delay in the presentment for acceptance or payment is excused if the delay is caused by circumstances beyond the control of the holder, and not imputable to his default, misconduct or negligence. When the cause of delay ceases to operate, the presentment must be made within a reasonable time (Sec. 75A).

☛ When Presentment is Unnecessary

Under Section 76, no presentment for payment is necessary, and the instrument is dishonoured at the due date for presentment, in any of the following cases:

(a) If the maker, drawee or acceptor intentionally prevents the presentment of the instrument;

(b) If the instrument is payable at the place of business of the maker, drawee or acceptor, and he closes such place of business on a working day during the usual business hours;

(c) If the instrument is payable at some other specified place, and neither he nor any person authorised to pay it attends at such place during the usual business hours;

(d) If the instrument, not being payable at any specified place, he cannot, after due search, be found;

(e) If he has engaged to pay notwithstanding non-presentment, the presentment is not necessary as against any party sought to be charged therewith;

(*f*) As against any party, if after maturity, with knowledge that the instrument has not been presented, he makes a part payment on account of the amount due on the instrument, or promises to pay the amount due thereon in whole or in part, or otherwise waives his right to take advantage of any default in presentation for payment; and

(*g*) As against the drawer, if the drawer does not suffer damage by reason of non-presentment.

Under an exception to Section 64, no presentment is necessary of a promissory note payable on demand and not payable at a specified place to charge the maker thereof.

☛ Position of Paying Banker

The position of a paying banker is different from that of a collecting banker, and is more secure than that of the latter because of two reasons:

(*i*) if a cheque is properly drawn and is otherwise regular in form, a banker is bound to honour it in the absence of express notice that the customer is committing a fraud;

(*ii*) the element of negligence does not enter into the consideration of the matter of all.

If he is acting as a paying as well as a collecting banker, in his position as a paying banker, the element of negligence would become immaterial; but as a collecting banker, it would be a decisive factor.

RESERVE BANK'S INSTRUCTION TO BANKS

The Reserve Bank of India has advised the banks to avoid delay in the collection of outstation instruments and to adopt new systems and procedures, infrastructure arrangement, etc., to ensure quick collection of such instruments. In 1995 the Bank also prescribed a new time frame for affording credit to the customer as follows:

(1) Immediate Credit of Cheques

Banks are required to give in the normal course immediate credit up to ₹ 5,000 to a customer for local as well as outstation cheques, subject to the satisfactory operation of the customer's account.

(2) Time Limit for Collection of Outstation Cheques

In the four metropolitan centres having MICR cheque clearing system, the amount of a cheque drawn on a bank located at any of the other three metropolitan centres and presented for collection on any day in a week should be credited in the customer's account latest by the same day in the following week.

In case of State capitals and other centres with more than 100 bank offices, credit to the customer's A/c should be given within 10 days and customer allowed to withdraw the amount. These facilities are to be provided to the customer even if the collection advices are not received by the banks concerned.

In the case of local cheques, customer's A/c should be credited latest by the third working day from the date of acceptance of the cheques at the counter.

For the above facility banks are prohibited from charging any additional charge. But if the cheques are returned unpaid, banks are permitted to charge interest at commercial rate on the overdrawn amount from the date of the withdrawal till the amount is reimbursed by the customer.

To limit the risks involved in the above, Reserve Bank has advised the banks to extend the facility of giving credit to the accounts for outstation cheques only to: (*i*) satisfactory operated accounts and (*ii*) up to a maximum amount of ₹ 10,000. If one or more cheques for the value of more than

₹ 10,000 are deposited for collection on a single day or on subsequent days, withdrawal can be allowed up to a maximum of ₹ 10,000 only. Thus, bank's exposure will be to the extent of ₹ 10,000 only against any individual customer. Reserve Bank has further authorised the banks to ensure that where delay occurs, the accountholders should be paid penal interest without their requesting for it.

☛ Liability of the Collecting Banker in Respect of its Agent Appointed for Collection

The collecting banker collects the amount of the cheque from the paying banker through its own branch at the place of the paying banker, if there is no branch of the collecting banker at that place, it appoints another banker having a branch at that place, as its agent for collection. The status of such agent banker — as a sub-agent or a subsitute agent — and the liability of the collecting banker in respect thereof was decided by the Bombay High Court in the *Punjab National Bank Ltd., Gondia vs. Ishwarbhai Lalbhai Patel & Co*. (A.I.R. 1971, Bombay 348). Brief facts of the case were as follows:

The firm Ishwarbhai Lalbhai Patel & Company presented to Punjab National Bank, Gondia, a cheque drawn in its favour on the Lakshmi Bank, Bhandara, with the instruction to credit the amount to its account, after realisation. P.N. Bank had no branch at Bhandara and, therefore, sent the cheque to Lakshmi Bank, Gondia, for collection. The cheque was sent by Lakshmi Bank, Gondia, to its Bhandara branch, which passed it for payment and issued a payment order to the P.N. Bank to receive payments at its Gondia branch. The payment order was presented twice, but no payment was made and by that time the Lakshmi Bank had suspended payment. The suit was filed by the firm on the P.N. Bank for the realisation of the amount of the cheque.

The Bombay High Court pointed out that in the case of property appointed sub-agent, the agent is responsible to the principal for the acts of the sub-agent which in case of substitute agent, *i.e.*, a person named by the agent holding an express or implied authority to act for the principal in the business of agency, the principal is responsible.

Dealing with the facts of the case the High Court observed that the nature of the business of the collecting banker, namely, agency to collect the amount on behalf of the customer, was such that the collecting banker had to appoint another person for the purpose of realisation. Since the collection of the amount would have been facilitated by appointing the Gondia branch, the collecting banker had implied authority to appoint the said branch, which would be a substituted agent and not a sub-agent. The High Court, therefore, held that the acts of Lakshmi Bank, Gondia, as substituted agent, would be bringing on the customer and P.N. Bank would not be responsible to the customer unless it had received the amount in its hands and credited the same to the accounts of the customer.

Payment of Cheques

☛ Duty

One important aspect of the banker-customer relationship is the banker's obligation to honour his customer's cheques. According to Section 31 of the Negotiable Instruments Act, 1881, the liability of the banker in regard to payment of cheques is as follows:

"The drawee of a cheque, having sufficient funds of the drawer in his hands, properly applicable to the payment of such cheque, must pay the cheque when duly required to do so and in default of such payment must compensate the drawer for any loss or damage caused by such default."

Thus, it is the duty of a banker to pay cheques properly drawn by his customer, provided he has sufficient funds of his customer to meet them.

☞ Liability

(1) In case the banker dishonours such cheques in spite of sufficient funds of the customer, he is liable to pay damages for breach of the banker's implied contract to honour such cheques.

(2) The banker is liable for non-payment of such cheques if, although there are insufficient funds of the customer in account, he has otherwise contracted to honour them, *e.g.*, by an arrangement with his customer for an overdraft or by a direct promise to pay the cheque.

(3) The banker is also liable if he dishonours a cheque after misleading the customer into believing that there were sufficient funds to meet the cheque. *(Holland vs. Manchester & Liverpool District Banking Co. 1909).* In this case, it was held that entries by a banker in his customer's pass book, although they are subject to adjustment, are *prima facie* evidence against the banker of the amount to the credit of the customer's account and the customer who draws a cheque relying on such entries can recover damages, in the absence of fraud, for the dishonour of such a cheque. The customer's right of action in such a case is not upon the cheque itself but is either for negligence on the part of the banker or for damages for breach of his implied contract to honour cheques. The cheque in such cases must be drawn or endorsed in favour of a third party and presented by the holder and not by the customer himself. *(Kuilan vs. Ulster Bank, 1928).*

☞ Risks

A banker's position in regard to payment of cheques is full of risks. If he honours a cheque through oversight, when there are no funds in the customer's account, he may lose his money; and if he dishonours it through inadvertence, he may be called upon to pay damages for wrongful dishonour. Moreover, he must either honour the cheque or refuse its payment at once, without even a chance to consult his legal adviser, customer or anyone else.

☞ Statutory Protection

Section 85 of the Negotiable Instruments Act, 1881, as amended by the Amendment Act of 1934, lays down that *"where a cheque payable to order purports to be endorsed by or on behalf of the payee, the drawee is discharged by payment in due course".*

☞ Crossed Cheques

In the case of crossed cheques, Section 128 amplifies the protection given to the paying banker by Section 85 of the Negotiable Instruments Act, 1881. Section 128 says:

"Where the banker on whom a crossed cheque is drawn has paid the same in due course, the banker paying the cheque, and (in case such cheque has come to the hands of the payee) the drawer thereof, shall respectively be entitled to the same rights, and be placed in the same position in all respects as they would respectively be entitled to and placed in if the amount of the cheque had been paid to, and received by, the true owner thereof."

When a cheque is crossed "Account Payee" or "Payee's Account", the banker should not collect it except on behalf of its payee, and it is not incumbent upon the paying banker to satisfy himself that the cheque is being collected for the benefit of the payee's account.

☞ Payment in Due Course

Section 10 of the Negotiable Instruments Act explains payment in due course as follows: *"Payment in due course means payment in accordance with the apparent tenor of the instrument in good faith and without negligence to any person in possession thereof under circumstances which do not afford a reasonable ground for believing that he is not entitled to receive payment of the amount therein mentioned."*

The following elements are essential for payment in due course:

(i) Payment in accordance with the apparent tenor of the instrument;

(ii) Payment in good faith;

(iii) Payment without negligence;

(iv) Payment to a person in possession of the instrument entitled to receive payment.

Precautions to be Taken While Making Payments

☞ Crossed Cheques

Sections 126, 127 and 129 of the Negotiable Instruments Act lay down the duties of and the precautions to be taken by a paying banker as regards crossed cheques.

Section 126: "When a cheque is crossed generally, the banker on whom it is drawn shall not pay it otherwise than to a banker. Where the cheque is crossed specially, the banker on whom it is drawn shall not pay it otherwise than to the banker to whom it is crossed, or his agent for collection."

Section 127: "Where a cheque is crossed specially to more than one banker, except when crossed to an agent for the purpose of collection, the banker on whom it is drawn shall refuse payment thereof."

Section 129: "Any banker paying a cheque crossed generally otherwise than to a banker, or a cheque crossed specially otherwise than to the banker to whom the same is crossed, or his agent for collection, being a banker, shall be liable to the true owner of the cheque for any loss he may sustain owing to the cheque having been so paid."

Thus, it is necessary for the banker to pay the cheques according to the direction of the crossing on it. If a cheque is paid in a manner contrary to the directions of crossing —

(i) the banker cannot debit the customer's account;

(ii) according to Section 10, such payment is not a "payment in due course", hence the banker will not be entitled to the statutory protection provided for in Section 129.

☞ Effect of Double Crossing

According to Section 127 of the Negotiable Instruments Act, unless one of the two banks named in the crossing acts as an agent for collection of the other bank, the cheque should not be honoured. If the words "Yourselves" are given in the crossing, the cheque is considered as a specially crossed cheque. If a cheque crossed specially to a bank is returned unpaid for any reason and is presented again through another bank, it should not be honoured unless the crossing in favour of the first bank is properly cancelled.

☞ Office of Payment

Cheques drawn on a particular branch or office should be paid by that very branch or office, unless previous permission has been given to draw cheques on some other branch. Precaution should be taken by the banker to see to it that cheques drawn on that branch are honoured.

☞ Mutilated Cheques

A banker should also be very careful when honouring mutilated, torn or cancelled cheques. If he honours a cheque which is torn by the customer in such a way as to give sufficient evidence of his intention to cancel it, the banker cannot debit the customer's account with the amount of the cheque.

If a cheque is accidentally torn by the drawer, he must confirm it in the following manner:

Torn by me by mistake
Mutilation confirmed
Ram Sharan Sinha

If a cheque is accidentally torn by the collecting banker, he must confirm it in the following manner before presenting it to the paying banker:

Accidentally torn by me
Mutilation confirmed
For the Central Bank of India
H.P. Shori, Agent.

☞ Correctness of Form

The banker should also take such precautions about the proper form of the cheque as would ensure that the instrument confirms to the legal definition of a cheque. In this connection, he should pay special attention to the following:

(i) Use of Printed Form: Though money can be withdrawn by writing on a piece of paper, the banker should accept only the printed forms supplied by him for withdrawals to avoid risks.

(ii) Complete: A cheque should be complete, *i.e.*, all the entries must be filled up when it is presented to a banker for payment.

(iii) Date: The date is an important entry on a cheque, and is written at the time of the writing of a cheque. If the date is not mentioned on a cheque, the banker should return it without payment. A bank is bound to make payment of a cheque only up to six months after the date of the writing of the cheque. After six months, the cheque becomes stale. If a later date is written on a cheque, it is post-dated cheque; and if the banker makes payment of such a cheque, it is done at the banker's own risk because of the following reasons:

(a) An order may be made by the customer to stop payment from his account.

(b) Payment from the customer's account is stopped in case of insolvency, insanity or death of the customer.

(c) In the case of payment by a banker of a post-dated cheque, due to insufficiency of funds, if some other cheque of the customer is dishonoured, the banker will be liable for wrongful dishonour.

(d) The greatest risk to the paying banker is that the payment of a post-dated cheque is not considered as payment in due course, hence the paying banker is not entitled to the statutory protection provided under Section 128 of the Negotiable Instruments Act, 1881.

(iv) Payee's Name: Before making payment, a banker should be careful about the name of the payee. Payment can be made to any person in case of bearer cheques. But the payee should be a definite person.

(v) Amount: A cheque will not be considered to be in order if the amount is not specific. The amount should be the same in figures as well as in words.

(vi) Signature of the Drawer: A specimen signature of the customer is taken by the banker before a new account is opened. It is one of the foremost duties of a banker to verify the signature of the customer before making any payment. In case of payment of a cheque on which signature of the customer is forged, the banker will be held liable. The legal position of a banker has been clearly stated in *Abbu Chettiar vs. Hyderabad State Bank, 1924:*

(a) It is for the customer to establish affirmatively that the signature on the disputed cheque is not that of the customer but a forgery.

(b) If the drawer's cheque is forged or unauthorised, however clever the forgery is, the banker cannot debit his customer's account in case he pays the same, unless he establishes adoption or estoppel.

(c) What amount to adoption or estoppel is dependent upon the circumstances of each case.

(d) In order to make the customer liable for the loss, the neglect on his part must be, or intimately, connected with the transaction itself and must have been the proximate cause of the loss.

(e) The banker cannot set up either estoppel or adoption if his own conduct or negligence has occasioned or contributed to the loss, the well-settled principle being that where one of two innocent parties must suffer for the fraud of a third, that party should suffer whose negligence facilitated the fraud.

(viii) Scrutiny of Endorsements: The banker should satisfy himself, whether or not the cheque presented to him requires to be endorsed, and if so, whether the endorsements on the same are in order.

"Once a bearer, Always a bearer": Where a cheque is originally expressed to be payable to bearer, the drawee is discharged by payment in due course to the bearer thereof, notwithstanding any endorsement whether in full or in blank appearing thereon and notwithstanding that any such endorsement purports to restrict or exclude further negotiation.

The banker must see to it that an endorsement on order cheques is regular; otherwise, the payment made may not be regarded as payment in due course.

☞ Hours of Payment

The banker is required to honour cheques if they are presented on a working day and during banking hours.

☞ Material Alterations

A cheque with material alterations make the instrument null and void. Therefore, if a cheque without any apparent but with material alteration is paid by a banker, he will not get the protection provided by Sections 80 and 82 of the Bills of Exchange Act, 1882.

An alteration is material which in any way alters materially or substantially the operation of the instrument and the liabilities of the parties thereto, irrespective of whether or not the change is prejudicial to the payee. Material alterations include the alteration of the date, crossing, place of payment, amount and name of the payee. As discussed in *Gourchandra Das vs. Prasanna Kumar Chandra,* 33 Calcutta 812, 816: "Any change in an instrument which causes to speak a different language in legal effect from that which it originally spoke or which changed the legal identity or character of the instrument either in terms or in relation of parties thereto is material alteration". Material alterations may be in the following forms:

(i) Alteration of date;

(ii) Alteration of place of payment;

(iii) Alteration of amount;

(iv) Alteration in the names of parties;

(v) Alteration of the word "bearer" in place of "order";

(vi) Alteration of crossing.

According to Section 87 of the Negotiable Instruments Act, "any material alteration of a negotiable instrument renders the same void as against anyone who is a party thereto at the time of making such alteration, and does not consent thereto, unless it was made in order to carry out the common intention of the original parties; and any such alteration, if made by an endorsee, discharges his endorser from all liability to him in respect of the consideration thereof".

The above discussion makes it clear that a material alternation makes a cheque void. Therefore, a banker should not honour such a cheque. However, a material alteration made with the consent of the parties shall not make the instrument void. The paying banker should, therefore, see to it that material alterations are confirmed by the signature of the drawer. In case of cheques signed by more than one person, material alterations should be confirmed by the signatures of all the persons. Where either party to a joint account has authority to sign cheques alone, the signature of one is sufficient and that need not necessarily be the one who originally signed the instrument. In the case of corporate bodies, alterations should be confirmed not only by the Secretary but by all the signatories unless the Secretary alone has the power to issue and sign cheques for the corporate body.

As a general rule, a banker cannot debit to a drawer's account, without the drawer's confirmation, a cheque which has been materially altered. However, this general rule is subject to one important qualification. A banker is justified in honouring a cheque that bears a non-apparent alteration. Further, if the drawer has, by his own negligence, facilitated the alteration, he may be precluded from denying that the alteration was made without his authority. *(Macmillan, Arthur vs. London Joint Stock Bank Ltd.,)*. Here, the drawer facilitated the alteration of the amount by leaving blank spaces before and after the amount. He was charged with negligence and precluded from denying that the alteration was made without his authority. The learned judge observed: "A cheque is a mandate to the banker to pay the amount according to the tenor of the cheque. The customer is bound to exercise reasonable care to prevent the banker from being misled. If he draws the cheque in a manner which facilitates fraud, he is guilty of a breach of duty between himself and he is responsible to the banker as a natural and direct consequence of this breach of duty. The customer is bound to take usual and proper precautions to prevent forgery."

In the case of a dispute about a material alteration, the burden of proof is on the person who seeks to enforce the negotiable instrument.

☞ Forgery of Drawer's Signature

A cheque with the forged signature of a drawer must not be paid by the banker. The payment of such a cheque is deemed as payment without the authority of the customer. The paying banker is not given any protection under law on the payment of a forged cheque. The banker's liability remains, even if the signature is cleverly forged and it is difficult to detect it with reasonable care, or if the customer is negligent about keeping the cheque book under lock and key as required by the rules of the bank.

In case of forged cheques, the banker cannot escape from liability, even if, the customer was negligent in keeping the cheque book under the lock and key as required by the rules of the bank. It was held by Allahabad High Court in *Lala Prabhu Dayal vs. Jwala Bank Ltd.,* (AIR 1938, All. 374) that "it is the duty of the employees of the bank to be able to identify the signature of the customers and if they fail to discharge their duty and thereby suffer loss, there is no reason why the customer should make good that loss."

Customer also has some responsibility in this regard and he should take the necessary precaution to save the banker from any loss which may arise because of his own acts. For example, if a banker seeks confirmation from the customer about the genuineness of his signature and the customer confirms the signature to be his own, then later on the customer will be estopped from denying the validity of his signature. Similarly, if a customer believes or has a reasonable doubt that a cheque with his forged signature is likely to be presented for payment, he should inform the banker otherwise, he will be estopped, later on, from denying the validity of the cheque.

In case of joint accounts, the signatures of all the accountholders must be genuine. The banker should not make payment if any of the signature is forged. It was decided in *Bihta Cooperative Development and Cane Marketing Union Ltd., and Others vs. Bank of Bihar and Others* (AIR 1967, Supreme Court, 389), that if one of the joint accountholders forges the signature of the other one, and the banker makes payment of the cheque, he will be liable to the other one. In the above case a sum of ₹ 11,000 was withdrawn by a cheque on which the signature of the Joint Secretary of the co-operative union was genuine but the signature of Treasurer was forged. It was held by the Supreme Court that since one of the signatures on the cheque was forged, there was no mandate to the bank at all. The bank was negligent in ascertaining whether the signature on the cheque is genuine.

☞ Stopping of Cheques

The stopping of a cheque is a mandate on the banker from his customer in much the same way as a cheque, when drawn on a banker, is a mandate from his customer to pay the same. If a banker negligently pays a cheque notwithstanding the fact that payment has been countermanded by the customer, he cannot debit the amount to the customer's account. *(Syd. Mohammed Yakub vs. Imperial Bank of India 1940).* If another cheque of the drawer is dishonoured due to the payment of the countermanded cheque, the drawer would be entitled to claim damages for the wrongful dishonour of the second cheque.

The mandate from the customer ordering the banker to stop his cheque operates only if it reaches the latter before the amount is actually paid out. In case the banker receives a telegram purporting to have come from his customer, he would be quite justified, if he has any doubts, in postponing the honouring of the cheque, pending enquiry. He should, however, be cautious because if he pays the cheque in spite of the telegram, he may be liable to make good that amount.

Only the drawer of a cheque can effectively countermand payment. Therefore, if the banker is advised by the holder of a cheque that he has lost it, the holder should be requested by the banker to approach the drawer and obtain written instructions countermanding the payment of the lost cheque. If, in the meantime, the lost cheque is presented, the banker must make very minute inquiries into the holder's title before paying it. The better course would be for him to postpone payment as he would in the case of telegraphic instructions to stop payment.

The banker must also stop payment when he has a notice of an available act of the bankruptcy of his customer or that of his death or insanity.

When a Garnishee order has been served upon a banker, the balance in the customer's account is attached, and the banker cannot honour a cheque drawn on that account.

☞ Payment by Mistake

When a banker makes payment of a cheque through a mistake of fact, he would naturally like to recover the amount so paid; and he can do so when the person to whom the amount was paid knew of the mistake. However, where there is a duty on the banker not to make mistake but to inform the payee of the true state of the account, the money cannot be recovered in case the payee has altered his position. (This has been discussed under the heading, "Wrong Entries in Pass Book.")

However, money cannot be recovered when payment has been made on a negotiable instrument (although endorsement or acceptance is subsequently proved to be a forgery) to an innocent holder after such an interval of time as to prejudice his rights against previous parties. The money can be recovered when notice of dishonour of the instrument has not been given to anyone and there is no negligence on the part of the payer indicating that the holder should have given credit and that, within a reasonable time, notice of mistake had been given.

According to Section 72 of the Indian Contract Act, a person to whom money has been paid or anything delivered by mistake or under coercion, must repay it. But this rule is qualified by the doctrine of equity. This doctrine, disfavours unjust enrichment. If a payee has not been enriched unjustly, he cannot be required to repay. In other words, if the position of the payee has not been altered to his detriment, he must repay the money to the buyer. But if the position of the payee has been changed to his prejudice, and thereafter the mistake has been detected, he cannot be held liable.

☞ Estoppel

Estoppel is a rule of law by which a party is estopped from denying that which he previously asserted to be true either orally or in writing or by a deed or in evidence in a court of law. A maker of a promissory note, or the drawer of a bill of exchange or cheque, or an acceptor for honour, is estopped from denying the validity of the instrument made or drawn to a holder in due course. A maker of a note, or an acceptor of a bill payable to the order of a specified person, is similarly estopped from denying the payee's capacity on the date of the note or bill to endorse it. An endorser of a negotiable instrument is not permitted to deny either the signature or the capacity to contract of any prior party to a holder in due course (Sections 120 and 121 of the Negotiable Instruments Act).

☞ Dishonour of Cheques

When a cheque is presented to a bank and not paid by the banker, it is called dishonour of a cheque. There are two situations in which a cheque can be dishonoured by a banker:

(i) *Compulsory Dishonour:* In the case of compulsory dishonour a banker has no choice but to dishonour the cheque. In the following cases the banker has to dishonour a cheque compulsorily:

   (a) The countermanding of payment by the customer;

   (b) On receipt of a Garnishee order;

   (c) In case of death of customer;

   (d) In case of insanity of customer;

   (e) In case of insolvency of customer.

(ii) *Dishonour at the Willingness of the Banker:* A banker may also dishonour a cheque when:

   (a) it is not properly written;

   (b) endorsement or crossing is not proper;

   (c) there is insufficiency of funds in the customer's account;

   (d) in case of doubt of the right of holder.

☞ Banker's Liability in Cases of Wrongful Dishonour

Before dishonouring a cheque on the ground of the customer's credit not being sufficient, or with the remark that the customer has "insufficient funds", the banker should be very careful, for here he would be running a great risk if the step taken by him proves to be erroneous. If the customer happens to be a businessman, the position would be worse and the banker would be liable to pay heavy damages, because the credit of a businessman is a delicate and valuable possession. Here the principle applicable to damage would be: "The smaller the cheque, the greater the damage", because it is obvious that the dishonour of a cheque for a very large amount would not damage the credit and standing of a customer to the extent it would if a cheque for a very small amount is dishonoured. It is pertinent to mention here the provision of Section 31 of the Negotiable Instruments Act, 1881: "The drawee of a cheque, having sufficient funds of the drawer in his hands, properly applicable to the payment of such a cheque, must pay the cheque when duly required to do so, and in default of such payment, must compensate the drawer for any loss or damage caused by such default".

☞ Usual Answer on Non-payment

The usual answers given by a banker in case of non-payment of cheques are:

(i)	E.I.	(Endorsement Irregular)
(ii)	W. and F.D.	(Writing and Figures Differ)
(iii)	R.D.	(Refer to drawer)
(iv)	N.S.F.	(Not sufficient funds)
(v)	N.A.	(No account)
(vi)	Requires Confirmation	(Vernacular signature)
(vii)	E.N.C.	(Effect not cleared. Please present again tomorrow)
(viii)	Not arranged for	
(ix)	Drawer's signature	incomplete
		differs
		required
(x)	Cheque is	mutilated
		post-dated
		out of date
(xi)	D.D.	drawer deceased
(xii)	Payment stopped by drawer	
(xiii)	Irregularly drawn.	

The remark "no account" is the most dangerous if passed through an error. It would mean that the customer was a cheat who drew a cheque on a bank in which he had no account. When the endorsement is forged, though the banker is justified in returning a cheque with the remark "endorsement false", he should avoid taking this risk. It would be judicious to state instead: "Endorsement requires verification". If a cheque is presented through the post, it should be returned at the close of the day, or the next day; if received through the local exchange, before the close of the date of presentation. In case a crossed cheque is offered across the counter, the answer whether the same is to be paid or not should be given immediately. The banker usually maintains what is called a "Stop Register", in which notices of countermand are entered, properly describing the cheque which is sought to be stopped. It is also the duty of the banker to inform other branch offices of this countermand of payment in the interest of his own customer and with a view to avoiding necessary unpleasantness with him.

☞ Discharge of a Negotiable Instrument

A negotiable instrument can be dishonoured by non-acceptance or non-payment.

A bill of exchange is said to be dishonoured by non-acceptance when the drawee, or one of several drawees who are not partners, makes default in acceptance upon being duly required to accept the bill, or where the presentment is excused and the bill is not accepted.

Where the drawee is competent to contract, or the acceptance is qualified, the bill may be treated as dishonoured (Sec. 91).

A promissory note, bill of exchange or cheque is said to be dishonoured by non-payment when the maker of the note, acceptor of the bill or drawee of the cheque makes default in payment when he is duly called upon to do so (Sec. 92).

☞ Rules Regarding Notice of Dishonour

When a promissory note, bill of exchange or cheque is dishonoured by non-acceptance or non-payment, the holder thereof, or some party thereto who remains liable thereon, must give notice that the instrument has been so dishonoured to all other parties whom the holder seeks to make severally liable thereon, and to some one of several parties whom he seeks to make jointly liable thereon (Sec. 93).

A notice of dishonour may be given to a duly authorised agent of the person to whom it is required to be given, or if he has died, to his legal representative, or if he has been declared an insolvent, to his receiver. It may be oral or written; if written, it may be sent by post, and may be in any form; but it must inform the party to whom it is given, either in express terms or by reasonable intendment, that the instrument has been dishonoured, and in what way, and that he will be held liable thereon; and it must be given within a reasonable time after dishonour, at the place of business or, if such party has no place of business, at the residence of the party for whom it is intended.

If the notice is duly directed and sent by post and miscarries, such miscarriage does not render the notice invalid (Sec. 94).

Any party receiving notice of dishonour must, in order to render any prior party liable to himself, give notice of dishonour to such party within a reasonable time, unless such party otherwise receives due notice as provided under Section 93 (Sec. 95).

When the instrument is deposited with an agent for presentment, the agent is entitled to the same time to give notice to his principal as if he were the holder giving notice of dishonour, and the principal is entitled to a further like period to give notice of dishonour (Sec. 96).

When the party to whom a notice of dishonour is despatched is dead, but the party despatching the notice is ignorant of his death the notice is sufficient (Sec. 97).

☞ When Notice is not Necessary (Section 98)

No notice of dishonour is necessary:

(a) When it is dispensed with by the party entitled thereto;

(b) When he has countermanded payment in order to charge the drawer;

(c) When the party charged does not suffer damage for want of notice;

(d) When the party entitled to the notice cannot, after due search, be found, or the party bound to give notice is, for any other reason, unable to give it without any fault of his own;

(e) When the acceptor is also the drawer;

(f) When a promissory note is not negotiable; and

(g) When the party entitled to notice knows the facts and promises unconditionally to pay the amount due on the instrument.

In addition, no notice to the maker of the dishonoured promissory note or the drawee or acceptor of the dishonoured bill of exchange or cheque is necessary (Sec. 93).

Solved Problems

Payment of Cheques

Q. 1. Shri Careless has an overdraft limit of ₹ 50,000 with your bank. On Monday, when the debit balance in the account is ₹ 47,200 a cheque of ₹ 5,000 drawn on the account is presented for cash payment by a third party. Will you pay the cheque and why? Which of the following is appropriate answers and why? Give reasons for not choosing the alternative.

(a) Funds expected

(b) Effects not cleared, present again

(c) Exceeds arrangements

(d) Refer to drawer.

Ans: The given limit is ₹ 50,000, and if the cheque of ₹ 5,000 as is further paid it will exceed the limit by ₹ 2,200 [*i.e.* 50,000 – (47,200 + 5,000)]. Therefore, the banker should not make the payment.

While returning the cheque the banker must give an appropriate answer according to the circumstances of the case. The fittest answer would be "exceeds arrangements", because overdraft arrangement does not permit excess payment. "Refer to drawer" indicates shortage of funds, whereas 'funds expected' and effects not cleared, 'present again' is not applicable as the banker cannot predict the future nor does it have any cheque for collection.

Q. 2. Answer the following:

(i) What will be the due date of the bill dated 28th Nov. 2001, payable 90 days after date.

(ii) Can the balance be paid, in respect of a current A/c in the joint names of X and Y, to be operated upon by both of them jointly, when X dies.

(iii) When a customer calls at the bank's branch after business hours to cash a cheque drawn in his favour by another customer of the same branch, can it be paid?

(iv) Is introduction necessary for opening a saving bank A/c.

Ans: (i) The due date will be:

It is calculated as follows:

Nov. 2 days + Dec. 31 days + Jan. (2002) 31 + Feb. 26 + 3 lag days = 1st March 2002.

Note: If it is a leap year (*i.e.*, any year exactly divided by 4) Feb. will be taken as 29 days for e.g., 1968, 1972, etc.)

(ii) Yes, the balance is payable (on demand of the survivor) if one of the joint A/c holder dies because of the *(a)* Law of Devolution and *(b)* Banking conventions.

(iii) No. The banker should not make the payment of the cheque being presented after working hours (business hours) of the bank because if any mishappenings take place, for e.g., countermanding the payment or Garnishee order of the court, the bank stands liable for the loss.

(iv) Generally, banker requires an introduction of the person applying for the opening of a Saving Bank A/c. But if he does not request for the cheque book facility, introductions may not be insisted upon by the banker.

Q. 3. The payee of a cheque informs the bank on which it is drawn that the cheque drawn in his favour is lost and requests the bank to stop payment of the cheque pending an advice from the drawer. But before the stop-payment instructions are received from the drawer, the cheque is presented through the clearing. How should the drawer bank act?

The drawee bank should send the cheque back with a remark, "reported lost, confirmation awaited". Because the intimations by the payee about the loss of the cheque serves a sufficient cause to doubt the possession and presentations of the cheque. The instructions to stop payment of a cheque can be served on the banker by the drawer only. The banker should, therefore, contact the drawer and seek the confirmations. If the banker pay the cheque, he cannot avail of the statutory protections available to the paying banker.

Q. 4. A cheque of ₹ 2000 drawn by your customer is presented in the clearing on the 26th of February 2002 for payment when the balance in the account is ₹ 1,500 only. The customer happens to have a Fixed Deposit with the bank for a sum of ₹ 500. It is however observed that the cheque is dated standing, the **** How will you act in the circumstances?

Ans: The banker should not make the payment remarking "funds insufficient" as the Fixed Deposit account of a customer is a separate A/c and its amount is payable after the specified period is over. The banker, thus cannot make payment of the cheque on the basis of fixed deposit receipt.

Q. 5. In the body of the cheque the words "Rupees seventy-nine; twenty-two paise are written whilst the figures read ₹ 71.22 p. How should the paying banker deal with such a cheque on presentation?

Ans: Section 18 of the Negotiable Instrument Act, states that if the figures and words on the body of the cheque differ, the amount stated in words shall be the amount ordered to be paid. Thus, the banker may treat the amount in words to be correct. But bankers usually return such type of cheques with remark "amount in word and figures differ" and seek the drawer's confirmation.

Q. 6. A customer of a bank draws a cheque for ₹ 300 inadvertently leaving blanks before the amount both in words and figures. The amount is fraudulently raised by the payee to ₹ 3,300 and the cheque is presented and cashed. Discuss the positions of the bank.

Ans.: The paying banker has to pay the amount directed by the drawer. If the alterations is clear or could be noticed for e.g., overwriting or corrections in figures and words, the banker would be liable for paying the amount fraudulently raised. If the banker is negligent in this regard he will not be protected u/s. 89.

But, if the alterations is not clear and the banker makes payment in good faith without negligence, the banker can justifiably debit his customers A/c. By such negligence the drawer committed a breach of duty towards the banker to exercise due care while drawing the cheque.

☞ Questions

1. What do you understand by "statutory protection" under the Indian Negotiable Instruments Act? Describe the circumstances in which a banker may lose it.
2. Explain the term "collecting banker". What are his duties and responsibilities in the collection of his customer's cheques? Does the law afford him any protection in this connection?
3. What are the rules governing presentment for payment of Promissory Notes, Bills of Exchange and Cheques? When is such presentment unnecessary?
4. What is the legal position of a banker if:
   (a) he pays a cheque after business hours;
   (b) he irregularly dishonours a cheque drawn by his customer?
5. As a paying banker, how would you deal with the following cases;
   (i) In the body of a cheque, the words "Rupees One Thousand Nine Hundred and Ninety" are written, while the figures read as "₹ 1,909".
   (ii) A cheque drawn on you is found to be crossed specially by two banks.
   (iii) A cheque for ₹ 25,000, drawn on an ordinary piece of paper by a customer resident in another town, is presented across the counter for payment.

6. As a paying banker, how would you act in any three of the following situations? Give reasons.
   (i) An order cheque payable to a minor bears his endorsement and is presented for payment by a third person.
   (ii) A cheque, bearing the special crossing of two banks, is presented through clearing for payment.
   (iii) A customer has a credit balance of ₹ 1,500 in his current account in your branch. Three cheques for ₹ 1,200, ₹ 1,000 and ₹ 700 respectively are simultaneously presented for payment through clearing.
   (iv) Yesterday, you had received a letter from your customer A, stopping payment of his cheque bearing No.2175 for ₹ 5,000 favouring B. Today, a cheque drawn by A, bearing No. 2174 for ₹ 5,000 in favour of B, is presented to you for payment.
   (v) A cheque, which had originally been crossed, carries below the crossing a remark "crossing cancelled" and is presented to you for cash payment across the counter.
7. A crossed order cheque drawn by C Bank is collected by D Bank for the latter's customer in whose favour it had been endorsed by the payee. Discuss, with reference to the provisions of the Negotiable Instruments Act, the position of the paying bank and the collecting bank —
   (i) if the signature of the drawer of the cheque has been forged, and
   (ii) if the endorsement of the payee has been forged.
8. When is a negotiable instrument considered dishonoured? Explain the rules for giving notice of dishonour. When is notice of dishonour unnecessary?
9. *(a)* Comment on the statement: "The main risk the banker runs in collecting a cheque for a customer is that of conversion".
   (b) A crossed cheque, which has been stolen, is paid in good faith and without negligence by the bank on which it is drawn to the bank whose crossing stamp it bears. On whom will the loss fall and why?
10. *(a)* Discuss the responsibilities of a payee or holder of a bill in regard to presentment for payment.
    (b) What action should a banker take when a bill is dishonoured either by non-acceptance or payment?
11. A customer pays into credit of his account a cheque payable to his order but incorrectly endorsed by him. The paying bank returns the cheque with the remark: "Endorsement irregular, will pay on collecting bank's confirmation". The endorsement is confirmed by the collecting bank, but it does not inform its customer. The cheque is re-presented but is returned unpaid with the remark: "Refer to Drawer". The collecting bank returns the cheque to its customer, debiting his account.
    (a) What the right of action does the customer have against the collecting bank?
    (b) Discuss the liability of the paying bank by reason of the remark: "Endorsement irregular, will pay on collecting bank's confirmation".
12. Give ánswers, with reasons, setting out the correct position in respect of the following:
    (i) Can a banker evade the consequences of his paying a "Stopped" cheque, if he gives the customer notice when receiving the "Stop" instruction that he will not hold himself responsible for any loss that may be incurred following inadvertent payment?
    (ii) A has current accounts with the Head Office of a Bank and also with its Market Branch. A Garnishee Order is received at the banker's head office, attaching all moneys due to A. What is the position of the account with the Market Branch subsequent to the service of the Garnishee Order on the head office?
    (iii) The Dadar branch of the Working Bank Ltd., is open for business on Sundays but is closed on Wednesdays. Rajaram, a customer of the branch, gives a cheque to Sitaram who goes to the branch on a Wednesday to cash the cheque but finds it closed. Discuss the position of Sitaram *vis-a-vis* the bank for non-payment of the cheque.
13. A draws a cheque for ₹ 1,000 in favour of B at Mumbai. The cheque was a bearer crossed cheque. B sends the cheque to C at Ahmedabad. C again sends the cheque by ordinary post to his Agent F in Mumbai for realisation

of the proceeds. The cheque was intercepted in transit, the crossing thereon removed and the amount of the cheque in words and figures altered in such a manner as not to be visible to the naked eye. The cheque was presented thereafter to the holder and the amount was paid over the counter. Subsequently, A came to know of this payment from his pass book, when he found that a sum bigger than that drawn by him was debited to his account. A filed a suit against the bank for having been wrongly debited for a higher amount. What defence can the banker offer under the Negotiable Instruments Act? Has C any remedy against A's bankers?

14. A joint account is opened by a husband and wife, each having the power to sign cheques. A cheque is presented in the handwriting of and signed by the wife, and altered and initialled by the husband. Is this correct?

15. As a branch manager, how will you deal with the following cases? Give your reasons.
    (*i*) Your customer sends a crossed order cheque drawn by A in favour of your bank, to be credited to his (the customer's) account with you.
    (*ii*) D presents for encashment an uncrossed cheque payable to him or bearer and refuses to endorse the cheque. Will it make any difference if the amount is small?
    (*iii*) A bill dated 29th January, 1968, payable after one month (without grace), remain unpaid on the 28th February, 1968.
    (*iv*) Smt. Radha P. Patel sends you a cheque drawn in favour of Smt. R.P. Patel and endorsed by her as Smt. Radha Patel to be credited to her account with you.
    (*v*) A firm, having A, B and C as partners, enjoys an overdraft limit of ₹ 1 lakh with the bank. A communication is received by the bank that A died on 20th April, 1970, two cheques, signed by the deceased partner on 18th April, 1970, are presented for payment.

16. (*a*) Is the position of the paying banker in India, in regard to legal liability on the ground of negligence, the same as that of the collecting banker? Give reasons for your answer.
    (*b*) Define conversion. Give examples of the circumstances in which an action for conversion would be against a banker in the course of collection of:
        (*i*) Cheques;
        (*ii*) Bills; and
        (*iii*) In the course of any other transaction.

17. A cheque drawn on your branch favouring Krishna and Company and crossed 'Not Negotiable' is endorsed by the payee but presented by Ram & Co. through X bank in clearing. Would you pay the cheque or return it? Give reasons. *[I.I.B., Part I]*
[I.I.B., Part II]

18. As a paying banker, how will you act in the following situations:
    (*i*) A cheque which had originally been crossed is presented to you for payment at the counter bearing the remark "crossing cancelled" below the crossing under the drawer's initials.
    (*ii*) An order cheque payable to a minor aged 17 years bearing his endorsement is presented to you for payment by a third party.
    (*iii*) A customer has a credit balance of ₹ 2,000 in his current account at your branch. Three cheques for ₹ 1,000, ₹ 500 and ₹ 1,200 respectively are simultaneously presented for payment through clearing.
    (*iv*) A cheque is drawn payable to Ramakant Patel or order (the word bearer on the cheque form is crossed out and changed to order). At the request of the payee the word order is crossed out by the drawer under his initials. Should the cheque be considered payable to bearer? *[I.I.B., Part I]*

19. Your accountholder finds, on scrutiny of the entries in his pass book one entry of ₹ 10,000 representing payment of a cheque. According to him the cheque was for ₹ 1,000 only. On examination of the cheque under ultra violet

machine, by a bank, it is observed that the amount was altered from ₹ 1,000 to ₹ 10,000. Your customer demands refund of ₹ 9,000. *[I.I.B., Part I]*

20. How will you deal with the following:
   (a) Mr. Malhotra has been sanctioned a clean overdraft limit of ₹ 40,000, for a period of 12 months from 1st January, 1982. On 1st March, 1982 you are informed of the death of Mr. Malhotra. His account shows a debit balance of ₹ 20,000 on that day. A cheque for ₹ 5,900 payable to the Reserve Bank of India A/c Income Tax Department and dated 25th January, 1982 is presented for payment through clearing.
   (b) A cheque for ₹ 1,000 dated 5th January, 1982 drawn by your customer Mr. X is paid by you on the 18th January, 1982. Your customer on seeing the debit entry in his pass book immediately rushes to the bank and informs you that his signature on the cheque is forged and the bank should not have paid the cheque. He asks you to credit the amount in the account.
   (c) An open bearer cheque for ₹ 10,000 favouring Natraj & Co. Ltd., is presented for cash payment at the counter by an unknown person. Will you, as a banker, pay it or not? Would it make any difference if the cheque is endorsed in blank by the company?
   (d) A wrong credit is shown in the pass book of a customer. Relying on the balance, he draws cheques. Meanwhile the bank finds the mistake. Should the Bank return cheques drawn against such credits? *[I.I.B., Part I]*

21. As a Branch Manager, how would you deal with the following:
   (a) An open bearer cheque for ₹ 1,000 issued by your customer is presented for cash payment. The cheque is in order in all respects except that the amount is written in words only and the amount in figures is omitted.
   (b) A firm having A, B and C as partners, enjoys a clean overdraft facility of ₹ 15,000 with your Branch. A communication is received by the Branch that A died on 20th June, 1977. On 22nd June, 1977 two cheques for ₹ 2,000 and ₹ 3,000 signed by the deceased partner on behalf of the firm on 18th June, 1977 are presented for payment. *[I.I.B., Part I]*
22. Explain the circumstances under which a collecting bank gets protection in collection of cheques under Negotiable Instruments Act. *[I.I.B., Part I]*
23. Define 'Negligence' as contemplated in Section 85 and Section 131 of the Negotiable Instruments Act. Bring out cases of negligence of Banks under the above sections separately. *[I.I.B., Part I]*
24. Your valued customer deposits on 1st March, 1987 a cheque crossed 'Not Negotiable' for ₹ 25,000/- drawn on a nationalised bank in Madras. The cheque is collected by you on 10th March, 1987 and the amount is credited to the account of your customer. After 10 days you received a letter from one Mr. A.B. Desai informing you that the cheque for ₹ 25,000/- collected by you for your customer was stolen from his house. He requests you not to credit the amount of the cheque to your customer's account and directs you to pay the amount to him. What is your legal position as a collecting banker? Give reasons for your answer. *[I.I.B., Part I]*
25. A teacher deposits into his account an outstation cheque for ₹ 800 issued by State Education Authorities. He demands immediate credit in his account against the cheque. Explain your reply. *[I.I.B., Part I]*
26. *(a)* A cheque for ₹ 10,000/- marked 'Account Payee' bearing two different endorsements (one of a payee) is presented for payment in clearing. Would you pay or not? Give reasons.
   (b) Mr. Rao maintains a current account with the upcountry branch of your bank. He approaches you with a crossed cheque for ₹ 5,000/- in his favour drawn on your branch, requesting you to issue a crossed 'Account Payee' demand draft on that upcountry branch. Would you agree or not? Give reasons.
   (c) Whether a cheque in favour of a limited company can be negotiated and credited to an individual's account or to another limited company's account? Give reasons. *[I.I.B., Part I]*

PART - VI

LENDING BY BANKS

CHAPTER 15

Principles of Good Lending

Part-A

Principles

Lending money to different kinds of borrowers is one of the most important functions of a bank. Lending is a risky business. The borrowers from a bank range from individuals to partnership firms, joint stock companies, institutions, societies, corporations, etc., engaged in such activities as farming, transport, business and industry, etc. The nature of their economic activity, the location of business, financial stability, earning and repaying capacity, purpose of advance, security for advance — all differ. To do this business of lending successfully and profitably, a banker has to follow certain principles, some of which are considered below:

☞ Safety

The very survival of a banker depends on the safety of his loans and advances. The ideal position is when all the advances are fully secured. But due to keen competition among bankers, they have to, particularly for Five Year Plans, advance loans which may not be secured. Here, a banker has to use his discretion and judgement about the customer. Therefore, to maintain a banking concern in a sound condition, it is very essential that, the safety of its advances to customers should be its first principle. Care should be taken to ensure that the funds advanced are not subject to any risk of being lost.

☞ Purpose of Advance

Another important point to be studied by a banker before lending is the purpose for which a loan is required and the resources from which the borrower is expected to repay. Loans may be required for productive purposes, trading purposes, agriculture, transport, self-employment. If a loan is required for a non-productive or speculative purpose, the banker should be very cautious in entertaining such a proposition. Even in cases of good business propositions, if they are contrary to national interest or to priorities of the Five Year Plans, the applications for loans may be turned down. The banker should advance loans only for the purposes determined to be worthwhile by the Reserve Bank and the Government. Nowadays, there is a certain amount of official control on bank advances, and a bank has to keep within the limits of such control. For example, Section 21 of the Banking Companies Act, 1949, empowers the Reserve Bank, *inter alia,* to determine the policy to be followed by banks and to give directions as to the purposes for which advances may or may not be made. These powers are used by the Reserve Bank through selective credit control measures.

☞ Borrower — His Character, Capacity, Standing and Means

Wherever a banker lends money, he must carefully consider the chances of his being repaid by the borrowers, which depend upon the character, capacity, standing and means of the borrowers. The banker may sometimes allow a considerable unsecured loan to a substantial customer in whose integrity and honesty he has complete confidence. It is extremely difficult to judge the character of a borrower. Generally, he sincerely wants to repay the bank loan; at the time of maturity, however, he may not be in a position to return it. In the last few years, due to official control by the Reserve Bank and Government's policy to finance self-employed persons, transporters, *e.g.,* taxi drivers, autorickshaw operators, and small farmers and businessmen having no means or standing, the lending bankers have had varied types of experience. But some of the borrowers were not honest; and though they had the capacity to pay the loan instalments, they did not do so. Others, though their capacity and means were not good, some how managed to meet their loan obligations. Character and honesty are subjective, and they can be judged in each case by bank officials on the basis of the information they have and other factors. The standing and means of the borrowers can be known from their bank accounts, business record, market goodwill, etc. The repaying capacity of farmers is always uncertain for their economic well-being depends on the vagaries of nature. The repaying capacity of small businessmen is not easy to assess, for it depends on many factors, *viz.,* the nature of business, purpose of advance, the amount of loan, the period of advance and the source of repayment.

☞ Nature of Business

A business may be subdivided into many categories, *e.g.,* manufacturing business, trading business, import and export business, wholesale and retail business, a business having a monopoly of the market or a business having a keen competition in the market, a business having a tremendous scope for increase in demand or a business having not much scope for increase in future demand. It may be seen here that there may be innumerable types of business and the repaying capacity of a borrower depends, to a great extent, on the nature of the business he is engaged in.

☞ Security

The security offered against the loan may be various. It may vary from gold and silver to stock exchange securities, goods, documents of title to goods, insurance policy and immovable property. The security accepted by a banker to cover a bank advance must be adequate, readily marketable, easy to handle and free from any encumbrance. There may be cases where there is no security except the personal security of the debtor. Whatever be the security, a banker must realise that it is only a cushion to fall back upon in case of need, and its adequacy alone should not form the sole consideration for judging the suitability of a loan. A detailed discussion about the securities has been undertaken in a separate Chapter.

☞ Location of Business

The location of a business largely influences the type of security that may be offered for a bank advance. In big industrial cities like Kolkata, Mumbai, Delhi, Kanpur, Chennai, etc., the banker would naturally be offered a large quantity of shipping documents, or other documents of title to goods as security for advances. In the countryside and in the interior, the security may be the produce of an agricultural area which has to be financed for the purpose of being taken to various centres of consumption. Title deeds of property for the purpose of raising temporary loans are also handled in almost every locality, whether it is in a commercial town or the countryside. In industrial areas the ready goods as well as raw material would be offered as security against advances. A bank, which has a large number of branches, is undoubtedly in a favourable position, because the securities on which its money is advanced are well spread out.

☞ Liquidity

The banker, while making advances, must see to it that the money lent is not locked up for a long time. Liquidity of capital is another important principle of good lending. If a banker advances for the fixed assets requirements of a business, which are of a long-term nature, there is no likelihood of his being able to recall such loans in time to meet the demands of his depositors, in case a general withdrawal of deposits takes place. This is an important aspect of banking, which distinguishes it from insurance finance or industrial finance. Of course, industrial banks, which have a large capital of their own and which borrow funds for long periods generally by the issue of bonds and debentures, can safely lend the required amount for fixed assets, for they can afford to wait for a long time for the repayment of their advances, since their liabilities do not mature on demand or at short notice.

In recent years, Indian commercial banks have also entered the field of industrial finance because of refinance and credit guarantee facilities.

☞ Safe Margin

When a security is offered to cover a bank advance, the banker has to consider two aspects. The first is economic, consisting of an estimate of the probable market value of the security at the time of its realisation, and the second is the legal aspect, that is, the validity of the security offered and the difficulties that may arise in its enforcement. The principle generally followed in these cases, with a view to arriving at the maximum amount which could be safely advanced, is to take the market value of the security offered and leave a sufficiently safe margin, both for fluctuations in value and interest accumulation. The banker should take care to ensure that not only its valuation is accurate but that, in the case of securities of a speculative nature which are subject to heavy fluctuations, the margin of safety is maintained in the form of a much higher percentage than it is in other cases. Moreover, if there is a subsequent fall in the market prices of the securities deposited with the banker, it would be necessary to call for more margin.

☞ National Policy Objectives

In a developing society like India, Banks are also required to fulfil some social responsibilities. After the nationalisation of banks in 1969, a major thrust in the lending policies of banks has been to provide credit facilities to the so far neglected sectors of the economy. Banks are now playing an active role in serving the development needs of the economy in conformity with the national policy and objectives. With the changing perspective, the attitude of banks in following the principle of security in lending to the weaker sections of society has changed. Security for the advances is not demanded exclusively in the tangible assets of the borrower, but banks also rely on the technical competence, managerial ability, honesty and integrity of the borrower. In recent years banks have been providing finance on a large-scale to agriculturists, small industrialists, professional persons, transporters, self-employed, etc., under 'priority sector' and '20-point programme'. Some advances to weaker and underprivileged sections are given at concessional rate of interest. The Deposit Insurance and Credit Guarantee Corporation guarantees such loans. But it may be noted that despite changes in the lending policies, the banks follow the basic principles of sound lending which are fundamental. However, the methods of lending are from time-to-time modified to suit the present needs of the society.

PART-B
Analysis of Financial Statements

When a borrower approaches a bank with a credit proposal, the banker should thoroughly investigate the following before granting any credit:

(i) An appraisal of the credit proposal;

(ii) An evaluation of the borrower's creditworthiness; and

(iii) An analysis of financial statements.

The first two aspects of the investigation have been discussed elsewhere in this book. In this Chapter, we propose to discuss the third aspect, *viz.,* analysis of financial statements. The two most important financial statements of a business are its profit-and-loss account and its balance sheet. The profit-and-loss account shows the financial results of the working of an enterprise over a period of time. This statement summarises the transactions which together result in a profit (or loss) for a specific period of time. The balance sheet is a statement of the financial position of a business enterprise. Since every accounting transaction influences a balance sheet, this statement may be regarded as a fundamental accounting report for any business enterprise. The balance sheet accomplishes the function of stating the financial position of a business by listing separately the resources owned by it and the equities of creditors and owners in these assets. Modern management has developed techniques for analysis and interpretation of financial statements from the point of view of credit appraisal.

The rules for the study and interpretation of financial statements are generally the same for a sole trader, a firm and a joint stock company, except that in the case of a sole trader, his balance sheet may be unreliable owing to the absence of the legal obligation regarding its form or its audit. It is more important to study the profit-and-loss account of a sole trader rather than his balance sheet. Such a study would show the scale of his operations, whether profits are in excess of drawings, and whether the business is progressing. Because the liability of partners is unlimited, the banker may, in case of necessity, call upon the personal assets of all the partners for the redemption of the loan advanced to them. That is the reason why the balance sheet of a partnership firm is generally conservative and accurate. In the case of a limited liability company, it must conform to the requirements of the Companies Act, and must be audited by a Chartered Accountant, and is, therefore, very reliable.

☞ Reserve Bank's Guidelines

While granting advances to big enterprises for amounts exceeding ₹ 6 crore, the commercial banks were required to seek prior sanction of the Reserve Bank under the Credit Authorisation Scheme. The Reserve Bank granted its permission after duly considering all aspects of the credit proposal of the borrowing concern. For this purpose the banks are required to furnish to the Reserve Bank detailed financial data relating to the borrowing concern. With effect from March 1, 1976 the Reserve Bank requires, *inter alia*, analysis of balance sheets and profit and loss accounts for four years, *i.e.,* actuals for the last two years, estimates for the current year and projections for the following year. For this purpose it has designed appropriate proforma which has been revised with effect from March 1, 1976 and has issued necessary guidelines for collecting and interpreting the required data. The Reserve Bank has also advised the banks to follow the practice of financial statement analysis for their own purposes in respect of appraisal of larger individual credit proposals so that the credit appraisal may be placed on more organised footing. We shall follow the appraisal procedure suggested by the Reserve Bank to the banks under its credit Authorisation Scheme.

☞ Analysis of Balance Sheet

A balance sheet represents the financial status of a business entity, and is often titled as a *"Statement of Financial Position"* or a *"Position Statement"* or a *"Statement of Sources and Use of Funds"*. The balance sheet of a company may be evaluated in two stages. *Firstly,* by an analysis of different assets and liabilities given in the balance sheet. *Secondly,* by determining and interpreting the numerical relationship between the different items in the balance sheet. This type of analysis is called *ratio analysis.*

☞ Classification of Assets and Liabilities

The first step in the analysis of a balance sheet is the study of various assets and liabilities and their classification into various categories.

☞ Assets

Assets are things of value owned by a business and acquired at a cost which is measurable. An asset must be: *(i)* valuable to the business; *(ii)* owned by the business; and *(iii)* acquired at a measurable cost. When it is difficult to determine the exact cost of an asset, the best course of action is to use the best possible estimate of value that can be made on the basis of available information. All assets may be divided into four categories; *(i)* Current Assets; *(ii)* Fixed Assets; *(iii)* Miscellaneous Assets; and *(iv)* Intangible Assets.

☞ Current Assets

In accounting statements, current assets include cash and other things of value, which can be realised in cash or which can be consumed or sold during the normal operating cycle of a business. The normal operating cycle of a business is the time required to complete a cash-to-assets and from assets-to-cash cycle. In a manufacturing enterprise, cash or credit is used to purchase raw materials and other services, which are then processed or manufactured into semi-finished goods. The finished goods are then sold either for cash or on credit. At intermediate stages within the cycle, the enterprise may hold things of value. Such assets are regarded as current assets. Therefore, in order to qualify as a current asset, an item must be convertible into cash within the normal operating cycle of a business. These assets are also called *circulating assets.* Current assets are important because they signify the liquidity position of a business. The larger the quantum of current assets, the greater are the possibilities of the repayment of loans which are repayable on demand or at short notice. Some of the items included under the head "current assets" are given below:

(i) Cash and Bank Balance: Cash and bank balances represent funds available for immediate disbursement. Cash consists of coins and notes, while the bank balance represents the amount in the firm's account with the bank. Cash and bank balances ensure liquidity and repaying capacity but they should be kept within a reasonable limit because they are non-earning assets.

(ii) Stocks (Inventory): Stocks, also called inventories, may consist of raw materials awaiting manufacture or processing, semi-finished products or work-in-progress awaiting sale. The types of inventories held depend on the nature of the business. A manufacturing enterprise may hold all the three kinds of inventories; a grocer or provision store, on the other hand, holds only finished or packaged goods for sale. Following basic accounting conventions, stocks are valued at cost or market value, whichever is less.

Inventories held by an undertaking should have a proper relation with sales. If the inventory-sales ratio is high, the banker should ascertain the reasons thereof.

(iii) Investments in Securities: Many a times surplus funds with a business undertaking are invested in marketable securities. Such investment may be either in Government securities or in shares and debentures of other business entities. The specific investments to be made depend on the entity's preference between liquidity, income and risk. For example, investment in a fixed interest-bearing Government security may yield a lower return than investments in equity shares of a company; but the Government security may be safer than company shares. Investments in securities strengthen the liquidity position of an undertaking because these assets are easily and quickly realisable.

It may be noted here that only those securities which can be easily sold in the market are deemed to be current assets. In the case of partly paid-up securities, the investor is responsible for the payment of uncalled money.

(iv) Sundry Debtors (Book Debts): Sundry debtors and bills receivable which are outstanding for not more than six months are treated as current assets. The banker should scrutinise these and if the book debts are realisable, he should compare the amount of book debts with the total credit sales effected.

☞ Fixed Assets

Fixed assets are tangible things of value owned by an undertaking for carrying on production operations over a long period of time. These assets are real and can be seen and touched, and are owned by a business undertaking because it expects to use them for the production of goods and services over a long period of time. The length of time for which a fixed asset is useful depends on the nature of the asset. Land, for instance, is assumed to be permanently useful. The useful life of plant and machinery, on the other hand, depends on the physical characteristics of the assets and technological and economic usefulness. Following the concept of cost basis of valuation, fixed assets are shown on the balance sheet at original cost. From this original cost, accumulated depreciation is deducted, leaving the assets on the balance sheet at net value or depreciated value.

☞ Miscellaneous Assets

Investments in the securities of subsidiary companies may not be marketable and are, therefore, placed in the category of miscellaneous assets. In the case of book debts, the receivable debts and bills which are outstanding for more than six months are included in the category of miscellaneous assets. According to the Companies Act, debt due and outstanding for more than six months (miscellaneous assets) are shown separately in the balance sheet.

☞ Intangible Assets

Intangible assets include goodwill, trade marks, patents and similar things of value owned by a business. Intangible assets are non-physical and intangible in nature, but have quite a long period of usefulness to the business. A patent, for example, has a legal life ranging from seven to seventeen years. Before advancing a loan, a banker has to ascertain whether the total amount of intangible assets is unusually large because they have no realisable value and because the "tangible net worth" of an enterprise is reduced by the amount of such intangible assets.

ANALYSIS OF BALANCE SHEET
PART A — BALANCE SHEET SPREAD

Liabilities	*20...20...* *Last 2 years Actuals as per audited B/S*	*20...* *Current year's Estimates*	*20...* *Following years' Projections*
CURRENT LIABILITIES			
1. Short-term borrowings from banks (including bills purchased and discounted and the excess borrowings placed on repayment basis)			
(i) from application			
(ii) from the banks			
Sub-total (A)			
2. Short-term borrowings from others			
3. Deposits (maturing within one year)			
4. Sundry Creditors (Trade)			
5. Unsecured loans			
6. Advances/progress payments from customers, deposits from dealers, selling agents, etc.			
7. Interest and other charges accrued but not due for payment			
8. Provision for taxation			
9. Dividend payable			
10. Other statutory liabilities (due within one year)			
11. Instalment of term loans/deferred payment, credit debentures redeemed/preference shares due within 1year.			
12. Other liabilities and provisions (due within one year			
Sub-total (B)			
13. Total Current Liabilities (Total of items 1 to 12)			
TERMS LIABILITIES			
14. Debentures (not maturing within one year)			
15. Redeemable Preference Shares (not maturing within one year, but of maturity not exceeding 12 years)			
16. Term loans (exclusive of instalment payable within one year)			
17. Deferred payment credits (exclusive of instalments payable within one year)			
18. Term deposits (repayable after one year)			
19. Other term Liabilities			
20. Total Term Liabilities (Total of items 14 to 19)			
21. Total Outside Liabilities (items 13+20)			
NET WORTH			
22. Equity Share Capital			
23. Preference Share Capital (maturing after 12 years)			
24. General Reserve			
25. Development Rebate Reserve			
26. Other Reserves (excluding provisions)			
27. Surplus or deficits in Profit and Loss account			
28. Net Worth (total of items 22 to 27)			
29. Total Liabilities (items 21 plus item 28)			

Liabilities	*20...20... Last 2 years Actuals as per audited B/S*	*20... Current year's Estimates*	*20... Following years' Projections*
CURRENT ASSETS			
30. Cash and bank balance			
31.Investments (other than long-term investment, e.g., Sinking Funds, Gratuity Fund. etc.)			
(i) Government and other Trustee Securities			
(ii) Fixed deposits with banks			
32. *(i)* Receivable other than deferred and export receivables (including bills purchased and discounted by bankers)			
(ii) Export receivables (including bills purchased and discounted by bankers)			
33. Instalments of deferred receivables (due within one year)			
34. Inventory			
(i) Raw materials			
(a) Imported			
(b) Indigenous			
(ii) Stocks-in-process			
(iii) Finished goods			
(iv) Other Consumable Spares			
35. Advances to suppliers of raw materials, Stores, Spares, Consumables			
36. Advance payment of taxes			
37. Other current assets			
38. Total Current Assets (Total of items 30 to 37)			
FIXED ASSETS			
39. Gross Block (land and buildings), machinery, construction in progress, etc.			
40. Depreciation to date			
41. Net Block (item 39 minus item 40)			
OTHER NON-CURRENT ASSETS			
42. Investments, book debts, advance deposits which are not current assets.			
(i) (a) Investments in Subsidiary Companies/affiliates			
(b) Others			
(ii) Advances to Suppliers of Capital goods/spares and Contractors for Capital expenditure			
(iii) Deferred receivables (other than those maturing within 1 year)			
43. Non-consumable Stores and Spares			
44. Other miscellaneous assets including dues from directors			
45. Total other Non-current Assets (Total of items 42 to 44)			
46. Intangible Assets (Patents, Goodwill, Preliminary and formation expenses, Bad/Doubtful debts not provided for, etc.)			
47. Total Assets (total of items 38, 41, 45 and 47)			
48. Tangible Net worth (item 28 minus item 46)			
49. Net Working Capital (item 38 minus item 13)			

☞ Liabilities

Liabilities represent the claims of outsiders on the assets of a business undertaking or the amounts that a company owes to persons other than the owners of the company. Except in specific cases, liabilities represent a general claim of outsiders on all the assets of a company. Specific claims of outsiders on specific assets of a company arise when the company, for example, has mortgaged its plant and machinery in return for a long-term loan.

Liabilities are classified on the basis of: *(a)* contractual agreement, and of *(b)* time element.

☞ Contractual Agreement

Normally, a company enters into a specific contract when it obtains funds from outsiders by mortgaging its assets. No such contract for payment is entered into when creditors extend credit to a company for the purchase of inventories of supplies. This distinction in the nature of the contracts gives rise to the classification of liabilities as secured liabilities or unsecured liabilities.

☞ Time Element

It is normally assumed that a company will honour and discharge its obligations as and when they become due. But some commitments may become due for payment within one year, while others may have to be discharged after a period of one year. The distinction in timing leads to distinction between long-term liabilities (term liabilities) and current liabilities.

Long-term Liabilities

☞ Loans

Loans are promises for future payments. As distinguished from current liabilities, they have to be repaid in periods beyond a year and are therefore, long-term liabilities.

☞ Debentures

Debentures are issued by companies when additional funds are required to finance their business operations. A debenture is a promise to repay the debentureholder at a distant maturity date. Generally, a company's promise is evidenced by legal documents, and where debentures are secured by the mortgage or pledge of specific assets, such mortgage is disclosed in the balance sheet.

☞ Bank Overdraft

A bank overdraft is a credit facility provided to a company by commercial banks. Unlike debentures which have to be repaid on a certain date, bank overdrafts may be a continuing facility available to a company. While debentures issued by a company can be traded on the stock markets, no such trading facility is available on overdrafts. On some balance sheets, bank overdrafts are traced as current liabilities.

☞ Fixed Deposits

In India, joint-stock companies accept fixed deposits from individuals and other parties. A company pays interest every year on these fixed deposits with an added agreement to return the deposits on a specified date.

☞ Current Liabilities

Current liabilities are required or expected to be honoured or discharged within a period of one year through the use of current assets. The current liabilities portion of long-term liabilities is also included in this classification; for example, that portion of a long-term liability which has to be discharged within one year's period.

☞ Sundry Creditors

Sundry creditors represent the claims of suppliers or other parties. The liability owed to sundry creditors is not secured against any specific assets of the company but is generally discharged through the use of current assets.

☞ Provision for Taxes

Provision for taxes represents the estimated amount owed to Government for taxes. The figure is called a "provision" since it is only an estimate of tax liability. The exact tax liability is determined after a scrutiny of accounts and assessment by the income-tax authorities. Generally, income-tax liability is shown separately from other tax liabilities (like State and local taxes, sales tax, etc.), not only because of the size of the amount, but also because it constitutes an important information for the users of financial statements.

☞ Other Current Liabilities

Other current liabilities include payments due on expenses, interest on long-term loans and debentures and other charges, wages and salaries unpaid or unclaimed amounts of dividend, etc. Payment due on expenses are similar to payments due to sundry creditors since they are generally discharged within a period of one year through the use of current assets.

☞ Owner's Equity (the Net Worth)

In addition to the liabilities due to outsiders, other items on the liabilities side of the balance sheet consist of paid-up share capital and the retained profits kept in the form of general reserves or other general reserves. The credit balance in the profit-and-loss account (net profit) is a part of the owned funds. But reserves made for specific purposes like depreciation, bad and doubtful debts, etc., are treated as current liabilities and do not form part of the owned funds because these funds are to be spent for a specified purpose.

All the items of the owner's equity constitute the *net worth* of the company which can be found out by deducting from the net assets (*i.e.*, excess of assets over liabilities), fictitious or intangible assets such as goodwill, balance of suspense account, etc., as these assets may not realise their book value. The owner's equity or net worth of a company must be sufficient, considering the requirements of a company. For the creditors, the net worth of a borrowing company is significant, because it indicates the extent of the solvency of the borrower.

☞ Contingent Liability

Contingent liabilities are liabilities which do not exist at the time of the balance sheet but which may arise in future; for example, arrears of cumulative dividends, liability as a surety, gratuity scheme for staff, etc. Such liabilities are shown not in the balance sheet but in a footnote to the balance sheet. The banker should assess the extent of such liabilities in relation to the financial resources of the company.

The most important part of a business are its current assets because they earn the profits which provide an adequate return on the capital employed. Therefore, current assets should be a good proportion of the total assets, and a business should not be overloaded with fixed assets. Different types of business have different proportions of fixed assets to current assets. A business having a smaller amount of capital blocked in fixed assets and more in current assets is considered to be a healthier one. In addition to actual reserves shown in the balance sheet, there may be "secret reserves" which are created by overdepreciating the fixed assets, undervaluing stock, excessive provision for bad and doubtful debts, etc. This type of creation of secret reserves results in an understatement of the disclosed profits and a reduction in the book value of the assets concerned.

An important item of the balance sheet is "debtors", for it is a current asset which actually produces cash. The banker should demand from the borrower a full list of his debtors because it is not good if a large amount is outstanding against one party. The debt should be well spread among many parties. Two aspects have to be considered in ascertaining the creditworthiness of a borrower, *viz.*, *(a)* a reasonable certainty about loan repayment at the time of maturity, and *(b)* if not paid on maturity, the chances of being paid at all. To study the first part of creditworthiness, the banker should find out the relation of current assets to current liabilities. To judge the second aspect of creditworthiness, he should consider the relationship of fixed assets to permanent liabilities.

Entering into contracts beyond a person's capacity to finance is called overtrading. The banker should carefully scrutinise the balance sheet of his borrower to assure himself that the borrower is not guilty of overtrading, which results in difficulties for all the creditors. Some important indicators of overtrading are:

(a) A tendency for the debtor-creditor ratio to fall progressively, generally caused by the increasing difficulty in paying creditors as the debts fall due.

(b) Increase in borrowings from bank and creditors without a proportionate increase in production or sale.

(c) Reduction in bills receivable due to discounting.

(d) Excessive amount of bills payable and a gradual fall in liquid resources.

The most important advantage of the assessment of the profit-and-loss account and balance sheet of a borrower is that one can detect trouble at an early stage (before sanctioning the loan), so that the banker may not ultimately get involved in the borrower's insolvency.

☞ Ratio Analysis

Ratio analysis is a widely used tool of financial analysis. It is defined as a systematic use of ratios to interpret the financial statements so that the strengths and weaknesses of a firm, as well as its historical performance and current financial conditions can be determined.

A banker analyses and interprets the financial statements so as to evaluate the solvency or repayment capacity of the borrower, *i.e.,* financial soundness and stability. Apart from this, their concern is to know the profitability or the earning capacity of the concern.

Ratios make the related informations comparable. A single figure by itself has no meaning, but when expressed in terms of related figures, it yields significant inferences. Thus, ratios are 'relative figures' reflecting the relationship between related variables. Their use as tool of financial analysis involves their comparison as single ratios, like absolute figures, are not of much use. Three types of comparisons are generally involved namely: *(i)* trend analysis *(ii)* inter-firm comparisons, and *(iii)* comparison with standards or industry average.

☞ Liquidity Ratios

Liquidity ratios measure the ability of the firm to meet its short-term obligations and reflect its short-term financial strength or solvency. The important liquidity ratios are: *(a)* current ratio, and *(b)* quick or acid test ratio.

Current ratio is the ratio of total Current Assets (CA) to total Current Liabilities (CL). A satisfactory current ratio would enable a firm to meet its obligations, even if the value of CA declines. It is however, a quantitative index of liquidity as it does not differentiate among the components of CA, such as cash and inventory which are not equally liquid.

The quick or acid test ratio takes into considerations the differences in the liquidity of the components of CA. It represents the ratio between quick CA and the total CL. It is a rigorous measure and superior to the current ratio. However, both these ratios must be used as complementary to each other to analyse the liquidity position of a firm

☞ Types of Ratios

Ratios can broadly be classified into four groups. Liquidity, capital structure or leverage, profitability and activity or turnover ratio.

The main liquidity ratios are:

1. Net Working Capital (NWC) = Current Assets – Current Liabilities

2. $$\text{Current ratio} = \frac{\text{Current Assets}}{\text{Current Liabilities}}$$

3. $$\text{Acid Test or Quick ratio} = \frac{\text{Cash} + \text{Assets} - \text{Stock} - \text{Pre-paid expenses}}{\text{Current Liabilities}} \text{ or}$$

$$\frac{\text{Cash} + \text{Marketable Securities} + \text{Debtors}}{\text{Current Liabilities}}$$

4. $$\text{Super quick ratio} = \frac{\text{Cash} + \text{Marketable Securities}}{\text{Current Liabilities}}$$

☞ Capital Structure or Leverage Ratios or Solvency Ratios

These ratios throw light on the long-term solvency of a firm. This is reflected by its ability to periodic payment of interest, repayment of loan on maturity, etc.

1. $$\text{Debt equity ratio} = \frac{\text{Long-term debts}}{\text{Shareholder funds}}$$

2. $$\text{Debt to total funds ratio} = \frac{\text{Long-term debts}}{\text{Shareholder funds} + \text{Long-term debts}}$$

3. $$\text{Debt to total assets ratio} = \frac{\text{Total debt}}{\text{Total assets}}$$

4. Proprietory ratio $= \dfrac{\text{Owner's funds}}{\text{Total assets}}$

5. Capital gearing ratio $= \dfrac{\text{Preference share capital + Debentures + Other borrowed funds}}{\text{Equity funds (net worth)}}$

6. Interests coverage ratio $= \dfrac{\text{Earnings before interest and taxes (EBIT)}}{\text{Fixed interest charge}}$

7. Dividend coverage ratio $= \dfrac{\text{EAT (Earning after tax)}}{\text{Preference dividend}}$

The objective of computing these ratios is to measure the degree of protections enjoyed by long-term lenders.

Profitability ratios: These ratios are computed to measure the profitability of the firm. It is a measure of efficiency and control of management. Profitability ratios may be calculated on the basis of sales or on the basis of investment.

A. On the Basis of Sales

(a) Gross profit profit ratio $= \dfrac{\text{Gross Profit}}{\text{Net sales}} \times 100$

(b) Net profit ratio $= \dfrac{\text{Net Profit}}{\text{Net sales}} \times 100$

(c) Operating profit ratio $= \dfrac{\text{Operating profit}}{\text{Net sales}} \times 100$

(d) Operating ratio $= \dfrac{\text{Operating cost}}{\text{Net sales}} \times 100$

B. On the Basis of Investment

(a) Return on investment $= \dfrac{\text{EBIT}}{\text{Capital employed}} \times 100$

(Return on capital employed)

(Capital employed = Shareholder's funds + Long-term debts – fictitious assets)

(b) Return on Equity $= \dfrac{\text{Earning after interest and tax but before Preference dividend}}{\text{Shareholders funds}} \times 100$

(c) Earnings per share = $\dfrac{\text{Net profit available for eq. shareholders}}{\text{No. of eq. shares}}$

(d) Price earning ratio = $\dfrac{\text{Market price}}{\text{Dividend per share}}$

☞ Activity/Turnover/Efficiency Ratios

The last category of ratios is the activity or turnover ratios. They are also known as efficiency ratios such ratios, are concerned with measuring the efficiency in asset management. The efficiency with which the assets are managed/used is reflected in the speed and rapidity with which they are converted into sales. Thus, the activity ratios are a test of relationship between sales/cost of sales and assets. Depending upon the type of Assets, activity ratios may be: *(a)* Inventory or stock turnover *(b)* Receivables/debtors turnover, *(c)* Total assets turnover, and *(d)* creditors turnover.

Formulas:

(1) Raw material turnover = $\dfrac{\text{Cost of raw material used}}{\text{Average raw material inventory}}$

(2) Work-in-process turnover (WIP) = $\dfrac{\text{Cost of goods manufactured}}{\text{Average WIP inventory}}$

(3) Finished goods inventory turnover = $\dfrac{\text{Cost of goods sold}}{\text{Average finished goods inventory}}$

(4) Debtors turnover ratio (DTR) = $\dfrac{\text{Total credit sales}}{\text{Average debtors + Average B / R}}$

(5) Debt collections period = $\dfrac{\text{Months in a year or no. of days in a year}}{\text{Debtors turnover ratio (DTR)}}$

(6) Total assets turnover ratio = $\dfrac{\text{Cost of goods sold}}{\text{Average total assets (Fixed + Current)}}$

(7) Working capital turnover ratio = $\dfrac{\text{Cost of goods sold (COGS)}}{\text{Average net working capital}}$

(8) Creditors turnover ratio (CTR) = $\dfrac{\text{Net credit purchases}}{\text{Average creditors}}$

(9) Creditors payment period = $\dfrac{\text{No. of days or months in a year}}{\text{Creditors Turnover Ratio (CTR)}}$

(10) Stock turnover ratio $= \dfrac{\text{COGS}}{\text{Average stock}}$

$$\text{Average stock} = \frac{\text{Opening stock} + \text{closing stock}}{2}$$

$$\text{COGS} = \text{Opening stock} + \text{Purchases} + \text{Direct Expenses } (-) \text{ Closing stock}$$

PART – B
ANALYTICAL AND COMPARATIVE RATIOS

	20.......20...... *Last 2 years' Actuals as per audited B/S*	*20.....* *Current year's Estimates*	*20......* *Following years' Projections*
1. Net Sales			
2. % rise or fall in net sales during the year as compared to previous year			
3. Profit (before tax) or loss			
4. Net Profit (*i.e.,* after tax) or loss			
5. *(a)* Equity dividend declared			
(b) Equity dividend paid			
(c) Rate % of (a)			
(d) Rate % of (b)			
6. Retained profit			
7. Retained Profit % Net Profit			
8. Raw Materials (including Stores and other items used in the process of manufacture)			
(a) Imported			
How many months' consumption these represent?			
(b) Indigenous			
How many months consumption these represent?			
9. Stock in process			
How many months' cost of production these represent?			
10. Finished goods			
How many months' cost of sales do these represent?			
11. Other consumable spares			
What is the percentage of total inventory and how many months, normal consumption do these represent?			

	20.......20...... Last 2 years' Actuals as per audited B/S	20..... Current year's Estimates	20...... Following years' Projections
12. (a) Receivables other than deferred receivables and export receivables (including bills purchased and discounted by bankers)			
How many months' domestic sales other than sales on deferred payment basis do these represent?			
(b) Export receivables			
How many months' export sales do these represent?			
(c) Deferred receivables			
13. Sundry Creditors (trade)			
How many months' purchase do these represent?			
14. Net Working Capital			
15. Current Ratio (item 38/ item 13)			
16. Tangible Net worth (item 48)			
17. (a) Total outside Liabilities/tangible net worth (item 21/item 48)			
(b) Total terms liabilities/tangible net worth (item 21/item 48)			
18. (a) Bank Borrowings/Total outside liabilities (item 1/item 21)			
(b) Net Sales/Total tangible assets.			

☞ Comparison with Standards

Ratios will not be of much use unless they are compared with certain predetermined standards. In financial management, four common standards are used in ratio analysis. They are budgeted standard, horizontal standard, historical standard and absolute standard. The budgeted standard is prepared on the basis of the budget of a company. Financial ratios are planned in the budget (budgeted standard) and then they are compared with ratios developed from actual performance in order to evaluate the degree of accomplishment of the planned targets of the company. If properly prepared after taking external and internal conditions into account, the budgeted standard can be a very useful tool of financial analysis. In a *horizontal* or *external standard*, ratios of the company are compared with those of another company in the same line. But in this method of comparison of industry ratio with a company ratio, the greatest disadvantage is that no two companies are similar. The *historical* or *internal* standard involves a comparison of a company's own past performance as a standard for the present or future. The *absolute* standards are those which are generally recognised as being desirable regardless of the type of company, the time stage of the business cycle, or the objectives of the analyst.

Part-C

Term Lending

Banks in India have been providing only short-term loans to business houses; and this has been regarded as one of the defects of the Indian banking system. But in the last few years, Indian banks have started giving medium and long-term advances, popularly known as *term loans*. So far, the only source of term loans to business and industry were the specialised financial institutions set up for this purpose. But it was thought necessary that commercial banks should also start term lending because of their close association with customers and a well-organised network of branches throughout the country. Term lending, which is also known as *developmental banking*, is gradually developing in India, and a significant change is noticeable in the whole pattern of industrial financing.

☞ Term Loans

Term loans are given for medium and long periods, and loans are used for acquiring fixed assets or for modernisation and expansion of existing units. They may also be used for working capital requirements. An important feature of term loans is the fact that they are repayable in yearly or half-yearly instalments over a period of time. Payment is to be made according to a specified schedule, extending up to 15 years, which imposes a sort of financial discipline on the borrowing concern. The amortisation generally starts 2 or 3 years after the sanction of the loan. Together with the normal interest, a commitment charge of one per cent per annum is also levied on the unutilised portion of the loan. Term loans are secured by a first legal mortgage of the block assets of the borrowing concern. In some cases, an equitable mortgage and a second charge are also agreed upon. The basic point in term lending is that the borrower should utilise the amount in such a way as to repay the loan as well as the interest accruing thereon from the anticipated income earned by the use of that loan itself. This is the reason why before allowing a term credit, the banker evaluates the technical and economic viability of the project for which the loan is sought and also the repaying capacity of the borrowing concern.

In India, commercial banks extend term credit to business or industrial houses in collaboration with other banks and such specialised financial institutions as the Industrial Finance Corporation, the State Finance Corporation and the Industrial Credit and Investment Corporation. The Industrial Development Bank of India provides refinance facilities for term loans sanctioned by commercial banks. In term lending, the lending banker constantly evaluates the working of the borrowing institution because on its efficient and proper working depends the repayment of instalments of loan and interest.

☞ Appraisal of Term Loans

In term lending, the main task of the lending institution is to make sure that the income generated from the loan is sufficient to repay the loan instalments according to the terms and conditions of amortisation. The risk involved in term lending is much more than the risk in short-term lending because the loans are given to new undertakings, or for the modernisation and expansion of existing undertakings, and for long periods. Term loans are to be repaid, not by liquidating the assets but from the increased earnings of the borrowing concern, resulting from a higher level of utilisation of existing installed capacity or additional capacity built-up by the use of the loan. Therefore, before sanctioning any term loan, a banker should assure himself that the borrowing concern shall be able to earn sufficient income to pay the loan instalments. The methods of analysis and standards to be adopted for an appraisal of term loans are more similar to investment decisions than to short-term lending. The appraisal of term loans includes projection of future trends of output, sales, estimates of costs, returns and flow of funds. It is extremely difficult to have a clear-cut formula for the appraisal of term loans, since many factors have to be considered, such as the type of borrowing institution and its activities, the size of the company, its product and/or services, the market potential, its management, financial position, the amount of loan and the period of its repayment. Another important factor is whether to give weightage to profitability or to its broad economic significance in the development of the economy. The extent of Government support in the form of concessional land, electricity, power, transport rates, subsidy for export promotion and exchange regulations also needs consideration in an appraisal of term loan.

A term loan may be appraised by considering four different aspects of the proposal. They are: *(i)* Technical Feasibility; *(ii)* Economic Feasibility; *(iii)* Managerial Competence; and *(iv)* Financial or Commercial Feasibility.

(i) Technical Feasibility: Technical feasibility includes an assessment of two important factors:

(a) Technology or technical know-how to be used in the project; whether it is Indian or foreign know-how is to be imported; whether the technology to be used will be appropriate in Indian conditions. If the technology is too sophisticated, can it be usefully operated in India by Indian technicians?

(b) Availability of land, transport, raw materials, power, water, etc., for the project. These requirements are to be assessed in relation to the location of the firm. Highly competent and qualified technical personnel should be employed by the lending banker to appraise the technical feasibility of a project in the light of the factors mentioned above.

(ii) Economic Feasibility: While examining the economic feasibility of a project, an appraisal is made of the possible demand for the product to be manufactured by the undertaking seeking the loan. Several other diverse factors are to be considered in forecasting demand, and it is not always easy to make a correct forecast. But it becomes necessary to evaluate a project before it is started — whether the output will be usefully absorbed in the economy. If there is no demand for the new product, all the economic activity will go waste and the project or undertaking will become economically unfeasible.

(iii) Managerial Competence: The organisational and administrative set up of the borrowing undertaking is also appraised with a view to assessing whether this organisational structure is proper and scientific and whether those who occupy managerial positions are qualified and competent to handle the affairs of the company in a proper manner.

(iv) Financial Feasibility: Financial feasibility is concerned with an appraisal of the financial soundness of the project. In a financial appraisal, an evaluation is made of the different sources of finance, and an attempt is made to determine whether they will be adequate to cover the total needs of the whole project, whether the cost of calculations are realistic, and whether they will cover all the items of expenditure. Another important point to be evaluated is the effect of the term loan on the production, sale, earnings, costs, etc., of the borrowing concern.

On the basis of such financial appraisal, the financial position of the borrowing concern over a period of years is assessed, and the period of loan as well as the repayment instalments are determined accordingly. For a detailed financial feasibility study, the following types of data are required:

(i) The cost of project;

(ii) The cost of production and profitability;

(iii) Cash flow estimated during the period of the loan; and

(iv) Proforma balance sheet.

☞ The Cost of the Project

An appraisal of the cost of a project covers an examination of expenditure (already incurred and to be incurred) on different items, including estimates of contingent expenditure. The items included in the cost of a project are land, buildings, plant and machinery, transportation and erection of machines, preliminary expenses, technical know-how and consultancy fees, intangibles and provision for contingencies, etc.

The cost of a project is examined in relation to the various sources from which the total project is to be financed. Some of the normal sources of financing a project are ownership capital, reserves, borrowings, etc. The banker has to see to it that there is a proper balance between owned capital and borrowed capital (debt-equity ratio). After an evaluation of the cost of the project and the various sources of financing it, it is phased according to a specific time schedule, and arrangement is made to procure the funds from different sources according to this time schedule.

COST OF THE PROJECT
TOTAL TIME REQUIRED FOR THE COMPLETION OF A PROJECT

	Amount already incurred (₹ equivalent to Foreign Exchange)	*Amount to be incurred (₹ equivalent to Foreign Exchange)*
Land (incl. dev. charges)		
Buildings		
Machinery (incl. freight, transportation, erection, etc.)		
Technical know-how/ Consultancy Fees		
Preliminary Expenses		
Intangibles		
Contingent Expenses		
Total		
Working Capital requirements		
General Total		

☞ Cost of Production and Profitability

This statement includes an estimate of all the different types of costs to be incurred on the production, *viz.,* cost of raw materials, labour, power, repairs, overheads, selling and advertising expenses, depreciation, etc. An estimate of sales and other income is also given year-wise. When all the production expenses are deducted from the sales and other income, the balance will be the operating profit. The net profit may be ascertained after deduction of taxes from the operating profit. Then the ratio of operating profit to sales, sales to capital employed and profits to capitalisation may be calculated.

The table given below shows how information about the cost of production and profitability may be presented.

COST OF PRODUCTION AND PROFITABILITY

Particulars	*(Amount in Rupees)* *Installation/Construction*
	I yr II yr III yr IV yr V yr I yr II yr III yr IVyr
Production (Quantity of Production)	
Cost of Production	
Raw materials	
Labour	
Power	
Repairs	
Overheads	
Selling and Advertising	
Depreciation	

Other expenses	
Operating Profit	
Less: Taxes	
Net Profit	

Ratios: Ratio of Profit to Sales
Sales to Capital employed
Profits to Capital.

☞ Estimates of Cash Flow

In term lending, a banker has to know the time schedule of cash requirements for different purposes and also the sources from which such requirements will be met. These requirements of funds and the sources of funds are given in the form of cash flow estimates or cash flow statements. A cash flow statement shows the sources of funds and the application of funds over different periods of time. This is a very important statement. In the first place, it ensures sound financial planning. Funds should be available throughout the period a project is being executed according to the requirements at different times. Secondly, from the cash flow statements, the lending banker can have information which will enable him to determine the period of the loan he may want to offer and cash flow statement is prepared in two parts, one containing the sources of funds and the other indicating the use of funds. A specimen of a cash flow statement is given below:

CASH FLOW STATEMENT

(Amount in Rupees)

	I yr	*II yr*	*III yr*	*IV yr*	*V yr*
Sources of Funds					
(a) Co.'s own Sources					
Net Profit (before taxes and interest and after depreciation)					
(b) Outside Sources					
(i) Share capital increase					
(ii) Increase in long-term loans					
(iii) Increase in short-term loans					
(iv) Other sources					
Total					
Uses or Application of Funds					
(i) Fixed Assets (capital expenditure)					
(ii) Current Assets					
(iii) Repayment of Long-term Borrowings					
(iv) Repayment of Short-Term Borrowings					
(v) Interest on Borrowings					
(vi) Other Expenses					
Total					
(i) Opening balance of cash surplus/					
(ii) Deficit during the period					
(iii) Closing balance of cash at the end of the period					

☞ Proforma Balance Sheet

A proforma balance sheet contains estimates of liabilities and assets during the period of a term loan. A specimen proforma balance sheet estimate is given below:

PROFORMA BALANCE SHEET

(Amount in Rupees)

	I yr	II yr	III yr	IV yr	V yr
Liabilities					
Share Capital					
Reserves					
Sundry Debtors					
Current Liabilities					
Total					
Assets					
Assets (*Less*: Depreciation)					
Current Assets					
Investments					
Intangible Assets					
Total					
Debt-equity ratio					
Current ratio					

MANAGEMENT OF CAPITAL — RATIOS

1. Gross Assets turnover	Net Sales/Total assets	Effectiveness of the use of all assets, *viz.*, current and non-current.
2. Net Assets turnover	Net Sales/Total assets - current liabilities	Effectivess of assets employed on the assumption that current liabilities are available to the business as a matter of course, and will effectively reduce the assets required to be employed.
3. Inventory turnover	Net Sales or Cost Goods Sold/Average Inventories	Shows the number of times inventory replenishment is required during an accounting period to achieve a given level of sales.
4. Receivables turnover	Net Sales/average receivables	Amount of trade credit allowed and revolved during a year to achieve level of sales.
5. Average collection	$\frac{\text{Average Receivables}}{\text{Period}} \times 100$	Evaluates the effectiveness of the credit period granted to customers.

☞ Appraisal of Proposals for Advances to Small-scale Industries

The method of appraisal of proposals for advances to small-scale or cottage industries is almost the same as in the case of large industries. But certain important points need consideration before sanctioning any advance to small-scale or cottage industries. Some of the points which should be looked into by Bank executives are given below:

1. Whether the control and management is a one-man affair? In such units, in case of death of proprietor, the business is closed down and the bank may face difficulty in the recovery of the advance.
2. How much is the equity of the entrepreneur in the unit and the amount of margin he is capable of providing in the event of the bank considering the facilities?
3. Whether the project has been examined by any expert body of Government organisation?
4. What is the condition of machines and equipment (old or new), the location of the unit and whether raw materials, labour, water and power are easily available?
5. How the entrepreneur will market the product and whether the demand for the products is steady or flexible? and
6. Whether the industry is eligible for the Credit Guarantee Organisation's cover?

Financing of small-scale and cottage industries is a new challenge to banks and they have already made considerable strides in lending to that sector in a big way. Government has assigned special priority to the small-scale sector, and the appraisal of loan proposals from this sector is made by banks liberally and sympathetically. This does not mean that highly risky and speculative proposals are entertained by banks. But it is the duty and responsibility of the banks to select efficient and viable units for financing.

The Liquid Assets

Banks are financial intermediaries. They mobilise deposits from the public mainly for the purpose of lending and investment and to earn profit from such operations. The entire funds of a bank are, however, not employed in income-earning assets like loans and investments. A part of deposits is kept in cash and other liquid assets to enable the banker to meet his obligations towards the depositors. In allocating his funds into various uses income earning and otherwise a banker is guided by statutory requirements. Reserve Bank directives and many other considerations. The first deciding consideration is the nature of sources from which the funds have been mobilised.

☞ Sources of Bank Funds

The funds of a banking institution, like any other business enterprise, fall into two categories: *(i) the owned funds* consisting of paid-up capital, reserve fund, other reserves, etc., and *(ii) the borrowed funds*, consisting of deposits of various types and borrowing from other banks, and apex banking institutions, etc. The owned funds belong to the members of the company or the government in case of the nationalised banks; capital is contributed by them and the reserve fund is constituted out of the profits of the bank. A special features of the banking companies *vis-a-vis* other companies is relatively smaller proportion of the owned funds to the total funds of the banking companies. The share capital of the State Bank of India, its subsidiary banks and the nationalised banks in India has been increased during recent years. The government has contributed a sum of ₹ 1,900 crore towards the capital of 20 nationalised banks during 1985-90. The objectives is to strengthen the owned funds. The borrowed funds, mainly the deposits of the public, constitute the bulk of the bank's funds.

☞ Capital Adequacy Norms

In April 1992 Reserve Bank of India asked all banks in India with international presence to achieve the capital adequacy norm of 8 per cent by March 1994. Other banks were expected to achieve the capital risk assets ratio of 4% by March 1993 and 8% by March 1996. Under this scheme which is broadly on the lines of the Basic Committee framework, all balance sheet assets, non-funds items and other off-balance sheet exposure are assigned risk-weights according to the prescribed percentage and banks are required to maintain capital funds equal to the prescribed level of the aggregate of the risk-weighted assets and other exposures.

☞ Banker's Obligations to Depositors

Acceptance of deposits of money from the public is an essential function of a banker. By accepting deposits, a banker takes upon himself the following obligations towards the depositors:

(i) obligation to pay-back the amount of the deposit on demand or as per the terms of such deposits, and

(ii) obligation to pay interest on the deposits (except in current accounts) at prescribed rates.

Both of these obligations are significant and have an impact on the pattern of employment of a bank's funds. For example, if a banker, receives large amounts in current accounts, he is under no obligation to pay interest thereon, but he is duty bound to pay the principle as and when a demand is made by the customer. The obligation of a banker is quite different in the case of fixed deposits, *i.e.,* interest is payable at a higher rate but repayment becomes due only on the specified date. The pattern of deposits thus determines the pattern of employment of the bank funds.

☞ Significance of Liquidity in Banking

The term 'liquidity' has special significance in banking business. 'Liquidity is the word', says R. S. Sayers, "that the banker used to describe his ability to satisfy demand for cash in exchange for deposits". The banker should attach great significance to his obligation to pay his depositor's money on demand, because his inability to do so, for any reason whatsoever, will lead to disastrous consequences — the public may lose confidence in the bank and there might be a run on the bank. The banker must safeguard his position by maintaining sufficient cash with himself or with other banks or in the form of assets which can be readily converted into cash without any loss. Such assets are called the liquid assets and include: (1) cash in hand and balances with other banks, (2) money at call and short notice, and (3) investments in Government and semi-Government securities. The urgency of maintaining the liquid assets is recognised by the Banking Regulation Act, 1949, Section 24 of which requires every banking company to maintain such liquid assets of an amount not less than 25% of its net demand and time liabilities.

Some of the liquid assets, *e.g.,* cash in hand and balances with other banks in current accounts, are idle assets in the sense that the banker does not derive any income from them. On some other liquid assets, *e.g.*, money at call and short notice and investment, the return is lower as compared to other profitable uses of a bank's funds. In order to enable the bank to meet its obligation to pay interest on deposits and to earn adequate profits to itself, the bank must employ the remainder of its funds in more profitable channels, *i.e.,* by way of loans and advances. As the proportion of interest-bearing deposits (*e.g., s*avings and fixed deposits) to total deposits increase, the obligation of the banker to pay interest thereon also increases and necessitates employment of the funds in higher income yielding assets. Thus, a banker has to strike a balance between the two apparently conflicting considerations of liquidity and profitability in the employment of his funds. He has to allocate total resources at his command amongst the various assets — liquid, semi-liquid and income earning — in such proportions that his own objectives: (1) to earn maximum profits, and (2) to meet his obligation to repay the depositor's money are fulfilled.

☞ Questions

1. What are the basic principles of good lending?
2. What principles should a banker follow before advancing a loan to a customer?
3. In considering the loan application of a borrower, what is the importance of his character, standing and his repaying capacity?
4. Discuss the need, importance and method of the assessment of a profit and loss account and balance sheet of a company before the sanction of any loan.
5. Is it necessary for a banker to keep a safe margin between the securities offered by the borrower and the loan sanctioned by the bank? How is this margin determined?
6. State briefly the general principles which govern secured advances.
7. When considering a proposal for an advance to a limited company, a banker has to study its previous and latest balance sheets, and in that connection the following are some of the items which come up for examination. Explain each of these items with special reference to its significance to the lending banker, giving hypothetical examples to amplify your answer:
   (i) Net Worth
   (ii) Book Debts
   (iii) Current Ratio
   (iv) Intangible Assets
   (v) Debt-equity Ratio.
8. What is the importance to a banker of the cash flow statement of an industrial joint stock company? What are the items of a cash flow statement which represent internal cash accruals and the items which represent external sources of funds?
9. What do you understand by cash flow? *[I.I.B., Part II]*
10. What is the significance to a banker, of the cash flow statement of an industrial joint stock company? Explain the various items included in such statement. *[I.I.B., Part II]*
11. What is the significance to a banker of the cash flow statement of an industrial joint stock company? What are the items in a cash flow statement which represent internal cash accruals and the items which represent external sources of funds? *[I.I.B., Part II]*
12. What do you mean by fixed, current and fictitious assets? How are these viewed while analysing the Balance Sheet of a borrower?
13. What is meant by 'credit analysis'? How does the Balance Sheet serve a good tool of financial credit analysis?
14. What are the important observations to be made by a bank in the Balance Sheet of a borrowing company?
15. What is meant by cash reserves maintained by bankers ? What are the factors governing the maintenance of cash reserves by a shrewd banker ? *[Delhi, Bangalore]*
16. Explain the motive behind the investment policy of a commercial bank. Does the study of distribution of assets provide any clue as to soundness or otherwise of a commercial bank ? *[Andhra, Shri Venkateshwara]*
17. With the help of an imaginary balance sheet discuss the cardinal principle in the choice of assets by a commercial bank. *[Andhra]*
18. Analyse the basic principle in the choice of assets of a commercial bank.
19. When considering a proposal for an advance to a limited company a banker has to study the previous and latest balance sheet of the company and in that connection the following are some of the items which come up for examination. Explain each of these items with special reference to its significance to the lending banker, giving hypothetical examples to amplify your answer:
   (i) Net Worth *(ii)* Book Debts *(iii)* Current Ratio *(iv)* Intangible Assets *(v)* Debt-equity Ratio.
   [I.I.B., Part II]
20. The latest audited Balance Sheet and trading results of Plastic Products Private Ltd. are tabulated below:

Balance Sheet

Liabilities	₹	*Assets*	₹
Creditors	56,700	Cash	10,500
Loans from Directors	8,200	Debtors	18,000
		Stock	24,000
	64,900		52,500
Capital	5,500	Plant and Machinery	15,500
Profit and Loss Account	1,250	Prepayments	1,200
		Goodwill	1.500
		Preliminary	950
	71,650		71,650

Raw materials purchased 1,38,000; Sales ₹ 2,25,000.

Net Profit annual ₹ 5,250.

The company manufactures plastic containers and bags. It is managed by two of the directors who are capable and energetic with good knowledge and experience of the trade. The company's current account was transferred from another bank about three months ago and has been active with a satisfactory turnover. The credit balance fluctuates between ₹ 1,000 and ₹ 8,000.

The company makes an application for a cash credit limit of ₹ 25,000 against the hypothecation of stocks to finance a relatively large contract of ₹ 75,000 for supply of plastic products. Give a brief analysis of the financial position of the company as revealed by the balance sheet figures and comment on the proposal from the bank's point of view. *[I.I.B., Part II]*

21. *(a)* What is a Power of Attorney? A customer who has an account at your Branch has issued a Power of Attorney in favour of his representative, what are the main features of the Power of Attorney to which you, as a banker, should pay special attention?

    (b) A person with 5 years' experience in driving approaches a bank for a loan of ₹ 10,000 to buy an auto rickshaw. Please list out in proper sequence the entire procedure/requirements from the stage an application is submitted till the loan is sanctioned. What security/documents will be obtained?

    [C.A.I.I.B., Part I]

22. A public limited company engaged, in the manufacture of chemicals, having suffered losses, decides to go for diversification, with a view to take up profitable activity involving capital expenditure of ₹ 30 lakh. The Company approaches the Bank, from whom they have already taken a loan, with a request to finance capital cost of diversification and also to give further working capital finance for the project.

The salient features of Company's Balance Sheet as at 31st December, 1972 are asunder:

Paid up capital	₹	1,00,00,000
Development Reserve	₹	20,00,000
Long-term Loan from Bank	₹	1,00,00,000
Fixed Assets at Cost	₹	2,00,00,000
Borrowing from Bank against Stocks	₹	75,00,000
Inventory	₹	90,00,000
Accumulated losses	₹	30,00,000
Arrears of Depreciation provided for	₹	35,00,000

It may be noted that, the Company is in arrears of 4 instalments in the term loan account. Only if they take up diversification, this unit can become viable and pay the instalments of the present loan as well as new loan. At the same time, it may be noted that, due to the diversification, part of the existing inventory will be slow-moving but will not deteriorate in quality.

In brief the Company wants:

(a) New term loan of ₹ 30 lakh.

(b) Additional Cash Credit for Working Capital

(c) Rephasing of existing term loan.

As a credit manager, how will you view the above proposal? Please give reasons. *[I.I.B., Part 1]*

23 The balance sheet items of the company can be classified as follows:

Balance Sheet

Proprietors' Funds	₹ 1,20,00,000	(comprising Share Capital and Development Rebate)
Long-term Liabilities	₹ 1,00,00,000	(Term Loan)
Current Liabilities	₹ 75,00,000	(Loans from Bank)
Fixed Assets	₹ 2,00,00,000	
Current Assets:	₹ 90,00,000	
Other Intangible Assets:		
Accumulated Losses	₹ 30,00,000	
Arrears of Depreciation	₹ 35,00,000	

The term loan of ₹ 1 crore is secured by the fixed assets of ₹ 2 crore (less depreciation). Thus, on realisation the assets are likely to repay the term loan. The current liability is secured by the current assets. There is no other asset of the company (except the intangible ones, which are fictitious assets). The company has suffered losses in the past. Hence, the profitability of the company is uncertain. On these facts, the company does not deserve any further credit from the bank.

However, the banker should think over the proposal *on the basis of future prospects of the company as a result of proposed diversification*, which can improve the profitability of the company, and thereby its capacity to repay term loan and current liability. After satisfying himself about the viability and profitability of the proposed diversification the banker may accept the request of the company to provide a further term loan, and cash credit and to reschedule the repayment of the existing term loan.

The banker should ask the company to secure its interest by the following measures:

(i) to give a negative lien on its assets,

(ii) to issue debentures to the bank to the extent of its indebtedness, and

(iii) to mortgage the assets to be acquired by it with the proposed term loan.

24. The salient features of the Balance Sheet of L & M Ltd. as at 31st December, 1973 are asunder:

	₹
Paid-up Capital	1,00,000
Profit and Loss Debit Balance	40,000
Fixed Assets	50,000
Inventory	2,70,000
Creditors	1,30,000
Book Debts	2,00,000
Outside borrowings from Moneylenders	1,70,000
Deposits by directors	1,00,000
Annual Sales	3,00,000
Loss for the year 1973	10,000

The directors approach the Sound Bank Ltd. for advance facilities to repay the outside borrowings and sundry creditors against the security of fixed assets, stock and book debts.

As a branch manager of Sound Bank Ltd., how will you view the above proposal? Should you decide to grant the facilities, state the stipulation you will make. Please give reasons. *[I.I.B., Part I]*

After analysing the above figures we come to the following conclusions:

(1) The paid-up capital of the company is ₹ 1 lakh and there are no reserves. On the other hand, the debit balance in the Profit and Loss A/c (including the loss for the year 1973) amounts to ₹ 50,000. Thus, half of the share capital has been wiped off. It also indicates the inefficiency of the management.

(2) The current assets of the company amount to ₹ 4,70,000 (inventory ₹ 2,70,000 and Book Debts ₹ 2,00,000). The current liabilities amount to ₹ 3,00,000 (i.e., Creditors ₹ 1,30,000 + Outside borrowing from money-lenders ₹ 1,70,000). The deposits by directors are not included in the current liabilities. The current ratio is more than

1 and is satisfactory. The company desires to obtain an advance of ₹ 3 lakh from the bank to repay the outside borrowings and creditors. Obviously the purpose of the loan is not very convincing. However, if the banker decides to advance the loan, the present liabilities of the company will be substituted by its liability towards the banker and thus the current ratio will remain unaffected.

(3) Another unsatisfactory feature is the excessive amount of book debts as compared to total annual sales. The sales are for ₹ 3 lakh and the debtors owe to the company ₹ 2 lakh. It shows that the company is extending credit to its customers to a large extent or the company has been unable to realize its debts over longer periods which is undesirable.

As the current ratio is satisfactory, the manager may decide, despite other unsatisfactory features, to grant a loan to the company. The banker should impose the following stipulations in this regard:

(i) The company should be advised to reduce its share capital by writing off the loss of ₹ 50,000.
(ii) He should ask the company to mortgage its fixed assets (₹ 50,000) to the banker and to assign the book debts in its favour and pledge the inventory.
(iii) All the above-mentioned charges be registered with the Registrar of Companies under Section 125 of the Companies Act 1956.
(iv) The Company must create a negative lien on the deposits by the directors in order to prevent the directors to withdraw their deposits.
(v) The company should be required to reduce the amount of book debts and grant credit on reasonable terms only.
(vi) Personal guarantee of the directors may also be secured.

25. "Cork Manufacturers" are engaged in the manufacture of rubberised cork-sheet. They have 3 partners, *viz.*, Shri A.R Basu, Shri N.K. Taneja and Shri V.M. Apte. Although they have been maintaining an account for some years, they have not obtained any loan or other advances from the Bank.

They now approach you stating that they require following facilities:

(i) Loan against equitable mortgage ₹ 8 lakh
(ii) Cash Credit against stocks ₹ 5 lakh
(iii) Bills purchase ₹ 1 lakh

The Balance Sheet features are as follows:

Balance Sheet

Liabilities	₹	*Assets*	₹
Partners' Capital	4,00,000	Land and Buildings (after providing for depreciation)	2,50,000
Sundry Creditors for goods purchased	5,00,000	Machinery (original cost ₹ 5,00,000) at depreciated value	4,00,000
Deposits	10,000	Inventory	
Income tax payable	50,000	*(a)* Raw Materials	1,00,000
		(b) Stock-in-progress	10,000
		(c) Finished Stocks	1,00,000
		Sundry Debtors	2,00,000
Total	10,60,000	Total	10,60,000

Sales of last 3 years have been ₹ 8 lakh, ₹ 10 lakh and ₹ 15 lakh. Profit margin, on an average, was 10% on sales.

Out of proposed loan against equitable mortgage, they want to purchase new machinery worth ₹ 2 lakh.

They state: although depreciated book value of land and buildings and machinery is ₹ 6.50 lakh, real value of land has gone up very high and it will fetch ₹ 12 lakhs any time and, therefore, the Bank gets adequate security. Please state up to what amount you will consider their request.

Does the Bank get any guarantee in the event of default? *[I.I.B., Part I]*

The sales of the firm show satisfactory rising trend during the last three years. The profit margin of 10% on sales is also satisfactory. It shows that the firm has good prospects for further increasing its sales. Its request for a term loan is quite justified. It needs ₹ 2 lakh for the purchase of new machinery for further expansion, while it demands a term loan of ₹ 8 lakh on the security of its fixed assets. It seems to be an excessive demand. A term loan is a project-oriented loan. Hence, the banker should grant a term loan of ₹ 2 lakh for the purchase of new machinery on the security of machinery itself.

The firm's current liabilities are ₹ 5,60,000 (Sundry creditors ₹ 5,00,000 + Tax liability ₹ 60,000). Deposits not being treated as current liability. Its current assets amount to ₹ 4,10,000 only inventory + sundry Debtors. The current ratio, therefore, comes to less than 1, which is not satisfactory. It also shows lack of working capital, on account of which the dues to the trade creditors are on the higher side.

Keeping in view the rising trend of sales, satisfactory profitability, good prospects with the addition of new machinery and the acquaintance with the firm for the past few years, the banker should grant cash credit limit against stocks as well. But as the level of stocks on the date of the Balance Sheet is ₹ 2,10,000, the banker should not grant cash credit limit beyond ₹ 2 lakh. The banker may grant loan against the book debts as well. Working capital may also be provided. In part, in the form of term loan on the security of fixed assets to the extent of ₹ 2 lakh.

The firm is a manufacturing concern and the value of its plant and machinery (after including the proposed one) comes to less than ₹ 20 lakh. Hence, the concern will be treated as a small-scale industry and the guarantee cover provided by the Deposit Insurance and Credit Guarantee Corporation will be available to the banker in respect of the advances granted to the firm.

26. The latest audited balance sheet and trading results of Plastic Products Private Ltd. are tabulated below:

Balance Sheet

Liabilities	₹	*Assets*	₹
Creditors	56,700	Cash	10,500
Loans from directors	8,200	Debtors	18,000
		Stock	24,000
	64.900		52,500
Capital	5,500	Plant and 1machinery	15,500
Profit and loss account	1,250	Prepayments	1,200
		Goodwill	1,500
		Preliminary expenses	950
	71,650		71,650

Balance Sheet

Raw materials purchased ₹ 1,38,00; sales ₹ 2,25,500; net profit annual ₹ 5,250.

The company manufactures plastic containers and bags. It is managed by two of the directors who are capable and energetic with good knowledge and experience of the trade. The company's current account was transferred from another bank about three months ago and has been active with a satisfactory turnover. The credit balance fluctuates between ₹ 1,000 and ₹ 8,000.

The company makes an application for cash credit limit of ₹ 25,000 against the hypothecation of stocks to finance a relatively large contract of ₹ 25,000 for supply of plastic products. Give a brief analysis of the financial position of the company as revealed by the balance sheet figures and comment on the proposal from the bank's point of view. *[I.I.B., Part I]*

27. The following figures make up the Balance Sheet of M/s Chunnilal Shah and Co. (Pvt). Ltd. as at 31st December 1980. Please rearrange the figures in a proper Balance Sheet form:

Liabilities	₹	*Assets*	₹
Capital	1,00,000	Fixed Assets	60,000
Sundry Creditors	1,05,000	Sundry Debtors	1,50,000
Deposits from Directors	1,00,000	Stock	1,85,000
Deposits from Directors	1,30,000	Cash in Hand and at Bank	15,000
Market Borrowings	1,30,000		
Profit and Loss a/c (Dr).	25,000		

Their sales for the year 1980 is ₹ 2,50,000 and loss for the same year is ₹ 5,000.

The above company has approached you for advance facilities for ₹ 1.50,000 for repaying their market borrowings which are at high rate of interest and also for repaying some pressing creditors against the security of Fixed Assets. Stocks and Book Debts.

Please comment on the various aspects of Balance Sheet and state whether you could consider their request favourably. *[I.I.B., Part I]*

28. ABC Co. (Private). Ltd. manufacturers of stainless steel utensils, is an old established undertaking, enjoys good reputation in the market and has prospered under present management. The company's summarised Balance Sheet as on 31st December, 1982 appears asunder:

Balance Sheet

Liabilities	*(₹ in thousands)*	*Assets*	*(₹ in thousands)*
Capital	100,00	Cash	25,28
Reserve	52,80	Debtors	56,20
Profit and loss A/c	92,50	Stock	1,10,78
Creditors	32,81	Investments	2,500
Provision for Taxation	25,15	Free-held Property	35,20
Provision for Dividend	8.50	Plant and Machinery	59.30
Total	3,11,76	Total	3,11,76
Sales (1982)	5,20,00		
Profit (1982)	35,40		
Depreciation	9,80		
Directors' Remuneration	2.30		

The Company has been dealing with your bank for the last about 24 years. The Bank is requested to renew an unsecured overdraft limit of ₹ 20 lakh for use in case of need. No substantial capital expenditure is contemplated and the facility, if drawn upon, will be used to finance trading. The account has been all along conducted satisfactorily and very often the account runs in good credit. Please give your comments on the Balance Sheet of the Company and explain how you will deal with the request of the company. *[I.I.B. Part I]*

CHAPTER 16 Loans and Advances

The granting of advances is one of the most important functions of a bank; and the test of a banker's strength depends considerably on the quality of its advances and the proportion they bear to the total deposits. In the money lending business, the moneylender must carefully consider the chances of his being repaid by the borrower. He, therefore, does not normally depend on the obligation of the borrower alone but wants some tangible security to safeguard his advances in case the borrower is unable to meet his obligation. The most important qualification of a successful banker is, and always has been, his ability to judge the character and creditworthiness of his customer.

☞ Clean Loans and Advances

Ordinarily, advances given by a banker must be properly secured; but in exceptional cases, where he has complete confidence in the integrity and honesty of the customer, an unsecured overdraft for a short period may be allowed. An overdraft allowed without taking some tangible security is called a *clean overdraft.* As opposed to a secured loan, an unsecured loan is termed as a *clean loan.* In the case of a clean loan and clean overdraft, the banker relies entirely on the personal liability of the customer and has nothing to fall back on in case of default in the repayment of such a loan or overdraft. Therefore, as far as possible, the banker should not incur such a risk except in known and deserving cases or in consonance with the social objectives of the banking policy in force at that time. The Banking Regulation Act, 1949, prohibits unsecured as well as secured advances to directors of the banking company itself.

According to Section 5(*n*) of the Banking Regulation Act, 1949, **a secured loan or advance** means a, "loan or an advance made on the security of assets the market value of which is not at any time less than the amount of such loan or advance".

An **Unsecured Loan or Advance** means a loan or advance not so secured. A *partly covered loan or advance* is partly covered by the security of assets, the market value of such securities being less than the amount that has been lent or outstanding at any time.

The Reserve Bank of India does not permit other banks to give clean advance in excess of 15 per cent of their total outstanding advances, including 20 per cent of unsecured guarantees. For the purposes of calculating the clean advances level, the following types of advances are eligible for deduction from clean advances:

(i) Advances backed by guarantees of the Central Government, State Governments, public sector financial institutions, insurance companies, banks and in respect of credit to small industries, and the Credit Guarantee Organisation. However, guarantees furnished by insurance companies in connection with deferred payment arrangements should themselves be backed by an adequate tangible security.

(ii) Advances against supply bills drawn on the Central Government and State Governments which are accompanied by duly authorised inspection notes or receipted challans, provided that the bank holds an irrevocable power of attorney registered with the concerned authorities.

(iii) Advances in the form of packing credit for exports.

(iv) Advances against trust receipts.

(v) Advances against export D/A bills.

(vi) Advances against inland D/A bills drawn under letters of credit (from another bank).

(vii) Advances against bills drawn for machinery supplied on deferred payment terms which have been accepted by the purchaser's bank and advances to finance sales on hire purchase or deferred payment terms of machinery and equipment for agriculture, dairies, farming and fishing, as well as trucks and commercial vehicles.

(viii) Cheques and D/Ds purchased.

(ix) Advances against truck/lorry receipts issued by operators approved by the Indian Banks Association.

(x) Advances against deferred receivable payments such as excise drawbacks, cash subsidies to exporters and dividends receivable from the coffee pool, provided that the amounts are due from Government or under export promotion schemes approved by Government, and advances to exporters for payment of export duty.

(xi) Advances to farmers against hypothecation of crops.

(xii) Bad and doubtful debts fully provided for.

(xiii) The secured portion of a partly secured advance.

(xiv) Inland D/A bills (even where such bills are not drawn under a letter of credit) having a usance not exceeding 90 days.

(xv) Advances against bad debts which are not outstanding for more than six months and are due by companies.

Old private bankers knew their customers personally and knew up to what amount a loan could be safely given without security. The position, however, is quite different today; in a large administrative setup having a large clientele, very limited discretion is possible to the local agents who must strictly adhere to the rules and regulations laid down by the head office. Thus, in present-day modern banking, the question of security is most important.

STYLE OF CREDIT

Commercial banks finance working capital requirements of their customers. The main style of credit of systems of financing prevalent in our country are:

1. Cash credit system
2. Overdrafts

3. Loan system
4. Purchase and discounting of bills.

The terms and conditions, the rights and previleges of the borower and the banker differ in each case. In India, the categogy of loans, cash credits and advances accountants for the bulk of bank credit. Purchase and discounting of bills is not as popular a means of bank credit of India, as it is in foreign countries. Efforts have been made to popularise the use of bills of exchange for extending bank credit.

☞ Cash Credit

Cash credit is one of the most important methods of lending in India. Under this method, the banker fixes a limit for a customer, called the cash credit limit. The limit is generally specified after taking into account the important features of the borrowing concern, for example, production, sales, inventory, past credit limits, etc. The customer is allowed to withdraw money from cash credit account according to his requirements. Similarly, he may deposit money in the account as and when surplus funds are available with him. The cash credit account is, thus, an active and running account to which deposits and withdrawals may be effected frequently. But the customer has to provide tangible assets as security for the amount borrowed from the banker. The interest is charged on the actual amount utilised by the customer and it is calculated only for the period of actual utilisation only.

☞ Commitment Charge

Since banks have to keep funds idle up to the credit limits sanctioned to customers, they may levy a commitment charge on the unutilised limits of credit. Reserve Bank of India had made it obligatory for all scheduled commercial banks to levy a commitment charge @ one per cent per annum on the unutilised portion of the credit limits in excess of ₹ 10 lakh with effect from 1st April, 1970. This levy of commitment charge was withdrawn by the Reserve Bank of India with effect from 1st Nov., 1975.

With effect from January 1, 1991 commitment charge was reintroduced with two objectives, namely: (1) to bring about discipline in availing bank finance by borrowers, and (2) to facilitate better funds management by banks. The salient features of the directive given by the Reserve Bank to banks in this regard are as follows:

(i) It will apply to all borrowers with working capital limit of ₹ 1 crore and over.

(ii) It will be imposed @ 1% p.a. on the unutilised portion of working capital sanctioned to borrowers, subject to a tolerance level of 15% of the quarterly operating limit. It means that no charge is to be made if the operating limit specified by the borrower for a given quarter remains unutilised within the range of 15% only.

(iii) The "unutilised portion" of the operating limit shall be ascertained by the banks by calculating the average utilisation during the quarter after excluding therefrom utilisation in excess of the operative sanctioned limit. The difference between the average utilisation thus determined and the operative sanctioned limit, as the case may be, shall be treated as unutilised portion.

(iv) Where the unutilised portion (as determined above) exceeds the tolerance level of 15%, the charge is to be imposed on the entire unutilised portion of operative/sanctioned limit and not only on the portion in excess of the tolerance level.

(v) This charge will not be imposed on the following limits:

(a) Working capital limits sanctioned to sick/weak units

(b) Limits sanctioned for export credit and against export incentives

(*c*) Inland bill limits

(*d*) Credit limits granted to commercial banks, financial institutions and cooperative banks.

The above mandatory requirement to levy a commitment charge on unutilised portion of the Cash Credit limits was withdrawn with effect from July 1, 1996. The Reserve Bank has advised the banks to evolve their own guidelines to ensure credit discipline and levy a commitment charge. Thus, the commitment charge now depends upon the discretion of individual banks.

☞ Advantages of Cash Credit System

1. *Flexibility:* The borrowers need not keep their surplus funds idle with themselves. They can recycle the funds quite efficiently and can minimise interest charges by depositing all cash accruals in the bank account and thus keeping the drawals at the minimum level. The system thus ensures lesser cost of funds to the borrowers and better turnover of mind for the banks.
2. *Operative convenience:* Banks have to maintain one account for all the transactions of a customer. The repetitive documentations can be avoided.

☞ Weaknesses of the System

1. *Fixation of credit limits:* The cash credit limits are prescribed once in a year. Hence, it gives rise to the practice of fixing large limits than is required for most part of the year. The borrowers misutilise the unutilised gap in times of credit restraint.
2. *Bank's inability to verify the end-use of funds:* Under this system the stress is on security aspect. Hence, there is no conscious effort on the part of banks to verify the end-use of funds. Funds are diverted, without banker's knowledge, to unapproved purposes.
3. *Lack of proper management of funds:* Under this system the level of advances in a bank is determined not by how much the banker can lend at a particular time but by the borrower's decision to borrow at that time. The system, therefore does not encourage proper management of funds by banks.

These weaknesses of the cash credit system were highlighted by a number of committees appointed for this purpose in India. Guidelines have been issued by the Reserve Bank for reforming the cash credit system on the basis of recommendations of the Tandon Committee and the Chore Committee.

☞ Overdrafts

When a current accountholder is permitted by the banker to draw more than what stands to his credit, such an advance is called an overdraft. The banker may take some collateral security or may grant such advance on the personal security of the borrower. The customer is permitted to withdraw the amount as and when he needs it and to repay it by means of deposit in his account as and when it is feasible for him. Interest is charged on the exact amount overdrawn by the customer and for the period of its actual utilisation.

Generally, an overdraft facility is given by a bank on the basis of a written application and a promissory note signed by the customer. In such cases an express contract comes into existence. In some cases, in the absence of an express contract to grant overdraft, such an agreement can be inferred from the course of business. For example. if an accountholder, even without any express grant of an overdraft facility, overdraws on his account and his cheque is duly honoured by the bank, the transaction amounts to a loan. In *Bank of Maharashtra vs. M/s. United Construction Co. and Others* (AIR 1985 Bombay 432), the High Court concluded that there was an implied agreement for grant of overdraft or loan facility.

Banks should therefore, obtain a letter and a promissory note corporating the terms and conditions of the facility including the rate of interest chargeable in respect of the overdraft facility. This is to be complied with even when the overdraft facility might be temporary in nature.

☞ Loans on Guarantee

Section 126 of the Indian Contract Act, 1872, defines a **contract of guarantee** as *"a contract to perform the promise, or discharge the liability, of a third person in case of his default"*.

The person who gives the guarantee is called the surety; the person in respect of whose default the guarantee is given is called the *principal debtor,* and the person to whom the guarantee is given is called the *creditor*. A guarantee may be either oral or written.

Significance of guarantee as a security for loans granted has greatly increased in recent years. Since the introduction of social control on banks and specially after the nationalisation of major banks, greater attention is being paid towards augmenting bank advances for small and neglected borrowers who are unable to provide sufficient tangible assets as security. To safeguard the interests of the lending bankers arrangement has been made for providing guarantees in respect of such advances by the Deposit Insurance and Credit Guarantee Corporation of India.

Another contract, which appears analogous to the contract of guarantee, is the contract of indemnity. Section 124 of the Indian Contract Act, 1872, defines the **contract of indemnity** as *"a contract by which one party promises to save the other from loss caused to him by the conduct of any other person"*.

Like any other contract, the contract of guarantee must be supported by a consideration. According to Section 129 of the Indian Contract Act, 1872, "anything done, or any promise made, for the benefit of the principal debtor may be a sufficient consideration to the surety for giving the guarantee".

☞ Difference between Contracts of Indemnity and Guarantee

In the case of a contract of guarantee, there are three parties, *viz.,*

(i) The surety or guarantor;

(ii) The principal debtor; and

(iii) The creditor.

In the case of a contract of indemnity, there are only two parties, *viz.,*

(i) The promisor or the indemnifier; and

(ii) The party to be indemnified or insured.

In the case of indemnity contracts, the promisor undertakes to indemnify or make good the loss of the other party in certain circumstances. All contracts of insurance are indemnity contracts.

It will be seen, therefore, that in the case of a guarantee, the primary responsibility lies on the principal debtor and the surety's obligation depends substantially on the default of the principal debtor. It is necessary that contracts of indemnity and guarantee should be supported by a consideration like all other simple contracts. It would be a sufficient consideration if anything is done or promised by the creditor for the benefit of the principal debtor, surety or any other person. It may be noted here that the guarantor is *collaterally liable*, and, therefore, if he pays out the debt, the principal debtor is not released from his liability, but the guarantor steps in the place of the creditor.

☞ Precautions to be taken by Banker

The banker should never accept the guarantee of a minor or a lunatic because contracts with such a person are void. Although married women can give a valid guarantee which will bind their separate property (*stridhan*), a banker should avoid such a guarantee because to evade liability, a married woman may plead that when she signed the contract she acted under coercion or under the influence of her husband, particularly when he himself or a relative or a friend of his happened to be the principal debtor. A banker should also be very cautious before he accepts the guarantee of registered companies, for such a guarantee requires a careful scrutiny of the powers of the company as stated in its Memorandum and Articles of Association. In the case of a partnership standing as surety, all partners must join unless the giving of a guarantee forms part of the partnership business, or all copartners definitely authorise one particular partner to sign a particular guarantee. The banker should take care to see that the authority given by the copartners is in writing.

☞ Specific and Continuing Guarantee

A specified guarantee is a promise to be collaterally answerable only for one specific transaction, or one which comes to an end on the repayment of the advances for which it was given.

A continuing guarantee is a guarantee which extends to a series of transactions.

☞ Disclosure of Material Facts

An important factor in a guarantee contract is that the guarantor should enter into his agreement with the full knowledge of the facts and the nature of the responsibility of his undertaking. No alteration in the contract should be allowed to be made without due notice to and the consent of, the guarantor; otherwise the guarantor is freed from his liability. In the case of certain alterations, such as extension on credit, or a larger overdraft given than guaranteed, the banker would be safe if the power is taken by him in the guarantee bond; otherwise the guarantor should be a consenting party.

☞ Misrepresentation or Concealment of Material Facts

According to Section 142 of the Indian Contract Act, 1892, "any guarantee which has been obtained by means of misrepresentation made by the creditor, or with his knowledge and assent, concerning a material part of the transaction is invalid".

Section 143 of the same Act states that, "any guarantee which the creditor has obtained by means of keeping silence as to material circumstances is invalid". Thus, it becomes clear that a creditor must not misrepresent the material facts and also must not keep silent about any material fact.

The following point are to be noted in this regard:

1. It is important that the misrepresentation or concealment must relate to the material part of the transaction. What is material in a particular transaction will depend upon the circumstances of each case. However, it may be stated that any fact or information which may affect the willingness of the surety to enter into a contract of guarantee or not, is considered to be a material fact.
2. Under both the Sections, it is the creditor (rather than the debtor) who is required not to misrepresent or not to keep silence as regards any material fact.
3. The words "keeping silence" in Section 143 mean intentional concealment of facts. It means not disclosing a certain fact with the purpose to defraud the other party.

4. In order to avoid a contract of guarantee under Section 143, it is essential to prove that the guarantee was obtained by means of keeping silence as to the material circumstances. In other words, it is to be proved that the surety might not have entered into the contract of guarantee, if silence was not kept as regards material facts.

Example: Indian Bank grants a loan of ₹ 1 lakh to Y on the guarantee of Z, but without disclosing to the surety that Y had deceived the Bank in the past by giving false description of the securities pledged with the bank. A material fact was thus concealed. The contract of guarantee is invalidated.

☞ Joint and Several Guarantee

A guarantee may be given by more than one person, either jointly or jointly and severally, in which case the ordinary rules of joint and several contracts would apply. In a joint guarantee, the banker would have to sue the guarantors jointly and obtain a decree against them in order to make them all responsible, because if he chooses to select one or two in the first instance, and fails to get satisfaction for the whole debt out of the decree so obtained, he cannot sue the others for the balance. In a joint and several guarantee, however, he can sue each of them in rotation until his full claim is paid. The usual guarantee forms of bankers are joint and several.

☞ Death or Insolvency of Guarantor

The death or insolvency of a guarantor does not release his estate from liability for advances made by a banker. The banker should, however, as soon as he hears of either of the incidents, close the account guaranteed until a fresh guarantee bond is given. In the event of the insolvency of the guarantor, the banker, after closing the guaranteed account, should demand immediate payment from the debtor and, failing to recover the money, put in a claim on the estate of the guarantor, either fully or for any balance unrecovered. On the death or insolvency of a joint guarantor, his estate is freed from liability and the banker has to look to the remaining guarantors for the whole amount; but in the case of a joint and several guarantee, he can move against the estate of the insolvent or the deceased guarantor.

☞ Application of Law of Limitation

Where the creditor fails to sue the principal debtor within the period fixed by the Limitation Act, the surety is not discharged. This is according to the judgements of Indian Courts.

RIGHT OF BANKER AGAINST SURETY

☞ Lien

A banker can exercise his right of lien on the balance of the account of the guarantor in his possession notwithstanding the fact that his claim under the guarantee is time-barred. The right of general lien can be exercised only when the default has been made by the principal debtor, in which case the banker should immediately inform the guarantor that the former has exercised his lien on the latter's money or securities deposited with him.

☞ Rights of Surety

In case the principal debtor makes a default in the fulfilment of promise and the surety has to meet his liability to the creditor, the surety steps into the shoes of the creditor and acquires all rights of the creditor against the principal debtor. According to Section 140 of the Indian Contract Act, "where a guaranteed debt has become due, or default of the principal debtor to perform a guaranteed duty has taken place, the surety, upon payment, or performance of all that he is liable for, is invested with all the rights which the creditor had against the principal debtor." Regarding the surety's right to the benefit of the creditor's securities Section 141 states as follows, "A Surety is entitled to the benefit of every security which the creditor has against the principal debtor at the time when the contract of suretyship is entered into, whether the surety knows of the existence of such security or not; and if the creditor loses, or, without the consent of the security, parts with such security, the security is discharged to the extent of the value of the security".

According to the provisions of Section 145, the surety has a right to recover from the principal debtor the amounts which he has rightfully paid under a contract of guarantee, but he cannot claim the amounts which he has wrongfully paid. The surety has also a right to revoke at any time a continuing guarantee by giving a notice of such revocation to the creditor. But according to Section 130, the surety may revoke a continuing guarantee as to future transactions only; he remains liable in respect of the transactions which have already taken place. According to Section 131, "the death of surety operates in the absence of any contract to the contrary, as a revocation of a continuing guarantee, so far as regards to future transactions".

☞ Surety's Right to be Discharged

In the following instances, a surety is entitled to a complete discharge:

(i) According to Section 134 of the Indian Contract Act, 1872, if a creditor discharges the principal debtor, or acts in a manner the legal consequence of which is to discharge the principal debtor, the surety is discharged.

(ii) Section 135 of the Indian Contract Act, 1872, says that if a creditor without the consent of the surety, arrives at a compromise with or without promises not to sue the debtor, the surety is released.

(iii) Under Section 139 of the Act, if a creditor does any act which is inconsistent with the rights of the surety or omits to do any act which his duty to the surety requires him to do and thereby the eventual remedy of the surety against the principal debtor is impaired, the surety is liable.

(iv) In Anirudham vs. The Tom*o's Bank Ltd*,. (I.M. & J.S.C., p. 137), the point for consideration was whether the surety was discharged by reason of the principal debtor having altered the amount in a letter of guarantee without the concurrence of the surety. It was held that the surety was liable.

☞ Liability of the Surety

The liability of the surety is up to the same extent to which the principal debtor is liable to the creditor, provided the surety does not restrict his liability in the contract of guarantee. Section 128 of the Indian Contract Act states "the liability of the surety is co-extensive with that of the principal debtor unless otherwise provided by the contract". As regards the time when the liability of the surety arises, it may be noted that the liability of the surety arises as soon as the principal debtor makes a default, it cannot be postponed. The creditor need not exhaust all remedies against the principal debtor before recovering the amount from the surety. In the *Bank of Bihar Ltd., vs. Damodhar Prasad and Another* (Civil Appeal No.1109 of 1965) it was held by the Supreme Court that "the liability of the surety is immediate and cannot be deferred until the creditor has exhausted his remedies against the principal debtor." In case the guarantee of a debt is given by more than one person, the liability of the co-sureties is determined according to the provisions of Sections 146 and 147 of the Contract Act. According to Section 146 "where two or more persons are co-sureties for the same debt or duty either jointly or severally and whether under the same or different contracts, and whether with or without the knowledge of each other, the co-sureties, in the absence of any contract to the contrary, are liable, as between themselves, to pay each in equal share of the whole debt, or of that part of it which remains unpaid by the principal debtor." Provisions in Section 147 state that the co-sureties are liable to contribute equal amounts towards the liability of the debtor, provided, there is no agreement to the contrary; and they are co-sureties for the same amount of debt. It is immaterial whether the contract of guarantee was the same or separate between each of them and the creditor and whether they knew about the guarantee given by the other person or not.

☞ Termination of Guarantee

The guarantee may be terminated by:

(a) *Revocation:* (Under Section 130 of the Contract Act); or

(b) *Death of Surety:* In this case, the banker should stop the account so that the amount borrowed may not be wiped out by any further payment made by the customer to his credit. The same position obtains in the event of insanity of the surety.

The insolvency of a surety terminates his guarantee so far as further advances to the principal debtor are concerned.

If only one of the parties who has signed the guarantee jointly becomes insolvent, the banker can seek his remedy against the solvent guarantor as well as the estate of the insolvent.

☞ Reserve Bank's Guidelines on Personal Guarantees

A review of practices of commercial banks regarding personal guarantees taken from directors and other managerial personnel of borrowing concerns at the time of sanctioning loans conducted by the Reserve Bank revealed that in some cases, the guarantees had been taken essentially to make up for the insufficiency of tangible security offered or the weak financial position of the borrowing concern. In other cases, guarantees had been taken as matter of routine even where the financing institutions possessed the security of the company's tangible assets. Banks feel that with the signing of the guarantees, the personal interest of the directors and other managerial personnel in the company is strengthened and hence continuity of good management in future may reasonably be expected.

In the view of the Reserve Bank of India the practice of taking guarantees in all cases is not necessary because of the following changed circumstances:

(i) There has been gradual rise of an entrepreneurial class in place of the Managing Agency System and the managerial cadres have been professionalised:

(ii) Financially sound units are able to offer adequate security for meeting their banking needs; and

(iii) The techniques of financial and technical appraisal by the lending institutions have improved.

In 1970, the Reserve Bank of India had issued detailed guidelines to commercial banks as regards personal guarantees from the directors. Guarantee should be obtained only in circumstances absolutely warranted after a careful examination of the circumstances of each case and not as a matter of course. Detailed credit analysis should be undertaken by the banks to determine the need for guarantees. The following broad considerations may be taken into account in this connection:

(a) *Guarantees need not be considered necessary in the following cases:*

(i) Ordinarily in case of public limited companies no personal guarantee need be insisted upon if the lending institutions are satisfied about the management, its stake in the concern, economic viability of the proposal and the financial position and capacity for cash generation. In case of widely owned public limited companies, which may be rated as first class and which satisfy the above conditions, guarantees may not be necessary even if the advances are unsecured.

(ii) In case of companies — private or public — which are under professional management, guarantees may not be insisted upon from persons who are connected with the management solely by virtue of their professional/technical qualifications and not consequent upon any significant shareholding in the company concerned.

(iii) Where the lending institutions are not convinced about the above-mentioned aspects of loan proposals they should seek to stipulate conditions to make the proposals acceptable without such guarantees. In some cases, more stringent forms of financial discipline like restrictions on distribution of dividends, further expansion, aggregate borrowings, creation of further charge on assets and stipulation of maintenance of minimum net working capital may be necessary. The parity between owned funds and capital investment and the overall debt-equity ratio may have to be taken into account.

(b) *Necessity of Guarantee:* The Reserve Bank has indicated that guarantees may be considered helpful in the following cases:

(i) closely held companies — the guarantee should preferably be that of the principal members of the Group holding shares in the borrowing company;

(ii) in case of other companies in order to ensure continuously of management;

(iii) public limited companies other than first class companies where advances are on an unsecured basis;

(iv) public limited companies, whose financial position and/or capacity for cash generation is not satisfactory even through the advances are secured;

(v) in case where considerable delay in the creation of a charge on assets is likely;

(vi) the guarantee of parent companies in the case of subsidiaries whose own financial condition is not considered satisfactory, and

(vii) where the balance sheet or financial statement of a company concerns owned or managed by a group.

Other Instructions: (a) The guarantees should bear reasonable proportion to the estimate worth of the person.

(b) Banks should obtain an undertaking from the borrowing company as well as from the guarantor that no consideration in the form of commission, brokerage, fees, etc., will be paid by the company to the guarantor directly or indirectly.

Keeping in view the increasing loan losses being suffered by the banks on account of sticky or stagnant accounts due to industrial sickness, the Reserve Bank advised the banks (July 1986) as follows:

(a) The banks may, at their discretion, obtain guarantees from directors (excluding the nominee directors) and other managerial personnel in their individual capacities, whenever they consider necessary.

(b) In cases where a guarantee is not considered expedient by the bank at the time of sanctioning an advance, an undertaking should be obtained from individual directors and a covenant should be included in the loan agreement that in case the borrowing unit shows cash losses or adverse current ratio or diversion of funds, the directors would execute guarantees in their individual capacities. If required, by the banks.

(c) Banks may also obtain guarantees at their discretion from parent holding company, when credit facilities are extended to borrowing units in the same group.

The Reserve Bank further advised the banks that ordinarily banks need not insist on personal guarantees from professional managers/directors except in cases where they have a significant shareholding in the company. If the management commits serious malpractices, the right remedy would be to have them removed or replaced.

☞ LOAN

Loan is a method of lending under which bank gives credit to a borrower for a fixed period and for a specific purpose. Many a times, as a borrower needs funds for fixed assets or non-repetitive type of activities and thus, seeks money from the bank which is withdrawn in one lump sum. If the borrower needs again funds for such purpose, he has to negotiate with the bank for a loan again or to get his existing loan renewed. The loan amount is normally repayed in instalments. Loans may be short-term, medium-term or long-term. Long-term loans are generally taken for meeting the capital investment requirements. Such loans are also called "term loans". When a loan is meant for meeting both fixed capital and working capital requirements of a borrower, it is called a Composite Loan.

☞ Advantages of Loan System

1. *Financial Discipline on the Borrower:* As the time of repayment of the loan or its instalments is fixed in advance, this system ensures a greater degree of self-discipline on the borrower as compared to the cash credit system.
2. *Periodic Review of Local Account:* Whenever any loan is granted or its renewal is sanctioned the banker gets an opportunity of automatically reviewing the loan account. Unsatisfactory loan accounts may be discontinued at the discretion of the banker.
3. *Profitability:* The system is comparatively simple. Interest accrues to the bank on the entire amount lent to a customer.

☞ Drawbacks

1. *Inflexibility:* Every time a loan is required, it is to be negotiated with the banker. To avoid it, borrowers may borrow in excess of their exact requirements to provide for any contingency.
2. Banks have no control over the use of funds borrowed by the customer. However, banks insist on hypothecation of the asset/vehicle purchased with loan amount.
3. Though the loans are for fixed periods, but in practice they roll over, *i.e.,* they are renewed frequently.
4. Loan documentation is more comprehensive as compared to each credit system.

☞ Types of Loans

Banks grant loans for different periods — shorts, medium and long, and for different purposes. Broadly, the loans granted by banks are classified as follows:

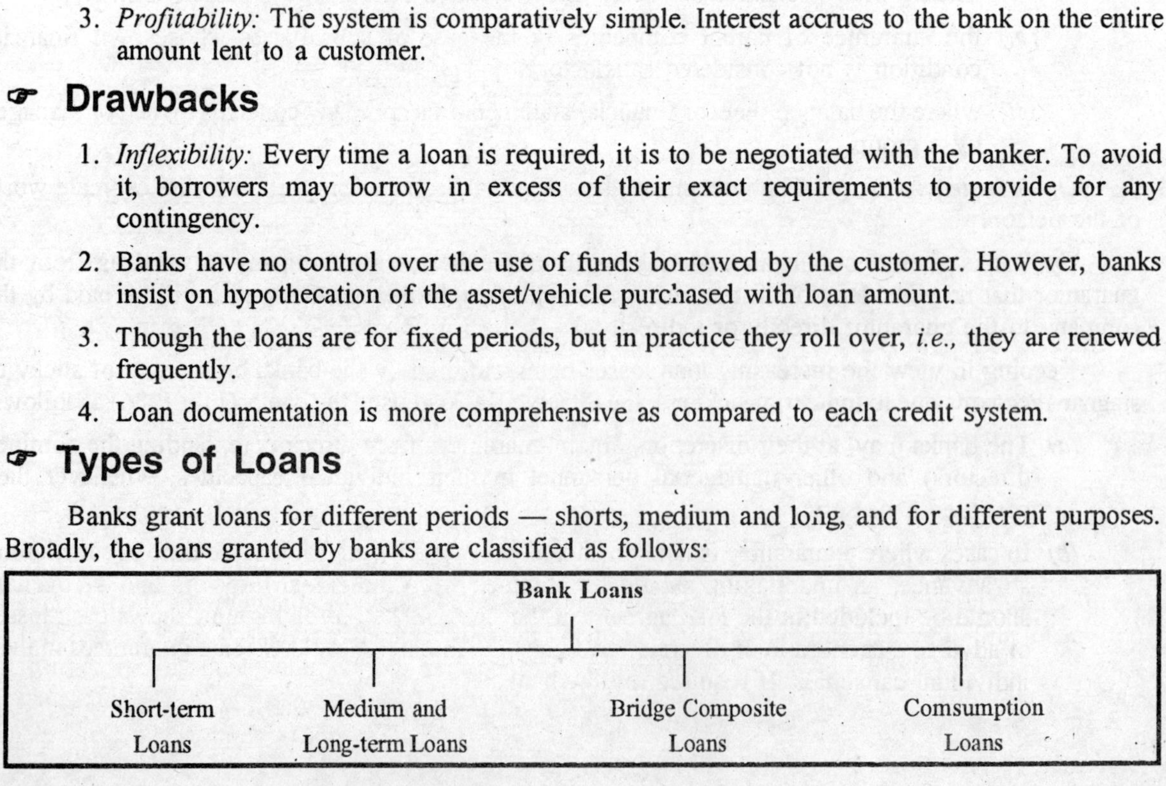

☞ Short-term Loans

Short-term loans are granted to meet the working capital needs of the borrowers. These loans are granted against the security of tangible assets — mainly the movable assets like goods and commodities, share, debentures etc. Since April 1995 Reserve Bank of India has made it mandatory for the banks to grant a portion of bank credit to big customers in the form of loans, which may be for various maturities. The Reserve Bank has also permitted the banks to rollover such loans, *i.e.,* to extend the loan for another period at the expiry of the tenor of the first loan.

☞ Term-loans

Medium and long-term loans are usually called Term Loans. These loans are granted for more than a year and are meant for purchase of capital assets for the establishment of new units and for expansion or diversification of an existing unit. Banks usually grant such loans together with specialised financial institutions like Industrial Finance Corporation of India, Industrial Credit and Investment Corporation, etc. Such loans constitute a part of the project finance which industrial enterprises are required to raise from different sources. These loans are usually secured by the tangible assets like land, buildings, plant and machinery, etc.

In recent years, Reserve Bank for India had encouraged banks to lend for projects as well. Exposure limits have been laid down at ₹ 200 crore for each bank lending to a project and ₹ 500 crores is the overall exposure limit for all banks to a single project.

☞ Bridge Loans

Bridge loans are essentially short-term loans which are granted to industrial undertakings to meet their urgent and essential needs during the period when formalities for availing of the term loans sanctioned by financial institutions are being fulfilled or necessary steps are being taken to raise the funds from the capital market. These loans are granted by banks or by financial institutions themselves and are automatically repaid out of amount of the term loan or the funds raised in the capital market.

In April 1995 Reserve Bank of India banned bridge loans granted by banks and financial institutions to all companies. But in October 1995 Reserve Bank permitted the banks to sanction bridge loans/interim finance against commitment made by a financial institution or another bank where the lending institution faces temporary liquidity constraint subject to the following conditions:

(i) The prior consent of the other bank/financial institution which has sanctioned a term loan must be obtained.

(ii) The term lending bank/financial institution must give a commitment to remit the amount of the term loan to the bank concerned.

(iii) The period of such bridge loans should not exceed four months.

(iv) No extension of time for repayment of bridge loan will be allowed.

(v) To ensure that bridge loan sanctioned is utilised for the purpose for which the term loans has been sanctioned.

☞ Composite Loans

When a loan is granted both for buying capital assets and for working capital purposes, it is called a composite loan. Such loans are usually granted to small borrowers, such as artisans, farmers, small industries, etc.

☞ Consumption Loans

Though normally banks provide loans for productive purposes only, but as an exception loans are also granted on a limited scale to meet the medical needs or the educational expenses or expenses relating to marriages and other social ceremonies, etc., of the needy persons. Such loans are called consumption loans.

☞ Classification of Loans and Advances: Secured and Unseured

The loans and advances granted by banks are broadly classified into:

(i) Secured, and *(ii)* Unsecured. According to Section 5 (a) of the Banking Regulation Act, 1949, a secured loan or advance means a loan or advance made on the security of assets, the market value of which is not at any time less than the amount of such loan or advance; and unsecured loan or advance means a loan or advance not so secured. Thus, the distinguishing features of the secured loan or advance are as follows:

(i) The loan must be made on the security of tangible assets like goods and commodities, land and buildings, gold and silver, corporate and government securities, etc. A charge on any such assets offered as security must be created in favour of the banker.

(ii) The market value of such security must not be less than the amount of the loan at any time till the loan is repaid. If the former falls below the latter because of decline in the market prices, the loan is considered as partly secured.

The distinction between secured and unsecured loan is made on the basis of legal title or charge created in favour of the lender. Under the traditional principles of lending, the borrowing capacity of the person is judged on the basis of the tangible assets in the possession of the borrower, *i.e.,* the larger is the creditworthiness of a borrower, if larger is the value of his tangible assets. However, it should not be understood that unsecured loans, also called clean loans and advances, are granted to persons without observing the above-mentioned criterion of creditworthiness. In fact, unsecured loans are also granted to persons of sufficient means, possessing tangible assets and with sound financial position, but no charge or right is created on any such assets of the borrower in favour of the banker. In such cases, the security happens to be the personal obligation of the borrower which is sometimes supported by a guarantee given by a third party regarding the repayment of the loan. Clean advances are obviously granted to parties enjoying high reputation and sound financial position. Unsecured advances are granted with caution and within certain limits only because in case of default by the borrower, the banker stands at par with other unsecured creditors.

In case of secured advances, the legal status of the banker is that of a secured creditor; he gets the first and absolute right to recover his dues out of the sale proceeds of the assets over which a charge is created in favour of the banker. Where money is advanced on (for the repayment of loan) is ruled out because that would frustrate the very purpose of taking security (*Central Bank of India vs. M/s. P.R. Garments Industries Pvt. Ltd.*, 1985 (2) xxvi Gujarat Law Reporter p. 919.)

PURCHASE AND DISCOUNTING OF BILLS

Another important method of lending by bank is purchasing and discounting of bills. There is a difference between collection of bills and purchase and discount of bills. In collection of bills, the bank collects the amount of the bill from the drawee/acceptor and credits the account of the customer. In purchase and discount, the bank credits the amount of the bill to the drawer's account before the realisation of the bill and, thus, lends money to the customer. All the bill purchased and discounted by bank are, therefore, shown in its Balance Sheet as part of loans and advances.

Bills are generally of two types — Demand bills and Usance bills. Demand bills are repayable on demand and there is no maturity. The banker can demand payment from the drawee on presentation. This is the reason the term used in regard to demand bills is known as 'purchase of the bills'. Usance bill matures after a period of time, the bank has to retain the bill till due date and realise the amount on the date of maturity. This practice is called discounting of the bill. In purchase and discount of bills, the banker credits the customer's account with the amount of the bill after deducting his charges or discount. Discount charge is higher than the charge made in case of purchase of a bill, because it includes the interest on the amount of the bill credited to the drawer's account besides the expenses incurred in realisation of the bill.

Purchase and discounting of bills is an important method of lending and has certain distinct advantages such as safety of funds, facility of refinance from Reserve Bank, certainty of payment, no risk of fluctuations in the value of the bill and profit to the bank.

☞ Collection of Bills

Just like collection of cheques, the banker collects the bills drawn by the customers from the debtors (drawees). When the drawer of a bill deposits with his banker for collection a bill drawn on his debtor, the banker acts as the agent of the drawer and makes its payment to him only on the realisation of the bill. In addition to cheques and bills the banker also receives bank drafts, dividend warrants, interest warrants, etc., for collection. A separate pay-in-slip is provided for the deposit of bill which contains the instructions of the drawn regarding the delivery of the documents (*i.e.,* documents against payment D/P or documents against acceptance D/A), to the drawee and getting and crediting the proceeds on realisation. The banker is bound to collect the bill according to the instructions of the drawer.

The bill is presented by the bank to the drawee either for acceptance or for payment. In case there is no branch of the collecting bank at the place of drawee, it is sent to the branch of some other bank with which the collecting bank has made such arrangement. The agent bank after recovering the amount of the bill remits the proceeds to the collecting banker who thereafter credits it to the account of the drawer. When a bill is dishonoured the bank informs the customer about it and is entitled to recover all the expenses incurred in this regard. In case of dishonour, the banker may present the bill to a drawee in case of need, if it is mentioned in the bill.

☞ Banker's Position in Collection of Bills

The banker's duty in collection and negotiation of bill on behalf of his customer was described by the Supreme Court in "*Keshari Chand vs. Shillong Banking Corporation*" (AIR, 1965, SC 1711) as follows:

"The banker is bound to act according to the directions given by the customer, and in the absence of such directions, according to the usage prevailing at the place where the banker conducted his business and applicable to the matter in hand. The banker is also bound to use reasonable skill and diligence in his work."

In *R.J. Mohammed Jacob Sahib and Others vs. Indian Bank, Madras and Another* (AIR 1975, Madras, 220), the Indian Bank negotiated the documents through State Bank to B and paid the price to A but the bank failed to deliver form "C" which was delivered by B to the State Bank of India at the time of clearance of documents. In the absence of form 'C', A had to pay sales tax at the rate of 7 per cent instead of 1 per cent. A claimed by way of damages the extra amount paid by him. The

Madras High Court held that the bank had not taken all the reasonable care in the delivery of form 'C' to A and consequently the suit was decreed with costs as against Indian Bank, State Bank of India merely acted for the purpose of negotiating the documents. Hence, there was no privity of contract between A and the State Bank. Suit against the latter was therefore dismissed.

☞ The Status of Bank — Owner or Agent?

In performing the activity of discounting of bills, whether the bank becomes the owner of the bill or acts as the agent of the customer? It is a question of fact whether a bill is taken by a banker for collection or as a security or for discount. The position of the discounting banker as owner or agent of customer was considered by *Madhya Pradesh High Court in Dena Bank vs. M.P. National Textiles Corporation* (AIR 1982, MP 85). In this case the bank purchased the bills with necessary documents for collection and credited the amount of the bills in the account of the company in accordance with the bill purchases facility granted to it. The documents were duly endorsed in favour of the banker. On the due date the bank could not realise the amount of the bills due to a fraud committed by a third party. Therefore, the bank reserved the entry in its books, debiting the account of the company with the amount of the bills and informed the company accordingly. The documents could not be returned back to the company and the company filed a suit against the bank.

The court held that if the bills and the relevant documents presented by its drawer were accepted by a banker with endorsement in its favour and the same were immediately discounted by the banker without waiting for their collection by giving full credit for the entire amount of the documents so presented, the banker itself becomes a purchaser and holder thereof for full value. Hence, the bank was not entitled to reverse the credit entry particularly when the documents were not returned.

☞ Advantages of Discounting of Bill

As a method of granting credit to the constituents, discount of the bills is a popular and profitable business of the banker. The following are the advantages of discounting of bills *vis-a-vis* granting loans and advances:

1. *Safety of Bank Funds:* A banker is primarily concerned with the safety of the funds he lends. Though the banker does not get charge over any tangible assets in case of discounting of bills, legal instrument bearing signatures of two parties is considered good for the amount of the bill. The banker can enforce his claim much more easily in the case of bills. If the acceptor of the bill fails to make payment on its due date, the banker has the remedy to claim the whole amount from his customer, the drawer of the bill. In case the bill is dishonoured, the banker debits the amount to his customer's account and sends him an intimation Thus, the banker is fully confident of recovering his money on the due date. To be on the safer side a banker should discount bills of exchange offered by parties of standing and good reputation.
2. *Certainty of Payment:* A bill of exchange is considered and ideal self-liquidating asset because it originates from an actual commercial transaction and the debtor meets the obligation to pay by disposing of the goods acquired from the creditor within a short period of time. As the bill of exchange matures within a 'short period of time' the banker recovers his money on the due date with certainty. The bills are therefore, called 'semi-liquid' assets. As the banker knows in advance the dates on which the discounted bills will mature, he can invest his funds in such a way that the same are profitably utilised to the maximum extent, without unnecessarily maintaining large cash balances. Thus, a banker is able to maximise his profit without taking any undue risk.
3. *Facility of Refinance:* When a banker is in need of funds, he can secure accommodation from the central bank of the country on the basis of eligible securities including the bills discounted.

The bills can also be rediscounted with the central bank or any other bank/financial institution and thus the need for cash balances can be met more easily and quickly.

4. *Stability in the Value of the Bill:* The value of the bills as a security does not fluctuate while the value of all tangible goods and securities is liable to fluctuations. The amount payable on account of a bill is fixed and the acceptor or the drawer is liable to pay the same in full. As the bill is a legally enforceable instrument, neither of these parties can subsequently dispute the validity of the banker's claim. These parties may be summarily sued for the payment of the amount of the bill.
5. *Profitability:* While discounting the bills the banker deducts interest (in the form of discount) from the amount of the bill. In case of other types of loans and advances, interest is payable by the debtor quarterly or half-yearly. Thus, the yield from discounting of bills is a little higher, if the rate of interest or discount remains the same as in the case of other loans, for example, if a bill of exchange for 1,000 payable after 3 months is discounted @ 6 per cent per annum, the banker pays ₹ 985 (₹ 1,000 – ₹ 15). The actual yield thus comes to 6.38 per cent per annum.

☞ Credit Limits for Purchase and Discounting of Bills

As already stated above, the purchase and discounting of bills is one of the methods of lending by banks to customers, banks take due precaution and fix annual credit limits for each borrower for the purchase and discounting of clean bills and documentary bills separately. Banks treat clean bills as unsecured advances, because, the realisation of such bills depend on the reputation and creditworthiness of the party. Documentary bills are treated as secured advances because documents of title to goods are attached with the bills. The credit limits for bills for a customer are renewed by the bank for another year on the basis of last year's utilisation, nature of business, creditworthiness of the party, etc.

Documentary bills may be drawn on either of the following two terms:

(i) Documents against Acceptance (D/A).

(ii) Documents against Payment (D/P).

In the former case, the banker is directed by the drawer to release the documents of title to goods to the drawer after he accepts the bill. But in case of the above (ii), the documents are handed over to the drawer when he makes payment of the bill to the banker. From the banker's point of view documentary bill on D/P basis are more safer than on D/A basis. A documentary bill is turned into a clean bill as soon as the drawer accepts the bill and takes delivery of the documents of title to goods from the banker. Thereafter, the banker depends on the acceptance of the drawee only. Hence, banks should take special care while purchasing/discounting bill on D/A basis. The banker should take the following points into consideration while sanctioning credit limit for purchase/discounting of bills.

(i) First of all, the banker should sanction a credit limit for this purpose very carefully, after considering the various aspects of the business of the customer. This limit should be on the safer side.

(ii) The banker should gather information about the creditworthiness of the customer from different sources. The credit limit for bills should be related to the financial soundness of the party concerned.

(iii) The liability of the drawee of the bill also arises after he accepts the bill and subsequently dishonours it on the due date. The banker should therefore, collect credit information about the drawee also. The amount of the bills should not exceed the safe limit as determined by his creditworthiness.

(iv) The credit limit should be prescribed after taking into account the quantum of business undertaken by the party, *viz.,* the total turnover during the year. Higher limits may be fixed in case of customers who have higher level of sales or despatches or goods to other centres.

(v) The banker should also ascertain that the business of the customer is not subject to any constriction or prohibition imposed by the government.

(vi) If a bill limit is to be granted to the endorsee of a bill, the banker should also ascertain the creditworthiness of such party.

(vii) The banker should grant the limits for various facilities gradually and carefully. In case of a new customer, documentary credit should be granted initially. Clean limits may be granted subsequently if the customer's conduct in respect of documentary bills proves to be satisfactory. In the beginning smaller credit limits may be prescribed to a new party. The limit may be raised gradually, as the need of the part increases and banker's experience in dealing with him proves to be satisfactory. D/A terms should not be granted liberally in the case of new customers.

☞ Precautions in Case of Bills Accompanied by Motor Transport Receipts

With the growth of road transport in recent years, bills accompanied by motor transport receipt (*i.e.,* Lorry Receipts) are presented to the banks for purchase/discounting. Such receipts have the following drawbacks:

(i) Motor Transport Receipts are not documents of title to goods under the Sales of Goods Act. The endorsee of the Receipt does not get a right to sue for the value of the goods.

(ii) Many motor transport companies deliver the goods to the consignee, even without the presentation of the Motor Receipt or an Indemnity Bond in lieu thereof.

(iii) Such receipt may be issued by bogus transport companies as well.

To overcome these drawbacks, the Indian Banks Association now maintains a list of approved motor transport companies. The receipt issued by such carrier must contain a clause that the company will not deliver the goods until the original Motor Receipt duly discharged by the banker is not presented to it. The Motor Receipt must be issued in the name of the seller and not the buyer. It must also contain an undertaking that the transport company shall reimburse the banks in respect of any damage caused because of its own negligence.

The banker should take the following precautions while purchasing/discounting bills supported by Motor Transport Receipts:

1. The Receipt is issued by an approved transport company. It contains the conditions stipulated by the Indian Banks' Association.
2. The Receipts must not be stale and it must not contain any alterations.
3. It must be issued in the name of the consignor, who must negotiate the bill with the banker or in the name of the bank. In the former case, the consignor must endorse it in the name of the banker.
4. The details given in the Receipt must be tallied with the details given in the invoice or any other documents attached with the bill.
5. The banker should immediately inform the transport company about its lien on the goods covered by the Receipt.

RENEWAL OF CREDIT LIMITS FOR BILLS

Credit limit for purchase/discounting of bills are sanctioned on annual basis. Requests are received by the banker for their renewal for another year. While dealing with such requests, the banker should take the following points into consideration:

(i) To what extent were the credit limits sanctioned for the previous/current year actually utilised, *i.e.,* the total amount of bills purchased/discounted during the year and the maximum, minimum and average outstanding balances. If the customer could not fully utilise these limits without valid reasons, the limits should be reduced accordingly. On the other hand, if the business of the customer is expanding, higher limits may be granted.

(ii) The banker should scrutinise the operations in the customer's account to find out —

(a) The name of the drawees of the bills and the total outstanding amount against each of them at any particular time. The banker may thus ascertain that the bills were drawn on real parties and that they were not accommodation bills.

(b) The nature of goods covered by the documents of title to goods, e.g., railway receipts and lorry receipts.

(c) The details of the bills which were returned dishonoured by the drawee and the reasons for such dishonour. What has been the experience of the banker in realising the amounts of such dishonoured bills from the drawer or the drawee on representation?

(d) With what periods the bills drawn by the customer were honoured by the drawees? Has there been any undue delay? The banker should also consider credit reports on the drawees as well.

If the experience of the banker regarding *(c)* and *(d)* has been satisfactory, the credit limits as requested may be renewed. If the bills were dishonoured frequently by one of the parties, it is an unsatisfactory sign and the banker should take note of it.

☞ Discounting of Bills in India

In the past discounting of bills as a method of granting credit was not as popular in India as in foreign countries. Though the amount of inland bills discounted/purchased by Indian scheduled banks increased from ₹ 134 crore in 1960-61 to ₹ 708 crore in 1970-71 but this accounted for less than one-fifth of the total outstanding bank credit in India. The Reserve Bank of india appointed a "Study Group on Enlarging the Use of the Bills of Exchange as an Instrument of Credit and the Creation of a Bill Market" on February, 1970. The Study Group considered the general question of enlarging the use of bills of exchange for providing credit. The usance promissory notes lodged by the customer under then existing Bill Market Scheme did not arise out of trade transaction but came into existence only to enable the banks to seek refinance from the Reserve Bank. The Study Group therefore, aptly remarked that these bills are not bills in the true sense nor is there a Market for them. It (the bill market scheme) is in effect an accommodation scheme on the basis of improvised bills. There has been paucity of sufficient trade bills which could be rediscounted with the Reserve Bank.

☞ Reasons for Insufficiency of Trade Bills

1. The preponderance of the overdraft and cash credit system of lending by the Indian banks is largely responsible for insufficiency of trade bills. A sizeable amount of short-term finance is provided by banks for sale of stock in the form of cash credit against the collateral of book debts.

2. The system of cash credit is preferred by the borrowers because of the opportunies to misuse it. This practice may in most cases result in an elongation of the period of bank credit as there is no discipline imposed on the purchasers to pay the dues within the stipulated period. As against this, the practice of credit sales by issue of usance bills imposes financial discipline on the purchasers and enables the suppliers to plan their financing commitments in a realistic manner.
3. The high rate of stamp duty on usance bills is also a discouraging factor. The rate of stamp duty for 90 days usance bill at present is 50 paise for ₹ 1,000. The Dehejia Study Group on the Credit Needs of Industry and Trade suggested to the Central Government to consider a reduction in the stamp duty on usance bills with a view to encouraging the development of bills market.

☞ Recommendation of the Dehejia Study Group

The Study Group came to the conclusion that "it would be advantageous to take steps to enlarge the use of bills of exchange as an instrument of credit and to create a bill market in the country where bill could be purchased or sold according to the requirements of the institutions concerned". It recommended the progressive use of the bills of exchange on a large-scale because of the following main advantages:

(i) In the absence of a bill market, the commercial banks heavily depend on the Reserve Bank while some banks have surplus fund which they are unable to make use of because the call loan market is not active throughout the country.

The Study Group, therefore, felt that the growth of bill market will make it possible for banks and others with surplus funds to be bills of various maturities and those in deficit to sell the bills in the market to meet their requirements. The eligible banks will thus approach the Reserve Bank of India only when they fail to obtain the requisite accommodation from the market. This will impart flexibility to the money market by evening out liquidity within the banking system and enable the Reserve Bank to exercise more effective control over the money market.

(ii) The lending banker will also be benefited by the discounting of bills as compared with the cash credit system because the repayment of the amount on a specified date will be definite and it will be possible for them to meet the requirements of cash easily by rediscounting bills either in the Bill Market or with the Reserve Bank of India.

(iii) The advantage to the borrower would be that a high class bill of exchange can normally be discounted at rates lower than those charged by banks on advances. Moreover, the use of bill would impose financial discipline on the purchases also as they will have definite obligation to pay the amounts on the due date.

(iv) In case of the large borrowers it would be possible that a single institution lends out the entire requirements by way of bills of appropriate maturities. Thereafter this institution may enable other institutions to participate in an indirect way, *i.e.,* by purchasing some of these bills. Thus, the difficulties inherent in a participation arrangement may be avoided.

☞ Rediscounting of Bills from the Reserve Bank

Reserve Bank of India provides refinance facilities to banks — vide Section 17 of the Reserve Bank of India Act, 1934, in the following two ways:

(i) By rediscounting the bills under Section 17(2) (a); or

(ii) By granting advances to eligible scheduled banks against the security of usance promissory notes of their customers under Section 17(4) (c). Two important schemes — The Bill Market Scheme, 1952, and the Bill Rediscounting Scheme, 1970, have been introduced by Reserve Bank of India to enable the banks to avail of the facilities of accommodation on the basis of bills of exchange.

BILLS REDISCOUNTING SCHEME

With a view to encourage the growth of a Bill Market in India the Reserve Bank of India introduced the Bills Rediscounting Scheme in terms of Section 17(2) (a) of the Reserve Bank of India Act with effect from November 1, 1970. In November 1981, Reserve Bank of India stopped to rediscount bills under the Scheme and permitted the Banks to rediscount the bills with one another as well as with approved financial institutions under the procedure laid down under the scheme. These financial institutions include Life Insurance Corporation, Unit Trust of India, Industrial Credit and Investment Corporation, Industrial Reconstruction Bank of India, Export Credit Guarantee Corporation of India, SBI Mutual Fund and Selected Urban Cooperative Banks. The main features of the scheme are as follows:

(1) *Eligible Banks:* All licensed scheduled banks (including the State Bank of India, its subsidiaries and the nationalised banks) are eligible to offer bills of exchange for re-discounting.

(2) *Fixation of Limits:* The eligible banks are required to apply to the Reserve Bank for sanction of limits for rediscounting of bills under the scheme giving their estimated credit requirements for 12 months ending October each year. Limits are sanctioned or renewed for a period of one year (1st November to 31st October).

(3) *Eligibility of Bills:* Following categories of bill are eligible for rediscounting under the scheme:

(*a*) Genuine trade bills which arise out of sale or despatch of goods and satisfy following conditions:

(i) The bills should have been drawn on and accepted by purchaser's bank or drawn on the purchaser and his banker jointly and accepted by them jointly. In case the purchaser's bank is not a licensed scheduled bank, the bill should, in addition, bear the signature of a licensed scheduled bank. The acceptance of the bill by the banker on behalf of the purchaser is intended to add to its value and make it acceptable for the purpose of rediscounting . In fact the entire basis of acceptability of a bill of exchange by a discounting agency is that it should contain at least one good signature besides that of the drawer. The signature of the licensed scheduled bank is treated as good signature.

(ii) The bill should normally have a maturity of not more than 90 days. A bill having a maturity up to 120 days is also eligible provided at the time of rediscounting it has a maturity of not more than 90 days.

Effective 29th April, 1995 a minimum period of 15 days has been prescribed for re-discounting of commercial bills and derivative usance promissory notes (explained ahead).

(iii) It should contain clause indicating the nature of the transaction out of which it has been arisen. For example:

"This bill of exchange has been drawn in connection with the sale of X bales of cloth covered by Railway Receipt

No.................. dated.....................

In case both the buyer and the seller are in the same city and the buyer generally indicates the receipts of goods by signing the relative invoice or receipted challan which accompany the other documents the bill drawn in respect of such sales should contain full particulars such as the number and date of invoice, or challan description and value of goods evidencing the sale.

(b) Bills drawn on and accepted by buyer under an irrevocable letter of credit and certified by the buyer's bank which has opened the letter of credit.

(c) Bills of exchange arising out of sale of goods of Government departments and quasi-Government bodies, statutory corporation and Government companies, provided such bills conform to the requirements of the scheme.

(d) Bills of exchange drawn on and accepted by the Industrial Credit and Investment Corporation of India Ltd., on behalf of its purchaser constituents singly or jointly with them provided an eligible scheduled commercial bank offers them for rediscount.

(e) Bills accepted by a licensed scheduled bank for a purchaser and discounted for a seller, if both are the clients of the same bank.

(f) Bills discounted at the instance of the drawee, provided discounting bank certifies the creditworthiness of the drawee and the genuineness of the signature.

(4) *The following categories of bills are not eligible for rediscounting:*

(i) Bill for sale and despatch of goods under the directives of Selective Credit Control.

(ii) Bill arising out of sale of services such as professional services/sale of goods on hire purchase basis.

(iii) Usance promissory notes executed by buyers in favour of sellers.

(iv) Bill drawn on mercantile agent for goods sent on consignment basis.

(v) Bill under Bill Rediscounting Scheme of IDBI.

(5) *Certificate by the Bank rediscounting the Bills:* While forwarding the bills for rediscounting, the bank is required to certify that —

(a) the bills arose out of bona fide commercial or trade transaction(s) relating to sale of goods.

(b) the drawers of the bills are financially sound, solvent, creditworthy and their signatures appearing on the bills are genuine and good signatures.

(c) the signature of the accepting bank appearing on the bill is genuine; and

(d) having discounted the bill for the full amount the discounting bank has full title to the bill.

The bank discounting the bill has to give the above certificate regarding the solvency and creditworthiness of the drawers of the bills. The bills are therefore, discounted on the creditworthiness of the drawers of the bills, though the signature of the banker of the drawee, who accepted the bill is also of significance.

Those bills are also rediscounted which are discounted by a bank at the instance of the drawee, who has accepted the bill as stipulated under the scheme, provided the discounting bank certifies that the drawee of the bill is financially sound, solvent and creditworthy and his signature on the bill is good.

Thus, the certificate of the discounting bank may be either in respect of the drawer or the drawee of the bill, who is considered creditworthy for the amount of the bill. Where the drawer of the bill is not a constituent of the bank, the bill is discounted on the strength of the creditworthiness of the drawee instead of the drawer. Such bills are called drawee bills.

☞ Lodgement of Bills/Derivative Usance P/N

Bill of exchange discounted by the eligible banks are to be endorsed in favour of the rediscounting institution and delivered to it at the time of rediscounting. The reserve process is required at the time of maturity of the bills. Banks face a lot of administrative difficulties in following this procedure, which result in waste of time and energy, besides the risk of losing the bills.

To overcome these difficulties discounting banks have been permitted to execute an agreement with the re-discounting institution for retaining the individual bills of the face value of ₹ 10 lakh and below as agent of the re-discounting institution. Bills over the face value of ₹ 10 lakh were till recently required to be physically lodged with the re-discounting institution.

The Reserve Bank further simplified the procedure of re-discounting in September, 1988 by dispensing with the necessity of physical lodgement of discounted bills. Under this procedure, the branches of a bank will intimate the head office the bills discounted by them. On the basis of such bills resting with the branches, the head office will prepare a derivative usance promissory note for suitable sums, say ₹ 5 lakh, ₹ 10 lakh etc. for suitable maturities up to 90 days and these derivative P/Ns can be re-discounted with any rediscounting institution. The Government of India have remitted the stamp duty on such P/Ns raised by banks. Such P/Ns should be backed by unencumbered usance bills of exchange of at least equal value. The discounting bank will hold and continue to hold such unencumbered bills till the date of maturity of the derivative P/N. If, in the meanwhile, any bill matures, it should be replaced by a fresh eligible bill of equal amount.

On the maturity of the promissory note, the amount payable by the issuing bank will be the value of the note.

The Bills Rediscounting scheme was introduced with a view to generate genuine bills, in the money market and to even out liquidity within the banking system. The ultimate objective is to have a broad-based bill market in which all institutions, financial and otherwise, should participate.

☞ Drawer and Drawee Bills

Bills of exchange discounted by bank are of two types: *(a)* Drawer bills, and *(b)* Drawee bills. The basic difference between the two is that in case of the former, the bill is discounted at the instance of the drawer and in case of the latter, at the instance of the drawee. In a business transaction, the seller draws a bill on the buyer whose bank accepts the bill and sends it back to the seller who can have it discounted with his bank. In some cases, the bank for the buyer and the seller may be the same. The buyer's bank grants an acceptance credit to the buyer and accepts bills up to such limit. The amount of goods purchased on credit under the acceptance limit are shown separately in the stock statements submitted by the buyer. There will be no drawing power against such unpaid stocks.

Under the drawee bills scheme, the buyer's bank itself discounts the bills and sends the proceeds to the seller, even if it is not the seller's bank. The rate of interest charged by the bank for discounting drawee bills is the same as that applicable to advances granted to the borrower against Pledge/ Hypothecation of stocks. In respect of drawee bills, the bank earmarks suitably the drawing power available against stocks after providing the prescribed margin. The drawer bills — also called sales bills, finance receivables and replace cash credit against book debts. The drawee bills, on the other hand, finance purchase of raw materials.

The Working Group to review the system of cash credit (Chore Committee) found in 1979 that though the use of sales bills was somewhat satisfactory, the system of drawee bills had not yet caught up. The Chore Committee recommended that banks should compulsorily extend at least 50 per cent of cash credit limit against raw materials to all manufacturing units by way of drawee bills. The objectives behind this suggestion were to:

(i) bring in financial discipline on the buyer in the purchase of raw materials,

(ii) to create a suitable short-term financial instrument to even out liquidity, and

(iii) to reduce dependence on the cash credit system to some extent.

In its guidelines issued in December 1980, the Reserve Bank advised the banks to implement the above recommendation of the Working Group.

RECENT MEASURES TO PROMOTE BILL FINANCING

In 1986 Working Group on the Money Market was appointed by the Reserve Bank of India under the chairmanship of Shri N. Vaghul. Accepting its recommendation, the Reserve Bank of India has taken the following steps to promote bill financing in India.

(1) Lowering of Bill Discount Rate

To encourage the use of bills, Reserve Bank prescribes the bill discount rate at a level lower than the rate charged on cash credit limits.

The maximum effective interest rate on the discounting of bills of exchange was brought down to 15.5 per cent with effect from April 1, 1987. This reduced the cost of bill finance by 1 or 2 percentage points.

Effective September 22, 1990 when the new lending rates were introduced, the effective interest rate on discounting of bills for borrowers with limits over ₹ 2 lakh was prescribed one percentage point below the minimum rate (16%) prescribed for them. As such the effective rate on discounting of bills for such category of borrowers was prescribed at 15% (minimum). It was raised to 16% effective April 13, 1991 when the minimum lending rate was hiked from 16% to 17% . The stipulation has been withdrawn with effect from Oct. 18, 1994.

(2) Abolition of Ceiling on Discount Rate

The ceiling on rediscount rate was raised from 11.5% to 12.5% with effect from April 1, 1987. This step was taken to attract additional funds from investing institutions into the discount market. With effect from May 1, 1989 this ceiling rate has been abolished.

(3) Drawing Power Against Receivables Reduced

In case of borrowers having aggregate credit limits beyond ₹ 5 crore while calculating the drawing power under cash credit and overdraft facilities against receivables, only 75 per cent of the receivable was eligible for financing, subject to the normal margin prescribed by banks. The remaining credit requiremets of such borrowers could be financed through demand or usance bills. In case of parties, where the proportion of receivables financing was already less than 75 per cent, this proportion was not to be increased. This was enforced with effect from April 1, 1988.

As the above directive was not fully complied with, Reserve Bank decided to impose a penal rate of interest effective January 1, 1991. Accordingly, in case of fund based working capital limits of ₹ 5 crore and above interest at 2 percentage points above the relevant cash credit interest rate was levied on that portion of the book debt finance which was in excess of the prescribed norm of 75% of limits — sanctioned to borrowers for financing inland credit sales.

This mandatory requirement was withdrawn with effect from July 1,1996.

(4) Stipulation on Bill Acceptances to Credit Purchases

Similarly all parties to whom (3) above applies are required to attain ratio of bill acceptance to credit purchases of 25% with effect from April 1, 1988. In case this ratio is below the required level, customers are required to progressively move towards attaining the 25% ratio. Where this ratio exceeds the 25% ratio, slippages would not be allowed.

According to Reserve Bank directive cases of these borrowers are now subject to post-sanction scrutiny by Reserve Bank. While sending such cases for Reserve Bank's scrutiny, banks are required to indicate in each case whether the minimum levels prescribed by the Reserve Bank under (3) and (4) have been achieved. If not, what steps have been taken for their compliance?

(5) Sanction of *Ad Hoc* Bill Limit

Banks have been given the discretion to sanction credit to above-mentioned parties a separate *ad hoc* bill limit for a period not exceeding three months up to an amount equal to 10% of the existing bill limit subject to a ceiling of ₹ 1 crore. Thus, additional funds may be made available to such parties in the form of bill finance.

STAMP DUTY ON BILLS REMITTED

On the recommendation of the Reserve Bank, the Government of India remitted the stamp duty chargeable in respect of usance bills of exchange, provided the following conditions are fulfilled:

(a) the bills of exchange are payable not more than three months after date or sight;

(b) the bills of exchange are drawn on or made by or in favour of a commercial bank or a co-operative bank; and

(c) the bills of exchange arise out of *bonafide* commercial or trade transactions.

The remission of stamp duty shall also apply to import and export bills of exchange, if the above-mentioned conditions are satisfied.

REDISCOUNTING FACILITIES WITH DISCOUNT HOUSE

As already noted, Finance and Discount House of India Ltd., (FDHI) has been established in 1988. Till then the bills, of exchange discounted by banks could be rediscounted with other scheduled banks and specified financial institutions. But such institutions were not allowed to further rediscount such rediscounted bills. Now, the FDHI stands ready to rediscount such rediscounted bills from any institution and also to sell such bills to them. Thus, an active discount market is intended to be established in India by promoting successive rounds of rediscounting of bills.

Consortium Advances

(Participation Financing or Joint Financing)

A new and important development in the field of bank lending in recent years in India is the granting of credit by commercial banks on a consortium basis. In case the credit needs of a borrower are very large, two or more banks join together to finance it jointly in proportion to their capacities. This collaborative financing by banks is also known as 'Participation Financing' or 'Joint Financing'. There are two important advantages of participation financing. *Firstly* banks may be able to participate in financing very large loans and *secondly,* banks may be able to diversify their risks. In recent years, banks have started financing through consortium basis not only working capital but term loans also.

There is a difference between consortium finance and multiple banking. In consortium finance, an advance is given by many banks to the borrower against a common security which is charged to all the banks for the total advance. One of the bank acts as a consortium leader and takes main part in loan processing, documentation and recovery. All the participating banks enter into an agreement about the terms and conditions of joint finance. In multiple banking, the customer borrows from a number of banks under separate agreements and provides separate security to each bank according to the amount of borrowing.

A Study Group under the chairmanship of Shri G. Lakshminarayanan was appointed by the Reserve Bank of India in 1973 to make recommendations about sharing of advances to units in private and public sectors, for participation amongst banks for revival of sick units and for better coordination and cooperation amongst banks, in respect of multiple banking. The Reserve Bank of India accepted the recommendations of the Study Group, and on that basis, suggested to the banks that, large credit limits by a bank to any single borrower in the public or private sector (including Electricity Boards) in excess of 1.5 per cent of its deposits should normally be extended on a participation basis. In cases, where a number of banks finance the working capital requirement of a borrower without consortium arrangements, all these banks should evolve a procedure of coordination among themselves to periodically exchange information, review of borrower's position and his credit requirements at the time of extension or renewal of credit limits or when borrower's performance shows signs of deterioration.

Reserve Bank of India issued further guidelines in 1978 to banks to be followed in lending for working capital under consortium agreements. According to these guidelines, banks are required to form a consortium, where the aggregate credit limits sanctioned by several banks to a single party amounted to ₹ 5 crore or more, the share of each participating bank in consortium was not to be less than 10 per cent of the total working capital limits sanctioned to the borrowers and the number of banks should not normally exceed five, except in case of very large credit limits. The terms and conditions should be uniform for all the participating banks.

In October, 1993 this threshold limit was raised to ₹ 50 crore. Reserve Bank also laid down other rules in this respect.

In October 1996, following the policy of liberalisation and deregulation in the financial sector, Reserve Bank decided that whenever a consortium is formed, either on a voluntary basis or on obligatory basis, the ground rules of the consortium arrangement would be formed by the participating banks in the consortium. These rules may relate to —

(i) number of participating banks.

(ii) minimum share of each bank.

(iii) entry/exit from the consortium.

(iv) sanction of additional/*ad hoc* limit in emergency situations contingencies by lead bank/other banks.

(v) the fee to be charged by the lead bank for the service rendered by it.

(vi) grant for any facility to the borrower by a non-member bank.

(vii) deciding timeframe for sanctions/renewals.

In April 1997, Reserve Bank decided that it would not be obligatory on the part of the banks to form a consortium even when the credit limits per borrower exceeds ₹ 50 crore. Thus, the need based finance required by a borrower may be extended by banks either entirely on their own or in association with other banks. But such bank shall have to observe the exposure limit prescribed by Reserve Bank, *i.e.,* credit to a single borrower should not exceed 25% of the net worth of the bank and to the borrowers' group not more than 50% of net worth.

☞ Participation Certificates

A participation certificate is an instrument through which a banker, which has granted credit to its borrowers, can share with other banks or financial institutions, having surplus funds, a part or whole of the credit given by it to its borrowers. The main advantage of participation certificate scheme is that it facilitates the inter-bank transfer of funds for short periods. The banks, thus, get funds from other banks or financial institutions, and have not to approach Reserve Bank for funds. To solve the problem of liquidity amongst banks and other financial institutions, this scheme was introduced in 1970. The Reserve Bank of India has prescribed the terms and conditions for the issue of participation certificates and banks can issue the certificates only on such terms and conditions which are as follows:

A bank may enter into participation arrangement with any other bank, Life Insurance Corporation of India, the Unit Trust of India, the General Insurance Corporation of India, the Industrial Credit and Investment Corporation of India, Export Credit and Guarantee Corporation and other institutions approved by the Reserve Bank from time-to-time. Banks may issue Participation Certificates against the working capital advances granted by them. Such advances may be earmarked in favour of the holder of the certificates and this should be noted on the certificates also. Accepting the recommendation of the Working Group on the money market the Reserve Bank has recently framed a scheme for Inter bank participations with a view to provide an additional instrument for evening out short-term liquidity within the banking system.

The Participation Certificates will be of two types, *viz.,*

(i) Inter-bank participations with Risk Sharing, and

(ii) Inter-bank participations without Risk Sharing.

The Certificates will be issued only to scheduled commercial banks and will not be transferable. Financial and investment institutions will remain outside their purview. The salient features of the two types of participations are as follows:

☞ Inter-bank Participation with Risk Sharing

The minimum period of such participations will be 91 days and the maximum period 180 days. The rate of interest will be determined by the issuing and participating banks but there will be a minimum rate of 14% per annum.

Banks will issue such participations only in respect of advances classified under Health Code No. 1 status (*i.e.,* advances to sound parties only). The aggregate amount of such participations of any account should not exceed 40% of the outstanding amount in the account at the time of issue. If later on the outstanding balance in such account falls short of the participations outstanding, the issuing bank will reduce the participations to the extent necessary. The issuing bank will normally repay the amount of participations, together with interest to the participant bank on the date of maturity. But when the risk has materialised, the issuing bank will take necessary action in consultation with the participating bank and share the recoveries proportionally.

The participating banks shall have to subscribe to the "Uniform Code for Participations' which contains their mutual rights and obligations in relation to the securities.

☞ Inter-bank Participation without Risk Sharing

Such Participations should be backed by Cash Credit Accounts of the borrowers. The maximum period of such participation will be 90 days. Rate of interest thereon will be determined by the two concerned banks, but there will be a ceiling rate of 12.5%.

On the date of maturity, the issuing bank will pay the amount of participations with interest to the participating banks, irrespective of the default, if any, in the advance concerned. The participations would be treated as part of the net demand and time liabilities and the net bank balances for purpose of statutory reserve requirements.

☞ Transfer of Borrowal Accounts

To increase competition amongst the banks, the Reserve Bank has also permitted all parties (including those enjoying credit facilities in excess of ₹ 5 crore) to transfer their accounts from one banks to another bank. There will be no need of a 'no objection' letter from the existing banker. The transferee bank will have to take over the entire liabilities of the party. If any industrial group maintaining more than one account with a bank seeks to transfer only a good account, leaving an unsatisfactory account with the existing bank, the latter may refuse to allow such transfer unless satisfactory arrangements are made by the party.

☞ Variation Clause in Loan Agreements

The schedule of interest rates on advances, prescribed by the Reserve Bank, is subject to changes made by it from time-to-time. To overcome the difficulty experienced by banks in implementing such changes in the interest rates, the Reserve Bank has directed the commercial banks invariably to incorporate in loan agreements and other relevant documents the following proviso in the clause relating to interest rates:

"Provided that the interest payable by the borrower shall be subject to the changes in the interest rates made by the Reserve Bank from time-to-time."

By inserting such a proviso, the banks retain the right to modify the rates of interest on the loans which are outstanding as on the date of revision of interest rates by the Reserve Bank. In other words, the revised rates become applicable, besides the new loans, to the existing loans also.

☞ No Scrutiny of Interest Rates by Courts

The Banking Laws (Amendment) Act, 1983 has inserted Section 21-A in the Banking Regulation Act, 1949 which provides that the rates of interest charged by banking companies are not to be subjected to scrutiny by Courts. According to the newly inserted section —

"Notwithstanding anything contained in the Usurious Loans Act, 1918 or any law relating to indebtedness in force in any state, a transaction between a banking company and its debtor shall not to be reopened by any court on the ground that the rate of interest charged by the banking company in respect of such transaction is excessive."

☞ Clause Prohibiting Diversion of Loan Funds

Loan amounts must be actually utilised for the purpose for which they are taken. Sometimes the funds are diverted towards some other use and the advance becomes sticky. To avoid such a situation, the Reserve Bank has advised banks to include a clause in the loan documents prohibiting the borrowers from deflecting the loan amount to a purpose other than the one for which it has been sanctioned. The clause should confer the right on the bank to recall the loan amount or a part thereof if the bank apprehends that the borrower has violated it or is violating this condition. This right will not be affected by any other condition contained in the loan agreement or any other agreement between the bank and the borrower. This clause will help the banks to ensure proper end-use of the loan amounts.

COMMERCIAL PAPER

Commercial paper is an additional source of raising short-term funds by highly rated corporate borrowers. The Reserve Bank of India has issued guideliness for this purpose. These guidelines, as amended from time-to-time, provide as follows:

(1) Companies which fulfil the following requirements are permitted to issue Commercial Paper in the money market:

(i) The minimum tangible net worth of the company is ₹ 4 crore as per the latest audited Balance Sheet.

(ii) The company has fund-based working capital limits of not less than ₹ 4 crore.

(iii) The shares of the company are listed at one or more stock exchanges. Closely held companies whose shares are not listed on any stock exchange are now also permitted to issue CPs provided all other criteria for issue of CP are met.

(iv) The company has obtained minimum credit rating of P_2 from Credit Rating Information Service of India Ltd., or A_2 from Investment Information and Credit Rating Agency or PR_2 from Credit Analysis and Research.

(v) The Company has been placed under Health Code No. 1 by the financing bank.

(vi) The company maintained the current ratio of 1.33:1 as per the latest audited Balance Sheet.

(2) The CPs will have to be issued in accordance with the following norms:

(a) The maturity of the CP would be from one month to one year.

(b) The minimum size of an issue to a single investor should be ₹ 50 lakh. The denomination will be in multiples of ₹ 10 lakh.

(c) CPs will be issued at a discount to face value and the discount rate will be freely determined by the issuing company.

(d) CPs will be freely transferable.

(3) The issuing company will have to bear dealers' fees, rating agency's fees, standby facility charges and any other relevant charges.

(4) The Reserve Bank of India has also laid down a limit on the maximum amount for which CPs can be issued by a company. Earlier, this ceiling was fixed at 30% of the company's working capital (fund based) limit from the banking system. Subsequently, it was raised to 75% of the cash credit limit. In April 1996, Reserve Bank, allowed companies with maximum permissible bank finance above ₹ 20 crore to issue CPs up to 100% of their cash credit component. But in case of borrower, with maximum permissible bank finance between ₹ 10 crore and 20 crore, the amount of CPs is restricted to 75% of the cash credit component. It must be remembered that the maximum permissible bank finance (MPBF) for a company is to be bifurcated into loan component and cash credit component as per RBI directions as follows:

MPBF	Loan Component	CC Component
₹ 10 crore to ₹ 20 crore	75%	25%
₹ 20 crore and above	80%	20%

With effect from October 19, 1996 the ceiling on the issue of CPs was removed. Companies are now free to issue CPs to any extent. But the amount of CP issued is to be deducted from the credit facilities available from banks. The quantum of CP will be first adjusted from Cash Credit component. If such amount is in excess of the Cash Credit component, the excess amount is to be adjusted against the loan component.

With effect from September 6, 1996 Reserve Bank has also permitted the Primary Dealers to raise funds by issuing CPs. But they are not allowed to rollover their issues and no grace period is allowed for repayment of CP. CP can be issued in parts or in one tranche. If the CP is divided into parts, all the segments must have the same maturity date. The CPs must meet the credit rating requirement as prescribed for the corporates. Thus, the Primary Dealers will have access to greater volume of funds for their operations.

☞ Interest Tax Reintroduced

The Government of India reintroduced interest tax on the income from interest accruing to the financial institutions with effect from October 1, 1991. Interest tax was first introduced in 1974 but was discontinued in 1978 and again remained in force during the period of 1980 and 1995. Its revival has been stated as an anti-inflationary measure, but in reality it is a revenue raising measure for the exchequer.

The tax is payable on the gross interest income of credit institutions which include banks, cooperative societies engaged in the business of banking (but excluding cooperative societies providing credit facilities to farmers and village artisans) public financial institutions, State Financial Corporations and financial companies.

Interest tax will be charged on commitment charges and discount on promissory notes and bills of exchange also. It will, however, not be charged on the following:

(i) Interest on deposits made by a bank with Reserve Bank of India as Statutory Reserve under Section 42(B) of the Reserve Bank of India Act.

(ii) Discount on Treasury Bills.

(iii) Interest earned by a credit institution on loans and advances made to another credit institution.

Interest tax is charged @ 2% of the gross amount of interest. Interest tax on sticky loans of banks shall be levied only during the year when such interest is actually received and credited to the profit and loss account by the bank. Interest Tax will be allowed as a deduction in computing the income of the credit institutions. The latter are permitted to reimburse themselves by making necessary adjustments in the interest charges. Interest tax is payable in advance in three instalments like the income tax.

☞ QUESTIONS

1. What are the general principles which should guide a banker in making loans and advances to a customer? *[Rajasthan]*
2. Explain the principles that guide the banks in granting loans and advances. *[Madras]*
3. What is the importance of the Principles of Diversification in commercial banking? How is it observed in the advances portfolio of a bank? *[Pune]*

4. What are secured and unsecured advances of the bank? What precautions should a banker take while making unsecured advances? *[Delhi]*
5. What are the different forms of banker's advances? Discuss the principles which govern secured advances? *[Bangalore]*
6. Discuss the various ways in which a commercial bank renders financial assistance to business. *[Delhi, B.Com. (Pass)]*
7. Write Explanatory notes on:
   (i) Participation Certificates.
   (ii) Commercial Charge. *[I.I.B., Part I]*
8. "Fundamental principles on which credit is generally based are Character, Capacity and Capital." Explain. *[I.I.B., Part I]*

CHAPTER

17 Secured Advances: Modes of Creation of Charge

In the preceding chapter, we have considered the question of advances against the personal security of the borrower. In the case of loans secured by a guarantee, the surety usually does not pledge any tangible security, but merely promises to pay the amount due from the principal debtor if the latter fails to do so.

The various methods by which a bank's advance may be secured are:

(i) Lien;

(ii) Pledge; and

(iii) Mortgage.

(i) Banker's Lien: The right to retain goods is known as lien. The phrase general lien is used to distinguish it from a *particular lien* of a craftsman on goods on which he has expended labour, time or money. The banker's general lien confers upon him the right to retain securities, etc., in respect of the general balance due from their owner to the banker. It is purely possessory and does not transfer the property or the right of ownership to the banker. By usage and statute, the banker's lien is an implied pledge conferring upon him the power of sale in certain events.

Negative Lien: Negative lien is to be distinguished from lien. Under the negative lien, the banker does not get the right to retain any asset of the borrower. The borrower gives a declaration to the banker that his assets mentioned therein are free from any charge or encumbrance. He also gives an undertaking that he shall not create any charge over them or dispose them of without the permission of the banker. The borrower cannot dispose of the assets or create any charge thereon without the consent of the banker. The banker on the other hand, is not entitled to realise his dues from the said assets of the customer. His interests are thus partly safe by securing a negative lien.

(ii) Pledge: A pledge is defined as a bailment of goods for security for the payment of a debt or performance of a promise. The ownership remains with the pledger, subject only to the qualified property which passes to the pledgee by virtue of the bailment to him. (Section 172 of the Contract Act).

Delivery is necessary before a pledge is deemed to have been completed. There is one distinction between a *lien* and a *pledge*, *viz*., in the case of a lien, the property, though in possession of the creditor, is still in the full ownership of the borrower. In the case of a pledge, however, not only the exclusive possession of the property is with the lender, but the lender also acquires the right or power to sell, without express agreement, by the end of a transaction after giving a reasonable notice to the pledger.

In the case of a pledge, there should be bailment of goods on behalf of a debtor or an intending debtor and the objective of such bailment should be to hold the goods as security for the payment of a debt or the performance of a promise. The person (customer) who offers the security is called the "pledger" — or "pawner" — and the bailee is called the "pledgee" or the "pawnee".

The banker as a pledgee has a right (vide Section 173 of the Indian Contract Act) to retain the goods pledged for the payment of the debt or the performance of the promise and also from the amount of interest due on the debt and the necessary expenses incurred by him in connection with the possession or for the preservation of the goods pledged. According to Section 174, this right is applicable only in case of a particular debt for which the goods are pledged in the absence of an agreement to the contrary. In case of default by the pledger, the banker as a pledgee has a right (vide Section 176) either to file a civil suit against the pledger for the amount due and retain the goods as a collateral security or to sell the goods pledged after giving a reasonable notice of sale to the pledger.

☞ Who can Pledge the Goods?

Goods can be pledged by any one who is in legal possession of the same, namely,

1. *The owner of the goods himself.*
2. *The mercantile agent of the owner*: According to Section 178, "Where a mercantile agent is, with the consent of the owner, in possession of goods or the documents of title of goods, any pledge made by him, when acting in the ordinary course of business of a mercantile agent, shall be as valid as if he were expressly authorised by the owner of the goods to make the same, provided that the pawnee acts in good faith and has not, at the time of pledge, notice that the pawner has no authority to pledge".
3. *Joint-owner with the consent of other co-owner*: If the interest of the pledger in the goods is to a limited extend only, he can pledge the same to the extent of his limited interest. But in such cases the rights of an innocent third party are well protected, if a second pledge is made to him.
4. If a person obtains possession of the goods by fraud, misrepresentation, coercion or undue influence, such contract is voidable at the option of the lawful owner. However, the former can create a valid pledge on such goods provided the following conditions are fulfilled:

   (a) The contract has not been rescinded before the contract of pledge is entered into.

   (b) The pledge acts in good faith and without notice of the defective title of the pledger.
5. If a buyer leaves the goods or documents of title to goods after sale in the possession of the seller, the latter may make a valid pledge of the goods provided the pledge acts in good faith and he has no notice of the sale of goods to the buyer.

   Similarly a buyer, who obtains possession of the goods with the consent of the seller, before the title of the goods passed on to the buyer, may also make a valid pledge.
6. A pledgee can himself repledge the goods but such repledge will be valid only up to the extend of his interest in the goods pledged.

☞ Rights of a Banker as a Pledgee

1. The pledgee has the right to retain the goods pledged for the payment of the debt or the performance of the promise and also for the amount of interest due on the debt and the necessary

expenses incurred by him in connection with the possession or for the preservation of the goods pledged (Section 173). This right is applicable only in case of particular debt for which the goods are pledged, in the absence of an agreement to the contrary (Section 174). The pledgee can also claim any extraordinary expenses incurred by him for the preservation of the security.

2. In case of default by the pledge to make payment of the debt, the pledgee has the right either—

(a) to file a civil suit against the pledger for the amount due and retain the goods as a collateral security; or

(b) to sell the goods pledged after giving the pledger reasonable notice of sale (Section 176).

The pledgee can resort to these steps only when the pledger defaults in making payment of the debt and not earlier. In case of loans repayable after a fixed period, default takes place if the loan remains unpaid after the expiry of the stipulated period. In case of a loan repayable on demand, default takes place if, on receipt of a notice from the creditor demanding the repayment of the loan by a specified date, the debtor fails to do so within the period allowed by the creditor.

3. The pledger is bound to disclose to the pledgee the faults, if any to the goods pledged which are within his knowledge and which materially interfere with the use to those goods or expose the pledgee to extraordinary risks. If the pledgee suffers any damage as a result of non-disclosure of such fault by the pledger, the latter shall be responsible for it.

4. If the title of the pledger to the goods pledged is defective and the pledgee suffers any loss due to this fact, the pledger shall be responsible for such loss.

5. If the pledgee has given his consent as a result of inducement by fraud or misrepresentation in this regard or in regard to pledger's interest in the goods, the contract would be voidable at the option of the pledgee.

6. A pledgee's rights are not limited to his interest in the pledged goods but he would have all the remedies that the owner of the goods would have against a third person for deprivation of goods or injury to them. In *Morvi Mercantile Bank Ltd., vs. Union of India*, the Supreme Court held that the bank (pledgee) was entitled to recover the full value of the consignment from Railways, namely, ₹ 35,000 and not only the amount due to it from the customer, namely, ₹ 20,000.

☞ Duties of the Pledgee

1. The pledgee is bound to return the goods on payment of the debt. It is the duty of the pledgee to restore the goods to the pledger or to deliver the goods according to the directions of the pledger as soon as the obligation to repay the amount is discharged.
2. The pledgee is responsible to the pledger for any loss, destruction or deterioration of the goods, if the goods are not returned by the pledgee at the proper time (Section 16).
3. The pledgee is bound to use the goods pledged according to the agreement between the two parties. If he violates any of the conditions of the pledge, the contract would be voidable at the option of the pledger. He is also liable to make compensation to the pledger if he suffers any damage due to the unapproved use of the goods pledged (Section 153).
4. The pledgee is also bound to deliver to the pledgee any increase of profit which may have accrued from the goods bailed in the absence of an agreement to the contrary (Section 163). In *M.R. Dhawan vs. Madan Mohan and Others* (A.I.R. 1969 Delhi 313), the borrower pledged certain shares with the banker. The right of the pledgee to the dividends and the rights and bonus shares issued in respect of pledged shares was disputed by the pledger.

5. The pledgee is bound to take as much care of the goods pledged as a man of ordinary prudence would, under similar circumstances, take of his own goods of the same bulk, quantity and value as the pledged goods (Section 151). If he has done so, he is not responsible for the loss, destruction or deterioration of the goods pledged (Section 152).

☞ Hypothecation

Another term analogous to the *pledge* is hypothecation. In the case of hypothecation, a charge is given on property or goods for the amount of the debt, the owner, however, retaining their ownership as well as possession. The pledge, as discussed above, implies the transfer of possession to the creditor. Where possession is not so transferred but a mere charge is given on property retained by the owner, the property is said to be hypothecated. The instrument which creates such a charge is known as the *letter of hypothecation*. In actual business practice, however, this term in used loosely. The memorandum giving a charge on documents of title pledged with a banker as security and authorising him to dispose of the goods if the pledge fails to meet his obligation is commonly known as a letter of hypothecation.

In *hypothecation* (which is also called an open loan), possession is not transferred to the banker, and, therefore, such an advance is no better than a clean loan. Such an advance is, therefore, granted only to a person in whose integrity the banker has full confidence. Moreover, certain other precautions should be taken by the banker; for example, he must ascertain the specific goods hypothecated; an undertaking should be taken from the borrower that he would not borrow elsewhere; insurance against all risks, including fire, should be effected on all the goods; it is necessary to have a regular periodical inspection of the goods as well as the books of accounts and the stock disclosed by the books should be verified with the stock on hand; a careful watch should be kept to ensure that the goods hypothecated do not stagnate or clog and become old and unsaleable.

In the case of a *pledge*, possession of goods and not ownership passes to the creditor (banker). This form of advance also calls for great care on the part of the banker who should make proper arrangements for the stocking of pledged goods in a godown. The godown must be properly insured. It is also necessary to ascertain that the borrower has a proper title to the goods pledged.

It was noticed by Reserve Bank of India that in practice many businessmen hypothecated same stocks with more than one bank. Many banks had granted loans to shopkeepers and small traders without verifying whether they were getting the benefit of similar credit facilities from other banks. This type of double financing was considered undesirable by the Reserve Bank, and the banks were advised* to observe the following precautions in this regard:

(a) Before sanctioning any credit limit, the bank should ensure that the applicant is not enjoying similar facilities with other banks. In case he is having credit facilities from any other bank/banks, detailed information should be called from by the bank from those banks. As far as possible, parties should be advised to restrict their borrowing to only one bank.

(b) The bank should obtain from the borrower a written application accompanied by a declaration about the existing credit arrangements and an undertaking that the stocks will not be hypothecated to any other bank without the prior approval of the bank. The undertaking should also be incorporated in the stock statements which the borrower is required to submit to the bank periodically. The terms of transaction should also stipulate that the advance will be recalled forthwith in case it is subsequently found that he has made a false statement in this regard.

(c) Before granting credit facilities to the party, as also during the pendency of the advance, an officer of the bank should inspect the stocks with a view to ensuring that the same stocks

*Report on Currency and Finance, 1970-71, p. 247.

have not been hypothecated to other banks. He should record such information in his report relating to his periodical inspection.

(d) In case the borrower is allowed to avail himself of credit facilities against hypothecation of stocks from various banks, it should be ensured that such stocks are segregated or demarcated in different godowns/shops and the same are properly recorded in separate stock books so as to facilitate easy verification by the bank officials.

GUIDELINES ISSUED BY RESERVE BANK AGAINST RISK OF DOUBLE FINANCING

In case of hypothecation of stocks, the same stocks may be hypothecated to more than one bank. The Reserve Bank of India noticed that some of the banks had granted advances to small traders, shopkeepers, etc., against the hypothecation of stocks, without ascertaining whether they were having similar credit facilities with other banks. The Reserve Bank felt this type of double financing as undersirable and advised the banks to observe the following precautions in this regard:

(a) Before sanctioning any credit limit, the bank should ensure that the applicant is not enjoying similar facilities with other banks. In case he is having credit facilities from any other bank/ banks, detailed information should be called for by the bank from those banks. As far as possible, parties should be advised to restrict their borrowings to only one bank.

(b) The bank should obtain from the borrower a written application accompanied by a declaration about the existing credit arrangements and an undertaking that the stocks will not be hypothecated to any other bank without the prior approval of the bank. The undertaking should also be incorporated in the stock statements which the borrower is required to submit to the bank periodically. The terms of transaction should also stipulate that the advance will be recalled forthwith in case it is subsequently found that he had made a false statement in this regard.

(c) Before granting credit facilities to the party, as also during the pendency of the advance, an officer of the bank should inspect the stocks with a view to ensuring that the same stocks have not been hypothecated to other banks. He should record such information in his report relating to his periodical inspection.

(d) In case the borrower is allowed to avail himself of credit facilities against hypothecation of stocks from various banks, it should be ensured that such stocks are segregatged or demarcated in different godowns/shop and the same are properly recorded in separate stock books so as to facilitate easy verification by the bank officials.

(iii) Mortgage: In Section 58 of the Transfer of Property Act, 1882, the term mortgage has been defined as, *"the transfer of an interest in specific immovable property for the purpose of securing the payment of money advanced or to be advanced by way of loan, an existing or future debt, or the performance of engagement which may give rise to a pecuniary liability".*

Except in the case of an equitable mortgage, a mortgage has to be effected by a registered deed, signed by the mortgagor and attested by at least two witnesses. Unlike a pledge, a mortgage does not necessarily involve the transfer of possession, although in certain forms of mortgage the creditor does, as a matter of fact, gain possession of the mortgaged property. Furthermore, unlike a pledge and a hypothecation which are in respect of movable property, a mortgage is effected always in respect of immovable property.

☞ Mortgage by Deposit of Title Deeds

Mortgage by deposit of title deeds is, in essence, a simple mortgage, whereby a charge in equity is created on the property, for it is provided under Section 96 of the Transfer of Property Act that the provisions as regards redemption of mortgages, which apply to simple mortgages, shall also apply to a mortgage by deposit of title deeds. The mortgage in this case is created by the deposit of documents of title along with a memorandum in which the debtor undertakes to pay a sum of money by a certain date, together with interest at the agreed rate. It is a mode of creating a legal mortgage under which the interest in the mortgaged property is transferred to the mortgagee.

☞ English Mortgage

Under Section 58 of the Transfer of Property Act, when the mortgagor binds himself to repay the debt on a certain date and transfers the mortgaged property *absolutely* to the mortgagee, but subject to the proviso that, he will retransfer it to the mortgagor upon repayment of the mortgage money as agreed, the right created is known as an English mortgage. Thus, an English mortgage is, in form, transfer of ownership to the mortgagee, with a covenant to repay the debt on a certain date and a proviso that, on this condition being fulfilled, the mortgagee will retransfer the property to the mortgagor. The remedy available to the mortgagee is a sale through the intervention of the court in a normal legal manner, but not a foreclosure (*i.e.*, forfeiture of the mortgaged property by way of appropriation by the mortgagee against the debt). This is because, in the case of a sale, the mortgagor has the right to the surplus in the sale proceeds of the mortgaged property left over after the appropriation of the debt.

☞ Equitable Mortgage

A bare deposit of title deeds, with an intent to create a security on the property comprised therein, amounts to an equitable mortgage of the property. Equitable mortgages have received statutory recognition in India.

☞ Simple Mortgage

In the case of a simple mortgage, the mortgagee has two rights:

(i) To sue the mortgagor personally on his personal covenant to repay; and

(ii) To recover the amount from the property itself which is virtually hypothecated with him.

Both these remedies may be resorted to at the same time or in succession. Here, the transfer is said to be that of the right of sale. A simple mortgage differs from a charge in this that a charge may not necessarily be given on a specific property but may extend over all the property, including movables, and it does not involve a transfer which is the essence of a mortgage.

☞ Mortgage by Conditional Sale

In the case of mortgage by conditional sale, the mortgagor ostensibly sells the mortgaged property on the condition that —

(i) the sale shall become absolute on default in payment of mortgage money; or

(ii) on payment of such money, the sale shall become void; or

(iii) that on such payment being made, the buyer shall transfer the property to the seller.

These conditions must be embodied in the document which effects or purports to effect the sale.

☞ Usufructuary Mortgage

In the case of a usufructuary mortgage, the repayment of the loan begins as soon as the mortgage is effected. Here the mortgagor delivers possession of the mortgaged property to the mortgagee, or expressly or impliedly agrees to do so, and authorises him to retain it until the repayment of the mortgage money. Meanwhile, he is authorised to receive the rents and profits accruing from the property or any part of it, in payment of interest or part of the mortgage money or both.

The main element in this type of mortgagee is the transfer of possession over the mortgaged property to the mortgagee, who is entitled to receive income accruing therefrom. By this arrangement the liability of the mortgagor is gradually reduced. In *Arumugam Pillai vs. Maruthakutti Gownder* (AIR 1973, Madras 242) the Madras High Court held that "when the mortgagor and mortgagee agree that the entire amount due for payment to the latter, should be recouped by the mortgagee by the enjoyment of the usufructs from the mortgaged property over a specified number of years, the documents may not refer to any interest payable on the principal, even though an element of interest and its rate and income from the property might have gone into their calculation. They may agree to limit the period of such enjoyment, and thereafter deliver the possession to the mortgagor. As the mortgagor binds himself personally to repay the mortgaged money, no suit for the repayment of the mortgaged money can be filed against him. The mortgagee has only one remedy, *i.e.*, to retain his possession over the property and to recover his dues from income accruing therefrom.

☞ Anomalous Mortgage

A mortgage which is not simple mortgage, mortgage by conditional sale, usufructuary mortgage, English mortgage or mortgage deposit of title deeds (Equitable mortgage) as per the provisions of Section 58 of the Transfer of Property Act is Anomalous mortgage. Even a slight variation from the terms prescribed in Section 58 for the different types of mortgages, a mortgage will be called Anomalous mortgage, *Shri Ram Dayal and Others vs. Bhanwar Lal and Others* (AIR 1973, Rajasthan 73) both the principal and interest were secured by the mortgage of the properties, the possession of which was handed over to the mortgagee, who in addition took personal liability for the payment of the interest which was the part of the mortgaged money and also secured by the mortgage of the property. The mortgage deed stipulated that if the rents and profits were less than the amount of interest, then the mortgagor would be liable to pay the balance every year and be liable for compound interest, if the amount was not deposited in time. The Rajasthan High Court held it an anomalous mortgage and not a pure usufructuary mortgage. In anomalous mortgage, the rights and liabilities of the parties are determined by their contract as evidenced in the mortgaged deed, and if such contract does not extend, by local usage, according to the provision of Section 98 of the Transfer of Property Act.

☞ Sub-mortgage

The mortgagee may himself like to sub-mortgage the property mortgaged to him by the mortgagor, for example, a company may mortgage its book debts to the bank for a loan. The need for such sub-mortgage may arise when a customer is unable to furnish any better security to the banker. The precautions to be taken by banker in cases of sub-mortgage include a notice to the mortgagor for confirmation of the amount due from him to the mortgagee. The banker should ask the mortgagor not to make payment to the mortgagee but to the bank. The banker should take the original mortgage deed and the title deed from the mortgagee. The sub-mortgage shall be subject to the terms and conditions stipulated in the original mortgage deed entered into between the mortgagee and the mortgagor.

☞ Rights and Liabilities of Mortgagor

The mortgagor has a right of redemption; that is, at any time after the principal money has become due, he has a right on payment or tender, at a proper time and place, of the mortgage money, to require the mortgagee to deliver to the mortgagor the mortgage deed and all documents relating to the mortgaged property which are in possession or power of the mortgagee to the mortgagor and at the cost of the mortgagor either to retransfer the mortgaged property to him, or to such third person as he may direct, or to execute and where the mortgage has been effected by a registered instrument, to have registered an acknowledgement in writing that any right in derogation of his interest transferred to the mortgagee has been extinguished. Provided that the right conferred by this section has not been extinguished by any act of the parties or by an order of a court. The right conferred by this section is called the right of redemption.

The right of redemption can be claimed only when the money becomes payable and due and cannot be insisted upon before that date. A mortgagor cannot be deprived of his right of redemption, and no clause in the mortgage agreement which impedes or prevents redemption would be allowed by a Court on the ground of its being oppressive and unreasonable.

☞ Implied Contracts by the Mortgagor

In the absence of a contract to the contrary, the mortgagor shall be deemed to contract with the mortgagee —

(i) that the interest which the mortgagor professes to transfer to the mortgagee subsists, and that the mortgagor has the power to transfer this interest;

(ii) that the mortgagor will defend, or if the mortgagee be in possession of the mortgaged property, he will be enabled to defend the mortgagor's title thereto;

(iii) that the mortgagor will, so long as the mortgagee is not in possession of the mortgaged property, pay all public charges that may fall due in respect of the property;

(iv) that where the mortgaged property is a lease for a term of years, the rent payable under the lease, the conditions contained therein and the contracts binding on the lessee have been paid, performed and observed up to the time of the commencement of the mortgage; and that the mortgagor will, so long as the security exists and the mortgagee is not in possession of the mortgaged property, pay the rent reserved by the lease, or if the lease is renewed, performs the contracts binding on the lessee, and indemnify the mortgagee against all claims preferred by reason of the non-payment of the said rent or the non-performance or non-observance of the said conditions and contracts; and

(v) that where the mortgage is a second or subsequent encumbrance on the property, the mortgagor will pay the interest that accrues from time-to-time on each prior encumbrance as and when it becomes due, and will, at the proper time, discharge the principal money due on such prior encumbrance.

☞ Mortgagor in Possession

A mortgagor in possession of the mortgaged property is not liable to the mortgagee for allowing the property to deteriorate; but he must not commit any act which is destructive or permanently injurious thereto, if security is insufficient or will be rendered insufficient by such act (Section 66).

☞ Rights and Liabilities of the Mortgagee

The mortgagee has the right of foreclosure or sale; but this right is restricted only to a mortgage by conditional sale and/or to an anomalous mortgage. He has the right to sue for mortgage money. In the case of a subsequent mortgage, the subsequent mortgagee has the right to pay-off the prior mortgagee. Further, the mortgagee has a right against prior and subsequent mortgagees.

☞ Precautions to be Taken by Banker in the Mortgage of Immovable Property

The banker, when dealing with mortgages and title deeds connected with immovable property, should take the following precautions:

(i) The title deeds should be immediately shown to a competent authority for a report as to their genuineness and correctness.

(ii) The property should be valued at frequent intervals. Certain classes of house property rapidly deteriorate in value if they are not kept in a proper condition of repair.

(iii) In dealing with lease-hold properties, allowance must be made for the fact that their value declines as the term of expiry approaches.

(iv) The customer should be required to produce a receipt for the ground rent of lease-hold property as soon as the period for payment has passed, for if this is not paid, the lease may be forfeited.

(v) All house property should be insured against fire, and the customer should produce for the banker's inspection the receipt for each annual premium as it falls due.

(vi) Second mortgages of all kinds should be avoided, for the first mortgage may elect to foreclose and a forced sale may leave nothing for the second mortgage.

☞ Sub-mortgage

The mortgagee may himself like to sub-mortgage the property mortgaged to him by the mortgagor. In certain cases, banks accept such sub-mortgages, when a customer is unable to furnish any better security. In accepting sub-mortgage the banker should take the following precautions:

(a) A notice should be given to the mortgagor who should be required to confirm the amount due from him to the mortgagee.

(b) The banker should direct the mortgagor not to make payment to the mortgagee but to the bank, being the sub-mortgagee.

(c) The sub-mortgage shall be subject to the terms and conditions stipulated in the original mortgage deed entered into between the mortgagee and the mortgagor. The banker should therefore scrutinise these terms very carefully.

☞ Assignment

Assignment is another mode of providing security to the lending banker. *"Assignment means transfer of a right, property or a debt-existing or future."* The customer of a bank may assign any of his rights, properties or debts to the banker to secure a loan. The transferer of such a right is called the "assignor" and the transferee the "assignee". The borrowers generally assign the "actionable claims" to the banker. Section 130 of the Transfer of Property Act, 1882 permits such assignment to anyone except to a judge, a legal practitioner or an officer of the court of justice. Section 3 of the Act defines, an "*actionable claim*" as a "*claim to any debt, other than a debt secured by mortgage of immovable property or by hypothecation or pledge of movable property, or to any beneficial interest in movable property not in the possession, either actual or constructive, of the claimant, which the civil courts recognise as affording ground for relief, whether such debt or beneficial interest be existent, accruing conditional or contingent.*" In banking business, a borrower may assign to the banker *(i)* the book debts *(ii)* money due from Government department or Semi-government organisation, and *(iii)* life insurance policies.

☞ Questions

1. What are the salient features of a guarantee? Which points should be borne in mind by a banker when granting an advance on the security of a guarantee?
2. Distinguish between a mortgage, a pledge and a lien, giving examples of each.
3. *(a)* What precautions does a banker take when advancing a loan against a guarantee?

   (b) A banker advances money on the security of a guarantee. The guarantor, learning that the principal debtor is in financial difficulties, deposits with the Bank the full amount of his liability under the guarantee and says that the security deposited by the customer with the bank may be surrendered to him. What should the bank do?
4. State the most important terms which bank guarantee forms usually contain. Distinguish between a contract of guarantee and a contract of indemnity. What is a continuing guarantee?
5. *(a)* The Friendly Bank Ltd. has granted an overdraft to A against the guarantee of Y, which covers all sums due to the bank from time-to-time, up to a limit of ₹ 10,000. The guarantee is terminable by one month's notice. One day, Y comes to the bank and states that as he is going on a long pilgrimage, he wants to payback immediately the balance of the overdraft outstanding and get relieved. How should the bank act and why?

   (b) A banker issues a guarantee on behalf of his customer and notes a lien on the latter's account to the extent of 25 per cent of the amount of the guarantee. A guarantee order is served on the balance of customer's account. How should the banker proceed?
6. As a lending banker who has to keep in mind, among other factors, the contingency of the principal debtor becoming insolvent, which of the following two forms of guarantee would you consider more advantageous to him?

   (i) A guarantee for a customer's liabilities, present and future, up to the extent of ₹ 10,000 Or

   (ii) A guarantee for a customer's liabilities, present and future, with a provision that not more than ₹ 10,000 shall be recoverable from the guarantor. Clarify your answer with reasons and examples. *[I.I.B., Part II]*
7. *(a)* A gives a guarantee to a bank for an overdraft granted to B. When the guarantee is invoked, A seeks to avoid liability on the pleas: *(i)* that when he signed the guarantee, the account of B was already overdrawn but the bank did not disclose this fact to him, and *(ii)* that the bank had not exhausted its remedies, against B before calling on him to pay. Discuss the merits of both these pleas.

   (b) A substantial customer, Shri Saha, who maintains an average credit balance of ₹ 20,000 in his current account, calls to tell you that he has been approached by his brother-in-law with request to guarantee a business transaction for ₹ 15,000. You consider your customer good for his liability. Saha added that he agreed to this request only because he found it difficult to refuse relative and hoped to preserve peace and quiet within his family.

   He understands that an enquiry will be made of his bankers as to his standing for the guarantee and when the enquiry is received he wants a reply to be given to the effect that his means are limited and he is considered unsatisfactory for the liability. He thinks that the guarantee will not then be taken up.
   Explain, giving reasons, how would you deal with the proposal. *[I.I.B., Part II]*
8. Your Bank has sanctioned a limit of ₹ 1 lakh to A against the guarantee of B. After about six months B writes to you saying that he wishes to terminate his guarantee on a date mentioned in his letter. This letter is received at your Bank but is misfiled and hence no action is taken on it. The letter is not even acknowledged. Sometime after the date mentioned by B in the letter you find that the advance cannot be recovered from A and hence you send a notice to B asking him to repay the advance as the guarantor. B calls your attention to his letter and refuses to pay. What is the position of your Bank? *[I.I.B., Part I]*
9. Answer whether following statements are true or false:

   (a) A limited company can borrow by pledging its own shares.

   (b) In equitable mortgage, possession of property is given to the bank. *[I.I.B., Part I]*

10. What constitutes a pledge? What are its advantages over other kinds of charges say, hypothecation and mortgage? *[I.I.B., Part I]*
11. What do you understand by a 'Mortgage'? Explain in brief three usual forms of mortgages to secure bank finance. *[I.I.B., Part I]*
12. An advance to a limited company against stocks is generally by way of hypothecation instead of pledge. Why? *[I.I.B., Part I]*
13. What is equitable mortgage? What is the procedure for creating such mortgage? What precautions would you take before accepting equitable mortgage as security? *[I.I.B., Part I]*
14. *(a)* It is considered that it is possible to give advance against hypothecation of stocks to a limited company than to a partnership firm or an individual. Do you agree with this view? Give reasons.
    (b) What are the precautions taken by the Banks to safeguard their interest for advances against hypothecation?
    (c) At the time of renewal of an advance against hypothecation, banks have discontinued the practice of obtaining fresh security documents. Instead they generally obtain the document — the so-called confirmation of balance and security every year. Please comment. *[I.I.B., Part I]*
15. A shortfall has occurred in the cash credit hypothecation account of one of your customer. You are apprehensive in regard to the full recovery of the outstanding balance and demand additional security from him. He replies that all he can offer is a sub-mortgage of the property. You are satisfied that he has no other security to offer and accordingly you decide to accept the sub-mortgage.
    (a) State the precautions you would take and the procedure you would follow for obtaining the sub-mortgage. *[I.I.B., Part II]*
16. A public limited company manufacturing electrical goods applies for cash credit limit against the hypothecation of its stock of raw materials, goods in-process and finished goods. What aspects of the proposal will call for your security before you accede to it?
17. Your branch has advanced ₹ 50,000 against pledge of cloth bales valued at ₹ 90,000. The cloth bales are stored in a godown in the business locality, The key of the godown is with the bank.
    (a) One fine morning it is reported to you by the borrower that the locks of the godown are broken and substantial quantity of the good is stolen.
18. Describe the various types of securities and methods of charging them to cover bank advance. *[I.I.B., Part II]*
19. What is meant by Charging of Securities? State and explain various modes of charging the securities. *[I.I.B., Part II]*
20. Messrs. Sharda Textiles have been sanctioned a clean bills purchase limit of ₹ 2 lakh and demand documentary bills purchase limit of ₹ 7 lakh for purchase of bills accompanied by Railway Receipts or Motor Transport receipts covering textile piece goods, for a period of one year. Before the expiry of the period, they approach you as Branch Manager for renewal of the said facilities for another period of one year. What are the various points you will consider before renewing the limits? *[I.I.B., Part I]*
21. *(a)* What are the different types of bills of exchange purchased/discounted by commercial banks? Explain the precautions you would exercise while purchasing/discounting bills at your branch level.
    (b) Explain why it is better to provide post-sale credit (finance) by discounting bills rather than against book debts. *[I.I.B., Part I]*
    (c) What is the difference between bills purchased and bills discounted?
    (d) Why advance against bills are preferred to Cash Credit against goods? *[I.I.B., Part I]*
    (e) State in brief the precautions you would take as a banker while discounting trade bills covered by Motor Transport Receipts and payable on demand. *[I.I.B., Part I]*

CHAPTER

18 Advances Against Collateral Securities

One of the most important functions of a bank is to advance money to its borrowers, and a bank's strength depends considerably on the quality of its advances and their proportion to total deposits. The lender must always consider carefully the chances of getting back the money advanced. Therefore, he should not normally rely on the obligation of the borrower alone but should take a tangible security from which he can obtain repayment in case the borrower is unable to meet his obligations. In the absence of such security, the money lending business would be far too speculative and a very high rate of interest would have to be charged. In making loans and advances, a banker also wants to secure himself by having a reliable security.

In exceptional cases, where the banker has complete confidence in the integrity and honesty of a customer, he may allow a considerable unsecured overdraft for a short period. But, ordinarily, all the advances must be properly secured. In olden times, when a banker knew his customers personally and intimately, he knew exactly up to what amount a loan could be safely given without a security. The position is quite different today. Big modern banks, having a large number of offices over a wide area, cannot allow much discretion to local agents, who must strictly adhere to the rules and regulations laid down by the head office. Thus, in present-day banking, the question of security is very important.

In a highly-developed modern banking system, many type of securities are offered to cover advances, and a banker can spread his advances over a large variety, thereby, reducing his risk. These securities may vary from gold and silver to stock exchange securities, goods of various types, documents of title to goods, immovable property (land, buildings, etc.), and life policies. As all these securities are of different types, they call for particular attention and care on the part of the banker, who has to see to it that the time he gets on them is not unsafe.

☞ Securities may be Classified asunder:

1. **Personal Security:** There is a personal right of action against the customer or a third party, *e.g.,* a promissory note, guarantee, etc.
2. **Impersonal Security:** Here, the secuiity can be realised by sale or transfer, *e.g.,* land, shares, goods, etc.
3. **Direct Security:** Here, the security is deposited by the customer himself.

4. **Indirect or Third-party Security:** Security deposited by another person, *e.g.,* guarantee by an elder brother for securing the younger brother's account at the bank.
5. **Continuing Security:** According to the rule in Clayton's case, the secured advance would be decreased by subsequent payments into the account and all payments to the customer would form new advances, unsecured by the above-mentioned security. In order to provide against this effect of the rule in Clayton's case, the form of the bank security should be so worded as to make it a continuing one, covering the liability of the customer to the bank.

☞ A Banker Usually Secures His Advance by:

(i) Stock exchange securities;

(ii) Bullion;

(iii) Goods;

(iv) Documents of title to goods;

(v) Immovable property; and

(vi) Life policies.

A banker can minimise his risk by spreading advances over a large variety of securities, deposited either by the borrower himself, or by someone else on his behalf as a guarantor. A **collateral security** is a security belonging to and deposited by a third party to secure a customer's account. These collateral securities are advantageous from the banker's stand-point because, the case of insolvency of the customer, he can prove for his whole debt in insolvency and receive from the customer's estate all he can in the course of distribution by the official assignee, and thereafter realise the securities with respect to the balance.

The usual practice should be to obtain a memorandum of deposit in a proper form. This is most essential because even though in law such a memorandum is not necessary, the banker, by using it, protects himself by inserting in it the clauses necessary for such protection. According to statute, a banker has a general lien on the cash and securities to his customer, which come into his possession in the regular course of his business for any debt that may be due to him. If, however, there is a specific agreement with the banker to the effect that he will not have a general lien or that he gives it up, this agreement will be binding on him. (*Kuham vs. Bank of Madras*). In the case of valuables or securities deposited only for safe custody, this lien does not arise. With regard to securities on which the banker is given the authority to collect interest and dividend, however, such a lien would extend to the dividend also, but not to the title deeds casually left with him on which he had previously refused to make an advance.

We shall now consider the banker's point of view on the various types of securities offered to secure advances.

Stock Exchange Securities: The term stock exchange securities include gilt-edged securities, such as Government loans, municipal, port trust and improvement trust bonds, and such other securities as are issued by a Government and public bodies, and shares and debentures of industrial and commercial companies, banks and insurance companies in which dealings take place on the stock exchange.

☞ Advantages

(i) *Reliability:* These securities are more reliable than a guarantee where the banker has to depend entirely upon the solvency of the security for the recovery of advance, in case the borrower makes a default.

(ii) *Valuation:* The market price of these securities is published in the daily papers and other economic journals. Hence, a valuation of these securities is comparatively easier.

(iii) *Ascertainment of Title:* It is easier for a banker to satisfy himself whether the title of the customer to the securities offered is good.

(iv) *Realisability:* Stock exchange securities are more easily realisable than those of certain other kinds, *viz.*, land, buildings and certain kinds of goods, because there is always a ready market for good stock exchange securities.

(v) *Stability in Prices:* Stock exchange securities are less liable to fluctuations than commodities such as cotton, sugar, etc.

(vi) *Transferability:* These securities can be more easily transferred than certain other partially negotiable securities or land and buildings.

(vii) *Portability:* The release of securities can be effected with a minimum of expense and formality.

(viii) *Reduction in Indebtedness:* These securities yield interest or dividend which, when received, reduces the borrower's indebtedness towards interest and often towards the principal as well.

☞ Disadvantages

(i) Partly Paid-up Shares: In the case of partly paid-up shares, the banker may be called upon to pay the uncalled amount.

(ii) Company's Lien: The Articles of Association of a company generally provide that its shares will be subject to its lien in case of default in the payment of calls on them or of any other amounts due to them. A banker may, therefore, find that he cannot get the full benefit of securities if he fails to give a proper notice of his charge on them to the company concerned.

(iii) Non-Negotiable Securities: If the securities are not negotiable, their transfer cannot give to the transferee a better title than his own.

(iv) Transferee's Liability: A banker renders himself liable as transferee to indemnify the company against any loss it may suffer, if the transferor's signature on the instrument of transfer turns out to be a forged one.

(v) Forged Scrips: Certain unscrupulous persons resort to the forging of scrips to obtain advances against them. In such cases, it becomes difficult for a banker to find out whether a particular scrip is genuine and in case of default, the advance may become difficult of realisation.

☞ Precautions to be Taken

A banker should take the following precautions if he is offered stock exchange securities as a cover for an advance:

(i) A banker should ascertain whether the shares are partly paid-up or fully paid-up. In the case of partly paid-up shares, he should make sure that no call has been made which the shareholder has failed to meet, because unpaid shares can be forfeited to the company. Moreover, by getting such shares transferred in his name, a banker makes himself liable to any calls that may be due on them. When he is only an equitable mortgagee, he has to find money for the payment of the calls on the shares to prevent their forfeiture.

(ii) With a view to eliminating the acceptance of undesirable securities, a banker has to be careful in selecting only those which he should accept as cover for his advances. He should consider the following factors in selecting securities.

(a) Study of Final Accounts: It is necessary for a banker to study the profit-and-loss account and balance sheet of a company for a number of years. Such a study gives him a reliable estimate of the future prospects of the company.

(b) Study of Market Prices: A banker should also carefully study the market prices of stocks and shares. The market prices of the shares which are frequently dealt in are far more reliable than those in which stray transactions take place.

(iii) Between shares and debentures, a banker should prefer debentures; and in choosing between different kinds of shares, he should prefer preference shares to ordinary shares. Cumulative preference shares are better than non-cumulative preference shares. A banker should also see to it that the shares selected as security are included in the approved list of one or two stock exchanges, and are freely dealt in; otherwise, it will become difficult for him to sell them in case of need.

(iv) A banker has to ascertain the market price of the securities offered against an advance. He should not always rely for the valuation of securities on the quotations given in daily or weekly papers. Particularly in the case of securities which do not appear in the "business done" column of the stock exchange quotation list. In the case of shares in which business is done very infrequently, it is better to ascertain from the secretary of the company the rate at which the last transfer of its shares was registered.

(v) The next problem before a banker is about the charge of securities. In the case of fully negotiable securities, the property in them can be transferred by mere delivery, if they are bearer securities. But in the case of securities payable to a certain person or to his order, the delivery, complete with the endorsement of the person, is essential for transfer of property in them. If a banker takes such securities in good faith and for value, he gets a good title to them.

(vi) There are occasions where a banker has to accept a blank transfer. In such cases, he should take the precaution to give an immediate notice to the company concerned, informing it of the pledge to its shares with him. This will protect the banker, if the debtor is not already indebted to the company at the date of the receipt of the notice, against subsequent indebtedness by giving him a priority, *i.e.,* in case of the subsequent debt with the company, the latter's lien will be deferred to that of the banker's claim.

☞ Negotiable Securities

Negotiable securities are of four kinds:

(i) Bearer bonds;

(ii) Scrips to bearer. The term scrip generally employed to denote provisional certificates or documents indicating the subscription to so much of a loan or to so many shares. When the allotment money is paid, a scrip or provisional certificate is generally issued. Bonds are issued after the payment of the final instalment. Scrips are held to be negotiable by the usage of bankers and dealers in public securities;

(iii) Shares or stock warrants to bearer generally;

(iv) Debentures payable to bearer generally.

☞ Non-negotiable Securities

These are:

(i) Inscribed Stocks: Inscribed stocks are so-called because the names of the holders of such stocks and the amounts of their holdings are "inscribed", *i.e.,* recorded, in the books kept either with the Government or with the corporation issuing them, or its agents. When such a stock is to be transferred, it is necessary for its owner or his duly constituted attorney to go to the office where the books for the transfer of the securities are kept, and authorise the transfer of the stock he has sold.

(ii) Registered Stocks and Shares: Most of the stock exchange securities belong to this category, *viz.,* registered stocks and shares. They are so-called because the registration of their transfer in the books of the issuing company is necessary before a legal title is acquired to them. They are evidenced by certificates given under the seal of the issuing body.

Government securities form an excellent and the most liquid security from a banker's standpoint. In the case of the Indian Government securities, an endorsement is necessary, for they are made out as payable *to order.* Bearer securities accompanied by a memorandum need only to be deposited with a bank. The actual credit may be in the form of either an advance, an overdraft or a loan at the option of the customer. In the case of registered stocks and shares, a bank has either to take a blank transfer for shares duly signed by the borrower, together with a memorandum of deposit and the share certificates, or get the shares transferred to it or to its nominee, stating that this transfer is effected by way of mortgage or pledge and that on the repayment of the loan, the shares would be retransferred to the borrower or his nominee. It would be better for a bank to adopt the latter course in the case of a blank transfer arrangement.

When the shares of a joint-stock company are offered as security for an advance, a banker should carefully study the nature of the business of the company, its past history, location, management and future prospects. Consideration should also be given to the type of shares offered and their marketability. From the banker's point of view, preference shares, especially cumulative preference shares, are safer than ordinary shares. Partly paid-up shares are not very safe as a security for an advance. The reason is the contingent uncalled liability on the shares, which sometimes results in sharp fluctuations in their value and also in the market value.

According to Section 19(2) of the Banking Companies Act, 1949, a banking company is not permitted to hold, whether as a pledgee, mortgagee or absolute owner, shares in any company (except of its subsidiary company) of an amount exceeding 30 per cent of the paid-up share capital of that company or 30 per cent of its own paid-up share capital and reserves, whichever is less. Section 19(3) further provides that, except in respect of a subsidiary, a banking company must not hold shares (whether as pledgee, mortgagee or absolute owner) in any company in the management of which any managing director or manager of the banking company is in any manner concerned or interested.

The shares of public utility companies (electricity, gas, tramways) are considered quite safe as securities for advances because their business is generally quite sound and because they have generally the monopoly of supplying a particular utility or product in a specified area.

☞ Advances Against Units of the Unit Trust of India

Banks make advances against the units of the Unit Trust of India up to 90 per cent of the current repurchase price by the Unit Trust of India. All the leading newspapers regularly publish quotations of the current repurchase price of the units. Except in special cases, units must be transferred to the bank's name before an advance is allowed against them.

☞ Advances Against National Savings Certificates, etc.

Customers often approach banks for small advances against National Savings Certificates, National Defence Certificates, Defence Deposit Certificates, etc. Whenever such advances are granted, they are considered a service to customers rather than a remunerative business in itself. In all cases, the surrender value of the certificates form the basis on which an advance is considered.

Before making an advance on the security of the National Savings Certificates, the banker should take an application in the prescribed form from the borrower in whose name the certificates stand. These certificates should then be sent to the concerned post office or the issuing authority for transfer to the lending bank's name. The banker should grant the advance only after the necessary endorsement by the post office or the issuing authority has been made on the certificates or after new certificates are issued in the name of the bank, if permitted by the rules. These certificates should be accompanied by a letter addressed to the postmaster of the concerned post office, authorising the bank to encash the certificates at anytime.

It may be noted here that, there are some restrictions on the transfer and surrender of these certificates. Bankers should acquaint themselves with the various rules governing their transfer, pledge, surrender, etc. It is advisable to obtain a copy of such rules for reference before granting an advance against these certificates. The procedure in respect of the transfer of National Defence Certificates, Defence Deposit Certificates, etc., to the lending bank is almost the same as in the case of the National Savings Certificates. The margin on the above advances is usually maintained between 10 per cent and 20 per cent.

☞ Advances Against Debentures

A debenture is a document issued by a company acknowledging its indebtedness to the person to whom it is issued. Debentures carry a fixed rate of interest payable at given periods. Interest is payable whether the company makes a profit or not. Debentures may be secured either by a fixed charge or a floating charge on the company's assets. If there is no such charge, debentures are clean or unsecured; these are sometimes called naked debentures. Debentures are accepted by banks as security if they are readily marketable. Their marketability, however, depends upon their safety and yield, the reputation and profits of the company and the public opinion about the integrity and capacity of company's directors. In considering the value of a debenture as security, it is necessary to know the terms on which it has been issued and the manner in which it has been secured. Unsecured debentures may be accepted by a bank as security only when the creditworthiness of the borrowing company is very good.

When considering debentures as a security against advances, the banker should take into account the following factors:

(i) The company's powers to issue debentures and restrictions on such powers, if any;

(ii) The financial position of the company;

(iii) The popularity and marketability of debentures;

(iv) The date of redemption, if debentures are redeemable;

(v) Regularity in the payment of interest;

(vi) Study of the Debenture Trust Deed (a debenture trust deed is a registered mortgage deed which is executed for the purpose of securing a charge on the assets of a company, against the specific security of which the debentures are issued. The names of the trustees are mentioned as mortgages in the debenture trust deed. The trustees hold the property in trust for the debentureholders);

(vii) Whether debentures are secured or unsecured.

A margin of 15 per cent to 25 per cent is usually maintained, provided that the debentures are marketable.

☞ Advances Against Goods

A modern banker does a large business in advances against goods. Divergent views are held by experts on the suitability of goods as security. A leading banking expert, while discarding this type of security, observes (according to Mr. Gilbert's, *Journal of the Institute of Bankers,* 1922):

"No banker should really make advances upon such securities. Now and then, they may take such a collateral security for an advance to a customer who is otherwise respectable, but if such customer requires such an advance frequently, not to say constantly, it shows that he is conducting his business in a way that will not ultimately be either for his own advantage or that of his customer."

Approximately two-thirds of the secured advances of the scheduled banks in India are against goods and commodities. The term *goods* is very broad in its connotation and refers to the following four categories of materials:

(i) Food articles;

(ii) Industrial raw materials;

(iii) Plantation products;

(iv) Manufactures and Minerals.

The prejudice against this form of security is based on the ground that as the value of these commodities is subject to constant fluctuations, they do not afford a sufficient protection to the lender. There is no doubt some justification for this attitude; but the modern tendency happens to be that, with due caution and care, this risk can be safeguarded against. Besides, it is argued that, under present conditions, a bank must come forward to finance agriculture, trade and small industry.

This type of security has the advantage of being a tangible security which is a better form of security than a guarantee or bill of exchange because a banker can rely upon something tangible in the case of the failure of the customer borrowing against such securities. Another advantage of this type of security is that goods can be sold more easily than certain other types of securities, such as land and buildings. Yet another advantage is that the price of goods can be more easily ascertained from the market than the price of certain other types of securities, *viz.,* immovable property, etc.

This type of security has certain disadvantages as well, for they are liable to deterioration and damage, and often to wide fluctuations in demand. Another important disadvantage of goods as security is that there is a greater risk of fraud both as regards the quantity and the quality of the pledged goods than in other types of securities. Moreover, the storage of goods in a godown entails risks about their deterioration as well as verification.

☞ Precautions to be Taken

(i) A banker should advance loans against the security of goods only to a person whose character is absolutely free from suspicion, for there will be many opportunities available to the borrower to practise fraud and deceit.

(ii) A banker should actively study the market in order to follow the price trends. During the period of a speculative rise or fall in prices, advances should not be made on the basis of the inflated value, and the margin should be increased in such cases.

(iii) Before accepting goods as security, the banker should ascertain the title of the borrower to the goods, say, by an inspection of the original invoices or cash memos.

(iv) If the goods are under pledge, extra care should be taken against pilferage, damage by insects, rain, and damage by passage of time because of the bank's responsibility as a pledgee.

(v) Goods should be fully insured against the risk of fire unless the cover may be safely waived; as, for example, in the case of such heavy steel goods as steel beams and girders. The godown should contain only goods which are pledged to the bank, unless all the goods are fully insured.

(vi) Godown-keepers and watchmen should be selected carefully. They should be honest and possess a high sense of responsibility.

(vii) In case of a hypothecation account, a written undertaking from the borrower should be obtained that the goods are not charged to any bank or creditor and will not be so charged till the account continues with the bank. Periodical certificates indicating the quantity and valuation of items should be received from the borrower and properly checked against the hypothecated stocks. The banker should tally the stocks hypothecated to him with the borrower's books.

(viii) In case of certain commodities, dealers are required to obtain a licence from the Government. The banker should verify whether the borrower has obtained the necessary license.

(ix) From time-to-time, the Reserve Bank of India issues directives, imposing restrictions on advances against certain commodities. Banks should observe, in letter and spirit, the conditions laid down in such directives. For example, the directive may stipulate a higher margin on advances against certain goods. The banker should not accommodate, on a clean basis, the borrower in whose account the margin has been raised and thus indirectly provide him with funds to meet the extra margin in the secured account.

The nature of the commodity offered as a security to cover a bank advance is an important factor to be borne in mind. Some commodities, *e.g.*, rice, become more valuable with the passage of time, while others deteriorate — their market value declines and it becomes difficult to see them when the occasion demands it. A banker should deal with the owner of goods or his authorised agent and should insist on taking possession of the goods before granting a loan. This is necessary in his own interest, for the transferee of goods, unlike the transferee of a negotiable instrument, cannot get a better title than that of the transferor except in the six cases dealt within Sections 27 to 30 and Section 54(3) of the Sale of Goods Act, 1930. These six exceptions are:

(i) Those who, having sold goods, continue in possession of the goods or the documents of title to goods [Section 30 (1)];

(ii) Those who, having bought or agreed to buy goods, obtain with the consent of the seller possession of goods or the document of title to the goods [Section 30(2)];

(iii) Those who have obtained possession of goods under a voidable contract which has not been rescinded at the time of the transfer [Section 29];

(iv) Part owners, who with the permission of co-owners, are in sole possession of the goods [Section 28];

(v) Mercantile agents who, acting in the ordinary course of business as mercantile agents, have, with the consent of the owner, possession of the goods or the documents of title to the goods [Sec. 54(3)];

(vi) Where an unpaid seller, who has exercised his lien or right of stoppage in transit, exercises his statutory right of resale, the second buyer gets a good title though the unpaid seller is neither the owner nor acting under the authority of the owner [Section 54(3)].

In all the six cases stated above, a good title to property can be passed on to all the *bonafide* purchasers or pledgees for value without notice.

☞ Documents of Title to Goods

Section 2 of the Sale of Goods Act, 1930, defines documents of title to goods as follows:

"A bill of lading, dock warrant, warehousekeeper's certificate, wharfinger's certificate, railway receipt, warrant or order for the delivery of goods and any other document used in the ordinary course of business as proof of the possession or control of goods, or authorising or purporting to authorise, either by endorsement or delivery, the possessor of the document to transfer or receive goods thereby represented."

To test whether a document is a document of title to goods is whether its possession is recognised by law or business practice as the possession of the goods, and whether, by endorsement or delivery (or both) of the document, the person in possession of the goods can transfer the goods represented thereby to any person so as to enable that person to take delivery of them in his own right.

As distinguished from the documents of title mentioned below, there are some other documents, for example, the warehousekeeper's non-transferable receipts, which are mere acknowledgements of goods. The possession of the receipt does not constitute possession of the goods. The distinction between documents which are recognised as documents of title to goods and those which are not is very important from the lending banker's point of view. If the banker is in possession of the documents of title to goods duly endorsed in his favour, where necessary, at the time of the customer's insolvency, such possession gives him a legal title to the goods and to take such goods "out of the order and disposition of the insolvent" under Section 52(2)(c) of the Presidency Town Insolvency Act, 1909, and Section 28(3) of the Provincial Insolvency Act, 1920.

By virtue of being in possession of such documents while the goods are in transit, the banker is entitled to take delivery of them on their arrival in his own right because the legal transfer of the documents has the effect of transferring the goods represented by those documents. Documents of title to goods can be effectively pledged either by the owner (*Morvi Mercantile Bank Ltd., vs. Union of India,* 1965, 35 Company Case 629) or by his mercantile agent, and an advance against the pledge of such documents is equivalent to an advance against the pledge of the goods themselves. (A mercantile agent refers to an agent who, in the normal course of his business as such agent, has the authority to sell goods, or to consign goods for the purpose of sale, or to buy goods, or to raise money on the security of goods. A broker, a factor or an auctioneer having such authority may be covered by the definition of a *mercantile agent*).

The following are the principal documents of title to goods:

(i) Bill of Lading;

(ii) Dock Warrant;

(iii) Warehousekeeper's Certificate or Warehouse Receipt;

(iv) Delivery Order; and

(v) Railway Receipt.

☞ Bill of Lading

In the case of a bill of lading, the goods are made deliverable to the bearer; they may be transferred by the original holder to anyone he chooses, and the transferee in his turn can also transfer it. The transfer can be made by endorsement or delivery, as the case may be, and the transferee acquires, by such a transfer, all the rights to goods shipped that the transferor had. He is also subject to the same liabilities as those of the transferor.

A bill of lading is not a negotiable instrument in the real sense of the term, though there are many points of resemblance between a bill of lading and a negotiable instrument, *viz.,* its transferability by delivery with or without endorsement, and without any notice to the person liable on it ; also transferee of a bill of lading can use it in his own name. Thus, some authors call it a quasi-negotiable instrument.

☞ Bill of Lading and Bill of Exchange

A bill of lading differs from a bill of exchange in point of negotiability, because in the case of bill of lading, a holder cannot give a better title than he himself has, whereas in the case of the bill of exchange, a holder in due course, who receives it for value and in good faith, receives it free from all defences as to defect in title that may have been successfully pledged against a previous holder, except, of course, forgery.

☞ Dock Warrant

A dock warrant is a document issued by a dock, warehousekeeper or wharfinger stating that the goods, as described therein, have been received and are deliverable to the person mentioned therein or his assigns, by endorsement.

☞ Warehousekeeper's Certificate or Warehouse Receipt

A warehousekeeper's certificate is a receipt certifying that the goods are held by the warehousekeeper, which is usually expressed to be non-transferable, though in some cases, it is transferable with an endorsement. This mere statement as to the holding of the goods on behalf of the owner in no sense makes it a document of title. It is for this reason that a bank does not consider this certificate to be a proper security for a loan.

Before making an advance against a warehouse receipt, a banker should see to it that the person approaching him for the advance is entitled to receive the goods in his own name and that he obtains, in addition, a declaration from the borrower that the goods mentioned in the receipt are his absolute property. The genuineness of the warehouse receipt should also be verified.

☞ Delivery Order

It is an order on the warehouseman from the owner to deliver the goods mentioned therein to a particular person. A banker before making an advance on such an order should see to it that the goods are transferred to his own name; otherwise the holder of a second delivery order for the same goods who has no notice of the banker's claim may obtain the goods by giving his copy to the warehouse.

Railway Receipt: Railway receipt is a document acknowledging the receipt of goods specified therein for transportation to a place mentioned therein. It is transferable but not a negotiable instrument. It can be transferred by endorsement and delivery. As the receipt is to be produced before the railway authorities to clear the goods at the destination advances sought against such receipts are for very short periods. Generally, the consignor of the goods draws a bill of exchange or a hundi on the consignee for the amount of the goods consigned and discounts the bill/hundi with the banker. The Railway Receipts is enclosed with the bill which is called a documentary bill. The banker releases the Railway

Receipt to the consignee against payment/acceptance of the bill. The Bombay High Court held that an endorsee of a Railway Receipt could not file a suit for damages for short delivery in consignment of the goods unless he had been shown to be the owner of the goods. Though this right of action is ordinarily vested in the consignor but the consignee, who is in possession of a railway receipt duly endorsed by the consignor, may maintain an action, but he could do so not because he is the consignee, but because he is the owner of the goods. A bare consignee who is not the owner of the goods could not maintain a suit for such compensation. The banker should take the following percautions in this connection:

(i) The consignor may give wrong description of the goods consigned. The banker should, therefore, discount only such documentary bill with Railway Receipt which are drawn by parties of repute.

(ii) Sometimes the goods are delivered by the railway authorities on the basis of Indemnity Bond furnished by a wrong party. In such circumstances, the banker shall have to file a suit in the court of law. To avoid such a situation, the banker should inform the railway authorities at the destination about his interest in the goods and ask them not to release the goods without the railway receipt duly discharged.

(iii) The railway receipt should be on railway risk and without any alterations. The banker should prefer "Freight Paid" railway receipt because he will not be required to pay the freight, if he is forced to take the delivery of the goods at the destination.

Trust Receipts: The goods or the documents of title to goods pledged with a banker as security for an advance are usually released by the banker on the repayment of the borrowed amount. Sometimes the borrower wishes to get the security released before he actually repays the loan. In such cases, the banker may at his discretion, allow the customer to get back the goods or documents and ask the latter to execute a Trust Receipt. By signing such receipt, the customer undertakes to receive the goods or the documents of title to goods in trust for the lender. The borrower promises to hold the goods or their sale proceeds as trustee for the banker and to pay the same to the latter as and when received.

The legal position of the Trust Receipt from the banker's point of view, however, remains unsatisfactory. As regards the ineffectiveness of a Trust Receipt as security for the banker, the Banking Commission, 1972 opined that: "The present position seems to be that advances against trust receipts do not create any trust, that goods released against trust receipt would be affected by the reputed ownership clause under the insolvency laws in India, that the borrower may validly create unauthorised pledge of the documents of title to goods released to him under a Trust Receipt and any wrongful dealing with the goods it may not be possible to prosecute the borrower".

The Commission, therefore, concluded that "from the banker's point of view, the trust receipt is considered practically valueless as a document creating a security interest in their favour". Banks treat advances against trust receipts as unsecured and grant this facility only to well established customers.

☞ Risks in Advances Against Documents of Title to Goods

There are certain risks in making advances against documents of title to goods, for these documents may be forged, or the number of bags or packages stated in the bill of lading or railway receipt may be fraudulently increased. Moreover, the documents of title are not negotiable securities, and title to the goods cannot, under any conditions, be acquired if the documents are stolen. But because such documents are transferable, they can be taken as security from the owner of goods, the transferee or the mercantile agent in possession of the documents as an agent.

☞ Precautions to be Taken

The banker should take the following precautions while advancing money against documents to title to goods:

(i) Advances should be given to only known customers who are honest and reliable.

(ii) The banker should always ask for a certificate of a reliable packer in order to ascertain the contents of the packages; or representative of the bank should be present to supervise the packing.

(iii) The banker should procure all the copies of a bill of lading. The captain of a ship is under no obligation to inquire into the title of the holder of the bill of lading, and will ordinarily give the delivery of the goods to the person presenting it, provided that he does not know that another copy is pledged with the banker.

(iv) The banker should get the bill of lading endorsed in blank by the consignee. In such a case, the liability for paying the freight falls on the customer and not upon the consignor.

(v) The banker should get the insurance policy in respect of the goods. It is not to have an open insurance policy, the insurance company should state that such and such goods are covered under that policy.

☞ Immovable Property

Though immovable property, *e.g.*, land and buildings, is legally a sound and valid security for advances by a bank, it is not popular because of the following reasons:

(i) Legal enactments have put some checks on such transfers, *e.g.*, a non-agriculturist cannot acquire agricultural land from an agriculturist.

(ii) Hindu and Mohammedan customs and laws relating to succession and transfer of property place serious obstacles in the way of the banker providing financial accommodation on the security of what is ordinarily considered to be a normal and sound security.

(iii) Another important difficulty regarding this security is about the ascertainment of the title of the customer.

(iv) The valuation of the property is also very difficult. The banker cannot rely upon his own judgement but has to depend on the valuation of experts.

(v) There are a variety of land tenures, *e.g., freehold, jazandari, sanedi, khoti, inami, toka, ryotwari, patidari,* and the banker has to take into consideration all these tenures.

(vi) Another problem is the delay and difficulty in the realisation of such security.

(vii) While accepting land and building as security for an advance, the banker expects to get some rent from the property; but there is always the difficulty of finding suitable tenants and collecting rent from them. The banker has also to incur costs on the repair and upkeep of the property.

Because of the difficulties discussed above, immovable property is not a popular security for bank advances.

☞ Life Policies

A life policy is a good security against advances on the basis of its surrender value. The other consideration for the banker is to make sure that the policy was effected by the person himself on his own life. In case the policy is effected on the life of some other party, it should be ascertained whether the party affecting this insurance had an insurable interest in the life insured.

☞ Insurable Interest

"Insurable interest is a certain pecuniary interest in the life of the person or thing insured. Mere natural love and affection will not suffice. The insured must stand in such relation with the subject matter of insurance that, in the event of its loss, he will sustain some pecuniary loss. It is essential that the interest should exist at the time the insurance is effected."

The banker should also see to it that premium receipts are deposited with him and that the policy is not allowed to lapse. The various clauses of the policy should be examined to find out whether there are conditions or clauses vitiating the policy as a form of security. It is better to obtain proof that the age of the assured has been admitted by the insurance company. If the policy has been assigned to someone, a reassignment in favour of the life assured and a subsequent assignment in favour of the banker should be secured.

A simple deposit of the policy with the banker as security for a debt does not constitute an assignment, but only gives him a lien. To create an equitable mortgage, it should be accompanied by a written agreement determining the purpose of a deposit. (A legal mortgage of a life policy is effected by a *deed of assignment*, the operative part of which includes a covenant by the borrower for the repayment of the principal and interest, and a statement regarding the assignment of the policy subject to a promise for redemption.

To protect his own interest, a banker should get the mortgage registered. The policy should also be taken possession of so that a subsequent mortgagee may not obtain a prior right of assignment by giving an earlier notice and obtaining possession of the policy concerned. A well-drawn deed of mortgage always contains a clause relating to the power to sell the policy in the event of a default.

☞ Fixed Deposit Receipt

A fixed deposit receipt is issued by a banker for a deposit made for a specific period. If, before the expiry of that period, the customer urgently needs money, he may take a loan from the bank on the security of the fixed deposit receipt. The banker should take the following precautions while making an advance against a fixed deposit receipt:

(i) He may advance a loan against the fixed deposit receipt issued by his own bank, but not against the fixed deposit receipt issued by another bank, because in that case the other bank possesses a paramount lien on the receipt.

(ii) If a fixed deposit receipt is in joint names and the loan is being sought by one of the depositors, the banker should get a letter of authority signed by all the depositors authorising the bank to sanction the loan against the receipt.

(iii) While receiving a fixed deposit receipt as security, the banker should have it signed by the depositor over a revenue stamp in the discharge of the instrument so that the bank gets the authority by appropriating the amount of the fixed deposit towards the repayment of the loan.

(iv) The banker should not grant a loan to a minor against a fixed deposit receipt, even though the receipt is in the name of the minor.

☞ Supply Bills

Banks are sometimes approached for advances against bills for goods supplied to government departments or agencies. Businessmen, who supply goods to these departments or agencies on the basis of previously submitted tenders, and contractors on partial or complete completion of contract, submit a bill for the amount of goods supplied or the contract work done in accordance with the terms and conditions of the contract. Such bills are referred to as *supply bills.* These bills are passed for payment by the appropriate authority only after verification that the goods supplied conform to the terms of the contract. The procedure, however, of checking and passing the bills takes a couple of months and sometimes even longer. During this period, the parties approach banks for advances against such supply bills.

Supply bills are not bills of exchange. They do not, therefore, enjoy the legal status of negotiable instruments. A supply bill, however, represents a debt arising out of a bonafide supply of goods, or contract work done. Such bills are endorsed for payment to the bank and have to be receipted on a revenue stamp. They are also accompanied by a separate letter of authority addressed to the concerned Government department or agency by the supplier or contractor to pay the amount directly to the bank.

In law, there can be valid equitable assignment of future debts, and such debts cannot be attached by another creditor to the detriment of a prior creditor who may have advanced money on their security (*Bharat Nidhi Ltd., vs. Takhtmal and Another,* 1969, 39, Company Case 114; also *Hindustan Commercial Bank Ltd., vs. Union of India and Others,* AIR 1965, Allahabad 474).

☞ Risk in Giving Advances Against Supply Bills

The banker incurs the following risks in granting loans against supply bills:

(i) The security available to a banker is by way of assignment of debts represented by supply bills. It suffers from the usual drawbacks of assignment of debts as security. There is always the possibility of a counter-claim or set-off against the debt.

(ii) The debtor, usually the government, might pay the amount direct to the creditor unless the assignment is registered with the debtor, and the debtor undertakes to pay the amount only to the assignee.

(iii) Generally speaking, the payments of such bills are made by the Government departments after a long time because of procedural delays.

(iv) The amount may be reduced or payment refused, if there is a default in observing the terms of contract by the supplier/contractor.

☞ Precautions to be Taken by the Banker

The bank should take precautions to ensure that he does receive payment on the supply bills.

(i) Advances against supply bills should be granted only to honest suppliers/contractors, having a long experience in the business.

(ii) The banker should thoroughly scrutinise the terms of the contract between the supplier/contractor and the government.

(iii) The banker should ask the supplier/contractor to execute an irrevocable power of attorney in his favour, authorising him to receive the amount of the bill. The power of attorney should be filed with the department to which the supply bill is submitted.

(iv) The banker should ask the supplier/contractor to give an undertaking to repay any amount received by the later directly from the Government department in respect of the bills entrusted to the banker for collection.

☞ Questions

1. Discuss the suitability of each of the following types of security as a cover for an advance:
   (a) Shares in joint stock companies;
   (b) Cotton;
   (c) Landed property.
2. Discuss the relative merits of the following securities which are offered by a customer as cover for a temporary advance:
   (a) An insurance policy on his own life in a first class insurance company;
   (b) The bank's fixed deposit standing in his name jointly with his wife and payable to either or survivor;
   (c) Preference shares standing in his name in a joint stock company quoted on the Bombay market.
3. Why does a banker look with disfavour on lands and buildings as security for an advance to such an extent that advances against security of this nature form a negligible proportion of his total advances? There are in existence special land mortgage banks. Why should they be able to advance money on such security when bigger and more influential banks avoid it?
4. Explain the principles underlying the rating of securities for banking investments and state the usual precautions taken by a bank when life insurance policy is offered as a security for an advance.
5. Describe in detail the various formalities to be observed and the precautions to be taken by a bank while making advances against immovable property.
6. Discuss the relative merits and demerits of advances against goods, debentures and life policies from the banker's point of view. What precautionary measures should be adopted by a banker while making advances on the security of goods?
7. A customer approaches his banker for a loan of ₹ 5,00,000 and is prepared to submit any one of the following securities:
   (a) A palace valued at ₹ 7,00,000;
   (b) A life insurance policy of ₹ 10,00,000;
   (c) Partly paid-up share of a joint stock company worth ₹ 12,00,000;
   (d) Wheat in a godown worth ₹ 8,00,000.
   Which security should the banker accept and why?
8. Discuss the suitability of the following types of security as cover for advances:
   (a) Debentures;
   (b) Partly paid-up shares in joint stock companies;
   (c) Oil seeds.
9. Mention the precautions to be taken by a banker in making advances against the security of goods.
10. (a) Discuss the merits and demerits of ordinary equity shares of a company as security for a banker's advances.
    (b) A borrower proposes to pledge with the Lending Bank Ltd., (the value of its paid-up capital and reserves is ₹ 1 crore) shares of the value of ₹ 1.50 crore of Business Co. Ltd., (The value of its paid-up capital is ₹ 2 crore and reserves ₹ 50 lakh) for a loan of ₹ 1.25 crore repayable in annual instalments spread over seven years. Examine and dispose of this application.
11. (a) Why are margins required to be maintained in the case of securities lodged with banks for advances? State whether a bank would charge a higher margin (i) for a pledge account or for a hypothecation account, and (ii) on an advance against immovable property or an unsecured advance. Give reasons in each case.
    (b) The Reserve Bank of India asks banks to maintain a margin of 50 per cent in respect of advances against raw cotton. Your bank's valued customer, who maintains a very satisfactorily conducted cash credit account secured by apledge of raw cotton for ₹ 50 lakh, applied for a clean limit of ₹ 10 lakh. Mention the factors you would take into consideration while disposing of this application.
12. (a) Enumerate the various documents of title to goods dealt with by a banker. What are the precautions to be taken by him granting advances against them?

(b) When pressed to adjust a loan account, your customer offers you as security a life policy taken by him in his own name for the benefit of his wife and children. As Branch Manager of the bank, how would you deal with this application?

13. What are documents of title to goods?
Indicate briefly some important documents of title to goods. What precautions should a banker take while making advances against the securities represented by the documents of title to goods?
[C.A.I.I.B., Part I]

14. You are the General Manager of Pioneer Bank Ltd., which has a paid-up capital and reserves totalling in all ₹ 1.50 crore. One of your customers applies to you for a loan of ₹ 25 lakh and offers as security the pledge of his shares in Progressive Engineering Company Limited whose paid-up capital and reserves are respectively ₹ 2 crore and ₹ 20 lakh. How would you deal with the application?
[I.I.B., Part II]

15. An advance of ₹ 75,000 is granted by a bank against stocks of cloth bales worth ₹ 1 lakh. The bank insists on insurance against fire up to the full market value of stocks, *i.e.*, ₹ 1 lakh, whereas the customer suggests insurance up to the amount of the advance.

16. Mr. A.B. Desai, your valued customer, approaches you to grant an overdraft facility up to ₹ 25,000 in his current account. He offers the following securities:
(a) 100 shares of Century Spinning & Weaving Co. Ltd. standing in the name of his wife.
(b) A Fixed Deposit Receipt for ₹ 50,000 standing in the name of his wife jointly with his son issued by another branch of your bank.
(c) His own Life Insurance Policy for ₹ 60,000 maturing in June 1980.
Which of the securities would you accept and why? What precautions would you take and what documents would you obtain for the advance? *[I.I.B., Part I]*

17. A limited company, manufacturing plastic goods (consumers' items), approaches you as a Banker for an advance of ₹ 2 lakh against hypothecation of raw materials, finished goods and stock-in-process. What precautions would you take as a banker in granting this advance? What documents would you obtain?

18. A person intends to start a retail shop with an initial investment of ₹ 10,000. For the investment he approaches a bank to grant him a loan of ₹ 10,000 against the security of his L.I.C. Policy. The Policy is 20 years Endowment L.I.C. policy for ₹ 20,000 on which premium of ₹ 11,000 is paid regularly during past 12 years. How will you process the loan application and what formalities will be necessary before disbursement of the loan?
[I.I.B., Part I]

19. A person calls at a branch office with a Fixed Deposit receipt for ₹ 5,000 issued in his name by the up-country branch of the bank. He requests for a loan of ₹ 3,000 against the F.D.R.
He represents that it is difficult for him to approach the branch which issued the F.D.R. as he is transferred from there to the place where he seeks a loan. How would you examine and decide. *[I.I.B., Part I]*

20. What are the merits of a Life Insurance Policy as a security for a bank's advance? Describe the formalities to be observed and the safeguards to be adopted when lending against this security. *[I.I.B., Part II]*

21. What are Supply Bills? Describe the procedure, documentation and precautions relating to advances against supply bills. *[I.I.B., Part II]*

22. Premier Engineering Co. Ltd., who are manufacturing light engineering goods and whose products command a wide market, approach your bank for credit facilities against their Book Debts. What are the procedures, formalities and precautions you will observe in granting them an advance against Book Debts?
[I.I.B., Part II]

23. Are Government supply bills normally drawn in the form of or accompanied by Bills of Exchange? State the precautions that must be taken and the practice generally followed by bankers when purchasing/discounting Government supply bills or granting advances against the security of such bills. What documents would you take for the purposes? *[I.I.B., Part II; I.I.B., Part I]*

24. Explain with reasons, the relative acceptability of the following as security for a loan by one of your constituents:
(a) Leasehold property with four years of lease unexpired.
(b) Shares in a private company.
(c) A second mortgage over freehold property. *[I.I.B., Part II]*

25. How would you consider an application for advances against:
(a) Book Debts
(b) Railway Receipts? *[I.I.B., Part II]*

26. A customer of your Branch approaches you for a loan facility against Fixed Deposit receipt for ₹ 5,000 of another bank issued in his favour. How would you deal? *[I.I.B., Part I]*
27. Explain:
    (*a*) The risks banks in India undertake in making advances against documents of title to goods. Enumerate the documents of title to goods and to safeguard banks take in accepting them as security for their advances.
    (*b*) Are book debts considered to be good security? What are the special aspects to be examined before granting an advance against book debts? *[I.I.B., Part II]*
28. Write short notes on:
    (*i*) Trust Receipts
    (*ii*) Surrender Value of Life Insurance Policy
    (*iii*) Book Debts *[I.I.B., Part I]*
29. State briefly the precautions to be taken and the procedure to be followed while granting advances against (1) Government Securities (2) Shares of Limited Companies: *[I.I.B., Part I]*
30. What is the meaning of the following:
    (*i*) Convertible Debentures
    (*ii*) Cumulative Redeemable Preference Shares *[I.I.B., Part I]*
31. Write short notes on —
    (*i*) Bearer Bonds
    (*ii*) Tax on Interest Earned by Banks *[I.I.B., Part I]*
32. What is the main difference between
    (*i*) Bill of Lading and Mate's Receipt
    (*ii*) Gilt-edged Security and Trustee Security. *[I.I.B., Part I]*
33. Bring the main difference between
    (*i*) Book Debts and Book Value
    (*ii*) Trust Receipt and Packing Credit
    (*iii*) Interest payable 'half-yearly' and with half-yearly interest. *[I.I.B., Part I]*
34. What are the main points to be looked into and what documents are to be obtained in the following:
    (*a*) When advances are granted against shares, National Savings Certificates, Rahat Patra, Indira Vikas Patra, etc. *[I.I.B., Part I]*
35. What documents would you obtain in case of cash credit against goods? Explain the purpose and importance of each document, giving the stamp duty required in each case. *[I.I.B., Part I]*
36. What precautions would you take for advances against bills in respect of supplies made to Government departments? *[I.I.B., Part I]*

CHAPTER

19 Letters of Credit

A letter of credit is a document or order by a banker in one place, authorising some other banker, acting as his agent or correspondent, in another place, to honour the drafts or cheques of a person named in the document, up to the amount stated in the letter and charge the total amount of the drafts so honoured or payments so made to the guarantor of the letter of credit. The particulars of all the drafts or cheques, drawn by the specified person against the credit, are required to be endorsed at the bank of the letter of credit so that it will be easy to find out how much of the credit allowed has been utilised, and how much is outstanding.

☞ Kinds of Letters of Credit

Letters of credit are of various kinds. They may be divided into two divisions, *viz.*:

(i) Personal Credit Letters or Travellers Facility Letters: A letter by which a banker requests another, to whom the said letter is addressed, to hold a certain sum at the disposal of a third person who is the holder of that letter and to pay to him such amounts as he requires against either cheques on the banker giving this letter or on the banker to whom the letter is addressed but not exceeding in total the whole amount covered by the said letter. This letter is generally taken when a customer wants to visit and spend most of his time at one particular place and wants to obtain funds during that period. Such credits are known as *encashment credits.*

(ii) Letters for Commercial Credit: These are letters of credit used for the purpose of financing shipments of goods imported into, or exported from, a country or for the movement of produce or manufactured goods from one place to another in the country itself.

☞ Personal Letters of Credit or Travellers Letters of Credit

A banker giving such a letter of credit asks another banker to whom it is addressed to place a specific sum of money at the disposal of or to the credit of one in whose favour the letter is issued. This type of credit aims at facilitating travellers or others temporarily resident in another country by allowing them to draw cheques on the branch offices or agencies of the bank concerned for the purpose of obtaining such cash as they may require in the course of their travel in, or residence at those places. When this letter is addressed to more than one banker, it is known as a *circular letter of credit* and the bankers to whom it is addressed have to endorse on the letter the amount paid by each one of them. With a circular letter, a letter of *indication* or *identification* is also issued to a customer which contains a specimen of his signature.

☞ Circular Notes

Sometimes, these letters of credit are accompanied by *circular notes* in the form of cheques of the value of denomination of such sums as may be convenient to the holder. The letter of credit then virtually becomes a letter of *indication* or *identification*, stating the numbers and the amount up to which the circular notes are due, and containing a specimen signature of the holder. The holder has to keep the letters of credit or indication, as well as the circular notes in separate boxes while travelling, and gradually cash the notes by producing the letter of credit as well as the signed circular notes at the various banks to which the letter of credit or indication is addressed.

☞ Circular Cheques

Instead of circular notes with letters of indication as mentioned in the preceding paragraph, it is more common nowadays to issue circular cheques without the letter of indication. These circular cheques are issued by banks to their agents abroad, are bound in the book form, and are drawn in the currency of the country in which the payment is to be made.

☞ Travellers' Cheques

Travellers' cheques are similar to circular cheques or circular notes but do not require a letter of identification. At the time of issue, the holder is required to place his signature on all the cheques issued to him and to pay for these cheques. At the time of encashment, he is required to sign once again. This facilitates identification, for the second signature is checked to find out whether it corresponds with the original signature placed at the time of issue before payment is made.

☞ Letters for Commercial Credit

This type of letter of credit is used to finance trading activities. The customer wishing to open such a credit approaches a banker with a request for a letter addressed to another person in a different city or country from whom he expects shipments of goods on credit. The total amount of such credit is settled with the banker after the later receives the requisite security to his satisfaction. The banker, by giving the said letter of credit, authorises the other party, who is to make the shipment, to draw a bill of exchange on him up to the amount mentioned in the said letter, which the banker giving the letter agrees to accept, provided it is drawn strictly in accordance with the terms and stipulations covered by the letter of credit. It is usual to stipulate in the said letter that the credit has to be made use of within the period stated in the letter, usually six months. If the banker undertakes to accept the bills drawn in accordance with such a letter without conditions, the document is called an *open* or *clean* letter of credit. If, on the other hand, the stipulation is that the documents of title to the goods covered by the bills drawn against shipments are to accompany the bills, the letter is called a *documentary letter of credit.*

☞ Documents Against Acceptance and Documents Against Payment

When documents are attached to a bill of exchange and are handed over to the drawee on his accepting the bill, the bill is called a D/A bill, *i.e., documents against acceptance bill.* If, on the other hand, the documents are only handed over or delivered not on acceptance, but on the actual payment of the bill, the same is known as *documents against payment bill* (D/P bill). In the first case, the drawee has to be given credit during the interval that the bill is accepted and the rate at which the bill is actually paid. In the other case, no credit is given because the documents are only deliverable on payment. It may be noted that, in commercial credits, the bills generally drawn are D/A (documents against acceptance) bills.

The possession of a bill of lading against acceptance would no doubt give a banker a good title to the goods. An agreement between him and his customer to the effect that bills of lading would be forwarded against acceptance would, on acceptance of the bill, give to the banker against his customer an equitable claim against the bill of lading which is good even against the trustee in bankruptcy or an official assignee *(Lutcher vs. Comptoir d'Escompe I.Q., B.D., 709)*. If a bill is accepted on the condition that it will be payable on delivery of the bill of lading, the banker is not liable to pay unless and until the bill of lading is casually handed over. The banker is thus a security for his acceptance in the bill of lading *(Ex-parte Breet,* L.R. 6, Ch. 838 at p. 84).

The law places on the banker who undertakes to negotiate a draft by his acceptance under a letter of credit granted by him the responsibility to properly protect the person on whose request he so acts, and that care is taken to ensure that all the conditions under which the said drafts are to be negotiated are fulfilled by the person to whom the said letter is addressed. The banker must also see to it that the person with whom he is dealing is a person to whom the letter has been issued. There was a case in which a bank negotiated a draft which was not accompanied by a Policy of Insurance in a proper form. It was held that the Bank was liable because it committed a breach of its contract with the party at whose request the letter was issued. *(Borthwick vs. Bank of New Zealand* (1900) 6 Com. Cases 1). Of course, here, the limit of the bank's obligation was to see that the documents presented along with the bill of exchange were actually the documents specified in the letter of credit. [*Basee and Selve vs. Bank of Australia* (1904), 20 T.L.R. 341].

CLEAN LETTER OF CREDIT

No. 11571

National & Grindlays Bank Ltd.,
14 Park Street,
London.

£ 1,00,000

February 15, 1976

To

Messrs. Prakash Wadhwani & Co. Ltd.,
Frere Road,
Bombay.

Dear Sir,

You are hereby authorised to draw drafts upon this bank at thirty days' sight to the extent on all of £ 1,00,000 (Pounds One Hundred Thousand only), and we hereby engage with the drawers, endorsers, and bonafide holders of all drafts drawn under and in compliance with the terms of this credit, that the same shall be duly accepted payable in London, UK, on presentation in order; and that they shall be duly honoured on presentation in order at maturity.

The credit will remain in force for six months from this date. The particulars of all drafts drawn against it must be endorsed on the back thereof, and the bills must specify that they are drawn that under credit No. 11751 dated the fifteenth day of February, 1976.

Yours faithfully,
For the National & Grindlays Bank
(Sd.) V. John
Manager

A confirming bank must not disburse moneys under a letter of credit except against documents strictly complying with the terms of the credit. Where a letter of credit is opened, the relationship between the instructing and the conforming banks is in the absence of a contract to the contrary that, of principal and agent. *[Bank Melli Iram vs. Barclays Bank* (1951) T.L.R. 1057].

DOCUMENTARY LETTER OF CREDIT

No. 305 $ 10,000	Lloyds Bank Ltd. 57th Street, 6th Avenue, New York, July 5, 1975.

To

Messrs. Alrich & Co. Ltd.
Colaba,
Bombay.

Dear Sir,

You are hereby authorised to draw drafts upon this Bank at thirty days' sight to the extent in all of $ 10,000 (Dollars Ten Thousand only) or invoice cost of goods to be shipped to Messrs. Alexander & Company of New York. This credit expires, unless previously cancelled, six months from the date. All drafts against it must be drawn and fully advised to us before that date, accompanied by invoices and bill of lading issued to the order of the shipper and endorsed in blank, together with marine insurance policies.

Particulars of all drafts drawn under this credit must be endorsed on the back thereof, and the bills must specify that they are drawn under credit No.305, dated July 5, 1975. We hereby engage with the drawers, endorsers, and bonafide holders of the drafts under and in compliance with the terms of this credit, that against surrender to this bank of the above-mentioned documents in order, the said drafts shall be duly accepted payable in New York, USA., on presentation in order; and that they shall be duly honoured on presentation in order at maturity.

Yours faithfully,
For Lloyds Bank Ltd.,
(Sd.) Samuel Smith
Manager

☞ Revocable and Irrevocable Letters of Credit

In the case of *revocable* or *unconfirmed* letters of credit, a banker issuing them can cancel the authority at any time he chooses; but he will still be liable for bills negotiated before its cancellation. An *irrevocable* or *confirmed* letter of credit cannot be cancelled unless it has run its full course or unless its beneficiary agrees to such cancellation. The opening of a confirmed letter of credit "constitutes a bargain between the banker and the vendor of the goods, which imposes on the banker an absolute obligation to pay, irrespective of any dispute which there may be between the parties on the question whether the goods are up to contract or not. A vendor of goods selling against a confirmed letter of credit is selling under the assurance that nothing will prevent him from receiving the price." [*Malas & Aur. (Trading as Hamzeh Males & Sons) vs. British Imex Industries Ltd.,* (1958) 1 All E.R. 262)].

In the case of *Cape Asbestos Co. Ltd., vs. Lloyds Bank Ltd.,* (1921) W.N. 274, it was held that in the case of revocable letters of credit, though the banker was not under any legal obligation to give notice before revoking, the practice of bankers in the usual course of business is to give such notice and that the said practice was the most prudent, reasonable and business-like practice. This means that though the bankers in the usual course do give notice as a matter of courtesy and as a matter of policy before they revoke a letter of credit, they are not bound to do so in law. That is the reason why Justice Bailhache observed in the case cited above that "an unconfirmed credit is practically useless". This is subject to the rule that as long as the credit happens to be in force and the documents are in order, the banker must accept the bill; otherwise he would be liable to damages. [*Urquhart Lindsay and Co., vs. Eastern Bank* (1922) I K.B. 318]

☞ Distinction Between Irrevocable Letter of Credit and Bank Guarantee

An irrevocable letter of credit also differs from a bank guarantee in *State Bank of India vs. The Economic Trading Co. S.A.A., and Others* (A.L.R. 1975, Calcutta 145), the Calcutta High Court observed that the more important point of distinction was the autonomy of an irrevócable letter of credit and the dependence of a bank guaranted on a contract between the beneficiary of the guarantee and a third party. Payment under an irrevocable letter of credit does not depend on the performance of obligations on the part of the seller except these which the letter of credit expressly imposes. In such cases the obligation is of the bank to the beneficiary and no third party comes into the picture. In the case of a bank guarantee by definition a third party is always on the scene. Unless there is some act of omission or commission on the part of the third party, payment under a bank guarantee does not become due. In other words, a bank guarantee does not enjoy the autonomy of an irrevocable letter of credit. In case of a guarantee there is always the question of a contingency on the occurrence of which the guarantee becomes enforceable.

OPENING OF LETTER OF CREDIT

As noted above the liability of the opening banker in respect of a letter of credit is absolute and firm. He should, therefore open a letter of credit with care and after having been satisfied with the standing and creditworthiness of the applicant, at whose request a letter of credit is issued. The following steps are taken in this regard:

(1) Application for Letter of Credit: The applicant fills a prescribed application form requesting the bank to issue a letter of credit in favour of the foreign supplier and gives an undertaking that the bills drawn under the letter of credit will be accepted and paid by him.

The applicant is required to give in the application all necessary particulars and terms, etc., on which the credit is to be opened, *e.g.,*

(a) The amount for which the credit is to be opened and the nature of credit — whether fixed or revolving, revocable, or irrevocable, 'with recourse' or 'without recourse' to the drawer.

(b) Details of the goods to be imported and their prices and other terms, e.g., f.o.r./f.o.b./c.&.f., c.i.f.

(c) Details of shipment — port of shipment and destination, time of shipment, last date of shipment. Whether partial shipment allowed or not; whether transhipment allowed or not.

(d) Full details of the shipping and other ducuments which are required to be attached with the bills of exchange. For example:

- *(i) Invoice*
- *(ii) Bill of Lading*
- *(iii) Railway Receipt/Air consignment Note, Post Parcel Receipt,* Forwarding Agent Receipt, showing the consignment of the goods.
- *(iv) Marine Insurance Policy or Certificate*

  The nature and extent of risks to be covered by the insurance policies should be clearly indicated.

(e) The tenor of the Bill and the name of the drawee of the bill to be drawn — whether the applicant or the opening bank — and whether the documents are to be delivered on D/A or D/P basis.

(f) Whether the letter of credit is to be opened by mail/air mail/cable.

(g) The date of expiry for the presentation of document for payment, acceptance or negotiation.

(h) Whether the letter of credit is to be confirmed by the advising bank. Who will bear the confirmation commission — buyer or seller?

(i) Details of the import licence.

All these details and instructions must be complete and very clearly indicated by the applicant in the application which should be duly signed and stamped.

(2) Scrutiny of the Application: The application submitted by the applicant must be carefully scrutinised by the opening bank to ascertain the following:

(a) that the means and standing of the applicant is good. In doubtful cases, banker should insist on the deposit of cash or approved securities.

(b) that the importer is in possession of the Import Licence granted by the Import Control authorities. In case the goods fall under an open general licence, its serial number and the particulars of the Import Trade Control Schedule should be noted. The banker should verify from the Import Licence that —

(i) the Import Licence is in the name of the applicant. If not, its use by the applicant should be authorised by the authorities;

(ii) the amount and the balance available under the licence is sufficient to cover the amount of the letter of credit applied for;

(iii) the import licence is valid. Validity period of a licence is one year plus 30 days of grace for the despatch of goods plus 15 days for the negotiation of documents;

(iv) the types of goods to be imported as mentioned in the licence conform to the details given in the application;

(v) the country of origin of the goods as given in *the licence is the same as given in the application.*

(c) that the goods to be imported under the letter of credit applied for should be readily marketable.

(d) the price of the goods to be imported should be approximate current market value and it should not be liable to wide fluctuations.

Margin: The opening banker decides the margin to be maintained by the applicant in the form of deposit of cash or securities. The extent of such margins decided keeping in view the standing and creditworthiness of the applicant. The amount deposited by them is kept in current account styled as "Margin on Documentary Credits" and interest thereon is also paid if demanded by the party.

Insurance: The importer should be asked to take usual marine insurance policies covering C.I.F. value plus certain percentage to cover profits. The policies should be in the joint names of the bank and the importer.

UNIFORM CUSTOMS AND PRACTICE FOR DOCUMENTARY CREDITS

The International Chamber of Commerce codified Uniform Customs and Practice for Documentary Credits in 1933. These Uniform Customs were revised in 1974 and have been adopted by a large number of countries. This document applies to all documentary credits and is binding upon all parties thereto unless otherwise expressly agreed. Besides general provisions and definitions, these Uniform Customs are divided into the following parts:

A — Form and Notification of Credits

B — Liabilities and Responsibilities

C — Documents

D — Miscellaneous Provisions

E — Transfer

The main provisions of this document are summarised as follows:

☞ General Provisions

After defining the documentary credits, as discussed earlier in this chapter, it is provided that such credits, by their nature, are separate transactions from the sales or other contracts on which they may be based. Banks are in no way concerned with or bound by such contracts. Credit instructions and the credits themselves must be complete and precise but excessive details be avoided.

☞ A — Form and Notification of Credit

Articles 1 to 3 deal with Revocable, Irrevocable and Confirmed Credits. Articles 4 to 6 deal with the notification of credits. When an issuing bank instructs a bank by cable, telegram or telex to advise a credit and intends the mail confirmation to be the operative credit instrument the cable, telegram or telex must state that the credit will only be effective on receipt of such mail confirmation. In this event, the issuing bank must send the operative credit instrument (mail confirmation) and any subsequent amendments to the credit to the beneficiary through the advising bank. The issuing bank will be responsible for any consequences arising from its failure to follow this procedure (Article 4). When a bank is instructed by cable, telegram or telex to issue, confirm or advise a credit similar in terms to one previously established and which has been the subject of amendments, it shall be understood that the details of the credit being issued, confirmed or advised will be transmitted to the beneficiary excluding the amendments, unless the instructions specify, clearly any amendments which are to apply (Article 5). If incomplete or unclear instructions are received by a bank to issue, confirm or advise a credit, the bank may give preliminary notification of the credit to the beneficiary for information only and without responsibility. Credit will be issued, confirmed or advised only when the necessary information has been received (Article 6).

☞ B — Liabilities and Responsibilities: Examination of Documents

Bank must examine all documents with reasonable care to ascertain that they appear on their face to be in accordance with the terms and conditions of the credit (Article 7). Payment acceptance or negotiation against such documents by a bank authorised to do so binds the party giving the authorisation to take up the documents and reimburse the bank which has effected the payment, acceptance or negotiation. If, upon receipt of the documents, the issuing bank considers that they appear on their face not to be in accordance with the terms and conditions of the credit, that bank must determine, on the basis of the documents alone, whether to claim that payment, acceptance or negotiation was not effected in accordance with the terms and conditions of the credit. If such claim is to be made, notice to that effect, stating the reasons thereof, must be given by cable or other expeditious means to the bank from which the documents have been received. The issuing bank shall have a reasonable time to examine the documents (Article 8).

According to Articles 9 to 11 banks assume no liability or responsibility for:

(i) the form, sufficiency, accuracy, genuineness, falsification or legal effect of any documents;

(ii) the general/particular conditions stipulated in the documents or superimposed thereon;

(iii) the description, quantity, weight, quality, etc., value or existence of goods represented by the documents;

(iv) the good faith or acts and/or omissions, solvency, performance or standing of the consignor, the carrier or the insurers of the goods or any other person;

(v) the consequences arising out of delay/loss in transit of any message, letters or documents or the delay, mutilation or other errors arising in the transmission of cables, etc.;

(vi) consequences arising out of the interruption of their business by strikes, lockouts, riots, wars, or other causes beyond their control.

According to Article 12, Banks utilising the services of another bank for the purpose of giving effect to the instructions of the applicant for the credit do so for account and at the risk of the latter. Bank assume no liability or responsibility, if the instructions they transmit are not carried out even if they have themselves taken the initiative in the choice of such other bank. The applicant for the credit shall be bound by and liable to indemnify the banks against all obligations and responsibilities imposed by foreign laws and usages.

☞ C — Documents

All instructions to issue, confirm or advise a credit must state precisely the documents against which payment, acceptance or negotiation is to be made (Article 14). Such documents fall under the following categories:

(i) Documents evidencing shipment or despatch (shipping documents). Article 18 states that a clean shipping document is on which bears no superimposed clause or notation which expressly declares a defective condition of the goods and/or the packing. Bank will refuse shipping documents bearing such clauses or notations unless the credit expressly states the clauses or notations which may be accepted.

(ii) *Marine bills of lading:* Article 19 provides that unless specifically authorised in the credit, Bills of Lading issued by forwarding agents, or those issued under and are subject to the conditions of a Charter Party or those covering shipment by sailing vessels, will be rejected.

According to Article 20, unless otherwise specified in the credit Bills of Lading must show that the goods are loaded on board a named vessel or shipped on a named vessel.

(iii) Other shipping documents, etc.

(iv) Insurance documents.

(v) Commercial Invoices.

(vi) Other documents.

☞ D — Miscellaneous Provisions Relate to

(i) *Quantity and amount:*

(ii) *Partial shipments:* Partial shipments are allowed, unless the credit specifically state otherwise.

(iii) *Validity and expiry date:* All credits, whether revocable or irrevocable, must stipulate an expiry date for presentation of documents for payment, acceptance or negotiation,

notwithstanding the indication of a latest date for shipment (Article 37). When the stipulated expiry date falls on a bank holiday, the period of validity will be extended until the first following business day (Article 39). But the latest date for shipment shall not be extended because of the extension of the expiry date.

(iv) Shipment, loading or despatch:

(v) Presentation: The credits must also stipulate a specified period of time after the date of issuance of the bills of lading or other shipping documents during which presentation of document for payment, acceptance or negotiation must be made. If no such period of time is stipulated in the credit, banks will refuse documents presented to them later than 21 days after the date of issuance of the bills of lading or other shipping documents (Article 41).

☞ E — Transfer

This section deals with transferable credits.

1. Marginal Letter of Credit

This kind of letter of credit is so named because the letter containing the terms of drawing and acceptance is to be found in the margin of the actual bill form used. The letter must not, however, be detached from the bill form and the document must be kept intact.

2. Red Clause Letter of Credit

It is a usual letter of credit wherein the issuing banker gives authority to the negotiating banker to grant advances to the beneficiary up to a specified amount at the responsibility of the issuing banker. The important feature of this letter of credit is a clause typed in red ink, known as 'red clause' which enables the customer to secure 'Packing Credit' from the bank. Packing credit is a type of credit needed by sellers or exporters to purchase raw material, process it into final product, pack and despatch the product to the buyer. The advance made under red clause letter of credit is for a short period and is recovered from the amount, payable by the negotiating banker to the beneficiary when the later negotiates the required documents under the letter of credit.

3. Revolving Credit

When a credit is issued for a specific sum to be availed of in a fixed period of time, a new letter of credit is necessary after the credit has been fully availed of. But in the case of revolving credit, the amount is automatically renewed after the bills negotiated under them are duly honoured, *e.g.,* where the revolving credit is for ₹ 10,000 and a bill for ₹ 5,000 is negotiated under the said credit, as soon as the said bill is honoured the amount of the credit is automatically restored to its original amount of ₹ 10,000.

4. Confirmed and Unconfirmed Letters of Credit

When the opening bank requests the advising bank in the exporter's country to add its confirmation to an irrevocable credit and the latter does so, it is called irrevocable and confirmed letter of credit. The advising banker, after he adds his name to the undertaking, is called the 'confirming banker'. Such confirmation constitues a definite undertaking on the part of the conforming bank either—

(i) that the provisions for payment or acceptance will be duly fulfilled, or

(ii) that in case of a credit available by negotiation of draft, the confirming bank will negotiate drafts without recourse to the drawer.

Such undertaking cannot be cancelled or modified without the agreement of all concerned. A confirmed irrevocable letter of credit provided absolute security to the beneficiary. The opener asks the issuing banker, at the request of the beneficiary to arrange confirmed credit. The confirming banker takes upon himself the liability similar to that of the opening banker.

If the advising banker does not add his confirmation the letter of credit remains an unconfirmed one. In such a case there will be no such obligation on the advising bank.

5. 'With' and 'Without Recourse' Credits

Bills of exchange may be drawn under the letter of credit with recourse to the drawer or without such recourse. In case of with recourse bills, the banker as the holder of the bill, can recover the amount of the bill from its drawer, in case the drawee of the bill fails to honour it. In order to avoid such liability, the exporter may ask the importer to arrange credit without recourse to the drawer. Under this type of credit, the issuing banker will have recourse to the drawee only and if he fails, to honour the bill, the banker can realise the amount by disposing of the goods (if it is a documentary credit and documents have not been handed over to the importer). The liability of the drawer of such a bill of exchange ends as soon as it is negotiated.

6. Transferable and Non-transferable Letters of Credit

Ordinarily, the beneficiary is authorised to draw bills of exchange under a letter of credit. But if the beneficiary is an intermediary in the transaction and the goods are actually to be supplied by someone else, the beneficiary may request the opener to arrange a transferable letter of credit. Under a transferable letter of credit the beneficiary can transfer his right to draw a bill to somebody else. *The Uniform Customs and Practice for Documentary Credits* define a transferable credit as "a credit under which the beneficiary has the right to give instructions to the bank called upon to effect payment or acceptance or to any bank entitled to effect negotiation to make the credit available in whole or in part to one or more third parties (second beneficiaries)". Thus, the credit may be transferred to one or more persons. But it can be done only if the credit is expressly designated as "transferable" by the issuing bank. The rules regarding transferable credit are as follows: (Article 46, *Uniform Customs*):

1. A transferable credit can be transferred only once.
2. Fractions of a transferable credit can be transferred separately, provided partial shipments are not prohibited and the aggregate of such transfers does not exceed the amount of the credit.
3. The credit can be transferred only on the terms and conditions specified in the original credit, with the exception of the amount of the credit, of any unit price stated therein, and of the period of validity or period for shipment. Any or all of these may be reduced or curtailed.
4. The name of the first beneficiary can be substituted for that of the applicant for the credit. But if the name of the applicant for the credit is specially required by the original credit to appear in any document other than the invoice, such requirement must be fulfilled.
5. The first beneficiary of a transferable credit can transfer the credit to a second beneficiary in the same country, but if he is to be permitted to transfer the credit to a second beneficiary in another country, this must be expressly stated in the credit.

The credit may be divisible also. The total amount may be split into more than one part and each part may be transferred to different persons.

7. Back-to-back Letter of Credit

When a beneficiary receives a non-transferable letter of credit, he may request a bank to open a new letter of credit in favour of some other person on the security of the letter of credit issued in his favour. Such letter of credit is called a Back-to-back Letter of Credit.

☞ Not a Negotiable Instrument

Letters of credit are not negotiable instruments, nor are they transferable. Therefore, a thief or any other person getting possession of them cannot make use of them in any form which would bind the banker who has issued them.

☞ Bank Guarantee and Letter of Credit

A distinction was made between a letter of credit and a bank guarantee in the case of *Sianson Teicher Corpn., vs. Oilcakes, etc., Co.,* (1954) 2 All E.R. 497, 501. It was pointed out that, under a letter of credit, a bank itself actually undertakes to pay against documents which are to be presented to it. If it is a confirmed irrevocable letter of credit, it creates a direct relationship between the banker and the seller, and the bank becomes directly liable to the seller for the fulfilment of the obligations which it has undertaken in the letter of credit. From the legal point of view, in a bank guarantee, the banker becomes liable only indirectly or secondarily as a guarantor if the buyer fails to fulfil his obligation.

☞ Precautions to be Taken by Banker in Negotiating a Bill Under a Letter of Credit

A banker who negotiates a bill under a letter of credit should satisfy himself about the following points:

(i) That the letter of credit is genuine and the signature of the officer signing the letter on behalf of the issuing bank corresponds to the specimen signature in the possession of the negotiating bank.

(ii) That the period of its validity has not expired. Letters of credit are issued for a specified period.

(iii) That the amount of the bill to be negotiated is within the unavailed balance of the amount given in the letter of credit.

(iv) That the terms of the letter of credit are satisfied. If the negotiating banker fails to satisfy himself in respect of the terms of the letter of credit, he may have no claim against the bank which issued the letter of credit.

(v) That the party whose bill the banker is asked to negotiate is the same as the one given in the letter of credit.

☞ Liability of Banker Issuing Letter of Credit

The banker issuing an irrevocable letter of credit gives a firm undertaking to the exporter that the bill drawn according to the terms of the letter of credit will be honoured. This commitment is subject to the fulfilment of the conditions laid down in the letter of credit itself. If, on the other hand, the exporter supplies inferior goods or equipments and violates his agreement with the importer, the liability of the issuing banker remains unaffected. This was decided by the Supreme Court in "*Tarapor and Company, Madras, vs. M/s. Shaw Tracto Export, Moscow and Another* (AIR 1970, SC 391). In this case, the Indian firm opened in favour of the Russian firm a confirmed, irrevocable and devisible letter of credit with the Bank of India for the entire value of the machinery to be supplied under credit; the bank was required to pay to the Russian firm 25% of the value on presentation of documents specified therein and the balance 75% on the expiry of one year. After using the machinery supplied by the Russian firm, the Indian firm complained about its unsatisfactory performance which caused considerable loss to the Indian firm. The Indian firm filed a suit to prevent the Russian firm from realising the balance of the amount payable under the letter of credit on appeal, the Supreme Court quoted with approval the following paragraph from the Halsbury's Laws of England (Volume 34, P. 185).

"The contractual relationship between the issuing bank and the buyer is defined by the terms of the agreement between them under which the letter opening the credit is issued; and as between the seller and the bank, the issue of the credit duly notified to the seller creates a new contractual nexus and renders the bank directly liable to the seller to pay the purchase price or to accept the bill of exchange upon tender of the documents. The contract thus created between the seller and the bank is separate from, although ancillary to, the original contract between the buyer and the seller, by reason of the bank's undertaking to the seller which is absolute. Thus, the banker is not entitled to rely upon terms of the contract between the buyer and the seller which might permit the buyer to reject the goods and to refuse payment thereof and conversely, the buyer is not entitled to an injunction restraining the seller from dealing with the letter of credit if the goods are defective."

The Supreme Court, therefore rejected the appeal and observed that "a letter of credit is independent of an unqualified contract of sale or underlying transactions. The anatomy of an irrevocable letter of credit is entitled to protection. As a rule courts refrain from interfering with that autonomy."

The principle cited in the above case is not applicable in a case where the seller commits a fraud in complying with the terms of the letter of credit. In *National Oils and Chemical Industries, vs. Punjab and Sind Bank Ltd., and Another* (AIR 1979, Delhi 9) the Delhi High Court held:

"There is no doubt that the principle is well established that a letter of credit is independent of the primary contract of sale between the buyer and the seller and that it must be allowed to be honoured free from interference by the courts, the banks being concerned only with the performance of the obligations which they themselves have confirmed. But this principle is not to be extended to protect an unscrupulous seller when there is a fraudulent transaction. The banks must examine all documents with reasonable care to ascertain that they appear on their face to be in accordance with the terms and conditions of the credit. The banker's right of reimbursement depends on its accepting from the seller a faultless tender. The accepting bank can only claim indemnity if the conditions on which it is authorised to accept are, in the manner of the accompanying documents, strictly observed, otherwise it acts at its own risk."

In this case, M/s. National Oils and Chemical Industries (buyer) filed a suit for issue of an injunction restraining the Punjab and Sind Bank from paying any amount on the basis of the letter of credit. The buyer alleged fraud by the seller in complying with the terms of the letter of credit on the following grounds:

(i) Under the terms of the letter of credit, the seller was required to submit a full set of clean "on board" ocean shipping company's Bill of lading and also the report of the recognised independent surveyor. But the bill of lading was not "on board" ocean shipping company's bill of lading.

(ii) The company signed the bill of lading as agents of the Master of the ship and not that of the shipping company.

(iii) The Certificate submitted by the seller was of an independent surveyor and not of a recognised surveyor.

The High Court confirmed the injunction restraining the bank from making payment.

In another case, *"Jai Hind Oil Mills Co., vs. Canara Bank and Others"* (1987 Bombay 304) the High Court ordered an injunction restraining the bank from making payments in terms of letter of credit, as the *prima facie* case of fraud had been established.

☞ Right of Banker Issuing Letter of Credit

The well established rule, regarding the liability of the banker issuing letter of credit, as discussed in the above paragraphs "is that if the seller has complied with the terms of the letter of credit, there is an obligation upon the banker to pay irrespective of any disputes there may be between the buyer and the seller as to whether the goods are up to contract or not".

In relation to this obligation the banker issuing letter of credit, gets the right to claim payment from the buyer of the goods. If the buyer wants to raise any objection regarding the non-compliance of the condition of credit, he must do so within a reasonable period after the presentation of the documents and not thereafter.

The buyer of the goods remains liable to reimburse the issuing banker even if the ship carrying the goods sinks and the insurance policy is in the joint names of the buyer and the banker. It is the buyer's business to pursue the claim against the insurance company. If the issuing bank has lodged a claim against the insurance company, it does not mean that the primary obligation of the buyer to pay the amount to the bank has ceased. The sinking of the ship will not absolve the buyers of their liability to the issuing banker. *(Lakshmi Commercial Bank Ltd., vs. Hira Lal & Sons and Others* (1983 Comp. Cases 313 Delhi).

☞ Advantages of a Letter of Credit to the Beneficiary

A Letter of Credit is an instrument which facilitates trade transactions between two parties who are not known to each other. The major advantages derived by the seller or the beneficiary of a letter of credit are as follows:

(1) Certainty of Payment and Avoidance of Risk: Though the exporter may be quite unfamiliar with the importer, the letter of credit provides him an absolute assurance that the bills of exchange drawn under the letter of credit will be honoured. The risk of dishonour of the bill is thus totally avoided because the financial standing and reputation of the opening banker (and also of the confirming banker, in case of a confirmed letter of credit) stands as an absolute security against any such risk. The exporter may execute the order with greater degree of assurance and certainty.

(2) Immediate Negotiation of the Bills is Possible Under Letter of Credit: Bills drawn under the letters of credit are readily negotiated by the advising/confirming banker or any other banker, because of the firm undertaking given by the opening banker. The seller (reexporter) is able to realise the amount of the bill immediately by negotiating it with any banker. In the absence of a letter of credit the bill may not be acceptable to a banker for negotiation or may be negotiated on the basis of the exporter's standing. If the bills are sent for collection, the exporter has to wait till the amount of the bill is actually realised from the importer.

The rate charged by the negotiating banker is also the minimum if the bill is drawn under a letter of credit.

(3) Security Against Exchange Restrictions: The opening banker issues a letter of credit after having been satisfied that the exchange control regulations of his own country do not impose any restriction on the transfer of money for the purpose in question. The availability of necessary foreign exchange in the importer's country for honouring the bill is taken for granted. The transfer risks are thus avoided and the exporter need not investigate into the foreign exchange regulations in the importer's country.

(4) Advance may be Obtained: The exporter may obtain an advance from the bank on the basis of a letter of credit for the purpose of procuring and processing or manufacturing the goods to be exported.

☞ Advantages of Letter of Credit to the Buyer (or Importer)

(1) The issuing banker lends the benefits of his own credit to the importer, who is enabled to import the goods which is otherwise not possible.

(2) The letter of credit gives an assurance to the importer that the bills of exchange drawn under the credit will be honoured only when they are strictly in accordance with the conditions laid down in the letter of credit and the documents required therein are duly enclosed.

☞ Questions

1. Explain the significance of opening credit. In this connection, clearly bring out the distinction between different kinds of letters of credit.
2. Differentiate between the following:
   (a) Acceptance credit and book credit;
   (b) Commodity credit and cash credit;
   (c) Travellers credit and circular notes;
   (d) Confirmed credit and revolving credit;
   (e) Documentary credit and London acceptance credit.
3. Define a Letter of Credit. Discuss the precautions which must be taken for negotiating a bill under a letter of credit.
4. Describe briefly the different kinds of letters of credit.
5. Distinguish between:
   (a) Revocable and Irrevocable Credit;
   (b) Travellers' Letters of Credit and Travellers' Cheques.
6. Explain the essential features of an irrevocable letter of credit. A customer approaches you for opening a letter of credit on his behalf for importing automobile spare parts from London. What considerations would weigh with you before you agree to open the credit. *[I.I.B., Part II]*
7. Write short note on "Red Clause letter of credit". *[I.I.B., Part I]*
8. Write short note on "Uniform Customs and Practices for Documentary Credit". *[I.I.B., Part I]*

CHAPTER

20 Agricultural Finance

India is predominantly an agricultural country. The agricultural sector is an important segment of the national economy because about 70 per cent of the people directly or indirectly depend on agriculture, for their livelihood, and because about 50 per cent of the total national income is derived from agriculture moreover, agricultural commodities comprise almost 80 per cent of the total consumer expenditure. Fluctuations in the levels of agricultural output directly affect the prices of consumer goods; and the general level of prices fluctuates with the rise and fall in agricultural prices. The purchasing power of a vast majority of people in India is thus linked up with fluctuation in the fortunes of agriculturists. Finance for agricultural purposes was generally provided by the cooperative banking system under the patronage of the State Governments and the Reserve Bank of India. It was only from 1955, when the Imperial Bank of India was converted into the State Bank of India, that commercial banks started financing for agricultural purposes.

Some other developments which have led to a more active involvement of the banks in the field of agricultural finance are:

(i) The establishment of the Refinance Corporation for Agriculture to provide refinancing facilities to cooperative, commercial and development banks for their agricultural advances;

(ii) The policy of the social control of banks imparted a new sense of direction to commercial banks which began to provide finance for agricultural purposes — something which they had not done before;

(iii) The Agricultural Finance Corporation was set up in 1968 to increase the commercial banks' participation in agricultural financing;

(iv) Fourteen major banks were nationalised in 1969 (six more were nationalised in 1980), which has led to a greater involvement of commercial banks in the financing of agriculture under the direction of the Reserve Bank and the Central Government.

☞ Objectives of Agricultural Finance

Some of the important objectives of agricultural finance are:

(i) To help increase agricultural production;

(ii) To help fill the existing credit gap in the field of agriculture;

(iii) To provide adequate and timely credit for viable agricultural schemes;

(iv) To help achieve the national plan objectives, with special emphasis on the weaker sections;

(v) To help in inculcating banking and saving habits among the rural people; and

(vi) To assist cultivators in adopting improved methods of agriculture.

It may be mentioned here that the financing of agriculture is the most important part of rural credit in India. The following chart indicates the various institutional channels of rural credit in this country:

Chart 1
INSTITUTIONAL CHANNELS OF RURAL CREDIT IN INDIA

Non-agricultural Credit	**Agricultural Credit** **NABARD (National Bank for Agriculture and Rural Development)**			
	State/Apex Co-operative Banks	**Scheduled Commercial Banks**	**Regional Rural Banks**	**State Cooperative Land Development Banks**
State/Central Industrial Cooperative Banks' Branches	District Central Cooperative Banks' Branches	Urban Rural Branches	Agricultural Development Branches	Branches
Primary Non-agricultural Credit Societies	Large-size Multi-purpose Societies Primary Agricultural Credit Rural Sector Agricultural and Non-agricultural Societies	Farmers' Service Societies (FSS) Societies	(a) S.F.D.A. (b) M.F.A.L. (c) PCS (d) FSS	Primary Cooperative Land Development Banks and Branches

The agricultural schemes covered under agricultural finance (indirect and direct) are:

☞ Indirect Finance

(i) Credit for financing the distribution of fertilisers, pesticides and seeds.

(ii) Loans to the Electricity Board for the expenditure already incurred by them to provide low tension connections from step-down points to individual farmers to enable them to energise their wells.

(iii) Loans to farmers through primary agricultural credit societies under the scheme introduced for the purpose.

(iv) Finance under hire-purchase schemes for the purchase of agricultural machinery and implements.

(v) Loans for the construction and running of storage facilities (warehouses, godowns, silos and cold storages) in the producing areas. If the loans to cold storages are covered by a guarantee of the Credit Guarantee Corporation, they should be classified under small-scale industrial advances.

(vi) Advances to custom service units managed by individuals, institutions or organisations which maintain a fleet of tractors, bulldozers, well-boring equipment, threshers, combines, etc., and

undertake work from farmers on contract basis. If these advances are covered by a guarantee of the Credit Guarantee Corporation, they should be classified under small-scale industrial advances.

(vii) Loans to individuals, institutions or organisations which undertake spraying operations.

(viii) Loans to cooperative banks to enable them to relend to cooperative marketing societies (provided that a certificate from the State Cooperative Bank in favour of such loans is produced).

(ix) Loans to cooperative banks of producers (for example, Aarey Milk Colony Cooperative Bank, consisting of licensed cattle-owners).

(x) Indirectly financing farmers through the cooperative system (otherwise than by subscriptions to bonds and debenture issues), provided that a certificate from the State Cooperative Bank in favour of such loan is produced.

(xi) Loans to Agro-industries Corporation.

(xii) Loans to State-sponsored Agricultural Credit Corporations.

(xiii) Advances to the Agricultural Finance Corporation Ltd.,

(xiv) The commercial banks also provide them finance through Primary Agricultural Credit Societies (PACS), Farmers Service Societies (FSS) and Large Sized Adivasi Multi-purpose Societies (LAMPS).

☞ Direct Finance

(i) Development loans (*i.e.,* the type of loans eligible for refinance from the Agricultural Refinance and Development Corporation) to traditional plantations, *viz.,* coffee, tea, rubber and spices, and short-term as well as development loans to other plantations, horticulture (including the growing of bananas, cashewnuts, coconuts, lemon, grass, oil, etc.), and bee-keeping.

(ii) Credit, secured or otherwise, provided directly to farmers to finance such production and development needs as are indicated in the following paragraphs.

(iii) Short-term loans for raising crops (crop loans), advance up to ₹ 5,000 to farmers against pledge/hypothecation of agricultural produce for a period not exceeding 3 months and medium and long-term loans for financing production and development needs.

I. Purchase of Agricultural Inputs and Machinery

(a) *Purchase of agricultural inputs:* Fertilisers, pesticides, insecticides, fungicides and weedicides and improved seeds, high-yielding variety seeds, manures, etc.

(b) *Purchase of agricultural implements:* Iron ploughs, harrows, hoses, land-levellers, bound formers, hand-tools, sprayers, dusters, hay-press, sugarcane crushers, thresher machines, etc.

(c) *Purchase of farm machinery:* Tractors, power-tillers, tractor accessories, namely, disc ploughs, etc.

(d) *Purchase of trucks, bullockcarts and other transport equipment, etc.,* to assist in the transport of agricultural inputs and farm products.

(e) *Purchase of farm animals* — cows, bullocks, buffaloes, poultry birds, pigs, bees, etc.

II. Development of Irrigation Potential

This is achieved through:

(*a*) The construction of shallow and deep tubewells, tanks, etc., and the purchase of drilling units;

(*b*) The construction, deepening and clearing of surface wells, boring wells; purchase of oil engines; and installation of electric motors and pumps;

(*c*) The purchase and installation of turbine pumps; the construction of field channels (open as well as underground);

(*d*) The construction of lift irrigation projects;

(*e*) The installation of the sprinkler irrigation system.

III. Reclamation and Land Development Schemes

The bounding of farm lands, levelling of land, terracing, conversion of dry paddy lands into wet irrigable paddy lands; the development of farm drainage; the reclamation of saline lands and the prevention of salinisation; the reclamation of ravine land; the purchase of bulldozers, etc..

IV. Construction of Farm Buildings and Structures

Bullock-sheds, implement-sheds, tractor and truck-sheds, farm stores, etc.

V. Construction and Running of Storage Facilities

The construction and running of warehouses, godowns, silos and cold storages.

VI. Production and Processing of Hybrid Seeds of Crops

VII. Payment of Irrigation Charges, etc.

Charges for hired water from wells and tubewells, canal water charges; the maintenance and upkeep of oil engines and electric motors; the payment of labour charges, electricity charges, marketing charges, service charges to custom service units; the purchase of poultry food; the payment of development cases, etc.

VIII. Development of Dairying and Animal Husbandry in all its Aspects

IX. Development of Fisheries in all its Aspects

(*a*) From fish-catching to exports;

(*b*) Financing of equipment necessary for deep-sea fishing;

(*c*) Rehabilitation of tanks (fresh-water fishing);

(*d*) Fish breeding, etc.

X. Development of Poultry and Piggery in all its Aspects

The erection of poultry houses and pig-houses, bee-keeping, etc.,

XI. Miscellaneous

The development and maintenance of stud farms, seri-culture, etc.,

☞ Types of Agricultural Finance

Agricultural credit may be provided in two ways:

(i) Short-term Credit or Seasonal Credit: This type of credit provides the farmers with the working capital to meet his seasonal requirements. This type of credit is normally repayable in one year.

(ii) Medium-term Credit: This credit provides the farmer with capital for the purchase of livestock, farm machinery, etc., or for undertaking improvements on land, etc. This is normally repayable in more than two years.

The credit provided by commercial banks to the agricultural sector may be divided into two categories:

(i) Direct Credit: This type of credit is provided to the farmers for the production and marketing of crops; and

(ii) Indirect Credit: This type of credit is granted to cooperative credit societies, marketing and processing societies, etc.

CROP LOANS

According to Reserve Bank guidelines, the banker should proceed in the matter as follows:

(i) Amount of Loan: The banker should determine the amount of loan to be sanctioned to a farmer on the basis of –

(a) the area to be cultivated by him, and

(b) the scale of finance for specific crops per hectare.

The scale of finance includes all expenses to be incurred by farmers for raising crops including costs all inputs, cost of operations/services and other charges. The scale of finance, once determined, should be reviewed periodically and revised if the cost of cultivation increases.

(ii) Disbursement: Short-term crop loans are generally divided into:

(a) Cash component to be disbursed in cash, and

(b) Kind component to be disbursed through the suppliers of seeds, fertilisers and pesticides.

Margin Money: In case of agricultural loans up to ₹ 10,000 (both short-term and long-term loans) banks should not take any margin.

Security: Banks are required to take security for agricultural loans as follows:

No collateral security by way of mortgage of land/charge on land or third party guarantee should be taken for crop loans up to ₹ 10,000 and terms loans up to ₹ 10,000 where movable assets are created. Only primary security by way of hypothecation of crops or movable assets should be taken. Where there are genuine difficulties in the creation of mortage/charge on land, wherever required, banks can take third party guarantee or any other security.

(iii) Rates of Interest: The Reserve Bank of India has prescribed concessional rates of interest on all advances granted by scheduled commercial banks and Regional Rural Banks up to ₹ 2 lakh.

Interest is payable only at the time of repayment of principal. Interest on current dues is not to be compounded.

(iv) Conversion into Term Loans: Banks are permitted to convert a crop loan into a term loan if the borrower is unable to repay it due to any natural calamities, his death or physical incapacity or any unusual circumstance beyond his control. Repayment period of the converted crop loan should be fixed keeping in view the losses suffered by him and his capacity to repay. Such a borrower may be given further crop loan for the next agricultural operations.

DEVELOPMENT LOANS

These loans are given in the form of term loans for the following purposes:

(i) Minor Irrigation, *i.e.,* sinking of new wells, renovation of old wells, installation of diesel/electric pumpsets;

(ii) Land improvement, *i.e.,* land reclamation, soil conservation, land levelling and shaping, laying out of field channels/drainage/ditch; and

(iii) Diversified purposes, such as:

(a) Purchase of tractors, threshers, farm machinery, agro-service centres.

(b) dairy, poultry, sheep-breeding, piggery, fisheries.

(c) plantation and horticulture development.

(d) construction of godowns and silos.

(e) market yards development.

(f) aerial spraying.

(g) forestry.

(h) setting up of gobar gas plants.

(i) purchase of work animals and animal driven carts, and

(j) seri-culture and bee-keeping.

☞ Period

These loans should be repayable in 3 to 10 years, ending the purpose of the loan, the borrower's capacity to repay other relevant factors.

☞ Security

Banks may take security for term loan as follows:

(a) Where the borrower creates movable assets out of loans: Such assets may be hypothecated with the bank in case the loan amount is up to the cost of economic unit where applicable or ₹ 5,000 whichever is lower. In case of loans exceeding ₹ 5,000, bank may also take a third party guarantee or mortgage of the land, at its own discretion.

(b) Where movable assets are not created out of loans: Bank should take only demand promissory note/loan aggreement if the amount of loan is up to ₹ 2,000. In other cases mortgage of land may also be taken at the discretion of bank. Bank may take a simple declaration by the borrower that a charge has been created on the land in favour of the bank. In those States where legislation on the lines suggested by the Talwar Committee has been passed.

☞ Margins

Banks are required to maintain margins as follows:

(a) Loans to cost of economic unit (where applicable) or ₹ 5,000, whichever is lower and loans up to ₹ 5,000 to small marginal farmers and agricultural labourers — no margin, if subsidy is available. If subsidy is not available margin @ 5%.

(b) For others, margin may vary between 15% and 25% depending on the purpose and amount of loan. The Reserve Bank has prescribed a minimum economic unit in respect of certain activities, *e.g.*, in case of purchase of milch cattle — 2 animals and in case of poultry — 90/100 layers.

Interest shall be payable only at the time of repayment of loan or instalments of principal as fixed. Where crop loans or instalments of term loans become overdue, banks can add the interest outstanding to the principal and compound the interest. However, the total interest debited to an account should not exceed the principal amount in respect of advances to small and marginal farmers.

☞ Repayment

If the borrower defaults due to his death, physical incapacity or natural calamity, etc., the repayment period may be extended and in suitable cases a fresh term loan may also be sanctioned.

Commercial banks provided mostly indirect credit to the agricultural sector before the imposition of the social control of banks. But, in recent years, they have started providing direct credits. Agricultural financing in India is full of risks, mainly because farmers depend mostly upon monsoon rains for their crops. Cultivation, moreover, is uncertain, and varies from year-to-year because of uncertain and unpredictable monsoons. The average Indian farmer is so poor that he is unable to provide any tangible security except land. Considering these impediments in the way of agricultural finance, the Reserve Bank and the Central Government have taken steps to ensure that commercial banks may play a more important part in agricultural financing. For this purpose, there are:

(i) The Reserve Bank's guidelines to commercial banks on agricultural finance;

(ii) Study Group on State enactments having a bearing on lendings by commercial banks to agriculturists;

(iii) The Agricultural Refinance and Development Corporation (A.R.D.C.);

(iv) The Agricultural Finance Corporation (A.F.C.);

(v) The Regional Rural Banks;

(vi) The Lead Bank Scheme;

(vii) The Small Farmers Development Agency (S.F.D.A.);

(viii) The Marginal Farmers and Agricultural Labourers' Development Agencies (M.F.A.L.); and

(ix) The Farmers' Service Societies.

(i) Reserve Bank's Guidelines to Commercial Banks on Agricultural Finance

In December 1970, the Reserve Bank of India issued guidelines to commercial banks, laying down clear policies and procedures to be followed in advancing agricultural loans.

☞ Objectives

The main objective of lendings by commercial banks for agricultural purposes is to help farmers to adopt improved practices so that they may move on to a higher technological plan of activity. Agricultural credit would have to be purposive and should be provided to already viable cultivators, to marginal farmers and to potentially viable cultivators. Banks should lend for productive purposes rather than for the purposes of maintenance and replacement of existing assets. Farmers using traditional methods of agriculture should be provided with all the banking facilities. At the same time, efforts should be made to encourage and help them to use improved methods with a view to increase their output and income. Funds should be made available to them at the right time and sufficient enough to meet their needs. Banks should maintain a close and regular contact with the borrowers for the purpose of timely recovery of loans. They should make all possible efforts to develop banking habits among farmers.

☞ Area of Operations

In their lending operations, banks should adopt the *area approach* method to avoid competition and overlapping in the same areas by two or more banks. Every bank should select a *command area* it proposes to serve. In general, a branch with one field officer/assistant attached to the agent, should serve an area within a radius of 10 miles. The norm of "one supervisor for 450-500 borrowers" may be adopted. In areas where the multiple cropping pattern prevails, two sets of officials may be considered — one for evaluating and scrutinising proposals and the other for effecting recoveries. Branch agents should be granted discretionary powers so that they may clear at least 80 per cent of proposals without reference to the central office.

☞ Norms of Credit

The branch agent should collect detailed information on the different types of crops grown in an area and then workout a rational scale of finance for the various crops. Short-term loans for crop raising should generally be divided into "cash" and "kind" components. Banks should ensure that the "kind" component of the loan is actually made directly by the bank. A list of approved dealers should be prepared for this purpose.

LENDING PROCEDURE

Banks should follow the following guidelines while granting direct agricultural advances:

1. Time for Lending: Agriculturists should be provided adequate quantity of credit at the right time. For this purpose banks should prepare a definite calendar of operations particularly for crop loans so that the applications for loans are collected and processed well in advance. Medium term credit may appropriately be disbursed in the off-season when the cultivators are not busy with their crops.

2. Availability of Ground Water: Banks should make their own arrangements to get information on ground water availability for grant of term loans for minor irrigation.

3. Completion of Application Forms: Banks staff should help the borrower in filling the forms. For illiterate small and marginal farmers and landless labourers, banks should arrange for their photographhs at their own cost.

☞ Area Approach

Banks should adopt area approach which aim at intensive and close coverage of the selected areas around a branch for meeting the total agricultrual credit needs of borrowers and for ensuring effective supervison over the use of credit by brorrowers. However, banks should also accept viable schemes received from places beyond their normal common areas, if they feel that they can service such loans effectively.

☞ Application Form

Loan application forms must be made available in all regional languages. These forms are in two parts. Form I contains basic data regarding the applicant and Form II covers the different purposes for which the loan is required. In Form II, the bank's supervisory staff will make recommendations on the loan proposal after making necessary enquiries from the applicant or by collecting information during their presanction visit to the applicant.

☞ Appraisal Form

If the application for loan is for a large amount, say ₹ 5,000 or more, the bank staff may collect more details for assessing the economic viability of the proposal. For this purpose banks may evolve an appraisal form with a brief check list of points to be verified in order to appraise the loan application. The form may include comments on —

(i) the quantum and period of loan with reference to the life of the asset to be acquired.

(ii) the possible improvement in income for deciding the repaying capacity of borrower, and

(iii) other relevnt details.

☞ Repayment of Loans

The repayment scheduled for both short- and medium-term loans should coincide with the time when the cultivator has sold his produce. Due dates for the repayment of the loans should be fixed accordingly.

GUIDELINES FOR RECOVERY OF AGRICULTURAL ADVANCES

The Reserve Bank of India has emphasized the need of prompt recovery of direct agricultural advances and has suggested to the commercial banks to follow the following guidelines in this regard:

(i) Credit provided by the banks should be related to production efforts. Banks should give low priority for financing of agriculture under traditional methods of cultivation or for maintenance and replacement of existing assets.

(ii) The scale of finance must be in consonance with the scale of inputs and cost of assets *vis-a-vis* incremental income.

(iii) The pre-lending appraisal system should be through and updated from time-to-time.

(iv) Loans should be disbursed promptly and in time, as far as possible, in the form of direct payment to suppliers. Cash component of the loan should not be large.

(v) To ensure that credit is used for productive purposes only periodical follow-up of the use of loan and condition of resultant produce is essential. Bank should carefully monitor the loan disbursement and should remain in contact with the borrower.

(vi) Repayment schedule for loans should coincide with the time when the cultivator generally sells his produce and is in possession of funds. The repayment period should not be a shorter one. It should be stipulated keeping in view the incremental income accruing to small farmer so that he may repay the loans within the prescribed period. A substantial portion of incremental income should be left with the borrower so as to enable him to meet his requirements of bare necessities in addition to repayment of loan instalment and interest.

(vii) The borrower should be informed about the due date soon after the crop is harvested.

(viii) Banks should appoint adequate and suitable field staff who would remain in touch with the borrowers and their agricultural operations, supervise the use of credit and sort out problems. Block-wise recovery campaigns should be organised in association with the officers of the State Government departments.

(ix) If the poor recovery performance is due to old overdues, banks should monitor the progress of current dues and arrears separately.

(x) In case of term loans the NABARD has indicated to banks the schedule of term loan repayment periods including the gestation periods to be given to small borrowers. Banks should adhere strictly to such repayment periods in the sanction letters.

(ii) Study Group on State Enactments Having a Bearing on Lendings by Commercial Banks to Agriculturists

Farmers can offer only land, a tangible asset, as a security for advances by commercial banks. But various State Govenments have enacted different laws relating to land tenure and tenancy reforms, ceiling on land holdings, agricultural debt relief, regulation of moneylending, etc. These enactments have made it difficult for commercial banks to participate in agricultural financing. Under the chairmanship of Shri R.K. Talwar, an Expert Group was, therefore, appointed by the Reserve Bank of India to examine the State laws having a bearing on the lendings by commercial banks to agriculturists. The Group submitted its report in 1970, recommending the enactment of a single legislation, incorporating the various amendments suggested by it to the different State laws, and prepared a Model Bill to enable the State Governments to take expeditious action on this recommendation. Some of the important recommendations of the Group are:

(i) The cultivator, having no right or restricted rights of alienation (transfer) in their lands or interest therein, should be vested with right to alienate land or interest in the land held by them in favour of banks in order to obtain agricultural finance.

(ii) The cultivators should receive the same concessions in respect of stamp duty, registration fees and charge for non-encumbrance certificates as was given to borrowers from co-operative societies.

(iii) Commercial banks should be exempted from the purview of moneylending and debt relief legislation.

(iv) Commercial banks should be exempted from legislation relating to ceiling on land, and should be permitted to acquire and hold land to facilitate recovery of loans.

(v) To help in the timely recovery of loans by commercial banks, a State Government should empower an official to issue orders, which have the force of a civil court decree, for the payment of dues to commercial banks by sale of mortgaged or charged property.

(vi) The general principle of priority as between institutional credit agencies in regard to the recovery of loans based on common security should be the same as is indicated in the Transfer of Property Act, 1882. This would ensure that the concept of first charge in favour of cooperatives does not adversely affect the commercial banks.

(vii) All institutional credit agencies should have priority of charge *vis-a-vis* private agencies. Moreover, the agency providing term loans for development purposes should have a priority of charge over the agency providing term loans for development purposes.

Many State Governments have enacted legislation on the lines of the Model Bill recommended by the Expert Group, and this has made it possible for commercial banks to undertake financing agriculture on a large-scale. Some State Governments have reduced the stamp duty payable by agriculturists on documents executed by them in favour of commercial banks. Many other cities have been added to the list where an equitable mortgage may be created. With these measures, some of the legal hurdles in the way of commercial bank financing agriculture have been removed.

(iii) Regional Rural Banks

Development of the rural economy was accepted as an integral aspect of the main strategy in the Sixth Five Year Plan. The case for the development of rural economy was urgent and pressing because it is the basis of social stability and economic growth with distributive justice. The concept of rural development is wider than that of agricultural development. In the rural sector, the credit requirements of village artisans, craftsmen and cottage industrial units have been neglected the most. The primary credit societies offer credit mostly to the agriculturist.

Credit is the most important and probably the most scarce input in Indian agriculture. Rural people are always unable to exhibit their latent potential and face difficulties in obtaining loans. It is generally believed that rural credit must be cheap so that even the poorest farmers and rural artisans may afford it.

Though there has been a commendable geographic extension in the operations of co-operative agencies, commercial banks, the State Bank of India and its subsidiaries and other financial institutions working in rural areas, a large part of rural India and many types of rural activities are still badly in need of finance and other assistance for their proper development. In order, therefore, that these financial institutions may be of greater assistance to small and marginal farmers, rural artisans, small and retail traders, self-employed persons, agricultural labourers and others in remote areas, and in order to identify their needs, the idea of regional rural banks was conceived.

In its report in 1972, the Banking Commission, which was constituted under the chairmanship of Shri R.G. Saraiya, recommended the setting up of rural banks which would extend banking facilities to rural areas and thus revolutionise rural finance. According to the Commission, the banking entity in rural areas should be essentially cooperative in character and provide a wider range of services than those which were provided by primary agricultural credit societies.

On 1st July, 1975, the Ministry of Finance, Government of India, constituted a Working Group to examine indepth the question of the setting up of new rural banks to cater to the credit needs of the rural people. The Group submitted its report on 30th July, 1975.

☞ Establishment

The Government of India accepted the recommendations of the Group and promulgated the Regional Rural Banks Ordinance on 26th September, 1975, for the establishment of regional rural banks. This ordinance was replaced by the Regional Rural Banks Act of 1976. In terms of Sub-section (1) of Section (3) of the Act, the Central Government may, by a notification in the *Official Gazette,* establish a regional rural bank, if requested to do so by a sponsoring bank.

☞ Capital Structure

The authorised capital of each RRB shall be ₹ 1 crore, which the Central Government may increase or decrease in consultation with the Reserve Bank of India and the sponsoring bank, subject to a minimum of ₹ 25 lakh. The issued capital of each RRB shall be ₹ 25 lakh, of which 50 per cent shall be subscribed by the Central Government, 15 per cent by the concerned State Government and 35 per cent by the sponsoring bank. There is a provision for an increase in issued capital by the Board of Directors of the RRB after consultation with the Reserve Bank and the sponsoring Bank and with the prior approval of the Central Government. The shares of a RRB shall be treated as trustee securities for the purposes of Section 20 of the Indian Trusts Act, 1882, and shall be treated as approved securities for the purpose of the Banking Regulation Act of 1949.

☞ Management

The general superintendence, direction and management of the affairs and business of RRB is vested in a Board of Directors. It has been specifically laid down in the Act that the Board, in discharging its functions, should act on business principles and should have due regard to the public interest, and that it shall be guided by such directions in regard to matters of policy involving public interest as the Central Government may give, after consultation with the Reserve Bank. Besides the chairman, the Board of Directors shall consist of not more than three Directors to be nominated by the Central Government (concerned) and not more than three Directors to be nominated by the sponsoring bank. The Central Government is empowered to increase the number of the members of the Board, up to a maximum of 15, and prescribe the manner in which the additional members may be appointed. The chairman of an RRB shall be appointed by the Central Government for a term not exceeding five years and shall hold office during the pleasure of the Central Government. He shall be eligible for re-appointment. The chairman is required to devote his whole-time to the affairs of the RRB. Subject to the superintendence, control and direction of the Board, he shall have the management of the affairs of the RRB entirely under his control. A Director shall hold office for a period of two years and is also eligible for renomination.

These regional rural banks are basically scheduled commercial banks but are different from the latter in the following respects:

(a) Their area of operations is limited to a particular region, comprising one or more districts in any State;

(b) They grant loans and advances, particularly to small and marginal farmers and agricultural labourers and rural artisans, small entrepreneurs and persons of small means engaged in trade and other productive activities in the area of the bank's operations;

(c) The lending rates of the bank shall not be higher than the prevailing lending rates of co-operative societies in any particular State;

(d) The salary structure of the employees of a regional rural bank is prescribed by the Central Government, having regard to the salary structure of the employees of the State Government and local authorities of comparable level and status in the area of operations of the bank;

(e) The area for which regional rural banks are set up shall be comparatively backward; or it shall be a tribal area or an area where coverage by commercial and cooperative banks is relatively poor.

☞ Functions

A regional rural bank undertakes all types of banking business which a scheduled commercial bank may engage in under Section 6 of the Banking Regulation Act of 1949. However, in terms of the provision of Sub-section 2(a) and (b) Section 18 of the Regional Rural Banks Act of 1976, the regional rural banks are particularly required to undertake the following types of business:

(a) The granting of loans and advances, particularly to small and marginal farmers and agricultural labourers, whether individually or in groups, and to cooperative societies, including agricultural marketing societies, primary agricultural credit societies of farmers service societies, for agricultural purposes or agricultural operations or for other purposes connected therewith;

(b) The granting of loans and advances, particularly to artisans, small entrepreneurs and person of small means engaged in trade, commerce or industry or other productive activities, within the notified area relating to the Regional Rural Banks;

(c) As regards loans, the Government of India have decided that, to begin with, the individual loans should be granted by these banks only to small, marginal farmers, landless labourers and artisans, etc. The rate of interest on loan charged by these banks should not be higher than that charged by cooperatives.

☞ Progress of Regional Rural Banks

The total number of Regional Rural Banks functioning in the country at the end of March 1990 was 196 covering 369 districts spread over 23 States. The deposits and advances of 196 RRBs aggregated to ₹ 4,419.35 crore and ₹ 3,501.84 crore respectively. The working of the RRBs was however, not satisfactory and as many as 162 RRBs had accumulated losses of ₹ 282 crore at the end of March, 1990.

REGIONAL RURAL BANKS IN INDIA

Sr. No.	*States*	*No. of RRBs*	*No. of Branches*	*No. of Districts*
1.	Andhra Pradesh	12	816	17
2.	Assam	5	223	10
3.	Bihar	20	1480	35
4.	Gujarat	9	175	15
5.	Haryana	3	181	7
6.	Himachal Pradesh	1	87	3
7.	Jammu & Kashmir	3	238	10
8.	Karnataka	12	818	18
9.	Kerala	2	247	5
10.	Madhya Pradesh	22	1132	39
11.	Maharashtra	7	354	14
12.	Manipur	1	16	8
13.	Orissa	9	689	13
14.	Rajasthan	13	683	26
15.	Tamil Nadu	1	130	2
16.	Tripura	1	64	3
17.	Uttar Pradesh	36	2247	44
18.	West Bengal	9	528	15
19.	Meghalaya	1	30	3
20.	Nagaland	1	4	7
21.	Punjab	3	79	6
22.	Arunachal Pradesh	1	4	4
23.	Mizoram	1	20	3
	Total	*173*	*10,245*	*307*

☞ Concessions by the Reserve Bank to Regional Rural Banks

With a view to ensuring the viability of the regional rural banks, the Reserve Bank of India has granted the following concessions to them:

(a) All the regional rural banks established under the Regional Rural Banks Act of 1976 are included in the second schedule of the Reserve Bank of India Act of 1934 from the date of their inception.

(*b*) In order to enable the regional rural banks in the initial stages to comply with the cash reserve requirements of Section 42 of the Reserve Bank of India Act of 134, the Reserve Bank has by a notification issued in the *Official Gazette,* exempted all the regional rural banks from the proviso to Sub-section (1) of Section 42 of the Reserve Bank of India Act of 1934 for a period of two years with effect from 2nd October, 1975. The cash reserve to be maintained by the regional rural banks, is therefore, at the rate of 3 per cent of their total demand and time liabilities as specified in Sub-section (1) of Section 42 of the Act as against the increased rate of 6 per cent at present applicable to other scheduled commercial banks.

(*c*) In order to enable the regional rural banks to comply with the liquidity requirements of Section 24 of the Banking Regulation Act of 1949, the Government of India has, by a notification dated 3rd October, 1975, notified all the nationalised banks, for the purpose of Sub-clauses *(ii)* and *(iii)* of the Sub-section (2A) of Section 24 of the Banking Regulation Act of 1949, that any balance, maintained in the current account by a regional rural bank with the State Bank of India and/or with any of the nationalised banks, shall be deemed to be cash for the purpose of compliance with the liquidity requirements of Section 24 of the Banking Regulation Act of 1949.

(*d*) Regional rural banks have been exempted from maintaining liquid assets at the enhanced rate of 33 per cent of their total demand and time liabilities under Section 24 of the Banking Regulation Act of 1949. The liquid assets to be maintained by these regional rural banks are therefore, 25 per cent. As many of the regional rural banks are still very young institutions it has been decided to continue this concession for the time-being.

(*e*) Regional rural banks are allowed to offer a rate of interest on deposits at one-and-a-half per cent more than that offered by scheduled commercial banks, subject to a ceiling of 10.5 per cent on term deposits.

(*f*) The Reserve Bank has formulated a scheme for the free transfer of funds between the head office of a regional rural bank and its different branches through the public sector banks operating in the areas covered by the former. Free remittance would be allowed in multiples of ₹ 5,000 subject to a minimum ₹ 5,000 at a time. All the public sector banks have been requested to give effect to the scheme from 1st January, 1977.

(*g*) For the purpose of the Income-Tax Act, 1961, or any other enactment for the time-being in force, the income, profits and gains of regional rural banks shall be deemed to be those of a cooperative society. A regional rural bank is not liable to tax under the Interest Tax Act of 1974.

☞ Insured Status

Regional rural banks are registered as insured banks with the Deposit Insurance Corporation. All the deposits, up to ₹ 20,000 per depositor in the same right and capacity in each bank, are accordingly, insured with the Deposit Insurance Corporation of India, thus providing protection to the depositors.

☞ Refinance Scheme for Regional Rural Banks

Regional rural banks shall be entitled to the facility of loans and advances under a scheme which came into force from 1st October, 1976. The total refinance limit for each regional rural bank is fixed on the basis of the prescribed formula at 15 : 50 : 35, indicating the proportion of the regional rural bank deposits, the Reserve Bank of India refinance and the sponsoring bank's advances respectively in the aggregate lending programme of each regional rural bank. The refinance is provided at 2 per cent below the bank rate, *i.e.,* at 7 per cent per annum at present.

☞ Steering Committee

At the national level, the Government of India has set up a Steering Committee to workout the details of the programme of the regional rural banks and to monitor their progress. The meetings of the Steering Committee are held periodically to discuss the problems of regional rural banks and to provide suitable guidelines to them.

☞ Training Facilities

It has been decided that the recruitment of managerial, supervisory and clerical staff of the regional rural banks should be from within the area of operations of each bank on such scales of pay and allowances as are applicable to the employees of a State Government. In order to help them to have a trained staff as early as possible, the Reserve Bank of India has undertaken the training of the chairman and branch managers of regional rural banks which is imparted to them at the College of Agricultural Banking (CAB), Pune. The training of the accountants, field officers and clerks is conducted at the training centres of the respective sponsoring banks under the overall supervision of the College of Agricultural Banking.

☞ Simplification of Loan Procedure

In order to minimise the procedural delays in making/withdrawing deposits, availing of loan facilities, etc., the Reserve Bank of India has set up a committee to suggest the simplified accounting and operational procedure to be followed by regional rural banks so that their rural clientele may feel at home in dealing with them. The report of the committee has already been issued for adoption by regional rural banks.

(iv) The Lead Bank Scheme

The Study Group appointed by the National Credit Council under the chairmanship of Prof. D.R. Gadgil to report on "The Organisational Framework for the Implementation of Social Objectives", had recommended *area approach* method in the preparation of plans and programmes for the development of the banking and credit structure. The Lead Bank Scheme, introduced by the Reserve Bank of India in December 1969, may be said to be the beginning of the implementation of the *area approach* method. The Study Group report revealed major territorial and functional gaps in the country and an uneven spread of banking offices and banking business in different States and population groups with a pronounced urban orientation. According to the report, there was a large flow of resources from smaller to large population centres and from rural to urban areas. It pointed out that there was an uneven distribution of credit to different economic sectors and that credit to certain types of borrowers was almost non-available. It, therefore, suggested that plans should be formulated for the extension of credit and banking facilities in the country on the basis of local conditions, and recommended the adoption of the *area approach* method for the formulation of plans and programmes for the development of the banking structure. It also suggested particular districts should be assigned to banks, which may act as pace setters for providing integrated banking facilities.

In August 1969, the Reserve Bank of India appointed a Committee of Bankers, with Shri F.K.P. Nariman as chairman, "to evolve a coordinated programme for ensuring the setting up of adequate banking facilities in the unbanked districts of the country". The Nariman Committee, among other things, recommended that "banks should be allotted specific districts where they would take 'the lead' in surveying the potential of banking development in extending branch expansion and expanding credit facilities". The Reserve Bank of India accepted these principles and evolved the Lead Bank Scheme. Under this scheme, all the districts in the country have been allocated to 22 public sector banks and

3 private sector banks. Almost the whole of India, except Greater Mumbai, Kolkata, Chennai, Delhi, Chandigarh and Goa, have been covered under this scheme.

☞ Functions of Lead Bank

The functions of a Lead Bank are:

(a) To survey the resources and potential for banking development in its district;

(b) To survey the number of industrial and commercial units and other establishments and farms which do not have banking accounts or which depend primarily on moneylenders;

(c) To examine the facilities for the marketing of agricultural produce and industrial production, storage and warehousing space, and the linking of credit with marketing in the district;

(d) To study the facilities for the stocking of fertilisers and other agricultural inputs and for the repair and servicing of equipment;

(e) To recruit and train staff who would offer advice to small borrowers and farmers and who would follow-up and inspect the end-use of loans;

(f) To assist other primary lending agencies; and

(g) To maintain contacts and liaison residually with government and quasi-government agencies.*

While other banks are not precluded from opening branches, the Lead Bank is expected to act as a consortium leader and invite the cooperation of other banks operating in the district in mobilising deposits, locating actual and potential credit needs, and catering for them.

☞ Progress of the Lead Bank Scheme

The first phase of the programme consists of the completion of impressionist surveys for the identification of centres which have a potential for bank operations and the opening of bank branches. Such surveys have been completed in almost all the districts.

In the second phase, area development programmes have to be formulated and implemented. Banks have so far prepared district credit plans for 377 districts, of which plans for 359 districts were launched by 30th June, 1978. The work relating to the preparation of credit plans of the remaining five districts was expected to be completed by 31st March, 1978.

In December, 1979, the Lead Banks were advised by the Reserve Bank of India to terminate the existing Credit Plans, and to prepare fresh plans for the period January 1980 — December 1982, along with annual action plans for 1980. To ensure uniformity in the coverage of the second round of the credit plans, detailed guidelines were issued by the Reserve Bank to all the Lead Banks. Up to June 1980, DCPs in respect of 357 out of 397 districts were prepared.

☞ Working Group to Review the Working of Lead Bank Scheme

A Working Group to review the working of Lead Bank scheme was set up in November, 1981, on the completion of a decade of working of this scheme. The terms of reference of the Working Group were:

(i) to review the working of the Lead Bank Scheme in regard to the preparation and implementation of the District Credit Plans (DCPs) and to suggest improvements for proper and effective coordination of activities among the various participating organisations, in the light of the recommendation of the "Committee to Review Arrangements for Institutional Credit for Agriculture and Rural Development (CRAFICARD);

* Reserve Bank of India, Annual Report, 1970, p. 63.

(ii) to review the role of the lead banks and to suggest measures to make them more effective and also to suggest measures to improve the organisational set up of lead and non-lead banks of the district and other levels;

(iii) to examine the role of the District Consultative Committees and Standing Committees and make suggestions for their more effective functioning;

(iv) to review the role of Lead District Officers of RBI;

(v) to consider the question of allocation of lead responsibility, particularly to banks which have been recently nationalised;

(vi) to consider measures to improve the flow of data under the information system;

(vii) to examine and review the existing arrangements for training of all officials concerned with the work relating to the scheme, with particular reference to the DCPs and consider what improvements would be necessary in this regard; and

(viii) any other matter germane to the aforesaid aspects.

☞ Guidelines for the Preparation of District Credit Plans (DCPs) 1983-85

The revised guidelines for the formulation of the DCPs covering the period January, 1983 to March, 1985 were issued by the Reserve Bank to the Lead Banks in February 1982. The DCPs to be prepared would be co-terminus with the balance of the Sixth Plan period. Programmes incorporated in the DCPs earlier were not always successfully implemented either because they were not tested for their feasibility or bankability or for want of adequate infrastructural support and forward and backward linkages. In terms of the new guidelines, only those programmes requiring bank assistance which are considered technically feasible and bankable would figure in the DCP. Further, not only are States required to indicate specifically the infrastructural support and other assistance they would provide for making various investment programmes indicated by them viable, but banks are also required to specify in the DCP document the implementing agencies in each case so as to facilitate monitoring of progress at the DCC meetings. A special feature of the new DCPs would be a separate chapter devoted to the special programmes, *viz.,* 20-point programme, IRDP, special component plan for the SC/ST, etc.

(v) Small Farmers' Development Agency (SFDA)

The All-India Rural Credit Review Committee (1969) recommended the establishment of the Small Farmers' Development Agency (SFDA). The main objective for the establishment of such an agency is to help those cultivators who have small yet potentially economically viable holdings. The small farmers have always been neglected by the unorganised as well as the organised sector of banking. Therefore, the establishment of the SFDA is a significant development in the field of rural finance, for it forms an important link in the chain of organised financial institutions through which money flows into the rural sector of the Indian economy.

SFDAs have been established in 46 selected districts on a pilot basis. These agencies:

(a) Identify small but potentially viable farmers in their areas;

(b) Find out the problems of such farmers; and

(c) Provide such farmers with institutional credit and inputs, and help them to improve their production capacity.

The SFDAs help potentially viable farmers in their areas in such a way that they become viable in three to four years. The schemes of these agencies are mostly production and credit oriented. Every

SFDA is supposed to help about 50,000 potentially viable farmers through assistance in subsidised irrigiation, land-levelling, soil conservation, storage, marketing and custom services facilities. Under this scheme, 25 per cent of the assistance is in the form of a subsidy; the balance is a loan, mainly from cooperative credit institutions.

(vi) Marginal Farmers' and Agricultural Labourers' Development Agencies (MFAL)

The Marginal Farmers' and Agricultural Labourers' Development Agencies have been established to help sub-marginal farmers and agricultural labourers. Marginal farmers with holdings up to one hectare and agricultural labourers who earn more than 50 per cent of their income from agriculture receive subsidised credit support for agriculture and subsidiary occupations under this scheme. This subsidised credit support is given for dairy-farming, poultry, fishery, piggery, sheep rearing, horticulture, etc. The MFAL schemes are based mainly in favour of employment and subsidiary occupation.

(vii) Role of Commercial Banks in SFDA and MFAL Project Areas

Commercial banks have involved themselves in financing the farmers under these projects. Banks assist the identified participants of the SFDA and MFAL projects in selected districts. The following steps have been taken by commercial banks in these areas:

(i) Opening of branches in the scheme areas.

(ii) Simplification of loan application procedure, and

(iii) Delegation of adequate discretionary powers to the branch agents.

(viii) Farmers' Societies

The National Commission on Agriculture (NCA), in its interim report in 1971, pointed out that the problem of agricultural credit was primarily the problem of providing credit and simultaneous organising facilities for the conversion of credit into various agricultural inputs and services. To convert this idea into actual practice, the NCA said that:

(a) The integrated credit service should be available to small and marginal farmers and agricultural labourers; and

(b) The organisation should cover not only a complete range of agricultural activities but ancillary occupations and artisans, and offer various types of services to the agricultural sector.

In accordance with these suggestions, some Farmers Service Societies have been organised in a few SFDA and MFAL areas by the commercial banks from 1973-74.

The basic objectives of the scheme of FSS have been to offer to small farmers a full package of services and technical guidance instead of just credit.

(ix) Crop Insurance Scheme

A crop insurance scheme was introduced by the Government of India in 1985. The basic objective of this scheme is to give financial compensation to the farmers in the event of crop failure which may occur due to drought or flood. Such a support will enhance the creditworthiness of the farmers. The salient features of the scheme are as follows:

(i) The scheme is applicable to farmers availing of crop loans from cooperative credit institutions, commercial banks and regional rural banks for growing rice, wheat, millet, oilseeds and pulses.

(ii) The General Insurance Corporation of India will operate the scheme with the active involvement of State Governments and Union Territories.

(iii) The Union Ministry of Agriculture will notify for each crop "defined areas" which may be a district, a tehsil, taluk, a block or a smaller contiguous area.

(iv) The sum insured for each farmer shall be 150 per cent of the loan disbursed to him during the insured season for the eligible crop. The cost of cultivation is estimated at 150 per cent of the present scale of financing.

(v) The insurance premium to be paid by the farmers is 2 per cent of the sum insured for rice, wheat and millets and one per cent of the sum insured for pulses and oilseeds. The insurance premium amount will be deducted at the time of disbursement of loans. In case of small and marginal farmers 50 per cent of the insurance premium will be subsidised by the Central and State Governments.

(vi) An insured farmer is eligible for indemnity under the crop loan scheme to the extent of shortfall in yield (*i.e.,* threshold yield less the actual average yield for the defined area) divided by the threshold yield and multiplied by the sum insured. The threshold yield of a crop is 80 per cent of the average yield per hectare in the defined area during the last five years (or a shorter period for a defined area).

(vii) Each bank will designate a nodal office at the district level. It will collect details of the crop loans disbursed from branches and will send to General Insurance Corporation a consolidated statement of loans along with premium every month.

Since the Kharif season of 1988, the sum insured has been reduced from 150 per cent to 100 per cent of the crop loan subject to a maximum of ₹ 10,000 per farmer. It is for the concerned State Governments to issue the necessary notifications for taking part in this scheme of the beginning of each kharif/rabi season.

(x) Service Area Approach

Service area approach to rural lending was introduced by the Reserve Bank of India with effect from April 1, 1989. The scheme aims to improve the quality of lending and to ensure that bank credit is used in increasing production, productivity and income levels of rural people. Under the scheme each bank branch in rural and semi-urban area will have a designated service area in which it will concentrate on productive lending and thus contribute to the development of the area. The main features of the Service Area Approach are as follows:

(a) Service Area Allocation: Specific areas comprising 15 to 25 villages will be allocated to all the rural and semi-urban branches of commercial banks and regional rural banks. Proximity to the branch and contiguity of villages will be the main criterion in allocation of villages. Fresh lending in villages should be done by the service area branch concerned; old loan accounts with the branches of other banks may either be transferred to it or continued till repayment.

(b) Village Surveys: Each branch has to undertake a survey of the allotted villages and prepare village profiles. These profiles include the following information about the village:

(a) Existing economic activities and potentialities for their expansion.

(b) Potentialities for undertaking new economic activities.

(c) Available infrastructure in the area.

(d) Existing skills of villagers and coverage of rural families by the credit institution.

(c) Village Credit Plan: Annual Credit Plan for the development of credit in each of the village in the service will be prepared by the branch manager. The plan should reflect the potentialities and the needs of the service area on the basis of the intimate knowledge gained by the branch manager. The present District Credit Plans (DCP) and Annual Action Plans (AAP) prepared under the Lead Bank Scheme should be kept in view for drawing up these plans.

(d) Branch Credit Plans: An Annual Credit Plan will be prepared by each branch by aggregating the village credit plans of all the villages allotted in the service area on an ongoing basis. This will comprise both priority sector and non-priority sector outlays. This plan will be the Performance Budget of the branch.

(e) Monitoring and Coordination: A block level banker's committee will be set up at each block under the chairmanship of a Lead Bank Officer, who will coordinate the activities of the banks as well as the Government officials in implementing the block credit plans. The branch credit plans will be aggregated at the block level after taking the credit component of co-operatives, land development banks and/or any other financing agency located in the block. Subsequently, these block credit plans are aggregated at the district level to form into Annual Action Plan.

(xi) Integrated Rural Development Programme (IRDP)

Increasing production and productivity in agriculture and other sectors in rural areas, creating substantial additional employment opportunities and making the rural families viable and self-sufficient, are the main objectives of the Integrated Rural Development Programme (IRDP) which is in operation in all the blocks of the country since October 1980. The programme seeks in particular to improve the lot of the poorest of the poor — small and marginal farmers, share croppers, agricultural labourers, rural artisans, scheduled castes/tribes and other weaker sections.

Under this programme, the lead banks were advised in January 1981, to prepare banking plans. Earlier they were prepared by Agricultural Refinance and Development Corporation (ARDC) to allocate the responsibility of financing the identified beneficiaries for different activities among the participating banks and integrate the same with the Annual Action Plans (AAPs) 1981. After a review by the Inter-Ministerial Committee of the Government of India in September 1981, the lead banks were advised to obtain complete details of village-wise distribution of physical programmes, subsidy, credit needs, etc. from the District Rural Development Agencies (DRDAs), incorporate the same in the AAPs from 1981 and ensure that the specified branches of the participating banks accept the responsibility for processing and sanctioning loan applications of the identified beneficiaries from the villages allocated to them.

The government gives subsidy ranging from 25% to 50% of the total capital investment depending upon the category of beneficiary. Total subsidy per year is estimated at about ₹ 300 crore and the expected credit support from banks not less than ₹ 600 crore. With a view to monitoring the progress made by cooperative banks in giving adequate credit support to the IRDP, a detailed information system was introduced in March 1982, and cooperative banks were advised to furnish data on a quarterly basis, in respect of their lendings under this programme.

(xii) National Bank for Agriculture and Rural Development (NABARD)

The National Bank for Agriculture and Rural Development (NABARD), a new statutory financial institution to operate as "Rural Reserve Bank" started functioning from 12th July, 1982. This national farm bank has now become the sole official instrunent of rural credit for economic growth. It has taken over the entire undertaking of the Agricultural Refinance and Development Corporation (ARDC) and has also taken the place of Reserve Bank of India in the matter of refinancing the State Cooperative Banks (SCBs) and the Regional Rural Banks (RRBs).

☞ Sources of Funds

1. NABARD has a share capital of ₹ 100 crore, contributed by the Union Government and the Reserve Bank on a 50:50 basis.
2. For its long-term operations, NABARD will draw funds from the Government of India, the World Bank and other multilateral and bilateral agencies and the market.
3. Another source of long-term operations will be 'National Rural Chit Fund' that NABARD will maintain and to which will be transferred the 'National Agricultural Credit (Long-term Operations) Fund of the Reserve Bank of India, with further contributions to the fund every year.
4. For the purpose of converting short-term loans into medium-term loans, funds will be drawn from National Rural Credit (Stabilisation) Fund to which will be transferred the National Agricultural Credit (Stabilisation) Fund of the Reserve Bank of India with further contributions made to it every year.
5. For its short-term operations, it will draw funds mainly from the Reserve Bank.
6. A 'Research and Development Fund' will be created and maintained through contributions from profits every year.

☞ Functions

The functions of NABARD can be divided into three categories:

(1) Providing credit facilities;

(2) Regulatory activities;

(3) Development activities.

1. Providing Credit Facilities

(a) It provides by way of refinance to the banks all kinds of production and investment credit to agriculture, small-scale industries, artisans, cottage and village industries, handicrafts and other allied economic activities in an integrated manner.

(b) It extends short-term credits, repayable over a maximum period of 18 months, to the State Cooperative Banks (SCBs) and the Regional Rural Banks (RRBs) and other Reserve Bank approved financial institutions for agricultural operations, marketing of crops, marketing and distribution of inputs required for farm and rural development, bonafide commercial and trade transactions and production and marketing activities of artisans, small-scale industries, tiny and decentralised sector industrial units, village and cottage industries, handicrafts and other rural crafts. There is a provision to convert these short-term loans granted to State Cooperative Banks and Regional Rural Banks into medium-term loans for a maximum period of seven years under drought conditions.

(c) It provides medium-term loans for a minimum period of 18 months and a maximum of seven years to SCBs and RRBs.

(d) It provides long-term credit not exceeding 25 years, including the period of rescheduling to SCBs and RRBs.

(e) NABARD extends loans and advances to State Governments for periods not exceeding 20 years to enable them to subscribe directly or indirectly to the share capital of cooperative credit societies.

(*f*) It gives long-term loans directly to any institution approved by the Government of India.

(*g*) It contributes to the share capital or invest in securities of any institution concerned with agricultural and rural development.

2. Development Activities

It formulates designs and aid, projects and programmes to suit the requirements of agriculture and rural development. Such projects will be aided from the Research and Development Fund. It will also monitor and implement the various projects and evaluate them for ensuring development of better projects.

3. Regulatory Activities

The Banking Regulation Act, 1949, empowers NABARD to undertake the inspection of RRBs and Cooperative Banks other than primary Cooperative Banks. Applications from these banks for opening new branches will be submitted to the Reserve Bank through NABARD, which will forward them with its comments.

☞ Administration

NABARD is managed by a full-time chairman and a separate managing director. It will have the following 16 regional offices under the control of regional managers — Hyderabad, Kolkata, Gauhati, Patna, New Delhi, Ahmedabad, Mumbai, Chandigarh, Jammu, Chennai, Trivandrum, Indore, Bangalore, Bhuvaneswar, Jaipur and Lucknow. But for operations on credit limits, Arunachal Pradesh, Assam, Manipur, Meghalaya, Nagaland, Tripura, West Bengal, Andaman and Nicobar, Island will be covered by the Kolkata office; Delhi, Himachal Pradesh, Jammu & Kashmir and Punjab by New Delhi Office; Maharashtra, Goa and Madhya Pradesh by the Mumbai Office; and Tamil Nadu, Kerala and Pondicherry by the Chennai Office.

☞ Questions

1. What are direct agricultural advances and indirect agricultural advances? Why are they so-called?
2. Write short notes on:
   (*a*) The Agricultural Finance Corporation.
   (*b*) The Agricultural Refinance and Development Corporation.
   (*c*) The Lead Bank Scheme.
   (*d*) The Mobile Bank.
   (*e*) NABARD.
3. It is said that there are too many institutions granting agricultural loans and advances. These are the Agricultural Credit Societies, the District Cooperative Banks, the State Cooperative Banks, the Land Development Banks, the Commercial Banks, the Agricultural Finance Corporation, etc.

   Please describe briefly the types of agricultural advances granted by various institutions and indicate the area in which a close co-ordination between the various agencies should be established.
4. Evaluate the assistance rendered to agriculturists by public sector banks under SFDA and MFAL schemes. Have they fulfilled their responsibilities?
5. What do you understand by:
   (*a*) Priority Sector Advances
   (*b*) Lead Bank Scheme

(c) SFDA and MFAL

(d) Farmers Service Societies

(e) Regional Rural Banks.

6. What steps has government taken to improve agricultural credit?
7. What are the objectives and functions of National Bank for Agriculture and Rural Development (NABARD)?
8. Write what you know about the National Bank for Agriculture and Rural Development (NABARD). What are its functions? *[C.A.I.I.B., Part I]*
9. Write short notes on:

   (i) Agricultural Finance Corporation

   (ii) Mobile Bank

   (iii) Crop Loans *[I.I.B., Part I]*
10. It is said that there are too many institutions for granting agricultural loans and advances. These are Agricultural Credit Societies, District Cooperative Banks, State Cooperative Banks, Land Development Banks, Commercial Banks, Agricultural Finance Corporation, etc.

    Please describe briefly the types of agricultural advances granted by various institutions and indicate what are the areas in which close coordination between various agencies should be established. *[I.I.B., Part I]*
11. What are direct agricultural advances and indirect agricultural advances? Why are they so-called? *[I.I.B., Part I]*
12. A farmer approaches you for a loan of ₹ 6,000 for installation of an electric pump set in the well (water being available) in his land of 5 acres. Explain the steps and safeguards you would like to take in granting the loan. What documents would you take? *[I.I.B., Part I]*
13. Write brief notes on any three of the following:

    (i) Marginal Farmers and Agricultural Labourers (MFAL) Agency.

    (ii) Scheme for financing Primary Agricultural Credit Societies by Commercial Banks.

    (iii) Farmers' Service Societies.

    (iv) Custom Service Centre.

    (v) Rural Banks. *[I.I.B., Part I]*
14. What are the different types of institutions for granting agricultural loans and advances in India. Name these institutions and mention their special objectives and features. *[I.I.B., Part I]*
15. Two small farmers, whose farms are adjacent, wish to install an electric pumpset on the well belonging to one of them, but situated near the border dividing the two farms. How will you deal with the request? What documents and securities will you take? *[I.I.B., Part I]*
16. A small farmer requests you to grant him a loan for purchase of a pair of bullocks. Will you entertain his application? If so, what precautions will you take? What procedure you will follow and what documents will you take? *[I.I.B., Part I]*
17. State briefly the salient features and functioning of Lead Bank Scheme. *[I.I.B., Part I]*
18. Discuss the background, structure, objectives and salient features relating the 'Lead Bank Scheme'. *[I.I.B., Part I]*
19. Discuss briefly 'Lead Bank' and Service Area Approach. *[I.I.B., Part I]*

C H A P T E R

21 Foreign Exchange and Export Finance

Foreign exchange operations and trade financing in India are significantly different from those of developed countries. Here, they are insulated from international markets by an elaborate system of foreign exchange and trade controls.

The term *foreign exchange* may be defined as a means of payment of an instrument of short-term credits for various countries with different monetary units, when looked at from the point of view of their purchase or sale against the national money, or that of their holdings as reserves. It refers to foreign money which includes notes, cheques, bills of exchange, bank balances and deposits in foreign currencies. It is often used to denote the process or system by which the currency of one country is converted into that of another country.

☞ Foreign Exchange Market

Foreign exchange transactions arise mainly from trade transactions among residents of different countries. The foreign exchange market is the clearing house through which the purchase and sale of foreign exchange are offset against each other. The main link between the buyers and sellers of foreign exchange in the foreign exchange market is the bank.

☞ Methods of International Payments

Payment by one country to another country may be made in the following ways:

(i) Telegraphic Transfer: A telegraphic transfer (TT) is a method of transferring money by telegram, cable or telex issued by a bank in one centre to another in a foreign centre. It is the quickest method of transmitting funds. Transfers of large amounts of money between banks are generally by TT.

(ii) Mail Transfer: A mail transfer is an order in writing sent by mail to pay cash to a third party. On receipt of an MT order, the receiving bank issues to the beneficiary its own cheque or makes payment to the beneficiary's account with itself or with another bank. An MT is similar to a cheque, but it is neither transferable nor negotiable. The purchaser of an MT pays cash in domestic currency immediately on its purchase; but the beneficiary receives the payment only after the arrival of the MT at the foreign centre.

(iii) Drafts and Cheques: A draft is a pay order issued by a bank on its own branch or some other bank abroad. It is payable on sight. The purchaser of a draft pays to the issuing bank money in local

currency. The funds in the foreign centre are available to him only after the presentation of the draft to the paying bank.

(iv) Bills of Exchange: A bill of exchange is an unconditional order in writing addressed by one person to another, requiring the person to whom it is addressed to pay a certain sum on demand or within a determinable date.

☛ Rate of Exchange

In simple words, the rate of exchange is the price of one currency in terms of another currency. It may be defined as the number of units of one currency that will be exchanged for one unit or a given number of units of another currency.

☛ Mint Parity under Gold or Silver Standard (up to 1914)

The rate of exchange may be determined on the basis of the gold or silver content in the currencies of two countries. If both the countries are on the gold standard or silver standard, this type of rate of exchange is known as *mint parity*. For example, if the currency of country A has twice as much gold content as the currency of country B, 2 units of currency B will be exchanged for 1 unit of currency A. In such a system, the exchange rate deviates from the mint parity only to the extent of the cost of shipping gold or silver from one country to another, including insurance, handling charges etc. The gold export or import points are known as *specie points.* They represent the exchange rates, below and above which it is more economical to use gold in settlement of international debts. If the rates move above or below the gold points, gold is imported or exported between the countries, which immediately brings about a readjustment in the exchange rate within the gold points.

☛ Purchasing Power Parity under Paper Currency (1918-1944)

Under the paper currency systems prevailing in different countries of the world, it is not possible to determine the rate of exchange on the basis of mint parity because there is no intrinsic value of the currencies. The rate of exchange is determined on the basis of the *"purchasing power parity theory"*, which was propounded by Prof. Gustav Cessel, a Swedesh economist, as an alternative method of arriving at a comparison of the values of two currencies. According to this theory, the basis for determining the exchange rates between currencies on paper currency standard is their relative purchasing power. The purchasing power parity between two currencies is defined as that amount of the currency of one country which endows the holder with the same amount of purchasing power, that is, command over goods and services — as would a stated amount of the currency of the other country. For example, if $ 1 in USA buys goods worth ₹ 7 in India, the exchange rate of U.S. $ and Indian rupee in a free market would be $ 1 = ₹ 7. This rate equalises the relative purchasing power of the dollar and the rupee.

The purchasing power parity theory has been criticised on the following grounds:

(i) The price indices of different countries do not reflect the true changes in the purchasing powers;

(ii) The prices of the commodities included for the computation of the index numbers change over a period of time in different countries;

(iii) The base period exchange rate may not be an equilibrium rate for use as the base rate; and

(iv) Tariffs, quotas, exchange restrictions, etc., may distort the demand and supply factors in both countries.

☞ Bretton Woods System (1946-1971)

During World War II (1939-1971), foreign exchange transactions were suspended by all the countries, and there was complete Government control on economic and trade activities. After the War, an international conference was convened at Bretton Woods in July 1944 with a view to establish a system of stable exchange rates and an orderly adjustment process to balance the payment's disequilibrium. In accordance with the agreement reached at Bretton Woods, the International Monetary Fund (IMF) was established in 1946. The main purpose of the establishment of the IMF, is known as the Bretton Woods system. The main features of this system are:

(a) Member countries of the IMF fixed the parities of their currencies in terms of gold or the US dollar.

(b) The pound sterling area countries, including India, fixed the parities of their currencies in terms of gold and pound sterling, while the UK alone in the sterling area fixed the parity of its currency in terms of gold and the US dollar.

(c) The USA fixed the parity of the dollar in terms of gold at $ 35 per ounce and undertook the obligation to convert the dollar balances, held by the central banks of different countries, freely into gold at the fixed rate, and thus maintain the stability of the price of the dollar in terms of gold.

(d) The exchange rates of all the currencies were stabilised in terms of the dollar by official intervention in the exchange market by the central banks of these countries.

(e) According to IMF rules, member countries are bound to maintain their exchange rates within a margin of one per cent above and one per cent below the fixed parity of their currencies.

(f) If there is a persistent and fundamental disequilibrium in the balance of payments position of a country, the declared parity of the currency of that country may be changed in consultation with IMF.

☞ Floating Exchange Rates

The massive balance of payments deficits, dwindling gold holdings, increasing dollar liabilities and accelerating inflation forced the US Government in August 1971 to stop the conversion of dollar balances into gold or other assets. As a result, the Bretton Woods system, which worked for about 25 years, came to an end.

After a brief period of realignment of currencies under the Smithsonian Agreement in December, 1971, major countries of the world adopted *floating exchange rates*. This present system of exchange rates is a mixture of:

(i) Limited floating rates; and

(ii) Pegged rates.

☞ Limited Floating Rates

The currencies of the United States, Britain, Canada, Italy, Japan, Switzerland, etc., are floating independently in world markets. This floating is, however, of a limited nature, because it is managed within certain limits, *i.e.,* the monetary authorities intervene in the market to keep the rates within nationally desirable limits.

Some other countries — Belgium, Denmark, West Germany, France, Norway and Sweden — float their currencies jointly under an arrangement called *snake in the tunnel.* Under this arrangement, member countries maintain fixed rates between their currencies with a maximum margin of 2½ per cent on either side of the parity in the official markets, while floating as a group against non-member currencies.

☞ Pegged Rates

Many countries peg their rates either to a single intervention currency or to a composite group of currencies. The main intervention currencies are the dollar, pound sterling and the French franc. For example:

(i) India, Pakistan, Bangladesh, Zambia, Guyana, Ireland, Mauritius and Sri Lanka have pegged their currencies to pound sterling;

(ii) Cameroon, Chad, Congo, Dahomey, Gabon, Ivory Coast, Mali, Niger, Senegal and Togo have linked their currencies to French franc;

(iii) Tanzania, Kenya, Uganda, Australia, Indonesia, Thailand and many Latin American countries have pegged their currencies to the US dollar;

(iv) Saudi Arabia, Kuwait, Fiji and Qatar have linked their currencies to Special Drawing Rights (SDRs).

The rates of the pegged currencies are maintained against the respective link currencies through official intervention in the domestic exchange market; but they float against their currencies in the international market together with the relative link currency. All the pegged currency countries avail themselves of the margin of 2¼ per cent permitted by the IMF since December 1971.

At present, the exchange markets of the world are highly unstable, and the rate movements are very high on a day-to-day basis. The worldwide inflationary trends and the massive current account deficits created by the rapidly rising oil prices have added more uncertainties to the already complex exchange market conditions. It is likely, therefore, that an agreement on a reform of the international monetary system may be reached in the near future.

☞ Exchange Rate of Indian Rupee

Under the Bretton Woods system, the par value of the Indian rupee was declared in terms of gold and the pound sterling was used as the intervention currency. The Reserve Bank of India maintained the par value of the rupee within the permitted margin of one per cent above and below the rate, and brought pound sterling, when there was an excess demand in the market, at fixed rates in order to keep the exchange rate of the rupee stable. When the rupee was devalued in June 1966, its par value was fixed at 0.118489 grams of fine gold per Indian rupee or ₹ 7.50 per US dollar. The corresponding rupee-sterling rate was ₹ 18 per pound sterling.

After the break down of Bretton Woods system in August 1971, when all the important countries switched over to floating rates, the pound sterling continued to be the intervention currency for the Indian rupee, and the rupee-dollar rate was kept stable. At the time of the realignment of currencies in December 1971, the rupee was delinked from the US dollar and linked with pound sterling. India decided to maintain the exchange rate stable within the wider margin of 2.25 per cent on either side of the central (*i.e.,* a total of 4.50 per cent margin). From June 1971 to September 1975, though the exchange rate of the rupee was kept stable in terms of pound sterling, it fluctuated with pound sterling against all the other currencies. During this period the pound sterling effectively depreciated by 29 per cent, and the effective trade weighted depreciation of the rupee was as much as 18 per cent against all the other currencies.

As the pound sterling was continuously showing signs of weakness and the rupee had already depreciated significantly with the pound sterling, the rupee-sterling link was not considered favourable to India at that stage. On 25th September, 1975, therefore, the rupee was delinked from the pound sterling and linked with a basket of currencies. The market value of all the units of the various currencies included in the basket at the time of delinking the rupee from the pound sterling was equal to £ 5.4620, which is the mid-point between the Reserve Bank's buying and selling rate for the pound sterling. As in the past, the intervention currency continues to be pound sterling. Whenever there is a change in the market value of the units of various currencies by more than 2.25 per cent against a standard unit of account, say, SRD, the rupee-sterling rate is altered suitably. The value of the rupee is maintained within a limit of 2.25 per cent on either side of the middle rate in terms of the basket of currencies.

☞ Quotations of Exchange Rate

The rate of exchange is the price of one currency expressed in terms of another currency. It is a rate at which the currency of one country is exchanged with the currency of another country. Any one currency may be selected as the standard against which the other currency is valued. Exchange rate quotations are of two types:

(i) Direct quotations;

(ii) Indirect quotations.

☞ Direct Quotations

In direct quotations, the exchange rate is expressed in variable units of the domestic currency for a fixed unit of a foreign currency. The domestic currency here refers to the currency of the centre from which the quotation emanates. For example, in the Bombay market quotations, the domestic currency is the Indian rupee.

Example:

Bombay Market Quotations

(a) ₹ 18.9678-18.9890 (per £)

(b) ₹ 7.1500-7.1550 (per $)

New York Market Quotations

(a) $ 2.3050-2.3060 (per £)

(b) $ 12.4550-12.4650 (per ₹ 100)

☞ Indirect Quotations

In an indirect quotation, the exchange rate is expressed in variable units of the foreign currency per fixed unit (S) of the domestic currency.

Bombay Market Quotations

£ 5.555 – 5.65 (per ₹ 100)

$ 12.4550 – 12.4650 (per ₹ 100)

New York Market Quotations

French Fr. frs. 4.81 – 4.91 (per US $ 1)

₹ 7.532-7.542 (per US $)

☞ Two-way Quotations

Exchange rate quotations are generally given in two ways — *i.e.*, buying rate and the selling rate.

☞ Buying Rate

The buying rate is the rate at which some dealers offer to buy foreign exchange.

☞ Selling Rate

The selling rate is the rate at which some dealers offer to sell foreign exchange. But these rates are applicable to the banks which are members of the foreign exchange market. The other customers of foreign exchange buy or sell at the customer rates quoted by the banks. These are different from the market rates, though they are based on market quotations.

☞ Forward Exchanges

Foreign exchange transactions may be divided into two categories:

(i) Spot or ready transactions; and

(ii) Forward exchange or future transactions.

☞ Spot or Ready Transactions

A spot or ready transaction is one in which the delivery of the foreign exchange takes place immediately after the deal is effected. In actual practice, however, the term spot delivery in international markets refers to delivery after two clear working days. For example, for a spot transaction entered into on 5th October, the delivery of the foreign exchange would be made on 8th October. In India, a spot transaction refers to a cash transaction or delivery of foreign exchange on the same day.

☞ Forward Exchange or Future Transactions

A forward exchange contract is a transaction in which foreign exchange is bought or sold for delivery at a future date as prearranged exchange rate. The currency is exchanged between the buyer and seller on the date of maturity. In international markets, however, the maturity date is two clear working days from the date of the contract plus the forward period. In India, the maturity date is calculated from the date of contract. For example, for a one-month forward contract entered into on 5th October, the maturity date will be 8th November. In India, the maturity date will be 5th November. The rate at which currencies are bought and sold is called the forward exchange rate or the forward rate, and is expressed in relation to the spot rate ruling at the time the forward rate is quoted.

There can be three possible relationships between the spot rate and the corresponding forward rate, namely:

(a) At par;

(b) At a premium; and

(c) At a discount.

The forward rate is at par with the corresponding spot rate if the forward exchange is worth as much as the spot exchange. If the forward exchange is worth more than the spot exchange, it is known to be at a premium. If the forward exchange is worth less than the corresponding spot exchange, it is said to be at a discount. The main advantage of the forward exchange is to protect import and export traders against the risk of changes in exchange rates. There is often a time gap between the signing of a sale contract and the receipt of payment by exporters and of the actual remittance of payments by importers. During this period, the exchange rate may change, and cause a loss to traders.

In India, only banks and other institutions licensed for the purpose by the Reserve Bank of India can deal in foreign exchange. Foreign exchange market operations are conducted within the framework of the foreign exchange regulations of India and the rules and procedures laid down by the Foreign Exchange Dealers Association of India (FEDAI). The FEDAI is an association of banks authorised to deal in foreign exchange. The latter's buying and selling rates, as well as their rates of commission, etc., are determined by the FEDAI in consultation with the Reserve Bank of India.

INTERNATIONAL LIQUIDITY (Special Drawing Rights)

☞ Definition

International Liquidity may be defined as the resources available to the monetary authorities of different countries for the settlement of net payments between national systems or currency areas with non-free exchange rates.

International Liquidity or International Money or International Reserves refers to all the resources available to the monetary authorities of a country which may facilitate the meeting of its balance of payment difficulties.

☞ Functions

The main functions of International Liquidity are:

1. to facilitate the settlement of international indebtedness, and
2. to act as a means of stabilising, or controlling the external value of domestic currency through intervention in the functioning of the normal foreign exchange mechanism.

☞ Components

The principal components of international reserves till 1969 were the following:

1. Gold.
2. National currencies of some countries used as international money, *e.g.,* in the last few decades US Dollar and pound sterling have been kept by many countries as foreign exchange reserves and they have been treated an1 accepted as near money assets.
3. Automatic drawing rights on the International Monetary Fund (IMF).

All the above three sources of reserves have not been found to be sufficient to meet the requirements of international indebtedness. This is not a new problem. First we will try to understand this problem of international liquidity.

THE WORLD LIQUIDITY PROBLEM

☞ Growth of International Trade

Due to rapid growth in international trade in the last few decades, the demand for acceptable means of international payments have been growing at a much faster rate than the development of possible international reserve assets to meet them. During 1950s world trade showed an annual growth rate of 8%, whereas the annual growth rate of reserves was 2.1%. During 1960s growth of world trade remained at 8%, the growth of reserves was 3.2%.

One of the most important factors responsible for the slow growth of international trade is the problem of international liquidity.

The old gold standard cannot cope with the world liquidity problems. In fact, the current output of gold is barely enough to meet a fraction of the demand for world liquidity.

Some of the measures which may help to create more liquidity are:

(i) Raising of IMF Quotas

Raising of quotas of member countries of IMF would be safe and effective method for raising the world liquidity.

(ii) Swap Arrangements

Swap arrangements are mutual arrangements between the central banks of two or more countries for the creation of necessary credit. Such arrangements have been tried from time-to-time and found satisfactory.

(iii) Special Drawing Rights (SDRs)

Another method to create large liquidity, through the issue of Special Drawing Rights to member countries of the IMF has proved quite successful.

SPECIAL DRAWING RIGHTS

An important factor responsible for the world liquidity problem is the emergence of developing economies in international trade. The developed economies have large surplus production to be sold in international market.

The developing economies have in recent decades started taking active participation in international trade mainly as buyers of goods produced largely in developed economies. Such large purchases have become necessary for the economic development of these economies. But this increase in international trade can be successfully achieved and operated only if it is well supported by a liberal state of international liquidity. In simple words, this means that the exporting economies should be able to recover the value of their exports, and the importing economies should have sufficient means (reserves) to meet these liabilities.

☞ Special Drawing Rights

"Special drawing rights are reserve assets allocated by the International Monetary Fund to its members as a supplement to existing reserve assets (Gold, foreign exchange reserves, IMF loans, etc.)." Special Drawing Rights (SDRs) scheme was introduced in January 1970, as a supplement to existing reserve assets.

☞ Salient Features

The salient features of the special drawing rights scheme are as follows:

1. SDR is a book entry (credit entry) in the name of the participating countries in the Special Drawing account of International Monetary Fund.
2. The scheme provides for the allocation to member countries of IMF, what are called Special drawing rights, created by an agreement amongst members as to the percentage of existing resources (quotas) with the IMF to be formed into SDRs.

3. The SDRs allocated and credited to a participant's account are owned by it for meeting deficits in its balance of payments only. Such a country can get an equivalent amount in the currency from other participating countries.
4. SDRs cannot be directly used for making international settlements. They can be transferred only within the "Special Drawing Account", to a designed participant for obtaining convertible foreign exchange which in turn can be used for settling international debts. In other words, the SDRs arrangement does not imply convertibility of SDRs into gold or any other form of international liquidity, because SDRs are not legal claims on any institution.
5. When any country wants to use its SDRs allocation, it requests the IMF to arrange conversion of its SDRs into foreign exchange. Some other countries are then designated by the IMF to accept the applicants SDRs and to provide specified currencies against transfer of SDRs to their account. There is no obligation on the part of a country which uses its SDRs allocation to restore its holdings or repay the obligations. However, it can restore its holdings by voluntarily purchasing SDRs from other countries.
6. All member countries of IMF are obliged to accept SDRs up to the point at which its holdings are three times its cumulative allocation. It means at any particular moment, a country's reserve may include an amount of SDRs that can vary from zero to 300% of its cumulative allocation or more with the members' agreement. The drawings from the "General Account" of the IMF have to be repaid, but SDRs once allocated continue in permanent existence.
7. Due to SDR scheme, for the first time, the total stock of reserves and its rate of growth are determined independent of the availability of gold to be held as official reserve and the accumulation of balances in key currencies.

☞ Mode of Allocation

All member countries of International Monetary Fund are participants in the SDR scheme. The fund allocates SDRs to participants in proportion to their quotas, *i.e.*, a member whose quota was 5% of the total quotas of participants in SDR scheme would receive 5% of each allocation. The time and amount of allocations are based on the recommendation of the Managing Director and are to be approved by the Board of Governors, voting with an 85% majority. The fund created SDR 9.5 billion over the three years 1970-72 which were allocated to 112 member countries. Total SDRs allocated up to now are as follows:

Date/Year	*Billion units of SDR Allocation*
1970-72	9.5
1979	4.0
1980	4.0
1981	4.0
	21.5

The total SDR allocations 21.5 billion units up to the end of 1981 constitutes 4.4% of the total world reserves, other than gold.*

The IMF has the authority to extend the range of official holders beyond its member countries. The World Bank, the International Development Association (IDA), Bank for International Settlement and six other financial institutions have been designated as "other holders" of SDRs. At the end of

* International Monetary Fund, Finance and Development, September 1982, p.32.

Dec.1981, SDR 16 billion were held by participants and SDRs 5 billion by the fund's General Reserve Accounts. Up to 1991, India's Reserve Trauche position was of SDR 487 million in the fund. The country also purchased SDR 1.27 billion under the IMF financing facilities.

☞ Valuation of SDR

Originally, the value of an SDR was expressed in terms of gold, but they were not redeemable in gold. With the advent of floating exchange rates between the major currencies in the early 1970s a new basis of valuation became necessary. With effect from 1st July, 1974, the standard basket technique was adopted under which the value of SDR was related to a basket of 16 currencies of the major world. From 1st January, 1981 the composition major of the basket was simplified by replacing the 16 currencies with those of currencies, *i.e.,* US Dollar, Deutsch Mark, Japanese Yen, French Franc and Pound Sterling.

Under the basket techniques, the SDR is valued as the sum of fixed amounts of several currencies. To ensure maximum stability for the exchange value of the SDR, the criterion used for the selection of the currencies in the basket in 1974, and again when the basket was reviewed in 1978, was that they should be those most widely used in international trade and payments. The weight each currency was given in the basket was intended to reflect its importance in trade as well as its importance in the financial markets.

☞ Importance and Use of SDR

The use of SDR as a unit of account outside the IMF has grown in importance in recent years. A growing number of international organisations use the SDR as unit of account. Some 15 countries peg their currency to the SDR. It has also gained acceptance as a unit of account in international financial markets, largely because of the automatic element of portfolio diversification entailed by its basket valuation. The reduction in the number of currencies in the valuation basket from 16 to 5 gave impetus to this use, particularly because it made it easier for banks to handle SDR denominated deposits. Time deposits denominated in SDRs are most important in terms of volume, but there is a wide range of other instruments, ranging from current accounts, through certificates of deposits and floating rate notes, to ten-year syndicated credits. However, a clearing system for private SDR payments has not yet developed. Such a system would facilitate further growth in the volume and type of SDR denominated financial instruments and might also encourage the use of the SDR as a unit of invoicing commercial transactions. Current use of the SDR for this purpose is minimal.

☞ Rate of Interest

The interest rate on SDR was set at 5% per annum on July 1, 1974, about half the combined market rate at the time. It was adjusted according to a formula every six months. Experience showed that the SDR rate, which the workings of the formula kept at about half the combined market rate, was too low, impairing the quality of the SDR as a reserve asset. Consequently, between July 1976, and May 1981, the SDR interest rate was raised in steps to the full combined market rate.

☞ SDR and the Developing Countries

A majority of the countries of the world (three-fourths of the members of International Monetary Fund) come in the category of developing countries. These countries because of their larger needs of reserves for developmental purposes are getting some relief and benefit from SDR scheme. It has strengthened their capacity to mitigate abrupt fluctuations in their export earnings and thus to meet on a continuous basis, their development-oriented import requirements. It also helps these countries in their balance of payment difficulties. However, the developing countries have a genuine case for receiving a larger share of the SDRs, and, if there is a technical hitch in doing so, it is very essential that the whole basis for the allotment of quotas in the IMF to different member countries should be revised. India has, time and again, stressed the importance of combining the creation of additional international liquidity with the provision of development finance, but it was never accepted by industrially developed countries.

EXPORT FINANCE

With the rapid increase in foreign trade, the demand for the financing of both import and export of goods has gone up. Like the financing of internal trade, foreign trade requires financing by banks. This is a specialised service and calls for not only technical expertise but also worldwide connections on the part of a banking company. For a very long time, foreign banks were financing India's foreign trade; but since the last few decades, Indian banks have a leading role in providing this service. They now finance exports by offering—

(i) Packing credit;

(ii) Loan against duty drawbacks and subsidy;

(iii) Advance against bills for collection;

(iv) Credit for purchase of export bills;

(v) Post-shipment term finance;

(vi) Guidance in exchange control formalities;

(vii) Export promotion measures; and

(viii) Documentation — shipping documents, uniform customs, etc.

Export finance includes pre-shipment finance or post-shipment finance or both.

☞ Pre-shipment Finance (Packing Credit)

An exporter may need finance to purchase raw materials and equipment to manufacture goods which may later be exported to foreign countries. Credit facilities required for these purposes are called packing credit or pre-shipment finance, which is generally short-term accommodation provided by banks.

☞ Post-shipment Finance

When an exporter loads the goods on to a ship and secures a bill of lading and insurance papers, etc., he seeks the help of a banker in realising payments from a foreign importer. In most cases, this is done through bills of exchange. Also called drafts, which are drawn by an exporter on the importer in a foreign country. These bills may be of two types:

(i) D/A — Documents against Acceptance;

(ii) D/P — Documents against Payment.

The bills are sent to the foreign importer (buyer) through a commercial bank. In the D/A bills, the documents of title to goods (bill of lading, insurance papers, etc.), are given by the bank to the importer following the acceptance of the bill drawn by the exporter. In the D/P bills, documents of title to goods are given by the bank of the importer on payment for the goods. This method of securing payment is common in cases where the foreign buyer is not known to the seller. When the buyer is not so known and the seller feels that there may be a risk in obtaining payment, the importer secures a letter of credit from a banker in his country. The bill of exchange drawn under a letter of credit may be negotiated with any banker or the banker named in such letter of credit. (By negotiation we mean the negotiating banker pays to the drawer the value of the bill on the assurance of the opening banker. By the opening banker is meant the banker who issues a letter of credit at the request of the importer in favour of the exporter on a bank in the exporter's country).

It may be noted here that, there is a difference between the negotiation of a bill and the purchase of an export bill. When the exporter knows the importer and the letter of credit is not thought necessary, a bill of exchange is drawn by the exporter on the importer and the payment is secured against documents. The bill may be drawn at the sight or payable after a stipulated period. In the latter case, it is retained by the bank and presented to the buyer for payment on the date of maturity. Such documentary bills are purchased by the banker. Normally, the exporter's bank gives immediate credit for these bills, and a discount or a fee or interest is charged by the bank for this service.

☞ Collection of Foreign Bills

The collection of a bill on behalf of a customer is done by a bank in the same way as it is in the case of home trade. Foreign bills are normally accepted for collection when the exporter is unable to negotiate them in the absence of a letter of credit or the exporter is unable to sell them to a banker.

☞ Medium-term Finance to Exporters

Banks also extend term loan facilities to exporters against the deferred instalments receivable from importers. The exporter normally furnishes to the financing bank the promissory notes executed by the importer or a guarantee from the importer's bank covering the deferred receivables.

Table 21.1
SDR VALUATION BASKET, 1974-81

Currency	July 1, 1974 – June 30, 1978		July 1, 1978 – December 31, 1980		January 1, 1981 to date		Sample valuation, November 6, 1981	
	Initial percentage weight	*Currency amounts*[1]	*Initial percentage weight*	*Currency amounts*[2]	*Initial percentage weight*	*Currency amounts*[3]	*Exchange rate*[4]	*US dollar equivalent*[5]
(1)	*(2)*	*(3)*	*(4)*	*(5)*	*(6)*	*(7)*	*(8)*	*(9)*
US Dollar	33.0	0.40	33.0	0.40	42.0	0.54	1.0000	0.540000
Deutsche mark	12.5	0.38	12.5	0.32	19.0	0.46	2.2225	0.206974
Pound sterling	9.0	0.045	7.5	0.42	13.0	0.071	1.8725	0.132948
French franc	7.5	0.44	7.5	0.42	13.0	0.74	5.6150	0.131790
Japanese yen	7.5	26.0	7.5	21.0	13.0	34.0	228.82	0.148588
Canadian dollar	6.0	0.071	5.0	0.070				
Italian lira	6.0	47.0	5.0	52.0				
Netherlands guilder	4.5	0.14	5.0	0.14				
Belgian franc	3.5	1.6	4.0	1.6				
Swedish krona	2.5	0.13	2.0	0.11				
Australian dollar	1.5	0.012	1.5	0.017				
Spanish peseta	1.5	1.1	1.5	1.5				
Norwegian krone	1.5	0.099	1.5	0.10				
Danish krone	1.5	0.11	—	—				
Australian Schilling	1.0	0.22	1.5	0.28				
South African rand	1.0	0.0082	—	—				
Saudi Arabian riyal	—	—	3.0	0.13				
Iranian rial	—	—	2.0	1.7				

US dollar value of SDR 1 = 1.60300
SDR value of US $ 1 = 0.861846

Source: IMF, Treasurer's Department.

— Indicates currency not included in SDR basket.

1 Derived from the initial percentage weights in column 2 using average exchange rates over the three months ending June 28, 1974, so that on that date the SDR's value was the same under the former valuation procedure and under the basket procedure.

2 Derived from the initial percentage weights in column 4 using average exchange rates over the three months ending June 30, 1978, so that on that date the SDR's value was the same under the former valuation basket (in column 3) and the revised basket (in column 5).

3 Drived from the initial percentage weights in column 6 using average exchange rates over the three months ending December 31, 1980, so that on that date the SDR's value was the same under the former valuation basket (in column 5) and the revised basket (in column 7).

4 Middle rate between buying and selling rates at noon in the London exchange market as determined by the Bank of England, expressed in currency units per U.S. dollar except for the pound sterling, which is expressed in US dollars per pound sterling.

5 The US dollar equivalents of the currency amounts in column 7 at the exchange rates in column 8 — that is, column 7 divided by column 8 except for the pound sterling, for which the amounts in the two columns are multiplied.

International Monetary Fund, Finance and Development/September 1982, p.32.

Table 21.2

CURRENCY UNITS PER SDR

Currency	*January*				*February*					
	26	*27*	*28*	*29*	*1*	*2*	*3*	*4*	*5*	*8*
Deutsche mark	2.19506	2.19621	2.18803	2.20203	2.22722	2.23026	2.24052	2.24518	2.25526	2.2495
French franc	7.40593	7.42617	7.4297	7.47044	7.53584	7.54803	7.58793	7.64924	7.64067	7.60633
Japanese yen	172.309	172.056	172.4	172.182	170.74	171.163	169.689	169.771	169.672	169.264
Pound sterling	0.903668	0.913463	0.916103	0.919904	0.938724	0.935776	0.95038	0.945742	0.940318	0.947112
US dollar	1.39183	1.38755	1.38808	1.38188	1.36866	1.36876	1.36351	1.36253	1.36064	1.36119
Argentine peso	—	—	—	—	—	—	—	—	—	—
Australian dollar	2.07118	2.0532	2.05611	2.03637	2.03035	2.02389	2.00959	2.00874	2.00951	2.02709
Austrian schilling	15.4479	15.4185	15.3813	15.4853	15.652	15.6969	15.7799	15.7767	15.8868	15.8279
Bahrain dinar	0.523328	0.521719	0.521918	0.519587	0.514616	0.514654	0.51268	0.512311	0.511601	0.511807
Bangladesh taka	54.2814	54.1145	54.1351	53.8933	53.3777	53.3816	53.1769	53.1387	53.065	53.0864
Belgian franc	45.1962	45.0919	45.0293	45.2738	45.7201	45.9424	46.3082	46.4282	46.5509	46.4098
Brazilian cruzeiro	20555.2	20742.3	21267.9	21437.	—	—	22014.3	22292.9	—	22868.1
Canadian dollar	1.7686	1.76191	1.76397	1.75513	1.72944	1.72779	1.72675	1.72074	1.7159	1.72068
Colombian peso	1139.57	1136.67	1137.68	1133.25	1123.04	1123.77	1119.91	1119.7	1118.73	1119.78
Danish krone	8.44075	8.42173	8.44508	8.48958	8.54933	8.59581	8.73669	8.72632	8.63394	8.60544
Finnish markka	7.36863	7.39203	7.59141	7.58652	7.64533	7.6062	7.72701	7.80389	7.70979	7.81323
Greek drachma	293.76	293.384	293.079	294.52	297.533	298.937	300.177	300.097	301.926	300.986
Indian rupee	—	36.3538	36.3677	36.2053	35.8589	35.8615	35.724	35.6983	36.6488	35.6632
Indonesian rupiah	2872.74	2863.9	2865.	2853.58	2826.28	2829.23	2818.38	2816.35	2813.8	2814.94
Iranian rial	92.3	92.3	92.3	92.3	92.3	92.3	92.3	92.3	92.3	92.3
Iraqi dinar	0.432661	0.43133	0.431495	0.429568	0.425458	0.425489	0.423857	0.423552	0.422965	0.423136
Irish pound	0.824446	0.836025	0.834032	0.84143	0.912075	0.915436	0.928316	0.933687	0.930289	0.923154
Italian lira	2015.68	2036.85	2053.44	2048.66	2065.08	2076.66	2084.62	2098.54	2084.8	2077.84
Korean won	1105.39	1102.13	1101.3	1095.97	1086.72	1089.26	1085.63	1084.85	1083.75	1085.41
Kuwaiti dinar	0.421947	0.421593	0.422504	—	0.419823	0.420606	0.418993	0.418692	—	0.418634

Libyan dinar	0.414286	0.414286	0.414286	0.414286	0.414286	0.414286	0.414286	0.414286	0.414286	0.414286
Malaysian ringgit	3.61041	3.6111	3.61595	3.62578	—	3.59341	3.58058	3.57255	3.57576	3.57966
Maltese lira	0.508896	0.50981	0.511113	0.509524	0.518236	0.517901	0.518012	0.519336	0.521918	0.520313
Nepalese rupee	60.1271	59.9422	59.9651	59.6972	59.1261	59.1304	58.9036	58.8613	58.7796	58.8034
Netherlands guilder	2.46396	2.47164	2.46481	2.48421	2.50478	2.51113	2.52277	2.54616	2.54453	2.5295
New Zealand dollar	—	2.68437	—	2.67082	2.65039	2.66244	2.64759	2.64364	2.64099	2.66065
Norwegian krone	9.31691	9.29728	9.3161	9.37744	9.46223	9.47182	9.55684	9.53635	9.54693	9.51676
Omani rial	0.535159	0.533513	0.533717	0.531333	0.52625	0.526288	0.52427	0.523893	0.523166	0.523378
Pakistani rupee	36.2083	36.097	36.1108	35.9495	35.6741	35.6767	35.6492	35.7193	35.6697	35.7251
Portuguese escudo	197.776	197.672	198.819	199.523	200.992	201.613	203.035	203.577	204.27	203.217
Qatar riyal	5.06626	5.05068	5.05261	5.03004	4.98192	4.98229	4.96318	4.95961	4.95273	4.95473
Saudi Arabian riyal	5.2124	5.19637	5.19836	5.17514	5.12563	5.12601	5.10634	5.10267	5.0956	5.09766
Singapore dollar	2.28789	2.27461	2.27381	2.26946	2.25364	2.25859	2.24747	2.2445	2.24914	2.24787
South African rand	4.24856	4.24937	4.24683	4.24652	4.22848	4.23563	4.23097	4.25041	4.24724	4.251
Spanish peseta	155.1	155.464	156.407	157.011	158.362	158.461	159.449	160.656	160.46	159.518
Sri Lanka rupee	64.5809	64.3823	64.4069	64.1192	63.6427	63.6473	63.4032	63.3576	63.2698	63.2953
Swedish krona	9.85555	9.82455	9.90881	9.99168	10.1397	10.1151	10.2066	—	10.1034	10.1368
Swiss franc	2.01676	2.02693	2.00716	2.03067	2.0571	2.06751	2.08208	2.08045	2.0811	2.08058
Thai baht	35.4221	35.327	35.3683	35.2241	34.9419	34.9855	34.8513	34.8126	34.7916	34.8056
Trinidad and Tobago dollar	5.93007	5.91183	5.91409	5.88767	5.83135	5.83177	5.8094	5.80523	5.79718	5.79952
UAE dirham	5.10941	5.0937	5.09564	5.07288	5.02435	5.02482	5.00545	5.00185	4.99491	4.99693
Venezuelan bolivar	112.529	112.364	112.504	112.14	111.204	111.349	111.058	111.114	111.096	111.209

Notes: 1. The value of US dollar in terms of the SDR is the reciprocal of the sum of the dollar values, based on market exchange rates, of specified quantities of the first five currencies shown. The exchange rates used for this purpose are noon rates in the London foreign exchange market. When the London market is closed, noon rates in the New York market are used. Frankfurt fixing rates are used when the New York market is closed.

2. The value in terms of the SDR of each of the other currencies shown above is derived from that currency's representative exchange rate against the US dollar as reported by the issuing central bank and the SDR value of the U.S. dollar, except for the Iranian rial and the Libyan dinar, the values of which are officially expressed directly in terms of the domestic currency units per SDR. Data: IMF Treasurer's Department

* IMF Survey, Feb, 22, 1993, p.54.

Apart from the normal risk involved in various types of lending by banks, the financing of exports involves certain other risks which may include those arising from the insolvency of the foreign buyer, exchange restrictions, currency regulations, and import controls, etc. Although in all such cases, the bank always looks to the exporter whom it has financed, this may not always help him to recover his dues and the bank, therefore needs some protection. In this connection, the establishment of the Export Risk Insurance Corporation Ltd., in 1956 was a welcome development. From January 1964, the Export Risk Insurance Corporation was merged into the Export Credit Guarantee Corporation. The services of the Corporation include covering risks of insolvency and default, of war and civil commotion, of transfer of money, of import/export restrictions, of diversion of goods, and any other risk which is caused by factors beyond the control of the exporter or the buyer which arise from events occurring outside the exporter's country such as CIF risks and inability to recover by sales, expenses incurred on market surveys, publicity and other promotional measures for the development of particular markets, etc.

☞ Insurance Policies to Exporters

The Export Credit Guarantee Corporation issue the following standard insurance policies to exporters:

(i) Shipments (comprehensive risks) policy;
(ii) Shipments (political risks) policy;
(iii) Contracts (comprehensive risks) policy;
(iv) Contracts (political risks) policy; and
(v) Packing credit insurance policy.

The contracts (comprehensive risks) policy protects the exporter, from the time he receives an order until he receives payment, against both political and commercial risks. Likewise, the shipment (comprehensive risks) policy covers both political and commercial risks from the date of shipment till the payment is received. Packing credit insurance policy covers pre-shipment risks on credit given against firm contract of sale. This policy covers the risks of insolvency of the exporter or his protracted default in repaying the advance. Risks involved in export-on-consignment basis are also covered by an appropriate endorsement. In addition to covering risks arising from events outside India, the corporation also covers additional risks arising out of cancellation of current export licences or impositions of restrictions on export licences or on the export of goods not previously subject to licences. The Corporation covers risk up to 80 per cent in the case of commercial risks and up to 85 per cent in the case of political risks. In the case of every buyer, the exporter has to get a credit limit fixed by the Corporation. Within that limit, he is free to export without reference to the Corporation. The insured exporters are required to cover shipments made by them to all the countries during a period of twelve months from the date of commencement of the policy, excluding shipments confirmed irrevocable letters of credit and those paid for in advance.

The benefits of these policies may also be assigned by exporters in favour of their banks. Such assignments can be of: *(a)* individual bills *(b)* exports to one country, or *(c)* the whole policy. The letter of authorisation signed by the exporter is an authority to the insurer to pay direct to the bank.

In addition to the five types of policies referred to above, the Export Credit Guarantee Corporation also issues the following policies:

(i) Manufacturers' Credit Insurance Policy;
(ii) Market Development and Market Survey Policies.

Some other functions of the Corporation include supply of status information about customers in other countries. The ECGC is a member of the Berne Union — an association of credit insurers in different countries — and is able to exchange credit information with insurers in other countries.

Financial Guarantees to Bankers

The Export Credit Guarantee Corporation now issues, besides the insurance policies, the following five types of financial guarantees direct to banks:

(i) Post-shipment export credit guarantee;

(ii) Export finance guarantee;

(iii) Export production finance guarantee;

(iv) Export performance guarantee; and

(v) Packing credit guarantee.

(i) The Post-shipment Export Credit Guarantee is issued to banks to indemnify them to the extent of 66½ per cent of any loss from purchase, discount or negotiation of an export bill arising from the continued default or insolvency of an exporter. An enhancement in the risk covered to 90 per cent was made in 1968 in respect of this guarantee covering advances to exporters of engineering and metallurgical products who secured large export orders involving medium-term and long-term payments.

(ii) The Export Finance Guarantee enables the exporter to obtain pre-shipment finance on the domestic value of his goods. The guarantee enables a bank to offer, on a selective basis, discounting facilities to exporters up to 125 per cent of the value stated in shipping documents, with a bank advance being guaranteed by the Corporation. The indemnity to banks is to the extent of 75 per cent of the loss incurred in the case of a loanee's insolvency or default.

(iii) The Export Production Finance Guarantee seeks to enable banks to make available pre-shipment credit to cover the value of goods plus the element of incentives accruable under various export promotion schemes.

(iv) Export Performance Guarantees are in the nature of counter-guarantees to the performance favouring foreign buyers.

(v) The Packing Credit Guarantee enables an exporter to obtain from his bank pre-shipment finance for the purpose of purchasing, processing and packing goods required to be sent to the export market. This guarantee is issued to banks and the Corporation indemnifies them up to 66$^2/_3$ per cent. During 1968, the Corporation increased the risk coverage under this guarantee to 90 per cent in respect of the exports of small-scale units.

Direct Finance for Exports by Industrial Development Bank of India

Exports from India have increased at a rapid rate in the last few years. It was, therefore, felt that commercial banks might not by themselves be able or willing to carry the whole risk and provide the entire term finance and guarantee facilities required by exporters. The Industrial Development Bank of India, therefore, introduced a new scheme from December 6, 1968, in terms of which a bank, in appropriate cases, enters into participation arrangements with eligible commercial banks with a view to providing term finance and guarantee facilities to industrial concerns, both in the public and private sectors, which export capital and engineering goods and services on deferred payment basis. The scheme provides for export credits both during the pre-shipment and post-shipment stages for periods over six months and for export performance guarantees on behalf of exporters. All licensed scheduled banks in India which are authorised dealers in foreign exchange are eligible for participation under this scheme. Normally, the Industrial Development Bank of India will charge on its portion of the export credit, a rate of 5½ per cent, while the participating bank will charge its own rate on its portion up to 7 per cent — the ceiling rate currently prescribed by the Reserve Bank of India.

☛ Refinance of Export Credit by IDBI

The Industrial Development Bank of India took over the business of the Refinance Corporation on September 1, 1964, under the provisions of the Industrial Development Bank of India Act. It has since been operating a scheme for refinancing medium export credit granted by commercial banks. Under this scheme, the IDBI grants to the eligible bank refinance to the extent of 100 per cent against their advances in respect of exports of capital and engineering goods. The eligibility for refinance covers all credits granted to those exporters in the public and private sectors who are manufacturers, recognised export houses and other exporters of standing. Construction projects executed by Indian firms are also covered by this scheme. Refinance is granted in respect of credits normally repayable after six months but before five years; the maximum period may be extended up to 7 years in deserving cases and up to 10 years in exceptionally deserving cases. The IDBI charges a uniform rate of 4½ per cent and the banks are required to charge the exporters not more than 6 per cent.

☛ Refinance of Export Credit by Reserve Bank

The Reserve Bank of India had, as early as June 1968, taken action in regard to the provision of forward cover in respect of long-term export contracts so as to minimise the risks of currency depreciation by providing rollover facilities, and enabling the authorised dealers to offer such a cover to exporters. The authorised dealers may in turn obtain forward cover from the Reserve Bank in respect of their sterling transactions. Similarly, the Reserve Bank had already exempted packing credit advances and post-shipment credit from the computation of the norm fixed in respect of *(a)* the credit-deposit ratio, and *(b)* unsecured advances and guarantees by banks. It has introduced the following schemes in regard to export finance:

(i) *Export Bill Credit Scheme:* The Export Bill Credit Scheme was introduced in March 1963. Under this scheme, the Reserve Bank grants advances to scheduled banks against their promissory notes payable on demand upon their declaration of holdings of eligible usance export bills drawn in foreign currencies or Indian rupees and purchased or negotiated by them.

(ii) *Pre-shipment Credit Scheme:* Under this scheme which was introduced from 1st February, 1969, the Reserve Bank makes advances to scheduled banks against their promissory notes, together with a declaration to the effect that they have granted pre-shipment loans to exporters.

(iii) *Export Credit (Interest Subsidy) Scheme:* The Export Credit (Interest Subsidy) Scheme was introduced on March 3, 1968, with the objective of reducing the cost of credit to exporters. Banks providing finance to exporters are given a subsidy of 1½ per cent on the total outstandings, provided that they charge interest from the exporters within the ceiling prescribed by the Reserve Bank.

☞ Documentary Credits and the Banker

Commercial transactions involving movement of goods from one country to another can be called the beginning of international trade. Importers and exporters are the two essential parties engaged in any business between two countries. But, unlike the domestic market there are many peculiar problems affecting the smooth conduct of foreign trade engagements. A few of them can be listed as problems of payment in terms of foreign currency, language, geographical separation by long distance, rules and regulations regarding import and export, political and commercial stability, problems in settling disputes between buyers and sellers and so many others. These are serious obstacles which frustrate any commercial activity. Also while the psychology of the seller is to hang on to the goods till he gets paid, the buyer will observe utmost care not to part with money till he receives the correct consignment under the contract. Of course, such a stubborn situation does not encourage any business. It creates stalemate in the dynamic commercial world of inter-dependence and mutual benefit. In this context, the role of banks is vital. Banks undertake to accommodate both buyers and sellers through the documentary credit operation which effectively means a reliable, fructuous intermediation so that the exporters and the importers get exactly what they want. Documentary credit is a brilliant discovery which acts as a nucleus around which all international commercial transactions revolve and bear positive results.

The revised edition of Uniform Customs and Practice for Documentary Credits (UCPDC) has come into effect from October 1, 1984. This new document (publication No. 400 of International Chamber of Commerce) has 55 articles which replaced the previous UCPDC of 47 articles. General provisions and definitions are discussed in articles 1 to 6, forms and notification of credits come under articles 7 to 14, liabilities and responsibilities are stipulated under articles 15 to 21, documents are dealt with in articles 22 to 42 (this is the section which has the maximum number of 21 articles out of 55 in UCPDC), miscellaneous provisions are mentioned in articles 43 to 53 and transferable credits by articles 54 and 55.

Article 3 of UCPDC says that credits by their nature are separate transactions from the sales or other contract(s) on which they may be based and banks are in no way concerned with or bound by such contract(s) even if any reference whatsoever to such a contract(s) is included in the credit. India is a country which has subscribed to adhere to the UCPDC as promulgated by the ICC and authorised dealers who are handling foreign trade in India are under the absolute control of RBI. Authorised dealers in India are concerned with sale contracts in the context of foreign transactions wherever it is applicable and a sale contract constitutes a basic document which should be made available to the banker. Banks insist on sale contracts which are legally enforceable, which are contracts not subject to any approval and which are not attached with any contingent conditions. Such documents or contracts are held as securities by banks where advance of many is involved.

Sale contract is the founding instrument which can be treated as the prime contract. From this prime contract originate three essential subsidiary contracts and some miscellaneous contracts. *First* subsidiary contract is a transport contract, *i.e.,* a contract of carriage. Under this a transport document evidencing consignment in transit has to be produced, namely, a bill of lading, or a combined transport document, or an airway bill, etc., which are covered by articles 22 to 24 in general and articles 25 to 34 in particular in UCPDC. *Second* subsidiary contract is an insurance contract which calls for an insurance policy to be submitted (articles 35 to 40). The *third* subsidiary contract is the financial contract. On the basis of the terms recorded in the prime contract it is decided whether a DC will be opened or not. By virtue of the financial contract a documentary credit is opened which is a contract of agreement between the buyer (opener) and the buyer's banker (issuing bank) favouring the seller (exporter). The exporter draws a bill of exchange for the value on the importer. The prime contract paves the way for bringing out the instrument of documentary credit which assures the exporter payment and ensures prompt delivery of specified goods to the importer. Miscellaneous contracts under the sale of contract deals with submission of miscellaneous documents such as commercial invoice (article 41), certificate of weight, certificate of origin, laboratory certificate, etc. (article 42).

Article 4 of UCPDC states that in credit operation all parties concerned deal in documents and not in goods, services and/or other performances to which the documents may relate. Here it is to be distinctly understood by all parties concerned with credit that the application and the protection available under UCPDC is extended only to those genuine documents handled by the banker and not for any document.

Articles 7 to 10 are concerned with different forms of credits such as revocable, irrevocable and confirmed irrevocable credits. Revocable credits are very cheap but not favoured by the sellers owing to the inherent unfavourable characteristics of the credit. Irrevocable credits are safe and the cost incurred is reasonable while confirmed irrevocable credits are costlier but safer. The utility of irrevocable credits are more in comparison to other credits.

Article 11 states that all credits must clearly indicate whether they are available by sight payment, by deferred payment, by acceptance or by negotiation. Although these four types of transactions are there in India, negotiation credits are maximum in use.

UCPDC have stipulated different types of general credits such as revocable, irrevocable, confirmed irrevocable and transferable credits, yet it is significantly silent on such special credits like red clause, revolving and back-to-back credits. It is very pertinent to note that Articles 54 and 55 of UCPDC deal with transferable credits in details while about back-to-back credits there is absolutely no reference at all. This speciality makes it interesting to study about transferable and back-to-back credits.

Generally, all documentary credits are opened by the buyer in favour of the seller. But in some situations the seller is not the actual producer or manufacturer of the goods to be exported. The beneficiary is an intermediary who purchases from one or more suppliers. In such cases to avoid additional transaction by buying required things from third parties and supplying the same to the importer, the beneficiary of the credit requests the buyer to arrange for a transferable credit, hence the buyer knows very clearly that the beneficiary is not the actual supplier of goods. Beneficiary under a transferable credit can be a person, a firm, a company, an export house or a trading house. Transferable credits are also opened where such sellers who cannot get a documentary credit opened in their favour of such sellers who are not exporters of the goods. But established exporters can easily arrange for credits which will help indirectly such suppliers.

In back-to-back credits the beneficiary receives a letter of credit in his favour. But he is not a manufacturer or producer of the goods and he does not wish to get a transferable credit as he does not want to feed any hint to the buyer regarding the procurement of goods from others for subsequent supply. The notable feature of a back-to-back credit is that unlike other credits, in this case the beneficiary of the credit requests the advising bank to open another letter of credit in favour of his suppliers on the strength of the first credit as security for the credits subsequently opened. Back-to-back credits are not covered by UCPDC, may be because this is a second credit transaction arranged by the seller through his bank in his country in favour of his suppliers. This transaction is also considered as a domestic credit arrangement between the bank and its customers. The advantage for the seller is that the suppliers of goods will not know about the ultimate buyer. It is also a point to note the comparing to the volume of transactions accounted through other kinds of documentary credits, operation by transferable credits are less and back-to-back credits are still less.

WORLD CURRENCY

Country	*Currency*	*Country*	*Currency*
Abu Dhabi	Dinar	Finland	Markka
Aden	Dollar	France	Franc
Afghanistan	Afghani	Gambia	Pound
Albania	Lek	Germany	Deutsche Mark
Algeria	Dinar	Ghana	New Cedi
Angola	Escudo	Greece	Drachma
Argentina	Peso	Guinea	Franc
Australia	Dollar	Hong Kong	Dollar
Austria	Schilling	Hungary	Forint
Bahamas	Dollar	Iceland	Krona
Bangladesh	Taka	India	Rupee
Bahrain	Dinar	Indonesia	Rupiah
Belgium	Franc	Iran	Rial
Bolivia	Peso	Iraq	Dinar
Brazil	New Cruzero	Ireland (Republic)	Pound
Brunei	Dollar	Israel	Pound
Bulgaria	Lev	Italy	Lira
Burma	Kyat	Jamaica	Dollar
Cambodia	Rial	Japan	Yen
Canada	Dollar	Jordan	Dinar
Central African Republic	Franc	Kenya	Schilling
Chile	Escudo	Korea (South)	Won
China (Mainland)	Yuan	Kuwait	Dinar
Colombia	Peso	Laos	Kip
Costa Rica	Colon	Lebanon	Pound
Cuba	Peso	Liberia	US Dollar
Cyprus	Pound	Libya	Pound
Czechoslovakia	Crown	Luxemburg	Franc
Denmark	Krone	Malaysia	Dollar
Dominican Republic	Peso	Malta	Pound
Dubai	Riyal	Mauritius	Rupee
Ecuador	Sucre	Mexico	Peso
Egypt	Pound	Monaco	Franc
El Salvador	Colon	Morocco	Dirham
Ethiopia	Dollar	Nepal	Rupee
Fiji Islands	Dollar	Netherlands	Guilder

Country	*Currency*	*Country*	*Currency*
New Guinea	Dollar	Sudan	Pound
New Zealand	Dollar	Surinam	Guilder
Nicaragua	Cordoba	Swaziland	Rand
Nigeria	Pound	Sweden	Krona (Kroner)
Norway	Krone	Switzerland	Franc
Pakistan	Rupee	Syria	Pound
Panama	Balboa	Tanzania	Schilling
Peru	Sol	Thailand	Baht
Philippines	Peso	Tunisia	Dinar
Poland	Zloty	Turkey	Pound
Portugal	Escudo	Uganda	Schilling
Rhodesia	Dollar	United Arab Emirates	Dirham
Romania	Leu	United Kingdom	Pound
Russia	Rouble	Uruguay	Peso
Saudi Arabia	Riyal	Vatican city	Lira
Senegal	Franc	Venezuela	Bolivar
Singapore	Dollar	Vietnam	Piaster
South Africa (Republic)	Rand	Yugoslavia	Dinar
Spain	Peseta	Zaire	Zaire
Sri Lanka	Rupee	Zambia	Kwacha

☞ Questions

1. What is Export Finance? State the various means of export finance.
2. Explain the role played by ECGC in making available export finance.
3. What is post-shipment finance? Explain the terms D/A and D/P.
4. Write short notes on:
   (i) Whole turnover packing credit policy of ECGC.
   (ii) Direct finance for export by IDBI.
   (iii) Refinance of export credit by IDBI.
5. What are the different methods of International payments?
6. Write short notes on:
   (i) Limited floating rates.
   (ii) Pegged rates.
7. Is the Indian rupee linked to the pound sterling? Explain how the exchange rate of the Rupee in managed.

[I.I.B., Part II]

CHAPTER

22 Credit to Priority and Neglected Sectors of Economy

Traditionally, commercial banks in India have been providing credit facilities to large commercial and industrial houses. The other sectors of the economy — namely, small traders, farmers, industrialists and self-employed professional persons — were almost totally neglected by them in matters of credit. In other words, their lending policies were highly imbalanced, providing credit facilities to only one or two sectors: the remaining sectors of the economy did not get any bank credit. Because of lack of credit facilities, many sectors of the economy remained backward.

For a long time, there has been a need for the nationalisation or control of commercial banking to ensure that it plays a more purposeful role in the economic development of the country. The Government started a scheme of Social Control of Banks in February 1969, which aimed at bringing about some changes in the management and credit policy of commercial banks. Under this scheme, a National Credit Council was set up to perform the following functions in regard to credit planning:

(i) An assessment of the demand for bank credit from various sectors of the economy;

(ii) A determination of priorities for the grant of loans and advances and for a consideration of the availability of resources and requirements of priority sectors; and

(iii) Coordination of the lending and investment policies of commercial banks, cooperative banks and other specialised agencies.

After the enforcement of social control, banks were required to provide a larger allocation of credit for three sectors which were designated priority sectors — agriculture, small industries and exports; and targets were laid down by the National Credit Council about the quantum of credit to be given to these sectors. In July 1969, fourteen leading commercial banks were nationalised; as a result, most of the banking sector came under the control of the Government. After nationalisation, the Government directed the banks to provide credit not only to the priority sectors but also to certain other sectors of the economy which were not getting any credit facilities from the banks till then. These sectors, called the neglected sectors, were traders, transport operators, self-employed persons and professional persons and students. One of the greatest advantages of the nationalisation of banks in India has been the provision of credit facilities to these priority sectors and neglected sectors of economy.

☞ Why these Sectors could not get Bank Credit in the Past?

Some of the reasons why these sectors did not get bank credit are:

(i) Prevalence of Urban Banking: Banking facilities were available only in urban areas. There were no branches of banks in villages and small towns.

(ii) Bankers' Apathy Towards These Sectors: Bankers were mainly interested in providing credit facilities to big industrialists and traders; they never cared to provide credit to priority and neglected sectors.

(iii) Security: The basis of lending by Indian banks has always been the security of some tangible assets. Thus, those sectors of the economy which were not in a position to provide a tangible security were deprived of bank credit. This was the reason why small borrowers could never get any credit from a bank and had to rely solely on indigenous bankers and moneylenders.

(iv) Priority and Neglected Sectors Unorganised: As compared to the well-organised industrial and trading sectors, the priority sectors were not well-organised. Due to the inadequacy of irrigation facilities, agricultural operations in India depend on rains, which are always uncertain. The business of small entrepreneurs and self-employed professionals is also full of risks — at least in the initial stages. Moreover, these sectors are not in a position to provide any tangible security to banks against advances. Banks, naturally, evaluate an application for an advance on the basis of the type of business conducted by those asking for loans, their repaying capacity, security to be pledged and their future prospects in business. No wonder credit propositions for most of the priority and neglected sectors were not attractive credit propositions for banks.

There were other reasons as well; the illiteracy of farmers and small traders, their ignorance of the rules and regulations governing bank credit and the forms to be filled up and of other formalities which had to be observed. They also did not know how to maintain proper accounts of their business transactions.

But after nationalisation of banks in 1969, the whole concept of bank lending underwent a change. Banks have abandoned their cautious, conservative and traditional outlook and methods. They have started providing credit facilities to new sections in the priority and neglected sectors. Instead of insisting on tangible security, they now advance money on the basis of a charge on the assets of the borrowers acquired from borrowed funds. Greater importance is now attached to *term loans*. In term lending, the banker examines the purpose of a loan, its economic viability, income-generation from the use of borrowed funds, etc. He has now started lending to some small sectors without security. But this change in a bank's credit policy has been made possible by the active direction and control of the Reserve Bank and of the Government, and by the establishment of the Institutional Guarantee Support system to cover the risks of banks in financing these neglected sectors.

☞ New Concepts and Criteria in Bank Lending

As a result of persuasion, directions and guidance of the Central Government and the Reserve Bank, the Indian banking community has adopted new concepts, techniques and criteria for lending to the priority sectors. Important developments in this field may be summed up as follows:

(1) Change in outlook: The outlook of the bankers in favour of the priority and neglected sectors has completely changed after the nationalisation of 14 major banks. The bankers are today committed to help the backward sectors. This change in their outlook and spirit has been a significant achievement.

(2) *The consideration of security has undergone radical change:* It is wrong to presume that the bankers do not observe the principle of safety and security while lending funds to the priority sectors and that they lend to all borrowers indiscriminately. They still judge the safety of funds lent as no modern banker can afford to ignore it. However, the concept of safety has undergone a significant change. Traditionally, the safety of funds is ensured by securities a charge over the tangible assets of the borrower, which may easily be liquidated in order to recover the loan in case of default by the borrower. Under the new concept of security, safety of funds is ensured in the following ways:

(a) A charge over the tangible assets is not altogether dispensed with. In practice, banks like to have a charge over the assets of the borrower as far as possible. If no tangible asset is available for this purpose, banks even grant unsecured advances depending upon the borrower's repaying capacity and ability to make use of the credit. It is to be noted that a charge is preferred on the tangible assets acquired with the borrowed funds and not necessarily over the asset already possessed by the borrower. Thus, a person without any tangible assets is also eligible to borrow provided he fulfils other conditions.

(b) The banker largely depends on the desirability of purpose and economic viability of the project for which credit is needed. The banker examines all aspects of the functioning of the proposed project of the borrower. The technical ability, managerial competence and integrity of the borrower are the valuable intangible assets on which the banker is now largely relying. The banks now grant credit facilities to really able and talented persons having plan for starting sound projects.

(c) Institutional guarantee system has been evolved to cover the risks of the banks in financing these neglected sectors. The advances granted to the priority sectors are guaranteed by the Deposit Insurance and Credit Guarantee Corporation of India. This institution guarantees the advances automatically and in bulk provided the conditions of eligibility are fulfilled. Thus, the bankers are enabled to take what is called "calculated risk". This system of institutional guarantee enables the banker to share his risks with the Guarantee Corporation.

(d) Follow-up measures are taken to ensure proper utilisation of the loans given for specific purposes. Adequate arrangements have already been made by the banks to ensure the success of the borrower's enterprise.

(e) Full information about the borrower and his business is sought by the banker in order to assess the desirability of the loan, the weak features of the working of his business, etc.

(f) Flexibility and not rigidity is what is required most. The branch managers are expected to dispose of the majority of cases themselves according to their judgement and discretion.

☞ The Priority Sectors

The concept of 'Priority Sector' was evolved at the time of introduction of Social Control on banks in 1968 and subsequent nationalisation of major banks in 1969. The scope of activities included in the term priority sectors has been gradually enlarged over the years. At present different segments of the priority sectors are as follows:

1. Agriculture
2. Small-scale Industries
3. Small Road and Water Transport Operators

4. Retail Trade
5. Small Business
6. Professional and Self-employed Persons
7. State-sponsored bodies for Scheduled Castes and Tribes
8. Education
9. Housing
10. Consumption Loans.

TARGETS FOR LENDING TO PRIORITY SECTORS

Reserve Bank has prescribed the targets for lending to the priority sectors by commercial banks as follows:

1. *Public and Private Sector Banks*

Total priority sector advances	40% of net bank credit
Total agricultural advances	18% of net bank credit
Advances to weaker sections	10% of net bank credit

2. *Foreign Banks Operating in India*

Total priority sector advances	32% of net bank credit
Advances to small-scale industries	10% of net bank credit
Export Credit	12% of net bank credit

It is to be noted that export credit forms part of the priority sector only for foreign banks operating in India. For such banks no sub-target for agricultural advances is prescribed. Instead sub-target is prescribed for small-scale industries.

Reserve Bank has also stipulated that if there is a shortfall in priority sector lending from the above targets and sub-targets the bank concerned should deposit an amount equivalent to the shortfall with the Small Industries Development Bank of India at an interest rate of 8% per annum.

In April 1997, Reserve Bank of India decided that out of funds available to all segments of the small-scale sector, banks should ensure that 40 per cent are made available for units with investment in plant and machinery up to ₹ 5 lakh 20 per cent for units with investment between ₹ 5 lakh and ₹ 25 lakh and the remaining 40 per cent for other small-scale industries.

Definition of Weaker Sections: Weaker sections in priority sector comprise:

(a) small and marginal farmers with land holdings up to five acres

(b) landless labourers

(c) tenant-farmers and share-croppers

(d) artisans

(e) village and cottage industries where individual credit requirements do not exceed ₹ 25,000

(f) beneficiaries of Integrated Rural Development Programme (IRDP) and Self employment Programme for Urben Poor (SEPUP)

(g) beneficiaries belonging to Scheduled Castes/Scheduled Tribes, and

(h) Differential Rate of Interest (DRI) beneficiaries whose family income from all sources does not exceed ₹ 3,000 per annum in urban and semi-urban areas or ₹ 2,000 per annum in rural areas.

☞ New Schemes of Bank Finance to Priority and Neglected Sectors

After nationalisation, most of the commercial banks have started new schemes to finance priority and neglected sectors which were undeveloped parts of the economy and were not in a position to provide the securities required. The banks now provide credit to these sectors under relaxed security conditions. Some of the important features of these schemes are:

(a) *Loans to Farmers for Agricultural Purposes:* Banks provide credit facilities to farmers for the purpose of seeds of high-yielding varieties, fertilisers, pesticides, dairy and farm animals, tractors and other farm machinery, installation of tubewells and pumpsets and for the development of land. Medium-term loans are also provided up to 75 per cent of the requirements for a period up to five years, and are repayable in half-yearly instalments.

Several banks have also introduced schemes for financing custom service units, under which they finance the purchase of agricultural machines for hiring out, for harvesting, ploughing, threshing, lifting water and other farm operations.

(b) *Credit to Small-scale Industries:* Small-scale industries get credit from banks for short periods or for medium terms on the basis of hypothecation of raw materials or semi-finished goods, or in the form of a charge on land, buildings, machinery, etc.

Finance provided to the small-scale industries falls in two categories — *(i)* Direct finance provided to small-scale industrial units *(ii)* Indirect finance provided to small-scale industrial units, and *(ii)* Indirect finance to small-scale industrial sector.

Direct finance: In the category of small-scale industries are included:

(i) artisans (irrespective of their location).

(ii) cottage/village industries in village and small towns with a population not exceeding 50,000 involving utilisation of locally available natural resources and/or human skills where individual credit requirements do not exceed ₹ 25,000, and

(iii) other small-scale industries as defined in the previous chapter.

The small-scale industrial units are those engaged in the manufacture, processing and preservation of goods and whose investment in plant and machinery (originally) does not exceed ₹ 3 crore. These units included those engaged in mining or quarrying, servicing and repairing of machinery in case of tiny sector the limit of investment of ₹ 25 lakh.

Indirect finance to small scale industrial sector includes —

(i) credit to agencies involved in assisting the decentralised sector in the supply of inputs and marketing of outputs of artisans, village and cottage industries.

(ii) credit to Government-sponsored corporations/organisations providing funds to the weaker sections in the priority sectors, and

(iii) loans for setting up industrial estates.

(c) *Aritisans and Self-employed Persons:* Artisans and self-employed persons also receive bank credit up to ₹ 3,000 for the purchase of machinery and raw materials on the guarantee of another person. For loan amounts exceeding ₹ 3,000, a bank may ask for the hypothecation of goods. Loans are to be repaid in instalments extending up to 36 months. The borrower is required to take out a Life Insurance Policy for the amount of the loan, banks, moreover, have special schemes to provide complete finance for a project prepared by a qualified entrepreneur or craftsman for the manufacture of a product. Such schemes are meant for those who have no finance but who have technical knowledge and ability, and they are processsed by the Small Industries Services Institute and certified technically feasible and economically viable. Financial assistance of ₹ 2 lakh to ₹ 3 lakh may be provided by a bank, depending upon the requirements of a project.

☞ Transport Operators

Banks also provide credit facilities for the purchase of a taxi or a scooter up to 75 per cent of the cost of the vehicle and for the purchase of a truck up to 70 per cent of its cost; the remaining part of the cost must be financed by the borrower. The vehicle will remain mortgaged to the bank till the loan is repaid, and its registration will be in the joint names of the bank and the borrower. In addition to a comprehensive insurance of the vehicle, the personal guarantee of a suitable person is required. The amount of the loan is to be repaid in 36 monthly instalments. The interest charged by the bank is at the rate of 9 per cent for cars and scooters and 9½ per cent for trucks.

A consolidated set of guidelines have been prepared by the Reserve Bank of India for priority sector lending. Reserve Bank also lays down targets for lending to the priority sectors as well as the weaker sections of the society. Important provisions of the guidelines are given below:

GUIDELINES

☞ Margin Money

For loans up to ₹ 25,000 no margin is to be maintained. In case of loans over ₹ 25,000, a margin of 15 to 25 per cent may be stipulated, depending on the purpose and quantum of loan. Where subsidy/margin money is available from Government and/or other agencies and is not less than 15% of loan, it should be considered sufficient margin.

The lower margins prescribed in respect of special schemes for technocrats, etc., may be continued. Margin may be introduced in stages as and when required. Bringing in such margin at the beginning of loan should not be insisted upon.

☞ Security

(i) In case of composite loans up to ₹ 25,000 given to artisans, cottage and village industries banks may require as security pledge/hypothecation mortgage of assets created out of the loans. Collateral security or third party guarantee should not be taken.

(ii) The above is applicable to credit loans up to ₹ 25,000 given to other small-scale industries. For limits over ₹ 25,000 bank may obtain security as decided by them on the merits of each case.

(iii) In case of advances over ₹ 25,000, collateral security or third party guarantee may be required only in cases where primary security is inadequate or for other valid reasons only (and not as a matter of routine).

(iv) Viable proposals should not be turned down merely for want of such collateral security or third party guarantee.

(v) Where feasible, equitable mortgage instead of registered mortgage should be taken.

Interest Rates should be charged as follows:

Composite loans up to ₹ 25,000 — 10% in backward areas
— 12% in other areas

Short-term loans — not exceeding 14% for loans up to ₹ 2 lakh
16.5% for loans over ₹ 2 lakh and up to ₹ 25 lakh
18% for loans above ₹ 25 lakh

Term loans for not less than 3 years — 12.5% in backward areas
13.5% in other areas.

Banks should provide finance to these categories of small units taking into account the following guidelines:

1. Credit limits up to ₹ 25,000 may normally be granted as composite term loans for purchase of machinery and equipment or working capital or both; alternatively they may be granted separately also.
2. Before granting composite term loans, banks should liberally assess the actual requirement of a borrower in a given period. Banks may grant 10 to 20 per cent additional credit also to meet any unexpected needs of funds due to operational difficulties or for some essential consumption needs.
3. At the end of each year, banks should review the sanctioned loans. The limits may be enhanced if the operation of the borrower has expanded or there has been increase in the costs.
4. Banks should not insist upon collateral security by way of immovable properties or third party guarantee as a matter of routine. Banks should be guided by the viability of projects. In fact banks have been asked to adopt a flexible approach towards margin requirement. A proposal, if otherwise in order, should not be rejected if the borrower is unable to provide margin money. In case of artisans and village industries, no margin mony is to be insisted upon.
5. Composite term loans are repayable in 7 to 10 years, or even longer. Actual repayment of composite term loans and payment of interest should commence only after 18 months from the date of loan disbursement. In case of borrowers who are already reasonably well established and who are expected to have sufficient viability to commence repayment earlier, this period is reduced to 21 months. The repayment schedule should be informed to the borrower at the time of grant of loans. The instalment payments should not normally be more than one per cent of the loan amount per month.

GENERAL CONSIDERATIONS

1. Timely Sanction of Credit: For all the borrowers in the small-scale industry, banks are expected to dispose of all loan applications up to ₹ 1 lakh within 30 days.

Branch managers are given the discretion to sanction loans up to ₹ 25,000 without reference to any higher authority. Alternatively, suitable administrative machinery may be set up at the district level itself for this purpose. For advances above ₹ 25,000 and up to ₹ 1 lakh, the appraisal should be taken up simultaneously at both the District Industries Centres and the Bank. All loan proposals need not necessarily be routed through these centres.

2. Guarantee cover is available on advances granted to small-scale industries, as we have already studied in the previous chapter.

3. Fire Insurance: Bank may waive the requirement of insurance cover against fire risk for securities from small-scale industries for advances up to ₹ 25,000 in respect of composite term loans, term loans and working capital advances against non-hazardous goods. For others this limit is reduced to ₹ 10,000. This will not apply to those cases where insurance is compulsory under the compulsion of any law.

OTHER BORROWERS IN PRIORITY SECTOR

☞ Small Road and Water Transport Operators

This category of borrowers includes operators of taxis, autorickshaws, cars, bullock-carts, other animal-driven carts, boats, barges, steamers and launches for carrying passengers or goods for hire. Those operators, who own not more than six vehicles, including the one which is proposed to be financed by the bank, can be granted bank loans for the following purposes:

(i) purchase of vehicles,
(ii) acquisition of spares,
(iii) periodical repairs of a major nature, and
(iv) working capital purposes.

A banker must take the following precautions while granting loans to transport operators:

☞ Precautions before Sanctioning a Loan

1. The applicant for a loan must be properly introduced to the banker. The banker-must try to know the background of the applicant, *i.e.,* his experience of driving the vehicle, his honesty, character, etc. His driving licence must be checked up to see whether it contains any endorsement regarding any accident. If the applicant has served as a driver with any employer, proper enquiry must be made with the latter about the former's conduct.
2. The banker should also ascertain the prospects of his proposed venture to know whether the applicant would be able to get enough business as a transporter. His estimated future profits should also be checked up to determine his loan repaying capacity within a stipulated period.
3. If the plying of vehicle, *e.g.*, truck, bus, etc., requires a permit from a competent authority, the banker must ascertain if the same has been actually granted or assured to the applicant.
4. The applicant should furnish a guarantee from a reliable party well-known to the bank. If the banker's findings regarding (1) and (2) above are satisfactory, guarantee need not be insisted upon.

☞ Precautions after Sanctioning a Loan

1. The banker must directly make payment to the dealer in vehicles on the basis of proforma invoice, to ensure that the loan is properly utilised.
2. The vehicle to be purchased must be hypothecated to the bank and the interest of the bank in vehicle must be noted in the Registration Book and a certificate to this effect must be issued by the Regional Transport Office.
3. The banker must insist that the borrower takes a comprehensive insurance policy on the vehicle in the joint names of the borrower and the banker for its full value. The policy must continue till the entire amount of the loan is repaid.

4. The loan must be paid in three/four years in monthly/quarterly instalments. The banker must ensure that the borrower pays the instalments regularly.
5. The banker must obtain the following documents:
   (i) a demand promissory note,
   (ii) a letter stating that the demand promissory note be regarded as a continuing security for the outstanding amount of the loan,
   (iii) an agreement of hypothecation,
   (iv) a letter of guarantee, and
   (v) a letter of loan.
6. Rate of interest on term loans for not less than 3 years is fixed at 12.5% for one vehicle and 15 per cent for two or more vehicles. The interest on short-term working capital is subject to a ceiling of 17.5%.

RETAIL TRADERS

☞ Eligibility

Retail traders in fertilisers are included in indirect finance for agriculture and retail traders in mineral oil under small business. Other retail traders are eligible to borrow under this category which includes advances granted to private traders dealing in essential commodities (fair price shops) and consumer cooperative stores.

☞ Purposes

For acquisition of fixed assets and tools and other equipments required for the trade.

SMALL BUSINESS

☞ Eligibility

Small business includes individuals and firms managing a business enterprise which provide services (other than professional services). The original cost of their equipments should not exceed ₹ 2 lakh and the working capital limit should exceed ₹ 1 lakh. These services include cycle hire shops, booking, clearing and forwarding of goods, beauty parlours, juice vendors, launderers, mobile restaurants and publishers-cum-booksellers. Such units should be eligible for cover provided by DICGC.

☞ Purposes

For acquisition of fixed assets and tools, etc.

PROFESSIONALS AND SELF-EMPLOYED PERSONS

This category includes loans granted to medical practitioners (including dentists), chartered accountants, cost accountants, lawyers or solicitors, engineers, architects, surveyors, construction contractors or management consultants or to a person who is trained in any other art or craft who holds a degree or diploma or to a person who is considered by the bank as technically qualified or skilled in his field. The borrowing limits of these persons should not exceed ₹ 2 lakh of which not more than ₹ 1 lakh should be for working capital requirements. Such loans should be eligible for DICGC cover also.

☞ Purposes

(i) For purchase of equipments, repairing or renovating of existing equipments, acquisition or repairing of business premises and purchase of tools, and (ii) for working capital requirements.

STUDENTS FOR EDUCATION PURPOSE

☞ Eligibility

Students or their parents/guardians of minor students and not the educational institutions.

☞ Purpose

For pursuing graduate and post-graduate studies, professional courses or job-oriented diploma courses in India or higher education abroad.

STATE-SPONSORED BODIES FOR SCHEDULED CASTES AND TRIBES

Such lands should be granted for the specific purpose of purchase and supply of inputs and/or the marketing of the outputs of the beneficiaries of these organisations.

HOUSING LOANS

(a) *Direct finance* includes loans up to ₹ 5,000 for construction of houses granted to Scheduled Castes/Tribes and the weaker sections of the society irrespective of DIGC cover.

(b) *Indirect finance* includes assistance given to any governmental agency for the purpose of constructing houses exclusively for the benefit of Scheduled Castes/Tribes and low income groups and where the loan component does not exceed ₹ 5,000 per unit. It also includes assistance to any governmental agency for slum clearance and rehabilitation of slum dwellers.

Realising the necessity to provide houses and improve housing facilities in the country, the commercial banks have been asked to provide fund for housing since 1979. Initially, they were expected to lend ₹ 150 crore annually, but the target was raised to ₹ 300 crore for the year 1989-90. For the year 1990-91 individual commercial bank's housing finance allocation was acquired to be computed at 1.5% of the incremental deposits on March 1990 over the corresponding figure of March 1989.

According to the guidelines issued by the Reserve Bank, bank's assistance to the housing sector (including rural areas) may be as follows:

(a) 30 per cent of the total housing finance allocation by way of direct assistance to individuals or group of borrowers, etc., out of which at least half should be given as direct housing loans in rural and semi-urban areas.

(b) 30% of the allocation for lending to HUDCO, Housing Development Boards, HDFC and other housing agencies for construction of houses.

(c) The remaining 40% of the assistance may be by way of subscription to the guaranteed bonds/ debentures of HUDCO, and National Housing Bank.

The term and conditions, etc., for housing finance have been liberalised to encourage the flow of credit for housing as follows:

(a) The loan can be used for purchase of a house or flat, construction of a house or tenement or for additions or extensions to an existing structure.

(*b*) The loan will be secured by mortgage of the property. Banks also accept security of adequate value in the form of the insurance policies, Government promissory notes, shares and debentures or gold ornaments.

(*c*) Term loans from banks to housing finance companies (other than HUDCO, HDFC and companies promoted by commercial banks) has been raised to three times their net owned funds in January, 1990.

(*d*) The repayment period will be spread over 15 years.

(*e*) The maximum amount of loan was earlier fixed at ₹ 3 lakh per individual. But this ceiling was withdrawn effective 11th Oct. 1989.

HOME LOAN ACCOUNT SCHEME

This scheme is being launched with effect from July 1, 1989 by the National Housing Bank with the cooperation of commercial and cooperative banks to provide housing loans to those who regularly deposit in this account for a period of 5 years. This scheme has been launched by the National Housing Bank to mobilise savings through the banks. The participating bank is required to accept deposits under the Scheme on behalf of the National Housing Bank and make use of these deposits by way of refinance under any scheme approved by the National Housing Bank. The excess of deposits over refinance may either by remitted by the bank to the Housing Bank or may be retained by it, subject to compliance with statutory reserve requirements.

The amounts deposited in Home Loan Accounts, together with interest thereon at 10% per annum, are eligible for tax concessions under Section 80(c) of the Income Tax Act.

(*i*) Any individual (including a minor) not owning a house anywhere in India can open a Home Loan Account. A Coparcener of a Hindu undivided family jointly owning a house and non-resident Indians can also open an account.

(*ii*) The account may be opened with any branch in India of designated scheduled banks.

(*iii*) The accountholder is expected to save regularly and deposit in the account in quartely, half-yearly or annual instalments, any amount subject to a minimum of ₹ 90, ₹ 180 or ₹ 360 respectively. The member may vary his contribution as and when it is convenient for him, but the contribution will be in multiples of 10.

(*iv*) The saving will earn interest @ 10% per annum which will be added to the account annually and treated as reinvested.

(*v*) The account is not transferable to others. Nomination facility is available for payment of accumulated saving.

(*vi*) After subscribing for a minimum period of 5 years, or any time thereafter, the member will be eligible for a loan from the bank to acquire a new house/flat. However, in the case of a minor, the loan will be admissible only after he attains majority. During this period of 5 years from the commencement of the Scheme the bank will give housing loans to members on a preferential basis on terms stipulated by the Reserve Bank. After 5 years, members will be permitted to withdraw the accumulated balance in the account for the purpose of acquiring a house/flat even if they do not avail of the loan facility.

(*vii*) After 5 years, the amount of loan to be given by the bank under the scheme will be a multiple of the amount of accumulated savings (including up to date interest). It will be 4 times the accumulated savings. If the built in accommodations is up to 430 sq.ft.:3 times if such accommodation is up to 860 sq. ft. and twice the accumulated savings in all other cases.

The amount of loan will, however, be limited to the repaying capacity of the beneficiary as assessed by the bank. The loan will normally not exceed 2½ times the annual income. The maximum amount of the loan will be ₹ 3 lakh.

The borrower under the scheme may avail of loan facilities from other sources also, including a loan from a bank on usual terms. The loan under the scheme will be subject to all other conditions laid down by the Reserve Bank for grant of housing loans by banks. Loan under this scheme will be an additional facility with assurance loan at a lower rate of interest.

CONSUMPTION LOANS

☞ Eligibility

Small and marginal farmers with land-holdings up to two hectares, landless labourers, rural artisans and other people of very small means, like carpenters, barbers and washermen.

The scheme to provide consumption loans to the poorer sections of the society has been in operation since 1976. Recently the scheme has been liberalised as follows:

(a) *Eligibility:* The scheme is now applicable to all the weaker sections of the community. "Weaker sections" means all IRDP beneficiaries, small and marginal farmers, landless agricultural workers, rural artisans and other people of very small means like carpenters, barbers and washermen.

(b) *Purposes and Ceilings for loans:* Loans may be granted for the following purposes within the ceilings prescribed per family.

1. General consumption	₹ 150
2. Medical expenses	₹ 500
3. Educational needs	₹ 200
4. Marriage ceremonies	₹ 500
5. Funerals, births, etc.	₹ 150
6. Certain religious ceremonies	₹ 150

The aggregate advance for 2 or more purposes should not exceed in cases where the loans are granted against the security of gold and silver ornaments. In such cases, the ceiling limits has been enhanced to ₹ 2,000 per family.

☞ Guidelines

Margin money: No margin is required in case of loans up to ₹ 25,000. For loans exceeding ₹ 25,000 a margin of 15 to 25 per cent may be maintained depending on the purpose and amount of loan. The margin for housing loans up to ₹ 5,000 to Scheduled Castes/Tribes and weaker sections is 20 per cent of the cost of construction. Where labour is contributed by the borrower himself, contribution in the form of labour could be taken as margin. Where subsidy/margin money is available and is not less than 15% of loan amount, no further margin should be maintained.

☞ Security

(i) For loans up to ₹ 25,000 pledge/hypothecation/mortgage of assets created out of loan is sufficient security. (Banks should not ask for collateral security or third party guarantee.)

(ii) In case of loans exceeding ₹ 25,000, the security to be taken may be determined by banks on the merits of each case. Collateral security or third party guarantee may be required only in cases where primary security is inadequate or for other valid reasons.

(iii) Mortgage of properties or government guarantee is adequate for housing loans.

(iv) Guarantee of one or more individuals or groups of persons may be obtained for consumption loans.

(v) Proposals otherwise viable should not be turned down merely for want of collateral security or third party guarantee.

(vi) Wherever feasible, equitable mortgage instead of registered mortgage should be taken to save stamp duty.

(vii) In case of clean loans for education, guarantee or collateral security may be taken on the merits of each case.

☞ Interest Rates

Interest is to be charged as follows:

(i) *Retail traders for distribution of fertiliser:* 11.5% for limits up to ₹ 5,000 not exceeding 14% for limits over ₹ 5,000 and up to ₹ 25,000, not exceeding 16.5%for limits over ₹ 25,000;

(ii) *Other retail traders:* 12.5% for loans up to ₹ 5,000, not exceeding 15% for loans up to ₹ 5,000, not exceeding 15% for loans over ₹ 5,000 and up to ₹ 25,000;

(iii) *Professionals and self-employed persons belonging to SC/ST and women entrepreneurs:* 14 per cent for loans other than term loans, 13.5 per cent for term loans;

(iv) *Education:* Not less than Bank rate for advances to indignant students for purpose of higher education in India and 14-16.5 per cent for other educational advances;

(v) *Housing:* 4 per cent for loans to SC/ST up to ₹ 5,000;

(vi) *Road transport operators:* 12.5 per cent for up to 2 vehicles and 15 per cent for more than 2 vehicles:

(vii) *Priority sectors not otherwise specified:* Not exceeding 16.5 per cent for short-term loans, 15 per cent for all term loans.

☞ Integrated Rural Development Programme (IRDP)

Integrated Rural Development Programme (IRDP) envisages capital subsidy and credit assistance generating assets to come up above the poverty line. The total term credit disbursed during 1991-92 by the banks was ₹ 1133.27 crore to 25.27 lakh beneficiaries.

☞ Self-employment Programme for Urban Poor (SEPUP)

The programme was launched by Govt. of India on 1st Sept., 1986 with the objective of encouraging families living below subsistence level in metropolitan, urban and semi-urban areas to undertake self-employment venture with the help of subsidy and bank credit. The programme covers cities and towns having population exceeding 10,000 as per 1981 census and all urban areas administered by municipal committees/town area committees notified area councils which are covered under IRDP, irrespective of their population.

Under the scheme, assistance up to ₹ 5,000 depending on unit cost is admissible to an eligible beneficiary for undertaking any of the eligible vocations. The borrowers are eligible for a capital subsidy of 25 per cent of the total amount of assistance. Applicant should have lived at least for three years in the city/town area. The family income of the beneficiaries should not have exceeded ₹ 600 per month.

During 1991-92, an amount of ₹ 48.86 crore was sanctioned to 1.11 lakh beneficiaries. The Self-employment Programme for Urban Poor (SEPUP) was merged with the Scheme for Urban Micro Enterprises (SUME) under the Nehru Rozgar Yojna (NRY) with effect from 1st April, 1992.

☞ Scheme of Urban Micro-enterprises (SUME)

The Scheme of Urban Micro Enterprises (SUME) was introduced on 15th June, 1990 with the objective of providing employment to the unemployed and underemployed poor in urban areas. It covers unemployed urban poor living below the poverty line with an annual family income of ₹ 11,850 and below for the Eighth Five Year Plan with effect from 1st of April, 1992 in metropolitan areas, cities and towns not covered by IRDP. The urban local bodies are primarily responsible for identifying beneficiaries. Maximum loan amount presently permitted is ₹ 15,000 in case of SC/ST and women beneficiaries and ₹ 4,000 for others. The subsidy is routed through the urban local bodies.

PRIME MINISTER'S ROZGAR YOJNA

This scheme was introduced on October 2, 1993 with the objective to provide sustained self-employment in micro enterprises to educated unemployed rural and urban youth. The salient features of the scheme are as follows:

(i) The youth should be in the age group of 18 and 35 years and his family income should be less than ₹ 24,000 per annum.

(ii) The beneficiary would bring in 5% of the project cost as margin money.

(iii) He will be entitled to a composite loan up to ₹ 1 lakh without a collateral security or guarantee and also a Government subsidy of 15% subject to a ceiling of ₹ 7,500.

(iv) Applicants who have formed a partnership concern are also eligible for loan/subsidy to each borrower does not exceed the prescribed ceiling. Total cost of the project should not exceed ₹ 5 lakh. Cooperative are not eligible for assistance.

(v) The rate of interest on loans granted under the scheme will be guided by Reserve Bank's directive.

(vi) The subsidy will be sent to the disbursing bank in advance and it will be treated as fixed deposit in the name of the beneficiary.

(vii) The beneficiary will be required to hypothecate/mortgage/pledge assets created out of the loan to the bank.

(viii) If no fixed assets are to be created from the loans above ₹ 50,000 banks should take extra care in scrutinising the case.

From April 1994, the earlier self-employment scheme for educated unemployed youth (SEEUY) was included in this scheme.

PRIME MINISTER'S INTEGRATED URBAN POVERTY ERADICATION PROGRAMME (PMIUPEP)

This scheme was introduced in January 1996. It has two components: *(a)* Self-employment Scheme (SES), and *(b)* Shelter Upgradation Scheme (SUS). The Scheme aims at eradicating poverty in targeted Urban areas in an integrated manner and is being implemented in over 400 urban areas. Its salient features are as follows:

(i) Urban poor including slums/pavement dwellers and street/destitute children, etc., whose household income is below ₹ 11,850 per annum and who are educated up to IX standard are eligible for assistance under the scheme.

(ii) Under Self-employment Scheme (SES) ---

(a) Projects up to ₹ 1 lakh would be financed.

(b) 5% of the project cost would be the margin money to be brought in by the borrower.

(c) Balance 95% would be provided as loan.

(d) The loan would be repayable in instalments spread over 3 to 7 years, after an initial moratorium of 6 to 18 months no collateral is required under this scheme.

(iii) Under the Shelter Upgradation Scheme (SUS) —

(a) 75% of the unit/renovation/repair cost (subject to a ceiling of ₹ 10,000 per household) would be financed.

(b) Remaining 25% (subject to a ceiling of ₹ 2,500) would be provided as subsidy.

(c) The repayment would be spread over 10 years.

(d) Appropriate guarantees required for loans under this scheme.

The applications for assistance under this scheme are to be forwarded by the Urban local bodies, which should satisfy themselves of the applicant's status and enclose a certificate to that effect with the application.

COMMON GUIDELINES

The following are the common guidelines applicable to all the advances in the priority sector:

(1) *Loan Disbursement:* As far as possible loan amounts should be disbursed directly to the suppliers of seeds, fertilisers, raw materials, implements, trucks, machinery, etc.

(2) *Repayment Schedule:* The schedule for the repayment of the loan should be filed on the basis of the following factors, *viz.*:

(a) sustenance requirements of the borrower,

(b) surplus generating capacity,

(c) break even point,

(d) life of assets, etc.

In respect of composite loans up to ₹ 25,000 to artisans, village and cottage industries, the repayment schedule may be fixed for term loan component only.

In case of default on account of national calamities like floods and drought, crop loans may be converted into medium-term loans of 3 to 5 years. In case of term loans extension or rephasement may be allowed.

Similarly, in case of borrowers affected by natural calamities, drawals exceeding the value of security may be converted into a term loan repayable over a reasonable period of time. Further working capital may be extended or rephased.

(3) *Guarantee Premium:* Banks should themselves bear the premium payable to DICGC in respect of the following advances:

(i) advances to weaker sections,

(ii) housing loans up to ₹ 5,000 to Scheduled Castes/Tribes and weaker sections, and

(iii) pure consumption loans.

In other cases the amount of premium may be passed on to the borrowers, but interest and premium together should not exceed 18 per cent.

(4) *Penal Interest:* No penal interest should be charged for loans up to ₹ 25,000. For others it may vary from 1 to 2.5 per cent over the normal rates of interest.

(5) *Inspection Charges* should be as follows:

(i) advances up to ₹ 5,000 nil

(ii) advances above ₹ 5,000 but ₹ 2.50 per inspection per borrower with a maximum up to ₹ 25,000 of ₹ 10 per year per borrower.

(iii) advances above ₹ 25,000 Reasonable charges.

(6) *Insurance Cover:* Where finance is provided for purchase of equipment and the credit facility covered under DICGC guarantee scheme does not exceed ₹ 10,000, requirement of insurance against fire may be waived. For other risks it may be waived for advances up to ₹ 5,000 covered by DICGC schemes.

Insurance cover against fire risk may be waived for securities taken for advances up to ₹ 25,000 granted to small-scale industries and covered under DICGC guarantee in respect of composite loans to artisans, village and cottage industries, etc., term loans and working capital advances against non-hazardous goods. In other cases, the insurance cover may be waived to the extent of ₹ 10,000 for SSI advances covered under DICGC guarantee. But where insurance vehicle, machinery or other equipment is compulsory under the provisions of any law, it should be waived in any case.

(7) *Borrower's Photographs* may be taken for purpose of identification. Banks should make arrangement for the same and also bear the cost in respect of weaker section borrowers.

(8) *Other Charges:* Only reasonable out of pocket expenses should be recovered from the borrower.

(9) *Loan Pass Books* in regional languages should be issued to all IRDP beneficiaries giving necessary details of the loan.

(10) *Disposal of Applications:* Applications for credit limit up to ₹ 25,000 should be disposed of within a fortnight and those for over ₹ 25,000 within 8 to 9 weeks. The case rejected by the Branch Manager should be verified subsequently by the divisional regional managers.

SPECIAL CREDIT SCHEMES

Many banks have formulated Special Credit Schemes with particular reference to employment potential. Banks should take into account the following points while granting advances:

(a) The credit given by banks should be sufficient to meet the total requirements of borrowers. The loan may be utilised for meeting the legitimate expenses for renovation of equipment, acquisition of spares and periodical repairs of major nature. Advances may also be granted for purposes like advertising and marketing surveys.

(b) Reasonable amounts should also be granted for meeting expenses for family maintenance in case of persons who commence business/practice and those who leave well-established jobs to take up self-employment.

(c) The banker should lay primary emphasis on the viability of the proposal. An applicant's skill, experience, integrity and ability to organise an activity or a business are also taken into account.

(d) Loans up to ₹ 500 are disbursed on the basis of demand promissory notes or simple loan agreement.

(e) If third party guarantee is not available and the quality of the proposal is otherwise satisfactory, loan should not be denied.

(f) Banks should help the borrowers in obtaining technical advice and guidance.

☞ Guarantee of Loans and Advances to Small-scale Industries

The seminar on the financing of Small-scale Industries organised by the Reserve Bank of India in July 1969 had come to the conclusion that bank lending to small business might be enlarged by enabling them to share the risks involved with some other agency set up especially for this purpose. Accordingly, the Government of India, in consultation with the Reserve Bank of India, prepared a Guarantee Scheme, the object of which was to enlarge the supply of institutional credit to small-scale industrial units by granting a degree of protection to the lending institutions against possible losses in respect of such advances. The scheme was administered by the Reserve Bank of India as an agent of the Government of India. A working group was set up in 1969 by the Reserve Bank to evaluate the scheme, which was amended in 1970 in accordance with the recommendations of the working group.

CREDIT GUARANTEE SCHEMES

The Deposit Insurance and Credit Guarantee Corporation (DICGC) has been empowered to guarantee credit facilities granted by any credit institution and to indemnify them in respect of such credit facilities. The term 'credit institution' has been defined so as to include commercial banks, including the nationalised banks, the Regional Rural Banks, the Cooperative Banks and the financial institutions as defined in Sec. 45(1) of the Reserve Bank of India Act 1934. The term 'Credit Facility' has been defined so as to include any financial assistance, including a loan or instalment credit and any guarantee other than a performance guarantee granted or issued in India by a credit institution at any of its offices in India. Like banks the DICGC is also under a statutory obligation to maintain secrecy about any information relating to an incurred bank or its customers or a credit institution and its customers, except in circumstances in which it is in accordance with law or practice or usages customary among bankers, necessary or appropriate for the Corporation to divulge such information.

The DICGC at present administers the following three Credit Guarantee Schemes:

(i) The Small Loans Guarantee Scheme, 1974.

(ii) The Small Loans (Small-scale Industries) Guarantee Scheme, 1981.

☞ Guarantee Fee

The Corporation charged a graduated scale of guarantee fee, which are weighted in favour of small borrowers till March 31, 1989. With effect from April 1, 1989 the rate of guarantee fee was enhanced to 1.5 per cent per annum uniformly. It is now payable in advance on an annual basis and is to be calculated on the amount of a bank's priority sector advances (less advances to small-scale industries), outstanding at the end of March every year as reported in the Annual Report. The fee may be paid on *ad hoc* or final basis by April 30 every year. In case of *ad hoc* payment, final payment may be made by July 31 with interest at Bank Rate on the amount of shortfall. If payment is made after July 31, interest rate will be 2% above the Bank Rate.

☞ Guarantee Cover

In respect of credit facilities granted/renewed/altered on or after 1st January, 1985, the guarantee covers 60% of the amount in default under all the schemes of the Corporation. On loans granted prior to January 1, 1985 the guarantee cover continues up to 75% of the amount of default.

All renewals or enhancements of credit limits sanctioned to borrowers are treated by the Corporation as fresh credit facilities granted. This step has been taken to avoid dilution in the quality of lending to small borrowers.

☞ Monetary Ceiling on Corporation's Claim Liability

Within the cover of guarantee, which is now 60% of the amount in default, in case of all types of borrowers at DICGC has laid down certain monetary ceilings on its claim liability which have been enhanced from April 1, 1989 as follows:

(i)	Transport operators	₹	1,50,000
(ii)	Retail Traders	₹	25,000
(iii)	Farmers and Agriculturists	₹	60,000
(iv)	*(a)* Crop Loans	₹	10,000
	(b) Development Activities	₹	20,000
	(c) Conversion Loans	₹	30,000
(v)	Professional and Self-employed persons	₹	50,000
(vi)	Indirect Finance for Agriculture	₹	60,000
(vii)	Housing – Indirect Finance	₹	60,000

The amount in default means an amount on account of any eligible credit facility, including interest and any other charge, which

(a) has become due and payable to the bank but has not been paid after the expiry of a period of one month from the date on which a notice of demand was served by the bank, and

(b) has been treated as bad or doubtful of recovery and has been provided or accounted for as such in the books of the bank. It is therefore, essential that a claim must be supported by such entries passed in the books of the bank.

If the external auditor of the banks does not consider the dues as bad or doubtful, the bank should immediately refund to the Corporation any amount received by it towards the claim.

☞ Invocation of Guarantee

Till March 31, 1989 banks were permitted to invoke the guarantee if the repayment was not made by the borrower on demand by the banker. But from April 1, 1989 the Corporation introduced a lock-in period of 3 years from the date of advance for the invocation of guarantee. It meant that banks were not allowed to file their claims within a period of three years from the date of the advance.

On the payment of a claim, the Corporation shall be deemed to have been discharged from all its liabilities on account of the guarantee. But the Corporation subrogated to the rights of the bank. If the bank subsequently recovers any amount from the borrower, it should be shared, after deducting expenses, if any, between the Corporation and the bank. Corporation's share of such amount must be paid within one month. Thereafter, interest at the Bank Rate shall be charged.

If no further recoveries are possible the balance in the borrower's account may be written-off after obtaining the Corporation's approval.

☞ Guidelines for the Bankers

The Guarantee Scheme also contains certain provisions for the guidance of the bankers so that they do not resort to any indiscriminate lending merely because of the availability of the guarantee cover from the Corporation. These provisions are not mandatory and if the banker considers it necessary, he may relax any of these provisions in a particular case or may even grant an unsecured loan. The guarantee shall not be conditional on the observance or enforcement of any of these provisions:

(a) Banks are expected to satisfy themselves about the integrity of the borrower and the genuineness of his requirements.

(b) The project or purpose should be productive or socially useful and should yield a surplus from which the loan can be repaid.

(c) Normally, a bank is expected to obtain any security which may be available such as goods or other assets, a life insurance policy or other collateral security, the guarantee of the third party or even a group guarantee under which small security is taken the bank may prescribe somewhat lower margins than usual.

(d) Clean loans and facilities can be granted and covered under the scheme, but only when no security can be offered by the borrowers.

(e) The bank should improve the security in respect of any facility, which may be granted, wholly or in part as clean or unsecured if and when the borrower becomes subsequently able to furnish any acceptable security covering the full amount of the facility.

(f) The bank is expected to obtain as a rule a charge on the goods or other assets created out of the loan or other credit facility granted by it and on any other goods or assets available with the borrower.

(g) The bank should take the necessary follow-up action to ensure that the loans are actually utilised for the purposes for which they are sanctioned.

☞ Credit Guarantee Corporation of India, Small Loans (Guarantee) Scheme, 1971

After the nationalisation of banks, there was an enormous increase in the credit to small borrowers, which necessitated some guarantee scheme for bankers to help them and facilitate their lendings to such borrowers. A working group was set up by the Government of India under the chairmanship of Mr. S.S. Shiralkar, which submitted its recommendations in 1969. On the basis of these recommendations, the Credit Guarantee Corporation of India Limited was established on January 14, 1971, as a limited company under the Indian Companies Act. Its authorised capital is ₹ 10 crore and paid-up capital ₹ 3 crore. The Reserve Bank of India holds 60 per cent of the capital, the balance being contributed by scheduled banks in the public and private sectors. The Credit Guarantee Corporation of India introduced a comprehensive guarantee scheme from April 1, 1971. Under this scheme, all the credit facilities given by banks to small traders, transport operators, traders in fertilisers and other goods, professionals and self-employed persons and farmers are covered by a guarantee of the Corporation.

☞ Scope of the Guarantee Scheme

All commercial banks are eligible for participation in the guarantee scheme after the execution of an agreement with the Corporation. The credit facility covered by the guarantee means any financial assistance, including a loan or an advance, cash credit, overdraft, bill purchased or discounted, a term instalment credit, a letter of credit or acceptance credit and any guarantee (other than a performance guarantee) granted by banks in India.

The following types of credit extended by banks shall not be covered by the guarantee scheme:

(a) Credit in respect of which risk is already covered by the Government or any general insurer;

(b) Any credit facility which is inconsistent with the provisions of any law or with any directive of the Reserve Bank;

(c) Any credit facility in respect of which the guarantee was extended previously and the borrower has not paid back any part of the loan guaranteed;

(d) Any credit facility granted to hire purchase financiers or to proprietors or publishers of newspaper and periodicals.

In the case of credit granted under the guarantee scheme, the liability of the Corporation to reimburse the banks is up to 75 per cent of the amounts of default. The remaining 25 per cent is to be borne by the Banks themselves. The fees charged by the Corporation is half per cent on the amounts outstanding on account of credit facilities, is payable quarterly, and is calculated on the total balances in individual accounts during the previous quarters.

☞ Special Provisions in Relation to Credit Facilities to Borrowers in Various Sectors

Till March 31, 1989, the Scheme contained special provisions in relation to credit facilities to borrowers covered under the Scheme. These provisions were classified into two categories: *(i)* essential for being eligible, and *(ii)* desirable.

Transport Operators: *Essential:* Transport operator must be an individual or an association of not more than six individuals owning and normally operating by himself, or themselves, a transport vehicle for carrying any passengers or goods for hire. The eligible borrowers will be those who own and operate not more than one vehicle. Loan sanctioned for: *(i)* meeting the cost of the vehicle of purchase, or *(ii)* for repairing or renovating the vehicle: and *(iii)* for working requirement are covered by the guarantee.

Desirable: The bank's interest as the financier should be recorded on the registration certificate and a comprehensive insurance policy be taken out by the transport operator with a clause assigning in favour of the bank such rights as do not belong or accrue to third parties under the policy operator must pay regulary taxes and other duties and keep the vehicle in reasonably good repair. The period of repayment of the loan should be 3-5 years which may be extended if necessary.

Retail Traders: *Essential:* The trader must be an individual or group of individuals, firm or registered cooperative society, trading in goods and should not have an annual sales turnover of more than ₹ 4 lakh.

Desirable: The loan is allowed only against merchandise which are readily saleable or against bills or book debts representing amounts receivable by the borrower on account of the sale of merchandise. Statements of stock-in-trade or the value of stocks are obtained from the borrower and the drawing power regulated according to the margin prescribed in the account.

☞ Dealers in Fertilisers and Mineral Oils

The dealer must be an individual, firm or a registered cooperative society trading in fertilisers or mineral oils and should not have an annual turnover of more than ₹ 5 lakh. The duration of the loan should not exceed 5 months in the case of a dealer who is not a cooperative society and 6 months if the dealer is a cooperative society.

Professionals and Self-employed Persons: Professionals and self employed persons include:

(a) Medical Practitioner;

(b) Dentists;

(c) Chartered Accountants;

(d) Cost Accountants;

(e) Lawyers;

(f) Solicitors;

(g) Engineers;

(h) Architects;

(i) Surveyors;

(j) Construction Contractors;

(k) Management Consultants.

They may also be such other persons as are trained in other arts or crafts, who hold a degree or diploma or otherwise are technically qualified or skilled. The amount of the loan or other credit facility should not exceed ₹ 1 lakh in the case of a doctor having a dispensary, or a nursing home or a clinic and for construction contractors; ₹ 50,000 in the case of engineering consultants and architects; and ₹ 20,000 in the case of other professionals and self-employed persons.

Small Business Enterprises: *Essential:* The business enterprise has been or is established by an individual or a firm and the original cost price of the equipment used for the purpose of the business should not exceed ₹ 2 lakh. The loan must be utilised for purchasing the equipment or for carrying on the business of the concern, which must render any services, other than professional services.

Desirable: The income from rendering the services or from any other sources regularly brought to account and recorded in the books of the borrower. Proper books of account must be maintained by the borrower. The current assets of the enterprise are reasonable by the borrower must be actually recovered within a reasonable period.

☞ Farmer and Agriculturists Essential

(i) The borrower may be an individual or Hindu undivided family or any group or association of persons, other than a company or a cooperative society. He may be the owner, tenant or lessee (including an oral lessee) of any land for agricultural or allied activities, like pisciculture, sericulture, animal husbandry, poultry farming, dairy farming, etc.

(ii) In case a loan is granted to a group or association of persons, every member of the group or association must be jointly or severally responsible to the bank for the entire amount of the loan.

(iii) The period of repayment should not exceed 24 months from the date on which it is first utilised in case it is sanctioned for financing sugarcane, 15 months for seasonal agricultural operations and 15 years for any other purpose.

PRECAUTIONS: THE BANK SHOULD AS FAR AS PRACTICABLE, ENSURE THE FOLLOWING

(a) The borrower is able to furnish satisfactory evidence to the bank that he is actually engaged in the cultivation of land, which bears a specified survey number or is otherwise identifiable or in any other activity for financing which the loan is granted.

(*b*) The land, farm, establishment or other business premises of the borrower can be visited or inspected. It must be located in a compact and contiguous area in which other borrowers have also been granted credit facilities or in area which is accessible to the bank and the Corporation.

(*c*) In case of credit facility for financing seasonal agricultural operations, the facility is utilised mainly for meeting through the bank or through sources known to or identifiable by the bank, the cost of fertilisers, pesticides, seeds or other agricultural inputs.

(*d*) In the case of credit facility for financing the reclamation and improvement of land, the construction of irrigation wells, the installation of pumpsets for drawing water, the purchase of machinery or equipment or the acquisition of any other capital assets, satisfactory evidence is furnished to the bank to the effect that the facility has been actually so utilised.

(*e*) The borrower avails himself technical assistance or other facilities available from any agency established in his area in connection with the utilisation of the facility.

☞ Credit Guarantee Scheme for Loans Granted by State Financial Corporations

Credit facilities provided by State Financial Corporations have also been eligible for guarantee from 1st July, 1971, under a new scheme formulated by the Credit Guarantee Corporation of India Ltd., known as the Credit Guarantee Corporation of India Small Loans (Financial Corporations) Guarantee Scheme, 1971. This scheme is similar to that applicable to commercial banks.

☞ Credit Guarantee for Small-scale Industries

The credit facilities provided by State Financial Corporations are already covered under the Credit Guarantee Scheme for small-scale industries, which is administered by the Industrial Finance Department of the Reserve Bank of India on behalf of the Central Government. This scheme was introduced in July 1960 to enlarge the flow of institutional credit to small-scale industries. It covers credit granted to small-scale units whose investment in plant and machinery does not exceed ₹ 7.5 lakh. The Guarantee Corporation charges a fee at one-tenth of 1 per cent per annum on a quarterly basis. The Guarantee Corporation shall pay 75 per cent of the amount in default or the amount guaranteed. Credit facilities granted to small-scale industrial concerns engaged in the following activities alone are eligible for guarantee under this scheme: (*a*) manufacture, (*b*) processing, (*c*) preservation of goods, (*d*) mining and quarrying, (*e*) servicing and repairing of certain types of machinery, and (*f*) customer service units.

As the State Financial Corporations are prevented by law from assisting any concern other than certain specified industrial firms as defined in the State Financial Corporation Act, 1951, the scope of its new scheme is limited to the residual categories of small borrowers, who include transport operators, hoteliers and small entrepreneurs engaged in generating or distributing power or in developing and managing industrial estates.

SMALL LOANS (SMALL-SCALE INDUSTRIES) GUARANTEE SCHEME, 1981

The Corporation operates this Scheme since April 1981 in respect of advances granted to small scale industrial units. Certain liberalisations and other changes have been effected in the scheme with effect from April 1, 1989. The salient features of the Scheme, as in force at present, are as follows:

1. Eligible Institutions: Commercial Banks, Regional Rural Banks, State Financial Corporations, certain Cooperative banks and Industrial Development Corporations, which provide loans to small-scale industries are eligible for guarantee cover.

2. Eligible Borrowers: Originally the small-scale industrial units were the eligible borrowers under the scheme. With effect from April 1, 1989 the 'priority sector' definition of Reserve Bank has been adopted for the purpose of extending the guarantee. Hence, indirect finance to small-scale sector and credit facilities to industrial estates have also become eligible for guarantee cover under the scheme. Thus, at present, the following borrowers are eligible for guarantee cover under the scheme.

(i) Small-scale Industries: Small-scale Industrial units are those units which are engaged in the manufacture, processing or preservation of goods and whose investment in plant and machinery (original cost) does not exceed ₹ 3 crore. These units also include units engaged in mining, quarrying, servicing and repairing of machinery. If an industrial unit acquires plant and machinery of the total original cost exceeding the above limits, it cannot qualify as a small scale industrial unit. Service-oriented enterprises having investment in plant and machinery not exceeding ₹ 2 lakh each and located in rural areas and towns with a population of 5 lakh or below are also eligible borrowers under the scheme. Such establishments provide personal or household services required in urban, semi-urban/rural areas such as laundry, zeroxing repair and maintenance of durables, etc.

(ii) Indirect finance to Small-scale Industrial Sector will include credit granted to —

(a) Agencies which assist the decentralised sector in the supply of inputs and marketing of outputs of artisans, village and cottage industries, and

(b) Government-sponsored corporation/organisation which provide funds to the weaker sections in the priority sector.

(iii) Industrial Estates: Loans granted for setting up industrial estates are now also eligible for guarantee cover under the scheme.

3. Compulsory Coverage: Till April 1, 1989, participation in the guarantee scheme by the eligible institutions was voluntary and they were required to enter into an agreement with DICGC for joining the scheme. Thereafter all of their eligible loans were automatically covered.

Now, the guarantee fee shall be payable on the entire priority sector advances as reported in the Annual Report of the banks. It implies that guarantee cover shall be applicable to all the priority sector advances of the eligible institutions.

4. Eligible Purpose and Credit Facilities: Loans granted for both of the following purposes are eligible for guarantee cover:

(i) For acquiring fixed assets and equipment such as land, building machinery, furniture, and vehicles, and for their repairs and replacement, and

(ii) For the purpose of working capital, *e.g.,* for production and marketing of products.

The banks are required to ensure that these loans are used only for genuine productive purposes and to examine the financial viability of th project and the integrity of the borrower. The guarantee cover is not provided in the case of the following:

(i) Performance guarantees.

(ii) Loans which are already covered under any guarantee given by the Government or general insurer or any person or association carrying on the business of insurance, guarantee and indemnity.

(iii) Credit facilities which do not conform to the provisions of any law of directives or instructions.

5. Extent of Guarantee Cover: DICGC provides guarantee cover on graduated scale. The extent of such cover as percentage of the amount in default is as follows:

(a) Small-scale Industrial Units having total credit facilities not exceeding ₹ 2 lakh	60%
(b) Small-scale Industrial Units having total credit facilities exceeding ₹ 2 lakh in —	
(i) Backward district specified by Government and other areas as may be specified by Government of India and DICGC	60%
(ii) Other Areas 50%	
(c) Agencies assisting the decentralised sector and Government sponsored corporations or organisations	60% in respect of credit facilities up to ₹ 2 lakh per borrowing unit. 50% in other cases.
(d) Loans for construction and running of Cold Storage/Loans to Custom Service units/ Industrial Estates	60% or 50% as stated above.

The ceiling on claim liability per borrower has increased from ₹ 10 lakh to ₹ 20 lakh per borrowing constitutent, which is equally and separately divided between term loans (₹ 10 lakh) and working capital loans (₹ 10 lakh). In respect of *(c)* above the monetary ceiling is ₹ 60,000 only per borrower. The higher ceiling limit shall be applicable to credit facilities granted on or after April 1, 1989. The maximum amount that can be claimed per borrower by all the financial institutions together has been fixed as above. If the total claims of all the financial institutions providing loans to a borrower exceed this limit, he shall have to share the maximum amount payable under the scheme on a pro rata basis.

6. Guarantee Fee: Till March 31, 1989 the DICGC charged a guarantee fee from the credit institutions at the following rates:

(i) 0.5% per annum on the amount outstanding in case of borrowers having eligible credit facilities up to ₹ 25,000, and

(ii) 0.75% in case of other borrowers.

The guarantee fee was payable in two half-yearly instalments (April-September and October-March). The fee was calculated with reference to the balance outstanding in the individual guaranteed accounts as on the last Friday of the preceding half-year. The rate of guarantee fee has been raised to 1.5 per cent per annum uniformly with effect from April 1, 1989 and is payable in advance on an annual basis (instead of on half-yearly basis). It is to be calculated on the amount of credit institution's priority sector advances (less advances to non-SSI sectors) outstanding as at the end of March every year. Guarantee fee is payable on *ad hoc* or final basis by April 30 every year. In case *ad hoc* payment is made by April 30, final payment must be paid by July 31, together with interest at Bank Rate on the amount of short fall. If payment is made after July 31, the rate of interest will be 2% above the Bank rate.

7. Invoking of Guarantee: Till March 31, 1989 a credit institution was permitted to invoke the guarantee if it fails to recover from the borrower the loan amount within one month from the date of issue of demand notice and if it treated the dues as bad and doubtful of recovery. But with effect from April 1, 1989, the lock-in period of 3 years from the date of advances for invocation of guarantee has been discontinued in April 1995 and rules as in the 1971 scheme were enforced.

8. Precuations: *(a)* The credit institution should not have suffered any loss in respect of the loan due to the –

(i) negligence of its employees in the observance of necessary safeguards in the appraisal, supervision and follow-up of credit facility.

(ii) any dishonesty on their part; or

(iii) decisions taken by them which are contrary to or in contravention of the instruction by their own institution or the guideliness advised by DICGC.

(b) The credit institution should take effective steps against the borrowers, and the sureties. The securities available should be realised for whatever amount is possible. Guarantee should, thereafter, be invoked for the rest of the amount.

☞ Credit Guarantee Scheme for Service Cooperative Societies

From 1st October, 1971, the Credit Guarantee Corporation of India Ltd., has started guaranteeing loans and other credit facilities to service cooperative societies, which may be serving small-scale industrial units. Cooperative societies which are not themselves engaged in any manufacturing, processing or other industrial activity, but assist their members in carrying on such activity by arranging the purchase and supply of raw materials, display and marketing of finished goods, procurement of orders and sale of finished goods, are eligible under this scheme.

☞ Differential Interest Rates

For a long time, it was felt that lower interest rates should be charged from certain sectors of the economy which need financial assistance but cannot get it from banks because of higher interest rates. The Reserve Bank of India appointed a committee under the chairmanship of Dr. R.K. Hazari to examine the question of differential interest rates. The terms of reference of the committee were:

(i) To review the scope and extent to which differential interest rates were already being charged by banks from borrowers in each sector;

(ii) To determine the criteria for identifying the borrowers who may be granted the benefit of lower interest rates in each sector;

(iii) To indicate the range of the differential rates that may be allowed in each sector; and

(iv) To examine if any other concessions should be granted either in lieu of, or in addition to, lower interest rates.

On the recommendations of this committee (which submitted its report in May 1971), the Government announced in March 1972, its decision to charge from low-income group persons uniform interest rates of 4 per cent. The Reserve Bank laid down certain criteria for eligibility for loans at differential rates under the scheme. The eligible sectors include scheduled tribes, scheduled castes and others engaged, on a modest scale, in agriculture and/or allied activities; people occupied in the collection, of elementary processing, of forest produce; people collecting fodder in difficult areas and selling it to farmers and traders; people physically engaged on a modest scale in rural cottage industries and vocations; students of merit going in for higher education; physically handicapped persons pursuing a gainful occupation; and orphanages and women's homes where saleable goods are made and for which there is no adequate and dependable source of finance. A person to be eligible for a loan under this scheme should not have a family income of more than ₹ 3,000 per annum if resident in an urban or semi-urban area or ₹ 2,000 per annum if resident in a rural area. In addition, he should not have land exceeding one acre if irrigated and 2.5 acres if unirrigated.

Term loan and working capital would be granted in accordance with the specific requirements of the borrower. In 1973, the ceiling for working capital loans to any single borrower was raised from ₹ 500 to ₹ 1,500 and for term loans from ₹ 2,500 to ₹ 5,000. Composite loans up to ₹ 6,500 may also be given to village artisans and persons engaged in village and cottage industries. In exceptional cases, particularly for students of merit, higher amounts may be considered. The Government of India has decided to allow the banks to determine the quantum of working capital term loan depending upon the nature and need to the activity of the borrower. But the overall ceiling of ₹ 6,500 shall be observed.

(a) **Margin:** Margin money is not to be insisted upon.

(b) **Security:** The assets purchased with the loan may be hypothecated to the bank. In appropriate cases loans to homogeneous group of borrowers, group guarantee may be accepted. Tangible security or third party guarantee is not insisted upon.

Each loan is to be covered under the credit Guarantee Scheme and the guarantee fee should be met by the banks. The cost of insurance of the assets charged to the bank, if considered necessary, should be borne by the bank.

(c) **Repayment of Loans:** The term loans are repayable within a period of five years including a grace period of up to 2 years. For each borrower a repayment schedule is worked out taking into account the nature of his activity and the surplus income he gets from the productive endeavour.

Supervision and Guidance: The banks will maintain continuous touch with the borrower to whom the benefit of the differential rate is extended and will arrange for necessary guidance and help in a number of ways either themselves or with the help of other recognised bodies which function in the area.

Lending Through Regional Rural Banks: The Government has permitted the commercial banks to lend through the Regional Rural Banks sponsored by them on a refinance basis. The RRBs are required to give preference to smaller borrowers amongst landless agricultural labourers, rural artisans, cottage and rural industries, beneficiaries of schemes for Scheduled Castes/Tribes and the weakest of the weaker sections. Refinancing is provided by the commercial banks to RRBs at two per cent per annum.

DISTRICT INDUSTRIES CENTRES

The Government has set up District Industries Centres at the district level. These centres provide all the services and facilities to the entrepreneurs at one place for setting up small and village industries. The centre renders various services required by small entrepreneurs including identification of a suitable scheme, preparation of feasibility report, arrangements for supply of machinery and equipment, provision of raw materials, credit facilities and inputs, marketing and extension services.

A District Industries Centre (DIC) is headed by a General Manager who is assisted by seven functional managers, each is a specialist in the following subjects:

1. Economic Investigation.
2. Machinery and Equipment.
3. Research, Extension and Training.
4. Raw Materials.
5. Credit.
6. Marketing, and
7. Cottage Industries.

Role of Credit Managers: The credit managers have been deputed by the banks to the DICs They provide all guidance, assistance and support required by entrepreneurs in obtaining the right type of credit in required amounts at the proper time from banks and financial institutions.

The credit managers are required to recommend the credit proposals of small entrepreneurs after due appraisal to the credit institutions. The entrepreneurs are therefore, not required to furnish the same particulars to banks again. The credit managers do not possess the authority to sanction loans nor are they responsible for the recovery of the loans. They act as liaison authority between borrowers on the one hand and the credit institutions on the other.

ADVANCES TO SMALL-SCALE INDUSTRIES

A small-scale industrial unit is one which is engaged in the manufacture, processing or preservation of goods and whose investment in plant and machinery (excluding land and buildings) does not exceed ₹ 7.5 lakh. Small-scale industry may be distinguished from village industries and handicrafts which are of a traditional nature and cater primarily to local markets. Small-scale industries may be classified into five main groups, *viz.,*

(i) *Manufacturing* industries producing finished products for direct consumption;

(ii) *Feeder* industries specialising in certain types of products and services, e.g., castings, electroplating, welding;

(iii) *Servicing* industries covering light repair shops which are essential for the maintenance of mechanical equipment;

(iv) *Ancillaries* to large-scale industries, producing parts and components for such light engineering products as cycles, sewing machines, diesel engines, machine tools;

(v) *Mining* and/or quarrying.

☞ Characteristics of a Small-scale Unit

Some of the important characteristics of a small-scale industrial unit are:

(i) Inadequate capital resources;

(ii) Obsolete machines and tools;

(iii) Lack of knowledge of modern methods of management, production and marketing;

(iv) Shortage of trained personnel;

(v) Scarcity of raw materials.

☞ Finance for Small-scale Industrial Units

Like any industry, small-scale units require land, buildings, plant and machinery and such ancillary services as water, power, transport. In addition to these fixed capital requirements, there are working capital requirements for the day-to-day running of the factory.

The main sources of finance for small-scale industries are:

(i) Proprietor's own capital;

(ii) Loans by State Governments and State Financial Corporations;

(iii) Finance by Commercial Banks;

(iv) Finance by National Small Industries Corporation;

(v) Finance by other agencies.

☞ Appraisal of Loan Proposals

In principal, there is rot much of a difference between the appraisal of a proposal for an advance to a small-scale industrial unit and a big industry. But, practice, the consideration of a proposal favouring a small-scale industry raises some problems of its own. An important aspect of the basic philosophy of a bank to assist a small-scale industrial unit is its commitment to meet its total needs, irrespective of the security which it is in a position to offer; provided that the unit is technically competent to produce marketable goods, notwithstanding the need-based approach rather than the security-oriented approach of traditional bankers. Many proprietors of small units may not be able to answer the standard questionnaire except with the guidance of the banker. Such guidance should always be provided. Some small units do not keep regular account books and are not in a position to submit audited balance sheets, which are essential for an appraisal of a proposal. The appraisal of a proposal involves many things, including the character of the proprietor, the quality of mangement, the financial strength of the enterprise, its technical and economic feasibility as well as an assessment of its credit requirements.

In appraising an advance proposal of a small-scale industrial unit, the following factors should be borne in mind:

(i) Proprietor (Management): The entrepreneur's honesty, efficiency and experience will be considered. If the unit is a one man show, the consequences of the unexpected death of the keyman in the running and progress of a unit will also be taken into account.

(ii) Finance: The financial strength of a unit may be assessed from a study of the statement of its assets and liabilities. It would be necessary to know the liquidity surplus or the available working funds determined out of the current assets and current liabilities because this is the quantum of free funds which will be utilised to provide a margin on the bank's advances as well as meet other overhead expenses. The unit's balance sheet or its statement of assets and liabilities should be studied to ascertain the sources from which funds shown as unsecured borrowings really belong to the proprietors of the enterprise and are likely to be retained in the business till it gains strength. Moreover, if there is any conflict in security, a study of the balance sheet would indicate whether the security proposed to be offered to the bank is free from prior encumbrances. From the statement of assets and liabilities, all the assets should be verified to determine the liquid surplus and the extent of the stake which the owners of the enterprise have therein. While no standard formula can be laid down, a 20 per cent to 25 per cent contribution to the cost of the entire project may be taken as a reasonable stake.

The working capital requirements of the unit may be assessed by anticipating the production in the next 12 months and the requirements of raw materials during the same period.

(iii) Technical Feasibility: It is necessary to investigate the capacity of a unit to produce goods. If a technical feasibility study has been made by some Government organisation or any other expert body, a copy of the report should be obtained and closely studied by the bank. The banker should also ascertain whether the machinery is second hand or new whether the factory is properly located, and whether spare parts, raw materials, labour, water and power are easily available.

(iv) Economic Feasibility: The banker should also determine the economic feasibility of the project to find out whether:

(i) a unit depends on raw materials which are easily available/or in short supply;

(ii) the products manufactured by it have a steady demand or a seasonal or fluctuating demand;

(iii) the type of marketing organisation the unit has adequate and satisfactory.

The Chart given here shows the various points to be considered by a bank while appraising a credit proposal before making an advance to a small-scale industry.

(v) Break even Analysis: *"The break even point of a manufacturing organisation is defined as that level of sales at which it recovers all its costs, and makes neither a profit nor incurs a loss."*

Therefore, a manufacturing unit (whether small-scale or large-scale) should aim at operating at or above its break-even point, if it is not to incur a loss and deplete its capital. Once a unit crosses its break even point, it generates a surplus. An assessment of the break-even volume of sales provides an effective index of the viable level of activity which ought to be achieved by a unit.

Chart Showing Advances to Small-scale Industries

CAPITAL APPRAISAL

- PERSON
  - Character
    1. Integrity
    2. Sincerity
    3. Reliability
    4. Motivation
    5. Age
    6. Health
    7. Initiative
  - Capacity
    - Knowledge
      1. Industry
      2. Pitfalls
      3. Systems
    - Skills
      1. Management
      2. Production
      3. Finance
      4. Marketing
  - Capital (Stake)
- PROJECT
  - Organisation
    - Key Functionaries
      1. Key Functional Areas
      2. Production
      3. Finance
      4. Marketing
  - Goods and Savings
    1. Availability
    2. Cost, Quality
    3. Accessibility
  - Market
    1. Market Study
    2. Production Planning
    3. Pricing
    4. Advertisement
    5. Sales Promotion
    6. Distribution
  - Finance
    - Estimate of cost
    - Sources
  - Profitability
    - Break even point
    - Different levels of activity
    - Time schedule

☞ Calculation of the Break even Point

The first step in calculating the break even point is to segregate the costs incurred by a firm into fixed and variable items of cost. Fixed costs would have to be met regardless of whether the firm operates or not. Examples of fixed costs are rent, taxes, insurance, depreciation, wages of permanent labour and salaries of the supervisory staff. In practice, fixed costs are not totally independent of the level of activity. They increase with an increase in activity. For example, fixed costs may be ₹ 4,000 per month for a production which ranges from 6,000 to 8,000 units per month, and ₹ 5,000 per month when production is between 8,000 and 20,000 units per month. The increase may be caused by the employment of more permanent labour and supervisors to handle a larger volume of production..

Variable costs, on the other hand, bear a definite relation to the volume of production. For example, the consumption of raw materials is directly linked to production. Power and interest on borrowings are other items of variable costs. Most overheads, in fact, are neither completely fixed nor completely variable, but consist of both the components of the costs — variable and fixed. For the sake of convenience, all costs, other than raw material costs, may be treated as fixed costs.

Once the fixed costs are known, the sales revenue at the break even point is easily calculated with the help of the following formula:

$$\text{Break Even Sales} = \frac{\text{Fixed Costs}}{1 - \dfrac{\text{Variable Costs}}{\text{Sales Volume}}}$$

Sales revenue less, variable costs, is defined as *contribution*, and is often expressed as a percentage of selling price. Thus, the break even sales are:

$$\frac{\text{Fixed Costs}}{\text{Contribution}}$$

☞ Example

A wooden toy manufacturer sells his toys at an average price of ₹ 5 per piece. The variable costs incurred on the manufacture of each toy are ₹ 3 per piece and the fixed costs are ₹ 25,000 per year.

Contribution =

$$\text{Sales at Break Even Point} = ₹\,\frac{25,000}{0.40}$$

$$= ₹\ 62,500$$

The break even sales volume = 12,500 toys per year.

The unit should, therefore, sell at least 12,500 toys per year to break even. In practice, it may not be possible to make an exact estimate of the fixed and variable costs. However, by treating all expenses other than raw material costs as fixed costs, the appropriate breakeven point can be calculated.

☞ Example

A leather shoe (Brand O) is sold for ₹ 25 per pair. Material costs (consisting of raw materials and packing) are ₹ 15 per price and fixed costs are ₹ one lakh per year.

$$\text{Break Even Sales} = ₹ \frac{1,00,000}{1-\frac{15}{25}}$$

$$= ₹\ 2,50,000$$

$$\therefore \text{ Break Even Sales Volume} = \frac{2,50,000}{25} = 10,000 \text{ shoes per year}$$

The break even point is, therefore, reached when 10,000 shoes are sold per year.

The calculation of the break even point becomes a slightly more complicated exercise when a firm manufactures a number of products, each with a different contribution margin. In such cases, the weighted average of the contribution margin has to be calculated to find out the break even point.

☞ Example

A company manufactures four products L, M, N and P. The contribution margins of the four products are 40%, 30%, 35% and 50% (defined here as sales revenue, less material costs) respectively. The company expects to realise 50%, 25%, 15% and 10% respectively. The fixed costs are ₹ 10 lakh per year.

Weighted Average of Contribution Margin

$$= (0.40 \times 0.50) +$$
$$(0.30 \times 0.25) +$$
$$(0.35 \times 0.15) +$$
$$(0.50 \times 0.10) +$$
$$= 0.3775$$
$$\text{or } 37.75\%$$

$$\therefore \text{ Break Even Sales} = ₹ \frac{10,00,000}{0.3775}$$

$$= ₹\ 26.49 \text{ lakh per year.}$$

While studying the loan proposals of small-scale industrial units from different angles, the bank should not lose sight of two broad matters of policy. In the *first* place, advances to small-scale industrial units are in the national interest, and bank should, therefore, take a little more than normal risk in approving them. *Second*, if a loss occurs in any case, the Government shares it with the banker through the credit guarantee organisation. But this does not mean that highly risky and speculative proposals should be entertained.

☞ Advances to Priority Sectors

Extension of credit to small borrowers in the hitherto neglected sectors of the economy has been one of the major tasks assigned to the public sector banks into the post-nationalisation period. To achieve this objective, banks have drawn up schemes to extend credit to small borrowers in sectors like agriculture, small-scale industry, road and water transport, retail trade and small business, which traditionally had very little share in the credit extended by banks. Taking into account the need to provide resource requirements of weaker sections, for specific needs, consumption credit (with certain limits) has been included in priority sectors. Similarly, small housing loans (not exceeding ₹ 5,000) to scheduled castes/scheduled tribes and other weaker sections are also classified as priority sector advances. Number of borrowal accounts with the public sector banks for these categories of borrowers increased from 2.60 lakh to 3.55 lakh between June, 1969 to September, 1990. Amount outstanding during the sale period increased from ₹ 441 crore to ₹ 39,833 crore. Public sector banks accounted for 42.7 per cent of the total bank credit by Sept., 1990. The following table shows achievements of the public sector banks in stepping up flow of credit in various priority sectors.

Table 22.1

PUBLIC SECTOR BANKS ADVANCES TO PRIORITY SECTORS*

Sector	*Amount outstanding (₹ Crore)*						
	June 1969	**Dec. 1985**	**Dec. 1986**	**Dec. 1987**	**Dec. 1988**	**Dec. 1989**	**Sept. 1990**
1. Agriculture							
(*i*) Direct finance	188.40	7415.13	8929.97	10341.38	12072.04	14020.29	14897.35
(*ii*) Indirect finance	—	1378.32	1377.49	1963.47	1498.42	1401.01	1286.43
2. Small-scale Industry	285.90	7470.70	8607.08	10190.20	12234.79	14281.40	15373.02
3. Road and Water transport operators	8.20	1882.70	1958.62	2016.30	2166.05		
4. Professional and Self-employed persons	0.30	453.29	833.68	991.93	1012.17		
5. Retail Trade and Small Business	—	1721.50	2122.49	2599.54	3137.99	7643.01	8275.76
6. Education	0.50	32.68	35.85	45.56	55.15		
7. Housing	—	63.80	106.06	167.01	228.94		
8. Consumption	—	21.07	18.91	30.00	24.44		
9. Other Priority Sectors	—	8.61	18.13	95.18	142.45		
	483.30	20647.88	20085.28	27940.57	32662.14	37345.71	39832.56

*India, 1991, p. 380.

☞ Credit to Weaker Sections (Differential Rate of Interest — DRI — Scheme)

To increase credit flow to small and poor borrowers, weaker sections comprising of small and marginal farmers, landless labourers, tenant farmers and share croppers, artisans, village and cottage industries, beneficiaries of Integrated Rural Development Programme, Scheduled Castes and Schedules Tribes, a Differential Rate of Interest (DRI) scheme has been evolved. This scheme was slated to receive not less than 10 per cent of net bank credit by March 1985. By Sept. 1990, weaker sections had received ₹ 9,961 crore and accounted for 10.7 per cent of aggregate advances of public sector banks.

☞ Questions

1. Define a small-scale industrial unit. Describe the various ways in which commercial banks extend credit to such units and the special features relating to bank credit to this sector of the economy. *[C.A.I.I.B., Part II]*
2. (*a*) What is the definition of a small-scale industrial unit for purposes of eligibility under the Credit Guarantee Scheme for small-scale industries administered by the Reserve Bank of India.

A small-scale industrial unit may need various types of credit facilities from its banker, e.g., working capital advances, term loans, deferred payment guarantees, packing credit or pre-shipment credit, as also facilities for the issue of performance guarantees on its behalf and limits of the negotiation of export bills. Are all these facilities eligible for cover under the Credit Guarantee Scheme? What types of facilities are specifically excluded as not being eligible for cover under this scheme?

(b) The Credit Guarantee Corporation of India provides guarantees in respect of small loans to borrowers in the priority and neglected sectors under its small loans guarantee scheme. What are the special provisions of this scheme and the extent of cover provided in relation to credit facilities extended by banks to:

(i) Transport operators, and

(ii) Professionals and self-employed persons? *[C.A.I.I.B., Part II]*

3. What is the rationale underlying the provision of concessional rate of interest to agriculture, small industries and under DIR scheme? Discuss. *[I.I.B., Part II]*
4. It is argued that in India the commercial bank credit has largely benefited large and medium industries and in the agricultural sector, large and medium farmers. Do you agree? Have any steps been taken recently to promote a more even distribution of credit? *[I.I.B., Part II]*
5. Write short notes on:

   (i) Differential Rates of Interest on Advances.

   (ii) Credit Guarantee Corporation of India. *[C.A.I.I.B., Part II]*
6. Write short notes:

   (i) Priority sector advances.

   (ii) Lead Bank Scheme. *[I.I.B., Part II]*
7. What is a small-scale unit? What are the credit facilities available to small-scale industry?
8. *(a)* What is the definition of small-scale industrial unit for purposes of eligibility under the Credit Guarantee Scheme for small-scale industries administered by the Reserve Bank of India? In what respect has the definition been recently revised?

   (b) You have granted the following limits to a firm of Construction Contractors and a firm of Engineering Consultants respectively.

   Firm of Construction Contractors: Limit of ₹ 75,000 for issuing performance guarantees in favour of Government department for due completion of contracts.

   Firm of Engineering Consultants: Limit of ₹ 60,000 by way of overdraft against the hypothecation of furniture and fixtures including the office car. State whether the above limits would be covered by the Credit Guarantee Scheme. *[I.I.B., Part II]*
9. An individual applies to you, as a Branch Manager, for a loan of ₹ 4,000 for the purchase of an autorickshaw. He wishes to ply the vehicle as a taxi. What precautions would you take before and after disbursement of the loan amount? What documents would you obtain for the purpose?

   After six months, if he defaults in the payment of monthly instalments and also does not respond to your letters of demand, what steps would you take to recover the Bank's dues?
10. Write short notes on:

    (i) Advances to neglected sectors. *[I.I.B., Part II]*

    (ii) Guarantee Scheme for Small-scale industries. *[I.I.B., Part II]*
11. A shoemaker in a village, who has mastered his art, approaches your bank for a loan of ₹ 1,000 for earning his livelihood. What points and factors will you take into account for granting the loan? What documents would you take from him? *[I.I.B., Part I]*
12. Will you, as a Branch Manager, entertain applications for loan from the following? If so what precautions will you take in each case?

14. A person from an urban area approaches a bank for a loan of ₹ 30,000 to set up a laundry unit. His requirements are stated to be ₹ 21,000 for furniture, ironing tools, washing machines, renovation of premises, etc., and ₹ 9,000 recurring expenses per month on washing materials, electricity bills, rent, labour charges, etc. He expects gross income of ₹ 500 per day. How will you process the proposal and arrive at final terms.
[I.I.B., Part I]
15. A transport firm consisting of three partners is doing transport business for the last three years. The firm has borrowed ₹ 1,50,000 against hypothecation of two trucks from another bank. Present outstanding is ₹ 1,00,000. The firm wants to purchase a new Telco truck. Its present bank refuses to grant further advance. The firm approaches you for a loan of ₹ 1,00,000. Would you agree to grant the advance? If so what precautions and what documents would you take?
[I.I.B., Part I]
16. Write short notes on:
    (a) Integrated Rural Development Programmes (IRDP)
    (b) Self-employment Scheme for urban poor. *[I.I.B., Part I]*
    (c) Service Area Approach in Rural lending. *[I.I.B., Part I]*
17. Over the past one-and-a-half decades, commercial banking in India has undergone a great deal of change both in outlook and in operations, with major thrust on the supplementary socio-economic programmes of the Govt. Please discuss in relation to any two of the following:
    (a) Integrated Rural Development Programme (IRDP).
    (b) Scheme for providing Self-employment to Educated Unemployed Youth (SEEUY).
    (c) Self-employment Programmes for Urban Poor (SEPUP). *[I.I.B. Part I]*
18. An old and valued customer of your branch maintains an average balance of ₹ 15,000 in his savings bank account with you for the last five years. He informs you that his son who has passed his B.E. degree in India has got admission for higher studies in USA. Total expenses for the course of two years would be ₹ 1.25 lakh. He requests for a loan of ₹ 1,00,000 to be disbursed in four instalments. He is agreeable to mortgage his flat worth ₹ 6 lakh as security. What formulations would you observe if your bank decides to sanction the loan?
[I.I.B., Part I]

CHAPTER 23 Electronic Banking and Internet Banking

The information technology has revolutionised various aspects of our life. The world at large is rapidly entering into the 'Net Age'. Internet or simply 'Net' is an interconnection of computer communication networks covering the whole world. The growth and expansion of Internet and Information Technology have facilitated the emergence of e-commerce.

E-commeree essentially is the paperless exchange of business information spread through computer devices like Electronic Data Interchange, e-mail, Electronic Bulletin Boards — in short the tools such as Internet, Intranet and Extranets created under the network-based technologies. Thus, e-commerce in today's context is a commercial transaction routed through Internet.

When the business and commerce tend to be on the electronic modes, banking can never remain isolated. When e-commerce refers to carrying on business transactions electronically, it covers any form of business including banking. Hence, e-banking implies performing basic banking transactions by customers round the clock globally through Electronic Media. Modern banking is more information based, speedy and boundary less due to the impact of e-revolution. Modern banks have to be well-versed in Information Technology–its users and applications. Banking divisions have to be IT-based, with the spread of digital economy. E-banking is more of a science than art. E-banking is knowledge-based and mostly scientific in using electronic devices of the computer revolution. When most business and commercial enterprises tend to become internet working organisations, banking has to be e-banking in the new century.

Today's banking is virtual Banking. Virtual banking denotes the provision of banking and other related services through the extensive use of IT, without direct resource to the bank by customers. The salient features of virtual banking are the overwhelming reliance on IT and the absence of physical bank branches to deliver banking services to customers. The rincipal types of virtual banking services include Automated Teller Machines (ATMs), shared ATM networks. Electronic Funds Transfer at point of sale (EFTPoS), smart cards, stored value cards, phone banking, home banking, internet and intranet banking. Thus, the practice of banking has undergone a significant transformation due to the adoption of e-banking.

☞ Traditional Banking vs. E-banking

In traditional banking, the customer has to visit the branch of the bank in person to perform the basic banking operations, *viz.,* account enquiry, funds transfer, cash withdrawals, etc. The brick and mortar structure of a bank is essential to perform the banking functions.

On the other hand, e-banking enables the customers to perform the basic banking transactions by sitting at their office or at homes through PC or LAPTOP. The customers can access the banks website for viewing their account details and perform the transactions on account as per their requirements. With e-banking, the brick and mortar structure of the traditional banking gets converted into a click and portal model, thereby giving a concept of virtual banking a real shape. Thus, today's banking is no longer confined to branches. Customers are being provided with additional delivery channels which are more convenient to customers and are cost-effective to the banks. These delivery channels include ATM, Tele Banking, Internet Banking, Mobile Banking, Home Banking, etc. Thus, e-banking facilitates banking transactions by customers round-the, clock globally.

Conventional banking is an art. But, e-banking is more of a science than art. e-banking is knowledge-based and mostly scientific in using the electronic devices of the computer revolution. When most corporates tend to become internet working organisations, banking has to be e-banking in the new century.

☞ Facets of E-banking

As said earlier, E-banking means the conduct of banking electronically. It calls for elimination of paper-based transactions and radical change in the banking operations. E-banking will operate through internet, extranet and intranet. E-banking is therefore a banking on the information superhigh-ways on the frontier of the Internet.

E-Banking must have at least the following dimensions:

(i) Customer-to-bank e-banking (EB)

(ii) Bank-to-bank e-banking

(iii) Electronic Central Banking

(iv) Intranet Procurement.

☞ Customer-to-bank E-banking

E-banking is basically Internet-based. Banking products and services such as deposits, remittances, credit cards, etc., as well as all important banking informations can be made available with easy access to customers on Internet. Customers can make use of these services with no restricted office hours, no queues, no tellers and no waiting. Several Network innovations for e-banking can be visualised such as smart card, Electronic Data Interchange, etc. Of course, the banking operations have to be guarded against unauthorised access by intruders.

☞ Bank-to-bank E-banking

This form of electronic banking is for transacting inter-bank transactions such as money-at-call, etc. This type of e-banking is driving extranets, which is restricted to banks only. Hence, it is well secured and unauthorised access is less.

☞ Electronic Central Banking

Under this E-central banking all banks within the purview of a central bank are interconnected on extranet to facilitate clearing of cheques, management of cash reserves, open market operations, discounting of bills etc. In fact, the central bank has to be connected with the Government treasury on extranet to carry out its functions as an agent of the Government. Again, the central banks of all countries can be inter-linked with the IMF. World Bank and other international financial institutions through extranets.

☞ Intranet Procurement

For the transactions that are internal to a bank, between the bank and its branches and subsidiaries, Intranet procurements of banking is required. On the other hand, extranet permits a bank to have full control over the users of intranet and the information to be transmitted.

The extranet-intranet-internet relationship that exists in the process of e-banking is presented in the following figure:

Figure showing Micro Model of e-banking

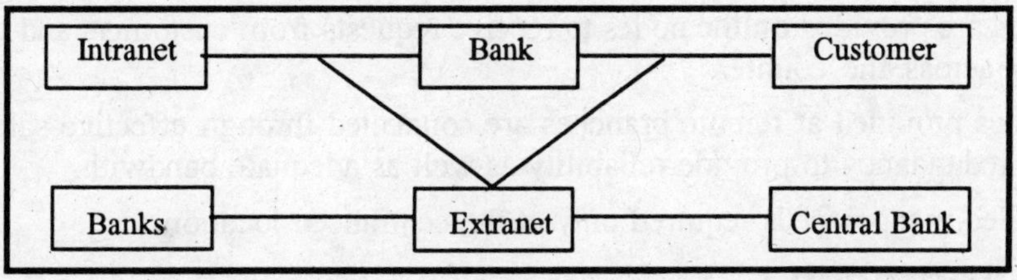

Extensive work is required to integrate internal and external communication of banking-related information through banking internet and intranet for the development of the financial sector.

☞ E-banking Transactions

Though any type of transactions can be handled through e-banking, in the initial phase most of the basic banking transactions can be performed conveniently through internet banking. The following are some of the basic functions:

- Account Enquiry
- Fund transfer
- Payment of Electricity
- Water, Telephone bills etc.
- Online payment for transactions actually performed through Internet
- Request for issuance of cheque book, draft etc.
- Statement of Accounts
- Access to latest schemes
- Access to rates of interest and other service charges.

☞ Models for e-banking

To implement effectively E-banking and augment the level of technology the following models have been suggested:

(i) Complete Centralised Solution (CCS)

(ii) Cluster Approach

(iii) High tech Bank within Bank.

☞ Complete Centralised Solution

This is an ideal branch network model on which e-banking activities can be implemented uniformly and efficiently. Under this model, the bank has to provide web-server and the requisite software which is connected to the main server. Once the required hardware and software are set in, the customers can access the web-server for their basic banking operations using any standard browser at any location.

☞ Features of CCS

The following are the features of complete centralised solution:

(i) The entire system software, data for the entire bank, etc., are stored in a centralised server with its hot standby server being placed at different location, and connected through high speed and efficient network.

(ii) Branches are provided online nodes to receive requests from customers and to provide them services across the counter.

(iii) The nodes provided at remote branches are connected through effective satellite links with enough redundancy to provide reliability as well as adequate bandwith.

(iv) The skilled manpower is required only at the centralised location.

☞ Cluster Approach

Under this model, computerised branches of each city are connected with regional Processor located at each such city which are then connected through reliable media to a centralised high end server. Under this approach, it is necessary that an integrated computerisation is available at all branches so that connectivity amongst various branches can be established through regional clusters. Most of the branches are computerised in an integrated way through Network/Unix Server.

Features: The following are the important features of the cluster approach:

(i) The entire branch network of the bank should be computerised through integrated software.

(ii) All these branches should be interconnected with regional servers through reliable network media.

☞ High-tech Bank within Bank

Under this model, complete computerisation of all branches is avoided. Within each bank, two different types of banks would function concurrently, *viz.*, High-tech Bank providing e-banking facilities through select branches and traditional bank offering traditional services through other branches. This approach enables the banks to play a balanced role to offer state-of-the-art service to ever demanding customers of major cities and simultaneously continue to offer traditional personalised services to the mass customers who still dominate the balancing scene.

Features: The following are the features of High-tech Bank within Bank:

(i) Out of the entire branch network of the bank, only certain branches are selected to offer e-banking depending upon the customer's needs, business potential, infrastructure facilities available etc.

(ii) The accounts of all the customers in those branches should be automated under a centralised system offering various electronic channels including internet banking.

(iii) The high network customers may be encouraged to use e-banking; services through these selected branches.

(iv) It would not impose any technological burden on customers who do not want to enjoy e-banking services.

(v) The banks could get a gestation period to cover more branches under the umbrella of High-tech Bank in a phased manner.

☞ Advantages of e-banking

E-Banking has the following advantages:

(i) Round-the-clock Banking

E-banking facilitates performing of basic banking transactions by customers round-the-clock globally. Worldwide 24 hours and 7 days a week banking services are made possible. In fact, there are no restricted office hours for e-banking.

(ii) Convenient Banking

E-banking increases the customers' convenience. No personal visit to the branch is required. Customers can perform basic banking transactions by simply sitting at their office or at home through PC or LAPTOP. Customers can get drafts at their door steps through e-mail call. Thus, E-banking facilitates home banking.

(iii) Low Cost Banking (Service)

The operational costs have come down due to technology adoption. The cost of transactions through internet banking is much less than any other traditional mode.

(iv) Profitable Banking

The increased speed of response to customer requirements under e-banking *vis-a-vis* branch banking can enhance customer satisfaction and, consequently can lead to higher profits via handling a larger number of customer accounts. Banks can also offer many cash management products for the existing customers without any additional cost.

(v) Low Cost Banking (Establishment)

Brick and mortar structure of banking gets converted into click and portal banking. Banks can have access to a greater number of potential customers without the commitment costs of physically opening branches. Hence, there is much saving on the cost of infrastructure. Moreover, requirements of staff at the banks get reduced to a greater extent.

(vi) Quality Banking

E-banking opens new vistas for providing efficient, economic and quality service to the customers. E-banking allows the possibility of improved quality and an enlarged range of services being made available to customers.

(vii) Speed Banking

The increased speed of response to customer requirements under e-banking will lead to greater customer satisfaction and handling a larger number of transactions at a lesser time. Thus, it increases the customers' convenience to a greater extent and facilitates better customer retention.

(viii) Service Banking

E-banking creates strong basic infrastructure for the banks to embark upon many cash management products and to venture in the new fields like e-commerce, EDI, etc. Instant credit, one day credit, immediate payment of utility bills, instant transfer of funds, etc., would be made possible under E-banking. In brief, it adds conveniences to the entire banking services apart from widening the range of services.

CONSTRAINTS IN E-BANKING

With the obvious benefits emerging out of e-banking mentioned above, the following factors contribute as major impediments in the smooth implementation of e-banking:

(i) Start-up Cost

Many banks have expressed their concern about the huge initial start-up cost for venturing into e-banking. The start-up cost includes:

(a) The connection cost to the internet or any other mode of electronic communication. The network should be robust, secured, efficient and scalable with inbuilt redundancy.

(b) The cost of sophisticated hardware, software and other related components including Modem, Routers, Bridges, Network Management System, etc.

(c) The cost of maintenance of all equipments, websites, skill level of employees, etc.

(d) The cost of setting up organisational activities to implement e-banking.

For a successful E-Banking, bankers need to develop a coherent perspective of the role of network technologies and advancement of their EFT-departments with a competitive introspection of their banking business.

(ii) Training and Maintenance

The introduction of e-banking involves 24 hours support environment, quality service to end-users and other partners which would necessitate a well qualified and robust group of skilled people to meet external and internal commitments. Hence, the bank has to spend a lot on training. What is more important is their retention in the organisation after necessary training. Moreover, the bank has to outsource certain functions and services to maintain the level of standards and state of readiness. The training and retaining of skilled manpower is a major cause of concern.

(iii) Lack of Skilled Personnel

It is a well-known fact that there is an acute scarcity of web developers, content providers and knowledgeable professionals to route banking trans-actions through internet. In a fast changing technological scenario, the obsolescence of technology is fast and hence there is always shortage of skilled personnel.

(iv) Security

In paperless banking transaction, many problems of security are involved. A security threat is defined as a circumstansive decision or event with potential to cause economic hardship to data or network resources in the form of destruction, disclosure, modification of data, denial of services, fraud, waste and abuse. There are chances that documents such as cheque, pass book, etc., can be modified without leaving any visible trace. Distortion of informations are also possible. Providing appropriate security may require a major initial investments in the form of application encryption techniques, implementation of firewalls etc. In spite of implementation of several security measures, the possibility of a security breach cannot be ruled out.

(v) Legal Issues

Legal framework for recognising the validity of banking transactions conducted through the 'Net' is still being put in place. Though initial legal framework has been devised for e-banking activities, it is uncertain as to what possible legal issues may pop up in future as banking on internet progresses. What may happen if a customer's sensitive data falls into the hands of a stranger or if his account shows a 'Nil' balance all in a sudden without his knowledge? The legal issues should cover unauthorised access, and unauthorised modification of data, wrongful communication, punishment to be meted out to combat computer crimes. To prevent computer crimes, the country's banking legislation needs to make suitable provisions with a thorough consultation and discussion among the legal as well as technical experts.

(vi) Restricted Clientele and Technical Problems

The user of e-banking needs a computer and time to log on to the site. It means that the target clientele is restricted to those who have a home PC or can access the 'Net' through the office or cybercafes. Moreover, phone connections are not always perfect and, on a home PC, the modem connection often breaks off, requiring another teditious log-on. Navigating around websites on home computers is often slow and frustrating. Moreover, local calls are not free generally and so the customer has to pay everytime he checks his balance.

(vii) Restricted Business

Not all transactions can be carried out electronically. Many deposits and some withdrawals require the use of postal services. Some banks have automated their front-end process for the customers, but still largely depend upon manual processes at the back-end. For example, the internet customers receive their statements online, but paper statements are also sent by mail. Mail and distribution costs are still necessary as the statements, cheques, etc., are still mailed.

(viii) Destruction of Pricing Mechanism

The internet may also destroy the basic business pricing models. The internet creates perfect market conditions where prospective consumers have access to more information and can more readily compare rates and financial products offerings. Now players in the field have lower costs than old banks. Hence, they can undercut the prices and provide stiff competition to established banks.

Moreover, banks marketing programmes and products are generally based on product or physical location. The web allows customers to easily compare all the products and their prices and sign-up for the products irrespective of location.

☛ Security Measures

Most of the problems mentioned above are in the nature of teething problems and hence they can be eliminated over a period of time. However, for venturing into e-banking, the following major controls must be ensured:

- Authenticity controls : to verify identity to individuals like password, PIN, etc.
- Accuracy controls : to ensure the correctness of the data flowing across the network.
- Completeness controls : to make sure that no data is missing.
- Redundancy controls : to see that data is travelled and processed only once and there is no repetitive sending of data.
- Privacy controls : to protect the data from inadvertent or unauthorised access.

- Audit trial controls : to ensure keeping chronological role of events that are occurred in the system.
- Existence controls : to make sure that ongoing availability of all the system resources is the same throughout.
- Efficient controls : to ensure that the system uses minimum resources to achieve the desired goal.
- Fire wall controls : to prevent unauthorised users accessing the private network which are connected to internet.
- Encryption controls : to enable only those who possess secret key to decrypt the cyber text.

E-banking is becoming immensely popular globally and India is no exception to it. The declining Internet rates, falling PC prices, broad bandwith access through cable and digital subscriber lines, accessing the NET through cable TV, etc., would definitely encourage the boom in e-banking in India. With the globalisation of business and services, our country cannot lag behind in niche areas of electronic banking. In the new global era of multi-currency, multi-legal and multiple regulatory systems, with the freedom of e-commerce, banks have to operate like multinational corporations to grow and survive by adopting e-banking.

INTERNET BANKING: ONLINE BANKING SERVICES

In this era of IT revolution, the NET is the future and the value-added services are increasingly used in the competitive banking world. The internet has already demonstrated in the West as to how effective it could be in the financial services industry. It has permanently altered the way the customers perceive service, how it is delivered, and the profit it can generate to the service providers. Financial Sector will be among the industries most profoundly benefited by the internet services, since the distribution of financial products doesn't require any physical exchange of goods. However, on account of internal and external constraints, the Indian banks have fallen far behind themselves in this area. The accomplishment of this task requires them to urgently and radically restructure their business model and strategies. Analysts predict that the Web would become the primary customer deliver channel in the near future and financial sector should recognize its significance in the coming years.

Internet banking may put an end to the usage of calculator and paper-based bank statements/bulky ledgers, thereby leading to greater savings in paper, postage and time. Internet services enable checking account statements and incorporate add-on features like 'funds transfer'. With their built-in security, accountability, low cost and efficiency, they are all set to replace the money in its conventional sense of trading. Apart from personal banking, there are a variety of organizations providing to the corporates the services such as-trade services, cash management, credit services, loans, etc. Providing these services online would definitely prove to be a boon to corporates, as also cost-effective for organization. Internet banking offers the lowest transaction cost among all the conventional electronic delivery channels including ATMs. A tech savvy bank customer can better manage his/her funds and payments than before. Most importantly, the customer will get all the financial data all the time, *i.e.,* 24 × 7 × 365. Anytime anywhere access to Internet Banking doesn't really need to be a bank. It can even be a group of innovative persons with no bank branch at all, just working through alliances and leading the field because of their superior capabilities through focus and innovation advantage.

☞ How to do Internet Banking

Customer submits a filled application form to the Bank either on-line or at its branch. The Bank will send customer a unique password for accessing to their WEB server. Customer through his PC and modem browses either with Netscape Navigator or Microsoft Internet explorer to the Bank site on entering his password for starting his financial activities. For example, ICICI Bank launched online banking INFINITY in October 1997, that provides remote banking facilities information such as account details, statement of account, allows various deposit options and funds transfer between two accounts. In Citibank, customers who logon to the bank's site can view/print their account balances and statements, order cheque books, transfer of funds and even pay bills for Electricity/Telephone. In IndusInd Bank and IDBI Bank, around 8,000/10,000 customers are availing this type of facility.

☞ Internet Banking and Strategic Implications

Internet banking would drive us into a new era. Established practices and procedures have undergone changes drastically. This is bound to change the nature of relationships of banks with their customers: Customers' supremacy will be a reality; customers would be no longer dependent on dedicated systems for each banking relationship. There would be increasing access to low cost electronic service and close integration of bank services with web-based E-Commerce services through direct electronic payments (E-cash). For performing international transactions, internet is more convenient due to lower switching cost, low prices that eliminate geographic boundaries. It would offer the opportunity of a new paradigm to the customers, both corporate and retail. All traditional channels would not die down in a day and indeed success would depend on how the banks generate synergy in these two vastly different channels.

Check points of Customer: Customers should ascertain the following:

(a) Whether the Banks provide online access or does it only offer electronic payment of bills.

(b) What type of online security it offers.

(c) Can you get electronic statement both in print and download formats.

(d) Can you transfer funds between two or more accounts?

(e) What are the freebies: toll-free number, online support, software support, stock quotes, newsletters and so on.

☞ Security aspect

Authentication: In the currently adopted traditional way of transaction being used in the banks, the only validity of the transaction is the 'Ink Signature' of the customer. But, how can an internet Transaction get validated? The answer is the Digital Signature. Each customer can be provided with Digital IDs. A transaction via his account can be done through this ID only (for the customers to access their accounts or sends payment instructions). It is not like a password that you generally use to get access into website or any other protected information. The strength of a digital ID is that it is available only with the customer and it is not available to the server (as is the case when you use a password). So, there is no chance that anyone gets this ID unless he himself discloses it to any one. This Digital Id is in an encrypted form, which gives maximum security by coding all the information as it travels over the Internet. Every time customer has to enter his ID (PIN) for connecting the bank, which provides better level of security in the transaction.

Secure the Website: The website needs to be certified by means of a Web Server Certificate which is available from and can be provided by only a globally accepted, and a reputed certified authority. Not only does a web server certificate provide organization with a globally trusted identity on the World Wide Web, but it also means that any information that rests on the server or is passed to and fro to this server over the Internet would remain secured thereby safeguarding the customers' information and taking care of his/her prime concern of security. Organization can secure web servers by means of 128 bit SSL web server certificates. This would thus enable your customers a safe, secure and a trusted means of transacting the web. Many organisations are using Digital certificate technology, *e.g.,* VeriSign.

Privacy: In order to access that only 'right person' for accessing data, 124 bit RSA, SSL and RCS technologies along with triple DES encryption are used while communicating. This encryption system is from RSA data security. From the customer system Data packets sends to Bank's server, which prevents people from snooping on a network connection and viewing information while in transit. Financial software programs enables with password features also.

Integrity: Message integrity is provided by SSL and RCS security technology so that the message received has not been altered after it left the sender.

Transaction Confirmation: All banks and software vendors provide a "special feature" that displays a list of instructions to be sent to the bank before going online and provide a record of all completed transactions.

How Banker Trusts the Customer: The digital IDs keep track of the transactions and bind the account holder for what he has transacted. It provides the authentication about the trustworthiness of the customer. This reduces the chances of frauds.

☞ Hurdles

1. Many people fear the technology and would rather let the banker's Teller or assistant do the needful.
2. Low density of telephone lines, power failures and computers in India, the process is slowed down.
3. Out of 65,000 branches in India only 9,000 are computerized.
4. Net banking on the assumption that it is more expensive than traditional method.
5. There are people tech-no-haters who do not want to do anything on the Net.
6. Banks would have to manage different product portfolios, at different yet competitive prices to different Corporates across the world.
7. The entry of multiple non-financial institutions and other non-traditional players would just fasten this whole process.

Key Aspects: Whatever be the strategy chosen and option adopted, certain key parameters would determine the Banks success on the Web technology:

(a) Adopting a web's mindset.

(b) Catching on the First Mover's advantage

(c) Recognizing the core competencies

(d) Ability to deal multiplicity with simplicity

(e) Senior management initiative to transform the organization from inward to outward looking.

(f) Aligning roles and value propositions with the customer segments

(g) Redesigning optimal channel portfolio

(h) Acquiring new capabilities through strategic alliances.

Indian Scenario: Throughout the country, the internet banking market is in the infant stages of development. Only 56 banks are currently offering any kind of internet banking services. In general, these internet sites offer only the most basic services. 55% are so-called "entry level" sites, offering little more than company information and basic marketing materials. Only 8% offer "advanced" transactional services, such as online funds transfer, transactions and cash management services. In general, the foreign and private banks are far ahead of Public Sector or Cooperative Banks in terms of the number of sites and their level of development. The private banks, with futuristic management and net-pro mindset seem all prepared to continue the pathfinder role in Indian internet banking. While the world has seen corporate banking as the first choice for net-bankers, India seems to be reversing the trend and most of the initial developments seem to be in retail banking area. Experts predict that the total number of users will touched 18 million in America by the year 2002. Indian banks are gearing up for retail banking in a big way. With world's second largest population and more than 5 million internet users, the number expected to grow at more than 200% in next two years, retail banking surely holds the key for India. Both prices and costs should come down as consumers migrate to online services. Operating efficiencies from online account servicing should reduce cost by 15-25% relative to regular accounts, but even greater savings are possible. *The customers would no longer be branch customers but rather the bank customers.* The unconventional net banks would try to lure the customers away from their current banks by offers like high deposit rates, which will lower overall net revenue for online accounts. Banks have to expand the range of their products and services offerings in internet. Apart from offering online accounts, the net-banks would have to tailor specific products for the internet, like online bill submission or credit cards with instant online approval, since today's value-added product could easily be tomorrow's commodity, success would depend more on product innovation than ever before.

These changes could prove to be ill for legacy banks that choose not to embrace new opportunities. Their asset base would diminish as customers would transfer accounts to banks that offer the convenience of online access, one-stop shopping, and better deposit rates. The profits would be squeezed and ultimately only those who would change to learn to change would survive. This because of the fact that multi-tiered distribution would be even more important in the future. Still, the notion that physical branches are an essential part of banking would be dispelled. Without the overhead of a bricks-and-mortar retail network, the operating costs would be greatly reduced and thus better pricing of services and products.

Banks must today at least hedge by experimenting with the web business model. But it calls for profound organizational changes if it is to be executed successfully. It needs banks to fundamentally reassess their opportunities for adding-value and hence redefine their roles in the new paradigm. Corporates realize how secure your customer and your organization can be by adapting to these tools for your online businesses.

Conclusion: Technological and market discontinuities are combining to generate rapid change and high uncertainty in banking. In such an environment, to apply the strategies of the past as a routine may be the riskiest option of all. The winners may not necessarily be traditional banks and the key to success would be the banks' readiness to change or adapt to fast changing customers' needs. Recognizing the core competencies and configuring value propositions would determine how well the bank faces this challenge? It is an opportunity for those who can harness the power of this technology to reduce costs and offset the squeeze of spreads by greater volume and new services. Those who would choose to ignore, and stay embedded within their old business models, would have bleak days ahead.

One must be well aware of the apparent benefits of online business in the banking industry — a trend that is fast catching on. Online business is most cost-effective and convenient, both to the bank as well as its customers. The need of the hour is to make the customer aware about the numerous benefits of online banking as also providing them the assurance of this being a very secure, trustworthy and satisfactory means of transacting their money.

The first thing the organization should do is to build trust and confidence among the customers. A trust that whatever information is shared by them with your organization during an online transaction would remain secure and confidential will generate confidence in adopting to this new, yet most practical and convenient way of banking. This trust and confidence in turn will lead to customer satisfaction which thereby would result into loyalty and this customer retention, needless to say would add to an increase in the business of the organization.

☞ Questions

Objective Type:

I. Fill up the blank with suitable word/words:

(a) .... refers to a banking transaction routed through internet.

(b) Banking without direct recourse to the bank is called................ banking.

(c) E-banking is basically .... based.

(d) Unauthorised users accessing the private network are prevented through .... controls.

(e) In paperless banking tr·· ɔaction, many problems of.............. are involved.

(a) E-Banking; *(b)* Virtual; *(c)* Internet; *(d)* Firewall; *(e)* Security.

II. Choose the best answer from the following:

(i) The important delivery channel of e-banking is:

(a) Home banking *(b)* Tele banking *(c)* Internet banking *(d)* Mobile banking

(ii) The click and portal model facilitates:

(a) Traditioral banking; *(b)* Paperless banking; *(b)* Virtual banking; *(d)* B and C together.

(iii) The biggest constraint in e-banking is:

(a) Start-up cost; *(b)* Maintenance cost; *(c)* Training cost; *(d)* Security cost.

[Ans: (i) C (ii) D (iii) A]

III. State whether the following statements are *True* or *False:*

(a) E-Banking facilitates paperless banking.

(b) 7 day banking is possible under traditional banking.

(c) Fire wall controls are used to prevent unauthorised users accessing the private network which are connected to Internet.

(d) Internet banking can be performed by accessing the NET through cable TV.

(e) Under High-tech. Bank model, the entire branch network of the bank is computerised.

[Ans: (a) True (b) False (c) True (d) True (e) False]

Short Answer Type:

(a) What is e-banking.

(b) Distinguish between Traditional banking and e-banking.

(c) Define virtual banking.

(d) List down the popular e-banking transactions.

(e) Explain in brief the Cluster Approach model for e-banking.

(f) "E-Banking involves many problems of security." — Discuss.

Essay Type:

(a) Discuss the features of e-banking and bring out its merits and constraints.

(b) Distinguish between conventional banking and e-banking and explain the various models for e-banking.

(c) Analyse the various issues involved in e-banking and suggest measures to overcome them.

PART - V

IMPORTANT TERMS, SHORT NOTES AND PRACTICAL PROBLEMS

Chapter 24

Important Terms

(1) A Bill of Exchange and Promissory Note

☞ Bill of Exchange

According to Section 5 of the Negotiable Instruments Act, *"a Bill of Exchange is an instrument in writing containing an unconditional order signed by the maker directing a certain person to pay a certain sum of money only, to, or to the order of, a certain person or to the bearer of the instrument".*

From this definition of a bill of exchange, it is obvious that, no condition shall be attached to it. But a promise or order to pay is not regarded as being conditional simply because the time for payment is expressed by reference to the occurrence of a specified event which is certain to occur, but which at the time could not be determined in advance, *e.g.,* by reference to death. The reference to an event which is not certain to occur (marriage of a certain person) would, however, involve a condition which would vitiate a bill of exchange.

The sum of money expressed in the bill of exchange must be certain, but that does not prevent the amount from being stated as inclusive of the amount of interest to be subsequently determined. The amount also is regarded as being "certain" even though it is expressed to be payable at a rate of exchange which will be determined subsequently.

A bill of exchange contains an order to pay; that is to say, a mere request to pay or the use of other polite words will not suffice. If a document, which purports to be a bill of exchange or a promissory note, fails to satisfy the necessary conditions, it can still be made use of as evidence of an ordinary contract, although it cannot be acted upon as a negotiable instrument. A bill of exchange or a promissory note payable to bearer on demand cannot be drawn.

☞ Promissory Note

According to Section 4 of the Indian Negotiable Instruments Act, *"a promissory note is an instrument in writing (Not being a bank note or a currency note) containing an unconditional undertaking, signed by the maker to pay a certain sum of money only to, or to the order of, a certain person, or to the bearer of the instrument".*

The main features of a promissory note are:

(i) There must be an undertaking to pay and not merely an acknowledgement of indebtedness. Therefore, an IOU is not a promissory note.

(ii) The promise to pay must be unconditional.

(iii) The promise must be to pay a specific sum of money.

(iv) The payee must be a definite person. The Reserve Bank of India or the Central Government cannot issue promissory notes payable to bearer.

(v) The promise to pay must be in writing, not verbal.

(vi) The instrument must be signed by the maker.

In the case of a promissory note, presentation for acceptance is not needed. A promissory note is payable on demand and not at any specified place; presentation is not necessary for fixing the liability on the maker because it is the duty of a debtor to seek out his creditor. However, in the following cases the presentation of a promissory note is necessary:

(a) When a promissory note is payable after a certain period after sight, it must be presented within a reasonable time and during business hours on a business day. (Section 64)

(b) A promissory note must be presented for payment, if it is a demand note, within a reasonable time, after it has been received by the holder, and in other cases within a reasonable time after maturity. (Section 74). Any delay in the presentation owing to unavoidable causes can be condoned. (Section 75)

(c) A promissory note which is payable in instalments must be presented on the due dates of instalments. (Section 67)

(d) A promissory note which is payable at a specified place must be presented for payment at that place. (Section 67)

☞ Differences Between a Bill of Exchange and Promissory Note

(a) A bill of exchange contains an order to pay, whereas a promissory note contains a promise to pay.

(b) In the case of a bill of exchange, the primary liability is that of the drawee after he has accepted the bill; the drawer's liability is secondary. In the case of a promissory note, the primary liability is that of the maker who signs the note.

(c) A bill can be drawn payable to bearer, provided it is not payable on demand. A promissory note cannot be made payable to bearer.

(d) In the case of a promissory note, the security for acceptance does not arise since the maker of the note is already liable upon it.

(e) Bill of exchange are sometimes drawn in sets; the position is not the same in the case of a promissory note.

(i) There must be an undertaking to pay and not merely an acknowledgement of indebtedness. Therefore, an IOU is not a promissory note.

(ii) The promise to pay must be unconditional.

(iii) The promise must be to pay a specific sum of money.

(iv) The payee must be a definite person. The Reserve Bank of India or the Central Government cannot issue promissory notes payable to bearer.

(v) The promise to pay must be in writing, not verbal.

(vi) The instrument must be signed by the maker.

In the case of a promissory note, presentation for acceptance is not needed. A promissory note is payable on demand and not at any specified place; presentation is not necessary for fixing the liability on the maker because it is the duty of a debtor to seek out his creditor. However, in the following cases the presentation of a promissory note is necessary.

(a) When the promissory note is payable after a certain period, it must be presented within a reasonable time and during business hours on a business day. (Section 64)

(b) A promissory note must be presented for payment, if it is a demand note, within a reasonable time, after it has been received by the holder, and in other cases within a reasonable time after maturity. (Section 74). Any delay in the presentation owing to unavoidable causes can be condoned. (Section 75)

(c) A promissory note which is payable in instalments must be presented on the due dates of instalments. (Section 67)

(d) A promissory note which is payable at a specified place must be presented for payment at that place. (Section 67)

(2) Cheque and Bill of Exchange

A cheque is a bill of exchange drawn on a specified bank and not expressed to be payable otherwise than on demand (Section 6, Negotiable Instruments Act). That is to say, it is a bill drawn on a banker and is payable on demand.

A bill of exchange is an instrument in writing containing an unconditional order signed by the maker, directing a certain person to pay a certain sum of money only to, or to the order of, a certain person, or to the bearer of the instrument. (Section 5, Negotiable Instruments Act).

☞ Essentials of a Cheque

(a) Instrument in Writing: A cheque must be an instrument in writing.

(b) Unconditional Order: A cheque must contain an unconditional order. It is not necessary that the word order or its equivalent must be used in the cheque. Generally, the order to a bank is expressed by the word pay.

(c) On a Specified Banker only: A cheque must be drawn on a specified bank. In other words, it should be drawn on a bank and not on any other person, and that the name of the bank should be specified, so as to avoid any mistake regarding the person or institution from whom or from which the payment of the cheque is to be demanded.

(d) Specified Sum of Money: A cheque must be an order to pay only a specified sum of money. In other words, the sum of money to be paid must be certain.

(e) Payable on Demand: A cheque must be an order to pay a certain sum of money on demand. It is not necessary that the words "on demand" or their equivalent should be used. When the drawer of an instrument asks the drawee to pay and does not specify the time for its payment, the instrument, according to Section 19 of the Negotiable Instruments Act, is payable on demand.

☞ Differences Between a Bill of Exchange and a Cheque

(i) In the case of a bill of exchange, the drawee may be any person, whereas in the case of a cheque, the drawee, *i.e.*, the person on whom the bill is drawn, must always be a banker.

(ii) A cheque is, as a rule, payable on demand and no days of grace are allowed.

(iii) In the case of a bill, notice of dishonour is usually required, whereas in the case of dishonour of a cheque, notice of dishonour is not necessary.

(iv) A bill cannot be drawn to bearer if it is made payable on demand, whereas a cheque can be drawn to bearer and made payable on demand.

(v) In the case of bills, presentation is sometimes required for acceptance, and it is always advisable to present them for acceptance even when it is not essential to do so. In the case of a cheque, it is not necessary to present it for acceptance.

(vi) Bills must be stamped according to law. Cheques are not required to be stamped in India. In several countries, cheques also are required to be stamped.

(3) Indemnity and Guarantee

☞ Contract of Indemnity

Section 124 of the Indian Contract Act, 1872, defines a contract of indemnity as, *"a contract by which one party promises to save the other from loss caused to him by the conduct of any other person"*.

☞ Contract of Guarantee

According to Section 126 of the Indian Contract Act, a contract of guarantee is, *"a contract to perform the promises, or discharge the liability, of a third person in case of his default"*.

The person who gives the guarantee is called the *surety*; the person in respect of whose default the guarantee is given is called the *principal debtor;* and the person to whom the guarantee is given is called the *creditor*. A guarantee may be either oral or written.

☞ Differences Between a Contract of Indemnity and a Guarantee

(a) In the case of a contract of guarantee, there are three parties, *viz.,*

(i) The surety or guarantor;

(ii) The principal debtor; and

(iii) The creditor.

In the case of a contract of indemnity, there are only two parties, *viz.,*

(i) The promisor; and

(ii) The party to be indemnified or insured.

In the case of indemnity contracts, the promisor undertakes to indemnify or make good the loss of the other party in certain circumstances. All the contracts of insurance are indemnity contracts.

(b) It will be seen, therefore, that in the case of a guarantee, the primary responsibility lies on the principal debtor and the surety's obligation depends substantially on the default of the principal debtor.

(c) The liability of the indemnifier is primary, whereas that of the surety is secondary.

(d) An indemnity contract comes into effect on the happening of a contingency, or the possibility of risk or loss. In the case of a contract of guarantee, there is an existing debt or duty which is guaranteed.

(e) In the case of an indemnity, the loss falls on indemnifier, except in certain special cases. In a guarantee, after discharge, the surety can proceed against the principal debtor.

(*f*) The indemnifier cannot sue in the transaction apart from the indemnity. In the guarantee contract, apart from the guarantee, the surety has no other interest in the transaction. This test is applied to find out whether a particular contract is a contract of indemnity or a contract of guarantee.

(*g*) The indemnifier has interest in his own right unless there is an agreement, but must bring the suit in the name of the indemnified, unless there is an assignment. In a guarantee contract, the surety, after payment, is entitled to file a suit in his own right against the principal debtor.

It is necessary that the contracts of indemnity and guarantee should be supported by considerations like all other simple contracts. It will be considered sufficient consideration if anything is done or promised by the creditor for the benefit of the principal debtor, surety or any other person. It may be noted here that the guarantor is *"collaterally liable"*, and, therefore, if he pays the debt, the principal debtor is not released from his liability. The guarantor steps in the place of the creditor.

☞ Precautions to be Taken by a Banker (in Accepting a Guarantee)

The banker should never accept the guarantee of minor or of a lunatic because contracts with such persons are void. Although married women can give a valid guarantee which will bind their separate property (*Stridhan*), a banker should avoid such guarantee because, to evade liability a married woman may plead that, when she signed the contract, she acted under the coercion or under an undue influence of her husband, particularly when he himself or a relative or a friend of his, happens to be the principal debtor. A banker should take great precaution in accepting the guarantee of registered companies and should carefully scrutinise the power of the company as stated in the Memorandum and Articles of its Association. When a partnership firm is standing as a surety, all the partners must join, unless the giving of a guarantee is part of the partnership business, or all the copartners should definitely authorise one particular partner to sign a particular guarantee. The banker should take care to see to it that the authority given by the copartners is in writing.

(4) D/A Bills and D/P Bills

A letter of credit is a document or order by a banker in one place, authorising some other bankers, acting as his agent or correspondent in another place, to honour the cheques of a person, named in the document, up to the amount stated in the letter, and charge the total amount of the drafts so honoured, or payments so made, to the guarantor of the letter of credit. The particular of the drafts or cheques, drawn by the specific person against the credit are required to be endorsed on the back of the letter of credit so that it will be easy to find out how much of the credit allowed has been utilised, and how much is outstanding.

The letters of credit are of various types, but all of them may be divided into two categories, *viz.*, (*i*) personal credit letters or travellers' facility letters, and (*ii*) letters for commercial credit. *Personal credit letters* aim at facilitating travellers or others temporarily resident in another country by allowing them to make use of the branch offices or agencies of the bank concerned for the purpose of obtaining such cash as they may require in the course of their travel or residence at these places by drawing cheques upon these branch offices or agencies.

Letters of commercial credit are letters of credit used for the purpose of financing shipments of goods imported or exported from a country or for the movement of produce or manufactured goods from one place to another in the country itself. In other words, this type of letters of credit is used to finance trading activities. A person, willing to open such a credit, approaches a banker with a request for a letter addressed to another person in a different city or country from whom he expects shipments or goods on credit. The total amount of such credit is settled with the banker and the requisite security is given to the latter's satisfaction, the banker, on his part, by giving the said letter of credit, authorizes the other party which is to make the shipment to draw bills of exchange on him according to the tender and up to the amount mentioned in the said letter, which the banker giving the letter agrees to accept, provided that they are drawn strictly in accordance with the terms and stipulation in the letter of credit. It is generally stipulated in the said letter that the credit has to be made use of within the period stated in it, which is usually six months. If the banker undertakes to accept bills drawn in accordance with such a letter without conditions, the document is called an open or clean letter of credit. If, on the other hand, the stipulation is that the documents of title to the goods covered by the bills drawn against shipment are to accompany the bills, the letter is called a *Documentary letter of credit.*

☞ Document Against Acceptance Bills (D/A Bills)

When documents are attached to a bill of exchange and are to be handed over to the drawer on his accepting the bill, they are called D/A bills, *i.e.*, documents against acceptance bills.

☞ Documents Against Payment Bills (D/P Bills)

When the documents are only to be handed over or delivered, not on acceptance but on actual payment of the bills, they are known as D/P bills, *i.e.,* documents against payment bills.

In the case of a D/A bill, the idea is that the drawer has to be given credit during the interval that the bill is accepted and the date on which the bill is actually paid.

In the case of a D/A bill, no credit is given because the documents are only deliverable on payment.

A documentary letter of credit is one which requires the beneficiary to submit the relevant shipping documents to the paying banker before he can draw any amount against the letter of credit. Sometimes a letter of hypothecation is also required to be executed by the beneficiary, when surrendering the shipping documents, so as to enable the banker to sell the goods if the importer fails to take delivery thereof. It will be obvious that the banker, when paying an amount against the letter of credit, will debit the branch of the banker at whose request the credit has been opened. The latter, in turn, will recover the amount from the person at whose request the facility has been arranged. In the meantime, he will hold the shipping documents and the letter of hypothecation, if any, as a security. To protect himself against the contingencies that the person who had opened the letter of credit might fall in the meantime the banker issuing the letter of credit would usually require a "marginal deposit" of 10 per cent to 25 per cent of the value of the credit to be kept with it.

(5) General Lien and Particular Lien

A lien is the right of a person to retain the goods which are in his possession until the debt due to him has been paid. But this lien, unless it is a banker's lien, does not confer any power of sale in respect of the property which is the subject of the lien.

There are two kinds of lien: Particular lien and general lien. A particular lien gives the right to retain goods in connection with which a particular debt arises. A general lien gives the right to retain goods in regard to the general balance due by their owner to the banker. Therefore, a particular lien is applied to one transaction on a particular transaction, whereas a general lien extends to all transactions arising in the course of dealings between the two parties.

The banker's lien is a general lien and is legally so recognised. It confers upon him the right to retain all the securities deposited by customer by a third person on a customer's account in respect of the general balance due to the customer. The lien is not limited only to fully negotiable instruments but extends to share certificates, insurance policies, etc. It is purely possessory and does not transfer the property or the right of ownership to the banker. Whatever be the nature of security, the lien can only be exercised when the goods have come into the banker's hands in the ordinary course of his business. Bills and other documents received for collection are part of the banker's ordinary business and he has a lien on them. The banker has a right of lien on bearer bonds and coupons, etc., received for the collection of interest or of the principal.

☞ No Lien

The banker has no right of lien in respect of the following:

(a) In case of discounting of bills of exchange for a customer on any credit balance in the account with respect to contingent liability on the bills not yet due, except where the customer is bankrupt.

(b) In respect of property which comes into the banker's hands by mistake or which is given to him with the object of securing an advance which did not materialise.

(c) Money paid in to meet specific bills accepted payable at the bank or for any other specific purpose. Securities for sale or money deposited to effect a purchase.

(d) Securities or other valuable property deposited with the banker merely for safe custody or for a special purpose and this on the ground that the limited and special purpose must be deemed to imply a contract to the contrary.

By usage and statute, a banker's lien is something more than an ordinary lien: it is an implied pledge conferring upon him the power of sale in certain contingencies.

(6) Not Transferable and Not Negotiable

☞ Negotiation

Negotiation means the transfer of the right, title and interest of the holder of a negotiable instrument, so that transferee may get a good title if he (the transferee) be a holder in due course, even though the transferor has a bad or defective title, except in the case of forgery of the holder's signature if the instrument is payable to order, or in the case of an instrument *void ab initio* or except in the case of an inchoate instrument completed and transferred after it is stolen and which was not at all delivered by the maker or drawer to anybody.

☞ Endorsement

According to Section 15 of the Negotiable Instruments Act, "when the maker or holder of a negotiable instrument signs the same, otherwise than as such maker, for the purpose of negotiation, on the back or face thereof, or on a slip of paper annexed thereto, he is said to endorse the same and is called the endorser". The purpose is to effect a transfer of the instrument. When it is so transferred, it is said that the instrument has been negotiated.

☞ Not Transferable

An instrument marked *not transferable* cannot be negotiated. In such cases only one person, *i.e.*, the payee of that instrument is entitled to the proceeds; no other person can get a title and thus the quality of negotiability is destroyed. A fixed deposit receipt (FDR) is a document which is not transferable. Therefore, an FDR is not a negotiable instrument. Transferability is one of the conditions of negotiability. A bearer instrument can be negotiated simply by transfer and an order instrument by transfer and endorsement.

Suppose the name of a payee in a cheque is written as pay to *Deepak Saran only*. The cheque in such a case will become a non-transferable instrument. The banker would pay such a cheque over the counter only to Deepak Saran. Should the cheque be presented through another banker, confirmation that the proceeds have been placed to the credit of the payee's account would be required.

☞ Not Negotiable

When a cheque is crossed with the words Not Negotiable, it does not mean that the instrument is not transferable; it only means that the transferee cannot acquire or give a better title than that of his transferor. If the endorser has a good title he can still transfer it with a good title; but if he has a defective title, his endorsee is effected by such defect, and the latter cannot claim the rights of a holder in due course by proving that he got the instrument in good faith and for value.

The most important feature of a negotiable instrument is that *bonafide* transferee for value obtains a good title despite a defect in the title of the transferor. For example, if an order cheque duly endorsed is stolen and the thief transfers it for value to one who was not aware of the situation, the latter, other things being in order, would obtain a good title. If the same cheque is, however, crossed "Not Negotiable" its quality of negotiability is destroyed, and the person receiving it cannot acquire a good title, even though he may have received it in good faith and for a consideration. The words "Not Negotiable" convey a warning to anyone to whom the cheque is offered, that if he takes it, he must take it subject to any defect there may be in the title.

(7) Pledge and Hypothecation

☞ Pledge

A pledge is defined in the Indian Contract Act (Section 172) as a bailment of goods kept as security for the payment of a debt or the performance of a promise on the implied understanding that the goods which are pledged shall be returned or otherwise disposed of, according to the directions of the pledger after the debt has been paid or the promise performed.

Delivery is necessary in order to complete a pledge. A pledgee has the right of lien over the goods which are pledged to him, as well as a limited right of sale in certain circumstances. There is one distinction between *lien* and a *pledge*, in the case of a lien, the property, though in complete possession of the creditor, is still in the full ownership of the borrower; in the case of pledge not only is the exclusive possession of the property with the lender, but the lender also acquires a right or power to sell it without express agreement by the end of the transaction after giving reasonable notice which, in the case of a lien, he does not generally possess. It is essential for a valid pledge that the pledger, transferring possession of the goods, should have a legal right or title thereto in some firm, though he may not have all the rights of an owner. Thus, a mercantile agent in lawful possession of the goods belonging to his principal can pledge the same.

☞ Hypothecation

Another term analogous to the pledge is *hypothecation*. In the case of a hypothecation, a charge is created on property or goods kept as security for a debt; the owner, however, retains ownership as well as possession. A pledge, as discussed above, depends on the transfer of possession to the creditor; where possession is not so transferred but a mere charge is created on the property retained by the owner, the property is said to be hypothecated. The instrument which creates such a charge is known as the *letter of hypothecation*. This term is, however, used loosely in actual business practice. The memorandum giving a charge on the document of title pledged with a banker as security and authorising him to dispose of the goods if the pledger fails to meet his obligation, is commonly termed as a letter of hypothecation.

A security in this form is particularly useful in the case of advances obtained against stock in trade or of raw materials; for in such cases, it is not possible for the borrower to part with their possession, without dislocating his business or industry. Moreover, the possession of the goods by the borrower is also advantageous to the creditor, for it facilitates the manufacture of the goods and their sale which helps in the repayment of the loan.

In the case of a pledge, there must be an actual or constructive delivery of possession of goods pledged to the pledgee; in hypothecation the goods need not be delivered. A pledgee can himself sell the goods pledged, after giving the pledger a reasonable notice; but a hypothecate cannot sell the goods which are the subject matter of hypothecation without a court decree.

(8) Stale Cheque and Post-dated Cheque

A stale cheque is one which is overdue and appears to be in circulation for a considerable period of time. It has not been defined as to what constitutes a considerable period of time. But the normal practice of bankers is to regard cheques which are presented six or more months after date as *stale* or *out of date*. The banker may refuse to honour such a cheque or may call for the drawer's confirmation before making the payment. If a stale cheque is negotiated it is subject to any defect of title affecting it. The transferee taking such a cheque cannot acquire or give a better title to it than that possessed by the person from whom he took it.

The validity of a cheque is not affected, whether it is ante-dated, post-dated on a Sunday. An ante-dated cheque is one which bears a date prior to the date of issue; a post-dated cheque is one dated later than the date of issue. The payee of a post-dated cheque cannot get payment on it from the bank before it is due for payment. A banker will lose his statutory protection if he pays a post-dated cheque before it is due for payment, and must bear any loss that arises out of his action. For example, if a banker pays a post-dated cheque and dishonours another cheque drawn by the customer, which would otherwise have been honoured, he will be liable for damage to the credit of his customer.

(9) Endorsement in Blank and Endorsement in Full

☞ Endorsement

Section 15 of the Negotiable Instrument Act defines endorsement as follows: "When the maker or holder of a negotiable instrument signs the same otherwise than as such maker, for the purpose of negotiation, on the back or face thereof, or on a slip of paper annexed thereto, or so signs for the same purpose a stamped paper intended to be completed as a negotiable instrument, he is said to endorse the same, and is called the endorser. The person in whose favour the bill is endorsed is called the endorsee."

An endorsement made on the face of an instrument is not wrong (Section 15 quoted above), but it is expedient in view of the time-honoured practice that all instruments should be endorsed on their back. According to Section 6 of the Indian Securities Act, 1886, an endorsement elsewhere rather than on the back of the security itself is not valid.

☞ Allonge

If the back of the instrument is filled up by endorsements the holder, in order to provide space for further endorsements, may paste on it a piece of paper called allonge, and subsequent endorsements may be made thereon.

The following are the different types of endorsements:

(i) Blank or General Endorsement: This type of endorsement contains only the bare signature of endorser, and no endorsee is specified. An instrument so endorsed becomes payable to bearer.

Example: B. N. Sahai.

(ii) Special or Full Endorsement: In this type of endorsement, in addition to the signature of the endorser, the person to whom or to whose order the instrument is payable is mentioned.

Example: Pay to S. Saran or order.
B. N. Sahai

(iii) Restrictive Endorsement: This type of endorsement has the effect of restricting further negotiation and transfer.

Example: Pay to G.D. Prasad only.
P. N. Sahai.

(iv) Conditional Endorsement: Such an endorsement contains an order to pay with a condition.

Example: Pay to G.D. Sahai on receipt of goods.
B. N. Sahai.

(v) Sans Recourse Endorsement: By adding these words after the endorsement, the endorser declines to accept any liability on the instrument to any subsequent party.

(vi) Sans Frais Endorsement: By adding the words *Sans frais* at the end of the endorsement, the endorser indicates that no expenses should be incurred on account of the instrument.

(vii) Facultative Endorsement: When the endorser desires to waive certain rights, words are added after the endorsement to indicate the fact, *e.g.*, "Notice of dishonour waived".

☞ Endorsement in Blank

In the case of a blank endorsement the endorser puts his signature on the back of the instrument without mentioning the name of any specified person in whose favour the endorsement is made. In this type of endorsement, the instrument is payable to bearer, and consequently, it can be negotiated by mere delivery.

☞ Endorsement in Full

In the case of a special or full endorsement, the endorser writes the name of the specified person and adds: order;

Example: Pay to Rajiv Kumar or order.
Rajesh Kumar.

According to Section 34 of the Negotiable Instruments Act, every endorser is liable to every subsequent party to that instrument, provided due notice of dishonour is given to or received by him. For example, if a cheque is written by "A" and is payable to "C" or order, and "C" endorses the cheque to "G" who in turn endorses it to "E" then, in case the cheque is dishonoured by the bank, the holder, *i.e.*, "E" has the right of action against all the preceding parties, *i.e.*, "D", "C" and "A". Similarly, "D" has a right against "C' and "A". The liability of endorsers of a negotiable instrument is sometimes explained on the basis that, whereas the drawer and the acceptor (*i.e.*, the primary parties) are the principal debtors, the endorsers (the secondary parties) are liable only as guarantors. Each preceding party is liable as a principal debtor to each succeeding party. Other preceding parties will be liable as sureties but not as co-sureties with rights of contributions.

(10) Holder in Due Course and Payment in Due Course

☞ Holder

The holder means a person who is entitled, in his own name to the possession of the instrument, and to receive or recover the amount due thereon from the parties thereto. If the instrument is lost or destroyed, its holder is the person who is so entitled at the time of such loss or destruction. A thief or a forged endorsee does not become a holder merely because of his being in possession of the instrument.

☞ Holder in Due Course

A person is a holder in due course who has taken a complete and regular negotiable instrument: *(a)* before the date of maturity, *(b)* in good faith, *(c)* for value, and *(d)* with due care, or without notice of any defect in the title of the person who negotiated it.

The holder of an instrument can be called "a holder in due course" if he satisfies all the four conditions mentioned above. A "holder in due course" has the following rights and privileges:

(a) Except where the instrument is obtained by fraud or is *void ab initio* a holder in due course gets a perfectly good title to the instrument, which may indeed be even better than the title of his transferors, for the holder's title is free from any defect attaching to the title of the transferor.

(b) The title of the holder "in due course" is protected even if the instrument is obtained by fraud or by an offence not caused by the holder himself. A holder does not have to prove that his holding was in due course, for he is normally presumed to be unless the contrary is established.

☞ Payment in Due Course

Section 85 of the Negotiable Instruments Act, 1881, as amended by the Amendment Act of 1934, lays down that —

"Where a cheque payable to order purports to be endorsed by or on behalf of the payee, the drawee is discharged by payment in due course."

By this Section, the banker gets statutory protection as regards payment of cheques. In case of crossed cheques, Section 128 amplifies the protection given to the paying banker, under Section 85 of the Negotiable Instruments Act, Section 128, provides that —

Where the banker, on whom a crossed cheque is drawn, has paid the same in due course, the banker paying the cheque, and (in case such cheque has come to the hands of the payee), the drawer, thereof, shall respectively be entitled to the same rights and be placed in the same position in all respects, as they would respectively be entitled to in case the cheque had been paid to, and received by the true owner thereof.

When a cheque is crossed "Account Payee" or "Payee Account", the banker should not collect such a cheque except on behalf of the payee and it is not incumbent upon the paying banker to satisfy himself that the cheque is being collected for the benefit of the payee's account.

Section 10 of the Negotiable Instruments Act explains payment in due course as follows.

"Payment in due course means payment, in accordance with the apparent tenor of the instrument in good faith and without negligence to any person in possession thereof under circumstances which do not afford a reasonable ground for believing that he is not entitled to receive payment of the amount therein mentioned."

The following elements are essential for payment in due course:

(i) Payment in accordance with the apparent tenor of the instrument;

(ii) Payment in good faith;

(iii) Payment without negligence;

(iv) Payment to a person in possession of the instrument entitled to receive payment.

(11) Inland Bill and Foreign Bill

According to Section 11 of the Negotiable Instruments Act, a promissory note, a bill of exchange or a cheque drawn or made in India and made payable in or drawn upon any person resident in India is deemed to be an inland instrument.

The requisites of an inland instrument are:

(a) that it must be drawn and payable in India, or

(b) that it must be drawn in India upon some person resident therein, though it may be made payable in a foreign country.

A bill is a foreign bill if it is drawn —

(a) outside India and made payable in or drawn upon any person resident in any country outside India;

(b) outside India and made payable in India, or drawn upon any person resident therein;

(c) in India and made payable outside India, or drawn upon a person resident outside India, but not made payable in India.

The special thing about foreign bills is that they must be protested for dishonour if such protest is required by the law of the place where they are drawn, but protest in case of an inland bill is optional.

(12) Travellers' Cheques and Banker's Drafts

A letter of credit is a letter by which one banker requests another, to whom the said letter is addressed, to hold a certain sum at the disposal of the third person who is the holder of that letter, and to pay him such amount as he requires against either cheques on the banker giving the letter or on the banker to whom the letter is addressed, but not exceeding in total the whole amount covered by the said letter. Such a letter is called a *personal credit letter or travellers' facility letter.* Its purpose is to facilitate travellers and others temporarily resident in other centres by allowing them to make use of the branch offices or agencies of the bank concerned for the purpose of obtaining such cash as they may require in the course of their travel in, or residence at, these places by drawing cheques.

When such a letter is addressed to more than one banker, it is known as a circular letter of credit. Sometimes these letters of credit are accompanied by *circular notes* in the form of cheques of the value or denomination of such sum as may be convenient to the holder; in which case the letter of credit becomes virtually a letter of indication, indicating their numbers, stating the amount up to which the circular notes are due, and containing a specimen signature of the holder.

Travellers' cheques are similar to circular notes but do not require a letter of identification. At the time of issue, the holder is required to place his signature on all the travellers' cheques issued to him and to pay for these cheques. At the time of endorsement, he is required to sign once again. This facilitate identification, for the second signature must correspond with the original signature placed at the time of issue before payment is made.

☞ Banker's Draft

A *banker's draft* is an order of one bank to another, or by one office of a bank to another office of the same bank, to pay a specified sum to a named payee, or to his order. Although it bears a close resemblance to a cheque, it is not regarded as one when the drawer and the drawee are branches or offices of the same bank. This is the position in the United Kingdom. In India, banker's drafts can be treated as cheques. If the drawer and the drawee are in different countries, banker's drafts are more or less similar to letters of credit, the only difference being that while the full amount of a banker's draft has to be paid on presentation, a letter of credit allows the drawing of amounts as and when required but not exceeding the amount stated in the letter of credit.

(13) NIBOR and LIBOR

Both these terms are associated with international lending and monetary transactions.

NIBOR — New York Inter-bank offered rate.

LIBOR — London Inter-bank offered rate.

The terms are used in case of international monetary transactions effected through euro-currency markets and offshore banking centres. The techniques adopted by the participating banks to recycle the euro-currencies to their clients are broadly classified into Syndicate Credits on fluctuating interest rates and fixed rate loans as euro-bonds. A major portion of euro-currency lending is in the form of syndicated medium-term loans. The terms NIBOR and LIBOR relate to the interest rate mechanism in syndicate credits. Inter-bank deposit market is the core of the medium-term syndicate which is in fact an inter-mediation market. The participating member banks purchase and sell euro-currency deposits among each other for periods varying from overnight to five years. In a syndicated credit strategy, a bank (designated as Lead Manager) constitutes a syndicate of a group of financial institutions after obtaining a mandate from the borrower. The basic objective is that the managing bank raises funds for the borrower without the necessity of entering into separate arrangements between the borrower and individual participating member banks. The interest rates are determined periodically on the basis of interest rates prevailing in the inter-bank part of the euro-currency market. Most of the loan agreements specify lending rates as a margin over the deposit rates of 'reference banks' which is usually taken to represent the London Inter-bank offered rate — LIBOR. A basic rate has to be determined because of the fluctuations in the interest rates according to the demand and supply of currencies in the international market. This basic rate is the average of rates at which a sample of three or more banks generally known as reference banks in a syndicated loan, offer funds for deposit in the inter-bank market. This average rate is rounded off to the nearest 1/8 per cent. In addition to the base rate margin which is technically known as banks' actual return on the loan. The basic rate as already stated is known as inter-bank offered rate which is always at the respective offshore banking centre. For example, in New York it will be — New York Inter-bank offered rate, whereas, in London it will be called London Inter-bank offered rate.

(14) Gift Cheques and Travellers' Cheques

Gift cheques are issued in different denominations printed on the cheque say ₹ 11, ₹ 21, ₹ 51, or ₹ 101. payee's name is inserted therein at the time of purchase. These gift cheques are the means of transferring money from one person to another person at some auspicious occassion. These are printed in attractive colours and designs. Full value of the cheque is paid by the purchase at the time of purchase. No surcharge is imposed to issue the cheque as well as no interest is paid to the purchaser on payee for the period for which the amount remains with the bank till the cheque is produced for payment. These cheques enable the banks to mobilise short-term deposit without any cost. These cheques are payable on demand and thus, the payee can get payment from any branch of the bank. In case of loosing a gift cheque, the other cheque will be issued on the submission of an indemnity bond.

These gift cheques are different than travellers' cheques in the sense that gift cheques are issued in small denominations while travellers' cheques are of bigger denominations.

Secondly, gift cheque can be paid only to an individual whose name is mentioned on it, while travellers' cheques are payable only to the purchase of the cheque, whose signature is taken thereon at the time of purchase. Thirdly travellers' cheques are accepted by various business establishment and traders from their customers in turn of discharge of their products and services while gift cheque does not perform this function and cannot be used for making payments.

(15) Travellers' Cheque and Credit Card

Credit card as well as travellers' cheque, both are issued from the bank. But they differ in their functions asunder:

(a) Consideration for travellers' cheques in deposit in the bank in advance at the time of issue. Thus, the amount against Traveller cheque remains with the bank till it is used, but the holder of credit card pays to the bank for the values of goods purchased and services availed after the specified period is over.

(b) Credit card facilitites holder to purchase goods and services on credit and to make payment afterwards. While travellers' cheque safeguards its holder from the risk of carrying cash and avoids the chances of loss of money in transit as well as enables him to encash the needed amounts only at a particular time.

(c) In case of credit card, the credit cardholder is charged with an admisstion fee, annual fee and also service charge of payments after, specified time. On the other hand travellers' bank issues travellers' cheque, free of cost.

(d) Transactions on credit card can be done for any amount while travellers's cheque are printed with fixed denominations like ₹ 50, ₹ 100, etc.

CHAPTER 25

Short Notes

(1) Joint and Several Liability

In joint liability, a creditor can bring only one action and not several. If the creditor sues one or more debtors but not all of the joint debtors and obtains judgement which is unsatisfied, his right of action against the remaining is debarred. But in joint and several liability, a creditor has as many rights of action as there are debtors. He may sue his debtors jointly or severally until his whole debt is satisfied; an unsatisfied judgement against one debtor will not be a bar to an action against the others. Under joint liability, the death or insolvency of one debtor leaves the creditor with recourse only against the survivors or solvent debtors; but under joint and several liability, the estate of a deceased or insolvent debtor can be held liable for the amount of the debt at the time of his death or failure, provided that such an amount is determined by breaking the account. Bankers generally see to it that a joint obligant to them shall also be severally liable, whether they are debtors, guarantors or makers of pronotes.

(2) Debentures

The word debenture has been derived from the Latin word *debere* which means to owe. A debenture is, therefore, an instrument issued under the seal of a company acknowledging indebtedness for the amount specified in it. As the debentures are creditorship securities, they do not confer the rights of ownership on their holders. According to Section 2(12) of the Companies Act, "debentures include debenture stock, bonds and any other securities of a company, whether constituting a charge on the assets of the company or not." Debentures can be of many types.

(a) Redeemable Debentures: Debentures that will be paid by the company at the end of a specified period, or by instalments during the existence of the company are known as redeemable debentures.

(b) Irredeemable Debentures: These are repayable at the option of the company after the expiry of a certain minimum period. They are also called perpetual debentures, and they become redeemable if the company fails to pay interest on these regularly.

(c) Mortgage Debentures: These are debentures which are secured by a fixed or a floating charge on the assets of the company.

(d) Simple or Naked Debentures: These are not secured by any charge on the assets of the company.

(e) Registered Debentures: These are entered in the register of the company. The transfer of such debentures requires the execution of a regular transfer.

(f) Bearer Debentures: These are transferable by mere delivery. The company keeps no record of debentureholders in this case. Payment of interest is made on the production of coupons attached to the debentures.

Debentureholders are entitled to a fixed rate of interest which is a necessary charge on profits and has to be paid whether or not the company makes profits. Debentures are generally covered by a charge on the assets of the company, which means that there is enough security for their redemption.

(3) Clearing Houses

A banker's clearing house is an institution of credit where reciprocal liabilities of local banks are counter-balanced against one another. The function of the settlement of the clearance balance between banks has been adopted by all the central banks as a part of their duty which has been laid down by law. In some countries where clearing arrangements had been made by the commercial banks themselves long before the establishment of a central bank, or where the central banks did not take the initiative in the matter in the beginning, there are independent clearing house institutions. But in these countries also, central banks, apart from being their members, have to perform the function of settling the difference among banks at the end of each clearing.

☞ Process of Their Working

The process of the working of a clearing house is simple. Suppose there are five clearing banks, namely, I, II, III, IV and V. Each of these banks keeps specially ruled sheets known as summary sheet of out-clearing, wherein a record of all the cheques or bills, which it has to realise from other banks, is kept. Thus, if Bank I, on sorting out the cheques and drafts in its possession, finds claims against Banks II, it will enter the same on the sheet; claims against Banks III, IV and V will be similarly entered. A separate sheet is used for each individual bank. After this, the cheques or drafts are carefully checked and bundled up separately. This is done by all the banks. These bundles are then taken to the clearing house and placed on the clearing desks of the five banks respectively. There, the clerks of the respective banks maintain their record in the *summary sheets of in-clearing*, in the same way in which the record had been kept in the *summary sheets of out-clearing.* If the total of out-clearing of Bank I against Bank II is greater than the total of its in-clearing from the other, it has to receive a balance, and *vice versa.* Then these balances are entered upon a list known as the general balance sheet of a particular bank. On this list are printed the names of the above banks, with debit and credit columns on the left and right side respectively. If an account is to be received from a bank, it is entered on the debit side against the particular bank's name, and *vice versa.* A balance is then struck off the debit and credit totals and instructions for transfer are given to the central bank. For instance, if Bank III has to receive a balance, it directs the central bank to transfer that amount from the clearing account, and *vice versa*. Thus, the entries in the accounts of the clearing banks with the central bank are made, also the entries in the account in the name of the clearing house.

☞ Advantages

A clearing house organisation is advantageous both to the bankers and the society at large.

(i) Bankers: They are not required to send their men to each bank separately.

(ii) They are not required to receive or pay in cash.

(iii) Because of the above two advantages, banks do not have to keep large sums in hand.

☞ Society

The clearing house system is advantageous to society as well, for it helps in the extension of credit following an increasing use of cheques, a practice which is encouraged by their settlement through this system.

(4) Equitable Mortgage

The term *mortgage* has been defined in Section 58 of the Transfer of Property Act, 1882, as "the transfer of an interest in specific immovable property for the purpose of securing the payment of money advanced or to be advanced by way of loan, or existing or future debt, or the performance of engagement, which may give rise to a pecuniary liability".

Except in the case of an equitable mortgage a mortgage has to be effected by a registered deed signed by the mortgagor and attested by at least two witnesses. Unlike a pledge, a mortgage does not necessarily involve the transfer of possession, although in certain forms of mortgage, the creditor does, as a matter of fact, gain possession of the mortgaged property. Furthermore, unlike the pledge and hypothecation, which are in respect of a movable property, a mortgage is effected always in respect of immovable property. Mortgages are of many kinds:

(i) Mortgage by deposit of title deeds;

(ii) English Mortgage;

(iii) Equitable Mortgage;

(iv) Simple Mortgage;

(v) Mortgage by conditional sale;

(vi) Usufructuary Mortgage.

☞ Equitable Mortgage

A bare deposit of title deeds, with the intent to create a security on the property comprised therein, amounts to an equitable mortgage of the property. Equitable mortgages have received statutory recognition in India, and are in vogue in Mumbai, Kolkata and Chennai. The effect of an equitable mortgage is the same as that of the mortgage of the properties themselves covered by the title deeds. It creates not merely a right in personem but a right which cannot be defeated by defence of *bona fide* purchase without a notice. Consequently, it will operate also against a subsequent legal mortgage of the same estate.

(5) Interest Warrant

This is an order for the payment of interest upon Government and debenture stocks and similar types of securities. Coupons are attached to the debentures representing the interest payable for a specified period. On the due date, the interest warrant is detached and presented for payment to the company which has issued debentures to its bankers.

(6) Revolving Credit

It is a type of letters of credit in which credit is issued for a specific sum to be availed of in a fixed period of time. A new letter of credit is necessary after the credit has been fully availed of, but in the case of revolving credit, the amount automatically revolves after the bills negotiated under it are duly honoured. For example, where the revolving credit is ₹ 10,000 and a bill for ₹ 5,000 is negotiated under the said credit, the amount of the credit is automatically restored to its original amount of ₹ 10,000 as soon as the said bill of ₹ 5,000 has been honoured.

(7) Marking of Cheques

If a banker certifies a cheque by writing on it words like *"approved"* or *"good"* or by initialling the cheques, such cheques are called *Marked Cheques.* Occasionally, cheques are marked or certified by the bankers on whom they are drawn. The marking of cheques, however, does not convert the banker into an acceptor or make him liable on the instrument; but it does constitute a representation by him on which he may be held liable that the cheque will be paid as drawn if presented within a reasonable time. The effect of the cheque is to give it additional currency by showing on its face that it was drawn in good faith on funds sufficient to meet its payment, and by adding to the credit of the drawer the credit of the banker on whom it is drawn.

The object and effect of a banker's marking of cheques is to facilitate the ready acceptance of the instrument by providing evidence on the face of it that it is drawn in good faith and that sufficient funds are available to meet it, and by adding the credit of the drawee bank to that of the drawer.

☞ Marking for a Drawer

In the case of a cheque marked or certified by the drawer at the request of the drawer, the banker can retain money to meet such a cheque and dishonour any cheque presented subsequently if the balance remaining after providing for the marked cheque is insufficient to cover these subsequent cheques.

☞ Marking for Another Banker

The marking between bankers is considered as a promise of undertaking to pay. It is, however, doubtful as to whether a banker has marked a cheque for another banker. The authorities seem to be conflicting on this point though, of course, the right of the customer to countermand payment previous to such a marking is clearly acknowledged.

☞ Marking for a Holder

Another type of marking can be by a holder or payee presenting a cheque to the banker and getting it marked. Such a marking constitutes nothing more than an intimation that at the time of marking the banker had a sufficient balance to the credit of the drawer and that there is no appropriation by the banker.

(8) Noting and Protesting a Bill

In the event of a promissory note having been dishonoured either by non-acceptance or by non-payment, or holder may have such a dishonour noted by a notary public either upon the instrument itself or upon a separate piece of paper annexed thereto or partly upon each. Such noting is required to be made within a reasonable time and such dishonour must contain the following particulars (vide Section 99 of the Negotiable Instruments Act):

(i) The date of dishonour and the reason adduced, if any, therefore;

(ii) If the instrument has not been expressly dishonoured, the reason why the holder treats it as dishonoured; and

(iii) The notarial charges.

☞ Protesting

Protest is a formally drawn up certificate of dishonour, signed by a notary public. According to Section 100 of the Negotiable Instruments Act, when the acceptor of a bill has become insolvent or his credit has been publicly impeached before the maturity of the bill, the holder may, within a reasonable time, cause a notary public to demand better security of the acceptor, and if such security is refused, he can, within a reasonable time, cause the bill to be protested for better security by the notary public. If a bill has been protested for better security it does not amount to a dishonour of the bill, and the holder, therefore, will have to wait till the time for the payment comes. If, on the date of payment, the amount is not paid, he can proceed as he would, when a bill is dishonoured.

The advantage of noting and/or protesting is that it constitutes a good and reliable evidence of dishonour which would be acceptable in a court of law, the Inland bills need not be noted and protested, although it is desirable to do so. But foreign bills must be noted and protested if they are dishonoured. Noting and protesting is also necessary in the case of acceptance or payment for honour.

☞ Notary Public

A notary public is legal practitioner appointed by the Government to exercise the powers and functions of attention of foreign documents, noting and protesting of bills, of promissory notes and other similar documents.

(9) English Mortgage

Under Section 58 of the Transfer of Property Act, when the mortgagor binds himself to repay the mortgage money on a certain date and transfers the mortgage property *absolutely* to the mortgagee, but subject to a promise that the mortgagee will retransfer it to the mortgagor upon repayment of the mortgage money as required, the right created is known as English mortgage. Thus, an English mortgage is, in form, a transfer of ownership to the mortgagee, with a covenant to repay the debt on a certain date and a promise that, on this condition being fulfilled, the mortgagee, will retransfer the property to the mortgagor. The remedy available to the mortgagee is a sale through the intervention of the court in the normal legal manner, but not a forecloser (*i.e.*, forfeiture of the mortgaged property by way of appropriation by the mortgagee against the debt). This is so because, in the event of a sale, the mortgagor has the right to the surplus in the sale proceeds of the mortgaged property left over after the appropriation of the debt.

(10) Hire-purchase Finance

The system of allowing extensive credit to consumers is a comparatively recent phenomenon. This type of finance has great social value because consumers who are not able to pay for goods and services fully at a time, are able to purchase and use them by paying for them in instalments. This phenomenon has an economic significance as well for it enables manufacturers to enhance their sales. The sales of radios, cars and refrigerators would be reduced by half if buyers are not allowed to pay for them in instalments. In a hire-purchase transaction, the parties agree that provided the hirer regularly pays the instalments of the price agreed upon the advance between the parties, the goods shall become the property of the hirer when the final instalment, is paid. Further, as long as all the instalments have not been paid, the goods remain the property of the seller, who is entitled to resume possession thereof on non-payment of an instalment or instalments which have fallen due. The hire-purchase agreement is both a contract of bailment and an option to buy. In other words, there is no agreement to sell; the hirer is only given the option to buy if he complies with certain conditions.

In Western countries, most commercial banks provide hire-purchase finance to traders and consumers. In recent years, Indian commercial banks have also started giving hire-purchase finance facilities. They provide loans to person in permanent employment for the purchase of radios, refrigerators, cars, scooters, and household equipment. The instalment money is deducted from the salary of the purchaser and deposited with the bank.

(11) Bill of Lading

A bill of lading is an instrument which is of the following purposes:

(a) A receipt for the goods which are loaded aboard a ship;

(b) A contract to deliver the goods, to a consignee;

(c) A document of title to the goods covered by it.

The following particulars are given in a bill of lading:

(i) The name of the consignor (exporter);

(ii) The name of the shipping company;

(iii) The date and place of shipment;

(iv) The name, nationality and class of ship;

(v) The description and weight of the cargo;

(vi) The freight, paid or payable;

(vii) An acknowledgement of the receipt and shipment of goods;

(viii) An undertaking that the goods shall be delivered in a good condition at the place of destination; and

(ix) A statement that the bill of lading has been issued under the Indian Carriage of Goods by Sea Act, 1928.

If a bill of lading contains any qualifications regarding the quality, condition or weight of the goods, it is considered to be a *qualified bill*. If a bill of lading contains no such qualifications, it is known as a *clean bill*. It is prepared in several sets which can be distributed to the different persons concerned — for example, to the consignor, the consignee, the clearing agents, bankers, etc.

A bill of lading is not precisely a negotiable instrument, but a quasi-negotiable instrument, and confers certain valuable rights upon the consignee named therein and upon the endorsee thereof. Moreover, its holder unlike the holder in due course of a negotiable instrument, does not acquire any better title to the goods than its transferor had. In other words, his title is subject to the defects and equities affecting the title of his transferor, and, to that extent, one of the essential characteristics of negotiability is absent. The other attributes of negotiability — for example, by endorsement and delivery — are present in a bill of lading. According to the provisions of the Bill of Lading Act, 1856, every consignee of goods named therein and every endorsee of the bill has the right of suit against the carrier to the same extent, and subject to the same limitations and liabilities, as the person with whom the original contract, represented by the bill, was made. Thus, a bill of lading confers more rights upon the consignee or endorsee thereof than a railway receipt does.

(12) Warehouse-keeper's Certificate or Warehouse Receipt

A warehouse-keeper's certificate is a mere receipt certifying that the goods are held by the warehouse-keeper, which are usually expressed to be non-transferable, though in some cases they are transferable by endorsement. The mere statement as to the holding of the goods on behalf of the owner in no sense makes it a document of title. It is for this reason that this certificate is not considered to be proper security for a loan by a bank.

Before making an advance against a warehouse receipt the banker should ensure that the person approaching him for the advance is entitled to receive the goods in his own name. It is also advisable for him to obtain a declaration from him that the goods mentioned in the receipt are his absolute property. The genuineness of the warehouse receipt should also be verified.

(13) Estoppel

An estoppel is a rule of law by which a party is estopped from denying that which he previously asserted to be true either orally or in writing or by a deed or by evidence in a court of law. A maker of promissory note, or the drawer of a bill of exchange or cheque, or an acceptor, for honour is estopped from denying the validity of the instrument made or drawn to a holder in due course. A maker of a note, or an acceptor of a bill payable to the order of a specified person, is similarly estopped from denying the payee's capacity to endorse it. An endorser of a negotiable instrument is not permitted to deny either the signature or the capacity to contract of any prior party to a holder in due course (Sections 120 and 121 of the Negotiable Instruments Act).

(14) Conversion

Conversion may be defined as unlawful taking, using, disposing or destroying of goods, which is inconsistent with the owner's right possession. According to Dr. Hart, "Conversion is a wrongful intermeddling with the good of another for the purpose of taking them away from the party entitled to them". (Hart's *Law of Banking,* 4th edition, p. 609).

Conversion is independent of intention or knowledge, and an innocent party, even as an agent for sale, may be held liable for conversion. (*Hollins vs. Fowler*).

It may be noted that, if there were no statutory protection, a banker would be liable for conversion if he paid a cheque on a forged endorsement or collected a bill, note or cheque bearing a forged endorsement. As banking business is vital to the economic life of a community, and as the doctrine of conversion exposes bankers to the risks and hazards of interminable claims, the purpose of the law has been to grant them a conditional immunity or concession, which is not enjoyed by the world at large. A banker, however, who takes as holder for value a bill or cheque marked *not negotiable*, will be liable in conversion because there is no protection, statutory or otherwise, in such a case.

(15) Dividend Warrant

Big joint-stock companies, generally, distribute dividends to shareholders by issuing dividend warrants. The amount mentioned in the dividend warrant can be drawn from the company's bankers. A dividend warrant is a cheque drawn by a company upon its banker in payment of dividends to its shareholders. They are quasi-negotiable instruments, and have acquired negotiability by custom. So far, no court judgment is available on the negotiability of dividend warrants; but on the evidence of custom, the court would recognise the fact of its negotiability.

(16) Acceptance for Honour

When a bill has been noted or protested for non-acceptance, or for better security, and every person accepts it to protect the honour of the drawer or of any one of the endorsers, such acceptance is called *acceptance for honour*, and the person who accepts is called *acceptor for honour.*

After the acceptor for honour has accepted the bill, the holder at the due date has to present it first to the drawer for payment. If it is dishonoured for non-payment by the drawee and noted and protested, it should then be presented to the acceptor for honour for payment.

A person desiring to accept for honour must, by writing on the bill under his hand, declare that he accepts under protest the protested bill for the honour of the drawer or a particular endorser who he names, or generally for honour when the acceptor does not indicate the person for whose honour it is made, it shall be deemed to be made for the honour of the drawer.

(17) Average Clause in Insurance

An average clause in a fire insurance policy lays down that if the property is under-insured (insured for a sum smaller than the value of the property), the insurer shall be liable only for that proportion of the actual value of property at the time of loss.

In marine insurance, marine losses may be divided into two categories — total loss and partial loss. A partial loss in marine insurance is called an *average loss.* An average loss may be either —

(i) A general average loss, or

(ii) A particular average loss.

A particular average loss is the one which has been accidentally caused by a maritime peril to property, *e.g.*, damage to cargo by sea-water. Such a loss is to be borne by the party on whom the loss originally fell.

A general average loss is a loss caused by a general average act. A general average act means any extraordinary expenditure or sacrifice, made at the time when a peril really existed, for the purpose of preserving the property imperilled in the common adventure. In the case of a general average loss, the party on whom it falls is entitled, subject to the conditions imposed by maritime law, to a rateable contribution from the other parties interested, and such contribution is called a general average contribution. For example, the captain of a ship may, in time of peril, throw overboard a part of the cargo to save the vessel. The loss would be incurred in the interest of the shipowners and the cargo-owners and, therefore, all must bear the loss rateably. If the goods of a particular cargoowners are sacrificed in their entirety, the particular cargoowner would be entitled to a general average contribution.

For the adjustment of a general average loss among different parties, a code of rules relating to it was adopted by maritime underwriters in 1890 (the rules were revised in 1924 at a Congress at Stockholm, Sweden). The code is known as "York Antwerp Rules". Every insurance contract contains an average clause.

(18) Export Credit and Guarantee Corporation

The Export Credit and Guarantee Corporation which is the successor of the Export Risk Insurance Corporation of India insures the exporter's credit risks and guarantees payment to him. It also furnishes guarantee to the financing bank to encourage credit facilities to exporters. With its head office in Mumbai, it has branches in Kolkata and Chennai. It is fully owned by the Government of India and works on a "no-profit-no-loss-basis".

The Corporation provides the following three types of covers:

(i) Policies to protect the exporters against the risk of trading with overseas buyers on credit terms;

(ii) Financial guarantees issued by banks against the risks involved in providing credit to exporters; and

(iii) Special policies.

Under its policies intended to protect the exporters against overseas credit risks, ECGC bears the main brunt of the risk and pays the exporter 80 per cent of his losses on account of commercial risks and 85 per cent on account of *political risks.* An exporter may either take a comprehensive risk policy covering both political and commercial risks or securing himself only against political risks, if he so desires. He can take the following types of policies:

(i) Contracts (Comprehensive Risks) Policy;

(ii) Contracts (Political Risks) Policy;

(iii) Shipments (Comprehensive Risks) Policy;

(iv) Shipments (Political Risks) Policy

☛ Financial Guarantees

In the sphere of financial guarantees, the Corporation undertakes to share the risks for the exporter with the lending bank. The beneficiaries under the guarantees given by the ECGC are not the banks alone but the exporters as well. These guarantees have been designed to assist and encourage banks to give liberal credit — both pre-shipment and post-shipment — for producing, packaging and exporting goods. The following three types of guarantees are given:

(i) Packing credit guarantee;

(ii) Post-shipment credit guarantee; and

(iii) Export finance guarantee.

These guarantees cover risks of non-payment by an export arising from his insolvency or default. The Export Credit and Guarantee Corporation pays the bank 69 per cent of the loss in the case of the packing credit and post-shipment credit guarantee and 75 per cent of the loss in the case of export finance guarantee.

To suit the various needs of the Indian exporter the ECGC has devised the following special policies:

(i) Manufacturer's credit insurance policy and exporters credit insurance policy; and

(ii) Market development policies.

The ECGC has also evolved a scheme under which foreign exchange credit is made available on a revolving basis to manufacturers-exporters for the import of essential raw materials for the manufacturer of goods destined for the export market.

(19) Term Loans

The short-term assistance provided by a bank may be converted into medium-term finance through renewal and extension from time-to-time. In other words, a cash credit or an overdraft may by converted into a medium-term loans. But there is the disadvantage of uncertainty in such arrangements. The renewal of extension of a short-term accommodation will depend on the bank's policy and the conditions in the money market.

Another method of securing medium-term assistance from a bank through a *term loan* for a duration of, say, 3 to 7 years. Indian banks always hesitate in extending such loans, but with the extension of the refinancing facility by the Refinance Corporation from 1958, banks have found it possible to engage in term lending to industrial enterprises. Under the refinance scheme, a bank can grant loans for periods ranging between 3 years and 7 years and get them refinanced by the Corporation at a relatively lower rate of interest. This avoids pressure on the short-term deposits of the banks. The refinance facility is now available from the Industrial Development Bank of India.

(20) The Deposit Insurance Corporation

To insure a bank's deposits, the Deposit Insurance Corporation was established on January 1, 1962. The aim of the Corporation is to provide a guarantee for the repayment of deposits up to a maximum fixed sum, if the insured bank goes into liquidation. The Corporation has an authorised capital of ₹ 1 crore, which is fully paid-up by the Reserve Bank of India. It is empowered to borrow up to ₹ 5 crore from the Reserve Bank. The general superintendence, direction and management of the Corporation vests in a Board of Directors consisting of five members.

All banks, which are notified as banks under Section 51 of the Banking Companies Act, shall be registered as insured banks. The maximum premium which the Corporation is empowered to charge the insured banks is 15 paise per annum for every ₹ 100 of the total amount of deposits (excluding the deposits by Central and State Governments, a foreign Government or a banking company).

The Act sets out in detail the manner of payment by the Corporation in the event of an insured bank ceasing to function. It is laid down that within three months from the winding up of a bank, the liquidator shall furnish to the Corporation a list of deposits in respect of each depositor and the amounts set off against them, in the case where a scheme of compromise or arrangement or of reconstruction or amalgamation has been sanctioned, in respect of an insured bank, the bank concerned (or the transferee bank, in the case of amalgamation) should furnish the corporation a list showing separately deposits in respect of each depositor, the amount set off against them, the amounts paid or credited to his account under the scheme. Within two months of the receipt of the list of depositors, the Corporation shall make the payment as required under the Act. Any amount to be paid by an insured bank, which has ceased to function, in respect of any deposit, shall be paid by it to the Corporation until the payments made by the Corporation in respect of that deposit are recovered in full.

A Deposit Insurance Fund is maintained by the Corporation, to which all amount of premium collected are credited, and the amount in this fund shall be utilised for payments of insured deposits. Borrowings from the Reserve Bank are exclusively for the purpose of the Deposit Insurance Fund and are repaid out of that Fund.

The Deposit Insurance Corporation is playing a very important role in strengthening and improving the banking and financial system of the country. It affords protection to depositors, specially small depositors, against the loss of their savings in the event of the failure of an insured bank. Such protection increases the confidence of depositors, reduces the incidence of panicky withdrawals, and generally contributes to the stability and orderly growth of the banking system as a whole as well as of individual banks. An assurance of safety of funds also assists in actively developing the banking habit of the community and facilitates the opening of offices on a large-scale, thereby mobilising the savings of the people, rich and poor.

(21) Material Alteration

According to Section 87 of the Negotiable Instruments Act, material alteration of a negotiable instrument renders the same void as against anyone who is a party thereto at the time of making such alteration and does not consent thereto unless, it was made to carry out the common intention of the original parties.

Section 87, however, does not specify what a material alteration is but specifies what are not material alterations, *e.g.,* filling in of an inchoate instrument (Section 20), conversion of a blank endorsement into a full one (Section 49), crossing of cheques (Section 125).

Section 62(2) of the Bills of Exchange Act specifies the following as material alterations:

(i) Alteration of the date;

(ii) Alteration of the sum payable;

(iii) Alteration of the time of payment;

(iv) Alteration of the place of payment;

(v) Alteration of the place of payment without the acceptors' assent where a bill has been accepted generally.

In addition to the above, the following are considered material alterations:

(i) Addition or elimination of parties to an instrument;

(ii) Alteration of the rate of interest;

(iii) Conversion of an "order", instrument into a "bearer" instrument, or alteration of material crossing by an unlawful party; and

(iv) Alteration in the currency or medium of payment.

The provisions of Section 87 of the Negotiable Instruments Act will apply only when the alteration is material. In other words, an alteration in order to come under the rule, must be a material alteration and the mere fact that it was made with a dishonest intention will not make the instrument void. Similarly, an alteration made by accident will not make the instrument void. In such cases the parties would have to show the circumstances under which the accidental alterations had come to be made.

The question as to whether an alteration is material or not will depend on whether the identity of the instrument has been affected. In the case of *Bank of Montreal vs. Exhibit and Trading Co. (1906)*, it was held that the name of the firm on a note payable to it could be altered to show its new entity, *i.e.,* a limited company into which the firm has converted itself, and such alteration would not be regarded a material alteration.

(22) Trust Receipts

If a banker has to part with a bill of lading or goods, without receiving the amount due from the customer, it is necessary and in the interest of the banker that he take a trust receipt signed by his customer, agreeing to hold the goods or their sale proceeds in trust for the banker, so long as the entire amount, due to the banker is not paid-off. The customer, who has signed such a trust receipt, will become liable for criminal breach of trust if he fails to hand over to the banker the sale proceeds of the goods sold.

(23) Registration of 'Charge' Under the Companies Act

According to Section 125 of the Indian Companies Act, joint stock companies are required to register certain types of securities charged by them. In this matter, companies are treated differently from individuals and firms. The above-mentioned section gives a list of charges that require registration — a floating charge, a charge on land, a charge made for securing an issue of debentures, etc. These charges must be registered within 21 days after the date on which they are actually signed or sealed, which may or may not be the same as the date of execution. In case a charge is not registered, it will make the security void against a liquidator and any creditor of the company. Further, a duly registered subsequent charge will get priority over the prior charge which has not been so registered, even if the person in whose favour the subsequent charge is created has expressed notice of the prior unregistered charge. *(Monolithic Building Company,* 1915, 1 Ch. 643).

(24) Banking Commission

The Government of India appointed a Banking Commission on January 29, 1969, with Shri R.G. Saraiya as Chairman to undertake a comprehensive review of the existing structure and organisation of a commercial banking system. The Commission issued a questionnaire to commercial banks in three instalments. It also constituted four groups to study in depth, the problems relating to banking costs, indigenous bankers, banking procedures and legislation affecting the banking. It also undertook many research projects relating to the field study of banking facilities, the range and quality of services to depositors and a survey of small-scale industries in selected centres.

The Commission submitted its report in 1972. Some of its important recommendations are:

Improvement in customer service by the extension of the Teller system; the opening of more clearing houses; making use of the regional language; simplification of credit procedures, and strengthening of the internal control system; decentralisation of administrative powers; the creation of specialised departments to ensure better organisation and management; the introduction of costing and budgeting techniques; the need for evolving a management information system which would serve not only the needs of the bank itself but also the Reserve Bank and the Government; rationalisation of recruitment, selection, promotion, and training of bank personnel and organisation of research in banking and allied subjects.

The Commission also suggested the creation of a Bank for facilitating inter-bank credit transfers, a phased programme of mechanisation, the establishment of a Credit Intelligence Bureau, the principle of one bank, one borrower, common inspection agency and uniform standards, and procedures for public sector banks, a five-day week for banks on an experimental basis, abolition of secret resources, more rational methods of covering risk assets, central agencies for cost and other surveys and processing and feedback of management information, a national banking service commission and increased reponsibilities for the National Institute of Bank Management which should work, more or less, as a Banking University.

The Commission has laid emphasis on the operational efficiency of banks. It has focussed attention on several areas of public dissatisfaction as well as areas where internal controls are required. It has highlighted the need for modernisation in the control areas relating to internal audit and inspection, periodical returns and inter-branch accounts.

As regards the Banking Companies Act, the main recommendations of the Commission relate to expeditious decisions to be taken by the Reserve Bank on the licensing of banking companies; enabling banks to undertake any form of business which the Reserve Bank may notify with the prior approval of the Central Government; formation of subsidiaries by banks for any purpose considered by the Reserve Bank, in consultation with the Government, proper grant of power to the Reserve Bank to revise the requirements of the maintenance of minimum liquid assets by banks within the range prescribed by the Central Government and grant of power to the Central Government to specify what percentage of bank profit should go into the reserves. The Commission has also suggested that the administration of banking regulations over financing institutes and deposit receiving institutions may be entrusted to an independent agency closely associated with the Reserve Bank or, alternately, the Reserve Bank itself may administer the regulations by opening offices of the concerned department in all the States. A comprehensive banking code should be enacted, which would contain provisions relating to different types of banking institutions, including firms and individuals.

The Commission has advocated uniform legislation for the State Bank and its subsidiaries and other nationalised banks in regard to the objectives, capital, management, forms of business they could engage in, and the conduct of Government business, etc. In particular, it has recommended that there should be a separate whole-time chairman and whole-time chief executive for each bank, that Government appointment of its representatives on the Boards of banks from farmers, artisans, depositors, etc., should not be by "election", but that the employee representatives should be chosen by secret executives, with adequate authority should be created for banks' adequate authority.

In addition, the Commission has made certain recommendations regarding secrecy of customer's affairs, the Banker's Book Evidence Act, the presentation of records and paid instruments, the disclosure of information, in public interest, the compilation and exchange of credit information, nomination facilities for depositors, borrowers, etc., punishing of wilful submission of incorrect financial statements by customers of banks, the tightening up of regulations applicable to moneylending and regulation of dealers in usance hundis. It has further suggested that a special machinery should be set up by the Government to make a constant review of the laws concerning and affecting banking.

(25) Bill Market Scheme of the Reserve Bank of India

A new bill market scheme came into operation from November 1970. This scheme is the outcome of the deliberations of the working group set up by the Reserve Bank of India in February 1970, which was constituted to go into questions relating to enlarging the use of the bill of exchange as instrument for providing credit and the creditor of a bill market in India. The working group came to the unanimous conclusion that it would be advantageous to take steps to enlarge the use of the bill of exchange as an instrument of credit to create a bill market in the country, for it would assist in the development of the practice of issue of usance bills and their acceptance for the purpose of trade credit and for securing discounting facilities against them.

The broad features of the new scheme are:

(i) The scheme is limited only to genuine trade bills; that is, to bills which evidence sale and/or despatch of goods.

(ii) The bills should be accepted by purchasers and bankers.

(iii) The bills should bear the signature of a licensed schedule bank as acceptor.

(iv) The bills should normally be of a usance not exceeding 90 days but may in exceptional cases, have usance up to 120 days, and in case of longer maturities, the rediscounting facilities will be available only in respect of bills which have to run for a period not exceeding 90 days at the time these are offered for rediscount to the Reserve Bank.

(v) The scheme would exclude bills of exchange arising out of sales of such commodities as may be indicated by the Reserve Bank of India from time-to-time.

(vi) The bills should contain a clause regarding the nature of the transactions out of which the bills have arisen.

Under the old bill market scheme which was in operation for nearly 20 years, the Reserve Bank of India provided refinance to eligible scheduled banks against usance promissory notes specifically created by their borrowers by converting their borrowings into usance promissory notes. These notes are not bills in the true sense, nor is there a market for them. The previous scheme has been in effect as an accommodation scheme on the basis of improvised bills.

(26) Blank Transfers

In order to effect a transfer of shares, the seller is required to make over to the buyer his share certificates together with a transfer deed duly stamped and signed by him. The transfer deed contains such particulars as the name of the company, the number of shares and their distinctive numbers, the consideration of money, the name of the seller and buyer, etc.

If, on a deed of transfer, all particulars have been filled in, including the signature of the transferor, except the name and signature of the transferee, it is called a blank transfer form. Share certificates accompanied by such blank transfers readily pass hands, for the real ownership transferred in his favour, the holder of documents is required to complete the transfer deed by inserting all the remaining particulars such as his name and signature as transferee, as well as to send the documents to the company concerned to have the change in the ownership registered. Such change in ownership will be recorded in the register of the company, and endorsements are made on the share certificates accordingly.

It is only after the completion of these formalities that the ownership in the securities will be deemed to have been legally transferred.

The justification for the existence and continuation of this method of blank transfers is:

(a) To ensure a free and quick circulation of securities from person-to-person by enabling the holder to sell them without first getting his name registered in the books of the company concerned.

(b) By investing in registered securities dealt in on a stock exchange, with the attributes of a negotiable instrument (i.e., passing of title by mere delivery), they facilitate in the obtaining of credit by being pledged.

(c) They facilitate the "budla" arrangements at the stock exchange, which are very necessary for long-term speculation and thereby help to stabilise the operations at the exchange.

On the other hand, blank transfers give rise to certain evils also which are:

(a) Blank transfers, by their very nature, encourage unhealthy speculation.

(b) Such transfers lead to the concealment of the identity of the true owner by keeping the holdings in the name of another and thus lead to evasion of taxes as well as to manipulation of holdings with a view to obtaining over companies. They also encourage the cornering of securities.

(c) As the shares continue to be kept on blank, holders escape payment of stamp duties on transfer of shares, and the registers of companies are rendered incorrect and incomplete.

(d) Transferor of partly paid shares continues to be liable to the calls made by a company as the name of the holder continues to appear in the register of members.

This method of blank transfers generated much controversy for a considerable time. It is now unanimously admitted that the blank transfers should not be allowed to continue in their present form.

One school of thought is in favour of abolishing blank transfers altogether; while another section favours limiting their tenure to a specified period of, say, six months or a year. The consensus of opinion favours the limitation of period and not outright abolition. This is because blank transfers have come to form an important and integral part of trading practices on the exchange and also have acquired a special significance in the credit mechanism. The Securities Contracts (Regulation) Act, 1956, has restricted the period of currency of blank transfers to a maximum period of six months.

(27) Budla Transactions or Carry-over

A speculator, who has bought or sold a security for forward delivery, may be either unable or unwilling to pay for it and take delivery or to deliver it on the settlement day and may desire the completion of the transaction to be postponed to the next settlement. The process by which bargains are continued from one account or settlement to another is termed as carry-over or *budla*. It consists, in the case of the buyer, in selling for the current settlement and simultaneously buying for the next; in the case of the seller, it is buying for the current settlement and selling for the next. It is allowed on the payment of some charges known as *contago*, or *backwardation* or the *budla* or *mandi budla*.

(28) Performance Budgeting

Performance budgeting is a technique of presenting an undertaking's operations in terms of functions, programmes, activities and projects. By a systematic classification of functions, the activities of an undertaking are sought to be identified in financial and physical terms so that a proper relationship between inputs and outputs could be established and performance budgeting is primarily a planning and control system.

The primary objective of performance budget is to provide a mechanism for a constant comparison of actual progress toward the attainment of objective. The technique of performance budgeting is used to draw up a plan of action, to evaluate periodically the variations with budgeted levels, and to apply appropriate corrective measures to bring the performance in line with the planned level of growth. The technique of performance budgeting, thus, assists the management to know what the management is performing, at what costs and with what consequences.

In the management of banks, performance budgeting is not only important but necessary.

According to Banking Commission, "Operational efficiency can be achieved through a proper planning of the years' activities sufficiently in advance and by fixing targets for performance of budgets and establishment of a good system of budgetary control". In a bank, in addition to the attainment of targets, performance budgeting ensures effective control over factors; involving incomes and costs, thus developing a sense of cost consciousness; helps in the identification of causes leading to the deviations from the targets and formulation or remedial measures; aids in the review of present policies and decisions about future course of action.

(29) Integrated Rural Development Programme

Integrated Rural Development Programme is in operation in all the blocks of the country since October 1980. The main objectives of the programme are:

1. to increase production and productivity in agriculture and other sectors in rural areas, and
2. to create substantial additional employment opportunities and make the rural families viable and self-sufficient.

The programme seeks in particular to improve the lot of the poorest of the poor — small and marginal farmers, share croppers, agricultural labourers, rural artisans, scheduled castes/tribes and other weaker sections. Under this programme, the Lead Banks have been made responsible to prepare banking plans (earlier prepared by Agricultural Refinance and Development Corporation) to allocate the responsibility of financing the identified beneficiaries for different activities among the participating banks and integrate the same with Annual Action Plans.

The Government gives subsidy ranging from 25% to 50% of the total capital investment depending upon the category of beneficiary. Total subsidy per year is estimated at about ₹ 300 crore and the expected credit support from banks not less than ₹ 600 crore.

(30) National Bank for Agriculture and Rural Development (NABARD)

The National Bank for Agriculture and Rural Development, a new statutory financial institution to operate as "Rural Reserve Bank" started functioning from 12th July, 1982. This National Farm Bank has now become the sole official instrument of rural credit for economic growth. It has taken over the entire undertaking of the Agricultural Refinance and Development Corporation (ARDC) and has also taken the place of Reserve Bank of India in the matter of refinancing the State Cooperative Banks (SCBs) and the Regional Rural Banks (RRBs).

NABARD has a share capital of ₹100 crore, contributed by the Union Government and the Reserve Bank on a 50:50 basis. For its long-term operations NABARD will draw funds from the Government of India, the World Bank and other multilateral and bilateral agencies and the market. National Agricultural Credit (Long-term operations) fund of the Reserve Bank of India will be transferred to "National Rural Chit Fund" to be maintained by NABARD. "National Agricultural Credit (Stabilisation)

Fund" of the Reserve Bank of India will be transferred to "National Rural Credit (Stabilisation) Fund" to be maintained by NABARD. A "Research and Development Fund" will also be created and maintained.

NABARD will provide refinance facilities to banks for all kinds of production and investment credit to agriculture, small-scale industries, artisans, cottage and village industries, handicrafts and other allied economic activities. It will provide short-term, medium-term and long-term credit. It will contribute to the share capital or invest in securities of any institution concerned with agricultural and rural development. It will formulate, design and aid projects and programmes to suit the requirements of agriculture and rural development.

NABARD will be managed by a full-time chairman and a separate Managing Director. It will have 16 regional offices under the control of regional managers.

(31) Small Farmers Development Agency (SFDA)

Small Farmers Development Agencies (SFDAs) have been established in 46 selected districts on an experimental basis to help those cultivators who have small yet potentially economically viable holdings. These agencies:

1. Identify small but viable farmers in their areas.
2. Find out the problems of such farmers.
3. Provide such farmers with institutional credit and inputs and help them to improve their production capacity.

The SFDAs help potentially viable farmers in their areas in such a way that they become viable in 3 to 4 years. The schemes of these agencies are mostly production and credit oriented. Every SFDA is supposed to help about 50,000 potentially viable farmers through assistance in subsidised irrigation, land levelling, soil conservation, storage, marketing and custom services facilities. Under this scheme 25 per cent of the assistance is in the form of a subsidy; the balance is a loan, mainly from cooperative credit institutions.

(32) Marginal Farmers and Agricultural Labourers Development Agencies (MFAL)

Marginal Farmers and Agricultural Labourers Development Agencies (MFAL) have been established to help sub-marginal farmers and agricultural labourers. Marginal farmers with holding up to one hectare and agricultural labourers who earn more than 50 per cent of their income from agriculture receive subsidised credit support for agriculture and subsidiary occupations under this scheme. This subsidised credit support is given for dairy farming, poultry, fishery, piggery, sheep rearing, horticulture, etc. The MFAL schemes are based mainly in favour of employment and subsidiary occupations.

(33) Farmers' Service Societies (FSS)

The National Commission on Agriculture (NCA), in its interim report in 1971 pointed out that the problem of agricultural credit was primarily the problem of providing credit and simultaneous organising facilities for the conversion of credit into various agricultural inputs and services. To convert this idea into actual practice, the NCA said that:

(a) The integrated credit service should be available to small and marginal farmers and agricultural labourers; and

(b) The organisation should cover not only a complete range of agricultural activities but ancillary occupations and artisans, and offer various types of services to the agricultural sector.

In accordance with these suggestions, some Farmers Service Societies have been organised in a few SFDA and MFAL areas by the commercial banks from 1973-74. The basic objectives of the schemes of FSS have been to offer to small farmers a full package of services and technical guidance instead of just credit.

(34) Duty Drawback Credit Scheme

The scheme is intended to benefit exporters who can avail of interest free finance from banks up to 90 days against shipping bills provisionally certified by the customs authorities towards refund of duty. The financing banks, in turn, are eligible to avail of interest free finance from Reserve Bank, pending final settlement of duty drawback claims of the exporters. During the period Nov. 1, 1981 to June 30, 1982, limits aggregating to ₹ 17.76 crore were sanctioned to 32 banks. As on June 30, 1982, these banks availed of refinance to the extent of ₹ 17.98 crore, and had an outstanding balance of ₹ 5.97 crore.

(35) Credit Authorisation Scheme

To ensure proper use of bank credit the Credit Authorisation Scheme was introduced by the Reserve Bank of India in 1965. Under the scheme, all the scheduled commercial banks are required to obtain the Reserve Bank's prior authorisation before sanctioning any fresh credit limits (including commercial bill discounts but excluding letters of credit and guarantee limits) of ₹ 2 crore or more in respect for private sector undertakings and ₹ 3 crore or more for public sector undertakings to a single party or any limit that would take the total limit enjoyed by such party from the entire banking system (including the cooperative sector) to ₹ 2 to 3 crore as the case may be on secured or unsecured basis. The system also covers individuals term credit exceeding ₹ 25 lakh as well, where the term of repayment exceeds three years, irrespective of the totality of credit limits available to the party from the entire banking system.

Term loans up to ₹ 50 lakh from the entire banking system in a period of a year (July-June) to a borrower engaged in industries listed under high-category for investment in capital assets would not require prior authorisation, irrespective of whether the party is covered under the credit authorisation scheme or not.

(36) Interest Tax

A tax on interest earned by commercial banks was imposed by the Government, known as Interest Tax, in the year 1974. This tax was withdrawn subsequently. But reintroduced from July 1, 1980. One of the objectives of Interest Tax is to increase revenues of the Central Government. Another objective is to make it an anti-inflationary measure, and, hence, its burden has been passed on the borrowers by adjusting the tax element upwards on a *pro rata* basis.

Besides the commercial banks, the scope of this tax has been extended to cover the interest earned by the all-India financial institutions like IDBI, ICICI, IDCI and IRBI. The rate of interest tax was 3.5 per cent (1983-84 budget). Chargeable interest of a previous year includes the total amount of interest accruing or arising to the bank on loans, and advances made in India. It includes discount on Promissory Notes and Bills of Exchange drawn or made in India. But the interest on loans and advances made to other scheduled banks and the interest earned on securities and discount on Treasury Bills are not included in the term interest.

(37) Factoring Services

☞ Definition of Factoring

A clear and succinct definition of factoring may be as follows:

"Factoring is a continuing legal relationship between a financial institution (the 'Factor') and a business concern (the 'client') selling goods or providing services to trade customers (the 'customers') on open account basis whereby the Factor purchases the client's book debts (accounts receivables), either with or without recourse to the client and in relation thereto, controls the credit extended to customers and administers the sales ledgers".

The meaning and significance of some of the words mentioned in the above definition are as follows:

(i) Clients/Customers

In the factoring context, the seller of goods is always referred to as a "client" and the buyers as the "customers".

(ii) On Open Account Basis

The distinctive feature of factoring service is that it facilitates greatly the conduct of business on open account basis. This feature will refreshingly be welcome to industry and trade, as against the other modes of payments, *viz.*, D/P, D/A and L/C.

(iii) Purchases

A factor finances a supplier, not by way of providing an advance, such as banker does, but by literally purchasing the book debts by making a pre-payment. It becomes the owner of the debts and thereby it assumes the onus of collecting the debts. If it is to be effective in its collections, it has preferably to assume control over the credit management of the supplier, including the maintenance of the sales ledgers. The significance of the words "in relation thereto", thus becomes clear.

☞ Factoring Services

The conventional services that a Factor offers are as under:

(a) Financing of Receivables

This is a key feature of factoring. The factor purchases the book debts of a client at a price. The debts are assigned in its favour.

The factoring could be with or without recourse to the client.

Being a purchase, and not an advance, a distinct advantage to the supplier is that his Balance Sheet shows an improved current ratio.

(b) Collection of Receivables

The Factor relieves the client of the onus of making the collections by itself assuming the responsibility. Resultantly the client gets the following benefits:

(i) Elimination or reduction in cost of collections in terms of savings of manpower as well as time and energy.

(ii) The client could concentrate better on the management of purchases, production, marketing, research and development, development of new products, etc.

One could legitimately ask whether the intervention of the Factor would not adversely affect the client's relationship with customers; also, how the factor would be more effective than the supplier himself in making the collections. The factor does not adopt stringent or coercive measures. It is equipped with trained and exclusive manpower. It has infrastructural aids such as access to communication network possibly dedicated. In other words, the follow-up of collections will be religiously systematic. As against this, very few organisations, even among larger ones, have separate or well organized credit management departments, exclusively devoted to collection matters. Units in the Small-scale industrial sector can ill-afford separate staff or infrastructural back-up.

(c) Credit Control and Sales Ledger Administration

Soon after concluding the factoring contract, the Factor steps in, through offer of his professional services, to control the credit extended and to be extended by the client. The Factor is able to provide quality services in this area as it builds up extensive information files on the financial standing and credit rating of individual customers and their track record for payments. Often a customer or a potential customer is also the customer of other clients. Based on the information files, a factor is able to advise its clients on whether at all to extend credit to a buyer, the amount of credit to be extended and for what period. Further, the Factor establishes credit limits for individual customers and indicates the extent to which it is prepared to accept the client's receivable on such customers.

It could happen that the Factor is in a position to advise its clients about the customers who could be extended more liberal credit terms or with whom it may not be desirable to do business. Thus, this specialised service of the factor enables the client to handle a far greater volume of business with confidence than would otherwise have been possible.

The client sends to the Factor copies of all invoices despatched to the customers. The factor maintains the individual sales ledgers in respect of the customers, on behalf of the client. The client is furnished by the Factor with periodical reports of the status of the receivables, together with age analysis and other useful information.

(d) Credit Protection

This refers to the insurance provided by the Factor to the client against default of payment by a customer. Where finance facility is provided, the credit protection is available only under a 'without recourse' arrangement. There could be cases where credit insurance is availed of, without resort to the finance facility as in the case of cash-rich companies.

The insurance covers only the debt defaults arising out of buyer's insolvency or financial inability to pay. Defaults occurring on account of commercial disputes such as those related to quality standards, faulty or delayed deliveries and other lapses in adhering to the terms of the sales contract are not covered.

Besides the above-mentioned conventional services, Factors also offer:

(e) Advisory Services

A Factor is in a position to render certain advisory services by reason of the specialised knowledge and experience of industries, the data bank and the information base it possesses: the skilled and technical personnel in its employment can extend financial and other industrial counselling services. It also provides to the client information on prospective buyers to facilitate market thrust.

(f) Other Innovative Services

In the USA and UK Factors do extend financial facilities over and above the prepayment made for the purchase of book debts. They are willing to facilitate opening of L/Cs by the client against their confirmation. Financial assistance, in some form or other, with or without security, is provided by the factor, to enable the client to tide over a temporary difficulty or a seasonal problem. This may even be to acquire inventories, *i.e.,* finance is provided even before a receivable is generated.

Factors to be set up in our country may not be expected to provide such innovative services before they stabilise and mature. Even Reserve Bank of India may be chary about so permitting them Even if a line is clearly drawn between the Factoring and banking services, yet it should be possible, in due course, in India as well, to merge to a state of liberalisation and progress, wherein with close association of a factor with a Bank, a client is rarely left to fend for himself in moments of temporary difficulties. However, it should be emphasised that nowhere in the world, Factors perceive their role as a provider of rehabilitation assistance. All the same, a client, with a support of a factor, is generally able to secure a more efficient management of its working capital which. in turn, helps in prevention of sickness.

Although a Factor offers a full range of services, some of the clients may not need all the services. A cash-rich supplier may not need funding services. A client selling to buyers of high standing and good payments track record may not need 'without recourse' factoring. A well-organised company with efficient credit management set-up, may not need sales ledger administration and collection services. It may, however, require the financial facility to have a smooth cash flow. It is of importance that the factor should identify the needs of the client and evolve a suitably tailored package of services so that factoring is perceived by the client as relevant to his business. After all, for each of the services, a price or fee has to be paid by the client.

Factoring services are not quite suitable for certain categories of business, *e.g.,* those undertaking job works, those where work-in-progress payments are involved and those prone to frequent disputes between sellers and buyers.

☛ Pricing of Services

Interest will be charged on the finance service normally at a rate not less than what banks charge for working capital finance. The charges for the administrative facilities will range from 1 per cent to 2.5 per cent /3.5 per cent. depending upon the services availed of, the credit sales turnover of the client, the number of invoices, the average amount of invoices, the creditworthiness and risk involved, etc.

The margin or spread will be low, considering the cost of funds to be raised and the competitive prices to be quoted *vis-a-vis* Banks. The turnover has therefore, to be large.

☛ Types of Factoring

The principal types of Factoring are:

(a) Full Factoring — Provides all four conventional facilities.

(b) Maturity Factoring — Prepayment is not made *ab initio*, but after an agreed period which is an estimated period of payment beyond the credit term.

(c) Undisclosed Factoring — Normally, the Factor's interest in the debt is notified directly to the customer. This is generally by way of imprinting a legend on the invoices sent to the customers, requesting them to make the payment directly to the factor. Some sellers may not want buyers to know of the factoring arrangement. In such a case, no notice of assignment of debt is given. Only finance, with or without credit protection, is extended. The client maintains the sales ledger and makes collections The Factor keeps a check on its risk by receiving from the client an age-wise analysis of the debts, at regular intervals.

(d) Invoice discounting — This is a variant of undisclosed factoring. The Factor purchases all or selected invoices of its client at a discount. The Factor does not maintain the sales ledger or undertake debt collection, the only function being to provide finance.

☞ The Organisation for Factoring

Any Factor to be set up should be well-equipped to handle a very large volume of transactions. This is necessary in view of the thin spread or low margins. The debtor-customers will be spread all over the country. It is, therefore, necessary for the Factor to have the back-up of the following infrastructure:

1. A large network of offices to reach far-flung customers for information, follow-up contact, recovery and remittance
2. Dedicated/integrated communication network for like purposes.
3. Extensive computer facilities, with on-line linkages.
4. A dedicated, knowledgeable and trained team of personnel, which includes financial analysts, computer specialists, legal experts and persons with intimate knowledge of particular industries and counselling capabilities.

Availability of sizeable funds to support large turnover is an important criterion. Only Banks, it is viewed, can command the funds of the order required and the high cost pre-requisite infrastructure mentioned. Banks can organise the purveying of the service through their subsidiaries or associates, rather than division of themselves, in order to achieve greater professionalism, better efficiency of operations and distinctive work culture.

☞ Factoring and Small-scale Industry

Small-scale industrial units have high expectations from Factors when set up. At the same time, they do have reservations whether they will be considered as creditworthy by the Factors.

In this context, it should be emphasized that Factors focus on assessing the creditworthiness of customers and will be in a better position to evaluate and accept the security of book debts even from SSI units as clients. In fact, on this basis, they may find SSI units relatively low risk as such units cater largely to established medium/large units.

For another reason too, Factors would look to SSI units for business. Factors cannot operate on viable lines, unless their volume of turnover is large. For this, they have necessarily, in their own interest, to exploit the vast market potential of this segment.

SSI Units cannot expect any directed credit finance allocation from Factors who will be operating strictly on commercial lines. They could, however, continue to enjoy the concessional finance under the tie-up arrangement between the Bank and the Factor.

SSI units would have access to periodical flow from Factors of analytical data on debtor-customers, present and potential. They would also have the benefit of timely and expert advice regarding problems faced, either generally by the industry or specifically by the units.

☞ International Factoring

International, factoring will greatly benefit exporters. Export trade is fraught with greater risks than the domestic trade.

International factoring generally operates on a two-factor system – an Export Factor (EF) in the exporter's country and an Import Factor (IF) in the importer's country. The Import Factor will provide the administrative services, *viz.,* credit protection, sales ledger administration and collection and remittance. There are what are called Factoring chains or groups which facilitate linking up of factors in various countries. The well-known ones are Factors International, International Factor's Group and Hellor's Group.

There is a trend world over to move away from L/C to non-L/C business. The interests of the exporter are no less protected under factoring than under L/C arrangement. Yet, sales are on open account basis. Factoring offers protection from risks such as currency devaluation and externalisation problems of importing countries, as pre-payment is made in rupees by the Export Factor.

The factors to be set up in India could start International factoring only after gaining experience in domestic factoring. The permission of the Reserve Bank of India (RBI) would be required under the Foreign Exchange Regulation Act (FERA) for commencing International factoring operations.

(38) Commercial Paper (CP)

Commercial Paper is a short-term negotiable money market instrument, consisting of unsecured promissory notes, with a fixed maturity, typically between seven days and three months, issued in a bearer form. Issues can be made on an occasional basis, or more generally, under a medium term revolving programme, with rollover facilities. Commercial Paper may be issued by many types of borrowers, including industrial and commercial companies, bank holding companies, etc. It is sold either directly by the issuer to investors, or placed by an intermediary bank or security dealers to investors like insurance companies, pension and provident funds, mutual funds, etc.

CPs differ from other short-term money market instruments such as banker's acceptances, in that it is the obligation of the issuer only, whereas acceptances are an obligation of both the drawer and the accepting bank. Another difference between CP and banker's acceptance is that issues of CPs do not have to be tied to a specific transaction, which is, in many circumstances, the case with the acceptances.

An important advantage of commercial paper is its simplicity. Documentation is minimum between the issuer and the investor and there is a flexibility with regard to the maturity of the instrument which can be tailored to the needs of both the issuer and the investor. A well rated company can diversify its sources of finance and raise short-term funds at somewhat cheaper rates than available from banks. This is more true of a financial system where reserve requirements of banks are compulsory. Investors can earn higher returns than what is obtainable from the banking system or on treasury bills. It also provides an incentive to the issuing companies to remain financially strong and efficient as it reduces the cost of borrowing. It also helps companies in raising long-term funds by becoming better known in the financial world. In the Indian context, CPs have another advantage of raising funds from the inter-corporate market, which are, at present, not under the control of monetary authorities.

The Working Group on the Money Market, set up by the Reserve Bank, in its report in 1987, recommended the introduction of Commercial Paper in India which is so popular in developed countries with the setting up of a Credit Rating Agency — the Credit Rating Information Services of India Ltd., (CRISIL), the stage was set for starting a Commercial Paper market.

In the light of the recommendations of the working group, the Reserve Bank announced its intention to introduce Commercial Paper in the Indian Market. Detailed guidelines for the purpose were issued in Dec. 1989 through Non-banking Companies (Acceptance of Deposits through Commercial Paper) Direction, 1989.

☞ Reserve Bank Guidelines for Issue of Commercial Paper

1. — A minimum tangible net worth of ₹ 10 crore.
   — A working capital of ₹ 25 crore (fund-based) or above
   — Listing on one or more stock exchanges
   — A PIT rating from CRISIL

— A minimum current ratio of 1.33

— The amount should be classified under health code No.1 by the financial banks.

2. The maturity of Commercial Paper should be minimum three months and maximum six months from the date of issue.
3. Each issue of CP (including rollovers) requires the approval of Reserve Bank.
4. The CP may be issued in multiples of ₹ 25 lakh, but the minimum amount to be invested by a single investor in the primary market shall be ₹ 1 crore of face value.
5. The aggregate amount to be raised by issue of CP is limited to 20 per cent of the company's working capital (fund-based) limit. The working capital limit of a company issuing the commercial paper is required to be correspondingly reduced by the bank once the issue is actually placed in the market. The intention is that CP would help reduce the cost of funds but not result in any increase in the overall resources.
6. CP is in the form of usance Promissory Notes, negotiable by endorsement and delivery, and issued at a discount to reflect the interest; the discount rate is to be freely determined by the issuing company. The company issuing CP has also to bear the expenses of the issue, including stamp duty, dealer's fee, rating agency fee, etc.
7. CPs will be issued to any person or corporate bodies (including banks) registered or incorporated in India as well as unincorporated bodies. Non-resident Indians can also invest, but on a non-repatriable basis and such a CP will not be transferable.
8. The issue of CP cannot be underwritten or co-accepted in any manner.
9. A company issuing CP is free to request its bankers to provide standby facility for an amount not exceeding the amount of issue for meeting the liability of CP on maturity.

A general permission has been granted by the Reserve Bank to all companies governed by Foreign Exchange Regulation Act, 1973 (FERA) to raise deposits by issue of CP. A company issuing CP is required to ensure that the relevant provisions of the various statutes such as Companies Act, 1956, the Income Tax Act, Negotiable Instruments Act, etc., are complied with.

☞ Further Liberalisation

With the issuance of these guidelines, several companies approached the Reserve Bank for issue of CP. In order to broad base the primary market and widen the scope for secondary market, the Reserve Bank made the following relaxations in the issue of CPs:

(i) The tangible net worth of the company eligible to issue a CP was reduced from ₹ 10 crore to ₹ 5 crore.

(ii) The minimum working capital (fund-based) limit was reduced to ₹ 15 crore from ₹ 25 crore.

(iii) The minimum credit rating from CRISIL was relaxed from P_{1+} to P_1.

(iv) The denomination in which the CPs could be issued was reduced to multiples of ₹ 10 lakh from ₹ 25 lakh earlier, while the minimum size of an issue to a single investor was reduced from ₹ one crore to ₹ 50 lakh (face value).

CPs have gained good market over the years. On June 28, 1991, outstanding amount of CPs issued by 50 Scheduled Commercial Banks was ₹ 4,556 crore (62.2 per cent of the limits of these banks). The typical interest rate for a three-month CP was in the range of 14 to 16 per cent per annum. For one year CP it was between 15 per cent to 16 per cent. At the end of Dec. 1991, the outstanding amount of CPs stood at ₹ 5,023 crore.

☞ Commercial Paper vs. Company Deposits

It is easier for companies to raise funds through public deposits. After the limit of public deposits is exhausted, the bank may go to Commercial Paper market to raise more funds. In India public deposits are raised for longer periods and are in small amounts of ₹ 5,000 to 10,000. Therefore, the cost of administration of public deposits is higher. Further, since for raising deposits no credit rating exercise is compulsory, investors may not like to place large sums with such companies. The threat to banks from commercial paper should not be more than that from company deposits, which are in some ways similar to Commercial Paper.

☞ Commercial Paper vs. Certificate of Deposits

Certificate of Deposits carry interest rate which is related to market rates and are not administered. Several banks offer up to 13 per cent interest to lure away deposits from other banks. In such a case, few investors will have the incentive to invest in Commercial Paper, because although the rate of return on certificate of deposits may be comparable, it does not carry any risk and banks are easy to react, while merchant banking institutions are few and not easy to reach.

The only problem with CDs is that, so far, they are limited to only 2 per cent of aggregate deposits of banks. Almost all banks have issued CDs up to the permissible limits. If this limit is raised, there will be a move away from Commercial Paper, unless the demand is so high that it spills over to CPs. It is surprising how banks, without any regard for their profitability, are going for Certificate of Deposits, when the cost is so high not only because the rate of interest on them is higher than even the maximum on fixed deposits, but also because certificate of deposits are subject to reserve requirements. It is, therefore, better for banks to encourage Commercial Paper rather than Certificate of Deposit.

TANDON COMMITTEE RECOMMENDATION

In July 1974, RBI constituted a study group to frame guidelines to follow-up of bank credit under the Chairmanship of Shri P.L. Tandon. The report submitted by the Committee in August 1975 is referred to as the Tandon Committee Report. The terms of reference for the Committee were:

1. Suggest guidelines for commercial banks to follow-up and supervise credit from the point of view of ensuring proper end-use of funds and keeping a watch on the safety of the advances and to suggest the type of operational data and other information that may be obtained by banks periodically from such borrowers and by the RBI from the lending banks.
2. Make recommendation for obtaining periodical forecasts from borrowers of:
    - Business/production plans, and
    - Credit needs
3. Make suggestions for prescribing inventory norms for different industries both in the private and public sector and indicate the broad criterion for deviating from these norms.
4. Suggest criterion regarding the sources for financing the minimum WC requirements.
5. Make recommendations as to whether the existing pattern of WC requirements by cash and if so, to safest suitable modifications.
6. Make recommendations on any other related matter as the groups may consider germane to the subject of enquiry or any other allied matter which may be specified referred to it by the RBI. The study group came up with a comprehensive set of recommendations.

☞ Norms for Inventory and Receivables

The committee has come out with a set of norms that represent the maximum levels for holding inventory and receivables in each of 15 major industries, covering about 50% of industrial advances to banks. As norms cannot be rigid, deviations from norms can be permitted under extenuating circumstances such as bunched receipts by raw materials, including imports, power cuts, strikes, transport bottlenecks, etc., for usually short periods. One normally restored is, the norms should become applicable. The norms should be applied to all industrial borrowers with aggregate limits from the banking system in excess of ₹ 10 lakh and extended to smaller borrowers progressively.

CHORE COMMITTEE

The various committees constituted by the RBI including the Tandon Committee had pointed out the drawbacks of the cash credit system. Tandon Committee had recommended for the bifurcation of the credit limit into a demand loan and a fluctuating cash credit component. The progress achieved in this respect had been very slow. Consequently, a small working group was set up by the RBI under the chairmanship of Shri K.B. Chore in April 1978 with specific terms of reference.

To review the operations of cash credit in recent years particularly with reference to the gap between sanctioned credit limits and the extent of their utilisation.

1. A modification in the system with the view to making the system more amenable to rational management of funds by commercial banks.
2. Alternate types of credit facilities which would ensure greater credit discipline and also enable banks to relate credit limits to increase in outputs or other productive activities and to make recommendations on any other related matter as the group may consider germane to the subject.

☞ Cash Credit Limits Against Book Debts

Sales are finalised either by allowing purchase/discount facilities of bills drawn by the seller or simply as cash credit facility against book debts. The facility of cash credit against book debts is to be discouraged and such limits are to be converted to bill purchase/discount facilities wherever possible.

For all borrowers enjoying aggregates fund based WC limits of ₹ 5 crore and more from the banking system a minimum of 25% of the limits sanctioned to such borrowers for financing inland credit sales must be in the shape of bill purchase/discount facilities.

Bifurcation of MPBF: The MPBF in respect of borrowers covered under the system will be bifurcated in two components as under:

➢ Cash credit component, and

➢ Loan component

In respect of borrowers with assessed MPBF of ₹ 20 crore and above cash credit component will be restricted to a maximum of 20% of MPBF only. The balance MPBF, if desired, can be availed only in the form of short-term loans repayable on demand for a stipulated period. A borrower may, however, avail short-term loan for WC purpose at a level of more than as the case may be, with corresponding reduction in cash credit component. To illustrate the system of bifurcation let us consider the following example:

Borrower with an assessed MPBF of ₹ 40 crore:

MPBF will be bifurcated as under:

Cash credit component – restricted to 20%, *i.e.,* ₹ 8 crore.

Loan component – ₹ 32 crore.

The borrower may avail higher loan component than indicated above in both the above cases with corresponding reduction in cash credit component. It shall further be noted that cash credit component is directly related to assessed MPBF and the loan component may or may not be availed by the borrower. The net effect of this bifurcation will thus reduce the quantum of total credit facilities available to the borrower in the shape of cash credit.

☞ Period of Loan

The introduction of this new loan system in the delivery of bank credit for WC purposes restricts cash credit to 20% of the borrower's credit limit. It does not however restrict the demand loan component to 80%. The borrower can avail more than 80% of his limit as demand loan component subject to his total limits. This helps to introduce credit discipline among borrowers and give banks the benefit of the certainty of utilisation of its funds by a borrower.

☞ Behaviour of Current Assets

The minimum level of current assets obtained by a company is more in the nature of fixed assets and hence can be regarded as permanent or fixed component of current assets, *i.e.,* cash receivables and inventory required to carry on the operations without break.

The level of current assets of the company can be looked upon as the permanent component of current assets super imposed by the fluctuating component. The behaviour of current assets in terms of fixed and fluctuating components, has an important bearing on the pattern of financing to be normally adopted. The level of current assets overtime is shown below.

The permanent current assets will go through the different stages of the operating cycle but are not locked up permanently as in the case of fixed assets. The permanent component needs to be financed from the long-term sources of finance available to a company such as internal accruals, ordinary shares, preference shares, debentures and to some extent term loans. The temporary or fluctuating component can be financed from the short-term sources such as accounts payable or trade credit, short-term bank borrowings or public deposits.

The sources which a company will have ready access to for financing the current assets during the normal course of business operations are referred to as spontaneous sources. These include accrued expenses, provisions and trade credit.

CREDIT CARDS

A credit card is an instrument which provides instantaneous credit facilities to its holder to avail a variety of goods and services at the merchant outlet. It is made of plastic and hence popularly called as 'plastic money'. Such cards are issued by banks to persons with incomes above certain minimum limits and are accepted by a variety of business establishments which are notified by the card-issuing bank. There are thus three parties to a credit card:

(i) the issuing bank,

(ii) the cardholder

(iii) the member establishments.

Leading Indian banks, such as the State Bank of India, Canara Bank, Bank of Baroda, Andhra Bank and a few foreign banks, *viz.,* Citibank, Hong Kong Bank and ANZ Grindlays Bank are the important issuers of Credit Cards in India. Some of them insist on the Cardholder being their customer while others do not. Similarly a few of them, specially Canara Bank, do not charge any fee for issuing credit cards, while others impose an initial enrolment fee and annual fee also. The eligibility conditions for issuing these cards prescribe certain minimum income ranges between ₹ 50,000 and ₹ 1 lakh per annum. The aim of the issuer bank is to provide this facility to the growing middle-income group and people above them. The cardholder is issued a plastic card on which is inscribed the name of the issuing bank, the card number, the name of its holder and his/her signatures.

The issuing bank enrolls member-establishments which agree to accept these cards for accepting payments for goods and services sold. They include various commercial establishments, shops, hotels, travel agencies, railways and domestic and international airlines.

When a cardholder makes purchases or avails of any services at a member-establishment, he signs a charge slip. For this purpose he is identified by his signature on the credit card. The member establishment gives one copy of the charge-slip to the customer, and presents the other to the respective issuing bank, which makes payment to the member establishment, after deducting its commission which may range between 2% and 4%. In turn the bank bills the cardholder for the full amount periodically, say monthly. The cardholder is allowed to make payment in full within a specified period, say 15 days. Thus, a cardholder avails of credit for a period ranging between 30 and 40 days. Some banks allow the cardholders to pay the bills in easy instalments; some require payment of 10% within the specified period and the balance later on. Some banks permit arrears up to three months involving a service charge of 2% p.a. The cardholder is thus allowed the facility of "revolving credit" at no extra cost. In fact, at the time of issuance of a credit card, a limit is also prescribed up to which the card-holder can avail credit on the card. As soon as a bill is paid by the cardholder, he can again avail of credit facility of similar amount.

Credit card business is a highly profitable business for the issuing banker. Their funds remain blocked up from the time they make payments to the member establishments till they realize the same from the cardholders. This cycle is complete within 40 to 45 days. As they get a commission up to 4% on each transaction, they earn about 40% p.a. on the capital employed by them in this business.

The member establishments are also benefited in a number of ways. Generally, they deal in high profit goods and services and hence larger turnover due to the facility of credit cards enhances their profits. They derive the advantage of larger sales on credit basis by paying a commission to the issuing banker, who guarantees to make payment for such sales. Thus, they pass on the risk of non-realization to the issuing banker.

☞ Other Advantages to the Cardholders

The business of credit cards is expanding in India. Banks are competing with each other by offering a number of additional benefits to the cardholders, some of which are as follows:

(i) Some of the card issuing banks enter into tie-up arrangements with other banks for issuing cards, e.g., Cancards of Canara Bank are issued by seven other member banks. Banks tie-up with other international credit cards.

(ii) Banks permit withdrawal of cash against credit cards at their branches also. The foreign banks have ATMs facilities for this purpose. The withdrawals are within specified limits only and nominal interest is charged thereon. The State Bank of India provides a specially designed cheque book to the cardholders, which could be used for withdrawing cash at any of its branch. The cheque leaf is of the denomination of ₹ 500 and goes up to ₹ 2,500.

(iii) Banks provide personal accidental insurance to the cardholders and their family members up to certain limits, say ₹ 3 to 4 lakh either free of cost or at discounted rates.

(iv) The credit cards also enable the cardholders to avail of other facilities such as booking of air tickets on phone.

(v) In case a card is lost the cardholder has a limited liability, usually up to ₹ 1,000.

☞ Difference Between Credit Cards and Traveller Cheques

Though both credit cards and traveller cheques are issued by the banks, they differ as follows:

1. The objective of a traveller cheque is to enable its holder to travel carefree without the risk of loss of money in transit and to encash them as and when he needs money. But a credit card enables its holder to purchase goods and services on credit and pay later.
2. The consideration for traveller cheques is paid to the bank in advance. Hence, the holder's money remains with the bank during the period such cheque remains in the possession of its holder. But a credit cardholder pays the value of goods purchased and services availed after the specified period is over.
3. Traveller cheques are issued by banks free of cost, but credit cardholders are charged an admission fee, annual fee and also service charge on delayed payments.
4. Traveller cheques are printed for fixed denomination like ₹ 50, ₹ 100, ₹ 500, etc., but transactions under the credit cards may be undertaken for any amounts within the specified limits.

STANDING INSTRUCTIONS

Banks render a useful service to their customers by complying with their standing instructions. Standing instructions are the instructions given by a customer to his banker which relate to certain financial dealings, (*e.g.,* receipts, transfers of payments of money) which the customer intends his banker to undertake on his behalf on regular basis. These instructions are meant either for a specific period mentioned by the customer or are to be carried out till a notice to the contrary is given by the customer. These instructions relate to dealings which are generally repetitive in nature. Some of these instructions are as follows:

1. Payments of life insurance premium to LIC periodically.
2. Payment of periodic membership fee/subscription to clubs, libraries, professional associations or charitable institutions.
3. Payment of other bills of the customer.
4. Transfer of specified amounts from one account of the customer to another account, *e.g.,* from savings account to Recurring Deposit account every month or to Fixed Deposit Account whenever the balance exceeds a certain amount.
5. Collection of dividends on behalf of customers.
6. Collection of pensions from Govt. Deptts.
7. Collection of interest on Government securities held in safe custody or otherwise.

On receipt of such instructions, bank should note the same on the ledger page of the concerned accountholder and also keep its record in 'Standing Instructions Register'. Bank should regularly comply with such instructions. In respect of payments, however, the banker bears no responsibility, if the customer's account does not possess the minimum amount required to carry-out the instruction. Hence, the customer's responsibility is to ensure sufficient amount in the account at a time when payment is to be made as per the standing instruction. In carrying out such instructions the banker acts as his customer's agent and hence may be held liable for the loss sustained by him due to his negligence by way of non-compliance or delayed compliance of the standing instruction.

GIFT CHEQUES

Banks issue gift cheques to the members of the public to enable them to present a specified amount to some friend or relation on some auspicious occasion. Thus, a gift cheque is a means of sending money by one person to another. These cheques are printed in attractive colours and designs. They are issued with counterfoils in different denominations which are printed there on, *viz.,* ₹ 11, 21, 51, or 101. Payee's name is inserted therein at the time of purchase. Neither a surcharge is imposed for its issuance nor any interest is payable to the purchaser/payee for the period for which the amount remains with the bank till the cheque is encashed. Thus, such cheques enable the banks to mobilise short-term deposits without any cost.

These cheques are payable on demand and hence the payee can claim the money at any branch of the issuing bank. If a gift cheque is lost, a duplicate one can be issued on submission of an indemnity bond.

☞ Difference Between Gift Cheques and Traveller Cheques

1. Gifts cheques are issued in small denominations, while traveller cheques are for relatively large amounts.
2. Traveller cheques are payable only to the purchaser, whose signature is taken thereon at the time of purchase, but a gift cheque is payable to an individual mentioned therein.
3. Traveller cheques are accepted by various business establishments from their customers in discharge of their obligations, but this is not possible in case of gift cheques.

TELLER SYSTEM

Some banks have introduced Teller system at some of their branches to expedite receipts of small amounts and payments of cheques, etc. Usually, when a cheque is presented for payment, it passes through a number of persons, *e.g.,* the ledger-keeper, accountant, cashier, etc., which takes time. To curtail such time, teller system has been introduced. Under this system one of the cashiers is designated as Teller who handles cash up to specified amounts immediately on presentation of cheque by the payee. He does not consult the ledger account or the specimen signature of the customer. He does so, only in case of doubt. Thus, payment of cheques is expedited. Banks prescribe maximum amount of payment and deposits to be dealt with by the Teller.

Besides the above a Teller also encashes Bank's rupee Traveller Cheques up to ₹ 2,500, Bank drafts up to ₹ 2,000 and gift cheques up to ₹ 2,000.

In some banks Prompt Payment Teller system has been adopted. Under this system, customers' accounts and specimen signatures are maintained in dublicate. One set is kept by the Teller, wherein customers' A/c is maintained on cards. He consults the A/c, makes entries therein and verifies the drawer's signature before making payments. Thereafter, the cheque is sent to the ledger-keeper who makes entries in the ledger account.

LIMITATIONS OF PRESENT CASH CREDIT SYSTEM NEW MODELS FOR REGULATING CASH CREDIT

The cash credit system is the main vehicle used by the banks for financing working capital requirement of industrial houses. The cash credit system follows a simple security based approach. The borrower provides security as stocks that are pledged or hypothecated to the bank. The bank deducts a specified percentage of the value of the security as margin and marks a drawing power in the cash credit account of the borrower. The borrower is now free to issue cheques and draw on his account to the extent of the drawing power. This system suffers from two important shortcomings.

1. The networking capital, *viz.,* the long-term funds available for financing the working capital requirements is usually based on projections submitted by the borrower. Many times the projected networking capital is based on an assumed profitability, which may or may not materialize. If the actual profitability turn out to be different from the projections the entire assessment may go wrong.
2. The limits are sanctioned on the basis of peak requirements. Most units work at below the peak levels for extended periods spanning several months each year. For example, consider a unit at its peak build-up of current assets as under:

(₹ in lakh)

Current Liabilities		*Current Assets*	
Bank borrowing	40	Stock	100
Sundry Creditors	50	Other current assets	20
	90		
NWC	30		
	120		120

On the basis of the peak requirements the unit is sanctioned a limit of ₹ 40 lakh. However, for a substantial part of the year, the need for the bank finance hovers at a lower level.

☞ New Models for Regulating Cash Credit

First Model: The simple drawings power model: The above problem can be tackled through a simple and ingenious method. At the time of sanction, the margin can be stipulated as a fixed amount or a percentage of the limit. Now the drawing power will be as under:

	At Peak	*Off Peak*
Stocks	100	80
Less: Margin	60	60
Drawing Power	40	20

Even by restricting the drawing power to ₹ 20 lakh, the borrower is able to draw just enough to meet his working capital needs. Since there is no extra drawing power available, the chances of diversion of funds are minimised.

Second Model: This system offer the following advantages over the existing approach:

(a) This is a need based approach and the drawing power correctly reflects the changing needs due to changes in inventory level as well as change in credit available in the market. The scope for diversion of funds is virtually eliminated.

(b) The calculation is simple and can be easily applied even to the smallest advances. The margin is fixed at the time of sanction/annual renewal at a level which allow the unit to draw the full amount sanctioned to him at the time of peak build-up of stocks.

(c) The approach is flexible as the margin can be refixed at the time of each renewal as well as whenever any excess drawings are granted.

The drawing power calculation will be now as under:

Stocks		100
Less: Sundry Creditors	65	
Add: Margins	10	– 75
Drawing Power		25

☞ New Paradigms

Bankers usually believe that sanctioning need based limits is enough to ensure end-use of funds. We have been able to show to paradigms where the calculation of drawing power itself can be need based. Such an approach, if adopted, may yield substantial benefits to the banks and is, at the least worth considering.

PERFORMING AND NON-PERFORMING ASSETS

Any amount of loan given by the Bank is termed as Performing Asset if the interest and loan instalments are being repaid regularly to the bank by the borrower.

In case interest and instalment of principal are in default for two quarters then this is termed as Non-performing Assets.

(39) SHORT NOTES

Stock Exchanges, BSE, NSE, OTCEI, Investment, Securities and Mutual Funds

STOCK MARKET

☞ Meaning

Business finance is concerned with the provision of funds for investment in business enterprise, whatever is invested in this way must be provided by an investor, and this means that the investor must forgo consumption and save to provide the funds. Savers and the users of their funds come together in the market for finance, where the normal rules of supply and demand apply unless there is government interference with interest rates. The price of money is the rate of interest paid for the use. If the demand for investment funds is greater than the funds offered for investment by savers, then the rate of interest will rise until people in the economy are induced to forgo consumption and make their savings available for investment.

The new issues of securities are made available in the *'primary market'*. The securities that are already outstanding and owned by the investors are usually bought and sold through the *'secondary market'*. Which are popularly known as *'Stock Market'*.

In the stock markets, the outstanding issues are permitted to trade. In this market, a stock or bond issue has already been sold to the public, and it is traded between current and potential owners. The proceeds from a sale in the stock market do not go to the issuing organisation but to the current owner of the security.

Once new issues have been purchased by investors, they change hands in the stock market. There are two broad segments of the stock markets: *(i)* The organised stock exchanges *(ii)* The over-the-counter (OTC) market. The primary middlemen in the stock market are brokers and dealers. The distinction between them is, the broker acts as an agent, whereas the dealer acts as a principal in the transaction.

Stock markets are said to reflect the health of the country's economy. On the other hand, major economic indicators determine stock market movements to a large extent. From a thorough analysis of the various economic indicators and its implications on the stock markets, it is known that stock market movements are largely influenced by broad money supply, inflation, credit/deposit ratio and fiscal deficit apart from political instability. Besides, fundamental factors like corporate performance, industrial growth, etc., always exert a certain amount of influence on the stock markets.

Because the stock market involves the trading of securities initially sold in the primary market, it is providing liquidity to the individuals who acquired these securities. The trends in stock market will have impact on the primary market.

The secondary market in India comprises of 23 stock exchanges on which 9,922 listed securities are transacted. A large volume of transactions on the secondary markets are put through the BSE and NSE. Presently, the BSE and NSE put together account for 83% of the total turnover as compared to 17% by the other stock exchanges. The BSE, which was originally established with 318 members in the year 1875, presently has 711 members. Its location, which originally was Mumbai, has now enlarged to many cities spread over the country through the satellite network. The National Stock Exchange of India (NSE), which was established in the year 1994 made rapid strides and has strength of 850 members in many cities spread across the length and breadth of the country. The NSE since inception was an electronic exchange.

Till recent past, floor trading took place in all the stock exchanges. In the floor trading system, the trade takes place through open outcry system during the official trading hours. Trading posts are assigned for different securities where buy and sell activities of securities took place. This system needs a face-to-face contact among the traders and restricts the trading volume. The speed of the new information reflected on the prices was rather slow. The deals were also not transparent and the system favoured the brokers rather than the investors.

Table 25.1

STOCK EXCHANGES: TURNOVER IN INDIA

	Total Turnover 2001-02 (₹ in crore)	*Total Turnover 2002-03 (₹ in crore)*	*Percentage Valuation*
Ahmedabad	14,843.54	15,458.64	4.1
BSE	3,07,392.3	3,14,073.2	2.2
Bangalore	70.2	0.0	NA
Bhubaneshwar	0.0	0.0	NA
Kolkata	27,074.7	6,539.9	–75.8
Cochin	26.6	0.0	NA
Coimbatore	0.0	0.0	NA
Delhi	5,828.0	11.1	–99.8
Guwahati	0.0	0.5	NA
Hyderabad	41.2	4.6	–88.8
ICSE	55.3	64.8	17.2
Jaipur	0.0	0.0	NA
Ludhiana	856.6	0.0	–100.0
Chennai	24.1	0.0	–100.0
Magadh	0.0	0.51	NA
Mangalore	0.0	0.0	NA

MPSE	15.9	0.0	-100.0
NSE	5,13,166.9	6,17,988.6	20.4
OTCEI	3.7	0.1	97.3
Pune	1,171.0	1.81	-99.8
SKSE	0.0	0.0	NA
UPSE	25,237.3	14,763.4	-41.5
Vadodara	10.1	2.59	74.3
Total	**8,95,817.4**	**9,68,907.6**	

NA: Not Applicable **Source:** SEBI Annual Report, 2002-03.

The setting up of NSE and OTECI with the screen based trading facility resulted in more and more stock exchanges turning towards the computer based trading. Bombay Stock Exchange introduced the screen based trading system in 1995, which is known as BOLT (Bombay On-line Trading System).

Madras stock exchange introduced Automated Network Trading System (MANTRA) on October 7, 1996. Apart from Bombay stock exchange, Vadodara, Delhi, Pune, Bangalore, Calcutta and Ahmedabad stock exchanges have introduced screen based trading. Other exchanges are also planning to shift to the screen based trading. The turnover and market share of the various stock exchanges are given in Table 25.1.

☞ Functions of Stock Exchange

Maintains active trading: Shares are traded on the stock exchanges, enabling the investors to buy and sell securities. The prices may vary from transaction-to-transaction. A continuous trading increases the liquidity or marketability of the shares traded on the stock exchanges.

Fixation of prices: Price is determined by the transactions that flow from investors' demand and suppliers' preferences. Usually the traded prices are made known to the public. This helps the investors to make better decisions.

Ensures safe and fair dealing: The rules, regulations and by-laws of the stock exchanges' provide a measure of safety to the investors. Transactions are conducted under competitive conditions enabling the investors to get a fair deal.

Aids in financing the industry: A continuous market for shares provides a favourable climate for raising capital. The negotiability and transferability of the securities helps the companies to raise long-term funds. When it is easy to trade the securities, investors are willing to subscribe to the initial public offerings. This simulates the capital formation.

Dissemination of information: Such exchanges provide information through their various publications. They publish the share prices traded on daily basis along with the volume traded. Directory of Corporate Information is useful for the investors' assessment regarding the corporate. Handouts, handbooks and pamphlets provide information regarding the functioning of the stock exchanges.

Performance inducer: The prices of stocks reflect the performance of the traded companies. This makes the corporate more concerned with its public image and tries to maintain good performance.

Self-regulating organisation: The stock exchanges monitor the integrity of the members, brokers, listed companies and clients. Continuous internal audit safeguards the investors against the unfair trade practices. It settles the disputes between member brokers, investors and brokers.

☞ Regulatory Framework

A comprehensive legal framework was provided by the Securities Contract Regulation Act, 1956 and the Securities and Exchange Board of India Act, 1992. A three tier regulatory structure comprising the Ministry of Finance, the Securities and Exchange Board of India and the Governing Boards of the Stock Exchanges regulates the functioning of stock exchanges.

Ministry of Finance: The Stock Exchange Division of the Ministry of Finance has powers related to the application of the provision of the SCR Act and licensing of dealers in the other area. According to SEBI Act, the Ministry of Finance has the appellate and supervisory powers over the SEB. It has power to grant recognition to the stock exchanges and regulation of their operations. Ministry of Finance has the power to approve the appointments of executive chiefs and nominations of the public representatives in the Governing Boards of the stock exchanges. It has the responsibility of preventing undesirable speculation.

The Securities and Exchange Board of India: The Securities and Exchange Board of India even though established in the year 1988, received statutory powers only on 30th January, 1992. Under the SEBI Act, a wide variety of powers is vested in the hands of SEBI. SEBI has the powers to regulate the business of stock exchanges, other security markets and mutual funds. Registration and regulation of market intermediaries are also carried out by SEBI. It has the responsibility to prohibit the fraudulent unfair trade practices and insider dealings. Takeover are also monitored by the SEBI. Stock exchanges have to submit periodic and annual returns to SEBI. SEBI has the multi-pronged duty to promote the healthy growth of the capital market and protect the investors.

The Governing Board: The Governing Board of the stock exchange consists of elected member directors, government nominees and public representatives. Rules, bye-laws and regulations of the stock exchange provide substantial powers to the Executive Director for maintaining efficient and smooth day-to-day functioning of the stock exchange. The Governing Board has the responsibility to maintain an orderly and well-regulated market.

The governing body of the stock exchange consists of 13 members of which: *(a)* 6 members of the stock exchange are elected by the members of the stock exchange *(b)* Central Government nominates not more than three members *(c)* the board nominates three public representatives *(d)* SEBI nominates persons not exceeding three, and *(e)* the stock exchange appoints one executive director.

One-third of the elected members retire at annual general meeting. The retired member can offer himself for election if he is not elected for two consecutive years. If a member serves in the governing body for two years consecutively, he should refrain from offering himself for another two years.

The members of the governing body elect the president and vice-president. It needs no approval from the Central Government or the Board. The office tenure for the president and vice-president is one year. They can offer themselves for re-election, if they have not held office for two consecutive years. In that case they can offer themselves for re-election after a gap of one-year period.

☞ The Stock Exchanges

The names of the stock exchanges are given below:

- Ahmedabad Stock Exchange
- Bangalore Stock Exchange
- Bhubaneshwar Stock Exchange
- Bombay Stock Exchange

- Calcutta Stock Exchange
- Cochin Stock Exchange
- Coimbatore Stock Exchange
- Delhi Stock Exchange
- Guwahati Stock Exchange
- Hyderabad Stock Exchange
- Indore Stock Exchange
- Jaipur Stock Exchange
- Kanpur Stock Exchange
- Ludhiana Stock Exchange
- Madras Stock Exchange
- Magadh Stock Exchange
- Mangalore Stock Exchange
- Pune Stock Exchange
- Saurashtra Stock Exchange
- Vadodara Stock Exchange
- NSE
- OTCEI
- Inter-connected Stock Exchange

INTRODUCTION

☞ BSE (Bombay Stock Exchange)

Bombay Stock Exchange Limited is the oldest stock exchange in Asia with a rich heritage. Popularly known as "BSE", established as "The Native Share and Stock Brokers Association" in 1875. It is the first stock exchange in the country to get permanent recognition in 1956 from the Government of India under the Securities Contracts (Regulation) Act, 1956. The Exchange's pivotal and pre-eminent role in the development of the Indian capital market is widely recognised and its Barometer Sensex, is tracked worldwide.

In terms of organisational structure, the Board formulates larger policy issues and exercises overall control. The committee constituted by the Board are broad-based. The day-to-day operations of the Exchange are managed by the Managing Director and a management team of professionals.

The Exchange has a nationwide reach with a presence in 417 cities and towns of India. The systems and processes Exchange are designed to safeguard market integrity and enhance transparency in operations. During the year 2004-05 the trading volumes on the Exchange showed robust growth.

The Exchange provides an efficient and transparent market for trading in equity, debt instruments and derivatives. The BSE's On-line Trading System (BOLT) is a proprietory system of the Exchange and is BS 7799-2-2002 certified. The surveillance and clearing and settlement functions of the Exchange are ISO 9001:2000 certified.

SENSEX — THE BAROMETER OF INDIAN CAPITAL MARKETS

☞ Introduction

For the premier Stock Exchange that pioneered the stock broking activity in India, 128 years of experience seems to be a proud milestone. A lot has changed since 1875 when 318 persons became members of what today is called, "The Stock Exchange Mumbai" by paying a princely amount of rupee one.

Since then, the country's capital markets have passed through both good and bad periods. The journey in the 20th century has not been an easy one. Till the decade of eighties, there was no scale to measure the ups and downs in the Indian stock market. The Stock Exchange, Mumbai (BSE) in 1986 came out with a stock index that subsequently became the barometer of the Indian stock market.

Sensex is not only scientifically designed but also based on globally accepted construction and review methodology. First compiled in 1986, Sensex is a basket of 30 constituent stocks representing a sample of large, liquid and representative companies. The base year of Sensex is 1978-79 and the base value is 100. The index is widely reported in both domestic and international markets through print as well as electronic media.

The index was initially calculated based on the "Full Market Capitalisation" methodology but was shifted to the free-float methodology with effect from September 1, 2003. The "Free-float Market Capitalisation" methodology of index construction is regarded as an industry best practice globally. All major index provides like MSCI, FTSE, STOXX, S&P and Dow Jones use free-float methodology.

Due to its wide acceptance amongst the Indian investors, Sensex is regarded to be the pulse of the Indian stock market. As the oldest index in the country, it provides the time series data over a fairly long period of time (From 1979 onwards). Small wonder the Sensex has over the years become one of the most prominent brands in the country.

The growth of equity markets in India has been phenomenal in the decade gone by. Right from early nineties the stock market witnessed hightened activity in terms of various bull and bear runs. The sensex captured all these events in the most judicial manner. One can identify the booms and busts of the Indian stock market through Sensex.

☞ National Stock Exchange (NSE)

The National Stock Exchange (NSE) of India became operational in the capital market segment on 3rd November, 1994 in Mumbai. The genesis of the NSE lies in the recommendations of the Pherwani Committee (1991). Apart from NSE, it had recommended for the establishment of National Stock Market System also. Committee pointed out five major defects in the Indian stock market. The defects specified are:

1. Lack of liquidity in most of the markets in terms of depth and breadth.
2. Lack of ability to develop markets for debt.
3. Lack of infrastructure facilities and outdated trading system.
4. Lack of transparency in the operations that affect investors' confidence.
5. Outdated settlement systems that are inadequate to cater to the growing volume, leading to delays.
6. Lack of single market due to the inability of various stock exchanges to function cohesively with legal structure and regulatory framework. These factors led to the establishment of NSE.

The main objectives of NSE are as follows:

- To establish a nationwide trading facility for equities, debt instruments and hybrids.
- To ensure equal access to investors all over the country through appropriate communication network.
- To provide a fair, efficient and transparent securities market to investors using an electronic communication network.
- To enable shorter settlement cycle and book entry settlement system.
- To meet current international standards of securities market.

Promoters of NSE: IDBI, ICICI, LIC, GIC, SBI, Bank of Baroda, Canara Bank, Corporation Bank, Oriental Bank of Commerce, Union Bank of India, Punjab National Bank, Infrastructure Leasing and Financial Services, Stock Holding Corporation of India and SBI Capital Market are the promoters of NSE.

☞ Innovations

NSE has remained in the forefront of modernisation of India's capital and financial markets, and its pioneering efforts include:

- Being the first national, anonymous, electronic limit order book (LOB) exchange to trade securities in India. Since the success of the NSE, existent market and new market structures have followed the "NSE" model.
- Setting up the first clearing corporation "National Securities Clearing Corporation Ltd.", in India. NSCCL was a landmark in providing novation on all spot equity market (and later, derivatives market) trades in India.
- Copromoting and setting up of National Securities Depository Limited, first depository in India.
- Setting up of S&P CNX Nifty.
- NSE pioneered commencement of Internet Trading in February 2000, which led to the wide popularisation of the NSE in the broker community.
- Being the first exchange that, in 1996, proposed exchange traded derivatives, particularly on an equity index, in India. After four years of policy and regulatory debate and formulation, the NSE was permitted to start trading equity derivatives three days after the BSE.
- Being the first exchange to trade ETFs (exchange traded funds) in India.

☞ Markets

Currently, NSE has the following major segments of the capital market:

- Equity
- Futures and Options
- Retail Debt Market
- Wholesale Debt Market

☞ Indices

NSE also set up an index services firm known as India Index Services and Products Limited (IISPL) and has launched several stock indices including:

- S&P CNX Nifty
- CNX Nifty Junior
- CNX 100 (= S&P CNX Nifty + CNX Nifty Junior)
- S&P CNX 500 (= CNX 100 + 400 major players across 72 industries)
- CNX Midcap (introduced on 18th July, 2005 replacing CNX Midcap 200)

Source: http://www.nse-india.com/content/indices/ind_majorindices.htm

☞ Certifications

NSE also conducts online examination and awards certification, under its programmes of NSE's Certification in Financial Markets (NCFM). Currently, certifications are available in 9 modules, covering different sectors of financial and capital markets. Branches of the NSE are located throughout India.

☞ Over-the-counter Exchange of India (OTCEI)

Over-the-counter Exchange of India was started in 1992 after the role models of NASDAQ (National Association of Securities Dealers Automated Quotation) and JASDAQ (Japanese Association of Securities Dealer Automated Quotation). The OTCEI was started with the objective of providing a market for the small companies that could not afford the listing fees of the large exchanges and did not fulfil the minimum capital requirement for listing. It aimed at creating a fully decentralised and transparent market. Over-the-counter means trading across the counter in scrips. The counter refers to the location of the member or dealer of the OTCEI where the deal or trade takes place. Every counter is treated as a trading floor for the OTCEI where the investor can buy and sell. The members or dealers of OTCEI counters are linked to the central OTCEI computer. The member should have the computer and telecommunication facility.

The promoters: OTCEI is incorporated as a company under Sec. 25 of the Indian Companies Act, 1956. As per the registration norms, OTCEI will be obliged to ploughback all its profits and will not be allowed declare dividends on its share capital. The promoters are as follows:

UTI	GIC
ICICI	SBI Capital Markets
IDBI	Canbank Financial Services
IFCI	LIC

Players in the OTCEI market: The players on the OTCEI exchange are the members and dealers. The activities of the members and dealers are:

1. Act as brokers, buy and sell securities according to the instructions of the investors.
2. Market-makers in securities, they quote the prices at which members are willing to buy and sell the specified number of securities.

Members can be the public financial institutions, scheduled banks, mutual funds, SEBI approved merchant bankers, banking subsidiaries, venture capital funds and other non-banking financial companies with minimum net worth of ₹ 2.5 crore. Members pay a one-time non-refundable admission fee of ₹ 10 lakh and ₹ 5 lakh after one year. The annual subscription fee is ₹ 1 lakh.

The dealers are: Individual, partnership firms and corporate entities with a minimum net worth of ₹ 5 lakh. They should have adequate office space and telecommunication facilities. They have to pay one-time non-refundable admission fee of ₹ 2 lakh and annual subscription fee of ₹ 5,000. OTCEI may collect additional security deposit if it consider necessary, depending upon the business experience of the applicant.

Scrips to be traded: Guidelines are issued for the companies whose scrips have to be traded in the OTCEI by the Government as per the guidelines.

INVESTMENT

Investment: As asset is usually purchased, or equivalently a deposit is made in a bank, in hopes of getting a future *return* or interest from it. Literally, the word means the "action of putting something into somewhere else" (perhaps originally related to a person's garment or *"vestment"*).

☞ Types of Investment

The major difference in the use of the term *investment* in economics and finance is that economists are usually referring to a real investment — such as a machine or a house — but financial economists usaully refer to a financial asset — money that is put into a bank or the market — which may then be used to buy a real asset.

➢ In *finance,* investment means buying *securities* or other monetary or paper (financial) assets in the *money markets* or *capital markets,* or in fairly liquid real assets, such as *gold as an investment, real estate,* or collectables. *Valuation* is the method for assessing whether a potential investment is worth its price.

➢ Type of financial investment include shares or other *equity investment,* and *bonds* (including bonds denominated in *foreign currencies*). These investments assets are then expected to provide income or positive future cash flows, but may increase or decrease in value giving the investor capital gains or losses.

➢ Trades in *contingent claims* or *derivative securities* do not necessarily have future positive expected cash flows — so are not considered to be assets, or strictly speaking, securities or investments. Nevertheless, since their cash flows are closely related to (or derived from) those of specific securities, they are often studied as or treated as investments.

Investments are often made indirectly through *intermediaries,* such as *banks, mutual funds, pension funds, insurance companies, collective investment schemes,* or even *investment clubs.* Though their legal and procedural details differ, an intermediary generally makes an investment using money from many.

➢ In many instances the term *saving* and *investment* are used interchangeably which confuses this distinction. For example, many *deposit accounts* are labelled as *investment accounts* by banks for marketing purposes. To help establish whether an asset is saving(s) or an investment you should consider where your money is invested. If the answer is cash then it is *savings,* if it is a type of asset which can fluctuate in value then it is *investment.*

☞ Concept of "Security"

The legal term "security" still means the legal right of the second party (usually a lender) to take the asset that backed the loan to satisfy the debt. An example would be a home loan which is secured by the house which was purchased with the loan proceeds. Because the original loan contract gave as part of consideration to the lender the *security interest* in the form of *mortgage*, the lender can take possession of the house if the borrower goes broke and cannot repay. If the right to repossess the house moved with the loan should the loan be transferred, then the loan secured by the mortgage claim is protected and would have a ready secondary market. It is in this light that the securitisation of loans enables a secondary market. And these secured loans could perform of the functions of *money* that modern securities do-today. They can be a store a value. For large denomination transactions, Treasury securities are so sound that they can be the basis of the medium of exchange. More recently, the term has also been extended to include units in *investment funds* and other forms of readily transferable investment.

The concept of "securities" should be distinguished from *"interests in securities"*. The latter are the assets of a client from whom an intermediary holds securities on an unallocated basis, commingle with the interests in securities of other clients. The distinction between securities and interests in securities is often overlooked in practice, although it is a source of *legal risk.*

☞ Classification

Securities are classified according to the following categories:

- Issuer
- Currency of denomination
- Ownership rights
- Term of maturity
- Degree of liquidity
- Income payments
- Tax treatment

USES OF SECURITIES

☞ For the Issuer

Issuers of securities include commercial companies, government agencies, local authorities and international and supranational organisations (such as the *World Bank*). Debt securities issued by the government generally carry a lower interest rate than corporate debt issued by commercial companies. Repackaged securities are usually issued by a company established for the purpose of the repackaging — called a special purpose vehicle (SPV).

New capital: Commercial enterprises have traditionally used securities as a means of raising new capital. Securities are an attractive option relative to bank loans, which tend to be relatively expensive and short-term. Another disadvantage of bank loans as a source of financing is that the bank may seek a measure of control over the business of the borrower via financial covenants. Through securities, capital is provided by investors who purchase the securities. In a similar way, government will raise capital from securities if taxation and other income are insufficient to meet public expenditure. This will result in a budget deficit.

Repackaging: In recent decades, securities have been issued to repackage existing assets. In a traditional securitisation, a financial institution may wish to remove assets from its *balance sheet* in order to achieve regulatory capital efficiencies or to accelerate its receipt of cash flow from the original assets. Alternatively, an intermediary may wish to make a profit by acquiring financial assets and repackaging them in a way which makes them more attractive to investors.

☞ For the Holder

Investors in securities may be *retail, i.e.,* members of the public investing other than by way business. The greatest part in terms of volume of investment is *wholesale, i.e.,* by financial institutions acting on their own account, or on behalf of clients. Important institutional investors include *investment banks, insurance companies, pension funds* and other managed funds.

Investment: The traditional economic function of the purchase of securities is investment, with the view to receiving *income* and/or achieving *capital gain.* Debt securities generally offer a higher rate of interest than bank deposits, and equities may offer the *prospect* of capital growth. Equity investment may also offer control of the business of the issuer. Debt holding may also offer some measure of control to the investor if the company is a fledging start-up or an old giant undergoing 'restructuring'. In these cases, if interest payments are missed, the creditors may take control of the company and liquidate it to recover some of their investment.

Collateral: Security Finance: The last decade has seen an enormous growth in the use of securities as collateral. Where A is owned a debt or other obligation by B, A may require B to deliver *property rights* in securities to A. These property rights enable A to satisfy its claims in the event that B becomes *insolvent.* Collateral arrangements are divided into two broad categories, namely security interests and outright transfers. Commonly, commercial banks, investment banks and government agencies are significant collateral takers.

☞ Debt and Equity

Securities are traditionally divided into debt securities and equities.

☞ Debt

The holder of a debt security, typically a bond, is owned a debt by the issuer and is entitled to the payment of principal and interest with other personal rights under the terms of the issue, such as the right to receive certain information. Debt securities are generally issued for a fixed term and redeemable by the issuer at the end of that term.

Government bonds are medium or long-term debt securities issued by sovereign governments or their agencies. Typically they carry a lower of interest than corporate bonds. In addition to serving as a source of finance for governments, treasuries are used to manage the money supply in the *open market operations* of central banks.

Supranational bonds represent the debt of international organisations such as the *World Bank, the International Monetary Fund,* regional *multilateral development banks* and others.

Corporate bonds represent the debt of commercial or industrial entities.

Money market instruments are short-term debt instruments, such as *certificates of deposit, commercial paper* and certain *bills of exchange.* They are highly liquid and are sometimes referred to as "near cash".

☞ Equity

An equity is an ordinary share in a company. The holder of an equity is a shareholder, owning a share, or fractional part of the issuer.

☞ Hybrid

Hybrid securities combine some of the characteristics of both debt and equity securities.

Preference shares form an intermediate class of security between equities and debt. If the issuer is liquidated, they carry the right to receive interest and/or a return of capital in priority to ordinary shareholders.

Convertibles are bonds which can be converted, at the election of the bondholder, into another sort of security such as equities.

Equity warrants are contractual entitlements to purchase shares on predetermined terms. They are often issued together with bonds or existing equities, but are detachable from them and separately tradeable.

SECURITIES MARKETS

☞ Primary and Secondary Markets

The securities markets can be divided into the primary markets and the secondary markets. Primary markets (also known as *capital markets*) comprise of new securities to their first holders. The issue of new equity securities is commonly known as an Initial Public Offering (IPO). Issuers usually retain investment banks to assist them in finding buyers for these issues, and in many cases, to buy any remaining interests themselves. This arrangement is known as *underwriting.*

Transferability is an essential characteristic of securities. This trading is called the after market or secondary market. Secondary markets often consist of what is called an exchange to facilitate the meeting of buyers and sellers. They are often referred to as stock exchanges, even though there are exchanges such as the Chicago Board of Options Exchange, where no stocks are traded. Many securities, including the majority of debt securities, do not trade on exchanges at all, even though they may be listed on exchanges. Rather, most debt securities trade in decentralised, dealer-based *over-the-counter* markets.

☞ Public Offers and Private Placements

In the primary markets, securities may be offered to the public in a *public offer.* Alternatively, they may be offered privately to a limited number of qualified persons in a *private placement.* Often a combination of the two is used. The distinction between the two is important to securities regulation and *company law.*

☞ Listing and OTC Dealing

Securities are often listed in a *stock exchange,* an organised and officially recognised market on which securities can be bought and sold. Issuers may seek listings for their securities in order to attract investors, by ensuring that there is a liquid and regulated market in which investors will be able to buy and sell securities.

Growth in informal electronic trading systems has challenged the traditional business of stock exchanges. Larger volumes of securities are also bought and sold "over-the-counter", (OTC). OTC dealing involves buyers and sellers dealing with each other by telephone or electronically on the basis of prices that are displayed electronically, usually by commercial information vendors.

☞ Mutual Funds

A mutual fund is a form of *collective investment* that pools money from many investors and invests the money in *stocks, bonds,* short-term *money market* instruments, and/or other *securities.* In a mutual fund, the fund manager trades the fund's underlying securities, realising *capital gains* or loss, and collects the *dividend* or *interest income*. The investment proceeds are then passed along to the individual investors. The value of a share of the mutual fund, known as the net asset value (NAV), is calculated daily based on the total value of the fund divided by the number of shares purchased by investors.

☞ Usage

Mutual funds can invest in many different kinds of securities. The most common are *cash, stock* and *bonds,* but there are hundreds of sub-categories. Stock funds, for instance, can invest primarily in the shares of a particular industry, such as *technology* or utilities. These are known as sector funds. Bond funds can vary according to risk (high yield or *junk bonds,* investment-grade corporate bonds), type of *issuers* (government agencies, corporations, or municipalities), or maturity of the bonds (short or long-term).

Most mutual funds' investment *portfolios* are continually adjusted under the supervision of a professional manager, who forecasts the future performance of investments appropriate for the fund and chooses the ones which he or she believes will most closely match the fund's stated investment objective. A mutual fund is administered through a parent management company, which may hire or fire fund managers.

Mutual funds are subject to a special set of regulatory, accounting, and tax rules. Unlike most other types of business entities, they are not taxed on their income as long as they distribute substantially all of it to their *shareholders.* Also, the type of income they earn is often unchanged as it passes through to the shareholders. Mutual fund distributions of tax-free municipal bond income are also tax-free to the shareholder. Taxable distributions can either be ordinary income or *capital gains,* depending on how the fund earned it.

☞ Net Asset Value

The *net asset volume,* or NAV, is a fund's value of its holdings, usually expressed as a per share amount. For most funds, the NAV is determined daily, after the close of trading on some specified, financial exchange, but some funds up date their NAV multiple times during the trading day. Open-end funds sell and redeem their shares at the NAV, and so only process orders after the NAV is determined. Closed-end funds may trade at a higher or lower price than their NAV; this is known as a *premium or discount,* respectively. If a fund is divided into multiple classes of shares, each class will typically have its own NAV, reflecting differences in fees and expenses paid by the different classes.

Some mutual funds own securities which are not regularly traded on any formal exchange. These may be shares in very small or bankrupt companies; they may be *derivatives;* or they may be private investments in unregistered financial instruments (such as stock in a non-public company). In the absence of public market for these securities, it is the responsibility of the fund manager to form an estimate of their value when computing the NAV. How much of a fund's asset may be invested in such securities is stated in the fund's prospectus.

TYPES OF MUTUAL FUNDS

☞ Open-end Fund

The term *Mutual Fund* is the common name for an open-ended investment company. Being *open-ended* means that at the end of every day, the investment management company sponsoring the fund issues new *shares* to investors and buys back shares from investors wishing to leave the fund.

Mutual Funds may be legally structured as *corporations* or *business trusts* but in either instance are classed as *open-ended investment companies.* Other funds have a limited number of shares, these are either *close-ended fund* or *unit investment trusts* neither of which are mutual funds.

☞ Exchange-traded Funds

A relatively new innovation, the exchange traded fund (ETF), is other formulated as an open-ended investment company. The way ETFs work combines characteristics of both mutual funds and close-ended funds. An ETF usually tracks a stock index. Shares are only created or redeemed by institutional investors in large blocks (typically 50,000 shares). Investors typically purchase shares in small quantities through brokers at a small premium or discount to the net asset value through which the institutional investors makes their profit. Because the institutional investors handle the majority of trades. ETFs are more efficient than traditional mutual funds and therefore tend to have lower expenses. ETFs are traded throughout the day on a *stock exchange,* just like close-ended funds.

☞ Equity Funds

Equity funds, which mainly consist of stock investments, are the most common type of mutual fund. Often times equity funds focus investments on particular strategies and certain types of companies.

☞ Mutual Funds vs. Other Investments

Mutual funds offer several advantages over stock investments, including diversification and professional management. A mutual fund may hold investments in hundreds or thousands of stocks, thus reducing risk of any particular stock. Also, the transaction costs associated with buying individual stocks are also spread around among all the mutual fund shareholders. As well, a mutual fund benefits from professional fund managers who can apply their expertise and dedicate time to research investment options. Mutual funds, however, are not immune to risks. Mutual funds share the same risks associated with the types of investments the fund makes. If the fund mainly invests in stocks, the mutual fund is usually subject to the same ups and downs and risks as the *stock market.*

☞ Selecting a Mutual Fund

Picking a mutual fund from among the thousands offered is not easy. The following is just a rough guide, with some common pitfalls.

1. Check with your tax adviser prior to investing in a tax-exempt or tax-managed fund.
2. Match the term of the investment to the time you expect to keep it invested. Money you need right away (for example, if your car breaks down) should be in a money market account. Money you will not need until you retire in decades (or for a newborn's college education) should be in longer-term investments, such as stock or bond funds. Putting money you will need soon in stocks risks having to sell them when the market is low and missing out on the rebound.
3. Expenses matter over the long-term, and of course, cheaper is usually better. You can find the expense ratio in the prospectus. Expense ratios are critical in index funds, which seek to match the market. Activity managed funds need to pay the manager, so they usually have a higher expense ratio.
4. Sector funds often make the "best fund" lists you see every year. The problem is that it is usually a different sector each year (interest funds, anyone?). Also, some sectors are vulnerable to industrywide events (airlines do come to mind). Avoid making these a large part of your portfolio.
5. Close-ended funds often sell at a discount to the value of their holdings. You can sometimes get extra return by buying these in the market. Hedge fund managers love this trick. This also implies that buying them at the original issue usually a bad idea, since the price will often drop immediately.

6. Mutual funds often make taxable distributions near the end of the year. If you plan to invest money in the fund in a taxable account, check the fund company's website to see when they plan to pay the dividend; you may prefer to wait until afterwards if it is coming up soon.
7. Research read the prospectus, or as much of it as you can stand. It should tell you what these strangers can do with your money, among other vital topics. Check the return and risk of a fund against its peers with similar investment objectives, and against the index most closely associated with it. Be sure to pay attention to performance over both the long-term and the short-term. A fund that gained 53% over a one year period (which is impressive), but only 11% over a five years period should raise some suspicion, as that would imply that the returns on four out of those five years were actually very low (if not straight losses) as 11% compounded over five years is only 68%.
8. Diversification can reduce risk. Most people should own some stocks, some bonds, and some cash. Some of the stocks, at least, should be foreign. You might not get as much diversification as you think if all your funds are with the same management company, since there is often a common source of research and recommendations. Too many funds, on the other hand, will give you about the same effect as an index fund, except your expenses will be higher. Buying individual stocks exposes you to company-specific risks, and if you buy a large number of stocks the commissions may cost more than a fund will.
9. The *compounding* effect is your best friend. A little money invested for a long time equals a lot of money later.

☞ Share Class

Many mutual funds offer more than one class of shares. For example, you may have seen a fund offers "Class A" and "Class B" shares. Each class will invest in the same "pool" (or investment portfolio) of securities and will have the same investment objectives and policies. But each class will have different shareholders services and/or distribution arrangements with different fees and expenses. As a result, each class will likely have different performance results.

A multi-class structure offers investors the ability to select a fee and expense structure that is most appropriate for their investment goals (including the time that they expect to remain invested in the fund).

Many mutual funds divide their assets up among multiple *classes* of shares. All of the assets of each class are effectively pooled for the purposes of investment management, but classes typically differ in the fees and expenses paid out of the fund's assets. These differences are supposed to reflect different costs involved in servicing investors in various classes, for example, one class may be sold through brokers with a front-end load, and another class may be sold direct to the public with no load.

☞ Criticism of Mutual Funds

The primary criticism of *actively managed* mutual funds comes from the historical fact that, over long periods of time, most have not returned as much as an *index fund* would.

There are also other criticisms levied against mutual funds as a consequence of the first criticism. One critique covers the concept of the sales commission, an upfront or deferred fee as high as 8.5 per cent of the amount invested in a fund. Critics point out high sales commissions represent a conflict of interest, as high commissions benefits the salespeople, but hurt the investors. High commissions can also cause salespeople to recommend funds that maximise their income.

Mutual funds are also seen by a some to have a conflict of interest with regards to their size. Fund companies charges a management fee of anywhere between 0.5-2.5 per cent of the funds total assets.

Theoretically this could motivate the fund managers, since a well performing fund would cause the amount invested in fund to rise and increasing the fee earned. It also could motivate the fund company to focus on advertising to attract more and more new investors, as new investors would also cause the fund assets to increase.

Many analysts believe, however, that the larger the pool of money one works with, the harder it is to manage actively, and harder to have good performance. Thus, a fund company can be focused on attracting new customers, hurting its existing investors' performance. A great deal of the funds costs are flat and fixed costs, such as the salary for the manager. Thus, it can be more profitable to the fund to try and allow it to grow as large as possible, instead of limiting its assets.

Other practices of mutual funds have been criticised from time-to-time, such as funds allowing *market timing.* More recent criticisms have focused on the fund managers accepting extravagant gifts in exchange for trading stocks through certain investment banks, who presumably overchange the fund compared to what another, non-gifting investment bank would charge.

☞ What does Grace/Interest Free Period Mean?

The number of days given to you on your card before the card issuer starts charging you interest is called grace period. Generally, the grace period is the number of days between the statement date and the due date of payment. Grace periods on credit cards are usually 2 to 3 weeks. However, there is likely to be no grace for balances carried forward from previous month and fresh purchases thereafter if any.

☞ What is Implied in Cash Advance?

Cash advances on credit cards are convenient and the easiest facility to utilise. Majority of the banks in India charge a transaction fee, as well as service fee/interest charge on cash advances. This service fee accrues from the date of the advance (as soon as you receive the cash) to the date of full payment. The charges varies from banks-to-banks. Cash advance facility is a part of the overall credit limit assigned to a cardholder. The limit of cash advance is always lesser than the borrowing limit or the credit limit.

➢ How to make payments from Dubai to the already existing Citibank cards in India. How to avail of the statements to know the current bank balance of each card. Is online facility available?

According to RBI "Resident Indians may be nominated as additional/add-on cardholders by non-residents. However, the non-residents from their foreign currency funds should meet claims arising out of use of such cards by residents only. In cases where the cards have been arranged by NRIs, these liabilities may be met out of NRE/FCNR accounts in India also. Under no circumstances will any remittance be allowed by residents from India to settle their claims against use of such additional/add-on cards". NRIs get rupee credit cards which are valid for use in India, Nepal and Bhutan.

➢ Can I use my Global credit card on the net to pay some US company for web hosting charges? or I have to obtain permission from RBI. If any permissions are needed, How to get them?

The RBI's exchange control manual mentions that International Credit Cards can be used for "Registration of Internet domain name, hosting charges for website/home pages overseas and access fees for Internet related services through website". Before using your Global Credit Card on the net for web hosting charges, you further clarify the aforesaid issue or seek permission from your card issuer, even get in touch with the card issuing bank or organisation directly for such clarifications.

☞ How will I know if my credit card application has got approved?

It is suggested to give your mobile number and e-mail id at the time of application for the credit card. This will help the issuer to intimate you either through SMS or through e-mail with the approved status of your application. You will also receive a letter by post informing you of the card approval. You should be receiving your card around the same time as the approval letter.

☞ How will I know if my credit card application has got declined?

You will receive a letter from the bank even if your application for card is not approved. If in case there is a further information of missing documents, you will be sent a letter asking for the same. Then you need to fulfil with the documents to the specified address.

☞ What to do if credit card is lost or stolen?

Report the loss or theft of your credit card to the card issuers at the earliest through their 24-hour helpline service. Follow-up your phone calls with a letter. Include your account number, when you noticed your card was missing, and the date you first reported the loss.

After doing these, check your homeowner's insurance policy to see if it covers your liability for card thefts. If yes, its fine, otherwise change your policy to include this protection.

Before the intimation, different banks have their own limit of loss bearing by the cardholder. After the intimation, it is the bank who bears the loss if any amount is spent.

☞ Mobile Banking in India

"The account that travels with you." This is needed in today's fast business environment with unending deadlines for fulfilment and loads of appointments to meet and meetings to attend. With mobile banking facilities, one can bank from anywhere, at anytime and in any condition or anyhow. The system is either through SMS or through WAP. (Check out for SMS banking under different head).

Mobile banking is the hottest area of development in the banking sector and is expected to replace the credit/debit card system in future. In the past two years, mobile banking users have increased three times, if we compare the use of either debit card or credit card. Moveover, 85-90% mobile users do not own credit cards.

Mobile banking uses the same infrastructure like the ATM solution. But it is extremely easy and inexpensive to implement. It reduces the cost of operation for bankers in comparison to the use of ATMs.

Using compact HTML and WAP technologies, the following operations can be conducted through advanced mobile phones which can be further viewed on channels such as the Internet via the Channel Manager.

- Bill payments
- Fund transfers
- Check balances
- And many more which is also availab!:: in SMS banking.

In countries like Korea, two SIM Cards are used in mobile phones. One for the telephonic purpose and the other for banking. Bank account data is encrypted on a smart-card chip. About 3.3 million transactions were reported by Bank of Korea in 2004.

☞ SMS Banking

Businesses are in move. So is to be your money. You may have to thank the banks which are providing banking at the send-of-your-SMS. The technology is at its highest level to move your money while you are on the move. If you are having non-WAP enabled mobile handset, you can use the facility of SMS services. The following operations can be easily used by the service provider:

- ➤ Balance enquiry
- ➤ Last three transactions
- ➤ Cheque payment status
- ➤ Cheque book request
- ➤ Statement request
- ➤ Demat — Free balance holding
- ➤ Demat — Last two transactions
- ➤ Bill payment

The SMS facility brings peace of mind to customers and opens doors to many more technological possibilities and innovative services. It is very similar to how an ATM works.

To use ATM, a card is necessary and to use SMS service, a mobile phone is needed. In both the cases, secret number is necessary to access.

SMS banking is also very much safe. First, one authenticates the mobile number with the authentication's key. Second, the customer uses secret Mobile Personal Identification Number (MPIN).

A new concept has been developed by Bank of Punjab Ltd. They call it "Mobile Wallet". With the support of this technology, a customer can make payment and receive payment of account of buy/sell (merchants) through SMS.

In this system, a buyer sends a message for buying and the bank in return sends a message confirming the purchase, both to the merchant as well as to the buyer. Debit card number is the key field which is used for the authenticity of the customer.

The processes of the service are simplified as under:

- ➤ Customer has to send "REG (one space) (Account Number) (one space) (Debit Card Number)" as an SMS to bank's mobile number 9810999992 for registration. For example, "REG 06SB11052122 5047531105000109109" Bank will confirm the registration with the return message.
- ➤ After that, customer will visit the nearest branch to collect the service brochure and get it filled.
- ➤ Registration will be a one time process. Once registered, customer would be able to buy things from any of the registered merchant of the bank.
- ➤ Customer need to send "PAY (one space) (merchant code) (one space) (amount) (one space) (Debit card number)" as an SMS on bank's mobile number 9810999992. For example, for making a payment of ₹ 56.16 to merchant BOPSTC from Card No.5047531105000109109, Send the following message "PAY BOPSTC 56.16 5047531105000109109".

- The transaction will be validated online and immediately funds will be transferred from customer account to merchant account.
- Bank would send transaction confirmation as a message to both merchant and customer (buyer).
- An SMS report will be sent to both merchant and buyer everyday stating the total number of transaction and total amount of transaction made during the (previous) one day.

Note: There is obviously a limit to the volume of transactions now.

☞ Some Useful Tips

Generally, with three invalid login attempts, SMS banking services are locked. Immediately contact the branch for unlocking the services. In case one forgets the password, obtain a new password from the branch. To log out, choose the "Log out" option in the handset and SMS banking session ends.

☞ Net Banking

Net banking is conducting one's banking or bank account on-line through a computer and a net connection. The system is up-dated immediately after every transaction automatically. In other words, it is said that it is up dated 'online, real time'. Through net banking one can check the status of his/her account, place queries and also can be facilitated with a wide range of transactions simultaneously.

In India, the regulatory body has not yet sanctioned virtual bank, in abroad there are banks like EGG Bank or NET Bank, which only have a virtual presence without any physical branches.

Net banking has three basic features. They are as follows:

- The banks offer only relevant informations about their products and services to the mass.
- Few banks provide interaction facility between the banks and its customers.
- Banks are coming up with arrangements of utility payments, like telephone bills, electricity bills, etc.

The current statistics show that hardly 10 per cent of Indian customers uses the Internet for banking. Among all the facilities provided, the maximum of them use only for checking balance or requesting for a cheque book. Very few customers use the advanced interactive services provided by the banks.

According to HDFC and ICICI Bank, 17 per cent of ICICI customers use the Internet for banking and 10 per cent of HDFC customers prefer it.

☞ Cost of Installation of Services

For basic features, the cost for providing such services to the banks come around ₹ 40 lakh to ₹ 50 lakh. For the third level service or sophisticated services, the investments mount to the tune of ₹ 4 crore to ₹ 5 crore.

These investments are just a fraction if compared to the operations of the bank using physical infrastructure.

☞ Services Provided by Net Banking

☞ Queries

- Check Balance
- See Statement

- Inquire about cheque status
- Ask for a Statement
- Ask for a Cheque Book
- Inquire about Fixed Deposit
- Inquire about TDS details
- See Demat Account
- Up date profile

☞ Transactions

- Stop a Cheque
- Pay Bills
- Ask for a Demand Draft
- Transfer funds between your accounts
- Transfer funds to a third party
- Request for a new Fixed Deposit
- Shop Online
- Pay Bank Credit Card Dues

☞ Advantages of Net Banking

- It removes the traditional geographical barriers as it could reach out to customers of different countries/legal jurisdiction. This has raised the question of jurisdiction of law/supervisory system to which such transactions should be subjected.
- It has added a new dimension to different kinds of risks traditionally associated with banking, heightening some of them and throwing new risk control challenges.
- Security of banking transactions, validity of electronic contract, customers' privacy, etc., which have all along been concerns of both bankers and supervisors have assumed different dimensions, given that Internet is a public domain, not subject to control by any single authority or group of users.
- It poses a strategic risk of loss of business to those banks who do not respond in time to this new technology, being the efficient and cost-effective delivery.

☞ Proxy Banking in India

Indian villages were miles away from mutual funds, insurance and even equity trading. Thanks to Internet kiosk and the ATM duo which has made it possible for rural India. This kiosk has been set up by ICICI Bank in partnership with network n-Logue Communications in remote villages of Southern part of the country. This is known as proxy banking. With the help of fibre optic cables, this kiosk works on wireless in local loop technology.

☞ Reasons for Setting Up of Proxy Banking

- 58% of rural households still do not have bank accounts.
- Only 21% of rural households have access to credit from a formal source.
- 70% of marginal farmers do not have deposit account.

- 87% households have no formal credit.
- Only 1% rural households rely on a loan from a financial intermediary.
- The loans take between 24 to 33 weeks to get sanctioned.
- Consumers bribe officials to get loans approved which varies between 10 and 20 per cent of the loan amount.
- Branch banking in rurals is loss-making.

☞ Benefits to Rurals

- Small loans given for buying buffaloes.
- Loans for setting up a tea shop.
- Life and non-life insurance provided.
- Whether insurance given to farmers.
- Insurance policies sold to farmers like groundnut, castor, soya, paddy crop, etc.

The proxy banking is an innovative approach to rural lending and will add to the government's expanding base of Kisan Credit Cards and the good old guidelines for agricultural lending.

(40) Crisil

CRISIL is the pioneer of independent credit ratings in India. In association with NSIC, CRISIL is now rating small-scale industries (SSIs) on a special rating scale, using criteria tailored for the small-scale sector. The fees for this rating are presently subsidised by the government, making it a unique opportunity for small enterprises to get themselves rated.

Rating Scale — CRISIL rating reflects CRISIL's opinion on the company's performance capability and financial strength. Ratings are assigned on the following rating scale:

	Financial Strength		
Performance Capability	*High*	*Moderate*	*Low*
Highest	SE 1A	SE 1B	SE 1C
High	SE 2A	SE 2B	SE 2C
Moderate	SE 3A	SE 3B	SE 3C
Weak	SE 4A	SE 4B	SE 4C
Poor	SE 5A	SE 4C	SE 5C

For example, a company with high performance capability and high financial strength will be rated 'SE 2A', while one with weak performance capability and how financial strength will be rated 'SE 4C'.

Benefits: When a SSI goes in for a rating from a credible agency, it improves its standing with bankers, customers, suppliers and employees. CRISIL rating brings the following benefits:

Credibility with banks: A good rating from CRISIL carries weight with lenders, and helps in getting faster and cheaper credit. The Indian Bank's Association (IBA) has endorsed the NSIC-CRISIL rating, and informed its member banks of the same. CRISIL has entered into a Memorandum of Understanding (MoU) with major banks including State Bank of India, UCO Bank, United Bank of India, State Bank of Travancore, State Bank of Mysore, Corporation Bank, Bank of Baroda and Canara Bank for rating their SSI customers at concessional fees.

Confidence building with business partners — CRISIL performance rating is an indicator of performance capability and financial strength. A good rating gives comfort to lenders, customers and suppliers.

Self-improvement tool — With its rating, CRISIL gives a detailed analytical report on company's strengths and weaknesses. The report helps to strengthen the operations and to improve the working of the company. This insightful, credible and independent feedback is supported by the strongest industry and company research in India.

Improved visibility: With the CRISIL rating, company gets a free listing in CRISIL's rating scan a publication that is used as a reference for lending decisions by bank. It also featured on CRISIL's website.

☛ Reasons for Choosing CRISIL

- **CRISIL – India's Leading Ratings, Financial News, Risk and Policy Advisory Company:** CRISIL leads the market indepth of analysis and sophistication of approach. A rating from CRISIL is a stamp of quality from the most renowned rating agency in India.
- **Association with Standard and Poor's:** CRISIL's majority shareholder is Standard and Poor's, the world's foremost provider of independent credit ratings, indices, risk evaluation, investment research and data. Leading corporations worldwide are rated by Standard and Poor's. S&P's Credit Risk Tracker (CRT) has analyzed about one million SMEs in Europe.
- **Value Driven Approach:** All CRISIL business operate on the core values of Analytical Rigour, Independence, Integrity, Innovation, and Commitment. CRISIL's consistent adherence to these principles is recognised by users of its ratings, and has been the key factor that makes CRISIL the leading player in the field.

☛ Rating Process Followed by CRISIL

- Receiving completed application form from the company
- Representatives visit company
- Short discussion with company managers by analysis of CRISIL.
- Rating report preparation and submission to company and NSIC

Whole process takes three to four weeks after receiving completed information from the company. In order to carry-out the process CRISIL charges its fees.

Eligible Units for CRISIL Rating

Any enterprise registered in India as an SSI unit can benefit from this rating. As a proof of eligibility, an SSI certificate issued by the concerned SSI registration authority is required by CRISIL.

List of Documents Required by CRISIL

1. SSI Registration certificate.
2. Partnership deed/Memorandum and Article of Association.
3. Authority letter to sign application.
4. List of all partners/directors with their age, address, net worth/income tax returns, qualifications and experience.
5. Copy of the audited accounts with schedules for the last three years (where accounts for the last year have not been audited, provisional accounts duly certified by a chartered accountant, along with two years audited accounts are to be submitted).
6. In case of new project/expansion, copy of the project report containing a brief profile, cost of project, source/means of finance.

7. Brief write-up about the products manufactured, end-users, marketing tie-up and orders in hand.
8. Details of subsidy, tax concession available to the applicant.
9. Quality certificates, export awards won, memberships of any association.
10. Any other information that would enable CRISIL to understand the business better.

CRISIL has its Head Office at Mumbai with its branches at Ahmedabad, Bangalore, Chennai, Hyderabad, Kolkata, New Delhi and Pune.

Website:- www.crisil.com

(41) Electronic Clearing Service (ECS)

Reserve Bank of India introduced this service in 1994 at four metropolitan cities. It was extended later to sixteen centres where clearing houses are managed by Reserve Bank of India. This scheme provides the facility of faster credit of dividends to the customer's account directly and thus avoids delays and frauds. Now this facility is extended even for the payments of bills like telephone bills of BSNL. In order to encourage the scheme, even suitable discount is also provided to the customer who adopts this system of payment.

In order to operationalise the scheme corporate bodies make payment of interest and dividends to their investors and shareholders without issuing payment warrant. Payment is credited directly into the accounts of the beneficiaries. Shareholders and investors are required to furnish details of their accounts standing to their credit in a bank, to corporate bodies. The corporate body in turn inform their bankers to make due payments.

The facility is optional and any shareholder willing to withdraw ECS facility can do it by giving 30 days notice before the due date of payment.

This scheme is advantageous in many ways. One who has opted for this scheme receives or pays his dues without delay. The time, otherwise, needed to produce the instrument at the bank and collection is saved. Chances of displacement of the voucher is eliminated, particularly for them who remain mostly on travelling or keep on changing their addresses due to transfers. Expenditure of corporates is also saved on printing, despatching and reconciling the paper instrument. The scheme may be availed to make or receive payments of ₹ 1 lakh per transaction.

(42) Stock Invest

It is an instrument available to the investors applying for shares and debentures. It is issued by banks. Stock Invest is obtained from the bank for the amount to the paid and it is attached with the application form. The amount is not debited immediately by the bank but creates a lien on his deposit account for the amount for which Stock Invest is issued. After the allotment of share Stock Invest is encashed by the share issuing company by presenting it to the banker of issuing company. In case share is not alloted, the issuer company returns it to the investor after cancelling it. The investor returns then cancelled Stock Invest to his banker. In this way the applicant does not suffer the loss of interest on his money for the period of processing of share application. Stock Invest is recognised by Government of India and Reserve Bank of India, as one of the instruments for paying application money. Stock Invest can be issued by the nominated banks by Reserve Bank of India.

Reserve Bank of India has framed certain rules for the banks athorised to issue the Stock Invest.

1. Bank's lien on deposit account of the investor for unused Stock Invest shall not be lifted for four months. However, the deposit amount under lien will earn interest in normal way.

2. Bank issuing Stock Invest will fill the name of the capital issuing company. The name of purchaser will be mentioned at the back.
3. It is for individual investors, corporate bodies, stock brokers, banks and financial institutions cannot avail this.
4. Stock Invest can be issued only against savings account, current account and term deposits.
5. Scheme was introduced from 5th June, 1997 with a ceiling of ₹ 50,000 per individual per capital issue.
6. Original Stock Invest is to be attached with application and not the photocopy or simply giving details of Stock Invest on the application form.

(43) Phishing

Phishing have become now a classic type of fraud, through which fraudsters attempt to obtain sensitive information such as user name, password, credit card details. It is not an attack on the Internet Banking site or other secured environment but on the key – in this event on the customer's personal and secret key to their finances.

A phishing e-mail means a bogus e-mail purporting to be an authentic e-mail from the bank and aimed at extracting a person's confidential data. Instances of phishing have long been a common place thing in the world.

➢ Usual techniques employed by fraudsters.
  - *False sender:* A customer receives an e-mail as if from their own bank on other sender as if related to the bank.
  - *Corporate style in e-mail:* An address such as "Dear valuable customers", the body of the message, a thank you note "Thank you for using bank service" and the closing text such as "sincerely, your bank" is worded with a view to imitate the bank's style as much as possible.
  - *Fake links:* The name of the link is made to look as much as possible like a genuine link or bank's activity, e.g., "Click here to up date your account" or "Go to Internet Banking, page," "but realety the link takes to a phishing website. It is just like when the link" "find out more" under an article in any website can take oneself to other webpage.
  - *Use of bogus webpage:* The deceptive links as described above normally takes one to a bogus webpage that imitates the genuine webpage and where the entered data becomes available to third parties and may be used for malicious purposes.
  - *Attempt to infect the computer:* In some cases, the fraudster will also try to infect the computer with a virus that may serve a malicious purpose.

➢ Precautions to be taken against phishing.
  - In case of any doubt or suspicion, promptly get in touch with the bank and verify the authenticity of the mail e-mail service.
  - Keep in mind the most important rule for financial safety on the web, which is also actively communicated by the bank.

A bank will never request customers to disclose any detail necessary for online banking.

Never e-mail or tell over the phone such data as.

➢ Internet banking passwords,

- Code card's or security token's codes in their entirety.
- Card number,
- Card expiry date
- PIN code
- Be alert and do "computer hygiene"
- Follows news offered by the bank and use bank's solutions and guidelines.

(44) Reverse Mortgage Scheme

The reverse mortgage scheme offered by some of the leading banks in India could bring answers to the suffering senior citizens.

Getting into oldage without proper financial support can be a very bad experience. The rising cost of living, health care, other amenities compound the problem significantly. No regular incomes, a dwindling capacity to work and earn livelihood at this age can make life miserable. A constant inflow of income, without any work would be an ideal solution, which can put an end to all such sufferings. Reverse mortgage scheme is to meet this requirement.

Most of the people in the senior age groups, either by inheritance or by virtue of building assets have properties in names, but they were not able to convert it into instant and regular income stream due to its liquid nature. The Union Budget 2007-2008 had a great proposal which introduced the 'Reverse Mortgage' scheme.

The concept is simple, a senior citizen who holds a house or property, but lacks a regular source of income can put mortgage his property with a bank or housing finance company (HFC) and the banker HFC pays the person a regular payment. The good thing is that the person who 'Reverse Mortgages' his property can stay in the house for his life and continue to receive the much needed regular payments. So, effectively the property now pays for the woner. So, effectively one continues to stay at the same place and also get paid for it. The catch is in the process of working of reverse mortgage. The way reverse mortgage works is that the bank will have the right to sell-off the property after the incumbent passes away or leaves the place, and to recover the loan. It passes on any extra amount to the legal heirs.

The whole idea is entirely opposite to the regular mortgage process where a person pays the bank for a mortgaged property. Hence, it is called reverse mortgage. The concept is more popular in West.

The draft guidelines of reverse mortgage in India prepared by RBI have the following salient features:

- Any house owner over 60 years of age is eligible for a reverse mortgage.
- The maximum loan is up to 60% of the value of residential property.
- The maximum period of property mortgage is 15 years with a bank of HFC.
- The borrower can opt for a monthly, quarterly, annual or lump sum payments at any point, as per his discretion.
- The re-evaluation of the property has to be undertaken by the Bank of HFC one every five years.
- The amount received through reverse mortgage is considered as loan and not income; hence, the same will not attract any tax liability.
- Reverse mortgage rates can be fixed or floating and hence will vary according to market conditions depending upon the interest rate regime chosen by the borrower.

The lender will recover the loan along with the accumulated interest by selling the house after the death of the borrower or earlier, if the borrower leaves the mortgaged residential property permanently. Any excess amount will be remitted to the bank to the borrower or his heirs.

Reverse mortgage thus, is very beneficial, for senior citizens who want a regular income to meet their everyday needs, without leaving their houses.

(45) Debit Card

Debit card in India was started by Citibank a few years ago in association with Mastercard in Mumbai. Nowadays debit card is quite popular for drawing money from a bank from one's own account.

Difference between credit card and debit card is that one can make as much purchases from his debit card as much balance is there in his account while credit cards facilitate oneself to make purchases on credit.

Debit card is thus a card serving purpose to make payments for purchases as well as withdrawing one's own money from ATM machines spread all over the region. Thus, one can draw cash from his own account at anytime round the clock and at any place where an ATM machine is available. One is thus not required to go to the bank counter everytime to withdraw his money. A debit card thus facilitates purchases and payments by the cardholder in the same way as credit card does with the difference that purchases are limited to his balance in his account. In case of debit card the desired amount is debited immediately from his account at the time of transaction itself. Additional security is provided in the form of personal identification number (PIN) which the cardholder punches on the electronic payment machine/ATM machine by himself. It is like a password.

(46) Know Your Customer (KYC)

Reserve Bank of India, issued in November 2004 the following guidelines vide its letter to all Commercial Banks under the title – Know Your Customer (KYC) Guidelines – Anti-money Laundering Standards.

'Know Your Customers' (KYC) Standards:

The objective of KYC guidelines was to prevent banks from being used, intentionally or unintentionally, by criminal elements for money laundering activities. KYC procedures also enable banks to know/understand their customers and their financial dealings better which in turn help them manage their risks prudently. Banks should frame their KYC policies incorporating the following four key elements:

(i) Customer Acceptance Policy

(ii) Customer Identification Procedures

(iii) Monitoring of transactions, and

(iv) Risk Management.

Customer for the purpose of KYC policy a 'customer' may be defined as:

- A person or entity that maintains an account and/or has a business relationship with the bank.
- One on whose behalf the account is maintained (i.e., the beneficial owner);
- Beneficiaries of transactions conducted by professional intermediaries, such as stock brokers, chartered accountants, solicitors, etc., as permitted under the law, and

- any person or entity connected with a financial transaction which can pose significant reputational or other risks to the bank, say, a wire transfer or issue of a high value demand draft as a single transaction.

☞ Customer Acceptance Policy (CAP)

(i) No account is opened in anonymous or fictitious benami name(s)

(ii) Parameters of risk perception are clearly defined.

(iii) Documentation requirements and other information to be collected.

(iv) Not to open an account or close an existing account where the bank is unable to apply appropriate customer due to diligence measures.

(v) Circumstances in which a customer is permitted to act on behalf of another person/entity.

(vi) Necessary checks before opening a new account.

Banks may prepare a profile for each new customer based on risk categorisation. The customer profile will be a confidential document and details contained therein shall not be divulged for cross-selling or any other purposes.

Banks may apply enhanced due diligence measures based on the risk assessment, thereby requiring intensive 'due diligence' for higher risk customers especially those for whom the sources of funds are not clear. Examples of customers requiring higher due diligence may include: *(a)* non-residents customers, *(b)* high net worth individuals, *(c)* trusts, charities, NGOs and organisations receiving donations, *(d)* companies having close family shareholding or beneficial ownership, *(e)* firms with 'sleeping partners' *(f)* politically exposed persons (PEPs) of foreign origin, *(g)* non-face-to-face customers, and (h) those with dubious reputation as per public information available, etc.

It is important to bear in mind that the adoption of customer acceptance policy and its implementation should not become too restrictive and must not result in denial of banking services to general public, especially to those, who are financially or socially disadvantaged.

☞ Customer Identification Procedure (CIP)

The policy approved by the Board of banks should clearly spell out the Customer Identification Procedure to be carried out at different stages, i.e., while establishing a banking relationship, carrying out a financial transaction or when the bank has a doubt about the authenticity/veracity or the adequacy of the previously obtained customer identification data. Customer identification means identifying the customer and verifying his/her identity by using reliable, independent source documents, data or information.

Monitoring of Transaction:

Ongoing monitoring is an essential element of effective KYC procedures. Banks can effectively control and reduce their risk only if they can understand of the normal and reasonable activity of the customer, so that they have the means of identifying transactions that fall outside the regular pattern of activity. However, the extent of monitoring will depend on the risk sensitivity of the account.

Banks should ensure that its branches continue to maintain proper record of all cash transactions (deposits and withdrawals) of ₹10 lakh and above. The internal monitoring system should have an inbuilt procedure for reporting of such transactions and those of suspicious nature to controlling/head office on a fortnightly basis.

Risk Management:

The Board of Directors of the bank should ensure that an effective KYC programme is put in place by establishing appropriate procedures and ensuring their effective implementation. It should cover proper management oversight, systems and controls, segregation of duties, training and other related matters. Responsibility should be explicitly collected within the bank for ensuring that the bank's policies and procedures and implemented effectively. Banks must have an ongoing employees training programme so that the members of the staff are adequately trained in KYC procedures.

Customer Education:

Implementation of KYC procedures requires bank to demand certain information from customers which may be of personal nature or which has hitherto never called for. This can sometimes lead to a lot of questioning by the customer as to the motive and purpose of collecting such information. There is, therefore, a need for banks to prepare specific literature/pamphlets, etc., so as to educate the customer of the objectives of the KYC programme.

Introduction of new technologies — credit cards/debit cards/smart cards/gift cards:

Banks should pay special attention to any money laundering threats that may arise from new or developing technologies including internet banking that might favour anonymity, and take measures, if needed, to prevent their use in money laundering schemes. It is also desirable that agents involved in promoting bank business are also subjected to KYC measures.

KYC for the existing customers:

KYC names are to be applied to all the existing customers in a timebound manner. Where the bank is unable to apply appropriate KYC measures due to non-furnishing of information and/or non-cooperation by the customer, the bank may consider the closing the account or terminating the banking/business relationship after issuing due notice to the customer explaining the reasons for taking such a decision. Such decisions are to be taken at a reasonably senior level.

Applicability to Branches and Subsidiaries Outside India:

The above guidelines shall also apply to the branches and majority owned subsidiaries located abroad, especially in countries which do not or insufficiently apply the Financial Action Task Force (FATF) recommendations, to the extent local laws permit. When local applicable laws and regulations prohibit implementation of these guidelines, the same should be brought to the notice of Reserve Bank.

Appointment of Principal Officer:

Banks may appoint a senior management officer to be designated as principal officer. Principal officer shall be located at the head/corporate office of the bank and shall be responsible for monitoring and reporting of all transactions and sharing of information as required under the law. He will close maintain, close liaison with enforcements agencies, banks and any other institution which are involved in the fight against money laundering and combating financing of terrorism.

(47) Nigerian 419 Scams

E-mail scams or popularly known as Nigerian 419 scams are being observed in increasing numbers. Incidents of such frauds is spreading nowadays. These e-mails generally carry tempting offers such as "lucrative job offers" or "winning a lottery". They ask to deposit some money which one gets tempted to deposit. Following precautions are to be taken with such e-mails.

- Not to be tempted by such 'too good to be true' offers. Such e-mails with unbelievable offers are to be ignored.

- ➢ One should not deposit money in an unknown person's account.
- ➢ Such mails if received are to be forwarded to one's respective bank, e. g., "antiphishing @ icicibank.com."

Reserve Bank of India has prohibited all remittances for such schemes under Foreign Exchange Management Act (FEMA), 1995.

(48) Ancillary Services Provided by Bankers

☞ Safe Deposit Lockers

Reserve Bank of India issued revised guidelines on safe deposit lockers in 2007 which superseded previous instructions. Salient points of revised guidelines are as under:

☞ Fixed Deposit as Security

At the time of allotment, banks may obtain a fixed deposit to ensure prompt payment of locker. Security would cover three years' rent and the charges for breaking open the locker, if needed.

Security

Bank is supposed to take due care and take necessary precaution for the protection of lockers. Security procedures should be in documented form and concerned dealing persons should be adequately trained.

If any locker is not operated for more than three years for medium risk category or one year for a higher risk category then bank is supposed to contact locker hirer with an advise either to open or surrender the locker. It is to be done even if the rent is being paid regularly. It is also required that locker-hirer should give in writing the reason for not operating the locker. If found that reason for not opening is genuine, then locker-hirer may allowed to continue his locker.

If locker-hirer fails to give genuine reason for the non-operation of the locker, bank should proceed to open the locker after giving him proper notice. At the time of allotment of the locker a copy of agreement should be handed over to the locker-hirer incorporating this clause. There should be a defined procedure for breaking open the locker and to take the stock of inventory.

Access to Safe Deposit Locker

Bank is supposed to follow the mandate at the time of allotment and take due caution before handing over.

(i) Care is to be taken to ensure the identity of survivor (s) or nominee (s) and the fact of death of the locker-hirer by taking proper documentary evidence.

(ii) To make diligent efforts to know that there is no orders from court restricting the bank to provide the locker.

(iii) Survivor(s) or nominee(s) should be made clear to them that access to locker for them is as a trustee. Reserve Bank of India has also instructed to banks that should not insist on production of succession certificate, letter of administration or to get bond of indemnity from survivor(s) or nominee(s).

In case there is no nomination, bank should in a customer-friendly procedure, provide access to legal heirs or representatives of the deceased.

Banks were also advised by RBI to develop a simplified policy or procedure for finalising the claims of their deceased locker-hirer.

Service Charge

RBI has deregulated the levy of service charges by commercial banks. These charges are left at the discretion of board of directors of the respective banks. Charges framed should be: *(a)* reasonable *(b)* consistent with the service provided *(c)* low value or low volume customers are not penalised.

RBI has also advised to ensure transparency in banking services, banks should display and up date the details of these charges on their website and should also be displayed in their branches in local language also.

(49) Guidelines to Banks Under Foreign Exchange Management Act,1999

Banks dealing in foreign exchange business come in the category of authorised dealers in foreign exchange. Under Section 11(2) of the FEMA Act, RBI is authorised to direct them to furnish such information as may be specified. RBI is also empowered to inspect their business in foreign exchange, as may be necessary. These authorised dealers (Banking Companies) shall have to produce to RBI, such books, accounts and other documents in their custody or to furnish any statement, information relating to the affairs of the authorised dealer [Section 12(2)].

(50) Cheque in Electronic Form

A cheque in electronic form means a cheque containing the mirror image of a cheque in paper form. This is generated, written and signed in a secure system ensuring the safety standards and using digital signature and asymmetric crypto system.

Negotiable Instruments (Amendment and Miscellaneous Provisions) Act was enforced in 2002. It has enlarged the definition of cheque. Definition of a cheque (Section 6) now also includes the electoninc image of truncated cheque and a cheque in the electronic form.

A truncated cheque is a cheque which is truncated in the course of clearing process, either by the clearing house or by the bank during payment or receiving payment, immediately on generating an electronic image for transmission and thus curtailing the physical movement of the written cheque.

CHAPTER

26 Practical Problems

☞ Relation of Banker and Customer

1. A customer draws a cheque on a branch where he has sufficient funds for the payment of it, but his account at another branch of the same bank is overdrawn. Has the banker any right to combine the accounts and dishonour the cheque on the ground that the balance of the accounts is not sufficient to meet it? Is a customer, who keeps an account at one branch, entitled to draw on another branch?

Ans.: Yes, the banker has the right (right of set-off and appropriation) to combine two accounts in the name of the same customer and to adjust the debit balance in one account with the credit balance in the other. He may exercise the right of set-off not only in the case of two accounts of a customer in the same branch of the bank, but also in the case of two or more accounts of the customer in different branches of the same bank.

The right of set-off may be exercised, subject to the fulfilment of the following conditions:

(i) The accounts of the customer must be in the same name and in the same right; for example, the funds in a trust account are deemed to be in different rights.

(ii) The right of set-off may be exercised by a bank only in respect of debts due and not in respect of future debts or contingent debts.

(iii) The right of set-off may be exercised by a bank only if there is no agreement to the contrary.

A customer who keeps an account in one branch is not entitled to draw on another branch. He has no right of set-off or appropriation. Although a banker has the right of set-off between two or more accounts of a customer before making any payment to him, the latter has no such facility of getting his two or more accounts considered before the banker pays the cheque.

2. What is meant by a banker's general lien? State the circumstances in which a banker may exercise this right. Is a banker entitled to a general lien in the following cases?

(a) X deposits a box containing ornaments for safe custody, but later on becomes indebted to the banker;

(b) A banker discounts a documentary bill for his customer B. On the dishonour of the bill together with the charges thereon. But the banker claims lien on the document attached to the bill for the other debts due from B;

(c) Where X who is indebted to the bank has a current account jointly with Y;

(d) A, B & Co., a firm of stock brokers, are indebted to the bank, and B. a partner of the firm carries a large credit balance in his current account;

(e) Dividend warrants are handed over to the banker for collection. On A's behalf, and A's account with the banker is overdrawn.

Ans.: A banker's general lien is his right to all the securities deposited with him by a customer unless there is an express contract, or unless there are circumstances showing an implied contract, which is inconsistent with the lien. The general lien of the banker is an implied pledge, and may be exercised by him on all bills, notes, cheques, bonds, coupons and dividend warrants. The right of sale extends to all the properties and securities belonging to a customer in the hands of the banker, except the title deeds of immovable property, which cannot be sold. But a banker has the right to retain even the title deeds.

A banker cannot exercise the right of lien on safe custody deposits, on deposits for a special purpose, on valuables left with the bank by mistake, on valuables left to cover an advance which was not granted, on securities handed over to the bank for sale, or on trust money with the customer.

(a) A banker is not entitled to a general lien on a box of ornaments kept for safe custody.

(b) The banker can exercise lien on the documents attached to the bill for the debts due from B.

(c) The lien cannot be exercised on a joint account of X with Y.

(d) If the liability of partners is joint as well as several, the bank can exercise the lien on the credit balance in B's A/c.

(e) The banker can exercise lien on A's dividend warrants given for collection.

OPERATION OF ACCOUNTS

☞ Fixed Deposit Accounts

3. A bank receives from its customer A, a credit containing, *inter alia*, a fixed deposit receipt of ₹ 5,000 duly receipted by the depositor. As A has obtained this receipt by false pretence from the depositor, and the receipt is marked "not transferable", would the bank be liable to the depositor?

Ans.: The bank will be fully liable to the depositor because a fixed deposit receipt is not transferable under any circumstances and the bank is liable only to the depositor.

4. A fixed deposit receipt (FDR) for two years is made out in the names of Shiv Saran, Ram Saran and Prem Saran and repayable to any one of them or survivor. After six months, Shiv Saran presents the FDR to the bank and asks for a loan against it. What documents should the bank take from Shiv Saran to safeguard its interests?

Ans.: Fixed deposits are frequently received by banks in the names of two or more persons and the conditions subject to which such deposits are accepted to regulate the manner of their withdrawal. According to the English law, payment to any one of the joint creditors gives a complete discharge to the debtor (*Wallace vs. Kelsall*). But considering the clear language of Section 45 of the Indian Contract Act, *Wallace vs. Kelsall* has no application in India and a debtor obtains a discharge only on payment to all the joint creditors. Therefore, in the above case, the banker should obtain the fixed deposit receipt from Shiv Saran duly signed by all the three parties, namely, Shiv Saran, Ram Saran and Prem Saran, before advancing any loan to Shiv Saran. In this way he would safeguard his interests.

5. On 5th January, 1978, Lakshmi Bank issued a fixed deposit receipt for ₹ 50,000 in favour of Premanand Lal and his son Gurdayal, the amount being payable on 5th January, 1979, to either or survivor. Subsequently, Gurdayal obtained an overdraft from the bank in his own name. On 5th January, 1979, he was indebted to the bank for ₹ 65,000. On that date, the bank credited the amount due under the fixed deposit receipt to the overdraft account of Gurdayal. When Premanand Lal demanded payment of the fixed deposit, the bank informed him of the adjustment made and refused to pay him, claiming that it had a general lien. Discuss the validity of the bank's action.

Ans.: In this case, the FDR has been issued by the bank in the joint names of Premanand Lal and his son Gurdayal, payable to either or survivor. Since Gurdayal has obtained an overdraft in his own name, the bank has no right to appropriate the amount of the overdraft from the fixed deposit and Premanand Lal can claim the amount of the fixed deposit on the due date. The bank cannot exercise its right of general lien on the FDR because the loan taken by Gurdayal was in his personal name, while the FDR was in the joint names of Premanand Lal and Gurdayal. If the loan had been jointly taken by Premanand Lal and Gurdayal, the bank could have exercised the right of general lien on the FDR. Since this was not so, it is liable to pay the amount of the fixed deposit to Premanand Lal. The banker could have exercised the general lien on the FDR if:

(a) Both Premanand Lal and Gurdayal had discharged the FDR by signing across a revenue stamp and handed over the FDR to the banker;

(b) Both of them had signed a request to the banker to sanction the overdraft.

In the present case, Premanand Lal had not authorised the bank to sanction the overdraft to Gurdayal.

6. An FDR for ₹ 10,000 dated 5th October, 1979, for one year, issued in the names of Shri Bhola Prasad and Smt. Kamla Prasad is payable to either or survivor. Shri Bhola Prasad died on 6th March, 1980. The amount is claimed by Smt. Kamla Prasad and one Prem Nath an uncle of the deceased.

Ans.: Banks accept the view, which is actually acted upon in practice, that in an account where the operation is by "either or survivor", the survivor is the only person who is entitled to the amount of the FDR after the death of one of the accountholders. This practice is based on the principle that the terms of operation form part of the contract of deposit. Therefore, in this case, after the death of Bhola Prasad, because the FDR is payable to either or survivor; and Smt. Prasad is the survivor.

7. A fixed deposit receipt had been issued in the joint names of A and B, with the "either or survivor" clause. Both the beneficiaries die before the due date. To whom is the amount payable?

Ans.: The amount will be paid to the persons nominated by A and B. A customer who has an FD A/c. in a bank may nominate any other person and such nominee has the right to take the amount of the fixed deposit in the event of the death of the holder(s) of the FDR. The customer(s) may also assign the FDR in certain circumstances and the assignee gets the right to the amount of the FDR in the event of the death of the customer(s).

The assignment can be made in the will of the customer or by a special agreement or contract. In the present case, the amount of the FDR will be paid to the nominee(s) or assignee(s) of A and B, as the case may be.

☞ Current and Other Deposit Accounts

8. A firm, XY & Co., has an overdrawn account with Hind Bank Ltd. X dies and Y admits O and M as partners in the same firm. What precautions, if any, has the bank to take in continuing the overdraft? What difference would it have made if X had retired instead?

Ans.: In the event of the death of a partner, the firm stands automatically dissolved, if an agreement to the contrary does not exist. If the firm's account shows a debit balance at the time of a partner's death, the latter's estate would be liable to pay the debts incurred by the firm before his death. Thus, to determine the liability of the deceased partner, the banker should close the account of the firm immediately after his death. If the banker defaults in doing so, the rule in Clayton's Case will apply. A new account should be opened in the name of the reconstituted firm with a fresh mandate and undertaking.

In the present case, on the death of X, Hind Bank should close the account of XY & Co., recover the amount from Y and from X's estate, and then open a new account in the names of Y, O and M. The bank should not continue the overdraft A/c but should clear this A/c before opening the new A/c.

In the event of the retirement of X instead of his death, the bank should close the A/c XY & Co., recover the overdraft from Y and X, and then open a new A/c in the name of the new partnership.

9. The bank A/c of a private limited company is operated upon by any two directors in terms of a resolution set forth in the customary mandate filed at the time of the account. There are three directors — A and B who are husband and wife, and C, their son, who is not of age. A falls ill and a resolution is passed conferring authority upon any director to operate the account and deal with all matters relating to the company's banking account. As C is a minor, what is the position of the bank if it honours cheques on the company's account signed by him alone? Can C make arrangements to borrow on the company's account? Will it make any difference if the bank is unaware that C is a minor?

Ans.: According to Section 26*(a)* of the Negotiable Instruments Act, "a minor may draw, endorse, deliver and negotiate a negotiable instrument". Therefore, it is clear that if a minor can validly draw a cheque, the bank would be bound to pay the same and be discharged by making the payment in due course. Relying on this principle, many commercial banks now open deposit accounts in the name of a minor operated upon by himself.

In the present case, since it is an A/c of a private limited company, the bank should not allow C, the minor director, to operate it. The bank may permit B, the wife, to operate the A/c as one of the directors.

In no circumstances, however, should it permit C to make arrangements to borrow on the company's A/c. C, being a minor, has no contractual capacity. In case the loan is not repaid, the bank would not be able to recover the loan amount from the company as well as from C.

The position will not be different if the bank is unaware that C is a minor. It is the liability of the bank to ascertain the correct age of the minor.

10. A, B and C maintain a current A/c with a bank. The A/c is jointly operated by A and C. All the three are jointly responsible for the overdraft in terms of the power of attorney executed by them. A also maintains a separate current account in his personal name in the same branch of the bank.

In this A/c, he maintains a steady balance of more than ₹ 40,000. The Branch Manager knows the position of the A/c maintained by A, and allows an overdraft of ₹ 10,000 in the joint A/c, relying on the balance in the personal A/c of A. Can the bank set-off the amount of overdraft against the balance maintained by A in his personal current account? Will it make any difference if the liabilities of the three persons are joint and several?

Ans.: The right of set-off is a statutory right which enables a debtor to take into account a debt owed to him by a creditor before the latter could recover the debt due to him from the debtor. A banker, like other debtors, possesses this right of set-off, which enables him to combine two accounts in the name of the same customer, and to adjust the debit balance in one account against the credit balance in the other.

One of the important conditions for exercising the right of set-off by a bank is that *"the accounts must be in the same name and in the same right"*. By the words "the same right" is meant that the capacity of the accountholder in both or all the accounts must be the same, *i.e.,* the funds available in one account are held by him in the same right or capacity in which a debit balance stands in the other account. The underlying principle involved in this rule is that funds belonging to someone else, but standing in the name of the accountholder, should not be made available to satisfy his personal debts.

In the present case, the bank account set-off the overdraft of ₹ 10,000 in the joint A/c of ABC from A's personal A/c, because the joint A/c of ABC and the personal A/c of A are not in the same name and in the same right. In the joint A/c, the three accountholders are jointly responsible for the overdraft; A is not individually liable for it.

But if the joint accountholders have specifically undertaken to be jointly and severally liable for the overdraft in the joint A/c to the banker, the latter can set-off ₹ 10,000 the overdraft in the joint account against the personal A/c of A.

11. X was maintaining a Current A/c and a Savings Bank A/c in a bank. The Current A/c showed a debit balance of ₹ 5,000 and the Savings Bank A/c a credit balance of ₹ 7,000 when X was declared a bankrupt. A cheque for ₹ 4,000 is presented by the trustees in bankruptcy of X for payment. What course of action should the bank adopt?

Ans.: The bank should set-off the debit balance of ₹ 5,000 in the Current A/c of X against the credit balance of ₹ 7,000 in his Savings Bank A/c before making any payment to the trustees in bankruptcy of X. Even if the banker receives a garnishee order in respect of the funds belonging to a customer, he has a right to exercise his right of set-off first and to surrender only the balance to the judgement creditor.

12. Electronic House, Udaipur, is a partnership concern. Shri Ganeshi Lal, one of the partners, died. His share capital in the business was ₹ 50,000. He had private property worth ₹ 4 lakh. All the properties are free from charge against any loan. But he had to pay ₹ 3 lakh to his private creditors. As against a bank loan of ₹ 3 lakh, the bank could realise from the firm and from the properties of other partners only ₹ 1 lakh. Now, can the bank recover ₹ 2 lakh from the private property worth ₹ 4 lakh of Shri Ganeshi Lal?

Ans.: The death of a partner has ordinarily the legal effect of dissolving the firm. If the firm has a debit balance, the account should be stopped to fix the liability of the estate of the deceased partner and to avoid the operation of the rule in Clayton's Case. In the present case, the bank can recover its loan of ₹ 2 lakh, which is outstanding against the firm of Electronic House, Udaipur, from the private property of one of the partners, Shri Ganeshi Lal. It should close the bank account of the firm and fix the liability of the firm from the estates of all the partners; and since it is mentioned that the bank could recover only ₹ 1 lakh from the estates of the other partners, the balance of ₹ 2 lakh can be claimed from the estate of the deceased partner, Shri Ganeshi Lal.

13. M/s. Shiv Saran & Sons is a partnership concern with four partners, each having contributed a share capital of ₹ 50,000. Shri Shiv Saran, one of the partners, maintains a current A/c in the bank in which the current A/c of the firm is maintained. The current A/c of Shri Shiv Saran shows a debit balance of ₹ 15,000. When the bank presses Shri Shiv Saran to liquidate the overdraft of ₹ 15,000, he draws a cheque for ₹ 15,000 as a partner of M/s. Shiv Saran & Sons and credits it to his individual current A/c. Will it be in order for the bank to accept the cheque in repayment of the overdraft?

Ans.: When Shri Shiv Saran draws a cheque for ₹ 15,000 on the firm's A/c to be credited to his individual current A/c to liquidate the overdraft, the bank should make an enquiry about it from the other partners and do so if it is satisfied, otherwise it will bear the risk of losing the statutory protection granted to the collecting banker under the Negotiable Instruments Act, 1881. The banker should be particularly careful in this regard if the partner sends such a cheque in response to a request from the bank to repay the overdraft taken by him from the bank.

☞ Drawing and Payment of Cheques and Bills

14. A cheque for ₹ 500, drawn in favour of Ram Chandra, is stolen. Ram Chandra notifies the loss to the bank and subsequently the cheque is presented for encashment. State the precautions which a paying banker should take to safeguard his own interest.

Ans.: When a banker receives instructions from a customer to stop payment on a particular cheque, he should clearly write these instructions on the customer's A/c and should not make payment on the cheque when presented. If payment on a cheque when it has been countermanded by its drawer, the banker may be compelled to reverse the entry made in this connection. In the present case, when Ram Chandra informs the bank about the stolen cheque, the latter should write clearly and prominently in red ink on Ram Chandra's A/c to stop the payment on the cheque. When the cheque is subsequently presented, the bank should refuse to pay this cheque and write the words "orders not to pay" or "payment countermanded by the drawer" at the time of dishonour.

15. A draft for ₹ 10,000 is issued to a customer M by the Jaipur branch of a commercial bank drawn upon the Head Office in Mumbai. The draft is handed over to P in settlement of a purchase; but before the presentation of the draft, M discovers that material facts have been withheld by P, which may constitute a fraud. M asks the bank to stop payment on the draft. In these circumstances, what is the right course of action for the bank?

Ans.: In case of a draft, its purchaser has no right to countermand its payment to its payee after its receipt by him, and the bank on which it is drawn is not bound to carry out his instructions (*Malik Barkat Ali vs. Imperial Bank of India*, A.I.R., 1945, Lahore, 213:1945). In the light of the above case, the bank will not carry out the instructions of M and make the payment of the draft to P on presentation.

16. Rajiv Kumar issued a cheque for ₹ 5,000 in favour of Rajesh Kumar on 1st October, 1980. Rajesh Kumar kept the cheque with other cheques in his office. The cheque was later removed by a person without his knowledge. This person approached Ramesh Kumar on 15th October, 1980 to negotiate the cheque, stating that he was in urgent need of money. Ramesh Kumar cashed the cheque and lodged it in his account for payment. The cheque was returned by the bank with reason: "Refer to Drawer". Is the cheque valid against the bank? Has Ramesh Kumar any right against Rajiv Kumar?

Ans.: The cheque is not valid against the bank and Ramesh Kumar has no right against Rajiv Kumar. The cheque was issued by Rajiv Kumar in the name of Rajesh Kumar and it was presented to the bank by Ramesh Kumar who was not the payee, but who had received it from a person who had stolen it from the true payee, Rajesh Kumar. Although Ramesh Kumar had received the cheque for consideration (after paying the amount of the cheque to the thief who had stolen it from Rajesh Kumar), he should have noticed that the cheque has not been endorsed in favour of the thief. Therefore, Ramesh Kumar can never get a good title on this cheque. Consequently, he cannot sue the bank for the amount of the cheque.

17. Ram Chandra, Avinash Chandra and Prem Chandra, partners in a partnership firm, have a current account in a bank. One of the partners, Ram Chandra, is authorised to operate the current account. On 10th January, 1979, Ram Chandra issued a cheque bearing No. 14721 for ₹ 1,550 in favour of M/s. Atma Ram & Sons. The agent of the bank received a letter from Prem Chandra, another partner, to stop the payment on the cheque, bearing No. 14721, for ₹ 1,550. On 11th January, 1979, the cheque was presented in clearing by the bank. Will it be in order for the bank to pay the cheque?

Ans.: A notice from one or more of the partners to the bank cancelling the authority of any one of the other partners would be sufficient notice to the banker to act upon. Similarly, one partner has an implied authority to stop payment on a cheque drawn on the partnership account by another, and the banker is bound to comply with the instructions issued by that partner.

In the above case, the bank is bound to comply with the instructions of Prem Chandra and to stop the payment on the cheque.

18. State the answers you would give for returning the cheques mentioned below, giving reasons for your action:

(i) Cheque dated February, 1970, presented on 1st March, 1970;

(ii) Cheque dated 3rd June, 1970, presented on 4th December, 1970;

(iii) Cheque dated 12th March, 1970, presented on 7th January, 1970;

(iv) Cheque dated 17th April, 1970, presented on 8th July, 1970.

Ans.: *(i)* The cheque will be returned with the remark "date incomplete", because this cheque does not bear the complete date. The date must comprise the number of the day, the month and the year

(ii) The cheque will be returned with the remarks "stale cheque — more than six months old", because it was issued more than six months before the date of presentment.

(iii) The cheque will be returned with the remarks "post-dated cheque". The payment on this cheque can be made on 12th March, 1970 or thereafter

(iv) The payment on this cheque will be made by the bank because it has been presented within the period of six months from its date.

19. Mr. J. Anthony and Mr. L. Srinivasan have a joint current account in a bank. The account showed a credit balance of ₹ 20,000 on 8th July, 1979. On 7th July, 1979, Mr. Srinivasan is reported dead.

The survivor, Mr. Anthony, draws a cheque for ₹ 20,000 to withdraw the whole amount and close the account. Can the bank pay the cheque, ignoring the representatives of the deceased?

In case the executors of Mr. Srinivasan claim the credit balance of ₹ 20,000 in the joint account on 8th July, 1979, what will be the course of action open to the bank?

Ans.: The persons opening a joint account are required to give a mandate in the application form about the person to whom the balance in the account shall be payable. A joint account may be payable to:

(i) Both or all of them or the survivor or survivors; or

(ii) Either or any one or more of them or the survivor or survivors.

In the event of the death of any one or more of the joint holders of the A/c, the balance becomes payable to the survivor or survivors without reference to the representatives of the deceased person or persons. Generally speaking, the banker asks the surviving accountholders to withdraw the balance in the joint A/c and deposit it in a new A/c opened in the names of the surviving joint accountholders.

Thus, the present legal basis for the bank permitting the opening of such type of accounts rests on the terms of the contract, express or implied, with the customers. But, in actual practice, banks sometimes face difficulties in giving effect to the terms of the contract, when there are conflicting claims about the balances held in the joint accounts. In *Nagarajamma vs. State Bank of Hyderabad* (A.I.R., 1962, Andhra Pradesh 260), the Andhra Pradesh High Court held, on the basis of the facts of the case, that the survivor was not entitled to the funds.

In *Krushandas Nagindas Bhate vs. Bhagwandas Ranchoddas and Others* (A.I.R. 1976, Bombay, 153), the Bombay High Court upheld the above decision, and observed:

"In respect of a joint account opened in the bank, the law seems to be well settled — that on the death of one, there is a resulting tiust in favour of the heirs and legal representatives, unless there are special facts and circumstances to show a contrary intention." The High Court further held that "if, from the facts and circumstances of the case, it could be held that the intention was to make the survivor the owner of the amount lying in the account, then he, and not the heirs, would be entitled to recover the amount. If the facts and circumstances of the case do not establish any such intention, although the holder of the joint account may be authorised to withdraw the amount, he would be bound to restore that amount to the heirs and legal representatives of the deceased joint holder. The bank may be discharged by payment to the survivor. But the survivor may, in the absence of an intention to make him the owner, be accountable to the heirs of the deceased joint holder." The High Court also rejected the practice of the State Bank of India in making the survivor in a joint account the absolute owner of the amount lying to the credit of that account.

In the case of accounts opened under *(ii)* above, if payment on an account is at any time forbidden by any one or more of the accountholders, the account will only be payable on the discharge of all the accountholders or the survivor or survivors.

In the present case, before giving the credit balance of ₹ 20,000 in the joint account to the survivor, Mr. Anthony, or the executors of Mr. Srinivasan, the bank would determine whether, at the time of opening the joint account, the accountholders had given any mandate in the application form regarding the person to whom the balance in the account should be payable. If the account is payable to either or survivor, the bank will pay the money to the survivor, Mr. Anthony. If the account is payable to both or survivors, the bank will have to ascertain the claims of the survivors, Mr. Anthony, and the executors of Mr. Srinivasan on the balance of ₹ 20,000, and pay the money accordingly.

20. Is the banker's action legally justified in the following cases? Give reasons:

(i) Requiring an introduction before opening a current account;

(ii) Returning and not collecting a cheque crossed to two banks;

(iii) Paying a cheque to B which is drawn in favour of A and marked "not-negotiable";

(iv) Not collecting a crossed cheque for a stranger, stating that it cannot be done under Section 131 of the Negotiable Instruments Act;

(v) Paying a cheque drawn on the customer's current A/c, when there is insufficient balance in it by making a lien on the shares held in the same customers's safe custody account.

Ans.: *(i)* The bank is legally justified in asking for an introduction before opening a current account. If an introduction is not taken before the opening of a current A/c, the bank will not be entitled to the statutory protection under Section 131 of the Negotiable Instruments Act on the ground of negligence in not establishing the true identity of his customer.

(ii) According to Section 127 of the Negotiable Instruments Act, when a cheque is crossed to more than one banker, the banker on whom it is drawn shall refuse payment thereof. But when the other banker is an agent of the first for the purpose of collection, the payment cannot be refused. Thus, a cheque bearing a double special crossing shall not be honoured by the paying banker. But the collecting banker cannot refuse to collect such a cheque. In the present case, the collecting banker is legally not justified in returning the cheque crossed to two banks.

(iii) A cheque marked "Not Negotiable" can be endorsed and is transferable. The only effect of the words "Not Negotiable" is that the transferee of such a cheque cannot get a title better than that of the transferor. These words, thus, constitute a caution to the transferee to accept the cheque only if he is well acquainted with the transferor. Therefore, a cheque drawn in favour of A can be paid to B irrespective of the words "Not Negotiable" marked thereon.

(iv) A bank is legally justified in not collecting a crossed cheque for a stranger, because if it opens an account for a stranger without a proper introduction, it is deemed to be negligent, and, therefore, it cannot avail itself of the statutory protection under Section 131 of Negotiable Instruments Act. Section 131 provides that "a banker who has in good faith and without negligence received payment for a customer on a cheque crossed generally or specially to himself shall not, in case the title to the cheque proves defective, incur any liability to the true owner of the cheque by reason only of having received such payment".

(v) The bank cannot exercise the right of general lien on the shares held in the customer's safe custody account because the shares have been kept with the bank for safe custody. The banker's position here is that of a trustee.

21. Alok Chand and Pramod Chand have a joint account, showing a credit balance of ₹ 10,000. A garnishee order of ₹ 6,000 is served on the bank, specifying Shri Pramod Chand as the judgement debtor.

It will be in order for the branch agent:

(a) To attach ₹ 6,000 because one of the joint accountholders, Pramod Chand, is a judgement debtor;

(b) Not to attach ₹ 6,000 because it cannot be ascertained by the bank that the share of Pramod Jain in the credit balance of ₹ 10,000 is ₹ 6,000;

(c) To attach ₹ 6,000 and advise the accountholders to secure withdrawal of the order from the court because non-compliance with a court order is contempt of court;

(d) Not to attach ₹ 6,000 and advise the solicitor acting for the judgement creditor to withdraw the order under intimation to the accountholders.

Ans.: When a garnishee order is received by a bank regarding a customer who has no individual account but a joint account in it, the joint account cannot be attached. But if both or all the joint account-holders are joint judgement debtors in any legal proceedings, the joint account can be attached. In *Herschoru vs. Evans* (1938), 2 KB, 801, where there was a joint account in the names of husband and wife, it was held that the joint account could not be garnished in execution of a decree obtained against the husband alone. It is not for the banker, however, to question the propriety of the court's order, nor can he, as a garnishee, be compelled to adjudicate upon conflicting equities.

In the present case, the bank will not attach ₹ 6,000 from the joint account because only Pramod Chand is the judgement debtor, while the account is in the names of Alok Chand and Pramod Chand.

22. There is a dormant Savings Bank A/c in your branch in the names of Shri J.B. Mahajan and Mrs. Ansuya J. Mahajan, payable to either or survivor, with a balance of ₹ 7,500 in 1965. The account was opened in 1953.

In January 1979, one Mr. Vasudev (aged 21 years), claiming to be the only son of Mr. J.B. Mahajan, approaches you and informs as under:

(a) He holds the Pass Book of this account;

(b) His mother Ansuya died in 1970;

(c) His father has left the house in 1960 and his whereabouts are not known;

(d) He has information that a safe deposit locker was also there in their names. The key of the locker is not traceable.

He requests you, as a branch manager, to make payment of the balance in the account to him and also to deliver the articles lying in the locker to him.

How will you deal with the matter?

Ans.: The persons opening a joint A/c are required to give a mandate, in the application form itself, about the person to whom the balance in the account shall be payable. In the event of the death of any one or more of the jointholders of the account, the balance becomes payable to the survivor/survivors (if any) or to the representatives of the deceased person or persons.

The joint A/c of Mr. and Mrs. Mahajan is payable to either or survivor. The branch manager will first of all see the mandate given by Mrs. and Mr. Mahajan at the time of opening the A/c to find out to whom the balance in the account is payable. If it is payable to the legal heir in case of the death of both the accountholders, Mr. Vasudev becomes entitled to claim the balance in the dormant A/c. The bank is bound to hand over the balance in the A/c to the heir and legal representatives of the deceased jointholders.

In the present case, Mr. Vadudev, the only son of Mr. and Mrs. Mahajan, possesses the pass book, and his mother died in 1970. After the death of his mother, the father becomes entitled to the balance in the A/c. But his father left the house in 1960 and his whereabouts are not known. Therefore, under the circumstances, the bank will ask Mr. Vasudev to furnish proof that both his father and mother are dead and a certificate that he is the only legal heir and entitled to the credit balance in the joint A/c.

☞ Safe Deposits

In the event of the death of the persons depositing valuables, the banker may deliver them to the personal representatives of the deceased on their producing evidence that the estate of the deceased has been probated or produce letters of administration, and obtain a receipt from them.

The bank manager should, therefore, ask Mr. Vasudev to produce proof of the death of both his father and mother and letters of administration before claiming the balance in the joint A/c as well as the articles lying in the locker. On production of these documents, the balance in the A/c and the valuables in the locker may be handed over to Mr. Vasudev.

Since the A/c has not been operated after 1965, and since, according to the rules of the Reserve Bank, accounts not operated for ten years become "dead accounts" and are accounts transferred to the Reserve Bank of India, Mr. Vasudev's claim, together with his evidence, should be forwarded to the Reserve Bank by the branch manager. When the money is received from the Reserve Bank, it should be paid to Mr. Vasudev.

23. As a branch manager, how would you deal with the following situations? Give reasons.

(a) Mr. A has a savings bank A/c with a balance of ₹ 25,000. Since he has not been in good health for the last two months, he writes to the bank to pay the balance in his A/c to his wife in the event of his death. He sends his wife's specimen signature duly attested by him. Will you accept such instructions? Why?

(b) A cheque for ₹ 1,000, drawn on your branch, is presented for payment with the amount in figures written in English and the other particulars in the regional language of the region in which the branch is located. The signature of the drawer on the cheque tallies with the specimen on your record. Will you pay the cheque?

(c) A cheque for ₹ 5,000, originally dated 6th April, 1979, and altered to 12th April, 1979, is presented for payment on 14th April, 1979, is presented for payment on 14th April, 1979. Will you pay the cheque? Does the bank run any risk in making the payment?

(d) A cheque for ₹ 1,000 payable to M/s. Anup Builders, is presented for cash payment. In the cheque, the words "or order" have been struck off and, in their place, the words "or bearer"

are written, duly initialled by the drawer. Will you pay the cheque? Does the bank run any risk in making the payment?

(e) An uncrossed cheque for ₹ 750, payable to "controller of stores (Govt.)" is presented for cash payment. The cheque is duly endorsed by the controller of stores and a letter of authority duly signed by him in favour of the presenter is produced. Will you pay the cheque? Why?

(f) Your branch has issued a Fixed Deposit Receipt for ₹ 10,000 in the joint names of Mr. and Mrs. M. B. Dalvi, payable to either or survivor, for a period of 12 months, maturing on 30th September, 1979.

Mrs. Dalvi approaches you on 11th December, 1978, with a request to issue a duplicate receipt since the original receipt has been lost by her. How would you deal with her request?

(g) A and B who have a joint current A/c payable to either or survivor, have granted a power of attorney in favour of C to operate the account. C usually operates the A/c. Yesterday, a notice was received by you, intimating to you the death of B. Today, a cheque for ₹ 2,500, drawn on the account and signed by C, is presented for payment. How would you deal with the matter?

Ans.: *(a)* The bank will accept the instructions of A nominating his wife to get the balance in his account in the event of A's death. This is a proper and legal nomination and there is nothing wrong in accepting such instructions.

(b) The amount of ₹ 1,000 would be paid because the amount written in words and figures is the same and the signature of the drawer of the cheque tallies with the specimen signature in the bank's record. Therefore, the cheque is valid in all respects.

(c) An alteration of the date of the cheque is a material alteration. An alteration is material, if in any way it materially or substantially alters the operation of the instrument and the liabilities of the parties thereto, irrespective of whether the change is prejudicial to the payee or not. According to Section 87 of the Negotiable Instruments Act, the Instrument (cheque), if altered, becomes void. When a material alteration has been made, the banker should satisfy himself that such alteration has been made with the drawer's consent or authority and is confirmed by his signature. In the present case, if the alteration in the date from 6th to 12th April, 1979, is made with the signature, the banker should pay the cheque without any risk.

(d) If in a cheque the words "or order" have been struck off and in their place the words "or bearer" have been written duly initialled by the drawer, the bank may pay the cheque across the counter without any risk, if it is not crossed.

(e) The payment of the cheque may be made by the bank because the cheque is not crossed and is duly endorsed by the payee, and is accompanied by a letter of authority duly signed by him in favour of the presenter.

(f) When an FDR is issued in joint names and is payable to either or survivor, a request by one of the jointholders to issue a duplicate receipt on the plea that original one has been lost should not be entertained by the bank. It should insist that the request should come from both Mr. and Mrs. M.B. Dalvi because in "In Innes vs. *Stephenson, Moore Rule 145*", by Lord Tenterden declared that where money is paid into a bank on the joint account of persons who are not partners in trade, the bank is not discharged by payment to one of those persons without the authority of others.

(g) On receipt of information about the death of B, the bank will close the joint account in the name of A and B, and the cheque presented for payment will not be paid. The balance in the account may be paid after consultations with A and the legal representative of B.

24. A issues an open "bearer" cheque for ₹ 5,000 in favour of B, who strikes out the words bearer and puts a crossing across the cheque. The cheque is thereafter negotiated to C, D and E. When it is finally presented by E's bankers, it is returned with the remark: "Payment countermanded by drawer". In response to legal notice from E, A pleads that: *(i)* the cheque was issued to B under threat from him and that *(ii)* the cheque was altered after it had been issued and, therefore, he (A) was not bound to pay the cheque. Discuss whether A's argument is valid or not.

Ans.: When the cheque is presented to the bank by E, it bears two alterations: *(i)* the word "bearer" has been struck off, and *(ii)* the cheque has been crossed. As both these alterations are not material alterations, the liability of any party, including the drawer, is not affected. Therefore, A is liable to pay the amount of the cheque to the holder.

The first argument of A is that "the cheque was issued to B under threat from him". This argument is to be examined in the light of Section 58 of the Negotiable Instruments Act, which provides that if an instrument is obtained from its market by fraud, etc., the possessor or his endorsee is not entitled to receive the amount, the instrument from its maker. But when the possessor or endorsee is the holder in due course, his right to receive payment is not at all effected. In the present problem, it has not been stated whether E is a holder in due course or not. If E is a holder in due course, he has the right to recover the money from A.

25. Ram Nath & Co., have issued an order cheque for ₹ 10,000 in favour of Girdharilal Sharma. The cheque bears the following endorsements when presented for payment:

(i) Pay to Murari Lal Shethi Girdharilal Sharma

(ii) Murarilal Shethi

(iii) Ratanlal Gupta.

Mr. Ratanlal Gupta does not maintain an account but is reasonably known to you as the owner of a cycle shop nearby, and so you pay the cheque to Ratanlal Gupta. After a few days, you receive a notice from Murarilal Shethi that the cheque was stolen from him and that his endorsement on the cheque was a forgery. Shri Murarilal Shethi claims the amount from the bank. Please discuss the position of the paying bank.

Ans.: Section 85 of the Negotiable Instruments Act grants statutory protection to the paying banker. The section lays down:

"Where a cheque payable to order purports to be endorsed by or on behalf of the payee, the drawee is discharged by payment in due course."

According to Section 16 of the Act, payment in due course refers to payment in accordance with the apparent tenor of the instrument, in good faith and without negligence to any person in possession thereof under circumstances which do not afford a reasonable ground for believing that he is not entitled to receive payment of the amount therein mentioned.

Thus, paying banks get statutory protection if: *(a)* the endorsement on the cheque is regular and *(b)* the payment has been made in due course. In the present case, both of these conditions have been fulfilled, *viz.,* the endorsement of Murarilal Shethi is regular (though it may not be valid) and the payment has been made by the bank to a person it knows, in good faith and without negligence. Therefore, under the circumstances, the paying banker can avail himself of the protection under Section 85 of the Negotiable Instruments Act, and is not liable to meet the claim of Murarilal Shethi.

26. X owes a certain sum of money to Y but he does not know the exact amount and hence he makes out a blank cheque in favour of Y, signs and delivers it to Y with a request to fill up the amount due from, and payable by him. Y fraudulently fills up an amount which is more than the amount due and payable by X, and endorses the cheque to Z in full payment of the dues of Y. The cheque of X is dishonoured. Discuss the rights of Y and Z.

Ans.: Section 44 of the Negotiable Instruments Act deals with the partial absence or failure of a money consideration. The present case should be examined in the light of the provisions of this section, which lays down:

"When the consideration for which a person signed a promissory note, bill of exchange or cheque consisted of money, and was originally absent in part or has subsequently failed in part, the sum which a holder, standing in immediate relation with such signer, is entitled to receive from him is proportionately reduced."

As Y, the payee, filled in a larger amount than was due from the drawer, the cheque drawn by X in favour of Y will be deemed to have been issued for consideration, a part of which the originally absent at the time of the issue of the cheque. As per the provisions of the cheque, Y, who is a party in immediate relation with the drawer of the cheque, is entitled to recover from X only the exact amount due from the latter and not the amount entered in the cheque. But the right of Z, who is a holder for value, is not adversely affected and he can claim the full amount of the cheque from Y.

27. *(a)* Your customer, Smt. Patel, asks you to stop payment on the cheque for ₹ 250 which she has issued to a salesman at the door as a deposit for a washing machine which he promised to deliver the next day. The machine has not arrived and the firm, whom the salesman claimed to represent, has no knowledge of him, has received no order through him and states that he has no authority to act on its behalf. The cheque which is crossed "not negotiable" is paid in at your branch by another customer of yours, a local cloth merchant, who had paid cash against it to the salesman.

Can the cloth merchant set up a valid claim to recover the value of the cheque? What is his position *vis-a-vis* Smt. Patel?

(b) Had you paid the cheque, after notice of a stop order from Smt. Patel, what would be your position *vis-a-vis* Smt. Patel? Give reasons stating what rights a bank may have against a customer whose cheque it pays in spite of specific instructions not to pay.

Ans.: (a) To understand this problem fully and clearly, we have to examine the provisions of Sections 43, 58 and 130 of the Negotiable Instruments Act. Section 43 (consideration) says: "A negotiable instrument made, drawn, accepted, endorsed or transferred without consideration, or for a consideration which fails to create no obligation of payment between the parties to the transaction. But if any such party has transferred the instrument with or without endorsement to a holder for consideration, such holder, and every subsequent holder deriving title from him, may recover the amount due on such instrument from the transferor for consideration or any prior party thereto."

In the present case, the salesman obtained the cheque from Smt. Patel on the promise to deliver the washing machine the next day. But the machine was not delivered and the consideration thus failed. Section 43 states that a consideration which fails creates no obligation of payment between the parties to the transaction. Therefore, the salesman gets no right to enforce its payment. But the cloth merchant, who paid cash against the cheque, becomes its holder for consideration and is entitled under Section 43 to recover the amount from the transferor.

Section 58 (fraud) states: "When a negotiable instrument has been lost, or has been obtained from any maker, acceptor or holder thereof by means of an offence or fraud, or for an unlawful consideration, no possessor or endorsee, who claims through the person who found or so obtained the instrument, is entitled to receive the amount due thereon from such maker, acceptor, or holder, or from any party to such holder, unless such possessor or endorsee is, or some person through whom he claims was, a holder thereof in due course".

In the present case, the salesman posed as a representative of the firm, which he was not, and, therefore obtained the cheque from Smt. Patel by fraud. According to the provisions of Section 58, the salesman has no right to receive the payment; but the cloth merchant, since he is a holder for value, has the right to receive payment.

Section 130 (Not Negotiable Crossing) states: "A person taking a cheque, crossed generally or specially, bearing in either case the words 'not negotiable', shall not have, and shall not be capable of giving, a better title to the cheque than that which the person from whom he had taken".

In the present case, the cloth merchant had received the cheque from the salesman who had no title to the cheque, and because the cheque was crossed "not negotiable", the cloth merchant cannot get a good title to the cheque according to Section 130. Therefore, the cloth merchant cannot recover the amount from the bank or Smt. Patel.

(b) If the bank pays the cheque in spite of the notice of "stop payment" from the drawer, the banker cannot debit the amount to the account of the drawer because the payment has been made without the authority of the drawer.

28. X is the Managing Director of a limited company, in which capacity he alone is authorised to operate the company's bank account which is kept with Y bank in Kolkata. X's personal account is with Z bank in Kolkata, where he has maintained an average credit balance of ₹ 5,000.

X draws a cheque on the company's account in favour of himself for ₹ 85,000 which he pays in at Z bank for credit to his personal account. The cheque is duly collected by Z bank and the proceeds credited to his account. Subsequently, the company goes into liquidation and the liquidator files a suit against Z bank for recovery of the money on the ground that there had been a fraudulent conversion.

What is the position of Z bank? Give reasons for your answer.

Ans.: In a situation given in the above case, the collecting banker may face the charge of fraudulent conversion. But Section 131 of the Negotiable Instruments Act gives statutory protection to the collecting banker against the charge of fraudulent conversion if the payment is received in good faith and without negligence.

Section 131 states: "A banker, who has in good faith and without negligence received payment for a customer of a cheque crossed generally or specially to himself, shall not, in case the title to the cheque by reason only of having received such payment.

In the present case, the charge of fraudulent conversion against the Z bank is valid because the banker was negligent in the collection of the said cheque. The reasons for such negligence are: first, the banker is presumed to know the true identity of his customers. When X issued a cheque on the company's account in favour of himself, it was a sufficient ground to arouse suspicion in the mind of the collecting banker to enquire about this. If the bank did not do so, it was negligent.

Second, X maintained an average credit balance of ₹ 5,000 in his account with the Z bank. A cheque for ₹ 85,000 was an abnormally big amount, and that too drawn by himself on the company account, was itself an abnormal transaction, which should have aroused the suspicion of the banker.

29. Smt. Saraswati, after opening a current account in her name with your bank, issues several cheques without providing funds in the account to honour them. Can the bank draw the attention of the lady's husband to the unsatisfactory conduct of the account? What steps should it take to close this account?

Ans.: The husband is not at all concerned with, or responsible for, the separate account of his wife. A married woman is fully competent to open and operate her bank account quite independently.

The banker is obliged to maintain secrecy in regard to a customer's account. Therefore, he cannot draw the attention of Smt. Saraswati's husband to the unsatisfactory position of her account.

But the banker has the right to close a customer's account after giving due notice if the account is not satisfactorily operated. In the present case, the banker requests Smt. Saraswati to conduct her account in a satisfactory manner. If Smt. Saraswati does not comply with the banker's request, a warning should be issued to her that the account will be closed if she does not operate it properly. Finally, a notice may be served on her informing her about the closing of the account.

30. Shri Traders purchases a demand draft for ₹ 10,000 from your Mumbai office, which is drawn on your Pune branch in favour of Shri Poonaman. After two days, the purchaser comes to the Mumbai office and reports that he has misplaced the draft. He wants a duplicate draft to be issued. What advice will you give him? What measures will you take to protect the bank's interest and why?

Ans.: A demand draft issued by a bank is an instrument drawn for consideration and has three parties:

(i) The drawer branch of the bank;

(ii) The drawee branch of the bank;

(iii) The payee of the draft.

After the issue of the draft, the purchaser is no longer a party to it. If he reports the misplacement of the draft, the drawer branch of the bank should immediately enquire from the drawee branch if the draft has been encashed. If it has not so far been encashed, the drawee branch should be instructed to be cautious in negotiating it. If the drawee branch informs the drawer branch that the draft has not so far been encashed, the latter should ask the purchaser to sign a stamped indemnity bond carrying the signatures of two guarantors of repute. Thereafter, a duplicate copy of the draft may be issued.

31. Shri Arjun Lal has an overdraft limit of ₹ 40,000 with your bank. On a Saturday, when the debit balance in the account is ₹ 38,200 a cheque for ₹ 5,800 drawn on the account, is presented for cash payment by a third party. Will you pay the cheque and why? If not, and if you return the cheque unpaid, discuss which of the following answers you will give and why? Explain also the reasons for not choosing the other answers.

(i) Funds expected;

(ii) Effects not cleared, present again;

(iii) Exceeds arrangement;

(iv) Refer to drawer.

Ans.: Shri Arjun Lal has an overdraft limit of only ₹ 40,000. If the cheque for ₹ 5,800 is paid by the banker, the debit balance in the account will go up to ₹ 4,000 (existing debit balance of ₹ 38,500 plus ₹ 5,800, the amount of the cheque). This will exceed the overdraft limit by ₹ 4,000. The banker should, therefore, not allow this limit to be exceeded, and the cheque should not be paid.

While returning the cheque, the banker should put the remark "exceeds arrangement", which is the most appropriate in this case, because the overdraft arrangement does not permit the payment of the cheque. The other remarks "funds expected" and "effected not cleared, present again" do not apply in the present case, because the banker has not received any cheque for collection. "Refer to drawer" also does not apply in this case because it implies insufficiency of funds.

32. As a branch manager, how will you deal with the following cases? Give reasons for your answers.

(i) Your customer sends a crossed order cheque drawn by A in favour of your bank, to be credited to his (the customer's) account with you.

(ii) D presents for encashment an uncrossed cheque payable to him or bearer and refuses to endorse the cheque. Will it make any difference if the amount is small?

(iii) A bill, dated 29th January, 1968, and payable after one month (without grace), remains unpaid on 28th February, 1968.

(iv) Smt. Radha P. Patel sends you for credit to her account, a cheque drawn in favour of Smt. R.P. Patel and endorsed by her as Smt. Radha Patel.

(v) A firm, having A, B and C as partners, enjoys an overdraft limit of ₹ 1 lakh with the bank. A communication is received by the bank that A died on 20th April, 1964. On 21st April, 1964, two cheques, signed by the deceased partner on 18th April, 1964, are presented for payment.

Ans.: *(i)* The amount of the cheque cannot be credited to the account of the customer because the cheque is drawn in favour of the bank. The banker is liable to pay the cheque as per the mandate of the drawer of the cheque.

(ii) While no endorsement is necessary in the case of an uncrossed bearer cheque, the customer presenting the cheque for encashment has to sign on the back of the cheque. This signature is actually a receipt for payment and not an endorsement. The banker can insist that the customer should give such a receipt before making the payment. In case the customer refuses to sign on the back of the cheque, the banker may ask him to give a separate receipt for the payment received by him. It will not make any difference, whether the cheque is of a large amount or small amount.

(iii) The bill dated 29th January, 1968 payable after one month (without grace) becomes payable on the corresponding day of the next month. Because the year 1968 was a leap year, the bill was payable on 29th February, 1968, and not on 28th February, 1968.

(iv) The payee or endorsee must endorse in the same name as is given in the cheque, otherwise the endorsement becomes irregular. Smt. Radha P. Patel must endorse the cheque drawn in favour of Smt. R.P. Patel in the same manner. The endorsement made by Smt. Radha P. Patel is, therefore, irregular.

(v) In the event of the death of a partner, the partnership account is closed and no payment is made by the bank from the partnership account. In the present case, the banker should not make a payment on the two cheques presented after receiving information about the death of the partner.

33. In reply to a question, a candidate, who appeared for Part I of the Indian Institute of Bankers Examination, gave the following answers:

(i) The due date of a bill dated 28th November, 1967 payable 90 days after date is 1st March, 1968.

(ii) In respect of a current account in the joint names of A and B, to be operated upon by both of them jointly, the balance cannot be paid to A when B dies.

(iii) When a customer calls at the bank's branch after business hours to cash a cheque drawn in his favour by another customer of the same branch, it cannot be paid in any circumstances.

(iv) No introduction is necessary for opening a savings bank account.

You are required to examine the answers critically and mention whether they are true or false and why?

Ans.: *(i)* The correct due date is 29th February, 1968. (1968 was a leap year).

November,	2 days
+ December,	31 days
+ January, 1968	31 days
+ February, 1968	26 days

90 days + 3 days grace = February 29, 1968

(ii) In the case of a joint account of A and B, the balance will be paid to A in the event of the death of B because of the law of devolution between the joint owners and established banking practice.

(iii) The bank should not pay the cheque after business hours because it is against the rules and there is risk in such payments. The drawer of the cheque may write to the bank to stop payment of the cheque or a garnishee order may be issued by a court after banking hours on that day. In such circumstances, the banker will not be entitled to debit the customer's account and shall have to bear the loss himself.

(iv) An introduction is necessary before a Savings Bank A/c is opened. But if a customer does not request that he may be given the cheque book facility, an introduction may not be insisted upon by banker.

34. A payee of a cheque informs the bank on which it is drawn that the cheque drawn in his favour has been lost and requests it to stop payment on the cheque pending an advice from the drawer. But before this "stop payment" instruction is received from the drawer, the cheque is presented through the clearing. How should the drawee bank act?

Ans.: Although only the drawer of a cheque can instruct the bank to stop payment on a cheque, the information by the payee should caution the bank about the right of the presenter of the cheque to receive payment. On receipt of information from the payee, the banker should contact the drawer before making the payment; otherwise, because of negligence, he will not get the statutory protection available to him.

35. A cheque for ₹ 1,000 drawn by your customer is presented in the clearing on 27th January, 1970 for payment when the balance in the account is only ₹ 501. The customer happens to have in the Fixed Deposit with the bank a sum of ₹ 500. The cheque is dated 25th January, 1970, which is a Sunday. How will you act in such a circumstance?

Ans.: When the balance in the customer's A/c is only ₹ 501, the banker should not pay the cheque for ₹ 1,000 on the basis of a Fixed Deposit A/c of ₹ 500 of the same customer. The Fixed Deposit A/c is a separate A/c and its amount is payable only after a specified period.

36. A drew a cheque for ₹ 20,000 in favour of B on 10th April, 1971, and gave it to him on the same day. B, who left the station immediately on a long pilgrimage tour, forgot about the cheque. When he returned and took it to the bank on 10th September, 1971, he found, to his dismay, that the bank had failed on the previous day. Discuss B's recourse against A and against the bank for recovering the amount.

Ans.: In this case, B presented the cheque after five months, which is not a reasonable time for presentation. Drawer A can be made responsible to Payee B only if the cheque is presented within a reasonable time, otherwise the drawer is discharged from his liability. The drawer is given this protection under Sections 72 and 84 of the Negotiable Instruments Act. According to Section 72, "In order to charge the drawer, a cheque must be presented at the bank upon which it is drawn before the relation between the drawer and his banker has been altered to the prejudice of the drawer".

According to Section 84(i), where cheque is not presented for payment within a reasonable time of its issue and the drawer or person on whose account it is drawn had the right, at the time when presentment ought to have been made, as between himself and the banker, to have the cheque paid and suffers actual damage through the delay, he is discharged to the extent of such damage, that is to say, to the extent to which such person is a creditor of the banker to a larger amount than he would have been if such cheque had been paid.

☞ Advances

37. Two brothers, P and Q, have a fixed deposit of ₹ 50,000 with your bank for a period of one year, bearing interest at 5½ per cent, the deposit amount being payable to either or survivor. Six months before the due date of the deposit, Q approaches the bank to get a loan against the deposit receipt for the maximum amount possible. In what manner can the bank assist him, and what are the formalities to be completed — that is: *(i)* Documents to be taken, *(ii)* Margin and *(iii)* Rate of interest?

Ans.: The loan may be granted by the bank against the fixed deposit receipt, provided that the following conditions are fulfilled:

(i) Since the deposit receipt is in the names of P and Q and since both are alive, it is necessary that both the brothers, P and Q, should discharge the receipt by signing across a revenue stamp and hand it over to the banker.

(ii) Both the brothers should sign a letter of request to the bank to sanction the loan. In the present case, however, only Q has approached the bank to get a loan. P should, therefore, authorise the bank to sanction the loan to Q. In general practice, the banks keep a margin of 5 per cent to 25 per cent in granting loans against the security of fixed deposit receipts because the latter is the safest security.

According to a directive of the Reserve Bank, the rate of interest chargeable on such loan shall be at least two per cent higher than the rate of interest payable on such deposit. The banker should, therefore, charge interest at not less than 7½ per cent per annum.

38. Mr. B has been sanctioned an advance limit of ₹ 1 lakh against the security of goods valued at ₹ 2 lakh. He proposes to insure the goods as required by the bank, but only to the extent of the bank's advance, *viz.*, ₹ 1 lakh. How will you react to the proposition and why?

Ans.: The banker should sanction the advance only on condition that the goods are fully insured. If he accepts the proposal of Mr. B about the insurance of goods only up to a value of ₹ 1 lakh, his interest may not be safeguarded in the event of the loss of goods. A fire insurance policy contains an "average clause", which lays down that if the goods or property is under-insured (*i.e.*, insured for a part of its value), the insurance company will pay the damages in the same proportion in which the total value stands to the amount insured. For example, if half of the goods worth ₹ 1 lakh is destroyed by fire, the insurance company shall be liable to pay half the value of the goods insured, *i.e.*, ₹ 50,000, and not ₹ 1 lakh.

39. Roshan Mehta has an overdraft arrangement with AB Bank Ltd., (a non-nationalised bank) on the usual terms and conditions. Roshan proposes to lodge the following shares, and desires to ascertain from the bank the drawing power there against:

10,000 fully paid shares of Tata Chemicals, standing in his own name.

5,000 fully paid shares of Associated Cement standing in his own name.

200 fully paid shares of A. B. Bank Ltd., standing in his own name.

200 fully paid shares of Ranbir Industries (P) Ltd., standing in his own name.

300 fully paid shares of Indian Dyestuff Industries, standing in his name, jointly with his wife.

100 fully paid shares of Century Spinning & Weaving Co. Ltd., in the name of Narayan Rao.

100 partly paid shares of Southern Petrochemicals, standing in his name.

(a) Would you, as a manager of A.B. Bank Ltd., accept the above shares for advances against them? If not, which shares would you consider ineligible and why?

(b) What documents will you take for the above advance?

Ans.: (a) The shares of Tata Chemicals & Associated Cement may be easily considered as eligible security. The shares of A.B. Bank Ltd., are not eligible as security because in terms of Section 20 (1)(a) of the Banking Regulation Act, 1949, a bank cannot grant a loan on the security of its own shares. The shares of Southern Petrochemicals, too, are not eligible as security because, according to a directive of the Reserve Bank, a bank shall not grant advances against the security of partly paid shares without the prior approval of Reserve Bank. The shares of Century Spinning & Weaving Co. Ltd., (which are in the name of Narayan Rao and not Roshan Mehta who is the borrower) may be accepted by the bank as security only if Narayan Rao signs the transfer form in the presence of a person known to the banker. Shri Narayan Rao should give up his right in favour of Shri Roshan Mehta by issuing a letter of renunciation, and authorising Shri Roshan Mehta to pledge the shares.

The banker should also consider the restrictions imposed by Section 19(2) of the Banking Regulation Act, 1949, on the acceptance of the shares of different companies as security. Section 19 (2) states: "No banking company shall hold shares in any company, whether as pledgee, mortgagee, or absolute owner, of an amount exceeding 30 per cent of the paid-up capital of that company or 30 per cent of its own paid-up capital and reserves, whichever is less".

(b) A charge on the securities may be created in favour of the bank in the following two ways:

(i) By giving it legal title; or

(ii) By creating an equitable title.

A legal title is secured by getting the name of the bank or its nominee registered in the books of the company as shareholder. The registration of transfer entails a certain amount of expenditure which is payable by the borrower. The bank may get the transfer form filled by Shri Roshan Mehta and get the name of bank registered as a shareholder in the books of the companies whose shares have been accepted as security.

As an alternative, the bank may take in its custody all the shares offered as security and take a bank transfer form filled (Memorandum of Deposit) by Shri Roshan Mehta. In the memorandum, the purpose of the deposit will be specified, and A.B. Bank will be authorised to sell the securities if Shri Roshan Mehta defaults in making payment or in maintaining the required margin.

40. Amrit, Balu and Chiman are three partners of Auto Traders, dealers in automobile spares. Amrit's personal friend, Dinesh, has an outstanding loan of ₹ 25,000 from your bank which the bank has recalled on the ground of inadequate security. At the request of Dinesh, Amrit has offered his firm's guarantee to the bank, which your bank accepts. The guarantee is signed by Amrit as partner of Auto Traders. Consider the position.

Ans.: The firm Auto Traders, deals in automobile spares, and giving guarantees, therefore, cannot be deemed to be the business of the firm. A partner can act as an agent of the firm for the purposes of carrying on its business. According to Section 19(1) of the Indian Partnership Act, "the act of a partner which is done to carry on, in the usual way, business of the kind carried on by the firm binds the firm", This is called the implied authority of a partner.

In the present case, Amrit has no implied authority to give a guarantee on behalf of the firm. Balu and Chiman, the other two partners, have not given any authority to Amrit to give such a guarantee for the outstanding loan of Dinesh on behalf of the firm. Therefore, the guarantee given by Amrit will not bind the firm or the remaining partners. In the circumstances, the banker should not accept the guarantee given by Amrit, unless Balu and Chiman authorise Amrit, in writing, to give such a guarantee on behalf of the firm and unless, in the partnership agreement there is a clause which provides that the firm can give guarantees for the loans taken by other parties.

41. A public limited company, engaged in the manufacture of chemicals, having suffered losses, decides to go in for diversification with a view to taking up a profitable activity involving a capital expenditure of ₹ 30 lakh. The company approaches the bank from which it has already taken a loan with a request for finance for the capital cost of diversification and also for working capital finance for the project.

The salient features of the company's balance sheet as on 31st December, 2005, are as under:

	₹
Paid-up Capital	1,00,00,000
Development Reserve	20,00,000
Long-term loan from bank	1,00,00,000
Fixed assets as cost	2,00,00,000
Borrowing from bank against stocks	75,00,000
Inventory	90,00,000
Accumulated losses	30,00,000
Arrears of depreciation not provided	35,00,000

The company is in arrears of four instalments in the term loan account. It is only if it goes in for diversification that it can become viable and pay the instalments of the present loan as well as the new loan. At the same time, it may be noted that, because of diversification, a part of the existing inventory will be slow-moving, but will not deteriorate in quality.

In brief, the company wants:

(a) A new term loan of ₹ 30 lakh;

(b) Additional cash credit for working capital;

(c) Rephasing of the existing term loan.

As a credit manager, how will you view the above proposal? Please give reasons.

Ans.: A classification of the balance sheet items of company may be made as follows:

Funds of Proprietor	₹	1,20,00,000	(Share Capital and Development Rebate)
Long-term liabilities	₹	1,00,00,000	(Term loan from bank)
Current liabilities		75,00,000	(Loan from bank)
Fixed Assets	₹	2,00,00,000	
Current Assets	₹	10,00,000	
Intangible Assets			
Accumulated losses	₹	30,00,000	
Arrears of Depreciation	₹	35,00,000	

The long-term loan of ₹ 1 crore, already taken by the company, is secured by fixed assets of ₹ 2 crore (less depreciation). These assets are sufficient to repay the existing term loan. The borrowings from the bank against stocks of ₹ 75,00,000 are secured by the current assets valued at ₹ 10,00,000. The other assets of the company are intangible assets which are fictitious assets. In the past years, the company has suffered losses; therefore, its profitability is uncertain. On the basis of these facts, the bank may refuse to give further credit to the company.

However, the proposal may be considered on the basis of future prospects of the company as a result of the proposed diversification, which may improve its profitability and, therefore, its capacity to repay the long-term loans and borrowings against stocks. If the banker feels satisfied about the viability and profitability of the proposed diversification, he may accept the request of the company for a further term loan and cash credit, and to reschedule the repayment of the existing term loan. The interest of the banker may be secured by requesting the company to issue debentures to the bank to the extent of its indebtedness, and to mortgage the assets to be acquired by it with the proposed term loan.

42. The salient features of the balance sheet of L and M Ltd., as on 31st December, 2006, are as under:

	₹
Paid-up Capital	1,00,000
Profit and Loss Debit Balance	40,000
Fixed Assets	50,000
Inventory	2,70,000
Creditors	1,30,000
Book Debts	2,00,000
Outside Borrowings from Moneylenders	1,70,000
Deposits by Directors	1,00,000
Annual Sales	3,00,000
Loss in 1973	10,000

The directors approach Sound Bank Ltd., for advance facilities to repay the outside borrowings and sundry creditors against the security of fixed assets, stocks and book debts.

As a branch manager of Sound Bank Ltd., how will you view the above proposal? Should you decide to grant the facilities, state the stipulations you would like to make? Please give reasons.

Ans.: The company's paid-up capital is ₹ 1,00,000 and there are no reserves. If the loss of ₹ 10,000 in 1973 is included, the debit balance in the profit and loss account will amount to ₹ 50,000. The loss of the company is, therefore, equivalent to half of its share capital, which clearly shows that the management is inefficient.

The current assets of the company (inventory ₹ 2,70,000 and book debts ₹ 2,00,000) are ₹ 4,70,000, and its current liabilities are (creditors ₹ 1,30,000 and borrowings ₹ 1,70,000) are ₹ 3,00,000. The current ratio is more than one and is satisfactory. The reasons which have impelled the company to request an advance of ₹ 3 lakh from the bank are not convincing because it proposes to repay the outside borrowings and sundry creditors with this advance. Even if the loan is sanctioned the current ratio will remain unaffected, because the present liabilities for the company will be substituted by its liability to the bank. The sales-debtors ratio of the company is not satisfactory. The sales are ₹ 3 lakh and the debts are ₹ 2 lakh, which means that the company has extended large credits to its customers for longer periods; and this is not desirable. But since the current ratio is satisfactory, the loan may be sanctioned despite the other unsatisfactory features. In granting the loan, however, the banker may impose certain stipulations. The company should be required to reduce the amount of debts and grant credit only on reasonable terms. It should be asked to reduce its share capital by writing off the loss of ₹ 50,000; to mortgage its fixed assets, pledge the inventory, and assign the book debts in favour of bank; and all these charges should be registered with the Registrar of Companies under Section 125 of the Companies Act, 1956. The company must create a negative lien on the deposits by the directors in order to prevent them from withdrawing their deposits. They may also be asked to give a personal guarantee for the lien.

43. Cork Manufacturers is engaged in the manufacture of rubberised cork sheets. It has three partners — Shri A. R. Basu, Shri A. R. Taneja and Shri V. M. Apte. Although they have been maintaining an account for some gears, they have not obtained any loan or other advances from the bank.

They now approach you, stating that they require the following facilities:

(a) Loan against equitable mortgage: ₹ 8 lakh

(b) Cash credit against stocks: ₹ 5 lakh

(c) Bills purchase: ₹ 1 lakh

The features of the balance sheet are:

Liabilities	₹	*Assets*	₹
Partners' Capital	4,00,000	Land and Buildings	
Sundry Creditors for Goods purchased	5,00,000	(after providing for depreciation)	2,50,000
Deposits	1,00,000	Machinery (original cost ₹ 5,00,000) at	
Income-tax Payable	60,000	depreciated value	4,00,000
		Inventory	1,00,000
	(a)	Raw Materials	1,00,000
	(b)	Stock-in-progress	10,000
	(c)	Finished Stocks	1,00,000
	(d)	Sundry Debtors	2,00,000
Total	**10,60,000**		**10,60,000**

The sales during the last three years have been ₹ 8 lakh, ₹ 10 lakh and ₹ 15 lakh. The profit margin, on an average, was 10 per cent on sales.

Out of the proposed loan against equitable mortgage, they want to purchase new machinery worth ₹ 2 lakh. They state: "Although the depreciated book value of land and buildings and machine is ₹ 6.50 lakh, the real value of land has gone up very high and it will fetch ₹ 12 lakh. Therefore, the bank gets adequate security." Please state up to what amount you will consider their request.

Does the bank get any guarantee in the event of default?

Ans.: The firm, Cork Manufacturers, has had a satisfactory sales and profit record during the last three years, and its future prospects are bright. The firm's request for a loan of ₹ 8 lakh against equitable mortgage appears to be very high. A term loan is generally a project-oriented loan. But a loan of ₹ 2 lakh for the purchase of machinery may easily be granted on the security of the machinery itself. The firm has requested a cash credit of ₹ 5 lakh. But the bank should grant cash credit up to ₹ 2 lakh only against the stocks of ₹ 2,10,000. A term loan of ₹ 2 to ₹ [illegible] lakh may also be sanctioned against the security of fixed assets to provide for the working capital needs of the firm.

The firm's current liabilities are ₹ 5,60,000 (creditors 5,00,000 + tax payable 60,000) and current assets ₹ 4,10,000 (Inventory 2,10,000 + Debtor 2,00,000). Therefore, the current ratio of the firm is less than one, which is not satisfactory. The amount of debts is also high, which shows that the firm lacks working capital.

Since it is a manufacturing concern and the value of its plant and machinery is less than ₹ 10 lakh, it will be treated as a small-scale industry and the guarantee cover provided by the Reserve Bank of India will be available to the banker in respect of the advances granted to the firm.

44. M/s. Star Electricals is a small-scale industry started by Shri Sunderajan, who is a qualified engineer. The bank has sanctioned a loan of ₹ 50,000 for it as well as a cash credit of ₹ 1,00,000 under the Technicians' Scheme.

Although the account is covered under the Guarantee Scheme for Small-scale Industries of the Reserve Bank of India, the bank has also obtained the personal guarantee of Mr. Krishnamurthy, who is the brother of Mr. Sunderajan and who is running his separate business in partnership with three other partners.

After about 6 months, Mr. Krishnamurthy calls on the bank and makes following requests:

(i) He asks you for information to find out whether the business of Star Electricals has been conducted satisfactorily;

(ii) He requests you to return his personal guarantee and offers to give you a guarantee of his partnership firm which is doing substantial business. The guarantee of his firm will be signed by him as a partner. Please discuss how you would deal with the above requests of Shri Krishnamurthy.

Ans.: The banker may give the required information to Mr. Krishnamurthy because he is a surety to the loan given to Star Electricals. When the borrower furnishes the name of a surety to the banker, his implied consent is presumed to disclose the state of affairs of his account. The banker should not accept the firm's guarantee in place of the personal guarantee of Mr. Krishnamurthy. According to Section 19(1) of the Indian Partnership Act, "the act of the partner which is done to carry on in the usual way, business of the kind carried on by firm, binds the firm". This is referred to as the implied authority of the partner. Mr. Krishnamurthy may not have an implied authority to bind the firm. The other partners of the firm have not given any authority to Mr. Krishnamurthy to give a guarantee on behalf of the firm in place of his personal guarantee. Therefore, the guarantee given by Mr. Krishnamurthy, will not bind the firm or the remaining partners.

45. Surendra & Co., is a partnership consisting of three partners. According to the copy of the partnership deed, which has been furnished to the bank while opening the account, the firm's profit or loss is to be shared among the partners as under:

1. Shri Surendra Motilal	50%
2. Shri Dharmendra Bansilal	30%
3. Smt. Vasanti Devi	20%

The firm has been granted a cash credit limit of ₹ 1,00,000. Of late, it has incurred losses, and the bank recalls the advance when the debit balance is ₹ 1 lakh.

The third partner requests you to discharge her from liability by accepting ₹ 20,000 from her on the ground that she has been sharing profit and loss in the firm to the extent of 20 per cent in terms of the partnership deed — a fact which is within the knowledge of the bank.

Please discuss whether the bank should accept the offer.

Ans.: The bank should not accept the request of Smt. Vasanti Devi, the third partner in the firm of M/s. Surendra & Co., having a share of 20 per cent in profits and losses, to discharge her from liability by accepting ₹ 20,000 for an advance of ₹ 1 lakh due to the firm. The liability of the partners is joint and several as well as unlimited. It means, therefore, that in case the bank is unable to recover the amount of loan from the assets of the firm, it can be recovered from the personal assets of all or any of the partners. It is not necessary that the partners should meet the liability of the firm in their profit-sharing ratio. In the present case, the banker has the right to recover the amount of the advance from any of the three partners or from all the partners of the firms. If the bank accepts the request of Smt. Vasanti Devi and discharges her from liability as a partner, it is just possible that he may not be able to recover the balance from the remaining partners. In that case, he would have to bear the loss. Therefore, the request of Smt. Vasanti Devi should not be accepted.

46. M/s. Zamania Electronics is a small-scale industry started by Shri Gur Dayal who is a qualified engineer. Bank has sanctioned them a loan of ₹ 50,000 and cash credit for ₹.1,00,000 under technicians scheme. The account is covered under the guarantee scheme of Reserve Bank of India for small-scale industries. But the bank has also obtained personal guarantee of Shri Anand, who is a relative of Shri Gur Dayal and who is running his separate business in partnership with three other partners.

After about six months Shri Anand comes to bank and requests you:

1. for information whether M/s. Zamania Electronics has been doing well, whether their account has been conducted satisfactorily,
2. to return his personal guarantee and offers to give you guarantee of his partnership firm which is doing substantial business. The guarantee of his firm will be signed by him as a partner.

Please discuss how would you deal with the above requests of Shri Anand.

Ans.: A guarantor is entitled, at any time during the currency of the guarantee, to call upon the banker to inform him of his liability under the terms of the guarantee. Under no circumstances should the bank supply the guarantor with any further information about the conduct of the borrower's account. Unless, of course, the customer gives his consent, for the relationship between the banker and his customer is a confidential one. (*Turner vs. National Provincial Bank Ltd.*, 1924, 1 KB 461). The banker should, therefore, accede to the request of Shri Anand.

Every partner is, in contemplation of law, the general and accredited agent of the partnership and may consequently bind all the other partners by his acts in all matters which are within the scope and objects of the partnership. Unless giving guarantee is one of the specified objectives of business of partnership in question or the proposal is expressly consented to by all the partners and Shri Anand given an authority to execute the guarantee, the banker will be ill-advised to accept the proposal in question.

47. An import-export firm of Chennai has requested you to book a forward exchange contract for Deutsche Marks 5,00,000 delivery "3 months".

Assuming Deutsche Marks are quoted in Tokyo market against US dollars as under:

Spot	US $ 1 = DM 2.3400 — 2.3450
3 months forward	.0400 — .0300 pm
6 months forward	.0360 — .0550 pm

and US dollars in the local inter-bank market as:

Spot	₹ 100 = DM	10.8500 — 10.8550
3 months forward	₹ 100 =	10.9500 — 10.9550
6 months forward	₹ 100 =	11.0500 — 11.0550

What will you quote to your customer bearing in mind that you are required to make an exchange profit of ¼% on the transaction?

☞ Solution

The transaction involves a sale of DM 5,00,000 to the customer delivering three months forward. The bank will arrange a cover for this transaction by buying DMs in Tokyo against US dollars, delivery three months forward at $ = DM 2.3000 (2.3400 minus premium of .0400 and the required US dollars from the local inter-bank market at ₹ 100 = US $ 10.9500).

Applying the chain rule the cover rate may be calculated as follows:

? DM = ₹ 100

if ₹ 100 = US \$ 10.9500

and if US \$ 1 = DM 2.300

$$X = \frac{100 \times 10.9500 \times 2.300}{100 \times 1} = 25.185$$

Cover rate	25.185
Less: Exchange Profit 1/4%	.063
	25.122

The contract will be booked at ₹ 100 = DM 25.12.

48. M/s. Ferguson & Co. Ltd., an export-import firm of Kolkata requests you to book a forward contract six months covering a 75 days sight bill on Paris under an irrevocable letter of credit for US \$ 3,25,000.

Assuming US dollars are quoted in the local inter-bank market as under:

Spot	₹ 100 = US \$ 1 10.80 — 10.81
One month discount	0.020 — 0.025
Two months discount	0.04 — 0.05
Three months discount	0.07 — 0.08
Six months discount	0.14 — 0.16
Twelve months discount	0.28 — 0.32

What rate will you quote to your customer bearing in mind the following factors:

Exchange profit half %
Interest for transit and usance period 12% p.a.
Transit period 30 days.

N.B. *(a)* Exchange profit must be included in the exchange rate.

(b) Exchange rate should be nearest to the third decimal as per FEDAI rules.

☞ Solution

The bill will be submitted for negotiation over the six months. Thereafter, the bill is to run for a total period of 105 days (usance period 75 days and transit period 30 days). The proceeds, therefore, are likely to be realised sometimes over 9th and 10th month. The rate of negotiation will, therefore, be ₹ 100 = US \$ 11.13 (*i.e.,* 10.81 plus 0.32 discount).

	US \$
Rate of negotiation	11.1300
Add: *(a)* Interest for 105 days of 12% p.a.	
$\frac{11.13 \times 105 \times 12}{365 \times 100} =$	0.03842

(*b*) Exchange profit @ 1/2% 0.5565

12.0707

Rounded off to the banker's advantage, the rate quoted to the customer will be ₹ 100 = 12.071.

49. On 28th February, your valued customer instructed you to retire a bill of exchange for US $ 5,00,000 drawn on him under an irrevocable letter of credit covering import of fibre glass from a British firm. Due to strike in the bank, the transaction could not be put through immediately but you effected the remittance on 3rd March.

Assuming that the rates of exchange were as follows, how much will the customer stand to gain or lose in terms of Indian ₹ by the delay in effecting the remittance?

28th Feb. ₹ 100 = US $ 12.00 – 12.20

2nd March London closing rate for US dollars

£ 1 = US $ 2.0500 – 2.0550

₹ – Pound Sterling Rate

₹ 100 = 6.0500 – 6.0800

No cushion or commission is to be adjusted in the rate and no forward cover was arranged for this transaction.

☞ Solution

The bank's spot selling rate for US dollars in London on 2nd March was ₹ 100 = US $ 12.00, and had the transaction been put through on that date, the customer's account would have been debited with:

$$\frac{5,00,000 \times 100}{12.00} = ₹\ 41,66,667$$

Taking into consideration the quotation for US dollars in London on 2nd March and ₹/Pounds Sterling rate for US dollars on 3rd March, may be calculated as follows:

? US $ = ₹ 100

if ₹ 100 = £ 6.0500

and if £1 = US $ 2.0500

$$X = \frac{100 \times 6.0500 \times 2.0500}{100 \times 1} = \text{US } \$\ 12.4025$$

Rounding off to the banker's advantage and conforming the quotation to the requirements of Rule 4 of FEDAI, the transaction was put through at ₹ 100 = US $ 12.40. The customer's account would thus have been debited with

$$\frac{5,00,000}{12.40} \times 100 = ₹\ 40,32,250$$

The delay in effecting the remittance has brought a benefit of ₹ 1,33,417 to the customer.

50. On 20th January, one of your branches booked a forward purchase contract for US $ 5,00,000 at ₹ 100 = US $ 12.30 for one month delivery, but failed to report the transaction to the Head Office. This came to light on 2nd February, when your head office had to cover this transaction by a sale to the Reserve Bank of India in order to square up the position.

Assuming US dollars were quoted in the London foreign exchange market on 2nd March as under:

Spot	2.0510 – 2.0550
Forward	.25 – .18, .38 – .28
	.50 – .40 C premium.

The buying rates of the Reserve Bank of India for Pound Sterling were:

Spot	6.0700
One month	6.0800
Two months	6.0850
Three months	6.0910

What would have been the loss suffered by the bank by not covering the transaction on the date of purchase. Show your working and give your answer in ₹.

☞ Solution

The purchase contract with the customer would be due on 20th February, and the bank's "Nostro Account" in New York would be credited on that date with US $ 5,00,000. In order to square up its position, therefore, the banker should sell a similar amount in London, delivery option over the first month, and the equivalent Pound Sterling to the reserve Bank of India, delivery option over the first month. The London markets buying rate for US dollars, delivery option over the first month, will thus be £ 1 = US $ 2.0550 and the Reserve Bank's buying rate for Pound Sterling, delivery option over the first month will be ₹ 100 = £ 6.0800.

The direct ₹ – US dollars cover rate may, therefore, be calculated as follows:

? US $ = ₹ 100

if ₹ 100 = £ 6.0800

and if £ 1 = US $ 2.0550

$$X = \frac{100 \times 6.0800 \times 2.0550}{100 \times 1} = 12.494$$

The banker had purchased US $ 5,00,000 from the customer at 12.30, delivery 20th February, and had to cover the transaction at ₹ 12.49. *i.e.*. at an adverse rate.

On 20th February, the entries will be recorded as follows:

Purchase of US $ 5,00,000 from the customer at ₹ 12.30 and credited his account with:

$$\frac{5,00,000 \times 100}{12.30} = 40,65,000$$

Sale of US $ 5,00,000 at ₹ 12.49 and received

$$\frac{5,00,000}{12.49} \times 100 = 40,03,203$$

The loss suffered by the bank on this transaction, therefore amounts to ₹ 61,797.

51. On 1st March, a dealer had the following position in French Francs:

	Francs
Balances with Bank France, Paris (cr)	2,00,000
Opening position oversold	50,000
Drafts issued, but not yet presented	1,00,000
TTs purchased	4,00,000
TTs sold	5,00,000
Cheques purchased but still in transit	6,00,000
Forward sales	4,50,000

What steps the dealer should take to keep his position square and maintain a credit balance of not more than 1,00,000 Francs with the Bank of France?

☞ Solution

	Purchases *Francs*	*Sales* *Francs*
Spot deals	2,00,000	50,000
TTs	4,00,000	5,00,000
Drafts, cheques, etc.	6,00,000	1,00,000
Forward sales		4,50,000
	12,00,000	11,00,000

The dealer is overbrought, spot to the extent of 5,50,000 Francs and oversold forward to the extent of 4,50,000 Francs. If he is to maintain a credit balance of 1,00,000 Francs with the Bank of France, the dealer should go in for a "Swap" deal, *i.e.*, combined deal at a margin, selling 4,50,000 Francs spot and buying a similar amount corresponding the delivery to the requirements of Forward contracts.

52. You have sold a TT to a customer for Deutsche Marks one million at 23.70. You wish to cover this transaction either through London or New York, whichever is more profitable.

Assuming that DMs are quoted in London of 4.5500 – 4.6250 and the quotation for DMs in New York is 1.1500 – 1.9510 and the local inter-bank rates for Pound Sterling and the US dollars are as follows:

Mumbai on London 5.5400 – 5.6450

Mumbai on New York 12.30 – 12.40

Please find out through which centre you will cover the transaction and what will be your profit in ₹? Ignore brokerage.

☞ Solution

If the transaction is covered through London, the dealer will purchase Pound Sterling in the local inter-bank market at the latter's selling rate, *viz.*, 5.5400 and, with the Pound Cterling so purchased, will purchase DMs in the London market at their selling rate, *viz.*, 4.5500. The direct cover rate may be calculated as follows:

? DM = ₹ 100

if ₹ 100 = £ 5.5400

and if £ 1 = DMs 4.5500

$$X = \frac{100 \times 5.5400 \times 4.5500}{100 \times 1} = \text{DMs } 25.20$$

If the transaction is covered through New York, the dealer will purchase US dollars in the local inter-bank market at the latter's selling rate, *viz.,* 12.30, and with the US dollars purchased, will purchase DMs in the New York market at their selling rate, *viz.,* 1.9500. The direct cover rate may be calculated as follows:

? DM = ₹ 100

if ₹ 100 = US $ 12.30

and if US $ 1 = DM 1.9500

$$X = \frac{100 \times 12.30 \times 1.9500}{100 \times 1} = \text{DM } 23.98$$

As the dealer gets a better rate by putting the transaction through New York, the cover will be arranged accordingly.

The dealer's profit may be calculated as follows:

(1) ₹ amount charged to the customer

$$₹ \frac{10,00,000 \times 100}{23.70} = 42,18,141$$

(2) ₹ amount chargeable against the cover

$$₹ \frac{10,00,000 \times 100}{23.98} = 42,03,410$$

Dealer's profit 1 – 2

₹ 42,18,141 – 42,03,410 = ₹ 14,731.

53. How is Domestic Bank Deposit Growth Estimated?

In most of our national and industry level analyses or comparisons we are familiar with growth rates of say 16% or 17% or 18% at which domestic deposits grow. Reserve Bank of India, which is the regulatory authority for monetary expansion in the country, announces the estimated growth of deposits year-after-year which is the barometer for many of our economic and banking operations. It is interesting to know how the average deposit growth is estimated.

Let's first take two major dimensions which compose the scenario for the deposit growth. These are:

(a) Macro Instruments

(b) Industry Level Determinants

Macro Instruments are:

(i) Economic Growth

(ii) Inflation

Of this, inflation is taken at 5% of economic growth.

Industry level determinants are:

(i) Interest rate on deposits

(ii) Rates on other instruments of savings

(iii) Branch network.

Projections or forecasts require not only quantitative accuracy but also qualitative variables and phenomena. Hence, macroeconomic variables are mainly necessary for projections. Industry level determinants are also important but they are less impacting in the long-run projections. Now the deposit growth estimates are as follows:

— **For every 1% growth in Real National Income, there is 1.5% growth registered in bank deposits.**

— **For every 1% growth in inflation, there is 1.3% growth registered in bank deposits.**

The tangible deposit growth in nominal terms is therefore less than in real terms.

Deducting from the above, we have to estimate the long-run growth of Real National Income and long-run expected inflation rate say over a period of five years. If the Real National Income growth is 5% then applying the deposit growth at 1.5 times of this, it will be 5% × 1.5 = 7.5%.

If the inflation rate is say 8% (over five years) then applying the deposit growth at 1.3 times of this it will be 8% × 1.3 = 10.4%.

Thus, the normal deposit growth would come to 7.5% + 10.4% = 17.9% or say 18%.

This satisfies the growth rate of banking industry which has been 18.1% between last Friday of March 88 and March 89.

In 1987 despite drought, the deposits grew at about 17% which has been compensated by higher inflation. The rate for 1989-90 has also been estimated at 18%.

When we project the deposits for say over next five years it would be average compound rate and this would be expressed as:

${}^{D}1995 = {}^{D}1990\ (1₹ + .18)^5$ = average should be 18% (where D is Deposits, .18 is annual deposit growth estimated at 18% and 5 is the number of years).

So far we have taken deposit growth expressed in relation to Real National Income + Inflation or Price Index.

Nominal National Income is composed of:

— Real National Income (P × Q) (where P is price of goods and services and Q is quantity of goods and services)

— Price Index (is Consumer Price Index).

The Consumer Price Index (CPI) is National Income Deflator of all goods and services in the economy and this National Income Deflator should be used for measuring the inflation rate.

Just 12 metropolitan centres in India, *viz.*, Mumbai, Kolkata, Delhi, Chennai, Hyderabad, Pune, Kanpur, Nagpur, Jaipur and Lucknow, not only account for as much as 40% of deposits but also 80% of stock/share market investments. This shows that the rate of deposit growth is much vulnerable to the changes in these commercial nerve centres.

54. Has the phenomenal branch expansion helped the deposits also grow phenomenally?

Not quite so. The over six-fold branch expansion between 1969 and 1989 in the post-nationalisation era is estimated to have contributed to just about 10% of total increase in deposits. This growth is treated as growing at glacial pace and not at phenomenal pace. But the population group-wise composition has of course undergone a change *inter se*. The rural and semi-urban categories of branches have gained at the expense of urban and metropolitan branches.

55. Is there disintermediation in banking business? If so, has it affected the deposit growth?

Yes. There is disintermediation of sorts in the banking business, because of growing capital and money market channels and instruments. But they are not outside the spectrum of banking channel. The funds have to be routed through banks only. Disintermediation affects at best the composition of deposits only. The increasing resort to capital market means, less dependence on bank advances. This is not to be attributed to disintermediation. With increasing economic activity, the existing bank clients' old limits and advances and new credit needs of new companies (small and medium) have still to be within the spectrum of bank funds. One of the steps to reduce the impact of disintermediation on banks is, through exploiting the **"Office Balance Sheet (OBS) Business"** reflected in merchant banking, investment banking, trading in securities, consultancy. This of course is the main challenge and opportunity for the banks in the nineties. This will not only prop up the profitability of the banks but also retain the "float money" channelised through the banks in between the gestation or lag periods of various types of economic activities as well as savings and investment aspects. The banks in India are more or less still in a protected environment and disintermediation is only at best causing small ripples but no major threat or impact. Otherwise, why and how the deposits are growing at an average annual rate of 18%?

During the next five years, the branch expansion is going to be at glacial pace only and hence more of consolidation will take place. With tab on manpower expansion also, by 1995 the profitability of branches is going to improve, of which a fair share of business is bound to be through improved intermediation of unconventional banking.

56. Does variation in interest rates affect the deposit growth?

Not quite so. Interest rates as an inducement for bank deposits have never been predominant in the banking industry, the worldover. Only the composition of deposits is expected to be affected by the variation in interest rates. The share of household savings which is at present 20.5% is expected to rise to 22.0% by Eighth Plan end and this is significant for bank deposit growth. For this, the banks have to indigenously improve their consumer banking efforts.

57. What does M_1, M_2, M_3, M_4 Connote?

These are money stock measures adopted by Reserve Bank of India, which is the monetary and regulatory authority of the country.

Various types of currency with the public and deposit money of public are segregated into four distinct money stock measures. They are:

M_1 : *(i)* Currency with the Public spread over:

(a) Notes in circulation.

(b) Circulation of rupee coins (including Two-rupee, Five-rupee and Ten-rupee also) and small coins.

(ii) Demand deposits with Banks.

(iii) Other deposits with RBI (excluding balances in IMF A/c,— 1, RBI EPF; Pension Fund and Cooperative Guarantee Fund, amounts under Addl. Emoluments (Compulsory Deposit) Act, 1974 and CDS (ITP) Act, 1974 and any extraordinary items).

M_2 : M_1 + Post Office Savings Bank Deposits.

M_3 : M_1 + Time Deposits with Banks.

M_4 : M_3 + Total Post Office Deposits.

All the figures are measured as at last Friday. The total money stock with the banks includes commercial and cooperative banks including Post Office deposits. Of the approximate total money stock (M_4) of ₹ 2,43,000 crore as at March 1990, the relevant portion of stock accounted by scheduled commercial banks (SCBs) is of the order of ₹ 1,73,000 crore (or 70%). About ₹ 12,000 crore (or 5% of the total money stock) is accounted by Post Office deposits and balance by cooperative banks. The M_1 stock excludes cash on hand with banks of approximately 1% of the total money stock.

M_1 is the most liquid. Though postal deposits do not come fully under RBI's reckoning of regulatory money stock, these are nevertheless included because they come under overall monetary system (*i.e.,* M_4). Further, this M_4 excludes monies held by Post Offices under National Savings Certificates (NSC).

In the US, the monetary stock measurement is much more complicated with one Federal Reserve System and 12 Federal Reserve Units (FRUs) operating and hence the measurement is even up to M_{17}.

58. What's the Operating Environment of Banks?

Banks are operating in a complex environment, composed of internal and external environment.

Internal Environment encompasses:

— Organisational structure.

— Management processes (Systems, procedures, leadership, organisational climate, etc.)

— Manpower.

External Environment is composed of Economic and Non-economic environment.

Economically, the factors influencing are:

— Macroeconomic (performance of the economy).

— Microeconomic (competition from non-bank financial institutions like companies, UTI, LIC, PFs, NSOs, Post Offices).

— Regulatory (periodical monetary measures through interest rate variations, SLR and CRR measures).

☞ Importance of Savings in the Bank's Environment

Gross domestic savings are the single largest component for banks and are accounted by:

— Household Sector (85%)

— Corporate Sector (10%)

— Public Sector/Govt. (5%)

Under Household Sector, the pattern of savings is 40% under physical assets and 60% under financial assets. The composition of financial assets, which embraces the banking/monetary system in a big way is, currency (10.1%), Bank deposits including coops, (43.5%), Non-bank deposits (5.2%), LIC and PF (24.0%), UTI (3.0%), Shares and debentures (3.8%) and claims on government excluding Govt. loans (10.4%).

Most of the cash is in rural areas, which is held partly due to liquidity reasons and partly due to lack of banking facilities.

While external environment has impact on the banks, the banks are susceptible to their own internal environment also. Thus, banks have to grapple with complex environmental impacting.

(The author would like to acknowledge valuable discussions he had with Dr. Ganti Subramanyam, Professor of Monetary Economics NIBM, Pune).

☞ The Banking Ombudsman Scheme

The concept of Ombudsman has gained importance in many countries like the United Kingdom, Australia and New Zealand as an effective means of customer grievance redressal. In India too, the RBI has introduced a similar scheme of Ombudsman from June 14th, 1995 to protect the interests of the customers as well as to redress their grievances. Indeed it is a landmark event in the history of Indian banking.

☞ Object of the Scheme

The main object of this scheme is to resolve complaints of customers relating to the provision of banking services and to facilitate the satisfaction or settlement of such complaints. This scheme is applicable to all commercial banks (excepting Regional Rural Banks) and Scheduled Cooperative Banks operating in India.

☞ Appointment of Ombudsman

The RBI may appoint one or more persons as Banking Ombudsman carry-out the functions entrusted to him under the scheme. The Banking Ombudsman must be a person of high standing in the legal, banking financial services and public administration. Generally, he will be appointed for a period of three years and he will be eligible for extension for a further period of two years subject to an overall age limit of 65 years.

☞ Powers and Duties of Banking Ombudsman

The powers and duties of the Banking Ombudsman may be classified under two heads namely:

(i) General powers and duties.

(ii) Specific powers and duties.

☞ General

The general powers of the Banking Ombudsman are:

(a) to receive complaints relating to the provision of banking services.

(b) to consider such complaints and facilitate their satisfaction, or

settlement by agreement or settlement by recommendation or settlement by an Award as the case may be in accordance, with the provisions under this scheme.

☞ Specific

To be more specific, the Banking Ombudsman can receive all complaints regarding deficiency in banking services such as:

(i) Non-payment or inordinate delay in the payment or collection of cheques, drafts, bills, etc.

(ii) Non-acceptance of small denomination notes without assigning any reason and for charging of commission in respect thereof.

(iii) Non-issue of drafts to customers as well as to outsiders.

(iv) Non-adherence to prescribed working hours by branches.

(v) Failure to honour guarantee or letter or credit commitments by banker.

(vi) Claims in respect of unauthorised or fraudulent withdrawals from deposit accounts.

(vii) Complaints relating to deposits such as delay in collection, non-credit of proceeds to parties' accounts, non-payment of deposit or non-observance of RBI's directives relating to rate of interest n deposits.

(viii) Complaints from Indian exporters regarding delays in receipt of export proceeds, handling of export bills, collection of bills, etc., provided such complaints pertain to the bank's operations in India.

(ix) Complaints of non-resident Indians relating to their remittances from abroad, deposits and other bank-related matters.

As far as the loans and advances are concerned, he can receive complaints such as:

(i) Non-observance of Reserve Bank Directives on interest rates.

(ii) Delays in sanction or non-observance of prescribed time schedule for disposal of loan applications.

(iii) Non-observance of any other directions of the RBI issued from time-to-time.

☞ Procedure for Redressal of Grievance

The procedure for redressal starts with the lodgement of a complaint. Any person who has a grievance against a bank may make a complaint in writing to the Banking Ombudsman either by himself or the authorised agent. The following conditions must have been fulfilled to file a complaint;

(i) The complainant should state clearly his name and address.

(ii) He should also state the name and address of the branch/office of the bank against which the complaint is made.

(iii) He should state clearly the facts giving rise to the complaint and it should be preferably supported by documents, if any.

(iv) He should also mention the nature and extent of the loss caused to him and the relief sought from the Banking Ombudsman.

(v) The complaint should be made to the Ombudsman only after making are presentation to the bank named in the complaint and the complaint should have been rejected or no reply should have been sent within a period of two months of the receipt of the complaint or the complainant should not have been satisfied with the reply given by the bank.

(vi) The complaint should be made within one year from the date of rejection or final reply given by the bank concerned.

(vii) The complaint should not be in respect of the same subject-matter already settled through the office of the Banking Ombudsman in any previous proceedings.

(viii) The complaint should not be in respect of the same subject-matter for which an order has already been passed by any court or tribunal or arbitrator or forum or any proceedings pending before such bodies.

(x) The complaint should not be frivolous or vexatious in nature.

☞ Power to Call for Information

On receipt of the complaint, the Banking Ombudsman may require the bank named in the complaint to provide any information or furnish certified copies of any document relating to the subject-matter of the complaint.

In case the bank fails to comply with the requisition, the Banking Ombudsman may presume that the information, if provided, would be unfavourable to the bank.

The Banking Ombudsman should maintain complete secrecy of any information or document coming into his knowledge or possession in the course of his functioning as Ombudsman and he should not disclose it to a person except with the consent of the person supplying such information. However, to render natural justice he can disclose it on reasonable grounds.

☞ Settlement by Agreement

On receipt of the complaint as well as the information from the bank concerned, the Banking Ombudsman shall try to promote a settlement of the complaint by means of an agreement between the complainant and the bank through conciliation or mediation.

For the purpose of promoting a settlement of the complaint, the banking Ombudsman may follow any procedure which he considers appropriate and at any cost, he shall not be bound by legal rule of evidence.

☞ Settlement by Recommendation

(i) If settlement by agreement is not possible within a period of one month from the date of receipt of the complaint (may be extended at the discretion of the Ombudsman) the Banking Ombudsman may make a recommendation on the basis of "what is fair in his opinion" by taking into consideration all the circumstances.

(ii) The copies of his recommendation must be sent to the complainant and the bank concerned.

(iii) If the complainant accepts all terms of the recommendation in full including the final settlement of his complaint, he must send his acceptance in writing within two weeks from the date of receipt of the recommendation.

(iv) Then, the Banking Ombudsman must forward a copy of the letter of acceptance given by the complainant to the bank. If the recommendation is also acceptable to the bank, it must immediately settle the complaint as per the recommendation and inform it to the Banking Ombudsman.

(v) If the recommendation is not acceptable to the bank, it must inform the Banking Ombudsman within a period of two weeks.

☞ Settlement by Award

(i) If the complaint is not settled by agreement or recommendation within a period of two months from the date of receipt of complaint (may be extended at the discretion of the Ombudsman), the Banking Ombudsman must inform the parties of his intention to pass an Award.

(ii) The complainant and the bank concerned can submit any further representations or evidence in support of their case within a period of 15 days from the date of notice for passing an Award.

(iii) The Banking Ombudsman must pass an Award after giving sufficient opportunities to the parties to represent their case. In passing an Award, he must be guided by the evidences, the principles of banking law and practice, directions/instructions/guidelines issued by the RBI from time-to-time and such other factors which he considers necessary in the interest of justice.

(iv) The Award must be in writing and it must state the directions to the bank for a specific performance of its obligations and the amount of compensation awarded to the complainant for the loss suffered by him. The Award must be supported by valid reasons also.

(v) The amount of compensation should not be in excess of that which is necessary to cover the loss suffered by the complainant or for an amount exceeding ₹ 10 lakh, whichever is less.

(vi) A copy of the Award must be sent to the complainant and the bank concerned.

(vii) The Award shall be binding on the bank only when the complainant sends a letter of acceptance of the Award to the bank within a period of one month from the date of the Award.

(viii) The bank concerned should comply with the Award within 15 days from the date of receipt of the acceptance letter from the complainant and it should inform it to the Banking Ombudsman.

(ix) Non-compliance of the Award by any bank must be duly reported to the RBI.

☞ Rejection of the Complaint

If, at any stage of the complaint, the Banking Ombudsman feels that the complaint is made without any sufficient cause or that it is not pursued by the complainant with reasonable diligence or there is no loss or damage or inconvenience suffered by the complainant, the complaint can be rejected immediately.

☞ Corporate Governance in Banks

According to *Wall Street Journal* "Corporate Governance, in principle, refers to *the joint responsibility imposed on the board of directors and management to protect shareholder rights and enhance shareholder value.* In practice, the board is the real representative of the shareholders and acts as a check against management. The board must ensure, among other things, that the company is accountable to shareholders, that it gives equitable treatment to all its 'owners', small as well as large, and that it acts transparently. Essentially, corporate governance determines whom the organisation is there to serve and how the purpose and priorities of the organisation is decided. Good Corporate Governance can be ensured if all participating parties play their role effectively, ethically and legally."

Corporate Governance must be based on acceptance by all involved in the management process, who should ensure the 'highest standards of integrity and ethical behaviour' in addition to ensuring transparency and consistency in all their actions. Given the degree of complexity involved, there are likely to be several conflicts of interest both between different stakeholder groups and for individual managers or directors as they try to balance these various interests. Separation of ownership and management has been found to be an effective way of improving performance, especially in large corporations. This is achieved through what is known as 'government body'.

Due to important differences in tradition between countries, there are differences regarding the role, composition and *modus operandi* of the board of directors. In UK and USA the widespread of shareholdings tend to bring the power of the individual shareholders and heighten that of intermediaries such as Pension Fund Managers.

In most other European countries, shareholding is more closely held and often minority led — perhaps by the founding family and financial institutions. In Japan, the board tends to be viewed as just one part of a multi-layered corporate decision-making process and hence is usually dominated by corporate executives. In India, in public sector banks, the majority shareholding shall continue to remain with the government. Although historically good governance in the banking sector has not been a major issue, in the era of deregulation, globalisation and competitiveness, the public sector banks have formidable task to perform. They need to take vital decisions on pricing of products, develop corporate strategies for managing various risks and designing products to meet the emerging needs of the customers. Because of competition in the marketplace customers have choices. Unless there is openness, fairness and transparency, customers will not have the confidence in the organisation.

An adequate institutional and legal framework is in place in India for effectively implementing a code of sound corporate governance in banks. The statutes have built in legal provisions that prohibit or strongly limit activities and relationships that diminish the quality of Corporate Governance in banks. As a major step towards strengthening Corporate Governance in banks, they have been advised to place before their Board of Directors the Report of the Consultative Group of Directors of Banks and FIs (Dr. Ganguli Group) set up to review the supervisory role of Board of Banks. The recommendations include the responsibility of the Board of Directors, role and responsibility of independent and non-executive Directors, fit and proper norms for nomination of Directors in private sector banks, etc.

Appendices

Appendix I

Specimen Form of Agreement for Cash Credit/Overdraft

In consideration of the United Commercial Bank, Udaipur, through their office at .... (hereinafter referred to as "the said bank" which expression shall include its assigns and successors in interest) allowing me/us. Messrs .... the undersigned (hereinafter called "the borrowers" which expression, unless repugnant to the context shall include my/our heir-executors, administrators, assigns and legal representatives), as advance by way of* .... up to the extent and limit of ₹.................. (₹ ....) (hereinafter referred to as the said limit) repayable to the said bank on demand being made by the said bank, the borrowers hereby jointly and severally agree as follows:

1. That the said bank shall not, under this agreement, be required to make advances to exceed the said limit. The borrowers shall, however, be responsible for the payment on demand of the entire amount that may, at any time, be due in this account although such amount may exceed the said limit.
2. That the interest at the rate of .... per cent per annum over Reserve Bank of India rate with a minimum of .... per cent per annum shall be calculated and charged on the last working day of each month and it will form part of the principal and will carry interest at the above-mentioned rate.
3. That the borrowers agree to pay incidental charges for every half-year or part thereof (according to labour involved) as fixed by the said bank from time-to-time during the time the account remains open.
4. That on demand being made by the said Bank, the borrowers shall pay to the said Bank the balance then outstanding and owing to the said Bank on the said account inclusive of interest at the rate mentioned above to the date of payment, together with all the charges and expenses charged or incurred by the said Bank as ascertained from the books of the said Bank, which the Borrowers agree to accept as sufficient proof of the correctness thereof without production of any voucher or paper.
5. That the amount due to the said Bank on this account shall be payable by the Borrowers at .... branch of the said Bank where the account is maintained or at the Head office of the said Bank of New Delhi and the said Bank shall be entitled to bring a suit against the Borrowers either at the place where the branch is situated or at New Delhi where the Head Office of the said Bank is located.
6. That the Borrowers will be liable for all costs of recovery incurred by the said Bank before filing a suit and also for all costs in connection with the suit till recovery of full amount.
7. That the Borrowers shall not be entitled to any interest for any sum which may be of any time stand to their credit in this account.
8. That the said Bank will always be at liberty to stop making fresh advance at any time without previous notice, which notice is hereby expressly waived and without assigning any reason even though the said limit has not been fully availed of.

*State here "credit" or "overdraft" as the case may be.

9. That the Borrowers agree that their liability to the said Bank for their dues on the said account shall be joint and several, with the authority and right to the said Bank to compromise and/or give indulgence to any of them reserving its rights and remedies against all or any of them.

10. That the Borrowers hereby agree to hold themselves liable as aforesaid on all confirmation letters signed by any one of them.

11. That the Borrowers do further agree and hereby give to the said Bank during the currency and for the payment of its dues, a general lien and right of set-off and charge on all movable property of every description coming into the possession of the said Bank on account of the Borrowers or any one of them, or for the time being held by the said Bank on behalf of the borrowers or any one of them, whether alone or jointly with others in India or elsewhere including, without prejudice to this generality, any money, bullion, deposits, deposit receipts for moneys, promissory notes, bill of exchange, hundis, stocks, goods and merchandise, bills of lading including railway receipts, Government bills with inspection notes and other bills in course of collection, articles in safe custody and other documents of title to goods, and any other negotiable or transferable instruments or securities, instruments and documents of title and mercantile documents of every description including hire-purchase agreement or contracts other than those affecting immovable property and requiring registration under the Acts or laws relating to registration and other documents evidencing the title of the Borrowers as creditors or members of any corporation, association, company or syndicate in India or elsewhere.

12. And it is hereby agreed that in the event of there being a surplus available after payment of all such principal and interest moneys and all charges and expenses as aforesaid of the net proceeds of such sale of security as aforesaid, it shall be lawful for the said bank to apply the said surplus as far as the same shall extend in or towards payment or liquidation of any other moneys due or to be due from the Borrowers or any one or more of them whether solely or jointly with any other person or persons, firms or company to the said bank by way of Loans, Discounted Bills, Letters of Credit, Guarantee charges or of any other demand, legal or equitable, which the said Bank may have against the borrowers or any one or more of them and whether the Borrowers or any one or more of them shall become or be adjudicated bankrupt or insolvent or be in liquidation or otherwise, and interest thereon from the date on which any and all advances in respect thereof shall have been made at respective rates at which the same shall have been so advanced.

13. That the Borrowers hereby agree that any notice in writing requiring to be served hereunder shall be sufficiently served if addressed to any one of them at their address registered in the said Bank or in the event of no such address being registered at their or of any one of their last known place of residence or business and left at such address or if forwarded to any one of them by post at the address or place aforesaid. And the Borrowers do hereby further agree that any demand hereunder may eventually be made by parole notice to any of them by any officer of the said Bank or by notice in writing under the hand of any such officer either served personally on the Borrowers or any one of them or left for or sent by post to any one of them at their usual or last known place of business.

14. In witness thereof I/we, the Borrowers, hereunto set my/our hand this .... day of ....one thousand nine hundred and eighty ....

Signed by the Borrower or Borrowers

Place of Execution ....

Address ....

Appendix II

Pledge of Goods to Secure Cash Credit

.....................Bank Ltd.,

....

No............................

Amount ₹...............

Name(s) ....

THE .... BANK LIMITED (hereinafter called "the Bank") having at the request of .... [hereinafter called "the Borrower(s)"] opened or agreed to open in the Books of the Bank at .... a Cash Credit Account to the extent of ₹. . . . with the Borrower(s) to remain in force until closed by the Bank and to be secured by goods to be pledged with the bank. It is hereby agreed between the Bank and the Borrower(s), the Borrower(s) agreeing jointly and severally as follows:

1. That the goods described in general terms in the Schedule hereto which have been already delivered to and the goods which shall be hereafter delivered to the Bank under this Agreement whether for the purpose of forming additional security for any sum already drawn or as security for any sum or sums to be drawn against the said Cash Credit Account, or by way of substitution for and in lieu of any goods which may from time-to-time have been delivered or may be delivered to the bank under this Agreement or otherwise howsoever (hereinafter called "the Securities"), are hereby pledged to the Bank or are to be deemed to have been so pledged as security to the Bank for the payment by the Borrowers of the balance due to the Bank at any time or ultimately on the closing of the said Cash Credit Account and for the payment of all debts and liabilities mentioned in the 11th clause hereof. The expression "the balance due to the Bank" in this and the subsequent clauses of this agreement shall be taken to include the principal money from time-to-time due to the said Cash Credit Account and also all interest thereon calculated from day-to-day at the rate hereinafter mentioned in the amount of all charges and expenses which the bank may have paid or incurred in any way in connection with the Securities or the sale or disposal thereof.
2. That the Borrower(s) shall not during the continuance of this Agreement pledge or otherwise charge or encumber any of the goods for the time being the subject or intended to be the subject of this security nor do or permit any act whereby the security herein before expressed to be given to the Bank shall be in anyway prejudicially affected.
3. That the Borrower(s) shall with the previous consent of the Bank be at liberty from time-to-time to withdraw from the bank any of the goods for the time being pledged to the Bank and forming part of the securities the subject of this Agreement, provided the advance value of the said goods is paid into the said account or goods of a similar nature to those mentioned in the schedule hereto, or any of the same, and of at least equal value, are substituted for the goods so withdrawn. Provided always that with the previous consent of the Bank the Borrower(s) shall be at liberty to withdraw from the Bank any of the goods for the time being pledged to the Bank without paying into the said Account such advance value as aforesaid substituting any goods as aforesaid provided the necessary margin required by the 6th clause hereof is fully maintained.
4. That all securities already and hereinafter delivered as aforesaid shall be insured against fire risk by the Borrower(s) with some Insurance Company or Companies approved by the Bank in the name of the Bank for the full market value of such securities and that all policies for and receipts for premia and on such Insurance shall be delivered to the Bank. Should Borrower(s) fail to so insure or fail

to deliver the policies or receipts for premia as aforesaid the Bank shall be at liberty to effect such insurance at the expense of the Borrower(s).

5. That all sums received under any such Insurance as aforesaid shall be applied in or towards the liquidation of the balance due to the Bank for the time being and in the event of there being a surplus, the same shall be applied as provided by the 11th clause hereof.

6. That the Borrower(s) shall make and furnish to the Bank such statements and returns of the cost and market value of the securities and a full description thereof and produce such evidence in support thereof as the Bank may from time-to-time require and shall maintain in favour of the Bank a margin of .... per cent between the market value from time-to-time of the securities and the balance due to the Bank for the time being. Such margin shall be calculated on the open market value of the securities as fixed by the Bank from time-to-time and shall be maintained by the Borrower(s) either by delivery of further security to be approved by the Bank or by cash payment by the Borrower(s) immediately on the market value for the time being of the securities becoming less than the aggregate of the balance due to the Bank plus the amount of the margin as calculated above.

7. The interest at the rate of .... per cent per annum shall be calculated and charged on the daily balance in the Bank's favour due upon the said Cash Credit Account until the same is fully liquidated and shall be paid by the Borrower(s) as and when demanded by the Bank.

8. That on demand by the Borrower(s) shall pay to the Bank Balance then due to the Bank on the said Cash Credit Account together with all further interest at the rate above-mentioned and the amount of all further charges and expenses (if any) to the date of payment provided that nothing herein in the clause contained shall be deemed to prevent the Bank from demanding payment of the interest for the time being due at the above-mentioned rate without at the same time demanding payment of the balance due to the Bank exclusive of such interest.

9. That if the Borrower(s) shall fail to maintain such margin as aforesaid or if the Borrower(s) fail or neglect to repay to the Bank on demand the balance then due to the Bank or in the event of the Borrower(s) becoming or being adjudicated bankrupt or insolvent or executing any Deed of Arrangement, Composition or Inspectorship or in the event of any distress or execution being levied or enforced upon or against any of the property of Borrower(s) whether the said property shall not be the subject of this security or [whether the Borrower(s) are or are not a Joint Stock Company] in the event of any person, Firm or Company taking any steps towards applying for or obtaining an order for the appointment of a Receiver of the Borrower(s) property or any part thereof or [in the event of the Borrower(s) being a Joint Stock Company] if any person, Firm or Company shall apply for or obtain an order for the winding up of the Borrower(s) or if any such order is made or any step be taken by any person, Firm or Company in or towards passing any resolution to wind up the Borrower(s), or if any such resolution be passed whichever may first happen, it shall be lawful for the Bank forthwith or at any time thereafter and without any notice to the Borrower(s), without prejudice to the Bank's right of suit against the Borrower(s), either by public auction or private contract absolutely to sell or otherwise dispose of all or any of the securities either together or in lots or separately and to apply the net proceeds of such sale in or towards the liquidation of the balance then due to the Bank.

10. That if the net sum realised by such sale be insufficient to cover the balance then due to the Bank, the Bank shall be at liberty to apply any other money or moneys in the hands of the Bank standing to the credit for or belonging to the Borrower(s) or any one or more of them in or towards payment of the balance for the time being due to the Bank; and in the event of there not being any such money or moneys as aforesaid in the hands of the Bank or in the event of such money or moneys being still insufficient for the discharge in full of such balance the Borrower(s) promise and agree forthwith on production to them of an account to be prepared and signed as in the 12th clause hereinafter

provided to pay any further balance which may appear to be due by the Borrower(s) thereon, PROVIDED ALWAYS that nothing herein contained shall be deemed to negative, qualify, or otherwise prejudicially affect the right of the Bank (which it is hereby expressly agreed the Bank shall have) to recover from the Borrower(s) the balance for the time being remaining due from the Borrower(s) to the Bank upon the said Cash Credit Account notwithstanding that all or any of the said securities may not have been released.

11. That in the event of there being a surplus available of the net proceeds of such sale after payment in full of the balance due to the Bank it shall be lawful for the Bank to retain and apply the said surplus together with any other money or moneys belonging to the Borrower(s) or any one or more of them for the time being in the hands of the Bank in or under whatever account as far as the same shall extend against in or towards payment or liquidation of any and all other moneys which shall be or may become due from the Borrower(s) or any one or more of them whether solely or jointly with any other person or persons, Firm or Company to the Bank by way of Loans, Discounted Bills, Letters of Credit, Guarantees, Charges or of any other debt or liability including Bills, Notes, Credits and other obligations current though not then due or payable or other demands legal or equitable which the Bank may have against the Borrower(s) or any one or more of them or which the law of set-off or mutual credit would in any case admit and whether Borrower(s) or any one or more of them shall become or be adjudicated Bankrupt or Insolvent or be in liquidation or otherwise and interest thereon from the date on which any and all advance or advances in respect thereof shall have been made at the rate or respective rates at which the same shall have been so advanced.

12. The Borrower(s) agree to accept as conclusive proof of the correctness of any sum claimed to be from them to the Bank under this Agreement a statement of account made out from the books of the Bank and signed by the Accountant or other duly authorised officer of the Bank without the production of any other voucher, document or paper.

13. That this Agreement is to operate as security for the balance from time-to-time due to the Bank and also for the ultimate balance to become due on the said Cash Credit Account and the said accounts not to be considered to be closed for the purpose of this security is not to be considered exhausted by reason of the said Cash Credit Account being brought to credit at any time or from time-to-time or its being drawn upon to the full extent of the said sum of ₹. .... if afterwards reopened by a payment to credit.

14. Provided always that this Agreement is not to prejudice the rights or remedies of the Bank against the Borrower(s) irrespective and independent of this Agreement in respect of any other advances made or to be made by the Bank to the Borrower(s).

15. In case the Borrower(s) shall be a firm or members of a firm no change whatsoever in the constitution of such firm or during the continuance of this Agreement shall impair or discharge the liability of the Borrower(s) or any or more of them thereunder.

IN WITNESS whereof the Borrower(s) have hereunto set his (their) hands this .... day of .... in the year One Thousand Nine Hundred and ....

SCHEDULE OF SECURITIES referred to in the foregoing Instrument.

Appendix III

Letter of Lien

.... 19....

To

The Manager,

.... Bank Limited,

....

Sir,

In consideration of your Bank having made an advance of ₹. .... or making advance to me/us (not exceeding ₹.................. in all), I/we hereby deposit and pledge with the Bank, goods, described in the Schedule hereto, of the value of ₹.................thus providing a margin of .... per cent therein in security for payment on demand of the said advances with interest thereon at .... per cent per annum or at such other rate as may be, from time-to-time, agreed upon with* .... rests together with Fire Insurance Premium and all Warehouse and other charges paid or incurred by the Bank in respect of the said goods.

I/we will be at liberty to remove goods from time-to-time on sufficient cash payments to the Bank, but so long as any money remains due to the Bank in respect of the said advances or any interest thereon or any Insurance Premium or charges on the said goods I/we hereby engage to maintain the above margin intact, i.e., the balance due to the Bank at any time will not have a larger proportion to the value of the goods in deposit with and pledged to the Bank than .... to 100.

In case the amount of the said advances with all interest and charges shall not be paid to the Bank on demand or in case I/we at any time fail to maintain the margin of security above stipulated between the sum due by me/us and market value of the security for twenty-four hours after being required in writing to do so, it shall be lawful for the Bank forthwith or at any time thereafter absolutely to sell and dispose of all or any said goods and to apply the net proceeds of such sale in satisfaction so far as the same will extend towards the liquidations of the amount due for principal and interest in respect of the said advances, together will all costs, charges and expenses incurred by the Bank and I/we agree to accept the Bank's account of such sale, signed by the manager, accountant or other duly authorised officer of the Bank as sufficient proof of the correctness of the amount realised by, and the charges and expenses in connection with such sale.

If the net sum realised by such sale should be insufficient to cover the full amount due in respect of the said advances with interest and charges as shown in the said account of the Bank, I/we agree to pay to the Bank forthwith on delivery of the said account any balance due by me/us on the footing thereof.

It is understood that the Bank's lien on the goods pledged under the agreement shall also extend to any other sum or sums of money for which I/we (or any or either of us) either separately or jointly with any other person or persons may be or become indebted or liable to the Bank on any other account.

On payment of all sums, including interest and charges payable hereunder, any part of the goods so deposited and pledged which may not have been sold shall be returned to me/us and any surplus of net proceeds of any such sale of the said goods shall be paid to me/us or as I/we shall direct.

....

Signature(s)

(On the reverse the following Schedule is printed)

SCHEDULE

Marks	*Date of Invoice*	*Bales or Packages*	*Description of Goods*

***Insert "half-yearly", or "monthly", as the case may be.**

Appendix IV

Trust Receipt

..........................2003

To

.... Bank, Limited.

....

In consideration of the Bank handing to me Shipping Documents for goods, as per particulars at foot, hypothecated to the Bank as collateral security for the due payment of the undermentioned draft drawn upon their office in .... by .... and accepted by their said Office, I/we hereby agree to land, store and hold the said goods as Trustee for and on behalf of the Bank, and the proceeds of the sales shall be received by me/us as Trustee for the Bank, and paid to the Bank as and when received, I/we at the same time specially advising the Bank of the account on which such payments made, and I/we undertake to provide the Bank, by this or other means, with sufficient funds to meet the said draft together with all charges and commission, not less than .... day before maturity.

I/we also undertake to keep the goods fully insured against fire, and to handover to the Bank all amounts received from the insurers, the policies of Insurance being, in the meantime, held by me/us as Trustee for and on behalf of the Bank.

Without prejudice to anything herein contained I/we will, on the Bank's written demand to be made at any time forthwith, either return to the Bank the said Shipping Documents, Fire Insurance Policies, or any of them, or deliver up to the Bank the said goods or any part thereof

PARTICULARS OF DRAFTS AND GOODS

Amount of Bills	*Due*	*Description of Goods*	*Marks and Nos.*	*Vessel*
₹ P.				

....

Signature

Appendix V

Mortgage Deed

This Indenture made the .... day of .... 19....... between .... of .... (hereinafter called the Mortgagor which expression shall be deemed to include his heirs, executors, administrators and assigns of the one part and the .... Bank, Limited a joint-stock Company incorporated under the Indian Companies Act and having its registered office at .... (hereinafter called the Bank which expression shall include its assigns) of the other part.

Whereas, the Mortgagor is the owner and the proprietor of the lands, heriditaments and premises described in the Schedule hereto and intended to be hereby mortgaged free from encumbrances and whereas the bank has agreed to the mortgagor the sum of ₹ .... only on having the repayment thereof with interest secured in the manner hereinafter appearing.

Now this Indenture Witnesseth as follows:

I. In pursuance of the said agreement and in consideration of the sum of ₹ .... paid on or before the execution of these presents by the Bank to the Mortgagor (the receipt whereof the Mortgagor hereby acknowledges) the Mortgagor hereby covenants with the Bank as follows:

1. That the Mortgagor will pay to the bank the said principal sum of .... by equal half-yearly instalments of ₹ .... on the first day of .... and the first day of .... each year commencing from .... and any interest due thereon so that the whole debt is paid in full on or before the ....
2. That the Mortgagor shall in addition pay interest on the principal sum secured by these presents at the rate of .... per cent per annum.
3. That the Mortgagor shall pay to the Bank interest at the rate stipulated in Clause 1 (2) with half-yearly rests on the .... and .... up to the date of realisation in case the Bank has to institute a suit for recovery of the principal and interest or any portion thereof that may be due to the Bank. And if at any time six months' interest payable under these presents shall remain owing and unpaid then the interest so in arrears shall be converted into principal and until paid-off shall carry interest at the aforesaid rate of .... per cent per annum with half-yearly rests.
4. That the Mortgagor shall and will during the subsistence of this security at his own costs and charges and expenses keep and maintain the said premises hereby mortgaged in good repair and tenantable condition.
5. It is hereby agreed and declared that in case any of the instalments of principal or interest payable under these presents be not satisfied on the dates hereinbefore appointed for the payments of such instalments of principal or interest then the whole amount of principal remaining unpaid together with interest due shall at once become payable to the Bank, and the Bank may forthwith enforce any of the remedies to which a holder of a simple mortgage is entitled under the Transfer of Property Act.
6. That the Mortgagor will within one month from the date of these presents insure and keep insured the building and such other part of the mortgaged premises as are of an unsuitable nature or any part or parts thereof from loss or damage by fire in the full value thereof in some insurance office to be approved of by the Bank in the joint names of the Mortgagor and the Bank as mortgagee (the relative policy to contain the agreed Bank clause of the Fire Insurance Association) and will duly pay all premiums and sums of money payable for that purpose and will deliver to the Bank the policy for such insurance and the receipt for every such payment

within seven days after it shall become due and in case the Mortgagor shall neglect or refuse to keep the said premises insured to the amount aforesaid or to deliver such policy and receipts as aforesaid then and in every such case it shall be lawful for the Bank to insure the same to the amount aforesaid or any less amount and all sums of money expended by the Bank in or about such insurance as aforesaid with interest for the same at the rate of ₹ .... per cent per annum (with half-yearly rests) computed from the time or respective times of advancing, the same shall be repaid by the Mortgagor to the bank on demand and in the meantime shall be a charge on the premises hereby mortgaged in addition to the principal sum and interest thereon.

7. That the Mortgagor agrees that sums of money awarded as compensation for any compulsory acquisition of any portion of the mortgaged property by any government, municipal or railway or district board authority shall be receivable by the Bank direct on behalf of the Mortgagor and that such money as well as moneys received under and by virtue of any such insurance as aforesaid shall at the option of the Bank either be forthwith applied in or towards substantially rebuilding, reinstating or repairing the said premises or in or towards the payment of the principal money, interest and costs for the time being remaining due on the security of these presents.

II. For the consideration aforesaid and in further pursuance of the said agreement the Mortgagor hereby grants and transfers by way of simple mortgage unto the Bank all the property described in the Schedule hereto together with all rights, easements and appurtenances thereto and all rights, title and interest in and to the said premises to the intent that all the said premises hereby mortgage shall remain and be charged by way of simple mortgage and free from all encumbrances as security for the payment to the Bank of the said principal money, interest and costs in accordance with the covenants hereinbefore contained.

III. That the mortgagor shall allow the Bank, its servants, agents and surveyors at all reasonable times to enter the said premises and view and examine the state and condition thereof.

IV. Provided always that the Mortgagor may at any time after giving the Bank thirty days' notice pay the Bank the whole of the principal sum and interest and costs that may due to the Bank.

In witness whereof the parties hereto have set their hands and seal on the .... day of 2003

(Schedule)

Signed in the presence of:

1. ....

2. ....

Appendix VI

Memorandum of Deposit by a Customer of the Title Deeds to Secure his own Account

Memorandum that I, the undersigned of .... hereby acknowledge that I have this day deposited with the .... Bank Ltd., (hereinafter called "the Bank", which expression shall include their successors and assigns) the documents specified in the Schedule hereto, with intent to create an equitable mortgage upon all my estate and interest in the property to which such documents relate, for the purpose of securing the payment to the Bank on demand for all moves now owing or which shall at any time hereafter be owing from me either solely, or jointly with any person or persons, to the Bank whether on balance of account or by discount, or otherwise in respect of bills of exchange, promissory notes, cheques and other negotiable instruments, or in any manner whatsoever, and including interest with half-yearly rests, commission and other banking charges, and any law costs incurred in connection with the account. And I hereby further agree whenever requested by the Bank at my own costs to execute to the Bank a valid legal mortgage of such property in such form and with such power of sale and other provisions as the Bank may require for recovering the repayment on demand of all moneys secured by this equitable mortgage. And I hereby also agree that so long as any money remain owing from me to the Bank to pay interest thereon to the Bank at the rate of .... per cent per annum. And I hereby declare that the documents now deposited are all that are in my possession or control, and that the property is not charged or encumbered in any way whatsoever.

As witness my hand this .... day of .... 2003.

The schedule above referred to

Witness (Customer's Signature)

....

Appendix VII

Bill of Lading

SHIPPED in good order and well condition by .... in and upon the good Steam Ship called the .... whereof......................... is Master for this present Voyage and lying in .... and bound for..

....

....

being marked and numbered as in the Margin and are to be delivered in the like good Order and well condition at the aforesaid Port of .... (the act of God, the King's Enemies, Fire, Machinery, Boilers and Steam and all and every other Dangers and Accidents of the Seas, Rivers and Steam Navigation, of whatever nature and kind whatsoever expected up to .... or to .... Assigns .... Freight for the said Goods .... with primage and average accustomed.

IN WITNESS whereof the Master or Persuer of the said Ship hath affirmed to .... Bills of Lading all of this Tenor and Date the one of which Bills being accomplished the others to stand void.

Dated in .... 2003.

....

For the Master

Weight and contents unknown.

Appendix VIII

Narasimham Committee Report on the Financial System, 1991 — Salient Features

The terms of reference of the Committee were as follows:

(i) To examine the existing structure of the financial system and its various components and to make recommendations for improving the efficiency and effectiveness of the system with particular reference to the economy of operations, accountability and profitability of the commercial banks and financial institutions;

(ii) To make recommendations for improving and modernising the organisational systems and procedures as well as managerial policies;

(iii) To make recommendations for infusing greater competitive vitality into the system so as to enable the banks and financial institutions to respond more effectively to the emerging credit needs of the economy.

(iv) To examine the cost, composition and adequacy of the capital structure of the various financial institutions and to make suitable recommendations in this regard;

(v) To review the relative roles of the different types of financial institutions in the financial system and to make recommendations for their balanced growth;

(vi) To review the existing supervisory arrangements relating to the various entities in the financial sector, in particular the commercial banks and the term lending institutions and to make recommendations for ensuring appropriate and effective supervision;

(vii) To review the existing legislative framework and to suggest necessary amendments for implementing the recommendations that may require legislative change;

(viii) To make recommendations on any other subject matter as the Committee may consider germane to the subject of enquiry or any related matter which may be specifically referred to the Committee by the Government of India.

The Committee submitted its Report to the Government on November 16, 1991.

The salient features of 'Narasimham Committee Report' are as under:

— Reputed banks may enhance capital through public issues

— No bar on new private sector banks

— Liberal policy towards foreign banks

— Four-tier banking structure

— Abolition of dual control

— Depoliticisation of chief executives' appointments

— Lower Statutory Liquidity Ratio (SLR) to 25 per cent

— Phasing out of concessional interest rates

— New system for provision of debts

— Transparent balance sheets

— Special tribunals for recovery of dues

— Scrapping of branch licensing

— No further nationalisation of banks

— RBI should be more liberal in allowing foreign banks to open branches.

The Committee's approach to the issue of financial sector reform is to ensure that the financial services industry operates on the basis of operational flexibility and functional autonomy with a view to enhancing efficiency, productivity and profitability. A vibrant and competitive financial system is also necessary to sustain the ongoing reform in the structural aspects of the real economy. The Committee believes that ensuring the integrity and autonomy of operations of banks and Development Financial Institutions (DFIs) is by far the more relevant issue at present than the question of their ownership.

The Indian banking and financial system has made commendable progress in extending its geographical spread and functional reach. The spread of the banking system has been a major factor in promoting financial intermediation in the economy and in the growth of financial savings. The credit reach also has been extensive and the banking system now caters to several million borrowers especially in agriculture and small industry. The DFIs have established themselves as a major institutional support for investment in the private sector. The last decade has witnessed considerable diversification of the money and capital markets. New financial services and instruments have appeared on the scene.

Despite this commendable progress, serious problems have emerged reflected in a decline in productivity and efficiency, and erosion of the profitability of the banking sector. The major factors responsible for these are: *(a)* directed investments; and *(b)* directed credit programmes. In both these cases, rates of interest that were available to banks were less than the market related rates or what they could have secured from alternate deployment of funds. There has been a deterioration in the quality of the loan portfolio which in turn has come in the way of banks' income generation and enhancement of their capital funds. Inadequacy of capital has been accompanied by inadequacy of loan loss provisions. The accounting and disclosure practices also do not always reflect the true state of affairs of banks and financial institutions. The erosion of profitability of banks has also emanated from the side of expenditure as a result of fast and massive expansion of branches, many of which are unremunerative especially in the rural areas, a considerable degree of over-manning especially in the urban and metropolitan centres and inadequate progress in up dating work technology. Both management weaknesses and trade union pressures have contributed to this. There have also been weaknesses in the internal organisational structure of the banks, lack of sufficient delegation of authority and inadequate internal controls and deterioration in what is termed 'housekeeping' such as balancing of books and reconciliation of inter-branch and inter-bank entries. The DFIs also suffer from a degree of portfolio contamination. This is more pronounced in the case of the State Financial Corporations (SFCs). Being smaller institutions the internal organisational problems of the DFIs have been less acute than those of the banks. However, both banks and the DFIs have suffered from excessive administrative and political interference in individual credit decision-making and internal management. The deterioration in the financial health of the system has reached a point where unless remedial measures are taken soon, it could further erode the real value of and return on the savings entrusted to them and even have an adverse impact on depositor and investor confidence. This diagnosis of the problems indicates the lines of solution which the committee proposes with a view as much to improving the health of the system as for making it an integral part of the ongoing process of economic reforms.

The Committee is of the view that the Statutory Liquidity Ratio (SLR) instrument should be deployed in conformity with the original intention of regarding it as a prudential requirement and not viewed as a major instrument for financing the public sector. In line with Government's decision to reduce the fiscal deficit to a level consistent with macro-economic stability, the Committee recommends that the SLR be brought down in a phased manner to 25 per cent over a period of about five years, starting with some reduction in the current year itself.

As regards the cash reserves ratio, the Reserve Bank should have the flexibility to operate this instrument to serve its monetary policy objectives. The Committee believes that given the Government's resolve to reduce the fiscal deficit, the occasion for the use of cash reserve ratio to control the secondary expansion of credit should also be less. The Committee accordingly proposes that the Reserve Bank consider progressively reducing the cash reserve ratio from its present high level. With the deregulation of interest rates there would be more scope for the use of open market operations by the Reserve Bank with correspondingly less emphasis on variations in the cash reserve ratio.

The Committee proposes that the interest rate paid to banks on their SLR investments and on Cash Reserve Ratio (CRR) in respect of impounded deposits above the basic minimum should be progressively market related while that on cash reserve requirement above the basic minimum should be broadly related to bank's average cost of deposits. However, during the present regime of administered interest rates, this rate may be fixed at the level of banks' one year deposit rate.

With respect to directed credit programmes, the Committee is of the view that they have played a useful purpose in extending the reach of the banking system to cover sectors which were neglected hitherto. Despite considerable unproductive lending, there is evidence that the contribution of bank credit to growth of agriculture and small industry has made an impact. This calls for some re-examination of the present relevance of directed credit programmes at least in respect of those who are able to stand on their own feet and to whom the directed credit programmes with the element of interest concessionality that has accompanied it has become a source of economic rent. The Committee recognises that in the last two decades banking and credit policies have been deployed with a redistributive objective. However, the Committee believes that the pursuit of such objectives should use the instrumentality of the fiscal rather than the credit system. Accordingly, the Committee proposes that the directed credit programmes should be phased out. This process of phasing out would also recognise the need that for sometime it would be necessary for a measure of special credit support through direction. The Committee therefore, proposes that the priority sector be redefined to comprise the small and marginal farmers, the tiny sector of industry, small business and transport operators, village and cottage industries, rural artisans, and other weaker sections. The credit target for this redefined priority sector should hence forth be fixed at 10 per cent of aggregate credit which would be broadly in line with the credit flows to these sectors at present. The Committee also proposes that a review may be undertaken at the end of three years to see if directed credit programmes need to be continued. As regards medium and large farmers, and the larger among small industries, including transport operators, etc., who would not now constitute part of the redefined priority sector, the Committee proposes that to further encourage banks to provide credit to these erstwhile constituents of the priority sector, the Reserve Bank and other refinancing agencies institute a preferential refinance scheme in terms of which incremental credit to these sectors would be eligible for preferential refinance subject to normal eligibility criteria.

The Committee is of the view that the present structure of administered interest rates is highly complex and rigid. This is so in spite of recent moves towards deregulation. The Committee proposes that interest rates be further deregulated so as to reflect emerging market conditions. At the same time, the Committee believes that a reasonable degree of macroeconomic balance through a reduction in the fiscal deficit is necessary for successful deregulation of interest rates. Premature moves to market determined interest rates could, as experience abroad has shown, pose the danger of excessive bank lending at high nominal rates to borrowers of dubious creditworthiness, eventually creating acute problems for both the banks as well as the borrowers. Accordingly, the Committee recommends that for the present, interest rates on bank deposits may continue to be regulated the ceilings on such rates being raised as the SLR is reduced progressively as suggested by the Committee earlier. Similarly, the interest rate on Government borrowing may also be gradually brought in line with market-determined rates which would be facilitated by the reduction in SLR. Meanwhile, the Committee would recommend that concessional interest rates should be phased out. The structure of interest rates should bear a broad relationship to the Bank rate which should be used as an anchor to signal the Reserve

Bank's monetary policy stance. It would be desirable to provide for what may be called a prime rate, which would be the floor of the lending rates of banks and DFIs. The spreads between the Bank rate, the bank deposit rates, the Government borrowing rates and the prime rate may be determined by the RBI broadly in accordance with the criteria suggested by the Chakravarty Committee so as to ensure that the real rates of interest remain positive.

The inadequacy of capital in the banking system is a cause for concern. While progress towards BIS norms is desirable, the Committee recognises that this will have to be phased overtime. The Committee suggests that the banks and financial institutions should achieve a minimum 4 per cent capital adequacy ratio in relation to risk weighted assets by March 1993, of which Tier 1 capital should be not less than 2 per cent. The BIS standards of 8 per cent should be achieved over the period of the following three years, that is, by March 1996. For those banks with an international presence it would be necessary to reach these figures even earlier.

The Committee believes that in respect of those banks whose operations have been profitable and which enjoy a good reputation in the markets, they could straightaway approach the capital market for enhancement of their capital. The Committee, therefore, recommends that in respect of such banks, issue of fresh capital to the public through the capital market should be permitted. Subscribers to such issues could include mutual funds, profitable public sector undertakings and employees of the institutions besides the general public. In respect of other banks, the Government could meet the shortfall in their capital requirements by direct subscription to capital or by providing a loan which could be treated as subordinate debt.

Before arriving at the capital adequacy ratio for each bank, it is necessary that the assets of the banks be evaluated on the basis of their realisable values. The Committee proposes that the banks and financial institutions adopt uniform accounting practices particularly in regard to income recognition and provisioning against doubtful debts. There is need also for adopting sound practices in regard to valuation of investments on the lines suggested by the Ghosh Committee on Final Accounts.

In regard to income recognition the Committee recommends that in respect of banks and financial institutions which are following the accrual system of accounting, no income should be recognised in the accounts in respect of non-performing assets. An asset would be considered non-performing if interest on such assets remains past due for a period exceeding 180 days at the balance sheet date. The Committee further recommends that banks and financial institutions be given a period of three years to move towards the above norms in a phased manner beginning with the current year.

For the purpose of provisioning, the Committee recommends that, using the health code classification which is already in vogue in banks and financial institutions, the assets should be classified into four categories, namely, Standard, Sub-standard, Doubtful and Loss Assets. In regard to Sub-standard Assets, a general provision should be created equal to 10 per cent of the total outstandings under this category. In respect of Doubtful Debts, provision should be created to the extent of 100 per cent of the security shortfall. In respect of the secured portion of some Doubtful Debts, further provision should be created, ranging from 20 per cent to 50 per cent, depending on the period for which such assets remain in the doubtful category. Loss Assets should either be fully written-off or provision be created to the extent of 100 per cent. The Committee is of the view that a period of four years should be given to the banks and financial institutions to conform to these provisioning requirements. The movement towards these norms should be done in a phased manner beginning with the current year. However, it is necessary for banks and financial institutions to ensure that in respect of doubtful debts 100 per cent of the security shortfall is fully provided for in the shortest possible time.

The Committee believes that the balance sheets of banks and financial institutions should be made transparent and full disclosures made in the balance sheets as recommended by the International Accounting Standards Committee. This should be done in a phased manner commencing with the current year. The Reserve

Bank, however, may defer implementation of such parts of the standards as considers appropriate during the transitional period until the norms regarding income recognition and provisioning are fully implemented.

The Committee suggests that the criteria recommended for non-performing assets and provisioning requirements be given due recognition by the tax authorities. For this purpose, the Committee recommends that the guidelines to be issued by the Reserve Bank of India under Section 43D of the Income Tax Act should be in line with our recommendations for determination of non-performing assets. Also, the specific provisions made by the banks and institutions in line with our recommendations should be made permissible deductions under the Income Tax Act. The Committee further suggests that in regard to general provisions, instead of deductions under Section 36 (1) (viia) being restricted to 5 per cent of the total income and 2 per cent of the aggregate average advances by rural branches, it should be restricted to 0.5 per cent of the aggregate average non-agricultural advances and 2 per cent of the aggregate average advances by rural branches. This exemption should also be available to banks having operations outside India in respect of their Indian assets, in addition to the deductions available under Section 36 (1) (viii).

Banks, at present, experience considerable difficulties in recoveries of loans and enforcement of security charged to them. The delays that characterise our legal system have resulted in the blocking of a significant portion of the funds of banks and DFIs in unproductive assets, the value of which deteriorate with the passage of time. The Committee, therefore, considers that there is urgent need to workout a suitable mechanism through which the dues to the credit institutions could be realised without delay and strongly recommends that Special Tribunals on the pattern recommended by the Tiwari Committee on the subject be set up to speed up the process of recovery. The introduction of legislation for this purpose is long overdue and should be proceeded with immediately.

While the reform of accounting practices and the creation of Special Tribunals are essential, the Committee believes that an arrangement has to be worked out under which part at least of the bad and doubtful debts of the banks and financial institutions are taken off the balance sheet so that the banks could recycle the funds through this process into more productive assets. For this purpose, the Committee proposes the establishment, if necessary by special legislation, of an Assets Reconstruction Fund (ARF) which could take over from the debts at a discount, the level of discount being determined by independent auditors on the basis of clearly stipulated guidelines. The ARF should be provided with special powers for recovery somewhat broader than those contained in Section 29-32 of the State Financial Corporation's Act, 1951. The capital of the ARF should be subscribed by the public sector banks and financial institutions.

It is necessary to ensure that the bad and doubtful debts of banks and financial institutions are transferred to the ARF in a phased manner to ensure smooth and effective functioning of the ARF. To begin with, all consortium accounts where more than one bank or institution is involved should be transferred to the ARF. The number of such accounts will not be large but the amounts involved are substantial to make a difference of the balance sheets of banks. Gradually, depending on the progress achieved by the ARF, other bad and doubtful debts could be transferred overtime. Meanwhile, banks and institutions should pursue recovery through the Special Tribunals. Based on the valuation given in respect of each asset by a panel of at least two independent auditors, the ARF would issue bonds to the concerned institution carrying an interest rate equal to the Government bond rate and repayable over a period of five years. These bonds will need to be guaranteed by the Government of India and should be treated as qualifying for SLR purposes. The advantage to banks of this arrangement would be that their bad and doubtful debts would be off their books though at a price but they would have in substitution of these advances bonds up to the discounted value with a certainty of interest income which would be an obviously important aspect from the point of view of income recognition, and further by making these bond holdings eligible for SLR purposes, banks' fresh resources could become available for normal lending purposes. The Committee emphasises that this proposal should be regarded as an emergency measure and not as a continuing source of relief to the banks and DFIs.

It should be made clear to the banks and financial institutions that once their books are cleaned up through this process, they should take normal care and pay due commercial attention in loan appraisals and supervision and make adequate provisions for assets of doubtful realisable value.

Selling these assets to the Fund at a discount would obviously mean an obligation on the bank/DFI is to write-off these losses which many of them are in no position to do now, given their weak capital position. The Committee proposes that to enable the banks to finance the write-off represented by the extent of the discount, the Government of India would, where necessary, provide, as mentioned earlier, a subordinated loan counting for capital. As far as the Government of India itself is concerned, the Committee believes that the rupee counterpart of any external assistance that would be available for financial sector reform could be used to provide this type of capital to the banks and DFIs.

The ARF would be expected to deal with those assets which are in the process of recovery. In respect of sick units which are under nursing or rehabilitation programmes, it is necessary to workout a similar arrangement to ensure smooth decision-making and implementation in respect of such nursing programmes. The Committee recommends that in respect of all such consortium accounts which are under a nursing programme or in respect of which rehabilitation programmes are in the process of being worked out, the concerned lead financial institution and/or lead commercial bank should takeover the term loan and working capital dues respectively from other participating institutions and banks. Such acquisitions should be at a discount based on the realisable value of the assets assessed by a panel of at least two independent auditors as in the case of transfer of assets to ARF.

In regard to the structure of the banking system, the Committee is of the view that the system should evolve towards a broad pattern consisting of:

(a) 3 or 4 large banks (including the State Bank of India) which could become international in character;

(b) 8 to 10 national banks with a network of branches throughout the country engaged in 'universal' banking;

(c) Local banks whose operations would be generally confined to a specific region; and

(d) Rural banks (including RRBs) whose operations would be confined to the rural areas and whose business would be predominantly engaged in financing of agriculture and allied activities.

The Committee is of the view that the move towards this revised system should be market driven and based on profitability considerations and brought about through a process of mergers and acquisitions.

The Committee is of the view that the structure of rural credit will have to combine the local character of the RRBs and the resource, skills and organisational/managerial abilities of the commercial banks. With this end in view the Committee recommends that each public sector bank should set up one or more rural banking subsidiaries, depending on the size and administrative convenience of each sponsor bank, to takeover all its rural branches and, where appropriate, swap its rural branches with those of other banks. Such rural banking subsidiaries should be treated on par with RRBs in regard to CRR/SLR requirements and refinance facilities from NABARD and sponsor banks. The 10 per cent target for directed credit which we have recommended as a transitional measure should be calculated on the basis of the combined totals of the present banks and their subsidiaries. The Committee proposes that while RRB should be allowed to engage in all types of banking business, their focus should continue to be to lend to the target groups to maintain at a minimum the present level of their lending to these groups. With a view to improving the viability of their operations, the Committee proposes that the interest rate structure of the RRBs should be in line with those of the commercial banks. The Committee would leave the option open to the RRBs and their sponsor banks as to whether the RRBs should retain their identity so that their focus on lending to the target groups is not diffused or where both the RRBs and the sponsor banks wish to do so they could be merged with the sponsor banks and the sponsor banks in such cases should take them over as 100 per cent subsidiaries by buying out the shares from other agencies at a token price, and eventually merge them with the rural banking subsidiaries which we have proposed. For those RRBs that retain their identity and whose viability would need to be improved, we propose that instead of investing in Government bonds as part of their SLR requirements, they could place the amount stipulated under SLR requirements, they could place the amounts stipulated under SLR as deposits with NABARD or some special federal type of agency that might be set up for this purpose. This would also be consistent with the statutory requirements in this regard and NABARD or this agency could pay interest on such balances by investing or deploying these funds to the best advantage on their behalf and thus help to augment the income of the RRBs.

The Committee proposes that Government should indicate that there would be no further nationalisation of banks. Such an assurance will remove the existing disincentive for the more dynamic among the private banks to grow. The Committee also recommends that there should not be any difference in treatment between the public sector and the private sector banks. The Committee would propose that there be no bar to new banks in the private sector being set up provided they conform to the start-up capital and other requirements as may be prescribed by the Reserve Bank and the maintenance of prudential norms with regard to accounting, provisioning and other aspects of operations. This in conjunction with the relevant statutory requirements governing their operations would provide adequate safeguards against misuse of banks' resources to the detriment of the depositors' interests.

The Committee recommends that branch licensing be abolished and the matter of opening branches or closing of branches (other than rural branches for the present) be left to the commercial judgement of the individual banks.

The Committee also believes that, consistent with other aspects of Government policy dealing with foreign investment, the policy with regard to allowing foreign banks to open offices in India either as branches or, where the Reserve Bank considers it appropriate, as subsidiaries, should be more liberal, subject to the maintenance of minimum assigned capital as may be prescribed by the Reserve Bank and the statutory requirement of reciprocity. Joint ventures between foreign banks and Indian banks could also be permitted particularly in regard to merchant and investment banking, leasing and other newer forms of financial services.

Foreign banks when permitted to operate in India should be subjected to the same requirements as are applicable to domestic banks. If, in view of certain constraints such as absence of branch network, the foreign banks are unable to fulfil certain requirements such as directed credit (of 10 per cent of aggregate credit) the Reserve Bank should workout alternative methods with a view to ensuring a level playing field.

The Committee is of the view that the foreign operations of Indian banks need to be rationalised. In line with the structure of the banking system visualised above, there would seem to be scope for one or more of the large banks, in addition to the SBI, to have operations abroad in major international financial centres and in regions with strong Indian ethnic presence. Pending the evolution of a few Indian banks with an international character, the Committee recommends as an interim measure that those Indian banks with the largest presence abroad and strong financial position could jointly set up one or more subsidiaries to takeover their existing branches abroad. The SBI operations abroad can continue and indeed be strengthened in the course of time. The Government may also consider the larger banks increasing their presence abroad by taking over existing small banks incorporated abroad as a means of expanding their international operations.

The Committee believes that the internal organisation of banks is best left to the judgement of the management of individual banks, depending upon the size of the bank, its branch spread and range of functions. However, for the medium and large national banks the Committee proposes a three-tier structure in terms of head office, a zonal office and branches. In the case of very large banks a four-tier organisation, as is the case with the State Bank, with head office, zonal office, regional office and branch may be appropriate. Local banks may not need an intermediate tier between the branch and the central office.

The Committee endorses the view of the Rangarajan Committee on Computerisation that there is urgent need for a greater use of computerised systems than at present. Computerisation has to be recognised as an indispensable tool for improvement in customer service, the institution and operation of better control systems, greater efficiency in information technology and the betterment of the work environment for employees. These are essential requirements for banks to function effectively and profitably in the increasingly complex and competitive environment which is fast developing in the financial services segment of the economy.

Consistent with the Committee's view that the integrity and internal autonomy of banks and DFIs is far more important than the question of ownership, the Committee makes the following recommendations regarding recruitment of officers and staff and appointments of chief executives and constitution of the boards of the institutions.

The Committee recommends that instead of having a common recruitment system for officers, individual banks should be free to make their own recruitment. Thus, there is no need for setting up a Banking Service Commission for centralised recruitment of officers not for their recruitment, as at present, through Banking Service Recruitment Boards (BSRBs). This will provide scope for the banks to scout for talent and impart new skills to their personnel. The Committee, however, predicts this recommendation on the assumption that the banks will set up objective, fair and impartial recruitment procedures and, wherever appropriate, they could voluntarily come together to have a joint recruitment system. As regards clerical grades, the present system of recruitment through BSRBS may continue but Committee would urge that the appointment of the Chairman of these Boards should be totally left to the coordinating banks.

The Committee believes that there has to be a recognition on the part of managements and trade unions that the system cannot hope to be competitive internally and be in step with the wide-ranging innovations taking place abroad without a radical change in work technology and culture and greater flexibility in personnel policies. The Committee has been reassured to know that organised labour is as much convinced of the importance of enhancing the viability and profitability of the banking industry and providing efficient customer service. It is equally incumbent on management of banks to adapt forward looking personnel policies which would help to create a satisfying work environment.

The Committee recommends that the various guidelines and directives issued by the Government or the Reserve Bank in regard to internal administration of the banks should be reviewed to examine their continuing relevance in the context of the need to ensure the independence and autonomy of banks. Such guidelines which relate to matters of internal administration such as creation and categorisation of posts, promotion procedures and similar matters should be rescinded.

The Committee believes that the Indian banking system, at present, is over-regulated and over-administered. Supervision should be based on evolving prudential norms and regulations which should be adhered to rather than excessive control over administrative and other aspects of bank organisation and functioning. The Committee would also like to place greater emphasis on internal audit and internal inspection systems of banks. The inspection by the supervisory authorities should be based essentially on the internal audit and inspection reports. Their main concern should be to ensure that audit and inspection machinery (which will cover the credit appraisal system and its observance) is adequate and conforms to well laid down norms.

The Committee is firmly of the opinion that the duality of control over the banking system between the Reserve Bank and the Banking Division of the Ministry of Finance should end and that the Reserve Bank should be the primary agency for the regulation of the banking system. The supervisory function over the banks and other financial institutions, the Committee believes, should be hived off to a separate authority to operate as a quasi-autonomous body under the aegis of the Reserve Bank but which would be separate from other central banking functions of the Reserve Bank. The Committee recognises that as long as the Government has proprietary interest in banks and financial institutions, it would be appropriate for the Ministry of Finance to deal with other Government departments and Parliament and discharge its other statutory obligations but not to engage in direct regulatory functions.

Central to the issue of flexibility of operations and autonomy of internal functioning is the question of depoliticising the appointment of the chief executive (CMD) of the banks and the boards of the banks and ensuring security of tenure for the CMD. The Committee believes that professionalism and integrity should be the prime considerations in determining such appointments and while the formal appointments have to be made by Government, they should be based on a convention of accepting the recommendations of a group of eminent persons who could be invited by the Governor of the Reserve Bank to make recommendations for such appointments. As regards the boards of public sector banks and institutions, as long as Government owns the banks, it would be necessary to have a Government director to take care of 'proprietorial' concerns but Committee believes that there is no need for the Reserve Bank to have a representative on the boards.

As regards development financial institutions, the main issue with regard to their operation are to ensure operational flexibility, a measure of completion and adequate internal autonomy in matters of loan sanctioning and internal administration. The Committee proposes that the system recommended for commercial banks in the matter of appointment of chief executives and boards should also apply to DFIs. The present system of consortium lending has been perceived as operating like a cartel. The Committee believes that consortium lending should be dispensed with and, in its place, a system of syndication or participation in lending, at the instance not only, as now, of the lenders but also of the borrowers, should be introduced. The Committee also believes that commercial banks should be encouraged to provide term finance to industry, while at the same time, the DFIs should increasingly engage in providing core working capital. This will help to enhance healthy competition between banks and DFIs. The Committee proposes that the present system of cross holding of equity and cross representation on the boards of the DFIs should be done away with. The Committee welcomes the removal of the tax concession enjoyed by IDBI as an important step in ensuring equality of treatment between various DFIs. As a further measure of enhancing competition and ensuring a level playing field, the Committee proposes that the IDBI should retain only its apex and refinancing role and that its direct lending function be transferred to a separate institution which could be incorporated as a company. The infected portion of the DFI's portfolio should be handed over to the ARF on the same terms and conditions as would apply to commercial banks.

In the case of state level institutions, it is necessary to distance them from the State Governments and ensure that they function on business principles based on prudential norms and have a management set up suited for this purpose. The Committee proposes that an action plan on these lines be worked out and implemented over the next three years.

As regards the role of DFIs in corporate takeovers, the Committee believes that DFIs should end support to existing managements who have a record of conducting the affairs of the company in a manner beneficial to all concerned, including the shareholders, unless in their opinion the prospective new management is likely to promote the interests of the company better. In doing so Committee would expect the institution to exercise their individual professional judgement.

The DFIs should seek to obtain their resources from the market on competitive terms and their privileged access to concessional finance through the SLR and other arrangements should gradually be phased out over a period of three years.

The last decade had witnessed a considerable growth in capital market operations with the emergence of new instruments and new institutions. The capital market, however, is tightly controlled by the Government whose prior approval is invariably required for a new issue in the market, the terms of the issue and its pricing. The process of setting up Securities and Exchange Board of India (SEBI) for overseeing the operations of the market is still not complete with the legislation for this purpose yet to be enacted. The Committee believes the present restrictive environment is neither in tune with the new economic reforms nor conducive to the growth of the capital market itself.

The Committee strongly favours substantial and speedy liberalisation of the capital market. Prior approval of any agency — either Government or SEBI — for any issuer in the market should be dispensed with. The issue should be free to decide on the nature of the instrument, its terms and its pricing. The Committee would recommend, in this context, that the SEBI formulate a set of prudential guidelines designed to protect the interests of investors, to replace the extant restrictive guidelines issued by the Controller of Capital Issues (CCI). In view of the above, the office of the CCI will cease to have relevance. In the Committee's view, SEBI should not become a controlling authority substituting the CCI, but should function more as a market regulator to see that the market is operated on the basis of well laid down principles and conventions. The capital market should be gradually opened up to foreign portfolio investment and simultaneously efforts should be initiated to improve the depth of the market by facilitating issue of new types of equities and innovative debt instruments. Towards facilitating securitisation of debt, which could increase the flow of instruments, appropriate amendments will need to be carried out in the Stamp Act.

In the last decade several new institutions have appeared on the financial scene. Merchant banks, mutual funds, leasing companies, venture capital companies and factoring companies have now joined hire-purchase companies in expanding the range of financial services available. However, the regulatory framework for these new set of institutions has still to be developed.

The Committee recommends that the supervision of these institutions which form an integral part of the financial system should come within the purview of the new agency to be set up for this purpose under the aegis of the RBI. The control of these institutions should be principally confined to off-site supervision with the on-site supervision being resorted to cases which call for active intervention. The SEBI which is charged with the responsibility of ensuring orderly functioning of the market should have jurisdiction over these institutions to the extent their activities impinge on market operations. In regard to mutual funds there is a good case for enacting new legislation on the lines obtaining in several countries with a view to providing an appropriate legal framework for their constitution and functioning. The present guidelines with regard to venture capital companies are unduly restrictive, and affecting the growth of this business and need to be reviewed and amended.

As in the case of banks and financial institutions there is need to lay down prudential norms and guidelines governing the functioning of these institutions. These prudential guidelines should relate, among other things, to capital adequacy, debt equity ratio, income recognition, provisioning against doubtful debts, adherence to sound accounting and financial policies, disclosure requirements and valuations of assets. The eligibility criteria for entry, growth and exit should also be clearly stipulated so that the growth of these institutions takes place on proper lines.

The Committee would like to emphasise that a proper sequencing of reforms is essential. Deregulation of interest rates can only follow success in controlling fiscal deficits. Asset reconstruction, institution of capital adequacy and establishment of prudential norms with a good supervisory machinery have to be proceeded within a phased manner over the next three to five years but, Committee believes, it is important that the process must begin in the current year itself.

The above set of proposals would necessitate certain amendments in existing laws which the Government should undertake expeditiously.

The Committee's approach thus seeks to consolidate the gains made in the Indian financial sector while improving the quality of the portfolio, providing greater operational flexibility and most importantly greater autonomy in the internal operations of the banks and financial institutions so as to nurture a healthy, competitive and vibrant financial sector. This will, above all else, require depoliticisation of appointments, implying at the same time a self-denial by Government and the perception that it has distanced itself from the internal decision-making of the banks and the financial institutions. The proposed deregulation of the financial sector and the measures aimed at improving its health and competitive vitality would, in the Committee's view, be consistent with the steps being taken to open up the Indian economy, enable the Indian financial sector to forge closer links with the global financial markets, and enhance India's ability to take competitive advantage of the increasing international opportunities for Indian trade, industry and finance.

Appendix IX

Securities and Exchange Board of India (SEBI) — Functions and Control

The Securities and Exchange Board of India (SEBI) has been authorised by the Government of India to oversee and regulate all Merchant Banking activity in the country. Suitable guidelines have been issued by the Government in this regard. The broad intention of the guidelines is that "those engaged in Merchant Banking should have necessary expertise, good financial standing, maintain a high standard or professional integrity and fairness in their transactions and take greater responsibility in disclosures about issues and post-allotments and refunds". SEBI will issue necessarily formats and also lay down procedures from time-to-time to ensure that Merchant Bankers actually function under the prescribed regulations. Existing Merchant Bankers are permitted to continue their activities but are required to obtain an authorisation from SEBI within a period of six months.

The gist of the government guidelines are as follows:

(i) Authorisation

Any person or body proposing to engage in the business of Merchant Banking would need authorisation by SEBI in their prescribed format. This will also apply to those presently engaged in Merchant Banking activity, including those acting as Managers, Consultants or Advisers to new capital issues.

(ii) Authorised Activities

- Issue management which will *inter alia* consist of preparation of prospectus and other information relating to the issue, determining financing structure, tie-up of financiers and final allotment and/or refund of the subscription;
- Corporate adviser services relating to the issues;
- Underwriting:
- Portfolio management services; and
- Managers, consultants or advisers to the issue.

(iii) Authorisation Criteria

SEBI will prescribe a code of conduct for merchant bankers. SEBI's authorisation criteria would take into account mainly the following:

- Professional competence;
- Personnel, their adequacy and quality and other infrastructure;
- Capital adequacy; and
- Past track record, experience, general reputation and fairness in all their transactions.

(iv) Terms of Authorisation

(i) Authorisation must be obtained from SEBI by all Merchant Bankers (including existing ones) within three months; the period may be extended by a maximum of three more months, at SEBI's discretion;

(ii) All merchant bankers to have a minimum net worth of ₹ 1 crore;

(iii) Authorisation will be for an initial period of three years;

(iv) SEBI may collect from the Merchant Bankers an initial authorisation fee, an annual fee and a renewal fee;

(v) All issues should be managed by at least one authorised Merchant Banker, functioning as the sole manager or the lead manager. Ordinarily, not more than two Merchant Bankers should be associated as lead managers, advisers and consultants to a public issue. In issues of over ₹ 100 crore, this number could go up to a maximum of four;

(vi) The specific responsibilities of each lead manager must be submitted to SEBI prior to the issue;

(vii) While directors/promoters authorising the issue of prospectus are fully responsible for the contents of the prospectus, Merchant Bankers shall exercise due diligence independently verifying the contents of the prospectus and reasonableness of the views expressed therein. Merchant Bankers to the issue shall certify to this effect to SEBI.

(viii) To ensure a direct stake of Merchant Bankers in the issue managed by them, lead managers would be required to accept a minimum of 5 per cent underwriting obligation in the issue subject to a ceiling. Details in this regard will be prescribed by SEBI.

(ix) The involvement of Merchant Bankers in an issue should continue at least till the completion of essential follow-up steps, which must include listing of the instrument and despatch of certificates/refunds. Even if any of these activities are handled by other intermediaries, Merchant Bankers shall be responsible for ensuring that these agencies fulfil their functions and must enable themselves to discharge this responsibility through suitable agreements with the issuer company.

(x) The Merchant Banker shall make available to SEBI such information, documents, returns and reports as may be prescribed and called for.

(xi) SEBI shall prepare and prescribe a code of conduct for Merchant Bankers which they should adhere to.

(xii) SEBI may suspend/cancel the authorisation of Merchant Bankers for suitable durations in case of violation of the guidelines. All such cases will be brought to the notice of the Controller of Capital Issues (CCI).

(xiii) The company, its functionaries or others are not exempted from any responsibility placed on them by any existing law, regulation or conditions imposed with any sanction by issue of the above guidelines.

Guidelines for Minimum Subscription

(i) The Union Government has decided that all rights and public issues of securities offered by companies from April 9, 1990 should not allot the shares and debentures unless a minimum 90 per cent subscription against the entire issue has been received.

(ii) If the subscription to this extent is not received, the entire amount collected with the applications should be refunded to the applicants at the end of 90 days from the closure of the issue and interest at 15 per cent p.a. should be paid if refunds are delayed by more than 10 days after the period.

(iii) Companies will be required to submit certificates to the regional stock exchange (with copy to SEBI and CCI), signed by the Merchant Banker and the Chief Executive/Company Secretary of the company to the effect that the issue has been subscribed up to 90 per cent of the total for getting approval of the stock exchange for allotment.

(iv) If there is a devolvement on the underwriters, subscription from them will have to be obtained within 90 days from the closure of the issue to achieve the minimum 90 per cent level.

(v) Promoters should make their subscriptions in advance before the public issue opens and also give a certificate to this effect to the concerned regional stock exchange.

(vi) Subscriptions received against rights/public issues will be kept in specific bank accounts and companies would not have access to such funds unless they have received the approval from the concerned regional stock exchange for allotment of the shares.

(vii) Where listing has been proposed on more than one stock exchange, no allotment or utilisation will be allowed till listing approval is available from each of the exchanges concerned.

SEBI Guidelines for Sick Units

According to the existing procedure, all sick companies which have not yet come under the purview of the Bank for Industrial and Financial Reconstruction (BIFR) have to submit their applications to SEBI seeking exemption from the provisions of Clause 40-B of the listing agreement of stock exchanges in respect of take-over offers. In order to enable SEBI to consider such cases in objective manner, protect the interest of public shareholders and help the lead financial institutions to prepare a complete application for exemption for consideration of SEBI, a set of guidelines has been recently prescribed by SEBI. These guidelines are basically intended to make the takeover or management changes in non-BIFR sick companies more equitable.

Control of Mutual Funds

It has also been reported that the Union Finance Ministry has agreed, in principle, that SEBI should be the apex body to deal with mutual funds. The mutual funds are presently regulated by either the Reserve Bank of India or the Finance Ministry. The reported move is a step in the right direction as it will end the dichotomy in rules governing mutual funds and all the players in the field will be deriving the same advantages and are subjected to the uniform rules and regulations.

Conclusion

Aggrieved parties with complaints regarding allotments/refunds relating to subscriptions in public issues may complain to SEBI who would take up the matter suitably to ensure speedy remedial action. It will, thus, be seen that SEBI exercises a wholesome and comprehensive control over the activities of merchant bankers and in several other important areas.

Appendix X

Report of the Goiporia Committee

The improvement in the customer service in banks has long been a concern of the Reserve Bank of India and the Govt. of India. In the past bank nationalisation era after 1969, this matter assumed greater importance and was examined by both the Banking Commission (Chairman: Shri R.G. Saraiya), 1972 and the working group on customer-service in banks (Chairman: Shri R.K. Talwar) 1975. To oversee the implementation of the recommendations made by the latter, a standing committee on customer-service in banks was also set up with representatives from the Government, the Reserve Bank of India, Banks and Indian Banks Association. Special drive was made to record and monitor the disposal of complaints made by the customers against services rendered by their banks.

In September, 1990, a new committee was set up by Reserve Bank of India under the Chairmanship of Shri M.N. Goiporia, Chairman, State Bank of India: *(a)* To look into the causes of below par customer-service in banks, *(b)* To identify structural and operational rigidities in the banking system, *(c)* Find ways and means to upgrade technology in banks, *(d)* Address deficiencies in bank service and suggest ways to improve work culture among bank employees. The Committee submitted its report on 6th Dec., 1991.

In its report, the Committee has observed that disservice to customer should be treated as delinquency and that an indifferent and casual approach to work should not go unnoticed. The report has identified quite a number of areas of customer-service which call for improvement. The major recommendations of Goiporia Committee are as follows:

(i) Extension of banking hours for all transactions except cash.

(ii) Change in the commencement of working hours for bank staff to facilitate timely opening of the bank counters.

(iii) Immediate credit of outstation cheques up to ₹ 5,000 as against ₹ 2,500 of present.

(iv) Enhancement of interest rate on savings account.

(v) Introduction of tax benefits against bank deposits.

(vi) Full use of discretionary powers vested in the bank staff at all levels.

(vii) Expeditious despatch of documents lodged for collection and regular follow-up with the foreign bank to facilitate timely realisation of export proceeds in the case of export finance.

(viii) Extension of teller's duties.

(ix) Modernisation of banks.

(x) Opening of specialised branches for different customer groups.

(xi) A new instrument in the form of Bank Orders, and

(xii) Introduction of restricted holidays in banks.

Appendix XI

Reserve Bank Guidelines for Follow-up of Bank Credit

(Based on the Reports of the Tandon and Chore Study Groups)

Apart from performing the traditional function of credit control, the Reserve Bank of India has also played during recent years a significant promotional role in bringing about desirable reforms in the system of bank tending. The ultimate objective of these efforts on the part of the central banking authority has been to establish a system of credit planning in the country. After the nationalisation of the major banks there has been a new sense of direction in bank lending and consequently advances to the priority sectors have stepped up. The task of credit planning becomes a difficult one because of the problem of potential imbalance in the demand for and supply of funds, which is accentuated by the manner in which the banks is determined not by how much a banker can lend at a particular point of time but by the borrower's decision to borrow at that time. Secondly, cash credit advances are repayable on demand only in name. They are rolled over and never fall below a certain level during the course of a year. To such an extent the business concerns employ bank funds on a quasi-permanent basis. Realising these drawbacks in the cash credit system, need was felt to review the existing system and effect changes in such a way that the borrower is induced to plan his credit needs and the banker is also enabled to plan his lending on the basis of his borrower's credit requirements. The Reserve Bank of India appointed in July 1974 a Study Group under the chairmanship of Shri P.L. Tandon to frame guidelines for the follow-up of bank credit —

(i) To suggest guidelines for commercial banks for the follow-up and supervision of credit from the point of view of ensuring proper end-use of funds and keeping a watch on the safety of advances and to suggest the type of operational data and other information that may be obtained by banks periodically from such borrowers and by the Reserve Bank of India from the lending banks;

(ii) to make recommendations for obtaining from borrowers periodical forecasts of —

(a) business/production plans, and

(b) credit needs.

(iii) to make suggestions for prescribing inventory for different industries both in private and public sectors and indicate the broad criteria for deviating from these norms;

(iv) to suggest criteria regarding satisfactory capital structure and sound financial basis in relation to borrowings;

(v) to make recommendations regarding the sources of financing the minimum working capital requirements, and

(vi) to make recommendations as to whether the existing pattern of financing working requirements by way of cash credit/overdraft system, etc., requires to be modified. If so to suggest suitable modifications.

The Study Group submitted its final report in August 1975. Accepting the major recommendations made by the Study Group, the Reserve Bank advised the banks as follows:

I. Norms for Inventory and Receivables

The Study Group suggested norms for 15 major industries. These norms represent the maximum levels for holding inventory and receivables in each industry. The norms suggested by the Study Group and accepted by the Reserve Banks are given on pages 535-36.

The Reserve Bank advised the banks as follows in regard to the implementation of these norms:

(i) These norms are to be applied in respect of both the existing and new borrowers with immediate effect. All fresh proposals (including those from the existing borrowers seeking enhanced credit facilities) may be regulated by these norms.

(ii) In the case of all existing borrowers (whether or not they seek enhancement in credit limits), at their levels of inventories and receivable are excessive on the basis of the suggested norms, the matter should be discussed with them and a programme for a phased reduction therein worked out.

(iii) In case the excess levels of inventories and receivables continue without justification, the banks should not abruptly stop operations in the borrower's account as it may upset his normal functioning. Instead, the bank may consider after a reasonable period of say, about two months, whether it should charge a higher rate of interest on the portion of the borrowings which is considered to be excessive. The banks exercise control with due flexibility and understanding of the circumstances which may warrant deviation from the norms for temporary periods. The banks may call for additional information for this purpose.

(iv) Initially, all industrial borrowers including small-scale industries with aggregate limits from the banking system in excess of ₹ 10 lakh should be covered. Borrowers with aggregate limits of ₹ 10 lakh or less should be covered progressively as early as possible. In the case of industries for which norms have not been specified by the Group, the purpose and spirit of the norms should be kept in view extending credit facilities.

SUGGESTED NORMS

Industry	*Requirements in terms of months*			
	Raw material	*Stock-in-process*	*Finished goods*	*Receivables and Bill purchased*
1. Cotton and Synthetic Textiles	2 to 3	$\frac{1}{2}$ to $\frac{3}{4}$	$2\frac{1}{4}$	
2. Man-made fibres	$1\frac{1}{2}$	$\frac{1}{2}$	$1\frac{3}{4}$	
3. Jute textiles	$2\frac{1}{2}$	$\frac{1}{4}$	1 to $1\frac{1}{2}$	$1\frac{1}{2}$
4. Rubber products	2			$1\frac{3}{4}$
5. Fertilisers	$\frac{3}{4}$ to 3	Neg.	1 to $1\frac{1}{2}$	$1\frac{1}{4}$
6. Pharmaceuticals	$2\frac{3}{4}$	$\frac{1}{2}$	2	$1\frac{1}{4}$
7. Dyes and Dyestuffs	$2\frac{3}{4}$	1	$\frac{3}{4}$	$1\frac{1}{4}$
8. Basic industrial chemicals	$2\frac{1}{4}$	$\frac{1}{4}$	1	$1\frac{3}{4}$
9. Vegetable hydrogenated oils	1	Neg.	$\frac{3}{4}$	
10. Paper	1	Neg.	$\frac{3}{4}$	
(a) Bamboo and wood	2 to 6			
(b) Chemicals	$2\frac{1}{4}$			

11. Cement	$\frac{3}{4}$ to $2\frac{1}{4}$	$\frac{1}{4}$		
12. Engineering automobiles and ancillaries	$2\frac{1}{4}$	$\frac{3}{4}$		$2\frac{1}{2}$
13. Engineering consumer durables	2	$\frac{3}{4}$		$2\frac{1}{2}$
14. Engineering ancillaries and component supplies	2	$\frac{3}{4}$		$2\frac{1}{2}$
15. Engineering machinery and other capital equipment suppliers	$2\frac{3}{4}$	$1\frac{1}{4}$		$3\frac{1}{2}$

Tandon Committee did not lay down any norms for electrical industry separately and those applicable to the engineering consumer durable industry were applied to it. But during 1986, following the recommendations of a subcommittee set up by the Committee of Direction, the Reserve Bank recommended the following norms for inventory and receivables for the electricals industry.

ELECTRICAL INDUSTRY CLASSIFICATION AND NORMS

Industry Classification	*Raw Materials including stocks and other items used in the process of manufacture (monthly consumption) Imp. Ind.*	*Stock-in-process (monthly cost of production)*	*Finished Goods (monthly cost of sales)*	*Receivable and bills purchased/ discounted (monthly sales)*
1. Bulbs, Fluorescent tubes and dry cell batteries	4	$2\frac{1}{2}$	$\frac{1}{2}$	3 (combined norms)
2. Storage batteries	4	$2\frac{1}{2}$		3 (combined norms)
3. Fans	3	1	$\frac{1}{2}$	4
			2	$2\frac{1}{2}$ (combined norms)
4. Transformers	$2\frac{1}{2}$	(combined norms)	$1\frac{1}{2}$	(combined norms)
5. Switchgears	$2\frac{1}{2}$	(combined norms)	$\frac{1}{2}$	$1\frac{1}{2}$ 2

Imp.= Imported Ind. = Indigenous

II. Approach to Lending

As regards the approach to lending the Study Group was of the opinion that the borrower should be expected to hold only a reasonable level of current assets in relation to his production requirements. The working capital gap has been defined as total current assets minus current liabilities other than bank borrowings. The working capital gap of the borrower could be bridged partly from his own funds and long-term borrowings and partly through bank borrowings. The Study Group has suggested that the banks should supplement the borrower's resources to enable the latter carry on acceptable level of current assets. In the light of the above approach, the group suggested three methods for working out the maximum permissible bank borrowings to meet the working capital gap. It is to be noted that each successive method is intended to increase progressively the involvement of lont-term funds comprising borrower's owned funds and term borrowings to support the current assets. The three methods are as follows:

(i) The banks can workout the working capital gap, i.e., total current assets, less current liabilities other than bank borrowings and finance a maximum of 75 per cent of the gap. The balance is to be met by owned funds and term loans.

(ii) The borrower to provide for a minimum of 25 per cent of total current assets out of long-term funds (*i.e.,* owned funds plus borrowings). A certain level of credit for purchase and other current liabilities will be available to the borrower and the bank will provide the balance. Total current liabiiities inclusive of bank borrowings will not exceed 75 per cent current assets.

(iii) The same as (ii) above but excluding core current assets from total current assets. The core current assets should be financed out of long-term funds.

The first method would give a minimum current ratio of 1:1 while the second and third methods give 1:3:1 and still higher ratio. Each successive method is intended to increase progressively the involvement of long-term funds comprising long-term borrowings and owned funds of the borrower to support the current assets. The level of bank borrowings would be reduced in stages and the current ratio would be strengthened.

Banks were asked to apply the first methods initially and to bring all the borrowers covered under the recommendations before September 1976.

III. Style of Credit

The Study Group also suggested the need to change the style of extending bank credit. As recommended by the Group, instead of making available the entire credit limit as cash credit, banks may bifurcate the accommodation into: *(a)* loan, comprising the minimum level of borrowing which the borrower expects to use throughout the year, and *(b)* a demand cash credit to meet the fluctuating requirements.

Both of these limits are to be reviewed annually within the overall availability. Bill limits may also be allowed.

The Group has also suggested that priority should be given to bill finance against seller's receivables over cash credit against book debts. The proposed system of lending may be extended to all borrowers with credit limits in excess of ₹ 10 lakh from the banking system and then extended progressively to others.

IV. Differential Lending Rates

With a view to bring about discipline in the use of bank credit, the study group also suggested a slightly higher rate of interest for demand cash credit component than for the loan component. Accepting this recommendation, the Reserve Bank of India asked banks to charge differential lending rates to implement the Study Group's credit norms. The Banks directed the banks that the interest rate on demand cash credit should be higher by 1 per cent than the rate on the loan component and that on term loan representing excess borrowing to be amortised, higher by half a per cent than on cash credit. Banks were required to start charging differential rates from the time borrower's accounts were bifurcated as described above or at the time of considering additional credit limits in case of borrowers seeking enhancement.

The above directive was based on the assumption that the lower rate of interest on the loan component will give borrower an incentive for more effective planning of his credit requirements.

V. Information System

The Study Group also devised an information system to be introduced by the banks. The Group has recommended for submission by the borrower an operating statement and funds flow statement for the whole year (i.e., ensuing year) as also a projected balance sheet as at the end of the next year. Any material change, say, around 10 per cent of the projected fugures, would require the banker's prior approval. Actual drawings within the sanctioned limits will be determined by the customer's quarterly funds flow statement, and the permissible level of drawings will be the levels as at the end of the previous quarter plus or minus the deficit or surplus shown in the funds flow statement.

VI. Follow-up and Supervision

The Reserve Bank of India attached considerable importance to streamline the system and procedures of banks in regard to follow-up and supervision of credit and ensuring proper end-use of funds lent. The Bank commanded the suggestions of the Study Group in this regard and drew the attention of the banks to the following:

(a) *Financial Follow-up:* A bank should follow-up and supervise the use of credit whether the assumptions on which the lending decision was taken continue to hold good, both in regard to the borrower's operation and the environment. It should verify from the periodical data whether there is any divergence calling for remedial action. Variations of around 10 per cent may be treated as normal and if they exceed this limit, the banker and customer should discuss the reasons. The periodical data obtained from the borrowers should also be examined to ensure that: (1) the relationship of the borrower's current assets to current liabilities, and (2) the respective shares of bank credit and the borrower's long-term funds in meeting the working capital gap, do not charge adversely.

(b) *Terms and Conditions:* The Reserve Bank agreed with the observation of the Study Group that since projected funds flow statement would form the basis for determining the overall credit limit, a banker would be justified in laying down a condition that any material change, say, around 10 per cent of the figure projected earlier, would require his prior approval. The banks are, therefore, advised to stipulate certain minimum terms and conditions relating to matter having impact on the funds flow of the borrower.

(c) *Stock-statements:* The Study Group recommended that the basis of valuation in the stock statements and financial statements should be uniform and that opening and closing stocks should be reconciled from month-to-month. The Reserve Bank suggested that the banks may review the proforma of their existing stock statements with a view, *inter alia,* to simplifying their structure and weeding out unnecessary details. This has been suggested keeping in view the financial reporting system to be introduced by banks.

VII. Norms for Capital Structure

Though it is not practicable to lay down absolute standards for debt-equity ratio, which may be looked at as funded debt-equity relationship or total outside liabilities–equity relationship, the banker should endeavour to persuade the borrower to strengthen his equity base as early as possible to reach the median for the industry.

VIII. Norms for Trade

While financing trade, banks should keep in view, *inter alia*, the extent of owned funds of the borrower in relation to the credit limits granted, the annual turnover, possible diversion to other units or uses and how much is being ploughed back from profits into business. Bank should avoid financing for goods which have already been obtained on credit.

IX. Need for Gearing the Organisational Set-up

The Reserve Bank of India reminded the banks that the system recommended by the Study Group will have far-reaching implications and that it cannot succeed without the total commitment of the top management in each bank to the new approach. It also emphasised the importance or gearing the bank's organisational set-up through delegation and decentralisation and also by providing adequate staff if necessary, and updating the credit appraisal skills of the bank's personnel on an extensive scale at different levels through suitable training programmes. Speedy appraisal, decision-making and flexible handling of the new system are the prerequisites for its success.

X. Need for Inter-bank Cooperation

The Reserve Bank of India also stressed the need for inter-bank cooperation and coordination in case of borrowers having multiple banking arrangements. In such cases, the appraisal and operational techniques, as suggested in the Report, cannot work successfully to a significant extent, unless there is proper liaison, sharing of information and coordination among the different financing banks. For this purpose, banks should enter into proper consortium /participation arrangements with one of the banks action as a lead bank. Where it is not possible, appropriate procedure for coordination amongst the financing banks through joint appraisal, joint review and follow-up may be evolved.

Other Recommendations of the Study Group

1. Stock Valuation and Verification: The stock statement need to be improved. The basis of valuation in the stock statement and balance sheet should be uniform. The stocks should be reconciled in the stock statements, showing the opening and closing stocks, quantity-wise and value-wise stock inspection poses problems particularly in large industries. The Group has, therefore suggested that where a banker feels, for special reasons, that a detailed stock verification is called for a regular stock audit may have to be arranged with the assistance of outside consultants.

2. Managerial Competence: Managerial competence is an important factor in the efficiency of operations, reflected in profitability and working capital and financial management. Banker should keep in mind that appraisal of management may be essential particularly because of new emphasis on viability and development rather than on security alone.

3. Inter-firm Comparison: To facilitate inter-firm and industry wise comparisons for assessing efficiency, companies in the same industry could be grouped under three or four categories, say according to size and the group-wise financial ratio compiled by the Reserve Bank for furnishing to banks.

Besides examining financial and operating ratios, certain productivity ratios may also be examined to determine labour efficiency, capital efficiency and fixed assets efficiency.

4. Borrower Classification: For the purpose of better control, there should be a system of borrower classification in each bank. This will facilitate easy identification of the borrowers whose affairs required to be watched with more than ordinary care and will also provide a rational base for the purpose of fixing rates of interest for the respective borrowers.

RESERVE BANK GUIDELINES ON CASH CREDIT SYSTEM

(Based on the Report of Chore Working Group)

In 1979 the Reserve Bank of India set up a Working Group to review the case credit system under the chairmanship of Shri K.B. Chore, Chief Officer in the Department of Banking Operations and Development. The Working Group made a number of recommendations which were accepted by the Reserve Bank with certain modifications. The salient features of the guidelines issued by the Reserve Bank in December 1980 are as follows:

1. *Annual Review of Accounts:* Realising the fact that the system of cash credit cannot for the present be totally replaced by any other system of lending, the Reserve Bank felt the necessity of streamlining the system with regular periodical reviews of limits to verify the continued viability of borrowers and to assess the need-based character of their limits. Banks are, therefore, required to review accounts of all the borrowers having working capital limits of ₹ 10 lakh and over from the banking system at least once in a year. Borrowers having working capital limits of ₹ 50 lakh and over from the banking system are required to submit quarterly statements.

2. *Bifurcation of Accounts Discontinued:* The Reserve Bank withdrew its earlier directive to the banks requiring them to bifurcate the cash credit accounts into demand loan and cash credit components and to charge differential rate of interest. In case of accounts already bifurcated, the differential rates were to be abolished immediately. This step was taken because the objective of assisting banks in their credit planning was sought to be achieved through the quarterly information system outlined below.

The Reserve Bank indicated the following four important measures to be enforced on all borrowers having total working capital limits of ₹ 50 lakh and over from the banking system.

(1) Peak Level and Non-peak Level Limits

Banks are required to fix credit limits for the normal peak level and non-peak level credit needs of the borrowers, wherever feasible. These separate limits are to be fixed on the basis of the utilisation of such limits in the past. The period during which they have to be utilised is also to be specified. Separate limits need to be fixed in case of all agriculture-based industries and consumer goods industries having seasonal demand. For others, only one limit is to be fixed.

(2) Withdrawal of Funds

After the credit limits are sanctioned as stated above, the borrower should be required to indicate before the commencement of each quarter, his expected requirements of funds in that quarter. Such limits are called the operating limits. Borrower is expected to withdraw funds from the bank within the operating limit on that quarter subject to a tolerance of 10 per cent either way. If a borrower draws more than or less than these tolerance limits, it must be considered as an irregularity in the account, which is the consequence of defective planning by the borrower. Banks should, therefore, take necessary corrective steps so as to avoid the repetition of such irregularity in future.

Submission of Quarterly Statements

Each borrower shall have to submit to his bank, the following two quarterly statements:

(1) Statement giving estimates of production, sales, stock position and current liabilities (to be submitted in the week preceding the beginning of a quarter).

(2) Statement showing actual performance in the quarter (to be submitted within six weeks from the end of the quarter).

On the basis of these statements, the banks are required to prepare the quarterly review of accounts.

Penalty for Default: If the borrower fails to submit any of the aforesaid statements in time, he shall have to bear penalties as follows:

(i) a penal interest of one per cent per annum may be charged on total outstanding for the period of default, and

(ii) at the same time, the borrower should be clearly told that if the default persists, the account may be frozen on the strength of the notice already served on him. If the borrower is financed by more than one bank, the bank freezing the account shall communicate its decision to other banks concerned. On receipt of such intimation, such banks shall not allow the borrower to operate the accounts with them. They will not grant fresh limit to the borrower, without getting clearance from the bank which has frozen the account.

In case of large borrower who is already enjoying credit limits with another bank/banks no bank shall grant any credit facility without the consent of the existing banker. Thus, concurrence of the main bank and/or the banks which have already sanctioned inventory limit is essential for opening new accounts or for sanctioning post-sales limits to a borrower.

(3) Temporary Limits

Banks should very carefully consider requests for *ad hoc*/temporary limits in excess of the sanctioned limits to meet unforeseen contingencies. Such limits should be allowed for predetermined short duration and may be in the form of a separate demand loan or non-operable cash credit account bearing an additional interest of one per cent over the normal rate. If the borrower in such a case is unable to provide corresponding additional contribution, bank may ignore the same.

(4) Borrower's Contribution

The Reserve Bank stressed the need to reduce the over dependence on bank credit by medium and large borrowers. They should be required to increase their contribution towards working capital. Banks should assess the maximum permissible bank finance of the borrower by adopting the second method of lending recommended by the Tandon Committee. Under this method, the borrower must contribute from: (1) his owned funds and (2) term loans an amount which should be at least 25 per cent of the total current assets. In other words, the borrower's contribution to working capital be increased from 25 per cent of the Working Capital Gap (under first method of Lending) to 25 per cent of total current assets. This will result in current ratio of 1.33:1 instead of 1:1.

Arrangement during Transition Period

If a borrower is unable to comply with the above requirements immediately, banks may segregate the excess borrowing and create it as Working Capital Term Loan (WCTL). This term loan should be repaid by the borrower in half-yearly instalments within a period not exceeding five years. Banks may, at their discretion, charge interest on such WCTL at a higher rate, not exceeding the ceiling, with a view to encourage early repayment and may even charge a penal rate if there is any default in the repayment.

Additional Credit Limits: Banks are permitted to grant additional credit limits to the borrowers. If such higher limits become necessary due to increased production. But they must insist on: *(i)* the incremental current ratio of 1.33:1, and *(ii)* no increase in the WCTL component.

Exemptions: Reserve Bank of India exempted the following categories of borrowers, who may be unable to switch over to the second method of lending from the compliance of this requirement:

(a) New companies floated prior to December 8, 1980.

(b) Companies showing signs of incipient sickness.

(*c*) Companies having finalised modernisation or expansion programmes prior to implementation of Chore Committee recommendations.

(*d*) Borrowers who are unable to pay the instalments/interest due to term lending institution, if the efforts to reschedule the instalments do not succeed.

In the aforesaid cases of borrowers, the Reserve Bank has advised banks to carefully examine the position on the basis of cash/funds flow statements and other relevant information and if they are satisfied on the merits of the case, they may assess credit requirements of the borrower without applying the second method of lending. Such relaxation may be permitted for a period not exceeding three years. Bank should impress upon the borrowers the desirability of change over to the second method as early as possible.

The Reserve Bank has clarified that the above-mentioned measures may not be made applicable to borrowers who enjoy aggregate working capital limits below ₹ 50 lakh from the banking system but exceed this level on account of sanction of additional credit limits for the temporary periods.

Banks are also advised to adopt a flexible approach in respect of exporters who are unable to bring in additional contribution for additional credit limits sanctioned for specific export transactions. If any borrowing unit exports a substantial part of its production and the working capital term loan (WCTL) has to be carved out of the existing packing credit banks may identify the WCTL on a notional basis only, i.e., the amount of excess borrowing may be identified but not transferred to a separate account so that the concessionaries rate of interest becomes available for the permissible time. The required contribution should be brought in by the borrower within five years.

BILL FINANCE

Reserve Bank of India also stressed the desirability of concerting cash credit against book debts (for financing sales) into bill finance, wherever possible. It has also had emphasis on increasing the use of bill finance for purchase of raw materials. Banks have been advised that at least 50 per cent of the cash credit limits given by them against raw materials to the manufacturing units in both public and private sector must be by way of drawee bills only. Banks should start this practice with borrowers having total working limits of ₹ 50 lakh and above from the banking system.

NEW MEASURES TO DISCIPLINE BORROWERS

In its credit policy for the busy season 1990-91, the Reserve Bank of India announced the following two measures to discipline big borrowers and reinforce the directives already issued:

(1) Commitment charge on unutilised quarterly operating limit

As noted above borrowers are required to indicate their expected requirement of funds within a quarter, which is called the quarterly operating limit. In 1991 Reserve Bank asked the banks to levy a minimum commitment charge of one per cent per annum on the unutilised portion of the quarterly operating limit, subject to the tolerance limit of 15% of the same. This was applicable to all borrowers with working capital limits of ₹ one crore and above. With effect from July 1, 1996, levy of this charge has been left to the discretion of the financing bank and it is now not mandatory.

(2) Penal interest on excess book-debt finance

To encourage the use of bills for financing receivables. Reserve Bank of India has prescribed that only 75% of the inland credit sales should be financed as advances against book-debts and the rest through the bills.

Now, it has been stipulated that interest at two percentage point above the relevant cash credit interest rate should be levied on that portion of the book-debt finance which exceeds the prescribed norm of 75% of limits sanctioned to borrowers for financing island credit sale. This applied to fund-based credit limits of ₹ 5 crore. This directive was withdrawn with effect from July 1, 1996.

REVISED NORMS FOR BANK LENDING FOR WORKING CAPITAL

On 28th October, 1993 Reserve Bank of India issued revised guidelines for bank lending whereby desired level of flexibility has been granted to the banks in their day-to-day operations. However, they will observe the prudential norms for lending prescribed by the Reserve Bank. The new instructions are as follows:

1. Norms of Inventory and Receivables

As noted above quantitative norms for each item of inventory and receivables are prescribed by the Reserve Bank of India for various industries. These norms are applicable to borrowers enjoying aggregate fund-based working capital limits of ₹ 10 lakh and above from the banking system.

Under the revised guidelines banks will make their own assessment of credit requirements of borrowers based on a total study of borrower's business operations, i.e., taking into account the production/processing cycle of the industry as well as the financial and other relevant parameters of the borrowers. The Reserve Bank would only advise the overall levels of inventory and receivables for different industries for the guidance of banks to serve as broad indication. This guideline will not apply to all borrowers enjoying aggregate fund-based working capital limits of ₹ 1 crore and above from the banking system.

2. Working Capital Limits for Village, Tiny and Other Small-scale Industries

Working capital limits for tiny industries and other small-scale industrial units enjoying aggregate fund-based working capital credit limits up to ₹ 50 lakh were already exempted from the inventory and receivable norms and first Method of Lending. For them such limits are computed on the basis of a minimum of 20% of their projected annual turnover. This facility has now been extended to all borrowers enjoying aggregate fund-based working capital limits of less than ₹ 2 crore from the banking system.

3. Method of Lending

Borrower enjoying fund-based working Capital Credit limit of ₹ 10 lakh and above and up to ₹ 50 lakh are required to follow first Method of Lending (with the exception of units falling under 2 above.)

Under the revised guidelines, for sanctions of credit limits to borrowers enjoying aggregate fund-based credit limits for amounts less than ₹ 1 crore from the banking system banks should enquire maintenance of minimum margin of 5% of the annual turnover of such borrowers as margin money.

For sanctioning aggregate fund-based working capital limits of ₹ 1 crore and above from the banking system banks are required to follow second method of lending.

4. Export Units

Under the existing guidelines, export units having export of not less than 25% of their total turnover during the previous accounting year, are not subject to secondly method of lending.

Under the revised guidelines, export units having export activities need not bring in any contribution from their long-term sources towards financing that portion of current assets as is represented by export receivables.

5. Sick/Weak Units

Sick/weak units under rehabilitation will continue to be exempted from the application of second method of lending.

6. Slipback in Current Ratio

Banks will continue permitting on merits slipback in current ratio for industrial units with a good track-record and sound current ratio, for the specified purposes and subject to the prescribed contributions.

7. *Ad hoc* Limits

Under the new guidelines, banks themselves will decide the quantum as also the period of any *ad hoc* credit facilities based on their commercial judgement and merits of individual cases.

For sanctioning of *ad hoc* limits, it will no longer be mandatory to charge additional interest of one per cent over and above the normal rate of interest.

8. Quarterly Information System

Under the revised guidelines banks must obtain from all borrowers enjoying aggregate fund-based working capital credit limit of ₹ 1 crore and more from the banking system the statements prescribed under the quarterly information system/monthly cash budget system (The cut-off rate was ₹ 50 lakh earlier).

Banks would continue to invariably charge penal interest of at least one per cent per annum of a period of one quarter on the outstandings under various working capital limits sanctioned to a borrower, who fails to submit any of the above referred statements.

In case the default is of a serious nature or continues for two consecutive quarters, banks may consider charging a rate of interest higher than the normal rate on his entire outstandings under the working capital limits sanctioned, until the position relating to timely submission of various statements is regularised.

MAXIMUM PERMISSIBLE BANK FINANCE

In October 1993, Reserve Bank of India slightly relaxed the method of calculation of maximum permissible bank finance. Hitherto the entire amount of term loan instalments falling due for payment during the next one year was reckoned as item of current liability for the purpose of arriving at the maximum permissible bank finance. Since Oct. 1993, only one-third of such instalments are to be treated as current liability, unless the loan has been rescheduled by the financial institutions/banks. Also the entire amount of term loan due within 12 months will continue to be current liability for the purpose of computing the current ratio. This will enhance the maximum permissible bank finance.

INSTRUCTIONS REGARDING MPBF WITHDRAWN

In April 1997, Reserve Bank of India withdrew all the above instructions relating to maximum permissible bank finance and permitted the banks to evolve their own methods of assessing the working capital requirements of borrowers within the prudential guidelines and exposure norms. The Bank has suggested the following alternatives:

(1) The turnover method for small borrowers may be continued as a tool of assessment for this sector.

(2) Banks may follow Cash Budget system for assessment of working capital finance of large borrowers.

(3) Banks may retain the present Maximum Permissible Bank Finance system with necessary modification, or

(4) Any other system.

The loan policy in respect of each broad category of industry shall be laid down by every bank with the approval of its Board.

Appendix XII

Subsidiaries of Banks and Mutual Funds

During recent years leading Indian commercial banks have set up their subsidiary companies to undertake the business permissible to them. Though Section 19 of the Banking Regulations Act, 1949 had already permitted the banks to establish subsidiaries, but the scope of the activities for which they can be established was a limited one till 1984. After the amendment to Section 19 of the Act in 1984, a banking company is now permitted to establish a subidiary company for any of the following purposes:

(a) For undertaking of any business which is permissible for a banking company to undertake under Section 6(I) clauses (a) to (o), or

(b) For carrying on the business of banking exclusively outside India, or

(c) For undertaking of such other business which the Reserve Bank may consider to be conducive to the spread of banking in India or to be otherwise useful or necessary in public interest.

The above amended section enlarged the scope of activities for the bank subsidiaries and enabled the banks to diversify their activities through their subsidiaries. Merchant banking commercial banks as a departmental activity, i.e., as a separate department within the bank. Apart from it, the Reserve Bank has during recent years permitted the banks to undertake the following activities:

(i) Equipment leasing

(ii) Housing capital

(iii) Venture capital

(iv) Mutual funds

(v) Factoring services.

Banks have commenced undertaking these activities by establishing separate subsidiaries, Mutual funds have been established as Trusts under the Indian Trusts Act. At the end of June 1996 there were 11 subsidiaries set up by banks in the field of equipment leasing, hire-purchase-cum merchant banking activities and 8 in housing finance.

Leasing and Merchant Banking Subsidiaries

Leading commercial banks have established such companies. The merchant banking business already undertaken by them departmentally has been entrusted to these companies. The main activities undertaken by them, popularly known as financial services, are as follows:

1. Management of Capital Issues: The companies manage the issues of private, joint and public sector companies by providing the following services:

(a) Designing the capital structure

(b) Drafting the prospectus

(c) Assistance in obtaining consent from authorities

(d) Obtaining approvals from Stock Exchanges

(e) Arranging institutional participation by way of private placement or market placement

(f) Arranging underwriting from brokers, banks and financial institutions

(g) Selection of bankers, brokers and issue houses

(h) Undertaking publicity for new issues.

2. Loan Syndication: Loan syndication means arranging finance from a number of banks and financial institutions. Its importance is felt when large amounts are to be raised. The merchant banking companies, therefore undertake the following businesses in this regard:

(a) prepare applications for assistance from financial institutions and undertake pre-sanction negotiations for sanction of facilities.

(b) tie-up working capital facilities from banks and facilitate consortium arrangements, and

(c) assist in completion of loan documentation.

3. Project Formulation and Consultancy Services: The merchant banking subsidiaries assist the entrepreneurs in formulating their project and offer the following services in this regard:

(i) Selection of appropriate technology

(ii) Collaboration arrangement

(iii) Project report preparation

(iv) Market surveys

(v) Advice on financing pattern

(vi) Assistance in obtaining various Government approvals.

4. Trusteeship: The merchant banking companies act as trustees on behalf of debentureholders, when companies' issues secure debentures. These companies execute documents for securing the debentures/bonds, register charge with appropriate authority and call information/reports to protect the interest of the debentureholders.

5. Investment Management: These companies manage the portfolios on behalf of their corporate/non-corporate clients, sale and purchase securities and provide market intelligence and advisory services.

6. Equipment Leasing: Equipment leasing is now gaining prominence as an alternative means of financing the acquisition of equipment by the clients. These companies provide on lease all type of industrial and non-industrial equipment.

7. Services for Sick Industrial Undertakings: To rehabilitate the sick industrial concerns, the merchant banking companies conduct diagnostic studies, prepare rehabilitation packages and arrange finance from financial institutions and banks.

8. Mergers and Amalgamations: The financial services companies also help in preparing and formulating schemes of financial reconstruction, mergers and amalgamations. They assist in obtaining necessary approvals from concerned persons/authorities.

9. Services for Non-resident Indians: The merchant banking subsidiaries help the non-resident Indians by way of project counselling for setting up industrial ventures in India, consultancy on investment opportunities and also provide portfolio management services.

FACTORING SUBSIDIARIES

Government of India notified factoring as a permissible activity for the banks in July 1990. According to the guidelines issued by Reserve Bank of India in this regard, banks are allowed to engage in purpose with prior approval of the Reserve Bank. They cannot undertake this business directly, *i.e.,* departmentally. They can either set up separate subsidiaries or invest in the factoring companies jointly with other banks. Such subsidiaries/joint venture factoring companies are permitted to undertake factoring business and other incidental activities, but they should not engage themselves in financing of other companies engaged in factoring. Further, the investment of bank in the shares of factoring companies, inclussive of its subsidiary carrying on factoring business, shall not in the aggregate exceed 10 per cent of the paid-up capital and reserves of the bank.

The commercial banks — State Bank of India and Canara Bank have joined Small Industries Development Bank of India (SIDBI) in promoting two factoring companies. SBI Factors and Commercial Services Pvt., Ltd., has been promoted jointly by State Bank of India and SIDBI to cater to the needs of the Western region, while Canbank Factors Ltd., has been set up jointly by Canara Bank and SIDBI to serve the Southern region. SIDBI has total shareholding of ₹ 7 crore in these companies. .

The importance of factoring services has recently been felt in India, specially because the small-scale industrial units face difficulties in realizing their book debts. Under the factoring services, a third agency, called the factor, purchases the book debts of the sellers and immediately pays either full value or a substantial part of a book debt. The factor, thereafter, realizes a debt from the buyers on the due dates. Factoring business may be undertaken: (1) with recourse, or (2) without recourse. Under the former arrangement, if the factor is unable to realize the book debt, it can realize the same from the seller. Such is not the case with 'without recourse' facility. Obviously, in the latter case the risk is borne by the factor.

MUTUAL FUNDS

Though the earliest mutual fund in India — the Unit Trust of India — came into existence in 1964, commercial banks began setting up mutual funds since 1987. The State Bank of India and the Canara Bank were the pioneers in this field, followed by Bank of India, Indian Bank and Punjab National Bank. Thus, five nationalised banks have set up the mutual funds, besides the LIC and the GIC.

A mutual fund is a term used to connote collective investment by a large number of investors. It aims at diversifying the risk in the investment in capital market and to optimise return therefrom. Thus, it is a major vehicle for mobilisation of saving particularly from the small and household sectors for investment in the stock market.

Mutual Funds in India are governed by the guidelines issued by the Reserve Bank and the Government of India. The latest guidelines were issued by the Government in February 1992. According to these guidelines, a Mutual Fund shall be established in the form of a Trust under the Indian Trusts Act and shall be operated only by separately established Asset Management Companies. All the five mutual funds by commercial banks have been set up as Trusts. These banks have appointed either their Merchant Banking Subsidiaries as the Managing Trustees of the Mutual Fund or themselves acting as such. Recently, efforts have been made to set up Assets Management Companies as the bank's subsidiaries for exclusively managing their mutual funds.

According to the guidelines the Assets Management Companies shall have a minimum net worth of ₹ 10 crore and at least 50% of the members of their Board of Directors should be independent directors not connected with the sponsoring organisation. It is specifically provided that AMC and Trustee should be two separate legal entities.

Schemes

Each mutual fund is allowed to float different schemes, which should have prior registration with Securities and Exchange Board of India. Mutual funds are allowed to have both the close-ended schemes and the open-ended schemes, but at least ₹ 20 crore and ₹ 50 crore respectively should be raised under each such scheme. Mutual funds are also required to provide continuous liquidity — close-ended schemes should be listed on stock exchanges and open-ended schemes should be listed on stock exchanges and for open-ended schemes, mutual fund shall sell and repurchase units at predetermined prices based on Net-assets value and such prices should be published at least once in a week.

The mutual funds set up by commercial banks in India have introduced a number of schemes — almost all of them are close-ended schemes (*i.e.,* the offer was open during a specified period only.) These schemes had different circumstances. Broadly, these schemes are classified into the following categories:

(*a*) Income Schemes

(*b*) Income-cum-growth Schemes

(c) Growth Schemes

(d) Tax Planning Schemes.

The objective of each scheme is different and is specifically spelt out at the time a scheme is announced. The pattern of investment consequently also differs from scheme-to-scheme.

Investment: According to guidelines, Mutual Funds are allowed to invest only in transferable securities either in the money market or in the capital market, including any privately placed debentures or securities debt. But such securities along with other unquoted debt instruments shall not exceed ten per cent in case of growth funds and 40% in case of income funds. Moreover, it is also required that all debt instruments must have been rated as investment grade by an approved credit rating agency. Mutual Funds are not allowed to give term loans for any purpose.

To ensure diversification of risk in case of investment in equity shares, the guidelines provide as follows:

(i) No individual scheme of the mutual fund should invest more than 5% of its corpus in any one company's shares.

(ii) No mutual fund under all its schemes taken together should invest more than 10% of its funds in the shares or debentures or other securities of a single company.

(iii) No mutual fund under all its schemes taken together should invest more than 15% of the funds in the shares and debentures of the specific industry such as cotton textile, tea, tyres.

Mutual funds are also required to take delivery of scrips purchased and give delivery in the case of scrips sold and in no case shall engage in short selling or carry forward transactions or badla finance.

The Assets Management Company shall charge the mutual fund with investment management and advisory fees and other expenses as per the guidelines. After charging these expenses, the net income is distributed amongst the unitholders as dividend.

The mutual funds in India have declared the minimum dividends as promised in case of income schemes and growing dividends in case of growth schemes. The close-ended schemes have to be terminated at the end of the prescribed period. The realized value of investments under the terminated scheme, after meeting all expenses, shall be distributed with priority amongst the unitholders.

Mutual funds have gained immense popularity amongst the Indian investors. Government has permitted mutual funds in the private sector also. The establishment of Money Market Mutual Funds has also been permitted by the Reserve Bank.

BANKS AND THE CONSUMER PROTECTION ACT

With the enforcement of the Consumer Protection Act, 1986 effective April 15, 1987, banks in India are now liable for additional liability towards their customers under this Act. The Act not only applies to the goods but is equally applicable to various services specified therein. By the term service is meant service of any description which is made available to potential users and included the provision of facilities in connection with banking, financing, transport, processing, supply of electrical or other energy, boarding/lodging or both, entertainment, amusement or the purveying of news or other information but does not include the rendering of any services free of charge or under the contract of personal service [Section 2(0)]. The Act thus has a much wider application than what is generally understood.

The Act provides an appropriate machinery for the redressal of the complaints of the consumers of various goods and services. Under the Act three consumer disputes agencies have been constituted, *viz.*, a Consumer Disputes Redressal Forum known as the District Forum, a Consumer Disputes Redressal Commission known as the State Commission and National Consumer Disputes Redressal Commission. The District Forums have the jurisdiction to entertain complaints where the value of goods or services and the compensation, if any, claimed is less than ₹5 lakh. The State Commission will bear complaints for claims above

₹ 5 lakh but up to ₹ 20 lakh and will consider appeals against the decisions of the District Forums. The National Commission will entertain complaints for claims above ₹ 20 lakh and will hear appeals against the verdicts of the State Commissions.

A complaint may be lodged with the appropriate authority under the Act by a consumer of the goods or services, any recognised consumer is defined as one who hires any service for a consideration which has been paid or promised or partly paid and partly promised or under any system of deferred payment and includes any beneficiary of such service, other than the person who hires for consideration.

A complaint in relation to a service may be filed if the service suffers from deficiency in any respect. The term deficiency has been defined in the Act as any fault, imperfection, shortcoming or inadequacy in the quality, nature and manner of performance which is required to be maintained by or under any law for the time being in force or has been undertaken to be performed by a person in pursuance of a contract or otherwise in relation to any service. The grounds on which a complaint may be lodged are quite wide.

The District Forum shall have the same powers as are vested in a civil court under the Code of Civil Procedure for trying the suits under the Act, if any of the allegations contained in the complaint about the service are proved, the Forum shall issue an order to the opposite party directing him to: *(1)* return the charges paid by the complainant, and *(2)* to pay such amount as may be awarded by it as compensation to the consumer for any loss or injury suffered by the consumer due to the negligence of the opposite party.

It is thus clear that the liability of the banker in relation to service rendered to the customer arises under the Act, provided the following conditions are fulfilled:

(i) the services has been rendered for a consideration and not free of charge.

(ii) the consumer suffers any loss or injury on account of any deficiency in the service rendered to him, and

(iii) the loss has been caused due to the negligence of the banker. The liability of the banker under the Act is an addition to the liabilities prescribed by other Acts affecting the bankers.

A banker renders various services to his customers (i.e., accountholders) as well as the general public. The Act applies to all the services rendered by a banker to both the categories of persons, provided the service is rendered for a consideration, i.e., a fee, commission or the like. So far as the main function of the banker is concerned (i.e., acceptance of the deposits or lending of money to customers) the banker-customer relationship is that of debtor-creditor or *vice versa*.

Any sort of payment received from a depositor is legally speaking a loan taken by the banker from the customer and when a customer draws a cheques on his deposit account, it is deemed as repayment of the loan taken by the banker. Similar is the legal position of the banker in relation to loans granted to the account holders. Hence in such transactions with the customers, a banker does not render a service for a consideration as envisaged in the Act. However, any negligence on the part of the banker in such cases do attract the provisions of this Act.

In a recent case, the cheque of an applicant for convertible debentures on rights basis, was unlawfully dishonoured by the payee banker on the ground of deficiency of funds. Consequently, no debentures could be allotted to him. The Consumer Forum awarded him compensation based on the market price of the shares that the applicant might have got on conversion of debentures, if the same were allotted to him.

In case of collection of cheques, drafts, bills, etc., from outstations, the banks renders this service for a consideration. Hence, any negligence on the part of the banker resulting in loss to the customer will make the banker liable for compensation under the Act. Reserve Bank of India has already directed the banks to pay interest in case of undue delays in the collection of outstation cheques. The compensation payable under the Act will be in addition to the interest payable under Reserve Bank's directive, provided negligence in the collection of cheque and the resultant loss to the customer are proved.

Recently a cheque for ₹ 42,515 was realised by a banker from outstation drawee banker after a period of four months. The District Forum granted a compensation of ₹ 2,000 for the physical and mental agony caused to the accountholder.

Negligence in taking all the necessary precautions by the banker in ensuring the safety of the safe deposit lockers/ safe custody lockers is another ground for action by the customer under the Act. Recently, the Consumer Disputes Redressal Commission of Maharashtra indicted one of the nationalised banks of negligence to render necessary service to safeguard the customer towards the cost of ornaments. Bank's plea that the relationship between the banker and the customer was that of landlord and tenant was rejected by the Commission and it was found guilty of gross negligence.

Banks issue demand drafts for a commission. At some of the branches the staff ask the customer to collect the draft after an hour or more. The customer might miss some important transaction in the meanwhile and thus make the banker liable for compensation. If the drafts are issued without the signature of the bank manager or his code number and the draft is dishonoured by the drawee branch on this ground, the customer may take recourse against the banker under the Act, if he suffers loss due to such dishonour.

In *Malti Bhat vs. State Bank of India* (1993 CPC 535), the Bank issued an unsigned draft for ₹ 200 to the purchaser, who was an applicant for sitting in the examination of the Institute of Engineers. As the draft was not honoured by the drawee branch the application was rejected. The District Forum held the Bank responsible for negligently issuing an unsigned demand draft, which resulted in loss of her career by six months, waste of her hardwork, great mental agony and anguish. The Forum rejected the plea of the Bank to invoke the principle of caveat emptor (*i.e.,* the buyer beware) and held that the said principle had no application at all in the present case. The Forum awarded compensation of ₹ 3,500 to the complainant.

The provisions of the Consumer Protection Act may also be made applicable in case of other services rendered by bankers. In case of a bank guarantee the bank charges a service charge from the customer and thus renders a service for a fee. If the customer does not fulfil his obligation, banker is bound to comply with the provisions of the guarantee given by him. The bankers must be conscious of their additional obligations and liabilities under the Act and bring about improvements in banking services.

The National Consumer Disputes Redressal Commission, New Delhi has given an important decision in *M/s. Special Machines, Karnal vs. Punjab National Bank* and Others. In this case the complainant alleged that due to failure on the part of the bank to provide timely financial services as promised by the bank, his business ran into serious difficulties and he suffered heavy losses as a result thereof. The Commission held that such failure on the part of the bank cannot form the subject-matter of adjudication under the Act since in the matter of grant or withholding of further advances and insisting on margin money, etc., the banks have to exercise their discretion and act in accordance with their best judgement after taking into account various relevant factors. Hence, mere failure to provide financial facility cannot be said to constitute deficiency in service.

In *Consumer Unity and Trust Society, Jaipur vs. Chairman and Management Director, Bank of Baroda, Calcutta and Another* (1995) 2 (SCC 150), the Supreme Court absolved the bank from any liability if the bank could not function and render any service to the customer due to illegal strike of the employees beyond the control of the bank. The Supreme Court held that the failure of the bank to render service could not be held to give rise to claim for recovery of any amount under the Consumer Protection Act, as there was no negligence on the part of the bank.

The scheme provides for expeditious and inexpensive solution of customer complaints. The Banking Ombudsman appointed under the scheme have the authority to look into the complaints.

(a) Concerning deficiency in service such as:

(i) non-payment/inordinate delay in the payment/collection of cheques, drafts, bills, etc.

(ii) non-issue of drafts to customers and others.

(iii) non-adherence by bank branches to prescribed working hours.

(iv) failure to honour guarantee/letter of credit by banks.

(v) claims in respect of unauthorised/fraudulent withdrawals from deposit accounts.

(vi) complaints regarding operations in accounts maintained with banks.

(vii) complaints from exporters in India.

(viii) complaints from non-resident Indians having accounts in India.

(b) Concerning loans and advances in so far as they relate to non-observance of Reserve Bank directives.

Procedures: If the bank concerned does not resolve the complaint of any customer relating to any of the aforesaid matters within a period of two months, he can approach the Banking Ombudsman. He will first try to promote a settlement between the parties. If no settelement is reached, he will make a recommendation which will become binding after being accepted by both parties. If his recommendation is not accepted he will proceed to make an award.

Imposition of minimum margin: In case of advances against commodities subject to selective control, higher margins are prescribed in order to restrict the borrowing capacity of the borrowers. With higher margin, a borrower can get less credit from banks against a certain quantity of stock and thus can finance only a smaller part of it through bank finance. Moreover, different margins may be prescribed for different types of borrowers against the security of some commodity. A higher margin is generally fixed for those however whose need for credit is not so urgent or larger flow of credit to whom is likely to aggravate the price situation. For example, minimum margins were prescribed for advances against foodgrains, pulses and oilseeds (w.e.f. 19th October, 87) at 45% for processing units/mills and against warehouse receipts and at 60% for others.

In case interest and instalment of principal are in default for two quarters then this is termed as Non-performing Assets.

Appendix XIII

KHAN COMMITTEE REPORT

In order to go into various issues relating to harmonising the roles and operations of Bank and Financial Institutions, the Reserve Bank of India set up a Working Group under the chairmanship of Shri S.H. Khan, the then Chairman of IDBI. The Group submitted its full report in May, 1998. As announced in the Credit Policy Statement of RBI, a 'Discussion Paper' is under preparation, which will contain RBI's views on Working Group's recommendations. The Khan Report has dealt with a few far-reaching changes such as:

(i) a gradual move towards Universal Banking

(ii) seeking the possibility of gainful mergers between sets of banks and DFIs on commercial considerations

(iii) speedy implementation of legal reforms to expedite debt recovery

(iv) consolidated supervision of banks and FIs

(v) gradual reduction of CRR, and

(vi) phasing out SLR. An attempt is made to put the 'Gist' of the Report before the readers.

I. Changes in Role, Structure and Operations

1. A gradual elimination of extant boundaries between Commercial Banks and Development Financial Institutions (DFIs), both on the assets as well as on the liabilities side, is necessary if Indian financial institutions and commercial banks are to prepare themselves to compete in a deregulated and increasingly global marketplace. The Group therefore recommends a progressive move towards universal banking and the development of an enabling regulatory framework for the purpose.
2. In particular, this implies that a full banking licence be eventually granted to DFIs. In the interim, DFIs may be permitted to have a banking subsidiary (with holdings up to 100%), while the DFIs themselves may continue to play their existing role.
3. A universal bank can have any of these structures: a single company, a holding company with individually capitalised but wholly-owned subsidiaries, a group of entities with cross holdings, or a flagship company with subsidiaries which may or may not have independent shareholders. The Group suggests that the appropriate corporate structure should be an internal management/ shareholder decision and should not be imposed by the regulator.
4. Size, expertise and reach are now deemed crucial to sustained viability and future survival in the financial sector. The Group therefore recommends that management and shareholders of Banks and DFIs should be permitted to explore and enter into gainful mergers. These mergers should be possible not only between Banks but also between Banks and DFIs and not only between strong and weak though viable entitles but even between two (or more), strong Banks and DFIs.
5. However, such restructuring/consolidation should be brought about in a market-oriented fashion and should be led by viability and profitability considerations alone. This would require the right and legal industrial relations environment to prevail so that optimum advantage can be derived from the proposed restructuring/consolidation through a process of rationalisation.
6. DFIs in India are already moving in the direction of universal banking and are increasingly operating on commercial as opposed to developmental considerations. However, if the DFIs are required to assume any developmental obligations, the Group recommends that the RBI/Govt. should provide an appropriate level of financial support to enable them to fulfil these obligations.

II. Changes in Regulatory and Legal Framework

7. The group recommends that the overall objective of regulation should be to facilitate free competition across traditional boundaries and to contain the impact of failure on the financial system rather than to prevent failure.
8. A function-specific regulatory framework must develop that targets activities, and is institution-neutral with regard to the regulatory treatment of identical services rendered by any participant in the financial system. This concept of neutrality should be applicable to both foreign and local entities.
9. No intermediary (such as a bank, financial institution, mutual fund or insurance company) should be relatively disadvantaged in performing an identical function *vis-a-vis* other intermediaries because of an unnecessarily high level of net regulatory burden being placed upon it. The latter must be determined solely by systemic efficiency and risk management concerns and, where necessary, the equalization of the net regulatory burden must be through a reduction of the burden on the over-regulated entity, not through an increase in burden on an adequately regulated entity. In particular, it must be kept in mind that any fresh regulatory burden that is imposed with a view to creating a level playing field must fulfil certain systemic and supervisory objectives and should not be driven merely by the need to equalize regulatory disadvantage.
10. In view of the increasing overlap in functions being performed by various participants in the financial system, the group feels that a measure of coordination among regulators is desirable. The group therefore recommends the establishment of a 'super regulator' to supervise and coordinate the activities of these multiple regulators in order to ensure uniformity in regulatory treatment.
11. The group's view is that, at a fundamental level, legal reform is called for in cases of enforcement of contractual obligations and dissolution of companies. In particular, a speedy implementation of legal reforms in the debt recovery area of Banks and Financial Institutions should be given top priority. Whilst several attempts have been made in the past to address this issue, it has fallen short of expectations for diverse reasons including the magnitude of cases pending in the various judicial fora. The Group recommends a thorough revamp of the 1993 Act on Recovery of Debts from Banks and DFIs on the suggested lines in this regard.
12. In addition, there is a need to redraft other codified laws impacting operations of DFIs/Banks enacted earlier, on the grounds of refundancy and/or incompatibility. This is essential to ensure that the legal environment moves in tandem with the emerging needs of the financial sector.
13. For effective computerisation of branches, the group recommends that amendments to the Banking Companies (period of reservation of Records) Rules, 1985 and other suitable enactments on the line of Electronic Fund Transfer Act in USA be examined for implementation.

III. Changes in Supervisory Practices

14. The Supervisory Authority should undertake primarily offsite supervision based on periodic reporting by the Banks or DFIs as the case may be. Onsite supervision should be undertaken only in exceptional cases, mainly to oversee the quality of self-regulation by financial sector participants. The assistance of statutory auditors may be taken by the Supervisory Authority to get special reports on selected areas of supervision every year. The emphasis of the supervisory system should be more on macro-management and health of the institution rather than on micro-level regulation at the individual transaction/account level.
15. Another essential element of the improved supervisory framework should be the ability of the supervisors to supervise the DFIs/Banks on a consolidated basis. This is one of the recommendations

of the Basle Committee on Banking Supervision, released in September 1997. Future accounting standards must consequently include rules on consolidated supervision for financial subsidiaries and conglomerates. Further, as domestic financial entities assume an international character, banking supervisors should adopt global consolidated supervision (instead of mere national regulation) adequately monitoring and applying appropriate prudential norms to all aspects of business conducted by banking organisations worldwide, primarily at their foreign branches and subsidiaries. A key component of such global consolidated supervision is establishment of contact and exchange of supervisory and financial information with other supervisors involved, primarily country supervisory authorities.

16. For meaningful consolidated supervision both domestic and global – the group recommends the development of a "risk-based supervisory framework" along the lines of the report of the Task Force on Conglomerate Supervision, published by the Institute of International Finance, in February 1997. The report addresses growing concerns among international financial regulators in the banking, insurance and securities markets that financial market globalisation and conglomerate corporate structure may increase systemic risk. It suggests that, for effective adaptation to global market trends, the international supervisory framework applicable to globally active financial institutions may be revised in a manner more consistent with firms' risk profiles rather than their corporate structures.

IV. Statutory Obligations

17. Any concerted move towards full-service universal banking, in the group's view, would have to be prefaced by a thorough examination and review of extant obligations. In particular, the provisions relating to —

    (a) the Cash Reserve Ratio,

    (b) the Statutory Liquidity Ratio requirement,

    (c) obligations relating to priority sector lending and other pre-emptions of resources (e.g., food advances), and

    (d) Rural Branches — even for existing entities would need to be reviewed. Its analysis leads the group to recommend that:

18. Given its twin importance as a standby liquidity support against premature withdrawals from a bank and also as an instrument of monetary policy, the application of CRR should be confined to cash and cashlike Instruments. Further, despite serial reduction in the initial phase of reforms, CRR in India is still very high by international standards. Besides, there will be intense pressure on margins with increased competition, both domestic and global. CRR should therefore be brought down progressively within a time-bound frame to international levels.

19. With the establishment of stringent asset classification and provisioning norms and the issuance of Government of India securities at market determined rates, the need for an SLR has declined considerably. It may, therefore, be useful to consider phasing it out in line with international practice.

20. The objective of placing a statutory minimum on the proportion of the advances to be given to certain sectors is to ensure that some of the sectors have access to funds at concessional rates and they do not suffer from a paucity of funds. Rather than impose this obligation on the entire banking system, the group's view is that there is a need for an alternate mechanism to be developed for financing these sectors. Such a mechanism will aim to balance the need for fund with the need to bring better suited structures and specialised skills to bear in dealing with the sectors. Whenever a need arises for concessional funding for certain sectors, the same can be provided by specifically targeted subsidies to that sector.

21. Since, in the interim, the existing obligation with respect to priority sector lending is expected to continue, the Group recommends that the following modifications may be made in its definition:

   (a) given the critical role of infrastructure in any future development of the Indian economy (in view of the serious bottlenecks that exist in the current infrastructure which hamper both the growth and competitiveness of Indian exports), the Group feels that infrastructure should be accorded the highest priority in financing. Therefore, if the concept of priority sector lending is to continue in its present form, it becomes necessary to modify its definition to reflect the growing importance of infrastructure finance. One clear alternative is to include infrastructure lending in the definition of priority sector. However, there is a concern that this may crowd out investment in other priority sectors and may relatively disadvantage those in the system who are not lending to the infrastructure sectors. It may therefore be preferable not to include infrastructure lending in the definition of "net bank credit" used in computing the priority sector obligations. This is absolutely imperative considering the large volumes involved in infrastructure financing (once it takes off) which would push up the overall credit quantum on which the priority sector lending is based, unnecessarily enlarging the latter obligation;

   (b) under the present stipulation, the priority sector obligation is linked to 40% of the net bank credit of the current financial year which hampers the process of credit planning. To facilitate efficient loan disbursals the priority sector obligation should be linked to the net bank credit at the end of the previous financial year;

   (c) at present, the classification of advances to priority sectors is determined mainly with reference to size. The Group is of the view that the definition of priority sector may be widened to enable the inclusion of a whole industry/class of activities. This would ensure that a sector which has been identified as priority is accorded due importance without imposing an additional restriction on account of the size of individual beneficiaries.

V. Re-Organisation of State-level Institutions (SLIs)

22. The Group recommends that the agenda for reform with regard to SLIs should incorporate the following:

   (i) Eventual merger of SFCs, SIDCs and SSIDCs in each state into a single entity. While the consolidation of SLIs should form part of the short-term agenda of reforms in the financial sector, an immediate-term imperative is the corporatisation of these entities to improve their competitive efficiency.

   (ii) Following restructuring/re-organisation, strong SFCs could be encouraged to go public by making IPOs. In the process, the State Government's holding in these Corporations may be allowed to be brought down to below 50%.

   (iii) Since the credit requirement of small-scale industries are being taken care of by Small Industries Development Bank of India (SIDBI) since its establishment in 1990, it would be desirable to transfer the present shareholding of IDBI in these SLIs to SIDBI. It should be vested with the overall responsibility for enacting policy and procedural guidelines with regard to the operations of SFCs.

   (iv) SIDBI should be accorded the same role and status as the nodal/coordinating agency for financing of small (and medium) industries as is now available to NABARD in the field of agricultural development. ownership in SIDBI should, as a logical corollary, stand transferred to RBI/Govt. on the same lines as NABARD.

   (v) SIDBI's role in the state-level institutions should be both as stakeholder as well as resource provider. For this purpose, SIDBI should have access to assured sources of concessional funding from RBI.

(vi) SLIs should be brought under the supervisory ambit of RBI.

(vii) With a view to fostering professionalism and efficiency, the CEO of the SLIs should ideally be a professional/technocrat, appointed by the Board and shareholders (for a fixed term) to whom he should be accountable. The CEO should be able to draw expert advice from an autonomous and professional Board of Directors, elected by shareholders. As an enabling measure, there should be suitable guideline for representation on these Boards.

VI. Harmonising the Role, Operations and Regulatory Framework of DFIs and Banks

23. The profile of asset creation of Banks and DFIs should be motivated by prudential requirements and asset-liability management considerations as well as the need for diversificatin of business risk through a wide range of products and services. Having regard to the need for large amount of funding required, the Group feels that both Banks and DFIs (and/or their subsidiaries) could play a role in working capital finance and long-term funding with different levels of emphasis on each segment. As a number of intermediate steps are needed before the universal banking model becomes a reality, the entire aspect of harmonising the roles of DFIs and Banks is being revisited on the premise that the basic functional differences would continue, at least for the present. Consequently, the recommendations that follow (Numbers: 24-30) are of an interim nature and must be viewed as such.

24. The considerable amount of overlap between the current business of Banks and DFIs necessitates close coordination and harmonisation of their lending policies. The objective of harmonisation is not to impede competition but to ensure that appropriate quantum of credit is made available to industry at a reasonable cost, there is proper supervision of accounts and a mechanism is built-up to detect incipient sickness and take prompt remedial measures in concert for better overall credit administration.

25. In order to achieve close coordination and harmonisation between DFIs and Banks on various issues of mutual interest, the Group recommends that a Standing (Coordination) Committee be set up on which Banks and DFIs would be represented.

26. Various restrictions have been imposed on DFI borrowings in terms of choice of instruments, maturity and interest rate, ceiling on short-term funding and also on their foreign currency operations. These disadvantages have introduced significant financial repression and have eventually contributed towards increased cost of long-term finance for clients. More recently, RBI has stipulated that bond issues by DFI with either a maturity of less than five years or maturity of five years and above but with interest rate exceeding 200 basis points over the yield on Government of India securities of equal residual maturity would require its prior approval. The Group feels that such restrictions run counter to the spirit of financial sector liberalisation and should therefore be withdrawn. Further, the Group recommends that the extant overall ceiling for DFIs' mobilisation of resources by way of term money bonds (having maturities of three-six months), Certificates of Deposits (maturities of one-three years), Term Deposits (fixed deposits from the public with maturity of one-five years) and inter-corporate deposits at 100% of net owned funds (NOF) of DFIs may be removed. The maturity ceiling of five years on deposits from the public, the capping of interest rate on deposits of DFIs at interest rates offered by SBI for similar maturities and the restriction relating to minimum size of deposits that may be accepted by DFIs may also be removed. The current restriction with regard to premature withdrawal not being permitted for two years may be reduced to one year. With the introduction of the above relaxations and having regard to the minimum maturiy of one year for fixed deposits from the public, the Group recommends that a suitable level of SLR may be stipulated for DFIs on increment outstanding fixed deposits raised from the public (excluding inter-bank deposits).

27. The Group recommends that CRR should not be applicable to DFIs under the present structure where they are not permitted to access cash and cash-like instruments.

28. The Group felt that there is an urgent need to activate the Term Money Market which would, in turn, assist in the rapid development of the rupee derivative Market. In this context, inter-bank/DFI investments and deposits should be free from reserve requirements.

29. In line with inter-bank deposits, a uniform risk weightage of 20% may be assigned for investment made by commercial banks in bonds of "AAA" rated DFIs.

30. The Group recommends that the Banks be permitted to exclude investments in SLR securities issued by a DFI while calculating the exposure to that DFI.

31. The Group feels that certain restrictions placed on DFIs' foreign currency operations would need to be removed. At present, DFIs operate in the forex markets under a restricted Authorised Dealer's licence which allows them to undertake specific types of foreign exchange transactions incidental to their main business. The Group recommends that the DFIs should be granted full Authorised Dealer's licence. This would help DFIs to manage their FC funds efficiently, offer better rates to clients and add liquidity and depth to foreign exchange markets.

VII. Organisation Redesign

32. A considered response to continuing liberalisation and greater external openness under CAC and WTO framework for an essentially service-driven financial sector implies going beyond mere paradigm shifts in the prospective role and operations of Banks and DFIs. They necessitate a complete transformation in the way these intermediaries do business, particularly in terms of their Organisation and Management Information Systems, Risk Management Practices and Human Resources Development. The Group was therefore asked to suggest suitable meaures for strengthening these aspects. The substantive content of reforms in these areas would, of course, vary, depending on the specific requirements of each institution. The Group's recommendations which follow are therefore largely indicative in nature.

33. Best practices in the area of corporate governance such as imparting full operational autonomy and flexibility to managements and Boards of Banks and DFIs should be implemented.

34. On organisational restructuring, the Group recommends that Banks/DFIs should principally target the following: a complete redesign of the business system, with the Top Management spelling out the strategic objectives for principal stakeholders (clients, employees, shareholders, etc.). The corporate culture must undergo an attitudinal change in favour of a pro-active relationship based approach, with Relationship Managers serving as the single contact point. A consensus-driven committee-based approach is recommended for loan sanctions to get the benefit of pluralistic views and at the same time eliminate individual biases. Finally, decisions on organisational structure should be allowed to be based purely on commercial judgement.

VIII. Risk Management

35. The increased menu of risks in the progressively deregulated and globalised scenario would require Banks/DFIs to assign primacy to risk management in its strategic initiatives. In this connection, the Working Group recommends a clear emphasis on the following as part of a prudent risk-return optimisation strategy.

    (i) There should be a clear strategy approved by the Board of Directors as to their risk management policies and procedures. The senior management should ensure that the structure of Banks/DFIs' business and the level of risk it assumes are effectively managed with a well-defined system and based on a clear definition of individuals/committees responsible for managing such risks.

(ii) An Integrated Treasury and a proactive Asset Liability Management (ALM), which considers both on-and off-balance sheet items, would be central to future prosperity of financial senior participants under the changed scenario.

(iii) Robust (internal) operational controls as well as strong firm-wide support functions — including audit — must be in place to ensure that risk management policies are being supported, controls are in effect and that complex areas are being appropriately dealt with.

IX. Information Technology and MIS

36. An upgraded Information Technology (IT) and a vastly improved and efficient Management Information System (MIS) are both mandatory to support the new organisational structures and redesigned processes. The Group is of the view that the following would facilitate the establishment of IT systems and MIS of international standards.

(i) Existing laws may not be adequate or have the clarity to deal with some of the key issues that are likely to emerge following introduction of computerisation and technologically advanced communications in banking. There is compelling logic to revisit the legal framework in this area and render it compatible with the requirements of a technology-driven banking environment.

(ii) DFIs/Banks should urgently establish, create employee/customer awareness and familiarity with e-mail, Internet and Intranet Banking, Smat Cards and Electronic Date Interchange (EDI) in a strategically sequenced fashion.

37. The Group considers that it would be worthwhile going into the details of the requirements and drawing up a perspective plan/blue-print for a robust automation in the financial sector. In particular, the Group is of the view that financial sector participants would need to implement computerised decision-support systems.

X. Human Resources Development

38. The Group feels that the success of any organisational change in a service-oriented industry like financial services will depend on the initiatives taken in the area of Human Resource Development. The Group therefore recommends that the reformed HRD agenda of DFIs/Banks should encompass the following.

(i) Present management and leadership, with accent on teamwork.

(ii) Broad-based recruitments both at entry level from campus as well as lateral entry of professionals at higher levels to full skill gaps, particularly in the areas of:

- Economic Research and Industry Analysis
- Risk Management
- Treasury and Financial Derivatives
- Investment Banking
- Human Resources Management
- Information Technology
- Relationship Management

(iii) Systematic training programmes (including exchange programmes), with focus on practical skills, and expertise linked to career development as well as real-time familiarisation of staff with the latest developments.

(iv) Skill-building and skill-upgradation, including moving staff across functions selectively to develop top management talent.

(v) Market-related compensation packages, with financial rewards for strong performance and superior skills.

(vi) Viable and enforceable exit option for employees who are unable to cope with the radical cultural and technological change. An enabling legal framework thus needs to emerge fairly early in the organised labour market area.

(vii) In order to facilitate proactive decision-making and make vigilance function more meaningful, a Special Vigilance machinery exlusively for the financial sector on the lines of Serious Fraud Office (SFO) of UK may be set-up.

Appendix XIV

Recent Changes — Legal Decisions

Reduction in Bank Rate

In its Mid-term Review of Monetary and Credit Policy announced on October 21, 2001, the Reserve Bank of India announced a half percentage point reduction in its Bank rate from 7% to 6.5% with effect from Oct. 23, 2001. The Bank rate now is the lowest rate since May 1973.

Reduction in Cash Reserve Ratio

Reserve Bank of India has reduced Cash Reserve Ratio by two percentage points from 7.5% to 5.5% in two stages — 5.75% with effect from Nov. 3 and further to 5.5% with effect from Dec. 29, 2001.

At the same time it has removed all exemptions available on CRR. (except the inter-bank liabilities) with effect from Nov. 3, 2001.

Interest Rate on Cash Reserve Ratio

Reserve Bank of India has linked the interest rate payable on eligible CRR balances with the Bank rate and thus it has been raised to 6.5% (equal to present Bank rate) with effect from November 3, 2001.

Loan System for Delivery of Bank Credit

In Oct. 2001, Reserve Bank of India granted the banks the freedom to change the composition of working capital advance by increasing the cash credit component beyond 20% for working capital limits of ₹ 10 crore and above if they so desire. This relaxation has been granted in view of the current environment when short term investment opportunities are available to both corporates and banks.

Credit to Women Borrowers

In August 2001 Reserve Bank of India advised all public sector banks to take immediate action to earmark 5% of their net bank credit for lending to women within three years, i.e., by March 31, 2004. It has also asked the banks to further simplify procedural formalities for loans to women.

Housing Finance Allocation

For the financial year 2001-2002, each bank has been asked to compute its share of the housing finance allocation at 3 per cent of its incremental deposits as on the last reporting Friday of March 2001 over the figure of the last reporting Friday of March 2000. Banks may grant housing loans exceeding this target if their resources permit.

Differential Rates of Interest Scheme

The target for lending under this scheme has been prescribed at one per cent of the aggregate advances of the previous year of the concerned bank.

Credit Guarantee Fund (Scheme) for Small Industries

This scheme is being implemented by Credit Guarantee Trust Fund for Small Industries set up by Government of India and the Small Industries Development Bank of India, who are the settlers to the Trust. During 2000-01 they have contributed ₹ 125 crore to the corpus of the Trust in the ratio of 4:1.

Initially loans and advances up to ₹ 10 lakh were guaranteed by the Trust. But subsequently this amount has been raised to ₹ 25 lakh per borrower. The guarantee extended by the Trust is up to 75% of the amount in default, which means a guarantee cap of ₹ 18.75 lakh per borrower.

Any credit facility sanctioned at an interest rate of more than 3 per cent over the Prime Lending Rate of the Lending Institution is not eligible for guarantee under the scheme.

Treasury Bills

Since May 14, 2001 the issues of 14-day Treasury Bills and 182-day Treasury Bills have been discontinued. The notified amount in each auction of 91-day Treasury Bills has been increased from ₹ 100 crore to ₹ 250 crore since May 18, 2001. The notified amount for each auction of 364-day Treasury Bills was raised from ₹ 500 crore to ₹ 750 crore effective from December 13, 2000.

- The Discount and Finance House of India Ltd., also provides a ready market for such bills, as it purchases the same as outright purchase or on repo basis.

Educational Loan Scheme

The Government of India, has accepted the model scheme for granting of educational loans, prepared by Indian Banks' Association. Reserve Bank has asked the banks to implement the scheme, which has the following features:

1. Need-based finance could be provided keeping in view the repaying capacity of the parents/ students. Maximum amount of loan could be ₹ 7.5 lakh for studies in India and ₹ 15 lakh for studies abroad.
2. No margin is required for loans up to ₹ 4 lakh. For loans of higher amounts, margin will be 5% for studies in India and 15% for studies abroad. Margin may be brought in on year-to-year basis.
3. No security is required for loans up to ₹ 4 lakh. For loans above ₹ 4 lakh, collaterally security of suitable value or co-obligation of parents/guardian/third party along with assignment of future income of the student for payment of instalments be obtained.
4. Rate of interest will be the Prime Lending Rate for loans up to ₹ 4 lakh and 1% over Prime Lending Rate for loans exceeding ₹ 4 lakh. Penal interest @ 2% be charged for loans above ₹ 2 lakh for the overdue amount and overdue period.
5. Repayments — The loan is to be repaid in five to seven years after the commencement of repayment. The repayment will start after the course period plus one year or six months after getting the job, whichever is earlier.

The interest accrued during the repayment holiday period should be added to the principal and repayment in equated monthly instalments (EMI) fixed.

LEGAL DECISIONS

Negligence of Banks

Banks have been held liable for negligence under the Consumer Protection Act, 1986 in the following two cases:

In Vimal Chandra Grover vs. Bank of India (AIR 2000 SC 2181) the Supreme Court quashed the decision of the National Consumer Commission and held the bank liable for negligence in providing service.

In this case the Bank of India had given overdraft facility to the appellant against the pledge of shares. Subsequently the appellant requested the bank to arrange for sale of 500 shares at a price indicated by him to clear the overdraft. The Bank referred the request to its Head Office, which denied holding of shares with itself. In fact, the shares were lying with the branch itself. In the correspondence much time was lost and in the meanwhile share price fell and the shares could not be sold at the price indicated by the borrower. The Supreme Court held, that the failure of the Bank to sell pledged shares within reasonable time causing loss to the customer amounted to deficiency in service and asked the Bank to pay the customer ₹ 5 lakh with interest to reimburse the loss caused to him.

In another case, the Consumer Forum at Delhi penalised state-owned Syndicate Bank for clearing cheques of a customer in spite of stop payment instructions from the accountholder. The clearing of these cheques resulted in dishonouring of subsequent cheques issued by the customer. The Forum directed the Bank to pay a token compensation of ₹ 500 and litigation cost of ₹ 500.

Pay Orders are also Cheques

In a recent case the Supreme Court has held that the Pay Orders issued by banks are also cheques and declined pay orders would also invite penalty under Section 138 of the Negotiable Instruments Act, (i.e., the law relating to offences involving bouncing of cheques). Rejecting the order of the Bombay High Court, the bench of the Supreme Court held a pay order was closer to a bill of exchange because of the unconditional order of its maker to the person concerned to pay a certain sum.

Appendix XV

REVIEW OF MONETARY POLICY FOR THE YEAR 2007-08

The Governor of the Reserve Bank of India announced the First Quarter Review of Annual Monetary Policy for the year 2007-08 on July 31, 2007, which consists of three sections:

Section I: Assessment of Macroeconomic and Monetary Developments

Section II: Stance of Monetary Policy

Section III: Monetary Measures

The present note brings out highlights of the Review Policy Statement, the Macroeconomic and Monetary Developments, the Stance of the Monetary Policy and the impact of Monetary Measures on the economy and the banking sector in India.

MAJOR HIGHLIGHTS OF THE POLICY

- Bank Rate (6%), Repo Rate (7.75%) and Reverse Repo Rate (6%) kept unchanged.
- The CRR applicable to banks increased by 50 bps to 7 per cent with effect from August 4, 2007.
- The ceiling of ₹ 3,000 crore on daily Reverse Repo under the LAF, which was fixed earlier, has been with drawn w.e.f. August 6, 2007.
- The second LAF, conducted between 3 p.m. to 3.45 p.m. is withdrawn from August 6, 2007.
- The GDP growth projection for 2007-08 retained at around 8.5 per cent.
- Inflation will be contained within 5 per cent in 2007-08.
- The acceleration in the growth of Money Supply (M3) is a matter of concern.
- Emphasis on credit quality and financial stability.
- Recent domestic financial market developments in India and unexpected uncertainties in global markets warrant a high priority in future monetary policy formulations.

I: MACROECONOMIC AND MONETARY DEVELOPMENTS

(A) Domestic Economy

Gross Domestic Product: Real GDP growth during the quarter January-March 2007 is placed at 9.1 per cent as against 10 per cent in the corresponding quarter a year ago. Real GDP growth for the Financial Year 2006-07 is revised upwards from 9.2 per cent to 9.4 per cent. In the revised estimate of 9.4 per cent growth, the GDP originating in agriculture, industry and services sectors increased by 2.7 per cent, 11 per cent and 11 per cent, respectively. This is in comparison to the growth rates of 6 per cent, 8 per cent and 10.3 per cent, respectively in 2005-06.

Agriculture: The progress of the 2007 south-west monsoon season has been satisfactory so far. Of the normal area of 71.9 million hectares under Kharif food grain crops, 30.1 million hectares were covered by sowing by July 20, 2007. The rainfall this year is expected to be normal to the extent of 93 per cent, which augurs well for the agricultural production.

Industrial Sector: The industrial production remained robust during April-May 2007 recording a year-on-year expansion of 11.7 per cent. The manufacturing sector remained the key driver of industrial activity with growth of 12.7 per cent. Electricity generation and mining activity increased by 9 per cent and 3 per cent, respectively. Within manufacturing sector, industries such as machinery and equipment, food products, basic metals and alloys and chemicals emerged as the growth drivers up to May 2007. The six infrastructure industries, (comprising nearly 27 per cent of the IIP) posted a higher growth of 8.1 per cent during April-May 2007 as against 7.2 per cent a year ago.

The Reserve Bank's Industrial Outlook Survey (May 2007) indicates that 60 per cent of the respondent revealed *status quo* in capacity utilization, working capital requirement and availability of finance.

The outlook for July-September 2007 appears to be optimistic with majority of the respondents expecting an improvement in the overall business situation on the back of the increase in production, order book and capacity utilisation.

Services Sector: The services sector activity has expanded in the first quarter of the current financial year by recording a higher growth of 8.1 per cent during April-May 2007, as compared with 7.2 per cent a year ago. The robust growth in services sector is mainly due to the growth in tourist arrivals, increase in new cell-phone connections, increase in passengers and cargo handled by civil aviation, increase in freight traffic, growth in banking and financial sector activity, etc.

Money Supply and Inflation: Growth in money supply (M3) at 21.6 per cent on a year-on-year basis on July 6, 2007 was above the projected trajectory of 17.5 per cent as indicated in the Annual Policy for 2007-08.

Inflation as measured by variations in the Wholesale Price Index (WPI), declined from 5 per cent at end-March 2007 to 4.4 per cent as on July 14, 2007. Inflation based on Consumer Price Index (CPI) for industrial workers was placed at 6.6 per cent as against 6.3 per cent in June 2007.

The Government Borrowings: Gross market borrowings of the Central Government during 2007-08 at ₹ 85,628 crore up to July 27, 2007 constituted 45.4 per cent of the budget estimates (BE), while net market borrowings at ₹ 46,047 crore constituted 42 per cent of the BE. Additional borrowings of ₹ 6,000 crore (through 182-day T-Bills) and ₹ 18,500 crore (through 91-day T-Bills) were undertaken in June 2007 to fund transfer of RBI's stake in State Bank of India to the Government of India.

(B) India's External Sector

Exports and Imports: During the first two months of 2007-08, export growth rose to 20.2 per cent from 19.2 per cent in the corresponding period of the previous year. Imports also posted a sharp rise of 33 per cent as compared with 16.9 per cent in the corresponding period of the previous year. Non-POL imports (petroleum, oil and lubricants) rose by 47.3 per cent, whereas oil imports remained broadly stable at the level recorded a year ago. As a result, the merchandise trade deficit widened to US$ 13.3 billion during April-May 2007 from US$ 8.2 billion in April-May 2006.

Foreign Capital Inflows: Net foreign capital inflows increased to US$ 44.9 billion in 2006-07 from US$ 23.4 billion in 2005-06. Sizeable increases in net inflows came from foreign direct investment (FDI), non-resident Indian (NRI) deposits, external commercial borrowings (ECB), external assistance and short-term credit. In respect of FDI inflows, manufacturing, construction, information technology services, financial and banking services were the main recipients in net inflows of US$ 8.4 billion in 2006-07. Net portfolio inflows were lower at US$ 7.1 billion as compared to US$ 12.5 billion in 2005-06. NRI deposits increased by US$ 3.9 billion as compared with US$ 2.8 billion in the previous year.

Foreign Exchange Reserves and External Debt: The foreign exchange reserves increased to US$ 222 billion as on July 20, 2007, an increase of US$ 22.9 billion over end-March 2007. India's external debt increased by US$ 28.6 billion to reach the level of US$ 155 billion at end-March 2007.

(C) Banking Sector

Aggregate Deposits: Aggregate deposits of SCBs increased by ₹ 1,05,534 crore (4 per cent) during 2007-08 up to July 6, 2007, as against an increase of ₹ 72,913 crore (3.5 per cent) in the corresponding period of the previous year. The accretion to bank deposits during the current financial year so far (April 1-July 6, 2007) is at a 14-year high. The year-on-year increase in aggregate deposits of SCBs at 24.4 per cent (₹ 5,31,881 crore) up to July 6, 2007, was higher as compared to the growth of 20.7 per cent (₹ 3,77,392 crore) a year ago.

Bank Credit: The year-on-year non-food credit growth of SCBs at 24.4 per cent (₹ 3,67,258 crore) on July 6, 2007 was lower than 32.8 per cent (₹ 3,70,899 crore) a year ago. On a financial year basis, non-food credit declined by ₹ 12,094 crore (0.6 per cent) during 2007-08 (up to July 6, 2007), in contrast to an increase of ₹ 36,654 crore (2.5 per cent) in the corresponding period of the previous year. Food credit registered a decline of ₹ 2,292 crore during the current year.

Provisional information on sectoral pattern of bank credit available up to March 2007 indicates some rebalancing of credit deployment, particularly in January-March 2007. The bank credit to agriculture recorded the highest growth (32.4 per cent), followed by services sector (31.0 per cent), personal loans (26.5 per cent) and industry (25.7 per cent). Growth in housing and real estate loans decelerated moderately to 24.6 per cent and 69.8 per cent, respectively. Within the industrial sector, sizeable credit offtake was recorded in respect of infrastructure (26.8 per cent), textiles (34.2 per cent), basic metals and metal products (26.7 per cent), petroleum (41.0 per cent), food processing (27.9 per cent), engineering (24.5 per cent), chemicals (14.2 per cent) and construction (46.7 per cent). Priority Sector advances grew by 24.0 per cent with a reduction in their share in outstanding non-food gross bank credit to 35.2 per cent in March 2007 from 36.4 per cent a year ago.

Bank Investments: Year-on-year basis, SCBs investments in shares, bonds/debentures and commercial paper declined by ₹ 809 crore (1 per cent) as compared with a decline of ₹ 9,961 crore (11.1 per cent) a year ago. On a financial year basis, such investments fell by ₹ 4,145 crore (5.2 per cent) during the current year up to July 6, 2007. Banks invested ₹ 45,048 crore in instruments issued by mutual funds as against only ₹15,902 crore in the corresponding period of the last year. On July 6, 2007, commercial banks' holdings of Government and other approved securities was 28.7 per cent of the total NDTL as against 31.5 per cent a year ago.

Deposit and Lending Rates: Banks increased their deposit rates by about 25-50 basis points across various maturities between March 2007 and June 2007, but reduced them during July 2007 especially in shorter maturities. The benchmark prime lending rates (BPL₹) of PSBs moved from the range of 12.25-12.75 per cent in March 2007 to 12.50-13.50 per cent in July 2007.

(D) Global Factors

According to the World Economic Outlook (WEO) of the International Monetary Fund (IMF) released in July 2007, the global real GDP growth expected to increase at 5.2 per cent in 2007 and sustain that level of growth in 2008 as well.

In the US, real GDP growth accelerated to 3.4 per cent in the second quarter of 2007 as compared to 2.6 per cent a year ago, mainly due to narrowing trade deficit and higher government spending. Nonetheless, there were several adverse factors to growth, *viz.,* weak growth in incomes and consumer spending and the continued weakness in the US housing sector.

In Asia, the Emerging Market Economies (EMEs) have continued to show robust economic growth in a favourable global setting, strong commodity prices and abundant global liquidity. However, global factors are posing threat to these economies.

Globally, headline inflation has picked up in the wake of increase in commodity prices and core inflation has also remained firm. The inflation outlook remains a matter of concern due to high energy and other commodity prices, increased capacity utilization rates in developed and major emerging economies and impact of rising wages on inflation in advanced industrial countries.

Perception of high inflationary pressures have prompted monetary authorities to tighten their policy rates. The central banks that have tightened their policy rates include the ECB; the Bank of England; the Bank of Japan; the Bank of Canada; Reserve Bank of Australia; Reserve Bank of New Zealand; People's Bank of China; Bank of Korea Banco de Mexico; and the Banco Central de Chile. Central banks in China and Korea have used supplementary measures for tightening, besides increasing the key policy rates such as increases in reserve requirements. Some central banks have paused in their policy cycles, particularly the US. The pause of the Federal Reserve since August 2006 came after seventeen increases by 25 basis points each (finally to 5.25 per cent in Fed rate) between June 2004 and June 2006.

Appendix XVI

Code of Bank's Commitment for Individual Customers Reserve Bank of India

www.rbi.org.in

This is a voluntary code, which sets minimum standards of banking practices to banks to follow when they are dealing with individual customers. It provides protection to you and explains how banks are expected to deal with you for day-to-day operations. In the code, 'you' denotes the customer and 'we', the bank the customer deals with.

1.1 Objectives of the Code

The code has been developed to: *(a)* promote good and fair banking practices by setting minimum standards in dealing with *(b)* increase transparency so that you can have a better understanding of what you can reasonably expect of the services, *(c)* encourage market forces, though competition, to achieve higher operating standards; *(d)* promote a fair cordial relationship between you and your bank; *(e)* foster confidence in the banking system.

The standards of the code are covered by the key commitments in Section 2.

1.2 Application of Code

Unless it says otherwise, all parts of this code apply to all the products and services listed below, whether they are provided by branches or subsidiaries across the counter, over the phone, by post, though interactive electronic devices on the internet or by any other method. However, all products discussed here may or may not be offered by all banks, *(a)* Current accounts, savings account, term deposits, recurring deposit, PPF accounts and all other deposit accounts. *(b)* Payment services such as pension, payment orders, remittances by way of Demand Drafts and wire traders. *(c)* Banking services related to Government transactions. *(d)* Demat accounts, equity government bonds. *(e)* Indian currency notes exchange facility. *(f)* Collection of cheques, safe custody services, sale deposit locker facility. *(g)* Loans and overdrafts. *(h)* Foreign exchange services including money changing. *(i)* Third party insurance and investment products sold through our branches. *(j)* Card products including credit cards, debit cards, ATM cards and services (including credit cards offered by our subsidiaries/companies promoted by us).

2. KEY COMMITMENTS

2.1 Our Key Commitments to You

2.1.1 To Act Fairly and Reasonably in all our Dealings with You By

(a) Providing minimum banking facilities of receipt and payment of cash/cheques at the bank's counter. *(b)* Meeting the commitments and standards in this code, for the products and services we offer, and in the procedures and practices our staff follow. *(c)* Making sure our products and services meet relevant laws and regulations in letter and spirit. *(d)* Ensuring that our dealings with you rest on ethical principles of integrity and transparency. *(e)* Operating secure and reliable banking and payment systems.

2.1.2 To Help You to Understand How our Financial Products and Services Work By

(a) Giving you information about them in any one or more of the following languages: Hindi, English or the appropriate local language. *(b)* Ensuring that our advertising and promotional literature is clear and not misleading. *(c)* Ensuring that you are given clear information about our products and services, the terms and conditions and the interest rates/service charges, which apply to them. *(d)* Giving you information on what are the benefits to you, how you can avail of the benefits, what are their financial implication and whom you can contact for addressing your queries and how.

2.1.3 To Help You Use Your Account or Service By

(a) Providing you regular appropriate up dates. *(b)* Keeping you informed about changes in the interest rates, charges of terms and conditions.

2.1.4 To Deal Quickly and Sympathetically with Things that Go Wrong By

(a) Correcting mistakes promptly and cancelling any bank charges that we apply due to our mistake. *(b)* Handling your complaints promptly. *(c)* Telling you how to take your complaint toward if you are still not satisfied (see para No. 7). *(d)* Providing suitable a'ternative avenues to alleviate problems arising out of technological failures.

2.1.5 To Treat all Your Personal Information as Private and Confidential

We will treat all your personal information as private and confidential subject to matters mentioned in para number 5 below.

2.1.6 To Publicise the Code We Will

(a) provide you (existing customer) with a copy of the code. *(b)* provide you (new customer) with a copy of the code when you open your account. *(c)* make this code available on request either over-the-counter or by electronic communication or mail. *(d)* make available this code at every branch and on our website; and *(e)* ensure that our staff are trained to provide relevant information about the code and to put the code into practice.

2.1.7 To Adopt and Practice a Non-discrimination Policy

We will not discriminate on the basis of race, gender, marital status, religion or disability.

3. INFORMATION

You can get information on interest rates, common fees and charges through any one of the following: *(a)* Looking at the notices in our branches. *(b)* Phoning our branches or helplines, *(c)* Looking on our website, *(d)* Asking our designated staff/ help desk; or *(e)* Referring to the service guide/tariff schedule.

3.1 Before You Become a Customer We Will

(a) give you clear information explaining the key features of the services and products you tell us you are interested in; *(b)* give you information on any type of products and services which we offer and that may suit your needs; *(c)* tell you if we offer products and services in more than one way (for example, through ATMs, on the internet, over the phone in branches and so on) and tell you how to find out more about them; *(d)* tell you what information we need from you to prove your identity and address, for us to comply with legal, regulatory and internal policy requirements.

3.2 When You Become a Customer We Will

(a) give you more information of the key features of the product, including applicable interest rates/fees and charges; *(b)* give you extra information on your rights and responsibilities especially regarding availing of nomination facility offered on all deposits accounts, articles in safe custody and safe deposit vaults; *(c)* automatically register your name under 'Do Not Call' Service. We will not inform/extend to you through telephone calls/SMSs/e-mails any new product/service unless and until you inform us in writing that you consent to avail of this information/service.

3.3 Interest Rates

We will give you information on.

(a) the interest rates which apply to your accounts, both deposit and loan. *(b)* when we will pay interest

on your deposits, or charge interest on your loan accounts. *(c)* how we apply interest to your account and method of calculation of interest.

Changes in Interest Rates

We will inform you when we charge interest rates on our products.

3.4 Tariff Schedules Fees and Charges

(a) We will display in our branches: *(i)* a notice about the tariff schedule and that you can ask to see this free of cost; *(ii)* a list of services which are rendered free or charge. *(iii)* A notice incorporating charges leviable for nonmaintenance of minimum balances in the savings bank account, collection of outstation cheques, issue of demand draft and cheque books, account statement, account closure and charges for deposit/withdrawal at ATM locations. *(b)* We will give you details in ourt tariff schedule of any charges applicable to the products and services chosen by you. *(c)* We will also provide you information about the penalties liable in case of non-observance/violation of any of the terms and conditions governing the product/ services chosen by you.

Changes in Fees and Charges

If we increase any of these charges or introduce a new charge, it will be notified one month prior to the revised charges being levied/becoming effective.

3.5 Terms and Conditions

(a) When you become a customer or avail of a product/service for the first time, we will advise you the relevant terms and conditions for the service you have asked us to provide. *(b)* All terms and conditions will be fair and will set out respective rights especially with regard to nomination facility and liabilities and obligations clearly and as far as possible in plain and simple language.

Changes to Terms and Conditions

(a) When you become a customer, we will tell you of changes to terms and conditions through any of the following channels: *(i)* Account statements/pass book *(ii)* ATMS *(iii)* Notice board at each branch *(iv)* Internet, including, e-mail and website *(v)* Newspaper, *(b)* Normally changes will be made with prospective effect giving notice of one month. *(c)* If we have made any change without notice and we will notify the change within 30 days. If such change is to your disadvantage, you may within 60 days and without notice does your account or switch it without having to pay any extra charges or interest. *(d)* If we have made a major change or a lot of minor changes in any one year, we will on request give you a copy of the new terms and conditions or a summary of the changes.

4. ADVERTISING, MARKETING AND SALES

(a) We will make sure that all advertising and promotional material is clear, and not misleading. *(b)* In any advertising in any media and promotional literature that draws attention to a banking service or product and includes a reference to an interest rate, we will also indicate whether other less and charges will apply and that full details of the relevant terms and conditions are available on request. *(c)* If we avail of the services of third parties support services, we will require that such third parties handle your personal information (if an available to such third parties) with the same degree of confidentiality and security as we would. *(d)* We may, from time-to-time, communicate to you various features of our products availed by you. Information about our other products or promotional offers in respect of our products/service, will be conveyed to you only if you have given your consent to receive such information/services either by mail or by registering to the same on our website or on our phone banking/customer service number. *(e)* We have prescribed a code of conduct for our Direct Selling Agencies (DSA) whose services we may avail to market our products/services which amongst other matters requires then to identify themselves when they approach you for selling our products

personally or through phone. *(f)* In the event of recent of any complaint from you that our representative/ courier or DSA has engaged in any in proper conduct or acted in violation of the code, we shall take appropriate steps to investigate and to handle the complaint and to make good the loss.

5. PRIVACY AND CONFIDENTIALITY

We will treat all your personal information as private and confidential (even when you are no longer a customer), and shall be guided by the following principles and policies. We will not reveal information or data relating to your accounts, whether provided by you or otherwise, to anyone, including other companies entities in our group, other than in the following exceptional cases. *(a)* If we have to give the information by law *(b)* If there is a duty towards the public to reveal the information. *(c)* If our interests require us to give the information (for example, to provident fund) but we will not use this as a reason by giving information about you or your accounts (including your name and address) to anyone else, including other companies in our group, for marketing purposes *(d)* If you ask us to reveal the information, or if we have your permission *(e)* If we are asked to give a banker's reference about you, we will need your written permission before we get it. *(f)* We will explain to you the extent of your rights under the existing legal framework for accessing the personal records that we hold about you, *(g)* We will not use your personal information for marketing purposes by anyone including ourselves unless you specifically authorise us to do so.

5.1 Credit Reference Agencies

(a) When you open your account, we will tell you when we pass your account details to credit reference agencies and the checks we may make with them. *(b)* We may give information to credit reference agencies about the personal debts you owe us; *(i)* You have fallen behind with your payments; *(ii)* The amount owed is not in dispute; and *(iii)* You have not made proposals we are satisfied with for repaying your debt, following our formal demand; *(c)* In these cases, we will initiate you in willing that we plan to give information about the debts you owe us to credit reference agencies. At the same time, we will explain to you the role of credit reference agencies and the effect the information they provide can have on your ability to get credit. *(d)* We may give credit reference agencies other information about the day-to-day running of your account. If you have given us your permission to do so. *(e)* We will provide you with a copy of the information that we have given to the credit reference agencies about you, or provide their lead lets that explain how credit referencing works.

6. COLLECTION OF DUES

Whenever we give loans, we will explain to you the repayment process by way of amount, tenure and periodicity of repayment. However, if you do not adhere to repayment schedule, a defined process in accountance withe the laws of the land will be followed for recovery of dues. The process will involve reminding you by sending you notice by making personal visits and/or repossession of security if any.

Our collection policy is built on courtesy, fair treatment and persuasion. We believe in fostering customer and long-term relationship. Our staff or any person authorised to represent us in collection of dues or/and security repossession will identify himself/herself and display the authority letter issued by us and upon request display(ing) to you his/her identity card issued by the bank or under authority of the banks. We will provide you with all the information regarding dues and will endeavour to give sufficient notice to payment of dues.

All the matters of the staff or any person authorised to represent our bank in collection or/and security repossession would follow the guidelines set out below:

(a) You will be contacted ordinarily at the place of your choice and in the absence of any specified place at the place of your residence and if unavailable at your residence, at the place of busir ess/occupation. *(b)* Identity and authority to represent would be made known to you at the first instance. *(c)* Your privacy

would be respected. *(d)* Interaction with you would be in a civil manner. *(e)* Normally, our representative will contact you between 0700 hrs and 1900 hrs, unless the special circumstances of your business or occupation require otherwise. *(f)* Your requests to avoid calls at a particular time or at a particular place would be honoured as far as possible. *(g)* Time and number of calls and contents of conversation would be documented. *(h)* All assistance would be given to resolve disputes or differences regarding dues in a mutually acceptable and in an orderly manner. *(i)* During visits to your place for dues collection, decency and decorum would be maintained. *(j)* Inappropriate occasions such as bereavement in the family or such other calamitous occasions would be avoided for making calls/visits to collect dues.

6.1 Security Repossession Policy Statement

We will know a security repossession policy in consonance with the law. A copy of the policy will be made available on request.

7. COMPLAINTS, GRIEVANCES AND FEEDBACK

7.1 Internal Procedures

(a) If you want to make a complaint, we will tell you. *(b)* How to do this *(i)* Where a complaint can be made *(ii)* How a complaint should be made *(iii)* When to expect a reply *(iv)* Whom to approach for redressal *(v)* What to do if you are not happy about the outcome. *(vi)* Our staff will help you with any questions you have. *(c)* When you become a customer, we will tell you when to find details of our procedure for handling complaints fairly and quickly. *(d)* If your complaint has been received in writing, we will endeavour to send you an acknowledgement/a response within a week. If your complaint is relayed over phone at our designated telephone helpdesk or customer-service number we shall provide you a complaint reference number and keep you informed of the progress within a reasonable period of time. *(e)* After examining the matter, we will send you our final response or explain why we need more time to respond and shall endeavour to do so within six weeks of receipt of your complaint and will led you how to take your complaint further if you are still not satisfied.

7.2 Banking Ombudsman Service

(a) We will display on our website and all our branches a notice explaining that we are covered by the Banking Ombudman Scheme, 2006 of the Reserve Bank of India. Copy will be made available on request at a nominal charge. *(b)* Within 30 days of lodging a complaint with us. If you do not get a satisfactory response from us and you wish to pursue other avenues for redressal of grievances, you may approach Banking Ombudsman appointed by the Reserve Bank of India under Banking Ombudsman Scheme, 2006. Salient features of the Banking Ombudsman Scheme are displayed in the branch notice boards and the scheme itself is displayed on our website. Our staff would explain the procedure in this regard.

8. PRODUCTS AND SERVICES

8.1 Deposit Accounts

You may open different type of accounts with us such as, savings accounts, term deposits, current accounts including 'No Frills' Account, etc., with us. You may open such accounts in the following styles:

(i) Single, *(ii)* Joint, *(iii)* Joint (Either or Survival) *(iv)* Joint (Former or Survivor), *(v)* Joint (Latter or suvivor), *(vi)* Or in many other style. The above may be operated by you with or without nomination facility. We will explain the implications of the foregoing accounts as also the nomination facilities at the time of opening of the account.

We will also inform you about liquid deposit facility, sweep account and similar types of products offered by us and their implications and procedures involved at the time of opening the account.

Account Opening and Operation of Deposit Accounts Before Opening any Deposit Account, We Will

(a) Carry-out due diligence as required under "Know Your Customer" (KYC) guidelines of the bank. *(b)* ask you to submit or provide necessary documents or proofs to do so. *(c)* obtain only such information to meet with or KYC, Anti-money Laundering or any other statutory requirements. In case any additional information is asked for, it will be sought separately and we will specify the objective of obtain such additional information. Providing such information will be voluntary *(d)* Provide the account opening forms and other materials to you. The same will contain details of essential information required to be furnished and documents to be produced for verification and/or for record for meeting the KYC requirements. *(e)* explain the procedural formalities and provide necessary clarification sought by you while opening a deposit account, f. at the time of opening of the account, make available to you the details of the insurance cover in force under the instance scheme, subject to certain limits and conditions offered by the Deposit Insurance and Credit Guarantee Corporation of India (DIGC).

Changing Your Account

(a) If you are not happy about your choice of current or savings account (except for term deposit account) within 14 days of making your first payment into the account, we will help you switch to another of our accounts or we will give your money back with any interest it may have earned. We will ignore any notice period and any extra charges. *(b)* If you decide to close your current/savings account we will close your account within five working days of receiving your instructions. *(c)* If you want to transfer your account to another branch of our bank we will do so. Your account at the new branch will be opernationalised within two weeks of receiving your request, subject to your complying within the required KYC formalities at the new branch. We will intimate you as soon as the account is on your standing instructions/direct details if any. *(d)* We will cancel any bank charges you would have to pay as a result of any mistake or unnecessary delay by us when you transfer your account to or from us.

8.1.1 Savings/Current Accounts

When you Open a Deposit Account, We Will

(a) Inform you about number of transactions, cash withdrawals, etc., that can be done free of charge within a given period. *(b)* inform you about the kind of charges, if any, in case of exceeding such limits. Details of the charges will be included in the tariff schedule. *(c)* inform you of the rate at which interest is paid on your savings deposits, how it is calculated and its periodicity.

Minimum Balance

The minimum balance to be maintained in the savings bank account will be displayed in our branches. For deposit products like savings bank account and current account or any other type of deposit account, we will inform you.

(a) About minimum balances to be maintained as part of terms and conditions governing operation of such accounts; *(b)* about charges which will be levied in case of failure to maintain minimum balance in the account by you. Details of the cheques will be included in the tariff schedule.

Charges

Specific charges for issue of cheque books, additional/duplicate statement of accounts, duplicate pass book, copies of paid cheques, folio charges debit card. ATM card, verification of signature, return of cheques for insufficient balance, change in mandate or style of accountent, etc., will be included in our tariff schedule. Concessions of relief given facts (such as perpetual waiver of renewal fee lifetime credit cards) will not be withdrawn during the original validity period of the concession relief.

Statements

(a) To help you manage your account and check entries in it, we will have a monthly statement of account, unless this is of appropriate for the type of account you have (like an account where you have a

pass book), *(b)* You can ask to provide you with account statements more often than is normally available on your type of account, at a charge. This charge will be indicated in the tariff schedule, *(c)* You will be able to see your last few transactions at the counter. You will also be able to see the transactions on ATM or through your internet account wherever such facilities are available with us. *(d)* We will also send you statement of accounts by e-mail, or through our secure internet service, if you so desire, provided we have such facility with us.

8.1.2 Term Deposits

Premature Withdrawal of Term Deposit

We will: *(a)* inform you the procedure for withdrawal of term deposit before maturity; *(b)* disclose the interest rates policy for premature withdrawal of term deposit.

Renewal Withdrawal of Term Deposit

We will tell you the interest rate applicable in case you renew the deposits after the date of maturity.

Advances Against Deposits

We will explain facility of loan/overdrafts available against term deposits.

8.1.3 'No Frills' Account

We will make available a basic banking 'No Frills' Account either with 'nil' or very low minimum balances. The charges applicable for various services/products in such an account will be indicated in separate tariff schedule. The nature and number of transactions in such accounts may be restricted which will be made known to you at the time of opening of the account a transparent manner.

8.1.4 Accounts of Minors

We will tell you if enquired how a minor can open a Deposit Account and how it can be operated.

8.1.5 Special Accounts

We will make our best effects to make it easy and convenient for our special customers like senior citizens, physically challenged persons and illiterate persons to bank with us. This will include making convenient policies, products and services for such applicants and customers. We will inform the procedure for opening of the account and the terms and conditions to blind/ offer physically challenged persons provided he/she call on the bank personally along with a witness who is known to both such person and the bank.

Normally no cheque book facility is provided to illiterate persons and blind persons. However, to meet periodic repayment of retail loans, utility bills, etc., we will consider issuing of cheque book with safeguards to protect your interest.

8.1.6 Dormant/Inoperative Accounts

We will: *(a)* tell you when you open your accounts, what period of inoperation of the account would render your account being classified as dormant/ inoperative account. You will also be informed three months before your account is classified as dormant, inoperative of treated as unclaimed account and the consequences including the charges for reactiviation thereof as per the tariff schedule *(b)* tell you the procedure to be followed if you want to activate the account.

8.1.7 Closing Your Account

Under normal circumstances, we will not close your account without giving you at least 30 days notice. Examples of circumstances, which are not 'normal' include improper conduct of account, etc. In all such cases, you will be required to make alternate arrangements to cheques already issued by you and desist from issuing any fresh cheques on such account.

8.2 Clearing Cycle/Collection Services

We will: *(a)* tell you about the clearing cycle for local instruments and the outstation instruments including details such as when you can withdraw money after lodging collection instruments and when you will be entitled to earn delayed interest as per our cheque collection policy, *(b)* provide details, if we offer immediate credit for outstation cheques, including the applicable terms and conditions, such as the limit to which instruments tendered by you can be credited operating accounts satisfactorily, etc. *(c)* proceed as per our cheque collection policy and provide all assistance for you to obtain a duplicate cheque/instrument in case a cheque instrument tendered by you lost in transit, *(d)* give the above information when your account and whenever you ask us. If there is any change in our policy the revised policy will be displayed on our website and at all our branches.

8.3 Cash Transactions

We will accept cheques/cash and dispense cash at counters wherever your account is maintained. We will exchange soiled/multilated notes and/or small coins at such of our branches as per RBI Directives.

For transactions above a specified amount we may require you to furnish your PAN Number.

8.3.1 Direct debts and Standing Instructions

We will: *(a)* at the time of opening the account tell you how direct debits/standing instructions work and how you may record/cancel them and the charges connected with them. Charges will be levied *(b)* act upon mandates given by you for direct details (say Electronic Clearing Services) (ECS) and other standing instructions. In case of any delay or failure in executing the mandate resulting in financial loss or additional cost, we will compensate as per the compensation policy of the bank. If the mandate cannot be executed due to insufficient balance in your account, we will levy charges as per the tariff schedule as amended from time-to-time; *(c)* Send a remittance advice to the efficient of the remittance at the time of making the remittance in case of Electronic Clearing Service (ECS) when we act as an agent of the remitter; *(d)* Refund your account with interest as soon as it is determined that it is unauthorisedly/erroneously debited from your account under a direct debit and compensate you as per the compensation policy of the bank.

8.4 Stop Payment Facility

We will: *(a)* Accept stop payment instruction from you in respect of cheques issued by you. Immediately on receipt of your instructions we will give a aknowledgement and take action provided these cheques have not already been cleared by us; *(b)* levy charges, if any, and the same will be included in the tariff schedule as amended from time-to-time; *(c)* In case, a cheque has been paid after stop payment instructions are acknowledged, we will reimburse and compensate you as per the compensation policy of the bank.

8.5 Cheques/Debit Instructions Issued by You

We will: *(a)* Keep original cheques/debit instructions paid from your account or copies or images of the same, for such periods as required by law; *(b)* Give you the cheque/debit instruction or a copy thereof as evidence as long as records are available with us. If there is a dispute about a cheque paid/debit instructions from your account, in case the request is made within a period of one year, no charge will be levied and beyond a period of one year charges will be levied as per the tariff schedule, *(c)* Tell you how we will deal with unpaid cheques and out-of-date (stale) cheques. We will charge for the cheques returned unpaid for want of balance in the account. The details of changes to be levied will be included in the tariff schedule as amended from time-to-time.

8.6 Branch Closure Shifting

If we plan to close our branch or if we move our branch, we will give you, *(a)* Notice of three months if there is no other branch of any bank functioning at your centre and inform you how we will continue to provide banking services to you; *(b)* Notice of two months, if there is a branch of any other bank functioning at your centre.

8.7 Settlement of Claims in Respect of Deceased Accountholders

8.7.1 We will follow a simplified procedure for settlement of accounts of deceased accountholders

(a) Accounts with survivor/nominee clause

In case of a deposit account of a deceased depositor where the deposits had utilised the nomination facility and made a valid nomination or where the account was opened with the survivorship clause ("either or suvivor", or "anyone or survivor" of "former or survivor"), the payment of the balance in the deposit account to the survivors (s) nominee of a deceased deposit accountholder will be made provided: *(i)* the identity of the survivor(s)/nominee(s) and the fact of the death of the accountholder, is established through appropriate documentary evidence; *(ii)* there is no order from the competent court restraining the bank from making the payment from the account of the deceased; and *(iii)* it has been made clear to the survivor(s)/ nominee that he would be receiving the payment from the bank as a trustees of the legal heirs of the deceased depositor, (i.e., such payment to him shall not affect the right or claim with any person may have against the survivor(s) nominee to whom the payments is made.

The payment made to the survivor(s)/nominee, subject to the foregoing conditions, would constitute a full discharge of the banks. In such cases, payment to the survivor(s)/nominee of the deceased depositors will be made without insisting on production of succession certificate letter of administrator or probate, etc., or obtaining any bond of identity or surety from the survivor(s)/nominee, irrespective of the amount standing at the end of the deceased accountholder.

(b) Accounts without the survivor/nominee clause

In case where the deceased deposit had not made any nomination or for the accounts other than those styled as "either or survivor" (such as single or jointly operated accounts), we will adopt a simplified procedure for repayment to legal heir(s) of the depositor keeping in view the imperative need to avoid inconvenience and undue hardship to the common person, keeping in view our risk management system, we will fix a minimum freehold limit, for the balance in the account of the deceased depositors, up to which claims in respect of the deceased depositors could be settled without insisting on production of any documentation other than a letter of identity.

(c) Premature termination of term deposit accounts

In the case of term deposits, we will incorporate a clause in the account opening form itself to the effect that in the event of the death of the depositor, premature termination of term deposits would be allowed. The conditions subject to which such premature withdrawal would be permitted would also be specified in the account opening form. Such premature withdrawal would not attract any penal charge.

(d) Treatment of flows in the name of the deceased depositor

In order to avoid hardship to the survivor(s)/nominee of deposit account, we will obtain appropriate agreement/authorisation from the survivor(s)/nominee with regard to the treatment of pipeline flow in the name of the deceased accountholders. In this regard, we will consider adopting either of the knowing two approaches:

(i) We could be authorised by the survivor(s)/nominee of a deceased accountholder to open an account styled as Estate of Shri ______________ the Deceased where all the pipeline flows in the name of the deceased accountholder could be allowed to be credited, provided no withdrawals are made.

OR *(ii)* We could be authorised by the survivor(s)/ nominee to return the pipeline flows to the remitter with the remark "Accountholder deceased" and to initiate the survivor(s)/nominee accordingly. The survivor(s)/nominee/legal heir(s) could then approach the remitter to effect payment through a negotiable or through ECS transfer in the name of the appropriate beneficiary.

8.7.2 Time Limit for Settlement of Claims

We will endeavour to settle the claim in respect of ceased depositors and release payments to survivor(s)/ nomimee(s) within a period not exceeding 15 days from the date of receipt of the claim subject to the production of proof of death of the depositor and suitable identification of the claim(s) to the bank's satisfaction.

8.8 Safe Deposit LockeRs

We will give you the complete details of the rules and the procedures applicable to the safe deposit lockers and also safe deposit of valuables, in case we offer the service.

8.9 Foreign Exchange Services

(a) When you buy or sell foreign exchange, we will give you information on the services, details of the exchange rate and other charges which apply to foreign exchange transactions, if this is not possible, we will tell you how these will be worked without. *(b)* If you want to transfer money abroad, we will tell how to do this and will give you; *(i)* A description of the services and how to use then; *(ii)* Details of when the money you have sent abroad should get there and the reasons for delays, if any; *(iii)* the exchange rate applied when converting to the foreign currency (if this is not possible at the time of the transaction, we will let you know later what is the rate is); *(iv)* Details of any commission or charges, which you will have to pay and a warning that the person receiving the money may also, have to pay the foreign bank's charges; *(v)* We will tell you the information provided by you for making payment abroad is adequate or not. In case of any discrepancies or incomplete documentation, we will advise you immediately and assist you to rectify/complete the same; *(vi)* If money is transferred to your bank account from abroad, we will tell you the original amount received and charges, if any levied. If the sender has agreed to pay all charges, we will not take any charges which we pay the money into your account; *(vii)* We will guide you about regulatory requirements or conditions relating to foreign exchange services offered by us as and when requested by you; *(viii)* In case of delay beyond the day when the amount is due for credit, you will be compensated *(a)* for any loss on account of interest for due period beyond the due date, and *(b)* also for adverse movement of forex rate as per the compensation policy of the bank, *(ix)* All certificates required to be issued under regulatory/statutory instructions will be issued free of charge.

8.10 Remittances Within India

If you want to remit money within India we will inform you how to effect and will.

(a) Give description of services and how to use them, *(b)* suggest to you the best way to send the money to suit your needs, *(c)* disclose the details of all charges including commission that you will have to pay for the service as per the tariff schedule as amended from time-to-time.

8.11 Lending

Before we lend you any money or increase your overdraft, credit card limit or other borrowing, we will assess whether you will be able to repay it.

If we cannot help you, we will communicate in writing the reason(s) for rejection where the amount of loan applied for does not exceed ₹ 2 lakh. If you want us to accept a guarantee or other security from someone for your liabilities, we may ask you for your permission to give confidential information about your finances to the person giving the guarantee or other security, or to their legal adviser. We will also; *(a)* encourage them to take independent legal advice to make sure that they understand their commitment and the possible consequences of their decision (where appropriate, the documents we ask them to sign will contain this recommendation as a clear and obvious notice); *(b)* tell them that by giving the guarantee or other security they may become liable instead of, or as well as, you, and *(c)* tell them what their liability will be.

8.11.1 Loan Products

Application for loans and their processing; *(a)* At the time of sourcing a loan product, we will provide information about the interest rates applicable, as also the fees/charges, if any payable for processing, pre-payment options and charges, if any and any other matter which affects the interest of the borrowers, so that a meaningful comparison with those of other banks can be made and informed decision can be taken by you; *(b)* Normally, all particulars required for processing the loan application will be collected by us at the time of application. In case we need any additional information we will contact you immediately; *(c)* We will convey you the credit limit along with the terms and conditions thereof; *(d)* We will supply authenticated copies of the loan documents executed by you at our cost along with a copy of each of all enclosures quoted in the loan document on request; *(e)* We will not discriminate on grounds of sex, caste and religion in the matter of lending. However, this does not prelude us from instituting or participating in schemes framed for different sections of the society; *(f)* We will process the request for transfer of borrowal account, either from the borrower or from a bank/financial institution, in the normal course.

8.12 Guarantee

Where you are considering to be a guarantor to a loan, we will tell you about: *(a)* your liability as guarantee; *(b)* the amount of liability you will be committing yourself to the bank; *(c)* circumstances in which we will call on you to pay up your liability; *(d)* whether we have recourse to you other monies in the bank if you fail to pay up as a guarantor; *(e)* whether your liabilities as a guarantor are limited to a specific quantum or are they unlimited; and *(f)* time and circumstances in which your liabilities as a guarantor will be discharged as also the manner in which we will notify you about this. We will keep you informed of any material adverse changes in the finance position of the borrower to whom you stand as a guarantor.

8.13 General Information

We will; *(a)* Give you information explaining the key feature of our loan and credit card products including applicable fees and charges while communicating the sanction of the loan/credit card; *(b)* Advise you what information/documentation, we need from you to enable you to apply. We will also advise you what documentation we need from you with respect to your identity, address, employment, etc., and any other document that may be stipulated by statutory authorities, (e.g., PAN details), in order to comply with legal and regulatory requirements; *(c)* Verify the details mentioned by you in the credit card application by contracting you at your residence and/or on business telephone numbers and/or physically visiting your residence and/or business address through agencies appointed by us for this purpose. if demand necessary by us; *(d)* If the other you want an overdraft, or an increase in your existing overdraft limit, we will tell you if your overdraft is repayable on demand or otherwise. We will also required advise about the method of calculation of overdrawn amount thereof and also the computation of interest on overdue loan amount.

8.14 Credit Card

8.14.1 General Information

(a) While you apply for card, we will explain the relevant terms and conditions such as fees and interest charges, billing and payment; method of computation of overdues renewal and termination procedures, and any other information that you may require about the card; *(b)* We will advise you of our targeted turnaround time while you are availing/applying for a produced/service; *(c)* We will send a service guide/member booklet giving detailed terms and conditions, losses on your account that you may be liable, if your card is lost/misused and other relevant information with respect to usage of your card along with your first card; *(d)* If you do not recognise a transaction, which appears on your card statement, we will give you more details you ask us. In cases, where we do not accept your contention we will give you evidence that you had authorised the transaction in question.

8.14.2 Insurance of Credit Card/PIN

(a) We will dispatch your credit card/PIN only to the mailing address mentioned by you or to the alternate address provided by you (if we are unable to deliver at the mailing address) through courier/post. Alternatively, if you desire we shall deliver your credit card/PIN at our branches after due identification. *(b)* We may also issue deactivated (not ready to use) credit card if we consider your profile appropriate for issuing credit card and such deactivated card will become active only after you take steps for activation as required and subject to such other conditions as may be specified. *(c)* We will extend a loan/credit facility/ enhance credit limit on your card only with your consent. *(d)* PIN (personal identification number) whenever alloted will be sent to you separately at your mailing address.

8.14.3 Credit Card Statements

(a) To help you manage your credit card account and check details of purchases/cash drawings using the credit card, we will offer you free of cost a facility to receive credit transaction details either via monthly mail and, if you so desire also through the internet. Credit card statement will be dispatched on a predetermined date of every month free of cost at your mailing address. *(b)* In the event of non-receipt of this information, we expect you to get in touch with us so that we can arrange to resend the details to enable you to make the payment and highlight exception, if any in a timely manner. *(c)* We will let you know/notify changes in schedule of fees and charges and terms and conditions. Normally, changes (other than interest rates and those which are a result of regulatory requirements) will be made with prospective effect giving notice of at least one month. The changes will be notified along with the monthly statement of account or copy thereof.

9. PROTECTING YOUR ACCOUNTS

9.1 Secure and Reliable Banking and Payment Systems

We will cooperate as an industry so that you enjoy secure and reliable banking and payment systems you can trust. We will install CCTV for close survelliance as part of security arrangements.

9.2 Keeping Up To Date

Please make sure you let us know as soon as possible when you change your: *(a)* Name, *(b)* Address; *(c)* Phone number; or *(d)* E-mail address (if this is how we communicate with you).

9.3 Checking Your Account

(a) We recommend that you check your statement or pass book regularly. If there is an entry which to be wrong, you should tell us as soon as possible so that we can investigate the same. Regular checks on direct debts and standing orders will help you to sure the money is going where you want to; *(b)* If we need to investigate a transaction on your account, you should cooperate with us and with the police other investigative agencies if we need to involve them.

9.4 Taking Care

The care of your cheques, pass book, cards, PINs and other security/information you, is essential to help prevent fraud and protect your accounts. Please make sure that you follow the active given below:

(a) Do not: *(i)* keep your cheque book and cards together, *(ii)* keep the blank cheque leaves signed, *(iii)* allow anyone else to use your card, PIN, password or other security information, *(iv)* write down or record you PIN, password or other security information, *(v)* give your account details password or other security information to anyone.

(b) Always: *(i)* write clearly the name of the person you are paying the cheques to if you send cheque through the post, it will help to prevent fraud. We will recommend that you write such cheques for instance with carbon, *(ii)* paper on the reverse to avoid chemical alternations; *(iii)* choose your new PIN carefully, if

you change your PIN, *(iv)* memorise your PIN, password and other security information, and destroy the written communication if any of the same as soon as you receive it, *(v)* take reasonable steps to keep your card safe in your personal custody and your PIN, password and other security information secret at all times, *(vi)* keep your card receipts safe and dispose them of carefully, *(vii)* write on the cheques the name of the accountholder (ABC Bank Account - XYZ), if you are paying a cheque into a bank account. You should draw a line through unused space on the cheques so unauthorised person, cannot add extra numbers or names.

(c) We will advise you what you can do to protect your card/cheque book, from misuse.

(d) In the event your cheque book, pass book or ATM/Debit card has been lost or stolen, or that someone else knows your PIN or other security information, we will, on your notifying us, take immediate steps to try to prevent these from being misused.

(e) It is essential that you feel as soon as you can if you suspect or discover that your cheque book, pass book, card has been lost or stolen or someone else knows your PIN, password or other security information.

(f) You could tell us about the loss by phone at our 24 hour toll free number given to you and send us written confirmation to that effect immediately. Alternatively, you may advise us by e-mail to the address we have given you for this purpose.

(g) You may be liable for misuses until the line that we have been notified.

9.5 Internet Banking

Online banking is safe and convenient as long as you take a number of simple precautions. Please make sure you follow the advise given below: *(a)* Visit our internet banking site directly. Avoid accessing the sale through a link from another site or an e-mail and verify the domain name displayed to avoid spool websites. *(b)* Ignore any e-mail asking for your password or PIN and inform us of the same to us to investigate the same. Neither the police nor we will ever contact you to ask you to reveal your online or payment card PINs, or your password information. *(c)* We advise you not to use cyber cafes/shared PCs to access our Internet banking site. *(d)* We advise you to up date your PC with latest anti-virus and spy ware software regularly. You may install security programmes to protect against hackers, virus attacks or malicious, 'Torian Horse' programmes. A suitable firewall installed in a computer to protect your PC and its contents from outsiders on the internet is recommonded *(e)* Disable the "File and Printing Sharing" features on your operating system. *(f)* Log off your PC when not using. *(g)* Do not store your ID/PIN in the Internet Export Browser. *(h)* Check your account and transaction history regularly *(i)* Follow our advice — our websites are usually a good place to get help and guidance on how to stay safe online..

9.6 Cancelling Payments

If you want to cancel a payment or series of payments you have authorised, you should do the following: *(a)* To stop payment of a cheques or cancel standing instruction given of a direct debt you must left us in writing. *(b)* To cancel a direct debt you inform us. We recommended that you inform the originator of the direct debit also. *(c)* It may not be possible to cancel payments if you do not give notice of your decision to cancel. *(d)* Cancellation of credit card payments will be subject to other terms and conditions as may be stipulated.

9.7 Liability for Losses

(a) If you act fraudulently, you will be responsible for all losses on your account. If you act without reasonable care, and this causes losses, you may be responsible for them. *(b)* Unless you have acted fraudulently or without reasonable case, your liability for the misuse of your card will be limited to the amount stipulated in the terms and conditions governing the issue of the card. *(c)* You may be liable for misuses on account of loss of your PIN or compromise of your password or of other secured information until the time that we have been notified and we have taken steps to payment issue.

10. MONITORING

The Banking Codes and Standards Board of India whose directors include members of the Governing Council monitor the code. The contact details are as follows:

The Bankng Codes and Standards Board of India

Reserve Bank of India Building, C-7, 4th floor, Bandra-Kurla Complex,
Mumbai-400 051.
Telephone: 26573716; Fax: 26573719
E-mail: ceo.bcsbi@rbi.org.in; Website www.bcsbi.org.in

11. GETTING HELP

If you have any enquiries about the code, you should contact us at our designated telephone help-desk or customer-service number or contact the Indian Banks' Association at the following address:

Indian Banks' Association

Stadium House, Block II and III, Veer Nariman Road, Mumbai-400 020.

Tel No. 022-22844999 Fax: 022-2283538

E-mail: ibastadium@vsnl.net

Website: www.iba.org.in<chttp://www.lba.org.in.

Or, contact the Banking Code/Codes and Standard Board of India at the address above.

11.1 We will have notices in all our branches and on our website explaining that copies of the code are available and how you can get one and that we will make a copy available to you on request.

12. REVIEW OF THE CODE

The code will be reviewed within a period of three years. The review will be undertaken in a transparent manner.

Appendix XVII

CONSUMER PROTECTION ACT, 1986 AND BANKING SECTOR

Social and economic justice is enshrined in the Constitution of India, of which consumer justice and protection is also a part. Towards this end, a number of legislations were passed by the Indian Parliament, *viz.*, Drugs (Control) Act, 1950, prevention of Food Adulteration Act, 1954, Essential Commodities Act,1968, Trade and Merchandise Marks Act, 1958, MRTP Act, 1969, etc. But these enactments failed to protect the interest of small consumers. The procedures under these enactments are cumbersome and litigations time-consuming and costly.

Meanwhile, the United Nations General Assembly passed a Resolution No. 39/248 dated 09.04.1985 adopting guidelines relating to consumer protection. These guidelines provided a framework for the government, particularly of developing countries for formulation of consumer protection policies and legislation.

In the above background, the Indian Parliament passed the Consumer Protection Act, 1986, as the name suggest to protect the interest of the consumers and to provide them a mechanism for easy, quick and cheap redressal of grievances against the mighty and unscrupulous producers, traders and service providers.

Consumer Protection Act, 1986

Following three-tier quasi-judicial machinery has been provided under the Act to deal with consumer complaints —

(a) District Forum – It operates at the district level and deals with consumer complaints pertaining to the value of goods or services and compensation not exceeding ₹ 20 lakh.

(b) State Commission – It operates at the state level and deals with complaints of the value exceeding ₹ 20 lakh but not exceeding ₹ 1 crore. It also hears appeals against the orders of the district forum.

(c) National Commission – It functions at the national level for the complaints of the value exceeding ₹ 1 crore and hears appeals against the orders of the State Commission.

Complaints in relation to any goods or services may be preferred before the above-mentioned for by the consumer himself or by any recognised consumer association where the consumer is a member or where there are a number of consumers having the same interest, one or more consumers on behalf or for the benefit of all the consumers so interested. Complaints may also be prefered by the the State Government.

As per Section 2 (1) (c), of the Act, following may form the subject matter of the complaint –

1. an unfair trade practice or a restrictive trade practice adopted by any trader;
2. defects in the goods purchased;
3. deficiency in the service;
4. overcharging of price;

In the context of the subject matter, it is important to note two important definitions given in the Act.

"Service" [Section 2(1) (o)] has been defined in the Act to mean service of description and includes the provision of facilities in connection with banking, financing, insurance, transport, processing, supply of electrical on other energy, etc., but does not include any service which is rendered free of charge or is under a contract of personal service.

Applicability of the Act.: "Consumer", according to Section 2 (1) (d) of the Act, includes a person who hires or avails of any service for a consideration. Thus, a customer of a bank who has a bank account with the bank or a person who purchases a bank draft, hires locker facility or objains bank garantee from a bank or all consumers can prefer complaints under the Act for 'deficiency in service' on the part of the bank or for 'restrictive trade practice' or 'unfair trade practice' adopted by the banks.

Examples

(1) *Vimal Chandra Gover vs. Bank of India* [2000 (2) CPJ 11 (SC): AIR 2000 SC 2181], it was argued before the Supreme Court on behalf of the bank that the appellant, who took overdraft facility from the bank by pledging shares, is not a consumer within the meaning of the Consumer Protection Act.

Supreme Court repelled the arguments of the bank and held that the bank is rendering service by providing overdraft facilities to a consumer, which is not without consideration. Bank is charging interest and other charges as well in providing the service. Provision for overdraft facility is certainly a part of banking and falls within the meaning of 'service' as provided in Section 2 (1) (o) of the Act.

(2) *Punjab and Sind Bank* vs. *Manpreet Singh* [1994(3) CPJ 532].

It was held by the Punjab State Commission that a savings bank accountholder is a consumer in the Act. It was observed that difference in the lending and borrowing rates is the consideration for rendering service by the bank. It was also deserved that even if the bank does not charge for providing cheque facility to the accountholder, it cannot be said that the same is given without consideration. Actually, the cheque book facility is obtained by the depositor in consideration of his putting funds at the disposal of the bank.

(3) *Shobhatai Daulatrao Talekar vs. Maharashtra Raja Shahakari Krishi and Gramin Development Bank* [2004(2)] CPJ 349].

The issue before the Maharashtra State Commission was the justifiability of the order of the district forum holding that the forum had no jurisdiction to entertain the dispute since the complainant was a member of the defendent bank which was registered under the Maharashtra Cooperative Societies Act, 1961 and that being so, the jurisdiction would lay before the cooperative court and not before the consumer court.

The State Commission did not agree with this view. It held that the nature of service hired by the complainant pertains to the banking business which is permissible by the bank to undertake under the provisions of the Reserve Bank of India Act and the Banking Regulation Act, 1949 and as such, would be squarely amenable to the jurisdiction of a consumer fora as per definition of 'service' under Section 2(1) (o) of the Act. The State Commission further held that the jurisdiction of the consumer fora is also not ousted in view of the provisions of Section 3 of the Act, which provides an additional remedy over the above those available in the other statutes to the parties jurisdiction ousted. In certain cases it has been held that Consumer Protection Act does not apply to banks. Some of such specific instances are given below.

Example

1. **Reserve Bank of India [1991 (1) CPJ 336 (NC)].**

A complaint was filed before the National Commission stating that the complainant was eligible for certain advantages in his foreign currency/rupee bank accounts but these facilities were denied by his bankers on the instructions from the RBI. The National Commission held that there was no contract of service between the complainant and the RBI was merely discharging its statutory function. Therefore, it was outside the purview of the Consumer Protection Act.

However, in *T.A. Abrahim vs. RBI* [2001 (3) CPJ 293], RBI also came within the purview of the Consumer Protection Act. The issue before the Kerala State Commission was that the complainant had applied for a loan under the Housing Facility Scheme of the RBI, of which he was an employee. He claimed that he suffered loss and inconvenience due to delay in sanctioning of loan, which amounted to deficiency of service and for which he was entilted to compensation. The disrict forum held that the complaint was not maintainable, but the State Commission before whom appeal was preferred by the complainant, held that availing a loan from an institution like RBI could be treated as 'service' within the meaning of Section 2(1) (o) of the Act as the opposite party's character as a banking institution cannot be in dispute. Further, as per the definition of 'consumer' in Section 2 (1) (d) (ii), it is not necessary that actual consideration should pass to the opposite party simultancously with the availing of service. The said definition envisages the consideration as the one, which is promised also. The State Commission observed that when a person applied for loan and get the loan on sanctioning the same, the amount would carry interest. The same should be treated as consideration.

Example

2. Aspirant to a post: ***IDBI vs. Krishendu Ghosh [1996(2) CPR 155]***

The issue before National Commission was that the complainant applied for the post of Deputy Manager (legal) along with a DD of ₹ 50 as examination fee. The interview letter was received by him on the same day on which the interview was to be held. The bank rejected the request for rescheduling. A complaint was filed claiming compensation for injury and mental shock. The National Commission held that payment of ₹ 50 as examination fee was not consideration for hiring on availing or the services of the bank. Therefore, complainant was not a 'consumer'.

Example

3. Employer-employees dispute. ***D. Yeshodharan vs. Canara Bank*** **[1994(3)CPJ 63].**

A complaint was lodged for denial of service benefits to an employee of the bank. National Commission held that the consumer court is not the correct forum for setting employer-employee dispute as an employee is not a consumer.

Example

4. Tenant landlord dispute:

UCO Bank vs. R. Chimanlal & Co. [1994(1) CPR 526], in a dispute with the bank. Landlord was sought to be settled under the Consumer Protection Act, which was turned down by the Commission.

Deficiency in Service

However, banks were held liable for deficiency in service. In large number of cases, banks have been pulled up for deficiency in service and compensation has been awarded to complainants by consumer courts. Some cases are being given below.

Example

1. ***SBI vs. N. Raveendran Nair.*** **[1992 (2) CPR 400] – Wrongful dishonour of bank draft.**

The issue before the National Commission was that the bank refused to encash the demand draft on the ground that the signature of one of the two officials of the bank was missing. The State Commission held that the dishonour of the draft was due to the fault of the bank and therefore, there was deficiency in service and mental agony caused. The National Commission dismissed the appeal of the bank against the judgment of the State Commission.

Example

2. ***Sovintory (India) Ltd., vs. SBI*** **[1999 (2) CPJ 4 (SC)]**

The issue before the Supreme Court was that the proceeds of the cheque deposited with the bank for collection were not credited to the account of the complainant though the same were collected by the bank. The State Commission awarded only interest of 12 per cent for withholding of the customer's money against the complainant's claim of 24 per cent interest and payment of compensation. The National Commission, on appeal by the complainant, confirmed the order of the State Commission. On further appeal before Supreme Court by the complainant, the Apex Court partly allowed the appeal by directing the payment of interest at the rate of 15 per cent but refused the claim of compensation on the ground that the allegation of negligence was not proved.

Example

3. ***Jilla Sahkari Kendriya Bank vs. Sarda Ram Nayak*** **[2004 (2) CPJ 534] Non-issuance of proper recipt.**

Where the bank did not adjust the loan repaid in its books nor issue proper receipt to the complainant, the award of compensation by the District Forum for deficiency in service was confirmed by the Chhattisgarh State Commission in this case.

Example

4. ***Abha Bhanthia vs. SBI*** **[2004(2) CPJ 138] – Payment of lower rate of interest.**

The complainant had made an FD with the bank, which carried interest at the rate of 11.25 per cent as per the receipt issued. On maturity, the bank paid lower interest @ 10.5 per cent. It was stated by the bank that the said rate of interest was the prevailing rate as per the directives of RBI. The District Forum held that there was no deficiency in service by the bank as it followed the RBI directive. On appeal by the complainant, the State Commission held that the bank was obliged and under liability to pay interest as agreed by it and any omission or inadvertence on the part of the bank employees would not adversely affect the rights of the appellant depositor.

Example

5. *UCO Bank vs. Surendra Kumar Bava* [2004(3) CPJ 472]. Default by bank's agent.

The issue before the Orissa State Commission was that the complainant had opened an account with the bank under a scheme called Laghu Bacht Yojna. An agent of the bank used to collect the deposits from the complainant periodically and make entries in the pass book issued by the bank under his initial. The agent of the bank misappropriated a part of the money. The Commission directed the bank to refund the amount misappropriated by its agent along with interest and also to pay compensation for mental agony, harassment and cost of litigation.

Example

6. *SBI vs. P. S. Krishnan* [2004(2) CPJ 579]. Interest not paid on excess amount deposited in violation of Public Provident Fund (PPF) rules.

In a rather interesting case the Tamil Nadu State Commission was asked to adjudicate upon a case where the complainant had deposited a sum of ₹ 8,50,000 in his PPF account during the financial year 1995-96. After a lapse of time, the bank informed the complainant that interest on the PPF account would be given on a total sum of ₹ 60,000 only. The bank returned ₹ 7,90,000 to the depositor without any interest. It was contended on behalf of the bank that the deposits in the PPF account are credited to the government account and do not form the part of the bank's the deposits. As per the rules of the PPF account, the maximum limit of deposit is ₹ 60,000. The bank is bound by the rules and is not liable for the alleged deficiencies in service.

It was held by the commision that the brochure issued by the directorate of small savings dearly stated that the deposits up to ₹ 50,000 will quality for deduction of income tax under Section 88 of the Income Tax Act and the interest on the balance held in the PPF account is absolutely free from tax. The act of bank in retaining a huge sum of ₹ 7,90,000 for nearly a year and returning it without interest is definitely an unjustified act. The commission also held that the banks entrusted with the public money are in a position of bailee and they have to function with caution and care that is expected of a bailee. Even if the complainant was ignorant of the rules, the bank authorities ought to have been more vigilant when such a huge deposit was received by them.

The Commission went to the extent of saying that the banking authorities had gone against the professional ethics in denying the interest, which the complainant was legitimately entitled to. The Commission also held that to retain one's money and deny that person the right of interest on that amount would definitely amount to 'unfair trade practice' and fall within the purview of Consumer Protection Act even otherwise.

Various judgment of the consumer courts reveal that they have not only been awarding the value of goods or services for the defect and deficiency in service but also the compensation for the mental agony and harassment. The provision in the Act enables a consumer to claim and empowers the Commission to redress any injustice done to him. The Commission or the Forum in the Act is thus entitled to award not only value of the goods or services but also to compensate a consumer for injustice suffered by him.

[CPR – Consumer Protection Reporter,

CPJ – Consumer Protection Journal

NC – National Commission.]